Elements of
Language

Fifth Course

Lee Odell

Richard Vacca

Renée Hobbs

Grammar, Usage, and Mechanics
Instructional Framework by

John E. Warriner

HOLT, RINEHART AND WINSTON

A Harcourt Education Company

Austin • Orlando • Chicago • New York • Toronto • London • San Diego

STAFF CREDITS

EDITORIAL

Executive Editor
Robert R. Hoyt

Program Editor
Kathryn Rogers

Project Editors
Randy Dickson
Eric Estlund
Ann Michelle Gibson

Copyediting
Michael Neibergall, *Copyediting Manager;* Mary Malone, *Copyediting Supervisor;* Elizabeth Dickson, *Senior Copyeditor;* Christine Altgelt, Emily Force, Julia Thomas Hu, *Copyeditors*

Project Administration
Marie Price, *Managing Editor;* Lori De La Garza, *Associate Managing Editor;* Christine Degollado, Janet Jenkins, *Editorial Coordinators*

DESIGN

Book Design
Joe Melomo, *Design Director;* Candace Moore, *Senior Designer;* Rina May Ouellette, *Design Associate*

Image Acquisitions
Curtis Riker, *Director;* Jeannie Taylor, *Photo Research Supervisor;* Rick Benavides, *Photo Researcher;* Sam Dudgeon, *Senior Staff Photographer;* Victoria Smith, *Staff Photographer;* Lauren Eischen, *Photography Specialist*

Media Design
Richard Metzger, *Design Director*

Cover Design
Bill Smith Studio

EDITORIAL PERMISSIONS
Susan Lowrance

PRODUCTION
Carol Trammel, *Production Manager;* Belinda Barbosa Lopez, Michael Roche, *Senior Production Coordinators*

MANUFACTURING
Shirley Cantrell, *Manufacturing Supervisor;* Mark McDonald, *Inventory Analyst;* Amy Borseth, *Manufacturing Coordinator*

Printed in the United States of America

ISBN 0-03-068669-5

1 2 3 4 5   048   05 04 03 02

LEE ODELL helped establish the pedagogical framework for the composition strand of *Elements of Language.* In addition, he guided the development of the scope and sequence and pedagogical design of the Writing Workshops. Dr. Odell is Professor of Composition Theory and Research and, since 1996, Director of the Writing Program at Rensselaer Polytechnic Institute. He began his career teaching English in middle and high schools. More recently he has worked with teachers in grades K–12 to establish a program that involves students from all disciplines in writing across the curriculum and for communities outside their classrooms. Dr. Odell's most recent book (with Charles R. Cooper) is *Evaluating Writing: The Role of Teachers' Knowledge about Text, Learning, and Culture* (1999). Dr. Odell is Past Chair of the Conference on College Composition and Communication and of the NCTE's Assembly for Research.

RENÉE HOBBS helped develop the theoretical framework for the viewing and representing strand of *Elements of Language.* A national expert in media literacy, Dr. Hobbs guided the development of the scope and sequence; served as the authority on terminology, definitions, and pedagogy; and directed the planning for the video series. Dr. Hobbs is Associate Professor of Communication at Babson College in Wellesley, Massachusetts, and Director of the Media Literacy Project. Active in the field of media education, Dr. Hobbs has served as Director of the Institute on Media Education, Harvard Graduate School of Education; Director of the "Know TV" Project, Discovery Networks and Time Warner Cable; and Board Member, The New York Times Newspaper in Education Program. She works actively in staff development in school districts nationwide. Dr. Hobbs has contributed articles and chapters on media, technology, and education to many publications.

RICHARD VACCA helped establish the conceptual basis for the reading strand of *Elements of Language.* In addition, he guided the development of the pedagogical design and the scope and sequence of skills in the Reading Workshops. Dr. Vacca is Professor of Education at Kent State University. He recently completed a term as the forty-second President of the International Reading Association. Originally a middle school and high school teacher, Dr. Vacca served as the project director of the Cleveland Writing Demonstration Project for several years. He is the co-author of *Content Area Reading; Reading and Learning to Read;* and articles and chapters related to adolescents' literacy development. In 1989, Dr. Vacca received the College Reading Association's A. B. Herr Award for Outstanding Contributions to Reading Education. Currently, he is co-chair of the IRA's Commission on Adolescent Literacy.

JOHN E. WARRINER was a high school English teacher when he developed the original organizational structure for his classic *English Grammar and Composition* series. The approach pioneered by Mr. Warriner was distinctive, and the editorial staff of Holt, Rinehart and Winston have worked diligently to retain the unique qualities of his pedagogy. For the same reason, HRW continues to credit Mr. Warriner as an author of *Elements of Language* in recognition of his groundbreaking work. John Warriner also co-authored the *English Workshop* series and was editor of *Short Stories: Characters in Conflict.* Throughout his career, however, teaching remained Mr. Warriner's major interest, and he taught for thirty-two years in junior and senior high schools and in college.

PROGRAM CONSULTANTS

The program consultants reviewed instructional materials to ensure consistency with current research, classroom appropriateness, and alignment with curriculum guidelines.

Ann Bagley
Senior Administrator for
Secondary English
Wake County Public Schools
Raleigh, North Carolina

Vicki R. Brown
Professor of Education
Grambling State University
Principal, Grambling Middle
School
Grambling, Louisiana

Beth Johnson
Supervisor of Language Arts
Polk District Schools
Bartow, Florida

Kathleen Jongsma
Associate Professor, Department
of Education Chair
Texas Lutheran University
Seguin, Texas

Lois King
Dallas Public Schools
Dallas, Texas

Bruce A. Marshall
Secondary Reading/Dyslexia
Teacher
Cypress Falls High School
Houston, Texas

Baird Neville
Principal Teacher,
Communications Arts High
School
San Antonio, Texas

Kaye Price-Hawkins
Language Arts Consultant
Abilene, Texas

Olga Samaniego
English Department Chair,
Burges High School
El Paso, Texas

CRITICAL REVIEWERS

The critical reviewers read and evaluated pre-publication materials for this book.

Patricia S. Bishop
Riverview High School
Riverview, Florida

Pamela A. Boggs
West Orange High School
Winter Gardens, Florida

Judy Champney
Science Hill High School
Johnson City, Tennessee

Rebecca D. Danello
Stafford County School District
Stafford, Virginia

Deborah F. Davis
Lynwood High School
Lynwood, California

Heidi Griffith
Bridgeport High School
Bridgeport, West Virginia

Gail L. Haddock
J. H. Rose High School
Greenville, North Carolina

Kay Hannum
Hobbs High School
Hobbs, New Mexico

Gail Hayes
South Florence High School
Florence, South Carolina

Phyllis S. Irby
Tri-Cities High School
East Point, Georgia

Erin Maynard Johnson
East Wake High School
Wendell, North Carolina

Heidi Juel
Roosevelt High School
Sioux Falls, South Dakota

Nancy Levi
Oakland High School
Murfreesboro, Tennessee

Dian Molinar
Montwood High School
El Paso, Texas

Cecilia R. Olan
Bel Air High School
El Paso, Texas

Jennie C. Otterman
Hamilton Southeastern High
School
Fishers, Indiana

Heidi M. Quintana
Robinson High School
Tampa, Florida

Troy Roberts
W. H. Burges High School
El Paso, Texas

Norm Rush
Chaffey High School
Ontario, California

Nedra Segall
Stillwater High School
Stillwater, Oklahoma

Linda Shepherd
Terry Parker High School
Jacksonville, Florida

Michelle Smith
Colleyville Heritage High School
Colleyville, Texas

Betty Templeton
Riverside High School
Greer, South Carolina

Debra Zupancic
Dripping Springs High School
Dripping Springs, Texas

Continued

Geri-Lee DeGennaro
Tarpon Springs High School
Tarpon Springs, Florida

Karen Dendy
Stephen F. Austin Middle School
Irving, Texas

Dianne Franz
Tarpon Springs Middle School
Tarpon Springs, Florida

Doris F. Frazier
East Millbrook Magnet Middle
    School
Raleigh, North Carolina

Shayne G. Goodrum
C. E. Jordan High School
Durham, North Carolina

Bonnie L. Hall
St. Ann School
Lansing, Illinois

Doris Ann Hall
Forest Meadow Junior High
    School
Dallas, Texas

James M. Harris
Mayfield High School
Mayfield Village, Ohio

Lynne Hoover
Fremont Ross High School
Fremont, Ohio

Patricia A. Humphreys
James Bowie High School
Austin, Texas

Jennifer L. Jones
Oliver Wendell Holmes Middle
    School
Dallas, Texas

Kathryn R. Jones
Murchison Middle School
Austin, Texas

Bonnie Just
Narbonne High School
Harbor City, California

Vincent Kimball
Patterson High School #405
Baltimore, Maryland

Nancy C. Long
MacArthur High School
Houston, Texas

Carol M. Mackey
Ft. Lauderdale Christian School
Ft. Lauderdale, Florida

Jan Jennings McCown
Johnston High School
Austin, Texas

Alice Kelly McCurdy
Rusk Middle School
Dallas, Texas

Elizabeth Morris
Northshore High School
Slidell, Louisiana

Victoria Reis
Western High School
Ft. Lauderdale, Florida

Dean Richardson
Scarborough High School
Houston, Texas

Susan M. Rogers
Freedom High School
Morganton, North Carolina

Sammy Rusk
North Mesquite High School
Mesquite, Texas

Carole B. San Miguel
James Bowie High School
Austin, Texas

Jane Saunders
William B. Travis High School
Austin, Texas

Gina Sawyer
Reed Middle School
Duncanville, Texas

Laura R. Schauermann
MacArthur High School
Houston, Texas

Stephen Shearer
MacArthur High School
Houston, Texas

Elizabeth Curry Smith
Tarpon Springs High School
Tarpon Springs, Florida

Jeannette M. Spain
Stephen F. Austin High School
Sugar Land, Texas

Carrie Speer
Northshore High School
Slidell, Louisiana

Trina Steffes
MacArthur High School
Houston, Texas

Andrea G. Freirich Stewart
Freedom High School
Morganton, North Carolina

Diana O. Torres
Johnston High School
Austin, Texas

Jan Voorhees
Whitesboro High School
Marcy, New York

Ann E. Walsh
Bedichek Middle School
Austin, Texas

Mary Jane Warden
Onahan School
Chicago, Illinois

Beth Westbrook
Covington Middle School
Austin, Texas

Char-Lene Wilkins
Morenci Area High School
Morenci, Michigan

CONTENTS IN BRIEF

CONTENTS

Informational Text

Narration/
Description

Defining Concepts **54**

Reporting Progress **104**

Informational Text

Exposition

Exploring Problems and Solutions

Analyzing a Novel 186

Exploring Historical Research

FOOD WILL WIN THE WAR
You came here seeking Freedom
You must now help to preserve it
WHEAT is needed for the allies
Waste nothing

CHAPTER

9

Informational Text

Persuasion

Evaluating Advertising 366

PART 3 Grammar, Usage, and Mechanics **482**

Parts of Speech Overview

Identification and Function **484**

CHAPTER **14**

CHAPTER

15

The Parts of a Sentence
Subjects, Predicates, Complements **512**

The Phrase

CHAPTER

16

Kinds of Phrases and Their Functions 534

The Clause

CHAPTER

17

Independent and Subordinate Clauses 556

Agreement

CHAPTER

18

Subject and Verb, Pronoun and Antecedent **576**

Using Pronouns Correctly

Case Forms of Pronouns **604**

Clear Reference

Pronouns and Antecedents **628**

Using Verbs Correctly

CHAPTER

Principal Parts, Tense, Voice, Mood **642**

Using Modifiers Correctly

Forms and Uses of Adjectives and Adverbs;

Placement of Modifiers

Symmetry Drawing E 22 by M.C. Escher.
© 1999 Cordon Art-Baarn-Holland. All
rights reserved.

A Glossary of Usage

Capitalization

Punctuation

Punctuation

CHAPTER

27

Other Marks of Punctuation 802

Spelling

CHAPTER

28

CHAPTER

29

Correcting Common Errors
Key Language Skills Review **874**

MODELS

STUDENT'S OVERVIEW

Elements of Language is divided into four major parts.

PART 1 — Communications

This section ties together the essential skills and strategies you use in all types of communication—reading, writing, listening, speaking, viewing, and representing.

Reading Workshops In these workshops, you read an article, a story, an editorial—a real-life example of a type of writing you will later compose on your own. In addition, these workshops help you practice the reading process through

- a Reading Skill and Reading Focus specific to each type of writing,

- Vocabulary Mini-Lessons to help you understand unfamiliar words, and

- Test-Taking Mini-Lessons targeting common reading objectives

Writing Workshops In these workshops, you brainstorm ideas and use the writing process to produce your own article, story, editorial—and more. These workshops also include

- Writing and Critical-Thinking Mini-Lessons to help you master important aspects of each type of writing

- an organizational framework and models to guide your writing

- evaluation charts with concrete steps for revising

- Connections to Literature and Connections to Life, activities that extend writing workshop skills and concepts to other areas of your life

- Test-Taking Mini-Lessons to help you respond to writing prompts for tests

Focus on Speaking and Listening
Focus on Viewing and Representing

This is your chance to sharpen your skills in presenting your ideas visually and orally and to learn how to take a more critical view of what you hear and see.

PART 2   Sentences and Paragraphs

Learn to construct clear and effective sentences and paragraphs—what parts to include, how to organize ideas, and how to write these essential parts of compositions with style.

PART 3   Grammar, Usage, and Mechanics

These are the basics that will help you make your writing correct and polished.

Grammar   Discover the structure of language—the words, phrases, and clauses that are the building blocks of sentences.

Usage   Learn the rules that govern how language is used in various social situations, including standard versus nonstandard and formal versus informal English.

Mechanics   Master the nuts and bolts of correct written English, including capitalization, punctuation, and spelling.

PART 4   Quick Reference Handbook

Use this handy guide any time you need concise tips to help you communicate more effectively—whether you need to find information in a variety of media, make sense of what you read, prepare for tests, or present your ideas in a published document, a speech, or a visual.

Elements of Language on the Internet

Put the communication strategies in *Elements of Language* to work by logging on to the Internet. At the *Elements of Language* Internet site, you can dissect the prose of professional writers, crack the codes of the advertising industry, and find out how your communication skills can help you in the real world.

As you move through *Elements of Language,* you will find the best online resources at **go.hrw.com.**

The Reading and Writing Processes

Do these situations sound familiar? While reading, you suddenly realize you have read the same sentences several times without gaining any meaning from them. While writing, you stare at the single sentence you have written, unable to think of anything else to write. When you find yourself stuck, step back and look at the processes of reading and writing.

Reading

The reading you do in school requires you to think critically about information and ideas. In order to get the most from a text, prepare your mind for the task before you read, use effective strategies while you read, and take time to process the information after you read.

TIP Reading and writing are both recursive processes—that is, you can return to earlier steps when needed. For example, you might make new predictions while you are reading a text or you might develop additional support for ideas when you are revising a piece of writing.

- **Before Reading** Get your mind in gear by considering your purpose for reading a particular piece of writing and by thinking about what you already know about the topic. Preview the text by skimming a bit and considering headings, graphics, and other features. Use this information to predict what the text will discuss and how challenging it will be to read.

- **While Reading** As you read, figure out the writer's point about the topic. Notice how the text is organized (by cause and effect or in order of importance, for example) to help you find support for that point. Connect the ideas to your own experiences when you can. If you get confused, slow down, re-read, or jot ideas in a graphic organizer.

- **After Reading** Confirm and extend your understanding of the text. Draw conclusions about the writer's point of view, and evaluate how well the writer communicated the message. Use ideas in the text to create a piece of art, to read more on a related topic, or to solve a problem.

Writing

A perfect text seldom springs fully formed from your mind; instead, you must plan your text before you write and work to improve it after drafting.

- **Before Writing** First, choose a topic and a form of writing, such as a poem or an editorial. Decide who your readers will be and what you want the text to accomplish. Develop ideas based on your knowledge and on research. Organize the ideas, and jot down your main point.

- **While Writing** Grab attention and provide background information in an introduction. Elaborate your ideas to support your point, and organize them clearly. Then, wrap things up with a conclusion.

- **After Writing** To improve a draft, evaluate how clearly you expressed your ideas. Ask a peer to suggest areas that need work. Then, revise. Proofread to correct mistakes. Share your finished work with others, and reflect on what you learned.

You may have noticed that the reading and writing processes involve similar strategies. The chart below summarizes these similarities.

The Reading and Writing Processes

Reading		Writing
■ Determine your purpose for reading. ■ Consider what you already know about the topic. ■ Preview the text to make predictions about what it will include.	— **Before** —	■ Identify your writing purpose and your audience. ■ Draw upon what you know about the topic, and do research to find out more. ■ Make notes or an outline to plan what the text will include.
■ Figure out the writer's main ideas. ■ Look for support for the main ideas. ■ Notice how the ideas in the text are organized.	— **While** —	■ Express your main ideas clearly. ■ Support them with details, facts, examples, or anecdotes. ■ Follow prewriting notes or an outline to organize your text so readers can easily follow your ideas.
■ Evaluate the text to decide how accurate it is and its overall quality. ■ Relate what you have read to the world around you by creating something, reading further, or applying ideas. ■ Reflect on what you have read.	— **After** —	■ Evaluate and revise your text. Use peer editors' comments to help improve your work. ■ Relate your writing to the world around you by publishing it. ■ Reflect on what you have written.

The Reading and Writing Workshops in this book provide valuable practice for strategies that will help you effectively use these related processes.

PART 1

Communications

Taking Tests: Strategies and Practice

Taking Reading Tests

You have been taking national and statewide **standardized tests** throughout your school career. These tests become increasingly important as you approach college applications and graduation. To improve your test scores, try the following strategies on standardized reading tests. These tests have brief **reading passages, multiple-choice questions,** and sometimes an open-ended **essay question.**

THINKING IT THROUGH — Reading Test Strategies

STEP 1 Watch the clock. Before you start, check the number of questions and estimate how long you can spend on each one. Then, pace yourself, checking frequently to see if you need to work faster.

STEP 2 Focus, focus, focus. Carefully read the directions and any introductions. Then, focus your attention completely on each reading passage, blocking out any distracting thoughts. If you can mark the test booklet, underline or circle key words and phrases.

STEP 3 Know what the question is asking. Watch out for words such as *not* and *except,* which require you to choose an answer that is false or opposite in some way. Also, beware of distractors, which make true statements but don't answer the question that's being asked. Don't choose an answer until you've considered *all* of the choices.

STEP 4 Trust your educated guess. Usually you can easily eliminate one or two answers that you know are wrong. Then, make an educated guess about the remaining choices.

STEP 5 Push ahead. Don't get bogged down on a difficult question. Skip the ones that bewilder you, and try again later if there's time.

STEP 6 Bubble with care. Make sure you carefully match each question's number to the same number on the answer sheet. If you skip a question, be sure to skip it on the answer sheet, too.

STEP 7 Review your work. Erase any stray marks on your answer sheet. If there's time, go back and try to answer any questions you skipped.

TIP Before a test, find out whether points are taken off for wrong answers. If not, answer every question. If wrong answers do count against you, answer only the questions you know and those you can answer with an educated guess.

Read the following passages carefully. Then, choose the best answer to each question.

Return of a Reptile

by Elizabeth G. Daerr

When most people conjure up the image of a crocodile, they may picture a large creature floating at the water's surface waiting to ambush an unsuspecting wildebeest[1] or a crocodile hunter wrestling a 15-foot beast in Australia. But Frank Mazzotti, a wildlife biologist at the University of Florida who has studied the American crocodile in Everglades and Biscayne national parks for 23 years, has a different image.

"They're really a gentle species," he says. "I've captured them and prodded them in the most invasive ways [for research], and they just lay there." Mazzotti believes that education about the crocodile's passive nature is one of the best ways to help recovery of this endangered species.

Paul Moler, a wildlife biologist with the Florida Fish and Wildlife Conservation Commission, says that the American crocodile has been wrongly linked to the human-eating reputation of its African and Australian cousins. "There's a pervasive[2] misconception that crocodiles are more aggressive than alligators," which few people fear in Florida, he said. "There's never been a documented crocodile

---

1. **wildebeest:** an African antelope.

---

2. **pervasive:** prevalent, common.

attack; they are pretty much reclusive[3] animals." In fact, a large population lives in the 168 linear miles of cooling canals of a Florida Power and Light plant, where they are rarely bothered by humans and also have access to the protected waters of Biscayne Bay.

The species was listed as endangered in Florida in 1975 because of hunting for the animal's hide and the loss of habitat to development. Today, various scientists estimate that between 500 to 1,200 crocodiles live in Florida—up from approximately 200 to 400 more than two decades ago. Their U.S. habitat extends from Big Pine Key through Biscayne Bay and the Everglades, but they are also found south into Mexico, the Caribbean, and Ecuador.

Though the species resemble one another, crocodiles vary greatly from the more than 1 million alligators found in Florida. Crocodile color ranges from olive green to gray compared with the black hue of alligators, and their snouts are narrower. In addition, the crocodile's bottom and top teeth are visible from the side; only the upper teeth are seen on an alligator. Breeding seasons also vary, and between March and May, female crocodiles lay 20 to 50 eggs that incubate two to three months.

When the nine-inch hatchlings emerge, they disperse immediately into saltwater estuaries, where the survival rate for the first year ranges from 6 percent to 50 percent, depending on the availability of fresh water. Adequate rainwater is needed to dilute seawater because baby crocodiles cannot tolerate high salinity.[4] Crocodiles can live up to 50 or 60 years according to scientists.

As the American crocodile expands into its historic territory, alterations of key habitat continue to cause problems. Restricted fresh water flows through Everglades National Park, which provide irrigation[5] for agriculture and flood control, have made much of the area unsuitable for hatchlings. Development has also increased the number of human interactions with crocodiles, creating more calls to the state wildlife commission to remove animals.

The population is rebounding without much management, Moler said, and he believes that the species is on its way to being upgraded to threatened status. But neither he nor Mazzotti believes that the American crocodile can be removed entirely from federal protection because of human attitudes toward the creature. "If you don't solve the problem of human intolerance, your program will never be a success," Mazzotti said.

---

3. **reclusive:** withdrawn, solitary.

4. **salinity:** saltiness.

5. **irrigation:** water for soil.

1. The article's main idea is that
   A. people do not fear the American crocodile
   B. American crocodiles face problems caused by people's attitudes
   C. all crocodiles attack and eat humans
   D. U.S. crocodiles are as aggressive as alligators
   E. crocodiles are extinct in the U.S.

2. The author's purpose for writing is
   F. to explain how to distinguish between crocodiles and alligators
   G. to correct a mistaken view of U.S. crocodiles
   H. to advocate for changing state and federal wildlife laws
   J. to tell the story of a wildlife biologist studying crocodiles
   K. to describe the life cycle of the American crocodile

3. The word *habitat* (paragraph 4) refers to a plant's or animal's
  A. native environment
  B. means of defense
  C. repeated behavior
  D. life cycle
  E. ability to reproduce

4. Which was a factor in the decline of the crocodile population?
  F. having long life spans
  G. being reclusive
  H. appearing similar to alligators
  J. being hunted for their hides
  K. gaining new habitats

5. What evidence does Frank Mazzotti give to support his views?
  A. personal observations
  B. widely accepted facts
  C. other experts' opinions
  D. statistics
  E. He gives no evidence.

6. Mazzotti and Moler agree that the American crocodile is
  F. just like the African crocodile
  G. more aggressive than alligators
  H. not a threat to humans
  J. nearly extinct
  K. attracted by human activity

7. In paragraph 5, the author compares and contrasts crocodiles and alligators, which differ markedly in color, shape of snout, and
  A. size
  B. number of babies
  C. feeding habits
  D. life span
  E. visible teeth

8. If fresh water decreases in saltwater estuaries, the crocodile population will soon
  F. increase dramatically
  G. rapidly decrease
  H. outnumber alligators
  J. become more aggressive
  K. die of thirst

Write several paragraphs in response to *one* of these questions:

9. Using information from the article, write the autobiography of an American crocodile. Include information on the animal's life cycle and activities as well as its interactions with humans. Conclude by having the crocodile reflect on what the future might hold for it.

10. Imagine that you are a congressional representative. What legislation would you propose regarding the treatment of crocodiles? Consider what you think should be done if a crocodile appears in a park or on someone's property. Support your points with details from the article.

Turtles in Trouble

by Tina Adler

A fisherman caught a female sea turtle in Baja California, Mexico, in 1986. He gave her to scientists. For the next ten years, Adelita, as she was named, lived in captivity.

Adelita was a loggerhead[1], one of seven species, or kinds, of sea turtles. All are endangered. They live in the ocean but, like all reptiles, they have lungs and so they must surface to breathe.

Jay Nichols is one of the scientists studying Adelita and other sea turtles and their behavior. In 1996 he released Adelita into the Pacific Ocean with a transmitter on her back that allowed him to track her movements. Would she make it across thousands of miles of ocean to her nesting beach? What threats would she and other sea turtles face?

---

1. **loggerhead:** a type of sea turtle with a hard shell and a large head.

Baby sea turtles face so many dangers that it's amazing they survive at all. Even before hatching, eggs are sometimes eaten by ghost crabs or crushed by adult turtles digging other nests. If the eggs do hatch and the hatchlings head for the sea, all kinds of predators—birds, raccoons, fish—try to gobble them up.

But the most serious threats to sea turtles come from humans. Fishermen accidentally drown thousands of sea turtles that get caught in fishing nets. Dumpers pollute the ocean with garbage that is toxic to sea turtles. People crowd turtles away from their habitat: ocean beaches. They also build seawalls that can block turtles from nesting areas. People eat turtles, and even kill them to make decorative objects out of their shells. Turtles have been swimming the seas for millions of years, but their future is more uncertain now than ever before.

Concern for sea turtles' survival has led to many studies aimed at helping these endangered reptiles. Tracking Adelita is one such project. By finding out where sea turtles feed, travel, mate, and nest, scientists can recommend specific measures to protect those areas from development, poaching, or illegal hunting, pollution, and other activities harmful to sea turtle survival.

Turtle Protectors

People around the world want to protect sea turtles. In French Guiana[2] and elsewhere, volunteers patrol the beaches to scare off poachers when turtles are nesting. Sea turtles return to the beaches where they hatched to lay their own eggs. Scientists put tags on adults and newly hatched sea turtles to help track them—

learning more about sea turtles' sense of direction and movements.

In Baja California, Mexico, Nichols uses computers to keep a close eye on the turtles he studies. After he released Adelita, he says, "I would rush to my office . . . hoping every day that she would keep going." He used his computer to see whether her radio tag had sent any new information on her speed and location. When Adelita swam to the surface, the transmitter sent signals to an orbiting satellite, which relayed them to computers back on land.

Right after Nichols put Adelita in the water, he got some good news. She was heading for Japan. Nichols felt certain that Adelita had hatched on a beach in Japan. He predicted that she'd head back to that beach to lay her own eggs. But how did she know where to go?

Hatchling turtles float around as if they have no sense of direction. Because the babies haven't learned how to dive or swim against currents yet, "they act just like tiny buoys that go where the currents take them," explains Nichols. In laboratory studies of hatchlings, however, scientists discovered that they can detect the angle and intensity of the Earth's magnetic field—the force that causes a compass to point north. As adults, sea turtles navigate, or find their way, using that magnetic field.

One year after her release, Adelita reached Japan. She had navigated 6,000 miles alone. She proved that sea turtles do indeed find their way "home" again.

Unfortunately the last signals received from Adelita's transmitter suggest that she was captured by the crew of a fishing boat. She may no longer be alive, but she provided useful information that will help scientists like Nichols as they try to save other sea turtles.

---

2. **French Guiana:** a French territory on the northeast coast of South America.

Sad Display

Law enforcement officials have seized enough illegal sea turtle items from international travelers to fill the shelves of a government crime lab in Ashland, Oregon. "Some people pay a lot of money for sea turtle parts and products such as stuffed turtles, turtle eggs, turtle-shell jewelry, turtle steaks, suntan lotion made with turtle oil, and even turtle shell guitars," says Ken Goddard, director of the lab. "The high demand could easily result in the extinction of sea turtles."

11. According to this article, the turtle's greatest danger comes from
   A. natural predators
   B. natural disasters
   C. human activity
   D. global warming
   E. storms at sea

12. The author captures the reader's attention and interest with
   F. facts and statistics
   G. her own personal experiences
   H. a logical argument
   J. the story of Adelita
   K. a startling quotation

13. Sea turtles find their way to their nesting beaches by using
   A. transmitters on their backs
   B. well-marked turtle seaways
   C. the moon and the stars
   D. compasses that point north
   E. the earth's magnetic field

14. You can infer that turtles are becoming more endangered because
   F. they have trouble navigating their way home
   G. human activities that harm them are increasing
   H. more predators are eating them
   J. their beaches are disappearing
   K. tracking devices keep them from surfacing

15. From the tone of the article, you can infer that the intended audience is
   A. professional biologists
   B. first-graders
   C. ordinary adult readers
   D. turtle experts
   E. congressional representatives

16. The writer's purpose is to
   F. entertain
   G. describe
   H. inform
   J. persuade
   K. criticize

continued

17. Jay Nichols compares baby turtles to *buoys* in order to

    A. provide a definition of *buoy*

    B. describe what a buoy looks like

    C. point out features of both

    D. explain how the turtles move

    E. make clear the size of the turtles

Comparing the Passages

18. Both articles include which of the following types of support?

    F. statistics about the species' population

    G. anecdotal evidence from research scientists

    H. the story of one member of the species

    J. opinions of people opposed to protecting the species

    K. quotations from law enforcement officials

Write several paragraphs in response to *one* of the following questions:

19. If you were presenting a report on endangered species and could choose only one of these two articles as a source, explain which article you would choose, and why. Consider content, reliability, and currency. In a separate paragraph, summarize what you would say about the article.

20. Write a letter to the editor, arguing for or against a proposed law intended to protect the American crocodile or the sea turtle. State your proposed law, and support your opinion with details and information from the passages.

Taking Writing Tests

Standardized tests evaluate your writing skills in two different ways:

- **On-demand writing prompts** set up a situation and ask you to write a narrative, expository, or persuasive **essay** or a **letter** in a limited time.
- **Multiple-choice questions** test your knowledge of sentence construction and revision, as well as paragraph content and organization.

Usually, you have less than an hour to write your essay. Don't panic. Apply the writing process steps you have learned, and use the following strategies for on-demand writing prompts.

THINKING IT THROUGH — Writing Test Strategies

▶ **STEP 1** **Analyze the writing prompt.** Be sure you understand exactly what you're being asked to do. Circle all **key verbs,** such as *analyze, compare and contrast, summarize, discuss, explain,* which define and direct your specific writing task. Points will be deducted if you don't cover the entire writing task. (Before the test, review the chart of **key verbs that appear in essay questions,** page 1000.) Identify your audience, and plan to shape your essay to fit that audience.

▶ **STEP 2** **Think first.** If you have forty-five minutes, spend ten of them on prewriting. Take notes, using whatever prewriting strategy feels most comfortable—brainstorm ideas, do a cluster diagram, or make a rough outline. Then, decide on your main idea statement and how you'll support it. Think about the order you'll use to organize ideas.

▶ **STEP 3** **Start drafting.** Allow about two thirds of your time to draft your essay, making sure you address all parts of the prompt. Focus on writing a strong opening paragraph and a definite conclusion. Express your ideas as clearly as you can, adding details that support and elaborate your main points. Use your natural voice; sound like yourself.

▶ **STEP 4** **Edit and revise.** Re-read what you've written, and see if you can add transitions or combine sentences to tie ideas together more smoothly. If you add a word or sentence, insert it neatly.

▶ **STEP 5** **Proofread with care.** Try to find and correct every single error in grammar, usage, mechanics, and spelling. You'll lose points for not following these conventions of standard written English.

Narrative Writing

Sample Writing Prompt *Think of an incident that made you feel very proud—of yourself, someone you know, your school, or community. Describe what happened, and tell how you felt at the time. Then, look back at your experience and tell how you feel and what you think about it now.*

What three things does the prompt ask you to include in your narrative? Plan your essay in a story map like the one below.

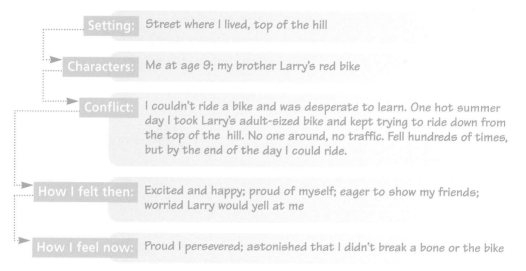

Setting: Street where I lived, top of the hill

Characters: Me at age 9; my brother Larry's red bike

Conflict: I couldn't ride a bike and was desperate to learn. One hot summer day I took Larry's adult-sized bike and kept trying to ride down from the top of the hill. No one around, no traffic. Fell hundreds of times, but by the end of the day I could ride.

How I felt then: Excited and happy; proud of myself; eager to show my friends; worried Larry would yell at me

How I feel now: Proud I persevered; astonished that I didn't break a bone or the bike

A good story begins with a bang and comes to a very definite conclusion. Help readers experience what you recall about the incident by adding plenty of specific, sensory details. Check to make sure you've answered all parts of the prompt.

Expository Writing

Sample Writing Prompt *Think of a problem that needs solving in your school, community, or the larger world. Identify the problem, and then propose a solution with specific details. Tell what the advantages and disadvantages of your solution are.*

Can you find the three key verbs (besides *think*) in this writing prompt? Your essay will have to cover all three parts of the prompt. You'll probably choose a problem you've already thought about. Before you start drafting, brainstorm specific details, examples, advantages, and disadvantages. State your main idea (identifying the problem) and solution in clear sentences.

Problem:	Voter turnout in the last citywide election was 32 percent of registered voters.
Solution:	Have a pre-election "Your vote counts" campaign (TV ads, posters; call registered voters to see who needs ride to the polls).
Advantages:	Voter turnout will increase. Maybe elected officials will become more responsive to voters' views and concerns.
Disadvantages:	Campaign will cost money and time. Not clear where funding will come from or who will organize it.

Persuasive Writing

Sample Writing Prompt *A respected educator recently proposed that standardized aptitude tests no longer be timed. All test takers, he believes, should have as much time as they need to answer test questions, since the test is intended to measure their aptitude, or abilities, not their speed. Consider the effects of "untimed" tests. Then, write a letter to the editor, clearly stating your opinion and supporting it with reasons.*

So what do you think? It's a good idea to consider both sides of a controversial issue—the pros and cons—before you make up your mind. Here's a list by a student who wants to keep tests timed and is trying to think of three good reasons to support her view.

<u>Cons</u>

Some students would take all day, wasting time that could be spent on other activities.

Confusion about what scores mean—would scores be reliable?

Speed at which a task can be done is sometimes important.

Like all persuasive writing, a letter to the editor demands clarity. Clearly state your opinion and then support it with your three strongest reasons, each in a separate paragraph. Elaborate each reason with facts, examples, anecdotes, and other kinds of evidence.

TIP Review the
strategies on page 3,
which also apply to
multiple-choice writing
questions.

Multiple-Choice Writing Questions

You may find a separate section of multiple-choice questions designed to test your understanding of sentences, paragraphs, and the conventions of standard English (grammar, usage, punctuation, capitalization, and spelling). Examples of some common types of multiple-choice writing questions are shown below.

Read the following two paragraphs. Then, choose the best answer for each question.

(1) That Americans are the worst thing that has ever happened to the English language has never been doubted by many Brits, from Prince Charles on down. (2) And while we are indeed responsible for the high quality of our slang and for an unfortunate predilection for using *like* as a form of punctuation, Americans, I am here to say, are not all bad for English. (3) The ultimate repository for the history of the language is greatly indebted to Americans for much of what makes the *Oxford English Dictionary (OED)* what it is: the citations, or the quotations of language that illustrate the use of every sense of every word in the *OED*. (4) "Every quotation," wrote Dr. Johnson in the preface to his great *Dictionary of the English Language*, "contributes something to the stability or enlargement of the language," and so for the *OED* finding good citations is its primary goal.

(5) While linguists now have phenomenal electronic resources, the need for skilled citation collectors is as strong as ever. (6) One reason is that many texts of interest—comic books, movie scripts, even modern novels—are simply not available electronically. (7) But the main reason is that most new usages and shifts in meaning can only be recognized by the human eye. (8) There is something new about the common word *so* in a sentence like "That *so* was a lame party" that a computer can't pick up, and even if you know to look for it, you would have to go through thousands of other examples of *so* to find the one you need.

From "On Language: Citations" by Jesse Sheidlower from *The New York Times Magazine*, September 9, 2001. © Copyright 2001 by **The New York Times Company**. Reprinted by persmission of the publisher.

Reference Note

For more on preparing for reading and writing tests, see the **Test-Taking Mini-Lesson** in each Part 1 chapter and **Studying and Test Taking** on pages 995–1010.

1. Sentence 1 begins with
  A. a prepositional phrase
  B. an infinitive phrase
  C. a gerund phrase
  D. a noun clause
  E. an adverb clause

2. In sentence 2, *predilection* means
  F. error in grammar
  G. difficult problem
  H. responsibility
  J. habit
  K. intense dislike

3. Which transition can replace *While* (sentence 5) without changing the meaning?
   A. Although
   B. Because
   C. If
   D. Since
   E. However

4. Which is the **best** supporting sentence for the topic sentence below?
   > Citations in dictionaries come from some surprising sources.

   F. That is why collecting citations is a full-time job.
   G. Popular culture is not considered a reliable source, however.
   H. They might be based on usage in TV shows, billboards, or conversations.
   J. Grammar books are the main source of dictionary citations.
   K. This is because changes in a word's meaning are difficult to document.

5. What is the purpose of the quotation in sentence 4?
   A. to mention a historical dictionary
   B. to note the importance of citations
   C. to provide a model of a quotation
   D. to make the article seem authoritative
   E. to give an example of British English

6. Which is the **best** thesis for the passage?
   F. Americans use *so* in unusual ways.
   G. The *OED* is an excellent resource.
   H. American English provides valuable citations.
   J. Electronic sources save linguists time.
   K. Dr. Johnson considered quotations important.

7. How should the sentence below be rewritten?
   > Please lie Eds dictionary on his desk.

   A. Please lay Eds dictionary on his desk.
   B. Please lay Ed's dictionary on his desk.
   C. Please lie Ed's dictionary on his desk.
   D. Please lie Ed's Dictionary on his desk.
   E. no change; correct as is

8. Which word is misspelled?
   > While <u>you're</u> <u>browsing</u> online, check
   >   **F**   **G**
   > out the *OED's* Web <u>cite</u> for a word's
   >   **H**
   > <u>historical</u> definitions. NO ERROR
   >   **J**   **K**

9. What is the **best** way to combine the following sentences?
   > The *OED* defines words. It also gives citations for their history.

   A. Defining words and giving citations for their history is the *OED*.
   B. The *OED* defines words, it also gives citations for their history.
   C. The *OED* defines words and also give citations for their history.
   D. The *OED* defines words; also gives citations for their history.
   E. The *OED* not only defines words, but also gives citations for their history.

10. Which of the following would provide the **best** information about differences between British and American English?
    F. an American English dictionary
    G. a British English dictionary
    H. a book on the history of English
    J. a U.S. news article on British English
    K. a Web site called "Ben's British-isms"

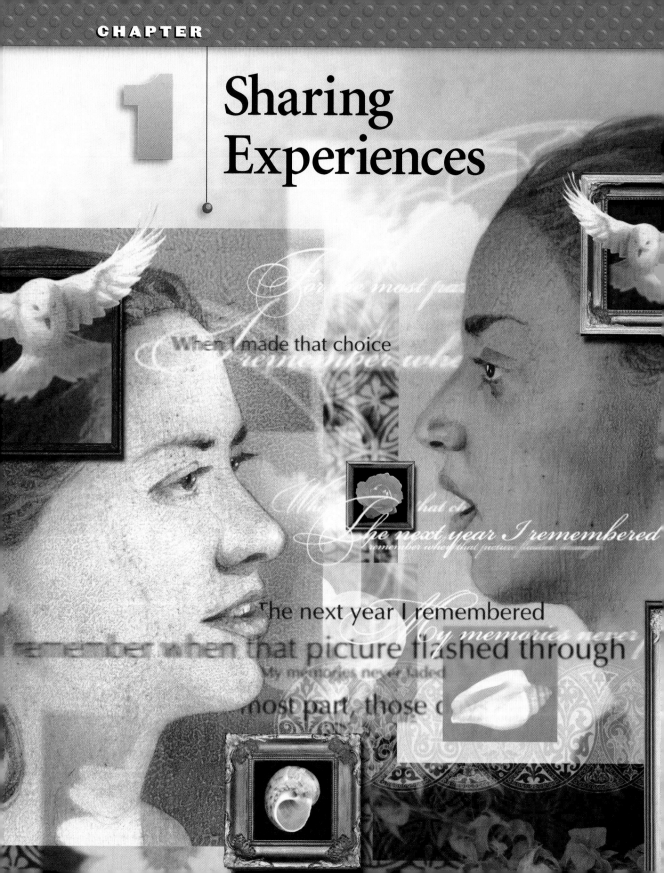

1

Sharing Experiences

Reading Workshop

Reading an Autobiographical Narrative

Writing Workshop

Writing an Autobiographical Narrative

Speaking and Listening

Creating an Oral History

Informational Text

Narration/
Description

Let's face it: We all are interested in one another. We want to know how a person became a teacher, a sports hero, or a president. We ask our friends what they did last weekend, and we tune in when survivors of a tornado disaster are describing their experiences on television. In short, we want to hear other people's stories. We also want to tell our *own* stories—about riding horseback through the Grand Canyon, for example, or about a comical moment at the school dance.

When these stories—often called **autobiographical narratives**—are written, they look a bit different from the stories we both hear and tell every day. They are more carefully crafted, for one thing. They guide the reader to see, hear, and feel the writer's experience truly. They are also more reflective, allowing the reader—and often the writer, too—to understand the meaning of the experience.

YOUR TURN 1
Brainstorming About Autobiographical Narratives

With two or three classmates, brainstorm the kernels of autobiographical narratives you might have heard during the course of one school day. Without revealing anything too personal, think about stories you have heard on television or overheard in the hallway. What anecdotes have your family and friends told? Discuss the differences between the narratives you have heard and others you have read. What kinds of experiences do you notice are *most* likely to be captured in writing?

internet connect

go. hrw .com

GO TO: go.hrw.com
KEYWORD: EOLang 11-1

Reading an Autobiographical Narrative

In this section, you will read an excerpt from an autobiographical narrative and learn to

- identify the narrative sequence
- analyze the narrative and descriptive details

Have you ever wanted to climb a mountain? As a twenty-three-year-old, Jon Krakauer climbed by himself to the top of Devils Thumb, a six-thousand foot peak rising out of the Stikine Ice Cap in Alaska. His autobiographical narrative—beginning on the next page—will show you how difficult and exciting the experience was at the time, and what it taught him about himself after it was over. Like many writers of personal essays, Krakauer's purpose is not solely to narrate the steps of his experience—he also wants to communicate its meaning.

Preparing to Read

READING SKILL ➤ **Identifying Narrative Sequence** When you ask the question, *What happened next?* you are asking about the **narrative sequence,** or the particular order of events in a narrative. Every experience actually occurs in **chronological,** or time, **order.** However, when authors want to *tell* about their experiences, they may alter the chronological order—with *flashbacks* or other techniques—to create a more dramatic narrative. As you read the selection on the opposite page, notice how the author tells you that time is passing. Look for dates and signal words such as *next, then,* or *after.*

READING FOCUS ➤ **Narrative and Descriptive Details** If the narrative sequence is the framework, or skeleton, of an autobiographical narrative, then **narrative** and **descriptive details** put muscle and sinew on that skeleton. These details are the tools that writers use when they want readers to *see,* to *hear,* and to *feel* the experience. Specific kinds of narrative and descriptive details include **sensory language,** language that appeals to the senses; the author's **thoughts** and **feelings;** and **dialogue,** or the exact speech of people depicted in the narrative. As you read "Reaching the Summit," look for narrative and descriptive details.

In the following excerpt from *Into the Wild,* author Jon Krakauer begins by recounting his love of climbing and his decision to climb Devils Thumb. However, because of the length of his tale, Krakauer's initial two attempts at climbing the mountain are omitted (signaled by a line of asterisks after paragraph three). In both cases, Krakauer failed because of the icy rock and the terrible storms. Beginning in the fourth paragraph, Krakauer narrates his third, successful attempt to reach the summit, starting out from his base camp on the northeast side of the mountain. As you read, jot down answers to the active-reading questions.

from INTO THE WILD

REACHING THE SUMMIT

BY JON KRAKAUER

As a youth, I am told, I was willful, self-absorbed, intermittently reckless, moody. . . . If something captured my undisciplined imagination, I pursued it with a zeal bordering on obsession, and from the age of seventeen until my late twenties that something was mountain climbing.

I devoted most of my waking hours to fantasizing about, and then undertaking, ascents of remote mountains in Alaska and Canada—obscure spires, steep and frightening, that nobody in the world beyond a handful of climbing geeks had ever heard of.

> **1. How does the writer's first sentence get your attention?**

> **2. What are the writer's thoughts and feelings about mountain climbing and his younger self?**

Some good actually came of this. By fixing my sights on one summit after another, I managed to keep my bearings through some thick postadolescent fog. Climbing *mattered.* The danger bathed the world in a halogen glow that caused everything—the sweep of the rock, the orange and yellow lichens, the texture of the clouds—to stand out in brilliant relief. Life thrummed at a higher pitch. The world was made real.

In 1977, . . . I got it into my head to climb a mountain called the Devils Thumb. An intrusion of diorite sculpted by ancient glaciers into a peak of immense and spectacular proportions, the Thumb is especially imposing from the north: Its great north wall, which had never been climbed, rises sheer and clean for six thousand feet from the glacier at its base, twice the height of Yosemite's El Capitan. I would go to Alaska, ski inland from the sea across thirty miles of glacial ice, and ascend this mighty *nordwand*. I decided, moreover, to do it alone. . . .

* * * *

I knew that people sometimes died climbing mountains. But at the age of twenty-three, personal mortality—the idea of my own death—was still largely outside my conceptual grasp. When I decamped from Boulder [Colorado] for Alaska, my head swimming with visions of glory and redemption on the Devils Thumb, it didn't occur to me that I might be bound by the same cause-and-effect relationships that governed the actions of others. Because I wanted to climb the mountain so badly, because I had thought about the Thumb so intensely for so long, it seemed beyond the realm of possibility that some minor obstacle like the weather or crevasses or rime-covered rock might ultimately thwart my will.

At sunset[1] the wind died, and the ceiling lifted 150 feet off the glacier, enabling me to locate my base camp. I made it back to the tent intact, but it was no longer possible to ignore the fact that the Thumb had made hash of my plans. I was forced to acknowledge that volition[2] alone, however powerful, was not going to get me up the north wall. I saw, finally, that nothing was.

There still existed an opportunity for salvaging the expedition, however. A week earlier I'd skied over to the southeast side of the mountain to take a look at the route by which I'd intended to descend the peak after climbing the north wall, a route that Fred Beckey, the legendary alpinist, had followed in 1946 in making the first ascent of the Thumb. During my reconnaissance,[3] I'd noticed an obvious unclimbed line to the left of the Beckey route—a patchy network of ice angling across the southeast face—that struck me as a relatively easy way to achieve the summit. At the time, I'd considered this route unworthy of my attentions. Now, on the rebound from my calamitous entanglement with the *nordwand*, I was prepared to lower my sights.

> **3. What words show time order in this paragraph?**

On the afternoon of May 15, when the blizzard finally abated, I returned to the southeast face and climbed to the top of a slender ridge that abuts the upper peak like a flying buttress on a Gothic cathedral. I decided to spend the night there, on the narrow crest, sixteen hundred feet below the summit. The evening sky was cold and cloudless. I could see all the way to tidewater and beyond. At dusk I watched, transfixed, as the lights of Petersburg[4] blinked on

---

1. **At sunset:** At this point, bad weather has just thwarted Krakauer's second attempt to reach the summit of Devils Thumb, and he is moving back down the mountain toward base camp.

2. **volition:** self-will; a conscious intent to act.

3. **reconnaissance** (ri•kän´ə•səns): exploration of unknown territory, or a search for information.

4. **Petersburg:** an island fishing village about twenty-five miles away from the base camp. Earlier, a bush pilot had airdropped supplies to Krakauer—the human contact he refers to in the following sentence.

in the west. The closest thing I'd had to human contact since the airdrop, the distant lights triggered a flood of emotion that caught me off guard. I imagined people watching baseball on television, eating fried chicken in brightly lit kitchens. . . . When I lay down to sleep, I was overcome by a wrenching loneliness. I'd never felt so alone, ever.

4. Why does the writer include his thoughts about what other people are doing?

That night I had troubled dreams. . . . I heard someone whisper, "I think he's in there. . . ." I sat bolt upright and opened my eyes. The sun was about to rise. The entire sky was scarlet. It was still clear, but a thin, wispy scum of cirrus had spread across the upper atmosphere, and a dark line of squalls was visible just above the southwestern horizon. I pulled on my boots and hurriedly strapped on my crampons. Five minutes after waking up, I was climbing away from the bivouac.[5]

I carried no rope, no tent or bivouac gear, no hardware save my ice axes. My plan was to go light and fast, to reach the summit and make it back down before the weather turned. Pushing myself, continually out of breath, I scurried up and to the left, across small snowfields linked by ice-choked clefts and short rock steps. The climbing was almost fun—the rock was covered with large, incut holds, and the ice, though thin, never got steeper than seventy degrees— but I was anxious about the storm front racing in from the Pacific, darkening the sky.

I didn't have a watch, but in what seemed like a very short time, I was on the distinctive final ice field. By now the entire sky was smeared with clouds. It looked easier to keep angling to the left but quicker to go straight for the top. Anxious about being caught by a storm high on the peak and without shelter, I opted for the direct route. The ice steepened and thinned. I swung my left ice ax and struck rock. I aimed for another spot, and once again it glanced off unyielding diorite with a dull clank. And again, and again. It was a reprise of my first attempt on the north face. Looking between my legs, I stole a glance at the glacier more than two thousand feet below. My stomach churned.

Forty-five feet above me the wall eased back onto the sloping summit shoulder. I clung stiffly to my axes, unmoving, racked by terror and indecision.

---

5. bivouac (biv´wak´): a tent camp or a temporary shelter set up in the open.

5. What problem does the writer overcome to reach the summit?

Again I looked down at the long drop to the glacier, then up, then scraped away the patina[6] of ice above my head. I hooked the pick of my left ax on a nickel-thin lip of rock and weighted it. It held. I pulled my right ax from the ice, reached up, and twisted the pick into a crooked half-inch fissure until it jammed. Barely breathing now, I moved my feet up, scrabbling my crampon points across the verglas.[7] Reaching as high as I could with my left arm, I swung the ax gently at the shiny, opaque surface, not knowing what I'd hit beneath it. The pick went in with a solid *whunk!* A few minutes later I was standing on a broad ledge. The summit proper, a slender rock fin sprouting a grotesque meringue of atmospheric ice, stood twenty feet directly above.

The insubstantial frost feathers[8] ensured that those last twenty feet remained hard, scary, onerous. But then suddenly there was no place higher to go. I felt my cracked lips stretch into a painful grin. I was on top of the Devils Thumb.

Fittingly, the summit was a surreal, malevolent[9] place, an improbably slender wedge of rock and rime no wider than a file cabinet. It did not encourage loitering. As I straddled the highest point, the south face fell away beneath my right boot for twenty-five hundred feet; beneath my left boot the north face dropped twice that distance. I took some pictures to prove I'd been there and spent a few minutes trying to straighten a bent pick. Then I stood up, carefully turned around, and headed for home . . . .

Less than a month after sitting on the summit of the Thumb, I was back in Boulder, nailing up siding on the Spruce Street Townhouses, the same condos I'd been framing when I left for Alaska. I got a raise, to four bucks an hour, and at the end of the summer moved out of the job-site trailer to a cheap studio apartment west of the downtown mall.

It is easy, when you are young, to believe that what you desire is no less than what you deserve, to assume that if you want something badly enough, it is your God-given right to have it. When I decided to go to Alaska that April, . . . I was a raw youth who mistook passion for insight and acted according to an obscure, gap-ridden logic. I thought climbing the Devils Thumb would fix all that was wrong with my life. In the end, of course, it changed almost nothing. But I came to appreciate that mountains make poor receptacles for dreams. And I lived to tell my tale.

6. What has the writer learned about himself after his climb?

---

6. **patina** (pat´n•ə): thin coating.

7. **verglas** (ver•glä´): thin layer of ice on rock.

8. **frost feathers:** frozen fog deposits.

9. **malevolent** (mə•lev´ə•lənt): wanting to bring harm to others.

Narrative Sequence

Following the Trail   Sometimes, tracking the events in a *narrative sequence* can be a little like playing detective—you must be alert for subtle clues and twists in the trail. This is true because **narrative sequence,** or the precise order in which events are presented, can vary from straight chronological order to one using **flashbacks** (jumps backward in time) and **flash-forwards** (jumps forward in time). Still, no matter how the writer chooses to order events, you can use specific clues to keep track of narrative sequence. Look at the following chart for some of these clues.

Clues	Examples
Time Signals: Time signals are words or phrases that explain how the events are hooked together in time. Think of them as road signs that tell you when, and how far, the narrative is moving forward or backward.	**Time Signal Words:** *before, after, then, next, when, meanwhile, first, finally, eventually, at last, thereafter* **Time Signal Phrases:** *in the meantime, a week earlier, at dusk, in 1998*
Verb Tenses: Writers use verb tense (the form of the verb that indicates time) to indicate when events occurred, whether in the present, past, or future. In autobiographical narratives, which usually reflect on past events, you will notice that many verb tenses point to the past. In flashbacks and flash-forwards, verb tenses can indicate an abrupt jump in time.	**Past:** I *wanted* to be in the marching band more than anything. **Flashback:** Now, finally on the field with my band mates, I was reminded of what *had happened* at band tryouts three months earlier. **Flash-forward:** No one standing there during the first quarter suspected what *would happen* later that night.

TIP It is sometimes hard to trace the sequence of events in autobiographical narratives because background information, description, and reflection often interrupt the narrative flow. While such interrupting passages do not advance the action of the narrative, they are vital parts of autobiographical writing. Their purpose is to deepen the reader's understanding of the writer's experience. In the first two paragraphs of the reading selection, for example, an older Jon Krakauer describes his younger self so that the reader will understand why climbing the Devils Thumb was so important to him then. As a result, the step-by-step narration of the climb takes on an added meaning.

THINKING IT THROUGH Understanding Narrative Sequence

Use the following steps to help you make sense of narrative sequences.

▶ **STEP 1** Identify all time signal words or phrases, such as *after, by now, no longer, when, a month earlier, on Friday.*

▶ **STEP 2** Be on the lookout for changes in verb tense. Note any tense changes as possible indicators of a flashback or flash-forward.

▶ **STEP 3** Create a time line like the one below. This kind of graphic organizer will allow you to visualize complicated narrative sequences.

| Event 1 | Event 2 | Event 3 | Event 4 |

YOUR TURN 2 Identifying Narrative Sequence

Using the three steps above, identify the correct sequence of the following statements about Jon Krakauer's experience in "Reaching the Summit." Jot your answers on your own paper.

1. returns to Boulder, Colorado
2. resolves not to let his failed climbs stop him
3. spends night alone on a ridge
4. crosses an ice field
5. takes photographs
6. notices darkening clouds for the first time
7. reaches the summit proper
8. skis to southeast side of mountain and notices another route to the summit
9. decides to climb Devils Thumb
10. uses axes to climb steep incline

Narrative and Descriptive Details

What Makes It Real?   A carefully plotted sequence of events is not enough to communicate an experience fully. Would you have truly understood Krakauer's experience if he had not recounted in detail what he saw, felt, and thought? To make events come alive for their readers, writers use *narrative* and *descriptive details.* The following chart illustrates the range of these details.

Narrative Details	Examples
• tell about **specific events** and **actions**	"I didn't have a watch, but in what seemed like a very short time, I was on the distinctive final ice field."
• suggest **thoughts** and **feelings**	"I was anxious about the storm front racing in from the Pacific."
• often include **dialogue,** or the exact words of a speaker	"I heard someone whisper, 'I think he's in there. . . .'"
Descriptive Details	**Examples**
• use **sensory language** (language that appeals to sight, hearing, touch, smell, and taste)	"Life thrummed at a higher pitch." (sensory detail that appeals to hearing)
• use **figurative language,** such as **similes** and **metaphors**	"The summit proper, a slender rock fin sprouting a grotesque meringue of atmospheric ice, stood twenty feet directly above." (metaphors comparing the ridge to a fish's fin and the ice to meringue, or a frothy egg-white topping)
• focus on the **factual** and **spatial** details of people, places, and objects	"It was still clear, but a thin, wispy scum of cirrus had spread across the upper atmosphere, and a dark line of squalls was visible just above the southwestern horizon." (spatial description that describes the sky from top to bottom)

Narrative and descriptive details are especially important in autobiographical writing because the writer's goal is to *share* his or her experience with a reader—to allow the reader to see and feel the experience as it unfolds. (This is true for biographies and fiction, too.) Narrative and descriptive details underscore the meaning of the experience for the writer and the reader.

TIP Writers do not use *all* of the details presented in the preceding chart in every autobiographical essay they write. They choose the ones most appropriate for their purposes. Using dialogue, for example, allows readers to overhear a key conversation, making the narrative more immediate and realistic. Using figurative language allows readers to visualize important images. Using factual details underscores an essay's authenticity and convinces readers of the truth of the experience.

YOUR TURN 3 Analyzing Narrative and Descriptive Details

Identify at least five narrative and descriptive details from "Reaching the Summit," beginning on page 19. Try to find a range of details, and be ready to discuss your examples. You might use a graphic organizer like the one below.

Narrative/Descriptive Details	Examples
Figurative language	"I hooked the pick of my left ax on a nickel-thin lip of rock and weighted it." ("Nickel-thin" is a metaphor.)

DILBERT reprinted by permission of United Feature Syndicate, Inc.

VOCABULARY

Context Clues for Specialized or Technical Terms

In "Reaching the Summit," several specialized terms are defined in footnotes. When this is not true, you can make an educated guess about the meaning of the unfamiliar term by looking at its **context**—the surrounding sentences and phrases in the passage.

One particular kind of **context clue** especially helpful with specialized terms is a **key word** (or **key phrase**): A key word is a word that you know and that functions as an anchor as you determine the meaning of any unfamiliar terms. The key word or key phrase may be found in the same sentence as the term or in the surrounding sentences within the paragraph.

THINKING IT THROUGH   **Using Key Word or Key Phrase Context Clues**

Look at the italicized word in this sample passage from "Reaching the Summit." Then, use the steps following it to discover the word's meaning.

Example:
I pulled on my boots and hurriedly strapped on my *crampons.* Five minutes after waking up, I was climbing away from the bivouac.

1. **Re-read the passage surrounding the unfamiliar word.** The writer is describing his hurried preparations to begin climbing.

2. **Identify a key word or key phrase in the passage,** such as *boots* and *climbing.*

3. **Determine the relationship between the key word or key phrase and the unfamiliar word:** *Crampons* are strapped onto the *boots* before climbing.

4. **Substitute a familiar word or phrase for the puzzling one, or make an educated guess at the word's meaning.** *Crampons* could be "specialized ice-climbing equipment for the feet" because of the term's association with boots and climbing.

5. **Check your dictionary to confirm the accuracy of your educated guess:** *Crampons* are "a pair of spiked iron plates fastened onto shoes to prevent slipping."

PRACTICE

Use the steps above to find out the meaning of the italicized words below.

1. I had thought about the Thumb so intensely for so long, it seemed beyond the realm of possibility that some minor obstacle like the weather or crevasses or *rime*-covered rock might ultimately thwart my will.

2. I pulled my right ax from the ice, reached up, and twisted the pick into a crooked half-inch *fissure* until it jammed.

3. I would go to Alaska, ski inland from the sea across thirty miles of glacial ice, and ascend this mighty *nordwand.*

4. I aimed for another spot, and once again it glanced off unyielding *diorite* with a dull clank.

5. It was still clear, but a thin, wispy scum of *cirrus* had spread across the upper atmosphere, and a dark line of squalls was visible just above the southwestern horizon.

Answering Vocabulary Questions

You probably encountered several unfamiliar words in "Reaching the Summit"—words you had to figure out in order to understand the piece as a whole. Many state and national tests will also test your knowledge of **vocabulary** by asking you about the meaning of a word within the context of the passage. If you do not immediately recognize the word, **context clues** can help you make an educated guess at the word's meaning.

Look at the following **reading passage** and the question that follows it.

Rulers in the ancient Hellenistic kingdom, which included Egypt, Persia, and all of Greece, generally pursued careful policies to encourage economic growth. For example, they maintained and repaired   5
roads to make travel and trade easier. Both manufacturing and trade increased dramatically. A new merchant and *artisan* class began to emerge in the Hellenistic cities, which further increased trade in   10
goods such as pottery, glass, and perfume.

1. In line 8, which of the following answers best captures the meaning of the word artisan?

  A. important woman

  B. artist

  C. politician

  D. store owner

  E. craftsworker

THINKING IT THROUGH **Answering Vocabulary Questions**

To determine the best possible answer, use the following steps.

1. Re-read the passage after reading the question and all of the answers.

2. Use context clues to identify the word's meaning (prefixes and **suffixes** are often helpful, too). In the passage above, **key word context clues** in the surrounding sentences are *economic, policies, trade,* and *manufacturing.*

3. Consider each answer. For example, *important woman* **A** is perhaps the answer because *pottery, glass,* and *perfume* are associated with traditionally female roles. The paragraph, however, is about economic growth, not male and female roles. *Artist* **B** has the same root as *artisan,* but artists don't usually "manufacture" their

artwork in large quantities—*artist* may be a decoy to fool readers who look for easy answers. A *politician* **C** doesn't make or trade things, so this answer seems incorrect. *Store owner* **D** may be a good guess, since the word may be a synonym for *merchant; trade* (associated with *merchant*) and *manufacturing* (associated with *artisan* perhaps) are two separate activities. A *craftsworker* **E** is different from a merchant, and is certainly involved in creating goods for market—this may be right.

4. Insert the answer you think is correct into the passage's sentence to check for accuracy in the context. When you try *craftsworker* in the passage, it makes sense—the answer is **E.**

Writing an Autobiographical Narrative

WHAT'S AHEAD?

In this section you will write an autobiographical narrative. You will learn to

- recall and arrange details about an experience
- reflect upon the meaning of your experience
- use dialogue correctly
- revise to include vivid details
- correct run-on sentences

Some discoveries, like the detection of a distant solar system, make headlines around the globe. Autobiographical narratives are discoveries, too, although they are announced in more quiet ways. Still, these discoveries are important to their authors—and to many readers, too.

Just think about the last time you wrote a diary entry or a letter to a friend. Did writing about the events of your life—that first day of your summer job or learning to drive under the watchful eye of your big brother—let you reflect on your experience in a new way? Now, think about significant events that you have read about in other people's autobiographical writing: Did you better understand the hardships of slavery when you read Frederick Douglass's autobiography? Could you relate to the Olympic athlete's description of winning the race? In this workshop you will narrate an experience and reveal its significance for your own readers.

Prewriting

Choose an Experience

Sifting Through Memories   Of course you cannot relate every meaningful experience of your life in the space of this essay—you will have to pick just one. Deciding upon an experience to write about may be a challenge at first, especially if you think your range of experiences has been limited by age or circumstances. Remember that your experience need not be a "life-or-death" one. Any experience, as long as it is significant to you, is a possibility. Journals or diaries are excellent places to look for topics. If you do not keep a journal, try the following idea-generating activities.

TIP   Remember to pick an event that is not too private to share. We all have experiences that should be explored only within the pages of our journals or diaries.

- **Fill in the blanks.** Jot down responses that complete such statements as *If only I had known . . .* or *I learned more about . . . that day than ever before* or *I never felt prouder than when . . .* or *Somehow I felt different after. . . .*

- **Go to a movie.** With other students, watch a video or movie about a youthful character whose "coming-of-age" experiences might prompt you to think about similar experiences of your own. Discuss your ideas collaboratively.

- **Listen to music.** Listen to your favorite song and write down the memories the song's lyrics or music suggest.

- **Follow a road map.** Draw a road map of your life from birth to the present. Mark several experiences as the signposts along your journey.

TIP If you think your experience is too trivial to write about, think again about the everyday experiences related in autobiographical narratives you have read. Henry David Thoreau, for example, discovered something about the importance of work as he hoed a row of beans. He later used that ordinary experience in some extraordinary writing. What you *think* about your experience—and how the experience has changed you—is more important than the events themselves.

After you have generated some possible topics for your essay, narrow your list by asking yourself the following questions:

- Which experience do I remember vividly?
- Which one feels important?
- Which experience has made me who I am?
- Which one shows the "real me"?

Then, look over your remaining possibilities and choose the one you would most like to explore in writing.

Consider Your Purpose and Audience

KEY CONCEPT

Knowing You, Knowing Me Your primary purpose for writing an autobiographical narrative is to express and explore your thoughts and feelings. Another important purpose is to share your experience and its meaning with others.

Who, then, is your **audience?** Of course, the first audience of your autobiographical incident is yourself. As you write, you may discover things about yourself you may not have realized before. What you know or discover about yourself, however, may not be so obvious to your readers. As you consider your wider audience, you must anticipate their questions and find ways to communicate the significance of your experience. Ask yourself the following questions.

- **What and how much background information do readers need in order to understand my experience?** Establish a context for your experience by inserting background information within your narration. If you were writing about running for the student council, for example, you might explain the campaign process and even mention that you lost in last year's election. This information would clarify your narrative and communicate its importance to your readers.

- **How can I make readers truly participate in my experience?** Illustrate the most dramatic or significant moments of your experience. *Show* the details of the events, rather than *tell* about them. Instead of talking about the hard-nosed football coach, for example, describe how he barks orders from the sidelines. Use specific names of people, places, and objects to show readers that your experience is real.

- **How can I share with readers how my experience felt and what it means?** Include your thoughts and feelings. If your hair stood on end or you felt a lump in your throat, tell your readers so. Also, point out the significance of your experience with specific comments about its meaning. If you wish, make a comment about human experience in general.

TIP An autobiographical narrative is usually an informal piece of writing, so its **tone**—the feeling the writer's words express—should be informal as well. Write in the first person (using the personal pronouns *I, my, me*) and use everyday vocabulary and sentence structure to create a natural, conversational **voice.**

Recall and Record the Details

Let Me Make This Perfectly Clear   Now that you have focused on an experience and thought about your audience and purpose, gather the **details** that will bring your experience to life. **Events** are the large details, specific points within an autobiographical narrative that, each in turn, answer the question *What happened next?* You might think of them as the backbone of the essay. **Narrative and descriptive details provide a more detailed picture: they flesh out the sequence of the events.**

KEY CONCEPT

Narrative Details	- tell about **specific events** and **actions** - suggest or reveal **thoughts** and **feelings** - often include **dialogue,** or the exact words of a conversation
Descriptive Details	- use **sensory language**—that is, language that appeals to the five senses (sight, hearing, smell, taste, and touch) - focus on **factual** and **spatial details** of places, objects, and people

Reference Note

For more help with **narrative** and **descriptive details,** see page 25.

Recall the Details   If you need help recalling the events and details of your experience, use your memory to "travel back in time." To take yourself back, try the following strategies:

- **Think about it.** Close your eyes and visualize the scene, replaying the events in your mind.
- **Talk about it.** Ask the others who shared your experience what they remember.
- **Return to it.** If possible, return to the place where the experience happened, and jot down a detailed description.
- **Dream about it.** Sort through your collections—scrapbooks, photographs, old ribbons, medals, songs, yearbooks.

Is All This Really Necessary?   One way to evaluate your details—to identify which are necessary and which are unimportant to your autobiographical narrative—is to ask yourself if a detail

- makes the experience clear
- adds necessary background information
- makes the experience seem more real
- clarifies the experience's overall meaning
- adds insight to your experience

If your details do not do any of these things, they probably are not necessary.

Record the Details   The following chart shows how one writer combined some of the events and details she recalled about a spring break experience. Notice that the events are listed in chronological order and that thoughts and feelings are listed beside the other narrative and descriptive details.

Events in the Experience	Narrative and Descriptive Details	Thoughts and Feelings About Events
1. Secretary at retirement home briefs me on my volunteer job	"Get Pierre out of his cage." Pierre, the pet parrot, will help me start conversations. Pierre: blue, green, yellow, orange feathers; wicked black eyes; messy; bad-tempered; a great favorite of the residents. He squawks.	Initial surprise for such an unusual request. I think Pierre is the most disgusting bird I've ever seen. I sigh at how long the week is going to feel. I think things like this are always happening to me.

| 2. Meet Mrs. Anderson, a retired schoolteacher, on the very first day | Curly hair, eyes crinkled with age, great laugh, warm and friendly; has had a car wreck like mine, but paid a fine instead of doing volunteer service with an awful parrot. | "I know just how you feel," she says. I really like her. Thinking of my friends at the beach—hot, sunburned; surprised by new friend; relieved it hasn't been such a bad week. |
| 3. After school is out for the summer, I return to the retirement home. | Red stars, blue streamers, huge straw hat on Mrs. Anderson's door. "Come in, Amy." She remembers me. | Anxious, guilty that I haven't had time to visit; nervous because I really like her; learned friendship from her, despite our differences. |

YOUR TURN 4 — Choosing an Experience and Recalling the Details

If you have not settled on a topic so far, work through the steps on page 29 and choose an experience for your essay. Remember to

- think about your purpose and audience
- recall and record the details of your experience. You might use a chart like the preceding student example.

Arrange the Details

Shuffling the Deck Most narratives, including autobiographical narratives, use **logical progression;** that is, they move forward in **chronological,** or time, **order** from the first event until the last. Many good writers, however, arrange the parts of their narrative sequence to build tension or to create interest in one particular part of the experience. Often, in order to heighten interest, writers begin with a particularly dramatic event—a moment of decision, for example—and then relate events leading up to it. Other times—when describing a place or person, for example—writers may arrange details **spatially** or in **order of importance.** Flashbacks (jumps back in time), flash-forwards (jumps forward in time), extended descriptions, and passages of reflection are common ways to interrupt straight chronological sequence. Look at the chart on the next page to see how one writer arranged the narrative events and details of her spring break experience to create a more interesting narrative sequence.

Reference Note

For more information about **chronological order, spatial order,** and **order of importance,** see page 461.

| Begin with most recent visit to retirement center. Add thoughts and feelings. | → | Flashback to first day at retirement center last fall. Give background of why I had to be there. | → | Event 1: Secretary asks me to sign in and get the parrot, Pierre. Add dialogue about Pierre. | → | Event 2: Meet Mrs. Anderson, describe her, tell of our conversation about tickets and car wrecks. | → | Thoughts and feelings about entire spring break experience. Explain why it was valuable. |

TIP Sometimes, simply arranging details is not enough to create an interesting and well-paced narrative. Often, you will have to cut out less important sections altogether.

Reflect upon Meaning

The Heart of the Matter   When you reflect upon the ways your experience has affected you, you take the long view. Recalling details has already given you the short view: an up-close examination of what happened and of the people, places, and objects that were part of the experience. Now, step back and think about what it all means.

In taking the longer view of your experience, you consider what you have learned about yourself as you look back upon a younger you. Ask yourself the following questions.

- What have I learned about myself from this experience?
- What have I learned about others from this experience?
- How did the experience cause me to change or to think differently about things?
- How have my goals changed because of this experience?
- What feelings does this experience raise in me?

TIP   Remember: A reflection upon meaning is not just tacked onto your narrative at the end. Reflecting upon meaning helps shape your entire essay. When you sit down to write a first draft of your essay, always keep the larger meaning of your experience in mind.

YOUR TURN 5   **Arranging Your Details and Reflecting on Your Experience**

Before you begin writing a first draft, plan how you will arrange the details of your experience and jot down some notes about the meaning the experience has for you.

Using Dialogue

We love to hear each other speak and why not? Talking is a uniquely human activity. In an autobiographical narrative, readers "hear" people talk through written **dialogue**—the exact words speakers have used during the events. Used well, dialogue makes an autobiographical experience seem more *real.* Consider the following examples. The first sentence is okay, but boring. The second sentence engages readers in the writer's experience more directly.

Flat   When I knocked on her door, Mrs. Anderson called out for me to come in and bring my parrot with me.

Vivid   "Mrs. Anderson, are you in there?" I asked softly.

"Come in, Amy," called out Mrs. Anderson, in answer to my knock on her door. "I was hoping you would bring that pesky parrot by to talk to me today."

You may use dialogue at any place in your narrative.

- At the beginning, dialogue immediately engages the reader's attention.
- Inserted in the middle, dialogue breaks up long sequences of events.
- Used carefully to close an essay, dialogue can make a dramatic impact or leave your reader with a final message.

To punctuate dialogue in your autobiographical incident, use quotation marks around the exact words of your speakers. You should also indicate clearly who the speaker is and start a new paragraph with every new speaker when two or more people are exchanging dialogue. Remember that dialogue tags (*he said, Juan shouted, Monique muttered*) add meaning, too—they tell your readers *how* the words are spoken. (For more information on **punctuating dialogue,** see page 818.)

PRACTICE

Try to transform the following bland sentences into lively dialogue. Rewrite the sentences so that two people speak to one another, and remember to identify the separate speakers. Be creative in suggesting dialogue tags. (Note: When a dialogue tag interrupts a sentence, the first word after the tag usually is not capitalized. Example: *"Oh no," I groaned, "not another ticket."*)

1. When I called my mother to tell her I had had a wreck, she told me that she was very upset.

2. The police officer asked to see my driver's license and my insurance card, but I said I couldn't find them at the moment.

3. After the courtroom clerk called out my name, I answered that I was present.

4. The judge asked me to step to the front of the courtroom and stand there while he questioned me about my wreck. I politely told him that I would.

5. I telephoned the secretary at the retirement center and asked permission to work there as a community service volunteer during my spring break from school. She told me that they had a job for me.

The Autobiographical Narrative

Framework	**Directions and Explanations**

Introduction
- Grab your reader's attention.
- Provide background information.
- Include possible hint at meaning.

Begin with a dramatic piece of dialogue This kind of opening arouses immediate interest.

Include background information early Background information helps your readers better understand the importance of your experience.

Hint at the meaning of your experience An early hint prepares your readers for your final reflections.

Body
- Write about your first event (including details).
- Continue with event two, and so on, varying your sequence.

Add narrative and descriptive details Such details make each of the events more vivid.

Vary your sequence of events Flashbacks, flash-forwards, and descriptive passages often add variety or dramatic tension to a strict chronology.

Gradually reveal more and more of the experience's significance Providing clues about the experience's larger meaning gives your essay coherence.

Conclusion
- Reveal the final outcome.
- State meaning of experience.
- Draw your paper to a close.

State what happened as a result of your experience Readers look for a conclusion.

Reflect upon your experience Show your readers that you recognize the meaning of your experience.

Use a final quotation or statement about human experience in general A dramatic or thoughtful end spells out the connection between your experience and the lives of your readers.

 Writing a First Draft

Using the framework above, write the first draft of your autobiographical narrative. Read the Directions and Explanations section of the chart for additional help. You might also read the Writer's Model on the next page to see an essay that follows this framework.

A Writer's Model

The following short essay, which is a final draft, closely follows the framework on the previous page.

A Spring Break Surprise

"Are you in there, Mrs. Anderson?" I called, after knocking on her open door at the Summerdale Retirement Center. The staff at the center had decorated the hallways for the Fourth of July. On Mrs. Anderson's door hung an enormous white straw hat, its brim wrapped with shiny red and blue strings of stars, its crown trailing red, white, and blue streamers down to below the door handle. I let the streamers run through my fingers as I remembered how much I had learned from the person inside the room. I had missed her since the week I had spent with her in the spring.

"Why, Amy!" she laughed. "Is that you again, coming back to see me? I thought I smelled your perfume. And I was sure I heard that pesky parrot squawk."

Even though it was midsummer, Mrs. Anderson still remembered me. A week at the retirement center had not been my first choice of recreation for my spring break. I would have preferred to be at the beach with my Long High School friends, working on an early tan and meeting other people my age. Unfortunately, however, I had gotten a traffic ticket the previous fall for failure to yield right of way. In my court appearance, the judge had assigned me twelve hours of community service to be completed within a four-month period instead of a hefty fine. Of course my schoolwork had kept me so busy that my only time to fulfill his requirement was during my spring break. I was not at all happy with the prospects for the week's entertainment.

The day I arrived at the center, the secretary said, "Sign our volunteer register first. Then, get Pierre out of his cage."

"Pierre?" I asked. "What's a Pierre?"

Pierre, I found out, was the pet parrot kept in a cage by the front office. He had beautiful blue and green feathers on his back, golden feet, yellow breast feathers with streaks of orange, and a wicked looking black eye. He talked. He also nipped my ear, cracked sunflower seeds into my shirt pocket, dug his claws into my shoulder, and thoroughly made a nuisance of himself. The residents, however, loved him. My volunteer job, the secretary told me, was to carry this cranky, unpleasant bird on my shoulder around the halls, stopping to talk to residents who were

(continued)

Attention-grabbing quotation and event one

Description

Hint at meaning

Dialogue

Background

Dialogue and event one of flashback

Description

(continued)

outside their rooms or in the recreation areas. All I could think was "This is going to be a long week."

On that first day, however, I also met Mrs. Amelia Anderson. She had curly hair, smooth skin, and eyes crinkled with age. Even though she sat in a wheelchair most of the time because of her chronic back trouble, she had the most pleasant personality and sweetest smile of anyone there. She reminded me of my grandmother who had died the preceding year. When I told her why I was there at the center, she clucked her tongue in sympathy. "I know just how you feel," she said.

It seems that Mrs. Anderson had had an experience similar to mine. She had also had a wreck in a blinding rainstorm, at an impossible-to-see-clearly intersection, in 5:00 P.M. traffic. The police officer had also given her a ticket, even though he just as fairly could have given it to anybody else involved. We began to laugh over our similar experiences, especially since she told me that, as an adult, she had been given no choice but to pay the hefty fine. I should feel lucky, she said, because all I had to do was dodge Pierre's flapping feathers. From that moment on, we became friends. We really did not even need Pierre to start our conversations. Every day we shared stories about our families. She was interested in my friends and schoolwork. I became interested in her life as a former high school teacher.

When the week was up, I returned to my life as a student, listening to my friends' tales of fishing at the beach, sunburn, sandy clothes, and seafood suppers. My friends were full of excitement at the new people they had met, who had promised to write and call. I thought of Mrs. Anderson, sitting in her wheelchair, waiting for someone to bring Pierre by to talk, waiting for the day when the girl who got a ticket returned to tell her what she had learned: that vacations do not always turn out the way a high school student might think. Sometimes you get a spring break surprise—a new friend.

Pesky Pierre!

A Student's Model

Notice the dramatic opener, the use of flashback, and the author's thoughts and feelings in the following autobiographical narrative written by Joseph T. O'Connor. This essay originally appeared in *Newsweek* when O'Connor was a student at Lee High School in Staunton, Virginia.

A View from Mount Ritter

"I hate this," I thought. We were on our way to the top of Mount Ritter in northeastern California. You would think everyone, near one of the tallest ridges in the Sierra Nevadas, would be in high spirits. But on this particular day the rain fell in torrents. Quarter-size hailstones pelted our protective helmets as thunder echoed through the canyons.

Thoughts and feelings

Description

It was the second week of my mountain expedition in California. The first week there had not been a cloud in the sky, but on Tuesday of week two, a dark cover crept in from the west, painting the sunlit, blue sky black. The storm came in so fast we didn't even notice it until our shadows suddenly disappeared.

Background

"Here it comes," our guide warned. As if God himself had given the order, the heavens opened, just a crack. Huge drops began falling but abruptly stopped, as if to say, "You know what's coming; here's a taste." As we began searching for shelter, a bolt of lightning ripped open the blackish clouds overhead and in unison thunder cracked, leaving everyone's ears ringing. We were in the midst of a huge July thunderstorm. Ethan, our guide, had said that during the summer in the high Sierras it might rain twice, but when it does, it's best not to be there. Suddenly lightning struck a tree not twenty feet from where I was standing.

Event one

"Lightning positions!" Ethan yelled frantically. A little too frantically for my taste. I thought he was used to this kind of thing. As scared as I was, squatting in a giant puddle of water and hailstones, with forks of lightning bouncing off the canyon walls around me, I couldn't help chuckling to myself at the sight of Ethan's dinner-plate-size eyeballs as he panicked like an amateur. Soon after the lightning died down some, we hiked to the shelter of nearby redwoods to put on rain gear. While we prayed for the rain to subside, I watched the stream we stood beside

Description

Event two

(continued)

(continued)

grow into a raging, white-water river. Another expeditioner, Mike, and I were under a full redwood donning our not-so-waterproof equipment when I realized we were standing on a small island.

Dialogue

"Mike! Let's go!" I yelled, my exclamation nearly drowned out by the roar of water surrounding us and another roll of thunder.

"I'm way ahead o' ya!" he screamed in his thick New York accent, and his goofy smile broke through the torrents. "Ya ready?"

"Yeah!" I yelled back, and jumped from our island into the knee-deep water. He followed as we slopped through the storm, losing our footing every few feet.

Event three

Narrative sequence time signals are highlighted

The unforgiving downpour lasted all day and into the night as we stumbled down the rocky cliffs seeking the driest place to set up camp. It was dusk before we found a small clearing in a pine forest, and began what was to be the worst night of my life. We constructed our tents in the dark, fumbling with the ropes with our frozen hands and finishing just as a stiffness like rigor mortis set in. We lay awake all night, shivering in our wet sleeping bags while rain poured down and a small stream made its way through our tent.

Background

It's funny how these memories keep coming back to me as if it was just yesterday. All this happened last summer, after my junior year in high school. . . .

Reflection on meaning

The wonder of all I'd experienced made me think seriously about what comes next. "Life after high school," I said to myself. "Uh-oh." What had I been doing for the last three years? I was so caught up in defying the advice of my parents and teachers to study and play by the rules that I hadn't considered the effects my actions would have on me. . . .

Thoughts and feelings

Thanks to that morning's conversion, I am a new person. Now, I know I'll have to work hard. The sun streaming over the eastern Sierras wiped out the dark clouds that blurred my vision. Jonathan Harker in Bram Stoker's *Dracula* must have felt exactly the same way when he wrote in his journal: "No man knows 'till he has suffered from the night how sweet and how dear to his heart and eye the morning can be."

Quotation

Revising

Evaluate and Revise

Did I Say That? To polish your writing, read through your paper twice. The first time, read for content and organization, following the chart below. Read the second time to revise for style, according to the guidelines on page 42. Get the most from both readings by **collaborating** or having a **writing conference** with a classmate.

☞ **First Reading: Content and Organization** Use the following chart to help readers understand your meaning. Ask yourself the questions in the left-hand column. Then, use the middle column for practical tips. To revise your paper, use the suggestions in the right-hand column.

Autobiographical Narrative: Content and Organization Guidelines for Peer and Self-Evaluation

Evaluation Questions	▶ Tips	▶ Revision Techniques
❶ Does the introduction capture the reader's attention and provide background? Is there a hint about meaning?	▶ **Bracket** any attention getter and background sentences. **Underline** the sentences that hint at the meaning of the experience. If you do not bracket or underline any sentences, revise.	▶ **Add** dialogue or a quotation as a first sentence. **Add** details that help explain events, people, and places. **Add** a hint of the meaning of the experience.
❷ Are events, people, and places vividly portrayed?	▶ **Circle** the sentences that help readers experience the events, people, and places. If you do not circle any, revise.	▶ **Add** or **elaborate** on narrative details of action and speech and descriptive details appealing to the five senses.
❸ Are the events in an order that makes sense?	▶ **Place a check mark** over words signaling narrative chronology—dates, times, and transitional words and phrases. Then, using these words, **number** each event. If you do not see any signal words or the events are not in logical order, revise.	▶ **Rearrange** events to make your chronology clear. **Rearrange** descriptive details in spatial order and order of importance. **Add** transitional words or phrases, if necessary.
❹ Does each event add to the meaning of the autobiographical narrative?	▶ **Draw a wavy line** under each event. **Bracket** sentences that reveal your thoughts and feelings about each event. If some events do not help to develop your meaning, or your thoughts and feelings are not presented, revise.	▶ **Delete** unnecessary events and details that do not contribute to your meaning. **Elaborate** upon events that point to your meaning by providing your thoughts and feelings.
❺ Does the last paragraph make the meaning of the experience clear?	▶ **Circle** the sentences that state the meaning of your experience. If you do not see any, revise.	▶ **Add** details that illustrate meaning or a general statement about the larger significance of your experience.

ONE WRITER'S REVISIONS Here's how one writer used the content and organization guidelines to revise some sentences from the Writer's Model on page 37. Study the revisions and answer the questions that follow.

add dialogue

> The day I arrived at the center, the secretary ~~told me to~~ said, "sign ~~the~~ our volunteer register first then, get Pierre out of his cage."
> "Pierre?" I asked. "What's a Pierre?" Pierre, I found out,
> ~~I wondered what kind of animal Pierre was, He was a parrot.~~
> was the pet parrot kept in a cage by the front office.

add narrative details

PEER REVIEW

Ask a classmate to read your paper and to answer the following questions.

1. What parts would you like the writer to describe more fully?

2. After reading the essay, did you understand what the writer's experience meant to him or her? Why or why not?

Analyzing the Revision Process

1. Why do you think the writer makes the revisions above?
2. What effect do the changes have on the paragraph?

YOUR TURN 7 **Focusing on Content and Organization**

Revise the content and organization of your autobiographical narrative using the guidelines in the chart and in the example revisions.

COMPUTER TIP

Use a computer's cut and paste features to rearrange the events in your narrative sequence.

> **Second Reading: Style** In your first reading, you thought about the content of your essay and how you organized your experience's events and details. In the second reading, you will look at how you have expressed your experience and its meaning—you will look at your style. In autobiographical narratives, it is a common mistake to summarize an experience with abstract descriptions of events, rather than to use descriptive details that specifically name and situate people, places, and objects. It is also very common to rush through without including enough details that appeal to the senses. Use the following style guideline to help you make your descriptions more vivid and less abstract.

Style Guideline

Evaluation Question	▶ Tip	▶ Revision Technique
Are there places where details are too general or dull?	▶ **Bracket** descriptions of people, places, and things. Revise if these descriptions are not specific enough to let a reader see the details of the scene.	▶ **Elaborate** on given details by including specific names or sensory language.

Vivid Details

Sometimes writing seems dull and vague because the descriptions present a fuzzy, gray picture of what is happening. Readers will not want to keep reading about you if your word choices do not spark their imagination. **Sensory language** enlivens writing with images of sight, sound, smell, taste, and textures. **Specific names** allow readers to visualize the scene more precisely.

ONE WRITER'S REVISIONS Here is how the writer of the Writer's Model on page 37 used the guidelines above to make her descriptive details more vivid.

BEFORE REVISION

The [staff] at the [center] had decorated [the hallways] for

[the holiday]. On Mrs. Anderson's [door] hung [red, white,

and blue decorations].

people, places, and objects bracketed

AFTER REVISION

The staff at the center had decorated the hallways for the Fourth of July. On Mrs. Anderson's door hung an enormous white straw hat, its brim wrapped with shiny red and blue strings of stars, its crown trailing red, white, and blue streamers down to below the door handle.

add specific name

add sensory language

Analyzing the Revision Process

1. To what senses do the new sensory details appeal? Are there other ways the writer might have appealed to the senses here?

2. What effect do the writer's revisions have on the sentence?

COMPUTER TIP

You can use a computer program's thesaurus for suggestions to replace flat words.

YOUR TURN 8 Focusing on Vivid Details

Revise the style of your autobiographical narrative, using the guideline and the sample revisions as a model.

Add Visuals to Your Narrative   Adding pictures or photographs to your autobiographical narrative can often make your experience seem more *real.* Whether they are your own photographs or hand-drawn illustrations or maps, visual images can clarify your narrative, set a scene, or suggest a mood. Below are some tips to help you choose images for your essay.

- **Choose the right you.** If your essay describes an experience you had when you were five, do not include a photo of you at sixteen. Your readers will want to see how you looked back *then.*

- **Select a point of view.** The angle from which you represent your subject can communicate how you feel about it almost as well as words can. For example, close-up shots often indicate a sympathetic feeling and faraway shots indicate a more detached point of view. If you are writing about an experience when you were seven years old and facing your neighbor's Rottweiler, you might communicate your fear by drawing the dog as if you were looking *up* at its stocky frame or by focusing on its huge teeth.

- **Watch for unintentional contradictions in point of view and placement.** If you want to illustrate what you saw from the top of a mountain, you could include a panoramic image of the landscape below, not a photo looking *up* at the mountain. Likewise, if you want to include a photo of your five brothers, it should align next to the section about them, and not near the section in which you describe your favorite teacher, Mrs. Martinez.

- **If necessary, use captions.** Captions can provide context or explanation for things—specific places, people, dates, and times—that *are* represented in your photos but *are not* specifically explained in your essay. For example, if you were writing about your travels to Yellowstone National Park, you might illustrate your chance encounter with a bear by inserting the following photographs and captions.

Bear at Rest

Bear at Attention

Publishing

Proofread Your Essay

Checkmate or "Check, Mate"   Proofread your paper—individually or collaboratively—checking for grammar, punctuation, and spelling errors. In particular, make sure you have avoided run-on sentences. Rushing from one sentence to the next without correct punctuation or capitalization may confuse your readers.

Reference Note

For more about **run-on sentences,** see page 875.

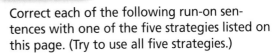

Avoiding Run-on Sentences

Run-on sentences, often written when the writer is hurriedly composing a draft or stretching to combine sentences, destroy a clear sequence. For readers, run-on sentences create confusion and make your prose muddy.

There are two kinds of run-on sentences: the **fused sentence,** which has no punctuation at all between two or more sentences, and the **comma splice,** which contains just a comma between two or more complete sentences.

Examples:
Fused Sentence: From that moment on, we became friends we really did not even need Pierre to start our conversations.

Comma Splice: From that moment on, we became friends, we really did not even need Pierre to start our conversations.

To correct run-ons, try one of these strategies:

- **Make two sentences:** From that moment on, we became friends**. We** really did not even need Pierre to start our conversations.

- **Use a comma and a coordinating conjunction:** From that moment on, we became friends**, and** we really did not even need Pierre to start our conversations.

- **Use a semicolon:** From that moment on, we became friends**;** we really did not even need Pierre to start our conversations.

- **Use a semicolon and a conjunctive adverb:** From that moment on, we became friends**; therefore,** we really did not even need Pierre to start our conversations.

- **Change one of the independent clauses to a subordinate clause. After we became friends,** we really did not even need Pierre to start our conversations.

PRACTICE

Correct each of the following run-on sentences with one of the five strategies listed on this page. (Try to use all five strategies.)

1. The best day of my life was the day I got my dog, Duke, he was the biggest, tallest, brownest Great Dane in the store.

2. Because I ran cross-country for my high school, my day began early Duke was right beside me on the streets, jogging away.

3. One early rainy morning, the traffic was particularly heavy, the cars came around a sharp curve too fast for the road conditions.

4. Duke always jogged on my right-hand side as if he needed to protect me this morning he, in fact, did.

5. Duke suddenly dragged me onto the curb away from the swerving car, Duke had saved my life.

TIP If you have not already settled on a title, choose one before you finish your essay. What is your narrative's most memorable phrase? Often, it can be used as a title. Remember, your title should be something that reflects your essay's tone and meaning.

Publish Your Essay

Let Me Tell You All About It   Here are a few ways you might share your autobiographical narrative with an audience:

- If other people were involved in the experience, send a copy of your essay to them.
- Submit your essay to your high school's literary magazine.
- If one of your local radio stations broadcasts a program devoted to listeners' essays, send in your essay.
- With a group of classmates, compile an anthology of essays and donate it to an English class a grade or two below your own.
- Stage a group reading at your school or at your community library. Invite family and friends to come.
- Publish your essay on your school's Web site as an example of autobiographical writing.

Reflect on Your Essay

PORTFOLIO

If I Had It to Do All Over Again   Write a short response to each of the following questions. Keep your answers in your portfolio, along with the final version of your essay.

- How did you choose an experience for your essay? Why was the experience you finally chose the best one?
- Did writing about your experience change your thoughts and feelings about the experience itself? How?
- What would you do differently if you were to write again about this experience—or about another personal experience? Why?

YOUR TURN 9 **Proofreading, Publishing, and Reflecting on Your Essay**

Review each of the proofreading, grammar, publishing, and reflecting steps in this section. Before you turn in your essay,

- be sure to proofread
- consider your publishing options
- reflect upon your essay by answering the questions asked above

Life

Writing a Narrative for an Application

Will you ever have an occasion, outside of the classroom or the pages of your diary, to write an autobiographical narrative? Yes. You will often use autobiographical writing in practical, real-world situations when you submit application forms for colleges, scholarships, internships, trade schools, art institutes, or employment. You may be asked to attach an autobiographical narrative to your résumé or to an application form in order to provide a more complete view of who you are or how your experiences have shaped your ambitions. Many of these narratives are written in response to a writing prompt, such as

■ *What experience have you had that would show your ability to contribute to our com-*

pany's (university's) commitment to excellence? or

■ *Write about a special experience that reveals your character.*

To write an autobiographical narrative for an application, follow the same steps in the composition that you used in the Writing Workshop: Do some brainstorming and planning; then, draft your essay, revise it, and proofread. Remember to consider your purpose to tailor your autobiographical narrative to your specific audience. The following chart will give you additional tips.

Tips for Writing a Narrative for an Application
Underline key words in the writing prompt or question. Noting important words and then repeating them in your essay shows readers that you are clearly responding to the question being asked.
Answer *only* the questions asked. Stay focused on the question without launching into a narration of your entire life. Include all relevant material, but avoid trying to prove your encyclopedic knowledge.
Use your own voice. Choose a respectful but natural voice. To make a good impression, avoid slang and colloquialisms. Also avoid overly formal, stilted language.
Choose a genuine experience. Write a narrative about an experience that has strongly affected you. Prewriting techniques such as freewriting may help you to come up with a suitable experience to use as the topic of your writing. Avoid manufacturing an experience in an attempt to create a more favorable impression on your readers—fake experiences will not ring true with your readers.
Create an interesting angle. Consider how you can approach a topic in a way that is different from the way your peers will approach their responses to the topic. The angle you choose may reveal your special qualities—the things that make you *you*.
Begin with an anecdote. Pick an opener that will intrigue readers immediately. Avoid beginning your essay with such an overworked expression as "I have always wanted to be a. . . ."

(continued)

(continued)

Limit your response to the required length. Edit your writing until you meet the required length. Avoid submitting a twelve-page essay, or a half-page essay, when the writing prompt asked for two pages. The best responses are those that use the space limits requested in the directions.

Avoid personal biases. Walk a fine line here. Communicate your own thoughts and feelings, but eliminate any attempts to persuade your readers to adopt your feelings about religion, politics, or other areas of debate.

Proofread. Correct any mistakes in grammar and spelling before you draft your final copy. You might even ask a teacher, parent, or friend to proofread your composition a second time. Then, submit a clean essay, not one that has stains or handwritten corrections.

In the chart below, one student has sketched out a plan for a narrative in response to the writing prompt *Explain why you would make a trustworthy and reliable summer intern at Good Credit Bank.* The student chose to narrate the experience of finding a billfold and returning it to its owner because the incident would reveal the student's honesty in dealing with another person's valuables.

Key Words	Experience	Interesting Angle	Beginning Anecdote
trustworthy, reliable	returning student's billfold I found in cafeteria	the trouble I had in locating the new student (it took one week)—ironic twist that his locker was ten down from mine	begin with last event in narrative: new student's relief and surprise at having billfold returned

YOUR TURN 10 Writing a Narrative for an Application

Use a similar chart to plan your own narrative for an application question. To prepare, you might pool sample application questions from job, internship, and college applications that you and your classmates have collected. You might ask your high school counselor or teachers for their suggestions about typical application questions. You may also make up some questions of your own—for example, *What in your past experience has prepared you for the responsibilities of job X?* Then, write a one-page response to the question that most appeals to you.

Creating an Oral History

Talk   Listen

What was it like to live through the Depression? How did people entertain themselves before television? If you have ever listened to older relatives or friends talking about things like this, you have heard **oral history.** Together, these kinds of stories—ordinary people narrating ordinary events in their lives—create social history, a kind of history based on peoples' private lives rather than on a nation's political and military events or leaders. You may have read or heard about some of the many oral history collections already in print. The Ellis Island Project, for example, has collected hundreds of personal accounts from people who immigrated to the United States in the early twentieth century.

No matter whose stories they are, individual life stories, collected and written down by someone else, offer insight into the question *What was it like to live back when. . . ?* In this workshop, you will add your own contribution to history by writing an oral history.

WHAT'S AHEAD?

In creating an oral history, you will learn to
- interview your subject
- transcribe your material
- edit your information into a focused presentation
- write an introduction

Who Has a Story to Tell?

You can find an interesting person to interview by asking yourself questions. For example, *Who were the people who won all the trophies in my high school display case and where are they now? What could my friend Satori's grandmother tell me about her early life in Japan? What would my elderly neighbor tell me about my neighborhood fifty years ago?* In choosing a subject, think about what you want to learn from him or her.

Preparing for the Interview

Educate Yourself   Before you interview your subject, read some background material—books, magazines, and newspaper articles—to prepare questions for the interview. You are not trying to become an expert on, say, World War II or the history of cattle ranching, but you do want to have some informed questions to ask your subject.

TIP If you plan to ask complicated or especially focused questions, send a copy of your interview questions to the subject before the scheduled interview.

Compose Possible Questions   Draft a set of questions for your interview, but feel free to ask others that occur to you in your conversation. Look at the following types of interview questions.

Types of Questions	Examples
Fact questions ask for specific answers.	▪ *When and where did you serve in the navy?* ▪ *What was your rank when you entered?*
Open questions have no set answer, and may inspire your subject to talk freely.	▪ *What were you doing when you were drafted?* ▪ *What kinds of duties did you have?*
Follow-up questions request more information when an earlier answer doesn't completely explain something.	▪ *What other maneuvers did you perform that might be considered dangerous?* ▪ *I didn't understand what you meant by _____. Could you explain further?*

Reference Note

For more information on **conducting an interview,** see page 986.

Conducting the Interview

However you conduct your interview—in person, over the telephone, or via e-mail—the following tips will be helpful:

▪ Set up a specific time and date at your subject's convenience.

▪ Ask permission to record your subject on audiotape or videotape.

▪ For the personal and telephone interview, take notes. Listen actively, and be alert to such signal words as *next, then,* and *after.*

▪ Ask your subject to comment upon the short- and long-term meaning of the experience.

▪ When the interview has ended, review your notes as soon as possible and summarize your impressions of the material covered.

▪ Shortly after the interview, write a thank-you letter. Later, when you have polished the oral history, send a copy to your subject, too.

TIP Active listening may involve one or all of the following types: *appreciative* (listening for enjoyment), *empathetic* (listening for the speaker's feelings), and *reflective* (listening for connections to your own experience). For more on the types of listening, see page 991.

    To get the most out of your interview, practice being an **active listener,** not a passive one. Think as you listen, look for meaning in what you are hearing, and be ready to respond to your interviewee. Use the following techniques to help you with your active-listening skills:

▪ **Reflect as you listen.** Compare what you are hearing with your own experience, and use your knowledge to understand the speaker better.

▪ **Take notes.** You do not have to write down every single word, but listen for important points that you may use to ask follow-up questions. Focus on the key points of the speaker.

- **Provide feedback.** Use your body language, such as eye contact and nods of your head, to let your interviewee know you are understanding. Ask questions, but do not interrupt the flow of your interviewee's thoughts. Wait courteously until a natural pause occurs in the conversation.

Preparing and Editing a Transcript

Crafting an oral history requires two steps: *transcribing* and *editing*. A **transcript** is a written document of the exact words your subject has used. It is the raw material you will shape into the final, edited piece.

Transcribing   Follow these procedures for creating a transcript:

- Listen to the audiotape or videotape, writing down the exact words of the subject.
- Omit the subject's stammers or filler words, such as *uh* or *hmmm*, unless you think they contribute to the flavor of the speech.
- Include, in brackets, any unspoken responses such as subject's laughter or gestures.

An interview transcript may look like this.

Interviewer's Question:	What was Broadmoor High School like when you arrived as its first football coach?
Coach "Wow" Wowjohwiscz's Answer:	When I came to Broadmoor in 1950, the school had just been built, but the athletic department was not finished. We had no offices, no equipment rooms, no gym, no bleachers, no football field, no yard lines, no goal posts, no nothing. And we were supposed to play our first game two weeks after school started. [Laughter.] It was a great start for a season.

Editing   Preparing an oral history also involves shaping, while not distorting, your subject's story. Follow these steps to organize and edit your interview transcript or e-mail printout.

Narrow your focus. Think back over your interview. What comments stand out as representative of your subject or the events your subject described? Using your impressions and memory as guides, mark those sections that form a unique and coherent portrait of your subject and his or her story.

Choose a style of presentation. Present your interview in one of the following formats:

- **Question and Answer** Identify each speaker (the interviewer and the subject) and begin new paragraphs for each speaker's comments. Remember to use ellipses when you omit parts of your subject's answers in order to focus on more memorable sections. For example:

Interviewer's Question:	When did you begin teaching at Broadmoor High School?
Coach "Wow's" Answer:	I began teaching in 1950, . . . when we didn't even have a school song, much less an athletic program.

- **Summary** Weave together the responses the subject has made into a more traditional paragraph form. Insert explanatory comments within brackets, and use ellipses to note material that has been omitted. For example:

When asked about the early days at Broadmoor High School, the school's first football coach explained, "In 1950, the school had just been built, but the athletic department wasn't finished [on time for the start of school]. . . . And we were supposed to play our first game two weeks after school started."

Making Introductions

Finally, introduce your oral history in a paragraph that includes your subject's background information: name, age, occupation, city, date of interview, and any other important facts. If possible, explain the meaning of the subject's experience both for him or her at the moment, and in the broader view. Provide some context for your readers by explaining how your subject's story reflects the cultural concerns of the past or present.

YOUR TURN 11 **Creating an Oral History**

After reviewing the steps to create an oral history, conduct your own interview. Then, transcribe the interview into print, and shape and introduce the interview for publication.

Choices

Choose one of the following activities to complete.

▶ **LITERATURE**

1. "I am," I said. Mark Twain mastered the art of the autobiographical narrative both in print and on the lecture circuit. Twain's work has been performed in live productions and on audiotape and videotape. Read Twain's autobiographical *Life on the Mississippi*—or read another author's autobiographical narrative—and in a **short essay** compare the printed narrative to its audio or audiovisual version. If the students in your class are reading different autobiographical narratives, compare and contrast these narratives.

▶ **VIEWING AND REPRESENTING**

2. Let Me See That Again. Present your autobiographical narrative without using text. Take original photographs or cut out pictures from magazines to represent the events and arrange them to tell your story visually. When you have finished, exchange **visual narratives** with a classmate. Can you identify each other's experiences and their meanings?

▶ **MEDIA AND TECHNOLOGY**

3. Spin a Webful of Stories. Create a **Web site** for your class's collection of oral histories.

Provide an introduction for the collection and supplement the Web site with photographs. Be sure to receive written permission from your interviewee before placing the story and pictures on the Web site.

▶ **CAREERS**

4. Put Your Experience to Work. Create a **résumé** that includes an autobiographical experience or choose the experience presented in your autobiographical narrative, if appropriate. Discuss with a partner the possible jobs for which your résumé might be useful.

▶ **CROSSING THE CURRICULUM: SCIENCE**

5. How in the World Did *That* Happen? Work with a partner or in small groups. Choose one person to be an interviewer, and one person to be a famous scientist responsible for a major scientific discovery. Research the discovery in the library. Draft a series of questions and answers that will reveal how the scientific discovery occurred and how the scientist—and the world— reacted. **Videotape** the interview for presentation.

PORTFOLIO

TIP For more information on **writing a résumé,** see page 1043.

CHAPTER

2 Defining Concepts

Reading Workshop

Reading an Extended Definition

Writing Workshop

Writing an Extended Definition

Speaking and Listening

Oral Interpretation of a Poem

Viewing and Representing

Comparing and Contrasting Media Coverage of an Event

Extended Definition

Imagine one of these scenarios:

- During a heated argument, a friend demands to know if you really understand the meaning of the word *loyalty*.

- After weeks of back-to-school shopping, you receive a form letter announcing guidelines for what school officials call "appropriate attire."

Sometimes a dictionary definition is all you need to understand or explain a word's meaning. Other words, especially when they stand for complex concepts, may need an extended definition to fully convey their meanings. For instance, a dictionary simply defines "rock" music as "a form of popular music, characterized by a strong and regular rhythm." An extended definition would flesh this definition out, discussing specific characteristics that define rock—perhaps its reliance on electric guitars, its tendency to be played fast and loud, the sometimes brash attitude of its performers, and so on. For people in all walks of life, reading or writing extended definitions is a way of digging deeper into the meanings of words.

> **Informational Text**
>
> Exposition

YOUR TURN 1 — Brainstorming About Extended Definitions

With a classmate, brainstorm a list of terms that are difficult to define. Try to include a mix of abstract words (like *love*) and other terms with specialized or complicated meanings (such as *antivirus software*). After you have listed a dozen words or more, jot down brief explanations of why each term could benefit from an extended definition.

internet connect

go. hrw .com

GO TO: go.hrw.com
KEYWORD: EOLang 11-2

Reading an Extended Definition

Has anyone ever invited you to "meet online"? Have you ever spoken (or typed) a sentence such as "I'll see you in the chat room"? If so, you've had firsthand experience with the potentially mind-bending concept known as *cyberspace*. The article on the next page—"Welcome to Cyberspace: What Is It? Where Is It? And How Do We Get There?"—explores various aspects of this space that isn't really a place. As the article's author provides an extended definition of cyberspace, he considers the ways people use the vast and powerful network of computers that lies "behind" cyberspace.

Preparing to Read

READING SKILL

Main Idea and Details The **main idea** of an essay is the author's most important overall point. In well-written essays, this central point is supported by a variety of **details**—facts, examples, statistics, anecdotes, descriptions, and so on. The following article is constructed around an extended definition of the word *cyberspace*. In an extended-definition essay, the main idea takes the form of a statement that most clearly defines (or sums up) the subject. However, if an essay's main idea is implicit, readers need to add up—and reflect upon—details in the essay to discover the author's implied message. Beginning with the title, try to home in on Philip Elmer-DeWitt's main idea as you read the article. Taking notes on supporting details may help you refine your notion of the main idea.

READING FOCUS

Classifying as a Definition Tool An apple is a fruit, and *The Great Gatsby* is an American novel. Even these simple definitions begin by **classifying** a subject or term as part of a larger category, or class. Once you establish that the term *apple* belongs to a larger grouping, for example, you can begin to understand how an apple differs from, say, a mango. Classifying helps writers and readers define concrete terms such as *sleet,* as well as abstract words such as *embarrassment*. As you read the following article, pay special attention to the way the author classifies *cyberspace*.

What exactly *is* cyberspace? See if you can clarify what people mean when they use this term. As you read, jot down answers to the numbered active-reading questions.

from Time

Welcome to Cyberspace:

What Is It? Where Is It? And How Do We Get There?

by Philip Elmer-DeWitt

It started, as the big ideas in technology often do, with a science-fiction writer. William Gibson, a young expatriate American living in Canada, was wandering past the video arcades on Vancouver's Granville Street in the early 1980s when something about the way the players were hunched over their glowing screens struck him as odd. "I could see in the physical intensity of their postures how rapt the kids were," he says. "It was like a feedback loop, with photons coming off the screens into the kids' eyes, neurons moving through their bodies and electrons moving through the video game. These kids clearly believed in the space the game projected."

That image haunted Gibson. He did not know much about video games or computers—he wrote his breakthrough novel *Neuromancer* (1984) on an ancient manual typewriter—but he knew people who did. And as near as he could tell, everybody who worked much with the machines eventually came to accept, almost as an article of faith, the reality of that imaginary realm. "They develop a belief that there's some kind of actual space behind the screen," he says. "Some place that you can't see but you know is there."

Gibson called that place "cyberspace," and used it as the setting for his early novels and short stories. In his fiction, cyberspace is a computer-generated landscape that characters enter by "jacking in"—sometimes by plugging electrodes directly into sockets implanted in the brain. What they see when they get there is a three-dimensional representation of all the information stored in "every computer in the human system"—great warehouses and skyscrapers of data. He describes it in a key passage in

> **1. What observations led William Gibson to coin the term "cyberspace"? What is cyberspace within Gibson's fiction?**

Neuromancer as a place of "unthinkable complexity," with "lines of light ranged in the nonspace of the mind, clusters and constellations of data. Like city lights, receding. . . ."

In the years since, there have been other names given to that shadowy space where our computer data reside: the Net, the Web, the Cloud, the Matrix, the Metaverse, the Datasphere, the Electronic Frontier, the information superhighway. But Gibson's coinage may prove the most enduring. By 1989, it had been borrowed by the online community to describe not some science-fiction fantasy but today's increasingly interconnected computer systems—especially the millions of computers jacked into the Internet.

2. What do people in the online community mean when they use the word "cyberspace"?

Now, hardly a day goes by without some newspaper article, some political speech, some corporate press release invoking Gibson's imaginary world. Suddenly, it seems, everybody has an e-mail address, from Hollywood moguls to the Holy See.[1] . . .

All this is being breathlessly reported in the press, which has seized on cyberspace as an all-purpose buzzword that can add sparkle to the most humdrum development or assignment. For working reporters, many of whom have just discovered the pleasures of going online, *cyber* has become the prefix of the day, and they are spawning neologisms as fast as they can type: *cyber*philia, *cyber*phobia, *cyber*wonk. . . .

What is cyberspace? According to John Perry Barlow, a rock-n-roll lyricist turned computer activist, it can be defined most succinctly as "that place you are in when you are talking on the telephone." That's as good a place to start as any. The telephone system, after all, is really a vast, global computer network with a distinctive, audible presence (crackling static against an almost inaudible background hum). By Barlow's definition, just about everybody has already been to cyberspace. It is marked by the feeling that the person you're talking to is "in the same room." Most people take the spatial dimension of a phone conversation for granted—until they get a really bad connection or a glitchy overseas call. Then they start raising their voice, as if by sheer volume they could propel it to the outer reaches of cyberspace.

3. Why is a telephone conversation a good example of a visit to cyberspace?

Cyberspace, of course, is bigger than a telephone call. It encompasses the millions of personal computers connected by modems—via the telephone system—to commercial online services, as well as the millions more with high-speed links to local area networks, office e-mail systems and the Internet. It includes the rapidly expanding wireless services: microwave towers that carry great quantities of cellular phone and data traffic; communications satellites strung like beads in geosynchronous[2] orbit; low-flying satellites that will soon

---

1. **Holy See:** Roman Catholic Church's seat of authority; the Vatican.

2. **geosynchronous** (jē´ō·siŋ´krə·nəs): revolving at a rate of speed simultaneous with that of the earth's rotation.

crisscross the globe like angry bees, connecting folks too far-flung or too much on the go to be tethered by wires. . . . Our television sets may be part of cyberspace, transformed into interactive "teleputers" by so-called full-service networks like the ones several cable-TV companies are building along the old cable lines, using fiber optics and high-speed switches.

But these wires and cables and microwaves are not really cyberspace. They are the means of conveyance, not the destination: the information super-highway, not the bright city lights at the end of the road. Cyberspace, in the sense of being "in the same room," is an experience, not a wiring system. It is about people using the new technology to do what they are genetically pro-grammed to do: communicate with one another. It can be found in electronic mail exchanged by lovers who have never met. It emerges from the endless debates on mailing lists and message boards. It is that bond that knits together regulars in electronic chat rooms and newsgroups. It is, like Plato's plane of ideal forms,[3] a metaphorical space, a virtual reality.

But it is no less real for being so. We live in the age of information, as Nicholas Negroponte, director of M.I.T.'s[4] Media Lab, is fond of pointing out, in which the fundamental particle is not the atom but the bit—the binary digit, a unit of data usually represented as a 0 or 1. Information may still be delivered in magazines and newspapers (atoms), but the real value is in the contents (bits). We pay for our goods and services with cash (atoms), but the ebb and flow of capital around the world is carried out—to the tune of several trillion dollars a day—in elec-tronic funds transfers (bits).

Bits are different from atoms and obey different laws. They are weight-less. They are easily (and flawlessly) reproduced. There is an infinite supply. And they can be shipped at nearly the speed of light. When you are in the business of moving bits around, barri-ers of time and space disappear. For information providers—publishers, for example—cyberspace offers a medium in which distribution costs shrink to zero. Buyers and sellers can find each other in cyberspace without the benefit (or the expense) of a marketing cam-paign. No wonder so many business-men are convinced it will become a powerful engine of economic growth.

At this point, however, cyberspace is less about commerce than about community. The technology has unleashed a great rush of direct, person-to-person communications, organized not in the

4. What are some of the components, or parts, of cyberspace?

5. Do you agree that cyberspace is a communica-tions "experi-ence"? What other things fit in this category?

6. What main idea does the author develop in this and the following two paragraphs?

---

3. **Plato's plane of ideal forms:** The philoso-pher's theory that ideal things exist only as ideas in the mind.

4. **M.I.T.'s:** *M.I.T.* is the common abbreviation for the Massachusetts Institute of Technology.

top-down, one-to-many structure of traditional media but in a many-to-many model that may—just may—be a vehicle for revolutionary change. In a world already too divided against itself—rich against poor, producer against consumer—cyberspace offers the nearest thing to a level playing field.

Take, for example, the Internet. Until something better comes along to replace it, the Internet *is* cyberspace. It may not reach every computer in the human system, as Gibson imagined, but it comes very close. And as anyone who has spent much time there can attest, it is in many ways even stranger than fiction. . . .

Although graphics, photos, and even videos . . . show up, cyberspace, as it exists on the Internet, is still primarily a text medium. People communicate by and large through words, typed and displayed on a screen. Yet cyberspace assumes an astonishing array of forms, from the utilitarian mailing list (a sort of junk e-mail list to which anyone can contribute) to the rococo[5] MUDS, or Multi-User Dungeons (elaborate fictional gathering places that users create one "room" at a time). All these "spaces" have one thing in common: They are egalitarian to a fault. Anybody can play (provided he or she has the requisite equipment and access), and everybody is afforded the same level of respect (which is to say, little or none). Stripped of the external trappings of wealth, power, beauty and social status, people tend to be judged in the cyber-space of the Internet only by their ideas and their ability to get them across in terse, vigorous prose. On the Internet, as the famous *New Yorker* cartoon put it, nobody knows you're a dog. . . .

The Internet is far from perfect. Largely unedited, its content is often tasteless, foolish, uninteresting, or just plain wrong. It can be dangerously habit-forming and, truth be told, an enormous waste of time. Even with . . . point-and-click software such as Netscape and Mosaic, it is still too hard to navigate. And because it requires access to both a computer and a high-speed telecommunications link, it is out of reach for millions of people too poor or too far from a major communications hub to participate.

But it is remarkable nonetheless, especially considering that it began as a cold war postapocalypse[6] military command grid. "When I look at the Internet," says Bruce Sterling, another science fiction writer and a great champion of cyberspace, "I see something astounding and delightful. It's as if some grim fallout shelter had burst open and a full-scale Mardi Gras parade had come out. I take such enormous pleasure in this that it's hard to remain properly skeptical."

There is no guarantee, however, that cyberspace will always look like this. The Internet is changing rapidly. Lately a lot of the development efforts—and most of the press attention— have shifted from the

> **7.** How has the development of the World Wide Web changed cyberspace?

---

5. rococo (rə·kō´kō): overdone, excessively elaborate.

6. postapocalypse (pōst´ə·päk´ə·lips): period following an apocalypse, a catastrophic event.

rough-and-tumble Usenet[7] newsgroups to the more passive and consumer-oriented "home pages" of the World Wide Web—a system of links that simplifies the task of navigating among the myriad offerings on the Internet. The Net, many old-timers complain, is turning into a shopping mall. But unless it proves to be a total bust for business, that trend is likely to continue. . . .

An even trickier question has to do with the so-called upstream capacity of the network. Everybody wants to build a fat pipeline going into the home; that's the conduit by which the new information goods and services will be delivered. But how much bandwidth[8] needs to be set aside for the signal going from the [home] borne back into the network? In some designs that upstream pathway is quite narrow—allowing just enough bits to change the channel or order a zirconium ring. Some network activists argue that consumers will someday need as much bandwidth going out of the home as they have coming in. Only then can ordinary people become, if they choose, not just consumers of media but producers as well, free to plug their camcorders into the network and broadcast their creations to the world.

How these design issues are decided . . . could change the shape of cyberspace. Will it be bottom up, like the Internet, or top down, like broadcast television? In the best case, says Mitch Kapor, cofounder (with John Perry Barlow) of the Electronic Frontier Foundation, we could collectively invent a new entertainment medium, one that taps the creative energies of a nation of midnight scribblers and camcorder video artists. "In the worst case," he says, "we could wind up with networks that have the principal effect of fostering addiction to a new generation of electronic narcotics."

If Kapor seems to be painting these scenarios in apocalyptic terms, he is not alone. There is something about cyberspace that sets people's imaginations blazing. Much of what has been written about it—in the press and on the networks—tends to swing from one extreme to the other, from hype and romanticism to fear and loathing. It may be that the near-term impact of cyberspace is being oversold. But that does not mean that real change is not in the works. As a rule of thumb, historians say, the results of technological innovation always take longer to reach fruition[9] than early champions of change predict. When change finally comes, its effect is likely to be more profound and widespread and unanticipated than anyone imagined—even the guys who write science fiction.

> **8.** Why do some activists think more bandwidth should go *out* of the home? Do you agree? Why or why not?

> **9.** What concerns do some people have about the future of cyberspace? Do you share these concerns? Why or why not?

---

7. **Usenet:** large set of online discussion groups covering a variety of subjects.

8. **bandwidth:** the range of frequencies within a radiation band required to transmit a particular signal.

---

9. **fruition** (froo·ish´ən): coming to fulfillment; realization.

READING SKILL

Main Ideas and Details

The Heart of the Matter   Like all nonfiction essays, extended definitions contain two types of **main ideas**—an overall idea and several smaller ideas that support the larger idea.

■ The **thesis statement** is a sentence (or two) that encompasses the main idea, or central point, of the essay as a whole. The thesis is the core—the "big idea" developed by every paragraph in the extended definition. The thesis sentence often appears at the beginning of articles, but it may appear later, too; sometimes it is not stated outright until the very end.

■ A **topic sentence** is a sentence within every body paragraph that announces the idea of the paragraph. While a topic sentence is often the first sentence in a paragraph, it may also appear in the middle or at the end.

Note that main ideas, whether contained in thesis statements or topic sentences, are always different from topics. A **topic** is what a reading is generally about—whether computers, baseball, or the War of 1812. In contrast, a main idea is what the writer specifically has to say about the topic—for example, "Computers should be more accessible in schools."

Reference Note

For more information on **implied main ideas,** see page 152.

TIP   Often an author states his or her main idea **explicitly**—that is, directly in a single thesis statement. Often, however, an essay's main idea may be **implicit,** or unstated. Occasionally, like the thesis, the main idea of a body paragraph may be implied, too. In cases like these, the reader must use details to infer a main idea.

In an extended definition, all main ideas are supported or illustrated by details. **Details** are the facts, statistics, anecdotes, quotations, descriptions, and examples that explain a larger idea. In an effort to define cyberspace, for example, the article you've just read uses a wide variety of details: quotations from science fiction writer William Gibson, descriptions of how people communicate in cyberspace, facts about how the Internet is constructed, and so on. All these details contribute to the author's main idea. (You will decide for yourself what that main idea actually is a bit later.)

THINKING IT THROUGH | **Identifying Main Ideas and Details**

As you read extended definitions—and other types of nonfiction essays—you can use the following steps to identify main ideas and the details that support them. First, read the paragraph from the reading selection below; then, look at how one student used the steps to analyze the paragraph's main idea and details.

> Cyberspace, of course, is bigger than a telephone call. It encompasses the millions of personal computers connected by modems—via the telephone system—to commercial online services, as well as the millions more with high-speed links to local area networks, office e-mail systems, and the Internet. It includes the rapidly expanding wireless services: microwave towers that carry great quantities of cellular phone and data traffic; communications satellites strung like beads in geosynchronous orbit; low-flying satellites that will soon crisscross the globe like angry bees, connecting folks too far-flung or too much on the go to be tethered by wires. . . . Our television sets may be part of cyberspace, transformed into interactive "teleputers" by so-called full-service networks like the ones several cable-TV companies are building along the old cable lines, using fiber optics and high-speed switches.

▶ STEP 1 **Answer the question, "What main point does the writer want me to understand?" Then, look for a sentence that is similar to your answer.** The main point is that cyberspace is larger than a phone call—this idea is stated in the first sentence.

▶ STEP 2 **Identify examples, facts, anecdotes, descriptions, or statistics presented in the passage.** Keep an eye out for terms like *for example* and *also,* which often signal the presence of supporting details. It may be helpful to jot down details in a two-column chart, like the one shown on the following page.

Main Idea:	Details:
Cyberspace is bigger than a telephone call.	• millions of connected computers • wireless services conveying data and cellular phone calls • communications satellites • TV sets transformed into "teleputers"

▶ **STEP 3** **Ask yourself if the details prove or support the main idea you identified in Step 1.** If so, you have correctly identified the main idea and details that support it. If not, check the piece again to make sure you have correctly pinpointed the main idea. Also, make sure you haven't restated the main idea too narrowly; try rephrasing how you have written it to encompass *all* the details. *Each of my facts and examples shows a specific way in which the paragraph's main idea is true—in other words, they all support the main idea.*

▶ **STEP 4** **If you didn't find an explicit main idea, ask yourself, "What do the details reveal about one idea or concept?"** If the main idea is not stated explicitly, you should examine the details and decide what larger idea they reveal. Sometimes, however, paragraphs do not have single, coherent ideas. When that is true, keep reading; perhaps the article's main idea will be stated further down or additional details will clarify the article's thesis.

YOUR TURN 2 **Identifying Main Ideas and Details**

Use the steps above to identify the main ideas and details of the following three paragraphs in Elmer-DeWitt's article: The paragraph beginning "Although graphics, photos, and even videos . . . " (page 60); the paragraph beginning "An even trickier question . . . " (page 61); and the last paragraph of the article (page 61). Then, use the same steps to figure out the thesis of the essay. How do the main ideas and details from various paragraphs work together to support a single main idea? Be prepared to explain your answers.

Classification as a Definition Tool

One of These Things Is Not (Exactly) Like the Others   Classi-fication—a method of organizing information so it can be easily under-stood—is an especially important part of extended definitions. When writers classify an idea or object, they show how it fits into a larger category and explain what makes the subject unique within that category. Look at the diagram below, which classifies the subject *figure skating* in order to define it.

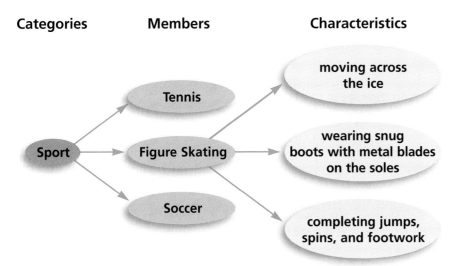

Categories   **Members**   **Characteristics**

- Sport
- Tennis → moving across the ice
- Figure Skating → wearing snug boots with metal blades on the soles
- Soccer → completing jumps, spins, and footwork

The left-hand side of the diagram shows that figure skating can be classified within the larger category *sport*. The diagram's center column illustrates that tennis and soccer are two other subjects that could appear within this category. The right-hand side of the diagram shows that figure skating has certain characteristics that distinguish it from tennis, soccer, and other sports. An extended definition of figure skating would include many of these characteristics.

As you read extended definitions, you will discover that writers commonly use several methods to present a subject's unique characteristics.

Classification Techniques

Explaining how something is distinct within a larger class. For example: "Figure skating differs from other sports because it involves wearing snug boots with metal blades on their soles, moving across ice, and completing jumps, spins, and other footwork."

Comparing and contrasting two or more things. For instance, an extended definition might compare and contrast the skills of figure skaters, ice hockey players, and speed skaters to clarify what makes figure skating unique.

Dividing a subject into several components to illuminate the whole. For example, the subject *figure skating* could be divided into parts such as pair skating, individual skating, skills and training, types of movements (such as turns, spins, and jumps), equipment, and the effect of judges on performance in competitions.

TIP Subjects within a category often share several characteristics. For instance, both figure skating and ice hockey involve moving over ice and wearing snug boots with metal blades on the soles. In cases like these, it is necessary to identify **defining characteristics**—ones that show how the subjects are *different* from all the other subjects within the category. For example, the types of movements in figure skating are defining characteristics, as are the hockey stick and puck in ice hockey.

THINKING IT THROUGH   Classification as a Definition Tool

How can you identify the methods an author uses to classify a subject? The following steps will show you. As you work though these steps in your own reading, you may find it useful to fill in a diagram like the one shown on the previous page. The example responses below illustrate one student's analysis of how the word *bit* is classified in the reading selection. If you want to refresh your memory, re-read the two paragraphs that discuss *bit,* beginning "But it is no less" on page 59.

▶ **STEP 1 Identify the subject's larger category.** (Often you can find a sentence in which subject and category are linked by a word such as *is*.)
My subject is bit—in paragraph ten of the reading selection, the writer says that the bit is the "fundamental particle" of the information age.

▶ **STEP 2 Look for descriptions of the subject's specific characteristics.** Jot down these characteristics and descriptions.
A bit is a "binary digit, a unit of data usually represented as 0 or 1." It is used to convey information across time and space.

▶ **STEP 3 Look for places where the author uses comparison and contrast to explain how the subject is distinct within its class.** Comparison may be signaled with clue words such as "like," "unlike," "similar to," "different from," and so on.
The atom is another fundamental particle—the fundamental particle of matter. Bits are different from atoms because they are weightless, easy to reproduce, and unlimited in supply. They can also be "shipped" at nearly the speed of light.

▶ **STEP 4 Does the author divide the subject into components? Note how this classification helps you see what is unique about the subject.**
Bits can carry many different types of information. Some carry words, like the bits that carry e-mailed essays to and from magazine publishers. Others carry monetary value, which enables people to make electronic financial transfers.

Follow the steps on the previous page to identify how Elmer-DeWitt classifies "cyberspace" throughout his article. Look for places where he divides his subject, explains its characteristics, or compares or contrasts it with another subject. Jot down your ideas on your own paper. You might want to fill in a diagram like the one shown below. When you are finished, you might think about whether the characteristics you identified in Elmer-DeWitt's article are *defining* characteristics—ones that are unique to cyberspace or that show how it is different from other members in the larger category. Then, compare your ideas with a classmate's. Did you identify the same things?

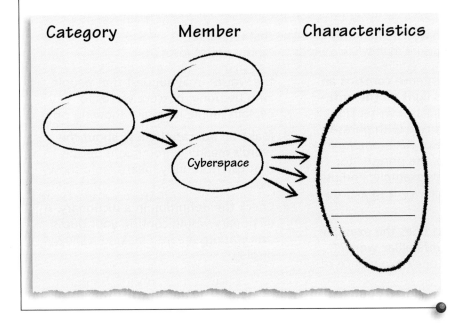

Category   Member   Characteristics

Cyberspace

HORSES ARE RELATIVELY EASY TO TRAIN..MULES ARE EASIER TO TRAIN THAN DONKEYS..IT TAKES PATIENCE TO TRAIN A DONKEY...A MULE IS ONE-HALF DONKEY AND ONE-HALF HORSE..

DON'T ALWAYS FEEL IT'S NECESSARY TO MAKE CONVERSATION, MARCIE..

PEANUTS reprinted by permission of United Feature Syndicate, Inc.

8-23

SCHULZ

Using Example Context Clues

Extended definitions *define* words by discussing them in relation to other words and concepts. In much the same way, readers can figure out the meaning of an unfamiliar word by examining its **context**—the words, phrases, and sentences that surround it. Sometimes a word's context includes an **example** that illustrates the meaning of the word.

THINKING IT THROUGH **Using Example Context Clues**

Use the four steps below to infer the meaning of the example italicized word.

> George loves to behave *ostentatiously* in online chat rooms; for instance, he uses obscure multisyllabic words to express simple ideas.

1. **Determine if the sentence contains an example that sheds light on the unfamiliar word.** Sometimes a writer signals an example context clue with phrases such as *for instance* or *for example.* In the sentence above, the phrase "for instance" signals this example: "he uses obscure multisyllabic words to express simple ideas."

2. **Ask yourself, "What does the example tell me about the unfamiliar word?"** The example—and one's experience of the world—may suggest that people who use long, obscure words to explain simple ideas are showing off.

3. **Make an educated guess about the word's meaning.** You might decide that ostentatiously means "in a showy manner."

4. **Check the definition in a dictionary.** A dictionary would confirm your guess; *ostentatious* means "making a showy display."

PRACTICE

Use the steps above to find the meanings of the boldfaced words in the following sentences.

1. When William Gibson saw young video game players bent over their screens with unwavering eyes, he understood how **rapt** the kids really were.

2. "For working reporters, many of whom have just discovered the pleasures of going online, *cyber* has become the prefix of the day, and they are spawning **neologisms** as fast as they can type: *cyber*philia, *cyber*phobia, *cyber*wonk. . . ."

3. "The telephone system, after all, is really a vast, global computer network with a distinctive, **audible** presence (crackling static against an almost inaudible background hum)."

4. There are **myriad** forms of Internet communication. For example, Internet users can communicate through e-mail, MUDs, Web pages, and even online greeting cards.

5. Many parts of the Internet are essentially **egalitarian,** since anyone who has the right equipment can use them.

Analogy Questions

In definitions, analogies are used to clarify a thing's qualities. On standardized tests like the SAT, **analogy questions** ask you to identify a particular relationship between a pair of words, called the **stem word pair,** and then identify another pair of words that has the same relationship. Take a look at the analogy below:

FLOOR : BUILDING :: step : staircase

You would read this analogy this way: "Floor is to building as step is to staircase." (In analogy questions, the symbol : means "related to," while :: means "equals" or "is equivalent to.")

The following examples illustrate three different types of analogies commonly seen on standardized tests.

Word to Synonym (One word is paired with a similar, but usually not identical, word.)
HOT : SCALDING :: fragrant : aromatic

Agent to Acted Upon (This type pairs something with another thing that is directly affected by it.)
PENCIL : PAPER :: chalk : chalkboard

Part to Whole (One word is paired with the whole to which it belongs.)
SCENE : MOVIE :: chapter : book

On tests, analogy questions contain multiple-choice answers, as in the following example.

1. STEERING WHEEL : CAR :: _____
   A. waiting room : hospital
   B. mouse : computer
   C. apple : seed
   D. physician : patient
   E. speaker : audience

THINKING IT THROUGH **Answering an Analogy Question**

Follow the steps below to find the answer to an analogy question. The responses are based on the sample question above.

1. **Analyze the relationship between the words in the stem word pair and create a sentence explaining that relationship.** A steering wheel is part of a car.

2. **Identify possible answers that contain the same relationship.** A waiting room **(A)** is part of a hospital. A mouse **(B)** is part of a computer. An apple is *not* part of a seed, so **C** can be eliminated. A physician is *not* part of a patient, just as a speaker is *not* part of an audience, so both **D** and **E** can also be eliminated.

3. **If you still have more than one possible answer, revise your sentence to describe more precisely the relationship in the stem word pair.** A steering wheel is the part that people use to control or operate a car.

4. **Analyze the remaining possible answers to see if they fit your new sentence. Eliminate all pairs that don't fit.** People do *not* use a waiting room **(A)** to operate a hospital. However, the mouse *is* the part that people use to operate a computer—the correct answer is **B**.

Writing an Extended Definition

WHAT'S AHEAD?

In this workshop, you will write an extended definition. You will also learn to

- choose and define a term
- extend an initial definition
- use analogy as a definition strategy
- eliminate lazy qualifiers
- punctuate sentences with essential and nonessential clauses

What is a *video game*? No doubt your answer to that question is pretty succinct. Would you answer as briefly if someone asked you, What is *happiness*? or What is *success*? Some words require longer definitions than others.

In everyday situations, people use three distinct types of definitions to convey the meanings of words. When people generally agree about what a word means, it can be defined with a **short definition,** also known as a dictionary definition. *Video game* can be defined this way. Other words have a range of meanings. In these cases, people offer **personal definitions** that differ somewhat from the general understanding of the word. Sometimes, for instance, you'll hear people say, "What I mean when I use the word *generosity* is. . . ." Finally, some words call for **extended definitions,** lengthy explanations that include short definitions, personal definitions, and other strategies of definition: examples, classification, and comparison-contrast, among others.

In the past year or so, you have probably seen extended definitions in the literature assigned in your English class.

- What does *self-reliance* mean?

- What is *civil disobedience?*

- Is a person ever really *free?*

You may remember questions like these from class discussions or essay tests. Definition questions are favorites of teachers and test designers because they require students to grapple with complex or abstract terms. Sometimes they even help us trace how a word's definition has changed over time. Just think: The words *school* and *work* probably meant something very different to people in the seventeenth century than they did to people in the twentieth century.

Choose a Term to Define

Look Right Under Your Nose   How do you choose a word to define? Think of words you use or hear every day, and make a list of possibilities. Avoid words that have simple definitions. Instead, focus on complex, harder-to-define words about which you want to write more than one sentence. You might think of those words as members of one of the following categories:

- difficult or exotic words you will *explain* for readers
- abstract words that have *personal meaning* and relevance for you

What, for example, do you think of when you hear the word *family*? *country*? *relationships*? Do you know any words that mean different things to different people? Write them down.

   If you are having trouble coming up with ideas, you might try some of the following activities:

- **Listen**   Do your family and friends describe things as *cool* or *awesome*? Have you learned any technical terms—such as *Boolean search* or *contrapuntal*—during classes and extracurricular activities? TV and radio are some other great places to pick up interesting words. Sometimes news stories feature words that have specific cultural meanings, such as *Kwanzaa* or *Cinco de Mayo*. Keep your ears open.

- **Read**   American literature is full of essays that define abstract terms, particularly character traits, such as *self-reliance* and *independence*. Think about recent novels you have read. Have you been startled or impressed by the way a work of fiction developed a picture of *courage, responsibility,* or *selflessness*? Also, check newspapers and magazines for terms as wide-ranging as *charter schools, celebrity,* and *fiscal responsibility*.

- **Think and Question**   What does the word *curfew* mean to you? Or the word *allowance*? Ask family, friends, and classmates for their definitions of familiar words that touch on fascinating or debatable issues. Then, do some research on the words' origins by studying their etymologies in a good dictionary. (If you cannot find histories in a regular dictionary, check the *Oxford English Dictionary.*)

TIP   The term you choose should interest a wide audience. Avoid any terms that will interest only a select few of your classmates. You might even have an **occasion,** a real-world reason, to choose a particular word.

Think About Purpose, Audience, and Tone

Keep Your Eye on the Goal   In an extended definition, your **purpose,** or goal, is already decided: to inform, explain, or communicate knowledge about the meaning of a term. Sometimes you may also want to prompt your audience to reflect on a term's meaning. To help people see your serious purpose, express your ideas in a fairly formal **tone**, even if you are defining informal or slang words.

Knowing your **audience,** the people who will read your extended definition, is also very important. Usually the main reader of your extended definition is a teacher, who will use it to gauge how well you understand an important historical or literary concept, such as *democracy* or *Romanticism.* In a sense, however, *you* are the first audience for your extended definition; writing and revising it will help you clarify your ideas about the word you chose to define. Who else will read your essay and learn from it?

THINKING IT THROUGH Analyzing Audience

Use the steps below to identify your audience. Note also how one student analyzes the potential audience for her paper.

▶ **STEP 1 Ask yourself, "Who will read this extended definition?"**

Aside from my teacher, my classmates may read it. I also want to submit it to a local club's essay contest.

▶ **STEP 2 Ask, "What does my audience already know about this term? What do they *need* to know?"** If the term is technical or obscure, you may have to provide some background information.

My term, "courage," is widely known—I won't have to provide much background. Since I want to define it in an uncommon way, though, my examples will have to be very clear.

▶ **STEP 3 Ask, "Does my audience already have a different definition in mind?"** If your definition will depart from a commonly held definition, your audience will expect you at least to acknowledge the more common definition.

With "courage," everyone just thinks of soldiers and people who help in disasters. I'll have to acknowledge these typical examples.

YOUR TURN 4 Identifying a Term, Purpose, Audience, and Tone

Now that you have completed some brainstorming exercises, list five terms you would like to explore further. With a partner, discuss the reasons why these words interest you. Think about the audience, purpose, and tone you would use in an essay on each word. Then, choose the one word from your list that you are most interested in exploring.

Define Your Term

Revising the Dictionary "If you don't know the meaning, look it up." How often have you heard that? Actually, looking a word up in the dictionary is a good way to begin gathering ideas for an extended definition. A dictionary definition, especially for a noun, basically does two things:

- identifies the class or category to which the term belongs
- lists characteristics that distinguish the term from other terms in its class or category

For instance, a dictionary definition of *canoe* is "a narrow, light boat with its sides meeting in a sharp edge at each end." The definition identifies the category (boat) and three characteristics that distinguish canoes from barges, yachts, ocean liners, ferries, and aircraft carriers.

KEY CONCEPT

After finding a short definition for your term, you can begin to extend the definition, or elaborate upon it, by using examples, descriptions, comparisons and contrasts, illustrations, opinions, and personal experiences. Each of these methods can help you fill out the dictionary definition and uncover the word's deeper meanings. You may even want to challenge parts of the dictionary definition and give examples to show why they may be misleading. When you finish, your extended definition will be too long for a dictionary definition, but it will give you and your readers a sense of the word's richness.

THINKING IT THROUGH Defining a Term

To begin writing your extended definition, ask yourself the following questions and consult a dictionary as needed. Jot down answers to the questions in your notebook. (Also, look at how one student answered the questions for a paper on snowboarding.)

▶ **To what larger class does the term belong? (What is it?)** Answering this question puts your term in a category with similar terms. *The larger class snowboarding belongs to is "winter sports."*

▶ **What are its characteristics? (What is it like?)** By answering this question, you will find the qualities or features of your term—the things that make it unique among the other members of its class. *Snowboarding is an individual sport. Someone travels down the side of a mountain with both feet attached to a single board, one foot in front of the other.*

▶ **How can the definition be extended? (What are some examples?)** There is no single *right way* to extend a definition. There are many methods for defining, and each one adds a different kind of information to a definition. The best extended definitions combine several methods to define a term. Some of these methods include illustrations,

TIP You may wish to work collaboratively with a group to define your term. Others often can supply examples and descriptions that are different from yours.

opinions, examples, quotations, comparisons, descriptions, and personal anecdotes and feelings. *Compare and contrast snowboarding and skiing, illustrate snowboarding with my own personal experiences and feelings, get opinions about it from my friends, describe the history of snowboarding, describe the necessary equipment, find quotations on the Internet from famous snowboarders.*

Another terrific tool for defining a term is a **definition map,** a kind of conceptual map that gives you a clear visual image of how an extended definition is constructed. A definition map is an extremely flexible tool. You can make it fit your particular needs. Below is a definition map for the term *courage,* which is defined in the Writer's Model on page 81. Notice that the map defines courage not only by listing its properties and providing examples of courageous acts, but also by saying what courage is not.

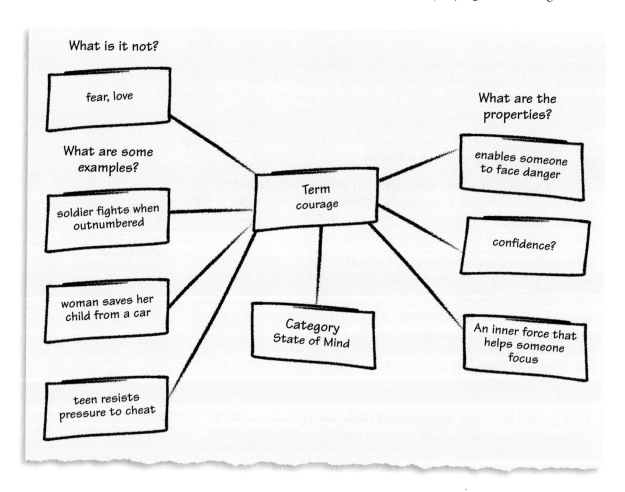

CRITICAL THINKING

Defining Through Analogy

What happens when you compare and contrast two things—for instance, a grape and an orange? First you notice the differences in their appearance, texture, and taste. Then you might note differences in the way they grow. No matter what you notice, one thing is certain: After observing them for a little while, you begin to get a very clear picture of the qualities that make them unique.

Comparing and contrasting something with another member of its class is a popular method of definition. This method is called **analogy,** and it often helps writers come up with very detailed characteristics of a term. Analogy can be especially helpful when you are trying to define abstract terms (like feel-ings or attitudes), since these subjects lack physical characteristics. It helps you look beyond surface similarities and differences to discover the essential ways that two things differ from each other. Remember, however, that the two subjects in an analogy must belong to the same category. If you compare things that are *too* different from each other, you won't locate the specific information that helps extend your definition.

In creating analogies, it often helps to list the similarities and differences between the two words in a chart like the one below. In the following example, the writer is defining the word *conceit*, and he has chosen the word *self-respect* (another character trait) to use in an analogy.

Similarities	Differences
Both are attitudes about one's personal value.	Conceit is an overblown sense of self-respect.
Both may be related to appearance or skill.	Self-respect is a sign of emotional well-being; conceit is often a sign of insecurity.
Both generally motivate people to achieve.	Conceit feeds on the sense of being "better" than others; self-respect doesn't rely on comparisons.

By using an analogy, the writer turned up several distinctive characteristics of the term *conceit*; he was also reminded that conceit and self-respect are somewhat closely related (conceit is self-respect run amok). As you develop analogies yourself, don't forget to note the similarities between terms. After all, a word cannot be defined thoroughly by saying only what it is *not*.

PRACTICE

First, identify a word that could be compared and contrasted with each of the following terms. Then, list at least two similarities and two differences between each pair of subjects.

1. health food
2. dependence
3. humor
4. amusement park
5. corruption

Research Your Term

TIP When you include formal and informal research in your paper, cite your sources. For more information about how to **cite sources** properly, see page 268.

Fill in the Blanks   Look at your definition map. Do the example boxes on your map look empty? Has your brainstorming led you to topics about which you know little? If so, this is a good time to gather some new information. There are two kinds of research you might try: *formal research* and *informal research.*

Formal research is investigation done with primary and secondary sources—encyclopedias, textbooks, historical documents, and periodical articles that offer specific information about your term. If your term relates to fields such as history or science, you will need to do formal research to verify that all the information you present is factual. For instance, if you are defining the historical term *Depression,* your extended definition should include information about the events that led up to the Depression and any other facts you think your audience will expect.

If you are defining a more abstract term, such as *vanity,* you might find it helpful to do **informal research,** investigative work in which you look at a wide variety of materials you may not normally think of as sources: interviews with friends, song lyrics, advertisements, films, and so on. In researching *vanity,* for example, you might ask a number of friends to share with you their ideas about what vanity is, including specific examples of vanity they have witnessed. Or you could describe the portrait of vanity presented by a recent film or made-for-TV special. These sources will offer fresh details to help you broaden your perspective.

It is important to have a rationale when deciding which kinds of research—formal, informal, or both—are appropriate for your definition. The following chart gives examples that will help you decide what kind of research is appropriate for your topic.

Determining Research Methods		
Example of term	nova	loyalty
Type of term	scientific	abstract
Research method required	formal	informal
Research rationale	scientific term relates to factual information found only in primary and secondary sources	little or no factual information on topic; yet everyone knows it when they see it, and there are portrayals of it all around us
Example of research results	A nova becomes several thousand times its original brightness in a short time period—a few hours or days (Encyclopedia).	A kidnapped cat escapes and travels 1,000 miles to find its owners (last Friday's movie).

Here is a chart that the author of the Writer's Model on page 81 created to plan her research method and keep track of the results:

Term	courage
Type of Term	abstract
Research Method	informal
Places to Search	Look for portraits of courage in books, TV programs, and song lyrics; interview friends and relatives.
Results	Lucia described her story about resisting pressure from her friends to cheat on a test.

Identify a Thesis

What's the Point? **After you find enough ideas and examples for your extended definition, you need to decide what your thesis, or main point, will be.** In a very general sense, the main point of all extended definitions is to give readers a thoughtful, detailed definition of a term—one that goes far beyond the simple dictionary definition.

KEY CONCEPT

One way of developing a thesis is by showing that a term can mean one thing, despite the fact that many people think it means something else. In the following thesis, the writer uses the word *although* to indicate the contrast between her definition and a more common one. *However* is a similar signal word.

Most people think that monster movies are a form of visual entertainment that scares people. Although that is true to some extent, I think they are also designed to make us laugh at the stupidity of the main characters and feel smart and safe by comparison.

Another way to develop a thesis is to show how a term's extended definition differs from its short definition. For instance, the author of the Writer's Model begins her introduction by stating a dictionary definition of *courage*—a state of mind that "enables one to face danger with self-possession, confidence, and resolution." Then, after she gives several examples of courageous behavior, the first part of her thesis, which appears on the next page, pinpoints ways in which these examples diverge from the dictionary definition. The second part of her thesis goes on to explain other ways her definition will improve upon the dictionary's.

I think that these examples actually show that confidence is <u>not</u> a necessary part of courage. Moreover, in order to understand courage better, one needs to think about what "danger" means and what courage feels like.

A reader of this thesis has a clear picture of how the essay will proceed. As you develop your thesis, try to give your audience the same sense of clarity.

Organize Ideas

Everything in Its Place   By now you probably have many different kinds of information about your term, information that you must present in an organized and coherent way. Your thesis will give your essay its overall structure, but how are you going to arrange everything else? That depends on the kind of information you have gathered. The most common way to organize an extended definition is in **logical order,** the order that makes the best sense.

There's one hitch: Different kinds of information call for different kinds of order. If your information is historical or anecdotal, the logical order to present it in is **chronological,** the order in which things happened. So, if you are tracing the way the definition of a term such as *citizen* has changed over time, present the meanings from earliest to latest—or latest to earliest, if that helps you make your point more clearly. If you are defining a quality, such as *selflessness,* it may be more effective to present different aspects of that quality through **order of importance**—either from most important (or essential) quality to least, or least important to most. If your extended definition includes a physical description of your subject, you may need to use **spatial order** to arrange your information. With spatial order you start at a particular point and move in a consistent direction—east to west, left to right, top to bottom, or near to distant, for example.

Other possible arrangements for data in an extended definition include

■ from dictionary definition to personal definition (when you want to show that your definition is richer and more accurate than the one in the dictionary)

■ from negative definitions to a positive definition (when you want to surprise readers or get their attention). This organization is also effective when you want to cast a positive light on a term commonly seen as solely negative.

- from personal anecdote to what others say, or vice versa (when you want to compare or contrast opinions)
- from least convincing (or simply convincing) to most convincing (when you want to really drive your point home)

The chart below shows how the writer of the essay on *courage* used several different methods to organize her extended definition. Notice how she considers her readers—and what will convince them most effectively—as she plans each section.

Information	My Intention	Method of Organization
Dictionary definition of "courage"	To show that my definition is fuller and more subtle	Dictionary definition to personal definition—This order lets readers compare my definition to the dictionary's and see how mine improves it.
The firefighter who rushes into a fire to save people, the soldier who fights when outnumbered, and the mother who runs out into traffic to save her child	To show that none of these instances of courage involves confidence	From convincing to most convincing—I'll put the example of the mother last because I think it supports the point more convincingly than the other two examples.
My description of how courage felt (the story about trying out for the musical)	To show the various stages of my emotions and how differently courage felt from fear	Chronological order—Readers need to see my fear before they can appreciate how courage affected me.

YOUR TURN 5 **Define, Research, Identify the Thesis, and Organize**

Use the steps on pages 73–79 to
- define the term you have selected
- do research to gather more information about the term
- create a thesis by thinking about the main idea of your essay and the way you will develop it
- create a plan like the one above to organize your supporting information in a way that your readers can read and understand easily

 # Writing

Extended Definition

Framework	Directions and Explanations

Introduction

- Use an attention grabber.
- Supply necessary background information, including your subject's larger category.
- Provide a clear thesis.

Get Your Readers' Attention Draw readers into your essay with an interesting quote or angle on the dictionary definition of your term, a striking example of the quality or thing you are describing, or an arresting statement or question.

Build Background Give readers the information they need to understand and appreciate your definition. Make sure they know the larger category of the term. If you have not already explained the brief or common definition, mention it now.

Get to the Point State your main point and indicate what makes your definition different from others. Hint at how you will develop your essay.

Body

- Discuss the first example, illustration, anecdote, or analogy.
- Discuss the second example, and so on.

Offer Some Support Provide details that support your thesis by explaining or illustrating the characteristics of your term.

Organize Your Ideas Organize supporting information in the most logical and effective pattern. Use more than one pattern, if necessary.

Conclusion

- Summarize the definition.
- Briefly explain the importance or relevance of the extended definition.

Sum it Up Give a brief overview of your extended definition, concentrating especially on the ways it differs from the dictionary or common definition.

Provide Your Opinion Why is this extended definition important? Remind readers why it is more accurate or useful than the brief or common definition.

 YOUR TURN 6 Writing an Extended Definition

Using the framework and explanations as your guide, write the first draft of your extended definition. Also, take a look at the Writer's Model, which follows the framework's guidelines.

A Writer's Model

This extended definition follows the framework on the previous page. The notes in the margin identify the elements of the framework that appear in this model.

What Is Courage?

We all know courage when we see it. It is the "special something" that enables firefighters to run into burning buildings to save people. It prompts a soldier to rush headlong into a losing battle or a mother to dash into a busy street to whisk her child out of traffic. In all of these examples, people take action despite physical dangers, and they seem self-possessed and resolved when they do. Believe it or not, however, their behavior does not fit the common definition of courage. The American Heritage Dictionary defines courage as "a state or quality of mind" that differs from others because it "enables one to face danger with self-possession, confidence, and resolution." I think that these examples actually show that confidence is <u>not</u> a necessary part of courage. Moreover, I think that in order to understand courage, one needs to think about what "danger" means and what courage feels like.

It may help to first examine the confidence of the soldier and the firefighter. Both have been thoroughly trained to meet the physical dangers and psychological challenges of their assignments. They recognize the risks that go along with their jobs, and they assume that their training will help them face those risks. To that extent, they are confident. Nevertheless, both of these people have moments on the job when they do not feel confident about what they have to do. In fact, both can be confronted by situations that defy confidence. Still, an inner strength—courage—sustains them, and they act <u>despite</u> their lack of confidence.

Confidence is trust, not just in oneself but in a situation. The soldier who lands on a beach where his army is outnumbered four to one may have confidence in his training, but he may not have much confidence that his situation will turn out for the best. He fights to protect his squadron (and perhaps even to defend an idea, like "liberty"), even as he doubts that he and his colleagues will live. No one I know would dare say he acts without courage just because he acts without confidence. Similarly, when a firefighter dashes into a building that has been burning for a long time, he hopes rather than trusts that he and the people trapped in the fire will emerge safely. He chooses to disregard his lack of confidence and tries to save people anyway.

INTRODUCTION
Attention grabber

Striking examples

Dictionary definition, including category

Thesis

BODY
Examples

TIP Although this is a formal paper, you may use the first person when discussing your own experiences.

(continued)

(continued)

Example

Now, consider the case of the mother dashing into traffic to save her child. She does not have time to experience an emotion like confidence. Like any parent in that situation, she acts instinctively. Yet if asked, most people would call her action courageous. This case particularly demonstrates that confidence is not a necessary part of courage.

Another false assumption about courage is that it always involves meeting physical danger. Many times it does, but more often courage is what lets people risk being hurt emotionally. Take, for instance, the case of my cousin Lucia, who resisted peer pressure to cheat on a test. When she told her friends she would not do it, she was pretty sure that they would not overtly call her a wimp. However, she suspected that they would not talk to her in school the next day and that they might convince other students to avoid her, which would make her feel miserable. In fact, Lucia's friends did not reject her, but it took courage for her to speak her mind when she knew how she would feel if they had rejected her.

Anecdote

Another important thing about courage—one that may be different for each person—is how it feels. I had my most vivid experience of courage last year, when I tried out for the school musical. I had never sung in front of a group before. As I waited in the wings, I was sure I would forget the words to "Edelweiss" or that my voice would crack on all the high notes. I could not stop thinking about what a laughingstock I would be by lunchtime the next day. My mouth went dry and my throat got tight. When at last my name was called, an inner force pushed me to the center of the stage. It must have been courage. I remember feeling focused and thinking, "It's now or never," and then I opened my mouth to sing. I felt strong and clearheaded, and suddenly none of my fears mattered at all. Other people may experience courage differently, but that is how it felt to me.

Anecdote

CONCLUSION

In conclusion, I think we need to stop thinking of courage as a state of mind that requires confidence. Not every person who acts heroically can honestly say, "I am confident that everything is going to be all right." Sometimes, people who act heroically are acting on instinct and not thinking anything at all. Other times, they lack confidence but push aside their doubts and fears to do what they <u>need</u> to do. Also, we should consider that acting with courage does not always involve putting your life on the line. More often, it means taking an emotional risk because you believe you must do so. By understanding more thoroughly the characteristics of courage, we can appreciate that most of us have the capacity to be courageous (at least a little bit) every day of our lives.

Summary of definition

Statement of definition's importance

A Student's Model

The following excerpt from an extended definition essay was written by Natalie Grissinger, a student at East Wake High School in Wendell, North Carolina. Notice how she uses quotations to define the concept of friendship.

The Meaning of Friendship

My grandfather once said, "When you get out of high school and can count your real friends on one hand, consider yourself lucky." He was speaking of good friends, however. There are also bad friends. They are the ones who do not stick around when life gets to its toughest nor do they respect the personal obligations that present themselves in one's life. These are the "friends" who drag you down. Bad friends everyone can live without, but good friends share; they share their virtues, loyalty, and trust. These are the important and real qualities of a good friend, the kind everyone needs.

Good friends share their moral excellence. The ancient Greek philosopher Aristotle defined friendship in this way: "We may describe friendly feelings toward anyone as wishing for him what you believe to be good things, not for your own sake but for his, and being inclined, so far as you can, to bring these things about." In other words, being friends does not require doing what your friend wants you to do. Rather, it requires doing what you believe is best for your friend. This will inevitably add virtuous qualities to your friend's character. For example, one of my best friends always let her boyfriend copy her homework, quizzes, and even tests. She always complained about how he needed to pay attention and do things on his own, but he never listened. One day, my friend decided to cover her paper on the exam day. Her boyfriend was pretty angry that he ended up failing, but it was not my friend's responsibility to help him pass. As a friend, it was her responsibility to share her virtues with him. He may not have liked the way or the day she chose to teach him to stay awake in class and to do his own homework, but in the end, he appreciated the fact that his girlfriend did what she believed was best for him. By her sharing with him and adhering to her "good things," as Aristotle put it, she helped bring about what was best for him.

Attention-grabbing opening

Differentiates subject from others in category

Thesis statement

Distinguishing characteristic of subject

Supporting quotation

Elaboration on distinguishing characteristic

Example of distinguishing characteristic

Revising

Evaluate and Revise Your Draft

Tinkering and Adjusting   Take a deep breath and read your paper from beginning to end—not once, but twice. The first time, look for organizational weaknesses and confusing content. The second time, focus on style, using the guidelines on page 86.

TIP   Working collaboratively to refine your essay is often helpful. A fresh pair of eyes may see things you have missed.

▶ **First Reading: Content and Organization**   With a peer or on your own, use the chart below to examine the content and organization of your extended definition. Read each question, and follow the tips to see if you need to make revisions.

Extended Definition: Content and Organization Guidelines for Peer and Self-Evaluation

Evaluation Questions	▶ Tips	▶ Revision Techniques
1 Does the introduction provide an attention-grabbing opener and identify the term and its category?	**Bracket** the attention grabber. **Circle** the term to be defined, and **draw a rectangle around** the category. If any of these are missing, revise.	**Add** an attention grabber. If necessary, **add** the term to be defined and its category.
2 Is there any necessary background information and a clear thesis?	**Underline** any background information. Draw a **wavy line** underneath the thesis. If there are no marks, revise.	**Add** any necessary background information. **Add** or **elaborate** on your thesis.
3 Do the body paragraphs develop the thesis with a variety of examples, illustrations, personal anecdotes, descriptions, or analogies?	Put a **check mark** next to each example, illustration, and so on. **Circle the check marks** for every detail that shows that the thesis is true. If there are no circled check marks, revise.	**Elaborate** on the thesis by adding more supporting details. **Delete** any details that do not support your thesis or define your term.
4 Are the details in an order that makes sense?	In the margin, **write** the name of the order used in each paragraph or group of paragraphs: chronological, dictionary definition to personal definition, and so on. If an order is confusing, revise.	**Rearrange** details in the most logical order—chronological, order of importance, and so on.
5 Does the conclusion summarize the definition?	**Highlight** the summary of the definition. If there is nothing to highlight in the conclusion, revise.	**Add** a brief synopsis of the definition.

ONE WRITER'S REVISIONS Look at the way one writer used the guidelines in the chart to revise her paper. Then, answer the questions below.

We all know courage when we see it. It is the "special something" that enables firefighters to run into burning buildings to save people. It prompts a soldier to rush headlong into a losing battle or a mother to dash into a busy street to whisk her child out of traffic. In all of these examples, people take action despite physical dangers, and they seem self-possessed and resolved when they do. Believe it or not, however, their behavior does not fit the common definition of courage. The American Heritage Dictionary defines courage as ~~something that~~ "a state or quality of mind" that differs from others because it "enables one to face danger with self-possession, confidence, and resolution." I think that these examples actually show that confidence is <u>not</u> a necessary part of courage. *Moreover, I* think that in order to understand courage, one needs to think about what "danger" means and what courage feels like.

Add

Add/Elaborate on thesis

Analyzing the Revision Process

1. Why did the writer add "'a state or quality of mind'"?
2. Why did the writer add the final sentence?

YOUR TURN 7 **Revise Content and Organization**

Using the guidelines in the chart and the revision model, make any necessary changes to the content and organization of your extended definition.

PEER REVIEW

Read a classmate's extended definition, and answer the questions below.

1. What have you learned about the meaning of the word?
2. What additional way to extend the definition would you recommend to the author? Why?

⟶ **Second Reading: Style**   Now that you have revised the content and organization of your paper, it is time to focus on style. In writing a first draft of an extended definition, writers are so concerned with getting ideas down on paper or disk that they choose the first words that come to mind. Some of these may be qualifying words, such as *very* or *kind of,* that are imprecise and can make an essay seem cluttered. As you read your extended definition for a second time, pay special attention to the qualifiers you used.

Style Guidelines

Evaluation Question	▶ Tip	▶ Revision Technique
Are many of your qualifying words imprecise or unnecessary?	▶ Select five lines from each paragraph. **Circle** all the *qualifiers*— words that limit or intensify the meaning of the words that follow them.	▶ **Eliminate** every unnecessary qualifier—that is, every qualifier that makes the message hesitant or unclear.

Word Choice

Eliminating Lazy Qualifiers

Like any definition, an extended definition should use precise language, even when it describes an abstract word. That's why it is important to make sure there are no lazy qualifiers in your definition. Qualifiers are words that weaken or intensify the meaning of the words that follow them. When used properly, qualifiers make ideas clearer. However, lazy qualifiers make writing sound hesitant and unconvincing, as if the writer is not sure of the subject. Words such as *sort of, kind of, very, certainly, rather, sometimes,* and *more or less* frequently have this effect. Consider the following sentences:

> We were *sort of* lost.
> We were lost.

Instead of making the idea clearer, *sort of* makes the meaning fuzzy. The second sentence drives the point home by eliminating the lazy qualifier.

ONE WRITER'S REVISIONS   Using the style guidelines above, the writer of the model on page 81 eliminated lazy qualifiers in the following way. Study the revisions on the next page, and answer the questions that follow.

BEFORE REVISION

My mouth went (really) dry and my throat got (sort of) tight. When at last my name was called, (some kind of) inner force pushed me to the center of the stage. It must have been courage. I remember feeling (very) focused and thinking, "It's now or never," and then I opened my mouth to sing. I felt strong and clearheaded, and suddenly none of my fears mattered at all. Other people may experience courage differently, but that is how it felt to me.

Qualifiers are circled

AFTER REVISION

My mouth went dry and my throat got tight. When at last my name was called, an inner force pushed me to the center of the stage. It must have been courage. I remember feeling focused and thinking, "It's now or never," and then I opened my mouth to sing. I felt strong and clearheaded, and suddenly none of my fears mattered at all. Other people may experience courage differently, but that is how it felt to me.

Lazy qualifiers are eliminated

Analyzing the Revision Process

1. Does "My mouth went dry and my throat got tight" sound stronger? Why is "very" unnecessary before "focused"?

2. Is "an inner force" clearer than "some kind of inner force"? Would you argue in favor of keeping "some kind of"? Why or why not?

YOUR TURN 8   Eliminating Lazy Qualifiers

Read your essay again, focusing on its style. Using the style guidelines and revision model, revise your extended definition by getting rid of all extraneous modifiers.

Creating Charts Have you ever noticed how many charts appear in textbook chapters, magazines, and newspapers? Writers frequently use charts to communicate ideas clearly to readers. Charts enable readers to see at a glance the links between important ideas. In extended definitions, charts are a good way to show the relationship between a term and its category, individual terms within the category, and characteristics of one or more of those individual terms. If you choose to include charts in your definition, here are a few conventions you should follow.

- Use rectangles to represent terms, characteristics, and categories. Label each rectangle clearly with the idea it represents.

- Link the rectangles with lines so that the connections between ideas are obvious.

- Use a pyramid shape and let the top box represent the broadest concept (the category). The second level should show terms that can be classified within that category, and the third level should show the characteristics of those terms. If necessary, a fourth level might provide an illustration of the term in action.

The following chart illustrates these tips.

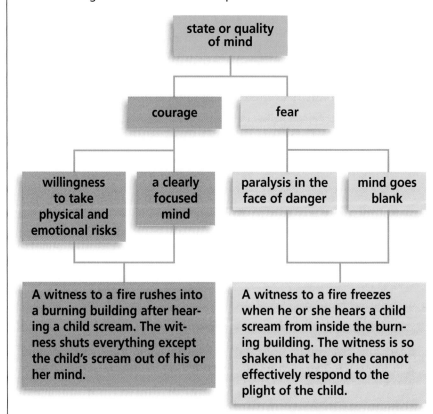

Publishing

Proofread Your Essay

Fit to Print   Can you imagine finding a spelling error in the dictionary—or finding a problem with grammar or punctuation? Such a discovery would be highly unlikely. After all, the dictionary is the resource people check to find out about correct usage. If there are spelling, grammar, or punctuation errors, readers may also wonder whether the definitions are accurate and reliable. The same is true of extended definitions. Proofread your essay to find any errors in spelling, grammar, and punctuation. Specifically, make sure you have punctuated essential and nonessential modifiers correctly.

Reference Note

For more information on **essential** and **nonessential modifiers,** see page 788.

Grammar Link

Punctuating Essential and Nonessential Modifiers

Within any extended definition, many smaller definitions are made, even within single sentences. Many of these definitions are made through **modifiers,** which may take the form of a word, a phrase, or a clause. To be sure any message you write will be clear, it is important to know how to punctuate these modifiers.

In particular, two kinds of modifiers need to be punctuated carefully: *nonessential* modifiers and *essential* modifiers. A **nonessential modifier** contains information that is not necessary to understand the main idea of the sentence. By contrast, an **essential modifier** is one that cannot be left out without changing the meaning of the sentence. Look at these examples:

| Nonessential | Anika Smith, **who joined our class this year,** offers good feedback on essays. |
| Essential | The students **who interviewed people** gathered many additional details. |

In the first sentence above, the fact that Anika joined her class this year is not essential to the main idea—that she offers good feed-back on essays. Because it is not necessary, that information is set off from the rest of the sentence with commas. However, in the second sentence, "who interviewed people" is necessary because it tells readers *which* students gathered additional details. Because that information *is* necessary, it is not set off by commas.

PRACTICE

Punctuate the following sentences correctly. If a sentence is correct as is, write *C* for correct.

1. The project, completed by students in Miss Heinz's class, earned honorable mention in the school contest.

2. Writers, who finish their essays before the bell rings, should go back and proofread.

3. Jonah seeing that my hands were full offered to close my locker.

4. The actors, rehearsing in the auditorium, attracted a crowd of curious students.

5. The Teacher of the Year award was presented by Mr. Chism our principal.

Publish Your Essay

TIP Before you publish, make sure your final essay is legible and free of spelling errors, and that it adheres to the standard conventions of punctuation and capitalization.

Get the Words Out   Now that you have finished proofreading your extended definition, it's time to share it with other readers. Think of the ways you can make sure an audience sees your work, as well as that of your classmates:

- Collect definitions that are school-related and put them in a handbook for entering freshmen.
- Create a *Dictionary of Difficult Terms* on the World Wide Web. Enter your class's definitions on different pages, and create links between terms that belong to the same category.
- If you have defined a controversial term, submit your essay to the school newspaper's editorial section.
- Send a copy of your paper to a friend, relative, or teacher with whom you have discussed the term.

PORTFOLIO

Reflect on Your Essay

A Quick Look Back   What lessons have you learned from writing an extended definition? Jot down answers to the following questions, and keep them in your portfolio along with the final draft of your essay.

- During the planning stages of this assignment, what useful things did you learn about the writing process?
- What part of the definition was the most challenging to write? Why?
- If you are asked to write another extended definition, what will you do differently?
- In what other classes might you apply the skills for writing a definition? Explain.

If you decide to include this essay in your portfolio, attach your reflections.

 YOUR TURN 9   Proofread, Publish, and Reflect

Read your extended definition from beginning to end. Correct errors in grammar, spelling, and punctuation, and pay special attention to the punctuation of essential and nonessential modifiers. Find a way to publish your extended definition for an audience, and then reflect on what you have gained from this writing experience.

Writing a Poem That Defines

Believe it or not, poems are a lot like definitions. They define concepts, feelings, and objects. A poem can take an abstract word like *infatuation* and show us very clearly what it means. A poem can also help us see the beauty of a person we've never met by comparing him or her to something we understand. For instance, when we read, "My love is like a red, red rose that's newly sprung in June," we understand the beauty of the person the poet calls "my love," because we know how beautiful the first rose of summer is. That's how most poems define: They use *metaphor*, a special kind of analogy.

Understanding Metaphors   To write a poem that defines, you need to become comfortable with writing metaphors. Writers traditionally use two basic kinds of metaphors to write poems. Some metaphors say that one thing *is* another. Others use the words *like* or *as* to compare two things. (Strictly speaking, metaphors that use *like* or *as* are called **similes.**) The examples below show these different methods of comparison.

Metaphor	"Much Madness *is* divinest sense—"
	—Emily Dickinson
Simile	"his brown skin hung in strips / *like* ancient wallpaper"
	—"The Fish," Elizabeth Bishop

Along with simply comparing one thing to another, you may occasionally want to twist a metaphor cleverly—by comparing an object to all the things it is *not* like. William

Shakespeare did this when he wrote, in Sonnet 130, "My mistress' eyes are nothing like the sun; / Coral is far more red than her lips' red. . . ." By explaining all the things his beloved is *not* like, Shakespeare narrows the scope of his readers' vision to help them imagine what she *is* like. He also defies readers' expectations, since even in his day there was a long-standing tradition of comparing women's features to the sun, moon, stars, and other beauties of nature.

Consult Your Muse   How do you choose a topic for a poem that defines? To come up with an idea:

- **Open Your Eyes**   Find a place to sit and watch the world for a while. Take stock of the things around you—animals, people, rain, skyscrapers. Notice color, movement, and texture. Any surprises?
- **Now, Close Them**   Try seeing with your ears. Listen to the squirrels rustling in the leaves or people laughing in the street. What do those sounds remind you of?
- **Get Close**   Find a small object, like a rock, flower, or china cup. What does it smell like? feel like? look like?

After you finish exploring, sit down and brainstorm. Did you find yourself comparing the objects you saw to other things? Jot down some notes about possible analogies.

Put the Pieces Together   Writers have a number of devices that help them turn their simple analogies into poetry. Take a look at the list on the next page.

- **Speaker**   Every poem has someone that tells it, a narrative voice. Usually that voice is the author's, but it doesn't have to be. You may decide to use a stethoscope as a narrator to define *death,* for example. Just make sure the voice is consistent throughout.

- **Diction/Tone**   Diction, or word choice, is very important because it helps set the poem's mood or tone. Tone is the attitude expressed in the poem. Is it light or serious? Angry or peaceful?

- **Imagery**   Imagery is language that appeals to the senses and draws readers into a poem. A blood-red sky, a flower unfurling its petals to the sun—images like these catch readers' attention and help create a poem's meaning.

- **Figurative Language**   Figurative language includes all words and phrases that are not meant to be taken literally. Metaphors and similes are figures of speech. So are phrases that give human qualities to objects, like "The daffodils nodded their heads in the breeze."

- **Sound Effects**   You can use sounds to create effects in a poem. For instance, the repetition of the *s* sound may make readers think of a serpent or of running water.

- **Rhyme Scheme**   Many poems have a repetition of vowel sounds in accented syllables and all succeeding syllables. Rhyme usually occurs at the end of a line of poetry, but it may also occur elsewhere.

A Sterling Example   In the following poem, Emily Dickinson defines the concept of human intelligence; notice how she uses metaphors to define the brain. The annotations point out key elements.

> The Brain—is wider than the Sky—
> For—put them side by side—
> The one the other will contain
> With ease—and You—beside—
>
> The Brain is deeper than the sea—
> For—hold them—Blue to Blue—
> The one the other will absorb—
> As sponges—Buckets—do—
>
> The Brain is just the weight of God—
> For—Heft them—Pound for Pound—
> And they will differ—if they do—
> As Syllable from Sound—
>
> —*Emily Dickinson*

Metaphor—The brain is compared to the sky.

Tone—Direct language creates a matter-of-fact, almost scientific tone.

Imagery—The picture of the sponge absorbing a bucket of water catches the reader's attention.

Rhyme—The second and fourth lines of each stanza rhyme.

YOUR TURN 10   Writing a Poem That Defines

Draft a poem that defines a person, place, thing, or concept. Use metaphors to help readers understand your topic and see it in a new light. Then arrange a time to read your poem aloud to your class or family.

Oral Interpretation of a Poem

Talk   Listen

Like a word, a piece of literature may have many meanings. One way to define the special meaning a piece of literature holds for you is to create an oral interpretation of it. **Oral interpretation** is the art of making meaning of a literary work and translating it to an audience through a spoken word performance. Though ideally a finished performance (a kind of final draft) looks relaxed and natural, such performances rarely happen spontaneously. Rather, they are the result of careful preparation.

WHAT'S AHEAD?

In this section, you will learn to

■ **select and analyze a poem for oral interpretation**

■ **prepare and present an oral interpretation of the poem**

Select and Analyze a Poem

Finding a Match   Poetry, with its roots in the oral tradition, is a natural for oral interpretation. However, for this **task,** be sure to choose a poem that inspires and interests you. If you truly enjoy or relate to a literary work, you will be better able to communicate its meaning and atmosphere. As you read and reflect on various poems as potential performance pieces, take into consideration the following tips:

■ Choose poems dealing with **universal themes**—love, individuality, the power or beauty of nature, or the impermanence of life, for example; they are likely to touch a wide range of listeners.

■ Most literary artists set out to express unique **ideas and insights.** Look for poems that invite you to view some aspect of life from a fresh perspective.

■ Poems that have **emotional appeal** are good choices for oral interpretation.

■ The content and tone of a poem should be **appropriate for the occasion and setting**—in this case, a classroom assignment.

■ The **length** of a poem is crucial: You must be able to perform the work in the time allotted. Some long poems can be excerpted, as long as you don't disturb the work's dramatic structure.

> **TIP** You might even choose a poem you have written yourself; it will be a challenge to see if you can convey its sound and sense to an audience. If you are having trouble choosing a poem, your teacher may be able to suggest several appropriate pieces. As you narrow your choices, avoid works with which you just can't "connect."

It may help to collaborate with others in analyzing the poem you've chosen. In a **group discussion,** try comparing and contrasting one another's interpretations. Be sure to ask questions for clarification and to make relevant contributions to the discussion, including offering suggestions for planning the presentation.

Taking It Apart to See How It Works   You must understand a poem thoroughly before you can interpret it for others. Because poets compress thought and language in ways that can be ambiguous or oblique as well as dazzling, you need to take poems apart slowly and study their workings. Here are some brief suggestions for analyzing a poem.

- Determine the identity—and characteristics—of the **speaker.** In narrative poems, think about the **character development** of the speaker and other figures.
- Think carefully about the poet's **syntax** and **diction,** including the **connotations** of words. Take time to clarify the meanings and pronunciations of unfamiliar words in a dictionary or encyclopedia.
- Identify any **figurative language** and other striking **imagery.** Visualizing such images will enhance your ability to evoke them with your voice.
- Get a feel for the poem's rhythm and other **sound devices.** Is the verse especially musical? Does the poet use **rhyme,** repetition, or alliteration to convey mood or meaning?
- As you analyze the poem's **structure,** note how the poet uses punctuation to signal places where you could pause, stop, or inflect your voice in certain ways.
- To test your grasp of the poem's overall meaning, find a way to state its **theme** in a single sentence.

As you work, paraphrase each and every line. If at any point you struggle to find your own words, go back to the poem and clarify the meaning of the corresponding passage in your mind.

Create and Rehearse Your Interpretation

Usually there is more than one way to interpret a literary work. A successful oral reading helps listeners understand *your* particular interpretation.

Crafting a Performance   Now you need to discover ways to give voice to the poem's main idea as well as to its music. Begin by saying the poem in your most relaxed and expressive speaking voice. Speak the poem aloud over and over until you grow comfortable with how the words feel and sound coming out of your mouth. Experiment with different ways of delivering certain phrases or lines. Then, take a step back and think about words or passages that might require particular **verbal strategies.**

- Would any sections become clearer with adjustments of **volume, pitch,** or **tone?**
- How well does your normal **rate** of speaking suit the poem's internal rhythm, as well as the poem's mood and meaning? Do you need to slow down or speed up at all?
- Should you **stress** certain words or phrases—perhaps key images, symbols, or juxtapositions—by inflecting your voice or by pausing?

Making decisions based on answers to such questions is how you begin to craft an oral presentation. At this point, it can be revealing to *listen* to your voice as you paraphrase lines or whole stanzas once again. Does your vocal quality change when you shift from the poet's words to your own words? If so, how might you invest the poet's words with your own natural intonations?

As you craft your oral interpretation, remember that punctuation marks are guides to meaning as well as sound. Since your audience can't see the punctuation, they will rely on you to convey its essence. Look for places where punctuation separates or connects ideas. By using a variety of vocal intonations and by pausing for various lengths of time, you can help your audience "hear" the punctuation and better understand the poem's meaning.

TIP As you prepare for your oral interpretation, it may be helpful to attend a professional dramatic reading or another **literary performance.** Many bookstores and community arts groups stage poetry readings. Alternatively, check the library for videotaped readings. As you listen, use the evaluation criteria on page 97 to analyze, evaluate, and critique the presentation.

Punctuation Marks	Oral Technique
Commas, semicolons, colons, dashes, periods	Commas require brief pauses; semicolons, colons, dashes, and periods need increasingly longer pauses.
Words in parentheses	Pause and use a softer volume.
Italicized or underlined words	Emphasize words by placing more stress on them or by speaking louder.
Question marks	Use a rising inflection.
Especially significant words, phrases, or lines	Vary pitch, volume, or rate to emphasize meaning.

Making Your Mark   As you craft and rehearse your oral presentation, it is helpful to use a working "script." On a double-spaced copy of the poem, make notes and markings to help you remember how to speak words, lines, and stanzas. (It is a good idea to mark a manuscript, even if you plan to deliver the poem from memory.) Here are some suggested markings:

- Use a slash (/) to indicate short pauses and a double slash (//) for longer pauses.
- Use arrows to indicate continuous speaking from line to line or stanza to stanza.
- Underline or circle key words, phrases, and lines, as well as unusual punctuation.
- Use brackets in the margin to link parallel constructions.

- Use phonetic spellings to help you pronounce troublesome words.
- Write concise notes about tone or content in the margins.

Look at the following short example to see how one well-known poem—Walt Whitman's "When I Heard the Learn'd Astronomer"—could be marked.

When I heard the learn'd astronomer, //

When the proofs, / the figures, / were ranged in columns before me, //

When I was shown the charts and diagrams, / to add, divide, and measure them, //

When I sitting heard the astronomer where he lectured with much applause in the lecture-room, //

How soon unaccountable I became tired and sick, /

Till rising and gliding out I wandered off by myself, /

In the mystical moist night-air, / and from time to time, /

The change from misery to wonder

Look'd up in perfect silence at the stars. //

You should rehearse your oral interpretation many times. Some sections may require more work—and more adjustments—than others. After several rehearsals, you may want to record yourself on videotape or audio-tape. Such recordings can help you to evaluate your performance and to discover opportunities for improvement. On videotape, pay special attention to such **nonverbal strategies** as facial expressions and hand gestures. Videotape often reveals how ineffective "dramatic" gestures and facial expressions can be. As a general rule, small, subtle gestures and facial expressions work better in an oral interpretation. If you do not have access to video equipment, ask a friend to watch you rehearse and offer some feedback on your performance; use your friend's praise and suggestions to improve your performance.

TIP Increasing the volume and force of your voice is vital if you deliver your oral interpretation in a theater or auditorium without a public-address system. Practice projecting your voice so that it can be heard in a large room.

Introducing Your Performance   It is a good idea to pique audience interest—and set the stage for your oral interpretation—with a brief introduction. You might identify the poem's author and title, provide helpful background information, or explain why you selected this particular poem. If you are reading an excerpt, it might be useful to summarize preceding sections or provide an overview of the poem. Remember, however, to be *brief*.

Deliver the Oral Presentation

Staying Loose and Focused   Nearly all performers—of all types and at all levels—experience nervousness before "going on." Since nervousness is natural, accept it in yourself and concentrate on the text. Thinking about the text instead of your anxiety will help you remain relaxed, and you can avoid the stilted, unnatural tones that result from tension. Challenge yourself to stay focused on conveying the text during *every instant* of your presentation. As continuously as possible, keep your eyes up and look at all sections of your audience. Finally, don't rush to finish: Hold the final moment of your reading for a beat before "dropping out of character" or turning to sit down.

Listen to and Evaluate an Oral Interpretation

Food for Thought   As you take the role of listener, use the following questions to help you evaluate an oral interpretation. Be sure to give **feedback** to the presenter.

- Does the introduction help a listener prepare for—or understand—the poem?
- Does the performer accurately reflect the attitude and personality of the poem's speaker?
- Does the performer emphasize important words and passages?
- Does the performer's voice indicate the connections between ideas?
- Does he or she vary pitch, tone, or rate of speaking in ways that convey meaning or mood?
- What is my overall reaction to the presentation of this poem?

TIP   As you listen to someone else's oral interpretation, be an **active listener.** Make eye contact and nod your head to show you are listening.

As you listen, you may also employ a variety of listening styles: critical, appreciative, and reflective, for example. Notice how the speaker appeals to your emotions, and consider how the poem reminds you of other pieces you have read or things you have experienced.

YOUR TURN 11   Creating and Performing an Oral Interpretation of a Poem

Choose a poem and prepare and perform an oral interpretation. Ask for feedback from listeners, and use it to set goals for future performances.

WHAT'S AHEAD?

In this section, you will learn to
- identify how different media forms shape news coverage
- analyze how two media cover the same event

Comparing and Contrasting Media Coverage of an Event

People see things very differently. It's a fact. Extended definitions wouldn't really be necessary if we saw—and *defined*—things exactly the same way. Consider this scenario: Two students, one a football player and one a brilliant math student, attend a pep rally. After the cheering and speech-making are over, they go back to class. The football player is walking on air—he feels the pep rally showed his classmates' support of the team. The mathematician, who has been prepping for an academic competition this weekend, wonders why the review session she attended was cut short to make room for a pep rally. To her, the pep rally was a waste of time. Does one of the students have the *right* way of looking at the pep rally? Not really. Their different reactions prove that people define things in unique ways that reflect their own experiences.

Like people, media define events in unique ways. In fact, every media message is shaped and limited by the technology and traditions of the medium itself. As an example, think about the strengths and weaknesses of covering an apartment fire on network TV news versus Web news.

Medium	Strengths	Weaknesses
Television news broadcast	Moving images and sound engage viewers' senses; cutting from one fiery image to another keeps attention on-screen; video and audio encourage emotional involvement of viewers—the sense of "being there."	Extreme time constraints—story lasts less than a minute; little discussion of fire's causes, other related information; "shocking" video footage overshadows substance of story. Viewers may wish they knew more.

World Wide Web news report	Interactive—viewers can use mouse to skip ahead or back in story; essentially a print form—audience reads text—so viewers can spend as much or as little time on story as they wish; great detail possible about fire's causes and effects.	Some Web sources unreliable—newsgroups may contain information from anonymous sources without supporting evidence; if Web report was provided by TV network, it might give just summary, no details.

As the chart indicates, our experience of the news varies according to the medium used to present it. People who want to get a complete picture of what happened frequently compare and contrast the way several media forms cover an event. Some aspects of news stories, like attention-grabbing techniques and emotional impact, are fairly easy to analyze and critique. Two points of comparison that are more subtle are the *sequence* of information in a story and the *complexity* of the story itself.

Sequence

What? When?   The **sequence,** or order in which information is presented, shapes a news story in several ways. Usually the most important information in a news story—whether a print, television, or radio story—comes at or near the beginning, in a statement called the *lead.* The **lead** is designed to attract viewers' attention. Sometimes the lead answers the questions *Who? What? When? Where? Why?* and *How?* Other times, the lead inspires curiosity by juxtaposing unusual information or facts. For example, the lead to a story about an unsuccessful mirror experiment on Space Station *Mir* might look like this:

> Russian officials scrapped the *Mir* Space Station's much-hyped space mirror experiment today after the metal object got stuck and failed to properly unfurl.

The lead is important because it helps the audience know what kind of story is coming and what kinds of details to expect. The lead about the mirror story lets readers know that it is a *problem* story (rather than a *hero* story, a *plea for help,* or a *humans versus nature/the environment* story). Then readers can ask themselves, "What kind of information generally appears in problem stories?" Most include causes, attempted solutions, and explanations about why the solutions failed. When readers know what type of story they are reading or seeing, they instinctively pay attention for the kinds of details that appear in that kind of story.

TIP   Just as different media give viewers different perspectives on an event, they also create different images of people who are running for public office. These images, in turn, have an effect on the **democratic process.** To get a more complete sense of who a candidate is and what he or she stands for, try comparing and contrasting stories about the campaign that appear in different media.

From Whose Point of View?   Writers and editors also manipulate the sequence of information to infuse a story with their **point of view**—a positive or negative opinion of the subject. To see how this is done, consider the sequence of information in the closing lines of this story:

> Russian space program officials had hoped the mirror would shed beams of light five miles wide on northern cities starved of sun during the long Arctic winter. Skeptics maintain the effort would have failed.

TIP   People who visit Web sites to get their news may feel that they are escaping the fixed sequence of TV news and the point of view of the people who create news stories. In one sense, they are right to think so. Web news is more interactive than TV news. Web users can use a mouse to scroll through information quickly or select different stories and images.

However, Web producers do in fact decide which story links and image links will be available on any given page of their news. Consequently, even though the sequence of information in a Web news story is more variable than a TV sequence, it is still determined by producers.

By ending with the skeptics' opinions, the author leaves readers with the impression that he sides with the skeptics. If the last two lines had been rearranged, the author might have expressed a hopeful point of view rather than a negative one.

Writers and editors manipulate sequence not only in newspaper and magazine articles, but also in television news, Web news, and radio news. In network news programs, reporters arrange video carefully to create particular effects. For instance, two TV news stories might both feature the same two clips: footage of space program officials looking depressed when the mirror malfunctions, and footage of one official expressing how proud he is of the space program and of the cosmonauts on *Mir*. An opponent of the mirror project might begin her story with the proud official, and then undercut the force of the official's words by featuring images and audio that stress the failures of the day. A proponent of the project would reverse the order, leaving viewers with the sense that the Russian space program will recover from this malfunction and move on.

Use the following questions to analyze how a story develops **sequence:**

- How does the story begin? How does the story end?
- From the beginning, what kind of story do you expect (problem story, plea for help, hero story, humans versus nature, and so on)?
- Based on the beginning, what kind of *details* do you expect to see in this story (eyewitness interviews, hard facts, or others)?
- Do you have a sense of the producers' or editors' point of view? How have words and images been manipulated to create that point of view?

Complexity

Below the Tip of the Iceberg   Behind any "just the facts" story, there is a *context*—background events in history and in the wider culture that have bearing on the story. Furthermore, in addition to any person's perspective on an event, there are always numerous other perspectives. Just think about it: In nearly every event, from a car accident to a political election, each participant has a different perspective. When news writers add context and additional perspectives to a story, they give it **complexity.**

Complexity helps readers understand a story's importance more completely and see how it fits together with other events, present and past. News reports of the mirror experiment, for instance, could provide complexity by reminding viewers that *Mir* has been plagued with problems, as well as by providing interviews with people who are affected by the mirror's malfunction—the Russian Space Program officials, the families of cosmonauts on *Mir*, and the Russians who had hoped to benefit from the mirror.

Use the following questions to analyze a news story's **complexity:**

- Which background details are included? Do they help you see how this event fits into a bigger picture?

- Which details and information are omitted?

- What types of sources are interviewed?

- Do the people interviewed represent a cross-section of all the people affected by the issue or event? If not, who is left out? Why might these people's perspectives be left out?

TIP Print media are usually better at providing context than radio and TV are. In Web news, for example, the page on which the story appears may include a sidebar with links to related stories and interviews that help readers broaden their understanding of the issue. By following links in those related stories as well, Web users can trace the seemingly endless complexity of a single story.

One Student's Discoveries

The chart below shows what one student discovered when he used the preceding analysis questions to compare how two stories developed sequence and complexity. One story was on network TV, and the other appeared on a news Web site. Both reported on an avalanche in the French Alps.

SEQUENCE	
Similarities	Differences
Both stories are set up as humans vs. nature stories. They focus on the devastation caused to towns and the effort to rescue trapped and unconscious skiers.	The network news story begins with peaceful Alpine views, then cuts to footage of the avalanche—shots of the devastation and rescue workers. It ends with a shot of heavy afternoon snowfall and a warning that time is running out. The Web news story begins with a brief description of the avalanche and then focuses on the rescue effort. Links in the text connect to photographs of rescue workers and survivors.

(continued)

COMPLEXITY	
Similarities	Differences
Both stories featured interviews. Both informed readers that this particular area of the Alps is prone to avalanches. Both showed the site of the avalanche on a map of Europe.	The TV story provided clips from an interview with an American couple who had been rescued earlier that day. The Web news story included this, too, and it also included interviews with the head of the rescue operation and with local merchants worried about the effects the avalanche may have on business. The Web news story's sidebar provided links to several articles on related topics, such as previous avalanches in the area, their cumulative effect on the local economy, and steps taken to prevent and prepare for avalanches.

One Student's Critique

Once you have taken stock of the ways two stories are similar and different, ask the tough question: *Why?* How did their different media forms shape them? Here is how the student who wrote the chart above brainstormed about the complexity of the two stories.

When I compare the Web story to the TV news story, I really see that the Web story was more complex—in particular, it provided a lot of context. The rescue effort was an important part of it, but the story went on to examine how the avalanche might affect the economy of the town. The sidebars gave more context about the economic effects of avalanches and what people have been doing to prevent them. The TV news story had more fixed time restraints, and so it focused on <u>this particular</u> avalanche and rescue mission. It provided "action" footage—like shots of the rescue effort. It also made use of shock value by showing us the devastation and made it feel "local" by including an interview with young Americans.

YOUR TURN 12 — Comparing and Contrasting Media Coverage of an Event

Choose an event and locate two news reports about it—whether television, Web, radio, or print reports. Then, write a **brief essay** or give an **oral presentation** about how the media may have shaped the message. Be sure to use the questions in this section to analyze the stories' sequence of information and complexity.

Choices

Choose one of the following activities to complete.

▶ **CAREERS**

1. Crack the College Code
Create a dictionary of important words to define for yourself and your family as part of the college application process. Ask your high school counselor to help you research the meanings of words such as *financial aid* and *preregistration*. Create a **pamphlet,** and put a copy in your school library.

▶ **CREATIVE WRITING**

2. The Domino Effect Write a **short story** about the chain of events that occurs when two characters understand the same word differently. The tone of your story can be comic or tragic, but it should explain the chain of events clearly and eventually reveal the characters' different definitions of the word.

▶ **CROSSING THE CURRICULUM: SCIENCE**

3. Teach Simply Choose any scientific process and write an **extended definition** of it for a child. Explain what the phenomenon is and why it is important. Then, to describe how it works, devise a metaphor and extend the metaphor as far as logically possible. Look up necessary informa-

tion in the library or on the Internet, or ask your science teacher for help.

▶ **CROSSING THE CURRICULUM: ART**

4. Say It with Pictures
Choose an abstract term, like *trust* or *hope,* and create a **collage,** clipping images that define it from magazines and newspapers. (Or draw your own images.) Arrange the images on a piece of poster board, and display it in a prominent place in your classroom. Decide whether you want to write the word on the poster board itself or let viewers guess what word your collage defines.

▶ **MEDIA AND TECHNOLOGY**

5. Get It on Tape Borrow a video camera, and interview various people about their definition of an abstract word, such as *success, friendship,* or *work.* Create an introduction for your **video** that explains why you think it is useful to collect and examine these definitions. Finally, in your conclusion, summarize the most interesting or important points of the definitions and explain how talking to people has affected your definition of the word.

PORTFOLIO

3 Reporting Progress

Reading Workshop

Reading a Progress Report

Writing Workshop

Writing a Progress Report

Speaking and Listening

Writing and Delivering an Informative Speech

Viewing and Representing

Analyzing Media Stereotypes

Informational Text

Exposition

A newspaper reporter keeps an editor up-to-date on an important story. A team of scientists explains its efforts to find a new vaccine. A teacher describes a student's work over the course of a semester. What do these events have in common? In each case, someone is making a *progress report.*

Progress reports explain how much work has been done on a specific project over a specific period of time. To explain fully, progress reports must look *back* at all the steps taken so far and look *ahead* to the necessary steps for reaching the final goal. You might think of progress reports as formal responses to the question *How are things going*?

Readers—whether teachers, architects, or the governor of your state—use progress reports to see how well a project is advancing and whether the plan needs to be adjusted. You use progress reports, too—when you explain the progress of your science project or hear someone announce how the school recycling drive is coming along.

YOUR TURN 1 **Brainstorming About Progress Reports**

Imagine that you are a medical researcher, a lawyer, or a member of another profession. With a few of your classmates, brainstorm the kinds of activities on which you might have to report progress. Discuss why your progress reports would be important and to whom they would be addressed. If you wish, also think about projects in your own life. What kinds of progress reports are necessary for your part-time job, summer plans, college hunt, or school activities? Be prepared to share your brainstorming ideas with the class.

internet**connect**

go.hrw.com

GO TO: go.hrw.com
KEYWORD: EOLang 11-3

Reading a Progress Report

Progress reports have to keep two things in view at once: the end goal and all the small steps that must be taken to get there—or the whole and the parts. According to one Chinese proverb, a journey of a thousand miles begins with a single step. In the newspaper article on the opposite page, which reports on student test scores, see if you can figure out the big goal and the "steps" along the way.

Preparing to Read

READING SKILL

Summarizing   As you read the article on the next page, you will probably ask yourself, "What is this really about?" or "How do things stand overall?" **Summarizing,** or boiling something down to its main ideas, can help you answer those questions; when you restate and condense something in your own words, you are bound to understand it better and to remember what you have read. To summarize accurately, readers must keep an eye out for key words and phrases that may signal main ideas. (In progress reports such as the one following, key words are often *improvement, increase, decrease, progress,* and similar words that indicate trends.)

READING FOCUS

Measurements of Progress   In progress reports, readers expect to see *concrete* evidence of progress, not vague statements like "Everything is coming along fine." To explain how everything is progressing in a project, progress reports include **measurements of progress**—specific markers of how much has been done to reach a goal and what is left to do. Often these markers are quantities, either exact numbers of steps or statistics such as percentages. If, for example, an article reports on a fund-raising drive, you might expect it to tell you that *25 percent* of the monetary goal has been raised. If your school counselor publishes a list for you to follow in preparing for next year's graduation, you might learn that you had completed five of the ten steps on the list. See if you can identify measurements of progress in the article ahead.

The article below appeared in *The New York Times* in September 1997. As you read, jot down answers to the numbered active-reading questions.

from THE NEW YORK TIMES

Students' Test Scores Show Slow but Steady Gains at Nation's Schools

by PETER APPLEBOME

Despite the pervasive[1] sense that the nation's schools are mired in decline, [the results of] three major tests of educational achievement released over the last month indicate that more than a decade of attention to student achievement seems to be paying off in modest, but significant, continuing improvements in student scores.

The progress is better in math and science than in reading and writing. It is more gradual than dramatic. And overall figures obscure the enormous variety of the nation's schools and the alarming shortcomings in its worst schools and school systems.

Examining long-term trends in the College Board's reasoning tests (the S.A.T.) and the American College Testing college-entrance tests (the A.C.T.), as well as the nation's broadest elementary and high school tests (the National Assessment of Educational Progress), which are given to a cross section of students, analysts are increasingly coming to see advances not only in test scores but, perhaps not surprisingly, in the contents of course work as well.

The progress comes at a time when students tend to be more diverse ethnically and poorer than in the past—which has been associated with lower achievement—and when college preparatory tests are being taken by a broader segment of the student population.

Coming as an array of critics call for revolutionary changes in American educa-

---

1. **pervasive** (pər·vā′ siv): spread throughout; generally accepted.

1. What main idea do the title and first two paragraphs present?

2. Why does the writer mention this particular background information here and in the previous paragraph?

tion, like vouchers and charter schools, the recent findings are likely to provide ammunition to those who counter that what is needed is not radical systemic reform but sustained, concerted attention to basics like teacher training, adequate resources, higher standards, and better tests.

"What leaps out at me is that we've got steady progress, and we have steady progress for all the major subgroups, whites, blacks, and Hispanics," said Marshall Smith, Acting Deputy Secretary of Education. "And that's exactly what you want in education. I don't think the word is getting out, because most people think test scores are still going down, but we have a positive story in the way progress is steady and significant."

And, in a tantalizing sidelight to the National Assessment of Educational Progress scores, which were released on Saturday, indications are the biggest improvement may be coming in the nation's belea-

3. Why does the writer use this quotation?

4. What two time periods show a continuous rise in scores?

guered public schools, not its private ones.

The first of the recent results was the A.C.T., taken by nearly 60 percent of America's entering college freshmen, predominantly in Western and Midwestern states. Scores announced in August rose for the fourth time in the last five years, only the second time since A.C.T. scores were first reported in 1960 that the national average increased four times in five years. The earlier period was 1984 through 1988.

"We're certainly seeing a different pattern in A.C.T. scores than we did 20 or 30 years ago," said the A.C.T. president, Richard L. Ferguson. "This period of stable or increasing scores coincides almost exactly with a nationwide effort beginning in about 1983 to improve the education we offer our young people."

5. What goal was established in 1983? Why might this goal be impossible to achieve completely?

6. What advances do the test results show?

Scores on the College Board's tests, taken by 1.1 million students, rose in math to the highest level in 26 years but were flat in English. Officials say the results, released last week, take into account the recentering[2] of test scores that produced a rise in scores two years ago.

The national assessment tests have shown significant progress in science and math over the last two decades, with less progress in reading and writing, according to a report of long-term trends released Saturday.

Similarly, Michael Casserly, head of the Council of the Great City Schools,

---

2. recentering: In 1995, the national average used as a marker for the mathematical and verbal sections of the College Board exam was changed, or recentered, based on the performance of students on the 1990 exam. When mathematics was recentered, the average score rose 20 points; when the verbal section was recentered, the average rose almost 80 points. The effects of recentering are still being debated.

7. Is this lack of progress explained? What additional information would you like?

8. What do these numbers measure? How do they support the point in the previous paragraph?

9. What does this quotation suggest about the future progress of test scores?

which represents the 50 largest urban school districts, said several districts, including New York, Chicago, Houston, Milwaukee, Philadelphia, San Francisco, and Seattle, have shown improvements on various standardized tests.

Still, experts say that the improvements are modest overall and that achievement results still range from encouraging to dismal. For instance, the most recent national assessment test of fourth-grade reading showed 40 percent of students did not score at even the lowest of three possible levels.

"There has been some improvement, and that's to be welcomed," said Chester Finn, an education expert at the Hudson Institute and a proponent of vouchers and charter schools. "But after spending more money and putting ourselves through all kinds of hoops, if we'd had zero payoff, it would have been pretty depressing."

One intriguing sidelight to the national assessment scores is that the greatest progress apparently has been made in public schools. Private-school students still outperform public-school students at all levels, however.

Yet, in mathematics, for example, between 1982 and 1996, scores of students in public schools improved nine points for 17-year-olds, six points for 13-year-olds, and thirteen points for 9-year-olds on a scale of 500 points. For private schools, 17-year-olds and 13-year-olds gained five points and 9-year-olds gained seven points.

Officials at the National Center for Education Statistics said that because of a small sampling, the individual differences for each grade and subject area could not be shown to be statistically significant, but because ten of twelve measures—four subject matters at three age levels—show public schools gaining more than private ones, the overall pattern appears to be statistically valid.

Analyses of all three tests indicate that one factor helping to push up results is that students are taking more rigorous courses.

"I think we're all tapping into the same mother lode and coming up with essentially the same results, with the trends seeming to be reasonably positive, less in verbal/reading than in math," said Donald M. Stewart, president of the College Board. "I think it has something to do with students working harder, taking harder courses. But looking cautiously at what for us is a self-selected group of students, things seem to be moving in the right direction. I guess that's called cautious optimism."

First Thoughts on Your Reading

Work with a partner to answer the following questions.

1. In your own words, what does the article say about the most recent national test scores? What progress or lack of progress do they show?

2. The writer discusses national test scores from three different tests. How do such scores indicate progress among students?

3. Who are some of the various people or groups that would be interested in reports such as this one? Why?

| READING SKILL

Summarizing

Now, for a Brief Recap . . .   When you **summarize,** you restate and condense a writer's main ideas and essential details. Summarizing is an important skill because it helps you think critically. To summarize accurately, you must distinguish between the most important ideas and details in a piece and those that are less important.

TIP **Summarizing** is especially important for *writers* of progress reports, too. To present a clear picture, they must often summarize complicated indicators of progress, presenting only the most essential ones. In the selection you just read, for example, the writer summarized information from three separate national tests.

Look at the short article below. Then, notice how one student condensed the material in the summary that follows the article.

Test Scores Soar in Charles County
by Rudy Gomez

Charles County administrators are patting themselves on the back and congratulating students for their dramatic increase in college placement test scores. Three years ago, the long-range planning committee of area high schools set the goal of raising student performance on standardized tests by 15 percent. It looks as if their hard work and dedication have paid off magnificently.

This year, test scores on two major standardized tests are 20 percent higher than they were three years ago. On average, students have raised their performance six points for the ACT and twenty-one points for the SAT. Mrs. Sabra Delmonico, counselor for Midway High School, sums up the feelings of area administrators and teachers: "We are thrilled at the results. The students certainly benefited from an after-school vocabulary-building class and the better practice booklets and audiotapes the district purchased."

In his article "Test Scores Soar in Charles County," Rudy Gomez reports that the college placement test scores for area high school seniors have risen dramatically in the last three years. Students this year scored six points higher on the ACT and twenty-one points higher on the SAT—a 20 percent average increase. The rise pleased school administrators, who had set a goal of a 15 percent increase three years ago. Two factors contributed to the rise in student performance: better practice materials supplied by the district and a special after-school vocabulary-building class.

THINKING IT THROUGH Summarizing

To summarize a reading selection, use the following steps. Look also at the notes made by the student writer of the summary above.

▶ **STEP 1 Skim the piece, noting all key ideas, words, and phrases, as well as the author and title.** It often helps to look at each of the topic sentences.

Key ideas: Charles County test scores up; school personnel "thrilled"; exceeded district goal

▶ **STEP 2 Then, try to capture the piece's main idea in its most complete, or broad, sense.** One way to identify the main idea is to ask yourself what statement would be supported by *all* of the key ideas in the article.

Main idea: County college placement scores have risen dramatically in last three years, pleasing school personnel.

▶ **STEP 3 Re-read the piece more carefully to gather details essential to the meaning of the piece.** Be sure to jot down important names, dates, statistics, and places, but avoid examples and description.

20 percent gain since three years ago, when 15 percent goal was established; more specific gains important, too: six points on ACT and twenty-one points on the SAT

▶ **STEP 4 Express the main idea of the piece and its most important support in your own words. Then, double-check your understanding.** Have you accurately captured the main idea and *all* essential details?

I forgot to include why gains occurred: district provided after-school vocabulary class and booklets and audiotapes. (Practice booklets and audiotapes can fit under the category "practice materials.")

TIP Remember that when you summarize, you are trying to determine the most direct and accurate answer to the question "What is this piece of writing about?" Make sure to *condense* the article instead of *retelling* it. Also, make sure that you have withheld all personal judgments about the article. A summary is a distillation of the author's ideas, not your own.

TIP When possible, also condense details into broader categories; for example, if it is not important to mention the SAT and ACT individually, just use the term "college placement tests" for both.

Using the four steps previously outlined, summarize a three-paragraph section from the article "Students' Test Scores Show Slow but Steady Gains at Nation's Schools." Start with the paragraph beginning "One intriguing sidelight" and include the two paragraphs immediately following it.

READING FOCUS

TIP Some projects or programs have **open-ended goals,** and the progress report may reflect that open-endedness. In the reading selection, for example, the goal of student improvement on test scores is ongoing.

Measurements of Progress

Are We There Yet? Progress reports are a bit like road maps; they show how much distance has been covered in a project or program and how much distance remains to reach the goal. **Measurements of progress**—like distance markers on a map—provide precise, concrete information about what has been done in a project and what is left to do. Of course, progress is measured in a variety of ways, depending upon the project and the goal. The following chart shows some of the possible ways that progress can be measured.

Ways to Measure Progress	Examples
Test Scores	Since the introduction of the tutoring program, students' test scores have risen an **average of fifteen points**.
Percentages and Fractions	The goal for Project VOTE is to increase voter turnout in this district by **25 percent** for the next national election.
Amounts	The student council plans to raise **$20,000** for area charities.
Frequency	Survey results show that the health unit on dental hygiene has persuaded students to visit a dentist **twice every year**.
Performance	Kate has studied piano for only two years, but **she can already play a difficult piece by Chopin**.
Mastery of Knowledge	After participating in the program, **each student could name the capital of every state in the United States**.
Tasks	With two weeks left before the group project is due, the students in Group A **have completed five of the seven preparation tasks** they were assigned.

Analyzing Measurements of Progress

To analyze what measures have been used in a progress report—and what they show—use the following steps.

▶ **STEP 1 Define the goal in the report.** Toward what final result is the progress moving?

▶ **STEP 2 Identify the time frame (days, months, years) for completion of the project.** Can you identify a completion date, or is the progress open-ended? When did the progress begin? When was the last time progress was identified or measured?

▶ **STEP 3 Identify the ways progress is being measured.** Is progress measured by a specific number of steps, or is some other measure used?

▶ **STEP 4 Decide how much progress has been made between the last measurement of progress and the current report.** How much is still left to do? If it would be helpful, create a time line or bar graph.

Progress ────────┼──────────────┼──────────────┼──────── Goal
　　　　　　Measurement　　　Measurement　　　Measurement
　　　　　　　　#1　　　　　　　　#2　　　　　　　　#3

▶ **STEP 5 Be sure to note if the goal is abstract or ideal, and explain why the ideal may never be reached.** Even if the goal is unreachable, ask yourself if the progress is limited, steady, or substantial. If you can see no progress, does the report explain why, or does it describe the obstacles in the way of the progress?

TIP Progress is moving toward a result—the completion of a project, the final goal, the end of a program. A report of progress explains how close or how far away from completion the project is, and it uses various measuring tools to determine what's been done and what still needs to be done. It helps to keep this definition in mind as you read.

The following chart shows how one student began to analyze the measurements of progress for the first reading selection on student test scores.

Step 1: The progress is toward improved student test scores. The final result would be perfect scores.

Step 2: The time frame is open-ended, but the progress actually began in 1987.

YOUR TURN 3 Analyzing Measurements of Progress

Use Steps 3–5 outlined in the Thinking It Through to complete the rest of the student chart above. (Use your own paper.) Look back at the reading selection on page 107 to develop your analysis. Then, discuss your chart with a small group of classmates.

MINI-LESSON VOCABULARY

Cause-and-Effect Context Clues

In progress reports, the steps or markers toward a goal are sometimes linked by cause and effect. If one step cannot be accomplished, then the next step cannot be achieved either. In progress reports, as well as other kinds of writing, readers can usually determine the meaning of an unfamiliar word if they understand its cause-and-effect relationship with the rest of the sentence or passage. To do this, readers use **cause-and-effect context clues,** words that signal how the unfamiliar word is affecting (or being affected by) something else.

THINKING IT THROUGH   Using Cause-and-Effect Context Clues

Take a look at the example sentence below and the steps following it.

Since public-school test score gains are so dramatic, parents of public-school children have reason for *optimism* about their children's education.

▷ **STEP 1** **Look for clue words that suggest a cause-and-effect relationship, such as** *because, consequently, determines, reasons, thus,* **and** *since.*

▷ **STEP 2** **Ask what kind of cause-and-effect relationship the context clue word suggests.** In the example above, *since* indicates that test score gains caused the parents' optimism. Because test score gains would be seen as positive by parents, *optimism* must have positive connotations, too—maybe "encouragement" or "hopefulness."

▷ **STEP 3** **Check your definition of the word in place of the unfamiliar word in the sentence. Check your guess in a dictionary also.** "Hopefulness" works in the sentence; the dictionary defines *optimism* as "taking a hopeful view of matters or expecting the best outcome."

PRACTICE

Determine the meanings of the italicized words in the following sentences.

1. Public outrage at poor student performance on standardized tests has resulted in a *beleaguered* public-school system.

2. The school district established more teacher training and higher standards, built better facilities, and provided extra resources; consequently, public education in the area has enjoyed *systemic* improvement.

3. He was so embarrassed by his many wrong answers on the test that he answered the teacher's questions with *diffidence.*

4. As a result of several self-improvement strategies, public schools no longer seem *mired* in problems.

5. Because students took college *preparatory* courses, they were ready for the academic challenges of higher education.

Logic Questions

Standardized reading tests such as state tests and the SAT will often ask a logic question, one that asks you to identify the logical relationship between details in a passage—that is, how two or more details fit into an overall pattern. For example, a logic question about a progress report might ask you how the steps work together chronologically to achieve a certain result. When you answer a logic question, pay special attention to words and phrases that show the particular relationship between the details, such as *despite* and *on the other hand* (for contrast); *likewise* and *in the same way* (for comparison); *therefore* and *as a result* (for cause and effect); and *before* and *subsequently* (for chronology).

Here is a typical **reading passage** and its logic question:

> In a January poll 224 students indicated they would be interested in volunteering to "adopt" the school's riverside trail. Fifty-three people then organized the "Trail Guardians Club" with Mrs. Felicia Gonzales of the science department as the sponsor. The club's first official meeting was scheduled for early February.
>
> During the first meeting, the members elected officers and discussed the goals of the club. They decided one important goal was to hold a Trail Day on May 7. Students, teachers, and parents will be invited to explore the trail using an interpretive map designed by the club. In the remaining three months of the school year, however, volunteers must first clean up the trail and design the map. The members then drafted a plan of work and assigned tasks.

1. In the passage above, "Trail Guardians" will hold a Trail Day

   A. before spring, as a public service

   B. at the February meeting

   C. after they have cleaned up the trail and devised a map

   D. once a month for the last three months of the school term

   E. before gaining a club sponsor

THINKING IT THROUGH   Answering Logic Questions

Keep the following steps in mind as you answer a logic question.

▶ STEP 1 **Read the question carefully and locate the specific details within the passage.** The information about the Trail Day is in the second paragraph.

▶ STEP 2 **Identify words or phrases that signal what kind of relationship the details have with the rest of the passage.** The words *during, first,* and *then* are words that show a chronological relationship.

▶ STEP 3 **Survey the passage again to avoid answers that are drawn from surrounding sections or that show inaccurate relationships.** All of the answers use chronological signal words, but only **C** correctly reflects the relationship between the Trail Day and the club's previous actions.

Writing a Progress Report

WHAT'S AHEAD?

In this workshop, you will write a progress report. You will also learn to

- recall and record progress
- analyze accomplishments
- design graphs to illustrate progress
- vary sentence lengths
- use the correct sequence of verb tenses

Imagine that you are working on a big project that is important to you, a project that requires many specific steps—learning to play the guitar well enough to be in a band, building a doghouse, or planting trees for a semester-long biology project. How can you show someone the progress you have made on this project? How can you yourself know how much you have accomplished and how much work there is left to be done?

When you want to demonstrate to someone—even to yourself—that you have made progress on a project, you can write a *progress report*. A **progress report** shows the amount of work done over a specific period of time in order to reach a goal. "Work done" can refer either to tasks you have accomplished on a project or to your results or findings so far. In the workplace, progress reports are written for people who need to be kept informed about a project so that they can decide whether the project should be continued, modified, or even halted. Since progress reports are generally written at fixed intervals—every week, once a month, or periodically during the year—they also serve as a record of the project after it is completed.

Prewriting

Choose a Topic

Mission *Not* Impossible   Often, progress reports are assigned by teachers who want to check on the status of lengthy class projects. When you are free to choose your own topic, however, try these ideas:

- **List your main interests and hobbies.** Are you training for a triathlon? planting a garden? collecting stamps? preparing for an orchestra performance? If so, what goal have you established for yourself?

- **Examine the different areas of your life,** such as your school, home, and community involvement. Can you think of an ongoing effort that you could use for a progress report?
- **Look for "triggers."** Browse the World Wide Web, read special-interest magazines, or watch TV "how-to" shows to find subjects that are related to your own experience. Look for something that makes you think, "That's what I am trying to do, too."

When you have found a few possible subjects, jot them down and circle the one for which you can most clearly explain progress.

TIP Try to keep your subject limited in scope; remember, you are writing a short report, not a book. Instead of reporting on what you have learned by taking care of animals, for example, focus on the process of raising one specific animal for a school or area livestock show.

KEY CONCEPT

Think About Purpose, Audience, and Tone

Who Wants to Know? **Remember that the purpose of a progress report is to inform an audience about the work done on a project.** You will explain your accomplishments so far, describe any problems you have encountered, and present your plan for reaching your goal.

The **audience** for your report may be teachers, classmates, partners working on different parts of the same project, or someone who doesn't know anything about your subject. How much background and explanation you include in your progress report often depends heavily upon who will read the report.

TIP Your **voice**—the way you talk to your readers in your report—should be natural, but you should avoid slang and overly informal expressions. Because you will be discussing your own efforts, use first-person pronouns such as *I, me, my,* and *we.*

THINKING IT THROUGH **Analyzing Audience**

Analyze your audience by asking yourself the following questions:

▶ **STEP 1** **To whom am I reporting?** What do they already know about the subject? Your English teacher, for example, may require more explanation of your physics project than your science teacher would.

▶ **STEP 2** **What does my reader *need* to know?** What details do I need to provide—either as background information or helpful tips for those working on a similar project?

▶ **STEP 3** **What kind of information—and how much—do I need to provide** to make the reader feel confident about the progress report's accuracy? Concrete, specific information often assures the more skeptical readers in your audience.

TIP Also think about **occasion,** an event or situation in the world that acts as a prompt for your essay. If, for example, your occasion for writing is an upcoming marathon, be sure to mention it specifically. You may pique the interest of those readers who will also take part.

TIP The format of a progress report depends on the complexity and time frame of the project. Progress reports can be written as memos, as letters, or as formal reports with title pages, summaries, tables of contents, and appendixes. Unless your teacher asks for one of these forms, write your progress report as a chronologically ordered narrative.

The **tone** of your report communicates your attitude about your subject to the audience. Because you want your audience to trust you, you should maintain a confident and optimistic tone, even when discussing setbacks. The following passages are examples of positive and negative tone. Notice the difference between these two approaches.

Negative   When the volunteer landscaping team from our biology class showed up to plant the trees in front of the school, we found that the nursery workers had not delivered the plants they had promised. We were very angry and confused.

Positive   Although the nursery workers had not delivered the trees as they had promised, the volunteer landscaping team spent Saturday afternoon cleaning out the flower beds. We rescheduled our tree planting day for the next Saturday, and assigned one person the job of contacting the nursery to make sure the trees would be delivered on time.

Recall Progress

How Did You Get Here from There?   In writing your progress report, you want to tell your audience how much you have accomplished and how long it has taken you. **To do this, you need to give your readers concrete, relevant information;** after all, vague statements like "Things are going smoothly" really do not communicate much of anything.

If you have taken any notes while working on your project, refer to them now to refresh your memory about your progress. If you have no written notes, make some mental notes about your accomplishments since your last report—or since the beginning of the project, if this report will be your first one. Jot down what has been done, as best you can remember. For a typical progress report, the following suggestions will help you note especially useful information.

KEY CONCEPT

COMPUTER TIP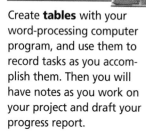

Create **tables** with your word-processing computer program, and use them to record tasks as you accomplish them. Then you will have notes as you work on your project and draft your progress report.

- **Identify the project and its purposes.**
- **Specify the time period covered by the report and the tasks accomplished** during that time.
- **Supply detailed data, results, or findings** that would be of use or of interest to your readers.
- **Note any unforeseen problems you encountered,** and explain how you are dealing with them. Your readers will feel confident about your honesty if you mention your problems and your plans for solving them.
- **Describe your plans for the immediate future** of your project.
- **List any additional resources, steps, or changes in procedure** needed to complete the project, and explain their effects upon the project's schedule.

Analyzing Accomplishments

Sometimes your accomplishments on a project are obvious, especially when they are tangible ones. Sometimes, however, accomplishments are not so apparent, especially when you have spent a lot of time planning your project or figuring out how to solve problems. By analyzing any of the steps you have taken in planning or solving problems, you can supply readers with the concrete evidence of progress they will want to see. Suppose you are on the planning committee for the Junior-Senior Prom, which is four months away. You may not think there is much to report, but look again. Breaking accomplishments into specific smaller steps often reveals the progress that has been made.

Topic: Planning the Junior-Senior Prom

Accomplishment: Established the need for a fund-raiser

Steps:
1. discussed the prom theme and budget with student council
2. discussed with principal possible sources of extra funds
3. designed, distributed, and analyzed surveys about options for prom, which showed students wanted a special party and would help with a fund-raiser

THINKING IT THROUGH **Analyzing Accomplishments**

Use these steps to analyze your accomplishments for your progress report.

1. **Make a list of your project's steps, breaking down each step into smaller steps.** Think also about the mental steps you took to plan the project. Use examples, facts, and numbers.

2. **Write down any problem you encountered.** For each problem listed, write the solutions you tried or that you will try. If you tried solutions that did not work, list your attempts and their results.

3. **Review your list and cross out any information that does not directly relate to the goal or accomplishment.** Avoid irrelevant details.

PRACTICE

In a small group, choose one of the following topics and break it into a set of possible tasks. Point out any possible problems.

1. Created a physical relief map for a geography class

2. Placed first in area high school band marching contest

3. Passed a driver's education course

4. Led a petition drive to request from the city council better bus service

5. Was hired for a part-time job

Saying Just Enough Plan to include enough—but not too much—detailed information about your progress. Although you may be tempted to include every tiny detail, too much information might make the report hard to follow. On the other hand, avoid supplying too little information—or information that is too general. Also, remember that concrete evidence is the only way your readers will completely understand the progress you have made.

TIP If, in jotting notes, you find yourself writing "this task is going smoothly" or "this step is on target," ask yourself *exactly* what you mean. When appropriate, include hard evidence such as facts, amounts, and statistics.

The chart below illustrates how one student recalled progress and analyzed accomplishments for a social studies project.

Project/Purpose/ Audience	Create a historical presentation on Cherokee Trail of Tears—the forced move of Cherokees from Georgia to Oklahoma in 1838—to take the place of the final exam and for possible display in library. Purpose of report is to inform social studies teacher about the status of my work.
Time Frame	Report is on project due in six weeks, on May 3. I've been working on project for six weeks.
Accomplishments or Findings	1. Used library to answer *who, what, when, where, why,* and *how* questions. Found out: Four different trails between Georgia and Oklahoma. 2. Wrote Cherokee Nation headquarters in Oklahoma for additional information, such as art and stories about Trail; received a reading list and copies of paintings about the experience.
Problems/Solution	Unsuccessful in finding one family's history on the Trail to use as example, but school librarian helped find a vinyl recording through interlibrary loan; also checked out books at local university with names of people on the march. When interlibrary loan sends the recording of stories, I will consider taping a portion for my presentation. Maybe I could also use Cherokee music, or drums to show the enduring strength of their culture.
Immediate Plans	1. Draw a map to show the four trails. 2. Devise a multimedia or 3-D presentation to show some aspect of Cherokee life, maybe what they lost, such as their homes in Georgia.
Other Resources	Our local nursery sells a flowering plant called a "Cherokee Rose." Perhaps I could learn how it got its name and use it in my presentation.

Choosing, Thinking, Gathering, and Analyzing

Review each of the preceding steps to plan your own progress report. Make sure to

- choose a specific topic on which to report progress
- think about your purpose, audience, tone, and voice
- recall your progress and analyze your accomplishments, jotting them in a chart like the previous one

"It seems some days like I make a little progress, then other days it seems like I'm not getting anywhere at all."

Organize Your Information

How Are Things Shaping Up?   Your progress report will need to be clear and direct in order to inform your audience about your project. Of course, you will begin by introducing your project, identifying the time frame, and explaining the goal. Then what? In progress reports, clear organization is the key. To communicate which steps have been done—and which are left to do—most writers use one of these two types of organization:

- **Chronological Order**   Chronological order is essentially time order; you use it when you want to present the steps and events since your last report (or since the start of the project) in the order in which they actually occurred.

■ **Logical Order**   This order is used when it makes more sense to group your material by tasks or findings than by time. Logical order is often used when your project requires you to carry out several different tasks at the same time.

The following chart shows how two different projects lend themselves to different organizational patterns.

LOGICAL ORDER	CHRONOLOGICAL ORDER
Social Studies Project: Cherokee Trail of Tears	**Fund–Raiser for Track Team**
Task 1: Did research at school: consulted reference books in school library; also used school's electronic library for Web sites and additional information.	**Week 1:** Scheduled "fun run" with city officials; coordinated event with other events on the city and school calendars.
Task 2: Mailed request for information: wrote the Cherokee Nation headquarters in Oklahoma to ask for information and to request copies of paintings.	**Week 2:** Wrote and printed registration materials.

Week 3: Began publicizing event: put ad in school paper, put posters up, passed out flyers. |
| **Task 3:** Did university library research: worked with school librarian to request vinyl recording from university archives through interlibrary loan. Also consulted books in university library. | **Week 4:** Assembled necessary equipment: tables for water stops, cones, signs to mark route, banners, stopwatches, start- and finish-line flags.

Week 5: Organized volunteers for race. |

Designing Your Writing

Creating Bar Graphs   You can show accomplishments visually in your progress report by including graphics. A particularly good way to display progress over time is in a **bar graph.** In a bar graph, quantities are shown side by side, so that a reader can compare the quantities quickly. In the following example, the bar graph gives immediate, visual evidence of the progress a runner has made in a seven-week training schedule.

TIP   Bar graphs are one of the most effective ways to represent numerical quantities. Because the length of the bars changes steadily, a bar graph also effectively displays trends over time.

Miles Run Each Week of Program

You may create bar graphs with computer software, or you may draw them by hand. In either case, keep the following suggestions in mind:

- **Decide whether to extend the measurement bars vertically or horizontally.** Experiment with each method; then, choose the one that best illustrates the progress you are reporting.

- **Draw horizontal and vertical axes, starting your measurements at zero or at the beginning of the project.** Use tick marks on one axis to indicate the quantities you are measuring—gallons, dollars, miles, and so forth. On the other axis, indicate the increments in which you are measuring the quantities—minutes, hours, days, weeks, and so on.

- **Label the horizontal and vertical axes of your graph,** and, if necessary, place labels next to each bar, too. In the example above, the axes are labeled "Miles Run" and "Weeks," and each bar is labeled by the number of the week ("1," "2").

- **Remember that your graph is supposed to be clear at a glance**—make sure you haven't left out any labels or confused any amounts. For clarity, give the entire graph a title, and, if necessary, use a key—a short guide to reading the graph correctly.

- **Refer to the bar graph in the text of your paper** and explain its purpose for your readers. Explain any variations or setbacks.

TIP Other graphic organizers such as tables, charts, or graphs are helpful if your progress report contains a lot of data. Introduce the graphic with a line of text summarizing the findings, or present your graphics separately from the main text in an appendix.

If you save graphics for an appendix, summarize the data within the body of your report and include a note that refers readers to the actual graphic. (For more information about **tables, charts,** and **graphs,** see page 931.)

YOUR TURN 5 **Organizing Your Information**

Review each of the prewriting steps. Before you begin writing your progress report, make sure to decide whether to organize your report in a chronological or logical order, and think about ways you might incorporate visuals such as bar graphs into your report.

Writing

Progress Report

| Framework | Directions and Explanations |

Framework

Introduction
- Introduce your project.
- Describe the time period covered by the progress report.
- State the purpose of your project.

Body
- Include background information and define terms.
- Explain the first significant accomplishment, and so on.
- Explain any problems.

Conclusion
- Provide an overall view of project.
- Confirm or revise the time schedule for completion of the project.

Directions and Explanations

Provide a Context To familiarize your audience with your project, briefly describe it or explain why you are working on it.

Announce the Time Frame Explain how long the project has been underway and how long you expect it to last. Give a specific target date for completion.

State Your Goal Explain what you hope to accomplish. Be specific, and use a confident tone.

Include Background Information Give your audience a fuller understanding of your project, its beginnings, and its direction. Also, define any specialized terms.

Organize Accomplishments Organize your accomplishments in the way that best suits your project, either in logical or chronological order. Use transitions such as *first, next, then,* and *finally.*

Explain Accomplishments Along with each accomplishment, give evidence that supports your claim of progress, such as specific examples or supporting statistics.

Explain Any Problems Discuss any problems you encountered. Emphasize the solutions you have used (or will use) in dealing with the problems. List any additional resources you may need, or any additional problems you must solve.

Sum Up Your Progress Restate your most important accomplishments. Briefly describe your plans for the future of the project.

Restate Your Time Frame Explain any changes to your time schedule, or confirm the completion date.

YOUR TURN 6 Writing a First Draft

Review the framework above and the Writer's Model that follows the framework. Then, write a draft of your progress report.

A Writer's Model

The following short essay, which is a final draft, closely follows the Framework on the previous page.

Progress Report for Final Project in Social Studies:
Presentation of the Cherokee Trail of Tears

For the past six weeks, I have been working on a project for my social studies class that focuses on the Cherokee Trail of Tears. The project will take the place of my final exam for the class, and the project is due in six weeks, on May 3. My project is designed to present the historical event in an interesting and thought-provoking way to my classmates, and I am hoping that our school librarian will display the finished project in the library.

The Trail of Tears was the forced removal of the Cherokee people from Georgia to Oklahoma in 1838. Even though the U.S. Supreme Court had ruled against the efforts of the U.S. government to take from the Cherokees the lands that past treaties had guaranteed them, President Andrew Jackson ordered the Cherokees to be removed from their homes. About fourteen thousand Cherokees were marched to Oklahoma in the winter. During the march the Cherokees were denied adequate food, clothing, and shelter, and over four thousand died before they reached their new home (hence the name "Trail of Tears").

During the past six weeks, I researched the specific routes the Cherokees took and found that there were four separate paths. To provide a visual of the Trail of Tears, I have also drawn a detailed, full-color map of the geographic area on a piece of poster board. The map shows the four paths—including a water route—from Georgia to Oklahoma.

I also requested information from the Cherokee Nation headquarters in Oklahoma and received a booklet, a reading list, and reproductions of several paintings about the Trail of Tears and of Cherokee leaders. I have chosen three of my favorite depictions to present in my project.

I want to give my classmates a sense of what was taken from the Cherokees. I found in my research that many of the Cherokees lived in houses in Georgia, and that some owned plantations, so I made a diorama that shows what a Cherokee house looked like back then. I will place it next to a model of the stockades in which the Cherokees were held before they began their march to Oklahoma. The diorama of the two structures will form the centerpiece of my presentation.

INTRODUCTION Project introduced
Time period
Goal
Background information
BODY First significant accomplishment
Evidence
Second significant accomplishment
Evidence
Third significant accomplishment
Evidence

(continued)

(continued)

Problem

Solution

My only problem has been finding specific information on the people who were actually moved. I wanted to show in my project that the people who suffered were individuals and not just numbers. With the help of our school librarian, I located some books at the local university that give names and drawings of the people in the march. I checked out several of the books and plan to include these in my presentation. We also found a listing of a vinyl recording of stories handed down through the generations by families of Cherokees who survived the march. This recording is held in the university archives, so we had to request it through interlibrary loan; this process usually takes two weeks, so I should receive the recording late next week. Then I will listen to it and determine whether I can include parts of it in my presentation.

CONCLUSION
Overall view of
project

Although I do not know exactly how the final presentation will look, I have the main components already in place. The map and paintings will take up the background, and the dioramas and the books with the names and drawings of the Cherokees who were in the march will be in the foreground. Here is a rough sketch of the layout:

I would like to add other Cherokee historical items such as an example of traditional clothing or perhaps a picture of the Cherokee rose, but I still have to do some research on them. I am confident that I will have the presentation ready by my deadline in six weeks, and I will be able to play parts of the vinyl recording I will receive in the next week to re-create the voices of the survivors.

Time schedule

A Student's Model

In the following essay, Chad Stoloff of Carson City, Nevada, explains the progress of a school food drive. His essay follows the framework on page 124. Notice how this student provides important background information and ends his essay with a personal note.

Progress Report: A Holiday Gift Drive

Over Christmas our English class decided to collect holiday food and other gifts for needy people because I came up with the idea from a previous project and mentioned it to my teacher. We decided to have a competition between Mrs. Anderson's English classes. Our goal was to contribute enough food for some needy families so they could have good meals over the Christmas holidays. The winning class of the competition would win a pizza party, and so both classes tried very hard to win.

A point system was set up for the food collected. We gave certain foods more points than others. For example, turkeys and hams were at the top of the list for points, while canned foods were at the bottom of the list with the least number of points.

Starting the competition two weeks before school let out for Christmas vacation gave us a good amount of time to get our items together. Along with many kinds of food, our class contributed bikes, clothes, and toys to the families that needed them. Several class members sold suckers after school; the money from that was used to buy much-needed clothes for the families.

The fund-raiser was for a good cause, and helping people out gave us a great feeling inside. Our class provided a large amount, while the other class contributed a lesser amount, but their effort was still very important to the needy. Every person in each class provided time and effort, and many also contributed money or items to help people out. The whole experience brought my classmates and me closer together.

Project introduced

Goals

Background information

Time period

Accomplishments

Evidence

Results of project

Revising

Evaluate and Revise Your Draft

Re-read to Revise   As you evaluate and revise your draft, you should do at least two readings. In the first reading, focus on the content and organization of your draft. In your second reading, revise for style.

➤ **First Reading: Content and Organization**   To revise the content and organization of your essay, ask yourself the questions in the first column below. Use the tips in the middle column, and make the changes suggested in the last column. If possible, work collaboratively with another student.

Progress Report: Content and Organization Guidelines For Peer and Self-Evaluation

Evaluation Questions	▶ Tips	▶ Revision Techniques
❶ Does the introduction identify the project and time period? Is the purpose or goal included?	▶ **Circle** the sentences that identify the project, time period, and the project's purpose or goal. If you do not find any, revise.	▶ **Add** a sentence that clearly identifies the project and the time period. **Add** an explanation of the purpose or goal of the project.
❷ Is background information given? Are unfamiliar terms defined?	▶ **Draw a box** around background information. **Underline** any unfamiliar terms. If you do not find background or definitions, revise.	▶ **Add** a statement near the beginning of the report that gives background information. **Add** definitions for any unfamiliar terms.
❸ Does the report give evidence and essential information for each accomplishment?	▶ **Draw a wavy line** under specific evidence of accomplishments. **Bracket** any evidence not directly related to the project's progress. If you do not find any wavy lines, revise; if you find any brackets, revise.	▶ **Add** facts, statistics, or examples that support your claims of progress. **Delete** sentences with unessential information.
❹ Is the information presented in an effective order? Have problems been addressed?	▶ **Number** the tasks discussed. **Place single check marks** over problems and **double check marks** over solutions.	▶ **Rearrange** the accomplishments to reflect either logical or chronological order. **Add** possible solutions for each problem mentioned if needed.
❺ Does the conclusion present an overall view of the project's progress? Does it describe future plans?	▶ **Circle** the sentence that summarizes the progress. **Bracket** comments on your future plans or changes in time schedule. If either one is missing, revise.	▶ **Add** a sentence that explains the scope of the project. **Elaborate** on your future plans or any adjustments to your time schedule.

ONE WRITER'S REVISIONS Here's how one writer used the content and organization guidelines to revise some sentences from the progress report on page 125. Study the revisions and answer the questions following the paragraph.

For the past six weeks,
∧ I have been working on a project for my social studies class   **add**

that focuses on the Cherokee Trail of Tears. The project will take

, and the project is due in six weeks, on May 3.
the place of my final exam for the class. ~~My~~ project is designed   **add**

in an interesting and thought-provoking way
to present the historical event ∧ to my classmates, and I am   **add**

hoping that our school librarian will display the finished project

in the library.

Analyzing the Revision Process

1. Why did the writer add material to the first and second sentences?

2. What did the writer add to the third sentence? What is the effect of the addition?

YOUR TURN 7 **Focusing on Content and Organization**

Revise the content and organization of your own progress report, using the guidelines on the previous page. Use the example revisions above as a model.

PEER REVIEW

Ask a classmate to read your progress report and to answer the questions.

1. Identify the report's goal and time frame. Are the steps toward the goal made clear? What else would you like to have explained?

2. Is the tone confident? Are the problems addressed positively or negatively? Explain.

Second Reading: Style You have already examined your work as a whole, looking at what your report says and how you organized your ideas. Just as important as content and organization is the way you describe your progress, or the *style* of your report. You may be tempted in a progress report to use the same sentence construction repeatedly: "I did this. I did that. I did something else." You can avoid boring, repetitive sentences by varying your sentence length. Your writing will become more interesting as a result. To refine your progress report's style, use the following guidelines to vary sentence length in your writing.

Reference Note

For more information on **varying sentence length** and **combining sentences,** see page 436.

Style Guideline

Evaluation Question	▶ Tip	▶ Revision Technique
Are most of my sentences just about the same length?	▶ **Underline** each sentence in your paper with a colored pen. Compare line length. If three or more lines in a row are about the same length, revise.	▶ **Combine** two sentences to make a longer one by using phrases. **Rearrange** sentences, if necessary, to combine by using compound verbs.

Focus on Sentences

Varying Sentence Length

Have you ever seen a film or TV show with a robot who speaks in clipped, repetitive sentences? Sometimes your writing style might also seem robotic, or repetitive and dry. Especially when you write an informative paper, you may feel tempted to state the facts, one after another, in the same fashion. To avoid distracting the reader with repetitive sentences and to add rhythm and variety to your sentences, make sure you **vary sentence length.**

Remember that there are different ways to vary the length of your sentences. Look for ways to combine your sentences, such as creating compound verbs or using phrases. Varying the length of your sentences makes your writing easier and more enjoyable to read. (For more information about combining sentences, see page 436.)

> **ONE WRITER'S REVISIONS** Here's how the writer of the progress report on page 125 used the guidelines above to vary sentence length.
>
> ### BEFORE REVISION
>
> I have researched during the past six weeks. I found the specific routes the Cherokees took. They called the routes the Trail of Tears. There were four separate paths. I have drawn a detailed, full-color map to provide a visual. The map fits on a piece of poster board. The map shows the four paths—including a water route—from Georgia to Oklahoma.

All these underlined sentences are of similar length.

AFTER REVISION

During the past six weeks, I researched the specific routes the Cherokees took and found that there were four separate paths. To provide a visual of the Trail of Tears, I have also drawn a detailed, full-color map of the geographic area on a piece of poster board. The map shows the four paths—including a water route—from Georgia to Oklahoma.

Combine sentences by using compound verbs.

Combine sentences by using phrases.

Analyzing the Revision Process

1. Why did the revisions improve the style of the sentences?

2. Give another example of the way some of the short sentences could have been revised into longer ones.

YOUR TURN 8 **Focusing on Varied Sentence Length**

Use the preceding style guideline on varying sentence length to revise your progress report.

© 1995 Creators Syndicate, Inc.

Publishing

Proofread Your Report

Reference Note

Some verbs have irregular forms for their past tenses. For more information on **irregular verbs** and on using the correct **sequence of verb tenses,** see page 646 and page 672.

A Final Check   Even if your project is right on track, your readers will doubt it if your progress report is filled with errors. Go over your report one last time to make sure its credibility is not weakened by any grammar, spelling, or punctuation errors. Try collaborating with other students in your class to check for the conventions of correct verb usage. Readers will have difficulty following your course of action if you shift needlessly between tenses.

Grammar Link

Using Verb Tenses Correctly

Progress reports rely on a variety of verb tenses: past tense to discuss tasks that are finished, present tense to assess the current state of the project, and future tense to describe what still needs to be done. When describing events that occur at the same time, always use verbs in the same tense. When describing events that occur at different times, use verbs in different tenses to show the order of events accurately. The following sentences are examples of incorrect and correct sequences of tenses. Note the confusion that the incorrect version could cause.

Confusing	After I *planted* the seeds, they *will grow* at the rate of an inch per week.
Clear	After I *planted* the seeds, they *grew* at the rate of an inch per week. [Both verbs are in past tense.]
Confusing	After I *received* the historical document, I *will have examined* it to determine whether to include it in my presentation.

Clear	After I *had received* the historical document, I *examined* it to determine whether to include it in my presentation. [The first verb is in past perfect tense; the second is past tense to indicate a completed action.]

PRACTICE

On your own paper, revise each of the following sentences to correct any incorrect verb tenses. If one is correct, write C.

1. After I finished the frame, I have measured and cut the wood for the walls.

2. After we notified the proper authorities, we will carry out our plan.

3. Before I present my findings, however, I wanted to prepare a bar graph.

4. When I assembled the completed model, I determined exactly what the building looked like in the past.

5. After I spoke to the club, I have an idea of the members' thoughts about my project.

Publish Your Progress Report

Present Your Findings   Now is the time to inform your readers of your progress. Here are some ideas:

- Prepare a panel presentation of the progress reports, grouping them according to common themes, such as hobbies or environmental concerns.
- Present your reports to a meeting of parents and teachers or to a group of classmates—whoever will have a natural interest in your findings.
- Assemble the class project reports in written collections, grouped by themes. You might display the collections in the school library, under a sign reading "Students Making Progress." Your work may inspire others to take up similar efforts.
- Present a copy of your report to the person who assigned the project, or to someone who has encouraged your efforts.
- Post your report to an Internet news group with an interest in projects like yours. You might also add a section in which you give some advice to others embarking on a similar project.

Reflect on Your Essay

PORTFOLIO

What Progress Have You Made?   Write answers to the following questions to build on what you have learned from this workshop. Keep your answers in your portfolio, along with the final version of your progress report.

- How has writing a progress report helped you look at your project in a different way? What have you learned about conducting a project?
- What might you do differently next time you write a progress report? What would you do the same way?

YOUR TURN 9 Proofreading, Publishing, and Reflecting on Your Report

Review each of the steps discussed in the sections above. Before you turn in your essay, make sure to

- proofread your progress report carefully
- consider publishing options
- reflect on your progress report by answering the questions above

Writing a Memo

Progress reports are often written in the form of a *memo*. A **memo**—the name is a shortened form of the word *memorandum*—is a brief note, written as a reminder or a record of events. It is a standard form of communication in many businesses. Because memos are intended to be understood completely at the first reading, they are concise messages—clearly organized and direct. Memos may announce or summarize meetings, request action, or provide important information.

Writing a memo is similar to writing any report—you tell the reader *who, what, when, where, why,* and *how.* Here are some tips to prepare your own memo:

- **Use the words** *Date, To, From,* **and** *Subject* **to provide important information** at the top of your memo.

- **State your purpose clearly and briefly.**

- **Include necessary background information** as concisely as possible. If you are requesting assistance on a project, tell your readers how far along it is and what essential steps have been completed.

- **Use a courteous, professional tone** since memos are for conducting business.

- **Include a deadline** if you are asking for action or information.

- **Include your phone number** so the recipient can call you if there are any questions.

- **Send a copy (*cc*) of the memo** to people who need to know about the memo but who are not addressed directly.

Electronic Messages It is no wonder that **e-mail** has become the most common way to send memos—e-mail memos are fast and easy to distribute. Still, many people find it a bit more difficult to read messages on-screen than on paper. If you are sending a memo by e-mail, here are some additional guidelines:

- **Break text into short paragraphs.** Readers will have difficulty digesting paragraphs that cannot be seen completely on one screen.

- **Insert blank lines between paragraphs.** "Chunking" the text of your memo will also make it easier to read.

- **Use bullets or numbered lists, when possible.** If you have four requests, for example, breaking them into a list will clarify them for your readers.

- **Use asterisks around words you wish to emphasize.** Since boldface and italics won't travel with your e-mail message, asterisks are one way to retain your emphasis on those words.

- **Remember to provide your e-mail address,** in addition to your phone number, in the text of your message.

- **Remember that e-mail is not private.** Since anyone can send your e-mail to anyone else with a few simple keystrokes, be sure to keep your message professional.

Note: Before you send your memo by regular or electronic mail, revise and proofread your draft. Include only essential information and follow the same general format as the following written sample.

U. R. Sports, Inc.
Memo

Date: November 18, 2001
To: All Employees
From: Frank Levy, Supervisor, Research and Design Department
            Extension 6444
cc: Joan Kincaid, Supervisor, Cardiac Hill Municipal Park
Subject: Request for Volunteer Testers

As you know, U. R. Sports is currently testing advance models of the company's new off-road in-line skates. The new models are sure to be a hit, but we need more testers in order to meet our production deadline of March 14, 2002.

Although product development began only last January, we have already settled on four possible final designs. The materials and components have been chosen. Manufacturers of the separate parts have already been researched and contracted.

Our only problem has been determining the proper brake for the skates. We would like to involve more people in the testing, in hopes that more data will allow us to choose and test thoroughly the superior brake system. Your input could determine the design that will hit the stores next summer.

If you are interested in participating in the testing, please sign up today or tomorrow at the R & D office. Testing will take place this Saturday and Sunday at Cardiac Hill, just west of town.

Thank you for your help.

Standard memo heading includes date, recipient, writer's name, name of person receiving a copy, and subject.

Text of memo should be clear and to the point; state purpose early.

Provide background information so that readers understand the ongoing project.

Establish a firm deadline for any request.

YOUR TURN 10 Writing a Memo

Use the memo above as a model in writing your own memo. Choose as your subject either the project you used in the Writing Workshop or another subject. Identify a real-life audience and purpose for your memo. Remember to follow the guidelines for printed or e-mail memos closely. Before sending your memo, be sure to revise and proofread.

Talk   Listen

Writing and Delivering an Informative Speech

A scientist speaks before an international forum about progress in cancer research. A park ranger tells a group of campers how a dramatic geyser was formed. A classmate in history reports on the progress of the international peace talks. What do they have in common? Each is delivering an *informative speech.* An **informative speech** presents information in ways that will help the listeners understand and remember what they are hearing. Of course the content is essential—whether it is an explanation of gravity or an overview of graduation requirements— but *how* that content is delivered is just as important. Because speeches are delivered live, you have only one chance to tell and show the audience what you want them to know; after all, audiences can't rewind the tape or turn back the page. In this workshop you will discover ways to give your own informative speech.

WHAT'S AHEAD?

In this workshop, you will make an informative speech. You will also learn to

- plan the delivery of your speech
- use verbal and nonverbal strategies
- evaluate and critique an informative speech

TIP If there are gaps in your knowledge of your subject, consult reference works and books on the topic, interview an expert, or conduct a survey. Remember that the more you know about your topic, the more you will be able to communicate to others.

Reference Note

For more information on **research strategies,** see page 76.

Plan the Content

This Is to Inform You . . .   To select a topic for your informative speech, choose something that you are interested in and is familiar to you. You can adapt the progress report you wrote in the Writing Workshop— progress reports are often given as speeches—or you can choose a new topic. Your speech may be **expository,** giving information about a specific subject, such as air pollution in your town; or it may be a **process** speech, explaining how to do something or how something works. You might want to discuss new topic ideas with a classmate to make sure you don't choose a topic that is too broad for a short speech.

Let Me Explain Further   Analyze your audience and tailor your speech to their interests and previous knowledge. If you think your audience already knows a lot about your topic—baseball, for example—try to present an interesting new perspective or little-known facts, such as an explanation of how vision-impaired people play baseball. Also, try to anticipate what your audience wants to do with the information. If you are telling your audience how to make an omelet, for example, make sure that by the end of the speech your listeners have all the information they need to make an omelet themselves. To make your explanations clear and concrete, be sure to include details, examples, facts, statistics, and anecdotes.

Let's Take It from the Top   Plan the main points of your speech and organize them so they are clear and easy to follow. Use the guidelines in the following chart to help you.

Introduction	• Capture your audience's attention with an interesting statement or question. • Gain listeners' interest by relating the topic to their experiences.
Body	• Organize main points in one of the following ways: • **Chronological order** If you are explaining a process, for example, it makes sense to present the steps in chronological, or time, order. • **Logical order** If you are supplying basic information on a subject, you may want to arrange your information in logical order, by groups or categories. • **Spatial order** If you are describing an arrangement—the arrangement of pilot controls in an airplane, for example—use spatial order.
Conclusion	• Refer to your introduction and summarize your main points; this kind of overview is an especially important way to reinforce your message for listeners. • End with a quotation, an anecdote, or a thought-provoking final statement.

TIP   Use the kind of language—informal, standard, or technical—that you need to match the *occasion* of your speech. (An **occasion** is a real-life event that acts as a prompt.) If your **task** is to explain something technical, be sure to define your terms.

TIP   Try opening with a **rhetorical question,** a question that does not require an answer. Asked at the beginning of your speech, such a question often gives your speech clarity, force, and aesthetic effect.

Plan the Delivery

May I Have Your Attention   Now that you have the content and organization down, choose one of the following three methods for delivering your speech.

- **Manuscript**   A manuscript speech is written out completely and read to the audience. This style allows the speaker to avoid making errors or leaving out important details; however, it often doesn't allow for as much eye contact or physical movement as other styles.

- **Memorized**   A memorized speech is written out completely—like a manuscript speech—but is then memorized and recited rather than read. Often, contestants in speech events use this "memorized" style so that the speech appears to be unrehearsed.

■ **Extemporaneous** An extemporaneous speech is outlined and rehearsed but not memorized; speakers may use an outline or note cards. Most professional speakers prefer this method in order to seem more spontaneous and to adapt their presentation according to their audience's various reactions.

Reference Note

For more information about **parallel structure,** see page 424.

Whatever kind of delivery you choose for your speech, you will probably want to use mnemonic (memory) devices, such as parallel structure or acronyms, so that your audience will remember your main points. You could, for example, have each recommendation in your speech on recycling correspond to the letters in the word *clean—C* is for "Clearing out old newspapers," and so on. Your audience would have an easy way to recall your speech.

I See What You Say, I Hear What You Look Like Listening to a speech is quite different from reading an article—what listeners *see* and *hear* affects how they think about the content. The following chart gives some tips for your spoken delivery and the nonverbal aspects of your speech.

TIP Remember: When you deliver your speech, follow the **conventions of oral language.** For example, if you are giving a formal speech, choose your words and sentences carefully, so that your speech does not sound like a conversation with one of your peers.

Delivery Strategies	• **Use your voice effectively** Vary your tone, rate, and volume to add emphasis and interest to your speech.
	• **Enunciate clearly** Speak distinctly to prevent slurring words or dropping word endings.
	• **Avoid vocalized pauses** Meaningless speech sounds, such as *uh, um,* and *you know,* are distracting. Use quiet pauses to emphasize important points.
	• **Be enthusiastic** Use your voice and word choice to show that you believe in your material; the audience will usually respond to your excitement.
Nonverbal Strategies	• **Dress appropriately** A neat, well-groomed appearance tells your audience you are serious and well prepared.
	• **Maintain eye contact with your audience** Give the audience the impression that you are speaking to each person individually.
	• **Use appropriate facial expressions and hand gestures** Concentrate on the interest you have in your subject.
	• **Use good posture** Stand up straight with both feet on the ground. Avoid rocking back and forth or pacing needlessly.

Bells and Whistles Audiovisuals can help you both clarify information and hold your audience's attention. For example, an audiotape of whale songs might bring life to your speech on whale migration. Likewise, a brief videotape of your new skateboard ramp will complement your progress report on the ramp's construction. Graphics such as charts, tables, and graphs will also help you underscore important data and statistics. Be sure to enlarge the graphics and mount them on poster board so that they can be seen easily.

Remember, however, that your audience will shift its focus from you to your audiovisual and that each audiovisual you use will take time to introduce, present, and explain. Keep these parts of your presentation simple, and don't allow them to take up more time than necessary.

> **TIP** Remember that you will not be able to control every variable when you give your speech. An annoying cough from an audience member or a chart dropped before you even begin may make you uncomfortable or distracted. The important thing, however, is to stay relaxed and keep your sense of humor. If the distraction is small, such as someone coughing, ignore it. If the distraction is too much to ignore—like having to pick up a dropped chart—mention it to the audience and go on. Remember, also, that even professional performers experience stage fright. If you concentrate on your material, you will do just fine.

Practice, Practice, Practice   Deliver your speech to a friend or to your family in exactly the same way that you plan to deliver it to your final audience. Ask your rehearsal audience for feedback on how to improve your speech, and incorporate their comments into your performance. Rehearsing your speech will give you an idea of how much time your speech will take, so that you can make sure you will not exceed a set time limit.

> **TIP** Practice with audiovisual equipment before you make your speech, so that you can use your allotted time efficiently.

Ask your rehearsal audience to use the following evaluation list—and use it yourself to evaluate and critique your own performance.

Organization and Content	• Did the introduction grab the audience's attention? • Was the speech tailored to the audience's knowledge and interests? • Were the purpose and the main ideas obvious to listeners? • Did the conclusion summarize the main ideas and provide a sense of completion?
Delivery	• Did the speaker seem relaxed and confident? • Did the speaker make eye contact? • Were facial expressions, gestures, and movements natural and used appropriately?

 YOUR TURN 11   **Writing and Delivering an Informative Speech**

Follow the steps outlined above to prepare, practice, and deliver your own informative speech.

Analyzing Media Stereotypes

WHAT'S AHEAD?

In this section, you will analyze characters in two thirty-minute situation comedies. You will also learn to

■ identify media stereotypes

■ evaluate the real-life effects of media stereotypes

Everything changes—and, despite the occasional setback, everyone makes progress. It's human. Still, much of what we see every day, especially on TV, doesn't mirror our complicated, changing selves. Think about it: After school, you turn on the television to relax. You perhaps flip through the channels, looking for those simple, often ridiculous characters you recognize because they make you laugh. After working hard all day, you want to be entertained—to be amused, to have your attention diverted from your "real life"—and those silly situation comedies, with their one-dimensional characters, do just the trick.

You know the format. Half-hour situation comedies have twenty-two minutes (without the commercials) to create a realistic or an improbable "situation," establish a conflict between the characters, generate a laugh every ten to fifteen seconds with visual jokes and one-liners, and then resolve the problem. (A drama follows the same format, but without the laughs.) To create a fast-paced comedy—all within a short time from finished script to filming "before a live studio audience"—most programs use stock characters, or **stereotypes:** one-dimensional characters, immediately recognizable and entirely predictable.

Identifying and Analyzing Stereotypes

To Cliché Is to Stereotype   Originally, **cliché** was the French technical term for using a solid, one-piece printing plate (called a stereotype) in printing presses. *Clichéd,* or *stereotyped,* meant "cast in metal from a mold." As we use the terms today, **clichéd** means "a fixed, worn-out, or hackneyed phrase"; and **stereotype** means "an unvarying form or pattern, something unoriginal." As a writer who cares about your words, you work hard to eliminate clichés from your writing, since they are ready-made phrases that block creative or complex thought. Similarly, if you care about people—real people, not television characters—you want to avoid the trap of accepting media stereotypes without question. After all, when you use clichés, you risk being unoriginal; but when you accept media stereotypes as reality, you risk the more serious error of prejudging people.

It is easy to see why the entertainment media (especially the television and film industries) might use stereotypes. These kinds of characters make telling stories faster and easier. In fact, you can usually pick out stereotypes pretty quickly—the well-educated person who has no practical knowledge or skills, the helpless elderly person, the irresponsible teenager. In situation comedies, especially, these stereotypes are "shorthand" characters, used in place of more realistic, complex figures.

Look at the following chart to discover how stereotypes are used.

TIP Stereotypes are also used because they are so identifiable. A character who is always clumsy or always mistaken is less realistic but quicker and easier for an audience to understand.

Methods of Stereotyping	Examples
Individual placed into a simplified category based on gender, physical appearance, cultural background, activities, or age, and so on	Dumb athlete, dizzy blonde, sarcastic teen, computer nerd
One characteristic of individual exaggerated; no other characteristics shown	A younger brother or sister—annoying and always smarter; the grouchy, older neighbor who only complains

To Know a Stereotype Is to See One   To see if your favorite television situation comedy uses stereotypes, first write down the names of the regular characters (those who appear week after week). Record information about such things as their **physical appearance, age, gender, cultural and family background, speech, major interests,** and **mannerisms.** Then, step back and take a more careful look at the characters. Are they complex and fully fleshed out, or are they stereotypes—one-dimensional characters, easily summed up with a single adjective? If they are stereotypes, what generalization is being made? If, for example, you decide that the gum-snapping, smart-aleck teenager is a stereotype, decide whether the underlying generalization is that teenagers don't respect adults. Finally, ask yourself what purpose the stereotypes serve in the program. To get started, look at the student chart below.

Character	Description	Possible Stereotype?
Fowler	Tall and skinny male, middle-aged, large nose, frightful red hair that stands straight up, clumsy, white socks, black shoes, gets into unusual predicaments, speaks very dramatically—he is never shown being calm or smart or emotionally complex	Yes, definitely. He is a clown, used mainly for physical comedy; there is even a pun on his name—he always fouls things up.

TIP Stereotypes, or stock characters, have been around as long as people have tried to entertain. Some stereotypes have not changed much over time. For example, a leading character in a comedy usually has a friend who is the opposite in temperament, physical appearance, and manner. The friend's purpose is to spark humor through his or her inevitable conflicts with the leading character.

Other stereotypes, however, *have* changed over time. In the 1950s, situation comedies usually portrayed mothers as women who stayed at home, solved their children's problems, and cooked—in high heels. In a 1990s situation comedy, a mother is often a professional career woman with problems of her own, and instead of cooking, she works out with her personal trainer. Consider how this new media stereotype (as well as the old one) matches the lives of the mothers you know.

I Would Rather See a Stereotype Than Be One   What do you think are the *effects* of media stereotypes? Of course, you probably know that in real life students skilled with computers are not "nerds," and that not all Texans wear boots and live on big ranches—as they might be stereotypically portrayed on television. However, what if you have never met a Texan, or know nothing about that person sitting next to you in class who comes from a different ethnic or social background? Do you generalize about people based on your television viewing habits? If so, perhaps a stereotype has intruded upon your judgment. To analyze how media stereotypes affect your own perceptions of others, try writing down answers to the following questions.

■ How is a real person that I know similar to the stereotypes I see on TV? How does this person look, act, or think like the stereotype?

■ How is the person different from the stereotype? List the ways that your real person is more complex than the stereotype.

■ How does the stereotype affect how you respond to this person? How might this person see *you* in a stereotypical way?

■ What occupations or cultural groups that are unfamiliar to you do you see depicted on television? How might media representations affect your expectations about these occupations or cultural groups?

YOUR TURN 12 Identifying and Analyzing Stereotypes

Follow the strategies given above to identify and analyze stereotypes in two half-hour television situation comedies. Do you see the same stereotypes in each, or different ones? If possible, choose one current sitcom and one older television program. Write a short explanation of your findings; be sure to consider whether these stereotypes are common in the wider world and what effects they may have.

Choices

Choose one of the following activities to complete.

▶ **VIEWING AND REPRESENTING**

1. A Film Diary Instead of writing a progress report, film one. Choose a student project such as the debate team's preparations for the big competition, and track the progress—the important accomplishments—on videotape. Then, edit your tape to include an introduction and a conclusion. Share the **film diary** with the participants in the project.

▶ **MEDIA AND TECHNOLOGY**

2. Now *That's* Progress! Create a **Web page** that shows the progress of an ongoing project of your choice. Include graphics and photos on your site, and update the information at frequent intervals. Be sure to include links to related Web pages.

▶ **LITERATURE**

3. Literature's Life Lessons In literature, a character or group of characters often experience growth or change—they make progress. Choose a literary work, and write a **report** from one character's point of view on the progress that character is making—the progress in growing up or in achieving a specific goal. Remember to record the progress as the character would judge it.

▶ **CAREERS**

4. Surveying the Field Choose a potential employer and do research in the library or on the Web about the business. If possible, conduct a personal interview with the business owner or the manager and a current employee. Ask what experiences and education you need that will be useful for this business. Write up your findings and then condense them into a **summary** or an *abstract*. An **abstract** briefly highlights, or summarizes, the main points of the material in a longer business report.)

▶ **CROSSING THE CURRICULUM: SCIENCE**

5. Conducting an Experiment Progress reports in science follow a rigorous system called the scientific method. If you are unfamiliar with the scientific method, research it and write an **essay** explaining how it has led to progress in the centuries in which it has been put to use. If you are familiar with the method already, put it to use yourself in an experiment of your own devising. Report on your findings.

PORTFOLIO

4

Exploring Problems and Solutions

Reading Workshop

Reading a Problem-Solution Article

Writing Workshop

Writing a Problem-Solution Essay

Viewing and Representing

Creating Graphics

Picture this: Your soccer team is playing the biggest game of the season on Saturday. Then you hear that your debate club has won a slot in the regional competition—yes, you guessed it—this Saturday. Obviously, you have a problem. What do you do?

Tough decision, right? Still, this is a problem you could probably solve on your own. How are more complex problems solved? It's true that when problems are large, or many perspectives are involved, things become more knotty—solutions must be agreed upon, and various alternatives weighed against each other. Usually, **explanations** are necessary. After all, if you can't explain a problem, how will others understand it?

When you think about it, explaining problems and offering solutions is something we do all the time—alone, and with others. This is how we all move forward in life. Otherwise, we would all be stuck in place, much like the snow-covered man in this cartoon.

Informational Text

Exposition

A man with no alternative plan.

THE NEIGHBORHOOD reprinted with special permission of King Features Syndicate, Inc.

YOUR TURN 1

Brainstorming About Problem-Solution Explanations

In what areas of our lives do you think problem-solution explanations are especially important? Brainstorm a list of examples and jot them down in your notebook. To get started, think about the problems you face daily in your own life; then, move outward to the wider world. When you are finished, discuss your list with a small group of classmates.

internet**connect**

go. hrw .com
GO TO: go.hrw.com
KEYWORD: EOLang 11-4

Reading a Problem-Solution Article

WHAT'S AHEAD?

In this section of the chapter, you will read a problem-solution article. You will also learn how to

■ analyze problem-solution structure

■ identify stated and implied main ideas

TV anchors report problems in measured tones. Bold, three-inch newspaper headlines shout them. Even homemade flyers stapled to telephone poles communicate them—"Help! Lost cat!" In fact, information about problems bombards us so constantly that particular messages can become lost in an incomprehensible blur. How do you make heads or tails of any one of these messages? The first step is to realize that, despite the different ways they are delivered, problem-solution messages all share some important features.

Preparing to Read

| READING FOCUS

Problem-Solution Structure   While no two problem-solution pieces are identical, the structure of such pieces usually is quite similar. That's because we all tend to think about problems with a certain natural logic. On paper, the process looks a little like this:

| Explanation of Problem | → | Possible Solutions | → | Best Solution or End Result |

As you read the article ahead, try to keep this basic pattern, or "big picture," in mind.

| READING SKILL

Stated and Implied Main Ideas   Problem-solution essays always contain a main idea, but sometimes it is *implied* rather than *stated*. While **stated main ideas** declare themselves in loud, clear voices, **implied main ideas** are more slippery. In fact, they really ask you to play detective—you must **infer,** or draw conclusions about, the main idea by gathering clues throughout the piece. As you read the article ahead, think about how it communicates a main idea. Is it stated outright or delivered more subtly?

As you read the article below, jot down answers to the numbered active-reading questions.

from **International Wildlife**

SINGLE, LONELY PARROT seeks companionship—
male Spix's[1] macaw, South American, mostly blue, last of his kind. Wants female for marital bliss, nesting. Open to blind dates arranged by scientists and bird collectors.

by MAC MARGOLIS

LATE ONE AFTERNOON in Curaçá, a sunbaked village in the northeast Brazilian backlands, a quiet vigil is under way. Three men sit on wooden stools in the back lot of a stucco and wattle farmhouse, their eyes fixed on the thin fringe of trees and bushes that lines a dried-up creek bed. The men scan the treetops, crown by crown. No binoculars are needed here. The men know well the habits of their anticipated visitor, the little blue, or Spix's, macaw, a species that has become as rare in the wild as a species can be, reduced to a lone male.

> **1. What problem can you infer from the headnote above and this first paragraph?**

In time they hear it, faint but unmistakable: *Kraw kraw arrrk*. "The macaw," says biologist Marcos Da Ré, the chief watchman here. He looks at his wristwatch. "Five sixteen," he announces, noting the time. Suddenly, a matte blue streak flashes against a powder blue sky. The macaw flies straight toward the tops of the caraibeira trees, where he will rest for the night.

At his side is a smaller, more brightly colored female maracana, or Illiger's macaw. The male, driven by loneliness or an instinctive need to establish social bonds, has become the constant companion of the maracana. They wheel and soar before disappearing among the leafy camouflage.

The world's 16 macaw species are scattered from Mexico to Argentina. A seventeenth became extinct around the turn of the century, and today nine are considered endangered, though none so gravely as the Spix's. Da Ré is a field biologist who has joined a scientific effort to save the Spix's from extinction, in part by locating a captive female as a potential mate for the lone wild male. If successful, the project will offer inspiration for similar projects around the globe.

The Spix's macaw first came to scientific recognition in 1819, when famed Austrian naturalist Johann Baptist von Spix shot one while visiting Brazil. The bird was not seen again in the wild until 1903, and scientists have

---

1. **Spix's:** *Spix* is pronounced shpēks.

observed it only rarely since. In 1986, Swiss scientist Paul Roth spotted a family of three on Melancia Creek, some 800 kilometers (500 mi.) inland from the coastal city of Salvador, near where Spix shot his specimen. But the wild-animal trade and habitat destruction by settlers had found them, too, and by 1988 naturalists thought that, with the exception of a few captive birds, the Spix's macaw was extinct.

Then in 1990, after a local farmer turned up with Polaroid snapshots of a large blue "parrot," a team of naturalists plunged into the backlands, coming upon a lone adult male Spix's near Melancia Creek. Scientists believe this bird is the last of his kind in the wild, living in the scrub that surrounds Curaçá.

Brazilians call this country the *caatinga*, a sun-scorched terrain of baked mud and dried-up riverbeds, cactus scrub and the occasional lofty caraibeira. This arid land provides habitat for three macaw species, including the Spix's.

But for Curaçá's stubborn male, the Spix's macaw would be a footnote of ornithology.[2] To save the species, a group of scientists in the late 1980s started a long and tricky campaign. Back then, they had a rough idea of who held the dozen or so captive Spix's, but locating and acquiring them posed a challenge. "We didn't know who had what birds, where they kept them all, much less what sex they were," says Iolita Bampi, currently the chief of the wildlife department of the Brazilian environmental authority, IBAMA. "We were starting in the dark."

In 1989, IBAMA turned the group of scientists into a formal entity, the Permanent Committee for the Recovery of the Spix's Macaw, which called upon the aid of conservationists[3] on three continents. Not knowing that any Spix's survived in the wild, the new committee focused on breeding the handful of captive birds with the intention of creating a reservoir of macaws for release into the wild. After discovery of the wild male, the committee hired Marcos Da Ré to conduct field research in the area where the wild macaw had turned up.

The committee's search was not only difficult but highly delicate. In addition to involving macaw specialists, environmental authorities, and diplomats, it also reached out to the private world of animal collectors and breeders. These collectors run legitimate concerns in their own countries, but in the past they have been the final customers in the netherworld of animal trafficking, which international law-enforcement agencies reckon moves more money than any other illegal activity except narcotics.

In Brazil, the capture, sale or purchase of wild animals is prohibited. But

2. Why do you think the author provides background information in this and the following paragraph?

3. What words or phrases in this paragraph indicate that the solution may be difficult? At this point, do you have a clear idea of the problem?

---

2. **ornithology:** the branch of zoology that deals with birds.

3. **conservationists:** people who advocate the care and protection of nature and natural resources.

demanding return of the collectors' macaws surely would have been a complex and drawn-out process, says Natasha Schischakin, who heads the committee's working group on captive breeding. What is more, many of the collectors possessed valuable expertise, such as the ability to reproduce Spix's in captivity. So the committee and the Brazilian government agreed that all holders could participate in the recovery program but would have to give up management of the macaws to the committee so the birds could be treated as a single population. To encourage collector participation, the Brazilian government promised that aviculturists[4] who helped out would be granted one-time amnesty[5] from prosecution for any macaws held illegally.

Apparently moved by the macaw's plight, five private breeders—one in the Philippines, one in Spain, one in Switzerland and two in Brazil—joined the project. The cooperation of these breeders was fundamental to success. All are now full partners in the program.

Even after the politics had been sorted out, the biological challenges remained daunting.[6] These included building up the captive Spix's into a breeding stock for future release and figuring out how to reintroduce a captive female macaw to the wild male and to the species' native habitat.

The committee located an eligible female Spix's in Recife, Brazil, and began to prepare her for release. Caught in the wild as an adult, she had been living a caged life for nearly seven easy years. "If we had released her cold into the wild, she would certainly have died," says Marcos Da Ré.

So she went to boot camp, with Da Ré as drill sergeant. He led her through an eight-month regimen of flying calisthenics and a Spartan, working-bird's diet. He logged the time she took to crack a pinhao nut, clocked her flights and even counted her wing beats.

The prep course worked. In mid-March, she left the cage. The researchers put food out for her to keep her near the cage while she adjusted to the wild. Soon, she flew away into the caatinga, but within a matter of weeks she turned up again, flying with the male Spix's and his maracana companion. The trio flew together for nearly six weeks, sometimes joined by other maracanas. Hope soared when, at night, the pair of Spix's roosted together.

Then, one day in June, the female Spix's disappeared. The field biologists suspect the maracanas split into two groups, with one Spix's macaw joining each group. Until the researchers are sure of the female's whereabouts, they are keeping a constant vigil for her, scouring a 2,000-square-kilometer (772-sq.-mi.) tract of terrain for a blue needle in an immense haystack. Meanwhile, the committee is attempting to boost Spix numbers in captivity. Seven

4. This and the preceding two paragraphs describe the committee's political solutions. What are they?

5. What is the main idea of this paragraph?

---

4. **aviculturists:** people who breed birds.

5. **amnesty:** pardon.

6. **daunting:** discouraging or intimidating.

birds hatched in 1995 brought the world total to 39.

Da Ré has discovered that protecting the endangered macaw means winning over the human community. So he has added helping the impoverished rural folk to his mission.

6. At this point, how do you think this new solution will help the Spix's macaw?

Years ago, Curaçá was a prosperous village of sheep herders and leather workers whose pastoral bounty paved broad streets, built sturdy buildings, even supported a flourishing theater troupe. Since then, Brazilian palates have turned from mutton to beef, and hides of better quality are imported from Africa or Argentina. As long as they were relatively prosperous, residents of the caatinga did no harm to the naturally rare and delicate local flora. But economic woes brought ecological decline as herders, desperate to make up for shortfalls, ravaged the scant surviving trees for firewood, farms and fences, leaving behind a denuded[7] landscape even more vulnerable to the cyclical dry spells. Now, like the macaw, Curaçá barely holds on.

But Da Ré has found friends here. "These people are my eyes, my scouts," he says. He has become as involved in their plight as they have in the fate of the little blue macaw. The interest is not just sentimental. Overgrazing and forest cutting have run down not only the Spix's habitat but the productivity of pastures and farms. So Da Ré and his team went to work building fences, teaching rotational grazing practices and replanting the caatinga, measures that protect the herders' fields and the macaw's feeding grounds.

Funding the fences, as well as school construction and cultural and sports activities, has not been easy. But the efforts made in behalf of the village have won respect and allies for the macaw. The whole community has become caught up in the effort to save the bird. The plight of the *ararinha azul*[8] has inspired poems, plays and songs and even a town pageant, where children paraded in blue-feathered costumes. The people of Curaçá follow the saga of the airborne dating game the way most Brazilians follow the prime-time *telenovelas*, or soap operas.

The case of the Spix's macaw, says Da Ré, shows how even a poor community like Curaçá, if given half a chance, can play a crucial part in conservation. And he expects the effort in Curaçá to reverberate elsewhere. "Through the Spix's macaw we are learning not only about the biology of this little-studied bird, but about the environmental history of the entire region," Da Ré says. "The macaw is also a flagship species, showing us the way to saving other endangered species."

7. How do the ideas in this paragraph support, extend, or contradict what you thought was the main idea of the article?

Mac Margolis is the Brazil correspondent for The Economist *and is a contributor to* Newsweek.

---

7. **denuded:** stripped.

8. *ararinha azul:* Portuguese for "little, blue bird."

Problem-Solution Structure

Checking the Map, Retracing Your Steps You began reading "Single, Lonely Parrot" with a simple map in your head. Now that you are finished reading, what do you think of that map? Did it account for all the landmarks you saw, the twisting trails you took? If not, you have shared a common experience for readers: basic structural patterns *do* help us anticipate the shape of an article, but they *don't* provide the detail and complexity that can only be found in the piece itself.

So then, if you drew a more accurate map for "Single, Lonely Parrot," what would it look like? One way to create a more detailed picture is to use a chart like the partially completed one on the following page. A chart like this contains the basic elements of the mental map you started with—problem, possible solutions, and so on—but it gives you a chance to stretch out and analyze them. You might think of the map you began with as a crude sketch and the more detailed chart as a painting that captures the finer distinctions of a problem-solution explanation.

TIP When complicated problems are presented, mapping them may get a bit tricky. Sometimes, for example, problems are broken down into several parts, which, in turn, have separate solutions.

TIP While analyzing structure, it may be helpful to think about how an essay that *proposed* solutions to the problem facing the Spix's macaw might differ from "Single, Lonely Parrot," which instead *described* solutions that have already been attempted. Usually, essays that propose solutions are written by people who are deeply concerned about the issue and who want to persuade their readers to accept the solution they recommend.

Descriptions, on the other hand, are primarily written by professional journalists who don't have as great a personal stake in the issue. In short, proposals and descriptions differ because they are written from different **points of view.** Among other things, point of view affects how much time writers spend explaining and defending a part of the problem, or a particular solution, which in turn affects the structure of the piece as a whole. Point of view also affects the tone writers adopt in speaking to their audience.

Analyzing Problem-Solution Structure

Complete the problem-solution chart below for "Single, Lonely Parrot." Then, jot some notes about the author's organization of ideas. Does this organization seem logical to you? Why or why not?

What is the central problem?

There is only one Spix's macaw remaining in the wild.

Why is it a problem?

Who has the problem?

Attempted Solutions	Outcomes

1. Political
   Example:
   Gave amnesty to breeders who had macaws illegally
	Able to create pool of macaws for recovery program

2. Biological Example:	
3. Local Community Example:	

Best Solution or End Result:

READING SKILL

Stated and Implied Main Ideas

Playing Detective A **main idea** always drives a problem-solution explanation, but *where* you actually find it may vary. If a main idea is **stated,** you are likely to find it right there on the page. If it is **implied,** a little more searching is required. One way to think about the difference is to imagine that a stated main idea offers a panoramic view of the article, as if from a mountaintop. In contrast, an implied main idea asks you to climb the mountain *yourself,* gathering clues as you move up the slope. Despite their differences, however, stated and implied main ideas are equally effective as controlling ideas for an entire piece.

Stated Main Idea   In many nonfiction pieces, the main idea, or **the-sis,** is **stated** outright. When this is true, you'll find the main idea neatly contained in a sentence or two, often near the beginning of an essay. In turn, the main idea of each paragraph or section supports the stated main idea of the article. Look at the diagram below to see how a stated main idea usually drives the structure of an essay, carrying its reader from general idea to more specific ideas and support.

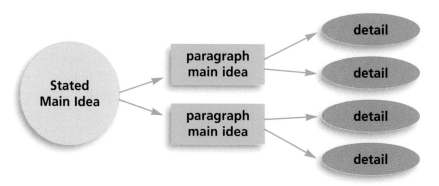

TIP   Sometimes, writers state their main ideas at the very end of a piece, often in an attempt to end with a bang. When this is the case, you will use the stated main idea to confirm the main idea you inferred as you moved through the article. Many good readers also scan the last paragraph of a piece for a stated main idea before they begin reading.

Implied Main Idea   An **implied main idea** is a bit more subtle than a stated main idea. Instead of announcing itself boldly in one particular statement, it lies concealed in a variety of clues that you must gather and interpret. That is, you must **infer** a main idea from the collective ideas, facts, key words, and details offered throughout the piece as well as the knowledge you already have about the topic being discussed. Often, an essay containing an implied main idea moves from one specific idea to another. The most general level is not on the page at all, but contained in the reader's mind. The graphic below may help you visualize this process:

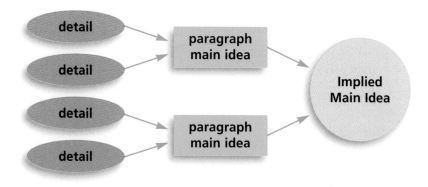

Above all else, a writer's decision to state or to imply his or her main idea affects *how* the reader grasps the meaning of the piece as a whole—either relatively quickly at the beginning or more slowly over the course of the article.

Take a look at how one student has identified stated and implied main ideas in the following two paragraphs:

> For the moment, at least, we are stuck with advising high schoolers that they must expect to take jobs they don't look forward to, because the interesting ones are too rare. Students want to be dental assistants, but St. Cloud, which has the appropriate program, gets three hundred applications for its forty places. Minnesota city dwellers may find it odd, but it is nonetheless true that to get into farming, you have to "know somebody." The good jobs, which by their nature are satisfying to sense and sensibility, are cruelly hard to land.
>
> Carol Bly, "To Unteach Greed"

Stated Main Idea: The first sentence states the main idea (and the last sentence restates it): Interesting jobs—and the slots in the training programs that lead to them—are too rare.

> All human beings have culture. It is the foundation on which all human achievements rest and is perhaps the defining characteristic of our species. But do animals have culture too? Not long ago, most scholars would have said "no," but in the last two decades a variety of research has challenged this view. For example, Jane Goodall discovered that chimpanzees living in nature not only use tools, but produce them first and then carry them to where they will use them.
>
> Herbert Tischler, "Introduction to Sociology"

Implied Main Idea: Though it's not presented in a single statement, everything in the paragraph supports the idea that animals have culture just as humans do.

THINKING IT THROUGH Identifying an Article's Main Idea

▶ STEP 1 **Before you begin reading any nonfiction article or essay, scan the piece for clues that might reveal its main idea.** For example, the title might hint at the main idea of the piece. Also, pay particular attention to the first and last paragraphs, as well as the first sentence of each body paragraph. Your scan—just a quick look, really—should lead you to form some hunches about the main idea; now you are primed to begin reading.

▶ STEP 2 **If you don't encounter a stated main idea in the first three or four paragraphs, prepare to identify an implied main idea.** To do this,

- **Break the selection into logical or manageable sections and extract a main idea from the details and supporting information in each section.** (In shorter pieces, each paragraph may be a section; in longer articles, you might group all the paragraphs that discuss the same topic into a section.)

- **Ask yourself how the sections connect to one another.** Do all of them connect to, or illustrate, an idea that is not stated but may be logically inferred? (Draw a cluster map if looking at the parts will help you visualize the whole.)

- **If a controlling idea is still not clear, then look closely at the ideas you have identified: Which seems the most important?** This step asks you to recognize which ideas the author spends the most time on, but it also requires you to use your own judgment and previous knowledge about the topic.

- **Compose a statement of the article's main idea** that takes into account the main ideas you identified in each section of the piece.

YOUR TURN 3 Identifying a Main Idea

With a partner, decide what you think is the main idea, or thesis, of "Single, Lonely Parrot." Is it stated or implied? Be sure to provide support for your answers. Also, discuss why the writer might have chosen to present his main idea this way.

Recognizing and Using Root Words

"Single, Lonely Parrot" contains a number of words that relate specifically to the natural world. While you may have already known some of them, others may have been unfamiliar—"aviculturalist," for example. Whenever you trip over a new word, identifying its **root word** can help you define it. Many root words had their beginnings in Latin, Greek, or older forms of modern languages; and once you know a root, you inevitably know a family of related words. Here's a brief list of root words that apply to nature:

arbor–	tree	*hydro–*	water
avi–	bird	*pisc–*	fish
astr–	star	*ornitho–*	bird
bio–	life	*terr–*	earth
helio–	sun	*zoo–*	animal

THINKING IT THROUGH **Using Root Words to Understand Meaning**

The first step in using roots to decipher the meaning of words is to identify and define the roots; the rest is relatively easy. Below is a checklist. In the right-hand column, look at how one student used these steps to understand the word "aviculturist."

► **STEP 1** **Break a word into its logical parts.** Then, identify the root or roots in the word and define them. (Identify prefixes and suffixes, too.)

aviculturist = avi- bird, cultur- care, ist- a person who practices

► **STEP 2** **Make an educated guess about the meaning of the word** using these definitions, your own previous experience with similar words, and the clues within the passage.

The passage is about bird breeders, so a possible meaning might be: aviculturist = a person who breeds or raises birds

► **STEP 3** **See if your definition makes sense** by placing it in the context of the sentence.

"...the Brazilian government promised that [people who breed birds] who helped out would be granted one-time amnesty from prosecution for any macaws held illegally." My definition seems to work.

PRACTICE

Try to work out the meanings of the following words, some of which are taken from "Single, Lonely Parrot." Then, confirm your definitions in a dictionary. Finally, list one or two other words that use the same root word(s). You may need to use a dictionary to find them.

1. biologist
2. arboretum
3. hydroelectric
4. terrain
5. astrophysics
6. aviary
7. zoology
8. heliocentric
9. piscivorous
10. ornithosis

TEST TAKING

Inference Questions

If you take a college entrance exam, you will no doubt run across multiple-choice questions that ask you to make an inference about a given passage. The words *imply* and *suggest* often signal inference questions. What these questions are really asking for is an educated guess; they want you to use information that is contained in the passage to make a logical guess about information that is not there. Look at the following **reading passage** from *Newsweek* magazine, and the accompanying inference question.

> The car culture of the 1920s didn't create new values. It simply expressed old ones (freedom, equality, individualism) in new ways. If people now traveled for fun, they needed new places to go. Farmers soon allowed motorists to pitch tents on bits of field. Then cabins sprouted. By the 1930s, the country had an estimated 15,000 cabin camps. However, travel made Americans crave the familiar, too. They didn't want every roadside meal or overnight stay to be a bad one. So arose the motel and fast-food chains whose appeal lay in standardization.
>
> As a parable of technology's power, the car has few rivals. After the Model T burst on the scene in 1909, cars quickly contributed to the erosion of the family, authority, and community by making it easier for people to pick up and go wherever and whenever they wished. For the same reason, it broadened their horizons and homogenized America by reducing the vast differences among regions.

1. The passage implies that:
   A. The car culture of the 1920s and 1930s represented freedom.
   B. Cabin camps and motels arose because people needed new places to go.
   C. Cars soon became the most destructive influence on American society.
   D. Motels and fast-food chains are still popular today.
   E. Before the car culture of the 1930s, many people hadn't traveled simply for pleasure.

THINKING IT THROUGH   Answering Inference Questions

Use the following steps to work through inference questions:

1. **Eliminate all answers directly stated in the passage.** Answers **A** and **B** are stated in the first paragraph of the passage, so they cannot be real inferences.

2. **Eliminate answers that are unsupported by the ideas in the passage.** Answer **D** may be a true statement, but nothing in the passage supports it; therefore, it is not the correct answer.

3. **Eliminate answers that overstate the ideas** in the passage. Answer **C** is related to the "erosion" of American culture mentioned in the second paragraph, but it exaggerates the point. (Beware of answers that use extreme words like *all, none,* and *always.*)

4. **Ask yourself, "Which, of the answers still remaining, is best supported by the ideas in the passage?"** The answer has to be **E,** since everything in the passage supports the idea that the rise of car travel in the 1930s represented a new form of entertainment.

Writing a Problem-Solution Essay

WHAT'S AHEAD?

In this workshop you will write a problem-solution essay. You will also learn how to

- investigate and analyze a problem
- investigate and analyze solutions
- compose interview questions
- improve sentence style by combining sentences
- correct subject-verb agreement problems

Global warming. Teen smoking. Unsafe toys. Heart attacks. Every-day—and everywhere—scientists, politicians, economists, and citizens identify problems and explore solutions. Often, solutions are easy to identify, or those involved in the problem feel passionately about how to solve it. Sometimes, however, problems are complicated or difficult to grasp. These problems must be approached with an open mind, carefully analyzed, and then *explained* to others who can help solve them. In the following writing workshop, this is just what you will do. Like a journalist from your local paper, you will identify a problem and explore its potential solutions; then, you will explain your findings to others.

As you think about the project ahead, remember two basic points about problems and solutions. First: Problems are often complex. Second: There is usually more than one solution to a problem. If you plan to write about the stress of completing college applications, for example, you cannot arrive at solutions until you break the problem down into parts: students' fears about going to college or about not being accepted at the "right" college, pressure from family and school counselors, and so on. Then, when searching for solutions, you should consider and describe several possibilities—not just the one you favor most. (You are a journalist now, remember?)

Prewriting

Choose a Problem

Problems, Problems—Everywhere You Look   How do you choose a manageable problem? World peace is much too large a topic to tackle in a short essay—so is pollution. On the other end of the spectrum, you don't want to choose a topic that is too personal or trivial—like why you almost have to dislocate your arm to open your locker. As you generate ideas, keep your eye on problems that you can thoroughly explain in the space of your paper. You should also choose a problem that others will want to know more about. Here are some ways to find a suitable topic:

- **Think about problems that affect many people in your school or community.** Focusing on your own frustrations about landing an internship is too personal a problem to explore, but it might provide the kernel of a good idea if you think others share this problem. You might transform the initial idea into a somewhat broader topic: How do teens find out about future career possibilities in your town?

- **Identify the local aspects of a national or international problem.** Instead of looking at the problem of low voter turnout in the U.S., narrow your focus to the reasons for low voter turnout in your city. Instead of tackling littering in general, zoom in on the efforts to decrease littering in your school or neighborhood.

- **Think about problems that interest you.** If biology is your favorite class in school, you might find out more about the ways scientists are combating the new "supergerms" that are resistant to antibiotics. That way, you will have a natural curiosity about uncovering the story. (You may also have some prior knowledge that will come in handy as you investigate further.)

After you have generated some ideas, review your list and pick—for now, at least—the problem that you would most like to explore further.

Think about Audience, Purpose, and Tone

Spelling It All Out Because your problem-solution essay will be primarily an *explanation* of a problem and its solutions, you will want your presentation to be clear, complete, and supported with concrete, trustworthy evidence. In short, your **purpose** is to inform. Your **voice**—the distinctive way you communicate to others—should be calm and authoritative, so you should adopt a **tone** that is objective and somewhat formal. (Stay away from emotional appeals and personal assertions—both are sure signs that you are trying to persuade your readers.)

Often you will have an **occasion** for writing, too. That means that you are writing because some recent event in the news or in your community prompted you to think about your topic. In other words, your problem has a context in the wider world. If possible, mention this occasion in your writing—it will make your paper relevant to your readers, too.

Your specific **audience** will partially determine how you present your problem, so you should think carefully about who your readers will be.

TIP One way to check the significance of a problem is to ask yourself the following questions:
- Does the problem affect a number of people?
- Is it important to the people it affects?

TIP One good way to identify the right **tone** is to examine the tone in newspaper and magazine articles that address problems. You will see that your writing can be stylish without using overly informal or emotional language.

Use questions like the ones below to help you write your essay with your audience's knowledge, interests, and attitudes in mind.

TIP As you continue exploring your problem and its solutions, you should keep your audience in mind, possibly returning several times during the process to ask yourself these questions again.

▶ **Who *are* my readers?** Are they your classmates, members of a community organization, or city officials? Once you have a mental picture of your readers, think about how your paper might acknowledge their concerns and viewpoints. How will you communicate the seriousness of the problem to them?

▶ **What do my readers already know about this problem?** If they know very little, plan to provide specific and detailed background information. If they know a great deal about the problem, you may be able to move on to a discussion of the solutions more quickly.

▶ **What if my readers believe that the problem is insignificant or that only one solution is worthwhile?** Then, think of some ways to explain why the problem is relevant to their lives or how several different solutions might be viable options rather than just one. Your purpose is not to persuade your readers to think in a particular way, but in order to report the story fully, you may have to break through some of your readers' preconceived ideas.

Define and Analyze the Problem

From the Ground Up   In order to write about a problem, you must know it inside and out. **The first step is to make sure you have pinned down the *real* problem**—the most brilliant solutions in the world will never make sense to your readers if you have not accurately diagnosed the problem.

| KEY CONCEPT

THINKING IT THROUGH **Describing a Problem**

To help you build a more precise understanding of your topic, use the strategies below.

▶ STEP 1 **Define the problem.** What is the problem, as concretely as you can state it? How far-reaching is it?

▶ STEP 2 **Tell a story about the problem.** Who or what caused the problem? What are the effects of the problem, and whom do they affect?

▶ STEP 3 **Compare and contrast the problem.** How is the problem like other problems? How is it different?

▶ STEP 4 **Evaluate the problem.** How serious is the problem? Why?

Take a Closer Look   Remember the warning about problems being complex? Sometimes even the simplest problems become complicated when you really examine them. Whatever problem you have chosen, breaking it into parts—or analyzing it—will help you reach beneath the surface and identify any underlying problems. Solving these hidden problems often eliminates the surface problem.

One good way to analyze a problem is to use the reporter's *5W-How?* questions (*Who? What? When? Where? Why? How?*). The following chart shows how one student interested in the problem of "Internet addiction" used the *5W-How?* questions to analyze the problem. Notice that *where?* is missing because answers to the question are not relevant to the student.

Who?	Kids, adults, teens—everybody. I know one girl who spends eight hours a day online.
What?	Problem is that people spend so much time online that they neglect schoolwork, jobs, family, friends, hobbies, exercise, and sometimes even food. Because the addiction increases over time, it's not seen as a problem by those who do it—this failure to see the connection between online time and stress or problems in other parts of life is part of the bigger problem.
When?	In evening, but some kids go online in morning, too. Some even stay home "sick" to stay online.
Why?	It's fun—you can play games, find out interesting information, and talk to others via e-mail or in chat rooms without feeling shy or judged.
How?	Usually, people have access at home and there's no one keeping track of how long they spend online.

At the end of your analysis, you should be able to write a clear statement of the problem. This kind of analysis can also alert you to parts of the problem you want to really focus on as you begin to look at solutions. The writer above, for example, became especially interested in the underlying problem of "denial," or the failure to recognize that there is a problem, among Internet overusers.

TIP   If you are having trouble pinning down your problem, do some research: Read about the problem in reference books or newspaper and magazine articles, conduct a search on the Web, or make some calls to experts or those affected by the problem. You might also do your own field research.

At this point in your prewriting,

■ choose a problem to investigate and think about your audience

■ define your problem carefully, researching it if necessary

Explore Solutions

With Problem in Hand   Once you understand the problem clearly, start exploring solutions. Remember, however, that you are writing as a journalist would—your search for solutions should not end with personal experiences and opinions. Instead, you will need to investigate solutions in a variety of outside sources. Of course library research is key, but also try the following pointers to gather information about solutions from other, nonprint sources. (Often, when you seek up-to-the-minute facts, the most current information has not yet made its way into print sources.)

■ **Interview Experts.** Find professionals working to solve your problem. You may send a letter or e-mail detailing your questions, or arrange to conduct a telephone or in-person interview. For example, if you are examining why fish are dying in your town's largest lake, interview someone in the nearest fish and game governmental office, or see if there is a biologist at the local university working on the problem.

■ **Observe Solutions.** If you learn that a solution is already in place somewhere near you, study the solution firsthand. For example, visit the local library to see how reading tutorials help combat community literacy problems.

■ **Research through the Web.** Using keywords, look for a Web site devoted to your problem and its solutions. For statistics about who is affected by eating disorders and how they can be helped, for example, look up *anorexia* and *treatment*.

Often when you are examining solutions, you will find out even more about the problem. Do not be afraid to refine or add to your knowledge at each step of the research process.

TIP   When researching, particularly in print sources, be sure to use reliable sources. *Reliable* means that the source is trustworthy—the information found there can be believed. Mainstream magazines and newspapers are generally reliable, as are experts who have studied the problem carefully and objectively.

Reference Note

For more on **evaluating sources,** see page 251.

TIP   As you investigate solutions, it helps to know about older attempts to solve the problem and why they failed. After all, successful solutions are usually built on a firm understanding of previous failures. If your problem has been around for awhile and you realize you don't know anything about prior attempts to solve it, take another look at print sources—they will probably give you some necessary history. This deeper knowledge will, in turn, make your essay more informative and credible for your readers.

Preparing Questions for an Interview

In writing this paper, you are working like a reporter, checking your sources and pinning down the facts. If you conduct interviews, you will likely use the four basic kinds of interview questions. Do you know what they are? Look at the descriptions and examples in the chart below. (For more on **conducting an interview,** see page 986.)

Type of Question	Description	Examples
Open Questions	encourage a person to talk freely, sharing feelings and thoughts	What are some solutions to Internet addiction?
Closed Questions	can be answered with "yes" or "no" or several words; used to pin down specific information	How many hours per week is a sure sign of Internet addiction?
Neutral Questions	don't unfairly cue the reader that the interviewer seeks a particular answer; instead, neutral questions imply that there is no "right answer"	How did you feel when you were spending so much time online?
Follow-up Questions	ask for additional information about a topic you have already discussed	Why do these solutions work? Tell me more about limiting time online.

In developing questions, you should be aware of a type of question that you should *not* use in an interview: a **leading question**—one that leads the person being interviewed toward a certain answer (*Aren't you dismayed that people abuse the Internet?*). This kind of question forces the person being interviewed, however subtly, to agree with the interviewer's preconceived ideas or opinions. When you catch yourself using leading questions, check to see if your own bias has crept into the interview.

PRACTICE

On your own paper, identify by type each of the following questions. (Hint: Some questions may be more than one type. Look for leading questions, too.)

1. What solutions would you consider for funding the school computer program?

2. Would students take advantage of after-school computer lab hours?

3. Was teen smoking a problem ten years ago?

4. You have mentioned requesting donations for the computer programs from local business and parents. Do you have other funding ideas?

5. Don't you think a new sports arena would solve a lot of the problems we have in our city?

Analyze Solutions

KEY CONCEPT

Stop and Think   While it is true that you are reporting on solutions rather than recommending one of them over the others, you still have an obligation to **analyze,** and even **evaluate** these solutions. Armed with your newfound expertise and your common sense, **you must explain to your readers which solutions are most practical and sound and which have the greatest possibility of success.**

To be as thorough as possible, think about all solutions. Don't let personal bias allow you to ignore or overlook one of them. For example, if the problem you are investigating is the lack of a theater program in your school, you should give attention to *all* of the various solutions: Mention the drama club's idea to ask a local theater company to sponsor them *and* the student council's proposal to redistribute the school's activities fund (even if you think the latter idea will never succeed). Despite the temptation to recommend one solution and ignore the rest, you *can* describe the strengths and weaknesses of each idea from an objective point of view.

To analyze the solutions (and also to evaluate them from an observer's point of view) ask yourself the following questions about the solutions you have gathered:

TIP   Jotting notes to these analysis questions may help you clarify and refine your ideas. It may also lead you to discover what else you need to learn before you can proceed.

- How can I categorize the solutions? Are some solutions similar to others in some ways? If so, in what ways do they overlap?

- Do some seem too superficial to be effective, some too difficult to implement?

- Will some solutions take longer to put in place? Do some solutions require fewer steps?

- Do any solutions offer a basic remedy for an underlying part of the problem?

As you analyze and evaluate solutions, remember that there are rarely perfect solutions. Often, pieces of two or more ideas are combined to fashion a compromise solution—or individual solutions must be implemented for each part of a complicated problem. Your task is to clearly and fairly describe the best solutions (or parts of solutions) available.

Look at the chart below to see how the writer working on Internet addiction assessed the solutions her research had uncovered.

Solutions to Internet Addiction	Analysis
1. Move the computer out of the bedroom to a public room—the kitchen or family room. 2. Place time limits on computer use.	The first two solutions seem to be simple physical or external solutions. The rest of the solutions are more complex, involving mental and emotional discussions and decisions.

3. Recognize that there is a problem by checking on the amount of time spent online, and what kind of online use the person favors.

4. Differentiate between kinds of online use—e-mail, chat rooms, games, research, and online homework sessions with real-life friends. Then, restrict time to school-related uses.

5. Prevent addiction in the first place by getting and/or staying involved in social activities with family and friends.

The third solution seems to be the most basic: the first step in solving the problem. If an online addict does not know there is a problem, he or she is probably not going to try to solve it.

The fourth solution seems useful, but most addicts probably can't restrict themselves.

The last solution is not really effective once the problem has begun; it may require another person to urge the "addict" to reconnect with others.

State the Thesis

Get to the Point   During the analysis of the problem and its solutions, a writer can often refine the topic of his or her essay. This refining process may end in a **thesis statement**. The writer studying Internet overuse would probably start with a thesis like this:

As computer use grows, one of the newest problems to crop up in students' lives is spending too much time online. The first step toward solving the problem is to help students become aware that it is a problem.

One way to create a thesis is to write a sentence or two that includes the problem and the solution (notice how the problem and the first step in solving it are mentioned in the thesis above). Even if the first attempt is a bit rough, this initial thesis statement will serve as an anchor as you plan the rest of the essay.

TIP   A thesis is often stated in one sentence, but theses can also be contained in two sentences, as is the case in the example above. Two sentences are used when it would be awkward or cumbersome to state the thesis in just one sentence. Remember, however, that despite its length, a thesis should always convey a specific idea that can be elaborated and supported.

Assemble and Evaluate Evidence

Getting Down to the Facts Your research has enabled you to define a problem carefully and analyze a range of solutions. Now, how will you present this detailed knowledge to your audience? After all, readers are usually a skeptical bunch—they will want to see **evidence: facts, examples, expert testimony,** even **statistics.** To decide which bits of evidence your audience will find useful and credible, you might begin by setting it all down in writing. Then, evaluate your evidence by asking these questions.

- How **concrete** is it? Can readers use it to understand precisely the problem or solutions?

- How **authoritative** is it? Will readers find it trustworthy?

Look at the following chart to see how one writer assessed some of the evidence she had gathered for the Internet addiction topic.

Evidence to define problem of Internet addiction	How concrete/authoritative?
Carnegie-Mellon study connecting Internet overuse with depression	Very authoritative—was done by researchers at a major university. Study was also widely reported in newspapers, a sign that professional reporters think it's trustworthy.
My friend Melinda's problem with constant Internet use	Not really "authoritative" because it doesn't involve professionals and it's just one example. Still, if I describe the way it affects Melinda's life, this example could be a concrete way to illustrate Internet abuse; in combination with the university study and other information, this piece of evidence helps show effects of problem.

TIP As you assemble your evidence in chart form, try to state each piece as precisely as possible. This way, you will have facts and figures at your fingertips as you draft. Notice the difference between the vague and precise statements below.

Vague: Many students have had car accidents.

Precise: Twenty percent of the Rollingwood junior class has had at least one minor car accident in the last year.

Organize Your Information

Make It Neat   When you analyze a problem and its solutions you really begin the organization process. After all, we tend to think about problems with a certain natural logic: First, we pin down the problem, and then we weigh and analyze the solutions. Articulating this process to readers requires a bit more planning; you have to structure information so your readers will truly understand it. In other words, you must create a **logical progression** for your ideas. Usually, this means that you must choose to order your information in **chronological order** (the order in which problems and solutions occurred, or will occur, in time) or in **order of importance** (from most important or successful solution to least, or vice versa, depending on the solution with which you want to conclude your essay). Use the following chart to help you to decide which is best for your essay.

Reference Note

For more about **chronological order** and **order of importance,** see page 461.

Chronological	Order of Importance
Does the problem have a history? How far back does my information go?	What aspect of the problem is most important or urgent?
Which solution was tried first? What were the results?	Which solution (or part of the solution) will work immediately?
What solution was tried next?	Which solution seems relatively minor?
Do I need to explain the steps to implement my solutions?	Which solution is most effective?

TIP   As you think about the order your essay should follow, try clustering various points, or creating an informal outline. This will allow you to see—and reorganize, if necessary—all the parts of your essay before you even begin drafting.

Problem-solution explanations can be quite complicated. You may need to use *both* chronological order and order of importance to explain a problem that has a long history; in cases like this, the problem and prior solutions might be described in chronological order, and then the current set of solutions related in order of importance.

YOUR TURN 5   Exploring Solutions and Planning Your Essay

Before moving on to the drafting stage, remember to

- explore and analyze solutions
- write a thesis statement that includes the problem and the solution
- assemble and evaluate your evidence
- plan how to organize your information

Problem-Solution Essay

Framework	Directions and Explanations

Introduction
- Create interest.
- Establish the problem.
- Include a clear thesis statement.

Get Readers Involved   To draw in your readers, begin with an attention-getting anecdote, a vivid description, or a pointed question directed at them.

Define the Problem   Give readers a clear idea of the problem your essay will address. If you think it is necessary, include a statement of the problem's seriousness or relevance to readers' lives.

Use a Complete Thesis   Be sure your thesis statement identifies the problem *and* mentions the solutions you will cover.

Body
- Present an expanded description of the problem.
- Discuss solutions in detail.

Describe the Problem and the Solutions   In a full explanation of the problem, describe all of its causes or parts. If it has a history, recall it for your readers, along with the past attempts to solve it; if there is a consensus about the problem's future, tell your readers about that, too. Display the fruits of your research by providing facts, examples, statistics, and statements from experts. (When necessary, introduce or cite your sources.)

Conclusion
- Restate the problem.
- Summarize the solutions.
- Provide an outlook for the future.

Organize your Points   Remember your organizational structure: chronological or order of importance (if you use both, clearly distinguish the two sections with introductions and/or transitional words and phrases).

Finishing Up   Without letting any personal bias color your judgment, let your readers know where you think the problem and its solutions are headed. If possible, refer back to your opening anecdote or description.

YOUR TURN 6   Writing a Draft

Follow the framework above to write the first draft of your problem-solution essay. Also look ahead at the models on the following pages.

A Writer's Model

As you read the following essay, use the margin notes to help you see where the elements in the framework from the previous page appear in this essay.

Too Much of a Good Thing

It is nearly 11 on a warm Tuesday night. While the majority of homes are dark, the home at 4817 Citrus Street remains an exception. A small, persistent blue glow shines through a back window; the light emanates from Melinda Key's computer monitor. The sixteen-year-old has been staring at her screen for the past seven hours, missing basketball practice, dinner, and her favorite television show. Though she is exhausted and her eyes are bloodshot, she is nowhere near quitting.

Is she beating a deadline for the school paper? Writing a novel? Hammering out an essay for her college application? The answer to all of these questions is a resounding "no."

Melinda is addicted to the Internet, and she is not alone. Like thousands of other teenagers and adults, she spends every moment of her free time online. As computer use grows, this is a problem that will affect increasing numbers of people. The reasons are obvious: Being online is fun, it provides an escape from everyday pressures, and even allows some to express part of their personality without feeling shy or judged. Yet, although friends and parents worry, many Internet abusers do not think there is anything wrong. The first step toward solving the problem is to recognize that there is a problem.

Unsubstantiated stories about people losing spouses, homes, and jobs while they remain glued to a computer screen are everywhere, but lately more scientific evidence of the problem has emerged. A team at Carnegie-Mellon University has recently done groundbreaking research connecting Internet use with increased loneliness and depression. Apart from the Carnegie-Mellon team, Dr. Kimberly Young, a clinical psychologist at the University of Pittsburgh, researches what she calls "Internet Addiction Disorder," or "IAD." She compares it to other forms of addiction because IAD involves an obsession with one thing (staying online) and neglect of school, work, family, friends, outdoor activities, hobbies, exercise, and even eating. Dr. Young believes IAD sufferers even experience some of the symptoms common to other kinds of addiction—sleep deprivation, cravings, and withdrawal signs, for example. Not all experts agree that

(continued)

INTRODUCTION

Anecdote creates interest

Statement of problem

Solution

BODY

Expanded description of problem, with evidence

Internet overuse results in physiological effects, but it seems likely that heavy, sustained Internet use to the exclusion of other aspects of life is not healthy and should be treated.

First solution

Although Melinda's high school offered a confidential Online Discussion Group where teens could speak to a counselor, it was discontinued earlier in the semester due to lack of interest. Melinda never attended. Her reaction is common—many people still do not believe that "Internet addiction" is a valid problem.

Outcome

Most important part of problem

Dr. Young and others in the field aim to change this perception with the aid of Web sites geared toward education. To help people decide if they are overusing the Internet, the sites offer quizzes with questions that range from, "Have you ever gone without sleep to spend extra time surfing the Net?" to "Do you constantly look forward to or even crave your next online session?"

Most basic solution

Once the problem is recognized, there are a number of solutions to try. Some are physical or external solutions; for example, moving the computer out of a bedroom and into a public room, such as the kitchen or the family room. This makes it possible for others to monitor Internet use. Also, time limits on computer use can be imposed by either the user or by a parent or friend.

Other solutions

The issue is not only the amount of time online, but also how that time is spent. Uses of the Internet vary widely. This is where solutions appealing to the mind can be put to use. For those who claim that the Internet is educational, it is important to point out that not all Internet use is necessarily educational. Recognizing the differences between spending time in chat rooms and using the Internet for online homework sessions, for example, could be a step in the right direction for someone who spends too much time online. The research group at Carnegie-Mellon points out that their report's conclusions about negative effects of Internet use does not apply to learning opportunities on the Internet.

More solutions

Of course, prevention is the best way to begin to solve the problem of online addiction. Staying involved with social activities, seeing friends, exercising regularly, and setting time limits (or limits on the kind of Internet use) will keep people out of the online obsession range. Yet prevention can only be a solution if one is already aware that Internet overuse can lead to addiction; those that have already crossed the line may need outside help to reconnect with real life. As one of Carnegie-Mellon researchers says, "The lesson is that one should not run away from friends and families and escape into cyberspace." If everyone heeds this lesson—and passes it on to others—then we will not see this problem rise in direct relation to mushrooming Internet use.

CONCLUSION
Problem restatement
Summary of solutions

Outlook

A Student's Model

The following excerpt by student writer Kerri Pelz of Viola, Kansas, consists of two introductory and six body paragraphs from a problem-solution essay. Notice that the writer uses parenthetical citations to document her sources. (For more on documenting sources, see page 268.)

Solid Waste in Sedgwick County

Each person in the United States throws away an average of 4.3 pounds of trash per day. Once thrown away, decomposition takes four weeks for a traffic ticket, 500 years for an aluminum can, and up to one million years for a glass bottle. At this rate, it is not surprising that our country's landfills are filling up. Over half of them could reach their capacities within the next ten years (Wallace 14). This includes Brooks Landfill, which services most of the Wichita area.

We must decide what to do with solid waste in Sedgwick County. Forty-one states presently have comprehensive solid waste reduction laws in effect. There are forty-four that have legislated or announced goals for waste reduction of up to 70 percent. Kansas presently has neither reduction laws nor goals for the management of solid waste (Brown 5). In Sedgwick County especially, we face the problem of too much trash and not enough space to dispose of it.

Until the late 1960s, when the public became increasingly concerned over air pollution, burning trash in backyard barrels and at the town dump was the most common way to dispose of waste. Incineration became popular again during the energy crisis of the 1970s as the Department of Energy experimented with ways to turn trash into electricity and steam. About 20 percent of the nation's trash is now being incinerated (Hays 6).

Incineration reduces the volume of waste and captures the energy content of the waste products. In waste-to-energy plants, trash is used to produce energy. One ton of trash yields the same amount of energy as 900 pounds of coal or seventy three gallons of fuel oil. The sale of this energy produced can pay for one third of the operating costs of a plant. Incinerators also have less potential to pollute ground water than a landfill and can be built on as

INTRODUCTION
Interesting opening

Problem stated

Elaboration of problem

Thesis statement

BODY
One solution

Advantages of the solution

(continued)

(continued)

little as an acre of land (Brown 19).

Disadvantages of the
solution

Unfortunately, incinerators generally cost more to build than landfills, which raises the cost of disposal to residents and businesses. The U.S. Supreme Court has ruled that cities have little control over where their trash goes, so some trash collectors take trash to cheaper landfills. This leaves cities to pay for an incinerator that is no longer needed. New air-pollution regulations adopted by the Environmental Protection Agency in 1995 could increase costs by as much as thirteen dollars a ton to reduce dioxin emissions. Property values near incinerators generally decline because of the fear of air pollution and the increased truck traffic and noise. Cities will still need to have a landfill or large storage area to take care of trash when the incinerator is out of operation (Hays 6).

More disadvantages
of the solution

Burning the 1,500 tons of trash a day that Wichita currently buries in its landfill would produce enough ash to fill fifty-three trash trucks a day. Disposing of this ash can run another $5.75 for every ton of trash burned. Currently the state has no regulations on how ash must be handled, but cities must test ash once a year for heavy metals and hazardous materials. Hazardous ash must be treated or disposed of in a hazardous-waste landfill, which costs as much as $75 per ton (Brown 19).

A second possible
solution

About sixty percent of the nation's trash is buried in landfills. At the current disposal rate of 1,500 tons of solid waste per day, Brooks Landfill will soon reach its legal capacity of 70 vertical feet (Brown 4). To continue to dispose of its trash in a landfill, Wichita would have to build a new one. Landfills are generally the cheapest forms of disposal. Some communities even raise money to fund their landfills by levying a tax on imported garbage. There would be greater financial support, and environmental improvements would be possible through state-of-the-art technology. Landfills are also more flexible than incinerators since they can easily be altered to accommodate fluctuating amounts of garbage (Hays 6).

Advantages of
second solution

Disadvantage of
second solution

Although they have their advantages, the number of landfills in both the nation and Kansas is dropping. One reason for this decline is the risk of ground water pollution. Landfill owners must test the ground water for pollution for 30 years after the landfill is closed. If pollution is found, it can lead to expensive cleanup.

Revising

Evaluate and Revise Your Essay

You Be the Judge Your revision process should include at least two readings. In the first reading, you should focus on whether you have thoroughly discussed the problem you chose, along with its solutions, and whether you have organized your information in a clear and accessible way. In the second reading, you should refine your style.

First Reading: Content and Organization Work **collaboratively** to **revise,** or **edit,** your essay. Respond to the questions in the first column below. Use the tips in the middle, and, if necessary, make the changes suggested in the third column.

Problem-Solution Essay: Content and Organization Guidelines for Peer and Self-Evaluation

Evaluation Questions	▶ Tips	▶ Revision Techniques
❶ Does the introduction pique the readers' interest?	▶ **Underline** any attention-grabbing opening sentences. If there are no underlined sentences, revise.	▶ **Add** an anecdote, a vivid description, or a provocative question that will interest your readers right away.
❷ Does the introduction have a thesis statement which clearly states the problem and mentions solutions?	▶ **Bracket** specific mentions of the problem and solutions separately. If there are no brackets, or only one set of them, revise.	▶ **Add** a statement of the problem, or solutions, or both. **Replace** vague statements with a tight, specific thesis.
❸ Is there an expanded description of the problem? Is the evidence about the problem (and solutions) authoritative and concrete?	▶ **Count** sentences that describe the problem. If there are fewer than three, revise. **Underline** descriptions of the problem and solutions. If they don't provide concrete or authoritative evidence, revise.	▶ **Elaborate** on the problem, using background information and evidence. **Add** separate discussions of the parts of the problem, if possible. **Add** evidence for each solution.
❹ Are the solutions discussed in a clear, organized way?	▶ **Number** the solutions in the order you have chosen. If a solution has several steps, number them separately. Revise if any set of numbers is not in sequence.	▶ **Rearrange** the solutions (or solution steps) to show clear chronological order or order of importance. If you are using both, make sure the sections are clear.
❺ Does the conclusion restate the problem, summarize the solutions, and present an outlook for the future?	▶ **Label** sentences in the conclusion showing each sentence's function. Use the labels "problem," "solution summary," and "outlook." Revise when a label is missing.	▶ **Add** the missing part of the conclusion without repeating word for word what you have previously written.

ONE WRITER'S REVISIONS Here is how one writer used the guidelines to revise some sentences from the problem-solution essay that appears on page 169.

Add

A team at Carnegie-Mellon University has recently done groundbreaking research connecting Internet use with increased loneliness and depression. Apart from the Carnegie-Mellon team,

∧ Dr. Kimberly Young, a clinical psychologist at the University

of Pittsburgh, researches what she calls "Internet Addiction

Disorder," or "IAD." She compares it to other forms of addiction

because IAD involves an obsession with one thing (staying

online) and neglect of school, work, family, friends, outdoor activ-

Elaborate

ities, hobbies, exercise, and even eating. ∧ *Dr. Young believes IAD sufferers even experience some of the symptoms common to other kinds of addiction—sleep deprivation, cravings, and withdrawal signs, for example.*

PEER REVIEW

Ask a classmate to read your draft and answer the following questions.

1. What explanations or descriptions helped you understand the problem presented in the essay?

2. Were the solutions presented clearly? List as many of them (and the steps to implement them) as you can remember.

Analyzing the Revision Process

1. Why did the writer add the first sentence?

2. What additional information, or elaboration, does the last sentence provide?

YOUR TURN 7 **Revising for Content and Organization**

Use the Content and Organization Guidelines on page 173 as you read through your draft for the first time. Revise your essay to make all aspects of the problem clear and all the solutions understandable.

▷ **Second Reading: Style** A problem and its solutions can involve some complex ideas. One way to communicate those ideas—and the relationships between them—is to **combine sentences by coordinating ideas.** Short, choppy sentences may give the impression that your ideas are not connected; in turn, this may weaken the overall impact of your essay. By showing a relationship between ideas at the sentence level, you can lend power to your writing and clarity to your ideas.

Evaluation Question	▶ Tip	▶ Revision Technique
Are there places in the essay where sentences are choppy?	▶ **Underline** all sentences with five to seven words. Also **underline** sentences that *sound* simple. They will sound abrupt rather than smooth.	▶ When two or more choppy sentences are grouped together, use coordinating or correlative conjunctions to **combine** sentences that have related ideas.

Coordinating Ideas Through Sentence Combining

Two sentences with equally important ideas can stand alone; however, if the ideas are related, they may be more powerfully or clearly expressed when combined into one sentence. You can also eliminate repetition by joining coordinate ideas with coordinating words, phrases, or clauses. Use coordinating conjunctions (*and, but, for, nor, or, so, yet*) or correlative conjunctions (*both—and, either—or, not only—but also*) when you combine sentences. For example, *and* can join ideas that are alike, while *but* joins two ideas that are opposite or different. You can also combine sentences by joining independent clauses with a semicolon.

Sentences

Reference Note

For more on **sentence combining,** see page 436.

ONE WRITER'S REVISIONS See below how the writer of the problem/solution essay on page 169 used the guidelines above to combine sentences in two different places in the essay, eliminating repetition and creating stronger statements.

BEFORE REVISION

1. Melinda is addicted to the Internet. Melinda is not alone.
2. One issue is the amount of time spent online. Also important is how time online is spent.

"Melinda" repeats—sounds choppy.
Need to relate ideas to one another more effectively.

AFTER REVISION

1. Melinda is addicted to the Internet, and she is not alone.
2. The issue is not only the amount of time online, but also how that time is spent.

One sentence has more impact.
Combining makes relationship more clear.

Analyzing the Revision Process

1. How does combining the sentences improve the flow?

2. What are other ways the sentences could be combined?

Reference Note

For more information on **conjunctions,** see page 505.

YOUR TURN 8 **Combining Sentences with Coordinating Ideas**

Revise your sentence style by looking for simple sentences with coordinating ideas and joining them. Remember: You need not combine any pair of simple sentences, but you should think about whether the ideas have a relationship that you can state better by using conjunctions.

Designing Your Writing

Using Bullets   Have you ever noticed that problem-solution articles in newspapers and magazines often use bullets to distinguish parts of the problem or to list separate solutions (or steps of the same solution)? Bullets emphasize main points and allow readers to read efficiently, moving through complicated information without confusion or unnecessary backtracking. If you choose to use bullets in sections of your essay, there are a few conventions you should follow:

TIP The viewing and representing section that follows this workshop (page 181) will give you pointers on using graphics, another valuable way to clarify the problems and solutions in your essay. Remember that many software packages can help you design graphics on a computer.

- **Make sure the bulleted items are parallel**—parts of the problem, separate solutions, or steps of one solution, rather than a jumble of all three.

- **Use a limited number of bullets.** If your essay were nothing but bulleted items, the bullets would lose the ability to break up and clarify information within a longer piece.

- **If it adds even further clarity, use a brief heading after each bullet.** Again, these headings should all be parallel—all statements, imperatives, key words, or questions, rather than a mixture. Often, such bullet headings are presented in boldface.

Look at the how the following passage illustrates these tips.

Example:
The student council has settled on a couple of possible solutions to the problem of speeding in the school parking lot:

- **Build speed bumps every thirty feet.** Although the cost would be substantial, this solution would be the most effective.

- **Institute an internal "ticketing" procedure.** The parking lot security guards would issue these tickets, and the student council would assign fines or penalties.

Publishing

Proofread Your Essay

Check and Check Again You have worked hard to explain your problem and its solutions. Now make sure that your paper is free of errors in grammar, spelling, and punctuation. After all, you do not want any minor errors to detract from your fine ideas and solid research.

Reference Note

For more information about **subject-verb agreement,** see page 578.

Grammar Link

Subject-Verb Agreement

Somewhere in your essay, in connecting people to problems and solutions, you have probably gotten tangled up in making subjects and verbs agree. You already know the fundamentals of subject-verb agreement:

1. A singular subject takes a singular verb.

Example:
Internet **addiction is** a common problem.

2. A plural subject takes a plural verb.

Example:
Chat **rooms are** a major draw for teens.

Things get a little more confusing when **intervening phrases and clauses** follow the subject. When you encounter intervening phrases, remember that the verb still must agree with the subject.

Incorrect The **study** of Internet users **reveal** that an increasing number of children are online.

Correct The **study** of Internet users **reveals** that an increasing number of children are online.

This rule also applies when the subject is followed by a phrase that begins with an expression such as *along with, as well as, in addition to,* and *together with.*

Incorrect The math **teacher,** as well as her students, **were** intrigued by the special mathematics Web site.

Correct The math **teacher,** as well as her students, **was** intrigued by the special mathematics Web site.

As you proofread, look for errors in subject-verb agreement, particularly when there are intervening phrases or clauses.

PRACTICE

On your own paper, correct the subject-verb agreement errors in the following sentences. If a sentence is correct, write C.

1. The variety of Internet newsgroups provide something for everyone.

2. The length of a typical online session are twenty-five minutes.

3. Those who "surf" the Web is growing in number every day.

4. Usually, the Internet "addict," together with family or friends, solve the problem in a relatively short time.

5. Many people accessing the Internet use it for sending e-mail and playing games.

Publish Your Essay

Spreading the News Once you have submitted your essay to your teacher, consider publishing it in one of the following ways:

- If your peers would be interested, submit your essay to your school's student newspaper.
- With some classmates, compose a newsletter made up entirely of problem-solution essays and distribute it to other classes, friends, and family.
- E-mail your essay to an Internet newsgroup that focuses on the problem.
- Send your essay to someone involved with the problem and its solutions— a local official, a member of Congress, or a community organization.
- With a group of classmates, publish your own online problem and solution magazine. Invite students from all over the world to submit essays for publication.

Reflect on Your Essay

PORTFOLIO

Take Another Look Once you have achieved some distance from your polished, final essay, read it again with fresh eyes. Then, jot down your responses to these questions:

- Why did you choose the problem you settled on?
- What was the most difficult task in writing this paper? What was the easiest? Why?
- Did you explain the problem and its solutions to your own and your audience's satisfaction?
- What might you do differently the next time you write a problem-solution essay?

If you wish to keep this essay in your portfolio, be sure to attach your answers to the above questions.

 YOUR TURN 9 **Proofreading, Publishing, and Reflecting**

Review the steps on this and the previous page. Before you submit your final essay, make sure to

- proofread it carefully
- consider publishing options
- reflect on your writing process by jotting answers to the questions above

Writing a Dramatic Scene

Comedy, drama, or musical—all plays have one thing in common: At their core, they contain a problem. After all, problems, or crises, move a plot forward. What obstacles will the characters overcome? What internal or external conflicts will they resolve? As you think about your own dramatic scene, keep problems in mind.

What's the Problem? To come up with ideas:

- **Spend a day listening and looking** What do you imagine the people on the street or in the grocery store dream of? What might their daily struggles be?

- **Peer into yourself** What internal conflicts have you felt? What obstacles have tested your mettle?

- **Set your imagination loose** You might think of two vastly different characters—a mild-mannered accountant and a space alien, for example—and imagine what would happen if they met.

Putting the Pieces Together Like stories and novels, the basic elements of drama include **plot, character,** and **setting.** Unlike fiction, however, a dramatic scene must communicate its meaning primarily through **dialogue,** the words the characters speak to one another on stage. To use these elements skillfully, take a look at the tips below.

- **Listen Up** You can gather tips on creating **dialogue** any time—it occurs all around you. Listen carefully to how people talk to each other in the cafeteria or at the park.

You might even strive to create speech patterns and word choices so unique to your characters that readers can recognize who is speaking even without seeing a name beside the line. (As you create speech, remember that gestures often replace speech in real life; people rarely say "no"—they nod their heads instead.)

- **What a Character!** Creating believable **characters** is always key. To spark ideas, use people you know as "models" while you flesh out their fictional counterparts. What do your characters look like? How do they act? What makes them happy, angry, or bored?

- **Behind the Scenes** **Set** and **stage directions** are written to guide the actors and director. These directions are not meant to be seen or heard by the audience, but rather shown with props and enacted with the actors' gestures. **Stage directions** describe how a certain line should be read, or what physical expression or position the actor should take; this type of direction appears in parentheses next to the dialogue or action it refers to. **Set directions** set a scene in a time and place; they may be general *(a large city; at night)* or specific *(the Ferris family's fourth floor apartment; a Saturday night in June, 1945).*

- **The Plot Thickens** Everything you know about **plot** from stories applies here, as well—a problem is introduced and the characters set out to resolve it, fight against it, or give up altogether. The only difference is that, in drama, you must *show* plot with dialogue and action.

Look and Learn Notice how the following annotated excerpt from Lorraine Hansberry's play *A Raisin in the Sun* demonstrates most of the key elements including conflict.

Set Directions give time, place, and general description of actors.

Time: Sometime between World War II and the present.

Place: Chicago's South Side

At rise: It is morning dark in the living room.

[TRAVIS appears in the hall doorway, almost fully dressed and quite awake now, his towels and pajamas across his shoulders. . . .]

Characters: In this scene they are obviously a mother and her young son. Their names precede the sections of dialogue they speak.

Ruth. Sit down and have your breakfast, Travis.

Travis. Mama, this is Friday. *(Gleefully)* Check coming tomorrow, huh?

Ruth. You get your mind off money and eat your breakfast.

Travis *(eating).* This is the morning we supposed to bring the fifty cents to school.

Plot—notice how the conflict between mother and son is shown through Ruth's gruff remarks and Travis's exasperated look.

Ruth. Well, I ain't got no fifty cents this morning.

Travis. Teacher say we have to.

Ruth. I don't care what teacher say. I ain't got it. Eat your breakfast, Travis.

Travis. I am eating.

Ruth. Hush up now and just eat!

Stage Directions, in italics and parentheses, tell how actors should move or deliver their lines.

(The boy gives her an exasperated look for her lack of understanding, and eats grudgingly.)

Travis. You think Grandmama would have it?

Ruth. No! And I want you to stop asking your grandmother for money, you hear me?

Dialogue—notice how Travis and Ruth have distinct voices: "gimme" and "gaaalee," for example, are a young boy's expressions; Ruth wouldn't use such phrases.

Travis. *(outraged)* Gaaaleee! I don't ask her, she just gimme it sometimes!

YOUR TURN 10 **Writing a Dramatic Scene**

Now that you have a sense of the elements of a good dramatic scene, try writing one of your own. Then, stage your scene for the class, or at home for family or friends.

Creating Graphics

You already know that visual messages carry meaning—in fact, images can communicate many kinds of information as effectively as texts can, sometimes even more effectively. Graphic artists and illustrators have as many ways of representing meaning as writers do.

A particular kind of image—a graphic—can be especially helpful with problem-solution explanations. Rather than describing in detail how pollution in Athens has caused the Parthenon to erode, for example, a magazine article might use a chart which lists the rate of erosion for each decade of this century—or a diagram comparing the number of cars in Athens today with the number fifty years ago.

You've probably "read" countless graphics like this, but what happens when you set out to design your own graphics? How do you determine which kind of diagram, chart, or map will best communicate your message?

Many kinds of graphics can accompany problem-solution essays, but some are used repeatedly because they especially suit the ways we think about problems—how we quantify, measure, or relate to them in our minds. These often-used graphics fit into two categories:

- graphics that represent parts of a whole
- graphics that represent change over time

WHAT'S AHEAD?

In this section you will learn how to create graphics that suit problem-solution explanations. In particular, you will learn about
- **graphics that show parts of a whole**
- **graphics that show change over time**

Representing Parts of a Whole

Problems are often represented by emphasizing parts of the "big picture." One way to think about this kind of graphic is to imagine a statistical "snapshot" that fixes a problem in the present moment so you can examine—and compare—all of its various elements.

Pie charts are a common way to show parts in relation to a whole. If, for example, you wanted to represent the tiny amount your county spent on schools last year, you might draw that percentage of the total budget as one slice, alongside slices for salaries, road upkeep, and so on. If your point were convincing, the slice for schools would be a mere sliver next to the other sections. (Remember, however, that you want to represent the truth, not manipulate it; your graphics should never falsify facts or statistics.)

TIP Pie charts are usually arranged by placing the largest wedge at the twelve o'clock position. The remaining wedges should then be placed clockwise in descending order.

The pie chart below represents how people responded to a poll asking them how aware of germs they were in their daily lives. Note how different shades of color are used to make distinctions.

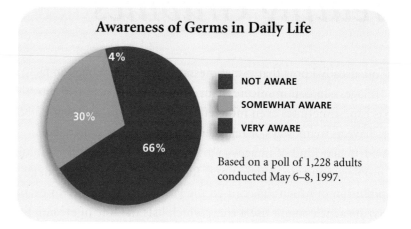

Awareness of Germs in Daily Life

- NOT AWARE
- SOMEWHAT AWARE
- VERY AWARE

Based on a poll of 1,228 adults conducted May 6–8, 1997.

The graphic below is another way to represent parts of a whole. It shows which states keep records of donations to political campaigns:

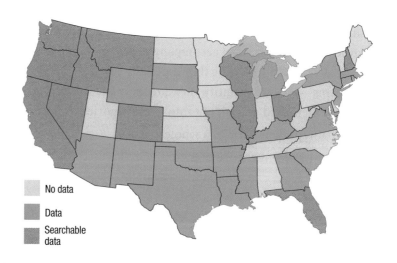

- No data
- Data
- Searchable data

THINKING IT THROUGH **Representing Parts of a Whole**

When you create a graphic that presents a "snapshot" like the ones illustrated above, try to

▶ **Distinguish the parts from one another.** You might use different colors, different type sizes or styles, or other distinguishing marks that make sense to you and will be clear to your reader.

- **Use labels or an easy-to-understand key.** After all, your graphic is meaningless if your reader can't decipher it.

- **Keep it simple.** You don't want to muddy your message with too many elements. Instead, make your graphic as clean and as manageable as possible by broadening your categories.

Representing Change over Time

Another common way to represent a problem is to track it over time. In this way, you can *show* a decline, an increase, a trend, or other developments. **Line graphs** and **bar graphs** are two of many kinds of graphics that can show change over time.

Look at the **bar graph** below, in which the decline in the use of public transportation by U.S. commuters is tracked from 1960 to 2000. In particular, note how the information is organized spatially: a vertical line for the measurements of public transportation use, and a horizontal line for the periods of time discussed.

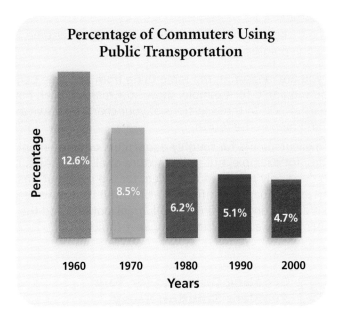

Percentage of Commuters Using Public Transportation

TIP Try to make your own bar graphs as square as possible, with the tallest bar extending to near the top of the vertical line. This is a convention that is commonly followed in line graphs, too. Also, remember to start your measurements at zero. Bar graphs that do not start at zero can often mislead readers by presenting exaggerated differences among the bars.

In the **line graph** on the following page, the same statistics that appear in the bar graph above are represented as a continuous line, along with a line that represents the decline over time in commuters who walk to work. Notice the way the two strings of information are distinguished from one another with solid and dashed lines.

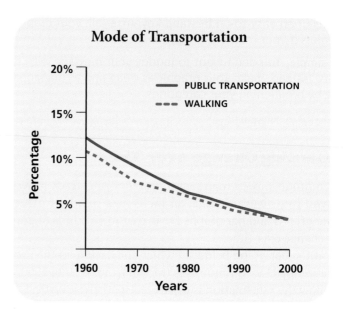

Mode of Transportation

- —— PUBLIC TRANSPORTATION
- --- WALKING

Percentage (y-axis): 20%, 15%, 10%, 5%

Years (x-axis): 1960, 1970, 1980, 1990, 2000

THINKING IT THROUGH **Representing Change over Time**

When you make a graphic that represents change over time, remember to follow the pointers given on page 183, *and*

▶ **Be sure you are measuring the same thing from one time period to the next.** You shouldn't, for example, show how many women have survived heart attacks in three sections of your chart, then switch to women and men in the fourth.

▶ **Present measurements for roughly equal units of time**—months, years, or decades, for example, but not a mixture of all three. Also, remember that you need only represent a problem for the period of time that you deal with in your paper, not from the time that records were started, or the beginning of time itself! (After all, graphs often need the same kind of narrowing and focusing that paper topics do.)

YOUR TURN 11 Creating Graphics for Your Problem-Solution Essay

If you think that a graphic or two would illustrate and clarify the ideas in the problem-solution essay you have just written, here's your chance to create them. Before you finalize your ideas for these graphics, however, meet with one or two classmates to discuss your plans. When you have completed your graphics, incorporate them into your essay and jot in your notebook a brief explanation of why you chose the particular graphics you used.

Choices

Choose one of the following activities to complete.

▶ CREATIVE WRITING

1. A Bird's Eye View Extend your reading of "Single, Lonely Parrot" through some creative writing. For example, you might write a **short monologue** written from the point of view of the last wild Spix's macaw and then give a **dramatic reading** to the class. (For inspiration, read one or two famous literary pieces about birds, such as Percy Shelley's "To a Skylark," or Ted Hughes's "Hawk Roosting.")

▶ ART

2. What's So Funny? Draw a **cartoon** that addresses a problem. First, look at a variety of editorial cartoons to see how other artists manage to be playful and funny, yet communicate a serious point.

▶ CAREERS

3. Different Perspectives With a small group, prepare a **multimedia presentation** to demonstrate how the same problem might be addressed by people working in different fields—education, psychology, film, and so on. Be sure to select the appropriate medium for each element of the presentation. Remember to break your presentation into separate sections, so each member of the group can participate.

▶ CROSSING THE CURRICULUM: SOCIAL STUDIES

4. Looking Back Identify a key conflict or trouble time in American history and research how it was resolved. Was it through military means or in another way? Prepare an **oral presentation** in which you describe the steps taken, and any alternative solutions that were not employed.

▶ VIEWING AND REPRESENTING

5. Sitcom Problems How do television characters solve problems? What types of conflict are most frequently shown? After viewing some programs with a critical eye, write a **short article** to share with the class.

▶ SPEAKING AND LISTENING

6. Loud and Clear Choose a radio or television news program, and listen for a particular report that presents a problem-solution explanation. As you listen, take notes or fill out a graphic organizer. Then, use your notes to write a **short analysis** in which you identify and explain the main idea, the problem, and the possible solutions.

PORTFOLIO

5 Analyzing a Novel

Reading Workshop

Reading a Literary Analysis of a Novel

Writing Workshop

Writing a Literary Analysis of a Novel

Viewing and Representing

Adapting a Scene from a Novel for Film

*T*o Kill a Mockingbird. The Red Badge of Courage. The Great Gatsby. *The Adventures of Huckleberry Finn.* Read the book? Seen the movie? Heard the audiotape? If so, then you probably remember a scene, a character, or a plot twist. Perhaps you have talked about these literary works in class and have learned that "hidden meanings" are not hidden at all, but are waiting for you to read, watch, hear, and *reflect upon.* Novelists write to tell a good story and to express their feelings about human experience. When you read a novel, or listen to a book on tape, you are drawn into thinking about the characters and their circumstances—how they relate to your understanding of life.

Often these first responses are simply *personal* responses—such as, "I loved that character" or "The plot was so real!" Later, we can move from a personal response to a more rigorous, more objective study of the work—a **literary analysis.** Literary analyses come from close, critical readings that usually focus on specific literary elements (character, setting, point of view, plot, symbol, imagery, and theme). Those literary elements might be the same ones that prompted your first response, or they might be ones you and your friends have discussed casually, but in literary analyses they are treated more formally and carefully.

Informational Text

Exposition

YOUR TURN 1 **Brainstorming Approaches to Literature**

Select an appropriate novel you have read. Brainstorm a list of things you could analyze in the novel. For example, consider a character from the story or the story's setting. Share your answers in a small group.

internet**connect**

go. hrw .com
GO TO: go.hrw.com
KEYWORD: EOLang 11-5

Reading a Literary Analysis of a Novel

WHAT'S AHEAD?

In this section, you will read a literary analysis. You will also learn to

- paraphrase
- recognize uses of literary evidence

Why are novels so popular? Some people say that they are especially satisfying because they are so rich in meaning. A novel often reflects the culture in which it was written, has vivid, unforgettable characters, or explores universal themes. If novels are so engaging, why, then, would you read a **literary analysis** of one? One reason is to hear the ideas of others. In listening, we grow to understand a piece of literature better and perhaps understand each other better. We become a community of readers held together by our interest in the novel's meaning. As you read the literary analysis of Nathaniel Hawthorne's *The Scarlet Letter*, think about the aspects of the novel the writer has chosen to discuss.

Preparing to Read

READING SKILL

Paraphrasing   When you **paraphrase,** you restate someone else's ideas or words in your *own* words. Paraphrasing is a good way to check that you understand the main point and details in what you are reading. In articles about literature, writers also use paraphrasing to explain passages in a literary work that may be too long or cumbersome to quote directly. As you read the following selection, try to find places in which the author, Nina Baym, has retold portions of *The Scarlet Letter*.

READING FOCUS

Support in a Literary Analysis   Like many other kinds of essayists, writers of literary analyses use **evidence** to support their ideas and interpretations. In other words, writers don't just tell readers about their ideas—they *show* them with details from the literary work itself. These details, called **literary evidence,** take the form of paraphrases, summaries, or quotations. (Direct quotations are cited with page numbers within the text.) The literary evidence—plus the writer's elaboration explaining the significance of the evidence—supports the writer's interpretations and insights. As you read the following selection, look for examples of how the writer uses support from the novel to show that her ideas are valid.

In the following selection, Nina Baym, a college English professor, focuses on Pearl, one of the characters in Nathaniel Hawthorne's highly symbolic novel, *The Scarlet Letter*. Pearl's mother, Hester Prynne, has been accused of adultery by her Puritan community and must wear the scarlet letter "A" as punishment. Despite her public shame, the letter links Hester to her illegitimate daughter and to the preacher Dimmesdale, Pearl's father. In this excerpt, taken from her book of literary criticism, Baym explains what Pearl represents in the novel. As you read, jot down answers to the numbered active-reading questions.

The Character of Pearl

by NINA BAYM

The character of Pearl is as much, or more, a symbolic function as she is the representation of a human child. In all the descriptions of Pearl, her affinity[1] with the scarlet letter is stressed. She is its symbol, its double, its agent: "It was the scarlet letter in another form; the scarlet letter endowed with life!" (102). Hester carefully dresses Pearl in clothing that mimics the color and embroidery of the letter; this gesture also stresses the way in which the child is her mother's creation. As such, she is both something that the mother produces deliberately, and something that reflects the mother despite herself. More particularly, she reflects the mother's deeds that gave her life (her life is never attributed to her father).

In one sense, the Puritan sense, that deed is equal to a broken law. "The child could not be made amenable[2] to rules. In giving her existence, a great law had been broken; and the result was a being, whose elements were perhaps beautiful and brilliant, but all in disorder" (91). Hester recognizes in Pearl's character "the welfare" of her own spirit during the months when she was pregnant: "She could recognize her wild, desperate, defiant mood, the flightiness of her temper, and even some of the very cloud-shapes of gloom and despondency that had brooded in her heart" (91).

In another sense, however, the child is beauty and freedom and imagination and all the other natural qualities that the Puritan system denies.

1. In what two ways does Baym describe the character of Pearl?

2. Which of Baym's main ideas do you think the two long quotations in the paragraph support?

---

1. **affinity** (ə•fin´i•tē): close association; kinship.
2. **amenable** (ə•mē´•nə•bəl): responsible, or able to be controlled.

Beautiful, intelligent, perfectly shaped, vigorous, graceful, passionate, imaginative, impulsive, capricious,[3] creative, visionary: these are only a sampling of the adjectives with which she is described. And these are all traits in Hester as well as in Pearl. Such descriptions suggest that Pearl is not an independent character so much as an abstraction of elements of Hester's character: a kind of "double," or "other self." This means that character analysis of Pearl is really analysis of Hester, and that the child's lawlessness shows how superficial Hester's quiet and subservient public demeanor is. And Hester's great love for the child signifies in part her refusal to disown her "sin" through a judgment that it was evil.

3. Besides her "lawlessness," what are some other traits that connect Pearl to Hester?

But Pearl is not simply a splitting off and intensifying of some aspects of Hester's character, a way of measuring Hester's attitudes. Quite apart from anything that Hester might intend consciously or unconsciously, Pearl seems to have a special, original relation to the letter. She is not only the letter as Hester might conceive it, but its agent in a scheme[4] that is quite independent of her. If, in Hester's scheme, the child represents elements of defiant and lawless beauty, in this other scheme the child represents a form of conscience. It is her role to enforce the mother's guilt as well as to represent her rebellion. She does this simply by making it impossible for Hester to forget the letter. The letter is the first object that Pearl becomes aware of as a baby, and she keeps the letter firmly at the center of Hester's life by keeping it firmly in her infant regard. We see this role as enforcer of the letter most clearly in the forest scene, the one and only time that Hester throws the letter away. Oblivious to the mother's resurgent[5] youth and beauty and happiness, Pearl refuses to join her until the letter is returned to its usual place. Only when she wears the letter is Hester her mother: And this, alas, is a true perception on Pearl's part. Should Hester repudiate[6] the letter, she will repudiate Pearl.

4. According to the writer, what two things does Pearl represent in her relationship to her mother?

Much in the depiction of Pearl is realistic; she is not all symbol and allegory.[7] Hawthorne used his journal entries about his first child, Una, as sources for elements of his depiction of Pearl. Wildness, caprice, imaginativeness are all traits consistent with the nature of a young child who is endowed with energy and creativity and allowed a great deal of freedom. She lacks reference and adaptation to the world into which she was born, Hester thinks (91); but

---

3. capricious (kə•prē´shəs): whimsical; given to sudden, impulsive behavior.

4. scheme (skēm): overall plan; a system of definite arrangement.

5. resurgent (ri•sʉr´jənt): returning; rising again.

6. repudiate (ri•pyo͞o´dē•āt´): get rid of publicly; refuse relationship with.

7. allegory (al´ə•gôr´ē): a story in which characters or objects have symbolic meaning.

kept apart from society as Pearl is, any child would find it difficult to adapt.

If we could separate Pearl from her symbolic tasks in the novel, we might take her simply as an unusual (for its time), unidealized, and unsentimental description of a real child. Her attraction to the letter is easily explained: The letter is colorful and shiny. Her equation of it with her mother is likewise comprehensible: Pearl has never seen Hester without it. And as for her behavior in the forest, Hester herself offers the explanation that the child is jealous. Her reflecting of Hester's moods may have nothing mysterious about it: Spending so much time with her mother, being completely dependent on her, and possessing an imaginative nature, Pearl would naturally be keenly attuned to Hester, even more than the preoccupied mother might be herself. Pearl's extreme restlessness during the last scene in the marketplace, the narrator says, was "played upon and vibrated with her mother's disquietude" (244).

> **5. Look closely at this paragraph and the preceding one. In what ways does the writer think that Pearl is a realistic character?**

However realistic she may be, there is no mistaking that at the end of the book (when she kisses her father)[8] Pearl becomes fully human for the first time.

> A spell was broken. The great scene of grief, in which the wild infant bore a part, had developed all her sympathies; and as her tears fell upon her father's cheek, they were the pledge that she would grow up amid human joy and sorrow, not for ever do battle with the world, but be a woman in it. Towards her mother, too, Pearl's errand as a messenger of anguish was all fulfilled (256).

So Pearl has been the letter's messenger (its angel, in the word's original sense) and the letter's incarnation;[9] and she has also been its victim. Her victimization has consisted in being denied a reality of her own. At the very moment when she becomes real, nevertheless—when her errand toward Hester is fulfilled—she ceases to be a character in the story.[10] Thus, the human character Pearl is not really part of *The Scarlet Letter*, and the character in the book is best thought of as a symbol and a function who is "naturalized" by being given a smattering of realistic traits.

> **6. In this paragraph, what point about Pearl does the long quotation support?**

---

8. **her father:** Dimmesdale, the preacher, who has never before publicly acknowledged he is Pearl's father and who has privately suffered great shame for allowing Hester to bear all the punishment. As Dimmesdale is dying, he calls out to Pearl for a sign of her affection (and forgiveness), and she kisses him.

9. **incarnation:** given a human body as a living example of something.

10. **she ceases . . . in the story:** From this moment on Pearl does not appear in the novel as a character. Her importance does not dim, but she is just not shown again.

| READING SKILL

TIP Paraphrasing is an especially helpful skill if the original text is written in poetic or elaborate language.

Reference Note

For more about how to write a **summary,** see page 958.

Paraphrasing

In Your Own Words   **Paraphrasing** is using your own words to recount the main idea and important details in a piece of writing. Note, however, that a written paraphrase is usually just about the same length as the passage it is paraphrasing. (A paraphrase differs from a **summary,** which restates the main points in a passage in a short, condensed way.)

People paraphrase for different reasons. For readers, paraphrasing is a tool for clarifying their understanding of the main ideas and details in a piece. Writers of literary analyses paraphrase when they want to refer to important moments in the work but do not want to quote them. For example, in "The Character of Pearl," Baym paraphrases in the following sentence: "Oblivious to the mother's resurgent youth and beauty and happiness, Pearl refuses to join her until the letter is returned to its usual place." Here, instead of quoting Hawthorne's account of the forest episode, Baym *describes* Pearl's response when Hester tries to throw the scarlet letter away.

The chart below shows how one student paraphrased a passage from *The Scarlet Letter.* In this passage, Pearl's father—the preacher Dimmesdale—is dying. He asks his daughter Pearl to kiss him goodbye.

The Scarlet Letter	Student Paraphrase
"My little Pearl," said he [Dimmesdale], feebly— and there was a sweet and gentle smile over his face, as of a spirit sinking into deep repose; nay, now that the burden was removed, it seemed almost as if he would be sportive with the child—"dear little Pearl, wilt thou kiss me now? thou wouldst not, yonder, in the forest! But now thou wilt?"	A weak Dimmesdale calls out affectionately to Pearl. He is smiling, with a pleasant look on his face, like someone relaxing. Because he feels unburdened, he seems almost playful with the child, calling again, asking her to kiss him. He reminds her of her earlier refusal when they were in the forest. Now he asks her again kindly, "Will you?"

Paraphrasing

Use the following steps to paraphrase a passage. Also, look at the notes made by the student who wrote the paraphrase on the previous page.

STEP 1 Read the entire passage carefully to get the overall meaning. Look up any words that are unfamiliar.

Dimmesdale seems very weak, but he still asks Pearl for a kiss. I think he asks her in a loving way—like a father would. Repose means "rest" or "peace of mind." Sportive means "playful."

STEP 2 Identify the main idea. Keep it in mind as you skim the surrounding text. How does the passage fit together with the sections before and after?

This scene comes near the end of the novel, after Dimmesdale has publicly confessed his own sin and shown his "scarlet letter." He is near death but wants some sign of affection (forgiveness?) from his daughter.

STEP 3 Identify the speaker. Is the author, a narrator, or a character speaking?

Dimmesdale is the speaker, asking Pearl for a kiss. A third-person narrator also describes how Dimmesdale looks and feels.

STEP 4 Write out your paraphrase in your own words. Use complete sentences and traditional paragraph form.

Describe what Dimmesdale says and how he says it. He does not seem serious and stern here, even though he is dying.

STEP 5 Check to make sure that your paraphrase expresses the same idea as the original.

Dimmesdale speaks in an old-fashioned way, using "wilt," "thou," and "wouldst." I will need to make sure I use modern English but still get the right meaning in my paraphrase.

TIP In paraphrasing passages from literary works, use the **literary present**—the present tense of verbs. With it, writers paraphrase, summarize, or analyze literary works that outlive their authors. In this paraphrase, for example, notice how the words "seems" and "asks" signal the literary present tense.

Reference Note

For more on the **literary present,** see page 217 in the Writer's Workshop.

YOUR TURN 2 **Paraphrasing**

Use the Thinking It Through steps and paraphrase the following two paragraphs from "The Character of Pearl": the paragraph beginning "The character of Pearl is as much, or more, a symbolic function" on page 189 and the paragraph beginning "Much in the depiction of Pearl is realistic" on page 190.

Support for a Literary Analysis

Don't Just Tell Me—Show Me!   What if you asked the writer of "The Character of Pearl," *How can you show that Pearl is a symbol more than a "representation of a human child"?* To answer your question, the writer would cite **literary evidence:** quotations, paraphrases, or summaries from *The Scarlet Letter* that clearly support her interpretations about Pearl. In fact, the writer has done just that in the article itself.

By recognizing literary evidence, readers can see that the writer has supported his or her ideas with the text. By itself, however, literary evidence does not *thoroughly* explain what the writer means. Such evidence must be introduced and then interpreted or elaborated upon to show how it relates to the writer's main idea or thesis about the work. When it is correctly presented, literary evidence is "sandwiched" between an introductory statement and an explanation of its importance. When reading analyses of literature, remember that **support in a literary analysis** usually requires three parts: an **introduction** to the quotation, paraphrase, or summary; the **actual quotation, paraphrase,** or **summary;** and an **elaboration** or interpretation of what the quotation, paraphrase, or summary means.

To visualize this three-part structure, remember the following equation.

Introduction to quotation, paraphrase, or summary

+

Literary Evidence: Quotation, paraphrase, or summary

+

Elaboration that ties the quotation, paraphrase, or summary to the main idea of the paragraph

=

Support in a Literary Analysis

The following chart shows how the three parts of the evidence "equation" work together to support another literary analysis of *The Scarlet Letter.* In this paragraph, the writer shows how Dimmesdale's passionate character is illustrated through his voice. (The literary evidence is underlined to point out its place in the three-part structure.)

Passage from a Literary Analysis	Annotations
When Dimmesdale preaches his last sermon, his voice reveals his passionate character. He communicates this passion, interestingly enough, in ways that do not need language—his tone and cadence. "Like all other music, [his voice] breathed passion and pathos, and emotions high or tender, in a tongue native to the human heart, wherever educated" (239). The sound of his voice—not his intellectual words or spiritual encouragements of his sermon—touches his listeners in general and Hester in particular with a powerful and moving testimony to Dimmesdale's own deep feelings.	Main idea (topic sentence) Support: Introduction Quotation Elaboration of quotation

TIP   **Elaboration** explains the meaning of a quotation and ties it to the main idea of the paragraph.

YOUR TURN 3   **Analyzing Literary Evidence**

Look back at "The Character of Pearl," and re-read the paragraph beginning "The character of Pearl is as much, or more, a symbolic function" on page 189. Identify the three parts of the support "equation" in the paragraph by completing the following chart on your own paper. Then, do the same for the paragraph beginning "But Pearl is not simply a splitting off and intensifying" on page 190.

	Paragraph 1	Paragraph 2
Main Idea	The character of Pearl is as much, or more, a symbolic function as she is the representation of a human child.	Quite apart from anything that Hester might intend consciously or unconsciously, Pearl seems to have a special, original relation to the letter.
1. Introduction		
2. Literary Evidence		
3. Elaboration		

MINI-LESSON VOCABULARY

Using Prefixes and Suffixes

In "The Character of Pearl," you may have run across words you did not recognize. Sometimes you can figure out the meaning of unfamiliar words from their word parts: **prefixes,** syllable or syllables at the beginning of a word; **suffixes,** syllable or syllables at the end of a word; and the **root**—or core—of a word. The list at right shows some common prefixes and suffixes and their meanings. (For more on **prefixes, suffixes,** and **common roots,** see page 970.)

Prefix/Suffix	Meaning
dis–	away, not, opposing
sub–	under, below
super–	over, above
–ed	having, characterized by
–ible, –able	able, likely
–ness	quality or state

THINKING IT THROUGH   Using Prefixes and Suffixes

To figure out the italicized word's meaning, take a look at the example sentence below and the following steps.

". . . Pearl would naturally be keenly attuned to Hester, even more than the *preoccupied* mother might be herself."

1. **Using your knowledge of prefixes and suffixes, break the word into its parts, and then define each part.** (Remember that adding prefixes and suffixes sometimes changes the spelling of the root word.)

   pre–occupi–ed; pre– = before;

   –occupy– = to fill up or keep busy;

   –ed = having; characterized by

2. **Determine the word's meaning by combining the separate meanings of the word's parts.** Preoccupied might mean "characterized by being busy with something else that has happened before."

3. **Use clues from the word's context to check your definition.** In the sentence Pearl is more keenly attuned to Hester than Hester herself is. People who are keenly attuned are paying attention, so preoccupied might mean "having something else on one's mind."

4. **Check your answer in the dictionary.** I was right—preoccupied means "wholly occupied or absorbed in one's thoughts."

PRACTICE

Using the steps above, define the following words. Note that some words have prefixes and suffixes.

1. superintendent
2. possible
3. subservient
4. premature
5. flightiness
6. predictable
7. discoverable
8. disown
9. victimize
10. thoughtfulness

Answering Sentence-Completion Questions: Figurative Language

Reading novels—and literary analyses about them—really puts your critical thinking skills to the test. These same skills will come in handy when you answer sentence-completion questions on state and national tests. Sentence-completion questions provide part of a sentence as the "question" and then ask you to decide which answer best completes the sentence. Their purpose is to test your ability to determine the relationship between ideas. In some sentence-completion questions, you can use **figurative language** (words and phrases that say one thing in terms of another) as clues.

For example, a sentence-completion question might include a **metaphor** (a suggested comparison between seemingly unlike things) as in the following sentence: "In the last moments, the field goal attempt sailed over the uprights, prompting an *earth-shattering* cheer from the 60,000 football fans." You can figure out that the crowd has made a tremendous amount of noise because the writer has used a metaphor that compares cheers to the effects of an earthquake. Here is a typical sentence-completion question that includes figurative language:

1. As the pressure from their constituents mounts, members of the United States Congress adopt a workhorse mentality; as a result, the members _____ .

   A. conduct all official government business while outside walking around Capitol Hill

   B. take frequent breaks and complain about going back to work

   C. plod along slowly but steadily

   D. become very difficult to work with

   E. threaten to resign

THINKING IT THROUGH **Sentence-Completion Questions: Figurative Language**

Keep the following information in mind as you work through the question:

▶ STEP 1 **Ask yourself if the sentence contains a metaphor.** Look for the ways in which one thing is compared to another. The example above, for instance, suggests that members of Congress and a workhorse have a similar way of looking at things or behaving.

▶ STEP 2 **Eliminate any answers that do not fit with the metaphor.** Workhorses, for example, are known for their reliability. They do not resist hard work or try to stop working; therefore, answers **B**, **D**, and **E** are not correct.

▶ STEP 3 **Ask yourself, "Which of the remaining answers is most logical?"** In answering the question above, you would note that answer **A** does not make sense—members of Congress officially conduct government business within the House and Senate chambers. Answer **C** does make sense, however, and inserting it to complete the sentence confirms that it is the correct choice.

Writing a Literary Analysis of a Novel

WHAT'S AHEAD?

In this workshop you will write a literary analysis of a novel. You will learn to

■ read and respond to a novel

■ identify literary elements

■ evaluate literary evidence

■ introduce quotations into your text

■ use the literary present tense of verbs correctly

Your first response to a literary work usually comes from your *feelings* about it. When you read a novel, you spend hours getting to know the characters and their experiences. As you close the book at its end, the characters still live on—perhaps not in the fictional time of the novel, but in your own mind.

When you write about the literary work, as you will do in this Writing Workshop, you build on your initial response. In addition to feelings, however, you use objective thinking. You re-read sections of the novel very carefully, and you notice details you missed the first time. You get a sense of how the different parts of the novel work together—how the characters represent a major theme, for example, or how the setting contributes to the mood. You think critically about the novel and take stock of all the different meanings that are available within it. The final essay—a **literary analysis**—shows the depth of your feelings *and* your understanding of the work.

Prewriting

Select a Novel

Pick and Choose If your teacher has not assigned a novel for the class, begin by selecting a novel that you like or one that prompts a strong reaction in you. If you have not yet read something that you want to write about, think about what kind of novels interest you, whether tales of the American frontier or more modern fare. Use the following suggestions to help you choose:

■ **Survey your literature book for excerpts or short stories that you especially liked.** Look for novels by the same author in your school or public library.

- **Ask friends, teachers, librarians, or your family members for recommendations.** Sometimes your teachers or librarians have lists of novels, selected especially for their interest to high school students.
- **Read book reviews in magazines, newspapers, or on the Web.** Would you want to read any of the books being reviewed and then discuss or explain them to other readers? Look for a novel serious enough for literary study.

Read, Respond, and Analyze

Read All the Way Through   As you read (or re-read) the novel you have chosen, try not to focus solely on your writing assignment; let yourself become immersed in the lives of the characters. Enter the fictional world of the novel as the confidante of the writer, who is telling you a story important enough to share.

Then, after you have finished the novel, respond to and question the text. **You should respond in two ways: personally and analytically.** Remember: A personal response reflects your emotional reaction; an analytical response reflects your thought processes. Both kinds of responses will help you settle on a topic for your essay.

Personal Response   As you jot down answers to the following questions, remember that each reader responds—feels, reacts, and thinks—differently, because he or she brings a unique background to the reading.

- How do you feel about the novel? Why?
- Which parts made you angry or happy or sad? Which sparked a moment of recognition in you?
- Were you surprised or confused by anything in the novel?

Keep your responses in mind as you move on to a more critical reading.

Critically Re-reading   Some people say that you cannot **analyze** a novel until you have read it twice. As you re-read (or skim) your novel, underline descriptions of characters, settings, or symbols; quotations you think are important; and sections which grab your attention. Then, make brief notes to yourself in the margin about your ideas. If writing in your book is not an option, use flags to mark pages, or record your notes in your writer's journal. Be sure to keep a list of the page numbers for this information so you can find it again later.

To guide your analysis, refresh your memory of literary elements from the list on the following page. Notice also the examples of analysis questions you may use. Asking yourself these questions and answering them on notebook paper or in your journal will help you get an overview of the novel and organize your thoughts.

TIP In searching for a suitable novel, you may encounter **"novellas"**—literary works that are longer than short stories, but shorter than novels. Novellas are often satirical and sometimes reveal a moral. Check with your teacher before selecting a novella for your literary analysis.

 **KEY CONCEPT**

TIP Remember: Different backgrounds produce different perceptions of the text. In personal responses, a number of different interpretations are possible. Sometimes, a **group discussion** among your peers will give you new insights into a text.

Literary Element	Analysis Questions
Character—a person (sometimes an animal or thing)	Who are the important characters in the novel? How do they think, talk, and act? Do their actions change over the course of the novel? Does the main character represent an abstract idea, such as honor or truth?
Setting—the time and place of the novel	Where and when does the story take place? What tone or mood does the setting suggest? How does the setting affect the development of the plot? Does the setting serve as a symbol?
Plot—the events that occur	What is the central problem or conflict in the story? How does the outcome of the story relate to the theme or meaning?
Symbol—an object (sometimes a person or animal) that has a meaning of its own but also stands for something else	Does any person, place, or thing seem to have symbolic value? If so, what?
Imagery—descriptions that evoke sights, sounds, tastes, textures, and smells	What feelings do descriptions of images, actions, and locations suggest?
Point of View—the perspective or vantage point from which the story is told	Is the story told by a first-person, or a third-person, narrator? How much does the narrator know? How does the narrator feel about the characters and events in the story?
Theme—sometimes called the "meaning" and often conveyed by other literary elements; the broad, overall idea or insight that the novel reveals about life or people	What truths about human nature, experiences, problems, or relationships does the novel express? What details or passages reflect the theme?

Notice in the following chart how one student responded critically by jotting down notes or questions about a passage from F. Scott Fitzgerald's *The Great Gatsby*, a novel set in the 1920s, during America's Jazz Age. Jay Gatsby, the main character in the novel, has made a great deal of money in order to impress Daisy Buchanan and convince her to marry him. In the novel's text, Jordan Baker is speaking to the first-person narrator, Nick Carraway.

Novel's Text	Notes and Questions
"Gatsby bought that house so that Daisy would be just across the bay."	Possible explanation of Gatsby's mysterious activities.
Then it had not been merely the stars to which he had aspired on that June night. He came alive to me, delivered suddenly from the womb of his purposeless splendor.	Perhaps Gatsby has shown off his wealth in the big, fancy parties he has given since June (the "purposeless splendor") to impress Daisy.

"He wants to know—" continued Jordan, *"—if you'll invite Daisy to your house some afternoon and then let him come over."*	Important—Gatsby must regard Nick as a friend if he will ask him for such a favor; he must trust Nick.
The modesty of the demand shook me. He had waited five years and bought a mansion where he dispensed starlight to casual moths so that he could "come over" some afternoon to a stranger's garden (83).	Nick's reaction. Note how long Gatsby has waited to meet Daisy again, and what he has done. I really like the phrase, "dispensed starlight to casual moths," because it describes the parties Gatsby has given and the kind of people who came.

 Read, Respond, and Analyze

Choose your novel, read it, and analyze it. Using the two preceding charts as guides, think critically about the novel you have chosen and jot down answers to questions you ask yourself about the elements.

Consider Your Audience, Purpose, and Tone

Who's Listening?   The primary **audience** for your paper is your teacher and classmates. Your **purpose** is to inform your audience of your insights about the novel, so your **tone**—the attitude you have toward your subjects—should be objective and formal. Your **voice**—the individual manner and style in which you express yourself—should show respect for your subject and your audience. Remember that an analysis is more than just a personal response: It reflects clear thinking about the novel and provides literary evidence to elaborate on its points.

TIP   Remember: Even if your audience has not read the novel you have selected, you should avoid retelling or summarizing the novel. Plan to provide only enough background information necessary to explain your main points.

Narrow Your Focus

Zooming in from Wide-angle to Close-up   If your teacher has not assigned a topic for your literary analysis, you will need to narrow your focus. In choosing a particular topic for your analysis

- Look back over your notes. Decide which of the elements of fiction has interested you the most or which element has the most information associated with it.

- Select no more than two of the literary elements—character, setting, plot, style, point of view, theme—to combine in a topic for your essay.

- Draft a preliminary statement of interpretation, or a generalization (which may become your thesis) about the role the literary elements play in the novel. This generalization will help guide you in developing your literary analysis.

Look below at the way one student narrowed her focus and wrote a preliminary statement of interpretation.

> The characters of F. Scott Fitzgerald's <u>The Great Gatsby</u> interest me. I think the characters help reveal the theme of the novel—the hollowness or corruption of the American Dream.
>
> My initial interpretation: I think that the characters in <u>The Great Gatsby</u>, by chasing dreams they will never realize, reflect the theme of an empty American Dream.

TIP Sometimes you can narrow your focus by comparing one literary element of a novel to the same literary element of another novel. For example, a comparison between the love triangles in *The Great Gatsby* and *The Scarlet Letter* shows that the characters Daisy and Hester Prynne share similar personality traits and life circumstances.

You may find that you can narrow your focus even more by considering how the literary elements that interest you are revealed in just one or two significant scenes from the novel.

Develop a Thesis

Where Are You Going?   Your **thesis,** which may at first be preliminary and can later be refined, is your interpretation or central idea about the novel. It holds your entire analysis together and lets readers know where you are taking them in your essay. A thesis is not a fact but a general statement—a considered judgment about the novel—that must be supported with literary evidence. For example, notice the difference between the following fact and thesis:

Fact: Gatsby wears white or pink suits and gives parties at his house.

Thesis: Three characters from <u>The Great Gatsby</u>—George Wilson, Jay Gatsby, and Daisy Buchanan—reveal by their empty lives the economic, spiritual, and moral desolation which results from chasing hollow dreams.

The first example, a specific statement about Gatsby's clothing and his parties, is composed of **facts** that can be supported by specific page references in the novel.

The second example is a **thesis,** not a statement of fact, because it shows the writer's interpretation. At no point in the novel does the narrator specifically say that the characters live empty lives and have hollow dreams. Instead, based upon a close reading of the novel, the writer of this literary analysis reaches a conclusion about the thematic meaning of the characters, as they reflect the hollowness of their culture in 1920s America. This conclusion, or thesis statement, becomes the basis of the rest of the essay.

Narrow, Consider, and Develop Your Interpretation

After considering your audience, purpose, and tone, narrow your focus. Then, draft your thesis. Remember: You can revise or refine your thesis as you continue planning your analysis; writing is always recursive.

Gather Evidence

Get Your Facts Straight   Now that you have a thesis, you need to support it. **The most important kind of support you can give is literary evidence, or evidence from the novel.** Literary evidence includes quotations, paraphrases, or summaries. When readers see literary evidence and your interpretation of it, they can decide for themselves if your thesis is well supported.

KEY CONCEPT

Most of the literary evidence you will use comes from the **primary source,** the work itself. However, you might also find evidence in **secondary sources**—reference materials such as encyclopedias, periodicals, or books about authors and their works. Sometimes evidence from a piece of literary criticism grants a writer's points some additional authority. Other times a critic has made a point in a precise and memorable way, and writers may want to pass that point on to their readers in a quotation.

To gather your own evidence, re-read the responses you jotted down in your writer's journal or noted in the margins of your novel. These responses will help you compile concrete support for your interpretation.

Then, to analyze how well your evidence supports your thesis, create a chart that looks something like the one below. In the chart, one student has begun to gather evidence to support her thesis.

TIP Record page numbers and take notes as you gather evidence from primary or secondary sources. Whenever you quote, you should enclose the direct quotation in quotation marks, and be sure you've copied the quotation exactly as it appears in the original.

Reference Note
For more information about **punctuating quotations,** see page 216.

Thesis: Three characters from The Great Gatsby—George Wilson, Jay Gatsby, and Daisy Buchanan—reveal by their empty lives the economic, spiritual, and moral desolation which result from chasing hollow dreams.

Character: George Wilson

Literary Evidence: "He was a blonde, spiritless man, anemic and faintly handsome. When he saw us a damp gleam of hope sprang into his light blue eyes." (p. 29)

Explanation: This quotation lets readers see George Wilson's appearance, and hints at his poor financial status, too. He looks at the narrator and his friends as if they will provide some kind of salvation.

Evaluating Literary Evidence

Before you use literary evidence, you must decide whether it will help you prove or support your thesis. Ask yourself:

■ **Does the quotation, paraphrase, or summary go beyond the thesis statement or merely repeat it?**

■ **Is the literary evidence actually relevant to the main idea in the thesis?**

Look first at the thesis and then at the unacceptable and acceptable uses of summary in the literary evidence below.

Thesis: Three characters from *The Great Gatsby*—George Wilson, Jay Gatsby, and Daisy Buchanan—reveal by their empty lives the economic, spiritual, and moral desolation which results from chasing hollow dreams.

Unacceptable: The narrator, Nick Carraway, sidetracked one summer from his intention to learn "the bond business," tells the story of three characters who pursue vacant dreams and reflect a hollow pursuit of the American Dream. [This comment about Nick Carraway is helpful, but the rest of the evidence merely repeats the thesis.]

Unacceptable: Many people today think that their lives are empty and directionless, because they have pursued a hollow American Dream. [While an interesting insight, this comment is not relevant to an analysis of the novel because it is off the topic the thesis introduces.]

Acceptable: Daisy is a character who has chosen riches over love by marrying Tom Buchanan, but money has not brought her happiness. [The literary evidence names a character and extends the thesis with a brief summary of events from the novel.]

PRACTICE

Read the following thesis statement. Then, with a partner, identify which numbered statements are acceptable and which are unacceptable as valid support for the thesis. If you think a statement is unacceptable, explain why.

Thesis: A turning point in Kate Chopin's novel *The Awakening* occurs when Edna learns to swim, because that moment defines her as a determined character who is gradually becoming independent.

1. At a dramatic moment in the novel, Edna learns to swim one summer night.

2. The comparison between Edna and a child just learning to walk reinforces the importance of this moment for her: It is a breakthrough, and she will never again be dependent upon others.

3. Robert, Edna's new friend, is a young man willing to spend time teaching her to swim, while Edna's husband prefers to read his paper.

4. Edna's "awakening" is the moment she learns to swim—she becomes more aware of her possibilities and power as a woman, and she begins to see her potential for independence.

5. Before Edna learns to swim, she experiences new feelings—that she has a place "in the universe as a human being"—and afterward, Edna feels thrilled with her "newly conquered power."

TIP When you use material from secondary sources, always document your sources to avoid **plagiarism.** Plagiarism is using other authors' words or ideas without giving them proper credit. In addition, all evidence from secondary sources must be correctly cited.

For more information about **plagiarism** and **citing sources,** see pages 254 and 268.

Arrange the Order of Ideas

Get Your House in Order How you organize your ideas will depend on your thesis. If, for example, you were examining how the title character of *The Great Gatsby* changes over time, you would probably find it easiest to track those changes by using **chronological order,** the order of events in the novel. Then again, if you were examining the characters as they represent a theme, you could discuss them in **order of importance.** You would begin with the most obvious meanings and work your way up to the most unusual and significant meanings, saving the best for last. Whatever order you choose, think about whether readers will find it logical and coherent.

Once you have picked the order that best fits your own paper, sketch a map (or outline) that shows the development of ideas. In the map below, one student has created a plan that uses order of importance for the first parts of her essay on *The Great Gatsby.*

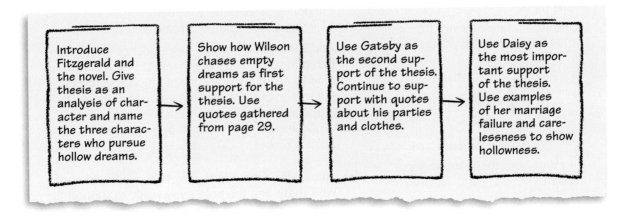

Introduce Fitzgerald and the novel. Give thesis as an analysis of character and name the three characters who pursue hollow dreams.

Show how Wilson chases empty dreams as first support for the thesis. Use quotes gathered from page 29.

Use Gatsby as the second support of the thesis. Continue to support with quotes about his parties and clothes.

Use Daisy as the most important support of the thesis. Use examples of her marriage failure and carelessness to show hollowness.

YOUR TURN 6 **Gathering Evidence and Arranging Ideas**

Create a chart like the one shown on page 203 to help gather support for your analysis. Then, pick an arrangement for your ideas and sketch a map for your analysis.

Writing

Literary Analysis

Framework	Directions and Explanations

Introduction

- Give the author and the title of the literary work.
- Note relevant background information.
- Include a clear thesis statement.

Give Important Background Information   To give readers a sense of the work's context, mention the book's author or his or her other works. You might even include something about the period or culture the work represents.

What's Your Main Point?   Even if your introduction is longer than one paragraph, provide a clear thesis. Your readers will then be able to judge for themselves how well your evidence supports or elaborates upon it.

Body

- Elaborate on the major points of the thesis.
- Include literary evidence from the text and/or secondary sources.

Support Your Thesis   The body is the place where you back up your thesis. Organize your major supporting points into several paragraphs, making sure each paragraph has a topic sentence related to one of the points. Also, order your points either in chronological order or by order of importance.

Add Some Facts   Use literary evidence—quotations, paraphrases, or summaries from the novel—to show readers exactly how the novel supports your points. (Be sure to provide citations when appropriate.) Introduce and elaborate upon your evidence by explaining the connection between it and the major point it proves.

Conclusion

- Restate your thesis and major points.

Sum It Up   Find a fresh way to remind readers of your thesis and the points you made to support it. End with a clincher—a statement about human nature, a dramatic quotation, or perhaps an important point from the novel.

 Writing a First Draft

Using the framework, write the first draft of your essay. Also, read through the Writer's Model and the Student's Model to see examples of essays that follow this framework.

A Writer's Model

The following essay closely follows the framework on the previous page.

Hollow Dreams—Empty Lives

Even before he wrote The Great Gatsby in 1925, F. Scott Fitzgerald was already the rising star of 1920s American literature with the publication of his first novel, This Side of Paradise. With his wife, Zelda, he lived the wild life of the early 1920s that he describes in his novel The Great Gatsby. To a post-World War I society, America seemed to promise unlimited financial and social opportunities for anyone willing to work hard—an American Dream. For some, however, striving for and realizing that dream corrupts the dream's promise, as they acquire great wealth only to pursue pleasure.

Even though the characters in Fitzgerald's novel appear to relish the heady atmosphere of the 1920s, their lives actually describe the folly and emptiness that result when wealth and pleasure become ends in themselves. Specifically, three characters from The Great Gatsby—George Wilson, Jay Gatsby, and Daisy Buchanan—reveal by their empty lives the economic, spiritual, and moral desolation which results from chasing hollow dreams.

One of the characters who chases an empty dream is George Wilson. He is "a blonde, spiritless man, anemic and faintly handsome" (29), the owner of a garage in the Valley of Ashes, a place apart from the wealthy social circles in the novel. Even though Wilson has gone into the business of buying, selling, and repairing cars with the hope of becoming rich, he has not been successful. Wilson thinks that if only Tom Buchanan, Daisy's very wealthy husband, will sell him a fancy car, he could then turn a nice profit by reselling it. When Tom and the narrator Nick Carraway meet Wilson one day at his garage, Nick describes Wilson's hope and the results of his attempts to do business with Tom:

When he saw us a damp gleam of hope sprang into his light blue eyes.

"Hello Wilson, old man," said Tom, slapping him jovially on the shoulder. "How's business?"

"I can't complain," answered Wilson unconvincingly. "When are you going to sell me that car?"

"Next week; I've got my man working on it right now."

"Works pretty slow, don't he?"

(continued)

INTRODUCTION
Title and author

Background information about the author and other works

Thesis statement

BODY
Major point: character #1

Literary evidence for first character

Long quotation

(continued)

"No, he doesn't," said Tom coldly. "And if you feel that way about it, maybe I'd better sell it somewhere else after all."

"I don't mean that," explained Wilson quickly. "I just meant—"

His voice faded off and Tom glanced impatiently around the garage. (29)

Elaboration on meaning

Wilson, looking pale and worn down, reveals that the car sale is very important to him. His eyes gleam with hope; he claims, unconvincingly, that he is doing well; and he weakly attempts to prod Tom to action. When Tom suggests he might sell the car to someone else, Wilson tries to assure Tom that he did not mean to be sarcastic, but Wilson's voice fades away. This brief exchange between Wilson and Tom suggests that Wilson has no real chance of either making a profit from Tom's car or realizing his dream of wealth. His dream of economic security is doomed to failure.

Major point: character #2

Literary evidence for second character

Background information from novel

Paraphrase

Elaboration on meaning

Another character who holds tightly to an illusion is the namesake of the book, Jay Gatsby. He believes that Daisy loves him even though she has been married to Tom Buchanan for four years. Before the war, Gatsby and Daisy had fallen deeply in love. Daisy's family, however, had prevented her from marrying Gatsby because, as a young soldier, he was penniless and could not support her. As a result, he has spent his years after the war becoming very rich, but he has done so by engaging in illegal activities. For Gatsby, the dream of wealth is tangled up with his idealized love for Daisy (117). For him, pursuing money is a spiritual quest to be loved by Daisy—the woman of his dreams denied him because of his earlier poverty.

Summary

Elaboration on meaning

When he has made his fortune, he moves near Daisy and puts on lavish parties in the hope that Daisy might stop in; and, being so awed by his mansion and success, she would leave her husband. Unfortunately, his newly acquired wealth does not necessarily bring respect or acceptance into a higher social class. Rumors about his tainted past circulate, even as the partygoers devour the extravagant food and drink he provides (48–54). He wears pink suits—too flashy to be respectable—and drives a bright yellow Rolls Royce, which Tom Buchanan derisively calls a "circus wagon" (128). Unlike the class of people who frequent his huge house, as he dispenses "starlight to casual moths" (83), Gatsby cannot make his money look like a natural part of him. He is the perennial outsider, and he fails to lure Daisy away from Tom. In a final conversation, Daisy cries out to Gatsby: "Oh, you want too much! " (139) She is right: Gatsby's desire to have it all—money, class, power, and Daisy, no matter the cost—has corrupted his spirit and proved his dreams to be empty.

Unlike Gatsby, Daisy Buchanan seems perfectly at ease in her wealthy social circle. Money, rather than love, has determined her choice of husbands. Despite her love for Gatsby, and despite her desperate tears on her wedding eve after receiving his letter, she forsakes him. She marries Tom Buchanan, who gave her "a string of pearls valued at three hundred and fifty thousand dollars" for a wedding gift (80). She obviously believes that comfort and security are the only true basis for finding happiness. Betraying Gatsby's love for Buchanan's money, Daisy is herself betrayed by her husband for another woman, a woman who is, ironically, crude, unattractive, grasping—everything Daisy is not. Well aware of her husband's moral corruption, Daisy—once described by Nick as "the king's daughter, the golden girl" (127)—then betrays her marriage vows to return to Gatsby.

When she and Gatsby are reunited, however, she is still unable to free herself from the constraints of her wealthy society, particularly from her husband, who sneers at Gatsby's background and wealth. The dream of happiness—the love she and Gatsby once shared—is doomed, because she believes that money is more important. Instead her wealth has become her prison. After Gatsby's murder at the end of the novel, Daisy retreats into her rich, loveless house. She seals herself off in the cocoon of wealth, having denied herself any bright, beautiful, happy, or desirable future. She, influenced by her husband Tom, has become what Nick calls a "careless" person, who "smashed up things and creatures and then retreated back into their money or their vast carelessness . . . and let other people clean up the mess they had made" (187–188). Such a lack of values, demonstrated further by her neglect even to send any message or flower to Gatsby's funeral, proves her own moral corruption.

Throughout the novel, Fitzgerald portrays a society that has corrupted the true meaning of the American Dream. The novel represents not only the hollow pursuits of wealth and love for Wilson, Gatsby, and Daisy, but also the moral rottenness of the very rich. Although George Wilson is not a part of the wealthy elite, he, as well as all of the other characters in the novel, reflects the emptiness surrounding them. If the characters in The Great Gatsby come from various classes of American society and seem to represent American culture more generally, then a major theme of the novel is that no one in 1920s America was safe from vacant dreams and desolation, whether it was economic, spiritual, or moral.

Major point: character #3

Literary evidence for third character
Summary

Elaboration on meaning

Quotation

Elaboration on meaning

CONCLUSION
Explanation of meaning

Restatement of thesis

Elaboration on meaning of thesis

Clincher

A Student's Model

The following passages from a literary analysis written by Jenny Lee, a student from Rolling Meadows High School in Rolling Meadows, Illinois, focus on Edith Wharton's use of imagery. Notice how the student includes quotations from the novel along with elaboration to support her main points.

Theme as Reflected Through Imagery

INTRODUCTION

Title and author

"Guess he's been in Starkfield too many winters" (7). This significant phrase describing Ethan Frome in the prologue of Edith Wharton's novel, <u>Ethan Frome</u>, provides insight into a major theme portrayed in this story, that of the harshness and despair of winter. In fact, the prologue introduces several of the novel's major themes, the most prominent being that of winter harshness. Hence, it foreshadows the major events in the book and provides insight into the personalities of the characters.

Thesis

BODY
Major point:
character #1

Zeena is a character often portrayed using harsh winter imagery. She is characterized as controlling, insensitive, and rather unattractive. This is evident in Ethan's perception of her prior to her doctor's visit when he says that she is sitting in "the pale light reflected from the banks of the snow" (64). The images of snow which first appear in the prologue symbolize this character's personality. The fact that Ethan connects his wife with the severity and strength of winter snow illustrates that he envisions her as stringent and powerful, characteristics he dislikes.

Literary evidence for
first character

Elaboration on
meaning

Throughout the novel, Ethan is attracted to true inner beauty, something he believes Zeena lacks. He considers his marriage a mistake and attributes it to the fact that he had met Zeena at a time when he felt isolated and alone. After his mother died one winter, he needed companionship and attached himself to Zeena. Ethan resents winter because he associates it with the death of a loved one. Due to his isolation, Ethan overlooks Zeena's true character when he decides to marry her. Also, the narrator connects the winter with the "deadness of the community" (8). He states, "It [winter] seemed to produce no change except that of retarding still more the sluggish pulse of Starkfield" (8). This statement in the prologue foreshadows Ethan's feeling of being trapped and dead when he is forced to stay in

Summary

Starkfield because of his wife. It again shows the connection made between winter and death and darkness.

Because of Ethan's longing for pleasant love like springtime, he attaches himself to Zeena's cousin, Mattie. All imagery of light, sunlight, and springtime represent the character of Mattie. This is contrary to the imagery used to describe Zeena. In the prologue there are contrasting images of the goodness of light shed on something not as good. An example of this is the description of Ethan's house when the narrator states his observation of, "A flash of watery sunlight exposed the house on the slope above us in all its plaintive ugliness" (20). This description indicates how the inner beauty of Mattie, the sunlight, illuminates the aspects disliked in Zeena, the ugly house, aspects which become evident later in the book.

Another reference to light is made regarding the sunset at the end of the prologue when the snow begins to fall. This is shown in the line:

> But at sunset the clouds gathered again, bringing
> an earlier night, and the snow began to fall
> straight and steadily from a sky without wind, in
> a soft universal diffusion more confusing than the
> gusts and eddies of the morning. (23)

This description indicates that at the end of the novel, the sun will fade and a changed snow will prevail. This happens when Mattie becomes crippled and the woman who appeared to be so harsh takes care of her. It is indeed a surprise that Zeena agrees to take care of Mattie after Zeena almost lost her husband to her.

The prologue also serves to foreshadow what Ethan becomes after the "smash-up." Ethan is essentially dead spiritually and the author uses the desolate imagery of wintertime to show this. The narrator also describes Ethan's appearance by saying, "He looks as if he was dead and in hell now!" (6) Ethan's world is dark despair after the accident. He realizes that there is no escape from Starkfield and the harsh reality of the dead winters. He is at the mercy of winter and is forced to see what his love, Mattie, has become. Ethan's appearance at the end of the prologue represents what he strives to avoid throughout the novel, a tragic end. . . .

Reference to thesis

Major point: character #2

Literary evidence for second character

Elaboration on meaning

Additional literary evidence

Long quotation

Elaboration on meaning

Major point: character #3

Literary evidence for third character

Elaboration on meaning

Transition to conclusion

Revising

Evaluate and Revise Your Draft

Do a Double Take To refine your writing, you will need to read through your draft at least twice. The first time, look critically at content and organization. The second time, use the guideline on page 214 to evaluate and revise style.

➤ **First Reading: Content and Organization** Can you see the parts of your paper that need revision? The following chart can help you whether you are reading your own paper or someone else's. Answer the questions in the first column. Use the tips in the middle column to plan your revisions. Then, make the changes suggested in the last column.

Literary Analysis: Content and Organization Guidelines for Peer and Self- Evaluation

Evaluation Questions	▶ Tips	▶ Revision Techniques
❶ Are the author's name, the novel's title, and details about the author or work given in the first paragraph?	▶ **Underline** the name of the author, the title of the novel, and any other details about the author or work.	▶ **Add** the name of the author or the novel's title. **Add** details about the author's life and his other works, if important.
❷ Does the introduction include a clear thesis that identifies the main point of the essay?	▶ **Bracket** the thesis. If there is no thesis, revise.	▶ **Add** a thesis sentence to state the main point of the essay.
❸ Do the body paragraphs support the thesis?	▶ Place a **check mark** in the margin next to topic sentences in each body paragraph.	▶ **Delete** sentences or paragraphs that don't support the thesis. **Elaborate** on the thesis as needed.
❹ Does the paper provide literary evidence to support each major point?	▶ **Put a jagged line** under any literary evidence from the text. If you do not find any, revise.	▶ **Add** quotations, paraphrases, or summaries from the novel. **Elaborate** on the meaning of the literary evidence.
❺ Are the main points of the paper and the literary evidence organized effectively?	▶ **Number** the sequence of development for chronological order. For order of importance, **underline** the most important point to make sure it is presented last.	▶ **Reorder** a chronological presentation in correct time order. For order of importance, **reorder** so the most important point is in the last body paragraph.
❻ Does the conclusion sum up the main points of the essay and bring it to a close?	▶ **Circle** the sentence or sentences that restate the focus of the essay.	▶ **Add** a sentence that restates the main idea. **Elaborate** with a closing, memorable statement.

ONE WRITER'S REVISIONS   Here's how the author of the
Writer's Model used the content and organization guidelines on page
212 to revise the concluding paragraph of her essay. Study the revisions and answer the questions following the paragraph.

*Throughout the novel, Fitzgerald portrays a society that
has corrupted the true meaning of the American Dream.*
∧The novel represents not only the hollow pursuits of wealth   Add

and love for Wilson, Gatsby, and Daisy, but also the moral rot-

tenness of the very rich. Although George Wilson is not a part of

the wealthy elite, he, as well as all the characters in the novel,
                                    If the
reflects the emptiness surrounding them. ~~The~~ characters in The   Elaborate
and seem to represent American culture more generally, then a
Great Gatsby come from various classes of American society. A

major theme of the novel is that no one in 1920s America was   Elaborate
                    whether it was economic, spiritual, or moral.
safe from vacant dreams and desolation∧

Analyzing the Revision Process

1. How does the information added at the beginning of the paragraph begin to draw the paper to a close?
2. What details of elaboration does the writer add to the last sentence of the essay? Why are those details important for the conclusion?

YOUR TURN 8   Focusing on Content and Organization

Revise the content and organization of your essay, using the guidelines on the previous page and the revisions shown above as a model.

PEER REVIEW

Ask a friend to read your essay and answer the following questions.

1. Do you agree with your classmate's analysis of the novel? Explain your answer.
2. Which point is developed best? Does the writer provide enough literary evidence? Why do you think so?

Second Reading: Style   In your first reading, you looked closely at *what* your paper says and *how* you ordered your ideas. Now, turn your attention to the *way* those ideas are expressed—the style of your paper. In literary analysis, introducing quotations is often a tricky stylistic matter. Any reader will tell you how hard it is to read a paper with quotations that have not been introduced—the quotations suddenly appear, as if they had dropped out of the sky. The results are choppy and distracting. So that you will not make this mistake yourself, use the following guideline.

Style Guideline		
Evaluation Questions	▶ **Tip**	▶ **Revision Techniques**
Is the quotation woven into the structure of the sentence? Does each quotation have an introduction?	▶ **Draw a box** around each quotation. **Put a check** if the sentence is not confusing. **Underline** the introduction of each quotation.	▶ **Reword** sentences that are not grammatically correct. **Add** a *sentence + colon* or a *brief clause* before quotations that need them.

Focus on

Sentences

TIP **Short quotations**—quotations of four lines or less—can be included as part of your text with no special treatment. Set off quotations that are longer than four lines by beginning on a new line and indenting the entire quotation ten spaces from the left margin. For more information on quotations, see Designing Your Writing on page 216.

Introducing Quotations

In writing a literary analysis, you need to give your audience signals when you repeat what someone else has said. These signals provide a clear transition from your own voice as a writer to the words you are using from someone else. Quotations may be introduced in two ways.

- Sometimes, writers like to weave quotations into their own sentence structure.

   George Wilson is "a blonde, spiritless man, anemic and faintly handsome" (29), the owner of a garage in the Valley of Ashes.

- Other times, writers introduce a quotation with an introductory sentence, followed by a colon.

   In a final conversation, Daisy cries out to Gatsby: "Oh, you want too much!" (139)

ONE WRITER'S REVISIONS   Here is how the writer of the model literary analysis on page 207 used the guidelines above to revise and place an introduction before a quotation.

BEFORE REVISION

Even though Wilson has gone into the business of buying,

selling, and repairing cars with the hope of becoming rich, he

has not been successful. Wilson thinks that if only Tom

Buchanan, Daisy's very wealthy husband, will sell him a fancy

car, he could then turn a nice profit by reselling it.

Drawing a box around this quotation identifies it, but there is no introduction to the quotation.

> When he saw us a damp gleam of hope sprang into his light blue eyes.
>
> "Hello Wilson, old man," said Tom, slapping him jovially on the shoulder. "How's business?"
>
> "I can't complain," answered Wilson unconvincingly. "When are you going to sell me that car?" (29)

AFTER REVISION

Even though Wilson has gone into the business of buying, selling, and repairing cars with the hope of becoming rich, he has not been successful. Wilson thinks that if only Tom Buchanan, Daisy's very wealthy husband, will sell him a fancy car, he could then turn a nice profit by reselling it. When Tom and the narrator Nick Carraway meet Wilson one day at his garage, Nick describes Wilson's hope and the results of his attempts to do business with Tom:

> When he saw us a damp gleam of hope sprang into his light blue eyes.
>
> "Hello Wilson, old man," said Tom, slapping him jovially on the shoulder. "How's business?"
>
> "I can't complain," answered Wilson unconvincingly. "When are you going to sell me that car?" (29)

Add an introductory sentence with a colon.

Analyzing the Revision Process

1. What information does the introduction supply?
2. Why is that information important?

YOUR TURN 9 **Focusing on Introducing Quotations**

Revise the style of your paper using the Style Guideline on page 214. Pay close attention to your use of quotations.

COMPUTER TIP

Word-processing programs offer many helpful features. For example, if you discover a name of a character or word misspelled in the title throughout your paper, use the "find and replace" feature to search for the misspelled word and correct it.

Designing Your Writing

Formatting Quotations   The conventions of style in quoting material from primary or secondary sources are an important part of a paper's overall design. These conventions have been formalized by the Modern Language Association of America (or MLA) in the following guidelines.

Quotations within sentences

- Incorporate all quotations of four lines or less within a grammatically correct sentence, and place the quotation inside quotation marks. The quoted material may begin or end a sentence, or it may fall in the middle. You may divide the quotation with your own words.
- Do not change the capitalization, spelling, or interior punctuation.
- Place the page reference for the quotation within parentheses, following the quotation mark, and before the final sentence punctuation.

> When Nick Carraway first sees the owner of a garage in the Valley of Ashes, George Wilson is "wiping his hands on a piece of waste" and appears as "a blonde, spiritless man, anemic and faintly handsome" (29).

Block Quotations

- Introduce a quotation of four lines or longer with a colon.
- Set off the entire double-spaced quotation one inch or ten spaces from the left margin. Do not enclose the quotation in quotation marks.
- For only one paragraph or part of one, do not indent the first line.
- If the paragraph uses dialogue, indent each piece of dialogue three spaces, and use quotation marks to indicate each speaker. Use brackets to identify speakers, if necessary.
- Put the citation in parentheses after the quotation's punctuation.

At an important moment in Zora Neale Hurston's novel *Their Eyes Were Watching God,* Janie's husband decides they must try to escape the hurricane and coming flood:

> [Janie's husband] saw that the wind and water had given life to lots of things that folks think of as dead and given death to so much that had been living things. Water everywhere. . . . He turned back to tell Janie about it so she could be ready to go.
>
>   "Git our insurance papers tuhgether, Janie. . . ."
>
>   "You got all de money out de dresser drawer, already?" [Janie asked.]
>
>   "Naw, git it quick . . . Us liable tuh get wet tuh our necks." (236–237)

TIP In a literary analysis, use quotations sparingly so that the design of your literary analysis does not look like a patchwork of other sources, stitched together with only a line or two of your own prose.

TIP You can best apply the one-inch or ten-space guideline when you type or handwrite your essay. If you use a computer with an adjustable spacing font, check with your teacher about the margins for a block quotation.

Reference Note
For more on using ellipses in **punctuating quotations,** see page 824.

Proofread Your Essay

To Err Is Human   All writers make mistakes. That is why it is so important to check your draft for grammar, spelling, and punctuation errors—individually and collaboratively—before you submit the final copy. With a literary analysis, you also need to be especially careful to use the **literary present,** the special verb tense writers use to write about literature.

Reference Note

For more on the **literary present,** see page 668.

Grammar Link

Using the Literary Present

When writing about literature, writers rarely use the past tense. Instead, they use **literary present**—the present tense of verbs. For example, in discussing one of Emily Dickinson's poems, you might write the following sentence:

In "Because I could not stop for Death," Dickinson **compares** death to a carriage driver.

The verb *compares* is in the literary present. Even though Emily Dickinson has been dead for many years, you still use present tense to talk about what Dickinson continues to do through her writing.

As with any rule, there are exceptions—times when you should not use the literary present to talk about literature. When you quote directly from a work, use the same tense the author uses, even if it is not the present tense. However, when you paraphrase the writer's ideas or draw your own conclusions about a work, use the literary present. Look at the following example.

Original:
Because I could not stop for Death—
He kindly **stopped** for me—
The Carriage held but just Ourselves—
And Immortality.

Incorrect Paraphrase	In Emily Dickinson's "Because I Could Not Stop for Death," Death **was** a carriage driver who **stopped** to pick up the narrator.
Correct Paraphrase	In Emily Dickinson's "Because I could not stop for Death," Death **is** a carriage driver who **stops** to pick up the narrator.

PRACTICE

Change all verbs that should be in the literary present and write the answers on your own paper. If the sentence is correct, write C.

1. Emily Dickinson used the metaphor of the carriage driver to make death concrete and familiar to her readers.

2. For her carriage ride, the narrator in the poem "Because I could not stop for Death" wore a gown made of thin material, even though the weather was chilly.

3. Stanza three used schoolchildren, fields of grain, and the setting sun as metaphors for three stages of life.

4. The narrator, looking at a grave site, tells how she "paused before a House that seemed / A swelling of the ground."

5. In the last stanza, the narrator suggested that time passes quickly for the dead.

Publish Your Literary Analysis

Get the Word Out   Here are some ways you might share your literary analysis with your audience.

- Submit it to your school newspaper or literary journal.
- Submit it for an essay contest run by your school or local library. (Most contests publish the winner's work.)
- Organize a literary night at your school. Choose several literary analyses from your class to read aloud. Alternate reading the essays with reading passages from the novels on which the essays are based.
- Collect the literary essays from your class into a resource booklet. Consult the resource booklet before writing another literary analysis.
- Create a bulletin board for your class. Arrange your literary analysis next to a photo of the novel's author. Add other supplementary material related to the novel or its author to catch a reader's eye.
- Find a Web site about the author of the novel you have analyzed. Send an e-mail message to ask the designers of the site if they will publish your essay there.

Reflect on Your Literary Analysis

PORTFOLIO

Get Some Perspective   Writing some short responses to the following questions will help you build on what you have learned in this workshop.

- How did you decide on a topic for your essay?
- What important revisions did you make to your draft? How did they improve it?
- How has writing the analysis deepened your understanding of the literary work?
- What will you do differently, if you write another literary analysis?

If you include this essay in your portfolio, attach your responses.

 YOUR TURN 10   **Proofreading, Publishing, and Reflecting**

Review each of the steps discussed on these last few pages. Before you turn in your essay, make sure to
- proofread it carefully
- consider your publishing options
- reflect on your essay by answering questions about the steps you went through to create it

MINI-LESSON TEST TAKING

Answering Open-ended Essay Questions

Test questions come in all shapes and sizes. Unlike a direct question about a particular selection, an **open-ended question** asks you to develop your own thesis about a piece of literature and even lets you decide which piece of literature to write about. Whether you are answering a question for your English final or for a national exam like the advanced placement test, it helps to have a strategy for composing your answer. Look over the sample questions below.

> Discuss the use of setting in a novel or play. (Pay special attention to changes in setting and how they contribute to the work's meaning.)

> Discuss a play or novel in which the protagonist's internal conflicts are more important than the external action of the work.

It is important to remember that both of these questions are asking two things:

- What does this work mean (thematically, not literally)?
- How does the author communicate that meaning (what devices or literary elements convey the meaning)?

If you keep these things in mind, you can easily turn your open-ended prompt into a clear, focused thesis sentence.

THINKING IT THROUGH   Developing a Thesis Statement

These steps will help you write a thesis statement for an open-ended question.

1. **Read the prompt carefully; underline the key phrases that identify the kind of work and the topic you should write about. Finally, bracket the key phrases that tell you what your essay should accomplish.**

   Prompt: Choose a novel or play that depicts a conflict between a parent (or a parental figure) and a son or a daughter. Write an essay in which you [analyze the sources of conflict and explain how the conflict contributes to the meaning of the work.] Avoid plot summary.

2. **Choose a work that addresses the prompt.** Death of a Salesman by Arthur Miller

3. **Use the underlined and bracketed material to create a thesis about the work you have chosen.** Be sure to include the **1) work's title; 2) the author's name; 3) information showing how the work fits the prompt** (note below how the thesis repeats "conflict"); **4) information on the device or literary element you will address** (theme is used below). In playwright Arthur Miller's Death of a Salesman, the conflict between the salesman, Willy Loman, and his son Biff dramatizes the central theme in this tragedy—that unrealized dreams of success result from self-deception.

Writing a Short Story

So far you have spent a lot of time thinking about literary elements—character, setting, plot, and so on—as a *novel* reveals them. Short stories, often brief enough to be read at one sitting, use these same elements, but in a sharper, more distilled way. This limited length makes writing short stories a bit like putting together a puzzle—you must carefully fit the pieces together so that, together, they mean something to your reader. In doing so, you become a writer of short fiction, rather than a writer who analyzes fiction.

Ease the Tension All stories begin in conflict and move toward some kind of resolution. To begin thinking of a possible conflict for your story, consider these options:

- **Oops!** Do you know the old saying, "Anything that can go wrong, will"? Think what would happen if, at a time when everything needs to go right—a wedding, the opening night of a play, or a shuttle launch—things begin to go very, very wrong.

- **Put up your dukes.** Take two traditional enemies—a Hatfield and a McCoy, or a Montague and a Capulet—and put them together. What would happen?

- **Truth or Dare.** Give a character an impossible task to accomplish in a short time. What will happen as he or she encounters obstacle after obstacle?

The Tools of the Trade Many novelists confess that often they begin a novel with an opening line or an image of a character, and then let their imaginations wander. In other words, they don't sit down and plot things out completely, from beginning to end. Short story writers, however, must pay fairly close attention to the development of action. While **character** (including **description** and **dialogue**), **setting, style, point of view,** and **theme** are all important elements in short stories, a tightly organized **plot** may be the most critical element of all. In thinking about the action of your short story, follow these steps:

- Establish the **conflict.** The conflict is the clash between two opposing forces—for example, parent and child, humanity and nature, or one character's desires and his or her external circumstances.

- Add one, but no more than two, **complications.** Complications are plot developments—often obstacles or minor conflicts—which allow the action to proceed.

- Develop the action toward a **climax,** or turning point. A short story's climactic moment is the moment of highest tension.

- Add a brief **resolution.** The resolution (or *denouement*) ties up all the loose threads of the plot and brings the story to its close.

One from the Short Story Master In the following excerpts, taken from the beginning, climax, and resolution of Edgar Allan Poe's short story, "The Fall of the House of Usher," notice the annotations that point out key literary elements. (Discussing the theme and style of Poe's short story with other students may also help you decide on plot elements for your story.)

During the whole of a dull, dark, and soundless day in the autumn of the year, when the clouds hung oppressively low in the heavens, I had been passing alone, on horseback, through a singularly dreary tract of country; and at length I found myself, as the shades of the evening drew on, within view of the melancholy House of Usher. . . . What was it—I paused to think—what was it that so unnerved me in the contemplation of the House of Usher?

This **character**, the narrator, rides alone. The first-person **point of view** adds to the sense of foreboding in the passage. The main **conflict** is the narrator's fear of the house itself. Words such as *dreary* and *melancholy* tell readers about the **setting**.

As if in the superhuman energy of his utterance there had been found the potency of a spell—the huge antique panels to which the speaker pointed, threw slowly back, upon the instant, their ponderous and ebony jaws. It was the work of the rushing gust—but then without those doors there *did* stand the lofty and enshrouded figure of the lady Madeline of Usher.

The appearance of Madeline, Roderick's strangely ill sister, who has escaped from her tomb, is the **climax**—the highest point of tension.

. . . I saw the mighty walls rushing asunder—there was a long tumultuous shouting sound like the voice of a thousand waters—and the deep and dark tarn at my feet closed sullenly and silently over the fragments of the "*House of Usher.*"

This is the **resolution**—the House of Usher, symbol of the doomed and dying family, collapses and disappears into the tarn (or water).

YOUR TURN 11 Writing a Short Story

Follow these steps as you plan and write your own story:

- Make sure your introduction includes details about setting and character and introduces the main conflict.
- Build suspense in the body. Add some complications that build steadily toward the climax.
- Write an ending that ties up all the loose ends. A good resolution should leave readers feeling satisfied—or in the case of "The Fall of the House of Usher," terrified.

After you have revised your story carefully, consider publishing it in a school magazine or a local literary journal, or hold a storytelling night.

Adapting a Scene from a Novel for Film

WHAT'S AHEAD?

In this section, you will adapt a scene from a novel for production in a film. You will also learn to

■ choose an appropriate scene

■ decide which parts of the scene should be filmed

■ write a script for the scene

■ create storyboards

All films adapted from novels—such as *Sense and Sensibility, Little Women,* or *The Natural*—begin with the printed word. Films, in the act of storytelling, actually share with fiction the literary elements of **character, plot, setting, point of view,** and **theme,** and the stylistic devices of **symbol** and **imagery.** In its particular kind of storytelling, however, film adds actual sights and sounds, elements which first must be described in print before they can be filmed—scene by scene. Your task in this workshop will be to take a scene from a novel and adapt it to film.

There are three major steps involved in making a movie: *preproduction* (preparing to film), *production* (filming), and *postproduction* (editing). This workshop will focus on the preproduction stage. You will write part of a **script,** which will require you to make choices about actions, dialogue, costume, lighting, and setting. Then, you will create a **storyboard** to serve as the visual representation of the shots you have devised in your script.

Choosing a Novel; Choosing a Scene

TIP Keep in mind that novels usually are divided into chapters. Each chapter may be a series of episodes or bits of action, and an entire chapter may still be too long to adapt as one scene in a film.

Some novels are better for adaptation than others. If your teacher has not assigned a particular novel, a novel you have already read and thought about would be a good choice. If the novel you choose has already been turned into film, a section that was omitted from the film could serve as the basis for your adaptation.

A scene adapted from a novel uses only a small part of the novel's action. A scene also has a structure of its own: a beginning, a middle, and an end. Usually the beginning marks a departure from the scene that came before it. The middle includes a climax, and the end is a resolution, or a winding-down period. Not every scene in a novel, however, is suitable for film. Writers who adapt novels to film usually leave out dozens of pages.

To help you choose a scene from a novel, follow these suggestions

- Limit your potential scene to two or three pages of a novel.
- Choose a section of the novel in which something significant happens, such as a turning point in the action of the characters.
- Select pages that also have interesting descriptions, dialogue, or characters.

Translating from Page to Screen

When you read a novel, you imagine what the characters look like, how they speak, and what setting they find themselves in. To translate what you have read into what an audience will see, take what you have imagined and describe how the same action might appear before a camera. *Show* what happens rather than narrate what happens. For example, if the narrator in a novel says that a character is stingy, demonstrate that trait visually. One way to *show* stinginess, for example, is to have a character ask a waiter for exact change from his lunch bill. Then, show him putting down a quarter tip, reconsidering, and then replacing the quarter with a dime.

The chart below shows a plan that one student created to adapt a scene from the first chapter of *The Great Gatsby*, when Nick arrives at Tom and Daisy's house to see them for the first time in years. The left-hand column describes parts of the novel's scene while the right-hand column shows the student's thoughts about how to adapt the scene for film. Notice the techniques the student uses for making the scene visually appealing, and note especially the parts of the novel cut for the film version.

Novel	Film
Tom is on the porch of his colonial red and white mansion. He is described as arrogant, aggressive, and physically powerful.	I can show Tom's aggressiveness and power by having him crush Nick's hand in a handshake. He's the kind of guy who would do that deliberately, just to show he's the "big man."
Nick and Tom talk a few moments on the porch. The conversation ends with Tom saying, "I've got a nice place here."	Insert dialogue here from conversations occurring later on in the chapter. Tom, after asking Nick about his current position as bond salesman, says he's never heard of Nick's company. This shows that Tom is insensitive, even dismissive. Keep "I've got a nice place here" to show Tom's proud, even snobby. Have them talk some about how long it has been since they've seen each other.
The men walk down a hallway to the room where Daisy and Jordan sit.	Cut this part. I can cut directly from the front porch to the room where the women sit.

Writing the Script

TIP Usually a film script leaves a wide right-hand margin for the production staff to record notes.

The real challenge of this project comes not in *organizing* the script but in *writing* it. What is a **script**? The script is a piece of writing, somewhat like a play, that includes all the dialogue of the movie but also notes about setting, costume, lighting, music, the kinds of shots to be used, and even details about characters' attitudes and mannerisms. It's like the skeleton of the movie—the structure behind the finished product. Here's an example of a film script written for a scene from Zora Neale Hurston's *Their Eyes Were Watching God*.

Center scene title
Capitalize film production information
Setting and time of day
Description of characters

All non-spoken references are justified on the left margin

Center and capitalize character's name
Stage directions for actors in parentheses

Cut = Sharp division between moving camera and still shots

Dialect used in novel picked up for film script

Indent all dialogue and justify on the right margin

SCENE ONE FROM CHAPTER 18

INTERIOR. *Midmorning, in rural South Florida, in 1920s. Janie (a tall, middle-aged, impressive black woman) stands at a primitive sink, washing the dishes in a basin. She looks out the kitchen window to see six Seminole Indians—three men in front and three heavily burdened women in back— walk silently and purposefully east along the road outside her cabin.*

CUT TO EXTERIOR. *Noon. Janie is sweeping the front porch of the cabin, one in a row of cabins. She stops, looks up, curious at the parade she sees coming up the road. Another group of Indians—two men and four women, three children and a dog—all walk silently in line up the road. They pass without looking or speaking in front of Janie.*

JANIE
(calling out to the Seminoles as they pass)
Where y'all goin'?

SEMINOLE LEADER
(Stops, turning deliberately, pauses, then speaks)
Going to high ground. Saw-grass bloom. Hurricane coming.

CUT TO EXTERIOR. *Night around cabin. In back, a large bonfire is blazing in the open field. Janie and her husband Tea Cake sit around it. Suddenly an old car pulls up out front and a young man—one of their friends from the Bahamas—hollers at them. They wander around front. Camera follows.*

YOUNG MAN
(looking as if in a hurry)
Hello, Tea Cake.

TEA CAKE
Hello, 'Lias. You leavin', Ah see.

YOUNG MAN
Mah uncle come for me. He say hurricane warning out in Palm Beach. Not so bad dere, but man, dis muck is too low and dat big lake is liable tuh bust.

TEA CAKE
Ah naw, man. Some boys in dere now talkin' 'bout it. Some of 'em been in de 'Glades fuh years. 'Tain't nothin' but uh lil blow. You'll lose de whole day tuhmorrer tryin' tuh git back out heah.

YOUNG MAN
De Indians gahn east, man, It's dangerous.

TEA CAKE
(Laughing off the young man's alarm)
You better stay heah, man. Big jumpin' dance tuhnight right heah, in back round the fire.

YOUNG MAN
(snorting out response and waving gaily a good-bye as car drives off)
Dis time tuhmorrer you gointuh wish you follow crow.

CAMERA PANS TO JANIE AND TEA CAKE, LEFT BEHIND. *(Janie looks thoughtful, in spite of Tea Cake's good humor.)*

SERIES OF CAMERA DISSOLVES. *Sounds of drums as dancers circle bonfire. Shots of rabbits scurrying through the cabins, Possums, skunks, snakes all slipping east through the quarters. Sounds of panthers' screams heard in back of exciting singing and music of the dance.*

CUT *to daybreak and sight of palm and banana trees blowing in the wind as it picks up.*

CAMERA PANS *back to show about ten or twelve buzzards swarming from the ground up, circling above the trees and then disappearing into the heavily darkening clouds.*

CAMERA PANS *back down to show Janie standing outside the cabin in the morning's chill, looking up at the sky.*

JANIE
(calling nervously)
Tea Cake! Tea Cake!

FADE TO BLACK.

Dissolve = Slow fading from one scene to another

Pan = Moving slowly from left to right, or vice versa

Fade = Going from focused shot to black screen.

This excerpt demonstrates two points you should keep in mind as you adapt a novel scene for film. First, notice how brief the actual dialogue in this scene is. Dialogue from a novel usually needs to be shortened, or excerpted, for films, because real people don't speak in perfect, lengthy paragraphs. Second, notice the way actions convey meaning. To build suspense, the writer has two groups of Seminoles parade silently by the cabin. The sense of dread increases with the shots of animals and trees and birds.

Creating Storyboards

You have probably been reading cartoons since you were too young to remember. That's great practice for creating storyboards. **Storyboards** are sketches of what a movie's director wants shots to look like. For this workshop, you can create a storyboard for your entire script or just for important shots. Then, make notes in your script referring to your storyboard. Don't worry if you're not the world's best artist. Stick figures will be fine.

When you sketch your shots, you will need to annotate them, too. To do this well, you need to know some of the basics about the different kinds of shots movie directors use. Look at the table on the next page.

TIP In filmmaking, storyboards are created as cost-saving tools in the preproduction process to help the director, cinematographer, set designer, costumer, and others "see" the scenes they will be filming later.

Shot	What is it?	Examples
Close-up shot	Focus tightly on the subject, so that the subject fills the screen.	A close shot of an actor's face can project his mood to the viewer.
Medium shot	Focus further away than a close-up shot—head and shoulders, a group standing close together	Medium shots are often used during dialogue between characters in a group.
Long shot	Focus on an object from far away so that it is tiny in the frame.	A long shot can set up a character's destination or show something coming toward him.
Full shot	Focus on a large object so that it fills the frame.	A full shot can be used to establish the setting for the action to come.
Low-angle shot	Take shot from below the subject, looking up at it.	A low-angle shot makes the subject look large and imposing or important.
High-angle shot	Take shot from above subject, looking down on it.	A high-angle shot makes the subject look small and unimposing or unimportant.

Look at the following sample storyboard.

Long shot of Nick walking away from camera toward Tom, who stands on the porch.

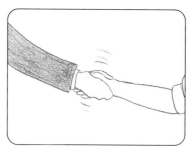

Close shot of Tom grasping Nick's hand—hard.

Close shot of Nick's face, wincing from the handshake.

TIP Filmmaking is a collaboration between agents, producers, directors, actors, set designers, location scouts, cinematographers, editors, musicians, and sound engineers. The credits at the end of a film show you how many people have worked together to bring a story from idea to screen.

Filming and Beyond

Once you complete your film script and storyboards, you have finished the preproduction process. If you want to take your script through the next stage—production—you will need to round up a crew and equipment. For now, however, try by sharing your production plans with classmates.

YOUR TURN 12 **Adapting a Scene from a Novel for Film**

Select a scene from a novel that you think will adapt well to film. Then, write the script and storyboards for your scene.

5 Choices

Choose one of the following activities to complete.

▶ **VIEWING AND REPRESENTING**

1. You're the Critic Watch a movie that has been adapted from a novel you have read. Select one scene from the film and re-read this scene in the novel. Look for the ways the literary elements of the novel have been translated to the screen. Then, present your findings in a **brief oral report** to the class.

▶ **CAREERS**

2. Those Who Can, Teach Create a **lesson plan** to teach the novel you analyzed in the Writing Workshop to students a year behind you in school. Highlight important information to present to them: background information, key scenes, and important literary elements—especially theme. Design activities that will help students understand the novel.

▶ **CROSSING THE CURRICULUM: SCIENCE**

3. Looking Through the Microscope Analyze an essay written on a scientific topic. Choose an article or chapter by a science writer, such as Stephen Jay Gould, who has written for non-scientists. Write a **short essay** explaining how the kind of evidence used in this essay is similar to and different from the support in a literary analysis.

▶ **SPEAKING AND LISTENING**

4. Do You Hear What I Hear? Listen to a reading of a piece of literature, either on an audiotape or in a live performance. Take notes on the performance. Ask yourself: How does the reader's inflection and tone enhance the literary performance? How does the reader's body language affect the audience's response? With this and other valid criteria, analyze, evaluate, and critique the literary performance. Write a **review** explaining your evaluation.

▶ **MEDIA AND TECHNOLOGY**

5. Lights! Camera! Computers! If you have access to a computer and drawing software, create the **electronic drawings** of the background scenery and props for your favorite moment from a novel. Alternatively, import designs, making choices about real or imaginary settings as backdrops for the action.

PORTFOLIO

6

Exploring Historical Research

Reading Workshop

Reading an Article about History

Writing Workshop

Writing a Historical Research Paper

Viewing and Representing

Evaluating Web Sites

Informational Text

Exposition

We are surrounded—sometimes bombarded—by information from books, magazines, billboards, radio, television, the Internet, speeches, and lectures. Although at times overwhelming, the wealth of information available can be a treasure-trove to someone with the desire to know more about a specific topic—what it is like to play rugby, for example, or why the Civil War began. Digging more deeply into a subject inevitably sends you into the world of information that surrounds us.

One fascinating kind of research—and the focus of this chapter—is historical research: finding out about people or events from the past. In this chapter, you will learn to read historical research and then do some research of your own. Perhaps you are curious about the hurricane that flattened your town twenty years ago or about when women were first admitted to college. Whatever the topic, your search might make you feel a bit like a detective, unlocking the secrets of history. Historical research also helps us gain a deeper understanding of today's world.

YOUR TURN 1 Brainstorming about Historical Research

With several classmates, consider things you have read or films you have seen that involve historical research—the film *Gettysburg*, for example. Then, answer these questions:

- What kinds of things did the author or creator have to find out? What kinds of sources might the creator have used?
- What kinds of research seem the most difficult or interesting? Why?
- How do these examples of historical research affect your life?

internet**connect**

go. hrw .com
GO TO: go.hrw.com
KEYWORD: EOLang 11-6

Reading an Article About History

WHAT'S AHEAD?

In this section, you will read an article about history and learn to

- **draw conclusions from what you read**
- **identify primary and secondary sources**

How could anyone question the appropriateness of the elegant Jefferson Memorial or the powerful Washington Monument? Why did people object to the Vietnam Veterans Memorial or to the depiction of Franklin D. Roosevelt in his memorial? Historical researchers, like the author of the following article, dig deeply into various sources to find answers to such questions; they may interview people, read documents, or look on the Internet. Then they pull the evidence together and draw conclusions about their findings. As you read the following article, notice where and how the author has done her own digging.

Preparing to Read

READING SKILL

Drawing Conclusions   A **conclusion** is a decision, or judgment, you make about an idea or subject in a text. You draw conclusions by combining information in the text with information you already know. In fact, most writers count on their readers to draw conclusions, or fill in gaps on their own. (Just think about how dull it would be to read an article in which *everything* was spelled out in excruciating detail.) As you read the article beginning on the opposite page, try to recall your knowledge of American history. Also, stop occasionally to ask yourself "What does this mean?" and "What do I know that will help me clarify these ideas?"

READING FOCUS

Primary and Secondary Sources   Usually sources of information can be divided into two categories—*primary* and *secondary*. A **primary source** is firsthand information, such as a letter, a speech, or a historical document. A **secondary source** provides indirect information that is at least one step removed from the original source. Examples of secondary sources include a biography or an article from a magazine, encyclopedia, or CD-ROM. Primary sources lie at the heart of much historical research, but secondary sources are also useful. As you read the following article, notice how the author uses both kinds of sources to highlight the controversies over the building of national monuments.

The style of the following article is informal; that is, it does not always use in-text documentation or provide a detailed list of sources. Nonetheless, the author still includes the facts and specific details that are important to historical research. As you read, jot down the answers to the numbered active-reading questions.

from *Smithsonian*

EVEN OUR MOST LOVED MONUMENTS HAD A TRIAL BY FIRE

BY ANDREA GABOR

Controversies like those swirling around the FDR Memorial are the rule when Americans try to agree on anything to be cast in bronze.

FDR never wanted a monument for himself. And who could blame him? It was he who watched with growing dismay, throughout the Depression and much of World War II, as battles raged over the proposed Jefferson Memorial. Today, that circular, domed edifice beside the Tidal Basin[1] seems a stately embodiment of the Republic itself. But back then, it was a lightning rod for critics, and when it finally seemed it would never get built, Franklin Roosevelt personally intervened.

Now a half century has gone by, and it's Roosevelt's turn to be honored. No surprise, then, that the FDR Memorial . . . caps a decades-long controversy that rivals not only the fight over the Jefferson Memorial but also those that engulfed other monuments and public sculptures—both major and minor—over the years.

Controversy has been as integral to public art in the United States as bronze and marble. In the nineteenth century, politicians and art critics sharpened their knives on everything from the now venerable Washington Monument to those seemingly innocuous lions outside the New York Public Library. In fact, trial by fire has been almost a rite of passage for even America's most beloved monuments

1. In what two ways is Franklin Roosevelt related to monument controversies?

---

1. Tidal Basin: the reservoir between the Potomac River and the Washington channel in Washington, D.C.

and memorials. "Never was a memorial yet erected that was not subject to criticism," lamented a besieged Representative John Boylan before Congress in 1937, as he sought to win backing for the Jefferson Memorial. Sixty years later, Bert Kubli, who ran the Art in Public Places section of the National Endowment for the Arts until retiring in 1995, countered: "If no one debates it, why have it? The process and the debate are very much a part of public art itself."

Of course, Americans haven't cornered the market on monumental controversies. Even Paris's signature structure, the Eiffel Tower, was deemed ugly when it went up. But the debates here often turn into high-stakes battles over our values and the very "definition of what it means to be American," writes Harriet Senie, co-editor with Sally Webster of *Critical Issues in Public Art.*

One reason for this long history of acrimony[2] is that, in many respects, monument building runs against America's democratic and puritanical grain. In the early years of the Republic, many Americans viewed any public sculpture as an extravagance. Also, although we have frequently had trouble agreeing on a common identity, nearly all of us have shared a discomfort with the old-world social and religious order depicted in classical sculpture.

> **2. What reasons does the author give to explain the history of controversies about public art?**

Finally, the costs and politics of getting a monument built often have led the advocates of a particular project to assume near-autocratic[3] powers.

The fight over the Jefferson Memorial spanned an eclectic[4] range of objections from art criticism to environmentalism. John Russell Pope's Pantheon-inspired design was derided as an "imitation classical building . . . [that] immortalized the very pomp and pretense [Jefferson] always fought." Joseph Hudnut, dean of the faculty of design at Harvard University, concurred: "This monument, when completed, will embody so grotesque a presentation of Jefferson's character as to make him, if such a thing is possible, forever ridiculous."

Meanwhile, the debate in Congress degenerated into what Representative Boylan called a "showdown" over the destruction of cherry trees around the Tidal Basin, where the memorial was to be located. In 1937, in one long and impassioned defense of the trees, Representative Allen Treadway proclaimed on the House floor: "I want the House at this time to understand that the people of the U.S. want the Tidal Basin and the cherry blossoms protected and we are going to have them protected by legislation if it is possible to do it." Boylan shot back that "not a single cherry tree [would] be disturbed."

In the spring of 1938, after wit-

---

2. **acrimony** (ak´ri•mō´ nē): bitterness of speech or manner.

3. **autocratic** (ôt´ə•krat´ik): in the manner of a dictator; using absolute power.

4. **eclectic** (ek•lek´tik): gathered from varied methods or materials.

nessing years of unproductive debate by Congress, a fed-up FDR approved both the site and a modified version of Pope's design, pushing through a $500,000 appropriation to begin construction. But the First Lady didn't share his enthusiasm. In what was almost certainly an act of defiance, in the April issue of *Reader's Digest* Eleanor Roosevelt wrote a paean[5] to the trees, which read in part: "I hope that neither ax nor water will harm them." The trees had become a cause célèbre,[6] as people chained themselves to the trunks in protest. When construction got underway, the National Park Service took to removing the trees at night; eventually, 150 were destroyed or moved.

> **3. What information illustrates the controversy over the Jefferson Memorial? Besides the *Reader's Digest*, what sources might the writer have cited?**

Ferocious as it was, the battle over the Jefferson Memorial was tame compared with the earlier, century-long war over the Washington Monument. As art historian Kirk Savage has observed, the effort to build a national monument in Washington's memory became "the most problematic undertaking in the campaign" to develop a national identity. You'd never guess that today; the 555-foot-tall stone shaft has become one of the nation's most recognizable icons.

Yet, when a monument to the first President was included in Pierre L'Enfant's[7] plans for the new capital city in 1791, Washington himself objected. He thought that government funds should not be spent for such a project. The trouble was compounded by the monument's original conception, an equestrian statue with Washington in Roman dress, a truncheon[8] held in his right hand. To many Americans, the design smacked of monarchism and ostentation, inappropriate for depicting the man who was a role model of republican citizenship.

After Washington's death, battle lines hardened. The proposed statue

---

5. **paean** (pē'ən): song of joy, thanksgiving, or praise.

6. **cause célèbre** (kôz' sə leb'): a famous controversy.

7. **Pierre L'Enfant** (1754–1825): the French engineer and architect who planned and designed Washington, D.C., after serving in the American Revolution.

8. **truncheon** (trun'chən): a staff or baton carried as a symbol of authority.

was championed by the federalists,[9] who favored a grand monument, and opposed by the republicans,[10] who questioned the very act of commemorating a single hero. As the decades wore on, haggling continued. In 1833, a private monument society was formed, bringing in gifts of money and blocks of marble from states and individuals. Fifteen years later, the cornerstone was laid on the monument's present site. The society had decided on a predictably grand design by Robert Mills: an obelisk[11] rising from a Greek temple, its colonnade encircling a vast rotunda that would house statues and murals of revolutionary heroes. The decision was made to build the obelisk first, and by 1854 the shaft stood at 152 feet. But, that year, progress came to a complete halt when Pope Pius IX donated a block of marble for the monument. Objecting to the "papist gift," members of the antiforeign, anti-Catholic American Party, known as the Know-Nothings (*Smithsonian*, November 1996), stormed the monument grounds, stole the papal rock, and, it is believed, threw it into the Potomac.

> **4. How does the author show that the controversy was less "tame" than the one over the Jefferson Memorial?**

The next year, a group of them broke into the society's offices and seized its records. The project was enmeshed in chaos, and with the onset of the Civil War, work stopped altogether.

The marble stump stood for a quarter century, a bleak rebuke to the young nation. In the early 1870s, with the centennial of the country approaching, Congress once again took up the issue of what to do with the unfinished obelisk. Some advocated tearing it down and starting over, and proposals flooded in for designs of towers ranging from English Gothic to Romanesque to a structure most closely resembling a Hindu temple.

The monument's completion in 1884, and its final design, owed much to the tenacity of Lieutenant Colonel Thomas Casey of the Army Corps of Engineers. As Congress bickered, Casey, who had been charged with supervising construction, drew up a new set of plans based on what had already been built. He envisioned a technological marvel equipped with electric lights and an elevator: an unadorned obelisk that would be the tallest masonry structure in the world. Somehow, this unsung hero persuaded the commission to dispense with the sculptural ornamentation originally planned for the base and, more amazing, to let him build the thing. A permanent reminder of the interrupted construction is the change in the shade of marble partway up—the original shade couldn't be matched. . . .

As a general rule, debate usually slows down the building of a monument, especially in Washington, D.C.,

---

9. **federalists:** a political party of the United States (1789–1816), which favored a strong, centralized government.

10. **republicans:** people who believed that the power of government should rest with the voting citizens.

11. **obelisk** (äb´ə•lisk): a tall, slender, four-sided pillar, which rises to a pyramidal point at its top.

where "debate as obstruction" is a high art form. In a notable exception, however, the most passionately contested monument in recent times—the Vietnam Veterans Memorial—was also built more quickly than any other in the city's history. The Vietnam Veterans Memorial Fund, announced by veteran Jan Scruggs in May 1979, attracted some powerful supporters, including a group of Vietnam veterans from West Point who enlisted the help of several key senators. But then the fund held a competition, in which a panel of art and architecture experts chose from among 1,400 entries submitted blind. Maya Lin's winning design, a polished, black granite wall inscribed with the names of those who died in Vietnam, was lambasted[12] by critics as a "black gash." . . .

5. **What kinds of evidence does the author use to show the different sides in the conflict over the Vietnam Veterans Memorial?**

Members of the selection panel were excoriated[13] by author Tom Wolfe as "mullahs[14] of modernism" responsible for the selection of this "enormous pit" as a memorial. . . .

It was a vicious debate, an argument that seemed to unleash years of pent-up rage and battling perceptions over the legacy of the Vietnam War. But, in the end, only 3½ years had passed from the beginning of fund-raising until

completion in 1982. In 1984, Frederick Hart's grouping of three soldiers, which was commissioned to mollify[15] those who wanted a representational memorial, was positioned to face Maya Lin's minimalist wall, as though the soldiers, too, are reading the names etched into it. Today, the Vietnam Veterans Memorial is the most visited monument in the country. According to Bert Kubli and other public-art experts, the memorial benefited from the debate that engulfed it. No other monument in America, says Kubli, is so clearly "the end product of a long, exciting, very democratic, and very American process."

6. **Why does Bert Kubli call the process of developing the memorial "democratic"?**

With the completion of the FDR Memorial, its builders hope that another spectacular round of controversy will come to an end. Since plans first were laid in the 1940s, this memorial has sparked many familiar debates. Critics have argued over its size (it now covers 7½ acres) and its cost (nearly $50 million). As the Depression and Roosevelt's stewardship during World War II faded from public memory, some questioned whether FDR deserved such a prominent tribute. The monument's design also came under fire. Two modernist plans of the 1960s—one of them derided as "Instant Stonehenge," and another an equally abstract and unpopular design by Marcel Breuer—were both jettisoned. Finally, in the

---

12. **lambasted** (lam•bāst´id): severely scolded or denounced.

13. **excoriated** (ek•skôr´ē •āt´id): harshly denounced.

14. **mullahs** (mul´əs): a title of respect for learned men, used ironically here.

15. **mollify** (mäl´ ə•fī´): to pacify or soothe.

1970s, the more traditional design of Lawrence Halprin, a San Francisco architect (*Smithsonian*, December 1988), passed muster with Washington's venerable Commission of Fine Arts, which reviews the development of all major monuments and public buildings in the nation's capital. Halprin designed a series of outdoor rooms, filled with figurative sculptures by Robert Graham, Neil Estern, George Segal, Tom Hardy, and Leonard Baskin.

But even Halprin's widely hailed plan was not immune to special-interest politics. . . . In another dispute, disability advocates are unhappy

that none of the sculptures of Roosevelt, who as a young man was stricken with polio, show him in a wheelchair. In Neil Estern's nine-foot-high sculpture, for example, a seated Roosevelt is draped in a cape. Estern says that, rather than hiding FDR's infirmity, the sculpture portrays it with subtlety; a pant leg slumping above the knee makes it clear that Roosevelt's thigh was withered. Elsewhere, in a bas-relief, the President is shown seated in a car. Curtis Roosevelt, FDR's oldest grandson, defends the designers' rejection of a blatant wheelchair depiction as consistent with what his grandfather would have wanted. "Even as a child," he says, "I would not have asked him about or made any reference to his paralysis." . . .

Lawrence Halprin says that he set out to design "not an object but an experience over time"; that he wanted to pay tribute to how FDR "faced challenges . . . and was able to effect solutions." In that endeavor, Halprin has surely been successful; the sylvan rooms ranged along the Tidal Basin are, indeed, a moving tribute to Roosevelt. But like George Washington, Roosevelt never wanted one. Four years before he died, FDR told Supreme Court Justice Felix Frankfurter that he would be happy with a memorial the size of his desk. "I want it to be plain, without any ornamentation," he told Frankfurter, "with the simple carving, 'In Memory Of . . .'"

> **7.** What would FDR's opinion probably have been about the memorial designed for him? Why?

First Thoughts on Your Reading

Work with a partner to answer the following questions about the article you have just read. Put your answers on your own paper.

1. **In your own words, what have you learned about some of our national monuments?**

2. **How do you know that the author has researched her topic?**

3. **Based on your reading of the article, what do you think might happen if someone wanted to create a memorial to a current political figure or veterans of a recent armed conflict? Why do you think so?**

Drawing Conclusions

READING SKILL

Putting Two and Two Together   Picture this scenario: You are standing on a corner waiting for the light to change so that you can cross the street. Suddenly you hear the wail of sirens. Seconds later two red trucks race through the intersection, sirens blaring and lights flashing. What do you conclude is happening? The evidence before your eyes and ears, combined with your prior experience and knowledge, leads you to conclude that somewhere in the vicinity there is a fire, and the people in the red trucks are on their way to fight it. If you read an article describing the same scene, you would come to the same conclusion, even if the article did not explicitly tell you this. The writer has trusted that with the text information and your own experience, you will make a particular kind of **inference,** or educated guess, called *drawing a conclusion.* In **drawing a conclusion,** you take the last step in a reasoning process—you combine information from the text with your own prior knowledge and experience to come to a decision or judgment about something that is not stated outright in the text.

TIP   Another kind of inference is a ***generalization,*** which also depends on your combining what you find in the text with what you already know. Unlike drawing conclusions, however, **generalizations** refer to the outside world rather than to the text. That is, a generalization is a judgment you make about the outside world based on what you have read and what you already know, while conclusions are drawn by using prior knowledge to make a judgment about the text in front of you.

Remember that drawing conclusions requires you to pay careful attention to the ideas and details in the text because, as you continue to read, you will gather increasingly more information. Be aware that your conclusions may change as a result.

Use the steps below to draw conclusions about what you read. Notice how one student used the steps to draw conclusions about the third paragraph of "Even Our Most Loved Monuments Had a Trial by Fire" (page 231).

▶ **STEP 1 Gather information or clues from the text about the idea or subject being discussed.** *Public art has always prompted controversy and arguments, especially among politicians and art critics. The text mentions a variety of particular monuments; also, the quotations cited span sixty years.*

▶ **STEP 2 Apply your personal knowledge and experience to the text information.** *People were up in arms about the statue of the school mascot planned for the courtyard at school; everyone had a different idea about what it should look like. I think that people want public art to reflect them and their particular ideas.*

▶ **STEP 3 Draw a conclusion. Remember, conclusions are decisions or judgments about what is in the text.** *I can conclude that the history of controversy over monuments in the United States indicates that people have truly cared about what represents them, the American people.*

▶ **STEP 4 Test your conclusion against the text. Does the information in the text support your conclusion?** *One quotation says that debate is an important part of public art; if no one debated it, that would mean no one cared about it. This statement reinforces my conclusion.*

TIP Sometimes despite careful research, two historians may draw different conclusions about the same information. This happens because they each apply different knowledge and experience to the information. When possible, try to identify and question any conclusions drawn by the writer of a historical piece. Ask yourself if the information actually supports the conclusion.

Arriving at the Right Conclusions   In historical research, historians do not have access to all possible information about the past; they must often draw conclusions about history from only the physical evidence, written accounts, and personal documents that have survived over time. In researching the article you have just read, for example, Andrea Gabor collected several different kinds of historical information that enabled her to draw the conclusion that controversy has been integral to public art in the United States. In turn, *readers* of historical research may have to draw conclusions about the writer's conclusions. To do this, they evaluate the author's evidence; that is, they judge the accuracy and reliability of the information the author used and decide whether it does, in fact, support the author's point. When you read, always look for trustworthy evidence within any text—but especially within historical interpretations—that supports the writer's conclusions. Ask yourself the following questions:

■ **What direct evidence has the writer given?** As you read, notice how writers support the conclusions they reach in their research. Do they use primarily one source or many, and do these sources really support or illustrate the author's conclusion? For example, in the Gabor article, look at the number of quotations from many different professionals that the author used as direct support for her conclusions about public art.

- **Is the evidence from a respectable or recognizable source?** Sometimes the evidence will be from books or magazines, or from well-known authors and authorities. In the article you've just read, for example, the author cited articles from *Smithsonian*—a nationally distributed magazine with an established standard of accuracy. In contrast, citing a Web site called "Joe's List of Fun Historical Facts" might prompt a bit of skepticism in readers.

- **Could I find similar information in other sources?** Material appearing in more than one source is usually more trustworthy than material found only in one place. In the monuments article, the author used both quotations and magazine references to support her conclusions. If you were interested in testing her conclusions, you could consult the sources the author supplied, using the publication dates of the magazine or the names of the people mentioned in the article to guide your investigation. You might also consult established reference sources, such as encyclopedias.

Reference Note

For more about **evaluating sources,** see page 251.

 Drawing Conclusions

Look back at the reading selection and re-read the paragraph on page 232 beginning "Meanwhile, the debate in Congress" and the next paragraph beginning "In the spring of 1938." Evaluate the author's use of evidence in concluding that the controversy over the cherry trees was a showdown. Then, explain the conclusion about presidential power you could draw from reading these two paragraphs. Write your answer on your own paper.

Identifying Primary and Secondary Sources

 READING FOCUS

On the Scene and After the Fact   Historical researchers use a variety of sources in their quest for information—both primary and secondary. A **primary source** is firsthand, original information, like a field recording, an interview, or a historical artifact. A **secondary source** is information derived from or about primary sources and even from other secondary sources. For example, a diary is a primary source; a magazine article about the diary's contents or a documentary film based on the diary is a secondary source. Use the chart on the next page to help you recognize and distinguish between the two types of sources. Notice that the chart shows the advantages and disadvantages of using each type of source for a researcher's work.

Sources		
	Primary	**Secondary**
Examples	letters, diaries, eyewitness accounts, historical documents, speeches, autobiographies, photographs, works of literature or art, court records, artifacts such as pottery shards	encyclopedias, CD-ROMs, documentary films, biographies, history books, newspapers and magazines that report on an event
Advantages	• allows researcher to make accurate observations • permits researcher to draw fresh, original conclusions	• provides an overview • allows researcher to profit from previous research • can lead researcher to related primary and secondary sources
Disadvantages	reliability might be affected by the feelings, memory, or perceptions of the author or creator of the primary source	reliability might be affected by author's bias (twisting information to support a point of view)

Sound historical research generally draws from both types of sources. For example, a historian researching the first manned moon landing might start with a review of secondary sources: an encyclopedia entry, a history of the space program, a biography of Neil Armstrong, and a magazine article or newspaper account about the event. After completing this introductory stage, the researcher might explore some primary sources: a transcript of the communications between NASA and the astronauts, an interview with Neil Armstrong, an unedited videotape of the moon landing, photographs, and diaries or autobiographical accounts from any of the people involved.

As a critical reader of historical research, be aware of the different types of sources that an article may contain. Generally, sources are easier to identify in formal research reports than in more informal reports or articles because **formal reports** cite their research sources parenthetically or in footnotes or endnotes. They do so primarily to validate their research for well-informed readers. Secondarily, these citations provide enough information so that readers may look up the sources on their own.

On the other hand, **informal reports,** written for a more general audience who may be reading for entertainment, usually omit formal citations. Because the purpose of most informal reports is to present research in an engaging manner, authors sometimes use phrases and clauses—"according to Bert Kubli," "Lawrence Halprin says"—within their sentences instead of using formal citations. The result is a lively style of writing, based on authentic research, but without clear distinctions between primary and secondary sources.

Should it matter to readers whether a source is primary or secondary? Sometimes this information provides a common-sense clue about the quality of the research. If, for instance, a book on the Civil War does not cite any of the thousands of secondary sources about that topic, you might doubt the book's scholarship. If, on the other hand, the same book cited no primary sources, you would have to question the depth and quality of the research. You would wonder how a book that relies entirely on secondary sources can provide new insights on the subject. Use the following tips to help you identify primary and secondary sources in any researched article:

- **Look for in-text citations and Works Cited lists.** If, for example, you see the title of a recent *Time* article in a parenthetical citation, you are probably dealing with a secondary source; if you see the word *interview* in a Works Cited list, the source is probably primary.

- **Examine how the author introduces the source information.** Remember, this strategy is important in informal research reports where citations are often absent. If, for instance, you read "Abraham Lincoln once wrote to his wife," followed by a direct quotation, common sense would tell you that the quotation is from a letter—a primary source—written by Abraham Lincoln. (Whether the article's author actually saw the letter or just saw parts of it quoted in a book is another matter.) If, on the other hand, you read "Newspapers reported that," common sense would tell you that the source of the information that follows is probably secondary.

TIP In informal research reports, readers must often **infer**—or make educated guesses about—whether the author's sources are primary or secondary. For example, near the end of the article on page 236, the author quotes FDR's grandson but gives neither the source of the quote nor any clue about where it was obtained. If the author had actually heard the grandson speak the words or read a transcript of the words, the source would be primary. If she had read the words in a newspaper or magazine article, the source would be secondary. In the absence of any documentation, readers can only use their best judgments about whether the source is primary or secondary.

YOUR TURN 3 **Identifying Primary and Secondary Sources**

Look back at the paragraph in the Reading Selection beginning "Controversy has been as integral to public art" (page 231). Using your best judgment, determine if the paragraph's sources are primary or secondary, and explain why you made that choice. Then, do the same thing for the paragraph beginning "With the completion of the FDR Memorial" (page 235). Discuss your findings with a partner.

Definition/Restatement Context Clues

Historians often clarify events in history by looking at similar happenings elsewhere. Likewise, you can determine the meaning of an unfamiliar word by examining its surroundings or context. Sometimes writers will actually define or restate the word, often using one of the following signals:

■ Commas, dashes, or parentheses

Example:
The castle's defenses included an enormous portcullis, a heavy iron gate forged by the local ironsmiths.

■ Words and phrases such as *called, known as, referred to as, or,* and *that is*

Example:
The castle's defenses included an enormous portcullis, *that is,* a heavy iron gate forged by the local ironsmiths.

■ Definition or restatement in a later sentence

Example:
The castle's defenses included an enormous portcullis. The heavy iron gate had been forged by the local ironsmiths.

THINKING IT THROUGH — Using Definition/Restatement Context Clues

Use the steps below to discover the italicized word's meaning.

Example:
The architect had designed a prize-winning *edifice,* a towering bank building whose ornate appearance overshadowed everything on the street.

1. **Re-read the passage, looking for punctuation marks, clue words, or any sentences that indicate definitions or restatements.** A comma separates "edifice" from "building."

2. **Substitute the definition or restatement** for the unfamiliar word or make an educated guess at the word's meaning. "The architect had designed a prize-winning building, a towering bank . . ."

3. **Check a dictionary to confirm your guess.** Edifice does mean "building."

PRACTICE

Use the steps above to figure out the meaning of the italicized words below. Write your answers on your own paper.

1. The controversy was beyond *banter,* that is, good-natured teasing.

2. The architect asked *advocates* of the new memorial to attend a meeting. He was hoping that these supporters would help him obtain approval.

3. The politicians spoke of the building as an *icon* of strength—a symbol of vigor.

4. Sitting on the hotel's *veranda,* or porch, the tourists talked about the tour.

5. The *garrulous* politician was called "the talkative senator" in the press.

Answering Questions About Rhetoric

Historians do not simply list events; instead, they craft their works by employing rhetorical strategies—special techniques to make a point, such as *argument by analogy* (showing a parallel between two similar situations), *historical allusion* (referring to a famous historical figure or event), and *appeal to authority* (quoting an expert as support for an argument.) On state or national tests you may encounter a question about the rhetoric rather than the content of a passage. For example, you might be asked why the author referred to a certain historical event or figure.

Read the following passage from an article about the famous pioneer woman pilot Amelia Earhart; then, look at the question about its rhetoric that follows.

[Amelia] Earhart and her navigator, Fred Noonan, were bound for Howland Island, a 2,556-mile journey and the longest leg of their flight around the world. [Although Charles "Lucky Lindy" Lindbergh had made his historic transatlantic flight in 1927,] no man had yet flown a plane around the world at its widest point, the equator, as Earhart was doing, nor had any woman pilot ever circumnavigated the globe.

Those who turned out that misty morning to watch her departure from Lae were the last ever to see Earhart or Noonan, the last to hear the poetry of the Lockheed's engines. Somewhere over the Pacific, the plane vanished. America had lost its Sweetheart of the Air, its lovely Lady Lindy.

1. The author of this passage calls Earhart "lovely Lady Lindy" in order to

   A. remind the reader that Earhart was a woman pilot

   B. suggest a parallel between two heroic pilots—Earhart and Charles Lindbergh

   C. challenge the idea that Earhart's accomplishments could equal Lindbergh's

   D. present a poetic description of Earhart

   E. hint at a personal connection between Earhart and Noonan

---

THINKING IT THROUGH Answering Questions about Rhetoric

To determine the best possible answer:

1. **Determine the kind of question about rhetoric being asked.** You might think, "The end of the passage refers to Charles 'Lucky Lindy' Lindbergh. The author makes a historical allusion.

2. **Consider each answer.** For example, exclude **A** because such a reminder would serve no purpose. Exclude **E** because the passage mentions no personal relationship with Noonan. Exclude **D** because while the description is poetic this is not its primary purpose. **B** and **C** refer to Lindbergh, but **C** suggests a challenge the passage does not support.

3. **Reevaluate your choice.** **B** is correct because it alludes to "Lucky Lindy," and the entire passage describes Earhart as a hero, like Lindbergh.

Writing a Historical Research Paper

A student traces the history of blues music to discover the roots of a guitar riff played in his favorite song. A public health scientist studies the conditions in a community to find out why so many people have contracted the same dreaded disease in the past ten years. An injured athlete looks for information about how athletes in ancient Greece dealt with similar injuries. In all these cases, people used historical research to find out answers to questions that intrigued them.

Historical research is research in which you explore a historical figure's life or find out about the connections between past events and your present concerns. What topics interest you? You might wonder, for example, why so many film directors use the classic movie *Citizen Kane* as a model for their own filmmaking or how American Indians played lacrosse three hundred years ago. In this workshop you will have the opportunity to dig deeply into a topic—to piece together bits of historical information in a new and meaningful way.

Prewriting

Develop a Research Topic

Travel to the Past Perhaps you have already identified a historical research topic—one with special significance that you want to explore in depth. If not, taking the time to find an appropriate one is well worth the effort. If your topic interests and excites you, the work ahead can seem like an adventure—a journey into the past. Use the following suggestions to help you identify a topic.

- **Consider your current interests.** What are your interests or hobbies? Does one of your interests have historical significance? How might a particular hobby have changed through the years and why?
- **Identify heroes.** What historical figure do you admire? What events might have shaped his or her life?
- **Think of fascinating places near and far.** What historical landmark have you always wanted to visit? The Gettysburg battlefield? The Little Bighorn? Yellowstone National Park? What history is associated with it? What local memorial or monument would you like to know more about?
- **Focus on current events.** What interests you in the news? What problems in the world concern you? How does the history of these problems and issues help to explain them?
- **Explore the library and media.** What subjects awaken your curiosity as you browse through books, magazines, the card catalog, a CD-ROM encyclopedia, or television listings? Are there interesting historical aspects to any of the subjects?

To get started, think about a historical topic in which you are interested. You may find that as you get further into your research, you will want to modify your topic or change it completely.

Narrow Your Topic

Zero In   The topic you have chosen may be too broad to be covered in a research paper. If so, you will need to narrow your focus to find a more specific aspect of the topic. You might start with an interest in the topic "the history of the people of Appalachia" and narrow that topic to something more manageable: "Appalachian coal-mining songs as they reflect the history of the region's people."

One way to narrow your focus is to look at subtopics. If you look in the sources listed below for the broad topic you have chosen, you may find subtopics that will give you ideas for a narrowed focus.

- card catalog
- *Readers' Guide to Periodical Literature*
- encyclopedias
- keyword searches and hyperlinks on the World Wide Web

Another method for narrowing your focus is to write down your initial idea and then to keep challenging yourself to make it more specific. The student chart on the next page shows how one writer narrowed a topic.

Subject:	I'm interested in the history of jazz.
More Specific:	Over time, jazz has gone through some major changes.
More Specific:	Jazz has changed because of the influence of individual musicians.
More Specific:	Charlie Parker is a musician who changed jazz.
Narrowed Topic:	Charlie Parker's major contributions to jazz changed the way it was heard and played from then on.

TIP Aside from being too broad, topics may also be too specific ("the weather on the day the Smoot-Hawley Tariff Act of 1930 was signed") or too personal ("my visit to Wounded Knee, South Dakota). If your topic is either too specific or too personal, move back up your narrowed chart to a more general idea.

THINKING IT THROUGH Choosing a Suitable Topic

▶ **Ask yourself: Can I find enough available information?** Make sure you can locate four to six different sources of information for your topic. For a topic like "Charlie Parker's debt to 1940s saxophone technology," you might be lucky to find even one article. Think about whether your own topic might be so specific or obscure that you can't find much information on it; if it is, be prepared to broaden your focus.

▶ **Ask yourself: Will I be able to add my own perspective to this topic rather than simply repackaging other people's ideas?** Of course, your personal experience should not be the basis for your report, but it is an important part of it. Will you be able to combine ideas in a way that reveals your unique point of view?

▶ **Ask yourself: Will the approach I take be interesting to others?** Almost any topic can be made interesting, so if your topic is not automatically appealing, decide on an approach that *would* interest your readers. In your essay on the history of rocket engineering, for example, you might use NASA space launches—something most people have seen on TV—as your central example.

Because your narrowed topic will eventually lead to your *thesis statement*—the main idea of your paper—it is wise to think about it carefully. Be sure to jot your topic down before you plunge into research.

Purpose, Audience, and Tone

Get the Big Picture   After you have narrowed your topic, think about **why you are writing** this paper, **for whom you are writing it,** and **what tone you will want to use.** In other words, consider your purpose, audience, and tone.

Purpose   Your **purpose** is to inform readers about some aspect of history through your research. You should not, however, just compile a collection of facts and expert opinions. **Your research paper should be an original synthesis (combination) of information, and it should include your own experience and knowledge.** To write this paper, you will have to think about what you discover and then pass along your insights.

KEY CONCEPT

Audience   You will probably be writing for your classmates and teacher. Therefore, you will have a good idea of how much background information you must give and how technical you can be. You want to be neither too elementary nor too complex. If you plan to write your report for another specific audience, then tailor your approach to them. How much do they already know about your topic? What explanations will they need?

Tone   The attitude and feeling that you convey to your audience through your writing is your **tone.** The tone of research reports may vary from somewhat informal to very formal depending on whether they are written for popular periodicals or academic audiences. The typical academic report, such as the ones that are required in school, and the typical professional report, such as the ones you may do for a job someday, are formal in tone. In this chapter, you are writing an academic report, and your audience will probably expect a formal tone. A formal tone usually has the following characteristics:

TIP   Your **voice** is your personality as expressed through your paper. It is the style that makes your writing you.

- **Third-person point of view**   Avoid the pronoun *I*.
- **Relatively formal language**   Formal language usually does not use slang, colloquial expressions, or contractions. Sounding stuffy is not your goal, but you should not be too casual.

Reference Note

For more information about **formal** and **informal language,** see page 941 in the Quick Reference Handbook.

YOUR TURN 4 Choosing and Narrowing a Topic

Choose and narrow a topic for your own historical research paper. Remember to judge the suitability of your topic using the questions on page 246 and to keep the audience, purpose, and tone of your final paper in mind.

Ask Research Questions

What Do I Want to Know? An initial research step is posing general questions that you want to answer. At this early stage, you cannot come up with *all* the important questions about your topic, but you can establish guides for exploration. You might try using the reporter's *5W-How?* questions (*Who? What? When? Where? Why?* and *How?*) to help you think of all the possible directions your questioning can take. Plan to investigate all aspects of your topic, including various viewpoints on it. The following example shows how one writer developed questions to focus research on Charlie Parker's influence on the history of jazz.

- **Who** influenced Charlie Parker's development as a jazz musician?

- **What** are the major contributions Parker made to jazz?

- **When** did Parker begin to influence other musicians?

- **Where** did Parker begin his career, and where did it take him?

- **Why** is Charlie Parker considered one of the two greatest influences on the development of jazz?

- **How** did Charlie Parker's influence change jazz permanently?

Gather Support

Picking Up the Scent After you have asked yourself possible questions about your topic, you will want to track down the answers. **You can begin by looking for sources of information—a book, a magazine, a site on the World Wide Web, an interview, or a videotaped documentary.** (Of course, just because a source gives you information does not mean that it is reliable. You will learn more about evaluating sources later in this workshop.)

Doing a Background Check Begin your research with a general reference work to get an overview of your topic, gain background information, and find other materials to use in your research. For this initial research step, you might consult a print or CD-ROM encyclopedia or search the World Wide Web for pages that contain related keywords.

TIP If your topic is narrowly focused ("the history of weather forecasting by supercomputer"), general reference works may not have an entry for it. Try looking for related or larger topics ("meteorology," "supercomputers"). If you already have a solid background in your topic, you can eliminate general reference works and go directly to the types of sources listed on the next page.

Following the Leads   Once you have an overview of your topic, you should move on to specific sources that match up with your interest in a more direct and detailed way. Do not restrict your thinking to print sources available at your school or community library. You might find your most valuable information by interviewing a historian, by visiting a museum, or by writing (or e-mailing) for information from a source outside your local area. Keep in mind that sometimes the most important role of a source is to lead you to other sources. Use the chart below to help steer you toward specific information sources in your library and community.

Reference Note

For more help on **using the library,** see page 942 in the Quick Reference Handbook.

INFORMATION RESOURCES	
Library	
Resource: Where to Look	Source of Information: What to Discover
Card catalog or online catalog	Books and audiovisuals (separate catalogs in some libraries)
Readers' Guide to Periodical Literature or online periodical indexes	Magazines and some journal articles
Newspaper indexes, specialized reference books, and CD-ROMs	Newspapers (often on microfilm), dictionaries, encyclopedias, bibliographies on particular topics
Microfilm or microfiche and online databases	Indexes to major newspapers, back issues of some newspapers and magazines
Community	
Resource: Where to Look	Source of Information: What to Discover
National, state and local government offices	Official records
Museums and historical societies	Exhibits, experts
Schools and colleges	Libraries, experts
World Wide Web and online services	Articles, interviews, bibliographies, pictures, videos, sound recordings
Television and radio, video stores	Documentaries, news, interviews, videos, instructional programs

COMPUTER TIP

If you have access to and know specifically what you want to find on the World Wide Web, you can make your search more efficient by using combinations of **keywords.** For example, if a computer search using the keyword *jazz* yields too much irrelevant information, you might narrow the search by trying *jazz + bebop.* Look for information on advanced searching strategies on the first screen of your search engine.

Reference Note

For more information on **conducting interviews,** see pages 50 and 163.

TIP An **interview** can also produce valuable research information, but planning ahead is essential for the interview's success. Prepare a list of specific questions—probably eight to ten—that you would like the subject to answer. You might use the *5W-How?* questions to help you prepare your list. If possible, you may also want to take a tape recorder with you to record your subject's responses.

The Hard Evidence   Most sources of information can be classified as either primary or secondary. A **primary source** is firsthand, original information, such as a letter, an autobiography, a work of literature or art, historical documents, or an interview with a person who participated in the experience being researched. A **secondary source** is information derived from, or about, primary sources, or even from other secondary sources. Examples include an encyclopedia or CD-ROM, a documentary film, a biography, history books, or an interview with a historian. If you are writing about post-Revolutionary America, for example, some primary sources might be the Articles of Confederation and Thomas Jefferson's letters; a secondary source might be a biography of Jefferson. (Your completed report may in turn become a secondary source for someone else to use.)

Although secondary sources are plentiful and essential to your paper and usually provide excerpts from primary sources, do not use them exclusively when primary sources are available. At the same time, don't assume that all primary sources are exempt from evaluation. Memory may be faulty or selective in an autobiography, and emotions may override facts in a letter. Research as widely as possible, so that you have a good basis for deciding what is accurate and what is slanted or biased. The general rule in research is to get as close as you can to the facts.

Reference Note

For a chart listing **primary and secondary sources** along with the advantages and disadvantages of each, see page 240.

MINI-LESSON CRITICAL THINKING

Evaluating Sources

Sound historical research is based on accurate, authoritative information. But how can you tell whether your sources contain such information? The following 4R test gives you particular qualities to look for in your sources. To judge, or evaluate, each of your sources, see if it meets the 4R test.

- **Relevant: Does the source's information relate directly to your narrowed topic?** For a book, check the table of contents and index. Skim magazine articles. Some nonprint sources include summaries; you may also find book reviews.

- **Reliable: Can you trust it?** A respected scholar, or a respected magazine such as the *Atlantic Monthly* or *Scientific American,* can usually be relied on for accuracy. Look for authors who are quoted frequently or who appear in most bibliographies on your topic.

- **Recent: Are you using up-to-date sources?** Information on many topics changes rapidly, so look for the most recent work on your topic. In dealing with historical topics, the information itself probably will not change over time, but the way it is presented will change. You will want to consider the most current interpretation of the information. (Looking at bibliographies of current works will quickly alert you to the older works that are still considered valuable by historians today.) Primary sources are, of course, never outdated.

- **Representative: Are you showing different points of view on a controversial topic?** You do not want a list of sources which all advocate a particular viewpoint or which all oppose it. Study, balance, and interpret the views on all sides.

Reference Note

For information on **evaluating Web sources,** see page 281 of this chapter.

PRACTICE

For the topic "Charlie Parker's influence on the development of jazz," evaluate, in a small group, the following possible sources by using the 4R test. If you feel uncertain about a source, explain what further information you would like to have about it. Be prepared to share your responses.

1. Cox, John H. *Folk-songs of the South.* Cambridge: Harvard UP, 1925.
2. Gammond, Peter. "Charlie Parker." *The Oxford Companion to Popular Music.* New York: Oxford UP, 1991.
3. *Celebrating Bird: The Triumph of Charlie Parker.* Dirs., Gary Giddins and Kendrick Simmons. Videocassette. Pioneer Artists. 1987.
4. Reese, Gustave. *Music in the Renaissance.* New York: Norton, 1954.
5. Williams, Martin. *The Jazz Tradition.* New York: Oxford UP, 1993.

Reference Note

For more information and examples of proper style for the **Works Cited** list, see page 270.

TIP Some teachers may ask you to list the articles you read for background information but did not use in the body of the paper. Those articles should appear in a separate **Works Consulted** list.

My Sources Inform Me . . . Keep accurate and complete source information about all of the articles you consult, even if you are not sure you will use them in your report. Your **Works Cited list**—the list of sources at the end of your report—must contain specific information in case readers want to consult your sources. Keep track of your sources by recording each one on a separate note card or in a separate computer file. With either method, you will save time if you list sources in the exact style required for the Works Cited list. Use the following guidelines and example to help you make source cards.

Guidelines for Making Source Cards

1. **Assign each source a number.**
   Later, when you are taking notes, it will save time to write a number instead of the author and title. (You might also use the author's last name as a source code.)

2. **Record full publishing information.**
   Record everything you might need: subtitles, translators, and volume and edition numbers. Getting all the necessary information at this stage will keep you from having to backtrack when you create your Works Cited list.

3. **Note the call number or location.**
   This information will help you relocate the source quickly.

Look at the example source card below.

Assign each source card a number.

⑤

Record full publishing information.

Hentoff, Nat. Jazz Is. New York:
    Random, 1976.

Note the location and call number.

School Library
785.4
HEN

TIP Besides the Modern Language Association (MLA) *Handbook,* your teacher may ask you to use *The Chicago Manual of Style* (CMS) or a manual published by the American Psychological Association (APA) to prepare your Works Cited list. Once you have chosen a style for documentation, follow it consistently. See also page 270.

YOUR TURN 5 **Gathering and Evaluating Information**

Begin your research by formulating a research question and gathering background information. Find at least four to six suitable sources, and make source cards for them.

Record Notes and Organize Information

Keeping Track   If you review and organize your sources before you begin to draft your paper, writing it will be significantly easier. You have already selected and evaluated your sources; now you are ready for the next step—**taking notes.** To get started, read or skim each source to be sure that you understand the overall meaning. (If you extract a sentence or two from an article or other source without understanding what the source is about, you may misrepresent your source and yourself.) Then, use the following guidelines for taking notes. Look at page 254 for a sample note card.

TIP "Do not rely on your memory" is the basic guide for all research activities. You may feel that keeping track of your sources makes the process harder, but you will be grateful for these records when you start writing your paper. Three extra minutes now can save you an hour (or more) later.

Guidelines for Taking Notes
1. Use a separate card, half-sheet of paper, or computer file for each source and item of information. Having separate cards will make rearranging and organizing your notes easier when you are getting ready to write.
2. Record the source number. In the upper right-hand corner of each note, write the number you have assigned each source. The numbers provide you with a shorthand system to show exactly where you got the information. (If you have decided to use each author's last name as a source code, use names here, too.)
3. Write a label or heading. In the upper left-hand corner of the card or file, identify the main idea of your note so that you do not have to re-read each note to remind yourself what it is about.
4. Write the page number(s). At the end of your note, write the page numbers from which the information comes. Page references, if available, are required for the documentation in your paper. You do not want to have to search for page numbers later.

TIP If an interview is part of your source material, remember to note specific historical facts your interviewee might mention. Ask the interviewee to repeat anything you might quote directly. Read such quoted material back to your interview subject to double-check its accuracy. Immediately after the interview, rewrite your notes into full sentences. If you have recorded the interview, be sure to transcribe the tape very carefully.

TIP Use the information you note to refine your topic and to ask additional questions about it.

Filling in the Blanks   There are two main **types of notes**—direct quotes and summaries or paraphrases—and you will probably use both. As you review the material you have gathered, you will come across phrases or whole sentences that are stated so powerfully you will want to use the exact words of the source—or a *direct quotation.* You will also come across important information that can be stated in your own words. For recording this type of information, you should use either a *summary* or a *paraphrase.*

Direct Quotation   To capture interesting, well-phrased passages or a passage's technical accuracy, quote an author directly. Use the same punctuation, capitalization, and spelling as in the original, and enclose the passage in quotation marks. Use ellipsis points to indicate omissions from the text and brackets to explain words changed for the sense of the sentence. Resist the urge to quote too much. Your task is to **synthesize** information, not stitch together a long series of quotes. The example note card below shows how to record a direct quotation.

Number matches source card	⑤
Main idea of passage	Musical significance in everything
Direct quotation; ellipsis points to show omission	"Everything had a musical significance for Bird . . . . Everything has a musical message for him. If he heard a dog bark, he would say the dog was speaking
Brackets for sense of sentence	. . . . or an expression on [a girl's face] would give him an idea for something to play on his solo."
Page number	page 179

Summaries and Paraphrases   In most of your notes, you will use *your own words* to record the author's ideas and facts. A **summary** is highly condensed—typically one fourth to one third the length of the original passage. (In notes, sometimes a summary can be as brief as jottings; look at the note card on the next page.) A **paraphrase** is a restatement of a passage in your own words that allows for more detail; often, a paraphrase is the same length as the original. Whether you summarize or paraphrase, you should recast the information in your own words and style. If you simply substitute synonyms for some of the words of your source, you run the risk of **plagiarizing,** or failing to give credit to an author whose words or ideas you have used. To be sure that you completely recast the information, try setting the passage aside and writing ideas from memory, using lists and phrases instead of complete sentences. Notice how the note card on the top of the next page summarizes information from a source.

Reference Note
For more information on **summaries,** see pages 110 and 958. For more on **paraphrases,** see pages 192 and 956.

(3) Number matches source card

Parker's contributions to jazz:

Main idea of passage

- new harmonies

- complex rhythms

List picks up key points of passage

- excellent technique

- willingness to experiment with music

- as influential in jazz as Louis Armstrong

page 445

Page number of passage

YOUR TURN 6 **Recording Information**

Review the steps in the Guidelines for Taking Notes chart on page 253. Take notes from your sources, and make sure that you write down quotations exactly. Use paraphrases and summaries whenever possible on your note cards.

TIP Remember, even a summary or paraphrase—if it expresses an author's original idea—must be credited in your final paper.

Write a Thesis Statement

What Is the Big Idea?   Once you have gathered your information, you need to re-read your research notes and draw some conclusions about what they mean. How do all these sources fit together? What larger point do they all support? Then, write a preliminary, or working, *thesis statement*. The **thesis statement** is a sentence or two expressing both your topic and the conclusion, or conclusions, you have drawn about it (the controlling idea). The thesis statement keeps you on track as you write your report (in your final version, it will also keep your reader on track). Of course, your thesis may change as your research and writing progress. The following are sample thesis statements for historical research papers. The topic of each is underlined once, the controlling idea twice.

TIP In most cases, you can write a thesis statement according to this formula:

topic + your idea or opinion about the topic = **the thesis statement**

Reference Note

For more help with writing **thesis statements,** see page 1027 in the Quick Reference Handbook.

Charlie Parker's music influenced jazz to change from music that entertains to music that expresses.

Mexican writer Sor Juana Ines de la Cruz became a noted intellectual in spite of both social and religious obstacles to her education.

Develop an Outline

Divide and Conquer Using your thesis statement as a guidepost, you can develop an **organizational plan**—an outline that will require you to review your information and to assess its usefulness. Because an outline provides an organizational overview, using one ensures that your ideas will flow in a **logical progression,** with adequate support for each idea.

Start by sorting your note cards or computer files into groups that have similar labels—the information you have written in the left-hand corner of each card. The way you group the labels may immediately suggest the main sections or ideas of your report. Then, you can decide how best to order ideas within groups and which supporting details to use. Although you may be able to order your information exclusively in one of the following ways, you will probably find a combination of the orders necessary.

Reference Note

For more information on **orders of organization,** see page 461.

- **Chronological order** gives events in the order they happen and is often used in historical research.
- **Logical order** groups related ideas together.
- **Order of importance** begins with the most important detail and moves to the least important (or in reverse).

Now you are ready to transfer information into outline form, first as a **working outline**—or early plan—in which you group details without arranging them into a more formal outline with numbers and letters. This is called a working outline because you are likely to change it several times as you find the best way to organize your ideas and information. In the following portion of an outline, see how one student organized information for a research paper on Charlie Parker's place in the history of jazz.

TIP Working outline entries may be words, phrases, or complete sentences. Another method to determine the organization of your research paper is to create a **concept map.** For more information about **mapping,** see page 1041 in the Quick Reference Handbook.

Introduction
    Thesis

Background of jazz: Dixieland revival and swing
    Commercial success
    Popular entertainment
    Audience-centered music

A new relationship with the audience
    Performer-centered expression
    Music to listen to
    Escape from entertainer's role

TIP **Subheadings** can be used within a research report to make the report easier to follow. The subheads, which often are written in boldface type, can be taken from the major points in your outline. Notice how the Writer's Model on pages 259–264 uses subheadings.

The **formal outline** is more refined than the working outline, and while you can change it if you need to, the changes you make will probably be minor. The formal outline has numerals and letters to identify headings and subheadings and indentations to show levels of subordination—important if you are trying to work out complicated sequences of information. In its final form, the formal outline is intended to give an overview of both the content and organization of your research paper. It can also serve as a table of contents. Here is part of a student's formal outline for a historical research report on Charlie Parker.

Reference Note

For more on **outlining,** see page 1037 in the Quick Reference Handbook.

I. Background of jazz: Dixieland revival and swing

    A. Commercial success

    B. Popular entertainment

    C. Audience-centered music

II. A new relationship with the audience

    A. Performer-centered expression

      1. Emphasized individual

      2. De-emphasized audience

TIP Note that there are no subordinate heads under the A, B, and C heads of Roman numeral I. This is because the information in these two paragraphs of the research paper is essentially background information about what jazz was like before Charlie Parker, the subject of the paper, changed jazz forever. The outline and the paper become more detailed when Parker's revolutionary influence is discussed beginning with Roman numeral II.

YOUR TURN 7 Writing a Thesis and Planning the Order of the Essay

After you have reviewed the steps above, write a thesis statement and arrange your note cards. Then, organize your information into a working outline.

Writing

The Historical Research Paper

Framework	**Directions and Explanations**

Introduction

- Draw readers into your research with an interesting opener.
- Give an overview of your research.
- Include your thesis statement.

Body

- Develop the first idea that supports your thesis.
- Develop the second idea that supports your thesis, and so on.

Conclusion

- Restate your thesis.
- Provide a final assessment of your ideas.

Grab your readers' attention right away   Use a vivid scene, interesting detail, or striking quotation. An intriguing title will also pique readers' curiosity.

Introduce your readers to your topic   Besides providing background information, you may want to explain the initial research questions you formulated and point to the answers you have found.

State your thesis   Incorporate a thesis statement smoothly into the introduction. In lengthy or complex research papers, an introduction may be longer than one paragraph.

Present your research   Be sure to

- Develop each idea with factual information from your note cards. Cite sources when necessary, and list them on your Works Cited list. Distinguish your own ideas from those of your sources' authors.
- Use a variety of primary and secondary sources.
- Arrange your ideas in a meaningful and sensible order. Consider using subheads as the paper on the opposite page has done.
- Make logical connections between your ideas. Use transitional words and phrases to move smoothly from one idea to another.

End your paper effectively   Reword your thesis statement, remind readers of the purpose of your research, draw final conclusions, and close with a memorable "clincher."

YOUR TURN 8 Writing a First Draft

Using the framework above, write the first draft of your historical research paper. Also, read the following Writer's Model and the Student's Model. Keep track of your sources as you write your rough draft. Then, put your citations in the correct parenthetical form.

A Writer's Model

The following historical research paper, which is a final draft, closely follows the framework on the previous page. Notice how facts, quotations, and summaries of ideas are incorporated. You will also see source information cited in parentheses throughout the report.

Beautiful Surprises from an Alto Sax:
Charlie Parker's Place in Jazz History

In mid-December 1949, Birdland opened, its big neon sign flashing "THE JAZZ CORNER OF THE WORLD." Named in honor of Charlie "Bird" Parker, the new music club, on Broadway near New York City's famed Fifty-second Street in Harlem, was filled with cages of exotic birds and the flights of musical improvisation from Charlie Parker's alto saxophone (Porter). Parker's own Kansas City bebop music had arrived in the Big Apple.

No other musician—except perhaps trumpet player Dizzy Gillespie—played bebop like Charlie Parker. From the time he was fourteen and a member of his junior high school band, Charlie Parker pushed himself musically to experiment with harmony and tempo. He practiced and performed, even when the result was not at first successful. In a defining experience, Parker recalls, "One time, when I was in my teens, jamming in a Kansas City club, I was doing all right until I tried doing double tempo on 'Body and Soul.'. . . Everybody fell out laughing. I went home and cried and didn't want to play again for three months" (qtd. in Hentoff 175). Playing double time and creating different chord harmonies, however, became Charlie Parker's trademarks. His resulting bebop music—named for its unique, staccato, two-tone phrasing—would revolutionize jazz with its new sound and tempo ("bebop"). Because of Parker's influence, jazz changed from a music of entertainment controlled by what the audience wanted to hear into a music of expression controlled by what the musician wanted to play—a music called modern jazz.

Background of Modern Jazz: Dixieland Revival and Swing

When Charlie Parker was born in Kansas City in 1920, there were two types of jazz: swing and Dixieland revival. Swing was commercially successful dance music (Berendt 16)—"background music for the innocent romances of its college audiences" (Green 648). Dixieland revival was also entertainment music—a "simplified and cliché-ridden" jazz that had popular appeal

(continued)

Interesting and informative title

INTRODUCTION
Attention-getting opener

Online source

Indirect source indicated by "qtd. in"

Overview of research
Thesis statement

BODY
Subheads introduce major sections

Direct quotation as support

Writer's conclusion	(Berendt 18). Audiences liked the familiarity of Dixieland and the danceability of swing.
Summary of source material	The swing bands and the Dixieland bands were not necessarily mediocre or lacking in inventiveness, but more often than not, original elements in music were slipped into a performance rather than showcased (Giddins 489). Setting their sights on popular appeal and a paycheck rather than musical inventiveness, many of the musicians who played Dixieland and swing music
Paraphrase of source material	satisfied customers with melodies and rhythm that required little audience concentration (Stearns 201). They played music that was danceable because the audiences wanted to dance and music that was familiar because audiences wanted to tap their feet and hum along.

A New Relationship with the Audience

Main idea: developed by order of importance	For Parker, however, jazz became a means of expression, rather than merely entertainment; he constantly searched for ways to communicate musically all that he felt inside (Feather 376). He saw his music not as an audience-centered performance, but as a performer-centered expression. "[His music] emphasized
Writer's additions in brackets	the individual, the solo; and it was existential in the sense that [he] would look for God, for meaning, on a personal level, in the music" (Braxton 328).
Author named in text	Novelist Ralph Ellison reflected that Parker struggled harder than any other jazzman "to escape the entertainer's role"
Point 1: Escaping the entertainer's role	(888). As a result, Parker played "music to listen to," rather than music to dance to or music to have in the background while laughing and talking. It was music, as Jean-Paul Sartre observed, "speaking to the best part of [the audience], the toughest, the freest, to the part which wants neither melody nor refrain, but the deafening climax of the moment" (711). Martin Williams observes that, to Charlie Parker, this change in the meaning of music was essential to the survival of jazz: "We will make it that, Parker seemed to say, or it will perish" (137).
Point 2: Changing musicians' stage presentation	The music was not the only thing that Parker helped to change; the stage presentation of the music also began to change. Lacking any acceptable traditions of performance to guide them, bebop musicians in general, and Parker in particular, were determined not to be the eager-to-please vaudevillians, the "grinning and eye-rolling" entertainers like earlier jazzmen, or stuffy, formal concert performers. In fact, the bebop musicians nearly

ignored the audience; in their performances "they sometimes refused to make even a polite bow to acknowledge the applause of their listeners" (Williams 149).

Of course, Parker did not set out to change the relation of the musicians to the audience. The changes that he made in "the language of jazz" were not self-conscious "impositions," but innovations that came from following "his own artistic impulses" (Williams 136). His musical expression came from "the depths of a tortured soul" (Berendt 89), as he played a "private music," something "more than entertainment" (Harrison, "Jazz" 573). Parker's style pushed bebop further and further away from popular taste, and as a result, Parker's new jazz was never popular in the way that swing and Dixieland were.

Despite Parker's insistence on self-expression, he did experiment with different background music for his solos, in the hope of placing himself in musical history alongside the greats of European tradition (Fordham 111). He tried a string section to give his music a classical aura (Berendt 90; Gammond 445). He even considered, but never carried through with, "a session with five or six woodwinds, a harp, a choral group, and full rhythm section" (qtd. in Hentoff 191).

Still, aside from what many considered these temporary lapses in musical judgment—his recordings with *doo-wah* groups backing him up, as another example—Parker was adamant throughout his career about playing what he wanted and how he wanted, without regard to respect or popularity. He said, "Music is your own experience, your thoughts, your wisdom. If you don't live it, it won't come out of your horn" (Celebrating Bird). An inner circle admired Parker's intensity; jazz pianist Hampton Hawes heard him at Berg's in 1945 and "couldn't believe what [Parker] was doing, how anyone could so totally block out everything extraneous, light a fire that hot inside him and constantly feed on that fire" (573).

However, the general public did not understand that Parker's music came from within. People familiar with Dixieland or swing did not expect "experience, thoughts, or wisdom" to be a part of the musical event. Orrin Keepnews, legendary producer of Riverside Records—the short-lived New York jazz label—says that Parker never learned how "to *sell* himself and his music. He just stood there and played" (qtd. in Berendt 90), and the audience, for the most part, stayed away.

(continued)

Transition to new paragraph

Point 3: Playing music as self-expression

Author of more than one work on Works Cited list

Support from two sources

Videotaped source

Primary source— autobiographical essay

(continued)

Legacy of Parker's Music: Experience the Passing Moment

(continued)

When he left Kansas City for New York in 1938, Parker told his first wife that he wanted to be "set free" so that he could become a great musician (Celebrating Bird). In that freedom, Parker was constantly looking for new forms of musical expression to translate "everything he saw and heard into terms of musical beauty" (Feather 376). Expression was the meaning of the music and the source of the music:

> Everything had a musical significance for Bird. . . . Everything had a musical message for him. If he heard a dog bark, he would say the dog was speaking. . . . or an expression on [a girl's face] would give him an idea for something to play on his solo. (Hentoff 179)

Musically, he never stood still. According to Benny Green this constant change is one of the determining factors of true jazz: At its core modern jazz is "essentially the musical experience of a passing moment, which cannot be repeated in quite the same way" (641). Even if a particular passage worked beautifully for Parker in practice or performance, the next time around he would play it differently. He would not repeat (Williams 134).

Bird was always improvising, always innovating, always experimenting, even on stage. When asked to define what he did, Parker said, "It's just music . . . trying to play clean and looking for the pretty notes" (qtd. in Levin and Wilson 70). To him, his music was always the most important thing, and the discovery of the "beautiful surprise was Charlie Parker's constant quest" (Davis 19).

Legacy of Parker's Music: Technical Contributions

Parker's most important contribution was elevating modern jazz from entertainment to art. In doing so, he also made enormous contributions to technique. His melodies, harmonies, and rhythms—which for decades musicians have tried to imitate—added new dimensions to jazz music.

Melodically, his unusual chord combinations seemed to "skim along the tops" of the original ones (Fordham 28). Harmonically, Parker adventured beyond familiar chord progressions. In his solos, he would sometimes play in harmony with parts of the song other than what the accompaniment was playing, producing "a large-scale effect of polyharmony" (Harrison, "Rare Bird" 208). Rhythmically, he "changed the face of jazz" by playing the saxophone part at "double the time of the tempo

Main idea: developed by logical order

Point 1: Finding new forms of musical expression

Long quotation, indented

Ellipsis points indicate omissions

Point 2: Developing his self-expressive style

Point 3: Always looking for the beautiful surprise of pretty notes

Source of title

Reference to thesis

being asserted by the rhythm section" (Green 647). He could put accents on "heavy beats, weak beats, and the various places between the beats." According to Martin Williams, he was the "most imaginative player rhythmically in jazz history" (139).

Lasting Impact

For some artists the times are right for exactly what they want to give. Some are willing to give exactly what the times invite. Others, like Parker, sacrifice popular reception of their art for the pursuit of personal artistic expression. Parker changed jazz—technically and emotionally. As he explored new territory, he left the audience behind and freed himself and jazz to become new (Green 647, "Bebop"). Because he shifted the performance from entertainment to expression, putting the expressiveness of music first, Charlie Parker was a musician who changed an era.

Works Cited

"Bebop." Britannica Online. Vers. 1994–99. Encyclopaedia Britannica. 11 Nov. 2000. <http://www.eb.com:180>.

Berendt, Joachim. The Jazz Book. Trans. Dan Morgenstern and Helmut and Barbara Bredigkeit. New York: Lawrence Hill, 1973.

Braxton, Anthony. "Anthony Braxton." Reading Jazz. Ed. Robert Gottlieb. New York: Pantheon, 1996. 325–335.

Celebrating Bird: The Triumph of Charlie Parker. Dirs. Gary Giddins and Kendrick Simmons. Videocassette. Sony. 1987.

Davis, Bob. "Golden Bird." Down Beat Dec. 1990: 16–19.

Ellison, Ralph. "On Bird, Bird-Watching, and Jazz." Reading Jazz. Ed. Robert Gottlieb. New York: Pantheon, 1996. 885–892.

Feather, Leonard. The Encyclopedia of Jazz. New York: Bonanza, 1960.

Fordham, John. Jazz. New York: Dorling Kindersley, 1993.

Gammond, Peter. "Charlie Parker." The Oxford Companion to Popular Music. New York: Oxford UP, 1991.

Giddins, Gary. "The Mirror of Swing." Reading Jazz. Ed. Robert Gottlieb. New York: Pantheon, 1996. 484–493.

Green, Benny. "Musical Forms and Genres: Jazz as a Social Force." The New Encyclopedia Britannica: Macropaedia. 15th ed. 1987.

TIP Research papers and their *Works Cited* lists are normally double-spaced. Because of limited space on these pages, A Writer's Model and A Student's Model are single-spaced. The *Elements of Language* Internet site provides a model of a research paper in the double-spaced format. To see this interactive model, go to **go.hrw.com** and enter the keyword **EOLang 11-6.**

(continued)

(continued)

Harrison, Max. "Jazz." The New Grove Dictionary of Music and Musicians. Ed. Stanley Sadie. Vol. 9. London: Macmillan, 1980. 561–579.

---. "A Rare Bird." The Charlie Parker Companion. Ed. Carl Woideck. New York: Schirmer-Simon, 1998. 204–225.

Hawes, Hampton. "At the Hi-De-Ho." Reading Jazz. Ed. Robert Gottlieb. New York: Pantheon, 1996. 573–576.

Hentoff, Nat. Jazz Is. New York: Random, 1974.

Levin, Michael, and John S. Wilson. "No Bop Roots in Jazz: Parker." The Charlie Parker Companion. Ed. Carl Woideck. New York: Schirmer-Simon, 1998. 69–79.

Porter, Bob. "Yardbird Suite: The Ultimate Charlie Parker Collection." 23 February 1999. <http://www.rhino.com/features/liners/722601in.htm>.

Sartre, Jean-Paul. "Jazz in America." Reading Jazz. Ed. Robert Gottlieb. New York: Pantheon, 1996. 710–712.

Stearns, Marshall W. The Story of Jazz. London: Oxford UP, 1958.

Williams, Martin. The Jazz Tradition. New York: Oxford UP, 1993.

TIP Some teachers prefer that the works cited begin on a new page. Be sure to find out what your teacher prefers.

SALLY FORTH reprinted with special permission of King Features Syndicate, Inc.

A Student's Model

The following excerpt from a historical research paper by student writer Ben Lopez of Bridgeport High School in Bridgeport, West Virginia, consists of the introduction and the body paragraphs developing the first main point.

A Lurking Beast:
Events That Caused the Great Depression

During the 1920s American morale was at its highest. A world of glittering automobiles, blaring radios, rambunctious parties, and seemingly general prosperity opened up to the citizens of the country as they scurried like busy ants to and fro in the streets of big cities. However, the Ford Model T Lizzies, the music and stock market reports of local radio stations, and the Prohibition parties were only the false outer appearance of a country nearly in ruin. Deep within the economic structure of the United States of America lay the beginnings of turmoil and despair. A beast—the Great Depression—was sleeping uneasily in the dark recesses of the U.S. economy and soon would rise to wreak havoc upon the nation and the world. What provoked the Great Depression to awaken in October of 1929? What events led to unemployment and a poverty-stricken world? Several factors disprove the popular belief that the Great Depression was caused *only* by a stock market crash (Thorkelson 344). Clearly, the Great Depression was caused by the country's poor management of foreign affairs, the unequal distribution of wealth among the people, the decline of the banking industry and an unnatural boom in the stock market.

Foreign Policy Folly

The United States failed to anticipate the consequences of its actions when dealing with foreign affairs after World War I. After the war ended, the Treaty of Versailles required monetary reparations for the countries devastated by the conflict. The treaty stated that Germany had caused the war and must pay approximately $33 billion, plus interest, to damaged countries, but this amount was more than Germany could pay (Ross 21). Since Germany could not repay all of the countries damaged in the war, the United States loaned a total of $15.7 billion to the Allies and Germany in hopes that their economies

Interesting and informative title

INTRODUCTION
Attention-getting opener

Thought-provoking questions

Overview from encyclopedia research

Thesis statement

BODY
Subhead introduces first point: foreign policy failure

Support

(continued)

(continued)

Correct in-text documentation

Synthesis of two sources

Transition to second main point

would prosper, and consequently, the U.S. would make back the money (Watkins 41). America also hoped that because Europe's economy would improve from the loaned money, foreign purchase of U.S. goods would be stimulated (Watkins 41). Despite the huge monetary sum the U.S. loaned to Europe, the plan failed because the repayment of the loans only drained European economies and rendered them fragile (Thorkelson 344), and Germany suffered terrible inflation (Ross 21).

Surrounding European nations followed Germany into inflation because of the closely knit trade patterns there (Schraff 15), and those countries, even those whose economies did not fail, ceased free trade internationally (Ross 21). In response to this action, U.S. Presidents Warren Harding and Calvin Coolidge both devised strict tariffs on foreign goods to keep them out of the country. Then, in 1922 the tariffs were increased again (Schraff 15). Since the European market was already delicate, "the loss of its American market accelerated the collapse of the European financial structure and the Great Depression swiftly became a worldwide disaster, not merely an American one" (Watkins 44). While government officials were unknowingly selecting unwise foreign policies and distributing money to other countries, the wealth in the U.S. was barely being distributed at all.

Works Cited

Ross, Stewart. Causes and Consequences of the Great
    Depression. Austin: Raintree, 1988.
Schraff, Anne E. The Great Depression and the New Deal:
    America's Economic Collapse and Recovery. New
    York: Watts, 1990.
Thorkelson, H. John. "Great Depression." Encyclopedia
    Americana. 1996 ed.
Watkins, T. H. The Great Depression: America in the
    1930s. Boston: Little, 1993.

Using Quotations

Who Said That?   Using direct quotations can add interest and authority to your historical research paper. If you use too many quotations, however, you leave little room for your own interpretation of the facts. In short, you let others write the paper. The following guidelines show the various ways quotations can be incorporated into your paper, either within sentences or as block quotations.

- **Quote an entire sentence, introducing it in your own words.**

  > Martin Williams observes that, to Charlie Parker, this change in the meaning of music was essential to the survival of jazz: "We will make it that, Parker seemed to say, or it will perish" (137).

- **Quote part of a sentence within a sentence of your own.**

  > Novelist Ralph Ellison reflected that Parker struggled harder than any other jazzman "to escape the entertainer's role" (888).

- **Quote one or more words within a sentence of your own.**

  > The changes that he made in "the language of jazz" were not self-conscious "impositions," but innovations that came from following "his own artistic impulses" (Williams 136).

- **Use ellipsis points (three spaced dots) to indicate omissions from quotations**—words that have been left out, or the continuation of a sentence from the text. (Note that in the example below, the song title is enclosed in single quotation marks because it appears within a quotation.)

  > "I was doing all right until I tried doing double tempo on 'Body and Soul.'. . . Everybody fell out laughing" (qtd. in Hentoff 175).

- **Use square brackets to surround any letters or words you might need to add to a quotation** to make its meaning clear.

  > "[His music] emphasized the individual, the solo" (Braxton 328).

- **Set off longer quotations as "blocks."** If longer than four typed lines, indent the entire quotation ten spaces from the left on a new line. Double-space and do not use quotation marks.

  > What the records . . . affirm is that the man called Bird was one of the protean eagles of jazz fiercely committed to improvisation as a way of musical life. Beautiful surprise was Charlie Parker's constant quest, and so each flight passed for the sake of the next. Except for those that happened to be recorded. (Davis 19)

TIP Too many block quotations will detract from the credibility of your paper as an original work. Use them sparingly.

Documenting Sources

Give Credit Where Credit Is Due The rules for *how* to document sources are clearly specified in whatever style guide you follow. The rules about *what* to document are not so clear. The following guidelines will help you avoid documentation pitfalls.

What to Document	
Yes	Each direct quotation (unless it's widely known, such as Cmdr. John L. Swigert's famous understatement on Apollo 13: "Okay, Houston, we've had a problem.")
Yes	Any original theory or opinion that is not your own, even if not directly quoted. Since ideas belong to their authors, you must, in all honesty, give the authors credit.
Yes	Sources of data from surveys, research studies, and interviews
Yes	Unusual, little-known, or questionable facts
No	Information that appears in several sources or in standard reference books. For example, you do not need to document that Charlie Parker was born in Kansas City because this information appears in many encyclopedias and other standard references.

Reference Note

For more information on the **placement and punctuation of citations,** see page 278 of this chapter.

Pointing the Way Sources of information enclosed in parentheses and placed within the body of your paper are called **parenthetical citations.** Their purpose is to point the way to the fuller reference found in the Works Cited list at the end of a historical research paper. The parenthetical citation should be as close as possible to the material it documents without disrupting the flow of the sentence—usually at the end of the sentence, as in the following example.

> Melodically, his unusual chord combinations seemed to "skim along the tops" of the original ones (Fordham 28).

Parenthetical citations should also be as brief as possible. **For most citations, the last name of the author and the page number are sufficient.** A few exceptions are given below.

- A **nonprint source** such as an interview or videotape will not have a page number.

- A **print source of fewer than two pages** (such as a one-page letter) will not require a page number.

- **For an author named in the sentence,** you need give only the page number (for print sources of more than one page) in parentheses.

> Novelist Ralph Ellison reflected that Parker struggled harder than any other jazzman "to escape the entertainer's role" (888).

■ **For an author who has more than one work in the Works Cited list,** you will also have to give a short form of the title so readers will know which work you are citing.

(Harrison, "Jazz" 571)
(Harrison, "Rare Bird" 208)

Sources do vary, and you will sometimes have to refer to guidelines for correct form for parenthetical citations. The following chart shows the forms for the most common kinds of sources. The examples assume the author or the work has not already been named in a sentence introducing the source's information.

Basic Content and Form for Parenthetical Citations		
Type of Source	**Content of Citation**	**Example**
Sources with one author	Author's last name and a page reference, if any	(Williams 135)
Separate passages in a single source	Author's last name and page references	(Ellison 88, 90–91)
Sources with more than one author	All authors' last names; if over three, use first author's last name and *et al.* (and others)	(Levin and Wilson 70) (Anderson et al. 313)
Multivolume source	Author's last name, plus volume and page	(Cattel 2: 214–215)
Sources with a title only	Full title (if short) or shortened version	(World Almanac 809) ("Birdland" 2)
Literary sources published in many editions	Author's last name, title, and division references (act, scene, canto, book, part, or line numbers) in place of page numbers	(Shakespeare, Hamlet, 3.4.107–108)
Indirect sources	Abbreviation *qtd. in* (quoted in) before the source	(qtd. in Hentoff 175)
More than one source in the same citation	Citations separated with semicolons	(Berendt 90; Gammond 445)

TIP Your teacher may want you to use a documentation style different from the parenthetical citation system above, such as footnotes or endnotes. **Footnotes** and **endnotes** are identical except that a footnote is placed at the bottom of the exact page where you use the source information, while endnotes are listed all together at the end of the report.

In either system, each note is numbered and a number also appears in the body of your report. The first note for a source gives full information; following notes are shortened. The example on the next page illustrates these guidelines.

Number in Body of Report:
For Parker, however, jazz became the way he expressed himself, rather than merely entertainment; he constantly searched for ways to communicate musically all that he felt inside.[2]

Full Form Note:
[2]Feather, Leonard, <u>The Encyclopedia of Jazz</u> (New York: Bonanza, 1960) 376.

TIP A **Works Consulted** list contains *all* the sources you have looked at for your report, whether you cited them or not. Be sure to ask if your teacher wants to see a Works Consulted list instead of, or in addition to, a Works Cited list.

Reference Note

For an **example of a Works Cited list,** see the Writer's Model on page 263.

Follow the Forms The **Works Cited** list contains all the sources, print and nonprint, that you credit in your report. (The term *Works Cited* is a broader title than *Bibliography*, which refers to print sources only.) You may have used other sources, such as general reference works, but if you do not name them in your historical research report, you do not include them in a Works Cited list. Use the following guidelines to prepare your list of Works Cited.

Guidelines for Preparing the List of Works Cited
Center the words *Works Cited*. Ask your teacher if she prefers that the list begin on a new sheet of paper.
Begin each entry on a separate line. Position the first line of the entry even with the left margin, and indent all other lines five spaces. Double-space all entries.
Alphabetize the sources by the author's last name. If there is no author, alphabetize by title, ignoring *A, An,* and *The* and using the first letter of the next word.
If you use two or more sources by the same author, include the author's name only in the first entry. For all other entries, add three hyphens where the author's name would normally be, followed by a period (---.).

The following sample entries, which use the Modern Language Association (MLA) style, are a reference for preparing your Works Cited list. Notice that you include page numbers only for sources that are one part of a whole work, such as one essay in a book of essays.

Sample Entries for the List of Works Cited
Standard Reference Works
If an author is credited in a standard reference work, cite that person's name first in an entry. Otherwise, the title of the book or article appears first. You do not need to cite the editor. Page and volume numbers aren't needed if the work alphabetizes entries. For common reference works, use only the edition (if listed) and the year of publication.

Print Encyclopedia Article

Green, Benny. "Musical Forms and Genres: Jazz." The New Encyclopedia
Britannica: Macropaedia. 15th ed. 1995.

"Parker, Charlie." Encyclopedia Americana: International Edition. 1987 ed.

Article in a Biographical Reference Book

"Parker, Charles Christopher, Jr." Encyclopedia of World Biography. 17
vols. Detroit: Gale, 1998. 105–106.

Books

One Author

Davis, Francis. Bebop and Nothingness: Jazz and Pop at the End of the
Century. New York: Schirmer-Simon, 1996.

Two Authors

Grossman, William L., and Jack W. Farrell. The Heart of Jazz. New York:
New York UP, 1956.

Three Authors

Bregman, Robert, Leonard Bukowski, and Norman Saks. The Charlie
Parker Discography. Redwood, NY: Cadence Jazz Books, 1993.

Four or More Authors

McCarthy, Albert, et al. Jazz on Record: A Critical Guide to the First 50
Years: 1917–1967. London: Hanover, 1968.

No Author Shown

Original Jazz Classics: Collector's Guide. Berkeley: Fantasy, 1995.

Editor of a Collection of Writings

Gottlieb, Robert, ed. Reading Jazz: A Gathering of Autobiography,
Reportage, and Criticism from 1919 to Now. New York: Pantheon, 1996.

Two or Three Editors

Ramsey, Frederic, Jr., and Charles Edward Smith, eds. Jazzmen. New York:
Harcourt, 1939.

Bibliography Published as a Book

Merriman, Alan P., and Robert J. Benford. A Bibliography of Jazz. 1954.
New York: Krause, 1970.

Translation

Berendt, Joachim. The Jazz Book. Trans. Dan Morgenstern and Helmut
and Barbara Bredigkeit. New York: Lawrence Hill, 1973.

(continued)

(continued)

Selections Within Books
From a Book of Works by One Author
Williams, Martin. "Charlie Parker: The Burden of Innovation." The Jazz Tradition. New York: Oxford UP, 1970. 120–137.

From a Book of Works by Several Authors
Feather, Leonard. "Yardbird Flies Home." The Charlie Parker Companion: Six Decades of Commentary. Ed. Carl Woideck. New York: Schirmer-Simon, 1998. 61–64.

Introduction, Preface, Foreword, or Afterword
Gillespie, John "Dizzy." Foreword. The Book of Jazz From Then Till Now: A Guide to the Entire Field. By Leonard Feather. New York: Horizon, 1965. vi–viii.

Articles from Magazines, Newspapers, and Journals
From a Weekly Magazine
Balliett, Whitney. "Jazz: The Bird Lives." New Yorker 6 Jan. 1992: 66–68.

From a Monthly or Quarterly Magazine
Davis, Bob. "Golden Bird." Down Beat Dec. 1990: 16–19.

Anonymous Author
"Jazz Explodes on Charts." Down Beat 14 July 1977: 12.

From a Scholarly Journal
Seeger, Charles. "Music and Class Structure in the United States." American Quarterly 9 (1957): 281–294.

From a Daily Newspaper, with a Byline
Horne, Elliot. "For Cool Cats and Far-Out Chicks." New York Times 18 Aug. 1957, sec. 6: 26.

From a Daily Newspaper, without a Byline
"N.Y.U. Will Teach Jazz." New York Times 15 July 1937: 16.

Unsigned Editorial from a Daily Newspaper, No City in Paper's Title
"Regulated Culture in Prague." Editorial. Christian Science Monitor 13 Mar. 1987: 17.

Other Sources
Personal Interview
Davis, Peter Jeffrey. Personal interview. 2 Dec. 1998.

Telephone Interview
Edwards, Charles. Telephone interview. 18 Oct. 1998.

Published Interview
Gillespie, Dizzy. Interview. Jazz Spoken Here: Conversations with Twenty-two Musicians. By Wayne Enstice and Paul Rubin. New York: Da Capo, 1994. 171–184.

Broadcast or Recorded Interview

Farmer, Art. Interview with Marty Moss-Coane. Fresh Air. Natl. Public Radio. WHYY, Philadelphia. 22 Jan. 1999.

Published Letter

Parker, Doris. "To Bob Reisner." 31 Dec. 1956. Letter in Bird: The Legend of Charlie Parker. By Robert George Reisner. New York: Da Capo, 1975. 172–177.

Unpublished Letter or E-Mail Message

Clinton, Katherine. Letter to the author. 22 Jan. 1998.

Reed, Peter. E-mail to the author. 9 July 1998.

Unpublished Thesis or Dissertation

Hansen, Chadwick Clarke. "The Ages of Jazz: A Study of Jazz in Its Cultural Context." Diss. U of Minnesota, 1956.

Sound Recording

Parker, Charlie. Charlie Parker: The Legendary Dial Masters. Jazz Classics, 1996.

Film or Video Recording

Celebrating Bird: The Triumph of Charlie Parker. Dirs. Gary Giddins and Kendrick Simmons. Videocassette. Sony, 1987.

Note: Always include the title, director or producer, distributor, and year. For video recordings, add a description of the medium (Videodisc or Videocassette) before the distributor's name.

Material Accessed Through the Internet

"Bebop." Britannica Online. Vers. 1994–99. Encyclopaedia Britannica. 11 Nov. 2000. <http://www.eb.com:180>.

Article from a CD-ROM Reference Work

Pen, Ron. "Jazz." The 1998 Groliers Multimedia Encyclopedia. CD-ROM. Danbury: Grolier Interactive Inc., 1998.

Full-Text Magazine, Newspaper, or Journal Article from a CD-ROM Database

"Why Jazz Music Will Never Die." Jet 16 Feb. 2000: 15–17. MAS FullTEXT Select Version 5.1. CD-ROM. EBSCO Publishing, 1996.

 YOUR TURN 9 **Documenting Sources**

Refine your parenthetical citations and add them to your research paper, if you haven't done so. Make sure they conform to MLA style or to the style your teacher has chosen. Then, prepare the Works Cited list for your paper. Follow the guidelines on page 270 and consult the sample entries on pages 271–273.

Revising

Evaluate and Revise Content, Organization, and Style

Twice Is Nice   To assess your writing effectively, work collaboratively to read through your paper at least twice. The first time, evaluate content and organization. Then, in your second reading, revise for style.

▷ **First Reading: Content and Organization**   The following chart can help you to determine whether you have clearly communicated your research. If you need help answering the questions in the first column, use the tips in the middle column. Then, revise your paper by making the changes suggested in the last column.

Historical Research Report: Content and Organization Guidelines for Peer and Self- Evaluation

Evaluation Questions	▶ Tips	▶ Revision Techniques
❶ Does the introduction grab the reader's attention, give an overview of the topic, and state the thesis?	**Underline** the attention-grabbing information; **bracket** the background information or overview of research; **circle** the thesis statement. If any of these elements is missing, revise.	**Add** a quotation or interesting detail to your first sentence. **Add** background information or **elaborate** on details that clarify your research. **Add** a sentence or two stating your thesis.
❷ Is the thesis developed by several main ideas? Are the ideas supported by factual information?	In the margin, **check** each main idea that develops the thesis. In the text, **double-check** at least one piece of supporting information for each idea. If there are not at least three ideas and support for each, revise.	**Add** main ideas to develop your thesis; consult your outline and note cards for ideas you may have missed. **Delete** ideas that do not support the thesis. **Elaborate** on each idea with material drawn from your research.
❸ Is some source material stated in the writer's own words? Are sources credited when necessary? Are the citations in the correct MLA format?	**Circle** all direct quotations. **Place stars** by direct quotations and facts that are not common knowledge. If direct quotations comprise more than half of the paper, or if sources are not documented (or incorrectly documented), revise.	**Replace** some quotations with paraphrases or summaries. **Add** documentation for quoted, summarized, and paraphrased material. Revise and correct citations.
❹ Are the ideas presented in an order that makes sense?	**Number** your main ideas. Revise if the order makes no sense or is unclear.	**Rearrange** the order of ideas for clarity. Try chronological or logical order.
❺ Does the conclusion restate the thesis?	**Bracket** the restatement of the thesis. Revise if the thesis is not restated.	**Add** a sentence that returns the readers to the purpose of the research.

ONE WRITER'S REVISIONS   Here is how one writer used the content and organization guidelines to revise some sentences which appear, in revised form, in the research paper on pages 259–264. Study the revisions and answer the questions following the paragraph.

Bird was always improvising, always innovating, always

experimenting, even on stage. ~~Dizzy Gillespie liked to play prac-~~   **delete**

~~tical jokes on stage.~~ When asked to define what he did, Parker

, *"It's just music . . . trying to play clean and looking for the*   **add quotation**

said ~~he looked for pretty notes.~~ To him, his music was always   **add documentation**

pretty notes" (qtd. in Levin and Wilson 70)

the most important thing, and the discovery of the "beautiful

surprise was Charlie Parker's constant quest" (Davis 19).

Analyzing the Revision Process

1. Why do you think the writer deleted the second sentence?
2. Why do the other changes improve the paragraph?

YOUR TURN 10   **Focusing on Content and Organization**

Revise your paper for content and organization using the guidelines in the chart. Use the example revisions shown above as a model.

Second Reading: Style   Your style, or the way you express your ideas, is important in a long and complex research paper. To succeed in your purpose of informing readers, you must keep their attention. One way to do so is to vary the way you begin your sentences. Using the following style guideline, work collaboratively to evaluate and refine your sentence beginnings.

PEER REVIEW

Ask a classmate to read your paper and to answer the following questions:

1. What was the most interesting information you learned from the writer's historical research?
2. Do you think the research sources are reliable? Why?

Style Guidelines

Evaluation Question	▶ Tip	▶ Revision Technique
❶ Do many of the sentences begin the same way?	▶ **Underline** the first five words of each sentence. If most subjects and verbs are underlined, revise.	▶ **Rearrange** or **combine** sentences to place dependent clauses at the beginning. Rephrase when necessary.

Focus on Sentences

Varying Sentence Beginnings

If all of your sentences start with a subject and verb of a main clause, your paper may seem boring. You can vary sentence beginnings by starting some sentences with a dependent clause, such as an adverb clause.

■ Rearrange an existing sentence to start with a dependent clause.

Before There were two types of jazz—swing and Dixieland revival—**when Charlie Parker was born in Kansas City in 1920.**

After **When Charlie Parker was born in Kansas City in 1920,** there were two types of jazz: swing and Dixieland revival.

■ Combine sentences and begin with a dependent clause.

Before Parker told his first wife that he wanted to be "set free." He told her this **when he left Kansas City for New York in 1938.**

After **When he left Kansas City for New York in 1938,** Parker told his first wife that he wanted to be "set free."

ONE WRITER'S REVISIONS Here is how the writer of the Writer's Model on page 259 used the above guidelines.

BEFORE REVISION

Parker changed jazz—technically and emotionally. He left the audience behind as he explored new territory and freed himself and jazz to become new (Green 647, "bebop"). He shifted the performance from entertainment to expression, putting the expressiveness of music first. Charlie Parker was a musician who changed an era.

All the sentences follow the same subject-verb pattern.

AFTER REVISION

Parker changed jazz—technically and emotionally. As he explored new territory, he left the audience behind and freed himself and jazz to become new (Green 647, "bebop"). Because he shifted the performance from entertainment to expression, putting the expressiveness of music first, Charlie Parker was a musician who changed an era.

Rearrange an existing sentence.

Combine using dependent clauses.

Analyzing the Revision Process

1. Why does the revised paragraph read more smoothly than the first one?

2. How does changing the sentence beginnings affect the clarity of the writing? Why?

YOUR TURN 11 **Varying Sentence Beginnings**

Revise your research paper for varied sentence beginnings, referring to the sample revisions as a model. Use the style guideline and the list of suggested sentence beginnings to help you revise.

Designing Your Writing

Using Subheads   Subheads can make a research paper easier to follow and help readers find specific information quickly. Subheads, which correspond to the major points in your outline, should concisely announce the main idea of the text that follows it. However, do not use a subhead for every paragraph in your paper, since this will prove confusing. Reserve subheads for larger sections of your research paper. In general, you should use phrases as subheads instead of sentences because phrases are easier to read. The following example of a subhead is from the Writer's Model on page 259.

> ### Lasting Impact
>
> For some artists the times are right for exactly what they want to give. Some are willing to give exactly what the times invite. Others, like Parker, sacrifice popular reception of their art for the pursuit of personal artistic expression.

Notice that the subhead above concisely announces the content of the section. Notice also that the subhead is flush with the left margin and written in boldface type. Try a different font size and typeface, if you wish. Remember, however, that a historical research paper is a formal, academic report, and its design must give that impression. Once you decide on a design, be consistent throughout your report.

TIP   Make sure your subhead phrases are parallel—all nouns, all gerunds—throughout your paper. For example, the subheads "Using an online database" and "Using CD-ROMs" are parallel, whereas the subheads "Online database" and "Using CD-ROMs" are not.

TIP   If you type or handwrite your paper, consider underscoring your subheads.

Publishing

Proofread Your Essay

Reference Note

For more on **proof-reading,** see pages 13 and 1044.

Show Off So that your readers will fully appreciate your historical research report, proofread it carefully to see that you have followed the standard conventions of formal writing. Work collaboratively with a classmate to check spelling as well as the correct use of conventions of punctuation such as italics, ellipses, and dashes. Pay particular attention to the placement and punctuation of citations. Whether you have typed or handwritten your report, make sure the final product is legible and error-free.

Grammar Link

Punctuating Citations Correctly

A citation in the text of your paper should provide just enough information to lead the reader to the full source listing in the Works Cited. Always place the citation as close as possible to the material being documented. The following guidelines for parenthetical citations are from MLA. Ask if your teacher requires a different form.

- **Always place the citation before the punctuation mark** within a sentence that contains the documented passage.

   "He just stood there and played" **(qtd. in Berendt 90),** and the audience . . .

- **When a quotation ends a sentence, put the citation after the quotation mark but before the period.**

   "It was his desire to devote his life to the translation of everything he saw and heard into terms of musical beauty**" (Feather 376).**

- **Place the citation for a block quotation two spaces after the final punctuation mark.**

   . . . to play on his solo. **(Hentoff 179)**

PRACTICE

Use the guidelines to the left to rewrite the following sentences on your own paper. Correctly place and punctuate the parenthetical citations. Write a C on your paper for correct citations.

1. A composer might have taken hours writing it, but "Parker simply stood up and improvised the chorus." (Williams 134)

2. Bebop "developed—at first in spurts—originally in Kansas City" (Berendt 16), then gained a wider audience in New York City.

3. The early bebop musicians "became quite clannish" about whom they played for and whom they listened to. (Barnet 169)

4. Band leader Jay McShann explains the impact of Bird's playing (qtd. in Giddins, "Bird Lives" 5): "You know the first time you hear Bird, you *hear* it—you've got to hear it."

5. Charlie Parker's first improvisations were rivaled only by those of Louis Armstrong in their "sheer fire, originality, and revolutionary influence (Fordham 111)."

Publish Your Paper

Everything You Wanted to Know About . . .   You have collected a great deal of information and tied it together. Here are some ways you might share your historical research paper with others, using a variety of formats.

- Save your historical research paper as a writing sample to submit for a college or job application.

- If you know a friend or relative who would be interested in the topic you have written about, add historical illustrations to your paper, bind it, and send it to the person as a gift.

- If the topic would be of interest to students in lower grades, send your paper to a teacher who teaches a related subject to those students.

- Submit your paper to a local historical club for a possible public reading.

- Surf the Web to discover sites related to your historical research topic, and submit your paper for possible online publication.

TIP   Before you publish, give your paper an interesting and informative **title.** Rather than "A Research Paper on Charlie Parker," search for a title that hints at your thesis and sparks curiosity, such as "Beautiful Surprises from an Alto Sax: Charlie Parker's Place in Jazz History." Sometimes the title is presented on a separate page; ask your teacher for the preferred format.

Reflect on Your Essay

PORTFOLIO

Taking Stock   Writing short responses to the following questions will help you to learn about yourself as a writer. Include these notes in your portfolio, along with the final version of your essay.

- How did you choose a research topic? What interested you the most about that topic?

- What did you learn about research strategies? What will you do differently the next time you conduct historical research?

- What did you enjoy about this project? What are you proud of?

- Did your research experience alter your attitude toward professional historians? How?

- How did your research experience affect your understanding of the study of history? How did it affect your understanding of your topic?

YOUR TURN 12   Proofreading, Publishing and Reflecting

Before you turn in your research report, review the steps in the previous section. Proofread your paper carefully, think about publishing options, and reflect on your work.

The Uses of History in Fiction

Writers of fiction often do historical research to write convincingly about the customs and concerns of people living in a previous time period. Many favorites from American literature, including *The Scarlet Letter, Moby-Dick, The Adventures of Huckleberry Finn,* and *A Raisin in the Sun,* have a historical context. Their authors tie historical fact to literature for various purposes, such as

- **to explore contemporary issues from a safe distance or to draw a parallel between past and present events** (In *The Crucible,* Arthur Miller uses the Salem trials as a way to explore the hysteria of the 1950s-era McCarthy hearings.)

- **to correct common thinking about a historical event** (John Steinbeck's, *The Grapes of Wrath* gives a human context to the miserable conditions of the 1930s Dust Bowl Oklahomans who migrated to California, hoping for a better life.)

- **to confront prejudice about a minority culture** (In *O, Pioneers!* Willa Cather celebrates as heroic figures those nineteenth-century immigrants who came from Eastern Europe to settle in the American Midwest.)

- **to depict the psychological effects of war** (In *Cold Mountain,* Charles Frazier explores the impact of the Civil War, as he tells the story of Inman, a wounded deserter.)

So why read history and fiction together? By doing so, readers gain valuable insights about both facts and emotions—how events happened and what it felt like to live through them. For example, reading the fictional *I Am Amelia Earhart* and a biography such as *Amelia: The Centennial Biography of an Aviation Pioneer* could be a fascinating journey into what we know about Earhart and also what she might have been thinking as she flew over the wide ocean. When reading history and fiction together, consider the following questions:

- How has reading history and fiction together broadened your understanding of a particular historical event, person, or era?

- How does the fictional work amplify, change or falsify the historical facts? Why do you think the author made the changes?

- What can fiction reveal better than straightforward histories? What can histories tell us about the past that fiction cannot?

YOUR TURN 13 Exploring the Uses of History in Fiction

Select a work of fiction that has a historical setting. Then, explore and analyze the author's use of history in the fictional work. Finally, prepare for the class a short presentation on your findings. You might want to use maps, photos, time lines, or diagrams to clarify historical events.

Evaluating Web Sites

I n their quest for information, historical researchers explore as many different sources as possible. Many turn to the World Wide Web—and its wealth of information—to get ideas for a research topic, to find authoritative information (including links to other Web sites), or to discover opinions (and possible quotations). Not just any information will do, however. Historical researchers look for **legitimate and reliable Web sites.**

Checking for Reliability

Stop. Think, "Is This a Good Idea?" The World Wide Web is like a global-sized filing cabinet, and *anyone* can slip *any kind* of file into it—in *any language* and for *any* reason. Because, at present, no gatekeeping or filtering system exists, you must first evaluate each Web site before you use it for your historical research. How can you distinguish a reliable Web site from an unreliable one? One way to begin is to recognize the various types of Web sites. Look, for example, at the following five categories:

- **Advocacy Web pages** support the goals of a particular organization. Because they aim to shape or sway public opinion, their information may be biased.

- **Commercial Web pages** primarily advertise or sell goods or services. Most search engines also place advertisements on their home pages.

- **Informational Web pages** often come from the servers of government or educational institutions, which use *gov* or *edu* in their URLs, or Web addresses. These Web sites might include information in the form of reports, schedules, directories, and encyclopedias.

- **News Web pages** come from news media organizations and report on current happenings. Their URLs usually contain *com* or *org* in the domain name. Many newspapers and nationally distributed magazines—as well as local and national radio and television networks—have online databases.

- **Personal home pages** are created by individuals for a variety of reasons—from sharing recipes to informing others about a rare disease. Their URLs often use a slash (/), a tilde (~), and perhaps a personal name attached to any of the above URL suffixes.

WHAT'S AHEAD?

In this section, you will learn to

- **evaluate Web sites for historical research reports**
- **use computer bookmarks to mark valuable sites**

TIP Currently, a URL (Uniform Resource Locator) from a college, university, or government agency does not *absolutely* guarantee that the site is reliable. Anyone associated with that organization can publish a site on its server. You must read the content of the Web page to understand who created the message and whether that source is reliable and objective.

Reference Note

To review the 4R **evaluation** criteria for traditional sources, see page 251 in this chapter.

For historical research reports, you most likely will search informational Web sites. The criteria for evaluating these Web sites are similar to the criteria for evaluating traditional sources—the author's credentials, the accuracy and quality of the information, and the date of publication. The following chart will also help you in your evaluation.

Criteria for Evaluating Web Sites	Related Questions
Coverage refers to the amount of information on the Web page and to the uniqueness of the information.	Is this the information I need? Is it complete enough to be useful? Is it available through more accessible sources such as library reference books?
Accuracy refers to the information's correctness. (Spelling and grammar errors generally indicate inaccurate information.)	Does the information on the Web site match information I have seen in other sources? Are claims backed by evidence? Are other reliable sources cited within the Web page?
Authority refers to the qualifications of the Web site's creator and publisher. Sometimes the authority is difficult to establish.	Has the Web site's creator shown any credentials that qualify him or her to write on this topic? Is the publisher respected in the field?
Currency refers to dates for creation, publication, and revision of the Web site. These dates—if available—usually appear at the bottom of the home page.	Is the information up-to-date? When was it last revised? Is the information likely to have changed since the page was updated?
Objectivity refers to the site's degree of bias—how much the author's feelings about the topic influences the information presented.	Is the Web site persuading you to adopt a certain point of view? Are both sides of an issue given? Who will benefit if the information is taken to be true?
Clarity refers to the visual dimensions of the Web page's design and the accuracy of its hyperlinks.	Can you easily navigate the site—is the design clear and the page uncluttered? Is the page logically organized? Do images load quickly?
Stability refers to how likely it is for the site to remain on the Web. (Web pages from educational institutions will probably last longer than pages published to advance a personal agenda.)	Will the site still exist if one of your readers wants to check your data or pursue your topic through your sources? (If you have doubts, be sure to make a hard copy of the appropriate pages.)

TIP As you evaluate a Web site, always think about who made it and why it was made. As you assess the site's clarity, also think about how design elements such as shape, line, and color contribute to the message.

TIP Librarians and other information specialists have accumulated many helps for evaluating Web sites and have published those helps on the World Wide Web. To find some of these documents, try typing in the keywords "evaluating web sites" into your favorite search engine.

While researching Charlie Parker's influence on jazz, the writer of the historical research report on page 259 found the following Web site, called Jazz Web, which is sponsored by the public broadcasting station on the campus of Northwestern University. Notice how the student used the criteria from the chart above to evaluate the Web site.

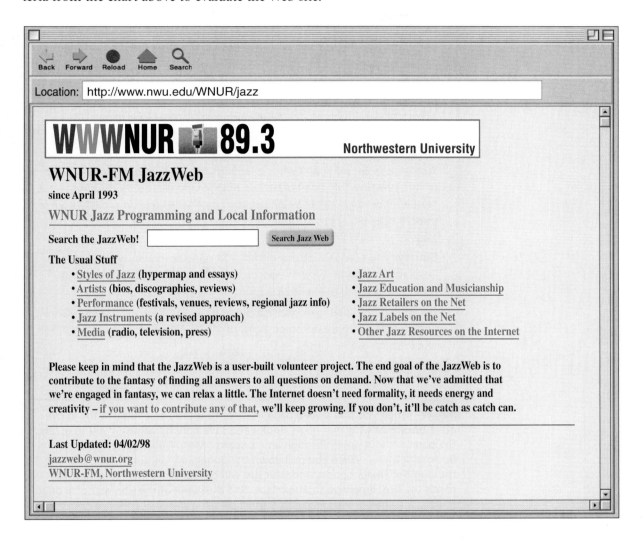

Location: http://www.nwu.edu/WNUR/jazz

WWWNUR 89.3   Northwestern University

WNUR-FM JazzWeb
since April 1993

WNUR Jazz Programming and Local Information

Search the JazzWeb! [   ] Search Jazz Web

The Usual Stuff
- Styles of Jazz (hypermap and essays)
- Artists (bios, discographies, reviews)
- Performance (festivals, venues, reviews, regional jazz info)
- Jazz Instruments (a revised approach)
- Media (radio, television, press)
- Jazz Art
- Jazz Education and Musicianship
- Jazz Retailers on the Net
- Jazz Labels on the Net
- Other Jazz Resources on the Internet

Please keep in mind that the JazzWeb is a user-built volunteer project. The end goal of the JazzWeb is to contribute to the fantasy of finding all answers to all questions on demand. Now that we've admitted that we're engaged in fantasy, we can relax a little. The Internet doesn't need formality, it needs energy and creativity – if you want to contribute any of that, we'll keep growing. If you don't, it'll be catch as catch can.

Last Updated: 04/02/98
jazzweb@wnur.org
WNUR-FM, Northwestern University

- **Coverage:** This site has several interesting hyperlinks, especially one to a map of jazz history. None of the hyperlinks had in-depth coverage, however. When I entered "Charlie Parker" as a search term, I found a quotation about Parker that I had not seen before.

(continued)

(continued)

- **Accuracy:** Many of the hyperlinks lead to names and quotations I know are accurate from my other research.
- **Authority:** The sponsoring University and FM radio station are reputable. The creators of the site are clearly identified, and while they may be students, they are obviously knowledgeable about jazz. For example, the hyperlink to the jazz map cites a noted author, whose name and book I recognize as authoritative.
- **Currency:** The last update of this site was 04 Apr 1998. This is not very current; but the lack of a more current update does not affect the usefulness of the particular information I'm seeking because this topic is about the 1940s and 50s.
- **Objectivity:** The note following the hyperlink list indicates that this Web site is an all-volunteer project intended as a complete source of information for jazz buffs. The site is sponsored by an educational site—the FM station on the Northwestern University campus. It doesn't seem to have a bias except that the members like jazz.
- **Clarity:** The site is well organized and easy to read—with hyperlinks and a box to type in search terms. One link I tried, however, resulted in a "Page Does Not Exist" message.
- **Stability:** The site has existed since at least 1993. Although it has not been updated since April of 1998, it will probably remain on the Web for some time.

TIP When you find a Web page that seems useful, you might want to create a **bookmark** for that page. Bookmarks save time by allowing you to access the page without going through a new search. Most Web browsers have a Bookmark Menu. When you pull down the *Bookmark* menu bar item, click on the *Add Bookmark* option, and your site will be marked. When you want to revisit the site, simply go to *Bookmark,* find the name of the site, and click on it.

 **YOUR TURN 14 Evaluating Web Sites**

Review the criteria for evaluating Web sites. On your own paper, write an evaluation of a Web site you used in preparing your historical research report. (If you did not consult a Web site in researching your paper, choose one now that is related to the same topic.)

Choices

Choose one of the following activities to complete.

▶ **CROSSING THE CURRICULUM: SCIENCE OR MATHEMATICS**

1. Life in Pieces Choose a famous mathematician or scientist, and use your research skills to prepare a **biographical poster.** In the center of the poster, draw or paste a picture of the person. Around the picture, write twelve short factual statements about the person's life. Write the name of your subject at the top of the poster and a significant quotation by or about the subject at the bottom. Document your sources.

▶ **VIEWING AND REPRESENTING**

2. Minute View Use a software application to prepare a two- or three-minute **multimedia presentation** on the subject of your historical research. Use images from the Internet, or scan in images to use in your presentation. Add appropriate music, commentary, and text. Be sure to document your sources.

▶ **CAREERS**

3. Top Three List three careers that interest you. Think of one that is possible but unlikely, one that you would love to do if it only paid well, and one that seems a very safe choice. Interview someone in each of these careers, using the interviewing techniques discussed on page 986 in the Quick Reference Handbook. Write a short **report,** and share what you learned with the class.

▶ **MEDIA AND TECHNOLOGY**

4. Technically Speaking Interview a professional (a technical writer, an academic writer, a lawyer, or a newspaper reporter, for example) about the writing strategies necessary for his or her profession. Make an **audiotape** or **videotape** of your interview. Then, present the information to your classmates and play selected portions of the audiotape or videotape to illustrate your major points.

▶ **SPEAKING AND LISTENING**

5. An Oral Version Use the information in your historical research report to create an **oral report.** Put main ideas and major supporting details on easy-to-handle notecards. Create visual aids, such as time lines and graphs, to make your oral presentation more compelling.

PORTFOLIO

Taking a Stand

FOOD WILL WIN THE WAR

You came here seeking Freedom
You must now help to preserve it

WHEAT is needed for the allies
Waste nothing

UNITED STATES FOOD ADMINISTRATION

**Reading
Workshop**

*Reading
an Editorial*

**Writing
Workshop**

*Writing
an Editorial*

**Speaking and
Listening**

*Writing and
Delivering a
Persuasive Speech*

**Viewing and
Representing**

*Creating a
Political Campaign*

Convincing Others

- Teenagers should not be allowed to drive until they are eighteen.
- Helmets should be required by law for all bicycle riders.
- Because of its inflated budget, the space station should not be built.

If you have a strong reaction to any or all of these statements, you may feel the urge to convince others to agree with your opinions. That feeling is the basis of **persuasion.** Whether you realize it or not, you are surrounded by messages trying to persuade you to do something or to think something. Many of these messages are trivial, such as which shampoo to buy. Others can have world-shaking consequences, such as whether one nation should take military action against another. This latter kind of message is often found in an **editorial,** an opinion essay published in a newspaper or a magazine or aired on radio or television. On a special page called the opinion-editorial ("Op-ed") page, or in a designated spot of airtime, the editorialist tries to persuade the audience to share a specific opinion on an important issue, and in many cases to take action.

> **Informational
> Text**
>
> **Persuasion**

YOUR TURN 1   Brainstorming About Editorials

With two or three classmates, brainstorm a list of ten current issues editorial writers might address. The issues may range from local to global. For each issue, suggest which media would be the most likely forum: school newspaper, local newspaper, national newsmagazine, specialized magazine, radio, local television, or national television. Why did you suggest certain media for certain issues?

internet**connect**

go.
hrw
.com
GO TO: go.hrw.com
KEYWORD: EOLang 11-7

Reading an Editorial

ditorial writers make an argument designed to change the opinions, beliefs, and actions of a large audience. Editorials may affect the opinions of ordinary readers, leaders in government and other fields, and even journalists, whose reporting may be subtly influenced by views they absorb from editorials. Reading editorials is one of the best ways to increase your understanding of current events, as long as you keep in mind that you are reading opinion, not fact. You should always read editorials critically to determine what the views of the writer are, what persuasive techniques he or she has used to try to convince you of those views, and how valid those techniques are.

Preparing to Read

READING SKILL

Point of View/Bias   No human being can be entirely objective; every writer's opinions about an issue are affected by his or her **point of view**—the way he or she sees things. Having a point of view on an **issue,** a topic about which people have opposing opinions, is not a bad thing. Sometimes, however, a strong, fixed, emotional view, or **bias,** on an issue causes a writer to paint an unfair picture either by omitting important facts that favor the other side, sneaking in faulty logic, or obscuring the issue with an overload of highly charged words. Recognizing the writer's point of view and any biases will help you evaluate an editorial argument. As you read the editorial on the next page, ask yourself what the writers' point of view is and whether it seems biased or fair.

READING FOCUS

Persuasive Appeals   To persuade you, editorial writers appeal to you in a variety of ways. They appeal to your mind by using **logic**—reasons supported by evidence. They appeal to your heart by choosing words that carry **emotion.** They appeal to **ethics**—your sense of right and wrong—by trying to gain your trust. Your responsibility as a reader is to recognize the effect these appeals have on you. Make sure you are not being convinced of something against your better judgment. As you read "Cleaning Up College Basketball," look for the appeals the writers use to try to convince you.

In the following editorial, the authors take a stand for reform in college basketball. Do they convince you? In your notebook, jot down answers to the active-reading questions.

from THE NEW YORK TIMES **OP-ED** Saturday, September 5, 1998

Cleaning Up College Basketball

by LEE C. BOLLINGER AND TOM GOSS

1. From the wording of the title, what can you determine about the authors' attitude?

ANN ARBOR, Mich.

Jim Delany, commissioner of the Big Ten, recently announced a proposal for major reforms in N.C.A.A. Division I men's basketball, a sport that has witnessed far too many scandals involving recruiting and player behavior. These reforms will not be readily embraced by N.C.A.A. members and the National Basketball Association—dramatic changes are always difficult to accept—but they must be adopted if we are to cure the ills that afflict this sport.

2. How does the phrase "if we are to cure the ills that afflict this sport" make you feel about the issue?

Many of college basketball's problems—and we've not been immune to some of them at Michigan—stem from the vast amounts of cash poured into the sport by shoe and apparel companies, money that has drastically changed the way colleges recruit high-school-age players.

Recruiting by the 310 members of the National Collegiate Athletic Association's Division I (the highest level of competition) used to be through contact with the players' high school coaches and their parents. But parents and coaches are no longer the primary influence for these young men in decisions about their futures.

3. What is the first reason the authors give as the cause of the problems involving players and recruiting?

Instead, a network of summer basketball camps bankrolled by shoe companies has taken over the recruiting process. Hoping to attract the loyalties of players with star potential, the companies spend more than $5 million a year on these summer programs. The young men in this system sometimes play 80 to 100 games outside of the high school season.

In addition, private coaches, also financed by shoe companies, favor certain players in their summer programs and control access to their star players. A pattern of behavior is established as early as junior high school in which players are wooed by agents, given free merchandise, and treated to other benefits that are forbidden at the college level.

Break the stranglehold of summer camps.

When players accustomed to such treatment reach college, where they must combine basketball with academics, it's not surprising that so many of them encounter difficulties. The commissioner's proposal to prohibit summer recruiting by college coaches and their staffs would take some of the power out of the summer camp machine and return the focus to the academic year and the high school basketball system, where it belongs.

Another troubling trend is the head-long rush by high school and college players toward professional careers. Increasingly these young men are focused not on getting a college education, but on how quickly they can get to the N.B.A., where big money beckons. From the minute they set foot on campus, their on-court performance is assessed in the coin of draft picks and signing bonuses. The graduation rate for men's basketball, 44 percent, is the lowest of any Division I sport.

Many of those who leave school after only one or two years fail to live up to their potential. Not only are their basketball skills underdeveloped, but so are their life skills. And without a college degree, these players have few career options if they are not successful at the professional level.

Two changes, both part of the commissioner's proposed reforms, must be made to turn college basketball back into an environment where student athletes are, first and foremost, concerned about being students.

First, freshmen should be ineligible to play on Division I basketball teams— as they were until the early 1970's. This would help limit the amount of time first-year students spend traveling to games and would give them a chance to focus on their studies and the adjustment to college life.

Second, the N.B.A., its owners and its players' union should voluntarily change the way players are drafted. A player who chooses to attend college should not be eligible to be drafted until completing at least three years (similar to the systems now used by baseball and hockey). These athletes would be closer to completing their degrees, and the N.B.A. would benefit because players would have better-developed skills and more maturity.

Critics will argue that these changes would raise the cost of running a Division I men's basketball program. But the additional cost would not be that high, not enough to prevent us from doing what is right. At stake are the futures of thousands of young men whose well-being we should have as our first priority.

Lee C. Bollinger is president of the University of Michigan, and Tom Goss is the director of athletics.

4. What is a stranglehold? How does the word "stranglehold" in this context make you feel? What do you think is the purpose of the pullout quotation?

5. How does the phrase "doing what is right" affect your image of the authors and your opinion on the issue?

6. Why might knowing the author's credentials be important?

Point of View/Bias

Where Are You Coming From?   Persuasive writers do not want to conceal or disguise their views. On the contrary, in most cases they directly state their position on an issue as a **position statement** or **opinion statement.** This statement often contains the word *should* or *must*. One useful strategy on first reading an editorial is to skim until you locate the opinion statement, the clearest and most concise presentation of the editorial's message. Be aware that an editorial writer will probably *not* tell you to what extent his or her point of view is **biased,** or unfair and unreasonable. You will need to figure that out for yourself, a task which involves evaluating the writer's support for his or her opinion.

The following chart shows various examples of techniques that signal biased writing. Finding these kinds of techniques in a piece of persuasive writing should raise a red flag about the writer's reasoning.

TIP   The term **point of view,** in this context, does not mean exactly the same thing as *point of view* in the narration of a work of fiction. In fiction, *point of view* refers to who is telling the tale. In persuasive writing, a point of view is an opinion or outlook. For more on point of view in fiction, see Chapter 5.

Techniques Signaling Biased Writing	Examples
One-sidedness: presenting only one side of an issue	When advocating mandatory recycling, the writer fails to mention the high cost of implementing such a program.
Name Calling: using a derogatory term to identify a person	In an editorial in favor of vegetarianism, the writer calls people who eat meat "murderers."
Bandwagon: implying that since other people are doing something, you should do it, too	To convince readers to buy a certain athletic shoe, the writer focuses on how popular the shoe is with the high school crowd.

(continued)

(continued)

TIP Often a bio-graphical note about the writer is included with an editorial. Use the information to help you identify the writer's bias or to gauge the credibility of the writer.

For example, if an article addresses whether or not marine mammals should be kept in amusement parks, you might trust a marine biologist with thirty years' experience more than you would trust an average citizen writing to the local newspaper or an owner of such an amusement park.

Half-truths: giving two linked statements, one of which is true and the other of which is false or misleading	To persuade people that Dallas needs transportation reforms, a writer states "Three Texas cities have close to or over a million people, and Dallas is the largest." The first fact is true; the second is not, for Houston is the largest.
Implication by Association: awarding praise or guilt simply by association	In an editorial or a political ad, a writer implies that a candidate is untrustworthy because a member of the same party has been convicted of a crime.
Loaded Words: using words that carry strong, emotional connotations, whether negative or positive	One political ad may describe its candidate as *upright* and *patriotic*. The opposition might say that the candidate is instead *self-righteous* and *extremist*.

THINKING IT THROUGH **Determining Point of View/Bias**

To determine the point of view and bias of a writer, you can use the following steps.

▶ **STEP 1** **Look for an opinion statement and for other direct statements of beliefs.** Opinion statements often include *should* or *must*. If you find no outright statement, ask yourself, "What does the writer want me to believe or do?"

▶ **STEP 2** **Identify any connotative or "loaded" language or descriptions of highly charged situations.** What attitude toward his or her subject does the writer's use of language reveal? Does the writer describe situations that tend to trigger strong emotional responses in people?

▶ **STEP 3** **Look for devices of biased writing, as shown in the chart above.** For example, does the writer present a series of one-sided statements without evidence?

▶ **STEP 4** **Consider what you know about the writer's background.** Might a personal interest in the issue cause the writer to be biased? For example, if the owner of an amusement park writes an editorial about the safety of amusement park rides, would you question his or her personal interest?

YOUR TURN 2 **Determining Point of View/Bias**

Use the steps outlined above to determine the point of view and possible bias of the authors of the editorial "Cleaning Up College Basketball." Meet with a partner to discuss your findings.

Persuasive Appeals

Heart, Mind, and Spirit Good persuasive writing uses a balance of different kinds of appeals in order to reach a variety of readers. **Emotional appeals** target the reader's feelings; **logical appeals** aim at the intellect; **ethical appeals** reach out to the sense of right and wrong. Reader X may be most impressed by logical appeals; Reader Y may be easily touched by emotional appeals. To win over skeptical Reader Z, every possible kind of appeal may be needed.

Emotional appeals Appeals to your feelings often use the connotations of words to push you in a desired direction. For example, most people are attracted to a leader with *bold vision* but suspicious of one with *reckless, unproven ideas;* yet these two phrases may describe the same thing. A writer is not necessarily being dishonest when using such loaded words, but you as a reader should be aware of the effects of these words.

Specific examples and vivid details may also appeal to readers' emotions. For example, in an attempt to persuade a warehouse owner to improve working conditions, a writer might describe how the freezing workers shiver uncontrollably and sniffle and sneeze constantly. Notice that many of the techniques listed in the chart on biased writing on pages 291 and 292 consist of emotional appeals.

Logical appeals Appeals to the intellect, or **logical appeals,** are intended to show that a writer's opinion is based on sound **reasons** supported by solid **evidence.** Usually, evidence takes the form of facts (data that can be proven such as statistics and examples) or expert opinions (statements by people considered authorities on the subject). Notice how the reasons and evidence in the following chart support the opinion statement.

Opinion Statement: Students at Hatchfield High School should be permitted to go off-campus for lunch.	
Reason: The seating area of the cafeteria is overcrowded.	**Evidence:** At least once a week, I wait for someone to finish eating so I can sit down. (example)
	Evidence: The fire marshal has warned that our cafeteria is close to exceeding safe seating capacity. (expert opinion)
Reason: Standing in line to be served uses a major portion of the lunch period.	**Evidence:** The average waiting time is 19 minutes, leaving only 26 minutes to eat, clean up, and get to class. (statistic)
	Evidence: I rarely have time for even a brief walk outside. (example)

Ethical appeals   Appeals to character or trust suggest that the action called for by the editorial is the right thing to do. Words such as *right, wrong, truth, justice, fairness, honesty, respect, responsibility, freedom,* and *equality* are often the signals of ethical appeals. Writers sometimes appeal to readers' sense of ethics by presenting both sides of the issue, thus showing they are fair-minded and balanced.

One of the most powerful forms of ethical appeal comes when a person identifies the opposing position—that is, admits something that is against his or her own self-interest; for instance, an executive of a tobacco company admits that smoking is harmful or an automotive engineer risks being fired by calling attention to safety problems. By contrast, some writers may appeal to readers' sense of ethics by **demonizing** the opposition—presenting the other side as monstrous or fanatical. Demonizing the opposition turns an ethical appeal into an emotional one and is often a sign of bias.

The following chart shows how one writer uses the three different appeals to support an opinion.

TIP   It is important to analyze the balance of the appeals when reading persuasive writing. Some issues really are primarily a matter of logic or primarily of right and wrong; however, even in those cases, emotional appeals can almost always be supplied for additional support. If an editorial does not use at least two kinds of appeals, its argument is probably not balanced.

Opinion Statement: A class in multicultural history should be a requirement for graduation from our high school.

Emotional Appeal	Logical Appeal	Ethical Appeal
A focus on history that leans unfairly toward the origins of one region—Europe—will cause over 80 percent of the student body to feel as if their heritage is somehow unworthy of study.	Our student body is multicultural. Presently, 50 percent is African American, 25 percent is Hispanic, 15 percent is Caucasian, and 10 percent is Asian.	By creating a history program that is more reflective of the entire world (not just a single region), we will be treating all cultures equally.

YOUR TURN 3   Analyzing Appeals

Identify the appeals used in the editorial "Cleaning Up College Basketball." Organize the appeals you find by listing them in a chart with three headings: **Logical Appeals, Emotional Appeals,** and **Ethical Appeals.** Then, analyze the balance—the number and range of types—of the appeals.

Prefixes Related to *Good* and *Bad*

Editorials often attempt to persuade readers that something is either good or bad; therefore, editorials often include words with the prefixes *bene–* or *mal–*. (A **prefix** is a word part added to the beginning of a word to change the word's meaning.)

The prefix *bene–* means "well, good," as in *benevolent* (meaning "doing good.") The prefix *mal–* means "bad, evil, ill," as in *malignant* (meaning "tending to produce death.")

Knowing these two prefixes will help you to figure out the meanings of unfamiliar words and can help you to determine a writer's stand on an issue.

TIP As you read, jot down words with prefixes meaning *good* or *bad*. A collection of such words and their meanings will be a storehouse you can dip into again and again, both as a reader of editorials and as a writer of them.

THINKING IT THROUGH **Using Prefixes Meaning *Good* and *Bad***

Take a look at the example below and the steps following it. Also, notice how one student used the steps to determine the meaning of *benign.*

The **benign** climate in the islands makes them the preferred vacation spot.

1. **Look for words with the prefixes *bene–* or *mal–*.** The prefix *bene–* is in **benign.**

2. **Determine the prefix's meaning.** *Bene–* means "*good.*"

3. **Make an educated guess at the meaning of the word. (If necessary, combine the meaning of the prefix with the meanings of other word parts.)** *Benign* might mean "*good or kind.*"

4. **Check to see if this meaning fits within the context of the sentence.** A good or kind climate would make for a wonderful vacation spot. The meaning fits.

PRACTICE

Use the steps above to determine the meanings of the boldface words in the following sentences. Put answers on your own paper.

1. The **malevolent** effects of the disease were terrifying to everyone.

2. The secret **benefactor** donated over a million dollars to the museum.

3. The newspaper **maligned** the man so much that he was embarrassed to be seen.

4. Because of the **beneficent** actions of the community, the four children were saved.

5. The veterinarian tried to determine the animal's **malady** from a long list of symptoms.

Answering Questions about Tone

Standardized reading tests often ask you to identify the **tone** of a passage—the language that indicates the writer's attitude toward the subject and reader. Because tone is implied rather than stated, try to determine the feelings of the writer rather than focusing on the argument given. Look for loaded or emotional words that convey the writer's attitude. For example, to say that a man has "unreasoned fears" or that a news story is "unreliable" reveals that the writer has a negative attitude—evident in the two adjectives *unreasoned* and *unreliable*.

Here is a typical reading passage and its question about tone:

Can surfing, snowboarding, and rock concerts save the environment? Surfrider—a conservation group based in Southern California—thinks so, and it is working to bring young, energetic outdoor enthusiasts into the activist fold. "There is a new type of environmental recreationist out there," says Pierce Flynn, the organization's executive director. "That's who we're aiming at."
    Surfrider started doing beach cleanups in the 1980s. From there, the organization broadened its perspective to fight water pollution. Based in San Clemente, Surfrider is now involved in a wetlands-restoration project at Doheny Beach, California, and is helping create the first map of storm-drainage areas in southern California to improve sewage management. A Surfrider representative sits on the Environmental Protection Agency's Ocean Stormwater Pollution Committee, and members have allied with grassroots activists from places as far-flung as the Baltic Sea, Guam, Puerto Rico, and Hawaii. Surfrider's current membership stands at 25,000, with forty chapters in four countries.

1. The author's tone in this passage can best be described as
   A. hostile and unapproving
   B. blindly adulatory
   C. neutral and objective
   D. admiring and enthusiastic
   E. sarcastic

THINKING IT THROUGH **Answering Tone Questions**

Keep the following steps in mind when answering tone questions:

1. **Look for descriptive words that might reflect the writer's attitude.** In the passage above, positive words such as *save, helping, allied, new, young, cleanups,* and *improve* indicate that the tone is not altogether neutral. Therefore, **C** is incorrect.

2. **Eliminate obviously incorrect answer choices.** The tone is not hostile or sarcastic. Answers **A** and **E** are incorrect.

3. **Examine the remaining choices and select the most appropriate answer.** **B** is an exaggeration, so the answer has to be **D.**

Writing an Editorial

The city council has passed a law setting a curfew for teenagers in your town. People under the age of eighteen will be barred from public areas after 10:00 P.M. on weekdays and after 11:00 P.M. on weekends. Violators will be fined or even jailed. Some of your friends favor the curfew; others oppose it. Neither you nor your friends, however, are old enough to vote. How can you make your voice heard? One way of making your opinion known is to write an *editorial* that can be published in the school or local newspaper. An **editorial** is an article written or approved by an editor that gives one writer's views. In an editorial, you try to *persuade* your readers to side with you on the issue—and to take action. To achieve this goal, you must provide convincing support for your own position and confront the arguments made by those with opposing opinions. In this Writing Workshop, you will learn how to create a convincing, well-supported editorial on any issue meaningful to you, from the future of the planet to the theme of the junior prom.

WHAT'S AHEAD?

In this workshop, you will write an editorial. You will also learn to

- focus on an issue
- gather support for persuasive writing
- avoid logical fallacies
- recognize euphemisms
- correct inexact pronoun references

Prewriting

Choose a Specific Issue

Add Incite to Insight   To find a good **issue** (a topic about which people have opposing opinions) for an editorial, look for a controversy on which your readers can take immediate action. They may be unaware of the issue before reading your editorial, but after reading it, they may want to do something to help solve the problem. Try at least two of the following issue-generating strategies:

- **Go for a walk** through your community. What issues concern your neighbors? What problems can you see around you?

- **Read a newspaper,** local or national. Pay special attention to the editorials and the letters to the editor. Do you find yourself agreeing or disagreeing strongly with a writer's position? Find a subject that makes you want to answer back.

- **Attend a meeting** of your student council or of a similar school organization. Take notes on new proposals and projects, and listen carefully when your fellow students share their views. What would you say if you were asked your opinion?
- **Learn about current issues** by browsing the World Wide Web, reading national newsmagazines, or watching TV news broadcasts. Whether an issue is big or small, consider how it affects your area. Keep in mind the slogan "Think globally, act locally."

When you have found a few issues you feel strongly about, list them and circle the ones that require swift action or that have special importance to your community.

Narrow Your Topic

TIP Your **occasion,** or prompt, for writing an editorial may be a real world event: Something has happened or an issue has arisen about which you have strong feelings.

Sharpen Your Focus   Take another look at the issues you have circled. Are any too complicated or too general to present in a short editorial? For example, the effects of industrial pollution on the formation of greenhouse gases may be too broad and complex a topic for an editorial. However, if you focus on the dangerous emission of pollutants from a specific factory in your area, your editorial will have a much tighter focus.

Ask yourself these questions about the issues you have circled:

- Is the issue important to you?
- Does the issue have clearly defined pro and con arguments?
- Can each side claim a strong case for its position?
- Do people care passionately about the issue?

If the answer to all four questions is yes, you have the makings of an arguable issue. Make sure, however, that the controversy is not simply a matter of taste, such as what flavor of yogurt is best or whether comedies are preferable to tragedies. Matters of taste can be argued only on the basis of personal opinion, not of evidence and logic. No amount of reasoning can convince a strawberry yogurt lover to switch to peach; on the other hand, even a person who deeply believes in public transit may be convinced that a monorail is unnecessary, given conclusive evidence. If you have trouble narrowing your choices to one issue, discuss the items on your list with a classmate. Choose an issue that you find compelling, controversial, and worthy of action.

Consider Your Audience

TIP If you know someone who disagrees with your position, keep that person in mind as a member of the audience you want to convince.

Whom Are You Convincing?   Do your readers know anything about the issue on which you are planning to write? Do they care about the issue? In fact, who are your readers, anyway? An editorial's readers are the consumers who buy a specific newspaper or magazine, who watch a certain television program, or who browse a specific Web site. Such an audience will probably not consist entirely of people who already agree with the writer. It will also contain people who disagree and—perhaps the largest group for many issues—people who are neutral. Thus, you need to use a **tone**—the attitude toward your subject and audience conveyed by your language—and other rhetorical strategies that will rouse this diverse group in the direction you want them to go. **You need to prepare your case by analyzing your audience.**

KEY CONCEPT

THINKING IT THROUGH | Analyzing Audience

Analyze your audience by asking yourself the following questions.

▶ **How much do my readers already know?** If your issue is obscure, don't assume your audience is as well informed as you. They may need to be filled in on the most basic points. If the issue is front-page news, on the other hand, readers will not welcome a rehash of common knowledge. The number of articles and letters on the subject in your local newspaper is one gauge of your audience's knowledge. Another is the knowledge of you, your friends, and your family.

▶ **How do my readers feel about the issue?** Determine whether your position is popular or unpopular. If it is unpopular, you will need to try very hard to sway readers by means of convincing support. If your position is popular, your focus may be more on persuading readers to take a specific action.

▶ **What is my readers' interest level on the issue?** Ideally, your audience will already care about the issue; if not, you will have to win their interest. The best way to convince readers that your subject is important is to show them how it affects their own lives.

▶ **How can I change my readers' minds?** Remember, you are not trying to convince people who already agree with you. Think carefully about the reasoning of people with opposing opinions: Why is their view different from yours? What weaknesses can you find in their arguments? Perhaps as importantly, what points can you agree on? Effective editorialists use a polite, respectful, and rational tone.

TIP As you prepare your argument, keep in mind that you must avoid language that would offend your audience. For example, if you were writing in favor of offering vegetarian lunches in the school cafeteria, it would be self-defeating to refer to people who eat meat as "heartless animal killers."

YOUR TURN 4 | Choosing a Topic and Considering Audience

Review each of the preceding steps to plan your own editorial. Make sure to choose a topic that is specific, compelling, and arguable. Also be sure to analyze your audience.

Write Your Thesis

TIP To show readers that you stand behind your opinion, state it assertively (but not bully-ingly). Avoid the use of qualifiers. For example, if you write, "I think that women's sports should probably receive about as much television air-time as men's sports," it sounds halfhearted, even uncertain. Removing the qualifiers creates a more assertive statement: "Women's sports deserve as much television air-time as men's."

State Your Opinion   The **thesis** of a piece of persuasive writing is a statement of the main opinion presented in the piece. Begin planning your editorial by jotting down this thesis, or **opinion statement,** as a single sen-tence. Sample opinion statements include "The city's new curfew for teenagers should be repealed" and "Standardized test scores should not be used as a factor in college admissions."

The thesis statement of an editorial is a statement of **opinion,** not of **fact.** The difference between a fact and an opinion is that a fact can be proven true. An opinion, however deeply held and strongly supported, is essentially a belief. Of the following statements, which is a fact and which is an opinion?

Standardized tests are required by most colleges.

Standardized tests should reflect aptitude rather than knowledge.

The first is a fact and cannot be argued. The second statement is a state-ment of opinion.

Gather Support

You'll Have to Convince Me!   Would you do something just because someone told you to do it, without giving you good reasons? **Your editorial will persuade no one unless it backs up your opinion statement with evidence.** Fortunately, there are many ways to provide support for your position:

KEY CONCEPT

- **Make logical appeals.** Give **reasons**—points that explain why your audi-ence should share your opinion. Amplify your reasons with **evidence**—facts, examples, and statistics that support the reasons. For example, if you are arguing against colleges' reliance on standardized test scores, one reason might be "High test scores are no guarantee of high performance in college." To make that reason more impressive, you could find **statistical evidence**—the actual numbers correlating test scores to college performance. **Expert opinions** from reliable authorities on your topic are another form of evidence. Remember to document each source.

TIP While editorials, along with other persua-sive essays, are best sup-ported by a combination of appeals, **formal arguments** rely exclu-sively on logic to prove or explain. The logical support for a formal argument must be impartial, and all avail-able evidence must be considered. Formal argu-ment is required in busi-ness proposals, scientific reports, research pro-jects, and some school essays.

- **Make emotional appeals.** Put **connotative language** (language that con-veys attitudes and associations) to work for you. The same facts can be placed in a positive or a negative light depending on the words you choose. For example, someone favoring a curfew might call it a "reason-able bedtime." Someone opposing it might call it a "nightly lockdown." You can also include **stories, analogies, examples,** and **details** that appeal to your audience's emotions. **Quotations** from people affected by or involved in the issue can also have strong emotional appeal.

- **Make ethical appeals.** Adopt a **reasonable tone** so that your audience trusts your intelligence and sincerity. **Demonstrate fairness** by conceding a point made by your opposition. Refer to ideals such as honesty, responsibility, and democracy. Mention any **special qualifications** that make you an authority on your issue. Do not ignore your opposition; instead, answer each opposing reason with your own reasons, called **rebuttals.**

Structure of Support   Imagine your editorial as having the structure of a pyramid, with your opinion statement at the top supported by many persuasive appeals. If the foundation is not sound, the pyramid may topple.

Make sure you can provide support for the opinion statement you choose. Different types of support are shown below.

TIP   Try to avoid a **biased** argument—one that is overly partial toward a particular point of view. If your readers feel manipulated by bias, you may lose their trust; therefore, be fair in acknowledging opposing points of view. Such an acknowledgment is called **conceding a point.**

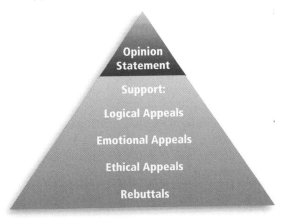

Opinion Statement

Support:

Logical Appeals

Emotional Appeals

Ethical Appeals

Rebuttals

Organize Your Support

Build Your Argument   Your editorial should lead the audience to your viewpoint as efficiently as possible. In your **introduction,** grab your audience's attention and present your opinion statement. In the **body** paragraphs of the editorial, develop your appeals with the support of evidence. In the **conclusion,** restate your position and give your audience a **call to action,** encouraging them to do something about the issue. Using this basic structure, order your support in **logical progression,** or a way that makes sense. Here are three basic strategies for ordering support:

- **Order of Importance**   You may want to begin with your strongest appeal in order to capture your audience's attention, or, alternatively, end with your strongest appeal in order to leave your audience with a powerful impression. When setting your appeals in order of importance, consider their importance to your *audience*—not just to you.

- **Chronological Order**   Your issue may include a series of events that happen one after another. For example, if your editorial takes a stand against smoking, you might describe the harmful effects of smoking in the order that they occur during a smoker's lifetime.

TIP   You can also organize an editorial using a modification of the order of importance. Save the strongest logical appeal and the rebuttal of the opposing argument for last. Place the weakest appeal in the middle, where stronger arguments buttress it on both sides.

■ **Logical Order** This is a good way of comparing and contrasting your views with those of the opposition. Either present all the opposing arguments and then give all your rebuttals, or provide a rebuttal for each opposing argument one at a time.

Your editorial should follow the basic structure of introduction-body-conclusion. The following chart shows how one writer organized the information for the editorial on page 305.

the editorial on page 305.

TIP In organizing your ideas, it may help to work collaboratively with another student. Discuss which order you each think will be most effective and why. Listening to another's ideas often helps to clarify your own.

	General points	Specific details
Introduction: Paragraphs 1 and 2	Attention-grabber Background Thesis statement	Popular event cancelled Background of curfew law Law should be repealed
Body: Paragraphs 3-7	Strongest reason	No effect on city's crime rate
	Weakest reason	City's police do not support
	Opposing argument/ rebuttal	Many cities have curfews
	Second strongest reason	School activities ignored
	Opposing argument/ rebuttal	Could lessen vandalism
Conclusion: Paragraph 8	Restatement of thesis Call to action	Repeal curfew law Contact city councilmember

TIP Editorials (and other essays) do not always have the same number of paragraphs. Length depends on how broad your thesis is and how much support you have for your thesis. You might have the typical five-paragraph essay: introduction, three body paragraphs, and a conclusion; you might also have a seven-paragraph essay: introduction, five body paragraphs, and a conclusion; or you might have as many paragraphs as it takes to support your position.

YOUR TURN 5 **Stating Your Thesis and Gathering Support**

Before you begin writing your editorial, write a thesis, or opinion statement, on your issue. Then, develop logical, emotional, and ethical appeals to support your thesis. Finally, test ways of organizing your editorial, and choose one way.

Avoiding Logical Fallacies

Because developing a convincing argument depends upon providing readers with sound reasons to support your position, you will want to be sure to avoid logical fallacies. **Logical fallacies** are statements that look and sound like reasons, but are actually errors in reasoning. Although these fallacies may work sometimes, they probably will not get past critical readers and listeners. Once detected, fallacies can undermine your position and your credibility. Two common logical fallacies to avoid when writing editorials are *begging the question* and *attacking the person.*

When you write your editorial, you may think some reasons are so obvious that you do not need to support them with evidence. If so, you have fallen into the trap of *assuming* a point that needs to be proved. This logical error is **begging the question.** For example, suppose you write, "The curfew should be repealed because discrimination against young people is wrong." If you don't follow this statement with convincing support, you

have merely taken it for granted that the curfew is a form of discrimination. This approach will appeal to readers who already agree with you, but what about readers who are not sure? To persuade them, you need to furnish proof that the curfew is discriminatory—and *then* remind readers that discrimination is wrong.

It is also easy to fall into the trap of emphasizing personalities. If you allow yourself to shift from the issue to the character or personality of the opposition, you are **attacking the person,** a fallacy informally known as "name-calling." The formal name is the *ad hominem* fallacy (literally, "to the person"). For example, you would be using this fallacy if you wrote, "Supporters of the curfew are too cowardly to search for alternatives." Instead of attacking individuals who oppose your position, concentrate on developing convincing support for your position.

For more on **logical fallacies,** see page 345 and page 386.

PRACTICE

On your own paper, write **B** for each of the following sentences that begs the question. Write **A** if the statement attacks the person. If the argument is valid, write **OK.** Be prepared to explain your choices.

1. Citizens who do not volunteer in their communities are self-centered.

2. Sixteen-year-olds should be allowed to vote because by sixteen a person should make his or her own decisions.

3. Schools should have shorter class days so that students will be forced to make the most of their learning time.

4. Only wealthy snobs want the public swimming pool to close.

5. Inmates should be given an education in prison so that they will be able to give something meaningful back to society when they are released.

**Writing**

Writing an Editorial

Framework	Directions and Explanations

Introduction
- Grab readers' attention.
- Give necessary background information.
- State your opinion clearly.

Attract Attention To draw your readers into your editorial, begin with an attention-getting statement, question, anecdote, fact, or quotation that will make them want to continue reading.

Describe Your Issue Give whatever background information you think your audience will need. If you have any special qualifications that increase your credibility on the issue, the introduction is a good place to state them.

State Your Position Introduce your thesis, stating your opinion as clearly and directly as possible.

Body
- Support your position.
- Rebut the opposition.

Present Your Appeals Use a combination of logical, emotional, and ethical appeals. Give convincing reasons and concrete evidence.

Organize Your Case Be sure to organize your ideas in a logical and coherent order.

Look at Both Sides Demonstrate fairness by conceding certain points made by the opposition; then, counter with your rebuttals.

Conclusion
- Restate your thesis.
- Call readers to action, if possible.

End with a Strong Impression Find a fresh way to restate your position on the issue.

Involve Your Readers If specific action on your issue needs to be taken immediately, call your readers to action. Otherwise, leave your audience with a question, anecdote, or idea as food for thought.

YOUR TURN 6 **Writing a First Draft**

Using the framework above, write the first draft of your editorial. Refer to the Writer's Model and Student's Model, which follow.

A Writer's Model

The following short essay, which is a final draft, closely follows the framework on the previous page.

TIP Examples of language that reveals the writer's opinion are highlighted.

Cancel the Curfew

This week, the Riverdale High School Student Council had to cancel its annual Charity Bowl-a-Thon—not because of a lack of interest or a shortage of funds or even a failure to sign up enough enthusiastic volunteers. The student council had to cancel the popular charity event because it would have violated the law.

Attention-grabbing introduction

The Riverdale City Council's new curfew law went into effect last summer in an attempt to crack down on a perceived rise in citywide crime committed by teenagers. Under the new law, anyone under the age of eighteen found in a public area after 10:00 P.M. on weekdays or 11:00 P.M. on weekends will be fined or jailed. While something should be done about youth crime, the measure is a reckless overreaction on the city council's part to the complaints of a few influential business owners and groups. Because the city's new curfew for teenagers is unfair and unnecessary, it should be repealed.

Background

Emotional appeal

Opinion statement

One of the most important reasons the law should be repealed is that it will have absolutely no effect on the city's crime rate. Most crimes are not committed by teenagers, a fact that is supported by the Riverdale Police Department's recent report on city crime, which places teenage crime at a mere 11 percent of the total. Of those offenses that are committed by teenagers, according to Dr. Theodore Chang in his study "Child Criminals," almost all occur between 4:00 P.M. and 9:00 P.M., which is before the curfew. If the curfew law aims to reduce youth crime, it mistakenly targets the wrong hours.

Second strongest reason
Evidence/Facts and expert opinions

Logical appeal

Another reason the curfew law should be repealed is that the city's own police force does not support it. Diane McCasland, the Riverdale Police Chief, admits herself that "the curfew won't do a thing, except to make my officers waste their time enforcing it." A recent poll of the police force shows support for the measure is weak. Only 5 percent of the police officers polled support the new law. When asked what would help stop city crime, 93 percent of the police officers polled replied that more officers and equipment were needed. Plainly, the police department already has its hands full trying to enforce the laws already on the books. Creating a new, unnecessary law only further stretches thin the strained resources of the department.

Weakest reason

Expert opinion

Evidence/Facts

(continued)

(continued)

Conceding a point

Rebuttal

Evidence/Facts

Emotional and
ethical appeal

Strongest reason

Conceding a point

Rebuttal

Establishing credibility

Emotional and
ethical appeal

Conceding a point
Rebuttal
Explanation

Restatement of thesis

Call to action

Emotional appeal

Although many other cities in the region have instituted curfew laws in the past twelve months, they have had very little success. According to the October 1 story "Evaluating the New Curfew Laws" in the Riverdale Gazette, neighboring Hillview's eight-month-old curfew law has had no effect on the city's crime rate, while Springdale's and Morgan's laws have been followed by an increase in overall crime. The new curfew law in Taylor, similarly ineffective, is currently under appeal by residents of that city as being a violation of its teenagers' constitutional rights.

The strongest argument against the curfew law is that it does not take into consideration school activities requiring late hours. For the most part, it is true that Riverdale's teens have no business being out at night at such late hours. There are, however, many exceptions, such as sports teams getting back late from athletic events, school-sponsored clubs attending competitions and festivals, and events such as the Riverdale High School Student Council's annual Bowl-a-Thon. As a senior and current president of the student council, I have been involved in three of these events that have raised a total of over $17,000 for local charities. As a member of the school's debate team, I have arrived back at campus from competitions well after curfew. Am I a criminal? I am only if staying out late is a crime. Do I believe these after-school activities should be dropped? Of course I don't. The price is too high, and the rewards too few.

It is true that a curfew could cut down on vandalism; however, it would be better if the city offered teenagers alternatives to committing crimes. For example, the city could build a recreation center where teens could go after school to play sports, work on computers, or discover new hobbies. The center could operate until 10:00 P.M.—during the peak hours for youth crime. Businesses could donate equipment and supplies, and their employees could be asked to volunteer their time. Operated in cooperation with the Riverdale Police Department, such a recreational center could be a constructive approach to youth crime.

Even if the city council's new curfew law were to withstand a legal challenge, it is clear that the measure is unneeded, misguided, and a waste of the police department's time and energy to enforce. I urge you to contact your city councilmember and ask that the law be repealed and that a constructive and creative solution such as a recreational center be put into place. Crime is not something that we can blame on just one group, but it is something that, united, we can fight.

A Student's Model

In the following excerpted editorial from *The New York Times*, Micah C. Lasher of Stuyvesant High School in New York, New York, attacks the issue of mandatory school uniforms. In the conclusion, which is not included in the excerpt, the author restates the thesis and summarizes the main points.

School Uniforms, the $80 Million Boondoggle

Last week, William C. Thompson Jr., the president of the New York City Board of Education, proposed "a mandatory uniform policy" for all public elementary schools in New York City. Later in the week, the schools chancellor and the mayor also jumped on the uniform bandwagon. But if enacted in New York, as proposed, the program could be a financial disaster.

While some claim that uniforms would reduce students' clothing expenses, each uniform would cost $100 to $200. The city would probably have to buy uniforms for families that can't afford them. About 75 percent of the 550,000 students in New York's elementary schools now qualify for the Federal free-lunch program. That's more than 400,000 students. The cost of outfitting them in uniforms could exceed $80 million. That's a hefty price to pay when school buildings are crumbling from disrepair and teachers remain badly underpaid.

Advocates of uniforms say that uniforms have been successful in other school districts. However, most of the evidence is anecdotal and unreliable.

Consider Long Beach, California. That school system has one of the oldest uniform programs, which has been praised for bringing about a dramatic drop in disciplinary problems. At the same time school uniforms were introduced, however, other, more traditional disciplinary measures, like having more teachers patrol hallways, also went into effect.

More positive initiatives like these will better promote discipline and academic success. More after-school programs, for example, may reduce youth violence. Internships in workplaces can bolster academic achievement. And the millions of dollars that Mr. Thompson wants to pump into uniforms could be used to repair school buildings, hire more teachers, and reduce class size.

Marginal annotations:

Background

Opinion statement

Conceding a point
Rebuttal

Evidence/facts

Emotional appeal

Conceding a point
Rebuttal

Explanation

Logical appeal

Examples

Reasons

Revising

Evaluate and Revise Your Draft

TIP As you revise, keep your **purpose, audience,** and **occasion** in mind. In other words, refine your writing to meet your readers' needs and attain your objectives as a writer.

Take Two Good Looks To evaluate and revise your editorial properly, you should do at least **two readings.** In the first reading, look for ways to make the content and organization more convincing. In the second reading, concentrate on achieving a more powerful persuasive style.

First Reading: Content and Organization The following chart will help you evaluate and revise the first draft of your editorial. Work **collaboratively** with another student to answer the evaluation questions in the left-hand column. Use the tips and techniques in the other columns to help you revise.

Editorial: Content and Organization Guidelines For Peer and Self-Evaluation

Evaluation Questions	▶ Tips	▶ Revision Techniques
❶ Does the introduction grab the audience's attention?	▶ **Circle** the question, detail, or anecdote that would interest the audience. If you don't see any, revise.	▶ **Add** an anecdote, question, or detail that would capture the audience's interest. **Delete** dull, flabby, or vague phrases.
❷ Does the introduction contain a clear opinion statement?	▶ **Underline** the opinion statement. If you don't see one, revise.	▶ **Add** an opinion statement near the beginning of the editorial. Make sure it *is* an arguable opinion.
❸ Does the paper include strong logical, emotional, and ethical appeals?	▶ **Circle** the logical appeals in the editorial. **Bracket** emotional and ethical appeals. If there are no circles and brackets, revise.	▶ **Add** logical, emotional, and ethical appeals, if necessary. **Elaborate** on support already given.
❹ Are the appeals well organized?	▶ **Number** the appeals from strongest to weakest, by chronological order, or by logical order. If there is no obvious order, revise.	▶ **Rearrange** appeals to reflect a logical progression of ideas.
❺ Is a rebuttal included?	▶ **Put a star** beside the paragraph that includes rebuttal information. Revise if there is nothing to star.	▶ **Add** information that acknowledges the opposition and counters its reasoning.
❻ Does the conclusion restate the thesis and give a call to action?	▶ **Underline** the restatement of the thesis and the call to action. If you do not see either, revise.	▶ **Add** a restatement of the thesis. You may also want to issue a call to action, though it is not required.

ONE WRITER'S REVISIONS Here's how one writer used the content-and-organization guidelines to revise some sentences from the editorial on page 305. Study the revisions and answer the questions following the paragraph.

> *Because*
> ∧The city's new curfew for teenagers is unfair and unnecessary.   **rearrange/add**
>
> The Riverdale City Council's new curfew law went into effect
>
> last summer in an attempt to crack down on a perceived rise in
>
> citywide crime committed by teenagers. Under the new law,
>
> anyone under the age of eighteen found in a public area after
>
> 10:00 P.M. on weekdays or 11:00 P.M. on weekends will be fined
>   *While something should be done about youth crime,*   **add**
> or jailed. ∧The measure is a reckless overreaction on the city
>
> council's part to the complaints of a few influential business
>
> owners and groups.∧It should be repealed.   **rearrange**

Analyzing the Revision Process

1. Why did the writer move the first sentence to combine it with the last sentence?

2. What did the writer add to the fourth sentence? What is the effect of the addition?

YOUR TURN 7   **Revising Content and Organization**

Revise the content and organization of your editorial, using the guidelines on the previous page. Use the example revisions above as a model.

PEER REVIEW

Ask a classmate to read your editorial and to answer the following questions:

1. How is the editorial organized? Is the organization helpful? Note any points at which the editorial is unclear.

2. What are the logical, emotional, and ethical appeals in the editorial? Are they effective? Why?

> **Second Reading: Style**   In persuasive writing, style is just as important as organization and content. A good writing style is a pleasure in itself: It makes the reader want to continue reading. An awkward style, on the other hand, distracts the reader; he or she may be less likely to accept the writer's viewpoint. Of the many ways to strengthen your style, one of the best is to write in plain English. Call things by their real names, not by weak substitute labels. Call garbage *garbage*, not "discarded material,"

Reference Note

For more on using **euphemisms,** see page 967 in the Quick Reference Handbook.

unless you have a sound reason for thinking that calling it "discarded material" will win converts to your cause. In other words, unless they work for your purpose, avoid **euphemisms,** words or phrases used as polite substitutes for more natural words or phrases. Use the following guidelines to identify and evaluate euphemisms in your writing.

Style Guidelines

Evaluation Question	▶ Tip	▶ Revision Technique
Are any euphemisms used in place of more direct terms?	▶ **Circle** every word or phrase that you think could be replaced by a more direct word or phrase.	▶ **Replace** each euphemism with a more direct word, unless the euphemism is necessary to persuade readers or to maintain a respectful tone.

Word Choice

Replacing Euphemisms

Have you ever downplayed the negative connotations of your words to avoid upsetting someone, for example, describing a friend's favorite music as *interesting* or *unusual* instead of *bizarre*? Have you ever seen an ad for a car that calls it *reconditioned* instead of *used*? If so, then you have used and seen **euphemisms.** Other examples of euphemisms that you hear often are given below:

Euphemism	Direct Term
correctional facility	prison
additional revenues	higher taxes
military action	war
memorial garden	cemetery
deceased	dead
strategic withdrawal	retreat

Euphemisms are fine to use if your intent is to avoid being unpleasant. In fact, many euphemisms are created for social situations. However, in most writing, euphemisms should be avoided. They can seem out-of-date and affected. Euphemisms can even make a writer seem unable or unwilling to face facts. Avoid beating around the bush; instead, say what you mean.

ONE WRITER'S REVISIONS This is how the writer of the editorial on page 305 used the preceding guidelines to revise his euphemisms.

BEFORE REVISION

Even if the city council's new curfew law were to withstand a legal challenge, it is clear that the measure is (perhaps not the most productive use) of the police department's time and energy to enforce. I urge you to contact your city council-member and ask that the law (be reconsidered in favor of) a constructive and creative solution such as a recreational center. (Antisocial behavior) is not something that we can blame on just one group, but it is something that, united, we can fight.

The circled euphemisms could be stated more directly.

AFTER REVISION

Even if the city council's new curfew law were to withstand a legal challenge, it is clear that the measure is unneeded, misguided, and a waste of the police department's time and energy to enforce. I urge you to contact your city councilmember and ask that the law be repealed and that a constructive and creative solution such as a recreational center be put into place. Crime is not something that we can blame on just one group, but it is something that, united, we can fight.

reword

reword

reword

Analyzing the Revision Process

1. How did each of the revisions improve the style and message of the paragraph?

2. How does a more direct wording help the writer's persuasive purpose?

YOUR TURN 8 **Focusing on Euphemisms**

Use the Style Guidelines on page 310 to help you identify and reword euphemisms in your editorial.

Pie Charts Editorials often rely on statistics, or numerical information, to support their positions. Such information can often be represented visually in the form of a pie chart. A **pie chart** is a circle in which percentage values are represented as proportionally sized wedges of a pie. Use the following steps to create a pie chart.

- **Draw a circle to represent the whole, and divide the circle into wedges.** Make the size of each wedge proportional to the amount of the whole that the wedge represents.

- **Arrange the wedges so that their relationship is clear.** You may want to arrange the wedges in descending order to make comparisons easy. It is common to place the largest wedge in the 12 o'clock position and arrange other wedges clockwise in order of their size.

- **Label the pie and each wedge.** Place the label inside or outside the circle, depending on the size of the wedge.

Remember to refer to the pie chart in the text of your editorial. Tell readers what the graphic shows and why it is there. In the example below, an excerpt from a magazine article, a pie chart reinforces and illustrates evidence about the problem of drunk driving by teenagers.

Example

Passing the driver's test is usually cause for celebration, an important day in the life of any teenager. Yet there is a darker side to this milestone: the problem of drinking and driving. The statistics are sobering, to say the least: Thousands of teenagers die each year in car crashes involving alcohol. The pie chart below, using information from the Illinois State Police, demonstrates the severity of the problem—seventeen percent of all alcohol-related fatal car crashes involve people under the age of twenty-one. Immediate steps, such as education and tougher laws, must be taken to resolve the problem before another life is lost.

COMPUTER TIP

If you have access to a computer, check to see if it is equipped with the software necessary to create graphics such as pie charts.

Drunk Driving Fatalities by Age Group

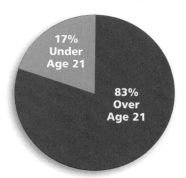

17%
Under
Age 21

83%
Over
Age 21

Publishing

Proofread Your Editorial

Polish Your ~~Apple~~ Appeal Since your issue is important to you, you have an extra motive for keeping your editorial error-free. Remember that you are appealing to the audience from a position of authority. Your credibility will be seriously weakened by any careless mistakes in grammar, spelling, or punctuation. Look in any newspaper and you will find a Corrections column; newspaper and magazine readers are sharp-eyed people, and those who disagree with your opinion are likely to seize upon your smallest errors.

> **Reference Note**
>
> For **Proofreading Guidelines,** see page 1044 in the Quick Reference Handbook. For more about **clear reference,** see page 628.

Grammar Link

Inexact Pronoun References

You have probably had the experience of saying something like, "Susan and Jenny used to be best friends, but then she moved," and then being asked, "Who moved—Susan or Jenny?" Confusion can arise when a sentence contains two or more nouns, one of which is later replaced by a pronoun. Whenever you use a pronoun, make sure the reader can tell what its antecedent is. (The **antecedent** of a pronoun is the word or phrase to which the pronoun refers.) Inexact pronoun reference in an editorial can cause some readers to misinterpret your position or to be left cold by what you hoped would be a strong persuasive appeal. You can resolve inexact pronoun references in two ways: by rearranging the sentence, or by reusing the noun instead of replacing it with a pronoun. Compare the inexact and exact pronoun references below to see examples of these techniques.

Inexact Tomás will feed the dog after he is finished running.

[Who is running—the dog or Tomás?]

Exact After Tomás is finished running, he will feed the dog.

Inexact Alice gave Lily the directions to the game she received for her birthday.

[Who received the game for her birthday?]

Exact Alice gave Lily the directions to the game Lily received for her birthday.

PRACTICE

Revise each of the following sentences to correct any inexact pronoun references.

1. Harold told Jamal that his neighbor offered to pay the boys money for trimming his trees.

2. When the owl grabbed the mouse, it emitted a loud shriek.

3. Anna and Felicia went for a walk before returning to work together to finish her science fair project.

4. The teacher explained to the student the importance of the painting she had chosen.

5. When Mr. Lee went to deliver the cookies to Mr. Butler, he saw that his dog had opened the box and had eaten almost all of them.

Publish Your Editorial

TIP If you have written your editorial for a general audience and now wish to publish it for a more specific audience—local experts on the topic, for example—you may need to refine your essay a bit. Always think about what your audience already knows about the topic and what will be convincing to them.

Take Your Cause to the Public   To persuade readers, you first have to reach them. Here are some ways you can bring your editorial to an audience.

- A natural choice for publishing your editorial would be the opinion-editorial ("Op-ed") page of your school or local newspaper. Check the guidelines for submissions to make sure your piece meets any necessary criteria, such as length. The maximum length for newspaper editorials is usually 750 words. Short editorials with strong appeals and a clear point of view are attractive to newspaper editors.

- If your issue is a specialized one, look for periodicals which cover that field, including newsletters and online magazines. A magazine or newsletter might wish to reformat your editorial as a feature article or a letter to the editor.

- You can also reach a wide audience by publishing your editorial on the World Wide Web. Post your editorial to an Internet newsgroup related to your issue.

PORTFOLIO

Reflect on Your Essay

Evaluate the Process   Professional editorial writers have daily practice in refining their craft. To refine yours, reflect on and write short responses to the following questions about this workshop experience.

- If you were beginning the workshop today, what decisions might you make differently about your issue choice and your organizational plan?

- Did your revisions strengthen your editorial's impact? If so, how? If not, what can you do about it?

- What do you think was the best part of your editorial? Why?

TIP Before you publish your essay, whether it is typed or handwritten, check to make sure it is neat and legible.

YOUR TURN 9   Proofreading and Publishing Your Editorial

Review the steps discussed on this and the previous page. Before turning in your editorial, make sure to
- proofread carefully
- consider the publishing options
- reflect on what the experience of creating an editorial has taught you as a writer

Writing Tests: A Persuasive Essay

Standardized writing tests often ask you to write a persuasive essay in which you state an opinion and provide support in response to a prompt. The **prompt** consists of two parts: **introduction of the topic** and **directions** for responding to the topic.

The most challenging part of writing a persuasive essay can be generating enough support to back up your opinion. A good way to trigger ideas for the different kinds of support is to memorize the acronym **F E E D C A T S.**

F = fact   **C** = causes/effects
E = example   **A** = anecdote
E = exaggeration **T** = testimony/quotation
D = detail   **S** = statistics

Before you begin the test, jot down this acronym on scratch paper—along with what each letter stands for—and refer to it as you are generating ideas in prewriting.

THINKING IT THROUGH   **Generating Support**

The following steps can help you generate supporting ideas for a persuasive essay written on demand. The student responses are based on the prompt below.

> Your school is considering a change from a closed campus (no one is allowed off the school grounds during school hours) to an open campus. Think about how this change might affect the students, the teachers, and the overall atmosphere of the school. Which option do you agree with— closed or open? Defend your opinion in an essay, supporting your opinion with examples.

1. **State your opinion.** Jot down a rough opinion sentence on the topic. *Our school should continue to have a closed campus.*

2. **Use the acronym F E E D C A T S to generate ideas by brainstorming. Fact:** *Last year, after Wilson High changed to an open campus, the number of students involved in off-campus traffic accidents increased.* **Anecdote:** *When my brother Ben was in high school, certain serious problems, such as truancy, were diminished when his school switched from an open campus to a closed one.* **Testimony/ Quotation:** *Senior Shawna Johnson comments: "I am afraid that an open campus might weaken the sense of unity the students feel with each other. Now, we spend free time at the library, on the sports field, or in the cafeteria, talking. Open campus would send kids all across the city to hang out in restaurants or at the mall, separating us from one another."* **Statistic:** *A recent school newspaper survey reported that 53% of the students are against the switch to an open campus.*

3. **Decide which of your reasons are best supported by the details.** Write your essay, using your best examples of support to defend your views on the topic.

Connections to Life

Writing a Sales Letter

Millions of dollars are spent each year using direct marketing to reach potential customers. This marketing often takes the form of sales letters and other promotional material sent to your home. Some people call direct marketing "junk mail," but knowing how to read a sales letter critically is a valuable skill. **Sales letters** are a lot like editorials in that they try to persuade a consumer to take action. In the following letter, the action is buying a product. (Sales letters also often use persuasive techniques, such as those given in the chart on page 384, that might not be appropriate to use in an editorial.)

```
Digital Dayz
4411 Electric Ave.
Reno, NV 89511
1-800-555-DAYZ

August 12, 2001

Dear High School Student Council:
```

Attention-getting opener

```
The new school year is just around the corner.
Do you know what it will bring? If you had a
new Digital Dayz preprogrammed electronic assist-
ant, you would have the whole school calendar at
your fingertips—from the big football game, to
the week of finals, to next summer's vacation.
The school directory is included, too!
```

Emotional appeal: bandwagon technique

```
Digital Dayz is excited to offer a special, low
rate of $45 per unit to high schools only.
Soon, everyone will need an assistant—and at
$45 apiece, this is your chance to get yours at
the lowest price ever! Anyone can use them—stu-
dents, parents, and teachers. Best of all, elec-
tronic assistants make great fund-raising items.

All you need to do is order a minimum of 300
units, paid in monthly installments throughout
```

the year. Send us your school's schedules, calendars, and directory, and we'll do the rest!
Delivery is guaranteed within six weeks—and for
reorders, only three weeks. So what are you
waiting for? Get your school organized—call   **Call to action**
1-800-555-DAYZ today.

Yours sincerely,

Marcus Zapp

Marcus Zapp
Owner
Digital Dayz Electronic Innovations, Inc.

Sales letters play an important part in busi-ness. For example, a potter might write sales letters to stores to convince them to buy his or her creations. A buyer for a store would read the sales letter critically to help decide whether the store will carry the pottery. Like editorials, sales letters appeal both to emotion and to reason. Unlike an editorial, a sales letter usu-ally does not concede any drawbacks of the product.

Letter Perfect One way to become a more critical reader of sales letters is to write one. To create a sales letter, you must first decide on a product to sell. Think about what makes the product you are writing about attractive, including **how it can help people, how much it will cost,** and **how it outperforms the competition.** It is also important to visual-ize your market: Who would be likely to buy the product? The letter itself should be organ-ized around the strongest sales points. After writing, it is a good idea to revise the letter so that you are sure it has an attention-getting opener, a number of appeals, and a call to action (*Buy now!*). Finally, proofread your let-ter: Carelessness with details can cause you to lose customers.

TIP If you have access to graphics or desk-top publishing software at home or at school, use it to create type styles, color, boldface, and bulleted lists for your letter. Design a letterhead for your company, or add an illustration of your product. Remember to integrate your graphics into the text of the letter.

YOUR TURN 10 **Writing a Sales Letter**

Write a sales letter for a product of your choice, either real or imagi-nary, with a specific audience in mind.

Talk Listen

WHAT'S AHEAD?

In this section, you will deliver a persuasive speech. You will also learn how to

- establish ethical standards for speaking
- use rehearsal strategies
- improve verbal and nonverbal delivery

TIP Another consideration in preparing your speech is the **occasion** of your speech. Occasion includes the time (date, time of day), place (location, seating arrangement, size of the room), and other conditions (time limit, availability of audiovisuals) that will affect your speech. Occasion also includes any real-life events that act as a prompt for your speech.

Writing and Delivering a Persuasive Speech

Many of the persuasive messages you encounter day-to-day are spoken ones—TV or radio ads, political speeches, sales pitches, and public health messages, to name a few. Persuasive speeches use many of the same persuasive techniques that are used in writing an editorial. A speech, though, allows you to use some tools available only to a speaker, such as varying tone of voice and using body language, gestures, and eye contact. These nonverbal tools help you to connect with your audience—to command their interest and to make your position clear.

Composing and Giving a Persuasive Speech

Master the Task   Planning, writing, and delivering a speech is a **task** with specific requirements. As a student, your task might be to give a persuasive speech that meets certain requirements set forth by your teacher. As student council president, your task might be to plan, write, and deliver a speech to persuade the student body to give up a Saturday morning to help clean up your campus. Recognizing your task is the first step in planning a speech.

Hot Topic   As you begin to think about a topic for your persuasive speech, keep in mind that you are more likely to deliver a convincing speech if you are speaking on a controversial, or arguable, topic about which you have strong feelings. If, for example, you are convinced that a proposed new freeway through your neighborhood will destroy the character of your neighborhood and you know that some of your neighbors disagree, you might have hit on a good topic for a persuasive speech. If a hot topic does not come immediately to mind, read the editorial page and the letters to the editor in your local newspaper or talk to neighbors and friends to see what issues concern them.

Pointed Persuasion   Once you have selected a topic, you need to remind yourself—in writing—of the **purpose** of your speech. Your general purpose is, of course, to persuade, or convince. Your *specific* purpose is what you need to put down on paper in the form of a complete sentence. Your specific purpose might look like this: "I want to persuade my neighbors to oppose actively the construction of a new freeway through our neighborhood." Once you have stated your specific purpose, you can write your **thesis statement,** a sentence that expresses your main opinion about your topic. For example, your thesis statement might read, "The proposed new freeway would destroy the peace and safety of a neighborhood of families by cutting the neighborhood in half, creating unsafe noise and air pollution levels, and bringing about traffic conditions dangerous to children."

Whom Are You Trying to Convince?   Your next consideration should be your **audience,** the target of your persuasive speech. Will most of the audience react favorably or negatively to your main idea? Will they be neutral? Will they care at all? If you believe most of your audience will react favorably to your ideas, you need to reinforce those feelings by persuading them that they are right. If you believe that most of the audience will react negatively, you have to convince them that you deserve a fair hearing—that what you have to say is worth hearing. A neutral audience will need to be convinced by your arguments. An apathetic audience will have to be shown that your topic is important to them.

> **TIP** Everything you have considered thus far—purpose, audience, occasion, and task—will determine how you use the **conventions of oral language** and what level of language, whether informal, formal, or technical, you will use. The conventions of oral language are the generally agreed upon rules that cover oral communications, including grammar, vocabulary, and style. For example, a speech at an outdoor rally in the park urging a group of neighbors to sign a petition against a proposed freeway would be much less formal in style and vocabulary than a speech delivered to the city council in their chambers at city hall.

Making Your Case   Your thesis statement presents your position. In hopes of convincing others, you must support that position with **claims,** or **reasons.** Three types of appeals can be used, in turn, to support these claims and validate your thesis statement.

- **Logical appeals** are rational appeals, or reasons supported by evidence in the form of facts and examples. Also called **logical points,** or **valid proofs,** these appeals can include statistics and expert opinions.

- **Emotional appeals** are statements that arouse strong feelings by using strong, vivid language (including images and sensory details), making personal references, and referring to specific people and incidents.

- **Ethical appeals** are appeals designed to make the audience think that you are trustworthy and that agreeing with you is the right thing to do.

Reference Note

For more on **evaluating sources,** see page 251.

You will probably need to do some research to gather evidence to support your claims. You may need to visit the library, conduct interviews, or search the World Wide Web. Be sure that the sources you use for support are recent, relevant, and reliable.

Maximizing Your Persuasive Powers   To make the most of your persuasive speech, you should use **effective language,** language that is appropriate for your purpose and audience. Because a speech is spoken language, the audience must be able to understand it immediately. You should, therefore, choose simple, familiar words that communicate your exact meaning in a straightforward manner. To emphasize a particular word or point, you can use the following **rhetorical strategies.** (Use them sparingly, however, or they will lose their desired effect.)

- **Repetition** is saying something more than once, for emphasis.
- **Restatement** is repetition of an idea or point using different words.
- **Parallelism** is the rhythmic repetition of words, phrases, or sentences to emphasize an idea. The following sentence uses a parallel phrase structure: "Safety is the issue here: safety in our homes, safety on our streets, and safety in our schools." Notice how the word *safety* precedes a prepositional phrase three times in the sentence; a parallel *structure* is often important in parallelism.
- **Announcement, or sign-posting,** is the emphasis of an important point by preceding it with a statement such as, "The most important thing to consider is this."

Deliver the Goods   Once you have written your speech, you will want to choose one of three methods to deliver it.

- You can **memorize** it word-for-word, but memorized speeches often sound wooden and dull.
- You can **use notecards** on which you write the main ideas and major supporting arguments, referring to the cards as you deliver your speech.
- You can **speak extemporaneously,** in which case you outline or make notecards and rehearse the speech. However, you do not memorize it or refer to notecards during the speech. The wording of the speech, then, is to some degree spontaneous, making the speech sound natural.

Whichever method you choose to deliver your speech, strive for **dynamism,** or enthusiasm, and communicate this feeling to your audience. Show your excitement in your appearance, your expressions, your gestures, and your tone of voice. *How* you say something and what you *show but do not say* can be almost as important as what you *do* say. The following tips can help you improve your nonverbal and verbal strategies.

TIP   An honest, **ethical presentation** is always best because people can detect dishonesty and unfairness. Ethical people do not try to confuse or mislead. If you twist the information or the evidence to sway your audience, they will lose trust in you and thus in your cause. If there is some merit to the opposing view, admit it but show how your view is better.

How to Improve Your Nonverbal Strategies	How to Improve Your Verbal Strategies
Dress appropriately. A neat, well-groomed appearance tells your audience you are serious and well prepared.	**Speak at a reasonable rate and volume.** Practice speaking at a consistent rate and not too fast; make sure all people in the room can hear you clearly.
Use natural gestures. Avoid excessive hand and arm movements, which can detract from your words.	**Maintain your natural pitch.** Pitch is the highness or lowness of the sound you make. If your pitch is higher or lower than normal, your voice will sound strained and unnatural.
Maintain eye contact with your audience. Give everyone in your audience the feeling you are speaking to him or her. Do not speak at the ground.	**Enunciate.** Don't slur your words or drop word endings.
Use appropriate facial expressions. One key to being expressive is to concentrate on your message, not on the fact that you are giving a speech.	**Avoid vocalized pauses** such as *uh, um,* and *you know.* If you must pause to collect your thoughts, pause silently or repeat a recent point in different words.
Use good posture. Do not slouch or shuffle your feet. If you use your hands excessively, place them behind your back.	**Choose the appropriate tone.** Your tone expresses your attitude toward your subject and your audience. You express tone through the sound of your voice and the language you choose.

TIP Visual materials, such as charts or graphs, can make your message clear to the audience. Make sure the visual is large enough for everyone to read and simple enough so that the audience does not get distracted trying to decipher it.

Perfect Practice Makes Perfect Practice is the best way to build your confidence—to eliminate any stage fright you might be feeling. Use the following **rehearsal strategies** to ensure the best delivery possible.

- **Rehearse by yourself.** Practice saying your speech in front of a full-length mirror. You may want to code your written speech with notes indicating word groupings, pauses, and voice inflection.

- **Rehearse before an audience.** Refine your presentation by collaborating or conferring with a peer. Get a trusted listener to comment on your speech. Ask for suggestions to improve content and delivery.

- **Videotape your rehearsals.** Then, watch the video critically to evaluate yourself. You can approach your own speech as a listener and incorporate both your own **feedback** and others' into your speech.

TIP If you have done something such as dropping a notecard on the floor, go ahead and pick it up. If you are unpleasantly interrupted or heckled, respond in a friendly way and wait until the distraction ends—the audience will admire you for responding gracefully.

Listening to a Speech

You will probably be part of the audience for your classmates' speeches. Remember that your skill in listening to a speech is just as important as your skill in giving one. Become a critical listener by not only comprehending the issues but also by testing the strength of the ideas. Use the following strategies for effective listening.

TIP Remember: Experts often use a technique known as **signposting**, identifying main points or reasons using transitional phrases such as "The first reason is. . . ." As a listening strategy, use these signposts to help you recognize the most important points as the speech progresses.

- **Identify the speaker's goal, his or her message or main ideas, and the supporting details of the speech.** Focus on content; try not to be distracted by the speaker's personality and delivery.

- **Be an active, not a passive, listener.** Ask questions for clarification, compare and contrast interpretations, and research points of interest and contention.

- **Take advantage of the speaker's nonverbal clues.** Weigh a speaker's behavior against his or her words. Nonverbal clues can help you understand the message better.

In order to analyze and critique persuasive speeches, use the following evaluation scale as a peer and self-evaluation form. Afterwards, jot any general comments you may have about the speech.

TIP When you get feedback about your own speech, use the suggestions and praise from your peers to improve the speech and set goals for any future speeches you might give.

Evaluation for Persuasive Speech			
Scale: 1 (poor)	2	3	4 (superior)
I. Organization			
A. Introduction gains audience's attention			___
B. Thesis indicates purpose of speech			___
C. Reasons and evidence develop thesis			___
D. Conclusion effectively closes speech			___
II. Delivery			
A. Uses visual materials effectively			___
B. Maintains eye contact			___
C. Uses good posture and gestures			___
D. Uses reasonable pitch, rate, and tone			___
E. Avoids vocalized pauses			___

 **YOUR TURN 11   Writing and Delivering a Persuasive Speech**

Follow the steps outlined in this section to prepare, practice, and deliver your persuasive speech.

Creating a Political Campaign

Voting is one of the greatest responsibilities a citizen of the United States has—and asking a person for his or her vote is a lot more serious than asking someone to purchase a product or to share an opinion.

In this workshop, you will create a political campaign by adapting some of the persuasive strategies you used in writing an editorial. You can choose a real candidate or issue—local, state, or national—or you can make up a fictional candidate or issue.

Persuading the Electorate

Selling an Unusual Product A **campaign** is a planned course of action for some special purpose. An ad campaign sells a product; a political campaign sells an idea or a leader. Since only adults can vote, political campaigns usually target an older audience and address adult concerns such as jobs, taxes, and raising a family, as well as universal concerns such as peace and the environment. When choosing a candidate or issue for your campaign, consider your own political passions. After all, your purpose is to influence votes. Your task should prove easier if your enthusiasm is real.

What's Your Angle? Politicians must appeal to voters' hearts and heads in competing for the attention of the public. When creating a political campaign, you have to decide on the main selling points of your candidate or issue. You have a limited amount of time to reach your target audience and to convey a message that will be remembered, so you must analyze your **audience** to determine the key issues on which to focus. For example, if your audience is concerned with your city's growing crime rate, a major focus of your campaign should be decreasing crime.

The campaign process also includes inventing a **slogan**—a short, catchy rallying motto—and choosing several different media (radio, TV, bumper stickers, for example) in which to publicize the slogan.

A vote for Emily Cook is a vote for integrity!
Pass Proposition 34: make ours a child-safe town!

TIP Because politics affect the way society is run, political campaigns often emphasize ethical appeals, such as honesty and leadership. Notice that the example slogans at left emphasize ethical, as well as emotional appeals. The **tone,** or attitude, of political ads is usually direct and serious.

TIP You can choose other media to convey a political message. For example, you might act out the issues in a brief dramatic scene, produce a multimedia presentation or music video, or write a campaign song. Each of these media uses elements similar to the ones in the chart to convey mood and message.

Special Delivery To effectively persuade your audience, you have to think about how to best deliver your message. You can reach your audience through **print media**—posters, banners, billboards, bumper stickers, Web pages, fliers, brochures, and ads that include photographs, artwork, or cartoons. You can also present your message through **nonprint media**—radio and television commercials. The way you present your information to the public is influenced by time, money, and your imagination.

Getting people's attention takes some creativity. Your message should have a visual impact on the audience. The chart below shows possible design elements and their effects in print and nonprint messages. Keep these elements in mind when designing your own campaign.

Design Elements in Print Media	
Visual Elements and Their Effects	**Examples**
Font: may convey mood, degree of formality, or degree of modernity	A typewriter-like font, such as that used in a newspaper, suggests that the message is factual and honest.
Color: may convey mood, degree of formality; may carry a theme	A bright red, white, and blue border is exciting and patriotic, as well as formal.
Layout: directs focus, conveys organization and mood	A neat layout with lots of white space focuses on the message and avoids looking cluttered.
Audiovisual Elements in Nonprint Media	
Camera techniques: focus attention, convey drama and mood	Close-ups at dramatic points play on audience's emotions.
Lighting: conveys mood	Soft lighting suggests a cozy sentimentality.
Editing: conveys mood	Quick cuts pick up the pace of the message and are exciting.
Sound: music conveys mood	Patriotic song may underscore theme.

YOUR TURN 12 Creating a Political Campaign

Create your own political campaign. First, decide on an issue or a candidate. Then, decide how you will present your campaign: Choose a message and the media for its delivery. Finally, produce and present your campaign to the public. If appropriate, you can adjust the topic of your written editorial for use in your political campaign.

 *Choices*

Choose one of the following activities to complete.

▶ CAREERS

1. Straight to the Source
Conduct an **interview** with a speech writer or an ad writer about the writing strategies he or she uses. For example, what persuasive techniques are considered most important? How is the audience analyzed? What percentage of time is spent on prewriting? Share your findings with your classmates in a class **panel discussion.**

▶ CROSSING THE CURRICULUM: HISTORY

2. The Struggle of Ideas Brought to Life Conflicts between nations or peoples have often been sparked by disagreements about the right way to live. The Declaration of Independence, for example, is partly a persuasive argument for a democracy instead of a monarchy. Martin Luther King, Jr.'s "Letter from Birmingham City Jail" persuasively condemns segregation but also reflects on what makes a law "just." Choose a historically significant document or speech, and write a **brief summary** of the persuasive case that was made for a specific idea. What rhetorical devices added to the impact of the writer's or speaker's points? How did persuasion affect history?

▶ LITERATURE

3. How Do I Persuade Thee?
It might be strange to think of a love poem as persuasive, but many poems and excerpts from romantic stories and plays are just that. The speaker tries to persuade the loved one of his or her love, and to persuade that person to love him or her back. Look through literature you have read for examples of romantic persuasion, and compile quotations and illustrations into a **scrapbook** of at least four or five pages. Good sources for material include Shakespeare's love sonnets and his plays, such as *The Tragedy of Romeo and Juliet.*

▶ VIEWING AND REPRESENTING

4. How Many Words Is a Drawing Worth? Analyze an editorial cartoon from a current newspaper. What is the cartoon's position? What are its appeals? Pay attention to the style and details of the drawing as you would to an editorial writer's literary style or to a persuasive speaker's gestures and tone. In a **short essay,** evaluate the cartoon's effectiveness in persuading the viewer. You may want to design your own **editorial cartoon** on the same or on a different topic.

PORTFOLIO

Reviewing Nonfiction

Reading Workshop

Reading a Book Review

Writing Workshop

Writing a Book Review

Viewing and Representing

Analyzing Television News Genres

> **Informational Text**
>
> Persuasion

Have you ever told a friend to buy a certain CD because the music was original? Urged someone to see a movie because the special effects amazed you? If so, you already have experience as a reviewer. Each time you make a judgment about a movie, a concert, a CD, a restaurant, or a book and then attempt to persuade someone to agree with your opinion, you are doing the job of a reviewer.

When reviews are written, rather than part of spoken conversation, a bit more is required than simple opinions. In addition to stating opinions and supplying reasons, written reviews must also establish that the writer has **evaluated** the subject thoughtfully. That is, written reviews must show that the subject was considered with some **criteria,** or standards, in mind. Would you, for example, trust a car review that did not evaluate how well the engine performed, or a review of a novel that did not mention how realistically the characters were depicted?

YOUR TURN 1   Analyzing Reviews

With two or three classmates, brainstorm the *types* of reviews that you use on a regular basis (such as movie, music, or restaurant reviews) as well as the *formats* in which these reviews appear (such as in newspapers or on television). Discuss which particular reviews, review writers, or formats you trust more than others. Why do you trust or prefer them? Be prepared to share your responses with the class.

internet **connect**

go. hrw .com

GO TO: go.hrw.com
KEYWORD: EOLang 11-8

Reading a Book Review

We all need advice from time to time. This includes advice about what book we should read next. Choosing one from the thousands that sit on library and bookstore shelves can be a bit overwhelming, like taking a long car trip without a map. This is one reason why book reviews are so popular—they are a little bit like maps, filled with information to help readers navigate the shelves. Part of that information is the reviewer's opinion of the book's quality; another part is details about the book's contents. Together, these pieces of information allow readers to select a book that matches their interests. In the review that follows, you will encounter a reviewer's opinion of the book *Volcanoes: Crucibles of Change*, as well as many interesting facts and anecdotes about volcanoes.

WHAT'S AHEAD?

In this section you will read a book review. You will also learn how to

- **distinguish between fact and opinion**
- **identify evaluation criteria for a nonfiction book**

Preparing to Read

READING SKILL

Distinguishing Between Fact and Opinion   Book reviews are made up of both the reviewer's *opinion* and a set of *facts* used by the reviewer to support this opinion. As a reader, you are free to debate, consider, and ultimately agree or disagree with the reviewer's opinion because an **opinion** is a value judgment or personal belief that *cannot* be proven absolutely true or false with hard evidence. On the other hand, you cannot agree or disagree with a reviewer's facts, since **facts** are truths, or statements that *can* be proven true with concrete information. As you read, see if you can recognize opinions, stated both directly and indirectly, as well as the facts that support the opinions.

READING FOCUS

Criteria for Evaluation   What makes a book or a CD good or bad? Professional reviewers do not base their opinions about these things on personal preferences alone. They base their opinions on certain **criteria for evaluation**—qualities the product must have to make it worth recommending. Of course, not everything can be judged by the same set of criteria. From sneakers to stereos, each thing has its own standards of excellence. As you read the book review that follows, try to figure out what criteria the reviewer might have used to evaluate the book *Volcanoes: Crucibles of Change*.

As you read the following review, try to determine what the reviewer's general opinion of the book is. Is he recommending the book or not? Also, try to note any facts the reviewer has included in this review, asking yourself why these particular facts might have been chosen. Jot down answers to the numbered active-reading questions as you read.

from **The New York Times Book Review**

HOT TOPIC

By **WILLIAM J. BROAD**

Many scientists believe we are entering a new dark age. Science budgets are down. The job market is bleak, with even senior researchers often making ridiculously low pay, given their high skills. Public comprehension of science appears to be virtually an oxymoron.[1] And there seems to be little hope of improvement. A decade ago there were more than one hundred newspapers with science sections; now there are about thirty. Neal F. Lane, director of the National Science Foundation, the Federal Government's top financial supporter of basic research, recently called on scientists to fight the overall decline. "Speak up, speak out, and speak English," he urged them. "We are not doing a service to the research community or the public if we do not help make the case about why science and technology matter in people's lives."

Few subjects would seem to be better suited to such an endeavor than volcanoes—among nature's most spectacular displays of fury, and objects of no little public fascination, whether portraits are credible or not. Consider the hit movie "Volcano," in which Los Angeles fills with fiery pandemonium as manhole covers blow sky-high.

Happily, a team of geologists has produced a vivid, insightful, heavily illustrated book that not only illuminates the wonder of incandescent rock and its constant reworking

> **1. Why do you think the reviewer begins with this background information? What do you think "Speak up, speak out, and speak English" means here?**

---

1. oxymoron: a figure of speech in which opposite and contradictory ideas or terms are combined.

of the planet's surface but deftly explains, as Lane has put it, "why science and technology matter in people's lives." Most important, *Volcanoes: Crucibles*[2] *of Change* is fun. The authors—Richard V. Fisher of the University of California, Santa Barbara; Grant Heiken of the University of New Mexico; and Jeffrey B. Hulen of the University of Utah—take us on a roller-coaster ride through centuries of volcanic thrills, keeping our attention riveted on the deadly fireworks while giving us just enough science to deepen our awe. And the science, which could get esoteric[3] in places, is made clear by revealing photographs and illustrations.

> **2.** Does the reviewer express a positive or a negative opinion about the book? What reasons does he give?

The focus of the book is on how volcanoes affect people. By its end, we come to realize that volcanic outbursts do much more than destroy. They turn out to be deeply creative forces that help make the earth habitable and regularly act as factories to aid in the production and transport of gold, diamonds, fossils and dozens of other items critical to the progress of civilization—not to mention cat-box filler. "Entrepreneurs take note," the authors remark. Volcanic clay sold as pet absorbent has "a very high profit margin."

The book opens with a striking contrast. It recounts the eruption of Mount Pelée in Martinique in 1902, which disgorged fiery debris that killed 29,000 people—the deadliest eruption of the 20th century. It then fast-forwards to Mount St. Helens in 1980, where the cataclysm resulted in only 35 confirmed dead. Science saves lives, the authors show in subtle detail. Volcano monitors, forecasts and alerts led to a series of evacuations and keep-out zones before the mountain blew. Scrupulously, the authors also show that even more lives might have been saved but for expert uncertainty and official indifference. Roadblocks were moved repeatedly in response to political pressures from towns and loggers.

> **3.** What specific words in this paragraph indicate the review's positive or negative view of the book? Explain.

In a paean[4] to basic science—the kind that pursues fundamental knowledge for its own sake with no clear vision of how it might be practically applied—the authors then demonstrate how decades of earth studies have improved forecasting of eruptions by illuminating how volcanoes work. Here the eruptions of Mount Pelée and Mount St. Helens are revealed as the latest acts in dramas "that started millions of years earlier" as oceanic crust collided with crustal plate and was pushed down into the planet's hot interior, where it was melted before it was lifted and spewed forth.

> **4.** How does this example demonstrate the reviewer's concept of "a paean to basic science"?

Volcanoes kill and maim in grisly ways. We learn how scientists, who used to think

---

2. crucibles: containers that can resist high temperatures.

3. esoteric: intended for or understood by only a chosen few.

---

4. paean (pē´ən): a song of praise.

that volcanic debris always flew upward, discovered that violent hurricanes of blistering hot gas, ash and rock can whirl laterally and downward at great velocities, burning and destroying as they go. In 1991, one such flow sped down the slope of Mount Unzen in Japan, killing 40 journalists and two French volcanologists (one volcanologist dies on the job every year or so.) "I had a terrible feeling of dread and decided to drive out of the area," recalled a prescient[5] expert who visited the site the day before the disaster.

Eyewitness accounts give a gripping intimacy to the book. "A tourist entwined with camera straps remarks, 'This has to be a preview of hell,'" as tour helicopters "pace back and forth in the sky" over a Hawaiian volcano. Here is Goethe[6] in a near-fatal escapade on the slopes of Vesuvius in 1787: "We tried to go half a dozen steps further but the ground under our feet became hotter and hotter and a whirl of dense fumes darkened the sun and almost suffocated us." And here is a pair of bold Russian scientists who in 1938 threw boulders into a lava river and gingerly stepped aboard, riding these makeshift boats more than a mile in order to study the incandescent rock: "We often had to balance one-footed like a stork" to cool overheated feet. The back of the book even has a tour guide for those interested in their own volcanic adventures.

5. Why do you think the reviewer includes these particular excerpts from the book?

The book's best section centers on volcanic benefits. Eruptions help produce not only cat litter but volcanic concrete (which made the ancient Roman roadbuilders so spectacularly successful), polishing compounds in toothpaste, the dikes in the Netherlands that keep the North Sea at bay, cobblestone streets, obsidian cutting tools used in eye surgery, gold deposits, gemstones and incredibly rich soils that are the secret behind many great wines and coffees. Even paleontologists benefit: rocks and soils rich in fossils (including human ones) are often that way because of ancient eruptions that killed, buried and preserved the dead en masse.

Alan Hale—co-discoverer of the Hale-Bopp comet, an out-of-work astronomer with two children who relies on his wife, a registered nurse, to provide most of the family income—recently denounced American attitudes toward science and discouraged present-day students from pursuing science careers "unless there are some pretty drastic changes in the way our society approaches science." These authors can take pride in having written a scientific book so stimulating and accessible that it might inspire some of those needed changes.

6. Why do you think the reviewer uses this real-world information about Alan Hale here?

7. In the conclusion, which reason for his opinion of the book does the author repeat? Why do you think he repeats it?

---

5. **prescient** (presh´ənt): having foreknowledge.
6. **Goethe:** Johann Wolfgang von Goethe (1749–1832), German writer of travel books, novels, poems, and the drama *Faust*.

William J. Broad is a science reporter for *The New York Times* and author of *The Universe Below: Discovering the Secrets of the Deep Sea*.

READING SKILL

Distinguishing Between Fact and Opinion

Good Advice   All types of reviews include two key elements: opinion and fact. An **opinion** is someone's judgment or belief, something that cannot be proven. A **fact** is something that *can* be proven or verified. Since you are most likely to read reviews when you are seeking advice (*Where can I find the best bakery in San Francisco? What type of bicycle helmet should I buy?*), it is important that you be able to distinguish between fact and opinion. Imagine if you were unable to do this; you might waste your energy debating or disagreeing with a fact, or you might even take an opinion as fact, when the statement *should* be questioned.

In a review, an opinion will often appear as the writer's thesis statement: *I recommend this book because it is fun, fascinating, and informative.* A fact, on the other hand, might appear as information about the writer or as a statistic about the book's subject: *In 1991, the Mount Unzen blast killed forty journalists.*

Look at the following examples of opinions and facts. What is the difference between them?

Opinions	Facts
People care less about science these days.	A decade ago there were more than one hundred newspapers with science sections; now there are about thirty.
People love to learn about volcanoes.	Consider the success and popularity of the movie *Volcano*, which made millions of dollars at the box office.
Volcanoes are great.	Cat litter is just one byproduct of an active volcano.

The following steps can help you to distinguish between fact and opinion.

▶ STEP 1 **Look for clue words that signal opinions** (many of these words are signals because they have strong positive or negative **connotations,** the feelings or associations connected with a word).

> **Judgment words:** best/worst, great/horrible, beautiful/ugly
>
> **Emotion words:** nervous/calm, peaceful/angry, frightened/soothed
>
> **Qualification words:** probably, perhaps, seems
>
> **Statements of Belief:** I think, I believe, as I see it, in my opinion

For example, in the sentence "The book's best section centers on volcanic benefits," the word *best* signals an opinion.

▶ STEP 2 **Ask yourself if the statement contains information that can be verified, tested, or proven.** If so, it is probably a fact. For example, the statement that Mount Saint Helens caused only thirty-five confirmed deaths can be verified by checking news reports or statistical data and is, therefore, a fact.

▶ STEP 3 **Be careful of words or phrases that seem to signal a fact but are actually opinions.** For example, when you see a strong assertion of a fact—*the truth is . . ., it is a fact that . . ., everyone knows that . . .,*—ask yourself if what follows is truly something that can be proven or that most people accept as true.

Love Is Not Enough   Of course, we express opinions every day of our lives—"Oranges are better than apples," "I hate my hair!" These opinions are usually spoken in passing and don't need to be defended or explained. Opinions in reviews, however, are a different matter; these opinions must be **valid.** That is, they must express more than a personal preference and must provide some support, or concrete reasons. In contrast, **invalid** opinions are usually short expressions of like or dislike that do not contain specific support. Look at the following examples of invalid and valid opinions:

> **Invalid:** This is an excellent book. I loved it!
>
> **Valid:** This is an excellent book because the subject is described with many details and entertaining anecdotes.

The first statement is invalid because it is based solely on an emotional response—"I loved it!"—and there are no reasons and evidence offered to support the opinion. In contrast, the valid opinion *does* contain specific

Valid opinion statements do not always contain the opinion and supporting reasons in the same sentence. When you see a statement of opinion standing alone, be on the lookout for reasons that support it—they should be close by. If not, the opinion may be unsupported and, thus, invalid.

support for the positive opinion—it says the book has many details and entertaining anecdotes. To decide whether an opinion is valid or invalid, ask yourself:

■ Is the statement based solely on an emotional reaction or a personal preference? If so, it may be invalid.

■ Does the statement contain concrete **reasons** and **evidence** that support the opinion? If so, it is probably valid.

(Support is easier to spot when a "because" clause follows the statement of like or dislike.)

YOUR TURN 2 Distinguishing Between Fact and Opinion

Read each statement below. Using the steps in this section, identify each fact by writing *F* beside the corresponding number. Then, identify the opinions in two ways: as either valid (supported by reasons) or invalid (not supported by reasons). Write *VO* by each valid opinion. Write *IO* by each invalid opinion. Put your answers on your own paper.

1. The production and transport of diamonds and gold is assisted by the action of volcanoes.

2. Volcanoes are especially fascinating to people in South America.

3. In 1902, an eruption of Mount Pelée caused the deaths of 29,000 people.

4. The best part of *Volcanoes: Crucibles of Change* focuses on volcanic benefits, featuring many well-written, colorful, and intriguing bits of information.

5. Volcanoes are terrifying because when my little sister visited one last year, she wouldn't even get out of the car.

Now, look back at "Hot Topic," and find five examples of facts and opinions (at least two of each). Be prepared to explain and share your examples.

READING FOCUS

Criteria for Evaluation

What's the Standard?   When writers review things, they work with a set of **criteria**, or standards, to decide whether or not they will recommend those things to their readers. This means that their recommendations are not based on preference alone, but on reasoned evaluations of how well the subjects fulfill—or fail to fulfill—the criteria. Criteria for a movie, for example, might include good acting, innovative cinematography, and an original script. An evaluation of a car would require a completely different set of criteria. Take a look at the following four common criteria for nonfiction books.

Common Criteria for Nonfiction Books
1. The book provides information that is important; it makes a contribution to its field of knowledge or to society.
2. The book includes accurate and comprehensive information gathered from authoritative sources.
3. Information is presented in a way that is accessible and engaging.
4. Information in the book is organized in a way that makes sense.

TIP It is important to remember that not all nonfiction books will meet *all* of the criteria, and that reviews of nonfiction books will most likely include at least one specialized criterion that is *not* mentioned here. After all, you wouldn't judge a biography with exactly the same criteria used to evaluate a computer manual.

Today's Special Is . . . Aside from the set of standard criteria used to judge most nonfiction books, reviewers often use **specialized criteria.** These criteria depend on the personal and professional standards of both the reviewer and the readers of the review. Like standard criteria, specialized criteria are often **implied** rather than stated outright. They must be figured out, or inferred, by looking at some evidence. One good way to identify any specialized criteria is to ask yourself:

- *Where* **does the review appear?** Is the periodical aimed at experts in a field or is it for a more mainstream audience? Is the periodical meant to entertain or inform? What might readers of this publication want or expect?

- *Who* **will be reading the review and why?** Will the readers know a lot about the subject or a little? Will they use the review to make an important choice in their lives? What is important to them?

- *How* **does the evidence in the review reveal the reviewer's criteria?** Evidence—examples, quotations—from the review itself can also be used to infer criteria. For example, if one review mentions a science book's helpful diagrams, clear graphics may have been a criterion for the review's author.

The chart on the next page shows how one student inferred the specialized criteria used in two reviews of the same nonfiction book—*Forever Surf.*

Periodical	Review Excerpt	Specialized Criteria
The Bookstore Times	"This lavishly illustrated hardcover has the potential to become a top seller. Large chains and small stores alike would be wise to stock up on books before the holiday rush. The eye-catching covers will look great in any holiday display."	I know that the readers of *The Bookstore Times* are bookstore owners. The excerpt also suggests that the reviewer's criteria are • the book will sell many copies • the book looks good on display and has the ability to draw customers into the store
The Surfing Journal	"*Forever Surf* is a must read for anyone who loves to surf. This gorgeously illustrated book takes the reader from the early origins of surfing in Hawaii into today's high-tech era."	Serious surfers read *The Surfing Journal*, so the reviewer's criteria have to include whether this book will interest and entertain anyone who is knowledgeable about surfing. The excerpt implies that great photos and a complete history are also criteria.

 Identifying Criteria for Evaluation

The following chart shows how one student used evidence from the review "Hot Topic" to identify one of the reviewer's criteria and his evaluation of whether the book meets this criterion. On your own paper, draw and complete a chart like the one below, using the remaining three criteria for nonfiction books (page 335) not shown in the model chart. For your own chart, be sure to find examples of evidence (examples or quotations) from "Hot Topic" to show whether the reviewer thought the criteria were fulfilled. (If you can't find support for a certain criterion, note this on your chart.)

Criterion	Reviewer's Judgment	Evidence from Review
Information is presented in a way that is accessible and engaging.	**Yes or No?** Yes, the reviewer definitely thinks that the book fulfills this criterion. **How?** Through great photos and language that anyone, not just a scientist, can understand.	"These authors can take pride in having written a scientific book so stimulating and accessible. . . ." "The science . . . is made clear by revealing photographs and illustrations." "[The book] . . . is fun."

MINI-LESSON VOCABULARY

Word Origins

Did you ever wonder where the word *volcano* comes from? In the same way that *you* have a personal history—a family tree that may include grandparents, great-grandparents, and so on—*words* also have histories. The study of word history, called **etymology,** involves tracing words back to their origins.

A dictionary is an ideal place to find a word's etymology, often listed immediately before the definition of the word. Note: You will find that the origin is usually given only for the base word (such as *visible*), not for forms that include prefixes or suffixes (such as *invisible*). Etymologies usually appear inside double brackets, like these: ⟦ ⟧. Within the brackets, abbreviations indicate the language from which the word is derived. The abbreviation *OE*, for example, indicates "Old English." Occasionally, the symbol < (meaning "derives from") is used to indicate another level of the word's history. Most dictionaries also have pages set aside in the front or the back for an etymology key.

THINKING IT THROUGH   Researching Word Origins

You can use the following steps to research the origin of a word.

▶ **STEP 1 Find the word's entry in a dictionary, and then locate the bracketed etymology that follows.** Look at the following etymology for the word *volcano*.

   volcano   ⟦It < L Volcanus, VULCAN⟧

▶ **STEP 2 Trace the word's history** from its most recent derivation through its most ancient, looking up any symbols you don't understand. The etymology indicates that *volcano* came through Italian, from the Latin word *Volcanus*, which is related to *Vulcan*. Vulcan was the Roman god of fire and metalworking.

▶ **STEP 3 Relate the word's history to its meaning.** Besides being interesting, this can help you understand why a word was chosen to represent a certain thing (and it may help you remember the word, too). The history of the word *volcano* suggests the actual character of this natural phenomenon—fiery and powerful.

PRACTICE

Use the steps above to research the origins of the following ten words that describe a variety of environmental phenomena. Write your answers on your own paper.

1. rain	**3.** inferno	**5.** hurricane	**7.** blizzard	**9.** tsunami
2. tornado	**4.** lava	**6.** thunder	**8.** frost	**10.** sleet

Evaluating Support

Whether it is a book review or a report on a scientific discovery, any article that you read will contain a main idea. The role of **support** (facts, details, examples) is also crucial, helping to establish the validity of the main idea. Some college-entrance exams will ask you to judge the relevance of support within a written piece. Here is a typical **reading passage** and test question:

   Currently, each adult in the U.S. consumes 150 pounds of sugar per year. It is no coincidence that while sugar consumption in the U.S. rises each decade, so do the number of adult-onset diabetes cases. The connection between too much sugar and diabetes works like this: When too many *refined* sugars (found in foods such as cookies and candy) are eaten and

rapidly digested, a large amount of glucose is released into the body, stressing it. Over time, this can result in a lowered sensitivity to insulin called *insulin resistance*. Scientists believe that insulin resistance is a major cause of diabetes.

1. Which of the following details is least relevant to the author's main idea?

A. Each adult in the U.S. consumes 150 pounds of sugar per year.

B. Consuming too much sugar can lead to insulin resistance, which, in turn, can lead to diabetes.

C. Consumption of sugar and recorded cases of adult-onset diabetes have both risen in the past few decades.

D. Cookies and candy contain refined sugar.

THINKING IT THROUGH **Evaluating Support**

Use the following steps to answer a test question in which you are asked to evaluate support.

▶ **STEP 1** **Identify what the author's *main idea* is**. To find an author's main idea, look for repeated phrases and an emphasis on one particular subject. If the main idea is stated, it is usually found at the beginning of the passage. In this case, the author's main idea is that consuming too much sugar can result in health problems—specifically, diabetes.

▶ **STEP 2** **Apply each possible answer to this main idea**. Ask yourself, does this answer choice *support* the main idea? By the process of elimination, you should end up with one answer that does not support the main idea. In this case, **A, B,** and **C** all support the main idea that eating too much sugar may cause health problems. Answer **D** also states an accurate fact, but it does not *directly support* the author's main idea about the link between sugar and diabetes. Therefore, it is the least relevant to the author's main idea.

▶ **STEP 3** **Review your choices**. If you have two answers left that seem irrelevant, apply them a second time to the main idea. Then, decide which one supplies the *least* amount of support.

Writing a Book Review

"**H**ave you read any good books lately?" Chances are, someone has asked you this question before. Your first response to it was probably an **opinion:** "I thought Jon Krakauer's *Into Thin Air* was great!" Then, perhaps, you offered **reasons** for your opinion: "The descriptions of his climb up Mount Everest were so vivid you could almost feel the freezing wind on your face." As you spoke, your main purpose was to make a convincing case for reading the book.

As you work through this Writing Workshop, you will be doing this again—using both evaluative and persuasive skills to review a book. In addition, your review may also provide a mini-lesson in the subject matter that the book explores. This is especially true in reviews of nonfiction books. It happens when the reviewer, in the process of trying to demonstrate why the book is worth reading, includes excerpts of information from the book, such as colorful anecdotes and interesting facts. Your final product, a nonfiction book review, will be something that you can publish and share with your classmates, friends, and community. Think of it as a written response to the question ". . . read any good books lately?"

WHAT'S AHEAD?

In this workshop, you will write a review of a nonfiction book. You will also learn how to

- **use criteria to make an evaluation**
- **gather text evidence as support**
- **recognize hasty generalizations**
- **use fresh adjectives**
- **punctuate quotations**

Prewriting

Choose a Book to Review

The Best of Books, the Worst of Books While it might seem like an obvious point—that the first step in writing a nonfiction book review is to choose a book—this is actually one of the most important parts of the process. By choosing a book about a subject that you are interested in, you can help guarantee your own enthusiasm and success.

Here are some tips to help you find a book that matches your interests:

- **Brainstorm a list of nonfiction books** that you have read and either enjoyed or disliked within the last year. Nonfiction includes histories, "how-to's," and biographies. If you haven't read a book you would like to review, ask friends, teachers, or family members for suggestions.

■ **Browse in the nonfiction section** of your local bookstore or library to look for books about subjects that are of special interest to you. For example, if you've always dreamed of traveling to Hawaii, you might search in the travel section of the bookstore or library for books about the origins of surfing, first-person accounts of life on a sugar-cane farm, or detailed histories about the Hawaiian people.

■ **Make a list of subjects** you want to learn more about. Once you have jotted these ideas down on paper, narrow the list to two or three topics. Then, go to the library and look up nonfiction books on these subjects. Choose the one that most piques your interest.

■ **Look in the newspaper for current issues** of interest (political, scientific, or cultural), and write down the ones that you are curious to learn more about. Keep an eye out for subjects that affect you in some way—anything from a recent medical discovery to air pollution to a new type of computer animation. Look for books on this subject in the "new books" section of your library or bookstore.

Now, look over the possibilities that you have discovered and choose the book that most interests you.

Consider Purpose, Audience, and Tone

Why and What For?   No matter which book you choose to review, it is important to remember that your **purpose** in writing this review is to persuade your audience either to read or avoid reading a particular book. If you have a particular **occasion,** or real-life impetus, to write a book review, your purpose may be more specific. For instance, you might find that peers are ill informed about their constitutional rights and might want to urge teenagers to read an eye-opening new book on the subject.

It is also important to consider who your **audience** is *before* you start writing. What persuades one person to accept your opinion might not persuade another. After all, the technique you use to persuade your parents to watch your favorite TV show is probably not the same one you would use to persuade your friends.

In the same way that you use a different speaking style with your friends than with your teachers, you use a different **tone** when writing for different purposes and audiences. For example, if you were writing a review for a literary journal, your tone would most likely be complex, serious, and formal, in order to best communicate ideas to a serious audience. If you were writing a review of the same book for a home page, newsletter, or zine, however, your use of a humorous or ironic tone or a unique format (writing the review as a poem or as dialogue between two people, for example) would appeal to readers interested in experimental writing.

Use the following steps to consider your audience. Pay close attention to how your review might change depending upon your answers.

▶ **STEP 1 Determine who will read your book review.** Then, tailor your writing (but not your opinion) to this audience's interests. For example, if your audience is made up primarily of teenagers, you could use a friendlier, more casual tone than if you were writing for teachers and parents.

▶ **STEP 2 Determine what your audience already knows about the subject of the book.** Are they experts on the subject, or will much of it be new information to them? If your book is extremely technical, you may need to define any complex terms or words that might be difficult for nonexperts to understand. For example, if you are writing about music for ordinary music *fans,* you may have to explain technical terms that readers of a publication aimed at *musicians* would already know. You may also need to provide any necessary background information about the subject.

▶ **STEP 3 Determine what your audience *wants* to know about the book.** For example, if your book is about the history of the city or region that you live in, you will want to focus on little-known facts that might surprise or intrigue your readers and avoid repeating common knowledge that most residents would already know. If you have trouble deciding what your audience might be interested in, try this idea-generating technique: Think back to recent conversations you have had at lunch, between classes, or with members of your family. What was discussed? What are your friends and family interested in right now?

TIP   One way to appeal to your audience is to allow your **voice,** the unique way that you express yourself, to add personality to your writing. In other words, be yourself.

Read and Take Notes

Noteworthy   The next important step is to read and take notes. Taking extensive notes will help you to form a valid opinion and to support that opinion with reasons and evidence from the book. Good notes can also save you a lot of work hunting back through the book later. One way to take helpful notes is to use the annotation tips listed in the chart on the following page. In the right-hand column of the chart on the next page, one student has made notes on *Undaunted Courage,* historian Stephen E. Ambrose's account of the Lewis and Clark expedition from Pennsylvania to Washington in the early 1800s.

Annotation Tips	One Student's Notes
1. Ask yourself what information in the book gives you new insight into its subject.	Once they were past St. Louis, Lewis and Clark had no maps to guide them and no way of communicating with the world they had left.
2. Make note of unanswered questions you have about the subject.	I would have liked to have known more about Sacagawea, the woman who traveled with them, and what her relationship with Lewis and Clark was like.
3. Jot down the main idea of each major section or chapter of the book. This will help you understand the organizational structure of the book.	The chapters are written in chronological order, with chapters spanning from 1774 to 1809. Important chapters include 10, 22, and 39.
4. Mark places where the book either bores or confuses you.	I didn't like when the author got off the subject of Lewis and Clark in Chapter 4, "Thomas Jefferson's America." I got a little bored reading about this subject when I really wanted to know more about the expedition.
5. Make note of sections and features you especially enjoy.	I loved the details about their daily lives, what they ate, what they wore, and what they were thinking. Especially good details are on p. 235 (Lewis curing himself of dysentery with chokecherry twigs) and on p. 319, the description of the exchange of Christmas gifts among the men.

 YOUR TURN 4   Choosing a Book and Taking Notes

If you have not already done so, choose a nonfiction book to review and think about your audience. Then, read and take notes.

Use Criteria to Make an Evaluation

You Can't Judge a Book by Its Cover   While it is true that your evaluation will make up the core of your book review, this evaluation must go beyond saying you like or dislike the book. **Evaluation—in a review or anything else—is always based on a set of criteria, or standards, that you use to guide your judgments.** For example, one criterion that you would use to evaluate a humor book is "the book is funny." Similarly, criteria for a novel might include an interesting plot, fully realized characters, and a satisfying conclusion. In deciding whether or not your book fulfills certain criteria, you create a reasonable, valid, and convincing review.

KEY CONCEPT

The criteria in the left-hand column below are generally considered the basic criteria for evaluating a nonfiction book. The questions on the right can be used to evaluate how the book meets each criterion. Use these criteria and questions to evaluate your own nonfiction book.

Standard Nonfiction Criteria	Evaluation Questions
1. The book provides important information; it makes a contribution in its field of knowledge or to society.	• Does the book provide new information on its subject? What is this new information? • Does the book approach its subject in a new way? How? • Does the book meet a need for readers?
2. The book includes accurate and comprehensive information gathered from authoritative sources.	• Is the author an expert on the subject? • Have a wide variety of knowledgeable sources been cited? • Are all important aspects of the subject discussed? If not, what has been left out?
3. The organization of information makes sense.	• Are sections or chapters logically ordered? • Do ideas within sections flow smoothly?
4. The presentation of information is accessible and engaging.	• Is the writing clear or confusing? Why? • Are specialized terms and technical or difficult words explained? • Does the book include interesting details and engaging anecdotes, or is it merely a dry recitation of facts?

TIP Not all nonfiction books can be measured against *all* of the four standard nonfiction criteria. In autobiographies, for example, the second criterion doesn't exactly fit; one expects the writer of an autobiography to be an "authority" on his or her own life.

TIP Aside from the standard criteria used to judge nonfiction works, there are also **specialized criteria,** or criteria that fit only a particular kind of nonfiction work. After all, the world of nonfiction is a pretty wide one—you wouldn't judge a history of jazz, a biography of George Washington, and a "how-to" book about golf in exactly the same way. Specialized criteria are applied more frequently when a reviewer knows a great deal about the subject. For example, a jazz buff might expect a history of jazz to mention all the major figures in jazz history. If the book didn't mention important jazz musicians like John Coltrane and Thelonious Monk, the jazz buff's review would probably be somewhat negative.

Look below at how one student answered two of the standard evaluation questions for his review of *Undaunted Courage.*

TIP As you consider whether your book meets various criteria, be sure to make definite decisions. Then, write "Yes" or "No" in your evaluation chart. If the book partially meets a criterion, write "Partially" and then explain what you mean. Clear decisions about each criterion will help you make an overall evaluation later.

Any new information? Does it approach subject in a new way?	Yes to both questions. With its focus on Lewis (his journal excerpts and chapters devoted to his youth and young adulthood) and use of new documents about Lewis, Undaunted Courage succeeds in providing new information for the reader, as well as a new approach, since it is Clark (rather than Lewis) who is most often written about.
Include interesting details and engaging anecdotes?	Yes, the book contains funny anecdotes from Lewis's journals and a wealth of vivid details (about illnesses and foods along with descriptions of things like hunting and making salt)—all of these things help bring the story to life.

State Your Opinion

Assert Yourself In evaluating your nonfiction book against criteria, you probably ended up with some positive judgments—cases in which criteria *were* fulfilled—and some negative judgments, or cases in which criteria were *not* fulfilled. To decide on an **overall evaluation,** or **opinion,** average the positives and negatives. For example, three positive judgments and one negative one would average out to a positive review. On rare occasions, the one negative judgment may be so striking that it outweighs the book's many positives, or vice versa.

TIP When writing your opinion statement, avoid using **weak qualifiers** such as "in my opinion" and "I think." Such statements are unnecessary—your audience will naturally understand that your opinion statement comes from you. Also, remember that you may revise and refine your opinion statement as you continue to plan your review.

Once you have established your overall evaluation, you can write it down as an **opinion statement.** In a book review, the opinion statement not only reveals the opinion, but also attempts to persuade readers to do one of two things: Read the book or ignore it. The opinion statement should include the topic of the review (the book's title, author, and subject) and its main idea (the reviewer's opinion of the book). Look at the example opinion statements below:

In a book that takes its title, *Undaunted Courage,* from Thomas Jefferson's description of Lewis, historian Stephen Ambrose skillfully and vividly chronicles each step of Lewis and Clark's journey.

Although Larissa Chang's *Yoga for Couch Potatoes* may have a catchy title, it completely lacks any kind of useful instruction for those who have no experience doing this type of exercise.

Hasty Generalizations

When you pick up the newspaper to read a review, you expect to see a balanced and fair presentation of judgments and views. You are trusting the reviewer to make a reasonable judgment, even about something that the reviewer dislikes. However, if the reviewer makes a **hasty generalization**—a conclusion based on insufficient evidence or one that ignores exceptions—you might feel uneasy about relying upon the reviewer's opinion.

Your readers will expect the same reasonable statements from *you*. Imagine, for example, if you wrote: "Action movies are always exciting; the car chases in *Fast Lane* make this clear." Right away, your readers could tell that your opinion—"action movies are always exciting"—was based on insufficient evidence because you mentioned only *one* movie. In short, you can't make a statement about *all* things if it's based on a limited sample.

One way to revise a hasty generalization is to use a qualifying word such as *most, some, many,* or *generally*. Look at these examples:

Hasty Generalization: Action movies have car crashes, fight sequences, limited dialogue, and quick, jumpy editing.

Acceptable Generalization: Many action movies have car crashes, fight sequences, limited dialogue, and quick, jumpy editing.

The first statement is unacceptable because it doesn't allow for any exceptions; the second statement allows for the possibility that not all action films have these qualities.

Overstatements, or exaggerations, are related to hasty generalizations because they are also too broad or rigid to appear reasonable. Instead of writing "This is the worst book ever written," you might write "This book has many faults, its lack of factual evidence the most glaring among them." The first statement seems like an overreaction (even if the book really *is* awful), while the second statement offers, in a reasonable tone, some evidence for the opinion expressed. Note, however, that writers sometimes use overstatements intentionally for comic effect, to emphasize a point, or to create an ironic tone. In this case the overstatement is not part of the logical argument, but rather an element of that writer's voice or tone.

PRACTICE

On your own paper, identify each of the following statements as either hasty generalizations (*HG*) or reasonable statements (*RS*). Be prepared to explain your answers.

1. No one has ever written a play this terrible before.

2. Although the prose and characters were captivating, the novel lacked the narrative thrust that keeps a reader turning pages.

3. Frances McKellen's new play captivates and engages with its deft blend of satire and drama.

4. Generally, many television news programs focus on violence and crime.

5. All of the food at Bill's Restaurant tastes awful.

Gather Support

Prove It!   You probably wouldn't buy a book or CD just because a friend said that it was great. You would want to know more: *Why* was it great? *What details* (evidence) could your friend cite to prove his opinion? Without reasons and specific evidence, you'd have to go on your friend's word alone—probably not quite enough to convince you. **To make your review authoritative and convincing, you will need to support your opinion statement.** Provide this support in the following ways:

KEY CONCEPT

- **Give reasons that are based on criteria.** You developed these reasons as you evaluated your book; now, you have to refine them, keeping your readers in mind.

- **Provide evidence to support your reasons.** Evidence includes examples and quotations from the book that clearly illustrate your reasons. Sometimes nonfiction book reviews also use evidence besides the book itself. Examples of this may include mention of the book's place in our culture, discussion of other books or movies on the same subject, or a quotation from an outside expert on the subject.

You can use a chart like the one below to gather reasons and to make sure you have concrete evidence from the book for each reason. In the following chart, one student prepares for his review of the book *Undaunted Courage*. His reason is based on criterion number 4—is the book accessible and engaging?

Reason Based on Criteria	Supporting Evidence from Book
The book is engaging because it includes interesting details and vivid anecdotes.	—Lewis's feelings about seeing the Rocky Mountains: "when I reflected on the difficulties which this snowey barrier would most probably throw in my way to the Pacific, . . . it in some measure counterballanced the joy I had felt in the first moments in which I gazed on them." (p. 227) —twenty-five spellings of "mosquito"

TIP   As you gather evidence for your own review, remember to jot down page numbers for each example. This allows you to double-check this evidence easily when you begin to draft your review.

Organize Your Support

Get It Together   Now, after gathering your support, how are you going to organize this information? You will want to present it in a way that maximizes its impact, thus making a more convincing argument for recommending or not recommending the book. In other words, make sure there is a **logical progression** of ideas. One way to do this is to rate your reasons from strongest to weakest, and then organize them according to rating. For example, use "1" for your strongest reason and "4" for your weakest, with the rest falling in between. The strongest reasons will be those you feel are most compelling or interesting, those which stand out from the rest.

Once you have rated your reasons, you can decide whether to lead with your best point, or to hold onto it so you can end your review with a bang.

If you have a couple of reasons that are equally strong, you might spread them out, so weaker reasons are sandwiched between stronger ones. In the chart below, look how one student rated some of his reasons for recommending *Undaunted Courage*; since he had two "very strong" reasons, he decided to begin his review with one and end with the other.

TIP In book reviews, the most common ways to organize support include

- listing evidence from strongest to weakest
- listing evidence from second strongest to weakest, placing the strongest piece of evidence last

Reasons	Rating	Organization
Offers new point of view (focuses on Lewis rather than Clark)	1 (very strong)	First
Vivid anecdotes about explorers	1 (very strong)	Last
Important perspective on American Indians	2 (not as strong)	Second
Historically accurate	3 (less strong)	Third

TIP As you organize your reasons and support, don't forget the importance of **background information** and a brief **summary** of the book. Reviewers usually include this information at the beginning of their reviews, so that readers can follow as the reviewer evaluates the book's qualities. To build credibility with your readers, try discussing your qualifications. For example, if you've hiked the Appalachian Trail, you are well qualified to review a book on hiking.

YOUR TURN 5   Evaluating Your Book and Gathering Support

Following the steps in this section, evaluate the nonfiction book you have chosen, develop an opinion statement, gather supporting evidence, and organize your ideas.

Nonfiction Book Review

Framework	Directions and Explanations

Framework

Introduction
- Hook your reader.
- Provide background information and a brief overview.
- State your opinion.

Body
- Provide first reason and its corresponding evidence.
- Provide second reason and supporting evidence.
- Provide additional reasons and evidence.

Conclusion
- Remind readers of your opinion and leave them with something to think about.

Directions and Explanations

Draw Readers In   Begin with a rhetorical device such as an attention-getting statement, a brief anecdote, a startling analogy, or a question. Making a connection to a current event is another way to grab readers' attention.

Lay the Groundwork   Provide background information about the book's subject, its author, or other comparable books. A brief summary or overview of the book's contents is also helpful.

Assert Yourself   Assert your opinion clearly. (Remember—your opinion statement should be both evaluative and persuasive.) Make sure the opinion statement includes the title of the book and the author's name.

Present the Reasons   Organize your paper in a logical way, keeping your readers in mind. Evidence should include examples and quotations.

Convince Them   For a convincing review, you should have at least three reasons for your opinion.

One Final Spark   In addition to restating your opinion, your conclusion might also pose a thought-provoking question, or tie your review to a current event or topical issue. In the review on the next page, the writer ends with the same analogy he opened with.

YOUR TURN 6 **Writing Your First Draft**

Using the framework above, write the first draft of your essay. For an example of an essay that follows this framework, read the Writer's Model on the next page.

A Writer's Model

The following final draft of a book review illustrates the framework on the previous page.

Meriwether Lewis: Portrait of an Explorer

INTRODUCTION
Attention-getting opener

Before setting out on his historic expedition, Meriwether Lewis knew less about the territory he was about to explore than Neil Armstrong knew about the moon. Yet in 1803, he and William Clark set out to cross the American continent with only a small group of men, a collapsible iron boat, the primitive weapons of the day, and some dry goods, including 193 pounds of Portable Soup. Once the explorers passed St. Louis, they would have no reliable maps and no means of communicating with the world they had left behind. Nonetheless, Lewis was anxious to make the trip. In *Undaunted Courage,* which takes its title from Thomas Jefferson's description of Lewis, Stephen Ambrose (himself a well-known historian and veteran of many trips down the expedition trail) skillfully and vividly chronicles each step of Lewis and Clark's journey.

Background and summary

Opinion statement (thesis)

One of the best qualities of this book is that, unlike many previous books about the Lewis and Clark Expedition, Ambrose presents the journey from Meriwether Lewis's point of view instead of Clark's. Frequent excerpts from Lewis's journals paint a complex portrait of the explorer. One excerpt, from June 18, 1806, shows a funny, opinionated Lewis describing a black morel mushroom he had eaten as ". . . truly an insippid taistless food." In fact, *Undaunted Courage* is as much a biography of Lewis as it is an account of the expedition, with chapters covering Lewis's youth and young adulthood, as well as his life after the journey's end. Ambrose's use of recently discovered material (some exclusive to this book) by and about Lewis also helps to make this book quite valuable. Many photos of Lewis's journal pages bring the man alive, showing his sketches of animals surrounded by detailed descriptions. Ambrose's affection and admiration for Lewis (whom he refers to as a father to his men) is expressed throughout the book, perhaps most eloquently in this quotation: "He walks you through his day and lets you see through his eyes; what he saw no American had ever seen before and only a few would see in the future."

BODY
First reason

Evidence: example

Evidence: examples

(continued)

(continued)

Second reason

While *Undaunted Courage* relates a well-known tale, it does so in a way that adds new insight and a fresh perspective. An example of this fresh perspective is the author's inclusion of vivid and sensitive descriptions of the interactions between the explorers and the American Indians. While this is by no means a story told from the American Indian point of view, Ambrose is sensitive to their perspective and acknowledges the harm done by explorers and settlers. For example, he calls Lewis's speech to the Otos in August of 1804 "an embarrassment" because it consisted primarily of a mixture of threats and coercion. Then, after describing Lewis's encounter with the Yankton Sioux, during which he made a similar speech and distributed U.S. flags as "presents," Ambrose notes of Lewis, "It never occurred to him that his actions might be characterized as patronizing, dictatorial, ridiculous, and highly dangerous." The role of the American Indian people to the expedition's success, particularly that of the female guide, Sacagawea, is also fully acknowledged. Throughout the book, mentions are made of her assistance, such as the time when a boat nearly overturned and Lewis praised her actions. She "caught and preserved most of the light articles which were washed overboard." Overall, the book provides a much more respectful treatment of American Indians than many previous books on the subject.

Evidence: example

Evidence: quotation

Evidence: quotation

Third reason

This book does not, however, take liberties with the facts in order to provide its fresh perspective. *Undaunted Courage* is carefully footnoted throughout and bases its information upon historical documents, such as Lewis and Clark's journals and letters, as well as on previously published scholarly works. When Ambrose does make something up, he lets the reader know. For example, in chapter nine, he speculates about the pre-trip meeting between Lewis and Clark, but then acknowledges, "Unfortunately, we don't have a single word of description of the meeting of Lewis and Clark." Ambrose manages to be faithful to the story, without being disloyal to history.

Evidence: example and quotation

Fourth reason

Another way in which Ambrose is faithful to the story is in his narrative approach. The book is organized in chronological order, with chapter titles that include the dates covered within the chapters. Chapters are initially organized by periods of

Lewis's life and later by segments of the expedition, such as "Over the Continental Divide, August 13–August 31, 1805." Seldom does Ambrose betray the chronology of events by jumping ahead in time. His chronological order maintains a tight narrative tension that keeps the reader turning pages.

Echoing the book's clear organization, the writing style is also straightforward; many sentences are as clear and simple as this one: "On the morning of December 8, Clark set out to find the best route to the ocean and to find a place for a salt-making camp." The footnote to this sentence also demonstrates Ambrose's willingness to explain any confusing or unknown terms. He explains the salt-making process clearly: "The method was to boil seawater in five large kettles until it evaporated, then scrape the sides for the salt."

The book also boasts a wealth of vivid details and anecdotes that bring the story and the explorers to life. For example, young Lewis's curiosity is illustrated with an anecdote: "when told that, despite what he saw, the sun did not revolve around the earth, Meriwether jumped as high into the air as he could, then asked his teacher, 'If the earth turns, why did I come down in the same place?'" Some of the details are funny as well, such as the examples Ambrose gives of the many (twenty-five in all) inventive spellings of "mosquito" to be found in Lewis and Clark's journals— "misqutr" and "musquetoe," among them. Finally, Ambrose includes many vivid and poignant excerpts from the journals that reveal the feelings of the explorers at historic moments. This one, from Lewis's journal, describes his first sight of the Rocky Mountains: "when I reflected on the difficulties which this snowey barrier would most probably throw in my way to the Pacific . . . it in some measure counterballanced the joy I had felt in the first moments in which I gazed on them."

Unlike Neil Armstrong's moonwalk, the moment that Lewis and Clark achieved their goal of crossing the continental United States to reach the Pacific Ocean is not recorded on film. Yet *Undaunted Courage* provides us with a clearly written account of their journey and of Lewis's life that is as vivid and compelling as any visual record could be.

Evidence: example

Fifth reason

Evidence: example and quotation

Evidence: quotation

Sixth reason

Evidence: example and quotation

Evidence: quotation

CONCLUSION

A Student's Model

The following excerpt from a nonfiction book review was written by Jon Novotny, of Piedmont, Oklahoma. The excerpt includes the introduction and first body paragraph of his review.

An Inventive Story

What exactly does it mean to "invent" something? It could mean to create a new idea or to mentally fabricate a form. It could also mean to physically bring something into existence. The various interpretations of the word "invent" seem to be the only barrier standing between partners Presper Eckert and John Mauchly and the recognition of building what is quite possibly the greatest single invention of the twentieth century—the first electronic multipurpose computer. In ENIAC: The Triumphs and Tragedies of the World's First Computer, Scott McCartney (author of several historical books and staff writer for The Wall Street Journal) accurately and candidly documents both the history of computers as well as Eckert and Mauchly's personal involvement in the technological triumphs and legal tragedies of their own great invention.

Opinion statement

Perhaps the most appealing element of this book is the extensive personal information provided about both Eckert and Mauchly. Primary facts such as schooling and job history are rightfully included and provide a thorough account of both men's lives before and after their creation of the ENIAC. However, it is the secondary details such as the sign over Mauchly's childhood bed that read "What should I be doing now?" and Eckert's affinity for "sketching radios and speakers" at the age of five that help create an almost friendly relationship between the reader and the two scientists. Through his inclusion of these intimate accessory details, McCartney is also able to supply the reader with a firm grasp of the relationship between the two men, a subject that has often been overlooked in previous accounts. The men are shown to be perfect complements of one another: "The lust for big ideas that drove Mauchly from engineering to physics gave the pair many problems to tackle, and the drive to build things that pushed Eckert away from physics to engineering gave the pair the ability to make fuzzy concepts real." Thus, this book is as much a biography of "a kid and a dreamer" as a record of their work on the ENIAC.

First reason

Evidence

Evidence: quotation

Revising

Evaluate and Revise Your Draft

Take a Second Look Remember, Rome was not built in a day, and no one writes a paper, review, or essay without revising it at least twice. The first time, use the guidelines below to help you evaluate and revise content and organization. Then, evaluate and revise your style.

First Reading: Content and Organization Work collaboratively to answer the questions in the first column. If you have trouble answering, use the strategies in the second column. Then, use the third column to make revisions.

Nonfiction Book Review: Content and Organization Guidelines for Peer and Self-Evaluation

Evaluation Questions	▶ Tips	▶ Revision Techniques
❶ Will the introduction "hook" readers and make them want to read the review?	▶ **Circle** the anecdote, attention-grabbing statement, or question that will engage readers. If there is not one, revise.	▶ **Add** a personal anecdote related to your experience reading the book. **Add** a link to current events. **Add** a vivid question or analogy.
❷ Is enough background information provided to help readers understand the review? Is there a brief summary of the book?	▶ **Draw a dotted line** under background information provided in the introductory paragraph. **Draw a wavy line** under the summary. If either is absent, revise.	▶ **Add** background information about the subject, author, and even your book's relationship to other books of its type. **Add** a brief (one to three sentences) summary of the book.
❸ Does the opinion statement include the topic and main idea of the review? Is it clear and assertive?	▶ **Bracket** the opinion statement, and **underline** the topic and then the main idea (the reviewer's opinion of the book). If either is missing, revise.	▶ **Add** an opinion statement that clearly states the topic and your evaluation of the book. **Cut** phrases (such as "I think") that make the statement less assertive.
❹ Is the opinion supported with three or more reasons and evidence? Are the reasons and evidence organized logically?	▶ **Number** each reason. **Draw arrows** from each reason to the evidence that supports it. If there aren't several of each, revise.	▶ **Add** reasons and evidence where necessary. **Elaborate** on reasons that are unclear by providing additional detail and information. **Rearrange** reasons in a logical way.
❺ Does the conclusion restate the reviewer's opinion and leave readers with something to think about?	▶ **Circle** the sentence in the conclusion that restates the opinion. **Draw a wavy line** under any final, intriguing question or statement.	▶ **Add** a sentence that expresses the opinion statement in a new way. **Add** a final question, quotation, analogy, or anecdote.

ONE WRITER'S REVISIONS   Here's how one writer used the content and organization guidelines to revise a sentence from the Writer's Model on page 349. Study the revisions and answer the questions that follow.

content and organization guidelines to revise a sentence from the Writer's Model on page 349.

no underlined statement of reviewer's opinion

In

∧ *Undaunted Courage,* which takes its title from Thomas

Jefferson's description of Lewis, ~~is written by~~ Stephen Ambrose

(himself a well-known historian and veteran of many trips
skillfully and vividly chronicles each step of Lewis and Clark's journey.
down the expedition trail).
∧

Analyzing the Revision Process

1. What important information does the second addition supply?

2. What effect do the words *skillfully* and *vividly* have on your understanding of the writer's opinion?

PEER REVIEW

Ask a classmate to read your review and answer the following questions.

1. Based on this review, would you read this book? Why or why not?

2. Which reason given by the writer to support his or her opinion was most persuasive? Why?

YOUR TURN 7   **Revising Content and Organization**

Revise the content and organization of your review using the guidelines on the previous page. Use the example revisions shown above as a model.

Second Reading: Style   Even if your review contains interesting material, readers may lose interest in it if the style is weak. As you revise for style, the presentation of your ideas will become clearer, too. One way to improve your style is to exchange stale adjectives for fresh, precise ones.

Style Guidelines

Evaluation Question	▶ Tip	▶ Revision Technique
Are stale, overused adjectives used? Are the adjectives as precise and meaningful as they could be?	▶ **Circle** all the adjectives in the review. If they are too general (such as "good" or "bad") or stale (such as "pretty"), revise.	▶ **Replace** overused or stale adjectives with more precise ones; use a thesaurus to find less common ways to capture your meaning.

Fresh, Precise Adjectives

In your review, you might be tempted to settle for the first adjective that springs to mind, even a dull one such as *nice* or *great*. Through overuse, these adjectives have lost much of their meaning; readers are so accustomed to seeing words such as *good* and *bad* that they are often skimmed over or even ignored. Your review will be much more engaging—and convincing—if it includes fresh, original adjectives such as *rotten, sublime, vivid,* and *colorful*. Remember, however, that not every adjective in your review should be replaced with an exotic new one. Using too many long, fancy words can make your writing seem stilted and pretentious. Instead, aim for the most precise term you can find.

Focus on

Word Choice

ONE WRITER'S REVISIONS Here is how the writer of the model book review on page 349 used the style guidelines on page 354 to revise some of his adjectives.

BEFORE REVISION

Finally, Ambrose includes many (excellent) excerpts from

the journals that reveal the feelings of the explorers at (important)

moments.

adjectives are circled

AFTER REVISION

Finally, Ambrose includes many ~~excellent~~ *vivid and poignant* excerpts from

the journals that reveal the feelings of the explorers at ~~important~~ *historic*

moments.

replace

replace

Analyzing the Revision Process

1. How did the new adjectives improve the sentence?
2. What other words could the writer have used to replace *excellent* and *important*?

Using the style guidelines, revise the style of your review. Use the example revisions shown on the previous page as a model.

Designing Your Writing

Two Column Formats   The next time you read a professional review in a newspaper or magazine, notice how the appearance of the review differs from the papers you turn in for school. For one thing, professional reviews are often set in a **two-column format.** (Two-column formats are used by some newspaper sections as well as magazines because people generally find it easier to read short lines than long lines.) To help make your own book review appear more professional, try imitating this two-column style. To do this:

- Use a computer program that will transform your text into two-column form; if you are working on a typewriter or with handwritten material, create narrow margins (usually about three inches) and then paste the columns of text side by side, leaving a small white space in between.

- To give the page some visual interest, set (or write) your title in larger, boldface letters and run it across the top of both columns. Whether you are working on a computer or with pen and paper, you might also experiment with different kinds of fonts, so the appearance of your review's title communicates something about the book you are reviewing. Is the subject no-nonsense, or is it cutting-edge? Choose a font—or "look"— that matches it.

- Don't forget the importance of white space. Leave a three-fourths to one-inch margin on both sides of your pages, as well as on the top and at the bottom. This will make your pages look clean and your review inviting. (When type takes up every available inch of a page, readers often feel overwhelmed.)

- Create a small box in which you give the book's title, author, publisher, and price, and set this box before your first paragraph or at the end of the review. If you are working without a computer, simply draw a box around the information. Such boxes, which help readers decide if they want to buy the book, often look like this:

Example:

> *Volcanoes: Crucibles of Change*
> By Richard V. Fisher, Grant Heiken,
> and Jeffrey B. Hulen.
> Illustrated. 317 pp.
> Princeton, N.J.: Princeton University Press. $35

Publishing

Proofread Your Review

Details, Details Before you publish your review, or even make a final copy, make sure to edit for grammar, spelling, and punctuation errors. Since you may have included quotations as evidence in your review, pay special attention to the use of quotation marks.

Reference Note

For more information on **punctuating quotations,** see page 815.

Grammar Link

Punctuating Quotations

Whenever you include someone else's exact words in your own writing, you must enclose their words in quotation marks. Study the following rules:

- **A direct quotation begins with a capital letter, but if only part of the original sentence is quoted, the quotation usually begins with a lowercase letter.**

  Ambrose notes that young Lewis "went barefoot, in the Virginia manner."

- **A direct quotation can be set off from the rest of the sentence by a comma, a question mark, or an exclamation point, but not by a period.**

  "As a boy and young man, he went barefoot, in the Virginia manner," notes Ambrose.

- **Commas and periods are placed inside quotation marks; semicolons and colons are placed outside.**

  "According to Jefferson," Ambrose notes, "the young Lewis hunted barefoot in the snow."

- **If you leave words out of the middle of a quoted sentence, you must replace those missing words with three ellipsis points, with a space before the first point. If you omit words at the end of a sentence, you**

must use end punctuation in addition to ellipses.

"On the morning of December 8, Clark set out . . . to find a place for a salt-making camp."

"On the morning of December 8, Clark set out to find the best route to the ocean. . . ."

PRACTICE

On your own paper, revise the following sentences to correct errors in the capitalization and punctuation of quotations. Hint: Not all of the sentences contain errors. If you think a sentence is correct, write C.

1. "Clark was accompanied by Twisted Hair, a Nez Percé chief", Ambrose explains.

2. Clark reported that Twisted Hair "had drawn him a map on a white elk skin of the country to the west".

3. "If Twisted Hair was right," Ambrose writes, "The expedition was . . a couple of weeks from the ocean."

4. When the Nez Percé considered killing the explorers, they were "dissuaded by a woman named Watkuweis."

5. "The expedition owed more to Indian women than either captain ever acknowledged." Ambrose points out.

Publish Your Review

Get Out There   There are many ways to publish your review so that it reaches a wider audience. Here are some possibilities:

- Submit your review to your school or local newspaper for publication.

- If you reviewed a book on a specific topic, send your review to a Web site, magazine, or journal that focuses on that topic. For example, if you reviewed a book about hockey, you could send your review to any one of many sports magazines or Web sites.

- Present your critical evaluation as an oral review of literature. As in your essay, evaluate the work based on criteria and state your opinion clearly. For listeners unfamiliar with the work, summarize significant events and details and explain the most important ideas and images in the work. Be sure to support your ideas with relevant examples and accurate and detailed references to the text. You may need to reorganize or eliminate some ideas to help your listeners understand your review.

- Create a "Readers Review" bulletin board to be displayed at your school or community library. Post your nonfiction book review there, and encourage others to do the same. Along with reviews, post other information relating to each book's topic—such as maps and photographs; also post professional reviews clipped from newspapers or magazines.

Reflect on Your Review

Looking Back   Writing is a way of discovering things about your topic and about yourself. Answering the following questions will help you in your process of discovery. If you include this review in your portfolio, attach your responses to it.

- How did you choose the book you reviewed? Are you glad you chose the book you did? Why or why not?

- Do you think you will read reviews in newspapers and magazines differently now? How?

- What did you learn about developing your opinions?

- Did you learn anything new or surprising about the subject covered by your book?

PORTFOLIO

TIP   Another way to reflect on your review is to compare your reviewing process to that of another writer. Contact someone who writes reviews for a local paper, and inquire about his or her writing strategies. How are they similar to or different from the ones you used?

YOUR TURN 9   Proofreading, Publishing, and Reflecting

Before you turn in your essay, be sure to proofread it carefully, consider publishing options, and reflect on your essay by answering the questions above.

Presenting an Oral Critique

- Your drama teacher asks you to share your review of a recent local theater production with the class.

- Your aunt, who admires your knowledge of computers, asks your opinion of a computer she is thinking of buying.

- During a summer internship at the newspaper, one of the graphic designers asks you to evaluate and present your views about the readability of a new page design.

These are just a few examples of situations in which you might be asked to make an oral critique. Knowing how to do this—to express your opinion in a clear, concise way—can make a big difference in how your employers, teachers, and others perceive you. It may also allow you to shape the opinion of your **audience,** as you did in your book review.

You Be the Judge To make an oral critique successful, you will first need to develop criteria, or standards, for evaluating. Criteria are the qualities that *must* be fulfilled to make your subject, whether it's a book, CD, film, or restaurant, worth recommending. To develop appropriate criteria, think about what you and your audience want from the thing you are critiquing. For example, if you are critiquing a new software program for use in the office at your part-time job, some criteria might be:

- the program is easy to use and easy to teach others to use

- the program is flexible enough to use for a variety of office tasks

    In judging your subject against criteria, you will inevitably come up with an overall opinion and reasons for that opinion; when planning an oral critique, it's wise to make careful notes during your evaluation because any audience will want to hear precise and well-supported reasons. Remember, however, that oral critiques usually last from five to ten minutes—they are much shorter than formal speeches—so you may only have time to critique your subject's most important features.

Signed, Sealed, Delivered Now, how will you deliver your critique? The way you present your evaluation has a lot to do with who your audience is and where your critique will be delivered. In contrast to formal speeches, short oral critiques are usually not read from prepared manuscripts; instead, they may be

- **memorized**—written out, then memorized and *told* (not read) to the audience, or

- **extemporaneous**—fully outlined on notecards and practiced (but not memorized), then delivered with periodic glances at these notecards.

Memorized critiques allow you to script the exact words you will use, while extemporaneous presentations allow for more spontaneity. As you prepare your critique for delivery, also consider the use of **props**—posters, handouts, slides, audio recordings, and videotape can all add emphasis or interest to your presentation.

    Oral critiques also often involve a personal connection between speaker and audience; the audience must trust the speaker and the speaker must show he or she is alert to the audience's perceptions. If you have special knowledge about the subject or expertise in the field, mention it to your audience. This special knowledge will establish your **credibility**—after all, listeners are more likely to trust your critique of the recent concert if they know you've played the guitar for ten years. Similarly, if you are delivering your critique to the very person who created or performed the subject of your review, be sure to mention good points along with your criticisms; also, suggest some *constructive* ways the subject might be improved.

To see how **voice** and **body language** can help or hinder your message, take a look at the following tips.

Tips for Presenting an Oral Critique
Make eye contact with the audience rather than continually looking down at notes.
Avoid distracting facial expressions by focusing on the content of your critique. This way, your expression will reflect, rather than contradict, what you are saying.
Avoid vocalized pauses, such as *uh, well, um, like,* and *you know.*
Enunciate clearly and loudly enough so that your audience will not have to struggle to understand.
Practice all of these things in front of a mirror or a friend before presenting your critique.

It Takes Two A successful oral critique requires more than a good speaker; it also needs a good listener to make it complete. Becoming a good listener is a skill, like speaking, that can be developed with practice. Here are a few strategies to help improve your skills as a listener.

- Think critically about what you hear, perhaps jotting down notes about comments that you wish to ask a question about later.

- If possible, connect what you are hearing to your own experience. Does your experience lead you to agree with the oral critique? If not, try to formulate exactly why you disagree. Also, think about how you might use this information in the future.

- Use body language to let the speaker know you are paying attention: Nod your head, make eye contact, and react when appropriate (laughing at a joke, for example).

YOUR TURN 10 **Preparing and Delivering an Oral Critique**

Prepare a critique on a subject of your own choice. Before delivering it to an audience, find a partner and present your critique, while your listener consults the chart above to evaluate your performance.

Analyzing Television News Genres

In writing your nonfiction book review, you probably spent some time thinking about why the author focused on this quote or that event—you might have even asked why the author chose to write about the subject at all. Now, think about the last time you saw a news broadcast on television. Did you ask yourself similar questions about the broadcast's content? Or did you assume that what you saw on-screen was a completely accurate representation of reality? Just as your nonfiction book was constructed by an author, each image and audio clip presented on the news has been carefully selected (by an editor, producer, or director) to shape the audience's perception of what's important. In general, reporters and producers use four criteria to decide whether a story is news. They ask whether it is

- **Unusual**   A cat walking down the street may not be newsworthy, but a stray elephant probably would be considered news.

- **Timely**   Is the event current? If it happened longer ago than yesterday, it is probably too old for the nightly news.

- **Of special interest to the audience**   Viewers are nearly always interested in events happening in their communities or in issues that may have an impact on their lives.

- **About important or famous people**   The doings of celebrities, world leaders, and other very well-known people are also considered news.

WHAT'S AHEAD?

In this workshop you will analyze the different genres of television news programs. You will also learn how to

- **identify the characteristics of three news genres: national news, local news, and news-magazines**

- **analyze visual and audio elements in individual news stories**

Hard-Boiled or Over Easy?

Of course, not every program provides an equal mix of stories about important events and those about movie stars. Some include more of the former, some the latter, according to the program's primary **purpose.** By nature, news provides **information**—but, in large part because of pressure to achieve high ratings for advertisers, news may also provide **entertainment.** News that aims to inform—whether it's coverage of an election or a story about crime in your city—is often called **hard news,** while news that aims

TIP   Documentaries—productions that focus on just one story, trend, or person—are another kind of news genre. For more about **documentaries,** see page 408.

to entertain—say, a story about a pie-eating contest, movie premiere, or stray elephant—is often called **soft news.** You might think of the difference between them as the difference between a message that touches your *mind* and one that touches your *heart,* or emotions. Many stories fall into both hard and soft categories. For example, hard news stories such as coverage of natural disasters often contain emotional elements.

© 1998, Washington Post Writers Group. Reprinted with permission.

Hard news and soft news are both seen in all kinds of news genres, but the growth of newsmagazines is directly related to the increasing appetite for more soft news stories. Look at how the following chart characterizes three common news genres: national news, local news, and newsmagazines.

Genre	Characteristics
National News	<ul><li>Length—half an hour</li><li>Stories usually last no more than three minutes</li><li>Focuses on hard news, although soft news stories (usually about managing finances and other consumer issues) may appear toward the end of the broadcast</li><li>Primary reporting by a main anchor often sitting behind a desk and reading stories from a teleprompter (a device that scrolls the story across a screen underneath the camera so the anchor can read while seeming to look straight at the audience)</li><li>Background of set usually consists of people sitting at computer screens, to emulate a working newsroom; graphics that accompany stories are often shown on a screen behind the anchor</li><li>Secondary reporting by reporters in the field; often these segments are prerecorded, then presented with a live introduction (this is called a "donut")</li><li>Program uses a logo, slogan, and theme music before and after breaks, and to open and close the broadcast, although network news guidelines prohibit using music during the broadcast</li></ul>

Local News	
	• Length—usually half an hour; many cities have two or more broadcasts beginning in the late afternoon
	• Stories usually three minutes or less
	• Mix of hard and soft news, with an emphasis on news that has an impact on the local audience
	• Reporting usually done by a pair of main anchors, field reporters, and in-studio weather and sports anchors. Again, anchors often sit behind a desk and read from a teleprompter; "donuts" also often used for stories, but live coverage is more frequent than in national news or newsmagazines
	• Background of set often consists of a screen on which graphics and shots of the local cityscape are shown
	• Program uses a logo, slogan, and theme music; again, most news guidelines prohibit using music during the broadcast
Newsmagazines	
	• Length—usually, an hour
	• Stories longer than nightly news stories (often ten minutes or longer); most stories prerecorded
	• Emphasis on soft news, especially on stories about individuals facing adversity
	• Story topics often less timely than those on nightly news; instead, premium is placed on how gripping or moving stories will be to audience
	• Main anchors introduce stories presented by other reporters
	• Stories may be composed of long interviews with experts or with the subjects of the story; reenactments, which are *never* used in national and local news, may also be used
	• Set may include a desk, but since it's less necessary to have set look like a workplace, set may be more "homey" and anchors may move around set more than on other news broadcasts
	• Program uses a logo, slogan, and theme music; music and sound effects often *do* accompany stories, often to add dramatic tension

Taking a Closer Look

Aside from examining the features listed in the chart above, how else can you identify news genres and determine whether their stories are intended to touch mind or heart? One way is to look closely at how individual stories are constructed. All television news stories—whether they are hard news or soft news, broadcast on nightly news or newsmagazines—depend heavily upon **images.** Producers carefully choose which images (or graphics) will accompany each story, always considering the power that visuals can have in shaping meaning. The chart on the following page demonstrates how different visuals can alter a story's meaning and its effect on an audience (these particular visuals accompany a story about a large ship that has had an accident, spilling oil into the Pacific Ocean).

TIP A chart like this one could also be used for **audio elements.** Keep in mind that what is *heard* can greatly affect the perception of what is *seen*.

Image	Effect
oil-covered birds	may create sympathy for birds and concern about damage to the environment
the ship's captain with his head bowed and family at his side	may create sympathy for captain, who is seen showing sorrow
graphic showing the square miles affected by the spill	transmits hard information about the spill; unlikely to provoke emotional response

The Medium and the Message

You are now prepared to view news with a more critical eye. You may ask why each story is considered newsworthy and what effect its presentation is supposed to have on you. Critical viewers always ask, "Why was this particular choice made?" To analyze television news, keep the following set of analysis questions in mind:

TIP Advertisements are another clue to the type and purpose of newscasts because they often signal the kind of audience the newscasts are targeting. Hard news programs are often interrupted by ads selling "serious" products—cars, headache medicine, banking services; such ads suggest an older audience interested in national affairs. Newsmagazines may contain more "fun" advertising for leisure products targeted to younger viewers.

- What types of topics are the focus of this program? Do they seem to be aimed primarily at the mind or at the emotions?
- Are music, voice-overs, or sound effects used? How often are they used? What is the goal of using these audio elements?
- What is the average length of each segment? What is the length of the entire program?
- Is the segment live, prerecorded, or a combination of the two? Which type of footage is more common?
- Are on-screen graphics or single photographs used? In what way are they used? What is their purpose?
- Who is reporting the news? What kind of set is used? What does the appearance of the reporters and set suggest about what kind of news will be presented?

YOUR TURN 11 **Analyzing Television News**

Watch one complete (preferably videotaped) broadcast of each of the following news genres: newsmagazine, nightly local news, and nightly national news. Then, take some notes about how much soft and hard news you see in each show and why you think it is hard or soft. When you are finished, discuss your findings with your classmates. In what areas do the broadcasts seem alike? In what areas are they very different? What conclusions can you draw?

Choices

Choose one of the following activities to complete.

▶ **VIEWING AND REPRESENTING**

1. ARTiculation Many newspapers publish reviews not only of books and films, but also of art. You could write such a review, either of a local art show or of an exhibit being shown at a nearby museum. You might focus on the exhibit as a whole or on one representative painting or sculpture. To evaluate a work of art, you will have to develop criteria for evaluation. What makes a work of art good? What is the role of art in society? Write a short **art review** for your local or school newspaper.

▶ **LITERATURE**

2. Historical Reviews Many books that are now considered classics received negative reviews when they were first published. For example, James Joyce's *Ulysses*, which is now widely considered to be one of the best novels of the twentieth century, was banned at the time of its publication. Choose a well-known book published twenty or more years ago and research reviews written at the time it was first published. What do the reviewers' opinions suggest about the values and tastes of that time period? Present your findings in a brief **oral report.**

▶ **CAREERS**

3. Job Seeker's Guide Have you ever wondered whether or not you would like a certain job? How can you know until you try? To save yourself time and energy applying for jobs you would not be interested in, get together with friends or classmates to compile a booklet of **job reviews.** Each person can review at least one job he or she has held. As you write your review, keep your audience— potential job seekers—in mind. What would they want to know about the job to decide whether or not they might like it?

▶ **CROSSING THE CURRICULUM: SCIENCE**

4. A Brave New World Not all technological and scientific developments are positive. For example, some might argue that advances in weapons technology are not advances at all. Choose a new (perhaps controversial) scientific or technological development, and write a brief **critique** of it in terms of its usefulness to society. What are the pros and cons of the development? What problems will it solve? What problems might it cause?

PORTFOLIO

Evaluating Advertising

Illustration:
viewed by 70%
of readers

Headline:
read by 30%
of readers

Read This, Read This

Subhead:
read by 15%
of readers

Maybe you should read this

Body copy:
read by 5%
of readers

If pigs had wings, I would consider reading this. If dessert had no calories, I might read this. There is a fat chance I will read this. If walls could talk, I would read this. If pigs had wings, I would consider reading this. If dessert had no calories, I might read this. There is a fat chance I

will read this. If walls could talk, I would read this. If pigs had wings, I would consider reading this. If dessert had no calories, I might read this. There is a fat chance I will read this. If walls could talk, I would read this.

Logo:
read by 10%
of readers

BRAND X

Reading Workshop

Reading a Critique of Advertising

Writing Workshop

Writing an Evaluation of an Advertisement

Viewing and Representing

Creating a Video Documentary

Informational Text

Persuasion

Advertising is so prominent in our world today that ads are actually part of our daily environment. Some experts say we may be exposed to as many as fifteen hundred promotional messages each day—including TV commercials, print ads, and promotional graphic designs on everything from T-shirts to trucks. Almost every space in our lives contains some message promoting a product or service. Some grocery stores even place little ads for video rental stores on stickers that go on fruit and vegetables. Look around you. What places or spaces do not contain commercial messages?

Advertising is also part of our cultural environment—the part of our environment that carries symbolic messages. Because advertising, like other symbolic messages, is everywhere, we tend not to pay much attention to it. Although most of us say advertising doesn't affect us, scholars who study persuasion have discovered that people are most likely to be persuaded when they are unaware of a message or when they are paying little attention to it.

YOUR TURN 1   **Noticing Advertisements**

In a small group, identify at least ten different places where you have seen ads, and write a brief description of an ad you have seen in each location. Afterward, jot down some notes about why ads may have been placed in these spots. What does the placement reveal about the product or the target audience?

🖅 internet**connect**

go. hrw .com

GO TO: go.hrw.com
KEYWORD: EOLang 11-9

Reading a Critique of Advertising

WHAT'S AHEAD?

In this section, you will read a critique of advertising and learn how to

- connect what you read to your personal experiences
- identify emotional appeals

Can you think of anyone whose life is free from advertising? Like it or not, you interact with advertising daily. Everyone has an opinion about advertising, too: Some people talk about their favorite commercials; others complain about the jingles that drive them crazy. The article on the next page, "Bananas for Rent," presents a powerful argument about advertising techniques and their expanding role in our culture. Reading the article may help you clarify your own opinions about advertising while you consider other points of view.

Preparing to Read

READING SKILL

Making Connections   One way to evaluate claims you read in persuasive writing is to compare those claims with your personal experiences. The writer of the article on the next page makes some strong claims about the negative impact of advertising on our culture. Before you read the article, think about your own experiences with advertising. Are you the type of person who puts the TV on mute during commercials, or do you think the ads are the best part? What events in your life have caused you to form opinions about the ways advertising works? As you read the article, ask yourself if the author's claims are in line with your own experiences.

READING FOCUS

Emotional Appeal   One technique writers use in trying to convince you to accept their opinions is called **emotional appeal.** A writer can appeal to the reader's emotions by using words with strong emotional overtones or by describing emotionally laden images. Emotions are very powerful, and when an argument taps into them, readers are more likely to ignore logical inconsistencies and be swayed to believe the argument. (When you think about it, advertising does the same thing.) As you read the article on the next page, take note of places where the writer uses emotional appeals. If you are not sure of a word's meaning, look up the word in a dictionary. It may be an emotionally charged word.

Has knowledge of advertisements become our cultural literacy? Do we need to be up on the latest commercials in order to be functioning members of society? The following article presents some forceful opinions about the effects of advertising on our culture. As you read, jot down answers to the numbered active-reading questions.

from

The New York Times Magazine

CULTURE ZONE

Bananas for Rent BY MICHIKO KAKUTANI

First rock-and-roll, then dead movie stars, and now fruit—is there anything that advertising hasn't co-opted?[1]

They are pervasive as roaches, as persuasive as the weather. . . . They adorn our clothes, our luggage, our sneakers, and our hats. They are ubiquitous on television, unavoidable in magazines, and inevitable on the Internet. The average American, it is estimated, is pelted by some 3,000 advertising messages a day, some 38,000 TV commercials a year.

> **1.** What feelings do you associate with roaches? Why do you think the word is used here?

Not so long ago, it was only race cars, tennis stars, and sports stadiums that were lacquered head-to-toe with ads. Nowadays, school buses and trucks rent out advertising space by the foot. There are entire towns that have signed exclusive deals with Coke or Pepsi. The dead, including Marilyn Monroe (Chanel No. 5), Gene Kelly

(Gap khakis), and Fred Astaire (Dirt Devil vacuum cleaners), have been hired as pitchmen. . . . Even bananas have been colonized as billboard space, with stickers promoting the video release of *Space Jam* and the "Got Milk?" campaign turning up on the fruit.

> **2.** Why is *colonized* a more effective word choice than *used*? What opinion about advertising does it imply?

As the scholar James Twitchell observes, advertising has become "our cultural literacy—it's what we know." Twitchell, author of a book called *Adcult USA* and a professor at the University of Florida, says his students share no common culture of books or history; what they share is a knowledge of commercials. When he questions them at random about concepts from *The Dictionary of Cultural Literacy,* he says he is likely to draw a blank. When, however, he recites a commercial jingle, his students

---

1. **co-opted:** made use of for one's own purposes, taken over.

3. What evidence does the writer give that today's students share no common culture of books or history? Do you agree with this statement? Why or why not?

"instantaneously know it, and they're exultant,"[2] he says. "They actually think Benetton ads are profound. To them, advertising is high culture." . . .

College students decorate their walls with poster-size reproductions of ads that are available from a four-year-old company called Beyond the Wall. Forget Monet and van Gogh. Think Nike, BMW, and Calvin Klein. As Brian Gordon, one of the company's founders, sees it, kids regard ads as "a form of self-expression." In today's "short-attention society," he reasons, ads are something people can relate to: They provide "insights into current culture," and they provide them in thirty seconds or less.

4. Do you think advertising can be a form of self-expression? Why or why not?

No doubt this is why entire *Seinfeld* episodes were built around products like Pez and Junior Mints. The popularity of Nick at Nite's vintage commercials, Rosie O'Donnell's peppy renditions of old jingles, the almost nightly commercial spoofs by Letterman and Leno—all have been testaments to the prominent role advertising has assumed in our lives. A whole school of fiction known as Kmart realism has grown up around the use of brand names, while a host of well-known songs . . . satirize[3] old commercials. It used to be that advertisers would appropriate a hit song (like the Beatles' "Revolution") to promote a product; nowadays, the advertising clout of a company like Volkswagen has the power to turn a song (even an old song like "Da Da Da," by the now defunct German band Trio) into a hit.

5. Why do you think that ads using songs to promote products are often effective?

So what does advertising's takeover of American culture mean? It's not just that the world has increasingly come to resemble the Home Shopping Network. It's that advertising's ethos of spin[4]—which makes selling a means and an end—has thoroughly infected everything from politics . . . to TV shows like *Entertainment Tonight* that try to pass off publicity as information. It's that advertising's attention grabbing hype has become, in our information-glutted age, the modus operandi of the world at large. "Advertising is the most pervasive form of propaganda in human history," says the scholar Mark Crispin Miller. "It's reflected in every esthetic[5] form today."

Miller points out that just as commercials have appropriated techniques

6. What feelings do you associate with the words *infected, hype,* and *pervasive*? Why do you think the writer uses these three words?

---

2. **exultant:** jubilant, triumphant.

3. **satirize:** to hold up to ridicule and contempt.

4. **ethos of spin:** a characteristic habit (ethos) of the mass media to manipulate the public's perception of events by presenting them from a specific point of view.

5. **esthetic** (es•thet′ik): of artistic form or taste.

that once belonged to avant-garde-film—cross-cutting,[6] jump-cuts,[7] hand-held camera shots[8]—so have mainstream movies and TV shows begun to ape the look and shape of ads, replacing character and story with razzle-dazzle special effects.

7. How do you think seeing the same techniques on film, on TV, and in advertisements might affect people?

For that matter, more and more film-makers, including Howard Zieff, Michael Bay, Adrian Lyne, and Simon West, got their starts in advertising.

Advertising has a more insidious[9] effect as well. Advertisers scouting TV shows and magazines are inclined to select those vehicles likely to provide a congenial (and therefore accessible or upbeat) backdrop for their products, while a public that has grown up in a petri dish of ads has grown impatient with any art that defies the easy-access, quick-study esthetic of commercials—that is, anything that's difficult or ambiguous. "People have become less capable of tolerating any kind of darkness or sadness," Miller says. "I think it ultimately has to do with advertising, with a

8. What support does the writer use to show the harmful effects of advertising?

vision of life as a shopping trip."

There are occasional signs of a backlash against advertising—the Vancouver-based Media Foundation uses ad parodies to fight rampant consumerism—but advertising implacably[10] forges ahead like one of those indestructible sci-fi monsters, nonchalantly co-opting the very techniques used against it. Just as it has co-opted rock-and-roll, alienation (a Pontiac commercial has featured an animated version of Munch's[11] painting *The Scream*), and Dadaist[12] jokes (an ad campaign for Kohler featured interpretations of . . . faucets by contemporary artists), so it has now co-opted irony, parody, and satire.

The end result of advertising's ability to disguise itself as entertainment and entertainment's willingness to adopt the hard-sell methods of advertising is a blurring of the lines between art and commerce. Even as this makes us increasingly oblivious to advertising's agenda (to sell us stuff), it also makes us increasingly cynical about everything else—ready to dismiss it, unthinkingly, as junk or fluff or spin, just another pitch lobbed out by that gigantic machine called contemporary culture.

9. Explain how spoofs or parodies of real ads might help fight consumerism.

---

6. **cross-cutting:** in film, the alternation of shots or scenes to suggest opposition.

7. **jump-cuts:** in a film, abrupt changes from one shot to another, without the use of a transition.

8. **hand-held camera shots:** film shots made without the use of a tripod or other stationary equipment.

9. **insidious** (in•sid´ē•əs): more dangerous than is apparent.

10. **implacably** (im•plak´ə•blē): relentlessly, unable to be pacified.

11. **Munch's:** Edvard Munch (ed´värt´ mooŋk) (1863–1944); Norwegian painter.

12. **Dadaist:** related to Dada; a follower of an artistic movement that thrived from 1919–1922 and whose members rejected all accepted conventions.

First Thoughts on Your Reading

1. **Explain why co-opting something, or taking something over, for the purposes of advertising can be an effective technique.**

2. **The writer of the article has some very critical things to say about advertising. What positive effects or qualities of advertising, if any, can you think of? Why are they positive? If you cannot think of any positive effects of advertising, write down two negative effects that the writer did not mention. Explain why they are negative.**

3. **Re-read the last paragraph and explain why the author thinks we should be concerned about the blurring of the lines between art and commerce. Do you agree or disagree? Explain your answer.**

READING SKILL

Making Connections

A Link in the Chain   In persuasive writing people will try to convince you of anything any way they can. The problem is, how do you know which claims to believe? Your **prior experience** can help you judge persuasive claims; it can be one of the best tools you have to avoid being influenced by every persuasive argument that comes your way.

TIP Making connections is a useful strategy when reading other things, too—everything from short stories to news reports.

THINKING IT THROUGH   **Making Connections**

Asking yourself the following questions will help you link your prior experience with whatever you are reading. Here is how one student made connections to an article she read about advertising and consumption.

▶ **STEP 1** **Ask yourself what subject the text is about.** The text is about how advertising leads to excess consumption.

▶ **STEP 2** **Ask yourself what experiences you have had with that subject.** I have bought things I really didn't need because the ads were so convincing or because all my friends were buying them.

▶ **STEP 3** **Ask yourself what the writer's opinion of the subject is. (If the text is an ad, ask yourself what underlying message is being communicated.)** The author is concerned about the issue. She claims excess consumption leads people to throw away perfectly good items, only to replace them with new items. She says this practice leads to overflowing landfills, which affect our environment and quality of life.

TIP If you have not had any direct experiences with the subject of the text, try to think of similar experiences you have had, or imagine how you would feel if you had experienced the subject.

▶| **STEP 4 Ask yourself if your experiences have led you to the same opinion of the subject.** It is fine if they have not—this just means that you will view the writer's argument more critically. *Sometimes I have bought a new thing simply because I was tired of the old one, even though it was still perfectly usable. I also know that my county has raised the rates on garbage pickup, because the landfill is filling up faster than city planners thought it would. City planners have not found a new site for expansion. Yes, my experience does fit with what the writer says.*

TIP You can use your **prior experience** not only to judge persuasive claims in articles and essays, but also to judge persuasive claims in advertising as well. Imagine, for example, an advertisement that implies you will become extremely popular if you buy a certain book bag. The magazine ads and free promotional posters are glossy and colorful. The book bag is also advertised on TV during your favorite program. The lively music, the crosscut shots, the attractive models looking happy and popular with book bags slung casually over their shoulders—everything about the ad says "Buy me and you'll be popular."

You are tempted to run right out and buy the book bag because the ad is really convincing and many of your friends are buying the bags. Then you remember other times you bought products—jeans, shoes, a wristwatch—that claimed they would bring popularity or respect. Some of your friends may have noticed and commented each time you wore a new product to school, but at the end of the day your total number of friends had not changed from the day before you bought the product.

By comparing an advertising claim, or any claim, to your prior experience, you can evaluate and critique its persuasive message effectively. Once you get through this step, you can make an informed decision whether or not to buy the product.

YOUR TURN 2 **Making Connections**

Making connections to "Bananas for Rent" will help you think more critically about the article. Answer the following questions, which correspond to the Thinking It Through steps on page 372, on your own paper.

1. What is "Bananas for Rent" about?
2. Being careful not to reveal anything too personal, write down a few sentences about your own experiences with this subject.
3. What is author Michiko Kakutani's opinion about the subject?
4. Use a few examples from your prior experience to explain why you agree or disagree with Kakutani's argument.

Emotional Appeal

A Heartfelt Strategy One persuasive technique that writers often use to convince you of their opinion is **emotional appeal,** also called pathos. Emotional appeals speak to your heart as well as your mind. They may convince you to buy an advertiser's product or believe a writer's argument by softening you up with vivid descriptions, touching anecdotes, and heartfelt narratives. For example, an ad for a charity might read *Have a heart: Donate money now.* A moving anecdote in a persuasive article might depict the suffering that will continue or the disaster that awaits us if we don't act now.

When you read persuasive writing in any form, be aware of appeals to your emotions. Emotional appeals can be used effectively to enhance a sound, logical argument. However, they can also be used to manipulate your feelings and distract you from your ability to think and reason.

Read the following quotation and the analysis below it.

> There are occasional signs of a backlash against advertising . . . but advertising implacably forges ahead like one of those indestructible sci-fi monsters, nonchalantly co-opting the very techniques used against it.

TIP Ads can persuade you by appealing to your head or your heart. When an ad appeals to your head, it uses **logical appeals,** information about the product's specific benefits or new features. When an ad appeals to your heart, it uses **emotional appeals,** inviting you to see the product in relation to some important feeling, emotion, or psychological need.

Quotation	Analysis of Emotional Appeals
"indestructible sci-fi monsters"	makes me think of a Godzilla-like creature destroying everything in its path
"implacably forges ahead"	makes me feel helpless when I picture the monster plowing its way onward with nothing to stop its progress
"nonchalantly co-opting"	makes me think that the monster of advertising is unconcerned about the consequences of taking over all other artistic expression

Here's how this sentence plays on my emotions: I think the writer wants me to feel scared or threatened by the influence of advertising on our lives.

Reference Note

For more information on **emotional appeals** and **logical appeals,** see page 293.

YOUR TURN 3 Analyzing Emotional Appeals

Find four other examples of emotional appeals in "Bananas for Rent." Write down these examples on your own paper, and explain how the author uses emotion in each example to further her persuasive aim. Put your answers in a chart like the one above.

Understanding Connotation and Denotation

Advertisers choose words not only for their **denotations** (the direct, specific meaning as defined in a dictionary) but also for their **connotations** (the feelings associated with a word). Some connotations convey double or multiple meanings that can subtly persuade people to buy a product or believe an argument.

For example, the words *odor* and *aroma* have similar denotations (they are both synonyms of *smell*) but different connotations. *Odor* can have unpleasant connotations such as the smell of a musty locker or a skunk. However, *aroma* is usually associated with a pleasant or savory smell. Which word would you use to persuade a finicky eater to buy your tasty soup?

THINKING IT THROUGH **Understanding Connotations**

Use the following steps to determine a word's connotations. (The example answers refer to the underlined word in the example sentence below.)

It's that advertising's ethos of spin . . . has thoroughly infected everything from politics . . . to TV shows like *Entertainment Tonight* that try to pass off publicity as information.

1. **Be sure you understand the denotation of the word.** If you do not know the word's meaning or if it seems to be used in a different way than you expect, check a dictionary. *Infected means "contaminated with a disease-producing agent."*

2. **List any words and phrases that are synonyms of the word.** Use a dictionary or thesaurus, if necessary. *Synonyms: corrupted, tainted, invaded*

3. **Based on whatever associations these words have for you, categorize the synonyms as having positive, negative, or neutral connotations, or undertones.** *All the synonyms have negative connotations.*

4. **Describe the connotation of the word and its effect on the passage.** *Infected has a negative connotation that is associated with disease. This word choice allows the writer to depict advertising's tactics as an unhealthy threat to our culture.*

PRACTICE

Use the steps above to identify the denotations and connotations of the italicized words in each of the sentences below. Write your answers on your own paper.

They are **(1)** *pervasive* as roaches, as persuasive as the weather. . . . They **(2)** *adorn* our clothes, our luggage, our sneakers, and our hats. They are **(3)** *ubiquitous* on television, unavoidable in magazines, and **(4)** *inevitable* on the Internet. The average American, it is estimated, is **(5)** *pelted* by some 3,000 advertising messages a day. . . .

Answering Main-Idea Questions

Advertising usually has a main idea: Buy *this*. Similarly, standardized tests often test your ability to find the main idea, or central point, of a reading passage.

Read the sample reading passage that follows. Then, use the Thinking It Through steps below to find the best answer to the multiple-choice question that appears after the passage.

Advertising is not always the low-level media form it is made out to be. An often overlooked genre of advertising is the public service announcement (PSA), which has the purpose of changing our perceptions and attitudes about public issues that concern everyone. Some PSAs, for instance, promote public safety. To convince people to wear seat belts, one catchy jingle urges viewers to buckle up before driving. Other

PSAs raise public awareness with cartoon characters whose slogans encourage us not to pollute or remind us that only we can prevent forest fires. Advertising is not only about making money, but also about making the world a better place where everyone benefits.

1. The author of the passage is primarily concerned with

   A. defending advertising in all its forms.

   B. showing how public service announcements help people be safe.

   C. disproving the idea that advertising is just about making money.

   D. describing types of public service announcements.

   E. describing advertising as harmful.

THINKING IT THROUGH **Answering Main-Idea Questions**

Use the following steps to find the main idea of a reading passage.

1. **Choose an answer that relates to the entire passage.** If you scan the entire passage, you see that **B** is only one detail that supports the main idea. Likewise, **D** does not state the main idea either. Types of public service announcements are only one piece of what the passage is about.

2. **Read every answer carefully.** Toss out answers that are obviously wrong. Choice **E** can be eliminated because the passage primarily discusses the benefits of public service announcements, a type of advertising.

3. **Beware of choices that overstate the answer.** Choice **A** is too inclusive. The writer does not defend *all* forms of adver-

tising. Be on the lookout for words such as *all, every, none, never,* and *always,* which can distort the truth of a statement.

4. **Look at the first and last sentences of the passage for a topic sentence that directly states the main idea. Check to see that other details in the passage support the main idea.** The last sentence states the main idea: Advertising's purpose is not only to make money, but also to benefit the public. The other details in the passage support this main idea. Choice **C** is the correct response, because it restates the main idea of the *entire* passage.

Writing an Evaluation of an Advertisement

WHAT'S AHEAD?

In this workshop, you will write an evaluation of an advertisement. You will also learn how to

- deconstruct an advertisement

- evaluate either-or reasoning and false analogy in ads

- evaluate and critique persuasive media techniques in an ad

- eliminate unnecessary *be* verbs

- correct sentence fragments

Can advertisements *force* you to buy a product or service? Some people think they can. That is because ads use a wide range of **persuasive techniques.** Most advertising is designed to connect a product or a service to a particular set of feelings—feelings like belonging, love, status, respect, or power. This approach is most common because exposure to an individual ad is so brief. A TV commercial may take up fifteen to thirty seconds of your attention, and a print ad may be seen for only one to three seconds as you flip by it in a magazine or newspaper.

There is no doubt that persuasive techniques in advertising are effective. They can raise your level of awareness about a product or issue—or change your attitude altogether. They can even affect your behavior itself, by convincing you to take action or to buy a product. In this workshop, you will **deconstruct,** or analyze, the persuasive techniques in an advertisement. Then, you will form your own opinion of that advertisement and support your evaluation of it.

Prewriting

Choose an Ad to Evaluate

Student Seeking Catchy Ad Before you can begin your analysis, you have to focus on just one ad. Look for an advertisement full of interesting information, such as illustrations of people or objects, engaging written or spoken copy, or an interesting background. As you choose your ad, think about who will be reading your essay. If you think your ad's content may not be suitable for a wide audience, choose another; when in doubt, ask your teacher. You might find a suitable advertisement in one of the sources on the next page.

- **Newspaper and magazine print advertisements** are good choices if you are interested in analyzing text and still images.
- **Television and radio commercials** are good choices if you are interested in audio/visual techniques and special effects.
- **Some Web pages** feature banner ads at the top and bottom of a page. Other entire Web sites are ads. Web ads are unique, since they can be interactive, requiring readers to "point and click" to receive information.
- **Buses, billboards, and posters** can display advertising. In fact, advertising can be found on just about any blank space including the sides of vehicles, walls, and bumpers. Outdoor advertising is usually designed to deliver a simple message quickly.
- **T-shirts, plastic cups, and other promotional products** can carry a message directly into the hands of a potential customer. Promotional products must make a simple and direct impression on their audience.

How's It Look? Once you have chosen an advertisement to evaluate, start by writing a detailed description of the ad. Focus on concrete details that will help someone who is unfamiliar with the ad be able to visualize—or hear—it. Also, make sure you summarize the slogan and claims that are made about the product, whether they are stated in words or visually demonstrated. Look at this student example:

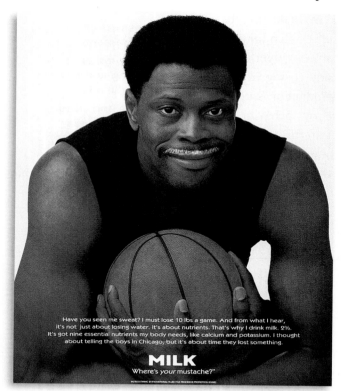

Have you seen me sweat? I must lose 10 lbs. a game. And from what I hear, it's not just about losing water. It's about nutrients. That's why I drink milk. 2%. It's got nine essential nutrients my body needs, like calcium and potassium. I thought about telling the boys in Chicago, but it's about time they lost something.

MILK
Where's *your* mustache?

> The ad I want to evaluate is for the "Milk. Where's your mustache?" campaign. The ad shows a photo of Patrick Ewing in a T-shirt, holding a basketball. He is looking up at the camera, smiling slightly, with a milk mustache painted on his upper lip. The ad's text is printed at the bottom of the page in white type over the photograph. The word "milk" is the largest word on the page and is centered over the rest of the slogan at the bottom of the ad.

Think About Purpose, Audience, and Tone

Taking Aim Every essay, whether it is for science class or for the school humor magazine, has to focus very specifically on its purpose and audience. Your **purpose,** or *why* you are writing this particular essay, should be to evaluate the effectiveness of an advertisement, to make your own value judgment of that advertisement, and to persuade your **audience,** the people you are writing for, of your opinion about that advertisement. Your audience, of course, is your teacher and your classmates, but you may also want to share your paper with a larger audience whose members are unfamiliar with persuasive techniques in advertising.

The purpose and the audience you choose will help you determine the tone and voice for your writing. **Tone** and **voice,** which communicate your attitude about your subject, have to do with the words you choose as you write. Some professional evaluations of advertisements are cynical and highly critical, while others can be light and humorous. If you choose to use a humorous tone, do not go too far. If your critique is too humorous, your audience will not take your opinions seriously. Follow these steps to determine your purpose, audience, voice, and tone.

THINKING IT THROUGH   **Thinking About Purpose, Audience, and Tone**

Asking yourself the following questions will help you clarify your purpose, audience, and tone.

▶ **Why are you evaluating this advertisement?** I think ads are very important in the decisions people make, especially about what they eat and drink. I want to evaluate how an ad for milk is persuasive and analyze whether it helps its audience make good health decisions.

▶ **Who will read your evaluation? How much background will they have—or need—about the subject or about advertising techniques in general?** My teacher and classmates will read my evaluation. It also might be read by people who are interested in learning more about nutrition. I'll probably have to explain something about diet. Although my audience knows a fair amount about ads, I'll want to explain the specific techniques used in the ad.

▶ **What tone and voice would be appropriate for your purpose and audience?** My tone and voice should be clear and straightforward, because I want my audience to understand how persuasion affects their health decisions. A cynical tone might alienate readers, while a humorous tone would undermine my message.

"Read" and Research the Ad

Snap Judgment   Advertising is everywhere in our society. Since there are so many ads competing for our attention, advertisers know they have to make a strong impression quickly. **Creators of ads focus on using simple, easily understood images and slogans to create a dominant impression.** Look at the ad you have selected to evaluate. Pretend it is the first time you have seen the ad. What is your overall impression? What "big message" do you think the advertisers had in mind?

> The overall impression I get from this milk ad is that milk is healthy. Patrick Ewing looks athletic and fit, so you're supposed to think that milk makes him so fit.

Prepare Yourself   To understand how your ad works, you will need to look at three important pieces that shaped its creation: the marketing purpose, the marketing strategy, and the "target" audience. The **marketing purpose** is the overall objective advertisers want the ad to accomplish. The **marketing strategy** is the plan that advertisers make to reach their goal and accomplish their purpose. The **target audience** is the group of people that an ad is focused to reach. You can get some information about all three things by closely reading and viewing your ad.

Identify the Marketing Purpose and Strategy   One purpose of many ads is obvious: to sell the product. Ads can also have other, more subtle, purposes, such as familiarizing you with a product's slogan. Once advertisers establish the ad's purpose, they develop a plan, or strategy, to reach that goal. Part of the marketing strategy involves creating a **campaign,** a series of several related ads that run over a period of time in a variety of media. The marketing strategy includes deciding what types of ads will run in the campaign—magazine ads, TV commercials, or billboards, for example—and how long they will run.

To figure out your ad's marketing purpose and strategy, research your ad in the sources listed below. (You may be surprised, for example, to find a newspaper article which specifically mentions the marketing purpose of your ad.)

■ Magazines about the advertising industry

■ Columns on advertising in national newspapers and magazines

■ Critiques of advertising in magazines, newsletters, and Web sites of nonprofit political and educational organizations

- Advertising agency and association Web sites
- Books on advertising

As you research these sources and closely examine your ad, take notes on what you find about the marketing purpose and strategy of your ad. Look at the way one writer jotted down findings about the milk ad.

According to an article from an advertising magazine, the purpose of the milk ad campaign is to increase sales of milk and revamp milk's image. The campaign's strategy uses print ads, including the one featuring Patrick Ewing, in many different magazines. The ad's slogan is also being promoted on T-shirts and cross-promoted on snack food packaging.

Analyze the Target Audience   Every ad is tailored for a target audience. Target audiences are determined by **demographics**—statistical characteristics of the population, including the tastes, occupations, and lifestyles of people in different geographic regions and age groups. For example, a lip balm ad may target middle-income skiers who live in snowy climates. By targeting a small audience, advertisers have the best chance of finding people most likely to buy a product.

TIP   If you have difficulty figuring out the target audience of your ad, try doing some research in the sources listed on page 380.

THINKING IT THROUGH   Analyzing Target Audience

The following steps will help you analyze an ad's target audience.

▶ **Look for context clues.** The location of an ad often reveals its target audience. Where did you first see your ad? Is there a particular group that the source appeals to? I think the audience for the milk ad is men and young people who like sports, because I found the ad in a men's sports magazine.

▶ **Analyze the headline or slogan.** Sometimes a slogan such as "You are over 50, but not ready to slow down yet" will state the audience—in this case, people over 50. The slogan "Milk. Where's your mustache?" could be used for any target audience; the headline could be aimed at anyone.

▶ **Examine the product and the product claims.** Ads usually appeal to the needs of a specific audience. Ask yourself, "Who uses this product? Who needs it?" Milk can be a drink for young people. The ad also mentions that milk can replace nutrients that an athlete loses. The target audience might be active, athletic teenagers and adults.

Analyze Persuasion in the Ad

KEY CONCEPT

Take It Apart Before you can **evaluate,** or make a judgment, about your ad, you have to **deconstruct** it. **Deconstructing an ad means analyzing its parts so that you can understand them and understand how they work together.**

TIP Make sure you take notes as you work through this section, since the details you discover now can be used as evidence to support your evaluation later.

Accentuate the Positive Effective ads convince you to buy products by playing up the positive and downplaying the negative. For example, you are more likely to buy a new pair of sneakers if an ad highlights how popular they will make you feel, rather than how expensive they are. Advertisers have three ways to emphasize the positive: **repetition, composition,** and **association.**

Repetition Effective ads repeat slogans or other messages to make the central ideas of the ads memorable; if you remember a product's slogan, you are more likely to buy that product. Looking at the campaign your ad came from can help you identify how repetition is used in your ad and ultimately how successful and effective your single ad is. Below are the notes one student took on the milk ad.

> The ad's message is repeated everywhere: on promotional products, in magazine ads, and in cross-promotions. Some people even trade and collect the ads. Repetition makes the ads seem like a natural part of our culture.

Composition It is hard to overestimate the amount of planning, money, and research that goes into **combining images and language** persuasively in an ad. Most ads begin with an attention-getter and then proceed to building the confidence of the audience, stimulating the desires of the audience, and tying those desires to the selling points of the product. All of the details in the ad, including **colors, shapes, line, and texture,** are designed with a specific goal in mind.

- **Colors add interest to ads,** as well as emphasizing or separating elements of the ad.

- **Lines add movement and direction to ads,** especially to flat ads, such as signs and print ads.

- **Textures and shapes help the audience interpret what objects are made of** and also add interest and emotion to ads.

   When you deconstruct a print ad, you need to focus on how the language fits in with the visual features to make a complete composition. Use the questions on the next page to examine the composition of an ad.

Language	■ What feeling does the slogan or the product name communicate?
	■ What needs, fears, or wants does the text of the ad appeal to?
Images and Visual Elements	■ How do the visual features and images contribute to the feeling of the advertisement?
	■ What font, or typeface, is used in the ad? What kind of impression do the fonts give you?
	■ How is the ad constructed? Does the ad use white space? What color scheme does the ad use? What impression does the layout of visual elements give you?
	■ Is the product pictured? Is there a product logo? Where are they placed? Why? What do they communicate to you about the product?
Advertisement as a Whole	■ What overall feeling does the advertisement have?
	■ What story does the ad tell? Who are the characters in the story? What is the setting and action? What is the point of view? Does the ad present a conflict and a resolution or a problem and a solution? What are they? What purpose do you think they serve?

If you choose to deconstruct a television commercial, you must also consider the elements that action, music, and special effects add to the advertisement. Begin by viewing your commercial several times. It may be helpful to tape it on a videocassette. Then, analyze each shot, or separate scene, in the commercial. Finally, ask the questions below about your commercial.

■ How is each scene framed? Is it a close-up, a medium shot, or a wide shot?

■ What camera angles and lighting techniques are used? For example, harsh light from above creates shadows under subjects' eyes and makes them look scary.

■ Where is the viewer of the ad positioned? For example, is the viewer outside of a house, looking in through a window? Positioning the viewer as an outsider can communicate that the viewer does not belong. (If, however, the viewer chooses to buy the advertised product, he or she will have all the things the people inside the house have.)

■ What computerized effects are used? For example, a commercial may use computerized effects to show the impossible, such as a flying dog.

■ What kind of music is used?

■ How do all of these effects contribute to the ad's power?

On the next page is an example of one way a student identified the strategies of image and language used in the composition of a milk ad. The ad's text is printed below.

> "Have you seen me sweat? I must lose 10 lbs. a game. And from what I hear, it's not just about losing water. It's about nutrients. That's why I drink milk. 2%. It's got nine essential nutrients my body needs, like calcium and potassium. I thought about telling the boys in Chicago, but it's about time they lost something."

TIP The physiology of the brain determines the power of text, sound, and image-based media messages. Images arouse the strongest emotions and are more persuasive than sound. This fact has given rise to a familiar cliché, "seeing is believing." Images and sound together, however, are more powerful than images alone.

Language	The text of the ad has a playful feeling, with Ewing even joking that he won't tell Chicago basketball players about the benefits of milk.
Images and Visual Elements	The white space in the photo and the typeface look modern, not distracting. The only milk in the picture is in the mustache on Ewing's face, and there is no logo other than the slogan. The ad feels personal—like Ewing and I are taking a break from a game of one-on-one—because Ewing is staring straight into the camera.
Whole Ad	The story of the ad is that milk makes this basketball player a winner.

TIP You have already been examining **persuasive techniques** such as *repetition* and *composition*. All of the persuasive techniques in the chart below fall into the category of *association*.

Association Effective ads associate, or link, the product being advertised with something familiar to the intended audience. Frequently, ads associate the product with an idea or object that is desirable. The chart below contains brief definitions of **persuasive techniques** (also called **propaganda devices**) used to establish association in ads. Use the questions in the center column to identify the technique in an ad, and consult the tips and examples in the right-hand column to understand each technique better. Keep in mind that not every technique will be used in every ad.

Persuasive Techniques	Questions	Tips and Examples
Glittering Generalities: associating a product with a "virtue" word to make a good impression without proof	Does the slogan or ad copy use words with strongly positive emotions?	Look for extremely positive words or phrases that are not supported by evidence. For example, "Sunrise Whole Wheat Biscuits: Bring the sunshine into your kitchen."
Symbols: associating the power and meaning of a cultural symbol with a product	Does the advertisement include any symbols such as flags, babies, or apple pie?	Look for images in the ad that are symbols. For example, an ad for chain-link fencing might show an American flag, a powerful cultural symbol in the United States, flying over the fence.
Transfer: linking the positive values of a person, place, object, or event to the product being advertised	Does the ad contain words or images with a positive value that are not directly connected to the product?	An example would be, "Like the Statue of Liberty, Veggie Vegetables has been around for over a hundred years."
Bandwagon: implies that everyone in a group is using or buying a product	Does the slogan indicate that *everyone* is using or buying the product?	Look at the slogan and ad copy for words or phrases like "join" and "be a part of"; for example, "Become a part of the Jump-Pro Sneaker nation!"

Testimonial: uses a spokesperson to advocate a product	Does the ad feature a celebrity, politician, or other respected spokesperson?	The testimonial may be from a single person or a group; for example, "I'm Maria Smiley, and as a dentist I recommend Glinty Toothpaste."
Snob Appeal: associating an attractive, desirable lifestyle with a product	Is the product identified with wealth, affluent people, or exclusive places?	Examine the ad for people, places, or things connected to affluence or status; for example, "I use only Lubricity Motor Oil in my collection of classic cars."
Use of Power Words: use of words such as "new," "fresh," or "improved" to make the product seem more powerful and desirable	Does the ad use words such as "fast-acting" or phrases that lend power and strength to the product?	Ads that use power words often claim to be improved without presenting proof; for example, "Zap! Detergent, with its new, fast-acting bleaching power, will zap your stains away!"
Appeals to "Scientific" Evidence: using scientific-sounding language to imply that a product is more effective or desirable	Does the ad contain scientific or technical language? Does the ad contain scientific-looking diagrams or illustrations?	Look for scientific claims not supported by evidence; for example, "Crystal Clean Water is 100% free of impurities such as chlorine or charcoal."
Nostalgia: an appeal to the good old days to make a product more appealing	Does the ad show images of the past or refer to the past in affectionate ways?	Look for affectionate references to the past, for example, "Remember camp outs, finger paints, and sandwiches in the kitchen? Let Mrs. Dee's Oatmeal Bread take you back to simpler days."

Here is how one student used the persuasive techniques chart to identify examples of association in the milk ad she was analyzing.

Persuasive Technique	Example from Milk Ad	Explanation
Bandwagon	"Milk. Where's your mustache?"	Implies that everyone is drinking milk. Milk is associated with acceptance.
Appeals to "Scientific" Evidence	Refers to nutrients that milk replenishes in our bodies.	Gives the message that milk is good for you. Milk is associated with health.
Testimonial	Famous basketball player Patrick Ewing is endorsing milk.	Makes milk seem like a part of Ewing's wealthy lifestyle. Milk is associated with success.

CRITICAL THINKING

Either-Or Reasoning and False Analogy in Advertisements

As you evaluate an advertisement, pay special attention to the advertiser's reasoning. Some ads contain a position and support, or a logical case that the advertiser wants potential customers to accept. Sometimes these ads contain sloppy thinking and **logical fallacies**—errors in reasoning. These fallacies may trick people who don't examine an ad carefully. When you evaluate advertising, look for logical fallacies such as *either-or reasoning* and *false analogy*. **Either-or reasoning** assumes that only two extreme alternatives exist—an unappealing one and the one the ad recommends. (Often either-or reasoning can be spotted by looking for all-inclusive words such as *only*, *never*, and *always*). Consider the following example.

Either-Or Reasoning: Truly Natural Water is the only healthy alternative to sugary, caffeinated drinks.

Logical Reasoning: Truly Natural Water is a healthy alternative to sugary, caffeinated drinks. Make it part of your healthy lifestyle.

Most ads are designed to make a point quickly. Analogies, or comparisons of two products or ideas, are a good way to make that point easily and clearly. **False analogy,** though, involves making a misleading or illogical comparison.

False Analogy: Using White Brite Bleach on your clothes is like buying new clothes every time you do the wash.

Effective Analogy: Using White Brite Bleach on your clothes makes them look like new every time you do the wash.

For more on **logical fallacies,** see page 303.

PRACTICE

Read the statements below and evaluate their reasoning. If the sentence contains either-or reasoning, write *E-O*. If the sentence is an example of false analogy, write *FA*. If the sentence contains logical reasoning, write *OK*. Write on your own paper and be ready to explain your answers.

1. The new IXP Laptop is your only connection to the great, wide world.

2. Educators say that imaginative play is an important step in a child's development. Get your child a Jolly Time playhouse today or a tutor tomorrow.

3. Eating Tom's Terrific Turkey is like running five miles every day.

4. Other shampoos with conditioners cost up to twice the price of Suds. If you don't buy Suds, you might pay more.

5. A Presley Frame makes your ordinary photograph a work of art.

6. If you buy a new car this year, make it a Roadly Coupe or you'll be left on the side of the road.

7. Don't let tax time creep up on you. Call RIA Tax Preparers.

8. A cup of Bryson's Applesauce every day will keep the doctor away. Stay healthy. Eat Bryson's Applesauce.

9. Let Cozy Soft blankets cover you like a blanket of pure white snow.

10. A bath with Ruffles Bubble Bath is as relaxing as a day on the beach.

On the Minus Side   Just as effective ads emphasize the positive, they also play down the negative through **omission, diversion,** and **confusion.** After all, who would buy candy if an ad admitted the candy rots your teeth? Up to now you have examined the language, sound, or images included in your ad; to find examples of omission, diversion, and confusion you may have to ask yourself "What's missing?" from your ad. To find out what's missing from your ad, you might compare and contrast your ad with another ad for the same product or even another ad in the same campaign.

Omission   Effective ads often downplay negative information to de-emphasize facts that may be harmful to the product's popularity. For example, an ad for an expensive product might not mention the product's price. Look at this student example.

> Looking back at the ad, I realize something is missing. When I compare the Ewing ad with another ad in which the Secretary of Health and Human Services advocates drinking fat-free milk, I see the Ewing ad omits the fact that two percent milk contains more fat than the average, nonathletic person needs. It omits information about the negative aspects of fatty milk.

Diversion   When necessary, some ads effectively shift attention from important issues to less important side issues in order to play down potentially negative information. For example, a junk food ad might divert attention away from the food's high sugar content by emphasizing the energy the food can give you. Use the questions below to find examples of diversion in your ad.

- **On what does the ad place priority?** What benefits or product claims are mentioned most? For example, does an ad for fire-engine red paint emphasize its low price?

- **Do the benefits mentioned in the ad match up** with the audience's priorities? For example, parents may place a priority on finding soothing, pastel-colored paint for the walls of their baby's nursery and not care how low the price of fire-engine red paint is.

- **Do the benefits mentioned in the ad represent the most important feature or effect** of the product? If not, what is the most important feature or effect of the product? For example, does a commercial for cookware explain all the things you will be able to cook with your new pots and pans, or does it focus on the "free" camera you will get if you buy the cookware?

Confusion   When necessary, effective ads use unclear words and claims to create confusion that may hide negative characteristics of the product. For example, an ad may claim that cereal can be "part of a balanced meal." This ad would confuse viewers into thinking the cereal itself is nutritionally balanced, when in fact the cereal is merely being added to an already nutritionally balanced meal. Use the questions below to identify examples of confusion in your ad.

- **Does the ad use "weasel" words:** words such as "great," "interesting," and "wonderful" that sound impressive but have little specific meaning? For example, "Buy Glitter Stars because they are really interesting."

- **Does the ad contain inconsistent or contradictory statements?** For example, "The Time-O Watch is absolutely free with your paid subscription."

- **Does the ad compare apples and oranges?** Are the comparisons fair and valid? For example, "Buying a Wheeley Bicycle is like winning the lottery."

YOUR TURN 4 **Choosing and Deconstructing an Advertisement**

Choose an ad, deconstruct its marketing purpose and goal and its target audience, and then jot down notes about the purpose, audience, and tone of your essay. Then, take notes on how your ad uses repetition, composition, or association to emphasize the positive and how it uses omission, diversion, or confusion to play down the negative.

Evaluate the Ad

You Be the Judge   Up to this point, you have taken apart your advertisement element by element. Now it is time to put the ad back together so that you can evaluate its overall effectiveness. Making an evaluation of an advertisement is not just saying whether you like the ad or not. It is a judgment based on a set of **criteria,** or standards. In this case, all of the criteria relate to how effectively the ad uses repetition, composition, association, omission, diversion, and confusion. To make a judgment about whether or not your ad is effectively persuasive, look over your notes on deconstructing your ad and ask the following questions:

- Does the ad effectively emphasize the positive through repetition, composition, or association? How?

- Does the ad effectively play down the negative through omission, diversion, or confusion? How?

On the next page is an example of how one student matched up her notes on an ad for milk with three of the evaluation criteria.

Repetition	The repeated use of the ad and its slogan in different magazines helps emphasize the positive.
Association	The testimonial technique associates being a star athlete with drinking milk. This strategy accentuates the positive qualities of milk. Also, the bandwagon technique—used in the slogan "Milk. Where's your mustache?"—associates drinking milk with being "part of the crowd." The appeals to "'scientific' evidence" in the ad's copy associate drinking milk with health and nutrition.
Omission	The milk ad omits negative information about the fat content of milk.
Evaluation	Based on the criteria of repetition, association, and omission, I know the milk ad is an effective form of persuasion.

Good-Bad/Fair-Unfair Put together all that you now know about the ad to make a **judgment** about its effect on people. Is the ad *good* or *bad*? Is it accurate or inaccurate? Even though an ad is effective at persuading people to purchase a product, you may not want to judge it favorably if the product is harmful to consumers. Before making a judgment of your ad, you should consider the ad's economic purpose and the value system it demonstrates.

Economic Purpose Almost every ad serves an economic purpose—*someone* will make money from the ad. As you examine persuasive techniques and product claims, don't forget the economic purpose of the ad. The student evaluating the milk ad did some research on the milk campaign to figure out the economic purpose of the milk ad.

TIP For suggestions of places to research background information about your ad, see page 380.

The economic purpose of the milk ad is to sell more milk. Apparently, milk sales had declined and milk producers wanted to drive them back up—milk producers will benefit from the ad's success.

Value System Every ad represents a value system that may or may not be in agreement with that of the audience, but the producers of an ad are always trying to appeal to something their audience values. To discover what values the ad demonstrates, ask the following questions:

- What does the ad say is the good life? What constitutes happiness in the ad?
- What does the ad say is bad or should be avoided?
- Does the ad use stereotypes? In what way? Is humor used? Who or what is the humor's target?

TIP Most ads are based on the value, or the idea, that people can find happiness and fulfillment through purchases.

Here are one student's notes about the value system represented in the milk ad.

When Ewing refers to the Chicago Bulls, the ad uses humor to draw people in and make them feel like Ewing is a friend. The ad uses a photograph of Ewing, an admired professional basketball player, to tap into the widely held notion that the good life is about winning and being a successful basketball player.

Big Picture   Now, what do you think of the value system the ad represents? What effect will it have on people who see the ad? Use the following questions to help you form a judgment about the potential effect of your ad on people.

- What impact do you think the message of the ad has on individuals and on society?
- Do you think the ad persuades consumers to act in their own best interests? Why or why not?
- Who, if anyone, benefits from the ad?
- Who, if anyone, is harmed by the ad?
- How do you think the ad or product affects and shapes attitudes and behavior?
- How do you think the ad reflects people's preexisting attitudes and behavior?

Here's how one writer made a judgment about the milk ad's effects on people.

I think that the milk ad is effective, but it is wrong to advocate using two percent milk without explaining the large number of fat grams and calories it has. The milk ad may have a negative effect on people. If people start drinking large quantities of two percent milk each day without altering the rest of their diet or increasing their daily amount of exercise, they may gain weight or have to deal with other weight-related health problems.

Write Your Thesis

Make a Statement   The thesis statement for your evaluation of an ad will have two parts. Since the purpose of your essay is to persuade readers to share your opinion of the ad, you should clearly state your opinion of the ad in both parts of your thesis statement.

- The first part of the thesis statement should state whether or not the ad is an effective form of persuasion according to the evaluation criteria.
- The second part of the thesis statement should contain your judgment of the ad's potential effect on people, including the impact of its economic purpose and the value system it represents.

Below is an example of a thesis about the milk ad.

This ad from the "Milk. Where's your mustache?" campaign effectively communicates the message that drinking milk will make you healthy, popular, and a winner. However, two percent milk may not be the most healthful choice consumers can make.

TIP Although thesis statements can sometimes be more than one sentence, try to make yours a complex sentence by using subordinate conjunctions such as *although* or prepositional phrases such as *along with* to join the two parts.

Organize Your Support

Put It All Together   Look over your notes. What three evaluation criteria are most strongly met (or not met) in your ad? What is your judgment of the ad, in terms of its effect on people? Your paper will require you to use evidence from the ad to persuade people of your opinion about the effectiveness of the ad and its potential effect on people. Look below at how one student found evidence to support one of her main points.

Evaluation Criteria	Support
Omission—The milk ad omits information about the fat content of milk.	The American Dietetic Association suggests buying lower fat versions of dairy products such as skim milk. The milk ad makes no mention of this.

TIP Be sure to gather support for every main point in your essay before you start drafting.

Once you have decided which of the evaluation criteria you will use for the main points of your essay, you will need to find a way to organize those points. There are two common types of organizational patterns for essays like this one: **Logical order,** or an order that makes sense, and **order of importance**—most important to least, or vice versa.

YOUR TURN 5   **Evaluating an Ad, Writing a Thesis, and Organizing Support**

Use the evaluation criteria to examine the effectiveness of your ad. Then, make a judgment about the ad's potential effect on people. Write a two-part thesis statement, and organize your support.

Writing

Evaluation of an Ad

Framework	**Directions and Explanations**

Introduction
- Open with an attention getter.
- Describe the ad and state the target audience.
- End with a thesis statement that shows your opinion of the ad.

Grab Their Attention   Start your evaluation with an attention-getting statement, statistic, or question.

Paint a Picture   To help your audience get a picture of your ad, describe the images, and the placement of text, slogan, and spacing. Also include a summary of the ad's written or spoken copy. Use the research you did about your ad to identify the intended target audience, as well as the marketing purpose and strategy.

Make Your Point   Include a two-part thesis stating your ad's persuasiveness and evaluating the ad's potential effect on people.

Body
- Include first main point based on the evaluation criteria, with evidence from the ad.
- Include second main point with evidence and so on.

Present Your Evidence   Use the notes you took during prewriting to provide proof, examples, and other evidence.

Explain Persuasive Techniques   Explain and illustrate the persuasive techniques you will discuss.

Draw a Comparison   Often, in illustrating one ad, it helps to draw a comparison to a more (or less) effective example. Such a comparison can elaborate or illustrate the features of the ad you are discussing.

Conclusion
- Sum up and reinforce the thesis.
- Restate your judgment about the ad's potential effect.

Restate the Thesis   Reinforce your main idea by restating the thesis and summing up your position.

Make a Judgment   State the potential effect the ad may have on individuals or on society.

YOUR TURN 6   Writing a First Draft

Use the framework and the directions and explanations above to help you write a first draft of your evaluation. On the following pages, a Writer's Model and a Student Model have been provided as examples.

A Writer's Model

The following is a final draft of an evaluation of an ad that closely follows the framework on the previous page.

What Is the Value of a Milk Mustache?

At first glance, the photograph of a smiling, physically fit Patrick Ewing holding a basketball would appear to be an advertisement for his basketball team, the New York Knicks. However, the milk mustache painted on his face and the slogan "Milk. Where's your mustache?" reveal that the photo of Ewing is in fact an ad for milk. The ad, part of a multiyear campaign to increase milk sales in this country, is designed to persuade teenagers, college-age students, and men in general to buy more milk. The ad's body copy suggests that two percent milk replenishes the nutrients that athletes like Ewing sweat off in a game. The copy also uses humor to suggest that drinking milk helps Ewing win basketball games. This ad from the "Milk. Where's your mustache?" campaign effectively communicates the message that drinking milk will make you healthy, popular, and a winner. However, two percent milk may not be the most healthful choice consumers can make.

The milk ad featuring Patrick Ewing is effectively persuasive because its slogan—"Milk. Where's your mustache?"—is repeated many times throughout a larger advertising campaign. Repetition of the slogan—through a multitude of ads, cross-promotions, and promotional products—has made the individual ads in the campaign recognized, and therefore effective. Repetition, a persuasive technique used to saturate the target audience with the ad's message, is effective because frequently repeated ads eventually root in the minds of the audience. The "Milk. Where's your mustache?" ad featuring Patrick Ewing, for example, appears in many different magazines, from business and news magazines to sports and health magazines, giving readers the impression that it is everywhere.

As repetition makes the audience used to the advertisement, the ad becomes a seemingly permanent part of our culture. For example, some teenagers are already collecting and trading original milk advertisements. The milk ad's slogan appears not only in magazines, but also in products for sale, including T-shirts, watches, and a book chronicling the creation of the ads. In addition to promotional products, you can find the "Milk. Where's your mustache?" slogan in cross-promotion on products ranging from snack food to oatmeal. By using repetition, the ad featuring

(continued)

INTRODUCTION

Attention getter
Description of the ad

Marketing purpose and strategy
Target audience

Description of the ad

Thesis statement

BODY

First criterion: repetition
Evidence for repetition

(continued)

Second criterion: association

Patrick Ewing—and the successful campaign it came from—have become a part of our everyday lives.

The milk ad is also effectively persuasive because it uses association. Association involves linking the product being advertised with something the ad's audience likes or appreciates. Association causes an ad's target audience to transfer their feelings and ideas about one item or idea to the product being advertised. The "Milk. Where's your mustache?" ad featuring Patrick Ewing uses the persuasive techniques of testimonial, bandwagon, and "scientific" evidence as forms of association.

Evidence for association

A testimonial is an endorsement by a famous person. As a spokesperson for milk, Patrick Ewing brings a healthy, athletic image to the campaign. His status as a talented professional basketball player causes readers to associate being a winner with drinking milk. The ad taps into its audience's desires to feel healthy, athletic, and successful. Since teenagers, especially young men, want to be winners like Patrick Ewing, they transfer these feelings and desires to the product, milk. Although simply buying a product like two percent milk can never fulfill all these needs, this advertisement is successfully persuasive.

Evidence for association

In another means of association, the ad's slogan "Milk. Where's your mustache?" persuades the ad's readers to join with celebrities and others who choose to drink more milk. This technique, called bandwagon, works by convincing the audience that "everyone is doing it." Bandwagon appeals to popularity and plays on the audience's desire to be "part of the crowd." The bandwagon technique is also an effective part of the "Milk. Where's your mustache?" campaign as a whole because so many different celebrities have posed for ads throughout the campaign. Since the ads seem to be everywhere, readers really do feel like everyone is drinking more milk.

Evidence for association

The milk ad also includes an appeal to "scientific" evidence. In the ad's copy, Ewing claims that because he sweats so much during games, his body is dehydrated and drained of important nutrients. The copy suggests that two percent milk replenishes these important vitamins and minerals. By using scientific terminology, the ad associates milk with health and good nutrition. Most consumers do not have the scientific background necessary to properly understand the ad's claims. By associating scientific language with milk, the ad's creators persuade the audience that milk, even two percent milk, is a healthful choice.

Third criterion: omission

One of the most subtle ways this advertisement persuades is by omitting negative information about the fat content of two percent milk. Omitting negative information, or giving people incomplete information, is effective because it can convince people to buy something that they might not otherwise buy. For most average consumers—those who may be more likely to watch basketball on TV than they are to play basketball—drinking large quantities of two percent milk may not be healthful. According to the American Dietetic Association (ADA), milk with two percent fat content has five grams of fat per cup. The ADA's tips for healthful eating suggest that consumers buy lower fat versions of dairy products such as skim milk. Yet the ad featuring Patrick Ewing specifically mentions two percent milk, which is not necessarily the best choice for most consumers.

Background

Evidence for omission

In contrast to the "Milk. Where's your mustache?" ad featuring Patrick Ewing, another ad featuring the Secretary of Health and Human Services promotes low-fat or fat-free milk. The Secretary agreed to do her ad as a free, health promotion activity. As a trustworthy advocate of and expert on health issues, the Secretary of Health and Human Services recommends drinking low-fat or fat-free milk, which may be more appropriate for an audience that does not exercise as much as Patrick Ewing does. Still, the ad featuring Patrick Ewing omits the potentially negative aspects of drinking two percent milk and therefore is effective in persuading readers to buy a product they might not otherwise buy.

Elaborate through comparison with another ad of its type

The ad featuring Patrick Ewing is successful in itself and as part of the larger "Milk. Where's your mustache?" campaign. The prevalence of the ads, the slogan, and the campaign-related products ensure that the ad's message is frequently repeated. By associating milk with a healthy winner, inviting readers to be like him, and citing scientific evidence that seems to back the ad's claims, the advertisers have created a very effective ad. Unfortunately, one of the ad's most effective techniques, omitting negative information about the fat content of two percent milk, is also one of its most questionable techniques.

CONCLUSION
Restatement of thesis

Consumers who are persuaded by this ad to buy and drink two percent milk may not be acting in their own best interest, especially if they engage in spectator sports more often than they exercise. Instead of creating advertisements that seem to promote health while omitting crucial nutritional information, the advertisers should focus on creating more ads, like the one featuring the Secretary of Health and Human Services, that promote a truly healthful lifestyle. And while they are at it, how about a new slogan: "Milk. Where's your fat-free mustache?"

Judgment of the ad's potential effect on people

The following evaluation of a car advertisement was written by Prita Chhabra, a student from Orlando, Florida.

You Are What You Drive

Attention getter

As consumers, we have been made to believe that we are what we drive. The car is a mode of transportation, but in our society, advertisements sell the car as a form of self-expression and personal style. With so many choices available, one automobile company has begun an ad campaign based on the concept of driving as an end in itself. The ads, which appear more frequently in upscale magazines, are aimed at people who can afford luxury cars but who also are interested in performance. One ad is a bright, colorful picture of a car in front of two different scenes which overlap. One scene is of a clear blue sky, rolling green hills, and a long winding road that ends in front of the car. The other scene shows a yacht club where expensive boats float on a pristine lake. At the top of this image are the words, "Luxury and performance come together like never before." Beneath the picture are two columns of information, one providing details about the performance of the car and the other about luxury. This ad proves to be very effective in persuading the consumer that driving can be enjoyable, but the ad's image of a car owner is not a very practical one for the general driving population.

Target audience

Description of ad

Thesis statement

First criterion: composition

This ad's composition is obviously well thought out. As the reader turns the page, his eyes immediately focus on the image of the car that is cleverly placed in the center of a black-framed page. The bright colors pop out at anyone who might be flipping through the magazine, compelling him to stop and look at the ad. Even if the reader does not stop to read the ad, the company logo is cleverly placed on the bottom right-hand corner where the page is flipped so that as he thumbs the page, he will still see the car's name and, the company obviously hopes, remember it later when buying a car.

Evidence for composition

The ad also uses effective language, such as like new, newly designed, and restyled, words that might attract people who want a distinctive car, and performance and luxury, words that might appeal to people who want one of the two or both. Because the ad is for a luxury car, one

Evidence for composition

might expect the price to be omitted since it might scare people away, but it is cleverly placed at the end of all the information given. On the one hand, those who do read to the end get a sense of the company's forthrightness, forming a sort of trust for the company.

To further entice readers to buy the product, the ad uses association, a technique that leads the reader to associate what he sees in the ad with himself. Because the theme is that luxury and performance make driving enjoyable, the scenes reflect those qualities. The single-lane road winding through the countryside evokes a sense of peace for people who just want to get away from the hectic lifestyle. The reader associates these pleasurable feelings with the car's ad and thereby subconsciously with the car itself. The driver of this car takes pleasure drives in the country, free of traffic, where he can really test the car's performance. Alternatively, he drives it, not to work, but to the yacht club, a place of leisure. The ad's readers associate the car with the scenes behind it. The ad seems to ask, "Don't you want to lead the life of wealth?" The answer is clearly, "Then drive this classy and sophisticated car and you will." Thus, the ad uses snob appeal.

While many ads leave out information about their product, this company provides many details, such as its audio system, engine size, and interior features. Although the ad gives a lot of information, it is guilty of omitting a comparison with other cars. People who do not know much about cars might believe that the features listed are exclusive to this model when in fact they may be able to find another car with the same features for a lower price.

The ad for this car is effective. The composition catches the reader's attention, and the copy provides information about both performance and luxury. Since some buyers are interested primarily in either luxury or performance while others are interested in both, this ad affects a larger audience than ads which concentrate on only one feature. While it is accepted that most people need a car for transportation, the car is marketed as more than transportation. Because this ad uses the clever technique of snob appeal, it may persuade people to buy a car that is more than their budgets comfortably allow. With thousands of cars being sold each day in the United States, a car manufacturer could do better in its ad campaign than play up the idea that people's cars determine their status.

Second criterion: association

Evidence for association

Evidence for association

Third criterion: omission

Evidence for omission

Restatement of thesis

Judgment of the ad's potential effect on people

Revising

Evaluate and Revise Your Draft

COMPUTER TIP

In your computer's word-processing program, try adjusting the line spacing and margins on a draft of your paper to make them larger. This will allow room for handwritten corrections on the hard copy.

Check It Twice When getting something right is really important, you check it not once but twice. You should carefully read your evaluation essay at least twice. During the first reading, focus on content and organization. On the second reading, concentrate on style.

➤ **First Reading: Content and Organization** The following chart will help you evaluate and revise your draft. Answer the evaluation questions in the left-hand column. Use the tips and revision techniques in the other columns to help you revise.

Evaluation of an Advertisement: Content and Organization Guidelines for Peer and Self-Evaluation

Evaluation Question	▶ Tips	▶ Revision Techniques
❶ Does the introduction have an attention-grabber, description of the ad, and background information about the ad?	▶ **Underline** the attention-grabbing beginning. **Put brackets** around the description of the ad. **Put a check mark** next to the background information.	▶ **Add** an interesting beginning statement, question, or statistic. **Add** or **elaborate** on a description of the ad. **Add** or **elaborate** on background information.
❷ Does the introduction contain a two-part thesis?	▶ **Write a number 1** over the part of the thesis that states whether or not the ad is effective. **Write a number 2** over the part of the thesis that has a judgment about the ad's potential effect on people.	▶ Revise the thesis to contain two parts: **add** a comment on the effectiveness of the ad according to the evaluation criteria on page 388 and **add** a judgment about the ad's potential effect on people.
❸ Does each body section discuss one type of criterion? Are body sections arranged in an order that makes sense?	▶ **Circle** a sentence in each section that tells what type of criterion that section discusses. **Number** each paragraph (or group of paragraphs) that discusses a different criterion.	▶ **Rearrange** information to support one type of criterion in each section. **Elaborate** on criteria. **Rearrange** sections in logical order or order of importance.
❹ Does the paper contain evidence and examples from the ad? Does it explain the persuasive techniques used in the ad?	▶ **Put a plus sign** by each sentence that contains evidence. **Put the letter P** next to each persuasive technique discussed.	▶ **Add** evidence from the ad or from research. **Elaborate** on existing evidence. **Add** information about the persuasive techniques used in the ad.
❺ Does the conclusion sum up the thesis? Does it make a judgment about the ad's potential effect on people?	▶ **Highlight** the sentence that restates the thesis. **Put a box** around the sentence that provides a judgment about the ad's effect.	▶ **Add** a sentence that restates the thesis. **Add** a judgment about the ad's potential effect on people, or **elaborate** on an existing judgment.

ONE WRITER'S REVISIONS Here is how one writer used the content and organization guidelines to revise part of the evaluation of an advertisement on page 393. Study the revisions, and answer the questions following the paragraph.

A testimonial is an endorsement by a famous person.
∧ As a spokesperson for milk, Patrick Ewing brings a healthy,   **add**

athletic image to the campaign. His status as a talented

professional basketball player causes readers to associate being a

winner with drinking milk. The ad taps into its audience's

to feel healthy, athletic, and successful
desires. Since teenagers, especially young men, want to be   **elaborate**
          ∧
winners like Patrick Ewing, they transfer these feelings and

desires to the product, milk.

Analyzing the Revision Process

1. Why did the writer add the information to the beginning of the paragraph?

2. Why does elaborating on information in the third sentence make the writing stronger?

YOUR TURN 7 **Focusing on Content and Organization**

Work collaboratively to revise the content and organization of your evaluation of an advertisement using the guidelines on page 398. Use the example revisions shown above as a model.

PEER REVIEW

Ask a classmate to read your paper and to answer the following questions:

1. Did the writer demonstrate whether or not the ad was effective? What evidence was most convincing?

2. Did you agree with the writer's judgment of the ad's potential effect on people? Why or why not?

▷ **Second Reading: Style** On your first reading, you focused on content and organization. The second time around, concentrate on refining style to suit your audience and your purpose. One of the most common stylistic errors is overusing *be* verbs. Why are such essential verbs thought of as clues to lifeless writing? Sentences built on forms of *be* verbs, including passive-voice verbs and state-of-being verbs, frequently carry unneeded baggage. Use the guidelines on the next page to evaluate and revise the use of *be* verbs in your paper.

Evaluation Question	▶ Tips	▶ Revision Technique
Are *be* verbs overused?	▶ **Highlight** all *be* verbs (not in a title or quotation). Count how many you have. If you have more than two per paragraph, check to see if you can revise.	▶ **Replace** unnecessary passive-voice verbs with active-voice verbs. **Replace** unnecessary state-of-being verbs with action verbs.

TIP Forms of the verb *to be* include *am, is, are, be, being, been, was,* and *were.* As you highlight *be* verbs in your paper, remember not to highlight *be* verbs in quotations.

Sentences

Eliminating Unnecessary *Be* Verbs

Start by eliminating unnecessary passive-voice *be* verbs. The passive voice combines a form of *be* with the past participle of another verb: *was given, is circulated, were updated.* In the passive voice, the subject of a sentence is acted upon instead of performing the action. As you can see in the following examples, the active voice is focused, clear, and concise, while the passive voice tends to be indirect, awkward, and wordy. In the sentence below, notice how making the subject perform the action of the verb eliminates the *be* verb and creates much livelier writing.

> **Passive:** The advertisement **was produced** by Tankersly Marketing.
>
> **Active:** Tankersly Marketing **produced** the advertisement.

Check also to see if you can eliminate unnecessary *be* verbs that are used as state-of-being verbs. State-of-being verbs connect the subject with a noun, pronoun, adjective, or adverb in the predicate. They show no action. State-of-being verbs often invade our writing without our knowledge, and when they do, they can bring the action of the sentence to a standstill. Think of state-of-being verbs as background music; no one notices them because they express so little. Often a potential action verb is hidden in a noun near the state-of-being verb. As you can see in the following example, replacing the state-of-being verb with an action verb not only puts life back into the writing but also tightens it.

> **State-of-being verb:** This advertising campaign **is** significantly different.
>
> **Action verb:** This advertising campaign **differs** significantly.

ONE WRITER'S REVISIONS Here is how the writer of the evaluation of an advertisement on page 393 used the Style Guidelines to eliminate unnecessary *be* verbs.

BEFORE REVISION

In another means of association, the ad's readers `are` persuaded by the ad's slogan "Milk. Where's your mustache?" to join with celebrities and others who choose to drink more milk. This technique `is` bandwagon, and it works by convincing the audience that "everyone is doing it." Bandwagon `is` an appeal to popularity and plays on the audience's desire to `be` "part of the crowd."

The paragraph contains four *be* verbs, one passive-voice verb and three state-of-being verbs.

AFTER REVISION

In another means of association, the ad's slogan "Milk. Where's your mustache?" persuades the ad's readers to join with celebrities and others who choose to drink more milk. This technique, called bandwagon, works by convincing the audience that "everyone is doing it." Bandwagon appeals to popularity and plays on the audience's desire to be "part of the crowd."

Changed passive-voice verb to active-voice verb.

Changed two state-of-being verbs to action verbs.

Analyzing the Revision Process

1. How did the writer's changes improve the paragraph?

2. Where do you think the writer got the idea for changing "is an appeal" to "appeals"?

YOUR TURN 8 **Evaluating and Revising for Style**

Revise your essay for style, particularly by eliminating unnecessary *be* verbs. Don't change every *be* verb, but make it a goal to get rid of all the *be* verbs that are unnecessary.

Reference Note

For more about *be* verbs, see page 666.

Writing Workshop 401

Publishing

Proofread Your Essay

Reference Note

For more information on **sentence fragments** see page 427. For the **proofreading guidelines** see page 13.

Make It Perfect Whenever you write, you want to be careful not to distract your readers with errors. Proofread your paper for errors in spelling, grammar, and punctuation. In particular, look for sentence fragments. Writers often write sentence fragments when they take notes. Unfortunately, some of those incomplete sentences make their way into essays without becoming completed thoughts.

Grammar Link

Fragments

A **sentence** is a group of words that expresses a complete thought. A sentence **fragment** is part of a sentence that has been punctuated as if it were a complete sentence. Fragments confuse your readers and make them wonder what you really meant to say. Sometimes fragments are created when subordinate clauses are capitalized and punctuated as a sentence. A **subordinate clause** has a subject and a verb, but it does not express a complete thought and cannot stand alone as a sentence. A subordinating conjunction, such as *because, that, since, who, which,* or *what,* signals a subordinate clause.

Fragment	That we had increased sales of fountain pens. [We is the subject and <u>had</u> <u>increased</u> is the verb, but this group of words doesn't express a complete thought.]
Complete Sentence	I told the manager that we had increased sales of fountain pens.

PRACTICE

Examine each of the following numbered groups of words, and decide if it is a complete sentence or a fragment. On your own paper, write a **C** if the word group is a complete sentence. If it is a fragment, rewrite the sentence to correct it. Be prepared to share your answers with the rest of your class.

1. The target audience for Playtime Popcorn which is primarily school-aged children.

2. Mothers who buy Playtime Popcorn.

3. That appeals to children's sense of fun and adventure.

4. The experts agree that Playtime Popcorn is 99 percent fat free.

5. Since this is a healthy nutritional snack for people from 5 to 105.

6. Because it can be served at sleepovers, camp outs, and movies with the family.

7. The ad shows children playing outside and digging their hands into a giant bowl of popcorn.

8. An ad that shows children's faces clean and smiling.

9. The typeface of the ad is pink with wavy letters.

10. Playtime Popcorn which is the most popular snack for school-aged children, teenagers, and even young adults.

Publish Your Essay

Getting the Word Out Now that you have revised, edited, and proofread your evaluation of an advertisement, it is time for your essay to reach its audience. Try one of these ideas to make sure your essay gets into the right hands.

TIP If you wrote your evaluation of an ad for a general audience, you will need to refine your evaluation in order to publish for a specific audience.

- If you evaluated a television commercial targeted toward young children, compile your essay with your classmates' essays to publish a viewing guide for parents. Pass it out at a local day-care center.

- Submit your essay for publication in a newsletter of a not-for-profit media education organization.

- With a few of your classmates, make an explanatory Web site about how to evaluate advertising. Include your favorite essays on the Web site.

DOONESBURY © 1995 G. B. Trudeau. Reprinted by permission of Universal Press Syndicate. All rights reserved.

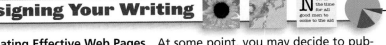

Designing Your Writing

Creating Effective Web Pages At some point, you may decide to publish your evaluation on the World Wide Web. By following a few steps, you can create an effective and interesting Web page.

- **Follow a simple and consistent design.** To create an effective Web page, you should plan the layout and design before you begin. Web pages usually have a title section, contents, navigational tools—such as hypertext and buttons you click on to move around the Web page—and a footer containing information about who created the Web page and when it was last updated. Make sure each of these elements uses a consistent font and color. The more consistent your design, the more readable and browsable your Web page will be.

- **Create useful navigational tools.** One of the most powerful features of the World Wide Web is hypertext—the ability to link pages. Make your links meaningful by including a description of the information being linked. Don't title your link "click here," but instead create links that say, "For more information, see Description of the Ad."
- **Use a standard footer.** Create a footer for the bottom of each page with standard information such as the date of the last update, an e-mail address for feedback, and links to other important pages. A standard footer helps your readers remember whose Web site they are visiting as they move from page to page.

Even if you do not have access to the Internet, you can use Web design principles to mock-up a paper version of a Web page. First, make a cover page that contains the most important information from your essay. Then, divide up the rest of your essay into sections and put each on a separate piece of paper with a title and a footer. "Link" the cover page to each section by including the page number where you can find each one.

PORTFOLIO

Reflect on Your Essay

Think About It   One way to become a better writer is by reflecting on your writing. Use the questions below to reflect on the essay you have just written—an evaluation of an advertisement.

- What do you think was the best part of your evaluation? Why?
- What was harder, deconstructing your advertisement or writing about it? Why?
- What would you change about your essay? What might you do differently the next time you write about advertising?
- How has writing about advertising affected how you view ads? What do you notice now that you didn't notice before?

If you intend to include your essay in a portfolio, attach your responses to your essay.

 YOUR TURN 9   Proofreading, Publishing, and Reflecting

Proofread your evaluation of an advertisement, paying close attention to any sentence fragments you may have accidentally included. Then, consider your options for publishing your essay. Reflect on your essay, and keep your reflections with your final draft of your evaluation essay.

Creating an Ad Campaign

Think about it: Have you ever seen just one ad for a well-known product? Probably not. Advertisers rarely create a single ad for a product. Normally, they create an **ad campaign**—several related ads that run over a period of time. Sometimes these ads carry a single story line throughout a series of ads, while others communicate different ideas related to the same basic **appeal,** or invitation to do or buy something. In addition, campaigns are organized around a single **target audience**—the group who might be most likely to buy the product. Ad campaigns may focus on a single medium, such as print, television, or radio, or combine several media forms.

Take Your Pick Work with a small group of classmates to create your own ad campaign. Your group will have to agree on a product and an appeal for the campaign. Have each student in your group create an ad for a different medium based on the product and appeal you choose. Each student will create only one ad, such as a TV commercial, a radio commercial, or a print ad. When you finish your ads, you will be able to put them together as a complete campaign.

To begin with, take a look at the ads your group members evaluated in the Writing Workshop (page 377), and pick one of the ads to revise for a new target audience. To whom else could you market the ad's product? (Consult the research and information gathered while writing the evaluation essay on this ad.) After you change the target audience, you will also need to change the appeal of the ad to meet the needs and desires of the new audience. (If you do not wish to use one of the ads your group members evaluated earlier, choose a new ad, and then decide how to adjust it for another audience.)

What if, for example, you tried to target an ad to sell a newspaper to an audience of young children? Since young children cannot read very well, your ad might emphasize the fun pictures on the comics page of the newspaper. Your ad might also omit information about the financial page, since that probably would not be interesting to children.

Once you have decided on a target audience and a basic appeal for your ad campaign, decide on a **format** and medium for the first ad in your campaign. (Remember, each group member should choose a different format for his or her ad.) This might be a full-page or a smaller, boxed announcement. You could even make a poster instead of a magazine or newspaper ad. If you choose to create a radio or TV ad, you will have to think about sound and video.

Also, think about where your target audience might see your advertisements most. If your campaign targets classmates at school, a poster and an ad in the school newspaper might get their attention. If your target audience is senior citizens, you could plan to take a small ad in a retirement newsletter and make a TV commercial to run during the national, nightly news. On the next page is an example of how one student planned to alter the milk ad discussed in the Writing Workshop to reach construction workers.

The Right Concept Once you have finished planning your approach, start planning the concept, layout, and written copy of the ad you will contribute to your group's campaign. The **concept** is the story or central creative idea that carries your appeal. Think about the ideas and emotions that you want to communicate as you create your ad's concept.

Set It in Stone The text or written copy for an ad often includes the following elements:

- **the headline or slogan**—a sentence or a few words that grab your audience's attention and present your audience with your appeal
- **the body copy**—a few brief, compelling arguments or persuasive facts that make the case for your appeal
- **the signature**—the name or logo of the company or organization whose product is being promoted

The student creating the milk ad wanted a headline that would appeal to a construction worker's desire to be strong. So, the student chose the headline "Milk. It's not only refreshing. It gives you strength, too."

Pay special attention to the headline, or slogan, since that will be read or heard first by your audience. Make it short and catchy. Tie the headline in to your concept, but also include an emotional appeal. If your headline affects your readers emotionally, they will be more likely to pay attention to your ad.

The text of your ad should include your best information and persuasive techniques. Choose words and techniques that will be especially appealing to your target audience. It can be tempting to put too much into your copy. Just remember that readers are not likely to read through a large block of text and listeners will tune out if they feel overloaded by words. For a print ad, position your copy below your headline so that your readers' eyes will naturally travel from the headline down.

Picture, Picture Illustrations draw your audience into your ad. Most people look at an ad's pictures before they read the headline or copy. Whether your illustration is drawn or photographed, make sure it is attention getting and relates to your overall concept.

Put together all of the elements discussed above to create the first ad in your campaign, but do not stop there. Go on to create more ads for your campaign. Note that you can use the general techniques above to create any type of ad. If you choose to create a radio commercial, remember you will have to think about how your slogan *sounds* as well as ways to describe orally the images you want the audience to picture. If you choose to make a TV commercial, you will need to create video storyboards.

Reference Note

For more information on making video **storyboards,** see page 413.

Here is an example of the student's concept for the milk ad.

The concept of the ad is that milk provides refreshment and strength other drinks cannot. The ad should show before-and-after pictures to demonstrate the effectiveness of milk. The ad should also use humor to get the audience's attention and make the ad memorable.

Here is an example of the copy one student wrote for the milk ad.

Copy: We all know that milk is good for you. It has nutrients that make you strong. What surprises some people, though, is how refreshing milk is. After you've had a hard day, pour yourself a glass of refreshment.

Here is one student's idea for how to illustrate the milk ad.

Show before-and-after pictures of construction worker. Before picture should show a tired worker sitting down at the construction site drinking a glass of milk. After picture should show construction worker looking happy and cool, performing a superhuman feat, like lifting a metal beam.

BEFORE   **AFTER**

Milk. It's not only refreshing. It gives you strength, too.

YOUR TURN 10 Creating an Ad Campaign

Using the previous steps, work with a group of classmates to create an ad campaign. Start by revising an ad for a new target audience. Then, have each group member use a different medium—such as newspaper, radio, TV, or a billboard—to create other ads for the same campaign. When you have finished, present all of the ads together to your class as a complete campaign.

Creating a Video Documentary

WHAT'S AHEAD?

In this section you will learn how to create a seven- to ten-minute video documentary about persuasive techniques in an advertising campaign. You will also learn how to

■ write a script

■ create storyboards

■ get feedback on your documentary

Advertisers use many persuasive techniques to convince consumers to buy their products. In your evaluation essay, you analyzed and evaluated an advertisement. Now it is time to broaden your topic and your audience. Expand your topic from one ad to an entire advertising campaign. Increase your audience by making a documentary.

Documentaries are informative, nonfiction films or videos that explore and analyze the real world. Since a documentary can be broadcast to many people at once, its message can reach more people in a shorter time than a single essay can. In this workshop, you will have the chance to create a video documentary that examines persuasive techniques in an advertising campaign. Creating a documentary on videotape requires research, analysis, and careful planning, just as writing an effective essay does. The difference is that in creating a video documentary, you use more than words to make your point: You use images and sounds as well.

Planning Your Production

Getting Down to Business   As you begin to plan your seven- to ten-minute documentary, remember that the first step drives all the rest. You have to choose an ad campaign to examine. Your documentary will examine the persuasive techniques used in a campaign, but which campaign? You could choose a real campaign, like the ad your essay evaluated, or an imaginary one, such as the one you may have created in the Connections to Life on page 405.

The Who and Why   Who will watch your documentary? What do you want it to accomplish? Deciding on your audience and purpose is vital to planning an effective documentary. The age of your intended audience, as well as the gender, economic status, and educational level, dictates the

TIP   Instead of choosing one ad campaign, you might choose two or more individual ads that use the same persuasive techniques. If you choose this option, your documentary will compare and contrast the ads' use of the techniques.

content and the tone of your documentary. Your **purpose** also affects your content. Do you want **to inform** people about how a specific persuasive technique, such as glittering generalities, works? Do you want **to entertain** people by creating a campaign for a fictitious product and then highlighting the persuasive techniques in that campaign? Do you want **to instruct** people on how to use persuasive techniques to create their own ad campaigns? Do you want **to persuade** people that persuasive techniques in advertising campaigns are deceptive and unfair to consumers? Most productions have more than one goal. What about your production?

Imagine this scenario: You have a younger brother who has just entered high school. In the last few months you have noticed your brother's preoccupation with "Milk. Where's your mustache?" campaigns. When he starts drinking seven or eight cups of whole milk every day without increasing his exercise routine, you become concerned that advertising is distorting his view of healthful living, so you decide to direct your documentary toward making him aware of how an advertising campaign works. The chart below shows how one student determined the **topic, purpose,** and **audience** for a documentary on a milk advertising campaign.

TIP As you plan your documentary, think about how media affect your perception of reality—that is, how you view the world. How specifically do you think your documentary will affect your audience's perception of reality?

Topic	the effects of the milk advertising campaign on people the age of my little brother
Purpose	I want to inform, entertain, and persuade my fourteen-year-old brother and his friends.
Audience	fourteen-year-old boys who are interested in the "Milk. Where's your mustache?" campaign

So, What's Your Point?   The next step in planning your documentary is to consider three important questions.

- **What persuasive techniques will your documentary address?** Ads and ad campaigns frequently use more than one persuasive technique. Since your documentary is only seven- to ten-minutes in length, you need to focus on just one or two techniques. Pick the techniques that are the most prominent throughout the campaign. For example, if you choose a campaign with different celebrities pictured in its ads, you might look for a persuasive technique such as testimonial. You would then need to explain in your video that the testimonial technique uses celebrity endorsements to entice consumers to buy a product.

- **How will your documentary engage the attention of your audience?** To get and hold an audience's attention, you must appeal to their emotions and give them ideas and images with which they can identify.

Reference Note

For more information on **persuasive techniques,** see page 384.

- **What will be the video content and what will be the audio content of your documentary?** The audio content, the words and background sound, helps the audience understand what it sees in the video content—the action sequences, interviews, and still photos.

Construction Zone Experts in the art of constructing television shows and films know that they not only have to attract the attention of audiences, but they also have to hold that attention. Here are some of the techniques professionals use to do both things.

Narrator or Voice-over	• Use an off-camera narrator to establish bridges between scenes. • Make sure the voice-over actually describes or highlights the video. The voice-over and the video should make sense together.
Action Sequences	• In every sequence include a combination of shots—from whole scenes to close-ups and from moving scenes to still shots. • Hold the camera steady or use a tripod so viewers don't feel seasick when they watch your video.
Transitions	• Use a **cut**—an instant transition achieved by stopping the filming of one shot and starting the filming of the next—to move from one shot to the next. A cut is one of the strongest types of transitions. • Use the **fade in/fade out** feature of the camera sparingly. This feature involves a two- to three-second transition from a full signal picture on the screen to a black screen and silence or vice versa.

TIP Set up a **preliminary meeting** with your interview subject before you film each interview. Your first meeting can give you a good idea of what your interviewee has to say so that you can get the best information on tape.

My Guest Tonight Is Another building block of documentaries is the interview. Since documentaries are about real people and events, interviews with experts can add a sense of authority to your documentary. To choose the best interview subject, find out about the local experts in your area. You might contact an advertising agency or even a local university to find interview subjects who are knowledgeable about persuasive techniques in advertising. Make a list of at least five people you might interview in your documentary. Keep the following tips in mind as you plan your interviews:

- Make sure everyone who is interviewed or videotaped signs a **release form,** a written consent to use a person's image and/or voice. You cannot use a person's likeness without his or her consent, even for a student production.

- Make frequent location and speaker changes to keep the audience's attention.

- Divide interviews into five- to ten-second segments.

- Make sure the interviewer asks only one question at a time and allows the interviewee to answer without interruption.

- Make sure interview questions are written so that they elicit lively (not yes or no) responses.

Reference Note

For more information about **interviewing,** see page 986 in the Quick Reference Handbook.

Learning the Lingo   Every profession or occupation has its own special language to refer to its unique ideas, techniques, situations, and concepts. Professional filmmakers have their special language, too—words and abbreviations that are written into scripts so that everyone involved in making a particular film or video will know what to do when. Some terms have already been defined in bold print for you. Here is a short list of other essential filmmaking terms and abbreviations.

Term or Abbreviation	Definition or Explanation
Angles	The angle of the camera in relation to the subject of the camera shot. For example, in a bird's-eye-view shot, the camera shoots from directly over the subject's head. Other common angles are high, low, eye-level, and canted (the camera is tilted to the side 25 to 45 degrees).
Close-up	The face of the subject fills the frame. This is the preferred shot for interviews because it shows facial expressions, which help the viewer understand the conversation.
Cover shot (also called a **master shot** or establishing shot)	A wide or long shot that establishes the overall scene for the viewer.
Full shot	A shot of a person from the feet to the top of the head.
Medium close-up	A shot of a person from the top of the head to the waist. Most of your shots should be medium close-ups.
Reverse angle	The camera shoots in one direction and then turns around 180 degrees to shoot in the opposite direction. For example, a camera operator might shoot the sun setting in the west and then turn around toward the east to shoot video of people watching the sunset.
Zoom in/zoom out	In a zoom in, the camera starts with a wide view and moves in to a closer view. The zoom out shot does the opposite.
Slow lap	A special effect in which images from two video sources momentarily overlap. It is used to provide transition between scenes.
EXT/INT	Exterior/interior.
MIC	Microphone other than a video camera's built-in microphone.
OS	Over-the-shoulder shot which shows the back of a person's head and possibly one shoulder.

(continued)

(continued)

OSV	Off-screen voice; the speaker is not visible.
POV	Shot taken from the point of view of a particular person.
FX or SFX	Effects (FX) or special effects (SFX), either for video or for audio, that are created during production to alter reality.
VO	Voice-over; narration heard over a video source and sometimes over music and other sound effects.

Get It in Writing   Scripting your documentary is the most important of your preproduction tasks. The success of your efforts will depend upon the quality of your script because it sets forth not only everything that you want your viewers to see and hear but also how you want them to see and hear it. Here are some basic rules to help you write for video.

- **Write short, concise sentences** in an informal, conversational style.

- **Appeal to your viewers' emotions.** Your viewers should care about the people and the content of your documentary.

- **Provide your viewers with structure.** Provide signposts that tell viewers where they are heading next, when they are seeing and hearing a key concept, and when a change of subject is about to take place.

- **Once you make an important point, illustrate it** or expound on it so that viewers can absorb it.

- **Keep in mind that viewers can absorb only so much information in a short period of time.** Do not give them more than they can handle. Take into account, too, that viewers are likely to be distracted, even in the space of your seven- to ten-minute time frame.

- **Remember the two critical parts of your documentary:** the beginning (where you want to grab your audience's attention) and the end (where you want to leave your audience with a positive impression).

TIP   If you are creating a script based on the essay you wrote in the Writing Workshop, remember to start with your thesis statement. (You may need to revise your thesis to match the topic and purpose of your documentary.)

TIP   You can use different typefaces to distinguish between your script's parts. Directions for the scene should be in italic print, or underlined, while special terms and abbreviations should be in italic boldface or all capital letters. Dialogue should be in regular print.

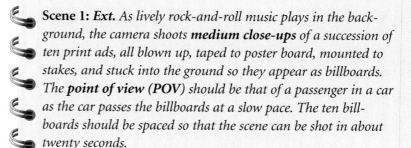

Scene 1: *Ext.* *As lively rock-and-roll music plays in the background, the camera shoots **medium close-ups** of a succession of ten print ads, all blown up, taped to poster board, mounted to stakes, and stuck into the ground so they appear as billboards. The **point of view (POV)** should be that of a passenger in a car as the car passes the billboards at a slow pace. The ten billboards should be spaced so that the scene can be shot in about twenty seconds.*

Picture Each Scene   The next preproduction stage is to create **story-boards**. These are the visual plans of the film footage you want to include in your documentary. You do not have to be a great artist to create story-boards. They are not works of art. Instead, they are simple sketches of what you want to film and how you want to film it. Once you have created the storyboards for each of your scenes, arrange and rearrange them until you are certain they are in the best order. Think about these questions as you create your storyboards.

TIP   You can use computer slide-show software to illustrate your storyboards.

■ What locations are appropriate for filming my documentary?

■ How many scenes do I want to include in my documentary?

■ What do I want to show in each scene?

■ In what order do I want to show these scenes?

■ How much dialogue do I want to have? Who will say what?

■ Do I want to use voice-over? How much?

TIP   There are many locations, such as malls and grocery stores, where you must get permission from authorities before you film. Before you shoot, ask a manager for permission to shoot. Have a one-paragraph description of your documentary available that contains your name, address, and phone number.

Here are a few storyboard cards from a student's documentary about the "Milk. Where's your mustache?" advertising campaign.

Scene 1: Rock-and-roll music in the back-ground. Camera moves over milk print ads.

Scene 2: Voice-over: You see them every-where—major celebrities with milk mus-taches. Milk is being touted as the latest health drink. How has the "Milk. Where's your mustache?" campaign convinced so many of us to begin drinking milk again?

Lights, Camera, Action   To be sure that you have everything just right, do a couple of dry runs before you shoot. Make sure you are able to take a high-quality image with good sound quality. Documentaries rely on communicating a lot of the message through language, so if your sound quality is poor, people will not be able to pay attention to your show. Practice using different kinds of microphones in different locations, such as outdoor locations and large auditoriums. The microphone in the camera may be appropriate for some kinds of shots, but usually will not be good enough when interviewing a source. When you are satisfied that everything is set up correctly and that your documentary will be within the seven- to ten-minute requirement, you are ready to shoot.

If you do not have film editing equipment, you may have to use in-camera editing. **In-camera editing** is not editing at all, but taping all your footage exactly in the order you want it to be seen. By carefully planning your shots and scripts ahead of time, you can get each scene right the first time. If you do make a mistake, correct it before you move on to the next scene by rewinding your tape and reshooting that scene. With careful pre-production planning, your video shoot will go smoothly and easily.

A Première Before Critics   Once you have finished taping your documentary, it is time to show it to your audience. Make a list of questions for your audience in advance of the showing. The feedback you receive could lead you to revise your script and reshoot your documentary. Here are some of the questions you might ask.

- What did you learn from this documentary?
- What was the strongest feature of this documentary? Why?
- What was the weakest feature of this documentary? Why?
- What one feature of this documentary would you change? Why?
- Will this documentary change the way you view ads? How? Why?
- Will it change your buying habits? Why or why not?

YOUR TURN 11   Making a Documentary

Follow the above guidelines to plan and to videotape a seven- to ten-minute documentary on persuasive techniques in an advertising campaign. Show the completed documentary to your classmates and others. Then, find out your audiences' reactions by asking them to respond to the items in your questionnaire. Finally, revise or reshoot your documentary based on your audiences' responses to the questionnaire.

Choices

Choose one of the following activities to complete.

▶ **CAREERS**

1. Survey Says Advertising is based on consumer research, and firms that conduct consumer research go where the consumers are: the mall. In fact, many malls and shopping centers have their own marketing research organizations. If there is a marketing research firm in your area, find out what kind of research they conduct. What information do their surveys ask for? Who uses this information? Conduct a brief **interview** with a representative of a marketing research firm and share your findings with the class.

▶ **LITERATURE**

2. Great Books Campaign Use the information you learned about creating ad campaigns to create a campaign for a classic work of literature. Select a target audience and brainstorm about their needs. For example, people who whitewash or paint fences for a living might feel overworked. You could get the attention of professional whitewashers with an ad that claims *The Adventures of Tom Sawyer* will teach them strategies for cutting their work time in half. Then, create a **print ad** or **commercial** that could con-vince people to pick up a great book and give it a try.

▶ **SPEAKING AND LISTENING**

3. On the Air Radio ads use many of the same persuasive techniques as print and TV ads. Listen to a commercial on the radio and take notes about any persuasive techniques you can identify. Then, prepare a brief **oral report** analyzing and evaluating the radio ad. Be sure to talk about the ways in which persuasion differs when you hear it from when you see it.

▶ **CROSSING THE CURRICULUM: MATH**

4. Adding It Up As you evaluated your ad, you probably noticed that much of advertising and marketing relies on demographics, or the statistical study of people's shopping habits, their media usage habits, their backgrounds, or other vital information about consumers. Do some research on what demographics are and how they are used. Then, prepare a **short report.** If you wish, share your report with your math teacher, in addition to your English teacher.

PORTFOLIO

Sentences and Paragraphs

10 Writing Clear Sentences

Ways to Achieve Clarity

GO TO: go.hrw.com
KEYWORD: EOLang

Have you ever adjusted a camera lens to bring an image into focus? Just as you can sharpen the focus of a camera to take a better picture, you can sharpen the focus of your writing to express your meaning more clearly. One of the best ways to achieve clarity is to write sentences that reveal the appropriate relationships between ideas. Usually, you reveal these relationships by adapting the structure of your sentences.

Coordinating Ideas

Equally important ideas in a sentence are called *coordinate* ideas. To show that ideas are coordinate, you can join them with a coordinating conjunction (*and, but, for, nor, or, so, yet*) or another connective. The connective tells your reader how the ideas are related; for example, *and* links equal and similar ideas, while *but* links equal and contrasting ideas.

In each of the following sentences, notice how the writer uses a coordinating conjunction to join two complete thoughts, or *independent clauses.* When you use coordination to link two independent clauses, the result is a *compound sentence.*

EXAMPLES   A colony of weaverbirds lived in a tree near his house, **and** he spent time watching them build and maintain their baglike nests.

Richard Preston, *The Hot Zone*

It is thrilling to be in touch with the world at all times**,** **but** it's also draining.

David Shenk, Data Smog

You can also form a compound sentence with a semicolon and a conjunctive adverb, or just a semicolon.

EXAMPLE　　But that L-shaped rip on the left sleeve got bigger**;** bits of stuffing coughed out from its wound after a hard day of play.

Gary Soto, "The Jacket"

NOTE　When you join two independent clauses with a coordinating conjunction, you usually put a comma before the conjunction.

We walked along the shore for a while**,** and then we dove into the ice-cold water.

However, a comma is not necessary if the clauses are very short and clear.

Shawna swam and I sunbathed.

Reference Note

For more about using commas with **coordinating conjunctions,** see page 505.

Sometimes you may have several equal, related ideas within a single independent clause. In addition to linking coordinate independent clauses, you can also use coordinating conjunctions to link coordinate words and phrases in a sentence.

EXAMPLES　　**Software piracy and component theft** alone are estimated to cost over $24 billion worldwide. [compound subject]

Mark Stuart Gill, "Cybercops Take a Byte Out of
Computer Crime," Smithsonian

Few people **knew or cared** about the dangers of such a policy. [compound predicate]

Malcolm E. Weiss, Toxic Waste

Anyone who had passed the day with **him and his dog** refused to share a bench with them again. [compound object of a preposition]

Kurt Vonnegut, "Tom Edison's Shaggy Dog"

Lifting her skirt, leveling her cane fiercely before her, like a festival figure in some parade, she began to march across. [coordinate verbal phrases]

Eudora Welty, "A Worn Path"

Reference Note

For more about **combining sentences by coordinating ideas,** see page 442.

Subordinating Ideas

Pennies, nickels, dimes—they are all units of money, but they are certainly not equal in value. Just as some coins have greater value than others, some of your ideas in writing are more important than others. However, the importance of an idea is not always as obvious as the worth of a coin. To make the main ideas stand out in your writing, you need to downplay, or **subordinate,** the less important ones.

You can subordinate an idea in a sentence by putting the idea in a subordinate clause. The subordinate clause elaborates on the thought expressed in the independent clause.

EXAMPLES   Maria, **who likes disaster movies,** saw the movie *Titanic* three times.

Titanic is a good example of the way historical events can be brought to life **because the story focuses on the relationships between people on the ship.**

Adverb Clauses

An **adverb clause** modifies a verb, an adjective, or an adverb in a sentence. You introduce an adverb clause with a subordinating conjunction (*although, after, because, if, since, when, whenever, where, while*).

EXAMPLES   **Although symbolic puns are relatively rare in dreams,** they do occasionally show up in surprising ways.

Keith Harary, "Language of the Night," *Omni*

This confession he spoke harshly **because its unexpectedness shook him.**

Bernard Malamud, "The Magic Barrel"

The controversy began simmering more than a year ago, **when Louis Sullivan, then Secretary of Health and Human Services, proposed a $400 million federal research program on violence.**

Anastasia Toufexis, "Seeking the Roots of Violence," *Time*

If there'd been any farther west to go, he'd have gone.

John Steinbeck, *The Red Pony*

The subordinating conjunction you use is important. It shows your reader the relationship between the ideas in the adverb clause and the independent clause. This chart lists the subordinating conjunctions you can use to express the following relationships of *time or place, cause or reason, purpose or result,* or *condition.*

Subordinating Conjunctions			
Time or Place	after as before since	until when whenever	where wherever while
Cause or Reason	as because	since	whereas
Purpose or Result	in order that	that	so that
Condition	although even though	if provided that	unless while

Exercise 1 **Selecting Appropriate Coordinating and Subordinating Conjunctions**

For each of the following sentences, choose an appropriate coordinating or subordinating conjunction to fill in the blank. The hint in parentheses tells you what kind of relationship the conjunction should express.

1. It is called a lake, _____ Moraine is really a three-acre pond located beneath a high, majestic ridge on Grapetree Mountain. (condition)
2. _____ we visited Lake Moraine, we heard wild geese and saw beavers building dams. (time)
3. We sat by the tent one summer evening _____ a snowshoe hare crept from behind the pine trees to eat lettuce from our hands. (time)
4. Lake Moraine, a wonderful, peaceful place, is now threatened _____ acid rains are destroying the brook trout that swim in its waters. (cause or reason)
5. _____ acid pollutants from factory fumes enter the atmosphere, they fall to the earth in rain and snow. (time)

STYLE   TIP

As you can see from the examples given, an adverb clause can make sense at either the beginning or the end of a sentence. Try a clause in both positions to see which sounds better to you. When you place an adverb clause at the beginning of a sentence, remember to separate it from the independent clause with a comma. Otherwise, you may confuse your reader.

EXAMPLE
The soils of boreal forests have high acid counts **because of the buildup of acidic tree needles.**

or

Because of the buildup of acidic tree needles, the soils of boreal forests have high acid counts.

Scientist taking water sample.

6. High-altitude ponds such as Lake Moraine get a heavy dose of acid rains _____ the mountains trap moisture-bearing air masses. (cause or reason)

7. _____ the acid pollutants end up in the mountain ponds, fish, especially trout, suffer and die in great numbers. (time)

8. Many remote trout ponds are encased in granite _____ little soil or organic matter exists to trap or buffer the acid rain. (purpose or result)

9. _____ it is possible to develop acid-tolerant strains of trout, such a program of selective breeding will likely take many years. (condition)

10. More and more isolated ponds like Lake Moraine will become trout graveyards _____ we don't find a way to combat the effects of acid rain. (condition)

Adjective Clauses

An *adjective clause* modifies a noun or pronoun and usually begins with *who, whom, whose, which, that,* or *where.*

EXAMPLES   I was camped near a creek **that emptied into the bay.**

> Timothy Treadwell and Jewel Palovak,
> *Among Grizzlies*

Chicago seemed an unreal city **whose mythical houses were built of slabs of black coal wreathed in palls of gray smoke,** houses **whose foundations were sinking slowly into the dank prairie.**

> Richard Wright, *American Hunger*

Before you use an adjective clause in a sentence, you need to decide which idea you want to emphasize and which you want to subordinate, or downplay. For example, suppose you want to combine these two ideas in one sentence:

> Advertising became big business in the 1920s. It fueled the demand for cars and other consumer goods.

If you want to emphasize that advertising became big business in the 1920s, put the information in the second sentence into an adjective clause.

> Advertising, **which fueled the demand for cars and other consumer goods,** became big business in the 1920s.

However, if you want to emphasize that advertising fueled consumers' demand for goods, put that information in an independent clause and the other information in an adjective clause.

> Advertising, **which became big business in the 1920s,** fueled the demand for cars and other consumer goods.

NOTE When using an adjective clause to transform two sentences into one, you may need to change the **word order** of the adjective clause to make the new sentence work. For clarity, be sure that you place the adjective clause next to the word it modifies.

STYLE **TIP**

Note that adjective clauses may be embedded within an independent clause or sentence.

Reference Note

For more about **combining sentences by subordinating ideas,** see page 444.

Exercise 2 Subordinating Ideas by Using Adjective Clauses

Change the emphasis in each of the following sentences. Emphasize the idea that is now in the subordinate clause, and subordinate the idea that is now in the independent clause. You may have to delete some words, change the word order, or use a different word to begin the new subordinate clause. Which version of the sentence sounds better to you? Why?

1. N. Scott Momaday, who writes eloquently about American Indian culture, won a Pulitzer Prize for the novel *House Made of Dawn.*
2. *House Made of Dawn,* which was published in 1968, focuses on an American Indian man's struggle to reconcile traditional tribal values with modern-day American life.
3. Momaday spent his boyhood on several different reservations, where he acquired extensive knowledge of American Indian history and culture.
4. Momaday's book *The Way to Rainy Mountain,* which gives a perceptive account of American Indian life, focuses on the history and culture of the Kiowas.
5. Momaday, who has also published two collections of poems, considers himself primarily a poet.

Correcting Faulty Coordination

Before you join ideas with a coordinating conjunction, it is important to make sure the ideas are of equal importance. Otherwise you may end up with *faulty coordination,* unequal ideas presented as if they were coordinate. Faulty coordination blurs the focus of your writing because it does not show the relationships between ideas. You can correct faulty coordination by putting the less-important ideas into phrases or subordinate clauses.

FAULTY   Norway's coastal waters are influenced by the warm Atlantic Ocean currents and the westerly winds, and the coastal waters stay ice-free, and they are ice-free all year.

REVISED   **Because Norway's coastal waters are influenced by the warm Atlantic Ocean currents and westerly winds,** they stay ice-free **all year.**

or

Norway's coastal waters, **which are influenced by the warm Atlantic Ocean currents and the westerly winds,** stay ice-free **all year.**

Using Parallel Structure

Like a comfortable bicycle ride, writing should have smooth movement; it shouldn't be a bumpy journey over mental potholes and gravel. You can make your writing smoother and clearer by checking your sentences for *parallel structure.*

You create parallel structure in a sentence by using the same grammatical form to express equal, or parallel, ideas. For example, you pair a noun with a noun, a phrase with a phrase, a clause with a clause, and an infinitive with an infinitive.

Use parallel structure when you link coordinate ideas.

NOT PARALLEL   Mrs. Silva prefers exercising and to paint. [gerund paired with infinitive]

PARALLEL   Mrs. Silva prefers **to exercise** and **to paint.** [infinitive paired with infinitive]

NOT PARALLEL   Our computer club promises that we will visit a college and a banquet. [noun clause paired with a noun]

PARALLEL   Our computer club promises **that we will visit a college** and **that we will have a banquet.** [noun clause paired with noun clause]

Use parallel structure when you compare or contrast ideas.

NOT PARALLEL   To think logically is as important as calculating accurately. [infinitive compared with a gerund]

PARALLEL   **Thinking** logically is as important as **calculating** accurately. [gerund compared with a gerund]

NOT PARALLEL   Einstein liked doing mathematical research more than to supervise a large laboratory. [gerund phrase contrasted with an infinitive phrase]

PARALLEL   Einstein liked **doing mathematical research** more than **supervising a large laboratory.** [gerund phrase contrasted with a gerund phrase]

Use parallel structure when you link ideas with the conjunctions *both . . . and, either . . . or, neither . . . nor,* or *not only . . . but also.* These pairs are called *correlative conjunctions.*

NOT PARALLEL   In a Puritan village of 1680, a girl had to help her mother not only as a maker of household remedies, such as palsy drops and pokeberry plaster, but also in cooking.

PARALLEL   In a Puritan village of 1680, a girl had to help her mother not only **as a maker of household remedies,** such as palsy drops and pokeberry plaster, but also **as a cook.**

When you use correlative conjunctions, be sure to place the conjunctions directly before the parallel terms. Otherwise the relationship between the ideas will not be clear.

UNCLEAR   The tornado not only destroyed the shed behind the store but also the water tower across the street.

CLEAR   The tornado destroyed **not only** the shed behind the store **but also** the water tower across the street.

> **Exercise 3** Revising Sentences by Using Parallel Structure

Some of the following sentences are out of balance. Bring balance to them by putting the ideas in parallel form. You may need to delete, add, or move some words. If a sentence is already correct, write *C*.

1. Sports fans may disagree about whether going to baseball games or to watch football is more fun, but few people can ignore the importance of sports in America.
2. Sports has always been a topic for friendly and not-so-friendly arguments.

STYLE   **TIP**

Parallel structure can add more than clarity to language—it can also add rhythm and emphasis. One good way to tell if your use of parallelism provides the emphasis you intend is to read the sentence aloud. Do you *hear* the similarities between the parallel ideas?

3. Some sports fans argue endlessly and with anger about whether football or baseball is truly the American pastime.
4. Baseball backers may insist that baseball is the more important game because it requires skill, dexterity, and to be fast.
5. On the other hand, football fans may praise a quarterback's speed, skill, and how agile he is.

Review A Revising Paragraphs for Clarity

Faulty coordination and faulty parallelism make the following paragraphs confusing. Using the methods you have learned in this chapter, revise each faulty sentence to make it clear and smooth. You may need to add, delete, or rearrange some words in the sentences. Remember to check the placement of correlative conjunctions.

Amy Tan is a Chinese American writer, and she writes skillfully about the lives of second-generation Chinese Americans. In her first two novels, The Joy Luck Club and The Kitchen God's Wife, she portrays family relationships both with humor and insightfully. These novels were praised by critics, and they deal with the difficulties mothers and daughters have in truly understanding one another.

In her third novel, The Hundred Secret Senses, Tan shifts to the relationship between sisters. The younger sister is embarrassed and has resentment of her older sister until the two travel to China together.

Tan seems like a natural-born storyteller, but she did not always plan to write fiction. In fact, her parents hoped she would become a neurosurgeon. Tan was working as a freelance business writer, and she decided to try her hand at writing short stories. She joined a writing workshop and submitted her first story. She was revising it, and the story grew, changed, and eventually to become the basis for her first novel. Once The Joy Luck Club was published, Tan became an instant celebrity. With her third novel, The Hundred Secret Senses, Tan has proven that she has an important subject and her talent is lasting.

Obstacles to Clarity

In the first part of this chapter, you had some practice at putting your ideas in proper relationship to one another. The next important step toward clarity is to check your sentences for completeness. As you revise, you need to be on the alert for two obstacles to clarity, *sentence fragments* and *run-on sentences.*

Sentence Fragments

A sentence should express a complete thought. If you capitalize and punctuate a part of a sentence as if it were a complete sentence, you create a **sentence fragment.**

FRAGMENT	Has large horns shaped like corkscrews. [The subject is missing. *What* has large horns shaped like corkscrews?]
SENTENCE	**A male kudu** has large horns shaped like corkscrews.
FRAGMENT	The kudu, a type of antelope, in Africa. [The verb is missing.]
SENTENCE	The kudu, a type of antelope, **lives** in Africa.
FRAGMENT	The kudu, a type of antelope, found in Africa. [The helping verb is missing.]
SENTENCE	The kudu, a type of antelope, **is** found in Africa.
FRAGMENT	While the kudu stands five feet high at the shoulder. [This has a subject and a verb, but it doesn't express a complete thought.]
SENTENCE	While the kudu stands five feet high at the shoulder, **with its long horns its total height can reach past ten feet.**

The meaning of a fragment you have written may seem clear to you because you know the information you have left out. Try looking at what you have written as though the information is all new to you. Ask what else a reader might need to know.

NOTE Experienced writers sometimes use fragments deliberately for effect. For example, in the following excerpt, Leslie Norris uses fragments to imitate the sounds of natural speech. Notice that the meaning of the fragments is made clear by the sentences that come before and after them.

> "This was an unusual goose," my uncle said. "Called at the back door every morning for its food, answered to its name. An intelligent creature. Eddie's sisters tied a blue silk ribbon around its neck and made a pet of it. It displayed more personality and understanding than you'd believe possible in a bird. Came Christmas, of course, and they couldn't kill it."
>
> Leslie Norris, "A Flight of Geese"

Fragments can be effective when they are used as a stylistic technique. You may want to experiment with using them in expressive and creative writing such as journals, poems, and short stories. You can also use fragments when an informal, shorthand style is appropriate—for example, in classified ads.

However, do not use fragments if they might interfere with your purpose or confuse your audience. For example, you would not use fragments in a research paper or a book report, since your readers expect formal, straightforward language in these types of informative writing.

Exercise 4 Identifying and Revising Sentence Fragments

Decide which of these word groups are sentences and which are fragments. If an item contains only complete sentences, write *C* for correct. If it contains a fragment, revise the fragment.

1. Many great Americans had little or no formal education. Among these are political leaders, writers, artists, scientists, and business executives.
2. Eleanor Roosevelt had little formal education. Susan B. Anthony the equivalent of a high school education.
3. When Abraham Lincoln was a young man, he worked in a general store. And at the same time studied books on law.

Susan B. Anthony

4. Although Carl Sandburg left school when he was thirteen years old. He later went on to Lombard College after serving in the army during the Spanish-American War.

5. Andrew Carnegie, who gave away many millions to charity, started to work at the age of thirteen. He did not go to high school.

6. Gordon Parks, who had a high school education, the World Press Photo Award in 1988.

7. Booker T. Washington walked two hundred miles to attend school at Hampton Institute. Later founded Tuskegee Institute.

8. One of the great letter writers of all time, Abigail Adams, had little formal schooling.

9. Ben Franklin, who became a printer's apprentice when he was only twelve. He taught himself to become a proficient writer by studying and imitating essays in *The Spectator*.

10. On the other hand, many famous Americans had excellent educations. As a child, Willa Cather, for instance, was taught Greek and Latin by a Nebraska shopkeeper.

Willa Cather

The Granger Collection, New York.

Phrase Fragments

One type of sentence fragment is a phrase fragment. A *phrase* is a group of related words that acts as a single part of speech and that does not contain a subject and a verb. Because a phrase does not express a complete thought, it cannot stand on its own as a sentence.

Often, you can correct a phrase fragment by attaching it to the sentence that comes before or after it.

FRAGMENT   **During her long and productive life.** Nina Otero-Warren excelled as an educator, writer, and public official. [prepositional phrase]

SENTENCE   During her long and productive life, Nina Otero-Warren excelled as an educator, writer, and public official.

FRAGMENT   **Descended from a long line of political leaders.** Otero-Warren became active in politics soon after she graduated from college. [verbal phrase—participial]

SENTENCE   Descended from a long line of political leaders, Otero-Warren became active in politics soon after she graduated from college.

Reference Note

The **types of phrases** include **prepositional, verbal, absolute, and appositive.** For explanations of these types of phrases, see pages 536, 540, 541, and 550.

FRAGMENT	She was one of the first Mexican American women. **To hold important public posts in New Mexico.** [verbal phrase—infinitive]
SENTENCE	She was one of the first Mexican American women to hold important public posts in New Mexico.

FRAGMENT	In 1917, she became superintendent of schools in Santa Fe County. **An unusual position for a woman at that time.** [appositive phrase]
SENTENCE	In 1917, she became superintendent of schools in Santa Fe County, an unusual position for a woman at that time.

FRAGMENT	**Her heritage being an important influence in her life.** Nina Otero-Warren wrote *Old Spain in Our Southwest,* a narrative account of the history and folklore of the Southwest. [absolute phrase]
SENTENCE	Her heritage being an important influence in her life, Nina Otero-Warren wrote *Old Spain in Our Southwest,* a narrative account of the history and folklore of the Southwest.

Subordinate Clause Fragments

A *clause* is a group of words that contains a subject and a verb. An *independent clause* expresses a complete thought and can stand alone as a sentence. However, a *subordinate clause* does not express a complete thought and cannot stand alone as a sentence. If you see a subordinate clause standing alone, it is another type of sentence fragment.

FRAGMENT	Felicia enjoyed watching the Comets' game. **Which was televised last Monday.**
CORRECT	Felicia enjoyed watching the Comets' game, which was televised last Monday.

FRAGMENT	Felicia hopes to play professionally. **When she graduates from college.**
CORRECT	Felicia hopes to play professionally when she graduates from college.

While checking over your work, you may find that two other constructions cause you trouble: items in a series and compound verbs.

FRAGMENT We had terrible weather. **Heat, drought, and thunderstorms.** [items in a series]

CORRECT We had terrible weather. **We had** heat, drought, and thunderstorms.

or

We had terrible weather**:** heat, drought, and thunderstorms.

FRAGMENT Tinesha tried to jog. **But could not tolerate the heat.**
[compound verb]

CORRECT Tinesha tried to jog**, but she could** not tolerate the heat.

Reference Note

If you have any questions about the **difference between independent clauses and subordinate clauses,** see pages 558 and 559.

Exercise 5 Revising to Eliminate Fragments

Some of the following items are sets of complete sentences, while others contain fragments. If an item has only complete sentences, write *C.* If it contains a fragment, revise it to include the fragment in a complete sentence.

1. Nat Love, who was born a slave in Tennessee, became a cowboy. When he was just fifteen years old.
2. Love being an expert horseman. He traveled throughout the West. Driving cattle on the open range.
3. After taking first prize in a riding, roping, and shooting contest in Deadwood, South Dakota, became known as "Deadwood Dick."
4. In 1907, Love published his autobiography, *The Life and Adventures of Nat Love, Better Known in Cattle Country as Deadwood Dick.*
5. The book both true stories and tall tales about Love and other famous characters of the Old West. Because Love did have many real-life adventures, it's difficult to tell which stories are fact and which are fiction.

Andrew Garcia

6. Another figure of the Old West. Andrew García, tells of similar exploits in his autobiography *Tough Trip Through Paradise.*

7. García describes some of the tough characters he met when he traveled with an outlaw band. One of the most notorious characters was the horse thief George Reynolds, better known as "Big Nose George."

8. Like many of the outlaws García knew. Reynolds died a violent death.

9. Although tempted to become an outlaw himself. García eventually settled down. And began writing his exciting account of his life.

10. García not living to see his memoirs published. The manuscripts, which he had packed away in dynamite boxes. Were discovered years after his death.

Run-on Sentences

When you are writing a draft, you may like to race full-speed ahead to get your thoughts down on paper. When you revise, however, it is important to know when to put on the brakes. Each complete thought should come to a full stop or be linked correctly to the next thought. If you run together two sentences as if they were a single thought, you create a ***run-on sentence.***

There are two kinds of run-on sentences. A ***fused sentence*** has no punctuation at all between the two complete thoughts. A ***comma splice*** has just a comma between them.

FUSED	Lightning speeds to our eyes at 186,000 miles per second thunder creeps to our ears at 1,087 feet per second.
COMMA SPLICE	We cannot hear and see the event at the same time, we sense it twice in different ways.

There are many different ways to correct a run-on sentence. Depending on the relationship you want to show between the two ideas, one method may be better than another.

1. You can make two sentences.

> Lightning speeds to our eyes at 186,000 miles per second. Thunder creeps to our ears at 1,087 feet per second.

2. You can use a comma and a coordinating conjunction.

> Lightning speeds to our eyes at 186,000 miles per second**, but** thunder creeps to our ears at 1,087 feet per second.

3. You can change one of the independent clauses to a subordinate clause.

> **While** lightning speeds to our eyes at 186,000 miles per second, thunder creeps to our ears at 1,087 feet per second.

4. You can use a semicolon.

> Lightning speeds to our eyes at 186,000 miles per second**;** thunder creeps to our ears at 1,087 feet per second.

5. You can use a semicolon and a conjunctive adverb.

> Lightning speeds to our eyes at 186,000 miles per second**; however,** thunder creeps to our ears at 1,087 feet per second.

NOTE You have probably noticed that well-known writers sometimes use run-on sentences in their works. You might wonder: If an expert writer uses run-ons, why can't I use them, too?

You *can* use run-ons occasionally in short stories, journal entries, and other kinds of expressive and creative writing. Run-ons can be especially effective in *stream of consciousness* writing, a style that imitates the natural flow of a character's thoughts, feelings, and perceptions. What is the effect of the run-on sentence below?

> The blue light from Cornelia's lampshade drew into a tiny point at the center of her brain, it flickered and winked like an eye, quietly it fluttered and dwindled.
>
> Katherine Anne Porter, "The Jilting of Granny Weatherall"

Always check your writing for unintentional run-ons. If you use run-ons for effect, make sure that your meaning will be clear to your reader.

Exercise 6 Revising Run-on Sentences

The following items are confusing because they are run-on sentences. Revise each run-on by using the method given in parentheses. (The examples above and on page 432 will help you.) If you have to choose a connecting word or subordinate an idea, make sure your revised version shows the appropriate relationship between the ideas.

1. The Victorian era was a time of extreme delicacy and tact in language, direct references to the body were considered offensive in polite society. (two sentences)
2. The word *limb* had to be used instead of *leg* or *arm* even a reference to the "leg" of a chair was considered impolite. (semicolon)
3. In reference to poultry, the thigh was called the second joint the leg was called the first joint or the drumstick. (comma and coordinating conjunction)
4. Delicate language was carried to an even greater extreme by some people, they referred to a bull as a "gentleman cow." (subordinate clause)
5. This kind of euphemistic language seems funny to us now, even today we use indirect language to replace words and phrases that might be considered offensive. (semicolon, conjunctive adverb, and comma.)

Review B   **Revising Paragraphs to Eliminate Fragments and Run-on Sentences**

Revise the following paragraphs to eliminate the fragments and run-ons. Add or delete words wherever necessary. Be sure to check your revised version for correct capitalization and punctuation.

War reports—both fact and fiction—have fascinated people since the first warriors and bards sat around campfires. Not all war literature is based on firsthand experience some comes out of imagination. One of America's most prominent war novelists, Stephen Crane, wrote about war before he ever saw a battle, Crane's short novel The Red Badge of Courage about a young soldier's reactions to fear during a major Civil War battle. Was written almost thirty years after the battle took place.

On the other hand, many of Ernest Hemingway's novels and stories were based on his own experiences during World War I before the United States entered the war Hemingway worked as an ambulance driver for the Italian army. His novel A Farewell to Arms. Which is often called the most important novel about World War I, follows the experiences of a young ambulance driver.

After World War II. Writer John Hersey introduced a journalistic technique to war fiction his book Hiroshima which describes the effect of the dropping of the A-bomb combines the literary techniques of fiction with the factual style of journalism. The Vietnam era produced several notable works of nonfiction. Including Ron Kovic's Born on the Fourth of July. A Vietnam veteran. Kovic describes how his feelings about war changed after he lost the use of his legs.

Recently, even historical books have been influenced by fictional and autobiographical accounts of war. Citizen Soldiers, a history of World War II. Recounts the experiences of ordinary soldiers in the field instead of focusing on the personalities of the generals or on battle strategies. Stephen E. Ambrose, the author of Citizen Soldiers, is able to provide gut-wrenching details usually found only in novels or memoirs, he gathered much of his material from the oral history accounts of soldiers who fought in the trenches.

World War II soldiers in the field

Memoirs of war also include diaries. Though not always the personal writing of soldiers. Mary Chesnut, wife of Confederate general James Chesnut, kept a diary. How war affected the daily life of people in the South. From ordinary people to generals and political figures, like Jefferson Davis, the president of the Confederacy. Her diary was first published as Diary from Dixie her words and observations used extensively in Ken Burns's documentary The Civil War.

Combining Sentences

internet connect

go.hrw.com

GO TO: go.hrw.com
KEYWORD: EOLang

Combining Sentences for Style

Revising is not just a matter of checking your writing for completeness and correctness. When you revise, you also look at your writing with an eye for style. It is important to notice how your sentences work together to shape each of your paragraphs. A short sentence may be fine by itself, but a long series of short sentences can make writing sound choppy and dull.

Read the following sentences. Does the writing style help hold your interest, or does it distract you from the meaning of the paragraph?

```
    There is an object at hand. It resembles a
fancy eggbeater. The eggbeater is fancy. It is
squat and top-heavy. It blends style with
utility. The style is Victorian, and the util-
ity is Industrial. It is an electric pen. The
pen is from Thomas Edison. He did not make it
for a while. He was 28 when he made it. He had
been granted patents. There were nearly 100 he
had been granted. He had spent most of his
adult life tinkering. He had been tinkering
with telegraphs.
```

The choppy sentences you just read are based on the following well-crafted sentences by journalist Bruce Watson. Notice how varying the length and structure of his sentences gives his paragraph a natural flow and rhythm.

> The object at hand resembles a fancy eggbeater. Squat and top-heavy, it blends Victorian style with Industrial Age utility. It is Thomas Edison's electric pen. By the time he got around to making it, Edison was 28. He had been granted nearly 100 patents and had spent most of his adult life tinkering with telegraphs.
>
> Bruce Watson, "A Wizard's Scribe," *Smithsonian*

Perhaps you have your own sentence style, one that is unique to your writing. No matter what your style, however, you can add rhythm and variety to your writing by balancing short sentences with longer, more detailed ones. Sentence combining helps you create this balance; it also helps make your sentences more precise by eliminating repeated words and ideas.

Combining Sentences by Inserting Words and Phrases

Often, you can combine related sentences by taking a key word or phrase from one sentence and inserting it into another sentence. The word or phrase adds detail to the other sentence, and repeated words are eliminated.

THREE SENTENCES   This barometer measures the pressure of the atmosphere. It uses a glass tube of mercury to do this. The barometer measures changes in pressure.

ONE SENTENCE   Using a glass tube of mercury, this barometer measures the changes in the pressure of the atmosphere.

or

With a glass tube of mercury, this barometer measures the changes in the pressure of the atmosphere.

Usually you will have some choice in where you insert a word or phrase. Just watch out for awkward-sounding combinations and ones that confuse the meaning of the original sentences. For example, avoid combinations like this one: *Changes in the pressure of the atmosphere,*

┌ TIPS & TRICKS ┐

When should you combine sentences for style? One good way to find out is to circle the first five words in each sentence in a paragraph. If the subject and verb are located within the circles in four consecutive sentences, combine two of the sentences using one of the techniques described in this chapter.

| COMPUTER TIP

If you are using a computer, you can use a word-processing program's cut and paste commands to move words, phrases, paragraphs, or blocks of text within a document. If you change your mind, you can always move the text again.

with a glass tube of mercury, this barometer measures. Be sure to read your sentence and make sure it is clear and grammatically correct.

Single-Word Modifiers

Sometimes you can take a word from one sentence and insert it directly into another sentence as a modifier. Other times you will need to change the word into an adjective or adverb before you can insert it.

Using the Same Form	
ORIGINAL	Timing is essential for performing magic tricks. The magician's timing must be excellent.
COMBINED	**Excellent** timing is essential for performing magic tricks.
ORIGINAL	Magicians guard the secrets of their tricks. They guard them carefully.
COMBINED	Magicians **carefully** guard the secrets of their tricks.

Changing the Form	
ORIGINAL	The famous magician Harry Houdini performed impossible escapes. The escapes only seemed impossible.
COMBINED	The famous magician Harry Houdini performed **seemingly** impossible escapes.
ORIGINAL	He escaped from a sealed crate that had been lowered into a river. He had handcuffs on.
COMBINED	**Handcuffed,** he escaped from a sealed crate that had been lowered into a river.

Prepositional Phrases

You can usually take a prepositional phrase from one sentence and insert it into another without any change in form.

ORIGINAL	Our English class is reading "Everyday Use." It is by Alice Walker.
COMBINED	Our English class is reading "Everyday Use" **by Alice Walker.**

You can also combine sentences by changing part of a sentence into a prepositional phrase.

ORIGINAL	A female narrator tells the story. Her tone is conversational.
COMBINED	A female narrator tells the story **in a conversational tone.**

Combining by Inserting Single-Word Modifiers and Prepositional Phrases

Combine each group of short, related sentences by inserting adjectives, adverbs, or prepositional phrases into the first sentence. You may need to change the forms of some words before you insert them. Add commas where they are necessary.

EXAMPLE   1. The Iroquois moved to the Northeast. They moved during the thirteenth century. They moved from the Mississippi region.

1. *During the thirteenth century, the Iroquois moved from the Mississippi region to the Northeast.*

Reference Note
For more on **using commas with introductory prepositional phrases,** see page 791.

1. The Iroquois formed a confederation. The confederation was powerful. The Iroquois formed the confederation in the Northeast region.
2. A central council of the confederation made decisions. The council made decisions unanimously.
3. Women nominated delegates. The women were from the confederation. They nominated delegates to the central council.
4. The Iroquois confederation subdued other groups of people. The groups of people were American Indians. The subduing of the groups was systematic.
5. The groups exchanged belts to ratify treaties. Their belts were of wampum. The treaties were important.
6. The Iroquois developed trade routes. The trade routes were extensive. The trade routes were along waterways and trails.
7. Hunting was an important activity. It was an annual activity in Iroquois society for the men. The hunt took place every fall.
8. The Iroquois also depended on farming. Their dependence on the farming done by the women was heavy.
9. Entire villages moved in search of soil. They were searching for soil that was richer. They needed the rich soil for farming.
10. The structure of Iroquoian life changed. The structure was complex. The change was considerable. The structure changed during the late seventeenth century.

Participial Phrases

A *participial phrase* contains a participle and any modifiers or complements related to the participle. The whole phrase acts as an adjective and, like other modifiers, adds concrete details to sentences.

Reference Note
For more on **participles and participial phrases,** see pages 540–541.

EXAMPLE   **Awakened by the uproar,** the group's guide, Simon Qamanariq, stumbled from his tent to find the bear between him and his *qamatiik,* the sledge **pulled by his snowmobile, where he kept his rifle.**

Paul Rauber, "On Top of the World," *Sierra*

Sometimes you can lift a participial phrase directly from one sentence and insert it into another sentence. Other times you will need to change a verb into a participle before you can insert the idea into another sentence.

ORIGINAL   Storm clouds revolve around a hurricane's calm center. The calm center is called the eye.

COMBINED   Storm clouds revolve around a hurricane's calm center, **called the eye.**

ORIGINAL   Hurricanes gather strength and size as they move over the water. They move westward initially.

COMBINED   **Initially moving westward,** hurricanes gather strength and size as they move over the water.

NOTE   Be sure to place a participial phrase close to the noun or pronoun you want it to modify. Otherwise, your sentence may end up with a meaning you did not intend.

MISPLACED   Broadcast by the National Hurricane Center, the town's residents listened to the forecast.

IMPROVED   The town's residents listened to the forecast **broadcast by the National Hurricane Center.**

Absolute Phrases

An ***absolute phrase*** consists of (1) a participle or a participial phrase, (2) a noun or a pronoun that the participle or participial phrase modifies, and (3) any other modifiers of that noun or pronoun. The entire word group is used as an adverb to modify the independent clause of a sentence. Absolute phrases are valuable tools for combining sentences. They bring in additional information and help to emphasize certain ideas.

EXAMPLE   **Excited sea gulls screeching in protest,** the men on horseback raced down the beach.

Exercise 2 — Combining by Inserting Participial and Absolute Phrases

Combine each of the following sentence pairs. First, reduce the second sentence to a participial or an absolute phrase, changing the form of the verb if necessary. Then, insert the phrase into the first sentence. Be sure to place a participial phrase next to the noun or pronoun it modifies.

EXAMPLE
1. Virtual reality is a simulated, three-dimensional environment. It is usually produced by a computer.

1. *Usually produced by a computer, virtual reality is a simulated, three-dimensional environment.*

1. Virtual reality systems can be used to train pilots, doctors, and engineers. These systems are seen most often in video games.
2. A head-mounted display is made of a headset with a screen for each eye. The display connects to a computer.
3. A tracking device senses the eye movements of the user. Tracking devices are usually built into the headset.
4. The computer creates an artificial world that seems real to the user. The images of the two screens are blended by the computer.
5. Some virtual reality systems include a small speaker for each ear. These systems use sound to enhance the illusion of the simulated world.

Appositive Phrases

Appositive phrases can also add detail to your sentences. An **appositive phrase** is made up of an appositive and its modifiers. (An appositive identifies or describes a noun or pronoun in a sentence.) Like a participial phrase, an appositive phrase should be placed directly before or after the noun or pronoun it renames. It should be set off by a comma (or two commas if you place the phrase in the middle of the sentence).

EXAMPLE
Tombaugh climbed up into the scaffolding of the sixteen-inch telescope, **a steel-and-glass affair that loomed up into the dark.**

Timothy Ferris, "Seeing in the Dark," *The New Yorker*

You can combine two sentences by placing one of the ideas in an appositive phrase.

TWO SENTENCES
Arna Bontemps wrote for the magazine *Opportunity*. Arna Bontemps was a major figure in the Harlem Renaissance.

HELP

Note that an absolute phrase is not obviously connected to the rest of the sentence, and the noun in an absolute phrase is always different from the subject of the sentence.

EXAMPLE
The **horse** standing and blowing in its exhaustion, the **knight** dismounted to kneel before his king.

If the noun of the absolute phrase is missing, the result is a dangling participle.

EXAMPLE
Standing and blowing in its exhaustion, the knight dismounted to kneel before his king.
[dangling participle]

ONE SENTENCE   Arna Bontemps, **a major figure in the Harlem Renaissance,** wrote for the magazine *Opportunity.*

or

A major figure in the Harlem Renaissance, Arna Bontemps wrote for the magazine *Opportunity.*

or

Arna Bontemps, **a writer for the magazine *Opportunity*,** was a major figure in the Harlem Renaissance.

Notice that the last combination emphasizes Bontemps's role in the Harlem Renaissance, while the first two combinations emphasize his work for *Opportunity.* In the last example, the ideas have been rearranged to change the emphasis, and the verb *wrote* has been changed to a noun, *writer,* to form the appositive.

Exercise 3   Combining by Inserting Appositive Phrases

Combine each pair of sentences by turning one of the sentences into an appositive phrase. You may see several ways to create the appositive; choose the combination that sounds best to you. Be sure to set off the appositive phrase with commas.

EXAMPLE   1. Calligraphy is an elegant form of handwriting. It requires a special pen or brush.

       1. *Calligraphy, an elegant form of handwriting, requires a special pen or brush.*

Brush

1. Calligraphy has been used for over two thousand years to decorate books and paintings. It is an ancient art form.
2. Chinese calligraphy is done with a brush. Chinese calligraphy is the oldest form of calligraphy.
3. In the 600s, Japanese artists learned calligraphy from the Chinese. The Chinese were the first masters of the art.
4. Islamic artists developed Kufic writing. Kufic writing is one of the most graceful styles of calligraphy.
5. In Islamic countries, you can see sentences from the Koran inscribed in beautiful calligraphy on buildings. The Koran is the Islamic holy book.

Pen

Reference Note

For more information on **coordination,** see page 418.

Combining Sentences by Coordinating Ideas

Sometimes you will want to combine sentences that contain *coordinate,* or equally important, ideas. You can join coordinate words, phrases, or clauses with coordinating conjunctions (*and, but, for, nor, or, so,* and *yet*) or correlative conjunctions (*both . . . and, either . . . or, neither . . . nor*). The relationship of the ideas determines which connective works best. When they are joined in one sentence, the coordinate ideas form compound elements.

ORIGINAL   Juan will work in the concession stand. Kinesha will work in the concession stand.

COMBINED   **Both Juan and Kinesha** will work in the concession stand. [compound subject]

ORIGINAL   Mrs. Braxton could sponsor our class trip. Mrs. Braxton could recruit parents to help her.

COMBINED   Mrs. Braxton **could sponsor our class trip or recruit parents to help her.** [compound predicate]

ORIGINAL   The class officers wanted to schedule the trip for May. Mrs. Braxton had already chosen June.

COMBINED   The class officers wanted to schedule the trip for May, **but** Mrs. Braxton had already chosen June. [compound sentence]

You can also form a compound sentence by linking independent clauses with a semicolon and a conjunctive adverb (*however, likewise, therefore*) or with just a semicolon.

EXAMPLE   You accept risk as part of every new challenge; it comes with the territory.

Chuck Yeager, *Yeager: An Autobiography*

┌ T I P S & T R I C K S ┐
Remember: When linking independent clauses, put a semicolon *before* a conjunctive adverb and a comma *after*.

Exercise 4 **Combining by Coordinating Ideas**

Combine each of the following sets of sentences by forming a compound element. Be sure to choose a connective that expresses the correct relationship between the ideas. You may need to add punctuation, too.

EXAMPLE   1. William Least Heat-Moon traveled across America. He wrote about his trip.

1. *William Least Heat-Moon traveled across America and wrote about his trip.*

1. William Least Heat-Moon's first name comes from an English ancestor. His last name was given to him by his Sioux father.
2. In 1977, Least Heat-Moon left his Missouri home. He began traveling across the country on back roads.

3. The title of his book *Blue Highways* does not refer to the actual color of roads. It refers to the blue lines that marked the back roads on his highway map.

4. Least Heat-Moon's trip began in the middle of the nation. On a map, his route appeared to be shaped like a jagged sideways heart.

5. Small, oddly named towns made his journey memorable. Friendly, helpful people made his journey memorable.

Combining Sentences by Subordinating Ideas

Reference Note

For more information on **subordinate clauses,** see page 559.

If two sentences are unequal in importance, you can combine them by placing the less-important idea in a subordinate clause.

EXAMPLES   He had a habit of pausing to fix his gaze on part of the con-gregation as he read, and that Sunday he seemed to be talk-ing to a small group of strangers **who sat in the front row.** [adjective clause]

Andrea Lee, "New African"

My luck ran out in mid-April **when a freak snowstorm moved in at midday and, in the next thirty hours, dumped eighteen inches of snow on the surrounding forest, the eagles' nest, and me.** [adverb clause]

Dr. Scott Nielsen, *A Season with Eagles*

What he had the most of was time. [noun clause]

Juan Sedillo, "Gentleman of Río en Medio"

Adjective Clauses

You can change a sentence into an adjective clause by replacing its subject with *who, whose, which,* or *that.* Then you can use the adjective clause to give information about a noun or pronoun in another sentence.

ORIGINAL   Aztec sculptures were used to decorate temples and other buildings. The sculptures were quite intricate.

REVISED   Aztec sculptures, **which were quite intricate,** were used to decorate temples and other buildings.

ORIGINAL   The Aztecs founded the city of Tenochtitlán. They prospered during the 1400s and early 1500s in what is now known as Mexico.

REVISED   The Aztecs, **who prospered during the 1400s and early 1500s in what is now known as Mexico,** founded the city of Tenochtitlán.

As with appositive phrases, you need to decide first which idea you want to emphasize and which you want to subordinate in the sentence. Be sure to keep your main idea in the independent clause.

NOTE How you punctuate an adjective clause depends on whether the clause is essential to the meaning of the sentence. If the clause is not essential, you need to set it off from the rest of the sentence with a comma or commas. If the clause is essential, no commas are necessary.

Reference Note

For more information on **punctuating adjective clauses,** see page 788.

NONESSENTIAL   The bicycle race, **which was sponsored by the student council,** will be the first activity on Saturday.

ESSENTIAL   Earlene entered the bicycle race **that Tyrone won last year.**

Adverb Clauses

An adverb clause modifies a verb, an adjective, or another adverb in the sentence to which it is attached. To make a sentence into an adverb clause, add a subordinating conjunction like *although, after, because, if, when, where,* or *while* at the beginning. The conjunction shows the relationship between the ideas in the adverb clause and the independent clause. It can show a relationship of time, place, cause or reason, purpose or result, or condition.

Reference Note

For more about **using adverb clauses to subordinate ideas,** see page 565.

ORIGINAL   The Spanish explorer Hernando Cortes landed on the east coast of Mexico. He and his men marched to the capital of the Aztecs.

REVISED   **After the Spanish explorer Hernando Cortes landed on the east coast of Mexico,** he and his men marched to the capital of the Aztecs. [time]

ORIGINAL   The baseball game was stopped in the seventh inning. Heavy lightning began.

REVISED   The baseball game was stopped in the seventh inning **because heavy lightning began.** [cause]

NOTE When you place an adverb clause at the beginning of a sentence, separate it from the independent clause with a comma.

Reference Note

For more about the **use of commas with subordinate clauses,** see page 788.

EXAMPLES   **Although I got up early this morning,** I was still tardy for school.

When I got home from school, I reorganized my English binder and set my new alarm clock.

Noun Clauses

You can make a sentence into a noun clause by adding a word like *that, how, what, whatever, who,* or *whoever* at the beginning of the sentence; you may also have to delete or move some words. Then, insert the clause into another sentence just as you would an ordinary noun.

ORIGINAL   Manuel has been asked to the *quinceañera*. Selena told me this fact.

REVISED   Selena told me **that Manuel has been asked to the quinceañera.**

Exercise 5 Combining by Subordinating Ideas

Combine each of the following pairs of sentences by turning one sentence into a subordinate clause.

1. Robotics is an important technology. Robotics deals with the creation of robots for use in industry, science, and other fields.
2. People worry that robots will take over the jobs of humans. There is evidence to contradict the belief.
3. Robots can perform small tasks like assembling watches. Robots are often used for tasks such as drilling and welding.
4. The robot usually follows a set of instructions. These instructions are entered and stored in the robot's computer.
5. Difficult and dangerous jobs need to be done. People can rely on robots.

Review A Combining Sentences by Coordinating and Subordinating Ideas

Use either coordination or subordination to combine each of the following pairs of sentences. You may see more than one way to combine a sentence pair. Just write the combination that sounds best to you.

1. Robert L. Ripley worked as a cartoonist for the *New York Globe*. He spent his life seeking incredible but true stories.
2. His unusual career started one day. He could not think of an idea for a cartoon.
3. To find an idea, he looked through his files. He hurriedly drew several items about unusual achievements.
4. Ripley's first collection of "Believe It or Not" was published in 1929. The collection was instantly successful.

┌H E L P┐

You may have to add, delete, or change some words in the sentences in Exercise 5. Add commas where necessary.

5. Eventually Ripley's features appeared in more than two hundred newspapers. Even more success lay ahead for him.
6. One of the categories was "Strange Coincidence." This was a category Ripley used as the basis of his features.
7. In one strange coincidence, an icehouse in Blanca, Colorado, burned to the ground. The ice inside did not melt.
8. In another, a horse named "Lucky Wonder" typed out a psychic prediction. The prediction foresaw the reelection of President Truman.
9. Two men playing golf together at a famous golf club in California, chipped simultaneously at the twelfth hole. Their golf balls collided and dropped into the cup.
10. Robert L. Ripley died in 1949. Today his work is carried on by the Ripley organization in Toronto, Canada.

Review B **Revising a Paragraph by Combining Sentences**

Using all the sentence-combining skills you have learned, revise the following paragraph for style. Use your judgment about which sentences to combine and how to combine them. Do not change the meaning of the original paragraph.

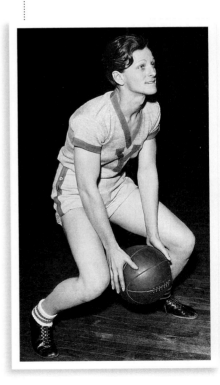

```
     Mildred "Babe" Didrikson Zaharias was born
in Port Arthur, Texas, around 1911. She was
considered one of the finest track-and-field
performers of all time. Babe gained national
attention in 1930. She competed in a track-
and-field meet in Dallas. She won two events.
She broke the world record in a third event.
The event was the long jump. Babe competed in
the Olympic Games in 1932. She entered the
high jump, the javelin throw, and the hurdles.
She set records in all of these events. They
were world records. Only two of these records
were made official. Babe's high-jump perform-
ance was disqualified. It was disqualified
over a technicality. Babe was a champion in
women's track and field for more than a decade.
She was a world champion in track and field.
Babe later became a world champion golfer.
```

12 Improving Sentence Style

Revising for Variety

Have you ever looked closely at an intricately woven tapestry or a beautiful oil painting? What catches your eye? Just as artists can use a variety of colors and textures to enrich their art, you can use a variety of sentence patterns to enrich your writing. This technique of varying sentence patterns applies to almost all writing, whether it is for school, business, or personal use.

As you read the following passage, notice how the sentences work together to form a smooth, effective paragraph.

GO TO: go.hrw.com
KEYWORD: EOLang

> Grace advanced her hand toward the nearest cobra. The snake swayed like a reed in the wind, feinting for the strike. Grace raised her hand above the snake's head, the reptile twisting around to watch her. As the woman slowly lowered her hand, the snake gave that most terrible of all animal noises—the unearthly hiss of a deadly snake. I have seen children laugh with excitement at the roar of a lion, but I have never seen anyone who did not cringe at that cold, uncanny sound. Grace deliberately tried to touch the rigid, quivering hood. The cobra struck at her hand. He missed. Quietly, Grace presented her open palm. The cobra hesitated a split second, his reared body quivering like a plucked banjo string. Then he struck.
>
> Daniel Mannix,
> *All Creatures Great and Small*

Mannix's carefully crafted sentences add style and interest to his writing. You can improve your own writing style by revising your sentences for variety.

Varying Sentence Beginnings

Have you ever heard or read a story that kept you on the edge of your seat? Chances are the sentence beginnings helped hold your attention. Instead of starting every sentence with a subject and a verb, the storyteller probably began some sentences with attention-grabbing words, phrases, and clauses such as *Suddenly . . .*, *At the bottom of the cliff . . .*, and *When she opened the door. . . .*

Varied sentence beginnings do more than hold a reader's attention. They also improve the overall style of writing. The examples in the chart below show how you can revise your sentences to open them with introductory words, phrases, and clauses.

NOTE When you vary sentence beginnings, you sometimes must reword the sentences for clarity. As you reword, be sure to place modifiers close to the words they modify; otherwise, you may create a misplaced modifier.

Sentence Connectives	
Subject First	Graphology is the study of how handwriting reveals a person's personality. Scientific handwriting analysis, though, determines the authenticity of a signature.
Coordinating Conjunction First	Graphology is the study of how handwriting reveals a person's personality. **But** scientific handwriting analysis determines the authenticity of a signature.
Subject First	Graphologists use size, direction, and regularity of letters to tell if a person is shy, quick-thinking, or independent. Graphology has not been recognized as a true science.
Conjunctive Adverb First	Graphologists use size, direction, and regularity of letters to tell if a person is shy, quick-thinking, or independent. **However,** graphology has not been recognized as a true science.

STYLE TIP

In your reading, you will frequently see coordinating conjunctions used to begin sentences. Because such usage is often considered informal, it is best not to use coordinating conjunctions to begin your sentences in formal, or academic, situations.

(continued)

(continued)

Single-Word Modifiers	
Subject First	The letters of Erica's signature are upright and elaborate and might suggest independence.
Single-Word Modifiers First	**Upright and elaborate,** the letters of Erica's signature might suggest independence.
Subject First	Angling letters to the left supposedly indicates shyness.
Single-Word Modifier First	**Supposedly,** angling letters to the left indicates shyness.
Subject First	Two people's signatures may show the couple's compatibility if the signatures are analyzed.
Single-Word Modifier First	**Analyzed,** two people's signatures may show the couple's compatibility.

Phrase Modifiers	
Subject First	Birds can close their eyes for sleep by raising the lower lid.
Prepositional Phrase First	**By raising the lower lid,** birds can close their eyes for sleep.
Subject First	The eyes of many birds are located on the sides of the head and provide peripheral vision.
Participial Phrase First	**Located on the sides of the head,** the eyes of many birds provide peripheral vision.
Subject First	Birds have a third eyelid beneath the upper and lower lids to blink and moisten the eyes.
Infinitive Phrase First	**To blink and moisten the eyes,** birds have a third eyelid beneath the upper and lower lids.

Clause Modifiers	
Subject First	Birds turn their heads instead of moving their eyes if they want to look at an object.
Adverb Clause First	**If they want to look at an object,** birds turn their heads instead of moving their eyes.
Subject First	Most nocturnal birds have very large eyes, but the New Zealand Kiwi's eyes are tiny.
Adverb Clause First	**Even though most nocturnal birds have very large eyes,** the New Zealand Kiwi's eyes are tiny.

Exercise 1 **Varying Sentence Beginnings**

Revise each of the following sentences by varying their beginnings. The hint in parentheses will tell you which type of beginning to use.

1. People have used signs and gestures to communicate their thoughts since prehistoric times. (infinitive phrase)
2. A system of commonly understood gestures often helped American Indian nations communicate with each other. (single-word modifier)
3. Nations in the Plains area spoke many different languages, so a well-developed sign language was essential for trading. (adverb clause)
4. The scope of the sign language grew as more groups settled on the Plains. (adverb clause)
5. One gesture was used to mean "peace" and was known by many nations. (participial phrase)

Varying Sentence Structure

You can also improve your style by varying the structure of your sentences. That means using a mix of simple, compound, and complex (and often even compound-complex) sentences in your writing.

Read the following short paragraph, which is made up of only simple sentences.

```
    The Bermuda Triangle is located between the
island of Bermuda, the coast of Florida, and
Puerto Rico. It is known for unexplained dis-
appearances. Ships have been disappearing in
the area since the mid-nineteenth century. It
got this reputation. A training squadron of
five U.S. Navy bombers disappeared in 1945.
This incident seemed to set the triangle's
reputation. Another ship is the nuclear-
powered submarine Scorpion. It disappeared in
this area in 1968. There have been disappear-
ances. These disappearances may have logical
explanations.
```

Now, read the revised version of the paragraph. Notice how the writer has used sentence-combining techniques to vary the structure of the sentences.

```
    The Bermuda Triangle, located between the
island of Bermuda, the coast of Florida, and
Puerto Rico, is known for unexplained dis-
```

Reference Note

For information about the **four types of sentence structure,** see page 569.

STYLE TIP

You may find that simple sentences work best in some of your paragraphs. Do not try to force sentences into compound or complex structures when simple structures sound better. However, if a paragraph sounds flat and dull, varying sentence structure may help improve it.

appearances. It got this reputation because ships have been disappearing in the area since the mid-nineteenth century. A training squadron of five U.S. Navy bombers disappeared in 1945, and this incident seemed to set the triangle's reputation. Another ship that disappeared in this area in 1968 is the nuclear-powered submarine *Scorpion*. However, these disappearances may have logical explanations.

Exercise 2 **Revising a Paragraph to Vary Sentence Structure**

Decide which sentences in the following paragraph would sound better with compound, complex, or compound-complex structures. Then, use sentence-combining techniques to vary the sentence structure. (You may need to change some wording to create smooth sentences.)

This person may look like a villain from a science fiction movie. He is actually a student of kendo. Kendo is an ancient Japanese martial art. It requires skill, concentration, and agility. The contestants fight with long bamboo swords called <u>shinai</u>. Kendo can be dangerous. The players must wear protective gear. The gear includes a mask, a breastplate, and thick gloves. Each match lasts three to five minutes. The first contestant to score two points wins. Kendo is a graceful, dignified sport. Respect for one's opponent is important. A contestant can even be disqualified for rudeness.

Revising to Reduce Wordiness

Read the following sentence. Could you remove a single word from it without changing its meaning or lessening its impact?

> At last I knelt on the island's winter-killed grass, lost, dumbstruck, staring at the frog in the creek just four feet away.
>
> Annie Dillard,
> *Pilgrim at Tinker Creek*

Skilled writers make every word count; they know that conciseness is essential for good style. You can make your own writing more concise by eliminating the clutter of extra words.

To avoid wordiness in your writing, keep these three points in mind.

- Use only as many words as you need to make your point.
- Choose simple, clear words and expressions over pretentious, complicated ones.
- Do not repeat words or ideas unless it is absolutely necessary.

The following examples show some ways to revise wordy sentences.

1. Take out a whole group of unnecessary words.

| WORDY | Every single individual in our class bought tickets to the concert. |
| BETTER | **Everyone** in our class bought tickets to the concert. |

| WORDY | At the edge of the river, we boarded a small boat that was floating there on the surface of the water. |
| BETTER | At the edge of the river, we boarded a **small boat.** |

2. Replace pretentious words and expressions with straightforward ones.

| WORDY | All attempts to mollify the male being in the early stage of life development and from an educational establishment were unsuccessful. |
| BETTER | All attempts to **soothe the young schoolboy failed.** |

3. Reduce a clause to a phrase.

| WORDY | Atul, who was the winner of the sportsmanship award, was asked to give a speech at the sports banquet. |
| BETTER | **Winner of the sportsmanship award,** Atul was asked to give a speech at the sports banquet. |

| WORDY | Tori, who is a computer expert, produced a program that detects computer viruses. |
| BETTER | Tori, **a computer expert,** produced a program that detects computer viruses. |

4. Reduce a phrase or a clause to one word.

| WORDY | Lenny contacted a reporter from Albania. |
| BETTER | Lenny contacted an **Albanian** reporter. |

| WORDY | The price that was confirmed will be honored by the dealer. |
| BETTER | The **confirmed** price will be honored by the dealer. |

Here is a list of wordy phrases and their simpler replacements. Watch out for these wordy phrases in your writing.

Wordy	Simpler
at this point in time	now
at which time	when
by means of	by
due to the fact that	because, since
in spite of the fact that	although
in the event that	if
the fact is that	actually

NOTE Sometimes no replacement is needed for wordy phrases—they can be cut altogether. "The fact is that," for example, is often unnecessary.

WORDY **The fact is that** I am turning seventeen in five months.
BETTER I am turning seventeen in five months.

Exercise 3 **Reducing Wordiness**

Some of the following sentences are wordy. Revise each wordy sentence to make it straightforward and concise. If a sentence does not need revision, write *C* for *correct*.

1. Good writing is precise and straightforward.
2. Have you ever read sentences that seem to ramble on and keep going forever?
3. Annie Dillard, who is a careful writer, revises heavily.
4. Redundant sentences are boring and repetitive.
5. Sentences that are longer than it is necessary for them to be may confuse your reader.
6. A sentence that has too many clauses that are subordinate becomes a mental maze for the unsuspecting reader.
7. Think of the sounds and rhythms of the writing you like best.
8. Sentences stuffed with extra, unneeded words resemble Saint Bernards squeezed into Chihuahua-sized sweaters.
9. The fact is that carefully crafted sentences are like well-tailored suits.
10. William Strunk, Jr., said, "Vigorous writing is concise."

| **COMPUTER TIP**

A word-processing program's search feature can help you look for wordy phrases such as those listed in the chart. The command can also find overused words. To choose synonyms for these words, use the thesaurus tool if the program has one.

Revising Sentences to Improve Style

Revise the sentences below as suggested in the parentheses.

1. Mary Kingsley set sail for Africa in 1893. (phrase beginning)
2. Kingsley equipped herself as a trader. She hired African guides. She set off into the bush of Gabon and the Niger Delta. (compound sentence)
3. Kingsley was a fearless and intrepid woman and was the first person to travel the route north from the Ogooué to the Rembwe River. (single word modifiers)
4. Kingsley brought back a variety of animal specimens. She donated them to the British Museum. (complex sentence)
5. Upon her return, Kingsley penned a prodigious tome, the title of which was *Travels in West Africa,* with the aim and purpose of convincing inhabitants of England that the traditions and customary ways of the peoples of the African continent were worthy of their respect and regard. (reduce wordiness)

Review B **Revising Paragraphs to Improve Style**

Revise the paragraphs below. As you revise, remember to vary sentence beginnings and sentence structure and to eliminate wordiness.

```
      Guglielmo Marconi invented wireless teleg-
raphy in the 1890s. Wireless telegraphy was the
forerunner of radio. There were many
problems with the first wireless messages. The
messages were full of static, noise, and unin-
telligible sounds. Also, they were not very
private as well due to the fact that anyone
could tune in and listen if he or she had the
proper receiving device.
      Several ships carried wireless technology by
1912. The famous ship Titanic was among them.
The Titanic struck an iceberg late at night
while on its first voyage, and its crew sent
out SOS messages on the ship's wireless. The
wireless operators on many other ships in the
area were no longer on duty, so the Titanic's
messages were not received by very many opera-
tors. The fact is that after the ship sank, the
U.S. government required wireless ship communi-
cations to be monitored at all times.
```

Wireless operator

The Granger Collection, New York.

Understanding Paragraphs and Compositions

GO TO: go.hrw.com
KEYWORD: EOLang

How Paragraphs and Compositions Fit Together

What do you see when you watch a good movie? Do you notice the *parts*—heroic characters, amazing sets, artful shots? Or do you see the movie as a *whole*—a work that has provided a satisfying, even thrilling experience? Paragraphs and compositions are a little like that movie; paragraphs are the parts that together form the composition, or whole.

The Parts of a Paragraph

Paragraphs come in all sorts of shapes and sizes. They can be as short as one sentence or as long as many pages; they can show a transition from one idea to the next or develop a single idea, and they can break up long passages to make them easier to read.

In thoughtful articles and other works of nonfiction, including essays that you write in school, paragraphs usually develop one **main idea.** These main-idea paragraphs are often made up of a **topic sentence, supporting sentences,** and a **clincher sentence.**

Parts of Paragraphs	
The Main Idea	▪ is the central focus of the paragraph
The Topic Sentence	▪ is a single sentence that states the main idea of the paragraph ▪ is often found in the first or second sentence of a paragraph (sometimes following a catchy, inviting first sentence) ▪ can be placed at or near the end of a paragraph, to create surprise or to summarize ideas
Supporting Sentences	▪ support, or prove, the main topic sentence ▪ use the following kinds of details: *sensory details*—images of sight, sound, taste, smell, and texture *facts or statistics*—A fact is something that can be proved true; a statistic is a fact based on numbers. *examples*—specific instances, or illustrations, of a general idea *anecdotes*—little stories, either biographical or autobiographical, used to illustrate a main idea
The Clincher Sentence	▪ is a final sentence that emphasizes or summarizes the main idea ▪ can help readers grasp the main idea of a longer paragraph ▪ sometimes is written in a bold or clever way, to close a thought with some pizazz

STYLE **TIP**

A paragraph may be developed with one type of supporting detail or with a combination of types.

STYLE **TIP**

Many paragraphs—even those that develop a main idea—do not use a clincher sentence. Clinchers are most often used with lengthy or complicated paragraphs, to remind the readers of the main idea.

NOTE   Not all paragraphs have or need topic sentences. In fiction, paragraphs rarely include topic sentences. Paragraphs in nonfiction works that relate sequences of events or steps also frequently do not contain topic sentences. (Paragraphs that do not have topic sentences often do not develop one main idea, either.) In the writing that you do in school, however, you'll find that topic sentences are useful. They provide a focus for your reader, and they keep you from straying off the topic as you develop the rest of your paragraph.

Putting the Parts Together

Look carefully at the parts of the following paragraph. Notice that the topic sentence at the beginning expresses the main idea.

Topic Sentence

    In the past forty years, however, anthropologists have done some very thorough digging into the life of the North American Indians and have discovered a bewildering variety of cultures and societies beyond anything the schoolbooks have

Supporting Sentences

taught. There were Indian societies that dwelt in permanent settlements, and others that wandered; some were wholly democratic, and others had very rigid class systems based on property. Some were ruled by gods carried around on litters; some had judicial systems; to some the only known punishment was torture. Some lived in caves, others in tepees of bison skins, others in cabins. There were tribes ruled by warriors or by women, by sacred elders or by councils. . . . There were tribes who worshiped the bison or a matriarch or the maize they lived by. There were tribes that had never heard of war, and there were tribes debauched by

Clincher Sentence

centuries of fighting. In short, there was a great diversity of Indian nations, speaking over five hundred languages.

Alistair Cooke, *Alistair Cooke's America*

NOTE Sometimes paragraphs are considered mini-essays; that is, their organization may be developed the same way you would compose an essay. Just as you want every paragraph to have some purpose in developing the main idea of your essay, so every sentence in a paragraph should be useful in developing the paragraph's main idea. In your own essays, having a clear idea or topic for each paragraph will help you in adding supporting details or clincher sentences.

Exercise 1   Identifying the Parts of Paragraphs

Try your hand at identifying the parts of paragraphs with the three paragraphs that follow. While all three of the paragraphs have a main idea, only two have topic sentences. First, state the main idea in each paragraph, and then identify the topic sentences in the two paragraphs that have them. Make up a topic sentence for the remaining paragraph. Then, identify the type of supporting sentences in each paragraph and determine whether any of the paragraphs have a clincher sentence.

HELP

For a sequence of events or actions, you can come up with a main idea and, in turn, a topic sentence by thinking of a one-sentence summary of what happens in the paragraph.

1. World War II brought economic and social changes that affected the big bands. Gasoline rationing impaired the constant touring that was one of their mainstays. The singers, whose popularity was first established through their work with the bands, became stars in their own right. After the war, the advent of television wrought fundamental changes in the ways people entertained themselves. Among the chief victims of the new stay-at-home trend was ballroom dancing. The big bands went into rapid decline, and only a handful maintained themselves, among them Ellington and Basie.

    "The Jazz Tradition," *The African American Almanac*

Count Basie

2. I attended more tournaments, each one farther away from home. I won all games, in all divisions. The Chinese bakery downstairs from our flat displayed my growing collection of trophies in its window, amidst the dust-covered cakes that were never picked up. The day after I won an important regional tournament, the window encased a fresh sheet cake with whipped-cream frosting and red script saying, "Congratulations, Waverly Jong, Chinatown Chess Champion." Soon after that, a flower shop, headstone engraver, and funeral parlor offered to sponsor me in national tournaments. That's when my mother decided I no longer had to do the dishes. Winston and Vincent had to do my chores.

    Amy Tan, "The Rules of the Game"

3.   He became a learner and teacher of men and in this life career what did he accomplish three hundred years ago? The simple unexplained record is in itself wonderful: he found the law of falling bodies; he invented the telescope; he discovered the moons of Jupiter; he explained the reflected light of planets; he laid down the laws of cohesion; he studied the law of the pendulum and applied it to the clock; and above all he adduced irrefragable proof of the correctness of the Copernican doctrine that the sun and not the earth is the center of our universe. Simply and barely stated this accomplishment is tremendous. To few human beings has it been given, in a life of four-score years, to advance so momentously the sum of human knowledge.

W.E.B. DuBois, "Galileo Galilei"

Qualities of Paragraphs

You wouldn't build a house without thinking about how the boards, bricks, and shingles fit together. Paragraphs need to be just as carefully constructed. A well-written paragraph has three major qualities: **unity, coherence,** and (often, but not always) **elaboration.**

Unity

Unity simply means that the paragraph "hangs together." In other words, all the supporting sentences work together to develop the main idea. A paragraph should have unity whether the main idea is stated in a topic sentence or is implied, or suggested. Unity is achieved in one of three ways:

- **All sentences relate to the main idea stated in the topic sentence.**

- **All sentences relate to an implied main idea.** Even when the paragraph does not have a topic sentence, all the sentences still support an implied main idea.

- **All sentences relate to a sequence of events.** In paragraphs that relate a series of actions or events, the main idea is often implied rather than stated. You can achieve unity in these kinds of paragraphs by providing all the steps in the sequence.

TIPS & TRICKS

When a main idea is implied, you have to *infer* it from the details contained in the paragraph. To do this, decide what you think is the main idea in the first sentence and then refine and adjust this idea as you read each additional sentence in the paragraph.

Coherence

Unity is not the only quality of a good paragraph; **coherence** is also important. In a coherent paragraph, the relationship between ideas is clear—the paragraph flows smoothly. You can go a long way toward making paragraphs coherent by paying attention to two things:

- the order you use to arrange your ideas
- the connections you make between ideas

Building Coherence: Types of Order		
Order	**When to Use**	**How It Works**
Chronological	• to tell a story • to explain a process • to show cause and effect	• shows how things change over time
Spatial	• to describe	• provides details according to their location—near to far, top to bottom, left to right, and so on
Order of Importance	• to inform or persuade	• arranges ideas and details from most important detail to least, or vice versa, according to which order the author considers more effective
Logical	• to explain or classify—often by defining, dividing a subject into parts, or comparing and contrasting	• groups ideas together in a way that shows the relationships between them

S T Y L E   **T I P**

Because chronological order is used with narration, it is often associated with fictional stories. However, nonfiction writing uses chronological order just as often—from accident reports to the step-by-step instructions for installing software on a computer.

S T Y L E   **T I P**

At times, multiple orders may be used to add variety to writing. In explaining an effect, for example, you may trace it **chronologically** from its cause. If one effect has four simultaneous causes, you would place these causes in **logical order** or **order of importance**.

In addition to presenting details in an order that makes sense, a paragraph that has coherence should also show *how* these details are connected. You can show connections by using **direct references** or **transitional expressions,** explained in the chart on the next page.

Building Coherence: Connecting Ideas	
Direct References	• refer to a noun or pronoun used earlier in the paragraph • repeat a word used earlier • use a word or phrase that means the same thing as one used earlier
Transitional Expressions	• compare ideas (*also, and, another, moreover, similarly, too*) • contrast ideas (*although, but, however, in spite of, instead, nevertheless, on the other hand, still, yet*) • show cause and effect (*as a result, because, consequently, since, so that, therefore*) • show time (*after, at last, at once, before, eventually, finally, first, meanwhile, next, then, thereafter, when*) • show place (*above, across, around, before, beyond, down, here, in, inside, into, next, over, there, to, under*) • show importance (*first, last, mainly, more importantly, then, to begin with*)

Elaboration

Elaboration is another important quality of many well-written paragraphs, along with unity and coherence. To *elaborate* is to refine, support, and develop an idea; a paragraph's **supporting sentences** elaborate the paragraph's main idea. When supporting sentences *do not* fully support or develop a paragraph's main idea, the reader is bound to be confused, skeptical—or both. Elaboration leads the reader to understand the writer's ideas more completely.

Looking at the Qualities of Paragraphs

Take a look at the following paragraph, which describes the process of hearing. The paragraph is unified because all of its sentences relate to and elaborate on the main idea stated in the topic sentence. Notice how the use of chronological order gives the paragraph coherence and how direct references and transitional expressions contribute to the paragraph's coherence. Note: All direct references are indicated with asterisks, and transitional expressions are highlighted.

What we call "sound" is really an onrushing, cresting, and withdrawing wave of air molecules that begins with the movement of any object, however large or small, and ripples out in all directions. First something has to move—a tractor, a cricket's wings—that shakes the air molecules all around it,* then the molecules* next to them* begin trembling, too, and so on. Waves* of sound roll like tides to our ears, where they* make the eardrum vibrate; this* in turn moves three colorfully named bones (the hammer, the anvil, and the stirrup), the tiniest bones* in the body. Although the cavity they* sit in is only about a third of an inch wide and a sixth of an inch deep, the air trapped there by blocked Eustachian tubes is what gives scuba divers and airplane passengers such grief when the air pressure changes. The three bones* press fluid in the inner ear against membranes, which brush tiny hairs that trigger nearby nerve cells, which telegraph messages to the brain: We *hear*. It* may not seem like a particularly complicated route, but in practice it* follows an elaborate pathway* that looks something like a maniacal miniature golf course, with curlicues, branches, roundabouts, relays, levers, hydraulics, and feedback loops.

Diane Ackerman, *A Natural History of the Senses*

Topic Sentence

Step 1

Step 2

Step 3

Step 4

Step 5

Step 6

Step 7

Clincher Sentence

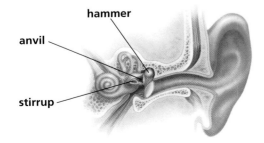

hammer

anvil

stirrup

The ideas in these two paragraphs are not arranged in an order that makes sense (some may even include information that detracts from the unity of the paragraph). Identify the type of order that would work for each paragraph, and then revise each paragraph by rearranging sentences into that order. To further improve unity and coherence, eliminate the sentences that are unrelated to the main idea and incorporate direct references and transitions. Finally, decide whether you think the paragraphs are sufficiently elaborated. Be prepared to explain your answers.

Rudolfo Anaya

1. Rudolfo Anaya, a well-known Mexican American writer, was born in Pastura, New Mexico, in 1937. In 1972, Anaya's first novel, *Bless Me, Ultima*, was published. *Bless Me, Ultima* is the story of a young boy who grows up in New Mexico during the time of World War II. Anaya's early life was marked by a loss of faith, which later became a theme in his novels. Together, three of Anaya's novels form a loose trilogy that depicts Mexican American life over several decades. Anaya was a public school teacher from 1963 to 1970. In 1979, *Tortuga*, Anaya's third novel, was published. In 1976, *Heart of Aztlan*, Anaya's second novel, was published. Rolando Hinojosa-Smith is also a Mexican American novelist.

2. These programs, which typically last from three weeks to two months, give students a chance to see what college life is like—from living in tiny dorm rooms to trekking across campus for an 8:00 A.M. biology class. Many colleges now have summer academic programs for high school students. Some colleges design special programs specifically for high school students. Some colleges have classes targeted to senior citizens. Like college itself, however, these programs often require that high school students fill out detailed applications. Many programs are quite expensive, some costing as much as $5,800. Colleges often use these programs as a way to recruit young students early. The applications usually ask for test scores, a personal essay, and letters of recommendation.

Review A Analyzing Paragraphs

Get together with two or three classmates, and as a group, gather several sample paragraphs. Try to pick paragraphs written for different purposes—to explain, to describe, to persuade, and so on. You might try such sources as popular magazine and newspaper articles; ads; CD liner notes; how-to manuals; and movie, book, and restaurant reviews. When you have gathered a range of paragraphs, identify each paragraph's parts (topic, supporting, and clincher sentences) and explain each paragraph's qualities (unity, coherence, and elaboration). Pay special attention to the order of ideas in each paragraph.

STYLE TIP

In your reading, you will find that many paragraphs and longer pieces of writing have more than one purpose. For example, writers often combine description with narration.

Paragraphs Within Compositions

In longer pieces of writing, or **compositions,** paragraphs are used to mark a movement from one idea to another. When you write your own longer pieces, you'll usually use paragraphs for the following reasons:

STYLE TIP

Sometimes, paragraph indentations do not mark a new idea; instead, they are used in convenient places to break up a long section simply to give a reader's eyes time to rest. Just think how difficult it is to read long stretches of uninterrupted text.

- to explain a different part of your subject or another step in a process
- to introduce another kind of support for your opinion
- to show a jump forward or back in time, or a change in location
- to show, in a story or a dialogue, that a different person or character is speaking

Remember these reasons as you read about compositions in the following section.

What Makes a Composition?

You have looked closely at paragraphs—at their parts, qualities, and purposes. When grouped together in a particular way, paragraphs form a *composition*—a longer piece of writing that, like a paragraph, usually focuses on a main idea.

Composition form is seen in nonfictional works such as articles, essays, and reports. Most compositions contain an **introduction,** a **body,** and a **conclusion.** (Although these elements are also found in fictional works, compositions use them in unique ways and for different purposes.) In this section, you will focus on aspects of composition form.

The Introduction

Many writers think the *introduction* of an article or composition is the hardest part to write; it is a critical time to capture your readers' attention and to let them know what your topic is. The length of an introduction may vary a great deal—from one sentence to several paragraphs. However, there are usually three things an introduction needs to accomplish:

- catch the audience's attention (otherwise they may not read on)

- set the tone, or show the writer's attitude, toward the topic (humorous, serious, critical, and so forth)

- present the **thesis** (sometimes at the beginning but often at the end of the introduction)

The Thesis Statement

When you write a composition, you have something specific to say about your topic. This is your *thesis,* and the sentence that you write to express this main idea is the *thesis statement.* The thesis statement helps you control the direction of your composition: The entire composition will support the ideas in this statement.

There are several different kinds of thesis statements. One kind simply states the topic, as in this example: "Central City collects millions of tons of garbage daily." Other thesis statements go further; they state what the writer will prove in the composition—for example: "Unless some innovative solutions are found quickly, there will be no place to put the millions of tons of garbage that Central City collects daily."

NOTE In the writing you do now, you will usually make the thesis statement a part of the introduction. However, experienced writers often use the thesis statement later in the composition. You will even find compositions (articles and essays) in which the thesis statement is implied, not directly stated.

Hints for Writing and Using a Thesis Statement

1. **Use your prewriting notes.** Before you begin to write, you will gather a great deal of information about your topic. Look over this information carefully. What one idea is most important? What one idea unifies the facts and details you have? Answering these questions will help you to focus your thinking—an important step in developing a thesis statement.

2. **State both your topic and your main idea.** Your thesis statement needs to make clear two things: your topic and your main idea. Remember: Your topic will be a limited (or manageable) one, and you will have a specific, unifying idea to state about it. When you first write out your thesis statement, underline your limited topic and circle your main idea to make sure you have included both.

   For example, think about this thesis statement: "If you want to be among the nearly eight million teens who are employed part time, the following tips on finding and landing a job may boost your chances of success." You can tell from this statement that the topic is the teen part-time job market and that the main idea is how to improve your chances of finding a part-time job.

3. **Avoid the following kinds of thesis statements:**
   - An obvious statement, such as "Basketball is played by two opposing teams of five players each." Statements like this don't need to be supported or defended.
   - A blanket thesis statement, such as "No matter what country they call home, all people desire material wealth." Because such statements are all-inclusive, they are almost always impossible to defend.

4. **Change your thesis statement if you need to.** To begin with, reword your thesis statement until it says clearly what you want it to say. Remember, however, that it is not written in concrete. If you get a different idea or decide to change the focus of your composition, just write a new thesis statement.

5. **Use your thesis statement to guide your writing.** Keep your thesis statement in front of you as you write, and be sure that all your ideas and details support it. Throw out any that do not, so that your composition will focus solely on your main idea.

NOTE The first draft of your thesis statement will probably be very plain and direct. However, an indirect statement of your thesis may be more interesting to your readers. Remember that one purpose of an introduction is to capture your reader's interest, and a catchy thesis statement can help. Try rewriting your thesis statement until it sounds interesting or exciting. Notice the difference in the following preliminary thesis statement after revision.

PRELIMINARY   In July 1997, after the *Mars Pathfinder* landed on Mars, the images captured by its camera-equipped rover began to answer many scientific questions.

REVISED   In July 1997, when the first grainy images were transmitted back to Earth from the *Mars Pathfinder*'s rover, they shed light on many mysteries of the red planet that have baffled scientists for centuries.

Exercise 3 **Analyzing Thesis Statements**

In the list below, find the four effective thesis statements: They each have a specific topic and a clear main idea. The remaining thesis statement is weak: It is missing a specific topic or a clear main idea. Rewrite it as needed to make it more effective.

1. Mexican Americans have made many important contributions to literature and music in the United States.
2. The study of volcanoes, whether on land or in the sea, has led to important knowledge about the inner workings of our planet.
3. The Internet, as well as other exciting new technology, has made it possible for millions of Americans to work at home.
4. Parks are important to city-dwellers.
5. Across the country, grass-roots campaigns are working to remind citizens of their responsibility to vote.

Techniques for Beginning a Composition

The following suggestions represent some of the techniques experienced writers use to capture their readers' attention. All of them are accompanied by sample introductions for a paper on the benefits of traveling, whether to another country or the next town over. As you look through them, keep in mind their primary purpose—to "hook" readers and make them want to keep reading. When you are trying to decide how to start a composition yourself, try one or two of these techniques.

1. **Begin by addressing the reader directly.** Statements such as "Welcome to the Grand Canyon!" or "If you could travel anywhere, where would you go?" involve the reader at once. This kind of introduction also sets an informal, friendly tone. (The Writer's Model on page 478 addresses the reader directly with "You're hired!")

2. **Begin with an interesting or dramatic quotation.** This kind of introduction piques your readers' curiosity—readers will want to keep reading as you explain or elaborate on the quotation.

> Of her travels abroad, the writer Miriam Beard has said, "Certainly, travel is more than the seeing of sights; it is a change that goes on, deep and permanent, in the ideas of the living."

3. **Begin with an anecdote or example.** Starting with an anecdote or example can immediately involve your reader, especially if the anecdote is humorous or mysterious.

> On my first morning in Japan, I learned a lesson I will never forget. My host family had picked me up at the airport the previous evening, and feeling overwhelmed by the sensation of being in a foreign place, I had gone to bed early. Now rested and excited, I went to greet Mr. and Mrs. Tsukada. They smiled and gestured toward the table where my breakfast was waiting. What was it? Hot dogs and sauerkraut! For breakfast! Slowly, I remembered that I had written on my student-exchange application that this was my favorite meal. My host family simply wanted me to feel at home. At that moment, I learned that "home" could be anywhere that people are kind.

4. **Begin with an unusual or enlightening fact.** Some new or unusual fact will often entice your audience to read on and learn more about your topic.

> There are now vacation tours in which you chase tornadoes with professional storm chasers, travel to the depths of the sea to see the wreckage of the ship *Titanic*, or go inline skating across the Netherlands. Soon, space travel will be available for the most adventurous tourists. If you have the money and the motivation, it seems, you can plan a very unusual vacation.

5. **Begin with a question or a challenge.** When you start with a question or a challenge, you immediately involve your readers. Even if they know the answer, they'll want to know what you have to say about the subject.

> What would you find if you traveled to the following three places: Aix-en-Provence, France; Deildartunguhver, Iceland; and Garland County, Arkansas? The answer may surprise you: hot springs.

6. **Take a stand on an issue.** When you are writing persuasively, you can begin with a statement that expresses a strong, even controversial, opinion. This will make your readers want to read on to see how you will support your opinion.

> Guided tours, whether they are at the Metropolitan Museum of Art or Yellowstone Park, are a bad idea. In fact, guides ruin the experience most travelers seek: to be on their own, seeing and learning things for themselves.

7. **Begin with an outrageous or comical statement.** An outrageous or comical statement will let your readers know to expect a humorous or satirical composition. Most readers are attracted to humor and will want to keep reading.

> If your family is planning a vacation this summer, I have one piece of advice for you—never, *ever* buy a souvenir that is bigger than your head! Lugging that three-foot, thirty-pound replica of the Empire State Building all the way home was no fun, and it didn't please my parents much, either.

8. **Begin with a simple statement of your thesis.** Often a well-written thesis statement is all you need to catch your reader's attention.

> Travel is a valuable experience because you learn how other people live; you also learn that in a lot of ways people in other places are just like the people at home.

The Structure of Introductions

As you learned in the previous section, you can begin an introduction in a variety of ways. Then what? How do you shape the *entire* introduction? In formal and informal writing alike, introductory paragraphs are frequently structured in a similar way: They move from general information to a more specific statement, which is frequently the thesis statement. You might think of the structure as an inverted triangle, with the flat top as the **general opening** and the pointed bottom as the **precisely stated thesis**—the main idea your composition will prove. Look at the graphic at the right.

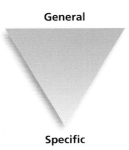

General

Specific

In the following example, which introduces an essay for a composition on literature, notice how the first two sentences grow increasingly specific and the third supplies the thesis. (Note, too, how this introduction supplies other important information, particularly the author's name and the title of the work.)

> John Steinbeck was both a great American novelist and a man firmly rooted in his time. His works reflect not only the hardships of people living during the Depression but also the influence of an increasingly important new art form—film. In *The Grapes of Wrath*, Steinbeck's descriptions are presented as if they are film sequences, one kind of shot quickly followed by another.

The following example is from a composition on a nonliterary topic. Note how it opens with two statements that seem to confirm commonly accepted knowledge. In the third sentence, however, the writer refutes the absolute truth of these statements and hints at the thesis statement that appears in the fourth sentence. This kind of introduction (sometimes called a "But" or "However" introduction) is a very effective way to capture your reader's attention.

You may think that forest fires are strictly harmful. After all, they can sweep over huge tracts of land, destroying trees that have grown for hundreds of years and killing great numbers of forest animals. Of course this is all true, but it is also true that forest fires have beneficial effects on the land. Fires are a part of a natural cycle that revitalizes the growth of many kinds of trees, including the lodgepole pine.

Exercise 4 Analyzing Introductions

Read the following three introductions written by professional writers, and then answer the following questions about each introduction.

- Which of the eight techniques (beginning on page 469) does the writer use in beginning the introduction?

- Does the technique work well enough to make you want to read the article? Explain your answer.

- What is the tone of the introduction—formal or informal? What words or phrases reveal the author's attitude toward the topic?

- Does the structure of the paragraph follow the pattern you learned about on page 471? How? If not, how does it differ from that pattern?

1. In 1984, two small clay tablets of vaguely rectangular shape were found in Tell Brak, Syria, dating from the fourth millennium B.C. I saw them, the year before the Gulf War, in an unostentatious display case in the Archeological Museum in Baghdad. They are simple, unimpressive objects, each bearing a few discreet markings: a small indentation near the top and some sort of stick-drawn animal in the center. One of the animals may be a goat, in which case the other is probably a sheep. The indentation, the archeologists say, is probably the number ten. All our history begins with these two modest tablets. They are—if the war spared them—among the oldest examples of writing we know.

Alberto Manguel, *A History of Reading*

2. Americans are a rootless people. Each year one in six of us changes residences; one in four changes jobs. We see nothing troubling in these statistics. For most of us, they merely reflect the restless energy that made America great. A nation of immigrants, unsurprisingly, celebrates those willing to pick up stakes and move on: the frontiersman, the cowboy, the entrepreneur, the corporate raider.

David Morris, "Rootlessness," *Utne Reader*

3. The best-known equation of the 20th century is $E=mc^2$, Einstein's statement linking energy, matter and the speed of light. But another formula— $V = c\ log_e{}^{Mi}/_{Mf}$ —has had at least as much impact on modern life. That's the equation relating the speed of a rocket to its other key characteristics: its weight and the efficiency of its motor. If you can get V up to 15,000 mph, you can hold a missile in suborbital flight long enough to hit a city halfway around the world. Get V up to 17,000 mph, and you can put a satellite into orbit. And if V goes to 25,000 mph, you can break free of Earth's gravitational pull and fly to the moon.

Russell Watson and John Barry, "Rockets," *Newsweek*

The Body

The **body** of a composition is the part where you develop your thesis statement. Each paragraph expresses a major point of your thesis and supports, or proves, it with details. These paragraphs should connect with one another and relate directly to your thesis statement. You can achieve these goals if the body has **emphasis, unity, coherence,** and **elaboration.**

NOTE Your thesis—along with your **purpose** for writing—always affects the kind of information with which you develop the body of a composition. For example, if you were developing a job description to train a co-worker, you would need different supporting evidence than if you were writing a letter describing your vacation to your friend.

TIPS & TRICKS

In writing the body of a composition, it is often helpful to draft a plan, whether an early plan (sometimes called a rough outline) or a formal outline.

Reference Note

For more information about **early plans** and **formal outlines,** see page 1037.

COMPUTER TIP

Use a word-processing program's outline view to organize your prewriting notes into an outline for the first draft of your composition. Some outline programs even include tools to help you create cluster diagrams.

Emphasis

To *emphasize* is to stress, and in most compositions you have some ideas that you want to stress because you think they are more important. The primary method for emphasizing ideas is to give them more attention, to devote more time and space to them. However, you can also emphasize an idea by discussing it first or last—the two positions that are most likely to draw the attention of the reader. The model composition on page 478 places more emphasis on applications and interviews, by giving them more space and attention, than it does on finding job leads.

Unity

Unity means "oneness." In a composition, unity means that every paragraph and every detail supports a single main idea. Each topic sentence for each paragraph should relate to the thesis statement of the composition. Similarly, each sentence in a paragraph should relate to the topic sentence of the paragraph.

Coherence

Coherence means "logical connection." A composition has coherence if all the ideas are connected in a sequence that readers find easy to follow. Sentences flow smoothly, and paragraphs connect sensibly. The best way to achieve coherence is to use **direct references** and **transitional expressions.**

Direct References

Reference Note

For more about **direct references** and **transitional words** and **phrases,** see page 462.

One way to link ideas is to refer directly to something that came immediately before. You can achieve coherence by using the following techniques:

1. Repeat key words or phrases from the preceding paragraph, or repeat or rephrase the last idea in that paragraph.
2. Use pronouns to refer to nouns already used.
3. Use synonyms or rewordings of ideas and key words.

Transitional Expressions

Transitional expressions, words and phrases such as *for example, of course, therefore, meanwhile,* and *later,* lead your readers from one sentence or paragraph to another. They help make relationships clear and create smooth connections among ideas.

> **NOTE** In a long composition or article, a short paragraph can be used to create a transition. Often such a paragraph is a single sentence acting as a bridge between the ideas in one paragraph and those in another.

Elaboration

Just as topic sentences need elaboration within paragraphs, thesis statements need to be elaborated within the body of a composition. *Elaboration*—in the form of details, reasons, and evidence—explains the thesis *completely*. When elaboration is not there, your reader has good reason to cast a skeptical eye on your thesis—after all, you haven't really proven your main idea.

TIPS & TRICKS

If you get stuck elaborating your thesis or main idea that is part of your thesis, use a freewriting technique such as clustering or listing to identify details you overlooked.

Exercise 5 **Analyzing Body Paragraphs**

Most writers really do use the techniques you have been reading about to write body paragraphs. (You will also use these techniques in your own writing.) In the following paragraph, identify the nouns, their direct-reference pronouns, and any transitional expressions. Then, explain whether the paragraph has unity and how the paragraph is ordered. Finally, determine whether there is sufficient elaboration of the paragraph's main point. Be prepared to explain your answers.

> The 369th Infantry Regiment, composed mostly of African American soldiers, established the best record of any U.S. Army infantry regiment during World War I. The regiment went to France in 1918 as a division attached to the French army. After training with the French, the men of the 369th fought in the trenches for 191 consecutive days. They did not lose any ground to the Germans throughout this period. After the war, the regiment received several awards for bravery from both the French and U.S. governments. In fact, Sergeant Henry Johnson was the first American, black or white, to win the French *Croix de Guerre*, a prestigious military honor. The battle in which he fought so bravely is now known as the "Battle of Henry Johnson."

The Conclusion

When you read a book or see a movie, you expect it to have a definite *conclusion,* or ending. Compositions should also have satisfying endings; readers need to feel that the ideas are tied together and presented completely. The following techniques are some options that experienced writers choose from to create effective conclusions.

1. **Refer to the introduction.** Use a phrase or image from your opening. This reminds readers where they started and provides a satisfying close to your composition.

> The next time you think to yourself, "Where do I want to go?" you can probably use the Web to find out.

The Writer's Model starting on page 478 also uses this technique, neatly wrapping up its main ideas with "You will be glad you did it right when you finally hear the words 'You're hired!'"

2. **Offer a solution or make a recommendation.** When you have taken a stand on an issue, you can stress your point by offering a solution or recommending a course of action in the conclusion.

> Sightseeing is about opening yourself to new experiences rather than having your first impressions forced into a particular mold. The next time you go somewhere new, try not to take the guided tour or pick up the historical pamphlet right away—first, just look around and ask yourself what *you* see.

3. **Restate your thesis.** Another good way to wind up your composition is to restate your thesis. Use different words to say the same thing, bringing your composition to an end that echoes the beginning. The example below restates the thesis illustrated in the eighth introduction on page 471.

> Traveling is a broadening experience because it lets you see how others live. Still, what is most valuable about traveling is learning that people share roughly the same dreams and have the same basic qualities—both good and bad—no matter where they live.

4. **Summarize your major points.** Another satisfying ending is a summary of the major points of a composition.

> The desire to experience the natural world is nearly universal. There simply would not be so many national parks and recreation areas if so many people did not need to get away from their everyday routines for a while, even just for an hour or two. These areas, set aside for us to play in or marvel at, also fulfill our desire for beauty. Natural landscapes let us know that there is a breathtaking world outside our office cubicles and crowded streets.

Other ways to conclude a composition include

- closing with an example of your main idea
- personally commenting on your topic
- posing a dramatic question or challenge
- ending with a thought-provoking or striking quotation
- describing a striking image or using a vivid figure of speech

Remember, however, that the most important thing is to tie your ideas together and leave your readers with the emotion you intended.

> NOTE In formal compositions, you will often conclude by summarizing your main points *and* restating your thesis. The shape of formal conclusions is often the reverse of introductions, which move from general to specific information (see page 471). In conclusions, writers frequently move from restating the specific points of the body of the essay to a more general final statement. The structure might be represented graphically by a shape like the triangle shown on the right.

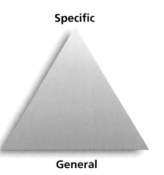

Specific

General

STYLE TIP

Oftentimes, descriptive and narrative compositions do not need distinctive conclusions separate from and following the body paragraphs. The description or experience is self-contained and does not require further elaboration or summarization.

Analyzing Conclusions

Get together with two or three classmates and look in books, magazine articles, and newspaper stories for at least three conclusions. Together, figure out which kind of techniques these conclusions use. Then, rewrite a new conclusion for each of the sample paragraphs, experimenting with different techniques. (You might also try rewriting the conclusion of the Writer's Model that appears on page 480.)

Using a Basic Framework

Below is a framework for basic composition structure. The Writer's Workshops within each chapter of this book will contain variations of this structure, tailored to specific types of writing. Still, most compositions follow this skeletal structure.

Framework for a Composition	
Introduction	Catches the reader's interest Establishes the tone Presents the thesis statement
Body	States the major points Supports the major points with details
Conclusion	Reinforces the main idea in the thesis statement Ties the ideas together Leaves the reader with a sense of completion

A Writer's Model

The following composition on teens getting part-time jobs includes the thesis statement on page 467. You might want to use this composition as a model as you write your own compositions.

INTRODUCTION

It Takes Work to Get Work

"You're hired!" These are exciting words to any anxious teen entering the job market for the very first time. If you want to be among the nearly eight million teens who are employed part time, the following tips on finding and landing a job may boost your chances of success.

Thesis statement

The first step is to find out what part-time jobs are available in your area. Some job leads come directly from employers: signs in store and restaurant windows, help-wanted ads in the newspaper, and listings at employment agencies or on company Web sites. Other leads can be developed by contacting potential employers yourself or by making use of contacts, such as friends, family members, business acquaintances, and your school counselor. The more leads you have, the more likely you are to find the job you want.

BODY
Major point: Job leads

Once you have a list of job leads, start applying for some jobs. In most cases, the first thing you will be asked to do is fill out a job application. This is the way an employer decides whom to interview. It is your first chance to show that you are qualified for the job.

Major point: Job applications

Here are some ways to use the job application to make a good first impression. First of all, neatness counts; use a pen and write clearly. Make sure you use standard English and avoid slang words. Spell words correctly and use good grammar. Finally, answer all questions honestly and clearly.

Above all, do not sell yourself short. Most job applications have a space to list special skills and accomplishments. Be honest, and try not to be shy. Does the job involve selling? Maybe you have sold ads for your school annual. Do you speak a second language? Many businesses need bilingual employees. Are you on the honor roll? Many employers know that people who work hard at school will also work hard at a job. Do you have job skills from completing courses in typing, computers, bookkeeping, or shop? Let your potential employer know.

(continued)

| STYLE | TIP |

Writers often wait until they finish their compositions before deciding on a **title.** When you write your own compositions, try to think of a title that lets readers know what to expect in subject and tone. (Note that it is not very wise to put a catchy, funny title on a serious essay, or vice versa—your readers will find this jarring or confusing.)

**Major point:
Job
interviews**

(continued)

After reviewing all the job applications, employers will choose some candidates to interview. An interview is the employer's chance to find out more about you and your chance to find out more about the job.

Arrive for the interview well-rested, clean, well-groomed, neatly dressed, and at least five minutes early. Have your Social Security card and a pen and pad of paper with you. During the interview, look the interviewer in the eye, smile, and remember to use the interviewer's name (always use Ms., Mrs., or Mr.—never first names). Be direct and honest, and be ready to answer questions. (Prepare yourself in advance by consulting employment booklets at the library that list some of the most commonly asked interview questions.) When the interview is over, express your interest in the job and thank the interviewer for his or her time.

**Major point:
Follow-up
letter**

Finally, that evening, type or neatly write a brief letter expressing your interest in the job and reminding the interviewer of the attributes that make you the perfect person for the job. Thank the interviewer for considering you. Address the envelope to the interviewer, and mail the letter the next day.

CONCLUSION

It may take a little time to prepare for and follow through with your job search, but it is worth the effort. You will be glad you did it right when you finally hear the words "You're hired!"

Review B **Writing an Informative Composition**

Using the following collection of facts, write a brief composition. You may not use all the information supplied, but be sure you use as much information as is necessary to write a complete composition. You may add other information, but limit your topic so that it can be covered in a short paper.

As you develop a thesis statement and draft your composition, consult the introduction, body, and conclusion sections of this chapter.

COMPUTER TIP

When writing on the computer, remember to save your work every ten to fifteen minutes. Turn on automatic save if you have it.

When you finish drafting, use the framework on page 478 to evaluate your composition, and then revise to achieve unity, coherence, and sufficient elaboration.

Soccer—the World's Game

1. The World Cup is a trophy granted to the world champion soccer team.
2. The first competition for the cup was organized by the Fédération Internationale de Football Association (FIFA) in 1930.
3. Uruguay, at that time the foremost soccer-playing nation, won the first match—with nearly 100,000 in attendance.
4. Since its beginning, the World Cup has been held every four years, except during World War II.

5. In 1970, the original trophy, made of solid gold and weighing nearly nine pounds, was permanently awarded to Brazil, at that time the only team to have won three competitions. A new trophy was introduced for future winners.
6. The World Cup competition consists of a series of tournaments that lead to a final elimination event made up of sixteen national teams.
7. World Cup teams are not limited to amateurs, so competition is truly among the world's best players.
8. Fans are a central part of World Cup events—and some fans' nationalistic pride has led to violent brawls.
9. Fans watch the World Cup games on TV in huge numbers worldwide; many also keep track through constantly updated Web sites (in 1998, there were more than seventeen sites devoted to the World Cup games).
10. Some soccer players—like Brazil's Pelé and Ronaldo—have become celebrities known all over the globe.
11. In 1998, the championship French team was said to symbolize France's diversity because it was composed of white and black players, both natives and immigrants.

PART 3

Grammar, Usage, and Mechanics

Parts of Speech Overview

Identification and Function

Diagnostic Preview

Identifying Parts of Speech

For each sentence in the following paragraph, write each italicized word or word group and tell how it is used—as a *noun, pronoun, adjective, verb, adverb, preposition, conjunction,* or *interjection.*

EXAMPLES   In parts of **[1]** *India,* for a **[2]** *few* weeks every year, it rains continually.

    1. *India—noun*

    2. *few—adjective*

After months **[1]** *of* drought, the **[2]** *storm* clouds build up in the **[3]** *sky* and the torrential deluge **[4]** *begins.* **[5]** *Well,* it is April in India, **[6]** *monsoon* season. In India **[7]** *and* neighboring Bangladesh, the monsoon **[8]** *usually* continues from **[9]** *late* spring to early fall. **[10]** *During* that time **[11]** *it* brings heavy rains **[12]** *that* are beneficial to crops, but **[13]** *some* monsoons **[14]** *can be* deadly if their **[15]** *rains* are abnormally heavy.

Monsoons are created **[16]** *when* there is a great difference **[17]** *between* the temperatures of hot air over the sea and cold air over the land. **[18]** *Southwesterly* winds carry warm, moist air up from the Indian Ocean and **[19]** *collide* with cooler air over the landmass. **[20]** *The* result is a downpour that can last for weeks.

The Noun

14a. A *noun* names a person, a place, a thing, or an idea.

Persons	architect	travelers	family	Kira Alvarez
Places	restaurant	islands	wilderness	Salt Lake City
Things	computer	sailboats	insects	Brooklyn Bridge
Ideas	education	beliefs	ambition	utopianism

Common and Proper Nouns

A *common noun* names any one of a group of persons, places, things, or ideas. A *proper noun* names a particular person, place, thing, or idea. Generally, common nouns are not capitalized unless they begin a sentence or are part of a title; proper nouns are capitalized.

Common Nouns	Proper Nouns
woman	Sylvia Bryan, Eda Seasongood, Queen Hatshepsut
nation	South Korea, Canada, Mexico, United States
event	World Series, Mardi Gras, World War II
holiday	Memorial Day, Thanksgiving Day, Fourth of July
language	English, Japanese, American Sign Language
painter	Pablo Picasso, Mary Cassatt, Jackson Pollock
athlete	Michelle Kwan, Michael Jordan, Vijay Singh

Reference Note

For more about **capitalization of nouns,** see page 753.

Concrete and Abstract Nouns

A *concrete noun* names a person, place, or thing that can be perceived by one or more of the senses (sight, hearing, taste, touch, and smell). An *abstract noun* names an idea, a feeling, a quality, or a characteristic.

Concrete Nouns	fire, garlic, cotton, horses, Liberty Bell
Abstract Nouns	self-confidence, strength, charm, ability, Zen

Exercise 1 Classifying Nouns

Classify each of the following nouns as either *concrete* or *abstract*.

EXAMPLE   **1.** satisfaction

　　　　　1. satisfaction—abstract

1. tradition	**6.** honor	**11.** palm trees	**16.** sand dune
2. flower	**7.** security	**12.** Mr. Nakamura	**17.** pencil
3. courage	**8.** lake	**13.** tears	**18.** commitment
4. cafeteria	**9.** happiness	**14.** suspicion	**19.** hope
5. dancers	**10.** bench	**15.** self-esteem	**20.** Mackinac Bridge

Collective Nouns

Reference Note

For information on using **verbs and pronouns that agree with collective nouns,** see pages 584 and 597.

The singular form of a **collective noun** names a group.

Collective Nouns				
audience	bunch	fleet	jury	pride
batch	cluster	flock	litter	set
bouquet	crew	group	pack	staff
brood	family	herd	pod	swarm

Compound Nouns

Reference Note

For information on words or word groups that may serve as nouns, see **prepositional phrases** (page 536), **verbals and verbal phrases** (page 540), and **subordinate clauses** (page 559).

A **compound noun** consists of two or more words that together name a person, a place, a thing, or an idea. A compound noun may be written as one word, as separate words, or as a hyphenated word.

One Word	sidewalk, tablecloth, Greenland
Separate Words	attorney general, telephone pole, Empire State Building
Hyphenated Word	daughter-in-law, jack-o'-lantern, great-grandfather

NOTE When you are not sure how to write a compound noun, look it up in a dictionary.

Review A **Classifying Nouns**

Classify the italicized noun in each of the following sentences as *common, proper, collective,* or *compound.*

EXAMPLE   **1.** Didn't you want a *treehouse* when you were a child?

   1. common, compound

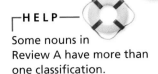

HELP

Some nouns in Review A have more than one classification.

1. *Republicans,* sometimes known as members of the Grand Old Party, use an elephant as their symbol.
2. After his term as the prime minister of Japan, Eisaku Sato was awarded the *Nobel Peace Prize* in recognition of his efforts toward nuclear disarmament.
3. Lamar and Yancy rowed to the middle of the lake to escape the *swarm* of mosquitoes on the shore.
4. Off the coast of Guam lies the deepest place in the ocean—the *Mariana Trench.*
5. Well, yes, I do enjoy the *Modern Jazz Quartet.*
6. *Reality* almost always falls short of ideals.
7. Standing regally in the shallow pool was a huge *flock* of flamingos.
8. Give me a *bunch* of those shasta daisies, please.
9. *Lucky* will never sit on command unless you train him.
10. Although the heritage and name of *boogie-woogie* may be African, that jazz sound is purely American.

The Pronoun

14b. A *pronoun* is a word used in place of one or more nouns or pronouns.

EXAMPLES   Angelo borrowed a hammer and some nails. **He** will return **them** tomorrow. [The pronoun *He* takes the place of the noun *Angelo.* The pronoun *them* takes the place of the nouns *hammer* and *nails.*]

Several of the students have entered the essay contest because **they** are extremely interested in the topic. [The pronoun *they* takes the place of the pronoun *Several.*]

The word that a pronoun stands for is called the ***antecedent*** of the pronoun. In the preceding examples, *Angelo* is the antecedent of *He; hammer* and *nails* are the antecedents of *them;* and *Several* is the antecedent of *they.*

Reference Note

For more information about **antecedents,** see page 593.

Personal Pronouns

A *personal pronoun* refers to the one speaking (*first person*), the one spoken to (*second person*), or the one spoken about (*third person*).

First Person	I, me, my, mine, we, us, our, ours
Second Person	you, your, yours
Third Person	he, him, his, she, her, hers, it, its, they, them, their, theirs

EXAMPLES   **I** hope that **you** can help **me** with **my** homework.

                  He said that **they** would meet **us** outside the theater.

NOTE This textbook refers to the words *my, your, his, her, its, our,* and *their* as possessive pronouns. However, because they can come before nouns and tell *which one* or *whose,* some authorities prefer to call these words adjectives. Follow your teacher's instructions regarding these words.

Reflexive and Intensive Pronouns

A *reflexive pronoun* refers to the subject of a sentence and functions as a complement or as an object of a preposition. An *intensive pronoun* emphasizes its antecedent.

First Person	myself, ourselves
Second Person	yourself, yourselves
Third Person	himself, herself, itself, themselves

REFLEXIVE   Kimiko wrote a note to **herself.**
INTENSIVE   Leonora **herself** organized the school's recycling program.

Demonstrative Pronouns

A *demonstrative pronoun* points out a specific person, place, thing, or idea.

this	that	these	those

⌐ TIPS & TRICKS ⌐

To determine whether a pronoun is reflexive or intensive, read the sentence aloud and omit the pronoun. If the meaning of the sentence changes, the pronoun is reflexive. If the meaning of the sentence stays the same, the pronoun is intensive.

EXAMPLE

I need a little time for **myself.** [*I need a little time for* doesn't make sense. The pronoun *myself* is reflexive.]

Did Paul prepare dinner **himself?** [Without *himself,* the meaning of the sentence stays the same. The pronoun *himself* is intensive.]

⌐HELP⌐

Do not use the nonstandard forms *hisself, theirself,* and *theirselves.* Use *himself* and *themselves* instead.

EXAMPLES   **This** is our favorite song by Ella Fitzgerald.

The apples I picked today taste better than **these**.

NOTE   The same words that are used as demonstrative pronouns can also function as *demonstrative adjectives.*

PRONOUN   Her best painting is **this.**

ADJECTIVE   Her best painting is **this** one.

Reference Note

For more information on **demonstrative adjectives,** see page 493.

Interrogative Pronouns

An *interrogative pronoun* introduces a question.

| what | which | who | whom | whose |

EXAMPLES   **What** is the answer to the last algebra problem?

Whose is this?

Relative Pronouns

A *relative pronoun* introduces a subordinate clause.

| that | which | who | whom | whose |

EXAMPLES   The house **that** you saw is a historical landmark.

She is the woman **who** is running for mayor.

Reference Note

For more information on **relative pronouns** and **subordinate clauses,** see page 560. For information on when to use *who or whom,* see page 619.

Indefinite Pronouns

An *indefinite pronoun* refers to a person, a place, a thing, or an idea that may or may not be specifically named.

all	each other	most	one another
another	either	much	other
any	everybody	neither	several
anybody	everyone	nobody	some
anyone	everything	none	somebody
anything	few	no one	someone
both	many	nothing	something
each	more	one	such

Reference Note

For information on the **agreement of indefinite pronouns with verbs,** see page 581. For information on **indefinite pronouns used with other pronouns,** see page 593.

GRAMMAR

EXAMPLES   I have packed **everything** we will need for the trip.

               Has **anyone** seen my binoculars?

NOTE   Many of the pronouns you have studied so far may also be used as adjectives.

whose basketball   **this** girl   **more** paper   **each** apple

Exercise 2   Identifying Pronouns

Identify the pronouns in the following sentences. Then, classify each pronoun as *personal, reflexive, intensive, demonstrative, interrogative, relative,* or *indefinite*.

EXAMPLE   1. Someone told me they had moved to Iowa.

                1. *Someone—indefinite; me—personal; they—personal*

1. Deven himself knew everyone who had a ticket or could get one for him at a low price.
2. Nobody has bought any of the CDs on sale at the discount store.
3. You won several of the events at the 4-H competition, I hear.
4. Those are photographs of some of the many contemporary politicians who are women.
5. What is the name of the large body of water that borders Ethiopia?
6. Althea Gibson stunned spectators but not herself when she took the singles and doubles titles at Wimbledon in 1957.
7. According to Buddhist belief, a soul detached from all of its desires enters nirvana, which is a state of consciousness, not a place.
8. Most of the participants purchased small souvenirs and such.
9. Either of their formats will work, but we prefer another.
10. According to this article, Sherlock Holmes never actually said "Elementary, my dear Watson."

Review B   Identifying Nouns and Pronouns

Tell whether each italicized word or word group in the following paragraph is a *noun* or a *pronoun*.

EXAMPLES   Tessellation is the filling of a plane with shapes so that [1] *each* of the [2] *shapes* touches the others without any space between them.

          1. *pronoun*

          2. *noun*

For centuries, cultures all over the world have used tessellated [1] *designs* to decorate fabrics, walls, floors, pottery, and many other everyday things. The [2] *Moors*, for example, were masters at creating intricate tiled walls and floors. Because their [3] *religion* did not allow [4] *them* to make images of any animals or [5] *people*, they worked with geometric shapes. Notice also that [6] *both* of the Moorish designs shown below (left and center) are symmetrical. One twentieth-century Dutch artist [7] *who* was inspired by designs like [8] *these* from Moorish buildings was [9] *M. C. Escher.* [10] *Many* of Escher's designs, however, feature birds, lizards, and other natural [11] *forms*. In addition, he often used asymmetrical [12] *shapes* in [13] *his* interlocking designs. The [14] *one* below on the [15] *right* consists of asymmetrical shapes. In this [16] *pattern* one [17] *kind* of creature interlocks with [18] *another*. In the design on the left—an amazing [19] *achievement* — a single, complicated shape interlocks in two ways with [20] *itself.*

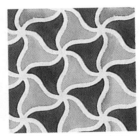

The Adjective

14c. An *adjective* modifies a noun or a pronoun.

To *modify* means "to describe or to make more definite" the meaning of a word. Adjectives modify nouns or pronouns by telling *what kind, which one, how many,* or *how much.*

What Kind?	Which One?	How Many?	How Much?
brown shoes	**those** cars	**ten** boxes	**some** water
English tea	**first** step	**several** books	**less** time
up-to-date look	**last** one	**many** students	**enough** money

Reference Note

For more information on **using modifiers,** see Chapter 22.

Adjectives usually precede the words they modify.

EXAMPLE The **wild** and **graceful** deer ran through the forest.

For emphasis, however, adjectives sometimes follow the words they modify.

EXAMPLE The deer, **wild** and **graceful,** ran through the forest.

Adjectives may be separated from the words they modify.

EXAMPLE The casserole was **delicious.**

NOTE The adjective in the example above is a predicate adjective. A **predicate adjective** is an adjective that completes the meaning of a linking verb and modifies the subject of the verb.

Reference Note

For more information on **predicate adjectives,** see page 525.

Articles

The most frequently used adjectives are *a, an,* and *the.* These words are called **articles.** *A* and *an* are called **indefinite articles** because they refer to any member of a general group. *A* is used before a word beginning with a consonant sound. *An* is used before a word beginning with a vowel sound. *The* is called the **definite article** because it refers to someone or something in particular.

EXAMPLES Jorge drew pictures of **a** pelican and **an** albatross.

For **an** hour I rode through **the** park in **a** horse-drawn carriage. [*An* is used before *hour* because *hour* begins with a vowel sound.]

Maple Avenue is **a** one-way street. [*A* is used before *one-way* because *one-way* begins with a consonant sound.]

The lion is often called "**the** king of **the** beasts."

Adjective or Pronoun?

A word may be used as one part of speech in one context and as a different part of speech in another context. For example, the following words may be used as adjectives or as pronouns.

all	each	more	one	such	those
another	either	most	other	that	what
any	few	much	several	these	which
both	many	neither	some	this	whose

Remember that an adjective modifies a noun or a pronoun and that a pronoun takes the place of a noun or pronoun.

ADJECTIVE   **Which** museum did you visit? [*Which* modifies the noun *museum.*]

PRONOUN   **Which** did you visit? [*Which* takes the place of the noun *museum.*]

ADJECTIVE   Leslie Marmon Silko wrote **these** stories. [*These* modifies the noun *stories.*]

PRONOUN   Leslie Marmon Silko wrote **these.** [*These* takes the place of the noun *stories.*]

NOTE   The words *this, that, these,* and *those* are called **demonstrative adjectives** when they modify nouns or pronouns, and they are called **demonstrative pronouns** when they take the place of nouns or pronouns.

Reference Note
For more information about **demonstrative pronouns,** see page 488.

Adjective or Noun?

Some words can be used as nouns or adjectives.

Nouns	Adjectives
business	**business** letter
saxophone	**saxophone** player
tuna	**tuna** salad
United States	**United States** government

Notice in the last example above that the proper noun *United States* is capitalized whether it is used as an adjective or as a noun.

NOTE   Some word groups make up compound nouns.

EXAMPLES   road map, blood bank, soap opera, country club, United States of America, Spanish moss, merry-go-round

By checking an up-to-date dictionary, you can avoid confusing an adjective with a word that is considered part of a compound noun.

Reference Note
For more about **compound nouns,** see page 486.

Proper Adjectives

An adjective that is formed from a proper noun is called a *proper adjective.*

Proper Nouns	Proper Adjectives
New Mexico	**New Mexican** food
Islam	**Islamic** teachings
Faust	**Faustian** bargain
Rubens	**Rubenesque** model
Christmas	**Christmas** tree

Exercise 3 Identifying Adjectives and the Words They Modify

Identify the adjectives and the words they modify in each of the following sentences. Do not include the articles *a*, *an*, and *the*.

EXAMPLE **1.** Put those aluminum cans in that empty box in the hall closet.

   1. *those, aluminum—cans; that, empty—box; hall—closet*

1. John lives on this street.
2. You need four cups of flour for this recipe.
3. Your new apartment, so spacious and sunny, certainly seems ideal.
4. The image of the eagle is quite powerful in many American Indian cultures today.
5. To which bookstore did you go?
6. All of the books on these shelves were written by eighteenth-century French writers.
7. Neither film was enjoyable.
8. The local stores open at 9:00 A.M.
9. Speaking of the space program, which astronaut do you admire more—Lt. Col. Eileen Collins or Dr. Mae C. Jemison?
10. Tomás bought a new tie for the dance.

Review C Identifying Nouns, Pronouns, and Adjectives

Tell whether each italicized word in the following sentences is used as a *noun*, a *pronoun*, or an *adjective*. If the word is used as an adjective, give the word it modifies.

EXAMPLE **1.** *Most* people do not realize the *tremendous* number of books the library has available for *them*.

   1. *Most—adjective—people; tremendous—adjective—number; them—pronoun*

1. Many *shop* owners decided to close *their* shops early.
2. *What* are the *other* choices on the menu?
3. The manuscript for Andrew García's fascinating autobiography was found packed in dynamite *boxes* under his bed five years after *he* had died.
4. We had a *family* reunion at my grandparents' house *last* summer.
5. As people encounter different *ways* of life, *they* gradually alter their speech patterns.
6. Thanks to the development of *digital* recording, symphony *performances* can now be recorded with higher fidelity.
7. *Oboe* players carry extra reeds with *them* because of the possibility that a reed might split during a performance.
8. *Alonzo* had never bought *that* brand before.
9. *Some* of the players felt nervous about the *athletic* contests.
10. *They* were penalized *ten* yards for holding.

The Verb

14d. A *verb* expresses action or a state of being.

In this textbook, verbs are classified as (1) action or linking verbs, (2) helping or main verbs, and (3) transitive or intransitive verbs.

Action Verbs and Linking Verbs

An *action verb* expresses either physical or mental activity.

Physical	travel	sit	arise	draw	build
Mental	remember	think	believe	consider	know

EXAMPLES   The ancient Egyptians **constructed** elaborate tombs for their rulers. [The verb *constructed* expresses physical activity.]

Do you **recall** the family we met on our vacation last summer? [The verb phrase *Do recall* expresses mental activity.]

A *linking verb* connects the subject to a word or word group in the predicate that identifies or describes the subject. Such a word or word group is called a *subject complement.*

Reference Note
For more on **subject complements,** see page 524.

EXAMPLES   Patience **is** the best remedy for many troubles. [The subject complement *remedy* identifies the subject *Patience*.]

He **became** a highly respected sculptor. [The subject complement *sculptor* identifies the subject *He*.]

The dessert **looks** delicious. [The subject complement *delicious* describes the subject *dessert*.]

Commonly Used Linking Verbs			
Forms of *Be*			
am	be	will be	had been
is	can be	could be	shall have been
are	may be	should be	will have been
was	might be	would be	could have been
were	must be	has been	should have been
being	shall be	have been	would have been

Other Common Linking Verbs			
appear	grow	seem	stay
become	look	smell	taste
feel	remain	sound	turn

Some verbs may be used as linking verbs or as action verbs.

LINKING   The soup **tasted** spicy.
ACTION   We **tasted** the soup.

LINKING   She **felt** good about her presentation.
ACTION   The explorers **felt** rain on their faces.

LINKING   The corn **grows** taller every day.
ACTION   Mr. Tahir **grows** pomegranates in his garden.

The forms of the verb *be* are not always used as linking verbs. They may be followed by words that tell *where* or *when*. Used in this way, *be* is referred to as a *state-of-being verb*.

EXAMPLE   My relatives from Ohio **will be** here tomorrow. [The verb *will be* is followed by *here*, which tells *where*, and *tomorrow*, which tells *when*.]

┌ TIPS & TRICKS ┐

To determine whether a verb in a sentence is a linking verb, substitute a form of the verb *be*. If the sentence makes sense, the verb is probably a linking verb.

LINKING
The milk **smelled** sour.
[The verb *was* can sensibly replace *smelled*: *The milk was sour*.]

ACTION
I **smelled** the milk to see whether it was fresh. [The verb *was* cannot sensibly replace *smelled*.]

Main Verbs and Helping Verbs

A *verb phrase* consists of at least one *main verb* and one or more *helping verbs* (also called *auxiliary verbs*).

EXAMPLES   John **will be arriving** at 3:00 P.M. [*Will* and *be* are the helping verbs; *arriving* is the main verb.]

She **should** not **have been told** about her surprise party. [*Should, have,* and *been* are the helping verbs. *Told* is the main verb.]

Commonly Used Helping Verbs				
Forms of *Be*	am	is	are	was
	were	be	being	been
Forms of *Have*	has	have	having	had
Forms of *Do*	do	does	doing	did
Modals	may	can	could	
	might	shall	should	
	must	will	would	

NOTE   Like a one-word verb, a verb phrase may be classified as action or linking.

EXAMPLES   I **have read** every book by Zora Neale Hurston. [action]

Is the koala **sleeping**? [action]

Sandra Day O'Connor **has been** a Supreme Court justice since 1981. [linking]

A *modal* is a helping verb that is joined with a main verb to express an attitude such as necessity or possibility.

EXAMPLES   We **must** be on time if we want to catch the plane. [necessity]

Uncle Rene said that the entire front of the house **may** need to be replaced. [possibility]

Reference Note

For more on using **modals,** see page 683.

FRANK & ERNEST reprinted by permission of Newspaper Enterprise Association, Inc.

Helping verbs may be separated from the main verb by other words.

EXAMPLES **Should** we **leave** immediately?

I **have** not **read** Nadine Gordimer's latest novel.

NOTE The word *not* and its contraction, *–n't*, are never part of a verb phrase. Instead, they are adverbs telling *to what extent.*

Reference Note

For more about **adverbs,** see page 499.

Reference Note

For more about **objects of verbs,** see page 521.

Transitive Verbs and Intransitive Verbs

A *transitive verb* has an *object*—a word that tells *who* or *what* receives the action.

EXAMPLES Everyone in the school **cheered** the football team during the championship game. [The object *team* receives the action of *cheered.*]

Nikki Giovanni **writes** poetry. [The object *poetry* receives the action of *writes.*]

An *intransitive verb* does not have an object.

EXAMPLES The gorilla **smiled** at its baby.

Suddenly, the child next to the door **screamed** loudly.

NOTE Some verbs can be transitive in one sentence and intransitive in another.

TRANSITIVE We **ate** our lunch quickly.
INTRANSITIVE We **ate** quickly.

TRANSITIVE Ms. Marino **measured** the boards carefully.
INTRANSITIVE Ms. Marino **measured** carefully.

⌐ **TIPS** & **TRICKS** ¬

Most dictionaries group the definitions of verbs according to whether the verbs are used transitively (v.t.) or intransitively (v.i.).

Exercise 4 **Identifying and Classifying Verbs**

Identify the verbs and verb phrases in the following sentences. Then, classify each verb or verb phrase as *transitive action, intransitive action,* or *intransitive linking.* Give the object(s) of each transitive action verb and the subject complement(s) of each linking verb.

EXAMPLE   1. The word *igloo* derives from the Inuit word *iglu,* which means "house."

 1. *derives—intransitive action*
    means—transitive action—"house" (object)

1. Throughout its history English has borrowed many words from other languages.
2. Because a newly borrowed word often sounds unfamiliar, people sometimes do not hear it correctly.
3. They will pronounce the word and will spell it as if it had come from other, more familiar English words.
4. The wrong spelling hides the true origin of the word and gives the false impression that its source is contemporary English, when its real source is something else entirely.
5. The word *woodchuck,* for example, might have come from two English words, *wood* and *chuck.*
6. Actually, *woodchuck* came from the Cree *otchek.*
7. Another interesting word of American Indian origin is the Algonquian word *musquash.*
8. When English-speaking settlers adopted the word, it became the animal name *muskrat.*
9. In a similar way, the Dutch word for cabbage salad, *koolsla,* became the English word *coleslaw,* and the French word for a kind of cart, *carriole,* led to the English word *carryall.*
10. Linguists generally know popular but inaccurate word histories as "folk etymology."

┌**HELP**──

In Exercise 4, look for verbs in subordinate clauses as well as in independent clauses.

The Adverb

14e. An *adverb* modifies a verb, an adjective, or another adverb.

An adverb tells *how, when, where,* or *to what extent* (*how much* or *how long*).

TIPS & TRICKS

Although many adverbs end in *–ly,* the *–ly* ending does not always signal that a word is an adverb. Some adjectives also end in *–ly:* the *daily* newspaper, an *early* train, an *only* child, a *friendly* person. Further, some words that do not end in *–ly,* such as *now, then, far, already, some-what, not,* and *right,* are often used as adverbs. To tell whether a word is an adverb, ask yourself these questions:

• Does the word modify a verb, an adjective, or an adverb?

• Does it tell *how, when, where,* or *to what extent*?

If you answer yes to both questions, the word is an adverb.

Reference Note

For information about **adverbs that are used to join words or word groups,** see relative adverbs (page 561) and conjunctive adverbs (page 570).

NOTE   Some adverbs can begin questions.

EXAMPLES   **Where** are you going?

When will they return?

Adverbs Modifying Verbs

EXAMPLES   Marian Anderson performed **magnificently.** [*how*]

Marian Anderson performed **earlier.** [*when*]

Marian Anderson performed **there.** [*where*]

Marian Anderson performed **widely.** [*to what extent*]

Adverbs Modifying Adjectives

EXAMPLES   The players are **exceptionally** skillful. [The adverb *exceptionally* modifies the adjective *skillful,* telling *to what extent.*]

The documentary about global warming was thorough **enough.** [The adverb *enough* modifies the adjective *thorough,* telling *to what extent.*]

Adverbs Modifying Other Adverbs

EXAMPLES   Cheetahs can run **extremely** fast. [The adverb *extremely* modifies the adverb *fast,* telling *to what extent.*]

André reacted to the news **rather** calmly. [The adverb *rather* modifies the adverb *calmly,* telling *to what extent.*]

Nouns or Adverbs?

Some words may be used as nouns or as adverbs.

NOUN   They returned to their **home.**
ADVERB   They returned **home** before noon.

NOUN   **Yesterday** was a good day.
ADVERB   The teacher reviewed what had been covered **yesterday.**

When identifying parts of speech, identify as adverbs words that modify verbs, adjectives, and adverbs.

Exercise 5 Identifying Adverbs and the Words They Modify

Identify the adverbs and the words they modify in the following sentences. State whether each adverb tells *how, when, where,* or *to what extent.*

EXAMPLE
1. We went to the museum today, but it was not open.
1. *today—went—when; not—open—to what extent*

1. Her calm, friendly manner always inspired confidence.
2. I understand now what he was saying.
3. The index lists all the book's topics alphabetically.
4. The guests have already left.
5. They thought that the decorations would be too expensive.
6. Maurice Hines and Gregory Hines tap-danced professionally when they were very young children.
7. The messenger said that she felt rather uncertain about which was the quickest route.
8. "Are you quite sure that this is the person you saw?" the detective asked the witness.
9. The teacher told the students, "Take your essays home for revision and return them to me tomorrow."
10. Visitors to China often bring back small figures that have been delicately carved from solid blocks of jade.

Review D Identifying Parts of Speech

Tell whether each italicized word in the following sentences is used as a *noun, pronoun, adjective, verb* or *adverb*. If the word is used as an adjective or an adverb, give the word or words it modifies.

EXAMPLE
1. *Is* the platypus *indigenous* to *Australia*?
1. *Is—verb; indigenous—adjective—platypus; Australia—noun*

1. He *announced* the names of *all* who had contributed *time* or money.
2. Jesse Owens *won* four gold medals in the 1936 *Olympics*.
3. In *ancient* Rome the new year began on March 1, and September *was* the *seventh* month of the year.
4. In 6000 B.C. the usual transportation for traveling long distances was the *camel* caravan, *which* averaged *eight* miles per hour.
5. The play received *generally* excellent reviews, but several critics were disappointed with the *rather* dull costumes.

STYLE TIP

To keep your writing fresh, try to avoid overusing adverbs such as *very, really,* and *so.* When you can, replace these words with more exact and descriptive words.

EXAMPLES
The lions were **ravenous** [not *very hungry*] after their unsuccessful hunt.

In the land of the Lilliputians, Gulliver appears **gigantic** [not *really tall*].

Hundreds of [not *So many*] people were waiting in line for tickets.

6. As *we* approached Santoríni, I saw sparkling white houses along the *steep* hillsides.

7. The teacher *posted* a list of students *who* would give *reports* about Sacagawea.

8. *Many* readers complained *angrily* about the editorial that appeared in yesterday's newspaper, but *others* found it amusing.

9. *Silently,* the drifting snow *blanketed* the narrow road.

10. I recall *vividly* that small town in the southern *part* of Texas.

Review E **Identifying Parts of Speech**

Tell whether each italicized word in the following paragraph is used as a *noun, pronoun, adjective, verb* or *adverb*. If the word is used as an adjective or an adverb, give the word or words it modifies.

EXAMPLES   I consider my aunt Laurette [1] *one* of my [2] *best* friends.

1. one—pronoun
2. best—adjective—friends

My aunt Laurette is just about the nicest [1] *grown-up* [2] *that* I know. I do [3] *not* get to see her [4] *very* often because she [5] *works* in Chicago, but when she comes [6] *here* to visit, I'm in heaven. [7] *What* do I like about her? For one thing, we share [8] *many* interests—both of us play the piano, [9] *sew* our own clothes, and love to make [10] *puns.* She is also a sympathetic listener and lets me tell about [11] *myself* without interrupting or criticizing me. Aunt Laurette shares [12] *her* own [13] *career* stories with me, and sometimes she even asks me for [14] *some* advice. A day with Aunt Laurette [15] *is* sometimes silly and sometimes [16] *serious,* but it's always a delight. I [17] *always* feel relaxed with my aunt Laurette. She's living proof that a person [18] *can* go through adolescence and [19] *still* emerge as a happy, [20] *highly* competent adult!

The Preposition

14f. A *preposition* shows the relationship of a noun or pronoun, called the *object of the preposition,* to another word.

Notice how the prepositions in the following examples show different relationships between the words *ran* (the verb) and *me* (the object of each preposition).

EXAMPLES   The playful puppy ran **beside** me.
            The playful puppy ran **toward** me.
            The playful puppy ran **around** me.
            The playful puppy ran **past** me.
            The playful puppy ran **after** me.
            The playful puppy ran **behind** me.
            The playful puppy ran **in front of** me.

A preposition, its object, and any modifiers of the object form a *prepositional phrase.*

"We the people, of the people, for the people, by the people, above the people, under the people, beside the people, behind the people..."

Overly thorough, lesser known Founding Father Clive Fishburne delivers his Preposition Proclamation.

THE QUIGMANS, by Buddy Hickerson, copyright 1993 Los Angeles Times Syndicate. Reprinted with permission.

Commonly Used Prepositions			
about	beneath	in	through
above	beside	inside	throughout
across	besides	into	to
after	between	like	toward
against	beyond	near	under
along	but (meaning	of	underneath
among	"except")	off	until
around	by	on	unto
as	down	out	up
at	during	outside	upon
before	except	over	with
behind	for	past	within
below	from	since	without

Reference Note

For more about **prepositional phrases,** see page 536.

Preposition or Adverb?

Some words in the preceding list may also be used as adverbs. Remember that an adverb is a modifier and does not take an object.

Reference Note

For more about **adverbs,** see page 499.

PREPOSITION   We drove **around** the parking lot. [The compound noun *parking lot* is the object of *around*.]

ADVERB   We drove **around** for a while. [*Around* modifies the verb *drove*.]

PREPOSITION   Vince went **inside** the house. [The noun *house* is the object of *inside*.]

ADVERB   Vince went **inside** when the rain started. [*Inside* modifies the verb *went*.]

Reference Note

For more information on **infinitives,** see page 674.

NOTE As a preposition, the word *to* has a noun or a pronoun as an object. Do not confuse a prepositional phrase with an *infinitive*—a verb form often preceded by *to.*

PREPOSITIONAL PHRASES   to the beach   to him and her

INFINITIVES   to remember   to read

A preposition that consists of two or more words is a *compound preposition.*

STYLE TIP

In formal writing and speaking, you should avoid ending a sentence with a preposition. However, prepositions are integral parts of many common English expressions, such as *come up with.*

INFORMAL
This is the solution that the committee has come up with.

Revising such a sentence to avoid ending it with a preposition may result in an awkward or pretentious construction.

AWKWARD
This is the solution up with which the committee has come.

In formal situations, therefore, it may be best to avoid such an expression altogether.

FORMAL
This is the solution that the committee has **proposed.**

Commonly Used Compound Prepositions

according to	because of	in spite of
along with	by means of	instead of
apart from	in addition to	next to
aside from	in front of	on account of
as of	in place of	out of

EXAMPLES   The young sculptor made a scale model of Mount Rushmore **out of** clay.

She placed a photograph of Mount Rushmore **next to** her clay model.

Exercise 6 Writing Prepositions

Supply an appropriate preposition for each blank in the following sentences. Do not use the same preposition twice.

EXAMPLE   1. ＿＿＿ the dark blue waters, whales played.

1. *Beneath*

1. Why does your cat always sleep ＿＿＿ my bed?
2. During the summer, the Dog Star, Sirius, shines ＿＿＿ the sky.
3. Everyone ＿＿＿ Julie, our guest of honor, knew about the party.
4. ＿＿＿ a long struggle, Lithuania won its independence from Russia.
5. Various pieces of electronic equipment were sitting ＿＿＿ the table.
6. The picnic was postponed ＿＿＿ rain.
7. ＿＿＿ the three-hour drive, my little brother took a nap.
8. Have you read ＿＿＿ the new videophones?
9. Little Turtle was true ＿＿＿ his word; he kept the treaty.
10. ＿＿＿ those days, mapmaking has become a much more exact science with multiple levels of precision.

The Conjunction

14g. A *conjunction* joins words or word groups.

Coordinating Conjunctions

A *coordinating conjunction* joins words or word groups that are used in the same way.

Coordinating Conjunctions			
and	for	or	yet
but	nor	so	

EXAMPLES   We found a bat **and** a glove. [The conjunction *and* connects two words.]

They may be hiding in the attic **or** in the basement. [The conjunction *or* connects two phrases.]

Will Rogers once claimed, "My forefathers didn't come over on the Mayflower, **but** they met the boat." [The conjunction *but* connects two clauses.]

Correlative Conjunctions

Correlative conjunctions are pairs of conjunctions that join words or word groups that are used in the same way.

Correlative Conjunctions	
both . . . and	not only . . . but (also)
either . . . or	whether . . . or
neither . . . nor	

EXAMPLES   **Both** athletes **and** singers must train for long hours. [connects two words]

We searched **not only** behind the garage **but also** under the pecan tree. [connects two phrases]

Either your fuel line is clogged, **or** your carburetor needs adjusting. [connects two clauses]

TIPS & TRICKS
You can remember the coordinating conjunctions as FANBOYS.
For
And
Nor
But
Or
Yet
So

Reference Note

For more information about **subordinate clauses,** see page 559.

Subordinating Conjunctions

A *subordinating conjunction* begins a subordinate clause and connects it to an independent clause.

Commonly Used Subordinating Conjunctions			
after	because	since	when
although	before	so that	whenever
as	even though	than	where
as if	how	that	wherever
as much as	if	though	whether
as though	in order that	unless	while
as well as	provided	until	why

EXAMPLES   We arrived late **because** our train was delayed.

Dr. Watson listened quietly **while** Sherlock Holmes explained his theory.

A subordinating conjunction does not always come between the groups of words it joins. It may come at the beginning of a sentence.

EXAMPLE   **While** Sherlock Holmes explained his theory, Dr. Watson listened quietly.

NOTE   Some words can be either prepositions or subordinating conjunctions.

PREPOSITION   **After** the basketball game, we celebrated.

SUBORDINATING CONJUNCTION   **After** we won the basketball game, we celebrated.

Review F   Identifying Prepositions and Conjunctions; Classifying Conjunctions

For each of the following sentences, identify every word or word group that is the part of speech indicated in parentheses. Then, classify each conjunction as *coordinating, correlative,* or *subordinating.*

EXAMPLE   1. Seeds were removed from short-staple cotton bolls by hand until Eli Whitney invented the cotton gin. (conjunction)

1. *until—subordinating*

1. Eli Whitney not only invented a new type of cotton gin but also manufactured muskets and other weapons. (*conjunction*)
2. Nowadays we take the idea of interchangeable parts for granted, but it was a revolutionary concept at that time. (*conjunction*)
3. For example, when a rifle is constructed with interchangeable parts, a defective part can be replaced quickly and easily with an identically made piece. (*preposition*)
4. Critical to any system using interchangeable parts is the standardization of parts, and Whitney himself took care of this task when he invented the first milling machine. (*conjunction*)
5. Like most great ideas, the idea of interchangeable parts was not solely one person's; others, Simeon North among them, also played pioneering roles in the Industrial Revolution. (*preposition*)
6. Even though this idea of interchangeable parts originated in Europe, it was Americans who made mass production the practical technique dubbed "the American System." (*conjunction*)
7. Before Eli Whitney introduced the idea of interchangeable parts, manufacturers had to employ many skilled workers. (*preposition*)
8. Although the new technology benefited manufacturers, it cost many workers their jobs. (*conjunction*)
9. Because of the simplicity of Whitney's system, unskilled workers could be used, for only repetitive actions are required by mass production. (*preposition*)
10. Could either Whitney or North have imagined the massive growth of industrialization and its consequences? (*conjunction*)

The Interjection

14h. An *interjection* expresses emotion and has no grammatical relation to the rest of the sentence.

EXAMPLES
| ah | hey | oops | uh-oh | whew |
| aha | oh | ouch | well | wow |

An interjection is often set off from the rest of the sentence by an exclamation point or a comma. An exclamation point indicates strong emotion. A comma indicates mild emotion.

EXAMPLES   **Ouch!** That hurts!

Well, I think you should apologize to her.

Determining Parts of Speech

14i. The way a word is used in a sentence determines what part of speech the word is.

EXAMPLES The coach decided that the team needed more **practice.** [noun]

The girls **practice** every Saturday afternoon. [verb]

They will have a **practice** session after school on Wednesday. [adjective]

Dublin, Ireland, was the **home** of the writer James Joyce. [noun]

The last **home** game will be played tomorrow night. [adjective]

We decided to stay **home.** [adverb]

Celine has won the citizenship award **before.** [adverb]

The two candidates debated each other **before** the election. [preposition]

Read the directions **before** you begin answering the questions. [conjunction]

Review G   **Identifying the Parts of Speech**

Identify the part of speech of each italicized word or word group in the following paragraphs.

EXAMPLE Playing on the radio was a [1] *piano* sonata by Beethoven.

   1. *piano—adjective*

Suddenly the radio announcer interrupted the [1] *musical* selection. "A [2] *funnel* cloud [3] *has been sighted.* [4] *All* people should take immediate [5] *precautions!*" [6] *Those* were the [7] *last* words Denise Moore heard [8] *before* the electricity went off and the [9] *terrible* roar came closer. [10] *She* and her two children [11] *ran* to the basement [12] *quickly.*

When they [13] *emerged* forty-five minutes later, [14] *they* weren't sure what they might see. [15] *Oh,* the terrible wind had [16] *truly* performed freakish tricks! It had driven a fork [17] *into* a brick up to the handle. It had sucked the [18] *wallpaper* from a living room wall [19] *but* had left the picture hanging [20] *there* intact. It [21] *had driven* a blade of grass into a neighbor's [22] *back.* Nevertheless, the citizens of the [23] *town* considered [24] *themselves* lucky because [25] *no one* had been seriously injured.

Chapter Review

A. Classifying Nouns

Classify the italicized noun in each of the following sentences as *common, proper, collective,* or *compound.* Some nouns have more than one classification.

1. Our new neighbors recently moved here from *Japan.*
2. Preston looked across the bay and saw the *fleet* of tall ships.
3. My father's favorite kind of music is *rock-and-roll.*
4. Please put the book on the *table.*
5. Isn't that the book that won the *National Book Award* last year?

B. Identifying Pronouns

Identify the pronouns in the following sentences. There may be more than one pronoun in each sentence.

6. Have you ever eaten paella, which is a typical dish of Spain?
7. Each of the sisters has her own computer.
8. We don't understand why Marta didn't do the work herself.
9. Akira Kurosawa was a Japanese filmmaker who made epic films.
10. What can Yung and he order that won't be too expensive?
11. This will be her first time to travel to the capital of Pakistan.
12. Everybody wants to answer the questions that are easy.
13. He insisted on preparing the meal himself.
14. Those tap shoes are mine, but whose are these?
15. That is the money they want to exchange for yen before leaving for Japan.

C. Identifying Adjectives and Adverbs

Identify each italicized word in the following sentences as an *adjective* or an *adverb.*

16. Edgar Degas, the *French* artist, was born in Paris in 1834 into a *well-to-do* family.
17. His art is *usually* classified with the *Impressionist* movement.

18. However, because he did not like to paint *directly* from nature, his style was unlike the styles of the other Impressionists.

19. Degas had an *extraordinary* ability to draw.

20. *This* ability was an *outstanding* characteristic of his art.

21. One of his *favorite* subjects was the theater, where he *frequently* went to observe people.

22. He also studied *Japanese* prints, which influenced his experimentation with *visual* styles.

23. When Degas was *older*, his eyesight began to fail, and he worked *increasingly* in sculpture and pastel.

24. In his sculpture, he was *quite successful* in capturing action.

25. When Degas died in Paris in 1917, he was *relatively unknown*.

D. Identifying and Classifying Verbs and Verb Phrases

Identify the verbs and verb phrases in the following sentences. Then, classify each verb or verb phrase as a *transitive action verb, intransitive action verb,* or *linking verb*.

26. After the first of the year, the weather will turn colder.

27. In art class last semester, Belinda painted a portrait of her parents.

28. Kenzo had thought hard about the question.

29. The baking bread smelled good.

30. I smell burning onions.

E. Identifying the Parts of Speech

Identify each italicized word in the following paragraph as a *noun*, a *pronoun*, an *adjective*, a *verb*, an *adverb*, a *preposition*, a *conjunction*, or an *interjection*.

Our English teacher gave us an **[31]** *unusual* writing assignment. He asked **[32]** *each* of us to rewrite a well-known **[33]** *saying*. **[34]** *Although* the sentences we wrote were quite **[35]** *unfamiliar*, we all knew the proverbs. **[36]** *These* are some examples of our work:

a. The feathered, egg-laying animal that is **[37]** *among* the first to rise invariably **[38]** *captures* the small, **[39]** *elongated*, and legless creature.

b. A person will not be able to retain possession of his or her sweet, baked **[40]** *batter* and devour **[41]** *it* also.

c. **[42]** *Never* place your total **[43]** *number* of small, oval objects that are laid by female birds **[44]** *into* a single receptacle made of woven material.

[45] *If* these sentences **[46]** *sound* strange, read the original versions.

a. The early bird catches the worm.

b. You can't have your cake **[47]** *and* eat it, too.

c. Don't put **[48]** *all* of your eggs in one basket.

[49] *Well*, the originals sound **[50]** *much* better!

Writing Application

Using Adjectives in a Paragraph

Specific, Vivid Adjectives   Your class is having Share the Music Week. Each person will bring in a tape of a favorite piece of music and a paragraph describing it. Write a paragraph describing any piece of music that you like. In your paragraph use at least ten adjectives. Make each adjective as specific as you can.

Prewriting   Write down the names of five pieces of music that you enjoy. Then decide which piece will make the most interesting topic for your paragraph. Listen to your selection several times. Sit quietly with your eyes closed, and think about how the piece sounds and makes you feel. While you are thinking, jot down any adjectives that occur to you.

Writing   As you write your first draft, include the adjectives that you jotted down. Try to give a clear description of the music. At the same time, imagine what specific details might persuade your class-mates to listen to this piece of music.

Revising   Re-read your paragraph, replacing vague, inexact adjectives with words that are more descriptive. Be sure you have included at least ten adjectives.

Publishing   Proofread your paragraph for any errors in grammar, usage, and mechanics. You might wish to gather the class's music descriptions and arrange them on a bulletin board titled *Share the Music!*

┌─ H E L P ───
Be sure to get your teacher's approval of your music selection.

The Parts of a Sentence

Subjects, Predicates, Complements

Diagnostic Preview

A. Identifying Subjects, Verbs, and Complements in a Paragraph

Identify the italicized word or word group in each sentence in the following paragraph as a *subject*, a *verb*, or a *complement*. If it is a complement, identify it as a *direct object*, an *indirect object*, a *predicate nominative*, a *predicate adjective*, or an *objective complement*.

EXAMPLE   **[1]** The National Science Foundation (NSF) is undergoing a great *surge* of growth.

       1. *complement—direct object*

    [1] The NSF is relatively *small* compared with other government agencies, such as the National Institutes of Health and the National Aeronautics and Space Administration. [2] However, it *has* always *accepted* new challenges. [3] In 1991, with funding of only $2.3 billion, the *foundation* began participating in several government programs. [4] *One* of these important programs investigates global climate change. [5] There is another *program* for which the NSF is developing sophisticated computer technology. [6] In a third project, the foundation supports *education* and *literacy* in science and mathematics. [7] How important the project *must have been* to the physicist Walter E. Massey, the foundation's director at that time. [8] Throughout his career,

Dr. Massey has shown *hundreds* of students the excitement of physics, chemistry, biology, and the other sciences. **[9]** In fact, in 1995 Dr. Massey returned to his alma mater, Moreland College, and its students, who historically have been *African Americans.* **[10]** As the school's president, Dr. Massey encourages these students to prove themselves *candidates* for either the NSF programs or some other career in science.

B. Classifying Sentences

Classify each of the following sentences as *declarative, imperative, interrogative,* or *exclamatory.* Then, supply an appropriate end mark after the last word in the sentence.

EXAMPLE   **1.** The school is five blocks from here

           1. declarative—here.

11. The umpire called a strike
12. Where did you park the car
13. His hard work earned him a promotion
14. Anita ran errands during most of the day
15. Why did Earl leave the party so early
16. Debbie Allen is a choreographer
17. What a wonderful day we had yesterday
18. Please hold my umbrella for a minute
19. The pear tree grew well in our backyard
20. Leave your classrooms quickly

Sentence or Fragment?

15a. A *sentence* is a word group that contains a subject and a verb and that expresses a complete thought.

A thought is complete when it makes sense by itself.

EXAMPLES   The weary executive had left her briefcase on the train.

           For how many years was Winston Churchill the prime minister of Great Britain?

           What extraordinary courage the early settlers in North America must have had!

           Wait! [The subject of the sentence is understood to be *you.*]

Reference Note

For information on the **understood subject,** see page 518.

| STYLE | ✏ | TIP |

Sentence fragments are commonly used in casual conversation, in written dialogue, and in advertisements. In these situations, the context usually clarifies any confusion caused by the sentence fragment. In formal speaking and writing, however, it is best to use complete sentences for greater clarity.

| COMPUTER TIP |

Many style-checking software programs can help you identify sentence fragments. If you have access to such a program, use it to help you evaluate your writing.

Reference Note

For information on **revising sentence fragments,** see page 427.

As you can see, a sentence begins with a capital letter and ends with a period, a question mark, or an exclamation point. Do not confuse a sentence with a *sentence fragment*—a word or word group that may be capitalized and punctuated as a sentence but does not contain both a subject and a verb or does not express a complete thought.

SENTENCE FRAGMENT	Athletes representing 160 nations.
SENTENCE	Athletes representing 160 nations competed in the Olympics.
SENTENCE FRAGMENT	The offices designed for high efficiency.
SENTENCE	The offices have been designed for high efficiency.
SENTENCE FRAGMENT	Plans every month for future growth.
SENTENCE	The board of directors plans every month for future growth.

Exercise 1 **Identifying and Correcting Sentence Fragments**

Some of the following word groups are sentence fragments. If a word group is a sentence fragment, revise it to make a complete sentence. If the word group is already a complete sentence, write *C.*

EXAMPLE
1. If a computer disk comes in contact with a strong magnet.

1. *If a computer disk comes in contact with a strong magnet, information on the disk likely will be lost.*

1. To have seen the Parthenon in its glory.
2. Between the towering mountain ridge and the wide ocean only a few miles away.
3. Engaging in endless discussions of pending legislation, especially the new tax bill.
4. One of the few who truly understood and took advantage of the opportunity for profit in personal computing.
5. Although it seemed unlikely, her prediction was soon fulfilled.
6. Not one but two deer appeared.
7. Than we had thought it would be.
8. I, to my surprise, enjoyed the ballet recital.
9. Beside the pool, children splashing each other and laughing at the antics of Uncle Tony.
10. Follow me!

The Subject and the Predicate

15b. Sentences consist of two basic parts: *subjects* and *predicates*. The *subject* tells *whom* or *what* the sentence is about. The *predicate* tells something about the subject.

Note in the following examples that the subject or the predicate may consist of one word or more than one word. Notice also that the subject may appear before or after the predicate or between parts of the predicate.

SUBJECT	PREDICATE
Lightning	struck.

SUBJECT	PREDICATE
Everyone	enjoyed reading *The Piano Lesson.*

SUBJECT	PREDICATE
All of the seeds	sprouted.

PREDICATE	SUBJECT
Into the sky soared	the young eagle.

PREDICATE	SUBJECT	PREDICATE
Where did	your family	go on vacation?

The Simple Subject and the Complete Subject

15c. The *simple subject* is the main word or word group that tells *whom* or *what* the sentence is about. The *complete subject* consists of the simple subject and any words or word groups used to modify the simple subject.

SIMPLE SUBJECT The **coach** of our hockey team used to play professional hockey.

COMPLETE SUBJECT **The coach of our hockey team** used to play professional hockey.

SIMPLE SUBJECT Supported by grants, **scientists** constantly search for a cure for cancer.

COMPLETE SUBJECT **Supported by grants, scientists** constantly search for a cure for cancer.

SIMPLE SUBJECT	The **scenes** that you see in these tapestries show the beauty of Pennsylvania in the 1700s.
COMPLETE SUBJECT	**The scenes that you see in these tapestries** show the beauty of Pennsylvania in the 1700s.
SIMPLE SUBJECT	The **Corn Palace** in Mitchell, South Dakota, is a popular tourist attraction.
COMPLETE SUBJECT	**The Corn Palace in Mitchell, South Dakota,** is a popular tourist attraction.

Reference Note

For more about **compound nouns,** see page 486.

Notice in the last example above that a compound noun, such as *Corn Palace*, may serve as a simple subject because together the two words name one thing.

NOTE In this textbook, the term *subject* usually refers to the simple subject unless otherwise indicated.

The Simple Predicate and the Complete Predicate

15d. The *simple predicate,* or *verb,* is the main word or word group that tells something about the subject. The *complete predicate* consists of the verb and all the words used to modify the verb and complete its meaning.

SIMPLE PREDICATE (VERB)	The puppy **chased** its tail frantically.
COMPLETE PREDICATE	The puppy **chased its tail frantically.**
SIMPLE PREDICATE (VERB)	Catalina **ran** swiftly across the field.
COMPLETE PREDICATE	Catalina **ran swiftly across the field.**
SIMPLE PREDICATE (VERB)	Today another space probe **was** successfully **launched**.
COMPLETE PREDICATE	Today another space probe **was successfully launched.**
SIMPLE PREDICATE (VERB)	**Did** Ethan ever **find** his history book?
COMPLETE PREDICATE	**Did** Ethan **ever find his history book**?

Reference Note

For more about **verbs** and **verb phrases,** see pages 495 and 497.

NOTE In this textbook, the term *verb* usually refers to the simple predicate (a one-word verb or a verb phrase) unless otherwise indicated.

The Compound Subject and the Compound Verb

15e. A *compound subject* consists of two or more subjects that are joined by a conjunction and that have the same verb.

The parts of a compound subject are usually joined by the conjunction *and, or,* or *nor.*

EXAMPLES   The **ship** and its **cargo** had been lost.

Will **Marva** or **Antonio** drive us to the track meet?

Neither the **sheets** nor the **blanket** should be washed with bleach.

Athens, Delphi, and **Nauplia** are on the mainland of Greece.

15f. A *compound verb* consists of two or more verbs that are joined by a conjunction and that have the same subject.

The parts of a compound verb are usually joined by the conjunction *and, but, or,* or *nor.*

EXAMPLES   We **chose** a seat near the door and quietly **sat** down.

Sandra **had gone** to the football game but **had left** at halftime.

For exercise I **swim** or **play** racquetball nearly every day.

Unfortunately, Eddie neither **relaxed** nor **did** anything productive this weekend.

Truth **enlightens** the mind, **frees** the spirit, and also **strengthens** the soul.

> **NOTE** Do not mistake a simple sentence containing a compound subject or a compound verb, or both, for a compound sentence. A simple sentence has only one independent clause. A compound sentence has two or more independent clauses.
>
> SIMPLE SENTENCE   **Kendra** and **I have taken** the Scholastic Aptitude Test but **have** not **received** our scores. [compound subject and compound verb]
>
> COMPOUND SENTENCE   **Kendra** and **I have taken** the Scholastic Aptitude Test, but **we have** not **received** our scores.

⌐ **TIPS** & **TRICKS** ⌐

When you are identifying compound verbs, be sure to include all parts of any verb phrases.

EXAMPLE
Should we **wait** for Ellen or **leave** a note for her?

Reference Note

For information on **independent clauses,** see page 558. For more about **simple and compound sentences,** see page 569.

How to Find the Subject of a Sentence

A simple way to find the subject of a sentence is to ask *Who?* or *What?* before the verb.

EXAMPLES   The **crew** of the racing yacht had worked hard. [Who had worked? *Crew* had worked.]

In their eyes shone **happiness.** [What shone? *Happiness* shone.]

Waiting at the harbor was a huge, cheering **crowd.** [Who was waiting? *Crowd* was waiting.]

Remembering the following guidelines will also help you find the subject of a sentence.

- The subject of a sentence expressing a command or a request is always understood to be *you*, although *you* may not appear in the sentence.

COMMAND   Turn left at the next intersection. [Who is being told to turn? *You* is understood.]

REQUEST   Please tell me the story again. [Who is being asked to tell? *You* is understood.]

The subject of a command or a request is *you* even when the sentence contains a word naming the one or ones spoken to—a ***noun of direct address.***

EXAMPLE   Chelsea, [you] close the door, please.

- The subject of a sentence is never in a prepositional phrase.

EXAMPLES   A **group** of students gathered near the main library. [Who gathered? *Group* gathered. *Students* is the object of the preposition *of.*]

One of the paintings by Vincent van Gogh sold for $82.5 million. [What sold? *One* sold. *Paintings* is the object of the preposition *of. Vincent van Gogh* is the object of the preposition *by.*]

Out of the stillness came the loud **sound** of laughter. [What came? *Sound* came. *Stillness* is the object of the preposition *Out of. Laughter* is the object of the preposition *of.*]

- The subject of a sentence expressing a question generally follows the verb or a part of the verb phrase.

TIPS & TRICKS

To help you find the subject and verb of a sentence, try crossing out any prepositional phrases.

EXAMPLE
The charcoal ~~in the grill~~ caught ~~on fire~~.
Subject: charcoal
Verb: caught

Reference Note

For information about **prepositional phrases,** see page 536.

EXAMPLES   Is the **dog** in the house? [What is? *Dog* is.]

When was **Madeleine Albright** appointed secretary of state of the United States? [Who was appointed? *Madeleine Albright* was appointed.]

- The word *there* or *here* is almost never the subject of a sentence.

EXAMPLES   There is the famous ***Mona Lisa.*** [What is there? *Mona Lisa* is there.]

Here are your **gloves.** [What are here? *Gloves* are here.]

In the two examples above, the words *there* and *here* are used as adverbs telling *where*.

NOTE   The word *there* also may be used as an ***expletive***—a word that fills out the structure of a sentence but does not add to the meaning. In the following example, *there* does not tell *where* but serves only to make the structure of the sentence complete.

EXAMPLE   There is a soccer **game** after school this Friday. [What is? *Game* is.]

FRANK & ERNEST reprinted by permission of Newspaper Enterprise Association, Inc.

Exercise 2 Identifying Subjects and Verbs

For each of the following sentences, identify the subject and the verb. Be sure to include all parts of a compound subject or a compound verb and all parts of verb phrases.

EXAMPLE   1. In ancient Japan, fierce samurai like the one shown on the next page ruled society with an iron hand.

1. *subject—samurai; verb—ruled*

1. The men, women, and children of the peasant class lived in terror of these landlord-warriors.

2. A samurai's powerful position gave him the right to kill any disobedient or disrespectful peasant.

3. Did anyone in Japan refuse a samurai's requests?

4. There was one dedicated group of rebels, called ninja, meaning "stealers in."

5. Off to the barren mountain regions of Iga and Koga fled the ninja people with their families.

6. There they could train their children in the martial arts of ninjutsu.

7. Lessons in camouflage, escape, and evasion were taught to children as young as one or two years of age.

8. The ninja sneaked down into the settled areas and struck at the samurai in any way possible.

9. In time, the ninja warriors gained a reputation all over Japan and were feared by the mighty samurai.

10. Hand me the book about Japan and the ninja warriors.

Complements

15g. A *complement* is a word or word group that completes the meaning of a verb.

Some sentences contain only a subject and a verb. The subject may be expressed or may be understood.

EXAMPLES

    S   **V**

Everyone participated.

    V

Stop! [The subject *you* is understood.]

Often, however, the predicate of a sentence also includes at least one complement. Without the complement or complements in the predicate, the subject and the verb may not express a complete thought.

          S   **V**

INCOMPLETE   Jose Canseco caught

          S   **V**   **C**

COMPLETE   Jose Canseco caught the **ball.**

        S **V**

INCOMPLETE   They sent

        S **V** **C**   **C**

COMPLETE   They sent **us** an **invitation.**

		S	V		
INCOMPLETE		The judges	named		

		S	V	C	C
COMPLETE		The judges	named	**Consuelo**	the **winner**.

	S	V
INCOMPLETE	Denzel Washington	is

	S	V	C
COMPLETE	Denzel Washington	is	an **actor**.

	S	V
INCOMPLETE	The players	seem

	S	V	C
COMPLETE	The players	seem	**weary**.

	V	S
INCOMPLETE	Is	this

	V	S	C
COMPLETE	Is	this	**what you want**?

As you can see in the preceding examples, a complement may be a noun, a pronoun, or an adjective and may consist of one word or a group of words.

> **NOTE** Do not mistake an adverb or an object of a preposition for a complement.
>
> ADVERB   Janna writes **well.** [The adverb *well* tells how Janna writes.]
>
> OBJECT OF A PREPOSITION   Janna writes for the school **newspaper.** [The noun *newspaper* is the object of the preposition *for.*]
>
> COMPLEMENT   Janna writes adventure **stories.** [The noun *stories* completes the meaning of *writes.*]

The Direct Object

15h. A *direct object* is a noun, pronoun, or word group that tells who or what receives the action of the verb or that shows the result of the action.

A direct object answers the question "Whom?" or "What?" after a transitive verb.

TIPS & TRICKS

Both independent and subordinate clauses contain subjects, verbs, and, sometimes, complements. In the last example to the left, the parts of the subordinate clause are as follows:

	C	S	V
	what	you	want

Reference Note

For information on **adverbs,** see page 499. For information on **objects of prepositions,** see page 502.

Reference Note

For information about **transitive verbs,** see page 498.

EXAMPLES   Drought destroyed **whatever we planted.** [Destroyed what? Whatever we planted.]

The journalist interviewed the **astronauts** before and after their flight. [Interviewed whom? Astronauts.]

Felicia invited **me** to the party. [Invited whom? Me.]

Do toads cause **warts**? [Do cause what? Warts.]

A direct object may be compound.

EXAMPLES   The dog chased **Eli** and **me** through the park.

Did Beethoven compose **sonatas** and **symphonies**?

NOTE For emphasis, the direct object may precede the subject and verb.

EXAMPLE   What a compelling **speech** he gave! [Gave what? Speech.]

The Indirect Object

15i. An *indirect object* is a noun, pronoun, or word group that precedes a direct object and tells *to whom* or *to what* (or *for whom* or *for what*) the action of the verb is done.

EXAMPLES   Ms. Cruz showed our **class** a great video about Moorish architecture. [Showed to whom? Class.]

The animal trainer fed the **bears** fish. [Fed to what? Bears.]

Their artistic skill won **them** honors. [Won for whom? Them.]

Will Julia buy her pet **terrier** a new rhinestone collar? [Buy for what? Terrier.]

NOTE Do not confuse an indirect object with an object of the preposition *to* or *for*.

INDIRECT OBJECT   The principal gave **her** the award.

OBJECT OF A PREPOSITION   The principal gave the award to **her.** [*Her* is the object of the preposition *to*.]

Reference Note

For information on **prepositional phrases,** see page 536.

An indirect object may be compound.

EXAMPLES   The architect showed **Mom** and **Dad** the plans for the new family room.

Are the judges giving **whoever finishes first** or **whoever does the best job** the prize?

The Objective Complement

15j. An *objective complement* is a word or word group that helps complete the meaning of a transitive verb by identifying or modifying the direct object.

An objective complement may be a noun, a pronoun, or an adjective.

EXAMPLES   The members elected Carlotta **secretary.** [The noun *secretary* identifies the direct object *Carlotta*.]

They considered all the prize money **theirs.** [The pronoun *theirs* identifies the direct object *money*.]

Years of hard work had made her **successful.** [The adjective *successful* modifies the direct object *her*.]

Only a few verbs take an objective complement: *consider, make,* and verbs that can be replaced by *consider* or *make*, such as *appoint, call, choose, elect, keep, name, cut, paint,* and *sweep.*

EXAMPLES   Many literary historians call [*or* consider] Shakespeare the greatest **dramatist** of all time.

The flood had swept [*or* had made] the valley **clean.**

Will the committee appoint [*or* make] her the new interim **leader**?

Children, keep [*or* make] it **quiet** in there.

An objective complement may be compound.

EXAMPLES   The Gibsons named their two cats **Bruno** and **Waldo.**

Charlena painted her old bicycle **black** and **silver.**

Cut my bangs **short** and **straight,** please.

NOTE   For emphasis, the objective complement may precede the subject, verb, and direct object.

EXAMPLE   What an exciting **adventure** our science teacher made the field trip!

┌HELP┐

Remember, a sentence containing either an indirect object or an objective complement must also contain a direct object.

Exercise 3 Identifying Direct Objects, Indirect Objects, and Objective Complements

Identify each complement in the following sentences as a *direct object*, an *indirect object*, or an *objective complement*.

EXAMPLE   1. Tutankhamen's tomb contained a candleholder.
          1. *candleholder—direct object*

1. Candles have tremendous appeal as decorative, religious, and utilitarian objects.
2. Every year candle makers use many tons of paraffin.
3. Before the invention of electricity, many people lit their homes with candles.
4. Candles on the dinner table can make even an average meal special.
5. Many of the early colonists in America made their own candles.
6. Nowadays, candle making offers hobbyists a relaxing and rewarding pastime.
7. These pictures show you the steps in candle making.
8. Incense mixed into the melted wax will give your candles a pleasant scent.
9. You can also dye candle wax various colors.
10. I like to make mine blue and white.

The Subject Complement

A **subject complement** is a word or word group in the predicate that identifies or describes the subject. A subject complement completes the meaning of a linking verb. There are two kinds of subject complements: *predicate nominatives* and *predicate adjectives*.

15k. A *predicate nominative* is a word or word group that is in the predicate and that identifies the subject or refers to it.

Reference Note

For a list of **linking verbs,** see page 496.

A predicate nominative may be a noun, a pronoun, or a word group that functions as a noun. A predicate nominative completes the meaning of a linking verb.

EXAMPLES   Adela Rogers St. Johns became a famous **journalist.** [The noun *journalist* refers to the subject *Adela Rogers St. Johns.*]

Of all the dancers, Marcelo was the most experienced **one.** [The pronoun *one* refers to the subject *Marcelo.*]

A reliable, fuel-efficient car is **what we need.** [The noun clause *what we need* refers to the subject *car.*]

A predicate nominative may be compound.

EXAMPLES   The two candidates for class treasurer are **Marco** and **I.**

Was that **oatmeal** or cold **cereal** Marilla had for breakfast?

South Dakota's chief crops are **corn, wheat,** and **oats.**

15l. A *predicate adjective* is an adjective that is in the predicate and that modifies the subject.

A predicate adjective completes the meaning of a linking verb.

EXAMPLES   The ocean is **calm.** [The adjective *calm* modifies the subject *ocean.*]

Does that orange taste **bitter**? [The adjective *bitter* modifies the subject *orange.*]

All of the astronauts look **confident.** [The adjective *confident* modifies the subject *All.*]

A predicate adjective may be compound.

EXAMPLES   Does this blouse look **pink** or **mauve** to you?

Most parrots are **noisy, colorful,** and **sociable.**

NOTE   For emphasis, a subject complement may precede the subject and verb.

PREDICATE NOMINATIVE   What an outstanding basketball **player** Michael Jordan was! [The noun *player* refers to the subject *Michael Jordan.*]

PREDICATE ADJECTIVE   How **talented** she is! [The adjective *talented* modifies the subject *she.*]

Reference Note

For more about **noun clauses,** see page 562.

TIPS & TRICKS

Do not assume that every adjective in the predicate is a predicate adjective. Ask yourself what the adjective modifies.

EXAMPLES

These Korean folk tales are **ancient.** [The adjective *ancient* is a predicate adjective because it modifies the subject *folk tales.*]

These Korean folk tales are **ancient** stories. [The adjective *ancient* is not a predicate adjective because it modifies the predicate nominative *stories.*]

Remember that a predicate adjective modifies only the subject.

GRAMMAR

Exercise 4 Identifying Linking Verbs and Subject Complements

Identify the linking verb and the subject complement in each of the following sentences. Indicate whether the complement is a *predicate nominative* or a *predicate adjective*.

EXAMPLE
1. Pluto is the smallest planet in our solar system.
1. *linking verb—is; subject complement—planet—predicate nominative*

1. The most common deer in India is a species of axis deer.
2. Many people feel concerned about the depletion of the world's natural resources.
3. Wilhelm Roentgen was the discoverer of the X-ray.
4. Is Jane Austen the author of *Pride and Prejudice*?
5. The violin solo sounded beautiful.
6. The animals grew restless at the sound of the crackling flames.
7. Harriet Tubman was active in the Underground Railroad.
8. Icy is the stare of the glacier.
9. Why does the spaghetti sauce taste too spicy?
10. What a massive work of carved stone the Great Sphinx is!

Review A Identifying the Parts of Sentences

For each of the following sentences, identify the sentence part indicated in parentheses. Be sure to include all parts of a compound subject, a compound verb, or a verb phrase.

EXAMPLE
1. (*simple subject*) The people of New Orleans are famous for their creativity with food as well as with music.
1. *people*

1. (*complete subject*) Both Creole cooking and Cajun cooking flourish in the kitchens of the city's French Quarter.
2. (*complete predicate*) Some visitors to New Orleans have trouble telling the difference between these two similar styles of food preparation.
3. (*indirect object*) My aunt, a restaurant critic, showed me the differences between Creole cooking and Cajun cooking.
4. (*verb*) The French founders of New Orleans developed the Creole style of cooking.
5. (*predicate nominative*) The *beignet*, a square doughnut, and *boudin*, a spicy sausage, are tasty local favorites from French cuisine.

6. (*simple subject*) In Creole dishes, there are also tangy traces of Spanish, African, and Caribbean cooking.

7. (*verb*) Cajun cooking is Creole's peppery country cousin and was born in the rural bayou areas surrounding New Orleans.

8. (*predicate adjective*) My aunt's favorite Cajun treat, alligator gumbo, is wonderfully thick and spicy.

9. (*direct object*) Don't those little red shellfish resemble tiny lobsters?

10. (*objective complement*) They're New Orleans crawfish, and I declare them the tastiest morsels that I've ever eaten!

Classification of Sentences

15m. Sentences may be classified according to purpose.

(1) A *declarative sentence* makes a statement and ends with a period.

EXAMPLES The lock on the front door is broken.

David Glasgow Farragut led Union naval forces against the Confederacy in 1864 in the Battle of Mobile Bay.

(2) An *interrogative sentence* asks a question and ends with a question mark.

EXAMPLES Have you seen a sculpture by Augusta Savage?

What is the capital of New Mexico?

(3) An *imperative sentence* makes a request or gives a command. Most imperative sentences end with a period. A strong command ends with an exclamation point.

EXAMPLES Please pass the salad. [request]

Call this number in case of an emergency. [mild command]

Watch out! [strong command]

Reference Note

For information on **classifying sentences according to structure,** see page 569.

Reference Note

For information about the **understood subject,** see page 513.

| STYLE   TIP |

Sometimes a writer will use more than one end mark to express intense emotion or a combination of emotions.

EXAMPLES

Bill yelled, "Pass me the ball**!!**" [intense emotion]

"They did what**?!**" gasped Irene. [combination of curiosity and surprise]

Using such double punctuation is acceptable in most informal writing and in writing fiction, especially in dialogue. However, in formal writing, such as essays and business letters, use only one end mark at a time.

NOTE The subject of an imperative sentence is always understood to be *you,* although *you* may not appear in the sentence.

(4) An *exclamatory sentence* shows excitement or expresses strong feeling and ends with an exclamation point.

EXAMPLES   What a great singer she is**!**

Ah, you have discovered the secret**!**

Ouch**!** That really hurt**!**

Exercise 5 **Identifying the Four Kinds of Sentences**

Identify each of the following sentences as *declarative, imperative, interrogative,* or *exclamatory.* Also, supply an appropriate end mark after the last word in each sentence.

EXAMPLE   **1.** In 1829, Louis Braille developed a system of writing for people with visual impairments

1. *declarative—impairments.*

1. Anyone with a little free time and a generous heart can help make the world of books available to people with visual impairments

2. Have you ever wondered how Braille schoolbooks are created for students with visual impairments

3. Imagine dozens and dozens of volunteers, all with their fingers flying across the keys of machines that look much like miniature typewriters

4. Different combinations of six keys on the machines make the raised-dot patterns that represent letters and numbers in Braille

5. First, Braille typists take a course to learn how to use the machines

6. Once you learn how, typing in Braille isn't difficult at all

7. If I participate, can I work at home in my spare time

8. What rewarding volunteer work this is

9. When I considered how much time I waste every week, I decided to use that time constructively by volunteering to help create Braille textbooks

10. If you know someone who might be interested in participating, help him or her find out how to get in touch with a Braille association in your community

Review B   Identifying Subjects, Verbs, and Complements

Identify the italicized word or word group in each of the following sentences as a *subject*, a *verb*, or a *complement*. If it is a complement, identify it as a *direct object*, an *indirect object*, an *objective complement*, a *predicate nominative*, or a *predicate adjective*.

EXAMPLES   **1.** *Sally* visited San Antonio last summer.
    1. subject

    2. The bull *cantered* across the field.
    2. verb

    3. Haven't you told *her* the news yet?
    3. complement—indirect object

1. Rondos are five-part *arrangements* of instrumental music in the form a b a c a b a, in which c is frequently replaced by a developmental passage.

2. Many modern movies are *incomprehensible* to me; I prefer musicals from the 1950s.

3. The prolonged drought last year *destroyed* a great number of crops throughout the Southwest.

4. In September 1998, the German people elected Gerhard Schroeder *chancellor of Germany*.

5. Ms. Villanueva, our art history teacher, showed the *freshman class* a video about the Mexican artist Diego Rivera.

6. The architect proudly displayed the *blueprints* for the new house to his prospective buyers.

7. After the trial, Justice Robinson declared herself *satisfied* with the jury's verdict.

8. On our trans-Sahara trek, we had a very experienced and capable *guide* whose talent was finding water.

9. Handing Mr. Stoddard his term paper, *Cameron* remembered that he had forgotten to include a bibliography.

10. What a remarkable *woman* Mother Teresa of Calcutta was!

Review C   Writing Sentences

Write your own sentences according to the guidelines on the following page. In your sentences, underline the sentence parts that are indicated by the italicized words. Also, use a variety of subjects, verbs, and complements in your sentences.

EXAMPLE   **1.** Write an imperative sentence with an *understood subject.*

   1. <u>(You)</u> *Stop right there!*

1. Write a declarative sentence with a *compound subject.*

2. Write an interrogative sentence with a *compound verb.*

3. Write an exclamatory sentence with a *direct object.*

4. Write an imperative sentence with a *compound direct object.*

5. Write a declarative sentence with an *indirect object.*

6. Write a declarative sentence with a *predicate nominative.*

7. Write an interrogative sentence with a *compound predicate adjective.*

8. Write a declarative sentence with an *objective complement.*

9. Write an imperative sentence with an *indirect object.*

10. Write a declarative sentence with a *predicate adjective.*

Chapter Review

A. Identifying Sentences and Sentence Fragments

Identify each of the following word groups as a *sentence* or a *sentence fragment*.

1. What the fastest-growing spectator sport in the United States is.
2. It is stock car racing, according to the National Association for Stock Car Auto Racing (NASCAR).
3. The sport in the 1930s on dirt tracks in the Southeast.
4. Did you know that today it's a two-billion-dollar-a-year industry?
5. That's a lot of money!

B. Identifying Subjects and Verbs

For each of the following sentences, identify the simple subject and the verb. Be sure to include all parts of a compound subject or a compound verb and all words in a verb phrase. If the subject is understood to be *you,* write *(you).*

6. The students, teachers, and staff of the school gathered in the auditorium.
7. The mechanic's knowledge of automobile repair is incredibly comprehensive.
8. Does someone in your family know French?
9. There were several loaves of bread on the windowsill.
10. The Ecology Club met in the park on Saturday and collected trash all morning.
11. Over the outfield fence flew the home-run ball.
12. Here at chess camp even casual players can learn useful chess strategies.
13. Professional athletes from baseball, hockey, and football joined forces for the charity fundraiser.
14. Both the director and the screenwriter offered opinions about the location manager's choices.
15. Please shut the door behind you.

C. Identifying Complements

In each of the following sentences, identify the italicized complement as a *direct object*, an *indirect object*, an *objective complement*, a *predicate nominative*, or a *predicate adjective*.

16. Please don't send any *samples* unless someone requests them.

17. Shirley Chisholm was the first *woman* to run for president of the United States.

18. The photographer gave *us* a picture she had taken of the school.

19. The director and the cast discussed the first *act* but decided not to change it.

20. The woman who called is an insurance *agent*.

21. At this point my plans for the future are quite *indefinite*.

22. Would you consider Maya *reliable*?

23. In her will, Ms. Vos left her *nurse* a share of the fortune.

24. Had Bob lost all *sense* of direction while wandering in the woods?

25. The table that we found in the basement was a valuable *antique*.

26. The people elected Jimmy Carter *president* in 1976.

27. Those dishes seem *worthless* to everyone except Ms. Lammers.

28. Kelly and I want to paint the room *blue*.

29. The Trans-Siberian Railroad is the world's largest *railway*.

30. The reporter asked the exhausted *survivors* too many questions.

D. Identifying the Four Kinds of Sentences

Identify each of the following sentences as *declarative*, *interrogative*, *imperative*, or *exclamatory*. Also, write the last word in the sentence, and supply an appropriate end mark.

31. What a spectacular sunset that is

32. I bought this Hawaiian shirt at a thrift store

33. Does it fit me well

34. Look out for the car

35. If Anna wants to apply to college, she should pick up some application information from the guidance counselor's office

36. Which '60s singing group is your favorite, the Beatles or the Beach Boys

37. How silly that all seems now

38. Judy asked Steve whether she should get her new cat declawed

39. Pick up your pack, and follow the guide

40. Was Cole Porter the composer of the song "Night and Day," or was it someone else

Writing Application
Combining Sentences in a Letter

Using Compound Subjects and Compound Verbs

You have just won the new car of your choice! All you need to do now is to decide what model and options you want. The car will be shipped to your local dealership. Write a letter to the sponsors of the contest thanking them for the prize and telling them what kind of car you want. Name six or more options that you've chosen for your car. Money is no object! In your letter, use at least three sentences with compound subjects and two sentences with compound verbs.

Prewriting   First, you will need to decide what kind of car you'd like to have. Then, list the options that you would like to have on the car. You can have as many options as you like. Choose wisely, though—don't pick options that you really wouldn't use.

Writing   Address your letter to an imaginary contest sponsor. Begin by thanking the sponsor for your prize. Then, describe your dream car as clearly and specifically as possible.

Revising   As you evaluate and revise your letter, you may think of more options you'd like to include. Check to see that your letter includes at least three sentences with compound subjects and two sentences with compound verbs. If it doesn't, you will need to combine or rewrite some sentences in the letter.

Publishing   Check the grammar, spelling, and punctuation of your letter. Be sure that your letter follows one of the standard business-letter forms. You and your classmates may wish to post your letters along with pictures of your "dream cars" on a bulletin board.

Reference Note

For information on **writing business letters**, see "Writing" in the Quick Reference Handbook.

CHAPTER

The Phrase
Kinds of Phrases and Their Functions

Diagnostic Preview

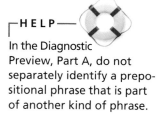

HELP

In the Diagnostic Preview, Part A, do not separately identify a prepositional phrase that is part of another kind of phrase.

A. Identifying Phrases

Identify the italicized phrase in each of the following sentences as a *prepositional phrase*, a *participial phrase*, a *gerund phrase*, an *infinitive phrase*, or an *appositive phrase*.

EXAMPLE   1. *Talking after the bell rings* is strictly forbidden.

     1. gerund phrase

1. *Working on the school newspaper* has taught me responsibility.
2. *Delayed by the snowstorm,* the flight from Chicago to Seattle was finally cleared for takeoff.
3. Today's crossword puzzle is difficult *to complete correctly.*
4. At the beginning of class today, we sang "La Marseillaise," *the French national anthem.*
5. If you want *to go to the concert tonight,* give me a call after school.
6. Preserving rare and valuable books and documents is one of the challenges *facing the Library of Congress.*
7. The emu, *a flightless bird from Australia,* is similar to the ostrich.
8. Franklin's history report was about Booker T. Washington, the founder *of the Tuskegee Institute.*
9. Refreshed by the cool breeze, I didn't object to *going back to work.*
10. The United States has been greatly enriched *by many diverse cultures.*

B. Identifying Phrases

Identify each italicized phrase in the following paragraph as a *prepositional phrase*, a *participial phrase*, a *gerund phrase*, an *infinitive phrase*, or an *appositive phrase*.

EXAMPLE   Here is an informative article **[1]** *about Charles Albert Bender.*

    1. prepositional phrase

┌─HELP─┐

In the Diagnostic Preview, Part B, do not separately identify a prepositional phrase that is part of another kind of phrase.

GRAMMAR

By **[11]** *being elected to the Baseball Hall of Fame in 1953,* Charles Albert Bender became a symbol of pride for American Indians. Bender, **[12]** *born in 1883 on White Earth Reservation, Minnesota,* was half Chippewa. He was better known to fans as "Chief," **[13]** *the nickname given to him by his teammates.* **[14]** *Pitching for the Philadelphia Athletics* was his first job in baseball. Although he played only briefly **[15]** *for a semipro team,* he pitched a four-hit victory in his first major-league game. He won twenty-three games and lost only five during the 1910 season, **[16]** *the best season of his career.* **[17]** *During that same year,* he had an earned run average of 1.58. If it was crucial **[18]** *to win a game,* Connie Mack, the Athletics' manager, would always send Bender to the mound. **[19]** *Finishing with a lifetime total of 212 wins and only 128 losses,* Bender led the American League three times in winning percentage. His last full active year as a pitcher was 1917, but he returned to the mound **[20]** *to pitch one inning for the White Sox in 1925.*

What Is a Phrase?

16a. A *phrase* is a group of related words that is used as a single part of speech and that does not contain both a verb and its subject.

VERB PHRASE	has been canceled [no subject]
PREPOSITIONAL PHRASE	before the party [no subject or verb]
INFINITIVE PHRASE	to buy bread [no subject or verb]

(NOTE) A group of words that has both a subject and a verb is called a *clause.*

EXAMPLES   the field trip has been canceled [independent clause]

              before the party started [subordinate clause]

Reference Note

For more about **clauses,** see Chapter 17.

Prepositional Phrases

16b. A *prepositional phrase* includes a preposition, the object of the preposition, and any modifiers of that object.

Reference Note

For a list of **commonly used prepositions,** see page 503.

EXAMPLES   The tall building **with the red roof** is our new library. [The noun *roof* is the object of the preposition *with.* The adjectives *the* and *red* modify *roof.*]

Next to it is the old library. [The pronoun *it* is the object of the compound preposition *Next to.*]

An object of a preposition may be compound.

EXAMPLE   The female cardinal is brownish red and has red markings **on its wings and tail.** [Both *wings* and *tail* are objects of the preposition *on.*]

The Adjective Phrase

16c. A prepositional phrase that modifies a noun or a pronoun is called an *adjective phrase.*

An adjective phrase tells *what kind(s)* or *which one(s).*

EXAMPLE   Many **of these books** include short stories **for young readers.** [*Of these books* modifies the pronoun *Many,* telling *which ones. For young readers* modifies the noun *short stories,* telling *what kind.*]

An adjective phrase generally follows the word it modifies. That word may be the object of another preposition.

EXAMPLE   Diego Rivera's experiments **with fresco painting on large walls** resulted in beautiful murals. [*With fresco painting* modifies the noun *experiments. On large walls* modifies the noun *painting,* the object of the preposition *with.*]

More than one adjective phrase may modify the same word.

EXAMPLE   Rivera developed a style **of his own with simplified figures and bold colors.** [The two phrases *of his own* and *with simplified figures and bold colors* modify the noun *style.*]

NOTE   If an adjective phrase is combined with a noun to form a compound noun, the entire group of words is considered a noun.

EXAMPLES   work of art   Habitat for Humanity

              hole in one   board of education

STYLE TIP

Prepositional phrases are handy for adding descriptive information to writing. Used excessively, however, these phrases can make writing wordy and stilted.

WORDY
With great care, Julia put on her blouse made of silk, fastened her necklace of pearls, and, with leisure, surveyed the results in the mirror.

REVISED
Carefully, Julia put on her silk blouse, fastened her pearl necklace, and leisurely surveyed the results in the mirror.

Reference Note

For more about **compound nouns,** see page 486.

Exercise 1 Identifying Adjective Phrases and the Words They Modify

Each of the following sentences contains at least one adjective phrase. Identify each adjective phrase and the word it modifies.

EXAMPLE   1. The small Scandinavian animal in this photograph is called a lemming.

         1. *in this photograph—animal*

1. Ordinarily, lemmings eat a diet of moss and roots.
2. Every few years, however, their population exceeds their food supply, and they ford streams and lakes, devouring everything in their path and leaving no trace of vegetation.
3. Legend tells us that when the lemmings reach the cliffs along the sea, they leap off and drown.
4. This pattern of behavior was puzzling because it contradicted the basic instinct for self-preservation.
5. Do these animals follow a pattern of self-destruction?
6. Recently, scientific study of these animals has revealed that this lore about them is untrue and that most lemmings become victims of predators or starvation.
7. Cozy homes underneath the ground protect young lemmings.
8. Bits of grass line their burrows' walls and floors.
9. Even growing numbers of hungry foxes and owls cannot significantly reduce the number of lemmings; second-year population increases by a factor of thirty are not unusual.
10. The cycle from plenty to starvation begins again every four years.

The Adverb Phrase

16d. A prepositional phrase that modifies a verb, an adjective, or an adverb is called an **adverb phrase.**

An adverb phrase tells *how, when, where, why,* or *to what extent* (*how long* or *how far*).

An adverb phrase may modify a verb.

EXAMPLE   **During the Civil War,** Louisa May Alcott worked **as a nurse in a hospital for six weeks.** [Each phrase modifies the verb *worked. During the Civil War* tells *when,* as *a nurse* tells *how, in a hospital* tells *where,* and *for six weeks* tells *how long.*]

┌─HELP─

Be careful not to confuse a prepositional phrase beginning with *to* with an infinitive or infinitive phrase beginning with *to* (*to swim, to know, to see*). Remember, a preposition always has a noun or pronoun as an object.

Reference Note

For more about **infinitives** and **infinitive phrases,** see page 546.

As you can see in the example on the previous page, more than one adverb phrase can modify the same word. That example also shows that an adverb phrase can precede the word it modifies.

An adverb phrase may modify an adjective.

EXAMPLE   Louisa May Alcott wrote *Little Women,* a novel rich **in New England traditions.** [*In New England traditions* modifies the adjective *rich,* telling *how rich.*]

An adverb phrase may modify an adverb.

EXAMPLE   Too late **for Alcott and other early suffragists,** United States voting laws were changed. [*For Alcott and other early suffragists* modifies the adverb *late,* telling *how late.*]

Exercise 2 Identifying Adverb Phrases and the Words They Modify

Each of the following sentences contains at least one adverb phrase. Identify each adverb phrase and the word or words it modifies.

EXAMPLE   **1.** Chinua Achebe's first novel, *Things Fall Apart,* was published in 1958.

    1. *in 1958—was published*

1. The trees were bent nearly double in the wind.
2. I got the twins ready for bed at 7:30 P.M.
3. In the classic Japanese movie *The Seven Samurai,* fierce professional warriors save a village from bandits.
4. They were assembled on benches for the presentation.
5. Especially for the children, the mariachi band played "The Mexican Hat Dance."
6. Fear sometimes springs from ignorance.
7. Is this outfit appropriate for a job interview?
8. The elephant dozed in the shade.

9. The first mass-produced car, the Model T, was built from 1908 until 1927.

10. Duncan is sitting in his chair, eating a bowl of oatmeal.

Review A **Identifying Prepositional Phrases**

For each sentence in the following paragraph, list all the prepositional phrases. Be sure to include any prepositional phrase that modifies the object of another preposition. Then, tell whether each prepositional phrase is an *adjective phrase* or an *adverb phrase*. Be prepared to give the word that each prepositional phrase modifies and to identify the word as a *noun*, a *pronoun*, a *verb*, an *adjective*, or an *adverb*.

EXAMPLE   **[1]** From what part of the world do these strange-looking objects come?

     1.   *From what part—adverb phrase; of the world—adjective phrase*

┌─HELP─
In the example for Review A, *from what part* modifies the verb *do come. Of the world* modifies the noun *part.*

[**1**] These items come from Africa, and they belong to the family of musical instruments called *mbira.* [**2**] Almost the size of a paperback book, these small *mbiras,* called *kalimbas,* are made of smooth, warm-colored wood. [**3**] The instrument is called a thumb box by some people because players pluck the steel keys with their thumbs to play melodies. [**4**] There is also a sound hole like the one on a guitar. [**5**] When players pluck one or more keys, the notes resonate inside the box. [**6**] The *kalimba* sounds like a cross between a small xylophone and a set of wind chimes. [**7**] It is easily carried in a pocket or backpack, and it is easy to play. [**8**] Nearly everybody enjoys the soft, light sound, even when a player hits a wrong note with both thumbs! [**9**] Instruments similar to the *kalimba* were noted by Portuguese explorers in the sixteenth century along the East African coast. [**10**] In 1586, Father Dos Santos, a Portuguese traveler, wrote that native *mbira* players pluck the keys lightly, "as a good player strikes those of a harpsichord," producing "a sweet and gentle harmony of accordant sounds."

GRAMMAR

Verbals and Verbal Phrases

Verbals are formed from verbs but are used as nouns, adjectives, and adverbs. The three kinds of verbals are the *participle*, the *gerund*, and the *infinitive*. A **verbal phrase** consists of a verbal and its modifiers and complements. The three kinds of verbal phrases are the *participial phrase*, the *gerund phrase*, and the *infinitive phrase*.

The Participle

16e. A *participle* is a verb form that can be used as an adjective.

Present participles end in *–ing*.

EXAMPLES   Esperanza sees the **singing** canary near the window.
[*Singing*, a form of the verb *sing*, modifies the noun *canary*.]

Waving, the campers boarded the bus. [*Waving*, a form of the verb *wave*, modifies the noun *campers*.]

We could hear it **moving** in the underbrush. [*Moving*, a form of the verb *move*, modifies the pronoun *it*.]

Most past participles end in *–d* or *–ed*. Others are irregularly formed.

EXAMPLES   The **baked** chicken with yellow rice tasted delicious. [*Baked*, a form of the verb *bake*, modifies the noun *chicken*.]

Confused and **frightened,** they fled into the jungle. [*Confused*, a form of the verb *confuse*, and *frightened*, a form of the verb *frighten*, modify the pronoun *they*.]

In your own words, define each term **given** below. [*Given*, a form of the verb *give*, modifies the noun *term*.]

The perfect tense of a participle is formed with *having* or with *having been*.

EXAMPLES   **Having worked** all day, Abe was ready for a rest.

Having been washed, the car gleamed in the sun.

NOTE   Do not confuse a participle used as an adjective with a participle used as part of a verb phrase.

ADJECTIVE   The Smithsonian Institution, **located** in Washington, D.C., is the largest museum in the world.

VERB PHRASE   The Smithsonian Institution, which **is located** in Washington, D.C., is the largest museum in the world.

Reference Note

For more information on the **forms of participles,** see page 644. For a discussion of **irregular verbs,** see page 646.

The Participial Phrase

16f. A *participial phrase* consists of a participle and any modifiers or complements the participle has. The entire phrase is used as an adjective.

EXAMPLES   **Speaking eloquently,** Julian Bond enthralled the audience. [The participial phrase modifies the noun *Julian Bond*. The adverb *eloquently* modifies the present participle *Speaking*.]

Nodding his head, the defendant admitted his guilt. [The participial phrase modifies the noun *defendant*. The noun *head* is the direct object of the present participle *Nodding*.]

Encouraged by his family, he submitted his book of poems for publication. [The participial phrase modifies the pronoun *he*. The adverb phrase *by his family* modifies the past participle *Encouraged*.]

Florence Griffith-Joyner, **sometimes known as Flo Jo,** held the U.S. national record for the women's 100-meter dash. [The participial phrase modifies the noun *Florence Griffith-Joyner*. The adverb *sometimes* modifies the past participle *known*. The adverb phrase *as Flo Jo* modifies *known*.]

The Absolute Phrase

An *absolute phrase* consists of (1) a participle or participial phrase, (2) a noun or pronoun that the participle or participial phrase modifies, and (3) any other modifiers of that noun or pronoun. The entire word group is used as an adverb to modify an independent clause of a sentence.

An absolute phrase has no direct grammatical connection to any word in the independent clause it modifies. Rather, the phrase modifies the entire clause by telling *when, why,* or *how.*

EXAMPLES   **The costumes having been made,** the actors prepared for their dress rehearsal. [The perfect participle *having been made* modifies the noun *costumes*. The absolute phrase modifies the independent clause by telling *when* the actors prepared for their dress rehearsal.]

Dark clouds threatening a storm, the hikers searched anxiously for shelter. [The participial phrase *threatening a storm* modifies the noun *clouds*. The absolute phrase modifies the independent clause by telling *why* the hikers searched anxiously for shelter.]

STYLE TIP

When writing a sentence with a participial phrase, be sure to place the phrase as close as possible to the word it modifies. Otherwise, the phrase may appear to modify another word, and the sentence may not make sense.

MISPLACED
Singing in the trees, the birdwatchers heard the wild canaries walking along the path.

IMPROVED
Walking along the path, the birdwatchers heard the wild canaries **singing in the trees.**

Reference Note

For more information about **misplaced participial phrases,** see page 712. For more about the **punctuation of participial phrases,** see page 788.

Exercise 3 Identifying Participial Phrases and the Words They Modify

Each of the following sentences contains at least one participial phrase. Identify each participial phrase and the word or words it modifies.

EXAMPLE   **1.** The Kentucky Derby, considered the first jewel in the Triple Crown of thoroughbred racing, is held each year on the first Saturday in May at Churchill Downs in Louisville, Kentucky.

   1. considered the first jewel in the Triple Crown of thoroughbred racing—Kentucky Derby

1. Known as Johnny Appleseed, John Chapman distributed apple seeds and saplings to families headed west.
2. Needing a sustained wind for flight, the albatross rarely crosses the equator.
3. At the reptile exhibit, we saw forty adders coiled together.
4. The salmon, deriving the pink color of its flesh from its diet, feeds on shrimplike crustaceans.
5. Having been aided by good weather and clear skies, the sailors rejoiced as they sailed into port.
6. Smiling broadly, our champion entered the hall.
7. I would love to see the hibiscus bursting into bloom in the spring; it must be quite a sight!
8. Sparta and Athens, putting aside their own rivalry, joined forces to fight the Persians.
9. Trained on an overhead trellis, a rosebush growing in Tombstone, Arizona, covers approximately 8,000 square feet of aerial space.
10. Searching through old clothes in a trunk, John found a map showing the location of a treasure buried on the shore.

Review B Identifying Prepositional and Participial Phrases and the Words They Modify

Identify each italicized phrase in the following sentences as a *prepositional phrase* or a *participial phrase.* Then, give the word or words each phrase modifies. Do not separately identify a prepositional phrase that is part of a participial phrase.

EXAMPLE   **1.** *Delighted by the play,* the critic applauded *with great enthusiasm.*

   1. Delighted by the play—participial phrase—critic; with great enthusiasm—prepositional phrase—applauded

1. Mahalia Jackson, perhaps the greatest blues *singer since Bessie Smith,* would sing only religious songs.
2. Her version of "Silent Night" was one *of the all-time best-selling records* in Denmark.
3. *Known for his imaginative style,* architect Minoru Yamasaki designed the McGregor Center, *located in Detroit.*
4. *Having been rejected by six publishers,* the story *of Peter Rabbit* was finally published privately *by Beatrix Potter.*
5. *Setting out in a thirty-one-foot ketch,* Sharon Sites Adams, a woman *from California,* sailed *across the Pacific Ocean* alone.
6. In 1932, Amelia Earhart, *trying for a new record,* began her solo flight *over the Atlantic Ocean.*
7. Maria Tallchief, an Osage Indian, was the prima ballerina *of the New York City Ballet company.*
8. *Dancing to acclaim in both the United States and Europe,* she was known *for her brilliant interpretation* of Stravinsky's <u>The Firebird</u>.
9. *Continuing her research on radium after her husband's death,* Marie Curie received the Nobel Prize *in chemistry.*
10. *First elected to the House of Representatives in 1968,* Shirley Chisholm was the first African American female member *of Congress.*

The Gerund

16g. A *gerund* is a verb form ending in *–ing* that is used as a noun.

SUBJECT	**Swimming** quickly tired us.
PREDICATE NOMINATIVE	Janetta's hobby is **knitting.**
DIRECT OBJECT	She has always loved **dancing.**
INDIRECT OBJECT	He gave **studying** all his attention.
OBJECT OF PREPOSITION	In **cooking,** use salt sparingly.

Do not confuse a gerund with a present participle used as an adjective or as part of a verb phrase.

GERUND	I enjoyed **volunteering** at the Special Olympics. [direct object of the verb *enjoyed*]
PRESENT PARTICIPLE	All students **volunteering** for the decorating committee should arrive one hour early. [adjective modifying the noun *students*]

Reference Note

For information on **subjects,** see page 515. For information on **predicate nominatives,** see page 524. For information on **direct objects** and **indirect objects,** see page 522. For information on **objects of prepositions,** see page 536.

PRESENT PARTICIPLE   Chamique is **volunteering** at the food bank this weekend. [part of the verb phrase *is volunteering*]

Reference Note

For information about **possessive forms,** see page 613.

NOTE   When writing a noun or a pronoun directly before a gerund, use the possessive form of the noun or pronoun.

EXAMPLES   **Rodrigo's** winning the contest surprised no one.

Mom was upset about **our** being late.

Everyone's arriving on time pleased us.

Exercise 4   Identifying Gerunds and Their Functions

Find the gerunds in the following sentences. Then, identify each gerund as a *subject*, a *direct object*, an *indirect object*, a *predicate nominative*, or an *object of a preposition*.

EXAMPLE   1. By reading the newspaper daily, you can become an informed citizen.

     1. *reading—object of a preposition*

1. Judging should be an exercise in objectivity.
2. Do you enjoy skiing?
3. I sometimes dream about flying.
4. Have you ever wished for a career in acting?
5. I have given camping a fair try, but I still do not like it.
6. Some of my friends work at stores in the mall, and others earn extra money by baby-sitting.
7. My doctor says that I should be more physically active, so my new exercise schedule includes jogging.
8. My favorite pastime is snorkeling.
9. Typing is a useful skill that could help you get a job next summer after you graduate.
10. My Navajo grandmother thinks that weaving would be a good hobby for me.

The Gerund Phrase

16h. A *gerund phrase* consists of a gerund and any modifiers or complements the gerund has. The entire phrase is used as a noun.

EXAMPLES   **Studying regularly** leads to better grades. [The gerund phrase is the subject of the verb *leads*. The adverb *regularly* modifies the gerund *Studying*.]

My brother likes **working at the travel agency.** [The gerund phrase is the direct object of the verb *likes.* The adverb phrase *at the travel agency* modifies the gerund *working.*]

Maya dreams of **becoming a well-known artist.** [The gerund phrase is the object of the preposition *of.* The noun *artist* is a predicate nominative completing the meaning of the gerund *becoming.*]

One important part of a healthy lifestyle is **eating fresh fruit.** [The gerund phrase is a predicate nominative identifying the subject *part.* The noun *fruit* is the direct object of the gerund *eating.*]

Review C **Identifying Participial Phrases and Gerund Phrases**

Identify the verbal phrase in each of the following sentences as either a *participial phrase* or a *gerund phrase.*

EXAMPLE   1. At what age did Se Ri Pak begin playing golf?

   1. *playing golf—gerund phrase*

1. Mary Shelley wrote *Frankenstein* after having a nightmare about a scientist and his strange experiments.
2. Dr. Mae Jemison became an astronaut by placing among the best fifteen candidates out of two thousand applicants.
3. Beginning with *Pippi Longstocking,* Astrid Lindgren has written a whole series of stories for children.
4. Marian Anderson was the first African American employed as a member of the Metropolitan Opera.
5. Fighting for women's suffrage was Carrie Chapman Catt's mission in life.
6. Appointed principal of the Mason City Iowa High School in 1881, Catt became the city's first female superintendent.
7. The Nineteenth Amendment to the Constitution, adopted in 1920, was largely the result of Catt's efforts.
8. Mildred "Babe" Didrikson, entering the 1932 Olympics as a relatively obscure athlete, won gold and silver medals.
9. Working for *Life* throughout her long career, Margaret Bourke-White was the first female war photographer.
10. Phyllis McGinley, a famous writer of light verse, began publishing her work while she was still in college.

The Infinitive

16i. An *infinitive* is a verb form that can be used as a noun, an adjective, or an adverb. Most infinitives begin with *to*.

TIPS & TRICKS

To find out if an infinitive is a noun, replace the infinitive with *what*.

EXAMPLES

To play the piano is relaxing. [*What* is relaxing? To play the piano is relaxing. The infinitive is a noun.]

He is anxious to begin tennis lessons. [He is anxious *what*? This sentence does not make sense. The infinitive is not a noun. It is used as an adverb modifying the adjective *anxious*.]

Infinitives	
Used as	**Examples**
Nouns	**To fly** was an ambition of humans for many centuries. [subject of *was*]
	Some fishes must swim constantly, or they start **to sink.** [direct object of *start*]
	Darius Freeman's dream is **to act.** [predicate nominative identifying the subject *dream*]
Adjectives	His attempt **to fly** was a failure. [adjective modifying the noun *attempt*]
	The one **to ask** is your guidance counselor. [adjective modifying the pronoun *one*]
Adverbs	With his dog Wolf, Rip Van Winkle went into the woods **to hunt.** [adverb modifying the verb *went*]
	Everyone in the neighborhood was willing **to help.** [adverb modifying the adjective *willing*]

Reference Note

For more information about **prepositional phrases,** see page 536.

NOTE Do not confuse an infinitive with a prepositional phrase that begins with *to*. An infinitive is a verb form. A prepositional phrase beginning with *to* ends with a noun or a pronoun.

INFINITIVES	to write	to forgive	to visit
PREPOSITIONAL PHRASES	to the game	to someone	to them

The word *to*, the sign of the infinitive, is sometimes omitted.

EXAMPLES Let's [to] **sit** down.

We wouldn't dare [to] **disobey.**

Please make him [to] **stop** that noise.

Thank you for helping me [to] **finish** the mural.

Exercise 5 Identifying Infinitives and Their Functions

Identify the infinitive in each of the following sentences. Then, tell whether it is used as a *noun*, an *adjective*, or an *adverb*. If the infinitive is used as a *noun*, indicate whether it is a *subject*, a *direct object*, or a *predicate nominative*. If the infinitive is used as a modifier, give the word it modifies.

EXAMPLE   **1.** Swans and geese are fascinating to watch.

      1. to watch—adverb—fascinating

1. To land on the moon became the national goal of the United States during the 1960s.
2. For me, one of the worst chores is to clean my room.
3. Karl "The Mailman" Malone slam-dunked the ball with one second to go!
4. In my spare time I like to read stories by James Thurber and Laurence Yep.
5. Did you find that book difficult to understand?
6. In our judicial system, the state makes the decision to prosecute the defendant in criminal cases.
7. I did not have time to watch the football game on television.
8. Anita's job was to interview all qualified candidates who had applied for the position.
9. I want to finish the dishes before I go to the movies.
10. Glad to help, Jennifer quickly found a paintbrush and a dropcloth and then started painting the shutters.

The Infinitive Phrase

16j. An *infinitive phrase* consists of an infinitive and any modifiers or complements the infinitive has. The entire phrase can be used as a noun, an adjective, or an adverb.

NOUN   **To finish early** is Peggy's plan. [The infinitive phrase is the subject of the verb *is*. The adverb *early* modifies the infinitive *To finish*.]

NOUN   Reginald wants **to go to the beach with us on Saturday.** [The infinitive phrase is the direct object of the verb *wants*. The adverb phrases *to the beach*, *with us*, and *on Saturday* modify the infinitive *to go*.]

ADJECTIVE	The team's desire **to win the game** was evident. [The infinitive phrase modifies the noun *desire*. The noun *game* is the direct object of the infinitive *to win.*]
ADVERB	Because of his sprained ankle, Chico was unable **to play in the football game.** [The infinitive phrase modifies the adjective *unable*. The adverb phrase *in the football game* modifies the infinitive *to play.*]

Reference Note

For information about other kinds of **clauses,** see Chapter 17.

Unlike other kinds of verbals, an infinitive may have a subject. An *infinitive clause* consists of an infinitive with a subject and any modifiers and complements the infinitive has. The entire clause is used as a noun. Notice in the second example below that the pronoun (*them*) used as the subject of the infinitive clause is in the objective case.

EXAMPLES	The director wants **Rebecca to star in the play.** [*Rebecca* is the subject of the infinitive *to star.* The entire infinitive clause is the direct object of the verb *wants.*]
	The sergeant commanded **them to march faster.** [*Them* is the subject of the infinitive *to march.* The entire infinitive clause is the direct object of the verb *commanded.*]

COMPUTER TIP

Some style-checking software programs can identify and highlight split infinitives. Using such a program will help you eliminate unnecessary split infinitives from your writing.

NOTE Placing words between the sign of the infinitive, *to,* and the base form results in a *split infinitive.* Generally, you should avoid using split infinitives in formal writing and speech.

SPLIT	The mayor wants to, as soon as possible, meet with her advisors.
REVISED	The mayor wants to meet with her advisors as soon as possible.

Sometimes, however, you may need to use a split infinitive so that the meaning of the sentence is clear.

UNCLEAR	The other team tried unfairly to influence the judges. [Does the adverb *unfairly* modify the verb *tried* or the infinitive *to influence?*]
CLEAR	The other team tried to unfairly influence the judges.

Review D Identifying Participial, Gerund, and Infinitive Phrases

Identify the participial, gerund, and infinitive phrases in the sentences in the following paragraph. For each participial phrase, give the word it modifies. For each gerund phrase, tell what part of a sentence it is. For each infinitive phrase, indicate what part of speech it is.

EXAMPLE **[1]** In Chinese communities all over the world, parading a huge paper dragon is a large part of the New Year's celebration.

1. *parading a huge paper dragon—gerund phrase (subject)*

[**1**] Dragons are a traditionally honored symbol of happiness to many Chinese people. [**2**] In ancient Chinese mythology, dragons are responsible for watching over people and bringing rainfall for the crops. [**3**] There are five different types of dragons, but it is the imperial dragon that is chosen to dance through the streets in traditional New Year's celebrations. [**4**] The dragon's role is to drive away bad luck and to bring good fortune for the new year. [**5**] Holding a stick with a white ball on the top, one dancer runs ahead of the dragon figure. [**6**] The ball symbolizes the highly valued pearl of wisdom, which the dragon chases. [**7**] The dragon's dance is accompanied by the beating of drums and gongs, the clashing of cymbals, and the popping of firecrackers. [**8**] The largest dragon figure in the world, similar to the one shown here, measured three meters tall and nearly one hundred meters long. [**9**] Decorated with thousands of mirrors and silk "scales," this dragon was truly impressive. [**10**] Because of its great weight and size, it took more than one hundred people, working in shifts, to carry it.

Link to Literature

Identify each italicized phrase in the following sentences as a *prepositional phrase*, a *participial phrase*, a *gerund phrase*, or an *infinitive phrase*. Do not separately identify a prepositional phrase that is part of another kind of phrase.

EXAMPLE
1. *Celebrating the strength of the human spirit,* Christy Brown's book <u>My Left Foot</u> tells the story *of his life.*

1. *Celebrating the strength of the human spirit*—participial phrase; *of his life*—prepositional phrase

1. Christy Brown, *born with cerebral palsy,* was unable *to speak a single word.*
2. Everyone, *including his family,* assumed he had very little intelligence, because he could not express himself *to anyone.*
3. Christy's left foot was the only limb he could control, and one day he succeeded in *grabbing a piece of chalk with it* and began *to write the word MOTHER on the wooden floor.*
4. Christy's family, *amazed at this remarkable achievement,* suddenly realized that *his leading a full, rewarding life* was not an impossible dream.
5. *Locked inside him,* a nimble intelligence and a mighty determination were waiting *to have their say.*
6. Not only was he capable of *understanding conversation* but he had also learned *to write and spell* all by himself.
7. *Looking into Christy's eyes that day,* his family might have felt that they were meeting him *for the first time.*
8. *With that one word,* his life changed, and the family made *helping him* a primary goal.
9. *Typing the entire manuscript with his left foot,* Christy Brown was eventually able *to tell his story in this inspiring book about his life.*
10. *Reading his book* will teach you much *about love and courage.*

Appositives and Appositive Phrases

16k. An *appositive* is a noun or a pronoun placed beside another noun or pronoun to identify or describe it.

An appositive usually follows the word it identifies or explains.

EXAMPLES   Both the Tewa and the Hopi are part of the American Indian group **Pueblo.** [The noun *Pueblo* identifies the noun *group.*]

The Hopi-Tewa artist **Dan Namingha** often paints abstract images of Hopi pueblos. [The noun *Dan Namingha* identifies the noun *artist*.]

Tony, did you know that she, **Martha,** won the race? [The noun *Martha* identifies the pronoun *she*.]

Aunt Sheila devotes Saturday mornings to her favorite hobby, **shopping.** [The gerund *shopping* identifies the noun *hobby*.]

Both the winners, **he** and **she,** will get mountain bikes. [The pronouns *he* and *she* identify the noun *winners*.]

For emphasis, however, an appositive may come at the beginning of a sentence.

EXAMPLE **Conifers,** both redwoods and sequoias bear their seeds in cones. [The noun *Conifers* refers to the nouns *redwoods* and *sequoias*.]

16l. An *appositive phrase* consists of an appositive and any modifiers the appositive has.

EXAMPLES Did Dan Namingha complete *Red Desert,* **one of his colorful acrylic paintings,** in 1980? [The adjective phrase *of his colorful acrylic paintings* modifies the appositive *one*.]

The Alaska moose, **the largest deer in the world,** inhabits the Kenai Peninsula. [The adjectives *the* and *largest* and the adjective phrase *in the world* modify the appositive *deer*.]

Remember the celebrations held on Monday, January 1, 2001, **the first day of the twenty-first century**? [The adjectives *the* and *first* and the adjective phrase *of the twenty-first century* modify the appositive *day*.]

Reference Note

For more information about **modifiers,** see Chapter 22.

Exercise 6 **Identifying Appositives and Appositive Phrases**

Identify the appositive or appositive phrase in each of the following sentences.

EXAMPLE 1. I enjoy reading about two colorful trickster figures, the Irish leprechaun and the American Indian Coyote.

1. *the Irish leprechaun and the American Indian Coyote*

1. Jose Saramago, a Portuguese novelist, won the 1998 Nobel Prize in literature.

2. Did Carrie Garcia write "Birds," one of her best-known songs, for her parents?
3. There goes the beautiful ship S.S. *Pericles,* bound for Greece!
4. "Aren't you Paolo Randazzo, the famous center-forward?" they asked excitedly.
5. Our teacher, Mr. Chun, overlooked the whole incident.
6. Sheila's grandmother Sra. Flores loves to listen to Tito Puente.
7. Their dog, a chocolate Labrador, chased a ball along the beach.
8. France is the home of the T.G.V., the fastest train in the world.
9. Ms. Ashoka teaches calculus at King High, a local magnet school.
10. A composer of Armenian ancestry, Aram Khachaturian was known for his exuberant music.

Review F Identifying Prepositional, Verbal, and Appositive Phrases

Identify each italicized phrase in the following paragraph as a *prepositional phrase,* a *participial phrase,* a *gerund phrase,* an *infinitive phrase,* or an *appositive phrase.* Do not separately identify a prepositional phrase that is part of another kind of phrase.

EXAMPLE   [1] *Packing effectively for a trip* requires careful thought.
            1. gerund phrase

Each year, thousands of Americans travel to hundreds [1] *of vacation spots in the United States and other countries.* [2] *Anticipating all kinds of weather and activities,* many eager travelers pack far too much clothing and equipment. The most effective way for these travelers to pack is [3] *to set out clothes for the trip* and then to put half of them back. For sightseeing trips, of course, travelers should give particular attention [4] *to walking shoes,* [5] *the most important item of apparel on such trips.* Experienced travelers pack only two or three changes of casual clothing, even if they plan [6] *to be away for some time.* [7] *Taking out the smallest piece of luggage they own,* they study its capacity. It is possible to pack enough clothes for three weeks in a small piece of luggage, [8] *perhaps a duffel bag or shoulder bag.* Passengers can carry such a bag onto an airliner and avoid [9] *waiting at the baggage claim area.* For many people, [10] *doing a bit of hand laundry every few days* is preferable to spending a vacation burdened with heavy suitcases.

Chapter Review

A. Identifying Prepositional Phrases

Write each prepositional phrase in the following sentences, and identify it as an *adjective phrase* or an *adverb phrase*. A sentence may include more than one phrase.

1. My family's cabin in the woods sits near the lakeshore.
2. During the intermission, Mr. Jackson played the pipe organ for the audience.
3. The oregano in the spice rack is fresher than the oregano in the pantry.
4. After the ball, the carriage in the palace courtyard became a pumpkin again.
5. The package arrived too late for Carmina's birthday.
6. Many of the cups on this shelf were made in Mexico.
7. After high school, my mother studied at Calvin College.
8. Add two cans of peeled tomatoes, a tablespoon of mild curry powder, and a cup of brown rice.
9. In *The Hobbit*, the hero of the story finds a magic ring.
10. Does your brother know anything about the history of railroads?

B. Identifying Verbal Phrases

Write each verbal phrase in the following sentences, and identify it as a *participial phrase*, a *gerund phrase*, or an *infinitive phrase*.

11. Off the coast of Australia, bottlenose dolphins have been observed with large natural sponges attached to their beaks.
12. Marian's attempt to rescue the cat was covered by a reporter.
13. Shiwonda wants to study law at Vanderbilt.
14. Archaeologists in Bulgaria unearthed a one-room tomb, hollowed out of two boulders, that contained frescoes.
15. Lee prefers swimming in water cooler than 72 degrees Fahrenheit.
16. Jamail spends plenty of time with his new puppy to accustom it to his voice and touch.
17. Mitsuyo's confidence was built up by winning the decathlon.

18. Preparing for the SAT took more time than I thought it would.
19. Shaking her head, Lisa indicated that she wasn't interested in the tour.
20. To learn the basics of French was Lina's main goal.

C. Identifying Appositive Phrases

Write each appositive phrase in the following sentences.

21. Sam, the youngest of Mimi's three cats, likes to climb.
22. Oscar Wilde, the author of *The Importance of Being Earnest,* was known for his sharp wit.
23. The band played "The Stars and Stripes Forever," a march.
24. They have the olive oil I like, the brand with the red label.
25. Winner of the Nobel Prize for literature, Toni Morrison is the author of such novels as *Beloved, Song of Solomon,* and *Paradise.*

D. Identifying Prepositional, Verbal, and Appositive Phrases

Identify each italicized phrase in the following sentences as a *prepositional phrase,* a *participial phrase,* a *gerund phrase,* an *infinitive phrase,* or an *appositive phrase.* Do not separately identify a prepositional phrase that is part of another phrase.

26. *Filling this order* will take at least two weeks.
27. Cuts and bruises, *minor injuries for most children,* are treated by the school nurse.
28. I have an appointment *to meet with the campaign committee.*
29. Ms. Behrman's only comment *on my paper* was that my handwriting was difficult to read.
30. He told me the story of Ta-sunko-witko, *a Sioux chief.*
31. His greatest joy was *seeing the latest science fiction movie.*
32. *Grabbing a sandwich,* René hurried off to join his friends.
33. Mom finally agreed *to buy me a new dress for the dance.*
34. On the top floor are three offices *connected by a hallway.*
35. Her attitude may seem indifferent *to you.*
36. In Israel, farmers use innovative agricultural methods to meet the difficulties of *growing food in a desert country.*
37. Woodrow Wilson, *the U.S. president during World War I,* tried to construct a lasting peace after the war.

38. During our vacation in Hawaii, we saw Mauna Loa, a volcano *rising two and a half miles above sea level.*

39. Withdrawing from the race, the candidate cited personal reasons for her unexpected decision *to return to private life.*

40. To conserve water, many farmers water only the roots of plants, using a series *of underground irrigation pipes.*

Writing Application
Describing a Business

Using Prepositional Phrases   Your school newspaper plans to publish a special careers issue. For a feature page, the editor has invited students to describe businesses they would like to own ten years from now. Think of your business, invent a name for it, and write a paragraph describing it. Use at least five prepositional phrases in your sentences.

Prewriting   Brainstorm ideas for three or four kinds of businesses you would enjoy owning and managing ten years from now. Then, jot down details about your product or service, your location, your equipment, and your customers.

Writing   As you write your first draft, think about your audience. What details about your business would interest your readers? Make sure that you include plenty of specific details.

Revising   Ask a friend to read your paragraph before you revise it. Can your friend clearly imagine your business? If not, add, cut, or rearrange details to make your paragraph clearer and more interesting. If your sentences sound choppy, combine them into longer, smoother sentences. Be sure that you have used at least five prepositional phrases in your paragraph.

Reference Note

For information on **sentence combining,** see Chapter 11.

Publishing   Check the grammar, spelling, and punctuation of your paragraph. You and your classmates may want to gather your paragraphs into a booklet to include in a class time capsule.

The Clause
Independent and Subordinate Clauses

Diagnostic Preview

A. Identifying Independent and Subordinate Clauses

Identify the italicized clause in each of the following sentences as *independent* or *subordinate.* If the italicized clause is subordinate, tell whether it is used as an *adverb,* an *adjective,* or a *noun.*

EXAMPLE   1. Miguel and Bette, *who were visiting us over the Labor Day weekend,* have returned to their home in Rhode Island.

1. *subordinate; adjective*

1. *Whenever Jorge practices the clarinet,* his neighbor's beagles, Banjo and Randolph, howl.
2. Advertisements encourage people to want products, and *many people cannot distinguish between their passing wants and their essential needs.*
3. In Ms. Weinberg's science class we learned *that chalk is made up mostly of calcium carbonate.*
4. Liliuokalani, *who was the last queen of Hawaii,* wrote "Aloha Oe"; she was an accomplished songwriter.
5. Does each of you know *how you can protect yourself* if a tornado strikes our area?

6. *If there is a tornado warning,* go quickly to the lowest level in your house, cover your head with your hands, and lie flat or crouch low until the danger is past.

7. The American Indians *who inhabited the area of Connecticut around the Naugatuck River* were called the Pequots.

8. *American music has been enriched by Ella Fitzgerald, Leslie Uggams, and Lena Horne, three well-known African American vocalists.*

9. *That the girls' volleyball team was well coached* was demonstrated last night when the team won the state championship.

10. *As you enter the school,* the principal's office is the third room on your right.

B. Classifying Sentences According to Structure

Classify each sentence in the following paragraphs as *simple, compound, complex,* or *compound-complex.*

EXAMPLE **[1]** In January 1991, Phoebe Jeter displayed leadership and courage.

1. *simple*

[11] Just who is this Phoebe Jeter from Sharon, South Carolina? [12] Phoebe Jeter, serving as a lieutenant in the U.S. Army, led a platoon during the Persian Gulf Conflict in 1991. [13] Jeter will always remember the tense January night when she heard the words "Scud alert!" [14] On her orders, thirteen Patriot missiles were fired, and at least two Scud missiles were destroyed. [15] When the Persian Gulf Conflict was over, Jeter had the satisfaction of knowing that she had successfully defended U.S. troops.

[16] That 40 percent of the women who served in the Gulf were African Americans may be an underestimate. [17] Figures have not been released by the Pentagon, but some say the actual number may have been closer to 50 percent. [18] The Persian Gulf Conflict tested the mettle of all female military personnel involved; throughout the conflict, women shared hazardous assignments, primitive living conditions, and various battle responsibilities with men. [19] The professionalism and courage of the women who served in the Gulf earned them considerable respect. [20] Perhaps now, because of soldiers like Phoebe Jeter, people will think differently about the role of women in the United States armed forces.

What Is a Clause?

17a. A *clause* is a word group that contains a verb and its subject and that is used as a sentence or as part of a sentence.

Every clause has a subject and a verb. Not every clause, however, expresses a complete thought. A clause that expresses a complete thought is called an *independent clause.* A clause that does not express a complete thought is called a *subordinate clause.*

SENTENCE   Lichens are plants that are composed of fungi and algae.

                   S   **V**

INDEPENDENT   Lichens are plants [complete thought]
CLAUSE

                   S   **V**

SUBORDINATE   that are composed of fungi and algae
CLAUSE   [incomplete thought]

HELP

A subordinate clause that is capitalized and punctuated as a sentence is a *sentence fragment.*

Reference Note

For information on **correcting sentence fragments,** see page 427.

The Independent Clause

17b. An *independent* (or *main*) *clause* expresses a complete thought and can stand by itself as a sentence.

                 S   **V**

EXAMPLES   **Ms. Martin explained the binary number system.**
[one independent clause]

                         S   **V**

In the binary system, each number is expressed in

                      S   **V**

powers of two, and only the digits 0 and 1 are used.
[two independent clauses joined by a comma and *and*]

              S   **V**   **S**

The binary system is a number system; however, it

V

is not the only number system. [two independent clauses joined by a semicolon, a conjunctive adverb, and a comma]

                 S   **V**

The binary number system is important to know

        S   **V**

because it is used by computers. [an independent clause combined with a subordinate clause]

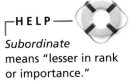

NOTE An independent clause used by itself is generally called a sentence. The term *independent clause* is generally used when such a clause is joined with at least one other clause (either independent or subordinate) to make a sentence.

The Subordinate Clause

17c. A *subordinate* (or *dependent*) *clause* does not express a complete thought and cannot stand by itself as a sentence.

Like a word or a phrase, a subordinate clause can be used as an adjective, a noun, or an adverb in a sentence.

EXAMPLES   that we had collected

   what Hui Su named her pet beagle

   when Roberto proofread his essay

The thought expressed by a subordinate clause becomes complete when the clause is combined with an independent clause.

EXAMPLES   Mr. Platero took the aluminum cans **that we had collected** to the recycling center. [adjective clause]

   Do you know **what Hui Su named her pet beagle**? [noun clause]

   When Roberto proofread his essay, he found several typographical errors. [adverb clause]

┌─**HELP**──
Subordinate means "lesser in rank or importance."

Exercise 1 Identifying Independent and Subordinate Clauses

Identify each italicized word group in the following paragraph as an *independent clause* or a *subordinate clause.*

EXAMPLE   **[1]** The photographs on this page and the next page show *how eggs are processed in a large processing plant.*

   1. subordinate clause

[1] Large plants like the one in the photographs are *where most eggs are processed today.* [2] After an egg is laid, *it gently rolls along the slanted floor of the cage to a narrow conveyor belt.* [3] These narrow conveyor belts converge into one wide belt *that runs directly into the processing plant.* [4] *As soon as the eggs reach the processing*

plant, they are automatically sprayed with detergent and water. [5] The eggs then pass through a specially lit inspection area, *where defective eggs can be detected and removed.* [6] After the eggs are weighed, *they are separated by weight into groups.* [7] Each group of eggs goes onto a separate conveyor belt, *which leads to a forklike lifting device.* [8] This device lifts six eggs at a time *while the empty egg cartons wait two feet below it.* [9] *The eggs are gently lowered into the cartons,* which are then shipped to grocery stores and supermarkets. [10] *What is truly amazing* is that no human hands touch the eggs during the entire process.

┌─ S T Y L E ✏ T I P ┐

Although the use of short, simple sentences is effective at times, overusing them will result in choppy writing. One way to avoid choppy sentences is to change some sentences into subordinate clauses. Furthermore, by using subordinate clauses, you can avoid the unnecessary repetition of words, such as *The Amazon River* in the following example.

CHOPPY
The Amazon River is about 6,276 kilometers in length. The Amazon River is the second-longest river in the world.

SMOOTH
The Amazon River, which is about 6,276 kilometers in length, is the second-longest river in the world.

The Adjective Clause

17d. An **adjective clause** is a subordinate clause that modifies a noun or a pronoun.

An adjective clause follows the word or words that it modifies and tells *what kind* or *which one.*

EXAMPLES   Dr. Charles Richter devised the Richter scale, **which is used to measure the magnitude of earthquakes.** [The adjective clause modifies the noun *scale.*]

Ferdinand Magellan, **who was the commander of the first expedition around the world,** was killed before the end of the journey. [The adjective clause modifies the noun *Ferdinand Magellan.*]

Didn't John Kieran once say, "I am a part of all **that I have read**"? [The adjective clause modifies the pronoun *all.*]

Relative Pronouns

Usually, an adjective clause begins with a **relative pronoun**—a word that not only relates an adjective clause to the word or words the clause modifies but also serves a function within the clause.

Common Relative Pronouns				
that	which	who	whom	whose

EXAMPLES   Grandma Moses, **who began painting at the age of seventy-six,** became famous for her primitive style. [The relative pronoun *who* relates the adjective clause to the noun *Grandma Moses* and also serves as the subject of the verb *began*.]

The treasure **for which they are searching** belonged to the Aztec emperor Montezuma II. [The relative pronoun *which* relates the adjective clause to the noun *treasure* and serves as the object of the preposition *for*.]

I have read nearly every novel **that Shirley Ann Grau has written.** [The relative pronoun *that* relates the adjective clause to the noun *novel* and serves as the direct object of the verb *has written*.]

An adjective clause may begin with *when* or *where*. When used to introduce adjective clauses, these words are called **relative adverbs.**

EXAMPLES   Uncle Chim told Lori and me about the time **when he backpacked across the island of Luzon.** [The adjective clause modifies the noun *time*.]

Pet birds should be kept in wide cages, **where they have room to fly.** [The adjective clause modifies the noun *cages*.]

Sometimes the relative pronoun or relative adverb is not expressed, but its meaning is understood.

EXAMPLES   The documentary **[that]** I watched yesterday was about Harriet Tubman.

We will never forget the wonderful summer **[when]** we stayed with our grandparents in Mayagüez, Puerto Rico.

Depending on how it is used, an adjective clause is either essential or nonessential. An *essential* (or *restrictive*) *clause* provides information that is necessary to the meaning of a sentence. A *nonessential* (or *nonrestrictive*) *clause* provides additional information that can be omitted without changing the basic meaning of a sentence. Nonessential clauses are set off by commas.

ESSENTIAL   Students **who are going to the track meet** can take the bus at 7:45 A.M. [Omitting the adjective clause would change the basic meaning of the sentence.]

NONESSENTIAL   Nancy Stevens, **whose father is a pediatrician,** plans to study medicine. [The adjective clause gives extra information. Omitting the clause would not affect the basic meaning of the sentence.]

Reference Note
For information on using **who and whom** correctly, see page 619. For information on using **who, that, and which** correctly, see page 740.

Reference Note
For more about **punctuating nonessential clauses,** see page 788.

Identifying Adjective Clauses and the Words They Modify

Identify the adjective clause in each of the following sentences, and give the noun or pronoun that it modifies. Then, tell whether the relative pronoun is used as a *subject, direct object,* or *object of a preposition* in the adjective clause.

EXAMPLE
1. Theo, who is the editor of the school newspaper, wrote an article about the inhumane treatment of laboratory animals.

1. *who is the editor of the school newspaper; Theo; subject*

1. Some of us have read *Native Son,* which Richard Wright published in 1940.
2. The book to which he referred was ordered yesterday.
3. Everyone in the stands at Wimbledon cheered for the player that had the better serve.
4. The fish that I caught yesterday weighed three pounds, but Sally's fish weighed five pounds.
5. The nominee for the prestigious award was a statesman whom everyone admired.
6. It's not easy to understand someone who mumbles.
7. They finally found my briefcase, which had been missing for two weeks.
8. Please indicate the people to whom we should go for help.
9. The guide advised those who enjoy Native American art to visit the new exhibit of Hopi weaving and pottery.
10. In March many countries have festivals that can be traced back to ancient celebrations of spring.

The Noun Clause

17e. A *noun clause* is a subordinate clause that is used as a noun.

A noun clause may be used as a *subject*, a *predicate nominative*, a *direct object*, an *indirect object*, or an *object of a preposition*.

SUBJECT	**That Jim Hynes is a talented writer** is an understatement.
PREDICATE NOMINATIVE	Another course in computers is **what the guidance counselor recommended.**

Reference Note

For more about **subjects, predicate nominatives, direct objects, and indirect objects,** see Chapter 15. For more about **objects of prepositions,** see page 536.

DIRECT OBJECT	The Greek astronomer Ptolemy believed **that the sun orbited the earth.**
INDIRECT OBJECT	The judges will award **whoever has the most original costume** a prize.
OBJECT OF A PREPOSITION	Grandmother Gutiérrez has a kind word for **whomever she meets.**

Common Introductory Words for Noun Clauses

how	whatever	whether	who	whomever
that	when	which	whoever	whose
what	where	whichever	whom	why

The word that introduces a noun clause may or may not have a grammatical function in the clause.

EXAMPLES Do you remember **who painted *Washington Crossing the Delaware*?** [The word *who* introduces the noun clause and serves as the subject of the verb *painted*.]

Ms. Eva Picard, an environmentalist, will explain **what the greenhouse effect is.** [The word *what* introduces the noun clause and serves as a predicate nominative completing the meaning of the verb *is*.]

Millicent said **that she would be late.** [The word *that* introduces the noun clause but does not have any grammatical function within the noun clause.]

NOTE Another type of noun clause is the infinitive clause. An ***infinitive clause*** consists of an infinitive with a subject, along with any modifiers and complements the infinitive has. The entire infinitive clause can function as the direct object of a verb.

EXAMPLE I wanted **her to tell the O'Leary twins the story about Mr. Omar.** [The entire infinitive clause is the direct object of the verb *wanted*. *Her* is the subject of the infinitive *to tell*. The infinitive *to tell* has an indirect object, *twins,* and a direct object, *story*.]

Notice that the subject of an infinitive clause is in the objective case and that the infinitive takes the place of a main verb.

Identifying Noun Clauses

Identify the noun clause in each of the following sentences. Tell whether the noun clause is used as a *subject*, a *predicate nominative*, a *direct object*, an *indirect object*, or an *object of a preposition*.

EXAMPLES **1.** Please address your letter to whoever manages the store.

      1. whoever manages the store—object of a preposition

      2. Do you know where the new municipal center is?

      2. where the new municipal center is—direct object

1. Would you please tell me what the past tense of the verb *swing* is?
2. I will listen carefully to whatever you say.
3. Whatever you decide will be fine with me.
4. Give whoever wants one a free pass.
5. That Jill was worried seemed obvious to us all.
6. Do you know why Eduardo missed the Cinco de Mayo celebration?
7. You can appoint whomever you like.
8. In biology class we learned about how hornets build their nests.
9. A remote desert island was where the pirates buried their treasure.
10. The teacher would like us to prepare the slides.

Review A **Distinguishing Between Adjective Clauses and Noun Clauses**

Identify the subordinate clause in each of the following sentences. Tell whether the subordinate clause is used as an *adjective* or a *noun*. Then, give the word that each adjective clause modifies, and state whether each noun clause is used as a *subject*, a *predicate nominative*, a *direct object*, or an *object of a preposition*.

EXAMPLE **1.** Until recently, scientists believed that the giant sequoias of California were the oldest living trees on earth.

      1. that the giant sequoias of California were the oldest living trees on earth—noun; direct object

1. Now, however, that honor is given to the bristlecone pine, which is a small, gnarled tree native to the western part of the United States.
2. Botanists estimate that some bristlecone pines are more than six thousand years old.
3. The oldest sequoias are only 2,200 years old, according to those who know.
4. Whoever respects hardiness has to respect the bristlecone.

5. The high altitude of the Rocky Mountains, the bristlecone's natural habitat, is what makes the tree grow so slowly.
6. Do you think that the bristlecone pine will win any beauty contests?
7. Judge by what you can see in the photograph on this page.
8. The bristlecone's needles last on the branches for fifteen to thirty years, a length of time that is extraordinary.
9. Botanists tell us that the bristlecone is a member of the foxtail family.
10. Like all members of this family, the bristlecone has needle clusters that resemble a fox's tail.

The Adverb Clause

17f. An *adverb clause* is a subordinate clause that modifies a verb, an adjective, or an adverb.

An adverb clause tells *how, when, where, why, to what extent,* or *under what condition.*

EXAMPLES   The pitcher felt **as though all eyes were on him.** [The adverb clause modifies the verb *felt,* telling *how* the pitcher felt.]

Frédéric Chopin made his debut as a concert pianist **when he was eight years old.** [The adverb clause modifies the verb *made,* telling *when* Frédéric Chopin made his debut.]

Ariel takes her new camera **wherever she goes.** [The adverb clause modifies the verb *takes,* telling *where* Ariel takes her new camera.]

Happy **because I had made the team,** I hurried home to tell my parents and older brother the news. [The adverb clause modifies the adjective *Happy,* telling *why* I was happy.]

The water in the lake was much colder **than we had expected.** [The adverb clause modifies the adjective *colder,* telling *to what extent* the water was colder.]

TIPS & TRICKS

Some of the words that introduce adverb clauses may also introduce adjective clauses and noun clauses. To determine what type of clause the introductory word begins, look at how the clause is used in the sentence.

ADJECTIVE CLAUSE
The day **when we got our puppy** was a Friday. [The clause modifies the noun *day.*]

NOUN CLAUSE
Does Jimmy remember **when we got our puppy?** [The clause is the direct object of the verb *remember.*]

ADVERB CLAUSE
Our older dog sulked a little **when we got our puppy.** [The clause modifies the verb *sulked.*]

If we leave now, we will avoid the rush-hour traffic. [The adverb clause modifies the verb *will avoid*, telling *under what condition* we will avoid the traffic.]

Reference Note

For more about punctuating **introductory adverb clauses,** see page 792.

> **NOTE** Notice in the example above that an adverb clause that begins a sentence is followed by a comma.

Subordinating Conjunctions

An adverb clause is introduced by a ***subordinating conjunction***—a word or word group that shows the relationship between the adverb clause and the word or words that the clause modifies.

Reference Note

The words **after, as, before, since,** and **until** may also be used as **prepositions.** See page 503.

Common Subordinating Conjunctions			
after	as though	provided that	until
although	because	since	when
as	before	so that	whenever
as if	if	than	where
as long as	in order that	though	wherever
as soon as	once	unless	while

The Elliptical Clause

17g. Part of a clause may be left out when its meaning can be clearly understood from the context of the sentence. Such a clause is called an ***elliptical clause.***

Most elliptical clauses are adverb clauses. In each of the adverb clauses in the following examples, the part given in brackets may be omitted because its meaning is clearly understood.

EXAMPLES Leilana finished her research sooner **than Marta** [did].

While [he was] **painting,** Rembrandt concentrated completely on his work.

Reference Note

For more information about the correct use of **pronouns in elliptical clauses,** see page 616.

> **NOTE** Often the meaning of an elliptical clause depends on the form of the pronoun in the clause.

EXAMPLES Martine asked her more questions **than I** [asked her].

Martine asked her more questions **than** [she asked] **me.**

Exercise 4 Identifying Adverb Clauses and the Words They Modify

Identify the adverb clause in each of the following sentences, and give the word or words that the clause modifies. Then, state whether the clause tells *how, when, where, why, to what extent,* or *under what condition.* If a clause is elliptical, be prepared to supply the omitted word or words.

EXAMPLE   1. Thao is quieter than Catherine.
   1. *than Catherine—quieter; to what extent*

1. When our school has a fire drill, everyone must go outside.
2. I visited the collection of Aztec artifacts because I wanted to see the religious and solar calendars.
3. She walked until she was too tired to take another step.
4. Because he was late so often, he bought a watch.
5. Gazelles need to be able to run fast so that they can easily escape their predators.
6. Return this revolutionary, new sonic potato peeler for a full refund if you are not completely satisfied.
7. As soon as you're ready, we'll leave.
8. You can set the table while I prepare the salad.
9. Your trip to New York will not be complete unless you see the Alvin Ailey American Dance Theater.
10. You understand the situation much better than I.

Review B Identifying Independent and Subordinate Clauses

Identify each italicized clause in the following paragraph as *independent* or *subordinate.* If the italicized clause is subordinate, tell whether it is used as an *adverb,* an *adjective,* or a *noun.*

EXAMPLE   [1] *When they think of American Indians,* many people immediately picture the Dakota Sioux.
   1. *subordinate—adverb*

   Do you know [1] *why the Dakota spring to mind?* I think the reason is [2] *that they are known for their impressive eagle-feather headdresses.* Until recently, [3] *if an artist painted or drew Native Americans of any region,* the people were often shown wearing Dakota headdresses, fringed buckskin shirts, and elaborately beaded moccasins. Even paintings of the Pemaquid people meeting the Pilgrims [4] *as they landed on*

┌─HELP─
In the example for Exercise 4, the word *is* is omitted from the elliptical clause.

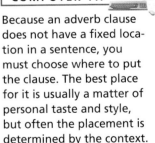

| COMPUTER TIP

Because an adverb clause does not have a fixed location in a sentence, you must choose where to put the clause. The best place for it is usually a matter of personal taste and style, but often the placement is determined by the context.

If you use a computer, you can easily experiment with the placement of adverb clauses in sentences. Create different versions of the sentence containing the adverb clause, along with the sentences that immediately precede and follow it. Read each version aloud to see how the placement of the clause affects the flow, rhythm, and overall meaning of the passage.

Photo: Charles Milton Bell (1890). From the collection of Kurt Koegler.

Photo: Carl Moon (1905). From the collection of Kurt Koegler.

Cape Cod sometimes show the Pemaquid dressed in the style of the Dakota, [5] *who lived far away in the northern plains region.* Artists apparently did not recognize [6] *that there are many different American Indian peoples.* Each group has its own traditional clothing, and [7] *the variety of Native American dress is truly amazing.* For example, [8] *compare the turbans and bearclaw necklaces of the Fox men above with the headband and turquoise jewelry of this Navajo boy.* [9] *While these images may not be familiar to you,* they are just as authentic as the image of the Dakota. To see other unique styles of dress, you might want to research the clothing worn by native peoples [10] *who live in different regions of the United States.*

Review C **Writing Clauses**

For each of the following items, supply the type of clause indicated in italics.

EXAMPLE   **1.** Do you know _____? (*noun clause*)

         1. *Do you know what the phrase "tip of the iceberg" means?*

1. _____, the entire audience stood as one to applaud them. (*adverb clause*)
2. You'd never know it, but the man _____ holds more than one hundred patents. (*adjective clause*)
3. They commanded _____. (*infinitive clause*)
4. I told them _____. (*noun clause*)
5. As we walked by a tall display of potatoes, _____. (*independent clause*)
6. Because the letter was in Chinese, Mrs. Mansfield took it to someone _____. (*adjective clause*)
7. Technology's advance has accelerated _____. (*adverb clause*)
8. In the tackle box were handmade flies _____. (*adjective clause*)
9. _____ should get a medal. (*noun clause*)
10. Africa's wildlife—indeed, animals all over the world—must be protected _____. (*adverb clause*)

┌**HELP**──

Remember that a clause must have both a subject and a verb.

Sentences Classified According to Structure

17h. Depending on its structure, a sentence can be classified as simple, compound, complex, or compound-complex.

(1) A *simple sentence* contains one independent clause and no subordinate clauses.

A simple sentence may contain a compound subject, a compound verb, and any number of phrases.

EXAMPLES   Uncle Alan taught me how to play the mandolin.

          The spotted owl and the golden-cheeked warbler are endangered species. [compound subject]

          Covered with dust and cobwebs, the old bicycle looked terrible but worked just fine. [compound verb]

Reference Note

⌐ **Sentences** may also be **classified according to purpose.** See page 527.

Reference Note

Independent clauses may be joined by a colon or a dash when the second clause explains or restates the idea of the first clause. For more about **colons** and **dashes** used this way, see page 806 and page 810.

Reference Note

For more information on using **semicolons** and **conjunctive adverbs** or **transitional expressions** to join independent clauses, see page 804.

(2) A *compound sentence* contains two or more independent clauses and no subordinate clauses.

The independent clauses in a compound sentence may be joined by a comma and a coordinating conjunction (*and, but, for, nor, or, so,* or *yet*), by a semicolon, or by a semicolon and a conjunctive adverb or a transitional expression.

EXAMPLES   Lorenzo's story sounded incredible, **but** it was true. [two independent clauses joined by a comma and the coordinating conjunction *but*]

Althea Gibson was successful at Wimbledon in 1957 and 1958; she won the doubles and singles championships both years. [two independent clauses joined by a semicolon]

The defeat of Napoleon at Waterloo was a victory for Britain; **however,** it brought to an end an era of French grandeur. [two independent clauses joined by a semicolon, the conjunctive adverb *however,* and a comma]

Common Conjunctive Adverbs		
also	however	nevertheless
anyway	instead	otherwise
besides	likewise	still
consequently	meanwhile	then
furthermore	moreover	therefore

Common Transitional Expressions		
as a result	for example	in other words
at any rate	in addition	on the contrary
by the way	in fact	on the other hand

NOTE Be careful to distinguish a simple sentence that has either a compound subject or a compound verb from a compound sentence.

SIMPLE SENTENCE   The archaeological discovery was made in the fall and was widely acclaimed the following spring. [compound verb]

COMPOUND SENTENCE   The archaeological discovery was made in the fall, and it was widely acclaimed the following spring.

(3) A ***complex sentence*** contains one independent clause and at least one subordinate clause.

EXAMPLES   Thurgood Marshall, who served on the United States Supreme Court for twenty-four years, retired in 1991. [The independent clause is *Thurgood Marshall retired in 1991.* The subordinate clause is *who served on the United States Supreme Court for twenty-four years.*]

         While we were on vacation in Washington, D.C., we visited the Folger Shakespeare Library, which is devoted to Shakespeare's legacy. [The independent clause is *we visited the Folger Shakespeare Library.* The subordinate clauses are *While we were on vacation in Washington, D.C.,* and *which is devoted to Shakespeare's legacy.*]

(4) A ***compound-complex sentence*** contains two or more independent clauses and at least one subordinate clause.

EXAMPLES   My mom just spoke to Mr. Kostas, who runs the neighborhood watch program, and he told her about last night's meeting. [The two independent clauses are *My mom just spoke to Mr. Kostas* and *he told her about last night's meeting.* The subordinate clause is *who runs the neighborhood watch program.*]

         Chelsea is only seven years old, but she can already play the violin better than her tutor can. [The two independent clauses are *Chelsea is only seven years old* and *she can already play the violin better.* The subordinate clause is *than her tutor can.*]

Exercise 5   Classifying Sentences According to Structure

Classify each of the following sentences as *simple, compound, complex,* or *compound-complex.*

EXAMPLE   **1.** Mr. Faust said that ancient Egyptians used the pith of the papyrus plant to make an early form of paper.

         1. complex

1. Charles Richard Drew researched blood plasma and helped develop blood banks.
2. Supposedly, if the month of March comes in like a lion, it goes out like a lamb.
3. Many Malaysians believe that sickness will follow the eating of stolen food.

COMPUTER TIP

Computers can help you get a better sense of your own sentence style. If you have style-checking software, run a style check on a paragraph or two (or more) of your writing. The style checker will analyze your writing sample and will provide information such as the number of sentences per paragraph, the kinds of sentences, the average number of words per sentence, and the lengths of the longest and shortest sentences.

If you discover that you tend to use only one or two sentence structures and that your sentences all tend to be of a similar length, you can focus your attention on revising for greater variety.

4. When World War I ended in 1918, many people thought that there would be no more wars; however, twenty-one years later, World War II began in Europe.
5. In his letter to Mrs. Bixby, Abraham Lincoln consoled her for the loss of several sons and hoped that time would ease her sorrow.
6. After the announcement of the final score, all of us fans cheered the team and clapped enthusiastically.
7. In England and Wales, salmon was once king, yet few salmon rivers remain there.
8. The English philosopher Thomas Hobbes once aspired to be a mathematician, but he never fulfilled this ambition.
9. As an older woman, Queen Elizabeth I always wore a dark red wig so that no one knew whether her own hair had grayed or not.
10. The professional tennis star Zina Garrison Jackson devotes time to training and encouraging young inner-city tennis players.

Review D **Writing a Variety of Sentence Structures**

Write ten sentences according to the following instructions.

EXAMPLE   1. Write a compound sentence containing a semicolon.
             1. *You rake the leaves, Janelle; I'll sweep the sidewalk.*

1. Write a simple sentence containing a compound subject.
2. Write a compound sentence containing the conjunction *but*.
3. Write a complex sentence containing an adverb clause modifying a verb.
4. Write a complex sentence containing an adverb clause modifying an adjective.
5. Write a complex sentence containing an adjective clause introduced by the relative pronoun *who*.
6. Write a complex sentence containing an adjective clause introduced by the relative pronoun *that*.
7. Write a complex sentence containing a noun clause used as the subject of the sentence.
8. Write a complex sentence containing a noun clause used as the direct object of the sentence.
9. Write a complex sentence containing an elliptical adverb clause.
10. Write a compound-complex sentence.

Chapter Review

A. Identifying Independent and Subordinate Clauses

Identify the italicized word group in each of the following sentences as an *independent clause* or a *subordinate clause*.

1. My older sister showed us *how she sketches human faces so skillfully.*
2. *Whenever Sue smells ginger,* she remembers her mother's kitchen.
3. *I know a boy* whose grandfather was one of the first astronauts.
4. *Whether the state government should raise the sales tax* was the issue before the legislature that afternoon.
5. *My uncle Leon,* who served in Vietnam, *is now a businessman.*

B. Identifying Adjective Clauses and the Words They Modify

Identify the adjective clause in each of the following sentences, and give the noun or pronoun that it modifies. Then, tell whether the relative pronoun in the adjective clause is used as a *subject,* a *direct object,* or an *object of a preposition.*

6. The lake, which is in Iowa, has swimming facilities.
7. Turn in at the green sign, which shows the way to the boat launch.
8. On the boat ride, wear one of the orange life vests that are available at no extra cost.
9. One lifeguard at the lake, about whom I've told you before, received a medal for saving two children.
10. Everyone whom the lifeguard has assisted is grateful for her training and her bravery.

C. Identifying Noun Clauses

Identify the noun clause in each sentence, and indicate whether it is a *subject,* a *direct object,* an *indirect object,* a *predicate nominative,* or an *object of a preposition.*

11. Did you know that the word *robot* originated from the Czech word *robota?*

12. The year 1921 was when the word was first used, in a play by the Czech playwright Karel Capek.

13. In many science fiction stories, robots and androids are used for whatever jobs humans are unwilling to do.

14. In *Star Trek: The Next Generation,* the android Data often gives whoever asks him a question a detailed response.

15. How robots will be used in the future remains to be seen.

D. Identifying Adverb Clauses and the Words They Modify

Identify the adverb clause in each of the following sentences, and give the word or words that the clause modifies. Then, state whether the clause tells *how, when, where, why, to what extent,* or *under what condition.*

16. The playwright left the stage after she had made her opening night speech to the audience.

17. Wherever she hiked that spring, Vera enjoyed seeing wildflowers.

18. The meeting ran a little longer than Marcia hoped it would.

19. The team captain played as if winning the championship depended entirely on her.

20. We stopped to eat at the Falafel Hut because we were in a hurry.

21. Whenever you want to rent a bike, ask for information at the bicycle shop.

22. Candida spoke as though she were speaking before a large convention instead of a small class.

23. Mr. Suzuki spread the grass seeds where they would do the most good.

24. The teacher distributed copies of the sheet music so that the class could follow along with the sonata.

25. If you're interested in coming to the movies, please let me know.

E. Classifying Sentences by Structure

Classify each of the following sentences as *simple, compound, complex,* or *compound-complex.*

26. I heard children shouting on the playground as the noise filtered into my room through the closed window.

27. Holding the freshly cut board carefully, Barbara pounded the nail into the wood.

28. Last summer Rita attended band camp, and she met a number of students who were interested in becoming musicians.

29. Last summer, I learned to keep financial records and to place merchandise orders; I also waited on customers.

30. No one will deny that it is the responsibility of a newspaper to report the day's happenings accurately.

Writing Application
Using Sentence Variety in a Guidebook

Sentence Structures The student council has asked your class to write a guidebook to inform new students and their families about your area. Write an entry for the guidebook, telling about a local attraction that people might enjoy visiting. Use a mix of sentence structures.

Prewriting Brainstorm points of interest in your city or area. Then, choose one attraction with which you are familiar. Be sure to jot down specific details, such as when the place is open to the public, how much admission is, and why it is worth a visit.

Writing Begin your guidebook entry by identifying the name, location, and significance of the attraction. Then, capture your readers' interest with a clear, vivid description of the place.

Revising Ask a friend or family member to read your paragraph. Add, cut, and rearrange details to include all important information. Use sentence-combining techniques to vary the structure of your sentences.

Publishing Proofread your paragraph for any errors in grammar, usage, and mechanics. Your class may want to compile a guidebook for your area. Double-check all the information included in your paragraphs. Then, type the paragraphs neatly and collect them in a binder. Place your guidebook in the library of your school so that anyone can read it, or make photocopies to give to new students.

Reference Note

For information about **sentence combining,** see Chapter 11.

CHAPTER 18

Agreement
Subject and Verb, Pronoun and Antecedent

Diagnostic Preview

A. Proofreading Sentences for Subject-Verb and Pronoun-Antecedent Agreement

Most of the following sentences contain errors in agreement. If a sentence contains an error in agreement, identify the incorrect verb or pronoun and supply the correct form. If a sentence is already correct, write *C*.

EXAMPLE   **1.** Each of the members of the school board are hoping to be reelected this fall.

         1. are hoping—is hoping

1. Half of the members of my history class this year is in the National Honor Society.
2. Over one thousand miles of tunnels travels through El Teniente, the largest copper mine in the world.
3. If she already has needle-nose pliers, she can exchange it for something else at the hardware store.
4. The etchings of Mary Cassatt, an impressionist painter, was definitely influenced by styles used in the prints of the Japanese artists Utamaro and Toyokuni.

5. Under the seat of the car were two dollar bills, seven quarters, and a handful of dimes, pennies, and nickels; they would buy enough gas to get us home.

6. If you see either Veronica or Sabrena in the cafeteria, will you please tell them that I won't be able to go to the mall?

7. Neither Adrianne nor Lillian expect to make the varsity softball team this year; nevertheless, both girls are trying out for it.

8. To learn more about our municipal government, our civics class is planning to invite a number of guest speakers to school.

9. Unfortunately, neither Mayor Ella Hanson nor Mrs. Mary Ann Powell, the assistant mayor, have responded to our invitations to the outdoor concert yet.

10. Try reading *The Borrowers* to your little brother; he'll love it.

B. Proofreading a Paragraph for Subject-Verb and Pronoun-Antecedent Agreement

Most of the sentences in the following paragraph contain errors in agreement. Revise each sentence containing an agreement error to correct the error. If a sentence is already correct, write *C*.

EXAMPLE   **[1]** My aunt runs Teresa's Treasures, which are next to the access road by the highway.

      1. *My aunt runs Teresa's Treasures, which is next to the access road by the highway.*

[11] Clothing, along with jewelry and household goods, are stacked or hung everywhere. [12] Everybody around here knows that they can get great deals there. [13] Ten dollars will buy more there than they will anywhere else in town. [14] I do little chores for Aunt T, and sometimes a few of my friends drops by and helps me. [15] She doesn't like doing the books, but mathematics are easy for me, so I also do the books for her. [16] Aunt T is a member of the Association of Taylor County Businesswomen and lets the group use her empty room for its meetings. [17] Ms. Lincoln, the owner of Acme Appliances, or Mrs. Abbot, the owner of a travel agency, usually brings their tape player. [18] The worst part of the job are the songs the ATCB plays; they're ancient. [19] Don't that old music get to you after a while? [20] Here's something: Yesterday I caught myself humming "A White Sport Coat and a Pink Carnation," and I didn't stop!

Number

Number is the form a word takes to indicate whether the word is singular or plural.

18a. A word that refers to one person, place, thing, or idea is singular in number. A word that refers to more than one is plural in number.

Singular	computer	half-hour	story	this	it
Plural	computers	half-hours	stories	these	they

Agreement of Subject and Verb

18b. A verb should agree in number with its subject.

(1) Singular subjects take singular verbs.

EXAMPLES   My **grandfather trains** dogs.

The **senator is** in favor of the bill.

She owns and **operates** a video store.

That is beautiful!

(2) Plural subjects take plural verbs.

EXAMPLES   My **grandparents train** dogs.

Many **senators are** in favor of the bill.

They own and **operate** a video store.

Those are beautiful!

In a verb phrase, the first helping verb agrees in number with the subject.

EXAMPLES   This **song was performed** by Bonnie Raitt. [singular subject and singular verb phrase]

These **songs were performed** by Bonnie Raitt. [plural subject and plural verb phrase]

Has the **dancer been rehearsing** since noon? [singular subject and singular verb phrase]

Have the **dancers been rehearsing** since noon? [plural subject and plural verb phrase]

Reference Note

For information on **finding the subject,** see page 518.

┌HELP─

Present-tense verbs, except *be* and *have*, add –s or –es when the subject is third-person singular. Present-tense verbs do not add –s or –es when the subject is a first-person pronoun (*I, we*), a second-person pronoun (*you*), or a third-person plural pronoun (*they*).

Reference Note

For information about **verb phrases,** see page 497.

NOTE A gerund phrase or an infinitive phrase used as a complete subject takes a singular verb. Do not be misled by any particular noun in the phrase. The gerund or infinitive serves as a singular simple subject.

EXAMPLES **Writing** verses for greeting cards **sounds** like an interesting job. [The singular verb *sounds* is used because the gerund *Writing*, not the noun *verses* or *cards*, is the subject of the verb.]

To compete in the 2004 Olympics **is** Monica's goal. [The singular verb *is* is used because the infinitive *To compete*, not the noun *Olympics*, is the subject of the verb.]

Reference Note
For information about **gerund phrases and infinitive phrases,** see page 544.

Intervening Phrases and Clauses

18c. The number of a subject usually is not determined by a word in a phrase or a clause following the subject.

EXAMPLES This **tape is** by the Boston Pops Orchestra.

This **tape** of songs **is** by the Boston Pops Orchestra. [*Is* agrees with the subject *tape*, not with *songs*, which is part of the prepositional phrase *of songs*.]

The **characters represent** abstract ideas.

The **characters** used in an allegory **represent** abstract ideas. [*Represent* agrees with the subject *characters*, not with *allegory*, which is part of the participial phrase *used in an allegory*.]

The **Great Barrier Reef lies** off northeastern Australia.

The **Great Barrier Reef,** which supports many marine animals, **lies** off northeastern Australia. [*Lies* agrees with the subject *Great Barrier Reef*, not with *animals*, which is part of the adjective clause *which supports many marine animals.*]

HELP
Remember that the subject of a sentence is never in a prepositional phrase.

USAGE

NOTE Do not be misled by a phrase that begins with a compound preposition such as *along with, as well as, in addition to,* and *together with.* Such a phrase does not affect the number of the subject.

EXAMPLES The **teacher,** as well as her students, **was fascinated** by the exhibit. [singular subject and singular verb]

The **students,** as well as their teacher, **were fascinated** by the exhibit. [plural subject and plural verb]

Exercise 1 Identifying Subjects and Verbs That Agree in Number

Identify the subject of the verb in parentheses in each of the following sentences. Then, choose the verb form that agrees in number with the subject.

EXAMPLE
1. The many varieties of American quilts (*reflect, reflects*) the spirit of the people who developed them.

1. *varieties—reflect*

1. During the colonial period, only women of means made quilts; however, by the mid-nineteenth century, women throughout the United States (*was making, were making*) quilts.
2. The abilities that someone needs to make a quilt (*include, includes*) patience, coordination, and a good sense of color and design.
3. A scrapbag full of colorful pieces of cotton and wool fabrics (*was put, were put*) to good use in making a quilt.
4. Usable fabric from worn-out shirts, as well as from other articles of clothing, (*was cut, were cut*) into pieces of various shapes and sizes.
5. The Amish people, known for their beautiful quilting, (*live, lives*) very simply.
6. Amish quilts, which are often brightly colored, (*seem, seems*) to convey the joyous spirits of their makers.
7. Several quilters, gathering at one person's home for a quilting bee, often (*work, works*) on a quilt together.
8. Quilts designed by the Amish usually (*include, includes*) only solid-colored fabrics and not patterned ones.
9. These quilts, which feature colors typical of Amish quilts, (*glow, glows*) with red, purple, blue, pink, and green.
10. In contrast, the clothing worn by Amish women (*is, are*) more subdued in color.

USAGE

Indefinite Pronouns

18d. Some indefinite pronouns are singular, some are plural, and some can be singular or plural, depending on how they are used.

(1) The following indefinite pronouns are singular: *anybody, anyone, anything, each, either, everybody, everyone, everything, neither, nobody, no one, nothing, one, somebody, someone,* and *something.*

EXAMPLES   **Everyone** in the Pep Club **is wearing** the school colors.

                One of the most beautiful places in North Carolina **is** the Joyce Kilmer Memorial Forest.

                Anything that makes yardwork easier **is** a good gift for Dad.

(2) The following indefinite pronouns are plural: *both, few, many,* and *several.*

EXAMPLES   **Both** of the games **were postponed.**

                Many of our words **derive** from Latin.

                Several of the juniors **have volunteered.**

(3) The indefinite pronouns *all, any, more, most, none,* and *some* may be singular or plural, depending on their meaning in a sentence.

These pronouns are singular when they refer to singular words and are plural when they refer to plural words.

EXAMPLES   **All** of the vegetable garden **has been planted.** [*All* refers to the singular noun *garden.*]

                All of the vegetables **have been planted.** [*All* refers to the plural noun *vegetables.*]

                None of the equipment **was damaged.** [*None* refers to the singular noun *equipment.*]

                None of the machines **were damaged.** [*None* refers to the plural noun *machines.*]

                Most of the food **has already been eaten.** [*Most* refers to the singular noun *food.*]

                Most of the sandwiches **have already been eaten.** [*Most* refers to the plural noun *sandwiches.*]

TIPS & TRICKS

Each, either, neither, and *one* can also be used as adjectives or as parts of correlative conjunctions. Used as these parts of speech, such words cannot function as subjects.

Reference Note

For information on **adjectives,** see page 491. For information on **correlative conjunctions,** see page 505.

COMPUTER TIP

If you use a computer when you write, you may want to create a help file containing lists of indefinite pronouns and their rules for agreement. Fill this file with information that will help you determine whether an indefinite pronoun is used correctly. Then, as you proofread your work, you can access the file whenever you have a question about the agreement between an indefinite pronoun and a verb or another pronoun.

USAGE

Identify the subject of the verb in parentheses in each of the following sentences. Then, choose the verb form that agrees in number with the subject.

EXAMPLE   1. Not one of the pears (*look, looks*) ripe.

            1. one—*looks*

1. Many of the recipes in this cookbook (*is, are*) adaptable to microwave cooking.
2. Neither of my parents (*has, have*) trouble using the metric system.
3. I know that all the workers (*was, were*) proud to help restore the Statue of Liberty.
4. Most of the English classes in my high school (*stresses, stress*) composition skills.
5. Few of the students (*was, were*) able to spell *bureaucracy* correctly.
6. (*Do, Does*) each of you know what you're supposed to bring?
7. None of the dessert (*remain, remains*), but we can still remember its wonderful taste.
8. Some of the word-processing software (*has, have*) arrived late.
9. Both of the paintings (*shows, show*) the influence of the work of Emilio Sánchez.
10. Everyone visiting Bob and Lynn (*notices, notice*) how well their new puppy behaves.

Compound Subjects

Reference Note

For more about
compound subjects,
see page 517.

A *compound subject* consists of two or more subjects that are joined by a conjunction and that have the same verb.

18e. Subjects joined by *and* usually take a plural verb.

EXAMPLES   **Basil** and **thyme are** plants of the mint family.

Following Julius Caesar's death, **Antony, Octavian,** and **Lepidus become** the rulers of Rome.

Subjects joined by *and* may name only one person, place, thing, or idea. Such a compound subject takes a singular verb.

EXAMPLES   The **secretary** and **treasurer is** Gretchen. [one person]

Grilled chicken and **rice is** the restaurant's specialty. [one dish]

USAGE

18f. Singular subjects joined by *or* or *nor* take a singular verb.

EXAMPLES   Neither **Juan** nor **Jeff wants** to see the movie.

Either **Felita** or **Terry sits** in the front row.

Has the **cat** or the **dog been fed** yet?

18g. When a singular subject and a plural subject are joined by *or* or *nor,* the verb agrees with the subject nearer the verb.

EXAMPLES   Neither the **players** nor the **coach was** ready to concede defeat. [The singular subject *coach* is nearer the verb.]

Neither the **coach** nor the **players were** ready to concede defeat. [The plural subject *players* is nearer the verb.]

STYLE   TIP

When possible, revise sentences to avoid awkward wordings like those in the examples for 18g.

EXAMPLE
The **coach was** not ready to concede defeat, and neither **were** the **players.**

USAGE

Review A   **Correcting Errors in Subject-Verb Agreement**

Most of the following sentences contain verbs that do not agree with their subjects. If the verb does not agree, give the correct form of the verb. If the verb already agrees with its subject, write *C*.

EXAMPLE   **1.** Each of the issues were resolved.

1. was

1. Emily Dickinson's imagery and verse structure has been analyzed and praised by many critics.
2. One or both of Shakespeare's plays about Henry IV is likely to be performed this summer.
3. The effective date of the new regulations for nuclear power plants have not yet been determined.
4. Each of the region's environmental groups are presenting its recommendations to the governor.
5. Spike Lee, whose movies tackle controversial social issues, has made a great contribution to the film industry.
6. The fact that compact discs do not wear out and do not have to be flipped over make them attractive.
7. The sales representative, with the help of her assistant, plan to expand her territory.
8. Not one of the speakers in the debate on South America appear eager to suggest a solution to the problem.
9. Neither the proposals of the air traffic controllers nor the report of the FAA's committee have been heeded.
10. James Baldwin, along with Richard Wright and Ralph Ellison, rank among the most important writers of the twentieth century.

Special Problems in Subject-Verb Agreement

18h. When the subject follows the verb, find the subject and make sure that the verb agrees with it.

TIPS & TRICKS

To find the subject when it follows the verb, invert, or rearrange, the sentence to put the subject first.

EXAMPLES
Your **gloves are** here.

A **message was** on her answering machine.

Arsenio is where?

The subject generally follows the verb in sentences beginning with *here* or *there* and in questions.

EXAMPLES   Here **is** the other **glove.**

Here **are** the **gloves.**

There **was** a **message** on her answering machine.

There **were** no **messages** on her answering machine.

Where **is Arsenio**?

Where **are Arsenio** and his **brother**?

NOTE   Contractions such as *here's, there's,* and *where's* contain the verb *is* (*here is, there is,* and *where is*). Use these contractions only with singular subjects.

NONSTANDARD	Here's your keys.
STANDARD	Here **are** your **keys.**
STANDARD	Here**'s** your **set** of keys.
NONSTANDARD	Where's the islands located?
STANDARD	Where **are** the **islands** located?
STANDARD	Where**'s each** of the islands located?

Reference Note

For more information about **collective nouns,** see page 486.

18i. A collective noun may be either singular or plural, depending on its meaning in a sentence.

The singular form of a *collective noun* names a group.

Common Collective Nouns			
army	club	family	squadron
assembly	congregation	group	staff
audience	fleet	herd	team
band	flock	number	troop

A collective noun is singular when it refers to the group as a unit and is plural when it refers to the individual members or parts of the group.

USAGE

SINGULAR	The tour **group is already** on the bus. [The group as a unit is on the bus.]
PLURAL	The tour **group are talking** about what they expect to see. [The members of the group are talking to one another.]

SINGULAR	A **flock** of geese **is flying** over. [The flock is flying as a unit.]
PLURAL	The **flock** of geese **are joining** together in a V-shaped formation. [The members of the flock are joining together.]

NOTE In the expression *number of,* the word *number* is singular when preceded by *the* and is plural when preceded by *a.*

EXAMPLES **The number** of students taking computer courses **has increased.**

A number of students taking computer courses **belong** to the Computer Club.

18j. **An expression of an amount (a measurement, a percentage, or a fraction, for example) may be singular or plural, depending on how it is used.**

An expression of an amount is singular when the amount is thought of as a unit and is plural when the amount is thought of as separate parts.

EXAMPLES **Five thousand bricks is** a heavy load for this truck. [The bricks are thought of as a unit.]

Five thousand bricks are scattered on the lot. [The bricks are thought of separately.]

Two days is the amount of time we will spend visiting each college campus. [one unit]

Two days of this month **are** school holidays, I believe. [separate days]

A fraction or a percentage is singular when it refers to a singular word and is plural when it refers to a plural word.

EXAMPLES **One fourth** of our high school's student body **is employed.** [The fraction refers to the singular noun *student body.*]

One fourth of the students **are employed.** [The fraction refers to the plural noun *students.*]

Seventy-five percent of the junior class **is** sixteen years old. [The percentage refers to the singular noun *class.*]

Seventy-five percent of the juniors **are** sixteen years old. [The percentage refers to the plural noun *juniors.*]

USAGE

Reference Note

For information on **when to spell out numbers** and **when to use numerals,** see page 854.

An expression of measurement (such as length, weight, capacity, or area) is usually singular.

EXAMPLES

Four and seven-tenths inches is the diameter of a CD.

Eight fluid ounces equals one cup.

Two hundred kilometers was the distance we flew in the hot-air balloon.

Exercise 3 Identifying Verbs That Agree with Their Subjects

Identify the subject of each verb in parentheses in each of the following sentences. Then, choose the verb form that agrees in number with the subject.

EXAMPLE   1. The band (*is, are*) tuning their instruments.
             1. *band—are*

1. How (*was, were*) the pyramids in Egypt built?
2. The stage crew (*is, are*) working together to make a rapid scene change for Rita Moreno's entrance.
3. Where (*is, are*) the other flight of stairs that go up to the roof?
4. On display in the entrance to the library (*is, are*) several paintings of famous local people.
5. The Hispanic population (*is, are*) one of the two fastest growing ethnic groups in the United States.
6. On our block alone, over two hundred dollars (*was, were*) collected for the American Cancer Society.
7. Of the world's petroleum, approximately one third (*was, were*) produced by the United States at that time.
8. Red beans and rice (*is, are*) sometimes served as a side dish at Cajun meals.
9. Thirty minutes of swimming (*serves, serve*) as a healthful way to get daily exercise.
10. A number of the seeds (*has, have*) failed to sprout.

18k. Some nouns that are plural in form take singular verbs.

The following nouns take singular verbs.

civics	genetics	measles	news
economics	gymnastics	molasses	physics
electronics	mathematics	mumps	summons

USAGE

EXAMPLES   **Measles is** a contagious disease.

The **news was** disappointing.

However, a few nouns take plural verbs even when they refer to single items.

binoculars	pants	shears
eyeglasses	pliers	slacks
Olympics	scissors	trousers

EXAMPLES   The **scissors are** in the sewing basket.

The first modern **Olympics were held** in Athens.

NOTE Many nouns ending in –*ics*, such as *acoustics, athletics, ethics, politics, statistics,* and *tactics,* may be singular or plural.

EXAMPLES   **Statistics is** a collection of mathematical data.

The **statistics are** misleading.

18l. Even when plural in form, the title of a creative work (such as a book, song, movie, or painting) or the name of a country, a city, or an organization generally takes a singular verb.

EXAMPLES   ***Those Who Ride the Night Winds* was written** by the poet Nikki Giovanni.

"The Birds" is a very scary story.

***Three Musicians* is** a collage painting by Picasso.

In the play *Our Town,* **Grover's Corners represents** the typical American town in the early 1900s.

The Philippines encompasses more than 7,000 islands.

NOTE The names of some organizations may take singular or plural verbs, depending on how the names are used. When the name refers to the organization as a unit, it takes a singular verb. When the name refers to the members of the organization, it takes a plural verb.

EXAMPLES   The **U.S. Marines is** a separate branch of the Department of the Navy. [The U.S. Marines as a unit is a branch.]

U.S. Marines are stationed all over the world. [Troops are stationed.]

┌HELP─

If you do not know whether a noun that is plural in form is singular or plural in meaning, look in a dictionary.

USAGE

USAGE

18m. A verb agrees with its subject, but not necessarily with a predicate nominative.

EXAMPLES **Han, Phuong Vu,** and **Mary are** Team B.

Team B is Han, Phuong Vu, and Mary.

The featured **attraction is** the exhibits showing how to build a biplane.

The **exhibits** showing how to build a biplane **are** the featured attraction.

18n. Subjects preceded by *every* or *many a* take singular verbs.

EXAMPLES **Every sophomore** and **junior is** participating.

Many a person supports the cause.

18o. The contractions *don't* and *doesn't* should agree with their subjects.

The word *don't* is the contraction of *do not.* Use *don't* with all plural subjects and with the pronouns *I* and *you.*

EXAMPLES Some **students don't** have access to a computer.

I don't know how to swim.

Don't you play in the school orchestra?

The word *doesn't* is the contraction of *does not.* Use *doesn't* with all singular subjects except the pronouns *I* and *you.*

EXAMPLES This **umbrella doesn't** belong to me.

Doesn't he attend Vanderbilt University?

Exercise 4 **Choosing the Correct Verb**

Choose the correct verb form in parentheses in each of the following sentences.

EXAMPLE 1. He (*doesn't, don't*) have a clue about the surprise party.

1. *doesn't*

1. The Girl Guides (*is, are*) a scouting organization that was founded in Great Britain.
2. (*Don't, Doesn't*) every boy and girl in the city schools vote in the student council elections?
3. My cousin's favorite comic-book duo (*is, are*) Batman and Robin.

4. In Michigan, I lived in Detroit and then Grand Rapids; Grand Rapids (*were, was*) my favorite place until I moved here.
5. "Seventeen Syllables" (*recounts, recount*) the story of a Japanese American family.
6. This (*doesn't, don't*) make sense to me.
7. Microelectronics, the area of electronics dealing with the design and application of microcircuits, (*have, has*) made possible many of the tremendous advances in computers and robotics in recent years.
8. There (*is, are*) many a slip between the cup and the lip, as my grandpa says.
9. When she is doing needlepoint, Aunt Ching's scissors (*hangs, hang*) around her neck on a red ribbon.
10. Gymnastics (*is, are*) a popular sport at our high school.

Review B **Choosing the Correct Verb**

Choose the correct verb form in parentheses in each of the following sentences.

EXAMPLE   1. How many of the foods shown on the next page (*is, are*) native to Central America and North America?

  1. *are*

1. Almost every one of the following sentences (*give, gives*) you a clue to the answer.
2. Popcorn, as well as peanuts, (*was, were*) introduced to European settlers by American Indians.
3. No one in Europe (*was, were*) familiar with the taste of pumpkins, blueberries, or maple syrup until explorers brought these foods back from the Americas.
4. One American food that helped reduce the famine in Europe (*was, were*) potatoes.
5. A field of potatoes (*produce, produces*) almost twice as much food in about half as much growing time as the same field would if it were planted with wheat.
6. News of tomatoes, sweet peppers, beans, and zucchini (*was, were*) received warmly in Europe, and now these foods are the heart and soul of southern Italian cooking.
7. At our school the Original American Chefs (*is, are*) a club that prepares and serves such American Indian foods as baked sweet potatoes and steamed corn pudding.

8. Statistics (*shows, show*) that three fifths of afl the crops now in cultivation originated in the Americas.

9. (*Doesn't, Don't*) it seem obvious by now that every one of the foods shown here was first eaten in the Americas?

10. *Indian Givers* (*is, are*) a wonderful book about all kinds of contributions that American Indians have made to the world.

Reference Note

For more about **relative pronouns** and **adjective clauses,** see page 560.

18p. When the relative pronoun *that, which,* or *who* is the subject of an adjective clause, the verb in the clause agrees with the word to which the relative pronoun refers.

EXAMPLES   Ganymede, **which is** one of Jupiter's satellites, is the largest satellite in our solar system. [*Which* refers to the singular noun *Ganymede.*]

I have neighbors **who raise** tropical fish. [*Who* refers to the plural noun *neighbors.*]

NOTE   When preceded by *one of* + a plural word, the relative pronoun generally takes a plural verb. When preceded by *the only one of* + a plural word, the relative pronoun generally takes a singular verb.

EXAMPLES   The dodo is **one of the birds that are** extinct.

Pluto is **the only one of the planets that crosses** the orbit of another planet.

Oral Practice 1 **Reviewing Subject-Verb Agreement**

Read each of the following sentences aloud, stressing the italicized words.

1. *Has either* of the essays been graded?

2. *Both* of these vegetables, green beans and broccoli, *are* nourishing.
3. Here *are* the *minutes* I took at the meeting.
4. The *salary* that he will earn at his new job *is* the minimum wage.
5. Not *one* of the student drivers *forgets* to fasten the seat belt.
6. Where *are* her *mother and father*?
7. The *coach doesn't* want us to eat sweets.
8. *Several* of the research papers *were* read aloud.

Review C **Choosing Verbs That Agree with Their Subjects**

Identify the subject of the verb in parentheses in each of the following sentences. Then, choose the verb form that agrees in number with the subject.

EXAMPLES
1. Both of the brothers (*play, plays*) in the zydeco band at the Cajun Cafe.
1. Both—play
2. One of the roads (*run, runs*) past the hospital at the edge of town.
2. One—runs

1. Neither the Litchfield exit nor the Torrington exit (*is, are*) the one you should take.
2. The president, after meeting with several advisors, (*has, have*) promised to veto the proposed tax bill.
3. A medical study of World War II veterans (*has, have*) concluded that the veterans have the same health prospects as nonveterans.
4. The list of the greatest baseball players of all time (*is, are*) dominated by outfielders.
5. Babe Ruth, Hank Aaron, Willie Mays, and Joe DiMaggio (*is, are*) all outfielders on the list.
6. The Mariana Trench, located in the Pacific Ocean near the Mariana Islands, (*remains, remain*) the deepest known ocean area in the world.
7. Styles in clothing (*seems, seem*) to change as often as the weather.
8. When (*do, does*) the new telescope at the observatory become operational?
9. Please find out whether the conference room next to the windows (*is, are*) available at 2:00 tomorrow afternoon.
10. These vegetables, which we bought at the market this morning, (*doesn't, don't*) look fresh.

Review D **Proofreading for Subject-Verb Agreement**

Most of the following sentences contain errors in agreement. If a sentence contains an error in agreement, identify the incorrect verb and supply the correct form. If the sentence is already correct, write *C*.

EXAMPLE   **1.** Don't the concept of child prodigies fascinate you?

         1. Don't—Doesn't

1. Prodigies, people who have immense talent, is born very infrequently.
2. One of the most interesting child prodigies of this century are young Wang Yani of China.
3. Two and a half years were the age at which Wang began painting.
4. How old do you think she was when this wonderful painting of frolicking monkeys were completed?
5. Neither of us were able to guess correctly that she was only five then.
6. It shouldn't surprise you to learn that *Little Monkeys and Mummy* are the painting's title.
7. The people of China has recognized Wang as a prodigy since she was four years old.
8. By the time she was six, she had painted four thousand pictures.
9. As you can see, wet ink and paint is freely mixed in Wang's pictures, producing interesting puddles and fuzzy edges.
10. Wang Yani is the youngest painter ever whose work have been displayed in a one-person show at the Smithsonian Institution.

Wang Yani. © Byron Preiss Visual Publications, Inc. & New China Pictures Company. Photograph: Zheng Zhensun © 1991. All rights reserved. Published by Scholastic, Inc.

Wang Yani, *Little Monkeys and Mummy.* © Byron Preiss Visual Publications, Inc. & New China Pictures Company. Photograph: Zheng Zhensun © 1991. All rights reserved. Published by Scholastic, Inc.

Agreement of Pronoun and Antecedent

A pronoun usually refers to a noun or another pronoun, which is called the pronoun's *antecedent.*

18q. A pronoun should agree in number, gender, and person with its antecedent.

(1) Singular pronouns refer to singular antecedents. Plural pronouns refer to plural antecedents.

SINGULAR   **Sammy Davis, Jr.,** made **his** movie debut in 1931.

PLURAL   The **hikers** took **their** canteens with **them.**

(2) Some singular pronouns indicate gender.

The singular pronouns *he, him, his,* and *himself* refer to masculine antecedents. The singular pronouns *she, her, hers,* and *herself* refer to feminine antecedents. The singular pronouns *it, its,* and *itself* refer to antecedents that are neuter (neither masculine nor feminine).

(3) *Person* indicates whether a pronoun refers to the one speaking (*first person*), the one spoken to (*second person*), or the one spoken about (*third person*).

FIRST PERSON   **I** need a transcript of **my** grades.

SECOND PERSON   Have **you** fastened **your** seat belt?

THIRD PERSON   **He** said **they** made **their** own costumes.

Indefinite Pronouns

18r. Some indefinite pronouns are singular, and some are plural. Other indefinite pronouns can be either singular or plural, depending on their meaning.

(1) Use singular pronouns to refer to the indefinite pronouns *anybody, anyone, anything, each, either, everybody, everyone, everything, neither, nobody, no one, nothing, one, somebody, someone,* and *something.*

These pronouns do not indicate gender. Often, however, the object in a prepositional phrase that follows such a pronoun indicates the gender of the pronoun.

Reference Note

For more on **antecedents,** see pages 487 and 630.

Reference Note

For information about **personal pronouns,** see page 488.

USAGE

You can often avoid the awkward *his* or *her* construction (1) by substituting an article (*a, an,* or *the*) for the construction or (2) by rephrasing the sentence, using the plural forms of both the pronoun and its antecedent.

EXAMPLES
Any interested **person** may send **a** résumé.

All interested **persons** may send **their** résumés.

EXAMPLES   **Each** of the **boys** brought **his** own mitt.

One of the **girls** left **her** sweater on the bus.

If the antecedent may be either masculine or feminine, use both the masculine and feminine pronouns to refer to it.

EXAMPLES   **Anyone** who is going on the field trip needs to bring **his or her** lunch.

Any interested **person** may send **his or her** résumé.

NOTE   In informal situations, plural pronouns are often used to refer to singular antecedents that can be either masculine or feminine.

INFORMAL   **Everybody** stayed late at the dance because **they** were enjoying **themselves.**

Such usage is becoming increasingly popular in writing. In fact, using a singular pronoun to refer to a singular antecedent that is clearly plural in meaning may be misleading in some cases.

MISLEADING   **Everybody** stayed late at the dance because **he or she** was enjoying **himself or herself.** [Since *Everybody* is clearly plural in meaning, the singular constructions *he or she* and *himself or herself,* though grammatically correct, are confusing.]

In formal situations, it is best to revise such sentences to make them both clear and grammatically correct.

EXAMPLE   **All** of the students stayed late at the dance because **they** were enjoying **themselves.**

(2) Use plural pronouns to refer to the indefinite pronouns *both, few, many,* **and** *several.*

EXAMPLES   **Both** of the debaters persuasively presented **their** arguments.

Several of these coins are worth more than **their** face values.

(3) Use a singular or plural pronoun to refer to the indefinite pronoun *all, any, more, most, none,* **or** *some,* **depending on how it is used in the sentence.**

EXAMPLES   **Some** of the computer terminology is difficult to understand; perhaps Ms. Alvarez can clarify **its** meaning. [*Some*
refers to the singular noun terminology.]

Some of the computer terms are difficult to understand;
perhaps Ms. Alvarez can clarify **their** meanings. [*Some* refers
to the plural noun terms.]

Oral Practice 2 **Using Correct Pronoun-Antecedent**
Agreement

Read each of the following sentences aloud, stressing the italicized words.

1. *Each* of the girls has prepared *her* presentation.
2. Has *anyone* brought *his or her* compass?
3. *Both* of the teams played *their* best.
4. *Neither* of the kittens has opened *its* eyes yet.
5. *Most* of the tires are on sale; *they* are 25 percent off the regular price.
6. *All* of the casserole is gone; *it* was delicious.
7. Have *many* of the eligible voters cast *their* ballots?
8. *Somebody* should speak up and give *his or her* opinion.

Compound Antecedents

18s. **Use a plural pronoun to refer to two or more antecedents**
joined by *and.*

EXAMPLES   If **Joann** and **Benjamin** call, tell **them** that I will not be
home until this evening.

Pilar, Kimberly, and **Laura** have donated **their** time.

Antecedents joined by *and* may name only one person, place,
thing, or idea. Such a compound antecedent takes a singular pronoun.

EXAMPLE   The **corned beef and cabbage** was delicious; I ate two
servings of **it.**

18t. **Use a singular pronoun to refer to two or more singular**
antecedents joined by *or or nor.*

EXAMPLES   Either **Renaldo** or **Philip** always finishes **his** geometry
homework in class.

Neither **Cindy** nor **Carla** thinks **she** is ready to audition.

USAGE

Using a pronoun to refer to antecedents of different number may create an unclear or awkward sentence.

UNCLEAR	Neither the backup singers nor the lead vocalist was satisfied with her performance. [*Her* agrees with the nearest antecedent, *vocalist*. However, it is unclear whether all the performers were dissatisfied with their own performances or all the performers were dissatisfied only with the lead vocalist's performance.]
UNCLEAR	Neither the lead vocalist nor the backup singers were satisfied with their performance. [*Their* agrees with the nearest antecedent, *singers*. However, it is unclear whether all the performers were dissatisfied with the entire group's performance or all the performers were dissatisfied only with the backup singers' performance.]
AWKWARD	Neither the lead vocalist nor the backup singers were satisfied with her or their performance.

It is best to revise sentences to avoid unclear and awkward constructions like the preceding ones.

REVISED	Neither the vocalist nor the backup singers were satisfied with **the** performance.
	All of the singers were dissatisfied with **their** performance.

STYLE ⟋ TIP

A sentence with singular antecedents joined by *or* or *nor* can be awkward or misleading if the antecedents are of different genders. Revise the sentence to avoid the awkward construction.

AWKWARD
Either Leo or Rose will give his or her report.

REVISED
Either **Leo** will give **his** report, or **Rose** will give **hers.**

Exercise 5 Supplying Pronouns That Agree with Their Antecedents

Complete each of the following sentences by supplying at least one pronoun that agrees with its antecedent. Use standard formal English.

EXAMPLE   1. Each of the girls took _____ turn at bat.
　　　　　1. *her*

1. Each student prepares _____ own outline.
2. One of the birds built _____ nest in our chimney.
3. Both Jane and Ruth wrote _____ essays about ecology.
4. If anyone else wants to drive, _____ should tell Mrs. Cruz.
5. Many of the students in our class have turned in _____ reports on the Frida Kahlo exhibit.
6. Not one of the students typed _____ research paper.
7. Neither Angela nor Carrie has given _____ dues to me.
8. Either Mark or David offered to take _____ car.
9. Each of the visitors filled _____ own plate with tacos and fajitas.
10. Everyone in the class has paid _____ lab fees.

Special Problems in Pronoun-Antecedent Agreement

18u. A collective noun can be either singular or plural, depending on how it is used.

A collective noun takes a singular pronoun when the noun refers to the group as a unit. A collective noun takes a plural pronoun when the noun refers to the individual members or parts of the group.

SINGULAR   The **committee** comprised three juniors and two seniors; **its** chairperson was Angelo. [Angelo was chairperson of the committee as a unit.]

PLURAL   The **committee** discussed **their** varied schedules. [The members of the committee had different schedules.]

18v. Some nouns that are plural in form take singular pronouns.

The following nouns take singular pronouns.

civics	gymnastics	mumps
economics	mathematics	news
electronics	measles	physics
genetics	molasses	summons

EXAMPLES   We bought several jars of **molasses.** Would you like to have a jar of **it**?

I'm looking forward to studying **physics** next year. **It** is my favorite subject.

However, a few nouns take plural pronouns even when they refer to single items.

binoculars	pants	shears
eyeglasses	pliers	shorts
Olympics	slacks	scissors

EXAMPLES   I have misplaced my **eyeglasses.** Have you seen **them**?

Wherever the **Olympics** are held, **they** attract athletes from all over the world.

Reference Note

For a list of commonly used **collective nouns,** see page 486.

USAGE

NOTE Many nouns ending in *–ics,* such as *acoustics, athletics, ethics, politics,* and *tactics,* may take singular or plural pronouns. Generally, when such a noun names a science, a system, or a skill, the noun takes a singular pronoun. When the noun names qualities, operations, activities, or individual items, the noun takes a plural pronoun.

SINGULAR   She has chosen to pursue a career in **politics**; she has always shown great interest in **it.** [Politics is thought of as a system.]

PLURAL   Some voters support her **politics,** while other voters oppose **them.** [Politics are thought of as activities or ideas.]

18w. Even when plural in form, the title of a creative work (such as a book, song, movie, or painting) or the name of a country or a city generally takes a singular pronoun.

EXAMPLES   I have just finished reading Nina Otero's **"The Bells of Santa Cruz."** Have you read **it**?

Star Wars is my favorite movie. George Lucas wrote and directed **it.**

The **Netherlands,** also called Holland, is situated on the North Sea; **its** capital is Amsterdam.

Located forty-two miles from the Rio Grande is **Las Cruces,** New Mexico. Not far from **it** is University Park, the home of New Mexico State University.

Avid golfers may enjoy dining at **Caddies** because **it** is designed to resemble a golf course and the menu has a golf theme.

NOTE The names of some organizations, though plural in form, may take singular or plural pronouns. When the name refers to the organization as a unit, it takes a singular pronoun. When the name refers to the members of the organization, it takes a plural pronoun.

SINGULAR   The **Evanstown High School Eagles** won all of **its** football games this year. [The team won as a unit.]

PLURAL   Wearing **their** new uniforms, the **Evanstown High School Eagles** posed for pictures for the yearbook. [The members of the team wore separate uniforms.]

18x. The gender and number of a relative pronoun (such as *who, which,* or *that*) is determined by its antecedent.

EXAMPLES   **Roseanne, who** knows everyone on **her** block, invited the Guerras to a cookout. [*Who* refers to the singular feminine noun *Roseanne*. Therefore, the singular feminine form *her* is used to agree with *who*.]

The **books that** have stains on **them** will be discarded. [*That* refers to the plural neuter noun *books*. Therefore, the plural neuter form *them* is used to agree with *that*.]

18y. An expression of an amount (a measurement, a percentage, or a fraction, for example) may be singular or plural, depending on how it is used.

EXAMPLES   **Five thousand bricks** is a heavy load; **it** almost ruined the truck's suspension. [The bricks are thought of as a unit.]

Five thousand bricks are scattered on the lot. **They** make walking dangerous. [The bricks are thought of separately.]

We have **ten minutes** to take the quiz; **it** is enough time. [The minutes are thought of as a unit.]

We wasted at least **ten minutes.** We spent **them** sharpening our pencils, asking questions, and putting our books away. [The minutes are thought of separately.]

Two thirds of the casserole is gone; **it** is delicious. [The fraction refers to the singular noun *casserole*.]

Two thirds of the apples are rotten; **they** should be thrown out. [The fraction refers to the plural noun *apples*.]

Exercise 6   Proofreading for Pronoun-Antecedent Errors

Each of the following sentences contains an error in pronoun-antecedent agreement. Identify and correct each error.

EXAMPLE   1. The Drama Club is preparing their annual show.

1. *their—its*

1. I read "Ali Baba and the Forty Thieves" and decided to create my own illustrations for them.
2. Bring those pants over here; I'll iron it.
3. We traveled through the Netherlands and across their border into the country of Belgium.

4. Here is where the United Nations meets; their fiftieth anniversary was celebrated in 1995.
5. The sales clerk continued, "Three hundred dollars may seem like a lot, but you'll get a lot of value for them."
6. Thomas is the one who finished their project early.
7. Measles has been held at bay by vaccines, but we must be constantly vigilant against them.
8. If your research requires either a CD-ROM drive or a World Wide Web connection, you will find them in our public library.
9. Around sundown, the herd comes to the river to drink, and they will stay until the lions appear.
10. The band played together for the first time last year, but it had known each other for many years before.

Review E Writing Sentences Demonstrating Agreement

Reference Note

For information on **verb tenses,** see page 664.

Write you own original sentences according to the following instructions. Use verbs in present tense only.

EXAMPLE   1. Write a sentence using singular subjects joined by *nor*.
     1. *Neither Alessandra nor Kim wants to leave the Mediterranean festival.*

1. Write a sentence using a compound subject joined by *and*.
2. Write a sentence beginning with *Many a*.
3. Write a sentence in which a pronoun refers to the noun *electronics*.
4. Write a sentence using a subject referred to by a relative pronoun.
5. Write a sentence using *Everybody* as the subject.
6. Write a sentence using an indefinite pronoun as the subject.
7. Write a sentence using a singular subject and a plural subject joined by *or*.
8. Write a sentence in which the pronoun *their* is used to refer to the subject.
9. Write a sentence using a gerund phrase as the subject.
10. Write a sentence using a singular subject followed by *as well as*.

Chapter Review

A. Identifying Subjects and Verbs That Agree

Identify the subject of the verb in parentheses for each of the following sentences. Then, choose the form that agrees in number with the subject.

1. Asthma, like other respiratory diseases, (*is, are*) made worse when the air quality is poor.
2. Neither of the ballplayers (*expect, expects*) to be drafted.
3. (*Has, Have*) any of the witnesses been sworn in yet?
4. If you have any questions, remember that either Lili or Roberto (*has, have*) experience with these computers.
5. My family (*is, are*) going to Thailand this summer.
6. In the village of San Ildefonso, two days (*is, are*) not considered a long time to spend polishing one piece of black pottery.
7. In recent years there (*has, have*) been many changes in farming.
8. Exactly one third of the students in my American history class (*is, are*) sophomores.
9. A pair of scissors (*was, were*) lying on the counter.
10. Neither the child nor her parents (*want, wants*) to be interviewed.
11. Cavities (*is, are*) one result of not brushing your teeth often enough.
12. *The Censors* (*is, are*) a book of stories by Luisa Valenzuela.
13. How (*do, does*) the wolf get his bad reputation?
14. The laws of physics (*tell, tells*) us that every action of force (*has, have*) an equal and opposite reaction.
15. John Lennon, Paul McCartney, George Harrison, and Ringo Starr (*was, were*) the Beatles.

B. Supplying Pronouns That Agree with Their Antecedents

Complete each of the following sentences by supplying at least one pronoun that agrees with its antecedent. Then, write the antecedent(s). Be sure to use standard, formal English.

16. Everyone has _____ reason for choosing to drive certain models of cars.

17. The words someone uses in daily conversation tell a great deal about _____ background.

18. If either Theo or Tommy calls, tell _____ I need help.

19. When Suzanne and Anita arrive, would you please help _____ find some good seats?

20. Only one of the girls has finished _____ project.

21. Could either Laura or Suzanne stop _____ before hitting the wall of the skating rink?

22. Anyone who wants to participate can leave _____ name with the secretary.

23. The new marching band made _____ debut at the game last night.

24. Just before the game, the director told the band that _____ new uniforms would arrive next week.

25. My aunt is a professor of economics, and she believes that _____ ought to be part of every student's curriculum.

26. Every turtle on the beach dug _____ own nest.

27. Half of the students had never heard of the book before, but _____ were looking forward to reading it.

28. Alfred Hitchcock's film *The Birds* was on television last night; _____ is one of the scariest movies I've ever seen!

29. Keith lowered the binoculars and handed _____ to me.

30. Neither Sean nor his brothers forgot _____ mother's birthday.

C. Choosing Correct Forms for Subject-Verb and Pronoun-Antecedent Agreement

For each sentence in the following paragraph, choose the word in parentheses that will complete the sentence correctly.

Kenny Walker was the only player in the history of the NFL who [**31**] (*was, were*) deaf. The Denver Broncos, my favorite team, [**32**] (*was, were*) smart to choose Walker in the 1990 football draft. Walker certainly [**33**] (*wasn't, weren't*) going to let his deafness keep him from being a great linebacker. Even today, not everyone [**34**] (*know, knows*) that spinal meningitis cost Kenny Walker his hearing when he was two years old. Sign language and lip reading [**35**] (*was, were*) taught to him at a special school, beginning when he was four years old. Because of his hearing impairment, most of the neighborhood boys [36] (*was, were*) unwilling to choose Walker to be on a team. After they saw him play, though, each of them wanted Walker on [37] (*their, his*) team! In all the time that Walker was a professional football player, neither he nor his coaches [38] (*was, were*) much bothered by his deafness. One of the accommodations the Broncos made [39] (*was, were*) to hire an interpreter to sign plays to Walker. Although he couldn't hear a sound on the field, Walker could feel the vibrations in his shoulder pads when the fans in the crowd cheered [40] (*them, him*).

Writing Application

Using Agreement in a Report

Pronoun-Antecedent Agreement   For your term project in history class, you've decided to poll people about what recent events they think will be among the most important events of the decade. Take a poll of at least ten people and write a brief report discussing your findings. Be sure that pronouns you use agree with their antecedents.

Prewriting   First, write down several specific questions that you will ask in your poll. Then, poll your subjects. Be sure to record the answers clearly and accurately and to identify your sources by their full names. After you take your poll, compile lists of the responses.

Writing   As you write your report, identify the answers people gave most frequently to each of your questions. Clearly identify your sources as well as the events you're discussing. You might wrap up your report with a paragraph telling what conclusions you've drawn from the results of the poll.

Revising   Make sure your report follows a clear, logical order. Also be sure you've accurately represented the responses to your poll.

Publishing   Check for pronoun-antecedent agreement, paying special attention to antecedents that are singular indefinite pronouns. Then, proofread your report for any errors in spelling, capitalization, and punctuation. You and your classmates may wish to compile all the responses gathered by your class and present the findings in an article in your school newspaper.

Using Pronouns Correctly
Case Forms of Pronouns

Diagnostic Preview

A. Proofreading Sentences for Correct Pronoun Forms

For each of the following sentences that contains an incorrect pronoun form, identify the error and then give the correct form. If a sentence is already correct, write *C*.

EXAMPLES **1.** Manuel and him are on the soccer team.

 1. him—he

 2. Did you know that he and she are the new captains of the soccer team?

 2. C

1. Debbie is planning a surprise party for Marita, Jorge, and she.

2. Please send Anna and me a copy of the rough draft that you and she wrote.

3. You and I should probably ask Mr. Beauvais because no one speaks French better than him.

4. Tamisha hopes it will be her and Pete who are appointed to the student council.

5. Us students feel much more confident about repairing cars after taking this course.

6. To who did Justin give that picture of Maria Tallchief?

7. Danielle and myself had our bat mitzvahs in the same month, and she and I both did very well reading from the Torah.

8. Mrs. Kitts says that our knowing facts is less important than our knowing where to find them.

9. I really appreciated you picking me up after school today, and I'm glad you can give me a ride tomorrow.

10. Seriously, whom did you expect would win the blue ribbon?

B. Proofreading a Paragraph for Correct Pronoun Forms

Identify each incorrect pronoun form in the following sentences, and then give the correct form. If a sentence contains no errors, write *C*.

EXAMPLES   [1] Meriwether Lewis hired me when him and William Clark set out to explore the Louisiana Territory.

1. *him—he*

[2] The two of them were already famous explorers when my cousin and I joined their expedition.

2. *C*

[11] My cousin John and me were proud to be included in the group that went along with Lewis and Clark. [12] Us cousins were jacks-of-all-trades; both of us did everything from loading pack animals to building campfires. [13] For John and I, one of the best things about the trip was getting to know the other members of the group. [14] Someone who we became good friends with was a strong, friendly man named York. [15] Everyone, including myself, found York to be one of the most fascinating members of the expedition. [16] Many people know that Sacagawea, a Shoshone woman, was an interpreter on the expedition, but York was in many ways as able an interpreter as her. [17] In fact, communicating with the American Indians would have been practically impossible without both Sacagawea and himself. [18] Whenever the expedition met with Native American peoples, Sacagawea would tell her French husband, Charbonneau, what was said between her and them. [19] Charbonneau would then repeat the message in French to York, who would translate the French into English for Lewis, Clark, and the rest of we expedition members. [20] When we needed food and horses, York himself did much of the trading with the Indians because him and them got along very well.

HELP

In Part B of the Diagnostic Preview, there may be more than one error in a sentence.

USAGE

Case

Case is the form that a noun or a pronoun takes to show its relationship to other words in a sentence. In English, there are three cases: *nominative, objective,* and *possessive.*

The form of a noun is the same for both the nominative case and the objective case. For example, a noun used as a subject (nominative case) will have the same form if used as an object (objective case).

NOMINATIVE CASE The **general** explained the strategy. [subject]

OBJECTIVE CASE The strategy was explained by the **general.** [object of the preposition *by*]

A noun changes its form in the possessive case by adding an apostrophe and an *s* to most singular nouns and only the apostrophe to most plural nouns.

Reference Note

For more about **forming possessive nouns,** see page 827.

POSSESSIVE CASE The **general's** explanation was both clear and concise. [singular noun]

Both **generals'** explanations were clear and concise. [plural noun]

Unlike nouns, most personal pronouns have three forms, one for each case. The form a pronoun takes depends on its function in a sentence.

NOMINATIVE CASE **We** listened closely to the directions. [subject]

The winners of the state championship are **they.** [predicate nominative.]

OBJECTIVE CASE The teacher gave **us** a vocabulary quiz. [indirect object]

Grandpa Worthington thanked **him** for picking the peaches in the orchard. [direct object]

Are those flowers for **her**? [object of a preposition]

POSSESSIVE CASE The teacher collected **our** papers. [possessive pronoun]

Within each case, the forms of the personal pronouns indicate *number, person,* and *gender.*

- *Number* tells you whether the pronoun is singular or plural.

- *Person* tells you whether the pronoun refers to the one(s) speaking (*first person*), the one(s) spoken to (*second person*), or the one(s) spoken about (*third person*).

- *Gender* tells you whether the pronoun is *masculine, feminine,* or *neuter* (neither masculine nor feminine).

Personal Pronouns			
	Nominative Case	Objective Case	Possessive Case
Singular			
First Person	I	me	my, mine
Second Person	you	you	your, yours
Third Person	he, she, it	him, her, it	his, her, hers, its
Plural			
First Person	we	us	our, ours
Second Person	you	you	your, yours
Third Person	they	them	their, theirs

Notice in the chart that *you* and *it* have the same forms for the nominative and the objective cases. All other personal pronouns have different forms for each case. Notice also that only third-person singular pronouns indicate gender.

The Nominative Case

The personal pronouns in the nominative case—*I, you, he, she, it, we,* and *they*—are used as subjects of verbs and as predicate nominatives.

19a. The subject of a verb should be in the nominative case.

EXAMPLES **We** ordered the concert tickets. [*We* is the subject of the verb *ordered.*]

Why does **she** think that **they** are too expensive? [*She* is the subject of the verb *does think. They* is the subject of the verb *are.*]

He, she, and Shelby have volunteered at the animal shelter. [*He, she,* and *Shelby* are the compound subject of the verb *have volunteered.*]

Ms. Chang said that **he** and **I** should audition. [*He* and *I* are the compound subject of the verb *should audition.*]

S T Y L E   T I P

Use the neuter pronoun *it* when referring to an animal unless the gender of the animal is made clear by another word in the sentence.

EXAMPLES
A stablehand led the horse to **its** stall.

That rooster is known for **his** bad temper. [The word *rooster* indicates that the animal is male.]

Eileen's cat, Melanie, kept an eye on the guests from **her** lookout post on top of the refrigerator. [The name *Melanie* indicates that the animal is female.]

USAGE

Reference Note
The **personal pronouns** in the nominative case may also be **used as appositives.** See page 550.

Reference Note
For more about **subjects of verbs,** see page 515.

To help you choose the correct pronoun form in a compound subject, try each form separately with the verb.

EXAMPLE

(*She, Her*) and (*I, me*) will make the piñata. [*She will make* or *Her will make? I will make* or *me will make?*]

She and **I** will make the piñata.

Reference Note

For more information about **predicate nominatives,** see page 524.

TIPS & TRICKS

Notice that the predicate nominative and the subject of the verb both indicate the same individual(s). To help you identify the correct pronoun form to use as a predicate nominative, try each form as the subject of the verb.

EXAMPLE

The only applicant for the job was (*he, him*). [*He was* or *him was?*]

The only applicant for the job was **he.**

Oral Practice 1 Using Pronouns as Subjects

Read each of the following sentences aloud, stressing the italicized pronoun(s).

1. *You* and *I* will go to the library this afternoon.
2. *We* and *they* have some research to do on Kiowa culture.
3. Either Terrell or *he* will select a topic about the environment.
4. Neither *they* nor *we* should use periodicals older than three months.
5. Both *she* and *I* will write about modern art.
6. Risa, Irena, and *I* might write about Georgia O'Keeffe.
7. Which playwright did Kaye and *she* select?
8. *She* said that *you* and *they* decided to go camping.

19b. A predicate nominative should be in the nominative case.

A **predicate nominative** is a word or word group in the predicate that identifies the subject or refers to it.

A pronoun used as a predicate nominative generally follows a form of the verb *be: am, is, are, was, were, be,* or *been.*

EXAMPLES   The chairperson of the prom committee is **she.** [*She* follows *is* and identifies the subject *chairperson.*]

The one who made the comment was **I.** [*I* follows *was* and identifies the subject *one.*]

A predicate nominative may be compound, with a pronoun appearing in combination with a noun or another pronoun.

EXAMPLES   The students who auditioned for the role were **he** and **Carlos.** [*He* and *Carlos* identify the subject *students.*]

The two new debaters are **she** and **I.** [*She* and *I* identify the subject *debaters.*]

Exercise 1 Using Pronouns in the Nominative Case

Complete the following sentences by supplying personal pronouns in the nominative case. For each pronoun you add, tell whether it is used as a *subject* or as a *predicate nominative.* Use a variety of pronouns, but do not use *you* or *it.*

EXAMPLE   1. When Charles L. Blockson was a child, _____ was eager to learn about African American heroes.

1. *he—subject*

1. When he told his teachers of his interest, it was _____ who said that there had been very few black heroes.

2. Certain that _____ must be wrong, Blockson started looking for African Americans in history books.

3. He began to collect books, and _____ showed him plenty of heroic black Americans.

4. Black people had not been inactive in shaping American history, he learned; in fact, _____ had played important roles in most of its key events!

5. When Blockson's great-grandfather was just a teenager, _____ had escaped slavery with the help of the Underground Railroad.

6. It was _____ who inspired Blockson's lifelong interest in the Underground Railroad.

7. It may have been my friends Latisha and _____ who read about Blockson's studies in a magazine article and then gave a report in history class.

8. Using Blockson's map as a source, _____ and _____ made this simplified map of the main Underground Railroad routes to freedom.

9. My ancestors escaped from slavery in Kentucky; therefore, as you can see, _____ must have followed one of the main routes to arrive in Detroit.

10. Latisha's great-great-great-grandmother traveled with her younger brother on the Underground Railroad from Virginia to Toronto, and later both _____ and _____ moved to Detroit to find work.

| STYLE | TIP |

Expressions such as *It's me, This is her,* and *It was them* incorrectly use objective case pronouns as predicate nominatives. Although common in everyday situations, such expressions should be avoided in formal speaking and writing.

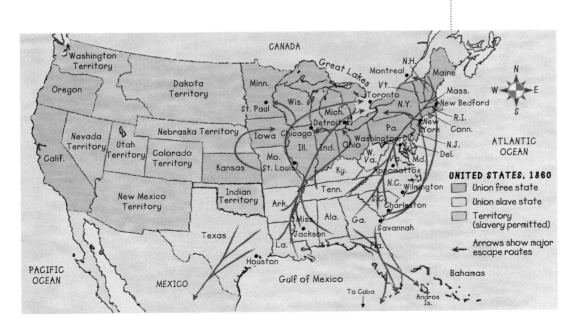

Reference Note

Personal pronouns in the objective case may also be used as appositives. See page 550.

Reference Note

For more about direct objects, see page 521. For more about indirect objects, see page 522.

The Objective Case

The personal pronouns in the objective case—*me, you, him, her, it, us,* and *them*—are used as direct objects, indirect objects, and objects of prepositions.

19c. A direct object should be in the objective case.

A *direct object* tells *who* or *what* receives the action of the verb.

EXAMPLES   My pen pal from Manila visited **me** last summer.

After the nails scattered all over the garage, we picked **them** up.

Can you drive the girls and **us** home from the game tonight?

19d. An indirect object should be in the objective case.

An *indirect object* often appears in sentences containing direct objects and tells *to whom* or *to what* or *for whom* or *for what* the action of the verb is done. The indirect object usually appears between the verb and a direct object.

EXAMPLES   The coach awarded **her** a varsity letter.

We gathered the chickens and gave **them** some feed.

Has Mr. Sims paid **Jason, Tracy,** and **her** their wages?

NOTE   Do not mistake an object of the preposition *to* or *for* for an indirect object.

INDIRECT OBJECT	Louise wrote **me** a letter.
OBJECT OF PREPOSITION	Louise wrote a letter to **me**. [*Me* is the object of the preposition *to.*]

┌ TIPS & TRICKS ┐

To help you choose the correct pronoun form in a compound direct or indirect object, try each form separately with the verb.

EXAMPLES
The new student asked Kelly and (*I, me*) for directions. [*asked I* or *asked me?*]

The new student asked Kelly and **me** for directions.

The editor in chief gave (*he, him*) and (*she, her*) an interesting assignment. [*gave he* or *gave him? gave she* or *gave her?*]

The editor in chief gave **him** and **her** an interesting assignment.

Oral Practice 2 Using Pronouns in the Objective Case

Read the following sentences aloud, stressing the italicized pronouns.

1. The judges chose Carmen and *me.*
2. Do you think that they will provide *us* with what we need?
3. Call either *her* or Rhea about the yearbook deadline.
4. *Him* I like, but don't ask *me* about the others.
5. These instructions confuse my brother and *me.*
6. Give the other girls and *her* the chemistry assignment.
7. Were they accusing *them* or *us?*
8. The success of the car wash surprised Mr. Kahn and *him.*

Exercise 2 Using Pronouns in the Objective Case

Complete the following sentences by supplying personal pronouns in the objective case. For each pronoun you add, tell whether it is used as a *direct object* or an *indirect object*. Use a variety of pronouns, but do not use *you* or *it*.

EXAMPLE 1. Marcia drove _____ to the civic center.

    1. *us—direct object*

1. Have you given Nick and _____ the reading list?
2. Did Bob show _____ his autographed copy of Amy Tan's latest book?
3. Mrs. Martin handed Lena, Chris, and _____ their notebooks.
4. Our teacher has already graded Latoya and _____ on our oral reports to the class.
5. Ms. Guerra has invited both _____ and _____ to the Independence Day Festival.
6. Would you please lend _____ and her the manual for the fax machine?
7. During practice today, the coach taught Patricia and _____ the proper form for the inward dive.
8. The play gave _____ some ideas for a skit.
9. My mother is picking up both you and _____.
10. Please tell _____ about the plans for the junior prom.

19e. An object of a preposition should be in the objective case.

The *object of a preposition* is a noun or pronoun that follows a preposition. The preposition, its object, and any modifiers of the object make a *prepositional phrase.*

EXAMPLES   for **me**   after **her**   next to **them**

    with **us**   beside **him**   between **you** and **me**

Reference Note

For more discussion of **prepositional phrases,** see page 536.

Exercise 3 Selecting Pronouns Used as Objects of Prepositions

For each of the following sentences, choose the correct form of the pronoun in parentheses.

EXAMPLE 1. The Irish terrier belongs to (*she, her*).

    1. *her*

1. Would you like to play baseball with Eugenio and (*me, I*)?
2. These photographs were taken by Dwight and (*she, her*).

TIPS & TRICKS

To help you choose the correct pronoun form in a compound object of a preposition, try each form separately with the preposition.

EXAMPLES
Please return these video-tapes to Mr. Mehta and (*she, her*). [*to she* or *to her?*]

Please return these video-tapes to Mr. Mehta and **her.**

They want to go camping with (*he, him*) and (*I, me*). [*with he* or *with him? with I* or *with me?*]

They want to go camping with **him** and **me.**

3. We can rely on Theresa and (*he, him*) for their help.
4. Would you like to sit next to Elaine and (*me, I*)?
5. There has been much cooperation between the Hispanic Chamber of Commerce and (*we, us*).
6. On the basketball court, teammates like Dave and (*he, him*) seem to read each other's minds.
7. The closing lines of the play will be spoken by you and (*she, her*).
8. We have been studying the early settlers from England and learning about the help that American Indian peoples gave to (*them, they*).
9. Most of the credit belongs to (*we, us*).
10. Steer the ship between the lighthouse and (*them, they*).

Review A **Choosing Correct Forms of Personal Pronouns**

For each sentence in the following paragraph, choose the correct form of the pronoun in parentheses. Then, tell whether the pronoun is used as a *subject*, a *predicate nominative*, a *direct object*, an *indirect object*, or an *object of a preposition*.

EXAMPLE   During our vacation in Mexico, my grandmother, her brother Luís, and **[1]** (*I, me*) visited the Oaxaca Valley.

1. *I—subject*

The state of Oaxaca is where **[1]** (*they, them*) and their two older brothers were born. As we drove through Arrazola, their village, Uncle Luís was amazed to find well-built brick homes where all of **[2]** (*we, us*) had expected to see bamboo houses. Turning to Grandma, **[3]** (*he, him*) exclaimed, "Something good has happened here, Nita!" After visiting Arrazola, my relatives and **[4]** (*I, me*) drove to the city of Oaxaca, which is the state capital, and strolled along its main street. I pointed out some painted woodcarvings to Grandma and showed **[5]** (*she, her*) and Uncle Luís the ones I liked best. I took this picture of a pair of carved dancing chickens and decided it would be **[6]** (*they, them*) or a wooden alligator playing a horn that I'd buy for a souvenir. While I was making up my mind, Uncle Luís spoke to the shopkeeper, asking questions of **[7]** (*he, him*) and his wife. It seems that not long before, a local man named Manuel Jiménez had started making colorful wooden figures and had been selling **[8]** (*they, them*) to tourists. Seeing his success, others in the Oaxaca Valley began carving, too, and within a few years **[9]** (*they, them*) and their fanciful woodcarvings had become famous. The imagination, skill, and hard work of Oaxaca's people have rapidly brought [**10**] (*they, them*) out of poverty.

The Possessive Case

The personal pronouns in the possessive case—*my, mine, your, yours, his, her, hers, its, our, ours, their,* and *theirs*—are used to show ownership or possession.

19f. The possessive pronouns *mine, yours, his, hers, its, ours,* and *theirs* are used in the same ways that the pronouns in the nominative and the objective cases are used.

SUBJECT	Your car and **mine** need to be washed.
PREDICATE NOMINATIVE	This yearbook is **hers.**
DIRECT OBJECT	We ordered **ours** yesterday.
INDIRECT OBJECT	Ms. Kwan gave **theirs** a quick look.
OBJECT OF A PREPOSITION	Next to **yours,** my Siamese cat looks puny.

19g. The possessive pronouns *my, your, his, her, its, our,* and *their* are used to modify nouns.

EXAMPLES   **My** watch is broken.

His first public performance as a concert pianist was in 1998.

Do you know **their** address?

19h. A noun or pronoun that precedes a gerund should be in the possessive case.

A *gerund* is a verb form that ends in *–ing* and functions as a noun. Since a gerund acts as a noun, the noun or pronoun that comes before it must be in the possessive case in order to modify the gerund.

EXAMPLES   We were all thrilled by **Joetta's** scoring in the top 5 percent. [*Joetta's* modifies the gerund *scoring.* Whose scoring? Joetta's scoring.]

His parents objected to **his** working late on school nights. [*His* modifies the gerund *working.* Whose working? His working.]

Their winning the state championship led to a week-long celebration. [*Their* modifies the gerund *winning.* Whose winning? Their winning.]

STYLE   TIP

As a matter of courtesy, first-person pronouns are placed at the end of compound constructions.

NOMINATIVE CASE
Nia and **I** went to the hockey game.

OBJECTIVE CASE
My aunt Evanda met Nia and **me** outside the hockey arena.

POSSESSIVE CASE
Aunt Evanda bought Nia's ticket and **mine.**

USAGE

Reference Note
For more about **gerunds,** see page 543.

The form of a noun or pronoun before an *–ing* word often depends on the meaning you want to express. If you want to emphasize the *–ing* word, use the possessive form. If you want to emphasize the noun or pronoun preceding the *–ing* word, do not use the possessive form. Notice the difference in meaning between the two sentences below.

EXAMPLES
The **pep squad's** dancing got the most applause. [emphasis on the gerund *dancing*]

The **pep squad** dancing got the most applause. [emphasis on *pep squad*, not on the participle *dancing*]

NOTE   Do not confuse a gerund with a present participle, which is also a verb form that ends in *–ing*. A gerund acts as a noun; a present participle serves as an adjective. A noun or pronoun that is modified by a present participle should not be in the possessive case.

EXAMPLE   We found him **sitting on a bench in the park.** [*Him* is modified by the participial phrase *sitting on a bench in the park.*]

Exercise 4 **Using Pronouns with Gerunds and Present Participles**

For each of the following sentences, identify the *–ing* word as either a *gerund* or a *present participle* and then choose the correct noun or pronoun in parentheses. Be prepared to explain your choices. [Hint: Some sentences may be correctly completed in more than one way.]

EXAMPLE   1. Jody saw (*us, our*) standing on the corner and waved.

1. *present participle—us*

1. Hao didn't see the huge, green wave until she felt (*it, its*) crashing over her shoulders.
2. I like my stepfather, but I just can't get used to (*him, his*) cooking.
3. The baby reached out to touch all the shiny (*ribbons, ribbon's*) decorating the gift.
4. (*He, His*) being sarcastic has ruined our chance to win the debate.
5. Do you mind (*me, my*) telling Dave that you entered the essay contest?
6. We could barely hear (*them, their*) singing over the music.
7. Pablo Neruda's political career didn't interfere with (*him, his*) writing.
8. Make (*you, your*) exercising a top priority.
9. Have you tasted the new (*chef, chef's*) cooking?
10. Several little (*boys, boys'*) dancing in traditional finery did their best to master the intricacies of the Zuni dance.

Special Pronoun Problems

Appositives

An ***appositive*** is a noun or a pronoun placed beside another noun or pronoun to identify or describe it.

19i. **A pronoun used as an appositive is in the same case as the word to which it refers.**

EXAMPLES   My best friends, **Raúl and she,** have been nominated for class treasurer. [*Raúl* and *she* are appositives identifying the subject *friends.* Since a subject is in the nominative case, an appositive identifying a subject is in the nominative case.]

My grandfather paid the two boys, **Mario** and **him,** for raking leaves. [*Mario* and *him* are appositives identifying the direct object *boys.* Since a direct object is in the objective case, an appositive identifying a direct object is in the objective case.]

To identify which pronoun form to use as an appositive, try each form in the position of the word to which it refers.

EXAMPLES   Two juniors, Erin and (*she, her*), conducted the survey. [*she conducted* or *her conducted?*]

Two juniors, Erin and **she,** conducted the survey.

The survey was conducted by two juniors, Erin and (*she, her*). [*by she* or *by her?*]

The survey was conducted by two juniors, Erin and **her.**

Reference Note

For more information about **appositives,** see page 550.

NOTE   Sometimes the pronoun *we* or *us* is followed by an appositive. To determine which pronoun form to use, try each form without the appositive.

EXAMPLES   (*We, Us*) students learned many interesting facts about our solar system. [*We learned* or *Us learned?*]

We students learned many interesting facts about our solar system.

The guidance counselor talked to (*we, us*) students. [*to we* or *to us?*]

The guidance counselor talked to **us** students.

Exercise 5   Using Appositives in Sentences

For each item, write a sentence using the given word group in the way specified in parentheses. Supply a pronoun in the correct case for each blank.

EXAMPLE   1. my neighbors, _____ and Steven (*indirect object*)
            1. *We gave my neighbors, her and Steven, a ride to the football game.*

1. the two star players, _____ and Kelly (*direct object*)
2. _____ and _____, the loudest fans (*subject*)

3. _____ Tigers boosters (*object of a preposition*)
4. _____ juniors (*predicate nominative*)
5. the world's best coaches, _____ and Mr. Gresham (*indirect object*)
6. _____ running backs (*predicate nominative*)
7. the head cheerleaders, _____ and _____ (*indirect object*)
8. _____ defensive linemen (*direct object*)
9. _____ and _____, the referees (*subject*)
10. Daniel and _____, the two band captains (*object of preposition*)

Pronouns in Elliptical Constructions

Reference Note

For more information about **elliptical constructions,** see page 566.

An *elliptical construction* is a word group, usually a clause, from which words have been omitted. The word *than* or *as* often begins an elliptical construction.

19j. A pronoun following *than* or *as* in an elliptical construction is in the same case as it would be if the construction were completed.

ELLIPTICAL   Jo said Ann was more frustrated **than he.**
COMPLETED   Jo said Ann was more frustrated **than he was frustrated.**

ELLIPTICAL   The assignment frustrated me as much **as him.**
COMPLETED   The assignment frustrated me as much **as it frustrated him.**

The pronoun form in an elliptical construction determines the meaning of the construction. Be sure to use the pronoun form that expresses the meaning you intend. Notice how the meaning of each of the following sentences depends on the pronoun form in the elliptical construction.

EXAMPLES   Dan misses New York more **than her.** [Dan misses New York more *than Dan misses her.*]

Dan misses New York more **than she.** [Dan misses New York more *than she misses New York.*]

Did Mr. Matsuda pay you as much **as I**? [Did Mr. Matsuda pay you as much *as I paid you?*]

Did Mr. Matsuda pay you as much **as me**? [Did Mr. Matsuda pay you as much *as he paid me?*]

Exercise 6 Selecting Pronouns for Elliptical Constructions

Add words to complete the elliptical construction in each of the following sentences. Include in the construction the appropriate pronoun form. Then, tell whether the pronoun is a *subject* or an *object*.

USAGE

EXAMPLE   1. Jo works longer hours than (*I, me*).

     1. *than I work—subject*

1. No one else in my class is as shy as (*I, me*).
2. The editors of our newspaper have written as much as (*they, them*).
3. Can you whistle as loudly as (*he, him*)?
4. If you want to sell more raffle tickets than Bradley, you should make more phone calls than (*he, him*).
5. My coach told me that I had more agility than (*she, her*).
6. We were all more eager than (*he, him*).
7. I am more interested in Spike Lee's films than (*she, her*).
8. Judges in the salsa dance contest presented Estella with a larger trophy than (*I, me*).
9. They sent Lois as many get-well cards as (*I, me*).
10. No one gave more time to good causes than (*she, her*).

HELP

Some of the elliptical constructions in Exercise 6 may be completed in more than one way; you need to give only one way of completing each.

Reflexive and Intensive Pronouns

Reflexive and intensive pronouns (sometimes called *compound personal pronouns*) have the same forms.

Reflexive and Intensive Pronouns		
	Singular	**Plural**
First Person	myself	ourselves
Second Person	yourself	yourselves
Third Person	himself, herself, itself	themselves

A ***reflexive pronoun*** refers to the subject of the verb and functions as a complement or an object of a preposition.

EXAMPLES   Bill is not **himself** today. [*Himself* refers to *Bill* and functions as a predicate nominative.]

I hurt **myself**. [*Myself* refers to *I* and functions as a direct object.]

The cat gave **itself** a bath. [*Itself* refers to *cat* and functions as an indirect object.]

She would rather be by **herself**. [*Herself* refers to *she* and functions as the object of the preposition *by.*]

Reference Note

The words *hisself* and *theirselves* are nonstandard forms. See page 734.

USAGE

19 j

Special Pronoun Problems **617**

Unlike a reflexive pronoun, an intensive pronoun may be omitted from a sentence without changing its basic meaning.

EXAMPLE
The children decorated the gym themselves. [*The children decorated the gym* makes sense without the pronoun. Therefore, the pronoun is intensive.]

HELP

If the sentence is imperative, the subject *you* may be understood.

An ***intensive pronoun*** emphasizes its antecedent and has no grammatical function in the sentence.

EXAMPLES   My grandfather and I restored the car **ourselves.** [*Ourselves* emphasizes *grandfather* and *I.*]

The weather **itself** seemed to be our enemy. [*Itself* emphasizes *weather.*]

19k. A pronoun ending in *–self* or *–selves* should not be used in place of a personal pronoun.

NONSTANDARD	Rena and myself mow lawns in the summer.
STANDARD	Rena and **I** mow lawns in the summer.

NONSTANDARD	Did Rosa make lunch for herself and yourself?
STANDARD	Did Rosa make lunch for herself and **you**?

Exercise 7 **Using Reflexive and Intensive Pronouns Correctly**

For each of the following sentences, identify the italicized pronoun as *intensive* or *reflexive*. Then, give the word or words that the pronoun refers to or emphasizes.

EXAMPLE   1. Ruthie taught *herself* how to make the special beads she wanted for her beadwork.

1. *reflexive—Ruthie*

1. Will the president *himself* preside at the welcoming ceremony for the foreign leaders?
2. Maria and Giorgio should be proud of *themselves.*
3. The store manager found the address of a lumberyard for us, but we had to order the materials *ourselves.*
4. To celebrate their anniversary, Mom and Dad bought *themselves* a couple of theater tickets.
5. I hurt *myself* building that fence.
6. Standing atop a hill all by *itself,* a full-grown stag can be a truly impressive sight.
7. Imagine *yourself* setting sail across the Ionian Sea.
8. Muriel *herself* replaced the shingles on the roof.
9. After I yelled at my little brother, I felt ashamed of *myself* and apologized.
10. The bear *itself* removed all the garbage from the dumpster and tossed the litter all over the ground.

Who and Whom

Like most personal pronouns, the pronoun *who* (*whoever*) has different case forms.

Nominative Case	who	whoever
Objective Case	whom	whomever
Possessive Case	whose	whosever

These pronouns may be used to form questions and to introduce subordinate clauses.

NOTE When *who*, *whom*, and *whose* are used to introduce adjective clauses, they are called **relative pronouns**.

EXAMPLES **Whom** did you get to take care of your cats while you were gone?

Who gave you that beautiful bracelet?

This prize will go to **whoever** collects the most items.

Yes, I am the one **who** wrote that poem.

In questions, *who* is used as a subject or as a predicate nominative. *Whom* is used as a direct object, an indirect object, or an object of a preposition.

NOMINATIVE **Who** played this role on Broadway? [*Who* is the subject of the verb *played.*]

Who could it have been? [*Who* is a predicate nominative referring to the subject *it.*]

OBJECTIVE **Whom** did the president recommend? [*Whom* is the direct object of the verb *did recommend.*]

Whom did you ask the question? [*Whom* is the indirect object of the verb *did ask.*]

For **whom** did E. E. Cummings write that poem? [*Whom* is the object of the preposition *For.*]

When choosing between *who* and *whom* in a subordinate clause, follow these steps:

STEP 1: Find the subordinate clause.

STYLE TIP

In informal English, the use of *whom* is gradually disappearing. In informal situations, it is acceptable to begin a question with *who* regardless of whether the nominative or objective form is grammatically correct. In formal speaking and writing, though, it is still important to distinguish between *who* and *whom*.

USAGE

STYLE TIP

Frequently, *whom* is omitted from subordinate clauses but is still understood.

EXAMPLE
The boys [*whom*] you met are brothers.

Leaving out *whom* tends to make writing sound informal. In formal situations, it is generally better to include *whom*.

Reference Note

For more information about **subordinate clauses,** see page 559.

STEP 2: Decide how the pronoun is used in the clause—as a *subject, predicate nominative, direct object, indirect object,* or *object of a preposition.*

STEP 3: Determine the case for this use of the pronoun.

STEP 4: Select the correct case form of the pronoun.

EXAMPLE Ms. Gonzalez, (*who, whom*) I greatly admire, operates a shelter for homeless people in our community.

STEP 1: The subordinate clause is (*who, whom*) *I greatly admire.*

STEP 2: The pronoun serves as the direct object of the verb *admire.* [I greatly admire (*who, whom*).]

STEP 3: A direct object is in the objective case.

STEP 4: The objective form of the pronoun is *whom.*

ANSWER: Ms. Gonzalez, **whom** I greatly admire, operates a shelter for homeless people in our community.

The case of a pronoun in a subordinate clause is not affected by any word outside the subordinate clause.

EXAMPLE The prize goes to (*whoever, whomever*) is the first to solve the riddles.

STEP 1: The subordinate clause is (*whoever, whomever*) *is the first to solve the riddles.*

STEP 2: The pronoun serves as the subject of the verb *is,* not the object of the preposition *to.* (The entire clause is the object of the preposition *to.*)

STEP 3: A subject of a verb is in the nominative case.

STEP 4: The nominative form of the pronoun is *whoever.*

ANSWER: The prize goes to **whoever** is the first to solve the riddles.

NOTE When choosing between *who* and *whom* to begin a question or a subordinate clause, do not be misled by an expression consisting of a subject and a verb, such as *I think, do you suppose, he feels,* or *they believe.* Select the pronoun form you would use if the expression were not in the sentence.

EXAMPLES **Who** do you think will win the Super Bowl? [*Who* is the subject of the verb *will win.*]

She is the one **whom** we believe they will elect. [*Whom* is the direct object of the verb *will elect.*]

Ed is the student **who** I feel will be valedictorian. [*Who* is the subject of the verb *will be.*]

USAGE

Exercise 8   Using *Who* and *Whom* Correctly

Choose the correct form of the pronoun in parentheses in each of the following sentences. Then, tell how the pronoun is used in the sentence—as a *subject*, a *predicate nominative*, a *direct object*, an *indirect object*, or an *object of a preposition*.

EXAMPLE **1.** Here are the names of some of the authors (*who, whom*) we will study this semester.

　　　1. *whom—direct object*

1. Betty Smith, the author of *A Tree Grows in Brooklyn*, was an obscure writer (*who, whom*) became a celebrity overnight.

2. Her novel is an American classic about a young girl (*who, whom*) she called Francie Nolan.

3. Francie, (*who, whom*) we follow through girlhood to adulthood, has only one tree in her city backyard.

4. Carson McCullers, (*who, whom*) critics describe as a major American writer, also wrote a novel about a young girl's coming of age.

5. (*Who, Whom*) could not be moved by *The Member of the Wedding*?

6. Do you know (*who, whom*) the actor was that played Frankie in the Broadway production of *The Member of the Wedding*?

7. Pearl Buck is a novelist with (*who, whom*) most Americans are familiar.

8. Pulitzer Prizes are awarded to (*whoever, whomever*) is selected by the panel of judges.

9. Gwendolyn Brooks, (*who, whom*) you told me won the Pulitzer Prize for poetry, also wrote a book called *Maud Martha*.

10. (*Who, Whom*) did you ask the question about who Maud Martha really is?

Review B   Selecting Correct Forms of Pronouns

Choose the correct form of the pronoun in parentheses in each sentence in the following paragraph.

EXAMPLE Ms. Kent talked with Jordan and **[1]** (*I, me*) about the artwork of some famous Impressionists.

　　　1. *me*

　Jordan and **[1]** (*I, me*) had thought of Impressionism as a French style of painting, and for the most part, we were right. Every artist, however, is influenced by other artists, regardless of **[2]** (*their, theirs*) nationality. If you have heard of Edgar Degas, you might know that

COMPUTER TIP

You can use the search function of a word-processing program to find each use of *who* and *whom* in a document. Then, you can double-check to make sure that you have used the correct form of the pronoun in each instance.

Link to Literature

USAGE

both [3] (*he, him*) and the American Impressionist Mary Cassatt were very much influenced by exhibitions of Japanese prints that came to Paris. At first glance, Impressionist paintings don't resemble Japanese works, but just look at [4] (*they, them*) placed side by side, and you can see strong parallels. This morning, Ms. Kent pointed out some of those stylistic similarities to Jordan and [5] (*me, myself*), using the paintings shown on this page. Neither of [6] (*we, us*) art lovers could possibly mistake the resemblance. "Just between you and [7] (*I, me*)," said Ms. Kent, "almost all of the Impressionists openly copied ideas from the Japanese." One of my favorite painters is Toulouse-Lautrec, [8] (*who, whom*) often used the Japanese technique of including a large object in the extreme foreground to lend a feeling of depth to a picture. Both Mary Cassatt and [9] (*he, him*) learned from the Japanese the principle of cutting figures at the edge of the canvas to achieve a snapshot-like quality. As you can see, the Japanese technique of juxtaposing different patterned fabrics appealed to Mary Cassatt, and this technique was used by Pierre Bonnard as well as by [10] (*she, her*).

Andro Hiroshige, *Branch of a Flowering Apple Tree.* Color woodcut. Paris, Galerie Janette Ostier/Giraudon/Art Resource, New York.

Toulouse-Lautrec, *Jane Avril* (1893). Albi, Musée Toulouse-Lautrec/Scala/Art Resource, New York.

Mary Cassatt, *The Letter.* The Metropolitan Museum of Art, Gift of Arthur Sachs, 1916.

Japanese woodcut. Victoria and Albert Museum, London/Art Resource, New York.

Review C Proofreading Sentences for Correct Pronoun Forms

For each of the following sentences that contains an incorrect pronoun form, identify the error and then give the correct form. If a sentence is already correct, write *C*.

EXAMPLE   1. Neither Karl nor myself could find the book.

     1. *myself—I*

1. I thought that Beth and her would make the best officers.
2. Both her father and herself have artistic talent.
3. I can't understand his dropping out of the marching band during his senior year.
4. The new exchange students from Switzerland, Michelle and her, already speak some English.
5. Robert's parents have no objection to him trying to get a job at the gas station after school.
6. Many farm workers voted for Cesar Chavez, who they knew would fight for their rights.
7. They have many more CDs than us.
8. The title of salutatorian goes to whomever has the second-highest grade-point average.
9. Who is supposed to sit in this empty seat between Lauren and I?
10. Who do you suppose won the traditional dance contest at the powwow?

Review D Selecting Correct Forms of Pronouns

Choose the correct form of each pronoun in parentheses in the following paragraph. Be prepared to explain your choices.

EXAMPLE   You have the same features in almost exactly the same positions as [1] (*I, me*), yet nearly anyone can easily tell our faces apart.

     1. *I*

[1] (*Whom, Who*) do you think the pictures on the next page represent? Reuben thought the one on the right was a woman, and I told him I was surprised at [2] (*him, his*) not recognizing [3] (*who, whom*) it is! You should give [4] (*yourself, you*) a round of applause if you guessed George Washington. Both of these pictures were created when a scientist named Leon D. Harmon asked [5] (*himself, him*) how much information people actually need to recognize a face. [6] (*He, Him*) and his

┌─HELP──
In the example sentence, the features *you have* are compared to the features *I* [have]. Adding the verb makes it clear that *I* is the subject and should be in the nominative case.

colleagues took photographs of famous portraits, divided each photo into squares, and then averaged the color and brightness inside each square into a single tone. The computer-generated image gives you and [7] (*I, me*) very little information—there are no features and no outlines, only a pattern of colored blocks. Although we can't see the eyes, nose, and mouth, the chances of [8] (*us, our*) recognizing a particular human face are very high. For the picture on the left, Reuben was a better guesser than [9] (*I, me*), especially when I held the page a few feet from his eyes. Suddenly, he saw the [10] (*Mona Lisa, Mona Lisa's*) looking back at him!

Ed Manning, Blocpix, Stratford, CT.

Ed Manning, Blocpix, Stratford, CT.

Chapter Review

A. Selecting Correct Forms of Pronouns

Choose the correct form of the pronoun in parentheses in each of the following sentences. Base your answers on standard, formal usage.

1. Because of the impending storm, (*us, we*) three decided to postpone our plans for the picnic.
2. It's easy to write about someone (*who, whom*) you know well.
3. The most difficult task remained for Lisle and (*I, me*).
4. No one worked harder on the campaign than (*she, her*).
5. Mr. and Mrs. Sandoval had duplicate photographs made for themselves and for (*me, myself*).
6. Vince and (*I, me*) have been classmates since kindergarten.
7. I saw (*you, your*) helping Ignacio in the kitchen.
8. (*Who, Whom*) did Elissa see in front of the theater?
9. I am certain that the scholarship winner will be (*him, he*).
10. Did you ask (*who, whom*) was at the front door?
11. This afternoon the talent committee will audition Tina and (*myself, me*).
12. As I waited for the elevator, I heard the receptionist say, "(*Who, Whom*) shall I say is calling?"
13. The best tennis players in school are my cousin Adele and (*he, him*).
14. I helped Two Bear and (*she, her*) take down the tepee.
15. We have the same kind of blender in our kitchen as they do in (*their, theirs*).

B. Proofreading Sentences for Correct Pronoun Forms

Each of the following sentences contains incorrect pronoun usage. Identify each incorrect pronoun. Then, write the form that is correct according to standard, formal usage. Some sentences may have more than one error.

16. Neither Lee nor me lost the tools.

17. Kyoko and I are the students whom our teacher says will represent our class in the competition.
18. Just between you and I, I think he gave the wrong answer.
19. The two whom could win the award are Carlos and him.
20. Will Michael and him cut the lawn today?
21. She encouraged the rest of we students to work harder.
22. Aaron and Rene, who I rely upon, are both home sick today.
23. Grandma lent Martin and I enough money that we could go Christmas shopping.
24. Jimi and her always finish their math assignments sooner than me.
25. I asked Fernando and she to go to the art show with me.
26. Because Alberto and them have taken dancing lessons, they were chosen to be in the chorus line.
27. Our math teacher strongly objects to us yelling out answers during class.
28. My great-grandmother taught we children about life in post-World War II Cuba.
29. Us student filmmakers should pool our resources and buy a camera.
30. When we were small, Ellie always got into more trouble than me.

C. Proofreading a Paragraph for Correct Pronoun Forms

The following paragraph contains errors in pronoun usage. Identify each incorrect pronoun form, and then write the form that is correct according to the rules of standard, formal usage. If a sentence is already correct, write *C*.

[31] Do you know whom won the Nobel Prize for literature in 1991? [32] The winner was Nadine Gordimer, my favorite writer. [33] She is a South African writer whose novels and short stories have brought herself much renown. [34] She winning the Nobel Prize helped to bring attention to the problem of apartheid in South Africa. [35] Few writers have been as skilled at exposing injustice as her. [36] In 1974, two writers, Stanley Middleton and her, won an important British literary award, the Booker Prize. [37] Her 1979 novel, *Burger's Daughter,* is the story of a young white woman and her activist father and how apartheid affects she as well as him. [38] After her father is imprisoned,

the daughter has mixed feelings about him opposing apartheid. **[39]** Gordimer's 1994 novel, *None to Accompany Me,* is about a woman who tries to achieve self-understanding through political activism in postapartheid South Africa. **[40]** Perhaps now you understand why my favorite writer is her.

Writing Application
Using Pronouns Correctly in a Letter

Who and Whom   Your school's newspaper is planning a special feature on outstanding students. Write a letter to the editor, describing a student at your school and explaining what makes him or her outstanding. In your letter, use *who* (or *whoever*) three times and *whom* (or *whomever*) twice.

Prewriting   Decide who you think is the most outstanding student at your school. Then, jot down some notes on the qualities and achievements that make this person special. Note a few specific examples of the person's behavior that illustrate these qualities.

Writing   Begin by naming the person and telling briefly why he or she should be featured in the newspaper. Then, give the examples you listed in your notes. You may also want to tell an anecdote that shows the person's special qualities.

Revising   Is your letter clear and convincing? If not, you will need to revise your examples or replace them with more engaging ones. Be sure each of your examples supports your description of the person.

Publishing   Does your letter follow one of the correct forms for a business letter? Proofread your paragraph carefully. Take extra care with pronouns, making sure that each of them is in the correct case. You and your classmates may want to create your own "Wall of Fame." Collect your letters and, perhaps, some photographs of the outstanding students about whom you have written, and arrange the letters and photos in a bulletin board display.

USAGE

Reference Note

For more information on **writing business letters,** see "Writing" in the Quick Reference Handbook.

Clear Reference
Pronouns and Antecedents

Diagnostic Preview

A. Correcting Faulty Pronoun References

The following sentences contain examples of ambiguous, general, weak, and indefinite references. Revise each sentence, correcting the faulty pronoun reference.

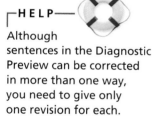

┌HELP─

Although sentences in the Diagnostic Preview can be corrected in more than one way, you need to give only one revision for each.

EXAMPLE   **1.** My grandparents walk five miles every day. It is one of the best forms of exercise.

    1. My grandparents walk five miles every day. Walking is one of the best forms of exercise.

1. If the phone rings again this evening, ask them please not to call anymore.
2. The German shepherds chased deer until they were quite exhausted.
3. We hiked almost fourteen miles to the campsite, pitched our tents, arranged our sleeping bags, and then made our supper. This was so exhausting that we immediately went to sleep.
4. Many of our presidents began their political careers as minor public officials, which is a good thing.
5. Maria told Joan that her bicycle had a flat tire.
6. In *Mama's Bank Account,* it describes how a Norwegian American family lives in San Francisco.
7. When we saw the flock of geese during the guided tour, they told us that they had flown all the way from northern Canada.
8. Jan liked the Wynton Marsalis tape but was disappointed that it didn't include her favorite one.

9. The shipwrecked men paddled their raft with their hands day after day, but this brought them no closer to land.

10. In northern regions, far away from city lights, you can frequently see the aurora borealis.

B. Correcting Faulty Pronoun References

Most of the following sentences contain ambiguous, general, weak, or indefinite references. Revise each faulty sentence. If a sentence is already correct, write *C*.

EXAMPLE   **1.** Carl Sagan praised Stephen W. Hawking after he wrote *A Brief History of Time.*

    1. Carl Sagan praised Stephen W. Hawking after Hawking wrote A Brief History of Time.

11. In Sagan's review of the book, it calls Hawking one of the greatest physicists of the twentieth century.

12. Hawking's 1988 book about physics and the universe became a bestseller, which was surprising.

13. Jaime told Rick that he should have read Hawking's chapter about black holes in space before writing his report.

14. Whenever Francine reads a good book about science, she always wants to become one of them.

15. According to Hawking, Galileo was a talented science writer. One of these was the work *Two New Sciences,* the basis of modern physics.

16. In this magazine article on Hawking, they tell about his personal battle with motor neuron disease.

17. Because the disease affects his speech and movement, Hawking wrote his book by using a voice synthesizer and a personal computer.

18. Even though Hawking carefully explains his theories on the thermodynamic and cosmological arrows of time, it still confuses some readers.

19. That Hawking apparently understands the applications of Einstein's theories to time and the universe does not seem astonishing.

20. One question Hawking has tried to answer is this: If you were to drop a book into a black hole, would the information in the book be destroyed?

USAGE

Reference Note

For more information about **pronouns and antecedents,** see page 487.

In most cases, a pronoun has no definite meaning in itself. Its meaning is clear only when the reader knows to which word or words the pronoun refers. This word or word group is called the *antecedent* of the pronoun.

20a. A pronoun should refer clearly to its antecedent.

In the following examples, arrows point from the pronouns to their antecedents.

EXAMPLES   Peg asked **Leonardo** to tell her what the surprise was, but **he** refused.

The math teacher gave **us** a problem that **we** couldn't solve.

After trying on the **dress,** Mary said, "**This** fits perfectly."

Ambiguous Reference

20b. Avoid an *ambiguous reference,* which occurs when any one of two or more words could be a pronoun's antecedent.

AMBIGUOUS   Colleen called Alicia while she was doing her homework. [The antecedent of *she* and *her* is unclear. Who was doing her homework, Colleen or Alicia?]

CLEAR   While Colleen was doing her homework, she called Alicia.

CLEAR   While Alicia was doing her homework, Colleen called her.

AMBIGUOUS   The ship's officer explained to the passenger the meaning of the regulation he had just read. [The antecedent of *he* is unclear. Who had just read the regulation?]

CLEAR   After the ship's officer read the regulation, he explained its meaning to the passenger.

CLEAR   After reading the regulation, the ship's officer explained its meaning to the passenger.

CLEAR   After the passenger read the regulation, the ship's officer explained its meaning to him.

Exercise 1   **Correcting Ambiguous References**

Revise each of the sentences on the next page to correct the ambiguous pronoun reference.

USAGE

EXAMPLE   1. When the ship struck the dock, it burst into flames.
            1. *When it struck the dock, the ship burst into flames.*
                                    or
                The dock burst into flames when the ship struck it.

1. The loyal forces fought the guerrillas until they were almost entirely destroyed.
2. The police officer told the sergeant that a button was missing from her uniform.
3. The guide explained to the tourist the value of the stone that she had found.
4. Leon told Carlos that his report would be better if he added more details about Cesar Chavez.
5. When Anna brought Lena to the conference, we asked her for her press credentials.
6. Since the show was scheduled for the same night as the intramural playoff game, it had to be postponed.
7. The manager told the dishwasher to be more careful because he would have to replace all the broken dishes.
8. When the ambassador joined the foreign minister, reporters thought he looked confident.
9. When the truck hit the wall, it was hardly damaged.
10. The Black History Month schedule was in my bag, but somebody took it.

┌─HELP─
Although sentences in Exercise 1 can be corrected in more than one way, you need to give only one revision for each.

USAGE

General Reference

20c. Avoid a ***general reference,*** which is the use of a pronoun that refers to a general idea rather than to a specific antecedent.

The pronouns commonly used in making general references are *it, that, this,* and *which.*

GENERAL   The gusts grew stronger, and rain clouds began rolling in from the distant hills. This prompted the campers to seek shelter.
           [*This* has no specific antecedent.]

CLEAR   The gusts grew stronger, and rain clouds began rolling in from the distant hills. These ominous conditions prompted the campers to seek shelter.

CLEAR   As the gusts grew stronger and rain clouds began rolling in from the distant hills, the campers sought shelter.

| GENERAL | More than 20 percent of those who enter college fail to graduate, which is a shame. [*Which* has no specific antecedent.] |
| CLEAR | That more than 20 percent of those who enter college fail to graduate is a shame. |

Exercise 2 Correcting General References

Revise each of the following sentences, correcting the general pronoun reference.

EXAMPLE
1. England invaded France in 1337. That began a series of wars known as the Hundred Years' War.

1. *England's invasion of France in 1337 began a series of wars known as the Hundred Years' War.*

or

When England invaded France in 1337, a series of wars known as the Hundred Years' War began.

1. On California's San Miguel Island, a ranger showed us around, and this made the visit especially interesting.
2. A great many young people have already left Hastings Corners to work in the city, which is unfortunate for this town.
3. My parents bought a new carpet and new curtains, and they hired someone to paint the walls and ceiling. That certainly improved the appearance of the room.
4. The guidance counselor asked me whether I wanted to take German, French, or Spanish, which was difficult to decide.
5. After the storm last weekend, the trail to the top of the mountain was washed out in some spots and was blocked in many places with fallen branches. It made the ascent nerve-racking.
6. The first part of the test will be on chemistry, the second on mathematics, the third on physics. This will make it very difficult.
7. Several of the eyewitnesses described the man as short, others said he was tall, and yet others said he was "about average." It confused the police investigators.
8. We hiked all morning and then went skiing at Gates of the Arctic National Park and Preserve, which made us all extremely tired.
9. The principal said that the play will have to be given in the old auditorium unless by some miracle the new auditorium can be completed ahead of schedule; that will surely be a blow to the Central High Drama Club.
10. I found out that three of my library books were overdue, which was a complete surprise.

HELP

Although sentences in Exercise 2 can be corrected in more than one way, you need to give only one revision for each.

USAGE

Most of the following sentences contain ambiguous or general pronoun references. Revise each faulty sentence. If a sentence is already correct, write *C*.

EXAMPLE
    1. Some people still haven't heard about the Civil Rights Memorial, which is unfortunate.

    1. *That some people still haven't heard about the Civil Rights Memorial is unfortunate.*

1. After Tonya saw the Civil Rights Memorial at the Southern Poverty Law Center in Montgomery, Alabama, she sent a postcard to Alice.
2. Morris S. Dees, cofounder of the Law Center, and other center officials wanted to find a top architect to create a special memorial. This led them to Maya Lin.
3. My mother remembers reading about Lin when she was chosen to design the Vietnam Veterans Memorial in Washington, D.C.
4. Before she made up her mind, Lin researched the history of the civil rights movement. That convinced her to accept the project.
5. As you can see here, the granite memorial consists of two distinct parts: a wall with an engraved quotation and a round, engraved tabletop. This makes a simple but striking effect.

┌─H E L P ──

Although sentences in Review A can be corrected in more than one way, you need to give only one revision for each.

USAGE

6. Whoever thought of engraving the events and names associated with the civil rights movement on the granite tabletop had an inspired idea.

7. Water flows down the wall and over the tabletop of the memorial, which adds a sense of calm and continuity.

8. Mrs. Bledsoe told Tamisha about some of the forty entries she had just read on the tabletop.

9. When the Law Center dedicated the memorial in 1989, it became a popular tourist attraction.

10. Nowadays, many people come to Montgomery especially to see the Civil Rights Memorial, which, of course, benefits the city.

Weak Reference

20d. Avoid a *weak reference,* which occurs when a pronoun refers to an antecedent that has been suggested but not expressed.

WEAK	Every time a circus came to town, my sister Erin wanted to become one of them. [The antecedent of *them* is not expressed.]
CLEAR	Every time a circus came to town, my sister Erin wanted to become one of the troupe.

WEAK	Kane is very talented musically. Two of these are singing harmony and playing the saxophone. [The antecedent of *these* is not expressed.]
CLEAR	Kane is very talented musically. Two of his talents are singing harmony and playing the saxophone.
CLEAR	Kane has many musical talents. Two of these are singing harmony and playing the saxophone.
CLEAR	Kane has many musical talents, two of which are singing harmony and playing the saxophone.

Exercise 3 Correcting Weak References

Revise each of the following sentences, correcting the weak pronoun reference.

EXAMPLE

1. Mom is very interested in psychiatry, but she does not believe they know all the answers.

1. *Mom is very interested in psychiatry, but she does not believe that psychiatrists know all the answers.*

┌HELP┐
Although some sentences in Exercise 3 can be corrected in more than one way, you need to give only one revision for each.

1. Sir Arthur Conan Doyle began his career as a doctor, and it explains his interest in careful observation.
2. She is a careful gardener, watering them whenever the soil gets dry.
3. They planned to eat dinner outdoors by candlelight, but a strong wind kept blowing them out.
4. For years after seeing the Alvin Ailey American Dance Theater perform, Leah dreamed of joining them.
5. Although rain was predicted on the night of the concert, Eric went because his favorite ones were scheduled to be played.
6. My brother has an anthology of Japanese literature for his college course, but he hasn't read any of them yet.
7. Although Bradley has always enjoyed reading poetry, he has never written one.
8. Sarah's uncle has a huge vegetable garden, and he keeps them supplied with fresh vegetables all summer long.
9. He spent more than an hour at the clothing store but did not try any on.
10. Deep-sea fishing isn't very enjoyable to me unless I catch at least one.

Indefinite Reference

20e. Avoid an *indefinite reference*—the use of a pronoun that refers to no particular person or thing and that is unnecessary to the meaning and structure of a sentence.

The pronouns commonly used in making indefinite references are *it, they,* and *you.* To correct an indefinite reference, revise the sentence to eliminate the unnecessary pronoun.

INDEFINITE   In the newspaper it reported that a volcano had erupted in the Indian Ocean. [*It* is not necessary to the meaning of the sentence.]

CLEAR   The newspaper reported that a volcano had erupted in the Indian Ocean.

INDEFINITE   At Yerkes Observatory in Wisconsin, they have the world's largest refracting telescope. [*They* does not refer to any specific persons.]

CLEAR   Yerkes Observatory in Wisconsin has the world's largest refracting telescope.

INDEFINITE In Shakespeare's time you could attend the performance of a play for a penny. [*You* does not refer to the reader or to any other particular antecedent.]

CLEAR In Shakespeare's time a theatergoer could attend the performance of a play for a penny.

NOTE The indefinite use of *it* in familiar expressions such as *it is snowing, it is early,* and *it seems* is acceptable.

Exercise 4 **Correcting Indefinite Pronoun References**

Revise each of the following sentences, correcting the indefinite use of *it, they,* or *you.*

EXAMPLE 1. In Japan they have the world's tallest roller coaster.

1. *Japan has the world's tallest roller coaster.*

or

The world's tallest roller coaster is in Japan.

1. In *The Diary of Anne Frank,* it shows a young Jewish girl's courage during two years of hiding from the Nazis.
2. I asked my aunt Shirley, who works for one of the largest architectural design firms in the city, what you have to do to become a licensed architect.
3. In some parts of Africa, they mine diamonds and sell them to jewelers to be cut.
4. In the sports sections of daily newspapers, it usually tells all about the previous day's events in sports.
5. When Grandpa was a child, you were supposed to be absolutely silent at the table.
6. In the movie guide, it states that *The Long Walk Home* is almost a documentary about civil rights.
7. On the book jacket, they say that the authors themselves had experienced these thrilling adventures.
8. The dancers, trying to keep up with the spirited pace of the music, had whirled so fast it made them dizzy.
9. One of the attractions of the tour was that they gave tour members free admissions to all the museums on the tour.
10. When the Neville Brothers come to town next week, it will be a sold-out show.

┌HELP──

Although sentences in Exercise 4 can be corrected in more than one way, you need to give only one revision for each.

Most of the following sentences contain weak and indefinite pronoun references. Revise each faulty sentence. If a sentence is already correct, write *C*.

EXAMPLE

   1. In the newspaper they ran an article about the late English actor Jeremy Brett, who played the detective Sherlock Holmes.

   1. The newspaper ran an article about the late English actor Jeremy Brett, who played the detective Sherlock Holmes.

1. Every time I see Sherlock Holmes reruns on public television's *Mystery!* series, I want to read some more of them.

2. In the article, they talk about Brett's authentic Holmes wardrobe, an example of which can be seen in the picture below.

3. Holmes is a very theatrical person. One of these is using disguises, such as that of a priest in "The Final Problem."

4. In the *Mystery!* series, Brett was given the opportunity to play Holmes as Conan Doyle himself had created the character.

┌─H E L P ─

Although sentences in Review B can be corrected in more than one way, you need to give only one revision for each.

USAGE

5. Throughout Conan Doyle's fiction, they present Sherlock Holmes as confident, fair, and dramatic but also as restless, temperamental, and moody.

6. When we heard that Brett had starred as Sherlock Holmes on the London stage, we wished we had seen it.

7. In the reviews of *Mystery!* they state that Brett is still widely considered the best Sherlock Holmes ever.

8. I joined the local chapter of the Baker Street Irregulars, which is a kind of Sherlock Holmes fan club.

9. From 1887 to 1927, Conan Doyle chronicled the life of Holmes, writing more than fifty of them.

10. In England around the end of the nineteenth century, you could read Sherlock Holmes stories in the *Strand* magazine.

Chapter Review

A. Correcting Faulty Pronoun References

Most of the following sentences contain examples of ambiguous, general, weak, and indefinite references. Correctly rewrite each sentence that contains a faulty pronoun reference. Although sentences can be corrected in more than one way, you need to give only one revision for each. If a sentence is already correct, write *C*.

1. In the magazine article, they explain how microprocessors are used in the electrical stimulation of paralyzed muscles.

2. Lucia wrote to Sara every week while she was visiting her aunt and uncle in Guadalajara, Mexico.

3. The star of the play was sick, two other actors had not memorized their lines, and the stage manager was out of town. This caused the director to cancel rehearsals.

4. Zack likes to browse in music stores but seldom buys any of them.

5. In Massachusetts between 1659 and 1681, you could not legally celebrate Christmas.

6. The architect discussed with the contractor the changes she had just made on the blueprint.

7. We could not ride the mules to Phantom Ranch at the bottom of the Grand Canyon, which was disappointing.

8. Even though it is raining again, the state highway crew is working to repair the bridge.

9. When the ceramic bowl landed on the glass table, it shattered.

10. He told many of his own original jokes, one of which was about a penguin on its first visit to Times Square.

11. Aaron had not yet seen the new aerobics video, so he had a difficult time doing any of them.

12. On the radio program it gave the time for the rally.

13. Before buying a season ticket to the film society, Glenn checked the society's schedule for his favorite ones.

14. Annie revised the first two chapters of her novel. That made the development of the characters clearer.

15. At the skating rink they have ice skates for rent.

HELP

Although sentences in Parts B and C of the Chapter Review can be corrected in more than one way, you need to give only one revision for each.

B. Correcting Faulty Pronoun References

Most of the following sentences contain pronouns without clear antecedents. Revise each sentence to correct any unclear pronoun references. If a sentence is already correct, write *C*.

16. Ferris studied the poet T'ao Ch'ien in his world literature class.

17. T'ao Ch'ien loved to work in his garden, which is evident in his poetry.

18. T'ao Ch'ien's topics came from his own simple life. One of these was worrying about his five sons.

19. In our literature book it states that the Chinese consider Tu Fu to be their greatest poet.

20. Many people admire poetry, but most people don't think they can be used for medicinal purposes.

21. In this book, it has a story about Tu Fu suggesting that his poetry could cure malarial fever.

22. That more than a thousand of Tu Fu's poems survive is amazing.

23. The poet Li Po liked to travel and to enjoy nature. This gave him many subjects for his poetry but little family life.

24. Alicia explained the meaning of the Li Po poem she had read.

25. Jay liked Po Chu-i's poetry, and he wanted to memorize one.

26. Darnell described the tragic love story related in Po Chu-i's narrative poem *The Song of Everlasting Regret.* It went by very quickly.

27. The world literature course could only scratch the surface of Chinese literature, and Ferris wanted to read more of them.

28. Ms. Johnson said some famous Chinese works were available in translation, and this prompted Ferris to check the library for them.

29. Ferris met Darnell in the library, where he found a copy of *Dream of the Red Chamber.*

30. In *Dream of the Red Chamber* it tells the story of the decline of a family during the Ch'ing dynasty.

C. Revising a Paragraph to Correct Faulty Pronoun References

Revise the following paragraph to correct each unclear pronoun reference.

    [31] The Millers went with the Ochoas to the Okefenokee Swamp when they were visiting. [32] The swamp covers a total area of about

684 square miles, which is amazing. **[33]** The Okefenokee is full of subtropical vegetation, and the two families saw quite a few of them. **[34]** In the information brochure, it stated that the swamp is a habitat for cypress trees, waterlilies, and brush vines. **[35]** The brochure also mentioned the swamp's connection to the Suwannee River and the Gulf of Mexico, into which it drains. **[36]** The Suwannee River has been an inspiration for many songwriters; two of these are Stephen Foster's "Old Folks at Home" and George Gershwin's "Swanee." **[37]** They say the name *Okefenokee* comes from an American Indian word meaning "trembling ground." **[38]** The Millers and Ochoas saw alligators in the water and flocks of birds flying overhead; they were delighted by this. **[39]** At one point, Lisa Ochoa called Suzette Miller's attention to a heron while she was looking into the distance. **[40]** The two families learned that most of the swamp has been designated as the Okefenokee National Wildlife Refuge to protect them.

Writing Application
Using Pronouns in Paragraphs

Clear Pronoun Reference   Your school's career counselor asks you to write about people you know who have different jobs. Making sure that your pronouns have clear and unambiguous references, write a paragraph about the jobs of three people you know.

Prewriting   Make a list of at least three people you know who have different sorts of jobs. Tell a little bit about each person, and describe what he or she does on the job.

Writing   While writing your first draft, be sure to include details that show how the jobs are different from each other.

Revising   Make sure that your rough draft shows a variety of jobs. If the jobs do not seem very different from each other, replace some examples or add new ones.

Publishing   Check for errors in grammar, usage, and mechanics. Make sure your pronoun references are clear. You and your classmates may want to read some of the paragraphs aloud in class and discuss how jobs differ from each other.

Using Verbs Correctly
Principal Parts, Tense, Voice, Mood

Diagnostic Preview

A. Proofreading Sentences for Verb Usage

Most of the following sentences contain awkward, informal, or incorrect verb usage. If a sentence has an awkward, informal, or incorrect usage, revise the sentence, using the verb form that is correct in formal, standard English. If a sentence is already correct, write *C*.

EXAMPLE   **1.** If I would have seen the accident, I would certainly have reported it.

          1. If I had seen the accident, I would certainly have reported it.

1. According to this news article, the concert last Saturday night is "a resounding success."
2. According to the latest census, more than 39,000 American Indians had been currently living in Wisconsin.
3. How many of us possess the skills to have survived on our own without using store-bought items?
4. If you would have taken the nutrition class, you would have learned how to shop wisely for food.
5. Wacky, my pet hamster, was acting as if she were trying to tell me something.

6. Yesterday, Dad's pickup truck was washed and waxed by my brother.
7. If modern society was an agricultural one, more of us would know about farming and about the difficulties faced by farmers.
8. Last week's concert has broke all attendance records here.
9. Because of the excessive amount of rain this spring, the water in the dam has raised to a dangerous level.
10. Working in the garden earlier this morning, Jim is now laying down for a rest.

B. Proofreading Sentences for Verb Usage

Most of the following sentences contain errors in the use of verbs. If a sentence has a verb error, revise the sentence, using the correct verb form. If a sentence is already correct, write *C*.

EXAMPLE   1. From our studies, we have concluded that women had played many critical roles in the history of our nation.

1. *From our studies, we have concluded that women have played many critical roles in the history of our nation.*

11. In Daytona Beach, Florida, Mary McLeod Bethune founded a tiny school, which become Bethune-Cookman College.
12. Jane Addams founded Hull House in Chicago to educate the poor and to acquaint immigrants with American ways; for her efforts she had received the Nobel Prize for peace in 1931.
13. In 1932, Amelia Earhart flown solo across the Atlantic Ocean.
14. Pearl Buck, a recipient of the Nobel Prize for literature in 1938, seeked to bring understanding and peace to people all over the world.
15. In 1964, Margaret Chase Smith, a senator from Maine, received twenty-seven delegate votes for the presidential nomination.
16. Lorraine Hansberry wrote the successful play *A Raisin in the Sun,* which had already been translated into at least thirty languages.
17. Has you ever heard of Belva Lockwood, whose accomplishments paved the way for women in politics?
18. In 1879, a short time after Lockwood was admitted to the bar, she became the first female lawyer to argue a case before the United States Supreme Court.
19. Although her name is not well known now, Lockwood gotten more than four thousand votes for the presidency in 1884.
20. By the time you leave high school, you will learn many interesting facts about history.

Reference Note

Depending on how they are used, verbs may be classified as **transitive verbs** or **intransitive verbs,** as **action verbs** or **linking verbs,** and as **main verbs** or **helping verbs.** For a discussion of these different kinds of verbs, see page 495.

The Principal Parts of Verbs

21a. The principal parts of a verb are the *base form,* the *present participle,* the *past,* and the *past participle.* All other verb forms are derived from these principal parts.

Base Form	Present Participle	Past	Past Participle
receive	[is] receiving	received	[have] received
join	[is] joining	joined	[have] joined
bring	[is] bringing	brought	[have] brought
sing	[is] singing	sang	[have] sung
hurt	[is] hurting	hurt	[have] hurt

HELP

The words *is* and *have* are included in the chart to the right because the present participle and past participle verb forms require helping verbs (forms of *be* and *have*) to form tenses.

Reference Note

For more information on **infinitives,** see page 546.

NOTE Some teachers refer to the base form as the *infinitive.* Follow your teacher's directions when labeling this form.

When the present participle and past participle forms are used as verbs in sentences, they require helping verbs.

Helping Verb	+	Present Participle	=	Verb Phrase
forms of *be*	+	taking	=	am taking
		walking		was walking
		going		have been going

Helping Verb	+	Past Participle	=	Verb Phrase
forms of *have*	+	taken	=	have taken
		walked		has walked
		gone		had gone

HELP

Sometimes the helping verb appears as part of a contraction.

EXAMPLES
He's running late.
We've already ordered.

Reference Note

For more information about **contractions,** see page 831.

Reference Note

For more about **passive voice,** see page 676.

NOTE Sometimes a past participle is used with a form of *be: was chosen, are known, is seen.* This use of the verb is called the *passive voice.*

All verbs form the present participle in the same way: by adding *–ing* to the base form. Not all verbs, however, form the past and past participle in the same way.

Regular Verbs

21b. A *regular verb* forms its past and past participle by adding
–d or *–ed* to the base form.

Base Form	Present Participle	Past	Past Participle
use	[is] using	used	[have] used
revise	[is] revising	revised	[have] revised
outline	[is] outlining	outlined	[have] outlined
watch	[is] watching	watched	[have] watched
happen	[is] happening	happened	[have] happened
trim	[is] trimming	trimmed	[have] trimmed

A few regular verbs have alternative past and past participle forms ending in *–t*.

Base Form	Present Participle	Past	Past Participle
burn	[is] burning	burned *or* burnt	[have] burned *or* burnt
dream	[is] dreaming	dreamed *or* dreamt	[have] dreamed *or* dreamt
leap	[is] leaping	leaped *or* leapt	[have] leaped *or* leapt

NOTE The regular verbs *deal* and *mean* always form the past and past participle by adding *–t: dealt, (have) dealt; meant, (have) meant.*

When forming the past and past participle of regular verbs, avoid omitting the *–d* or *–ed* ending. Pay particular attention to the forms of the verbs *ask, attack, drown, prejudice, risk, suppose,* and *use.*

NONSTANDARD	The firefighter risk his life to save the valuable artifacts.
STANDARD	The firefighter **risked** his life to save the valuable artifacts.

NONSTANDARD	We should have ask for directions.
STANDARD	We should have **asked** for directions.

Reference Note

Adding suffixes to the base forms of some verbs can pose spelling problems. For information on **adding suffixes,** see page 846.

USAGE

Reference Note

For a discussion of **standard and nonstandard English,** see page 723.

Exercise 1 Using Regular Verbs

For each of the following sentences, give the correct past or past participle form of the verb in parentheses.

EXAMPLE   1. As a rule, electronic equipment should be (*clean*) regularly.

1. *cleaned*

1. Haven't you ever (*bake*) clams on the beach before?
2. The rangers had often (*walk*) the five miles from their station down to the lodge.
3. By the end of the carnival, we will have (*raise*) more than ten thousand dollars.
4. You should have (*stir*) that lime sauce; now it has lumps in it.
5. Henry Ossawa Tanner (*paint*) Biblical subjects as well as everyday scenes from African Americans' lives.
6. For our service project this semester, our club (*remove*) the graffiti from the park walls.
7. Because the dates of the holidays often are (*print*) in red on calendars, we have the expression "red-letter day."
8. My grades in speech went up after I (*tape*) myself and then played the tape back to study my delivery.
9. The Sioux leader Sitting Bull had (*emerge*) victorious at the Battle of Little Bighorn.
10. One of the American Dance Theater's artistic directors, José Arcadio Limón, was born in Mexico; he (*dance*) his way to success.

Irregular Verbs

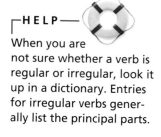

─HELP─

When you are not sure whether a verb is regular or irregular, look it up in a dictionary. Entries for irregular verbs generally list the principal parts.

21c. An *irregular verb* forms its past and past participle in some other way than by adding *–d* or *–ed* to the base form.

The best way to learn the principal parts of irregular verbs is to memorize them. No single usage rule applies to the different ways that these verbs form the past and past participle. However, there are some general guidelines that you can use. Irregular verbs form the past and past participle in one of these ways:

- changing vowels
- changing consonants
- changing vowels and consonants
- making no change

Base Form	Present Participle	Past	Past Participle
swim	[is] swimming	swam	[have] swum
bend	[is] bending	bent	[have] bent
teach	[is] teaching	taught	[have] taught
burst	[is] bursting	burst	[have] burst

When forming the past and the past participle of irregular verbs, avoid these common errors:

(1) using the past form with a helping verb

NONSTANDARD	I have never swam in this lake before.
STANDARD	I never **swam** in this lake before.

(2) using the past participle form without a helping verb

NONSTANDARD	She swum to shore to get help.
STANDARD	She **has swum** to shore to get help.

(3) adding –d, –ed, or –t to the base form

NONSTANDARD	We bursted into laughter as soon as we saw the comedian.
STANDARD	We **burst** into laughter as soon as we saw the comedian.

Common Irregular Verbs

Group I: Each of these irregular verbs has the same form for its past and past participle.

Base Form	Present Participle	Past	Past Participle
bind	[is] binding	bound	[have] bound
bring	[is] bringing	brought	[have] brought
build	[is] building	built	[have] built
buy	[is] buying	bought	[have] bought
catch	[is] catching	caught	[have] caught
creep	[is] creeping	crept	[have] crept
feel	[is] feeling	felt	[have] felt
fight	[is] fighting	fought	[have] fought

(continued)

STYLE TIP

Some verbs have two correct past or past participle forms. However, these forms are not always interchangeable.

EXAMPLES
He **shone** the candle into the cellar. [*Shined* would also be correct.]

I **shined** my shoes. [*Shone* would be incorrect in this usage.]

If you are unsure about which past participle to use, check an up-to-date dictionary.

(continued)

Common Irregular Verbs

Group I: Each of these irregular verbs has the same form for its past and past participle.

Base Form	Present Participle	Past	Past Participle
find	[is] finding	found	[have] found
fling	[is] flinging	flung	[have] flung
have	[is] having	had	[have] had
hear	[is] hearing	heard	[have] heard
hold	[is] holding	held	[have] held
keep	[is] keeping	kept	[have] kept
lay	[is] laying	laid	[have] laid
lead	[is] leading	led	[have] led
leave	[is] leaving	left	[have] left
lend	[is] lending	lent	[have] lent
light	[is] lighting	lit *or* lighted	[have] lit *or* lighted
lose	[is] losing	lost	[have] lost
make	[is] making	made	[have] made
meet	[is] meeting	met	[have] met
pay	[is] paying	paid	[have] paid
say	[is] saying	said	[have] said
seek	[is] seeking	sought	[have] sought
sell	[is] selling	sold	[have] sold
send	[is] sending	sent	[have] sent
sit	[is] sitting	sat	[have] sat
spend	[is] spending	spent	[have] spent
spin	[is] spinning	spun	[have] spun
stand	[is] standing	stood	[have] stood
sting	[is] stinging	stung	[have] stung
swing	[is] swinging	swung	[have] swung
teach	[is] teaching	taught	[have] taught
tell	[is] telling	told	[have] told
think	[is] thinking	thought	[have] thought
win	[is] winning	won	[have] won

USAGE

Exercise 2 Using the Past and Past Participle Forms of Irregular Verbs

For each of the following sentences, give the correct past or past participle form of the verb in parentheses.

EXAMPLE   **1.** Bob and Terri have (*lead*) our class in math scores for two years.

      1. led

1. The movie monster (*swing*) around and lurched into the woods.
2. Have you (*teach*) your little brother Stephano how to throw a curveball yet?
3. Mrs. Torres (*tell*) us yesterday that Mexican ballads are called *corridos*.
4. Ever since we met last year, Kitty and I have (*sit*) together in assembly.
5. When Larry and Dana got to the new video store at the mall, you had just (*leave*).
6. Unfortunately, Darlene has already (*spend*) most of her weekly allowance.
7. In an earlier scene, Tarzan had (*catch*) hold of a vine and used it to swing through the trees.
8. Those two paintings by Horace Pippin really (*hold*) our interest.
9. Not only had he juggled six oranges, but he had also (*spin*) two plates on sticks.
10. The tiger-striped cat (*creep*) down the hallway and into the room.

Exercise 3 Using the Past and Past Participle Forms of Irregular Verbs Correctly

Many people like to play with the English language. Some enjoy word games. Some, like the author of the following silly poem, break the rules of standard usage just for fun. Each couplet in the poem contains an incorrect past or past participle form of an irregular verb. For each incorrect form shown in italics, provide the correct form.

EXAMPLE   Bake, baked; make, **[1]** *maked*? Hold it—not so fast!
      Verbs that rhyme in the present may not rhyme in the past!

      1. made

Today we fling the same old ball that yesterday we flung;
Today we bring the same good news that yesterday we **[1]** *brung*.

And we still mind our parents, the folks we've always minded;
And I may find a dime, just like the dime you **[2]** *finded*.

┌─HELP─
The poem in Exercise 3 will no longer rhyme when it is corrected.

I smell the crimson rose, the very rose you smelled;
I tell a silly joke today, the same joke you once [3] *telled.*

You grin to hear me tell it now, just as last week you grinned;
You win our game of checkers, just as last week you [4] *winned.*

I peek into your closet now, and yesterday I peeked;
I seek my birthday present, as every year I've [5] *seeked.*

You reach to take my hand in yours; it was not I who reached;
You teach me to be friendly, as always you have [6] *teached.*

I beep my horn to warn you; I'm sure my horn just beeped;
I keep all my appointments, the ones I should have [7] *keeped.*

I scream all day, I yell all night, I've screamed and I have yelled
To sell all my newspapers, and today's batch I have [8] *selled.*

I wink my eye at you today, as yesterday I winked;
I think I like you very much, as yesterday I [9] *thinked.*

I lose my train of thought sometimes; my train of thought I've [10] *losed.*
But I can use my verbs with care; just see the ones I've used!

—HELP—

Notice that several of these verbs have alternate past or past participle forms.

Common Irregular Verbs

Group II: Most of these irregular verbs have different forms for their past and past participles.

Base Form	Present Participle	Past	Past Participle
arise	[is] arising	arose	[have] arisen
be	[is] being	was, were	[have] been
bear	[is] bearing	bore	[have] borne or born
beat	[is] beating	beat	[have] beaten or beat
become	[is] becoming	became	[have] become
begin	[is] beginning	began	[have] begun
bite	[is] biting	bit	[have] bitten or bit
blow	[is] blowing	blew	[have] blown
break	[is] breaking	broke	[have] broken
choose	[is] choosing	chose	[have] chosen
come	[is] coming	came	[have] come
dive	[is] diving	dove or dived	[have] dived

Common Irregular Verbs

Group II: Most of these irregular verbs have different forms for their past and past participles.

Base Form	Present Participle	Past	Past Participle
do	[is] doing	did	[have] done
draw	[is] drawing	drew	[have] drawn
drink	[is] drinking	drank	[have] drunk
drive	[is] driving	drove	[have] driven
eat	[is] eating	ate	[have] eaten
fall	[is] falling	fell	[have] fallen
fly	[is] flying	flew	[have] flown
forbid	[is] forbidding	forbade *or* forbad	[have] forbidden *or* forbid
forget	[is] forgetting	forgot	[have] forgotten *or* forgot
forgive	[is] forgiving	forgave	[have] forgiven
forsake	[is] forsaking	forsook	[have] forsaken
freeze	[is] freezing	froze	[have] frozen
get	[is] getting	got	[have] gotten *or* got
give	[is] giving	gave	[have] given
go	[is] going	went	[have] gone
grow	[is] growing	grew	[have] grown
hide	[is] hiding	hid	[have] hidden *or* hid
know	[is] knowing	knew	[have] known
lie	[is] lying	lay	[have] lain
ride	[is] riding	rode	[have] ridden
ring	[is] ringing	rang	[have] rung
rise	[is] rising	rose	[have] risen
run	[is] running	ran	[have] run
see	[is] seeing	saw	[have] seen
shake	[is] shaking	shook	[have] shaken
show	[is] showing	showed	[have] showed *or* shown
shrink	[is] shrinking	shrank *or* shrunk	[have] shrunk

USAGE

(continued)

(continued)

Common Irregular Verbs

Group II: Most of these irregular verbs have different forms for their past and past participles.

Base Form	Present Participle	Past	Past Participle
sing	[is] singing	sang	[have] sung
sink	[is] sinking	sank *or* sunk	[have] sunk
slay	[is] slaying	slew	[have] slain
speak	[is] speaking	spoke	[have] spoken
spring	[is] springing	sprang *or* sprung	[have] sprung
steal	[is] stealing	stole	[have] stolen
strike	[is] striking	struck	[have] struck *or* stricken
strive	[is] striving	strove *or* strived	[have] striven *or* strived
swear	[is] swearing	swore	[have] sworn
swim	[is] swimming	swam	[have] swum
take	[is] taking	took	[have] taken
tear	[is] tearing	tore	[have] torn
throw	[is] throwing	threw	[have] thrown
wake	[is] waking	waked *or* woke	[have] waked *or* woken
wear	[is] wearing	wore	[have] worn
weave	[is] weaving	wove *or* weaved	[have] woven *or* weaved
write	[is] writing	wrote	[have] written

Exercise 4 Using the Past and Past Participle Forms of Irregular Verbs

For each of the following sentences, give the correct past or past participle form of the verb in parentheses.

EXAMPLE 1. Aunt Barbara (*freeze*) fourteen pints of corn.
1. *froze*

1. Your friends have (*come*) to see you.
2. He (*do*) his best on the PSAT last Saturday.

3. Elizabeth has finally (*begin*) to understand the value of proofreading.

4. One of the poems I had (*choose*) to read was "Out of the Cradle Endlessly Rocking."

5. The tour group had (*see*) the ancient Pueblo dwellings.

6. Strong winds (*drive*) the Dutch galleon off its course.

7. The silence was (*break*) by a sudden clap of thunder.

8. West Side High's team easily (*beat*) its opponents.

9. Miguel (*blow*) up balloons and made decorations for his sister's *quinceañera* party, the celebration of her fifteenth birthday.

10. How long had the treasure (*lie*) undiscovered?

Review A **Using the Past and Past Participle Forms of Irregular Verbs Correctly**

In the following paragraph, decide whether each italicized verb form is correct. If it is not, give the correct verb form. If a verb form is correct, write *C*.

EXAMPLE   Even as a child, Midori never [1] *shrinked* from an audience.

        1. shrank

If you have [1] *seen* the maturity and intensity of performances by the young woman shown to the right, you know firsthand that she has [2] *stealed* the hearts of many music lovers. More than once, excited fans [3] *brung* down the house with applause and [4] *throwed* bouquets of roses at her feet. In fact, Midori has [5] *knew* the joys and struggles of being a professional concert violinist ever since she was a young girl. Whenever she has [6] *spoke* to the press, Midori has always [7] *showed* an outgoing and unaffected personality. Her violin teacher at the Juilliard School, Dorothy DeLay, also [8] *taught* such stars as Itzhak Perlman and Joshua Bell. When Midori was eleven, the famous conductor Zubin Mehta [9] *lead* her onstage as a surprise guest soloist with the New York Philharmonic. Ever since, Midori has [10] *finded* the concert hall a wonderful place; in fact, she says that she loves being there, whether she is on the stage by herself or with an orchestra.

Common Irregular Verbs

Group III: Each of these irregular verbs has the same form for its base form, past, and past participle.

Base Form	Present Participle	Past	Past Participle
burst	[is] bursting	burst	[have] burst
cost	[is] costing	cost	[have] cost
cut	[is] cutting	cut	[have] cut
hit	[is] hitting	hit	[have] hit
hurt	[is] hurting	hurt	[have] hurt
let	[is] letting	let	[have] let
put	[is] putting	put	[have] put
read	[is] reading	read	[have] read
set	[is] setting	set	[have] set
spread	[is] spreading	spread	[have] spread

Exercise 5 Using the Past and Past Participle Forms of Irregular Verbs Correctly

Most of the following sentences contain an incorrect verb form. If a verb form is incorrect, give the correct form. If a sentence is already correct, write *C*.

EXAMPLE   1. The concert ticket costed thirty dollars.
               1. *cost*

1. The crowded roots of the plant had bursted the ceramic flowerpot.
2. Nancy carefully sat the antipasto salad in the center of the dining table.
3. After we've cut the grass, we'll weed the garden.
4. The angry hornet stung me right on the end of my nose, and it hurted all afternoon.
5. Hasan spreaded his pita bread with a thick layer of tasty hummus.
6. Where have I putted my notebook?
7. You must have read the assignment too quickly.
8. As soon as the robin was well, we letted it go free.
9. How much money has owning a car costed you this year?
10. Both Felina and Fernanda hitted home runs in last week's game.

The following paragraph contains ten numbered blanks. For each
blank, choose an appropriate verb from the box below and give the
correct past or past participle form of the verb.

become	creep	make	spin
begin	find	see	spread
bring	let	seek	think

EXAMPLE   Suppose you were a farmer, and one morning you went out
to your fields and **[1]** _____ a 300-foot-long pattern of circles
and lines in the middle of your crops!

1. *found*

Many circular flattened areas like these **[1]** _____ to
appear in fields across southern England in the late 1970s.
The phenomenon soon **[2]** _____ one of the most popular
mysteries the world had ever known. People calling themselves "cereologists" insisted that no human being could have
[3] _____ these unusual patterns. The idea quickly
[4] _____ that the circles were the landing spots of UFOs
that had **[5]** _____ visitors from space. Respected scientists **[6]** _____ that the weird designs resulted from ball
lightning, whirling columns of air, or other strange
weather conditions. When it was reported that circle
researchers had **[7]** _____ public funding, two British
landscape painters came forward with the truth. David
Chorley and Douglas Bower confessed that they had
[8] _____ into the fields at night with a ball of twine
and a wooden plank and had **[9]** _____ the plank in a circle
to create the flattened areas of grain. Before Chorley and Bower spoke
up, millions of people had **[10]** _____ themselves believe that the crop
circles were formed by extraterrestrials—and even now, thousands of
diehards still do.

Review **C** Using the Past and Past Participle Forms of
Irregular Verbs

For each of the sentences on the next page, give the correct past or past
participle form of the verb in parentheses.

EXAMPLE   1. The pitcher (*strike*) out eleven batters in a row.

1. *struck*

1. Has Chelsea ever (*read*) anything by Gwendolyn Brooks, the poet laureate of Illinois?
2. We (*drink*) tomato juice with last night's dinner.
3. How many of you (*see*) Fernando Valenzuela pitch?
4. I thought my skates had been (*steal*), but then I finally found them.
5. He had (*write*) a play about his experience in Vietnam.
6. Garrett's dad has (*sing*) in a barbershop quartet for years.
7. If they had not (*cost*) so much, we would have bought one for everyone in the family.
8. Some of the authors who had been scorned ten years earlier had (*become*) quite popular.
9. Don't you think that the dough for the bread has (*rise*) enough to bake?
10. Mary says she has never (*ride*) on a roller coaster.
11. Have you ever (*fly*) a Japanese dragon kite?
12. I shivered and (*shake*) after I dented the front fender of Mom's car.
13. When Mrs. Isayama called my name, I (*swing*) around.
14. Have you (*forgive*) Christy for playing that practical joke on Marcia and you?
15. Wanda (*burst*) into the room to greet her friends.
16. Yesterday, Nguyen and I each (*hit*) about two hundred tennis balls.
17. Darius had (*fall*) as he went in for the layup.
18. The government class has (*go*) to observe the city council in session.
19. I was not aware that the telephone had (*ring*).
20. Have you (*have*) a taste of that delicious pea soup yet?

Review D **Using the Past and Past Participle Forms of Irregular Verbs Correctly**

For each of the following sentences, decide whether the italicized verb form is correct. If it is not, give the correct verb form. If a sentence is already correct, write *C*.

EXAMPLE   1. When the bagger at the supermarket asked me whether I wanted paper or plastic bags, I *telled* her, "Paper, please."

1. *told*

1. American shoppers have certainly *grew* accustomed to the convenience of paper grocery bags.

2. In recent years, many Americans have *went* right on using them—at the rate of forty billion bags a year!

3. Have you ever *thinked* about the history of the standard flat-bottomed grocery bag with pleated sides?

4. Someone must have *cutted* out and pasted together the first flat-bottomed paper bag.

5. Actually, I have *read* that the inventor of these bags was a man named Charles Stilwell.

6. After he had *fighted* in the Civil War, he returned home and began to tinker with inventions.

7. He created a machine to fold and glue brown paper into bags, a job that had previously been *did* by hand.

8. Earlier bags had V-shaped bottoms, which meant that they had not *standed* up by themselves.

9. I have certainly *putted* Charles Stilwell's bags to good use in my after-school supermarket job.

10. Many other everyday items that we have always *took* for granted, such as safety pins and eyeglasses, have interesting histories, too.

Review E **Proofreading Sentences for Correct Verb Forms**

For the following sentences, give the correct form for each incorrect verb form. If a sentence is already correct, write *C*.

EXAMPLE **1.** When my art class went to the Museum of African American Art, I seen some collages that Romare Bearden had maked.

    1. *saw; made*

1. Seeing the unusual medium of collage has leaded me to think about art in a new way.

2. Bearden growed up in North Carolina and then spended time studying in New York, Pittsburgh, and Paris.

3. His art career begun in the 1930s, and he soon gotten a reputation as a leading abstract artist.

4. Instead of specializing in painting or drawing, Bearden finded his niche in the somewhat unusual medium of collage.

USAGE

5. He fashioned his works of art out of pieces of colored paper that had been cutted or teared into small shapes.

6. Often, he gave his collages more variety by using pieces from black-and-white or color photographs.

7. If you examine his *Blue Interior, Morning,* you can see that Bearden built this composition around a family eating breakfast.

8. The materials that he assembled were chose for their textural harmony and for their ability to be woven into the color scheme.

9. In his work, Bearden often depicted universal human figures whose complex nature is clearly showed by their different-colored fingers or legs.

10. I could have swore it was nearly impossible to create a pleasing composition with all the figures way down in one corner, but Bearden certainly succeeded.

Review F Proofreading a Paragraph for the Correct Use of Irregular Verbs

Most of the sentences in the following paragraph contain an error in the use of irregular verbs. If a verb form is incorrect, give the correct form. If a sentence is already correct, write *C.*

EXAMPLE   [1] Thanks to James Beckwourth, crossing the Sierra Nevada becomed easier for wagon trains traveling to California.

1. *became*

[1] Pioneers on their way to California had always losed much time when they hit the rugged Sierra Nevada. [2] Wagon trains had turned and drived many miles out of their way, searching for a trail their oxen and horses could take through these mountains. [3] Then James Beckwourth, a frontiersman and explorer, finded an important route between the forbidding peaks. [4] Beckwourth Pass is shown on the map on this page. [5] Other routes, including Donner Pass, had already been discovered, but soon wagonmasters seen that Beckwourth Pass was the lowest in elevation and, therefore, the easiest to cross. [6] James Beckwourth was a versatile man; he been a trapper, trader, explorer, and mountain man. [7] He even fighted in the Second Seminole War as an army scout. [8] During the Gold Rush, he caught gold fever and spended some time prospecting in California. [9] Beckwourth always gotten along quite well with many American Indians—especially the Crow people, who adopted him. [10] By the end of his life, he had became such a good friend to the Crow that they gave him the chance to be a chief!

Review G Proofreading a Paragraph for Correct Verb Forms

Most of the sentences in the following paragraph have one or more errors in verb usage. For each error, write the correct form of the verb. If a sentence is already correct, write *C*. Be prepared to explain your answers.

EXAMPLE   **[1]** As a child, Frida Kahlo often thinked she would become an explorer.

     1. *thought*

┌HELP┐
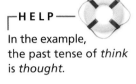
In the example, the past tense of *think* is *thought*.

[**1**] You have probably saw pictures of murals painted by Diego Rivera, the famous Mexican painter. [**2**] However, you may have never came across paintings by Frida Kahlo, his wife. [**3**] Kahlo was a powerful painter in her own right, although she often standed in the shadow of her more renowned husband. [**4**] She taked up painting during her recovery from a streetcar accident in which she had broke several bones. [**5**] Other medical problems arised from time to time throughout her life, and though sometimes she had to paint from her wheelchair, Kahlo always painted straight from her heart. [**6**] In fact, she gave this figure of speech literal expression in one of her paintings, in which she portrays herself using a heart as her palette. [**7**] Kahlo never forgetted her childhood dream of exploration and, instead of seas and mountains, she explored the territory of the human spirit.[**8**] Frida Kahlo striked people who met her as an elegant, intense, and talented woman. [**9**] Although she sometimes found life painful, she was full of fun, high spirits, and love. [**10**] Kahlo is especially noted for her self-portraits, in which she sometimes choosed to paint herself with a tiny portrait of Rivera on her forehead, as in the painting shown here.

Frida Kahlo (1907–54), *Self Portrait as a Tehuana (Diego on my mind)*. Oil on canvas (29 7/8" x 24") (76 cm x 61 cm). Private collection, Mexico City. Photo courtesy of The Metropolitan Museum of Art.

Six Troublesome Verbs

Lie and Lay

The verb *lie* means "to rest," "to recline," or "to be in a place." *Lie* does not take an object. The verb *lay* means "to put [something] in a place." *Lay* generally takes an object.

Base Form	Present Participle	Past	Past Participle
lie	[is] lying	lay	[have] lain
lay	[is] laying	laid	[have] laid

EXAMPLES   The printout **is lying** there next to the computer. [no object]

The secretary **is laying** a copy of the printout next to the computer. [*Printout* is the object of *is laying*.]

The holiday decorations **lay** in the box. [no object]

Martha carefully **laid** the holiday decorations in the box. [*Decorations* is the object of *laid*.]

My basset hound **has lain** in front of the fireplace since early this morning. [no object]

My basset hound **has laid** my slippers in front of the fireplace. [*Slippers* is the object of *has laid*.]

Exercise 6 Choosing the Forms of *Lie* and *Lay*

For each of the following sentences, choose the correct verb form in parentheses. Be prepared to explain your choices.

EXAMPLE   1. The workers are (*laying, lying*) the planks down.
           1. laying

1. The old stereoscope had (*lain, laid*) in the attic for years.
2. The interstate you want to take (*lays, lies*) north of town.
3. The rake is (*laying, lying*) in a pile of leaves.
4. Where has Roger (*laid, lain*) the keys this time?
5. Judy and Adrian (*lay, laid*) their books on the table.
6. She read *The Awakening* as she (*laid, lay*) in the hammock.
7. The key to success (*lays, lies*) in determination.
8. (*Lie, Lay*) here and relax before going on.
9. Ms. Collins (*laid, lay*) the study guides on the table.
10. I was (*laying, lying*) my beach towel on the sand just then.

Exercise 7 Writing Sentences Using the Forms of *Lie* and *Lay*

For each numbered item, use the given subject and verb form to write a correct sentence. Be sure to add an object for forms of *lay*. For participle forms, you will need to give helping verbs. When two forms

---

STYLE TIP

The verb *lie* has definitions other than the ones given here. One common definition is "to tell an untruth."

EXAMPLE
Don't **lie** to them, Irena.

In this use, *lie* does not take an object.

USAGE

HELP

The meaning of the verb in the example sentence is "to put"; therefore, the correct verb is *lay*, and the answer is *laying*.

are spelled the same, the information in parentheses tells you which form and meaning to use.

EXAMPLE

	SUBJECT	VERB FORM
1.	package	lying

1. *The package was lying on the doormat when we got home.*

	SUBJECT	VERB FORM
1.	detectives	lay (base form meaning "put")
2.	sparrow	laid (past form meaning "placed [something]")
3.	father	laying
4.	dog	lain
5.	children	lie
6.	butler	laid (past participle meaning "placed [something]")
7.	Mr. Hill	lay (past form meaning "rested or reclined")
8.	books	lying
9.	Miami	lies
10.	mechanic	lays

Sit and *Set*

The verb *sit* means "to be in a seated, upright position" or "to be in a place." *Sit* seldom takes an object. The verb *set* means "to put [something] in a place." *Set* generally takes an object.

Base Form	Present Participle	Past	Past Participle
sit	[is] sitting	sat	[have] sat
set	[is] setting	set	[have] set

EXAMPLES

May I **sit** here? [no object]

May I **set** the chair here? [*Chair* is the object of *May set*.]

The candles **sat** on the piano, where Karen left them. [no object]

Karen **set** the candles on the piano. [*Candles* is the object of *set*.]

The squirrel **has sat** on the sill awhile. [no object]

The squirrel **has set** a pecan on the sill. [*Pecan* is the object of *has set*.]

STYLE TIP

The verb *set* has definitions other than the one given here.

EXAMPLE
The sun **sets** in the west.

In this use, *set* does not take an object.

Complete each of the following sentences by using the correct form of *sit* or *set*.

EXAMPLE　　**1.** Carrie is _____ in the rocking chair and reading the newspaper.

　　　　　　　1. sitting

1. I _____ in the doctor's waiting room for an hour yesterday morning.
2. Yesterday, we _____ the seedlings on a table on the back porch.
3. _____ the carton down near the door.
4. We were _____ so high up in the theater that the stage looked no bigger than a postage stamp.
5. If we had _____ any longer, we would have been late for class.
6. Let's _____ that pot of hot-and-sour soup on the buffet.
7. Jonathan is _____ aside five dollars each week to buy a CD player.
8. You shouldn't _____ on the damp ground.
9. I hope that Trish and Brandon haven't _____ those plants too close to the radiator.
10. We have _____ around the campfire a long while.

Rise and *Raise*

The verb *rise* means "to go up" or "to get up." *Rise* does not take an object. The verb *raise* means "to lift up" or "to cause [something] to rise." *Raise* generally takes an object.

Base Form	Present Participle	Past	Past Participle
rise	[is] rising	rose	[have] risen
raise	[is] raising	raised	[have] raised

EXAMPLES　　She **rose** from the chair uncertainly. [no object]

She **raised** herself from the chair uncertainly. [*Herself* is the object of *raised*.]

The prices of fresh fruit and vegetables **have risen** considerably because of the drought. [no object]

The grocer **has raised** the price of fresh fruit and vegetables. [*Price* is the object of *has raised*.]

STYLE　　**TIP**

The verb *raise* has definitions other than the one given here. Another common definition is "to grow" or "to bring to maturity."

EXAMPLES
They **raise** sorghum.

She **raised** two foster children.

Notice that both of these uses also take an object.

Exercise 9 **Using *Rise* and *Raise* Correctly**

For each of the following sentences, decide whether the italicized verb form is correct. If it is not, give the correct verb form. If a sentence is already correct, write *C*.

EXAMPLE   **1.** Everyone *raised* for the pledge of allegiance.

        1. rose

1. The cost of a ticket to see a LeAnn Rimes concert *has raised*.
2. The student council president *had risen* the new flag.
3. The Bunsen burner flame *has raised* too high.
4. While fishing with my uncle Etienne in Louisiana, I saw an alligator slowly *raise* out of the mud.
5. The curling smoke *risen* from the pile of leaves.
6. The campers *had rose* early to climb Pikes Peak.
7. The woman who *is rising* now to address the audience has been nominated for vice-president.
8. *Has* the price of gasoline *raised*?
9. The price of a dozen eggs *has been raised*, but you can use this coupon.
10. *Has* the popularity of video games *risen*?

Review H **Choosing the Forms of *Lie* and *Lay*, *Sit* and *Set*, and *Rise* and *Raise***

For each of the following sentences, choose the correct verb form in parentheses. Be prepared to explain your choices.

EXAMPLE   **1.** I think I will (*lay, lie*) here and rest awhile.

        1. lie

1. They (*sit, set*) the yearbooks in Mr. Cohen's office.
2. The thermostat should have kept the temperature from (*rising, raising*).
3. Where was Emily (*sitting, setting*) at the end of *Our Town*?
4. Has the number of traffic fatalities (*raised, risen*)?
5. San Francisco (*lays, lies*) southwest of Sacramento.
6. Let's (*set, sit*) down and talk about the problem.
7. The price of citrus fruit (*rises, raises*) after a freeze.
8. Hours of driving (*lay, laid*) ahead of us.
9. A replica of Rodin's *The Thinker* had (*set, sat*) there.
10. The helium-filled balloon (*rose, raised*) into the air.

┌─HELP─
The meaning of the verb in the example is "to recline"; therefore, the correct verb is *lie*.

Review I Choosing the Forms of *Lie* and *Lay*, *Sit* and *Set*, and *Rise* and *Raise*

Many familiar expressions and sayings include a form of *lie*, *lay*, *sit*, *set*, *rise*, or *raise*. Complete each expression below by choosing the correct form from the pair given.

EXAMPLE   **1.** I just want to ____ the record straight. (*sit, set*)

        1. *set*

1. Let sleeping dogs ____. (*lie, lay*)
2. ____ down your burden. (*Lie, Lay*)
3. Those who would deceive the fox must ____ early in the morning. (*rise, raise*)
4. I'm ____ on top of the world. (*setting, sitting*)
5. If you can't ____ the bridge, lower the river. (*rise, raise*)
6. He who ____ down with dogs gets up with fleas. (*lies, lays*)
7. Cream always ____ to the top. (*rises, raises*)
8. ____ down—you're rocking the boat! (*Set, Sit*)
9. Whenever possible, ____ to the occasion. (*rise, raise*)
10. ____ high standards. (*Set, Sit*)

Tense

21d. The *tense* of a verb indicates the time of the action or of the state of being expressed by the verb.

The tenses are formed from the verb's principal parts. Verbs in English have the six tenses shown on the following time line:

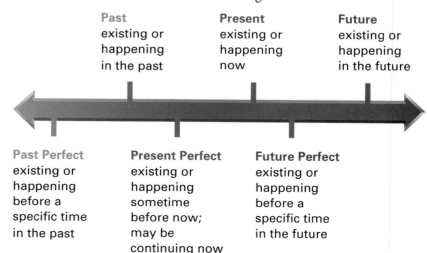

Past	Present	Future
existing or happening in the past	existing or happening now	existing or happening in the future

Past Perfect	Present Perfect	Future Perfect
existing or happening before a specific time in the past	existing or happening sometime before now; may be continuing now	existing or happening before a specific time in the future

Verb Conjugation

Listing all of the forms of a verb according to tense is called *conjugating* a verb.

Conjugation of the Verb *See* in the Active Voice

Present Tense

Singular	Plural
I see	we see
you see	you see
he, she, it sees	they see

Past Tense

Singular	Plural
I saw	we saw
you saw	you saw
he, she, it saw	they saw

Future Tense

Singular	Plural
I will (shall) see	we will (shall) see
you will (shall) see	you will (shall) see
he, she, it will (shall) see	they will (shall) see

Present Perfect Tense

Singular	Plural
I have seen	we have seen
you have seen	you have seen
he, she, it has seen	they have seen

Past Perfect Tense

Singular	Plural
I had seen	we had seen
you had seen	you had seen
he, she, it had seen	they had seen

(continued)

Reference Note

For a **conjugation of *see* in the passive voice,** see page 676.

STYLE TIP

Traditionally, the helping verbs *shall* and *will* were used to mean different things. Now, however, *shall* can be used almost interchangeably with *will*.

USAGE

(continued)

Conjugation of the Verb *See* in the Active Voice	
Future Perfect Tense	
Singular	**Plural**
I will (shall) have seen	we will (shall) have seen
you will (shall) have seen	you will (shall) have seen
he, she, it will (shall) have seen	they will (shall) have seen

The Progressive Form

Each of the tenses has an additional form, called the ***progressive form,*** which expresses continuing action or state of being. It consists of the appropriate tense of *be* plus the present participle of a verb. The progressive form is not a separate tense but another form of each of the six tenses.

Present Progressive	am, is, are seeing
Past Progressive	was, were seeing
Future Progressive	will (shall) be seeing
Present Perfect Progressive	has been, have been seeing
Past Perfect Progressive	had been seeing
Future Perfect Progressive	will (shall) have been seeing

STYLE TIP

The emphatic form is also used in questions and in negative statements. These uses do not place any special emphasis on the verb.

QUESTION
Do you **know** him?

NEGATIVE STATEMENT
They **do**n't [**do** not] **have** any.

The Emphatic Form

The present and past tenses have another form, called the ***emphatic form,*** which shows emphasis. In the present tense, the emphatic form of a verb consists of *do* or *does* plus the base form. In the past tense, the emphatic form consists of *did* plus the base form.

Present Emphatic	do, does see
Past Emphatic	did see

The Verb *Be*

The verb *be* is the most irregular verb in English. The chart on the following pages gives the conjugation of *be*.

Conjugation of the Verb *Be*

Present Tense

Singular	Plural
I am	we are
you are	you are
he, she, it is	they are

Present Progressive: am, are, is being

Past Tense

Singular	Plural
I was	we were
you were	you were
he, she, it was	they were

Past Progressive: was, were being

Future Tense

Singular	Plural
I will (shall) be	we will (shall) be
you will (shall) be	you will (shall) be
he, she, it will (shall) be	they will (shall) be

Present Perfect Tense

Singular	Plural
I have been	we have been
you have been	you have been
he, she, it has been	they have been

Past Perfect Tense

Singular	Plural
I had been	we had been
you had been	you had been
he, she, it had been	they had been

(continued)

USAGE

Conjugation of the Verb *Be*	
Future Perfect Tense	
Singular	**Plural**
I will (shall) have been	we will (shall) have been
you will (shall) have been	you will (shall) have been
he, she, *or* it will (shall) have been	they will (shall) have been

The conjugation of the verb *be* differs from that of any other verb. The progressive form of *be* is rarely used in any tenses other than the present and past tenses, and none of the tenses have the emphatic form.

The Uses of the Tenses

21e. Each of the six tenses has its own uses.

(1) The *present tense* expresses an action or a state of being that is occurring now, at the present time.

EXAMPLES   Martina **races** down the court and **shoots** the ball. [present]

        The fans **are cheering** wildly. [present progressive]

        Martina and her teammates **do look** confident. [present emphatic]

The present tense is also used

* to show customary or habitual action or state of being
* to convey a general truth—something that is always true
* to summarize the plot or subject matter of a literary work (such use is called *literary present*)
* to make a historical event seem current (such use is called *historical present*)
* to express future time

EXAMPLES   On Saturdays I usually **go** to the tennis court and **practice** my serve. [customary action]

        The gravity of the moon **pulls** on the earth's oceans and **causes** the tides. [general truth]

USAGE

The Dark Child **relates** the experiences of a boy growing up in an African village. [literary present]

In a surprise move, the Greeks **construct** a huge wooden horse and **leave** it outside the walls of Troy. [historical present]

The tournament that **starts** next Thursday **continues** for two weeks. [future time]

(2) The *past tense* expresses an action or a state of being that occurred in the past and did not continue into the present.

EXAMPLES   In the last lap the runner **fell** and **injured** his knee. [past]

He **was trying** to break the record for that event. [past progressive]

The injury **did prevent** him from competing in the relay race. [past emphatic]

NOTE   A past action or state of being may also be shown by using *used to.*

EXAMPLE   I **used to hate** spicy food.

(3) The *future tense* expresses an action or a state of being that will occur. The future tense is formed with the helping verb *shall* or *will.*

EXAMPLES   The president **will** not **return** to Washington today. [future]

We **will** (or **shall**) **be holding** a press conference at noon. [future progressive]

A future action or state of being may also be expressed by using

- the present tense of *be* followed by *going to* and the base form of a verb
- the present tense of *be* followed by *about to* and the base form of a verb
- the present tense of a verb with a word or phrase that expresses future time

EXAMPLES   My cousins **are going to visit** Japan in July.

Ms. Scheirer **is about to announce** the winners.

The boxer **defends** his title **next Friday night**.

BORN LOSER reprinted by permission of Newspaper Enterprise Association, Inc.

(4) The ***present perfect tense*** expresses an action or a state of being that occurred at an indefinite time in the past. The present perfect tense is formed with the helping verb *have* or *has.*

EXAMPLES   Miguel and Tim **have** already **entered** the information into the computer. [present perfect]

Who **has been using** this computer? [present perfect progressive]

The present perfect tense is also used to express an action or a state of being that began in the past and that continues into the present.

EXAMPLES   Mr. Steele **has taught** school for twenty-one years. [present perfect]

He **has been coaching** soccer since 1996. [present perfect progressive]

> **NOTE**   Do not use the present perfect tense to express a specific time in the past. Use the past tense.
>
> NONSTANDARD   They have bought a computer last week. [*Last week* indicates a specific time in the past.]
>
> STANDARD   They **bought** a computer last week. [past tense]

(5) The ***past perfect tense*** expresses an action or a state of being that ended before some other past action or state of being. The past perfect tense is formed with the helping verb *had.*

EXAMPLES   Paul **had traveled** several miles before he realized his mistake. [past perfect]

He discovered that he **had been misreading** the road map. [past perfect progressive]

> **NOTE**   Use the past perfect tense in an *"if"* clause that expresses the earlier of two past actions.
>
> EXAMPLE   If I **had used** the spellchecker, I would have corrected the spelling errors.

Reference Note

For more information about using **past perfect in *"if"* clauses,** see Rule 21g on page 673.

(6) The ***future perfect tense*** expresses an action or a state of being that will end before some other future occurrence. The future perfect tense is formed with the helping verbs *shall have* or *will have.*

EXAMPLES   By the time school begins in August, you **will have saved** enough money to buy the car. [future perfect]

By then, you **will have been working** here a year. [future perfect progressive]

Exercise 10 **Identifying the Six Tenses**

Identify the tenses of the italicized verbs in each of the following pairs of sentences. Be prepared to explain how these differences in tense alter the meanings of the sentences.

EXAMPLE   **1. a.** Mr. Olmos *taught* Spanish for thirty years.
b. Mr. Olmos *has taught* Spanish for thirty years.

1. *a—past tense; b—present perfect tense*

1. a. Channel 5 News *has reported* on how successfully Asian immigrants have adjusted to life in the United States.
b. Channel 5 News *is reporting* on how successfully Asian immigrants have adjusted to life in the United States.

2. a. I *took* piano lessons for three years.
b. I *have taken* piano lessons for three years.

3. a. We *will do* our research on Friday.
b. We *will have done* our research on Friday.

4. a. Jane *has studied* recent fossil discoveries.
b. Jane *had studied* recent fossil discoveries.

5. a. *Do* you *know* that voting by secret ballot originated in Australia?
b. *Did* you *know* that voting by secret ballot originated in Australia?

6. a. We *did send* out invitations.
b. We *are sending* out invitations.

7. a. I *will make* a time line of the Middle Ages before this weekend.
b. I *will have made* a time line of the Middle Ages before this weekend.

8. a. Ms. Wong *was* the club sponsor for five years.
b. Ms. Wong *has been* the club sponsor for five years.

9. a. *Did* the jury *reach* a verdict?
b. *Has* the jury *reached* a verdict?

10. a. I *think* that I *have seen* her somewhere before.
b. I *thought* that I *had seen* her somewhere before.

┌HELP──

The meaning of the first sentence is that Mr. Olmos used to teach but no longer does. The second sentence means that Mr. Olmos is still teaching now.

For each of the following sentences, change the tense of the verb according to the instructions in italics.

EXAMPLE

1. Do those blue jays still nest in the hedge? (*Change to present progressive tense.*)

1. *Are those blue jays still nesting in the hedge?*

1. Ivy roots made their way into the bricks. (*Change to present progressive tense.*)
2. By next June, Xavier will have studied piano for ten years. (*Change to future perfect progressive tense.*)
3. He runs for thirty minutes every morning. (*Change to past perfect progressive tense.*)
4. These scissors had been needing sharpening. (*Change to present emphatic tense.*)
5. A true samurai always follows *bushido,* a code of honor. (*Change to past emphatic tense.*)
6. A cool layer of air is holding the thermal inversion layer in place. (*Change to future perfect tense.*)
7. The heady scent of Mexican tuberoses filled the air. (*Change to past perfect tense.*)
8. Are you calling about the tickets? (*Change to past progressive tense.*)
9. By my birthday, I will have visited relatives in Arizona. (*Change to future progressive tense.*)
10. We were singing "Home on the Range." (*Change to present perfect progressive tense.*)

Special Problems in the Use of Tenses

Sequence of Tenses

21f. Use tense forms correctly to show relationships between verbs in a sentence. Do not change needlessly from one tense to another.

(1) When describing events that occur at the same time, use verbs in the same tense.

EXAMPLES   The coach **blows** the whistle as the swimmers **dive** into the pool. [present tense]

The coach **blew** the whistle as the swimmers **dived** into the pool. [past tense]

(2) When describing events that occur at different times, use verbs in different tenses to show the order of events.

EXAMPLES   She **plays soccer** now, but last year she **played** field hockey. [Because her soccer playing is occurring now, the present tense form *plays* is the correct form. Her field hockey playing occurred at a specific time in the past and preceded her soccer playing; therefore, the past tense form *played* is the correct form.]

Since the new band director **took** over, our band **has won** all of its contests. [Because the new director took over at a specific time in the past, the past tense form *took* is correct. The winning has taken place over a period of time and continues into the present; therefore, the present perfect tense form *has won* is used.]

The tense you use depends on the meaning that you want to express.

EXAMPLES   I **think** I **have** a B average in math. [Both verbs are in the present tense to indicate that both actions are occurring now.]

I **think** I **had** a B average in math. [The change to the past tense in the second verb implies that I had a B average sometime in the past.]

Lia **said** that she **lived** near the park. [Both verbs are in the past tense to indicate that both actions happened in the past.]

Lia **said** that she **lives** near the park. [The change to the present tense in the second verb indicates that Lia still lives near the park.]

21g. Do not use *would have* in "if" clauses that express the earlier of two past actions. Use the past perfect tense.

NONSTANDARD   If she would have handed in her application, she would have gotten the job.

STANDARD   If she **had handed** in her application, she would have gotten the job.

NONSTANDARD   If Felita would have asked her parents, she probably could have gone with us.

STANDARD   If Felita **had asked** her parents, she probably could have gone with us.

Exercise 12 Using Tenses Correctly

Each of the following sentences contains an error in the use of tenses. Identify the error, and give the correct form of the verb.

EXAMPLE   1. The holidays will begin by the time we arrive in Miami.

1. *will begin—will have begun*

1. Would you still have told that joke if we said we had already heard it?
2. Who found that the earth revolved around the sun?
3. By the time we get to the picnic area, the rain will stop.
4. In July my parents will be married for twenty-five years.
5. If the books have been cataloged last week, why haven't they been shelved?
6. I would have agreed if you would have asked me sooner.
7. Val claims that cats made the best pets.
8. After Sam had answered, Mr. Catalano says, "There were no rabbits."
9. Before leaving the house, we have closed the windows.
10. As a witness to the accident, Pam told the police what happened.

The Present Infinitive and the Present Perfect Infinitive

Infinitives have present and present perfect forms.

Reference Note

For more about **infinitives** and their uses, see page 546.

Present Infinitive	to see	to be	to change
Present Perfect Infinitive	to have seen	to have been	to have changed

21h. The ***present infinitive*** expresses an action or a state of being that follows another action or state of being.

EXAMPLES   Latrice hopes **to attend** the Super Bowl. [The action expressed by *to attend* follows the action expressed by *hopes.*]

Latrice had planned **to go** to the game with her brother. [The action expressed by *to go* follows the action expressed by *had planned.*]

21i. The ***present perfect infinitive*** expresses an action or a state of being that precedes another action or state of being.

EXAMPLES   The divers claim **to have located** an ancient sailing vessel. [The action expressed by *to have located* precedes the action expressed by *claim.*]

They claimed **to have spent** three weeks exploring the ship. [The action expressed by *to have spent* precedes the action expressed by *claimed.*]

The Present Participle, the Past Participle, and the Present Perfect Participle

Participles have present, past, and present perfect forms.

Present Participle	seeing	being	changing
Past Participle	seen	been	changed
Present Perfect Participle	having seen	having been	having changed

21j. When used as a verbal, the *present participle* or *past participle* expresses an action or a state of being that occurs at the same time as another action or state of being.

EXAMPLES **Gazing** through the telescope, I saw the rings around Saturn. [The action expressed by *Gazing* occurs at the same time as the action expressed by *saw.*]

Committed to the recycling project, the students work tirelessly to see it through. [The action expressed by *Committed* occurs at the same time as the action expressed by *work.*]

21k. When used as a verbal, *the present perfect participle* expresses an action or a state of being that precedes another action or state of being.

EXAMPLES **Having completed** her outline, Kate wrote the first draft of her research paper. [The action expressed by *Having completed* precedes the action expressed by *wrote.*]

Having proofread her research paper, Kate is typing the final draft. [The action expressed by *Having proofread* precedes the action expressed by *is typing.*]

Reference Note
For more about **verbals,** see page 540.

Reference Note
For more information about **participles** and their uses, see page 540.

USAGE

Review J Using Tenses Correctly

Most of the sentences on the following page contain an error in the use of verbs and verbals. Identify each error, and give the correct form of the verb or verbal. If a sentence is already correct, write *C*.

EXAMPLE   1. I would have taken more money on my trip to Japan if I would have known what the exchange rate was.

          1. *would have known—had known*

1. When you charge the battery in the car, be sure to have protected your eyes and hands from the sulfuric acid in the battery.
2. Deciding to attend the concert at Boyer Hall, we bought four tickets for Saturday night.
3. By the time Friday is over, we will hear some great music.
4. If I would have known about the free offer, I would have sent in a coupon.
5. My old skates are lying in my closet for the past two years.
6. I had hoped to have gone swimming yesterday.
7. Having sung the aria, Jessye Norman received a standing ovation.
8. If I had the address, I would have been able to deliver the package.
9. Dave goes to the dentist three months ago when his tooth began to hurt.
10. The volcano sent up a huge cloud of ash and smoke that will have closed the nearby airport for several hours.

Active Voice and Passive Voice

Voice is the form a verb takes to indicate whether the subject of the verb performs or receives the action. When the subject of a verb performs the action, the verb is in the *active voice.* When the subject receives the action, the verb is in the *passive voice.*

    The verb in a passive construction always includes a form of *be* and the past participle of a verb. Notice in the following conjugation of the verb *see* in the passive voice that the form of *be* determines the tense of the passive verb.

Reference Note

For more discussion of **transitive verbs,** see page 498.

Reference Note

The **conjugation of *see* in the active voice** is on page 665.

Conjugation of the Verb *See* in the Passive Voice	
Present Tense	
Singular	**Plural**
I am seen	we are seen
you are seen	you are seen
he, she, it is seen	they are seen
Present Progressive: am, are, is being seen	

Conjugation of the Verb *See* in the Passive Voice

Past Tense

Singular	Plural
I was seen	we were seen
you were seen	you were seen
he, she, it was seen	they were seen

Past Progressive: was, were being seen

Future Tense

Singular	Plural
I will (shall) be seen	we will (shall) be seen
you will (shall) be seen	you will (shall) be seen
he, she, it will (shall) be seen	they will (shall) be seen

Present Perfect Tense

Singular	Plural
I have been seen	we have been seen
you have been seen	you have been seen
he, she, it has been seen	they have been seen

Past Perfect Tense

Singular	Plural
I had been seen	we had been seen
you had been seen	you had been seen
he, she, it had been seen	they had been seen

Future Perfect Tense

Singular	Plural
I will (shall) have been seen	we will (shall) have been seen
you will (shall) have been seen	you will (shall) have been seen
he, she, it will (shall) have been seen	they will (shall) have been seen

USAGE

As the following examples show, transitive verbs in the active voice have direct objects and transitive verbs in the passive voice do not.

ACTIVE VOICE   Gloria Naylor **wrote** *The Women of Brewster Place.* [*The Women of Brewster Place* is the direct object.]

PASSIVE VOICE   *The Women of Brewster Place* **was written** by Gloria Naylor. [no direct object]

ACTIVE VOICE   The optometrist **adjusted** the eyeglasses. [*Eyeglasses* is the direct object.]

PASSIVE VOICE   The eyeglasses **were adjusted** by the optometrist. [no direct object]

ACTIVE VOICE   Carol **has adopted** the two puppies. [*Puppies* is the direct object.]

PASSIVE VOICE   The two puppies **have been adopted** by Carol. [no direct object]

PASSIVE VOICE   The two puppies **have been adopted.** [no direct object]

From the examples above, you can see how an active construction can become a passive construction. The verb from the active construction becomes a past participle preceded by a form of *be.* The object of the verb becomes the subject of the verb in a passive construction. The subject in an active construction may become the object of the preposition *by* in a passive construction. (As the last example shows, a prepositional phrase beginning with *by* is not always necessary.)

The Retained Object

A transitive verb in the active voice often has both an indirect object and a direct object. When such a verb is put in the passive voice, either object can become the subject. The other object then serves as a complement called a ***retained object.***

                   S   **V**   **IO**   **DO**
ACTIVE VOICE   Ms. Ribas gave each student a thesaurus.

S	**V**	**RO**

PASSIVE VOICE   Each student was given a thesaurus (by Ms. Ribas).

S	**V**	**RO**

PASSIVE VOICE   A thesaurus was given each student (by Ms. Ribas).

As you can see, the indirect object *student* in the active construction becomes the subject in the first passive construction, and the direct object *thesaurus* remains a complement. In the second passive construction, *thesaurus* is the subject, and *student* is the complement. Remember, a complement in a passive construction is a retained object, not a direct object or an indirect object.

The Uses of the Passive Voice

21l. The passive voice should be used sparingly. Use the passive voice in the following situations:

(1) when you do not know the performer of the action

EXAMPLES   Asbestos **was used** for making fireproof materials.

An anonymous letter **had been sent** to the police chief.

(2) when you do not want to reveal the performer of the action

EXAMPLES   Several flat notes **were hit** during the opening number.

The missing paintings **have been returned** to the museum.

(3) when you want to emphasize the receiver of the action

EXAMPLES   Penicillin **was discovered** accidentally.

This book **has been translated** into more than one hundred languages.

Exercise 13 Revising Sentences in the Passive Voice

Revise the sentences on the following page by changing the passive voice to active voice wherever the change is desirable. If you think the passive voice is preferable, write *C*. Be prepared to explain your answers.

EXAMPLE   1. A variety of cooking methods and utensils were invented by early humans.
            1. *Early humans invented a variety of cooking methods and utensils.*

USAGE

COMPUTER TIP

If you use a computer when you write, you may want to find out more about the different kinds of style-checking software programs that are available. At least one such program checks for overuse of passive voice. Remember, though, that the computer can highlight the passive-voice verbs it finds, but it cannot determine whether they are used for a particular reason.

HELP

In the example, the active voice is preferable because we know and want to reveal the performer of the action.

1. At first, roots and berries were gathered and eaten by these people.
2. The discovery that certain foods can be improved by cooking may have accidentally been made by them.
3. Slaughtered animals or piles of edible roots may have been left near the fire by hunters and gatherers.
4. It was noticed by them that when food was cooked, it tasted better.
5. The first ovens were formed from pits lined with stones and hot coals.
6. It wasn't long before ovens were built above the ground with some kind of chimney to carry away the smoke.
7. Primitive kettles were made by early humans by smearing clay over reed baskets and drying them in the sun.
8. Liquid foods could then be kept in such a basket for short periods without leaking out.
9. When a clay-coated basket was placed near the flames by a prehistoric cook to heat its contents, sometimes the clay was baked by the high temperature into a pottery shell.
10. Once the simple physics of making pottery was mastered by early people, they learned to create the pottery shell without the basket.

Mood

Reference Note

For examples of all of the **tense forms in the indicative mood,** see the conjugations on pages 680 and 1061.

Mood is the form a verb takes to indicate the attitude of the person using the verb. Verbs in English may be in one of three moods: the *indicative,* the *imperative,* or the *subjunctive.*

21m. The *indicative mood* expresses a fact, an opinion, or a question.

EXAMPLES   Andrei Sakharov **was** the nuclear physicist who **won** the Nobel Peace Prize in 1975.

All of us **think** that this baseball team **is** the best one in the entire state.

Can you **explain** the difference between a meteor and a meteorite?

21n. The *imperative mood* expresses a direct command or request.

The imperative mood of a verb has only one form. It is the same as the verb's base form.

USAGE

EXAMPLES   **Explain** the difference between a meteor and a meteorite.

Please **fasten** your seat belt.

Stop!

21o. The *subjunctive mood* expresses a suggestion, a necessity, a condition contrary to fact, or a wish.

Only the present and past tenses have distinctive subjunctive forms. The following partial conjugation of *be* shows how the present and past tense forms in the subjunctive mood differ from those in the indicative mood.

Present Indicative		Present Subjunctive	
Singular	**Plural**	**Singular**	**Plural**
I am	we are	(that) I be	(that) we be
you are	you are	(that) you be	(that) you be
he, she, it is	they are	(that) he, she, it be	(that) they be

Past Indicative		Past Subjunctive	
Singular	**Plural**	**Singular**	**Plural**
I was	we were	(if) I were	(if) we were
you were	you were	(if) you were	(if) you were
he, she, it was	they were	(if) he, she, it were	(if) they were

HELP
The use of *that* and *if* in the chart is explained on the next page.

USAGE

Notice in the above conjugation that the present subjunctive form of a verb is the same as the base form. For verbs other than *be,* the past subjunctive form is the same as the past tense form. The verb *be* has two past tense forms. As you can see, however, the past tense form *was* in the indicative mood becomes *were* in the subjunctive mood. Therefore, *were* is the only past subjunctive form of *be.*

GREETING CARDS · all occasions ·
I NEED A GET-WELL CARD FOR MY OLD ENGLISH TEACHER. DO YOU HAVE ONE THAT CAJOLES IN THE INDICATIVE MOOD RATHER THAN COMMANDS IN THE IMPERATIVE?

FRANK & ERNEST reprinted by permission of Newspaper Enterprise Association, Inc.

USAGE

(1) The *present subjunctive* expresses a suggestion or a necessity.

Generally, the verb in a subordinate clause beginning with *that* is in the subjunctive mood when the independent clause contains a word indicating a suggestion (such as *ask, request, suggest,* or *recommend*) or a word indicating a necessity (such as *necessary* or *essential*).

EXAMPLES Ms. Chávez suggested that he **apply** for the job.

The moderator at the convention requested that the state delegates **be seated.**

It is necessary that she **attend** the convention.

It is required that you **be** here on time.

(2) The *past subjunctive* expresses a condition contrary to fact or expresses a wish.

In general, a clause beginning with *if, as if,* or *as though* expresses a condition contrary to fact—something that is not true. In such a clause, use the past subjunctive. Remember that *were* is the only past subjunctive form of *be.*

EXAMPLES If I **were** you, I'd have those tires checked.

If he **were** older, he would be allowed to stay up later.

Because of the bad telephone connection, Gregory sounded as though he **were** ten thousand miles away.

Similarly, use the past subjunctive to express a wish—a condition that is desirable.

EXAMPLES I wish I **were** more patient than I am.

Reiko wishes that the summer **were**n't so hot.

> **Exercise 14 Identifying the Mood of Verbs**

For each of the following sentences, identify the mood of the italicized verb as *indicative, imperative,* or *subjunctive.*

EXAMPLE 1. I wish I *were* going with you to the Bahamas.
         1. *subjunctive*

1. Theo, *stand* back a safe distance while I try again to start this lawn mower.

2. Did you know that Tamisha's mother *is* the new manager at the supermarket?

3. Bradley says that if he *were* president, he would take steps to increase the minimum wage.

4. I suggest that these young maple trees *be* planted quickly, before they wilt.

5. *Were* you and your two brothers excited about visiting your birthplace in Mexico?

6. This Lenni-Lenape moccasin *was* found near Matawan, New Jersey.

7. Stay there and *be* a good dog while I go into the bakery, Molly.

8. When my dad saw the dented fender, he looked as if he *were* ready to explode.

9. "I wish that you *were* not moving so far away," muttered my best friend, Bao.

10. Mr. Darwin said that you *will be* the bus monitor on our next class trip.

Modals

21p. A *modal* is a helping, or auxiliary, verb that is joined with a main verb to express an attitude toward the action or state of being of the main verb.

The helping verbs *can, could, may, might, must, ought, shall, should, will,* and *would* are modals.

(1) The modals *can* and *could* are used to express ability.

EXAMPLES   **Can** you **repair** this necklace?

I **could** not **have solved** the problem without your help.

(2) The modal *may* is used to express permission or possibility.

EXAMPLES   **May** I **use** your computer? [permission]

You **may want** to add a little more garlic to the pasta sauce. [possibility]

(3) The modal *might*, like *may*, is used to express possibility.

Often, the possibility expressed by *might* is less likely than the possibility expressed by *may*.

EXAMPLE   The jury **might reach** its verdict today, but I doubt that it will.

Reference Note

For more about **helping (auxiliary) verbs** and **main verbs,** see page 497.

STYLE   TIP

Can is often used to express permission in informal situations. In formal situations, you should use *may*.

INFORMAL   Can I borrow your book?

FORMAL   **May** I borrow your book?

Mood   **683**

(4) The modal *must* is used most often to express a requirement.

Sometimes, *must* is used to express an explanation.

EXAMPLES   Antonio and I **must be** home by 7:00 P.M. [requirement]

You **must have overwatered** this plant, for many of its leaves have turned yellow. [explanation]

(5) The modal *ought* is used to express obligation or likelihood.

EXAMPLES   You **ought** to send her a thank-you note. [obligation]

The rehearsal **ought** to be over by 8:00 P.M. [likelihood]

(6) The modals *shall* and *will* are used to express future time.

EXAMPLES   I **will** (or **shall**) **be** eighteen years old next month.

When **will** the election results **be announced**?

(7) The modal *should* is used to express a recommendation, an obligation, or a possibility.

EXAMPLES   My guidance counselor told me that I **should take** the Scholastic Aptitude Test in October. [recommendation]

You **should have called** Ms. Langley as soon as you heard the news. [obligation]

Should you **decide** to go to the ceremony, please let me know. [possibility]

(8) The modal *would* is used to express the conditional form of a verb.

A conditional verb form usually appears in an independent clause that is joined with an *"if"* clause. The *"if"* clause explains *under what condition(s)* the action or state of being of the conditional verb takes place.

EXAMPLE   If I had known you were interested in the job, I **would have offered** it to you.

Would is used also to express future time in a subordinate clause when the verb in the independent clause is in the past tense.

EXAMPLE   Calista said that she **would meet** us at the restaurant at 6:00 P.M.

Additionally, *would* is used to express an action that was repeated in the past, an invitation, or a request.

USAGE

EXAMPLES   Every summer, my family and I **would go** camping in the Blue Ridge Mountains. [repeated past action]

Would you **like** to attend the arts and crafts festival? [invitation]

Would you please **help** Damon program the VCR? [request]

Exercise 15 **Writing Appropriate Modals**

For each of the following sentences, supply an appropriate modal.

EXAMPLE   **1.** Provided that the agreement is acceptable to all parties, I _____ draw up the contract.

1. *will*

1. Oops, the board is too short; I _____ have measured more carefully.
2. No, class, you certainly _____ not leave twenty minutes early today.
3. "I definitely _____ call you tomorrow," Eleanor promised.
4. It _____ rain; then again, it _____ not.
5. There are no exceptions: All students _____ complete two semesters of American government classes.
6. We were so close to the stage that we _____ touch the microphone.
7. Although the rules allowed a substitute, the judges _____ not allow it.
8. Explain this spreadsheet to me; I simply _____ not figure it out.
9. The committee _____ not have chosen anyone better than Esteban.
10. The word *kosher* denotes food that _____ be eaten according to Jewish dietary laws; these laws exclude shellfish and pork.

HELP

Although more than one response may be possible for each item in Exercise 15, you need to give only one answer for each.

USAGE

Review K **Proofreading Sentences for Correct Verb Usage**

Most of the following sentences contain informal or incorrect verb usage. Identify each informal or incorrect usage, and give the correct verb form. If a sentence is already correct according to the rules of formal, standard usage, write *C*.

EXAMPLE   **1.** After he had passed the jewelry store, he wished he went into it.

1. *went—had gone*

1. Do you think that she volunteer to help the victims of the flood?
2. The rock group had finished the concert, but the audience called for another set.
3. If Sherrie would not have missed the printer's deadline, the yearbook delivery would have been on time.

4. Although I thought I planned my trip down to the last detail, there was one thing I had forgotten.
5. If you would have remembered to bring along something to read, you would not have been so bored.
6. The smell from the paper mill laid over the town like a blanket.
7. Stephanie says she enjoyed working on the kibbutz in Israel last summer, but she hardly got a chance to set down the whole time.
8. By the time they had smelled the smoke, the flames had already begun to spread.
9. I hope to have the opportunity to revise my essay.
10. If Emiliano Zapata would have known the invitation was a trap, he would not have been ambushed.

Review L Proofreading a Paragraph for Correct Use of Verbs

Most of the following sentences contain awkward, informal, or incorrect verb usage. If a sentence has an awkward, informal, or incorrect usage, revise the sentence, using the verb form that is correct in formal, standard English. If a sentence is already correct, write *C*.

EXAMPLE [1] After he had lit the candle, Dad begun to recite the first principle of Kwanzaa.

1. begun—began

[1] Kwanzaa is celebrated by African Americans for more than a quarter of a century. [2] This holiday has been created in 1966 by Maulana Karenga, who is a professor of black studies at California State University. [3] Dr. Karenga wished that there was a nonreligious holiday especially for black Americans. [4] If he has not treasured his own background, we would not have this inspiring celebration to enjoy. [5] Professor Karenga has long believed that people's heritage should be celebrated by them. [6] Recently, more and more African Americans have began to reserve the seven-day period immediately following Christmas for Kwanzaa. [7] If you would have joined my family for Kwanzaa last year, you would have heard my grandfather's talk about family values and about African Americans who have fought for freedom and honor. [8] We all wore items of traditional African clothing and displayed a red, black, and green flag to symbolize Africa. [9] Mom lay out a wonderful feast each night, and we lit a candle and talked about one of the seven principles of Kwanzaa. [10] I wish I asked you to our house last year for Kwanzaa, and I will definitely invite you this year.

Chapter Review

A. Using Irregular Verbs Correctly

For each of the following sentences, identify the verb form in parentheses that is correct in standard, formal English.

1. These gloves have (*lay, laid, lain*) on the bureau all week.
2. If I (*knew, had known, would have known*) about the team tryouts, I would have signed up for them.
3. Only after I (*had went, had gone, went*) home did I remember my dental appointment.
4. My younger brother (*has took, taken, has taken*) my notebook.
5. The book (*laid, lay, lied, lain*) open at page 35.
6. Even though the sun had not yet (*rose, risen, raised*), my uncles were out fishing on the lake.
7. I suddenly knew what I had wanted (*saying, to say, to have said*).
8. I didn't notice that my pocket was (*teared, torn, tore*).
9. I would be careful with that if I (*had been, were, was*) you.
10. By this time next year, Lupe (*has began, will have begun, will begin*) classes at the University of Colorado.

B. Proofreading Sentences for Verb Usage

In each of the following sentences, identify the incorrect verb form, and then write the correct form. If a sentence is already correct, write *C*.

11. A beautiful oak tree raises above the meadow.
12. If you would have visited Mexico City, you might have seen the great pyramids of Tenochtitlán.
13. Sara wishes that she had went to the beach yesterday.
14. Edmundo ought to go to the Diez y Seis party yesterday.
15. One of the statues has fell off its base.
16. How long did it lie on the floor?
17. Since last September I missed only one day of school.
18. I predict that by next year Lorenzo will grow taller than his sister.
19. Fortunately, I have never been stinged by a bee.
20. The unusual pattern in this wool material was woven by Seamus MacMhuiris, an artist who uses bold geometric designs.

C. Proofreading Sentences for Verb Usage

Identify each incorrect verb form in the following sentences, and then write the verb form that is correct in standard, formal English. If a sentence is already correct, write *C*.

21. Sit this pitcher of lemonade on the table, please.

22. If Maya would have listened to the instructor, she wouldn't have made that mistake.

23. The mural *Sky Above Clouds* was painted by Georgia O'Keeffe.

24. Martin's teacher has suggested that Martin learns more about the history of his town before writing the essay.

25. When Maritza left the lecture, she knew she wanted to have studied the gray wolf.

26. Mr. Huang looked as if he was about to faint.

27. Mount Etna erupted in Sicily in 1669, and approximately 20,000 people are killed.

28. The Koslowski family use to have a Dalmatian.

29. By this time next month, the software company will ship a hundred thousand copies of its new game.

30. Bette studied economics for two years before she realized that she really wanted to make documentary films.

D. Revising Sentences in the Passive Voice

Revise the following sentences by changing the passive voice to active voice.

31. The rules of the game were explained to me by the coach.

32. The half-time show was enjoyed by the crowd.

33. It was noticed by the choir that Linda was quite a good singer.

34. The quilt that was made by me won second prize.

35. The ball that was thrown by me was caught by the dog.

E. Identifying the Mood of Verbs

For each of the following sentences, identify the mood of the italicized verb as *indicative, imperative,* or *subjunctive.*

36. What *is* the distance between the earth and the moon?

37. Mimi wishes that the winters in Michigan *were* not so long.

38. *Remember* to remove your shoes in a Japanese restaurant.

39. I strongly recommend that you *see* a doctor about that cough.

40. The members of the football team played as if they *were* unaware of the driving rain.

Writing Application

Using Verbs in a Story

Active Voice and Passive Voice A writers' club is holding a contest to find the most exciting opening of an adventure story. To enter the contest, write a two- or three-paragraph opening for an adventure story. Use active-voice verbs to make your sentences lively and concise. Use passive-voice verbs wherever they are needed for style or for emphasis.

Prewriting Brainstorm some ideas for an exciting conflict. Then, create a brief plot outline for a story based on the conflict you think would lead to the greatest adventure. Think of a way to begin your story. You may want to begin at an exciting point in the middle of the action, or you may want to tell the story as a flashback.

Writing Use your prewriting notes to help you write a first draft. Expand on your original ideas, adding details as you think of them. Remember that you are telling an exciting story and that you want to hold the reader's interest.

Revising Ask a friend to read your story opener. Is the opening interesting and exciting? Can your friend predict what will happen next? Write down any revision suggestions. Have you used active voice and passive voice effectively?

Publishing Check carefully for mistakes in grammar, usage, spelling, and punctuation. Be sure that you have used the correct forms of irregular verbs. Take turns reading your story openings aloud in front of the class. After everyone has read their openings, the class might vote on which story or stories they would like to hear continued.

Using Modifiers Correctly

Forms and Uses of Adjectives and Adverbs; Comparison

Diagnostic Preview

A. Using Modifiers Correctly

Most of the following sentences contain errors in the use of modifiers. If a sentence is incorrect, revise it to eliminate the error. If it is already correct, write *C*.

EXAMPLE   **1.** Steve is the most brightest student in the physics class.
          1. Steve is the brightest student in the physics class.

1. After listening to The Battle of the Bands, we thought that the jazz band performed even more better than the rock group.
2. When the treasurer presented the annual report, the statistics showed that the company had done badder this year than last.
3. Megan shoots free throws so good that she has already made the varsity team.
4. The more even you distribute the workload among the group members, the more satisfied everyone will be.

5. In 1949, Jackie Robinson was voted the Most Valuable Player in the National League.
6. Last night the weather forecaster announced that this has been the most wet spring season the area has had in the past decade.
7. This is the most tastiest piece of sourdough bread I have ever eaten.
8. After receiving a rare coin for my birthday, I began to take coin collecting more seriously.
9. Before taking a computer course, I couldn't program at all, but now I program very good.
10. When she danced at the Paris Opera, American ballet star Maria Tallchief was received enthusiastic by French audiences.

B. Proofreading for the Correct Use of Modifiers

Proofread the following paragraph, correcting any errors in the use of modifiers. If a sentence is already correct, write *C*.

EXAMPLE   **[1]** When in doubt, dress conservative rather than stunningly for a job interview.

      1. *conservatively*

[11] No matter whether three or three hundred candidates apply for a job, a smart employer tries to find the more qualified applicant. [12] If you heed the following simple guidelines, you will likely create a more favorable general impression than any candidate in your job market. [13] First, a well-prepared résumé always helps to make a better impression before the interview. [14] Second, a proper dressed candidate appears neat and well groomed during the interview. [15] Your clothes do not have to be fancier or more expensive than any other candidate's clothes, but they should look professional. [16] Third, before your interview, you should try to imagine the most common asked questions for your field. [17] There is no worst way to make a lasting impression than to provide poorly thought-out answers to an interviewer's questions. [18] Finally, learning all you can about a company is one of the effectivest ways to impress a future employer. [19] When two equally well-qualified candidates apply for the same position, often the one with the greatest knowledge of the company is hired. [20] If you follow these guidelines and still don't get the job, try not to feel too bad; instead, set your sights on succeeding at your next job interview.

Forms of Modifiers

A *modifier* is a word or word group that makes the meaning of another word or word group more specific. The two kinds of modifiers are *adjectives* and *adverbs.*

An *adjective* makes the meaning of a noun or a pronoun more specific.

Reference Note

For more information on **adjectives,** see page 491. For more information on **adverbs,** see page 499.

EXAMPLES   **strong** wind   **an** alligator   **two** cubes

             a loud voice   **the painted** one   **this** bit

An *adverb* makes the meaning of a verb, an adjective, or another adverb more specific.

EXAMPLES   drives **carefully**   **suddenly** stopped   **too** hot

             extremely low   **rather** quickly   **not** here

Most modifiers with an *–ly* ending are used as adverbs. In fact, many adverbs are formed by adding *–ly* to adjectives.

Adjectives	Adverbs
perfect	perfect**ly**
clear	clear**ly**
quiet	quiet**ly**
abrupt	abrupt**ly**
handy	handi**ly**

However, some modifiers ending in *–ly* are used as adjectives.

EXAMPLES   a **daily** lesson   an **early** breakfast   a **lively** discussion

A few modifiers have the same form whether used as adjectives or as adverbs.

Adjectives	Adverbs
a **hard** job	works **hard**
a **late** start	started **late**
an **early** arrival	arriving **early**
a **fast** walk	to walk **fast**

USAGE

Phrases Used as Modifiers

Like one-word modifiers, phrases can also be used as adjectives and adverbs.

EXAMPLES   It was a monument **to peace.** [The prepositional phrase *to peace* acts as an adjective that modifies the noun *monument.*]

Sweeping through the gulch, the wind scattered leaves and branches. [The participial phrase *Sweeping through the gulch* acts as an adjective that modifies the noun *wind.*]

She is the one **to invite today.** [The infinitive phrase *to invite today* acts as an adjective that modifies the pronoun *one.*]

Drive **to the lakefront in the morning.** [The prepositional phrases *to the lakefront* and *in the morning* act as adverbs that modify the verb *Drive.*]

This is easy **to do well.** [The infinitive phrase *to do well* acts as an adverb that modifies the adjective *easy.*]

Clauses Used as Modifiers

Like words and phrases, clauses can also be used as modifiers.

EXAMPLES   Toni Morrison is the author **who wrote *Beloved.*** [The adjective clause *who wrote Beloved* modifies the noun *author.*]

Because winter was coming, the butterflies flew south. [The adverb clause *Because winter was coming* modifies the verb *flew.*]

Uses of Modifiers

22a. Use an adjective to modify the subject of a linking verb.

The most common linking verbs are the forms of *be: am, is, are, was, were, be, been,* and *being.* A linking verb is often used to connect its subject to a ***predicate adjective***—an adjective that is in the predicate and that modifies the subject.

EXAMPLES   Our new computer system is **efficient.**

The governor's comments on the controversial issue were **candid.**

Reference Note
For more about different kinds of **phrases,** see Chapter 16.

USAGE

Reference Note
For more about **clauses,** see Chapter 17.

Reference Note
For more about **predicate adjectives,** see page 525.

22b. Use adverbs to modify action verbs.

Action verbs are often modified by adverbs—words that tell *how, when, where,* or *to what extent* an action is performed.

EXAMPLES   Our new computer system is operating **efficiently.**

The governor **candidly** expressed her point of view on the controversial issue.

Some verbs may be used as linking verbs or as action verbs. Notice the kinds of modifiers used after the verbs in the following examples.

EXAMPLES   Carmen looked **frantic.** [*Looked* is a linking verb. *Frantic* is an adjective modifying *Carmen.*]

Carmen looked **frantically** for her class ring. [*Looked* is an action verb. *Frantically* is an adverb modifying *looked.*]

Like verbs, verbals may be modified by adverbs.

EXAMPLES   Barking **loudly,** the dog frightened the burglar. [The adverb *loudly* modifies the participle *Barking.*]

Not fastening the bracket **tightly** will enable you to adjust it **later.** [The adverbs *Not* and *tightly* modify the gerund *fastening.* The adverb *later* modifies the infinitive *to adjust.*]

Reference Note

For more information about **linking verbs** and **action verbs,** see page 495.

Reference Note

For more about **verbals,** see page 540.

TIPS & TRICKS

To help you determine whether a verb is a linking verb or an action verb, replace the verb with a form of *seem.* If the substitution sounds reasonable, the original verb is a linking verb. If the substitution sounds absurd, the original verb is an action verb.

EXAMPLES
Carmen looked frantic.
[Since *Carmen seemed frantic* sounds reasonable, *looked* is a linking verb.]

Carmen looked frantically for her class ring. [Since *Carmen seemed frantically for her class ring* sounds absurd, *looked* is an action verb.]

Exercise 1   Selecting Modifiers to Complete Sentences

Select the correct modifier in parentheses in each of the following sentences.

EXAMPLE   1. When you look (*careful, carefully*) at the pots shown on the next page, you can see how tiny they are compared to the kernels of corn.

    1. carefully

1. Rosemary Apple Blossom Lonewolf is an artist whose style remains (*unique, uniquely*) among American Indian potters.
2. Lonewolf combines (*traditional, traditionally*) and modern techniques to create her miniature pottery.
3. In crafting her pots, Lonewolf uses dark red clay that is (*ready, readily*) available around the Santa Clara Pueblo in New Mexico, where she lives.
4. These miniatures have a detailed and (*delicate, delicately*) etched surface called sgraffito.

USAGE

5. Because of the (*extreme, extremely*) intricate detail on its surface, a single pot may take many months to finish.

6. The subjects for most of Lonewolf's pots combine ancient Pueblo myths and traditions with (*current, currently*) ideas or events.

7. One of her pots (*clear, clearly*) depicts a Pueblo corn dancer walking down a city street lined with skyscrapers.

8. Lonewolf uses such images to show that American Indians can and do adapt (*real, really*) well to new ways.

9. At first known only in the Southwest, Lonewolf's work is now shown throughout the United States because the appeal of her subjects is quite (*broad, broadly*).

10. Rosemary Lonewolf's father, grandfather, and son also are (*high, highly*) skilled potters.

COMPUTER TIP

Some word-processing software packages include a thesaurus. You can use the thesaurus to help you find precise modifiers to use in your writing. To make sure, however, that a modifier you choose from the thesaurus has exactly the meaning you intend, you should look up the word in the dictionary.

USAGE

Eight Troublesome Modifiers

Bad and *Badly*

Bad is an adjective. *Badly* is an adverb. In standard English, only the adjective form should follow a sense verb or other linking verb.

NONSTANDARD	If the meat smells badly, don't eat it.
STANDARD	If the meat smells **bad,** don't eat it.

NONSTANDARD	This shade of green looks badly on me.
STANDARD	This shade of green looks **bad** on me.

Good and *Well*

Good is an adjective. *Well* may be used as an adjective or as an adverb. Avoid using *good* to modify a verb. Instead, use *well* as an adverb, meaning "capably" or "satisfactorily."

NONSTANDARD	The school orchestra played good.
STANDARD	The school orchestra played **well.**

NONSTANDARD	Although she was extremely nervous, Aretha performed quite good.
STANDARD	Although she was extremely nervous, Aretha performed quite **well.**

NONSTANDARD	Did you do good on the quiz?
STANDARD	Did you do **well** on the quiz?

Feel good and *feel well* mean different things. *Feel good* means "to feel happy or pleased." *Feel well* means "to feel healthy."

EXAMPLES	Donating some of my time at the children's ward at the hospital makes me feel **good.**
	Frank went home because he didn't feel **well.**

Slow and *Slowly*

Slow is used as both an adjective and an adverb. *Slowly* is used as an adverb. In most adverb uses, it is better to use *slowly* than to use *slow*.

ADJECTIVE	Are sloths always that **slow**?
ADVERB	Do sloths always move that **slowly**?

ADJECTIVE	Take a few **slow,** deep breaths.
ADVERB	Breathe **slowly** and deeply.

USAGE

┌ S T Y L E ✏ T I P ┐

Although the expression *feel badly* has become common in informal situations, you should use *feel bad* in formal speaking and writing.

INFORMAL
I felt badly, so I apologized to her.

FORMAL
I felt **bad,** so I apologized to her.

┌ S T Y L E ✏ T I P ┐

The expressions *drive slow* and *go slow* are common in informal situations. In formal speaking and writing, however, use *drive slowly* and *go slowly.*

INFORMAL
Why is traffic going so slow this morning?

FORMAL
Why is traffic so **slow** this morning?

Why is traffic going so **slowly** this morning?

Real and *Really*

Real is an adjective. *Really* is an adverb meaning "truly" or "actually." Informally, *real* is used as an adverb meaning "very."

INFORMAL   Jamaal's report was real interesting.

FORMAL   Jamaal's report was **really** interesting.

INFORMAL   Most of the students seemed real eager to return to school after the winter break.

FORMAL   Most of the students seemed **really** eager to return to school after the winter break.

> **Exercise 2** Using *Bad* and *Badly, Well* and *Good, Slow* and *Slowly,* and *Real* and *Really*

Each of the following sentences contains an italicized modifier. If the modifier is used incorrectly or informally, give the form that is correct according to the rules of formal, standard English. If the modifier is already correct, write *C.*

EXAMPLE   1. When I painted the house, I fell off the ladder and hurt my right arm *bad.*

   1. *badly*

1. The renowned conductor Leonard Bernstein led the New York Philharmonic Orchestra *well* for many years.
2. Despite the immense size and tremendous power of this airplane, the engines start up *slow.*
3. I can hit the ball *good* if I keep my eye on it.
4. Before Uncle Chet's hip replacement surgery, his gait was *real* painful and slow.
5. After studying French for the past three years in high school, we were pleased to discover how *good* we spoke and understood it on our trip to Quebec.
6. Some of the experiments that the chemistry class has conducted have made the corridors smell *badly.*
7. During the Han dynasty in China, candidates who did *bad* on civil service tests did not become government officials.
8. Whenever I watch the clock, the time seems to go *slowly.*
9. The movie's special effects are *real* spectacular.
10. After hearing how her Navajo ancestors overcame many problems, Anaba felt *well* about her situation.

Review A Determining the Correct Use of Modifiers

Proofread the following paragraph, correcting any informal or incorrect uses of modifiers. If a sentence is already correct, write *C*.

EXAMPLES [1] Some volcanoes rest quiet for many years.
1. *quietly*

[2] When they erupt, however, they can be extremely violent.
2. *C*

[1] More than five hundred actively volcanoes exist on land, and thousands more are found in the sea. [2] Eruptions of these volcanoes are often spectacularly violent. [3] Hugely reddish clouds rise from the volcano, while bright rivers of lava pour down the mountainside. [4] Beyond the eerie, beautiful spectacle that the eye sees, however, is the tremendous destructive force of the volcano. [5] A volcano begins as magma, a river of rock melted by the extreme heat inside the earth. [6] The rock melts slow, forming a gas that, together with the magma, causes the volcano to erupt. [7] Lava flows from the eruption site, sometimes quite rapid, destroying everything in its path. [8] After a volcano erupts, observers usually feel badly because the heat and ash created by the eruption can seriously threaten not only the environment but also the lives and property of people nearby. [9] On the other hand, volcanoes can also have a positively effect on the environment. [10] Lava and volcanic ash gradually mix with the soil to make it wonderful rich in minerals.

Comparison of Modifiers

22c. Modifiers change form to show comparison.

There are three degrees of comparison: the *positive*, the *comparative*, and the *superlative*.

	Positive	Comparative	Superlative
Adjectives	large	larger	largest
	careful	more careful	most careful
	courageous	less courageous	least courageous
	good	better	best
Adverbs	soon	sooner	soonest
	clearly	more clearly	most clearly
	commonly	less commonly	least commonly
	well	better	best

Regular Comparison

(1) Most one-syllable modifiers form the comparative degree by adding *–er* and the superlative degree by adding *–est.*

Positive	Comparative	Superlative
soft	soft**er**	soft**est**
clean	clean**er**	clean**est**
fast	fast**er**	fast**est**
long	long**er**	long**est**
big	bigg**er**	bigg**est**

(2) Two-syllable modifiers may form the comparative degree by adding *–er* and the superlative degree by adding *–est,* or they may form the comparative degree by using *more* and the superlative degree by using *most.*

Positive	Comparative	Superlative
simple	simpl**er**	simpl**est**
funny	funni**er**	funni**est**
angry	angri**er**	angri**est**
cautious	**more** cautious	**most** cautious
freely	**more** freely	**most** freely
certain	**more** certain	**most** certain

S T Y L E 〰️ T I P

Most two-syllable modifiers can form their comparative and superlative forms either way. If adding *–er* or *–est* makes a word sound awkward, use *more* or *most* instead.

AWKWARD
  specialer, specialest

SMOOTH
  more special, most special

(3) Modifiers that have three or more syllables form the comparative degree by using *more* and the superlative degree by using *most.*

Positive	Comparative	Superlative
efficient	**more** efficient	**most** efficient
punctual	**more** punctual	**most** punctual
frequently	**more** frequently	**most** frequently
skillfully	**more** skillfully	**most** skillfully

(4) To show a decrease in the qualities they express, modifiers form the comparative degree by using *less* and the superlative degree by using *least.*

Positive	Comparative	Superlative
proud	**less** proud	**least** proud
honest	**less** honest	**least** honest
patiently	**less** patiently	**least** patiently
reasonably	**less** reasonably	**least** reasonably

Irregular Comparison

The comparative and superlative degree of some modifiers are not formed by the usual methods.

Positive	Comparative	Superlative
bad	worse	worst
ill	worse	worst
good	better	best
well	better	best
little	less	least
many	more	most
much	more	most
far	farther *or* further	farthest *or* furthest

HELP

A dictionary will tell you when a word forms its comparative or superlative form in some way other than by adding *–er* or *–est* or *more* or *most.* Look in a dictionary if you are not sure whether a word has irregular comparative or superlative forms or whether you need to change the spelling of a word before adding *–er* or *–est.*

HELP

The word *little* also has regular comparative and superlative forms: *littler, littlest.* These forms are used to describe physical size (the **littlest** piglet). The forms *less* and *least* are used to describe an amount (**less** lemonade).

USAGE

Exercise 3 **Writing the Comparative and Superlative Forms of Modifiers**

Write the comparative and the superlative forms of each of the following modifiers.

EXAMPLE   **1.** stubborn

   1. *more (less) stubborn; most (least) stubborn*

1. anxious	**8.** stealthily	**15.** jealous
2. hard	**9.** expensive	**16.** fresh
3. cheerful	**10.** enthusiastically	**17.** clearly
4. eager	**11.** late	**18.** silly
5. quick	**12.** safely	**19.** bravely
6. well	**13.** colorful	**20.** responsibly
7. cold	**14.** dangerously	

FRANK & ERNEST reprinted by permission of Newspaper Enterprise Association, Inc.

Uses of Comparative and Superlative Forms

22d. Use the comparative degree when comparing two things. Use the superlative degree when comparing more than two things.

COMPARATIVE   Both sisters are athletic, but the **younger** one works **harder.** [comparison of two sisters]

After reading *King Lear* and *A Winter's Tale,* I can understand why *King Lear* is **more widely** praised. [comparison of two plays]

SUPERLATIVE   Of the careers I have researched, I think marine biology is the **most appealing.** [comparison of many careers]

I sat in the front row because it provided the **best** view of the chemistry experiment. [comparison of many views]

STYLE **TIP**

In formal English the words *farther* and *farthest* are used to compare physical distance. The words *further* and *furthest* are used to compare amounts, degrees, and abstract concepts.

EXAMPLES
   The campers hiked **farther** up the mountain than they had planned. [physical distance]

   Excavation of the ancient ruins may provide **further** understanding of the reasons for the decline of the ancient civilization. [abstract concept]

STYLE **TIP**

In informal situations the superlative degree is sometimes used to compare only two things. Avoid such uses of the superlative degree in formal speaking and writing.

INFORMAL
   Which was hardest to learn, French or Spanish?

FORMAL
   Which was **harder** to learn, French or Spanish?

The superlative degree is also used to compare two things in some idiomatic expressions.

EXAMPLE
   Put your **best** foot forward.

USAGE

Problems Using Modifiers

Double Comparisons

22e. Avoid using double comparisons.

A **double comparison** is the use of two comparative forms (usually *–er* and *more*) or two superlative forms (usually *–est* and *most*) to modify the same word.

NONSTANDARD	This week's program is more funnier than last week's.
STANDARD	This week's program is **funnier** than last week's.

NONSTANDARD	In our school the most furthest you can go in math is Calculus II.
STANDARD	In our school the **furthest** you can go in math is Calculus II.

Comparison Within a Group

22f. Include the word *other* or *else* when comparing one member of a group with the rest of the group.

ILLOGICAL	Anita has hit more home runs this season than any member of her team. [Anita is a member of the team. Logically, Anita could not have hit more home runs than she herself did.]
LOGICAL	Anita has hit more home runs this season than any **other** member of her team.

ILLOGICAL	I think Jean-Pierre Rampal plays the flute better than anyone. [The pronoun *anyone* includes Jean-Pierre Rampal. Logically, Rampal cannot play better than he himself plays.]
LOGICAL	I think that Jean-Pierre Rampal plays the flute better than anyone **else.**

> **Exercise 4** Using the Comparative and Superlative Forms of Modifiers

Revise the following sentences by correcting the errors in the use of the comparative and superlative forms of modifiers.

EXAMPLE	1. It seems I spend more time doing my biology homework than anyone in my class.
	1. *It seems I spend more time doing my biology homework than anyone else in my class.*

1. Which is the most famous Russian ballet company, the Kirov or the Bolshoi?

2. When Barbara Rose Collins served as a state representative in Michigan, my aunt thought that Collins fought harder than anyone for key legislation to help minorities.

3. I read that Hurricane Andrew, which hit Florida in 1992, did more damage than any hurricane in the 1990s.

4. Both cars appear to be well constructed; I think that the most desirable one is the one that gets better gas mileage.

5. Which of these two hotels is farthest from the airport?

6. I know this shade of blue is a closer match than that one, but we still haven't found the better match.

7. In the dance marathon, Anton and Inez managed to stay awake and keep moving more longer than any other couple on the dance floor.

8. Of all the female singers of the 1960s and 1970s, Joan Baez may have participated in more peace rallies than anyone.

9. Lucinda has the most uncommonest hobby I've ever heard of— collecting insects.

10. The newscaster said that the pollen count this morning was more higher than any other count taken in the past ten years.

Clear Comparisons

22g. Be sure comparisons are clear.

When making comparisons, clearly indicate which items you are comparing.

ILLOGICAL   Katie's arguments in the debate were more persuasive than her opponent. [The sentence makes an illogical comparison between arguments and an opponent.]

LOGICAL   Katie's arguments in the debate were more persuasive than her **opponent's [arguments].** [The sentence logically compares Katie's arguments with her opponent's arguments.]

ILLOGICAL   The ears of the African elephant are larger than the Asian elephant. [The sentence makes an illogical comparison between ears and the Asian elephant.]

LOGICAL   The ears of the African elephant are larger than **those of** the Asian elephant. [By including *those of*, the sentence logically compares the ears of the two elephants.]

Use a complete comparison if there is any chance that an incomplete one could be misunderstood.

UNCLEAR	I baby-sit them more often than anyone else. [The comparison is unclear because the elliptical construction *than anyone else* may be completed in more than one way.]
CLEAR	I baby-sit them more often than **anyone else does.**
CLEAR	I baby-sit them more often than **I baby-sit anyone else.**

UNCLEAR	The director admired the stage crew as highly as the cast members.
CLEAR	The director admired the stage crew as highly as **the cast members did.**
CLEAR	The director admired the stage crew as highly as **she admired the cast members.**

Include all the words that are necessary to complete a *compound comparison,* which uses both the positive and the comparative degrees of a modifier. Avoid the common error of omitting the second *as* in the positive degree.

| INCORRECT | The meteorologist predicted, "The temperature tomorrow will be as high, if not higher than, it was today." |
| CORRECT | The meteorologist predicted, "The temperature tomorrow will be as high **as,** if not higher than, it was today." |

Absolute Adjectives

A few adjectives have no comparative or superlative forms; they do not vary in degree. Such adjectives are called *absolute adjectives.* In formal situations, avoid using absolute adjectives in comparisons.

Common Absolute Adjectives		
complete	equal	perfect
correct	eternal	round
dead	full	square
empty	impossible	true
endless	infinite	unique

TIPS & TRICKS

To make sure a sentence contains all of the words necessary for a compound comparison, try making a sentence using each part of the comparison separately.

EXAMPLES
The meteorologist predicted, "The temperature tomorrow will be **as high as** it was today."

The meteorologist predicted, "The temperature tomorrow will be **higher than** it was today."

INFORMAL	Lena's design was more unique than any of the other designs.
FORMAL	Lena's design was **more unusual** than any of the other designs.
FORMAL	Lena's design was **unique** among all of them.
INFORMAL	Of all the gymnasts' performances, Kyle's was the most perfect!
FORMAL	All of the gymnasts' performances were excellent, but Kyle's was **perfect**!

An absolute adjective may be used in a comparison if the adjective is accompanied by *more nearly* or *most nearly.*

INCORRECT	Yolanda's answer was more correct than mine.
CORRECT	Yolanda's answer was **more nearly** correct than mine.

Review B Making Correct Comparisons

The following sentences contain errors in the use of comparisons. Identify and revise each error.

EXAMPLE
1. Does Column A or Column B give the best estimate?

1. best—better

1. For many years, the observatory at Mount Palomar was larger than any in the world.
2. Macros make using a computer program more simpler.
3. Sound quality from a CD is generally most acute than that from a cassette tape.
4. Among these writers, Amy Tan certainly has the most unique point of view.
5. When Mrs. Garr decided between the two designs, she chose the one with the best access for wheelchairs.
6. Wow! Your brother Ricardo certainly handles a skateboard better than anyone!
7. This edition of the encyclopedia features the most complete index of subjects.
8. You always have the bestest ideas, Wendy.
9. Athens is older than any European capital.
10. The Bentley was the better of all the British racing cars manufactured between World War I and World War II.

STYLE TIP

Throughout the years the rules regarding absolute adjectives have changed, becoming alternately more and less strict. The trend nowadays is increasingly to allow comparisons of absolute adjectives. One historical precedent for this usage occurs in the preamble of the Constitution of the United States of America:

*We the People of the United States, in Order to form a **more perfect** Union, establish Justice, insure domestic Tranquility, provide for the common defense, promote the general Welfare, and secure the Blessings of Liberty to ourselves and our Posterity, do ordain and establish this Constitution for the United States of America.*

Follow your teacher's instructions regarding the use of absolute adjectives.

USAGE

Using Modifiers Correctly

Proofread the following paragraph, correcting any informal or incorrect uses of modifiers. If a sentence is already correct, write *C.*

EXAMPLE   **[1]** Of the two forts, this one is the oldest.

        1. *older*

    [1] St. Augustine, Florida, is the home of Castillo de San Marcos, the most oldest standing fort in the United States. **[2]** Earlier wooden forts were extremely difficult to defend, but Castillo de San Marcos was built of stone. **[3]** Before the construction of this fort, Spain had no strong military base that could withstand a real fierce enemy assault. **[4]** In fact, previous battles with the British had proved that of the two countries, Spain had the least defensible forts. **[5]** Begun in 1672, the building of Castillo de San Marcos went slow, taking several decades to complete. **[6]** Replacing the existing nine wooden forts in St. Augustine, the new stone fort fared good against attacks. **[7]** Today, no one is sure which fort was easiest to protect, Spain's Castillo de San Marcos or the British fort in Charleston, South Carolina. **[8]** However, Castillo de San Marcos, with its 16-foot-thick walls and 40-foot-wide moat, proved to be one of the most strongest forts in the South and was never taken by force. **[9]** When Florida finally did come under British control, the Spanish felt especially badly about leaving their impressive fort in the hands of their old enemies. **[10]** Castillo de San Marcos is now a national monument and stands today as a memorial to all those who fought so courageous to guard St. Augustine long ago.

Chapter Review

A. Using Modifiers Correctly

For each of the following sentences, identify the modifier in parentheses that is correct according to the rules of formal, standard English.

1. When Rosa and I had the flu, Rosa was (*sicker, sickest*).
2. Emilia watched the demonstration (*careful, carefully*).
3. As you approach the next intersection, drive (*cautious, cautiously*).
4. Our new car is roomier than (*any, any other*) car we have ever had.
5. The leaders of the Underground Railroad acted (*quick, quickly*) to help runaway slaves.
6. The smaller kitten is the (*healthier, healthiest*) one.
7. The candidate had prepared his answers (*well, good*).
8. That was a (*real, really*) bad movie.
9. You will drive more (*steady, steadily*) if you focus on the road.
10. Mr. Yan thinks that Jacinto Quirarte is the (*better, best*) of all authorities on Mexican American and pre-Columbian art.

B. Revising Sentences to Correct Modifier Errors

Most of the following sentences contain an awkward, informal, or incorrect use of a modifier. Revise the sentences to correct each such usage. If a sentence is already correct, write *C*.

11. I don't think this suitcase is any more heavier than yours.
12. After comparing my air conditioner with the one on sale, I decided that mine was most efficient.
13. Antonia cooks so bad that I was hesitant to taste her stew.
14. "I predict," said Gretchen, "that the backgammon final between Pearly and Katina will be won by the player with the better strategy."
15. The Indian physicist's theory about supernovas turned out to be more accurate than the Russian astronomer.
16. What is the most scariest movie you have ever seen?
17. She feels badly after losing the chess tournament.
18. After the game, Ian said that his team had played terrible.
19. Lena is the candidest and least pretentious person in our class.
20. Paco is quieter than any member of his debating team.

USAGE

C. Correcting Modifier Errors

Most of the following sentences contain at least one error in the use of modifiers. Identify each error, and then write the correct form. If a sentence is already correct, write *C*.

21. Mrs. Chiang seemed doubtfully when I promised to repair the damage right after dinner.

22. The house on the corner is the less attractive of all the houses on the block, but with a few repairs it could be the nicer.

23. Her perfume smelled even sweeter when she came nearer.

24. My aunt treats uninvited guests rather rude.

25. Dr. Black seems most capable than the other doctor in the clinic.

26. Though the car was in the repair shop for two days, it still does not run real good.

27. When Davis gave his speech, his tone was clearer than that of any other speaker in the class.

28. Your excuse sounds very convincingly.

29. Carry these dishes cautious.

30. Raul seemed even more nervouser about the test than I.

D. Proofreading a Paragraph for the Correct Use of Modifiers

Proofread the following paragraph, and identify any errors in the use of modifiers. Then, write the correct form of the modifier. If a sentence is already correct, write *C*.

[31] Malcolm and I went to visit Chicago's interestingest museum, the Museum of Science and Industry. [32] The museum houses more than two thousand displays, so we knew it would be totally impossible to see all the exhibits in one day. [33] To see certain special displays, we planned our day careful. [34] First, we walked through a really incredible model of a beating heart. [35] The thumping and swishing of the heart were the most greatest sound effects we had ever heard. [36] Next, Malcolm went to play computer games while I decided to explore more livelier happenings at the farm exhibit. [37] When we met later for lunch, I asked him which computer game was hardest to win, tic-tac-toe or solitaire. [38] As we headed for the Omnimax Theater to view the most advanced film projection system in the world, Malcolm admitted that he had not done good at either game. [39] We spent the

rest of the day looking at a submarine, a lunar module, and—the funniest thing of all—ourselves on television! **[40]** We both agreed that the Museum of Science and Industry is the better museum we have ever visited.

Writing Application

Using Modifiers in a Letter

Comparative Forms   Write one of the major television networks a letter pointing out how producers can better address the interests and concerns of teenage viewers. To support your opinion, draw a comparison between two current television shows–one that you and your friends like and one that you do not like. In your letter, use at least five comparative forms of modifiers.

Prewriting   Start by listing several current TV programs aimed at teenage audiences. Ask a few friends to tell you what they like or dislike about each show. Jot down your friends' responses along with your own opinions. Use your notes to help you identify the kinds of characters, situations, and themes that do and do not appeal to teenage viewers.

Writing   Begin your draft by explaining the reason for your letter and clearly stating your opinion. Then, use your notes to help you give specific examples to support your opinion. Be sure that you use the proper form for a business letter.

Revising   Revise your letter to make it as concise and direct as you can. Make sure your comparisons are organized in a clear and logical order.

> **Reference Note**
>
> See "Writing" in the Quick Reference Handbook for the proper form for a **business letter.**

Publishing   Proofread your letter for any errors in grammar, spelling, and punctuation. Pay special attention to modifiers, and revise any double comparisons. Mail your revised letter to a television network. First, find out the address of the network and, if possible, the name of the person to whom you should write. Then, retype or recopy the letter neatly. You and your classmates may want to collect your letters and send them all together, along with a cover letter.

Placement of Modifiers
Misplaced and Dangling Modifiers

Diagnostic Preview

A. Revising Sentences by Correcting Faulty Modifiers

The following sentences contain errors in the use or placement of modifiers. Revise each sentence so that its meaning is clear and correct.

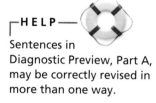

┌HELP┐
Sentences in Diagnostic Preview, Part A, may be correctly revised in more than one way.

EXAMPLE   1. Attached to my application, you will find a transcript of my grades.

1. *You will find a transcript of my grades attached to my application.*

1. Having eaten the remains of the zebra, we watched the lion lick its chops contentedly.
2. To reach the barrier island, the bridge must be crossed.
3. Snowing heavily, we couldn't see the road in front of us.
4. To do well on examinations, good study habits should be used.
5. We have almost seen every painting on the third floor of the modern art museum.

6. The leader of the photo safari promised in the morning we would see a herd of eland.
7. While running for the bus, my wallet must have dropped out of my pocket.
8. Catching the line drive with her usual skill, the crowd rose to their feet and cheered.
9. She traveled to Paris especially to see the *Venus de Milo* on the train last week.
10. After crumbling for hundreds of years, we hardly recognized the ruins as a castle.

B. Using Modifiers Correctly

Most of the following sentences contain errors in the use or placement of modifiers. Revise each faulty sentence so that its meaning is clear and correct. If a sentence is already correct, write *C*.

EXAMPLE   1. Using computer technology, last-minute changes in newspaper layout can be made more easily.

          1. *Using computer technology, people who lay out newspaper pages can make last-minute changes more easily.*

HELP———

Sentences in Diagnostic Preview, Part B, may be correctly revised in more than one way.

USAGE

11. Computer expert Kim Montgomery claimed in the computer resource center anyone can learn to master basic desktop publishing.
12. To prove Kim's point, we asked Terri, the editor of the school newspaper, to give desktop publishing a try.
13. Kim led Terri, a novice computer user, to an unoccupied terminal with an encouraging smile.
14. In a short tutorial session, Kim emphasized the need to practice adding, deleting, and moving paragraphs.
15. Enthusiastic, page layout was what Terri wanted to learn next.
16. Terri asked Kim to review the session's major points after a short break.
17. Creating illustrations, the sample pages looked terrific to Terri.
18. "To prepare professional-quality illustrations, a graphics package is what is needed," Kim said.
19. Finishing the tutorial, it was clear that desktop publishing would make the school paper even better than last year's.
20. Kim was pleased to see Terri confidently keyboarding information on the way to helping another student.

Misplaced Modifiers

A modifying word, phrase, or clause that seems to modify the wrong word or word group in a sentence is a *misplaced modifier.*

23a. Avoid using misplaced modifiers.

To correct a misplaced modifier, place the modifying word, phrase, or clause as close as possible to the word or words you intend it to modify.

MISPLACED Undaunted, the storm did not prevent the crew from setting sail as planned. [misplaced word]

CORRECT The storm did not prevent the **undaunted** crew from setting sail as planned.

MISPLACED Uncle Carmine saw a deer bounding across a meadow on his way to work. [misplaced prepositional phrases]

CORRECT **On his way to work,** Uncle Carmine saw a deer bounding across a meadow.

MISPLACED They were delighted to see a field of daffodils climbing up the hill. [misplaced participial phrase]

CORRECT **Climbing up the hill,** they were delighted to see a field of daffodils.

STYLE TIP

Be sure to place modifiers correctly to show clearly the meaning you intend.

EXAMPLES

Only Dr. Rufus reads the tests. [Dr. Rufus, not anybody else, reads the tests.]

Dr. Rufus **only** reads the tests. [Dr. Rufus reads the tests; he does not mark them.]

Dr. Rufus reads **only** the tests. [Dr. Rufus does not read anything else.]

USAGE

MISS PEACH courtesy of Mell Lazarus and Creators Syndicate. © 1991, Mell Lazarus.

MISPLACED	The coach praised his players for playing their best as he gave out the trophies. [misplaced adverb clause]
CORRECT	**As he gave out the trophies,** the coach praised his players for playing their best.
MISPLACED	A few years ago, a resident of our town bequeathed her entire estate to the animal shelter, which was valued at two million dollars. [misplaced adjective clause]
CORRECT	A few years ago, a resident of our town bequeathed her entire estate, **which was valued at two million dollars,** to the animal shelter.

Reference Note

For more about **phrases and clauses used as modifiers,** see Chapter 16, The Phrase, and Chapter 17, The Clause.

Squinting Modifiers

23b. Avoid misplacing a modifying word, phrase, or clause so that it seems to modify either of two words. Such a misplaced modifier is often called a *squinting,* or a *two-way, modifier.*

MISPLACED	The prime minister said yesterday her opponent spoke honestly. [Did the prime minister speak yesterday or did her opponent?]
CORRECT	**Yesterday,** the prime minister said her opponent spoke honestly.
CORRECT	The prime minister said her opponent spoke honestly **yesterday.**
MISPLACED	The manager told the two rookies after the game to report to the dugout. [Did the manager talk to the rookies after the game or were the rookies to report to the dugout after the game?]
CORRECT	**After the game** the manager told the two rookies to report to the dugout.
CORRECT	The manager told the two rookies to report to the dugout **after the game.**
MISPLACED	The mayor said when the city council met he would discuss the proposed budget. [Did the mayor make his statement when the council met or would he discuss the budget when the council next met?]
CORRECT	**When the city council met,** the mayor said he would discuss the proposed budget.
CORRECT	The mayor said he would discuss the proposed budget **when the city council met.**

USAGE

┌HELP─────

Sentences in
Exercise 1 may be correctly
revised in more than one
way.

Exercise 1 — Revising Sentences by Correcting Misplaced Modifiers

The following sentences contain misplaced modifiers. Revise each sentence so that its meaning is clear and correct.

EXAMPLE
1. To get some exercise during our vacation last summer, we almost played tennis every day.

1. *To get some exercise during our vacation last summer, we played tennis almost every day.*

1. Louise projected the photographs on a large screen that she had taken at the zoo.
2. Mr. Martínez promised in the morning he would tell an American Indian trickster tale.
3. I pointed to the fish tank and showed my friends the baby angelfish, swelling with pride.
4. Ralph Ellison said during an interview Richard Wright inspired him to become a writer.
5. I talked about the problem I had in writing my first draft with Megan, and she said she had the same problem.
6. My aunt had finally mastered the art of upholstering furniture, filled with pride.
7. Rested and refreshed, a night's sleep had energized them.
8. Mrs. Jennings sang some folk songs about working on the railroad in the auditorium.
9. There is a bracelet in the museum that is four thousand years old.
10. I found a good book about Virginia Woolf written by her husband Leonard at a garage sale.

┌S T Y L E   T I P┐

A few dangling modifiers
have become standard in
idiomatic expressions.

EXAMPLES
Generally speaking,
Americans now have a
longer life expectancy
than ever before.

To be honest, the party
was rather boring.

Notice in the examples
above that when a modify-
ing participial phrase or
infinitive phrase comes at
the beginning of a sen-
tence, the phrase is fol-
lowed by a comma.

Dangling Modifiers

A modifying word, phrase, or clause that does not clearly and sensibly modify any word or word group in a sentence is a ***dangling modifier.***

23c. Avoid using dangling modifiers.

To correct a dangling modifier, add or replace words to make the meaning of the sentence clear and sensible.

DANGLING   Determined, Christy Haubegger's plan was to publish a bilingual magazine for Hispanic women. [Was the plan determined?]

CORRECT	**Determined, Christy Haubegger planned** to publish a bilingual magazine for Hispanic women.
CORRECT	**Christy Haubegger was determined** to publish a bilingual magazine for Hispanic women.
DANGLING	Having selected a college, a trip to the campus was planned. [Who selected a college?]
CORRECT	**Having selected a college, my friend and I** planned a trip to the campus.
CORRECT	**After we selected a college, my friend and I** planned a trip to the campus.
DANGLING	After researching the African American oral tradition in Florida, the book *Mules and Men* was written. [Who was researching?]
CORRECT	**After researching the African American oral tradition in Florida, Zora Neale Hurston** wrote the book *Mules and Men.*
CORRECT	**After Zora Neale Hurston researched the African American oral tradition in Florida, she** wrote the book *Mules and Men.*
DANGLING	While wrapping the gifts, Murphy, my pet terrier, kept trying to untie the bows. [Was the terrier wrapping the gifts?]
CORRECT	**While I was wrapping the gifts,** Murphy, my pet terrier, kept trying to untie the bows.
CORRECT	**While wrapping the gifts, I** noticed that Murphy, my pet terrier, kept trying to untie the bows.

Reference Note

For information about using a **comma after an introductory word, phrase, or clause,** see page 791.

Exercise 2 Revising Sentences by Correcting Dangling Modifiers

The following sentences contain dangling modifiers. Revise each sentence so that its meaning is clear and correct.

EXAMPLE
1. Waiting at the bus stop, my older brother drove by in his new car.

1. *While I was waiting at the bus stop, my older brother drove by in his new car.*

1. Noticing the fresh lettuce, the rabbit's ears perked up and its nose twitched.
2. To interpret this poem, a knowledge of mythology is helpful.
3. All bundled up in a blanket, the baby's first outing was a brief one.
4. When performing onstage, the microphone should not be placed too near the speaker cones.

HELP

Sentences in Exercise 2 may be correctly revised in more than one way.

23
c

USAGE

5. To be a good opera singer, clear enunciation is extremely important.
6. To help colonial soldiers during the Revolutionary War, Haym Solomon's efforts raised money to buy food and clothing.
7. Before moving to Sacramento, Pittsburgh had been their home for ten years.
8. While reaching into his pocket for change, the car rolled into the side of the tollbooth.
9. Alone, the peace and quiet that followed the busy weekend was a welcome relief.
10. When discussing colonial American writers, the contributions of the African American poet Phillis Wheatley should not be forgotten.

Review A **Identifying and Correcting Dangling and Misplaced Modifiers**

─HELP─
Sentences in Review A may be correctly revised in more than one way.

Most of the following sentences contain a dangling or misplaced modifier. Revise each sentence so that it is clear and correct. If a sentence is already correct, write *C*.

EXAMPLE   1. Please put the grocery bags in the car on the counter.
           1. *Please bring the grocery bags in from the car and put them on the counter.*

1. Puzzled by the philosopher's statements, a forest of hands rose in the audience.
2. A painting of horses prancing around a stream by that artist hangs in our living room.
3. Vinnie, who had just turned three years old, saw his grandfather for the first time.
4. Before being admitted to the university, numerous forms must be completed and returned.
5. Having met the Dalai Lama in person, the memory would always be treasured.
6. Surprised, the announcement of the award left Heidi speechless.
7. Did you see a video about polar bears at summer camp?
8. To make accurate calculations, using a computer is helpful but not necessary for accountants.
9. Balloons flew to the ceiling above the children carried by helium.
10. While cleaning my room, a number of lost items appeared—a charm from my bracelet, my favorite socks, and my old journal from fourth grade.

The following sentences contain misplaced and dangling modifiers. Revise each sentence so that its meaning is clear and correct.

EXAMPLES

1. Taylor told me at tonight's concert Nicoletta would be singing a solo part in Prokofiev's cantata *Alexander Nevsky.*

1. *Taylor told me Nicoletta would be singing a solo part in Prokofiev's cantata* Alexander Nevsky *at tonight's concert.*

or

1. *At tonight's concert, Taylor told me Nicoletta would be singing a solo part in Prokofiev's cantata* Alexander Nevsky.

2. After washing and peeling the carrots, they were sliced lengthwise and added to the stew.

2. *After washing and peeling the carrots, I sliced them lengthwise and added them to the stew.*

1. Having deposited her paycheck at the bank branch in the supermarket, her checkbook could not be found until she looked in her shopping cart.

2. Afraid that the strong wind and enormous waves of the hurricane were going to sink his ship, the freighter was deliberately driven aground just south of the lighthouse by its captain.

3. To prepare us for the test on Monday, our English teacher encouraged us to watch the film version of *Much Ado About Nothing* directed by Kenneth Branagh at some point during the weekend.

4. Having admired the young pianist's first two recordings of Duke Ellington's tunes, the music critic's wish was that the artist would record a version of Ellington's "Take the A Train."

5. Ms. Beckinsale always ordered whatever new dish was placed on the menu of the Thai restaurant downtown before anyone else had tried it.

6. Kendra announced after reading through all the college and university catalogs she had decided to apply to three schools: the University of Michigan, the University of Texas, and Stanford University.

7. While trying to write a short story at my computer, my cat Sam insisted on walking back and forth across the keyboard.

STYLE TIP

A dangling modifier may occur when a sentence is in the passive voice. Rewriting sentences in the active voice not only eliminates many dangling modifiers but also makes your writing more interesting and lively.

PASSIVE VOICE
To improve your writing, good books must be read. [*To improve your writing* is a dangling modifier.]

ACTIVE VOICE
To improve your writing, you must read good books. [*To improve your writing* modifies *you.*]

Reference Note

For more about **active voice** and **passive voice,** see page 676.

HELP

Sentences in Review B may be correctly revised in more than one way.

USAGE

8. The research ship from the oceanographic institute discovered the wreck of an old Spanish galleon in the waters of the Gulf of Mexico that had sunk over three hundred years ago.

9. Concerned about the heat and the humidity, the annual marathon was canceled to protect the health of the runners.

10. Looking everywhere, even under the bed and at the back of the closet, the red shoes could not be found in time for the dance recital.

Review C **Revising Sentences by Correcting Faulty Modifiers**

Most of the following sentences contain errors in the use of modifiers. Revise each faulty sentence so that its meaning is clear and correct. If a sentence is already correct, write *C*.

EXAMPLE
   1. I showed all my friends the terrific photos I had taken on my trip to Hawaii when I got back.

   1. *When I got back, I showed all my friends the terrific photos I had taken on my trip to Hawaii.*

1. Visitors soon learn how important one person can be on vacation in Hawaii.

2. Born in the mid-1700s, the Hawaiian people were united under one government by Kamehameha I.

3. After capturing Maui, Molokai, and Lanai, the island of Oahu soon became another of Kamehameha's conquests.

4. Kamehameha assured the Hawaiian people when he became the ruler of the entire island they would see peace.

5. Kamehameha was certain by 1810 his conquest of the islands would be successful.

6. United, Kamehameha's victory over Kauai and Niihau brought prosperity to the Hawaiian Islands.

7. A hero to his people, Kamehameha's government ruled Hawaii for many years.

8. Thomas Gould crafted a statue honoring the great ruler.

9. While being transported by sea, the Hawaiian people lost their beloved statue.

10. Still resting at the bottom of the ocean, the sculptor made the duplicate shown here.

┌HELP─

Sentences in Review C may be correctly revised in more than one way.

KAMEHAMEHA I

Chapter Review

A. Revising Sentences by Correcting Misplaced Modifiers

The following sentences contain misplaced modifiers. Revise each sentence so that its meaning is clear and correct.

1. Min Li happened to see an albino squirrel on the way to school.
2. The teacher told Meg during the class to present her book report.
3. The race car driver said earlier his crew had performed well.
4. I saw an organ grinder and his monkey perform on a crowded sidewalk while sitting in a café on the Champs Élysées in Paris.
5. In costume, Elizabeth thought the dancer looked stunning.
6. The speaker of the house said after the final vote was taken he would speak to the press.
7. Tony was fascinated by a school of dolphins on the excursion boat.
8. Fearless, the bomb was defused by the special squad.
9. Ava counted the moons of Jupiter looking through the telescope.
10. The literary agent promised for the author to negotiate a fair royalty when the book was accepted.

B. Revising Sentences by Correcting Dangling Modifiers

The following sentences contain dangling modifiers. Revise each sentence so that its meaning is clear and correct.

11. When planning a vacation, Brownsville, Texas, is an interesting destination to consider.
12. Serving as a tourist gateway from the U.S. to Mexico, two bridges lead to Matamoros, Tamaulipas.
13. Located near South Padre Island, you can visit the best beaches in Texas without driving far from there.
14. To attend the Charros Days festival hosted by Brownsville and Matamoros, February is the time to go.
15. Before leaving the area, the Sabal Palm Grove Wildlife Sanctuary should be explored.

USAGE

C. Revising Sentences by Correcting Faulty Modifiers

Most of the following sentences contain errors in the placement and use of modifiers. Revise each faulty sentence so that its meaning is clear. If a sentence is already correct, write C.

16. The Alvarezes decided to visit the historic town of Williamsburg, Virginia, which has been painstakingly restored on the spur of the moment.

17. Decorated in colonial style, the family registered at a quaint inn.

18. After resting for an hour or so, the Governor's Palace and the Capitol were visited.

19. Joel snapped a shot of a candlemaker quickly focusing his camera.

20. A tour guide at DeWitt Wallace Decorative Arts Gallery explained how eighteenth-century costumes were sewn.

21. The tour guide said when the family asked she would be happy to go into greater detail.

22. Dressed in colonial garb, a woman at the Raleigh Tavern asked the family to imagine how eighteenth-century residents may have spread news.

23. Having seen enough for the day, a quiet dinner at the inn was enjoyed by the Alvarez family.

24. Kevin dipped his spoon into a bowl of peanut-butter soup filled with great apprehension.

25. With fond memories and many photographs, the trip to Williamsburg will not soon be forgotten.

D. Revising Sentences by Correcting Faulty Modifiers

Most of the following sentences contain errors in the use of modifiers. Revise each faulty sentence so that its meaning is clear. If a sentence is already correct, write C.

26. Racing across the screens, computer programmers use animation programs to show cartoon characters.

27. Grant and Lee rode to Appomattox Court House to make an agreement that ended the Civil War on horses.

28. To honor the inventor Jan Ernst Matzeliger, the U.S. Postal Service issued a new stamp in the Black Heritage Series.

29. Lue Gim Gong developed a type of orange that could resist frost in his laboratory.

30. Attacking at dawn, the Battle of Hastings was won by William the Conqueror in 1066.

31. The detective writer said on page one he would introduce a new villain.

32. In all departments of Huntsville's Marshall Space Flight Center, scientists have planned carefully to ensure that the International Space Station will soon be completed.

33. When proofreading on a computer, screen format should be checked as well as spelling.

34. The mayoral candidate said in a full-page newspaper advertisement an apology would be forthcoming.

35. Did you know that Navajo advisors helped to develop a system of codes that the U.S. Army used while fighting World War II in New Mexico?

Writing Application

Using Modifiers in a Restaurant Review

Making Comparisons You are the restaurant critic for a food magazine. Write a paragraph describing, evaluating, and comparing one meal at each of your two favorite restaurants. Make sure your modifiers are correctly placed.

Prewriting Think of two restaurants, either real or imaginary. Compare the restaurants in several categories—food, atmosphere, price, service. Read several columns by a magazine or newspaper restaurant critic to see how a professional writes about food.

Writing Use your prewriting notes to help you describe the meals as you write your first draft.

Revising Ask a classmate to read your paragraph. Are your descriptions clear? Did you include factual details to support your opinions? Revise any confusing or unclear sentences.

Publishing Check your paragraph for errors in grammar, usage, and mechanics. Your class may want to assemble your paragraphs and put together a guide to local restaurants.

A Glossary of Usage
Common Usage Problems

Diagnostic Preview

A. Correcting Errors in Usage

Most of the following sentences contain errors in the use of standard English. If a sentence contains an error, revise the sentence. If a sentence is already correct, write *C*.

EXAMPLE   **1.** Did we do alright, Terry?

        1. *Did we do all right, Terry?*

1. They said it was a awfully serious issue.
2. I inferred from what Julio said that he has excepted my apology.
3. Over eighty years ago my great-grandfather immigrated from Mexico.
4. The Seminoles of Florida piece together colorful fabrics to create striking dresses, shirts, skirts, and etc.
5. He talked persuasively for an hour, but his words had no affect.
6. The amount of hours I have spent studying lately has really helped my grades.
7. Are you implying that you noticed nothing unusual in the cafeteria today?
8. When Ruth, Tamisha, and I ate at the new Ethiopian restaurant, the food was served in communal bowls, and we divided it between ourselves.

9. The reason the book was so difficult to understand was because the writing was unclear.

10. If you kept less fish in your tank, they would live longer.

B. Correcting Errors in Usage

Each of the sentences in the following paragraph contains at least one error in the use of standard, formal English. Identify the error(s) in each sentence, and then write the correct form(s).

EXAMPLE　　**[1]** In-line skates provide such a smooth, fast ride that they give the allusion of ice-skating.

　　　　　　1. allusion—illusion

[**11**] Almost no one could of predicted the revolution that took place in skating equipment a few years ago. [**12**] Surprisingly, the very first in-line roller skates were invented somewheres in the Netherlands in the 1700s. [**13**] I read in the newspaper where in 1769 a London instrument maker and mechanic wore in-line skates with metal wheels to a party. [**14**] Playing a violin, he came gliding into the room on the skates, but he made a crash landing because he didn't have no idea how to stop. [**15**] Maybe that's why nobody really excepted the newfangled skates in them days. [**16**] Later, an American inventor devised the four-wheeled skate, which became popular, and it looked like in-line skates weren't never going to succeed. [**17**] Finally, in 1980, two Minneapolis brothers noticed that hockey players hated being off of the ice during the summer. [**18**] Being as in-line skates would be a perfect cross-training tool to help keep hockey players in shape all year, the brothers started making the new skates in their basement. [**19**] The idea might of stopped right there if other people hadn't found out that beside being a good training tool, in-line skating is just plain fun. [**20**] In-line skating offers a great low-impact aerobic workout, and it's safe—as long as skaters wear the right type protective gear and learn how to stop!

About the Glossary

This chapter provides a compact glossary of common problems in English usage. A *glossary* is an alphabetical list of special terms or expressions with definitions, explanations, and examples.

　　You will notice that some examples in this glossary are labeled *nonstandard, standard, formal,* or *informal.* The label **nonstandard** identifies usage that does not follow the guidelines of standard English usage. *Standard* English is language that is grammatically correct and appropriate in formal and informal situations. *Formal* identifies usage that is appropriate in serious writing and speaking, such as in compositions for school and in speeches. The label *informal* indicates standard English that is generally used in conversation and in everyday writing, such as in personal letters.

The following are examples of formal and informal English.

Reference Note

For a list of **words often confused,** see page 857. Use the index at the back of the book to find discussions of other usage problems.

Reference Note

For more about **articles,** see page 492.

Formal	Informal
unpleasant	yucky
agreeable	cool
very impressive	totally awesome

a, an These *indefinite articles* refer to a member of a general group. *A* is used before words beginning with a consonant sound. *An* is used before words beginning with a vowel sound.

EXAMPLES   "New African" is **a** poignant story about **a** young African American girl growing up in Philadelphia during the early 1960s.

Orchard Avenue is **a** one-way street. [The *o* in *one-way* is pronounced as if it were preceded by a *w*; therefore, the word begins with a consonant sound.]

The teacher read from the novel **an** excerpt that describes the grandfather as **an** honorable man. [The *h* in *honorable* is silent; therefore, the word begins with a vowel sound.]

accept, except *Accept* is a verb meaning "to receive." *Except* may be used as a verb or as a preposition. As a verb, *except* means "to leave out." As a preposition, *except* means "excluding."

EXAMPLES   Dawn is always eager to **accept** a challenge.

Ms. Liu will not **except** anyone from the deadline. [verb]

She typed everything **except** the bibliography. [preposition]

affect, effect *Affect* is a verb meaning "to influence." *Effect* may be used as a verb or as a noun. As a verb, *effect* means "to bring about [a desired result]" or "to accomplish." As a noun, *effect* means "the result [of an action]."

USAGE

EXAMPLES   Decisions of the United States Supreme Court **affect** the lives of many people.

Some of the decisions **effect** great social change. [verb]

Did you study the **effects** of the *Brown* v. *Board of Education of Topeka, Kansas,* decision? [noun]

ain't *Ain't* is nonstandard. Avoid using *ain't* in speech and in all writing other than dialogue.

all ready, already See page 857.

all right *All right* means "satisfactory," "unhurt," "safe," "correct," or, in reply to a question or to preface a remark, "yes." Although the spelling *alright* is sometimes used, it has not become accepted as standard usage.

EXAMPLES   There has been an accident, but everyone is **all right.**

All right, now save the document on your hard drive.

all the farther, all the faster Avoid using these expressions. Instead, use *as far as* and *as fast as.*

NONSTANDARD   Eight miles is all the farther we can hike in one day.
STANDARD   Eight miles is **as far as** we can hike in one day.

allusion, illusion An *allusion* is an indirect reference to something. An *illusion* is a mistaken idea or a misleading appearance.

EXAMPLES   The phrase *the golden touch* is an **allusion** to the myth of King Midas.

Illusions of being invincible can lead to tragedy.

The 3-D glasses created the **illusion** of depth.

a lot With the article *a, lot* may be used as a noun or as an adverb. As a noun, *a lot* means "a large number or amount." As an adverb, *a lot* means "a great deal" or "very much." Both uses are informal; avoid them in formal speaking and writing situations. *Alot* is a misspelling of the expression in either use.

INFORMAL   A lot [not *Alot*] of movies have been adapted from the works of Shakespeare. [noun]

They arrived a lot [not *alot*] earlier than I did. [adverb]

FORMAL   **Many** movies have been adapted from the works of Shakespeare. [adjective]

My guests arrived **much** earlier than I had expected. [adverb]

alumni, alumnae   *Alumni* (pronounced ə • lum´• nī) is the plural of *alumnus* (a male graduate). *Alumnae* (pronounced ə • lum´• nē) is the plural of *alumna* (a female graduate). Considered as a single group, the graduates of a coeducational school are referred to as *alumni*.

EXAMPLES   The **alumni** I mentioned are both Eagle Scouts.

Did the administration ask the **alumnae** how they felt about admitting men to the school?

Men and women from the first graduating class attended the **alumni** reunion.

> NOTE   In informal usage the graduates from a women's college are sometimes called *alumni.* In formal situations, however, the plural *alumnae* should be used.

among   See **between, among.**

amount, number   Use *amount* to refer to uncountable nouns. Use *number* to refer to countable nouns.

EXAMPLES   Pearl has a large **amount** of homework today. [*Amount* refers to the word *homework.*]

She must study for a **number** of quizzes. [*Number* refers to the word *quizzes.*]

and etc.   *Etc.* is an abbreviation of the Latin words *et cetera,* meaning "and others" or "and so forth." Since *and* is included in the definition of *etc.,* using *and* with *etc.* is redundant.

EXAMPLE   Arthur has already learned several dances: the two-step, the waltz, the grapevine, the mazurka, **etc.** [not *and etc.*]

STYLE TIP

In formal situations, it is generally best to avoid using *etc.*

anyways, anywheres   These words and similar words, such as *everywheres, somewheres,* and *nowheres,* should have no final *s.*

EXAMPLES   I couldn't take both band and art **anyway** [not *anyways*].

Are your grandparents going camping **anywhere** [not *anywheres*] this summer?

as   See **like, as.**

as if See **like, as if, as though.**

at Avoid using *at* after a construction beginning with *where.*

NONSTANDARD Where is the Crow Canyon Archaeological Center at?
   STANDARD Where is the Crow Canyon Archaeological Center?

a while, awhile Used with the article *a, while* is a noun meaning "a period of time." *Awhile* is an adverb meaning "for a short time."

EXAMPLES It's been **a while** since we've taken a vacation.

Michael Jordan played professional baseball for **a while.**

Let's rest **awhile;** I'm tired.

Exercise 1 **Identifying Correct Usage**

For each of the following sentences, choose the word or word group that is correct according to the rules of standard, formal English.

EXAMPLE 1. My mother and Ms. Wang, both (*alumnae, alumni*) of Pratt Institute, went there to see an exhibition of paintings.

1. *alumnae*

1. In 1988, the artist Chuck Close suffered spinal-artery collapse, and even though he never fully recovered, he kept painting (*anyway, anyways*).
2. Partially paralyzed, he learned to work from a wheel-chair, with (*a, an*) handy arrangement of straps to hold his brush in place.
3. As he had done before his illness, Close painted large portraits of friends, fellow artists, (*and etc., etc.*)
4. The picture here is an example of how Close generally painted before 1988, dividing a photograph of a person into a large (*amount, number*) of tiny squares.
5. He would first rule the canvas or paper into a grid, and then he would copy the photo's colors, bit by bit, into the small squares to create the type of (*allusion, illusion*) you see here.
6. A single painting might contain (*anywhere, anywheres*) from a few hundred to several thousand squares.
7. This explanation was perfectly clear to everyone (*accept, except*) me.

Chuck Close, *Alex* (1987). Oil on canvas (100" x 84"), John Back. Photo courtesy of The Pace Gallery, New York.

8. The photograph here shows Close in 1991 working on a self-portrait that has a similar (*affect, effect*); you can see that his style is bolder and more colorful.
9. At first glance, you may be surprised by his newer paintings and wonder where that computerlike quality (*is, is at*)!
10. However, you soon realize that Close had never really gone (*all the farther, as far as*) he could with his grid technique and that his recent paintings are a logical extension of his earlier style.

bad, badly   See page 696.

because   In formal writing and speaking, do not use the construction *reason . . . because*. Instead, use *reason . . . that*.

INFORMAL   One reason to use mulch on your garden is because it helps keep the weeds down.

FORMAL   One reason to use mulch on your garden is **that** it helps keep the weeds down.

being as, being that   Avoid using either of these expressions for *because* or *since*.

EXAMPLE   **Because** [not *Being as*] Flora is a good carpenter, she will be a great asset to the stage crew.

beside, besides   *Beside* is a preposition meaning "by the side of." *Besides* may be used as a preposition or as an adverb. As a preposition, *besides* means "in addition to." As an adverb, *besides* means "moreover."

EXAMPLES   He set the plate of sandwiches **beside** the bowl of fruit punch.

Besides fringe benefits, the job offered a high salary. [preposition]

I am not really hungry for popcorn; **besides,** the movie is about to start. [adverb]

between, among   Use *between* when referring to only two items or to more than two when each item is being compared to each other item.

EXAMPLES   The photography assignments for the next issue have been divided **between** Tanaki and Jeffrey.

Ms. Murray explained the differences **between** a neutron, a proton, and an electron.

Use *among* when you are referring to more than two items and are not considering each item in relation to each of the others.

USAGE

Chuck Close in his studio painting *Self Portrait* (1991). Oil on canvas (100"x 84"). Bill Jacobson Studio. Photograph courtesy of The Pace Gallery, New York.

EXAMPLE   The mother divided the broccoli casserole equally **among** the three children.

borrow, lend   *Borrow* means "to take [something] temporarily." *Lend* means "to give [something] temporarily." Its principal parts are *lend, (is) lending, lent, (have) lent.*

EXAMPLES   May I **borrow** your calculator?

I'll be glad to **lend** you the money if you want to buy the tickets.

bring, take   *Bring* means "to come carrying something." *Take* means "to go carrying something."

EXAMPLES   Please **bring** the results of your survey when you come to our next class meeting.

Please **take** the model of the Globe Theatre to the library tomorrow.

You may **take** my softball glove to school today, but please **bring** it home this afternoon.

bust, busted   Avoid using these words as verbs. Use a form of *break* or *burst*, or *catch* or *arrest*, depending on the meaning you intend.

EXAMPLES   One of the headlights on the van is **broken** [not *busted*].

A pipe in the apartment above ours **burst** [not *busted*].

I tried to sneak past Charley, but I got **caught** [not *busted*].

The police **arrested** [not *busted*] two burglars.

but, only   See **The Double Negative,** page 743.

can, may   See page 683.

can't hardly, can't scarcely   See **The Double Negative,** page 743.

could of   See **of.**

discover, invent   *Discover* means "to learn of the existence of [something]." *Invent* means "to bring [something new] into existence."

EXAMPLES   In 1610, Galileo Galilei **discovered** Jupiter's four large moons: Io, Europa, Ganymede, and Callisto.

The compact disc was **invented** in 1972.

STYLE   TIP

Loan, a noun in formal language, is often used in place of *lend* in informal situations.

INFORMAL
I'll be glad to loan you the money if you want to buy the tickets.

FORMAL
I will be glad to **lend** you the money if you want to buy the tickets.

USAGE

done *Done* is the past participle of *do*. Avoid using *done* for *did*, which is the past form of *do* and does not require a helping verb.

NONSTANDARD	He done all of his homework over the weekend.
STANDARD	He **did** all of his homework over the weekend.
STANDARD	He **had done** all of his homework over the weekend.

STYLE   TIP

Some people consider contractions informal. Therefore, in formal speech and writing, it is generally best to spell out words instead of using contractions.

Reference Note

For more information about **contractions,** see page 831.

don't, doesn't *Don't* is the contraction of *do not*. *Doesn't* is the contraction of *does not*. Use *doesn't*, not *don't*, with singular subjects except *I* and *you*.

EXAMPLES   She **doesn't** [not *don't*] like seafood.

The bookstore **doesn't** [not *don't*] have any copies of Faith Ringgold's *Tar Beach* in stock.

effect See **affect, effect.**

emigrate, immigrate *Emigrate* is a verb meaning "to leave a country or region to settle elsewhere." *Immigrate* is a verb meaning "to come into a country or region to settle there."

EXAMPLES   Thousands of people **emigrated** from Germany during the 1870s.

Most of the German refugees **immigrated** to the United States.

NOTE   The nouns that correspond to *emigrate* and *immigrate* are *emigrant* (one who goes away from a country or region) and *immigrant* (one who comes into a country or region).

etc. See **and etc.**

everywheres See **anyways, anywheres.**

except See **accept, except.**

fewer, less Use *fewer*, which tells "how many," to modify a countable noun. Use *less*, which tells "how much," to modify an uncountable noun.

EXAMPLES   **Fewer** students are going out for football this year.

I find that I have much more fun now that I spend **less** time watching TV.

good, well See page 696.

Exercise 2 **Identifying Correct Usage**

For each of the following sentences, choose the word or word group that is correct according to the rules of standard, formal English.

EXAMPLE   **1.** I need to (*bring, take*) these books back to the library.

 1. *take*

1. There isn't one state that (*doesn't, don't*) have numerous place names derived from American Indian words.

2. You will make (*fewer, less*) mistakes if you proofread your paper.

3. The assignments on classical Greek philosophers were divided (*among, between*) the juniors in the humanities class.

4. Please (*borrow, lend*) me your notes from yesterday.

5. Will you (*bring, take*) these books to Jonah when you go to his house?

6. (*Being that, Since*) she has passed all the tests, she should be a likely candidate for the military academy.

7. The reason the can burst is (*because, that*) water expands when it freezes.

8. Chen Rong was a famous Chinese artist who (*did, done*) many beautiful paintings of dragons.

9. (*Beside, Besides*) *The Scarlet Letter* and *The Red Badge of Courage*, we read *The Joy Luck Club*.

10. During the middle of the nineteenth century, many Asians (*emigrated, immigrated*) to the United States.

Review A   **Completing Sentences with Correct Usage**

Choose an item from the colored box to complete each of the following sentences correctly.

except	accept	held at	number
being as	busted	that	because
immigrate	alumni	alumnae	took
anywheres	held	amount	anywhere
brought	emigrate	since	broke

EXAMPLE   **1.** Two years ago, my uncle Koichi decided to _____ to this country.

 1. *immigrate*

1. Fortunately, he _____ along his marvelous kite-making skills and his keen business sense.

HELP—

Be careful!
Some of the items in the box in Review A are nonstandard usages.

A Glossary of Usage   **731**

2. At first it was hard for Uncle Koichi to _____ the fact that kite flying isn't as popular here as it is in Japan.

3. I did some research for him and found out where the big kite festivals are _____.

4. He decided to settle right here in Southern California _____ plenty of kite enthusiasts live here all year-round.

5. First, Uncle Koichi built a small _____ of beautiful kites, and then he started giving kite-flying lessons.

6. All three of my older brothers are enthusiastic _____ of Koichi's Kite College.

7. The reason that Uncle Koichi's shop is successful is _____ he loves his work and is very good at it.

8. My first kite _____ into pieces when I crashed it into a tree, but Uncle Koichi built me another one.

9. I took this photograph of his magnificent dragon kite, which takes _____ from three to five people to launch, depending on wind conditions.

10. My uncle's customers and friends all hope that he will never _____ from the United States and take his glorious kites back to Japan.

Review B Correcting Errors in Usage

Most of the following sentences contain errors in the use of standard, formal English. If a sentence contains an error or an informal usage, revise the sentence. If a sentence is already correct, write *C*.

EXAMPLE **1.** The five starting players have twenty fouls between them.

1. *The five starting players have twenty fouls among them.*

1. It don't look as if the rain will stop this afternoon.
2. Sometimes I can get so absorbed in a movie that I forget where I am at.
3. Would you bring your guitar when you come to visit us?
4. The drought seriously effected the lettuce crop.
5. You must learn to except criticism if you want to improve.
6. Being as the Black History Month essay contest ends next week, we need to submit our entries soon.
7. The reason that many Irish people moved to France and Argentina after the unsuccessful Irish rebellion in 1798 is because they refused to live under English rule.
8. Who first discovered computer chips?
9. The title of James Baldwin's *Notes of a Native Son* is an illusion to Richard Wright's famous novel *Native Son*.
10. Beside you and me, who is going on the hike?

Review C ## Proofreading a Paragraph for Correct Usage

Most of the sentences in the following paragraph contain an error in the use of standard English. Identify the error in each sentence, and then write the correct form. If a sentence is already correct, write *C*.

EXAMPLE [1] If you like to jump rope alot, find out if there's a branch of the American Double Dutch League near you.

1. *alot—a lot*

[1] Double Dutch is a fast-action rope-jumping style that has been popular on U.S. playgrounds for anywheres from fifty to a hundred years. [2] In Double Dutch, turners twirl two ropes alternately in opposite

USAGE

directions, creating an eggbeater effect. [**3**] Being that the two ropes are going so fast, jumpers have to jump double-fast. [**4**] Their feet fly at over three hundred steps a minute—about half that number is all the faster I can go! [**5**] To make things even more interesting, two jumpers often perform together to rhymes or music, doing flips, twists, cartwheels, and etc. [**6**] Besides competing in local meets, jumpers can participate in competitions organized by the American Double Dutch League, the sport's official governing body. [**7**] In competition, all teams must undergo the same amount of tests, including the speed test, the compulsory-tricks test, and the freestyle test. [**8**] The photo on the previous page isn't an optical allusion—the two jumpers are twins as well as a Double Dutch doubles team! [**9**] These girls not only won their divisional title in the American Double Dutch League World Championships but also were chosen to bring their sport to the Moscow International Folk Festival. [**10**] The late Olympic athlete Florence "Flo-Jo" Joyner enthusiastically supported Double Dutch, and it don't surprise me at all that she liked to jump Double Dutch herself!

had of See **of.**

had ought, hadn't ought Do not use *had* or *hadn't* with *ought.*

| NONSTANDARD | Your rough draft had ought to be finished by now. |
| STANDARD | Your rough draft **ought** to be finished by now. |

| NONSTANDARD | She hadn't ought to have turned here. |
| STANDARD | She **ought not** to have turned here. |

hardly See **The Double Negative,** page 743.

he, she, it, they Avoid using a pronoun along with its antecedent as the subject of a verb. Such an error is sometimes called a ***double subject.***

| NONSTANDARD | The computer system it is down today. |
| STANDARD | The **computer system** is down today. |

| NONSTANDARD | Fay Stanley and Diane Stanley they wrote a biography of the Hawaiian princess Ka'iulani. |
| STANDARD | **Fay Stanley and Diane Stanley** wrote a biography of the Hawaiian princess Ka'iulani. |

hisself, theirself, theirselves *Hisself, theirself,* and *theirselves* are nonstandard. Avoid using these forms in speech and in all writing other than dialogue. Instead, use *himself* and *themselves.*

hopefully *Hopefully* means "in a hopeful manner" or "it is to be hoped."

EXAMPLES   When the fog lifted, the mountain climbers **hopefully** resumed their ascent.

We will leave early, **hopefully** by six.

illusion See **allusion, illusion.**

immigrate See **emigrate, immigrate.**

imply, infer *Imply* means "to suggest." *Infer* means "to interpret" or "to draw as a conclusion."

EXAMPLES   The governor **implied** in her speech that she would support a statewide testing program.

I **inferred** from the governor's speech that she would support a statewide testing program.

in, into *In* means "within." *Into* means "from the outside to the inside." In formal situations, avoid using *in* for *into.*

INFORMAL   He threw the scraps of paper in the litter basket.

FORMAL   He threw the scraps of paper **into** the litter basket.

invent See **discover, invent.**

it See **he, she, it, they.**

its, it's See page 860.

kind of, sort of In formal situations, avoid using *kind of* for the adverb *somewhat* or *rather.*

INFORMAL   Jackie was kind of disappointed when she did not make the basketball team.

FORMAL   Jackie was **somewhat** [or *rather*] disappointed when she did not make the basketball team.

kind of a, sort of a In formal situations, omit the *a.*

INFORMAL   What kind of a car do you drive?

FORMAL   What **kind of** car do you drive?

kind(s), sort(s), type(s) With the singular form of each of these nouns, use *this* or *that.* With the plural form, use *these* or *those.*

EXAMPLES   **This kind** of gas is dangerous; **those kinds** are harmless.

These types of reading assignments are always challenging.

STYLE   TIP

Some authorities disapprove of the use of *hopefully* to mean "it is to be hoped." Avoid using *hopefully* in this sense in formal speech and writing.

INFORMAL
We will leave early; hopefully, we will leave by six.

FORMAL
We will leave early; **we hope to** leave by six.

USAGE

learn, teach *Learn* means "to gain knowledge." *Teach* means "to provide with knowledge."

EXAMPLES   I would like to **learn** how to play chess.

                  Will you **teach** me the fundamental rules of chess?

leave, let *Leave* means "to go away." *Let* means "to permit" or "to allow." Do not use *leave* for *let*.

EXAMPLES   Please **let** [not *leave*] them stay where they are.

                  They **let** [not *left*] Jaime have the flag that flew over the capitol.

lend See **borrow, lend.**

less See **fewer, less.**

lie, lay See page 659.

like, as *Like* is a preposition. In formal situations, do not use *like* for the conjunction *as* to introduce a subordinate clause.

INFORMAL   The stir-fry did not turn out like I had hoped it would.

  FORMAL   The stir-fry did not turn out **as** I had hoped it would.

Reference Note

For more information about **prepositions,** see page 502. For more about **subordinate clauses,** see page 559.

like, as if, as though In formal situations, avoid using the preposition *like* for the conjunction *as if* or *as though* to introduce a subordinate clause.

INFORMAL   That guitar sounds like it is out of tune.

  FORMAL   That guitar sounds **as if** [or *as though*] it is out of tune.

may, can See page 683.

might of, must of See **of.**

Exercise 3   Identifying Correct Usage

For each of the following sentences, choose the word or word group in parentheses that is correct according to the rules of standard, formal English.

EXAMPLE   **1.** What (*kind of, kind of a*) computer do you have?

              1. *kind of*

 1. (*These, This*) kinds of questions require more thought than (*that, those*) kind.
 2. I (*had ought, ought*) to check out a good library book.
 3. It looks (*like, as if*) we'll be able to attend the powwow.

4. Will the coach (*leave, let*) you skip soccer practice today?

5. He serves the ball exactly (*as, like*) the coach showed him.

6. I (*implied, inferred*) from Dad's remark about "slovenliness" that my sister and I ought to clean our room.

7. When Jay Gatsby walked (*in, into*) the room, everyone stared at him.

8. (*Leave, Let*) Rosetta explain the trigonometry problem.

9. Did Mr. Stokes (*imply, infer*) that he was pleased with my research paper on Mexican American authors?

10. What sort (*of, of a*) culture did the Phoenicians have?

no, none, nothing See **The Double Negative,** page 743.

nor See **or, nor.**

nowheres See **anyways, anywheres.**

number See **amount, number.**

number of, a/the See page 585.

of *Of* is a preposition. Do not use *of* in place of *have* after verbs such as *could, should, would, might, must,* and *ought to.*

NONSTANDARD	He could of had a summer job if he had applied earlier.
STANDARD	He **could have** had a summer job if he had applied earlier.

NONSTANDARD	You ought to of taken a foreign language.
STANDARD	You **ought to have** taken a foreign language.

Also, do not use *of* after *had*.

NONSTANDARD	If I had of known the word *raze,* I could have completed the crossword puzzle.
STANDARD	If I **had** known the word *raze,* I could have completed the crossword puzzle.

Avoid using *of* after other prepositions such as *inside, off,* and *outside.*

EXAMPLE	Meet me **outside** [not *outside of*] the auditorium at six o'clock.

off, off of Do not use *off* or *off of* in place of *from*.

NONSTANDARD	You can get a program off of the usher.
STANDARD	You can get a program **from** the usher.

or, nor Use *or* with *either;* use *nor* with *neither.*

EXAMPLES   Edwina will make **either** vegetable stew **or** bean burritos for the potluck dinner.

Before 1959, **neither** Alaska **nor** Hawaii was officially part of the United States.

ought to of See **of.**

raise, rise See page 662.

reason . . . because See **because.**

scarcely See **The Double Negative,** page 743.

she See **he, she, it, they.**

should of See **of.**

sit, set See page 661.

slow, slowly See page 696.

some, somewhat In formal situations, avoid using *some* to mean "to some extent." Instead, use *somewhat.*

INFORMAL   Wyatt's TV viewing has decreased some during the past month.

FORMAL   Wyatt's TV viewing has decreased **somewhat** during the past month.

somewheres See **anyways, anywheres.**

sort(s) See **kind(s), sort(s), type(s)** and **kind of a, sort of a.**

sort of See **kind of, sort of.**

supposed to, used to When writing the past form of *suppose* or *use,* especially before the word *to,* avoid omitting the *–d* ending.

EXAMPLES   Juan is **supposed to** [not *suppose to*] meet us at the restaurant at 6:00 P.M.

I **used to** [not *use to*] live on a farm in Nebraska.

take See **bring, take.**

teach See **learn, teach.**

than, then *Than* is a subordinating conjunction used in comparisons. *Then* is an adverb telling *when.*

EXAMPLES   He is a better cook **than** I am.

Reference Note

For information about forming the past tense of **regular verbs,** see page 645.

Reference Note

For information about **subordinating conjunctions,** see page 566. For more about **adverbs,** see page 499.

Let the sauce simmer for ten minutes, and **then** stir in two cups of cooked mixed vegetables.

that See **who, which, that.**

theirs, there's See page 865.

theirself, theirselves See **hisself, theirself, theirselves.**

their, there, they're See page 865.

them Do not use *them* as an adjective. Use *those.*

EXAMPLE All of **those** [not *them*] paintings are by Carmen.

they See **he, she, it, they.**

this here, that there Avoid using *here* or *there* after the demonstrative adjective *this* or *that.*

EXAMPLE **This** [not *This here*] story tells about the Hmong people of Laos.

this, that, these, those See **kind(s), sort(s), types(s).**

try and, try to Use *try to,* not *try and.*

EXAMPLE Let me **try to** [not *try and*] repair the pipes before you call a plumber.

type(s) See **kind(s), sort(s), type(s).**

type, type of Avoid using *type* as an adjective. Add *of* after *type.*

NONSTANDARD The trainer recommended a new type shoe.
STANDARD The trainer recommended a new **type of** shoe.

used to See **supposed to, used to.**

ways In formal situations, you should use *way,* not *ways,* in referring to distance.

INFORMAL We had to travel a long ways when we moved from Virginia to New Mexico.
FORMAL We had to travel a long **way** when we moved from Virginia to New Mexico.

well, good See page 696.

what Use *that,* not *what,* to introduce an adjective clause.

EXAMPLE One of the books **that** [not *what*] he recommended was Langston Hughes's novel *Not Without Laughter.*

Reference Note

For more about **adjective clauses,** see page 560.

A Glossary of Usage **739**

USAGE

when, where Unless you are defining a time or a place, do not use *when* or *where* to begin a definition.

NONSTANDARD	A spoonerism is when the beginning sounds of two words are switched.
STANDARD	A spoonerism is **a slip of the tongue in which the beginning sounds of two words are switched.**
NONSTANDARD	Claustrophobia is where you have an abnormal fear of enclosed spaces.
STANDARD	Claustrophobia is **an abnormal fear of enclosed spaces.**

where Do not use *where* for *that.*

EXAMPLE I read **that** [not *where*] Demosthenes learned to enunciate by practicing with pebbles in his mouth.

where . . . at See **at.**

who, which, that *Who* refers to persons only. *Which* refers to things only. *That* may refer to either persons or things.

EXAMPLES Isn't Nora the runner **who** [or *that*] won the gold medal?

The movie *La Bamba,* **which** was written and directed by Luis Valdez, received popular and critical acclaim.

Is Emily Dickinson the poet **that** [or *who*] wrote "Tell all the Truth but tell it slant."

Is this the film version of *Macbeth* **that** stars Orson Welles?

who, whom See page 619.

who's, whose See page 866.

would of See **of.**

your, you're See page 866.

Exercise 4 Identifying Correct Usage

For each of the following sentences, choose the word or word group that is correct according to the rules of standard, formal English.

EXAMPLE 1. Where did you get (*that, that there*) poster?
  1. that

1. I read in a newspaper article (*that, where*) some dogs are being trained to help people who have hearing impairments.

2. The first female novelist in United States literature who wrote frankly about women's concerns was neither Willa Cather (*or, nor*) Edith Wharton, but Kate Chopin.

3. Jack London must (*of, have*) led an adventurous life.

4. Our teacher assigned us (*this, this here*) chapter to read.

5. Joe had the flu last week, but he's feeling (*some, somewhat*) better.

6. As we passed Shreveport and crossed the Texas line, El Paso seemed a long (*way, ways*) away.

7. For advice, I go to Ms. Sanchez, (*which, who*) is a very understanding guidance counselor.

8. This (*type, type of*) short story has appealed to readers for many years.

9. Pass me (*them, those*) notes on the experiment, please.

10. He jumped (*off, off of*) the edge of the porch.

Review D Identifying Correct Usage

Each sentence in the following paragraphs contains at least one pair of italicized items. From each pair, choose the item that is correct according to the rules of standard, formal English.

EXAMPLE **[1]** While we were driving through the Appalachian Mountains, (*my father, my father he*) suddenly started chuckling and pulled over to the side of the road.

　　1. *my father*

[1] Dad said that we really (*had ought, ought*) to get out of the car and see the amazing mailbox that somebody had built. [2] Neither Ivy nor I was especially interested in mailboxes, but when we saw the fanciful metal figure that Dad was pointing to, we both smiled just (*as, like*) he had. [3] We jumped out to take the photo shown on this page, and while we were standing (*beside, besides*) the road, a man came out of the house. [4] He introduced himself as Charlie Lucas and said he had built the mailbox man by welding together scraps from (*broken, busted*) machinery. [5] We started chatting with him, and the next thing we knew, he had invited us (*in, into*) the house to see more of his figures. [6] The house was (*kind of, rather*) like an art museum: There were dinosaurs made from colorful twisted wire, a fiddle player with a head made from a shovel, and an alligator whose body (*might have, might of*) once been a crankshaft.

[7] "Dad, are these figures art?" Ivy whispered, and Dad's answer

Charlie Lucas, *Old Buddy.* Photo: Paul Rocheleau.

(*inferred, implied*) that they were. [**8**] He said that art (*don't, doesn't*) have to be stuffy and serious or made from bronze or marble and that true artists aren't always (*alumna, alumni*) of famous art schools. [**9**] (*Mr. Lucas he, Mr. Lucas*) agreed with Dad that (*these kind, these kinds*) of sculptures and all other kinds of folk art are of great value. [**10**] Folk art comes straight from the heart; it often recycles castoff materials that most people (*would have, would of*) considered junk; it offers a different perspective on life; and it makes people smile!

Review E   Identifying Correct Usage

Each sentence in the following paragraphs contains at least one pair of italicized items. From each pair, choose the item that is correct according to the rules of standard, formal English.

EXAMPLE   [**1**] Have you read (*where, that*) Vietnamese refugees are working hard to succeed in the United States?

1. *that*

[**1**] When Vietnamese immigrants stepped (*off, off of*) the planes that had brought them from refugee camps all over Asia, they didn't know what to expect in America. [**2**] However, like previous immigrants, they were people (*which, who*) managed to succeed against all odds. [**3**] Many of them neither spoke English (*or, nor*) knew much about life in the United States. [**4**] Often grateful just to be alive, they could (*of, have*) contented themselves with simple survival. [**5**] Instead, many of (*them, those*) Vietnamese families have encouraged their children to achieve academic excellence. [**6**] According to one study, half of the refugee children earn a B average overall and half also receive A's in math; (*that, that there*) study also places these students near the national average in English.

[**7**] One reason Vietnamese students do so well is (*because, that*) many believe that success comes from hard work, not from luck or natural aptitude. [**8**] Consequently, rather (*than, then*) watch television or go to the mall, many families spend weeknights doing homework together. [**9**] Parents who do not speak English well sometimes help by assigning (*less, fewer*) chores on weeknights. [**10**] Younger children get extra instruction (*from, off of*) older brothers and sisters, and all this effort is helping the Vietnamese become one of the most successful immigrant groups in the United States.

The Double Negative

A *double negative* is a construction in which two negative words are used to express a single negative idea. Although acceptable until Shakespeare's time and common in other languages, double negatives are now considered nonstandard English.

NONSTANDARD   She has not read none of Nadine Gordimer's books.

STANDARD   She has **not** read **any** of Nadine Gordimer's books.

STANDARD   She has read **none** of Nadine Gordimer's books.

NONSTANDARD   I do not know nothing about the Peloponnesian War.

STANDARD   I do **not** know **anything** about the Peloponnesian War.

STANDARD   I know **nothing** about the Peloponnesian War.

NONSTANDARD   Grandma said that she hadn't never seen another pumpkin that was as large as this one.

STANDARD   Grandma said that she **hadn't ever** seen another pumpkin that was as large as this one.

STANDARD   Grandma said that she had **never** seen another pumpkin that was as large as this one.

Common Negative Words		
barely	never	not (n't)
but (meaning "only")	no	nothing
	nobody	nowhere
hardly	none	only
neither	no one	scarcely

NOTE   Avoid the common error of using *–n't*, the contraction of *not*, with another negative word, especially *barely*, *hardly*, or *scarcely*.

NONSTANDARD   The film is so long that we couldn't scarcely see all of it in one class period.

STANDARD   The film is so long that we could **scarcely** see all of it in one class period.

The words *but* and *only* are considered negative words when they are used as adverbs meaning "no more than." In such cases, the use of another negative word with *but* or *only* is considered informal.

INFORMAL   Whenever I see you, I can't help but smile.

FORMAL   Whenever I see you, **I can't help smiling.**

"Confounded Double Negatives!"

© 1993 by Sidney Harris.

HELP

Although the sentences in Exercise 5 can be corrected in more than one way, you need to give only one revision for each.

Exercise 5 **Correcting Double Negatives**

Revise each of the following sentences to correct the double negative.

EXAMPLE 1. He hadn't no pencils on his desk.

1. *He had no pencils on his desk.*

1. Tom didn't have no time to buy the books.
2. Haven't none of you seen the dog?
3. Isn't nobody else interested in going to visit the pueblo at Tesuque this morning?
4. We haven't but one day to visit the fair.
5. She didn't contribute nothing to the project.
6. The lights were so dim that we couldn't barely see.
7. They said that they didn't have no time to go to the post office before tomorrow.
8. In the mountains you can't help but feel calm.
9. Can't none of them come to the party?
10. José Martí was sentenced to six years in prison, and he hadn't done nothing but write a letter that the Spanish government didn't like.

Review F **Correcting Errors in Usage**

Most of the following sentences contain errors in the use of standard, formal English. If a sentence contains an error, revise the sentence. If a sentence is already correct, write *C*.

EXAMPLE 1. Can't none of the staff sort the yearbook pictures?

1. *Can't any of the staff sort the yearbook pictures?*

1. A New Year's Eve Watch is when African Americans join together to welcome the new year by singing, chanting, and shouting.
2. We divided the confetti between the four children.
3. We should of paid closer attention to the instructions.
4. I wonder how many Americans realize the importance of the Minutemen, which were true champions of freedom during the American Revolution.
5. Being as my parents prefer CDs, they don't hardly ever play their tapes anymore.
6. A large amount of people contributed to the charity drive.
7. Swimming is a type of sport that requires daily training.
8. I don't think he knows where he is at.

9. Did Mr. Jackson mean to infer that we might have a pop quiz tomorrow, or was he just joking?

10. Some speakers make illusions to the "good old days."

Nonsexist Language

Nonsexist language is language that applies to people in general, both male and female. For example, the nonsexist terms *humanity, human beings,* and *people* can substitute for the gender-specific term *mankind.*

In the past, many skills and occupations were generally closed to either men or women. Expressions like *seamstress, stewardess,* and *mailman* reflect those limitations. Since most jobs can now be held by both men and women, language is adjusting to reflect this change.

When you are referring generally to people, use nonsexist expressions rather than gender-specific ones. Following are some widely used nonsexist terms that you can use to replace the older, gender-specific ones.

Gender-specific	Nonsexist
businessman	executive, businessperson
chairman	chairperson, chair
deliveryman	delivery person
fireman	firefighter
foreman	supervisor
housewife	homemaker
mailman	mail carrier
man-made	synthetic, manufactured
manpower	workers, human resources
policeman	police officer
salesman	salesperson, salesclerk
seamstress	needleworker
steward, stewardess	flight attendant

If the antecedent of a pronoun may be either masculine or feminine, use both masculine and feminine pronouns to refer to it.

EXAMPLES   **Anyone** who wants to apply should bring **his or her** application.

Any applicant may bring a résumé with **him or her.**

STYLE   TIP

Avoid using the awkward expressions *s/he* and *wo/man.*

You can often avoid the awkward *his or her* construction (or the alternative *his/her*) by substituting an article (*a, an,* or *the*) for the construction. You can also rephrase the sentence, using the plural forms of both the pronoun and its antecedent.

EXAMPLES   Any interested **workers** may submit **an** application.

All interested **workers** may submit **their** applications.

Exercise 6 Using Nonsexist Language

Rewrite each of the following sentences to avoid using gender-specific terms.

EXAMPLE   1. I had to stay home all afternoon to wait for the deliveryman.

1. *I had to stay home all afternoon to wait for the delivery person.*

1. Some of the visitors felt that the man-made objects detracted from the natural beauty.
2. Make sure those letters are ready to go by the time the mailman gets here.
3. The first business before the committee was to elect a chairman.
4. Among the speakers at career day were doctors, lawyers, and businessmen.
5. Are you certain we have enough manpower to get this project done on time?
6. If anyone wants to join us at the movie tonight, he should meet us out front at 7:15.
7. The salesman never stood a chance of convincing Father to buy a more expensive car.
8. If you need the stewardess, just press that button above your head.
9. Jaime's uncle was one of those few who followed through on his childhood dream of becoming a policeman.
10. Johnny's summer job involved calling housewives and asking them questions about laundry detergent.

USAGE

Chapter Review

A. Identifying Correct Usage

For each of the following sentences, choose the word or word group in parentheses that is correct according to the rules of standard, formal English.

1. The Polar Bear Club jumped (*in, into*) the icy lake.

2. The clap of thunder almost (*burst, busted*) my eardrums.

3. After hearing my grandmother's stories about World War II, I realized that she was more daring (*than, then*) I had ever imagined.

4. Rochelle read (*where, that*) flood waters reached the rooftops.

5. Leticia's temperature rose (*somewhat, some*) before noon.

6. Many students felt that the date for the prom should (*have, of*) been set in early June rather than in May.

7. Mr. Cronin wants to raise cattle (*like, as*) his grandfather did.

8. A large (*amount, number*) of students in my computer class are unfamiliar with spreadsheets.

9. Chan repeated that he preferred that (*type, type of*) backpack.

10. Alex thought the workshop on handcrafting paper was (*kind of, somewhat*) interesting.

B. Correcting Errors in Usage

Most of the following sentences contain errors in the use of standard, formal English. If a sentence contains an error or an informal usage, revise the sentence. If a sentence is already correct, write *C*.

11. All of the members of the budget committee accept, I believe, Representative Carpenter voted to retain the present tax structure.

12. The generosity of my grandparents has effected all of us.

13. I couldn't hardly believe my eyes when I saw a 90 on my paper.

14. This here paper glider was designed by Dr. Yasuaki Ninomiya.

15. Does this poem make an illusion to the *Iliad*?

16. Being that Jennifer had never learned to swim, she was afraid to go on the boat ride.

17. Two of my great-grandparents emigrated from Ireland and came to the United States.

18. When the singer recorded the CD of folk songs, he didn't have no way of knowing that it would sell thousands of copies.

19. Can't anybody see that she is doing her best?

20. The Gallaghers they have lived in this town for years.

C. Identifying Correct Usage

For each of the following sentences, choose the word or word group in parentheses that is correct according to the rules of standard, formal English.

21. Just (*like, as*) Devin had thought, the library was closed.

22. The lifeguard got down (*off of, from*) his high seat to help us.

23. The reason she was late was (*because, that*) the roads were blocked.

24. All of the teachers will (*bring, take*) their students to the park on the last day of school.

25. The new legislation attempts to (*effect, affect*) a change in the behavior of the stock market.

26. The trucker (*could of, could have*) avoided the accident.

27. Jahi and Aritha don't like (*those kinds, those kind*) of concerts.

28. He was so tired that he (*couldn't hardly, could hardly*) move.

29. (*Less, Fewer*) than fifty people attended the lecture.

30. (*Among, Between*) those invited to the governor's inauguration were Mr. and Mrs. Jackson.

D. Identifying Correct Usage

Each sentence in the following paragraph contains at least one pair of italicized items. From each pair, choose the item that is correct according to the rules of standard, formal English.

Whenever I walk into Montsho Books, I can't help [31] (*feeling, but feel*) proud to be black. Do you want to know where this bookstore [32] (*is at, is*)? I should have mentioned that it's in Orlando, Florida, just a short [33] (*way, ways*) from the Orlando Arena. Ms. Perkins, [34] (*which, who*) runs the store, told me [35] (*where, that*) *montsho* means "black" in an African language. [36] (*Anyways, Anyway*), when Ms. Perkins was a schoolteacher, she noticed that there [37] (*were, weren't*) hardly any children's books that featured African Americans. Ms. Perkins decided she [38] (*had ought, ought*) to open a store that sold books exclusively by blacks and about blacks.

[39] (*Beside, Besides*) poetry and fiction by African Americans, the shop offers all kinds of nonfiction selections. Montsho Books has become a **[40]** (*kind of, kind of a*) cultural center for Orlando's black community.

Writing Application
Using Standard English in a Letter

Writing a Local History   Dr. Yolanda Washington, a professor at the nearby community college, is compiling an informal history of your area. Write a letter to Dr. Washington, telling a true story about your block, your neighborhood, or your town. You may use dialect in direct quotations, but be sure to use standard English in the rest of your letter.

Prewriting   First, think of some of the stories you may have heard about your community. Then, choose the best story to send to Dr. Washington. Jot down as many concrete details as you can. Record a few good quotations and paraphrases that capture the local flavor of the story.

Writing   Begin your draft by greeting Dr. Washington and explaining that you would like to contribute to her local history project. Then, set the scene for your story by indicating the time period and setting. Write down the events of the story in a clear, straightforward order.

Revising   Have a classmate read your draft. Does the letter flow logically? Do the details and quotations capture the local flavor of your area? Add or revise details to make the story clear and vivid.

Publishing   Proofread your letter carefully for errors in grammar, usage, and mechanics. Be sure you have used the correct form for business letters. Check words and expressions in the Glossary of Usage to make sure that they are formal, standard English. If you have included quotations, check them for correct punctuation. You and other members of your class may want to compile an informal history of your community. You can publish your stories by collecting them in a booklet.

Reference Note

For more information about **punctuating quotations,** see page 815. For information on writing **business letters,** see "Writing" in the Quick Reference Handbook.

Capitalization
Rules of Standard Usage

Diagnostic Preview

Capitalizing Words Correctly

For each of the following sentences, correctly write the word or words that should be capitalized. If a sentence is already correct, write *C*.

EXAMPLE   1. The rotary club has invited congressman William Bashone to speak tonight at the annual banquet.

1. *Rotary Club; Congressman*

1. According to Zack Johnson, the company's representative, you should not buy just any car; you should buy a neptune.
2. One of the earliest cars made by Henry Ford was called the Model T; it had a four-cylinder, twenty-horsepower engine.
3. On our vacation we toured several states in the south.
4. Ridgewood bake shop and deli is just north of park ridge street on highway 143.
5. Before you can take this computer course, you must pass algebra II.
6. Aren't they planning a parade and party to celebrate Dr. Martin Luther King, jr.'s birthday?
7. Because we cheered so loudly at the special olympics, ms. Andrews made us honorary cheerleaders for her special-education class.
8. In a nationally televised press conference, the president warned that he would veto any tax increase.

9. The british poet Ted Hughes was married to Sylvia Plath, who was an american writer.

10. The only man in American history who was not elected vice-president or president—yet held both positions—is ex-president Gerald Ford.

11. My mother asked me to walk to the supermarket and buy a quart container of farmingbury milk and two pounds of dried beans.

12. When we toured eastern Tennessee, we visited the Oak Ridge National Laboratory, where atomic research was carried out during World War II.

13. The Spanish-american Club has planned a festival for late summer; it will be held at the north end of the city.

14. If you are looking for the best apples in the state, follow route 14 until you see the signs for Peacock's Orchard.

15. In a controversial debate over the Panama canal, the United States voted to relinquish its control of the canal to the government of Panama.

16. When aunt Janice visited England last summer, she toured buckingham palace and tried to catch a glimpse of queen Elizabeth.

17. Mayor-elect Sabrena Willis will speak to the public about her proposals to expand the city's literacy program.

18. Earl and Jamie were lucky to get tickets to see the garth brooks concert at freedom hall.

19. When spring arrives, I know it is time to start thinking about where to look for a summer job.

20. Although the east room of the White house is now used mainly for press conferences, it was once a place where Abigail Adams aired president Adams's laundry.

Using Capital Letters Correctly

In your reading, you will notice variations in the use of capital letters. Most writers, however, follow the rules presented in this chapter. In your own writing, following these rules will help you communicate clearly with the widest possible audience.

25a. Capitalize the first word in every sentence.

EXAMPLE   In 1985, Lynette Woodard became the first woman to play for the Harlem Globetrotters.

The first word of a quoted sentence should begin with a capital letter, whether or not the quotation comes at the beginning of your sentence.

EXAMPLE   Plutarch once said, "**T**he mind is not a vessel to be filled but a fire to be lighted."

When quoting only part of a sentence, capitalize the first word of the quotation if (1) the person you are quoting capitalized it or (2) it is the first word of your sentence.

EXAMPLES   What does the image "**a** fire to be lighted" suggest about the mind?

"**A** fire to be lighted" suggests the mind's potential.

NOTE   Capitalize the first word of a sentence fragment used in dialogue.

EXAMPLE   Selena asked, "Have you read Toni Morrison's new novel?" Bradley said, "**N**o, not yet."

Traditionally, the first word of each line of a poem is capitalized.

EXAMPLE
I peeled my orange
That was so bright against
The gray of December
That, from some distance
Someone might have thought
I was making a fire in my hands.

Gary Soto, "Oranges"

25b. Capitalize the first word in both the salutation and the closing of a letter.

EXAMPLES   **D**ear Mr. Ramirez: **M**y dear Sasha,

Sincerely yours,   **Y**ours truly,

25c. Capitalize the pronoun *I* and the interjection *O*.

The interjection *O* is usually used only for invocations and is followed by the name of the person or thing being addressed. Don't confuse it with the common interjection *oh*, which is generally not capitalized and which is followed by punctuation.

EXAMPLES   Walt Whitman's tribute to Abraham Lincoln begins, "**O** Captain! my Captain!"

What **I** meant was—**o**h, never mind.

Reference Note
For more information on using **capital letters** in **quotations,** see page 816.

HELP
Some writers do not follow traditional capitalization rules. When you quote from a writer's work, use capital letters exactly as the writer uses them.

Reference Note
For information on **writing letters,** see "Writing" in the Quick Reference Handbook.

MECHANICS

25d. Capitalize proper nouns and proper adjectives.

A *common noun* names any one of a group of persons, places, things, or ideas. A *proper noun* names a particular person, place, thing, or idea. A *proper adjective* is formed from a proper noun.

Common nouns are capitalized only if they

- begin a sentence (also, in most cases, a line of poetry)

  or

- begin a direct quotation

  or

- are part of a title

Reference Note

For more information on **proper nouns** and **common nouns,** see page 485. For more on **proper adjectives,** see page 493.

Common Nouns	Proper Nouns	Proper Adjectives
a **w**riter	**D**ickens	**D**ickensian characters
a **c**ountry	**C**hina	**C**hinese coastline
a **p**resident	**L**incoln	**L**incolnesque ideals
an **i**sland	**H**awaii	**H**awaiian climate
a **l**anguage	**A**rabic	**A**rabic letters
a **p**oet	**S**hakespeare	**S**hakespearean sonnet
a **r**egion	**N**ew England	**N**ew England chowder

In proper nouns made up of two or more words, articles, coordinating conjunctions, and short prepositions (those with fewer than five letters) are generally not capitalized.

EXAMPLES   Queen **o**f Spain

"America **t**he Beautiful"

"Tales **f**rom **t**he Vienna Woods"

American Society **f**or **t**he Prevention **o**f Cruelty **t**o Animals

NOTE Proper nouns and proper adjectives may lose their capitals after long usage.

EXAMPLES   **m**adras   **s**andwich   **w**att   **p**uritan

quisling   **b**oycott   **p**latonic   **h**amburger

When you're not sure whether to capitalize a word, look it up in a dictionary.

MECHANICS

Reference Note

For information on **abbreviations** such as *Dr.* and *Jr.,* see page 779.

(1) Capitalize the names of persons and animals. Capitalize initials in names and abbreviations that either precede or follow names.

Persons	Animals
Toshio **W**illiams	**S**ocks
Heitor **V**illa-**L**obos	**S**ecretariat
W.E.B. Du**B**ois	**L**assie
Dr. **A**retha **O**zawa	**S**hamu
Brian **G**oldblum, **Jr.**	**W**hite **F**ang

COMPUTER TIP

The spellings of personal names can challenge even the best spellchecking software. However, you may be able to customize the spellchecker you use. If the software allows, add to it any frequently used names that you have difficulty spelling or capitalizing.

NOTE Some names contain more than one capital letter. Usage varies in the capitalization of *van, von, du, de la,* and other parts of multiword names. When possible, verify the spelling of a name with the person whose name it is, or check in a reference source.

EXAMPLES **La F**ontaine **McE**wen **O'C**onnor **Va**n **D**oren

De **la M**er **I**bn **E**zra **S**mith-**T**yson **v**an **G**ogh

(2) Capitalize geographical names.

Reference Note

The abbreviations of names of states are capitalized. For information on using and punctuating such **abbreviations,** see page 780.

Type of Name	Examples	
Towns, Cities	**N**ew **O**rleans	**P**ortage la **P**rairie
	Tokyo	**S**an **J**ose
Counties, Parishes	**M**arion **C**ounty	**L**afayette **P**arish
Townships, Provinces	**S**askatchewan **P**rovince	**L**awrence **T**ownship
States	**W**isconsin	**O**klahoma
	New **H**ampshire	**N**orth **C**arolina
Regions	the **S**outh	the **M**iddle **E**ast
	the **S**unbelt	the **N**orthern
	the **W**est **C**oast	**H**emisphere

NOTE Words such as *north, western,* and *southeast* are not capitalized when they indicate direction.

EXAMPLES **e**ast of the river driving **s**outh **w**estern Iowa

Type of Name	Examples	
Countries	India Ivory Coast	United States of America
Continents	Australia Africa	South America Europe
Islands	Dauphin Island Greater Antilles	Isle of Wight Florida Keys
Mountains	Blue Ridge Mountains Sierra Nevada	Mount McKinley Humphreys Peak
Bodies of Water	Pacific Ocean Gulf of Mexico	Rio de la Plata Saint Lawrence Seaway
Parks, Forests	Point Reyes National Seashore	Lowden Memorial State Park
Streets, Roads, Highways	County Road 16 Interstate 10 Lancaster Turnpike	Downing Street Euclid Avenue Avenida de Mayo
Other Geographical Names	Cape Canaveral Perce Rock Mississippi Valley	Isthmus of Suez Crater of Diamonds Point Sur

STYLE **TIP**

Since *rio* is Spanish for "river," *Rio de la Plata River* is redundant. Use only *Rio de la Plata*.

Other terms to watch for are

- *sierra*, Spanish for "mountain range" [Use only *Sierra Nevada*, not *Sierra Nevada Mountains*.]

- *yama*, Japanese for "mountain" [Use only *Fujiyama* or *Mount Fuji*, not *Mount Fujiyama*.]

- *sahara*, Arabic for "desert" [Use only *Sahara*, not *Sahara Desert*.]

- *gobi*, Mongolian for "desert" [Use only *Gobi*, not *Gobi Desert*.]

MECHANICS

NOTE The second word in a hyphenated number begins with a lower-case letter.

EXAMPLE   Twenty-fifth Street

A word such as *city, island, street,* or *park* is capitalized only when it is part of a proper noun.

Proper Nouns	**Common Nouns**
a rodeo in Carson City	a rodeo in a nearby city
a ferry to Block Island	a ferry to a resort island
swimming in Clear Lake	swimming in the lake
along Canal Street	along a neighborhood street

Reference Note

In addresses, abbreviations such as *St., Ave., Dr.,* and *Blvd.* are capitalized. For information on **abbreviations,** see page 780.

Exercise 1 Capitalizing Words and Names Correctly

If one or more words in an item should be capitalized, write the entire item correctly. If an item is already correct, write *C*.

EXAMPLE   **1.** south american countries

　　　　　 1. South American countries

1. living in the west
2. a city north of louisville
3. bonneville salt flats
4. the cape of good hope
5. chris o'malley
6. hoover dam
7. southern illinois
8. lock the door!
9. the kalahari desert
10. the northeast
11. gulf of Alaska
12. mary mcleod bethune
13. a mountain people
14. tom delaney, jr.
15. hawaiian volcanoes state park
16. north american actor
17. san francisco bay
18. skiing on the lake
19. turned west at the corner
20. he said, "i am, too."
21. mexican gold
22. and, o Zeus, save us
23. west indian curry
24. decatur street
25. fifty-sixth street

(3) Capitalize the names of planets, stars, constellations, and other heavenly bodies.

EXAMPLES

Saturn	**R**igel
Centaurus	Little **D**ipper
Comet **K**ohoutek	**P**luto
Pisces	**C**anis **M**inor
Betelgeuse	**P**roxima **C**entauri
the **G**reat **N**ebula	**I**o
Antares	**V**ega
Sirius	**A**rcturus

NOTE The word *earth* is not capitalized unless it is used along with the name of another heavenly body that is capitalized. The words *sun* and *moon* are generally not capitalized.

EXAMPLES Recycling is just one way to help preserve the **e**arth.

The planet **J**upiter takes almost twelve **E**arth years to orbit the **s**un.

The **m**oon reflects light from the **s**un.

(4) Capitalize the names of organizations, teams, government bodies, and institutions.

Type of Name	Examples	
Organizations	League of Women Voters Habitat for Humanity	American Dental Association Franklin Key Club
Teams	St. Louis Cardinals Karr Cougars	Miami Dolphins Seattle Sounders
Government Bodies	Department of State National Institute on Aging	Congress North Carolina State Senate
Institutions	Duke University Newcomb College United States Air Force Academy	St. Jude's Children's Research Hospital Smithsonian Institution

Do not capitalize words such as *democratic, republican,* and *socialist* when they refer to principles or forms of government. Capitalize these words only when they refer to specific political parties.

EXAMPLES   The citizens demanded **d**emocratic reforms.

Who will be the **R**epublican nominee for governor?

(5) Capitalize the names of businesses and the brand names of business products.

Businesses	De Havilland, Ltd.	Motorola, Inc.	Kelley's Hardware
Product Names	Toyota Tercel® Kraft® cheese	Apple Macintosh® Quaker® oatmeal	Sanford Pink Pearl®

Notice that a common noun that follows a brand name is not capitalized.

(6) Capitalize the names of particular buildings and other structures.

EXAMPLES   **R**ialto **T**heater   **C**olumbia **S**eafirst **C**enter

Moore **H**igh **S**chool   **C**lark **M**emorial **H**ospital

---

STYLE   TIP

The names of organizations, businesses, and government bodies are often abbreviated to a series of capital letters.

EXAMPLE
American **T**elephone & **T**elegraph   **AT&T**

STYLE   TIP

The word *party* in the name of a political party may or may not be capitalized; either way is correct. However, you should be consistent within any piece of writing.

EXAMPLE
Democratic **p**arty
or
Democratic **P**arty

MECHANICS

Reference Note

For more on the differences between **common nouns** and **proper nouns,** see pages 485 and 753.

┌HELP─

Do not capitalize a word such as *building, monument,* or *award* unless it is part of a proper noun.

(7) Capitalize the names of monuments, memorials, and awards.

EXAMPLES   **N**avajo **N**ational **M**onument

              Craters of the **M**oon **N**ational **M**onument

              Mount **R**ushmore **N**ational **M**emorial

              Civil **R**ights **M**emorial

              Presidential **M**edal of **F**reedom

              National **S**ociety of **F**ilm **C**ritics **A**ward

(8) Capitalize the names of historical events and periods, special events, holidays, and other calendar items.

Type of Name	Examples	
Historical Events and Periods	**G**reat **D**epression **R**eformation **P**ax **R**omana **R**eign of **T**error	the **A**merican **R**evolution **R**enaissance **M**iddle **A**ges
Special Events	**C**areer **D**ay 2002 **N**ew **Y**ork **C**ity Marathon **S**pecial **O**lympics	**T**exas **S**tate **F**air **P**an **A**merican **G**ames
Holidays and Other Calendar Items	**M**onday **S**eptember **K**wanzaa	**C**inco de **M**ayo **M**emorial **D**ay **M**other's **D**ay

NOTE Do not capitalize the name of a season unless the season is being personified or it is used as part of a proper noun.

EXAMPLES   This has been a rainy **s**pring.

              Finally, **S**pring tiptoed in and kissed the chill away.

              This year's **S**pring **F**estival will feature folk dancing and arts and crafts.

┌ S T Y L E   T I P ┐

The words *black* and *white* may or may not be capitalized when they refer to races; either way is correct. However, you should be consistent within any piece of writing.

EXAMPLES

Black-owned businesses
or
black-owned businesses

(9) Capitalize the names of nationalities, races, and peoples.

EXAMPLES   **L**ithuanian   **H**aitian   **J**ewish   **A**sian

              Caucasian   **H**ispanic   **B**antu   **S**erbo-**C**roatian

(10) Capitalize the names of religions and their followers, holy days and celebrations, sacred writings, and specific deities.

Type of Name	Examples	
Religions and Followers	**C**hristianity **H**induism **J**udaism	**B**uddhist **M**uslim **P**resbyterian
Holy Days and Celebrations	**E**piphany **R**amadan **R**osh **H**ashanah	**E**aster **P**assover **Y**om **K**ippur
Sacred Writings	the **H**oly **B**ible the **K**oran the **T**almud	**R**ig-**V**eda **G**enesis the **P**entateuch
Specific Deities	**A**llah **B**rahma	**G**od the **H**oly **S**pirit

The words *god* and *goddess* are not capitalized when they refer to deities of ancient mythology. However, the names of specific mythological gods and goddesses are capitalized.

EXAMPLE   The Greek **g**od of the sea was **P**oseidon.

NOTE Some writers capitalize all pronouns that refer to a deity. Other writers capitalize such pronouns only if necessary to prevent confusion.

EXAMPLE   Through Moses, God commanded the pharaoh to let **H**is people go. [The capitalization of *His* shows that the pronoun refers to God, not to Moses or the pharaoh.]

(11) Capitalize the names of ships, trains, aircraft, spacecraft, and any other vehicles.

Type of Name	Examples	
Ships	*Monitor*	**R.M.S.** *Titanic*
Trains	*Zephyr*	*Orient Express*
Aircraft	*Flyer*	*Enola Gay*
Spacecraft	*Skylab*	*Columbia*

Reference Note

For information on when to **italicize names,** see page 813.

MECHANICS

NOTE The names of the make and model of a vehicle are capitalized.

EXAMPLES **T**oyota **C**elica®   **F**ord **R**anger®   **C**essna **C**onquest®

25e. Do not capitalize the names of school subjects, except course names that include a number and the names of language classes.

EXAMPLES **h**istory   **a**rt   **p**hysics   **g**eometry

Spanish   **L**atin   **A**lgebra I   **C**hemistry II

NOTE Do not capitalize the class name *senior, junior, sophomore,* or *freshman* unless it is part of a proper noun.

EXAMPLES The **j**uniors are planning a surprise for **S**enior **D**ay.

The **F**reshman **F**ollies was a big success.

TIPS & TRICKS

As a rule, a singular noun identified by a number or letter is capitalized.

EXAMPLES
Room 22   **F**igure A
Chapter 18   **E**xample B
Channel 11   **A**pt. 3C

However, the word *page* is not usually capitalized, nor is a plural noun followed by two or more numbers or letters.

EXAMPLE
Look at **m**aps A and B on **p**age 315.

MECHANICS

Exercise 2 Capitalizing Words Correctly

Write the following word groups, using capital letters where they are needed. If an item is already correct, write *C*.

EXAMPLE   1. tropicana® orange juice
1. *Tropicana® orange juice*

1. two juniors and a senior
2. north atlantic treaty organization
3. st. patrick's cathedral
4. *city of new orleans* (train)
5. the federal reserve bank
6. the normandy invasion
7. classes in auto mechanics
8. the world cup
9. the washington monument
10. cherokee history
11. midtown traffic
12. jones and drake, inc.
13. spaceflight to mars
14. on labor day
15. the boat *ariadne*
16. at holiday inn®
17. the louisiana world exposition
18. early summer
19. gold medal® flour
20. an american history class

Review A Proofreading a Paragraph for Correct Capitalization

For each sentence in the following paragraph, correctly write the word or words containing incorrect capital or lowercase letters. If a sentence is already correct, write *C*.

EXAMPLE **[1]** Even if you don't know much about Horses, you likely can appreciate the beauty of the arabian horse shown below.

1. *horses; Arabian*

[**1**] Perhaps no other breed of horses can conjure up such images of romance as these beautiful animals from Northern Africa. [**2**] Their distinctive and colorful trappings bring to mind the nomadic lives of wandering peoples and the exciting exploits of their bedouin chieftains. [**3**] Smaller and lighter than many other breeds, with relatively large hooves, these horses are perfectly suited to the hot sands of the Sahara or the Arabian desert. [**4**] Some evidence suggests that african peoples may have been breeding these horses as long ago as seven thousand years. [**5**] Arabians characteristically have elegant heads and necks as well as large, lustrous eyes, features that have been prized by breeders all over the Earth. [**6**] These horses have played a part in many historical events far from the Continent of Africa. [**7**] During the Revolutionary war, for instance, George Washington rode a gray horse said to be the offspring of a famous Arabian stallion. [**8**] America's love affair with the Arabian horse has continued from the early days of our nation right through to the Present. [**9**] Today, the Arabian Horse International association has thousands of names on its roster. [**10**] Some importers include W. R. Brown of Berlin, New Hampshire, and Spencer Bade of Fall river, Massachusetts.

25f. Capitalize titles.

(1) Capitalize a person's title when the title comes before the person's name.

EXAMPLES   **M**ajor Malone   **D**r. Ramírez   **P**resident Carter

              Mrs. Wilson   **P**rofessor Cho   **M**r. Scott

Generally, a title used alone or following a person's name is not capitalized. Some titles, however, are by tradition capitalized. If you are not sure whether to capitalize a title, look it up in a dictionary.

EXAMPLES   The city elected a new **m**ayor today.

              Sherian Grace Cadoria, a **b**rigadier **g**eneral, is the highest-ranking African American woman in the U.S. armed forces.

              The **S**peaker of the **H**ouse rose to greet the **Q**ueen of England.

Also, for special emphasis or clarity, writers sometimes capitalize a title used alone or following a person's name.

EXAMPLES   I recently met Frank Sanchez, our local **B**usiness **L**eader of the **Y**ear.

              Did the **P**resident veto the bill?

Titles used alone in direct address are generally capitalized.

EXAMPLES   Can you discuss your strategy, **G**eneral?

              We're honored to welcome you, **M**s. **M**ayor.

              Please come in, **S**ir [or *sir*].

NOTE Do not capitalize *ex–, –elect, former,* or *late* when using it with a title.

EXAMPLES   **e**x-Governor Walsh   President-**e**lect Chan

(2) Capitalize a word showing a family relationship when the word is used before or in place of a person's name, unless the word is preceded by a possessive.

EXAMPLES   **A**unt Amanda   **U**ncle Hector   **G**randmother Ross

              my **a**unt Amy   your **c**ousin   Thelma's **n**ephew

(3) Capitalize the first and last words and all important words in titles and subtitles.

Unimportant words in a title include

- articles: *a, an, the*
- short prepositions (fewer than five letters), for example: *of, to, in, for, from, with*
- coordinating conjunctions: *and, but, for, nor, or, so, yet*

Type of Name	Examples
Books	*The Way to Rainy Mountain* *Edgar Allan Poe: The Man Behind the Legend*
Chapters and Other Parts of Books	"Empires of the Americas" "Glossary of Literary Terms"
Periodicals	*Popular Science* *Louisville Courier-Journal & Times*
Poems	"Tonight I Can Write" "Most Satisfied by Snow"
Short Stories	"In Another Country" "The Catch in the Shadow of the Sunrise"
Plays	*Watch on the Rhine* *The Importance of Being Earnest*
Historical Documents	the Magna Carta Treaty of Versailles
Works of Art	*Woman Before a Mirror* *Prelude to Farewell*
Movies	*Lost in Space* *Free Willy*
Television and Radio Programs	*Adventures in Good Music* *Discovery: Barrier Reef* *Third Rock from the Sun*

(continued)

Type of Name	Examples
Videos, Video Games	*The Adventures of Mowgli* *Super Mario Brothers*
Musical Works	"Bridge over Troubled Water" *La Traviata*
Audiotapes, Compact Discs	*Celtic Twilight* *One Step at a Time*
Computer Games and Programs	*Titanic: Adventure Out of Time* *Microsoft Word*
Comic Strips	*For Better or Worse* *Wizard of Id*

Reference Note

For information about **which titles should be italicized and which should be enclosed in quotation marks,** see pages 813 and 820.

NOTE Capitalize an article (*a, an,* or *the*) at the beginning of a title or subtitle only if it is the first word of the official title or subtitle.

EXAMPLES **A** *Christmas Carol*   **t**he *Austin American-Statesman*

"**A**n Acre of Grass"   **T**he *New Yorker*

The official title of a book is found on the title page. The official title of a newspaper or other periodical is found on the masthead, which usually appears on the editorial page or in the table of contents.

Exercise 3 Capitalizing Correctly

Write the following items, using capital and lowercase letters where they are needed. If an item is already correct, write *C*.

EXAMPLE **1.** the story "the kind of light that shines on texas"

1. the story "The Kind of Light That Shines on Texas"

1. *the washington post*
2. ex-senator Margaret Chase Smith
3. the television program *soul train*
4. emancipation proclamation
5. the first chapter in *the grapes of wrath*
6. the painting *Holy Family On The Steps*
7. my poem "Black my Midnight Sight"
8. General Colin Powell

9. the song "Blowin' In The Wind"

10. for my Aunt Mary

> **Review B** **Proofreading Paragraphs for Correct Capitalization**

For each sentence in the following paragraphs, change lowercase letters to capitals and capital letters to lowercase as necessary. If a sentence is already correct, write *C*.

EXAMPLE   [1] Did mr. Lebowski explain the process of Vulcanization?

　　　　　　1. *Did Mr. Lebowski explain the process of vulcanization?*

[1] Among the many unusual scenes that captain Christopher Columbus witnessed in the Americas was that of the Tainos playing games with balls made of latex, a white liquid produced by plants like the rubber tree, guayule, milkweed, and dandelion. [2] Latex balls were also used by the maya, but unlike the ball games that you may have played with your Brother or Sister, many Mayan games were sacred rituals. [3] According to the *Book Of counsel,* an ancient Mayan document, some games reenacted the story of twins who became immortal. [4] Ball games were so important to the Mayan culture that, along with stately masks of their gods, Mayan artists rendered statues of ball players, and builders erected large stone stadiums for the games. [5] Besides columbus, other European explorers observed how the maya used latex; in fact, one explorer reported what is shown in the scene here—the Mayan practice of coating their feet with a protective layer of Latex.

[6] Latex does not hold up well in extreme temperatures, and it was used in europe only for erasing pencil marks until Charles Goodyear became fascinated with the substance and declared that "elastic gum" glorified god. [7] Goodyear's invention of vulcanization enabled the successful commercial production of rubber and earned him the public admiration of emperor Napoleon III. [8] In the next

decades, Brazil increased its rubber production thousands of times over, as Eric R. Wolf points out in *Europe And The People Without History.* [9] Indeed, rubber became such an essential part of our lives that the U.S. army once asked a young Major named Eisenhower to study the matter. [10] Wisely, the Future President Eisenhower advised the military to maintain its own source of this valuable commodity.

Abbreviations

25g. Generally, abbreviations are capitalized if the words that they stand for are capitalized.

An ***abbreviation*** is a shortened form of a word or phrase. Notice how capital letters are used in abbreviations in the following examples.

Personal Names

Abbreviate given names only if the person is most commonly known by the abbreviated form of the name. Capitalize initials.

EXAMPLES   Ida **B.** Wells   **T. H.** White

NOTE Leave a space between two initials, but not between three or more.

EXAMPLES **J.R.R.** Tolkien   **W.E.B.** DuBois

Titles

(1) Abbreviate and capitalize most titles whether used before the full name or before the last name alone.

EXAMPLES   **Mr.** Chris Evans   **Ms.** Sue Aiello   **Mrs.** Dupont

                Sr. (Señor) Cadenas   **Sra.** (Señora) Garza   **Dr.** O'Nolan

(2) You may abbreviate civil and military titles used before full names or before initials and last names. Spell them out before last names alone. Capitalize the title whether or not is it abbreviated.

EXAMPLES   **Sen.** Kay Bailey Hutchison   **Senator** Hutchison

                Prof. E. M. Makowski   **Professor** Makowski

                Brig. Gen. Norman Schwarzkopf   **Brigadier General** Schwarzkopf

MECHANICS

Reference Note

For information on **forming the plurals of abbreviations,** see page 833.

(3) Abbreviate and capitalize titles and academic degrees that follow proper names.

EXAMPLES   Hank Williams, **Jr.**   Peter Garcia, **M.D.**

> NOTE Do not include the titles, *Mr., Mrs., Ms.,* or *Dr.* when you use an abbreviation for a degree after a name.
>
> EXAMPLE   **Dr.** Joan West *or* Joan West, **M.D.** [not *Dr. Joan West, M.D.*]

Agencies, Organizations, and Acronyms

In formal writing, the names of agencies, organizations, and other things commonly known by their initials should be spelled out the first time the name is mentioned but may be abbreviated in later references.

EXAMPLE   My older sister encouraged me to sign up for the **Preliminary Scholastic Aptitude Test (PSAT).** She said that taking the **PSAT** is good practice for the standardized tests I will face in the next few years.

An **acronym** is a word formed from the first (or first few) letters of a series of words. Acronyms are written without periods. The abbreviations for many agencies and organizations are acronyms.

Abbreviations	Names
AMA	American Medical Association
IRS	Internal Revenue Service
NASA	National Aeronautics and Space Administration
UN	United Nations
USAF	United States Air Force

Geographical Terms

In regular text, spell out names of states and other political units whether they stand alone or follow other geographical terms.

EXAMPLES   Willa Cather spent her early years in **Winchester, Virginia,** and **Red Cloud, Nebraska.**

On our vacation in **Canada,** we visited **Edmonton,** the capital of **Alberta.**

HELP

Many common abbreviations are capitalized even though the spelled-out words are not. If you are not sure whether to capitalize an abbreviation, check a dictionary.

HELP

A few acronyms, such as *radar, laser,* and *scuba,* are now considered common nouns. They do not need to be spelled out on first use and are no longer capitalized. When you're not sure whether an acronym should be capitalized, check a recent dictionary.

MECHANICS

Reference Note

For more information on **geographical terms,** see page 780.

Abbreviate the terms in tables, notes, and bibliographies. Generally, you should use the same capitalization rules for the abbreviations as you use for the full words.

TABLE

| London, **U.K.** | Tucson, **Ariz.** |
| Victoria, **B.C.** | Fresno, **Calif.** |

FOOTNOTE   ³The Public Library in Annaville, **Mich.,** has an entire collection of Smyth's folios.

BIBLIOGRAPHY   "The Last Hurrah." Editorial. *Star-Ledger*
ENTRY   [Newark, **NJ**] 29 Aug. 1991:30.

In regular text, spell out every word in an address.

EXAMPLE   We live at 413 **West** Maple **Street.**

Send the package to Holmstead **Drive,** Santa Fe, **New Mexico.**

Such words should be abbreviated in letter and envelope addresses and may be abbreviated in tables and notes.

ENVELOPE   413 **W.** Maple **St.**

TABLE

Holmstead **Dr.**
Santa Fe, New **Mex.**

NOTE   Two-letter state abbreviations without periods are used only when the ZIP Code is included.

EXAMPLE   Cincinnati, **OH 45233-4234**

MECHANICS

COMPUTER TIP

Publishers usually set time abbreviations as small capital letters—uppercase letters of a smaller font size. If you use a computer, your word-processing software may offer small capitals as a style option. If it does not, or if you are writing by hand, you may use either uppercase or lowercase letters for time abbreviations as long as you are consistent within each piece of writing.

Time

Abbreviate the two most frequently used era designations, A.D. and B.C. The abbreviation A.D. stands for the Latin phrase *anno Domini,* meaning "in the year of the Lord." It is used with dates in the Christian era. When used with a specific year, A.D. precedes the number. When used with the name of a century, it follows the name.

EXAMPLES   In **A.D.** 476, the last Western Roman emperor, Romulus Augustulus, was overthrown.

The legends of King Arthur may be based on the life of a real British leader of the sixth century **A.D.**

The abbreviation B.C., which stands for "before Christ," is used for dates before the Christian era. It follows either a specific year number or the name of a century.

EXAMPLES   Homer's epic poem the *Iliad* was probably composed between 800 and 700 **B.C.**

The poem describes battles that occurred around the twelfth century **B.C.**

In regular text, spell out the names of months and days whether they appear alone or in dates. Both types of names may be abbreviated in tables, notes, and bibliographies.

TEXT   Please join us on **Thursday, March 21,** to celebrate Grandma and Grandpa's anniversary.

FOOTNOTE   **Thurs. Mar.** 21

Abbreviate the designations for the two halves of the day measured by clock time. The abbreviation A.M. stands for the Latin phrase *ante meridiem*, meaning "before noon." The abbreviation P.M. stands for *post meridiem*, meaning "after noon." Both abbreviations follow the numerals designating the specific time.

EXAMPLE   My mom works four days a week, from 8:00 **A.M.** until 6:00 **P.M.**

Units of Measurement

In regular text, spell out the names of units of measurement whether they stand alone or follow a spelled-out number or a numeral. Such names may be abbreviated in tables and notes when they follow a numeral.

TEXT   Dad prefers to drive at a steady sixty-five **miles per hour** [not *mph*].

The cubicle measured ten **feet** [not *ft*] by twelve.

TABLE

1 **tsp** pepper, 2 **tbsp** olive oil	97°**F**
12 **ft** 6 **in.**	2 **oz** flour

Notice that the abbreviation for the word *inch* is followed by a period to avoid confusion with the preposition *in*.

HELP

In your reading, you may come across the abbreviations *C.E.* and *B.C.E.* These abbreviations stand for *Common Era* and *Before Common Era*. These abbreviations are used in place of *A.D.* and *B.C.*, respectively, and are always used after the date.

EXAMPLES
Constantinople fell to the Turks in 1453 **C.E.**

Pharaoh Ramses the Great died in 1213 **B.C.E.**

MECHANICS

Rewrite the following sentences, correcting errors in the use and capitalization of abbreviations.

EXAMPLE   1. Charles Demuth was born in Lancaster, PA.

1. *Pennsylvania*

1. Tomorrow, the flight for NY departs at 11:15 A.M.
2. Julius Caesar was assassinated in the Roman Forum in B.C. 44.
3. Harun ar-Rashid, whose reign is associated with the Arabian Nights, ruled as caliph of Baghdad from 786 to 809 A.D.
4. The Mississippi River flows from Lake Itasca, MN, all the way to the Gulf of Mexico at Port Eads, la.
5. The letter was addressed to Mr. Nugent on Elm st. in New London, WI.
6. G. Washington was our country's first president.
7. The keynote speaker was dr. Matthew Villareal, Ph.D.
8. Congress has designated holidays to honor the memory of such great Americans as Abraham Lincoln and Dr. Martin Luther King, jr.
9. Gen. de Gaulle became president of France in 1958.
10. I think sr. Martinez is waiting for you in the front lobby.

"After working all day on my MBA, I hop into my BMW and race home to watch PBS on my VCR—OK?"

© 1990; reprinted courtesy of Bunny Hoest and Parade magazine.

MECHANICS

Chapter Review

A. Capitalizing Words and Names Correctly

If a word group in the following items has an error in capitalization, write the entire word group correctly. If an item is already correct, write *C*.

1. *The Return Of The Native*
2. Yellowstone National park
3. the Federal bureau of investigation
4. temple Beth Israel
5. a bar of Ivory soap
6. a hindu temple
7. *A Day in the Life: the Music and the Artistry of the Beatles*
8. the constellation cassiopeia
9. on Fifty-first Avenue
10. the Rocky mountains

B. Revising Sentences to Correct Capitalization

Rewrite the following sentences, correcting errors in capitalization.

11. My Uncle Roger sailed on the *star of India* from London to Cyprus and Turkey.
12. the film was in spanish, and english subtitles were provided.
13. Was Artemis the Greek Goddess of the hunt?
14. Pablo's favorite movie is *2001: a Space Odyssey.*
15. Have you seen *A raisin in the sun* yet?
16. Leora went to the store during her lunch hour and chose just the right card for Valentine's day.
17. My cat bartinka often chases my dog piper through the yard and into the garden.
18. Lucinda's new brother was born at Sparrow hospital.
19. Come see our fantastic selection of top-quality stereo equipment at thompson electronics, at our new location just south of interstate 4 and River road!
20. Name the country located to the North of Zambia.

C. Correcting Errors in Capitalization

Identify and correct the capitalization errors in the following sentences. If a sentence is already correct, write *C*.

21. The committee included Mrs. Alaria, dean Roget, and Mr. Wilson.

22. Last Winter, she took a short course in Psychology at the University of southern California.

23. After Labor day I will return to the West and continue my work.

24. The delegates stayed at the Conrad Hilton Hotel on Forty-seventh Street during the Democratic National Convention last August.

25. My Sister Francesca enjoyed reading "A Rose For Emily."

D. Using Abbreviations and Correct Capitalization

Rewrite the following sentences, correcting errors in the use of abbreviations and capitalization.

26. The author of the play *Twelfth night* is Wm. Shakespeare.

27. The first structures at Stonehenge, the ancient monument near Salisbury, eng., were constructed about B.C. 3100.

28. I'm proud to be able to address my aunt as dr. Lauren Wigen, m.d.

29. My family comes from the little town of dime box, TX.

30. Sen. Baxter went to the hospital and visited her mother in the icu.

E. Proofreading a Paragraph for Correct Capitalization

Proofread the following paragraph for errors in capitalization. Identify each error, and then write the correct form.

[**31**] Last year, in a special Ecology course at Charlotte High School, I found out about some endangered North American animals. [**32**] I learned that conservationists here in the south are particularly concerned about the fate of the Florida panther. [**33**] All of that classroom discussion didn't have much impact on me, however, until early one Saturday morning last Spring, when I was lucky enough to sight one of these beautiful creatures. [**34**] My Uncle and I were driving to Big Bass Lake for some fishing when I saw what looked like a large dog crossing

the road some distance ahead of us. **[35]** Suddenly, Uncle Billy stopped his old ford truck and reached for the field glasses in the glove compartment. **[36]** As he handed them to me, he said, "look closely, Chris. You probably won't see a panther again any time soon." **[37]** Standing in the middle of Collingswood avenue, the cat turned and looked straight at us. **[38]** When those brown eyes met mine, I knew I had the title for my term paper—"Hello And Goodbye." **[39]** Then the big cat leisurely turned and crossed the road and loped off into the woods east of Sunshine mall. **[40]** As the panther disappeared back into the wilds of Charlotte county, Uncle Billy said, "Good luck to you, pal."

Writing Application
Using Capitalization in a Letter

Proper Nouns and Proper Adjectives   You have just started corresponding with a teenager in Japan. Write a letter to your pen pal describing some custom or practice that is unique to American culture or special to your family. In your letter, follow the rules of capitalization given in this chapter.

Prewriting   List some typically American holidays, customs, and practices. For each item on your list, brainstorm as many descriptive details as you can. Choose one item from your list to describe.

Writing   As you write your draft, organize your information clearly. Add facts, examples, and details as you think of them. Use clear, straightforward language, and try to avoid colloquialisms and idioms that your friend may not recognize. Make sure you include at least three proper nouns and three proper adjectives, all correctly capitalized.

Revising   Be sure that you have followed the guidelines for writing personal letters. Also, make sure your description paints a vivid picture of American customs.

Publishing   Proofread your letter for errors in grammar, usage, and mechanics. Take special care with capitalization of proper nouns. You and your classmates may want to display your letters on a bulletin board or collect them in a binder.

Reference Note

For information about **writing personal letters,** see "Writing" in the Quick Reference Handbook.

Punctuation
End Marks and Commas

Diagnostic Preview

A. Using End Marks and Commas

Rewrite the following sentences, adding, deleting, or reordering end marks and commas as necessary. If a sentence is already correct, write *C*.

EXAMPLE   1. Sally asked, "Where do you want to go after the recital"?

           1. Sally asked, "Where do you want to go after the recital?"

1. Who said, "I only regret that I have but one life to give for my country?"
2. Startled, we heard a high-pitched, whining, noise just outside the living room window.
3. Any student, who has not signed up for the contest by three o'clock, will not be eligible to participate.
4. My friend Esteban, running up the stairs two at a time, yelled out the good news.
5. "Why does the telephone always ring just as soon as I sit down to work," she asked?
6. My parents are trading in their car a two-door model with a sunroof four-wheel drive and air conditioning.
7. I have drilled practiced trained and exercised for weeks.
8. "Well Coach I can promise you that I'll be ready for the game next week," Kit said.

9. James King an Iroquois guide used to conduct tours of the Somers Mountain Indian Museum in Somers Connecticut.

10. He answered, "The abbreviation for *California* is *Cal.*".

B. Proofreading a Letter for the Correct Use of End Marks and Commas

Add, delete, or replace end marks or commas to correct each numbered word group in the following letter.

EXAMPLE   **[1]** Dear Toni

          1. Dear Toni,

Dear Toni,

    [11] As she promised our friend Takara, and her family were waiting for us at the Osaka airport on Monday June 16. **[12]** I am very glad that you introduced us and that I could come to visit such a kind generous, and friendly family

    [13] Wow I love their house; it's quite different from any home that I've ever seen before and my favorite part of it is the garden **[14]** In the middle of the house and down one step a large rectangular courtyard lies open to the sun and air. **[15]** Rocks not plants and trees fill the space, and clean white sand not grass covers the ground **[16]** I wonder who carefully rakes the sand every day leaving small rows of lines covering the ground? **[17]** Takara told me that the sand represents the ocean the lines are like waves, and the rocks stand for islands. **[18]** I believe she is right for the garden is as peaceful as any deserted beach.

    [19] My flight by the way will be arriving in Portland in ten short days; if you're free would you please meet me at the airport.

    [20] Sincerely yours.

        Ramona

STYLE TIP

In speaking, the tone and pitch of your voice, the pauses in your speech, and the gestures and expressions you use all help to make your meaning clear. In writing, marks of punctuation such as end marks and commas tell readers where these verbal and nonverbal cues occur.

However, if the meaning of a sentence is unclear in the first place, punctuation usually will not clarify it. Whenever you find yourself struggling to punctuate a sentence correctly, take a closer look at your arrangement of phrases or your choice of words. Often you can eliminate the punctuation problem by revising the sentence.

MECHANICS

End Marks

Reference Note

For information on how **sentences** are **classified according to structure,** see page 569.

End marks—periods, question marks, and exclamation points—are used to indicate the purpose of a sentence.

26a. A statement (or *declarative sentence*) is followed by a period.

EXAMPLES The blue whale is the largest animal that has ever lived.

September 15 to October 15 is Hispanic Heritage Month in the United States.

The keyboardist showed us how she uses the synthesizer to create a wide range of sounds.

NOTE In a sentence ending with a direct quotation, the period at the end of a sentence should be placed inside the closing quotation marks.

EXAMPLE The teacher explained, "Hoping to learn the secret of everlasting life, Gilgamesh, the epic's hero, searches for Utnapishtim."

STYLE TIP

Some requests and commands are put in question form even though they are not actually questions. In informal writing, such requests and commands may be followed by either a question mark or a period.

EXAMPLES
Will you please complete this brief questionnaire?
or
Will you please complete this brief questionnaire.

26b. A question (or *interrogative sentence*) is followed by a question mark.

EXAMPLES Did you get the leading role?

When is your first performance?

Can you name the Seven Wonders of the Ancient World?

NOTE In a sentence ending with a direct quotation, a question mark should be placed inside the closing quotation marks when the quotation itself is a question. Otherwise, it should be placed outside the quotation marks.

EXAMPLES To avoid answering a personal question, simply reply, "Why do you ask?" [The quotation is a question.]

Did Mr. Shields actually say, "Your reports are due in three days"? [The quotation is not a question, but the sentence as a whole is.]

Do not use a question mark after a declarative sentence containing an indirect question.

EXAMPLE Katie wondered who would win the award.

26c. An exclamation (or *exclamatory sentence*) is followed by an exclamation point.

EXAMPLES   I can't believe that!

What an exciting race that was!

We're so happy for you!

NOTE In a sentence ending with a direct quotation, an exclamation point should be placed inside the closing quotation marks when the quotation itself is an exclamation. Otherwise, it should be placed outside the quotation marks.

EXAMPLES   "Down in front!" yelled the crowd.

Ms. Chen couldn't have said, "No homework"!

STYLE TIP

Do not overuse exclamation points. Use an exclamation point only when a statement or an interjection is obviously emphatic.

At the beginning of a sentence, an interjection is generally followed by a comma or an exclamation point.

EXAMPLES   Hey, you're a great dancer! [mild exclamation]

Hey! Don't do that again! [strong exclamation]

Instead of a comma or an exclamation point, another mark of punctuation—period, question mark, dash, or ellipsis points—can be used after an interjection, depending on the meaning of the sentence.

EXAMPLES   "Oh. Are you sure that's what Carmen said?" inquired César.

"Well? What do you think of my painting?" Gillian asked.

"Hey—never mind," said Kevin.

"Wow . . . I don't know what to say," Myron stammered.

26d. A request or command (or *imperative sentence*) is generally followed by either a period or an exclamation point.

Generally, a request or mild command is followed by a period; a strong command is followed by an exclamation point.

EXAMPLES   Close the door, please. [request]

Close the door. [mild command]

Close the door! [strong command]

Reference Note

For more information about **interjections,** see page 507.

Reference Note

For more about **dashes** and **ellipsis points,** see pages 810 and 824.

MECHANICS

For more about the **placement of end marks and quotation marks,** see Chapters 26 and 27.

STYLE TIP

Sometimes (usually in dialogue) a writer will use more than one end mark to express intense emotion or a combination of emotions.

EXAMPLES
The panicked passenger kept shouting, "Help‼"
[intense emotion]

"You told them what⁈" Mary Ann exclaimed.
[combination of curiosity and surprise]

Using double end punctuation is acceptable in most informal writing. However, in formal writing, use only one end mark at a time.

MECHANICS

NOTE In a sentence ending with a direct quotation, a period at the end of an imperative sentence or interjection should be placed inside the closing quotation marks.

EXAMPLE   The announcer requested, "Please stand for the singing of the national anthem."

An exclamation point should be placed inside the quotation marks when the quotation is a strong command or interjection. Otherwise, it should be placed outside the quotation marks.

"Hey!" exclaimed Mark. "I just can't believe the referee said 'Foul'!"

Exercise 1 Correcting Sentences by Adding End Marks

Write each word that should be followed by an end mark in the following sentences; then, add an appropriate end mark. If quotation marks should precede or follow the end mark, write them in the proper place.

EXAMPLES 1. Mom asked, "When did you receive the letter
         1. *letter?"*

         2. Terrific What a throw you made
         2. *Terrific!; made!*

1. When do you want to take your vacation
2. Andrew didn't think he had enough money to go to the movies
3. Wow Did you see that liftoff
4. Willie, are you ready to give your report on Thurgood Marshall
5. Carefully set the Ming vase on the display stand

6. Mom wants to know why you did not buy a newspaper on your way home
7. What a downpour we had last night
8. Leave the theater immediately
9. He yelled across the field, "Hurry
10. Didn't you hear her say "I'm not ready yet

Abbreviations

26e. Use a period after certain abbreviations.

An *abbreviation* is a shortened form of a word or phrase. Notice how periods are used with abbreviations in the examples in this part of the chapter.

Personal Names

Abbreviate given names only if the person is most commonly known by the abbreviated form of the name.

EXAMPLES   Daniel **P.** Moynihan   **P. J.** O'Rourke   **J.R.R.** Tolkien

NOTE Leave a space between two such initials but not between three or more.

Titles

Abbreviate social titles whether used before the full name or before the last name alone.

EXAMPLES   **Mr.** Ted Evans   **Mrs.** Anne Frears   **Ms.** Agnello

Sr. (Señor) Cadenas   **Sra.** (Señora) Garza   **Dr.** Kostas

You may abbreviate civil and military titles used before full names or before initials and last names. Spell them out before last names used alone.

EXAMPLES   **Gen.** Douglas MacArthur   **General** MacArthur

Sen. Margaret Chase Smith   **Senator** Smith

Prof. E. M. Makowski   **Professor** Makowski

Abbreviate titles and academic degrees that follow proper names.

EXAMPLES   Ken Griffey, **Jr.**   Joe Sears, **M.D.**

─HELP─

If a statement ends with an abbreviation, do not use an additional period as an end mark. However, do use a question mark or an exclamation point if one is needed.

EXAMPLES
Mrs. Cuellar visited her relatives in Edison, N.J.

How long did she stay in Edison, N.J.?

MECHANICS

Agencies, Organizations, and Acronyms

An *acronym* is a word formed from the first (or first few) letters of a series of words. Acronyms are written without periods.

AMA, American Medical Association	**USAF,** United States Air Force
NASA, National Aeronautics and Space Administration	**UN,** United Nations
FSA, Farm Service Agency	**PBS,** Public Broadcasting Service
NFL, National Football League	**DOC,** Department of Commerce

After spelling out the first use of the names of agencies and organizations, abbreviate these names and other things commonly known by their acronyms.

EXAMPLE   Tamara is interested in working for the **United Nations Educational, Scientific, and Cultural Organization (UNESCO).** She says that **UNESCO** promotes international cooperation.

Geographical Terms

In regular text, spell out names of states and other political units whether they stand alone or follow other geographical terms. You may abbreviate them in tables, notes, and bibliographies.

TEXT   Karen Blixen spent her early years in Copenhagen, **Denmark,** and in East Africa.

On our vacation in Mexico, we visited Guadalajara, the capital of **Jalisco.**

TABLE

Copenhagen, **Den.**	Tucson, **Ariz.**
Vancouver, **B.C.**	Guadalajara, **Jal.**

FOOTNOTE   ³The Public Library in Setauket, **N.Y.,** has an entire collection of Smyth's folios.

BIBLIOGRAPHY ENTRY	Wilson, E.O. <u>The Diversity of Life</u>. Cambridge, **Mass.:** Harvard University Press, 1992.

In regular text, spell out every word in an address. Such words should be abbreviated in letter and envelope addresses and may be abbreviated in tables and notes.

TEXT	We live at 413 **West Maple Street.**
	Send the package to **Holmstead Avenue, Santa Fe, New Mexico.**
ENVELOPE	413 **W. Maple St.**
TABLE	Holmstead **Ave.,** Santa Fe, **New Mex.**

NOTE Two-letter state abbreviations without periods are used only when the ZIP Code is included.

EXAMPLE   Golden, **CO** 80401-0029

STYLE TIP

Only a few abbreviations are appropriate in the text of a formal paper written for a general audience. In tables, notes, and bibliographies, abbreviations are used more freely in order to save space.

Time

Abbreviate the frequently used era designations. The abbreviation *A.D.* stands for the Latin phrase *anno Domini,* meaning "in the year of the Lord." It is used with dates in the Christian era. When used with a specific year number, *A.D.* precedes the number. When used with the name of a century, it follows the name.

EXAMPLES   Between **A.D.** 61 and **A.D.** 63, Queen Boadicea led a war against the Roman invaders in Britain.

The Romans finally defeated her and controlled Britain until the sixth century **A.D.**

The abbreviation *B.C.,* which stands for *before Christ,* is used for dates before the Christian era. It follows either a specific year number or the name of a century.

EXAMPLES   In 343 **B.C.,** Aristotle tutored a thirteen-year-old boy who would later be known as Alexander the Great.

Aristotle, one of the great philosophers of ancient Greece, wrote over 400 literary works during the fourth century **B.C.**

In regular text, spell out the names of months and days whether they appear alone or in dates. Both types of names may be abbreviated in tables, notes, and bibliographies.

STYLE TIP

In your reading, you may see the abbreviations *B.C.E.* (Before the Common Era) and *C.E.* (Common Era). These abbreviations should be placed after the year.

EXAMPLES
The famous Roman orator Cicero died on December 7, 43 **B.C.E.**

The Ottoman Turks took Constantinople in 1453 **C.E.**

MECHANICS

TEXT	Please join us on **Thursday, March 21,** to celebrate Grandma and Grandpa's anniversary.
FOOTNOTE	**Thurs., Mar.** 21
BIBLIOGRAPHY ENTRY	Bower, B. "Domesticating an Ancient 'Temple Town.'" Science News 15 **Oct.** 1988: 246.

Abbreviate the designations for the two halves of the day measured by clock time. The abbreviation *A.M.* stands for the Latin phrase *ante meridiem,* meaning "before noon." The abbreviation *P.M.* stands for *post meridiem,* meaning "after noon." Both abbreviations follow the numerals designating the specific time.

EXAMPLE	The dentist's office is open five days a week, from 7:00 **A.M.** until 4:30 **P.M.**

Units of Measurement

In regular text, spell out the names of units of measurement whether they stand alone or follow a spelled-out number or a numeral. Such names may be abbreviated in tables and notes when they follow a numeral. Abbreviations for units of measurement are usually written without periods. However, do use a period with the abbreviation for inch (*in.*) to prevent confusing it with the word *in.*

TEXT	Dad prefers to drive at a steady sixty-five **miles per hour** [not *mph*].
	The sinkhole measured ten **feet** [not *ft*] by twelve.

TABLE	

1 **tsp** salt	2 **tbsp** vinegar	79° **F**
2 **ft** 6 **in.**	1 1/2 **c** water	2 **oz** dried beans

Exercise 2   Using Abbreviations

Rewrite the following sentences, correcting errors in the use of abbreviations.

EXAMPLE   1. Mom was born in Waukesha, WI.
                    1. *Mom was born in Waukesha, Wisconsin.*

1. Tomorrow, the flight for Cincinnati departs at 11:15 A.M. in the morning.
2. The Athenian statesman Alcibiades died in B.C. 404.
3. Charlemagne ruled the Holy Roman Empire from 800 to 814 A.D.

4. The Mississippi River flows from Lake Itasca, MN, all the way to the Gulf of Mexico at Port Eads, LA.

5. The letter was addressed to Mr. Schenk on Pine St. in Boise, ID.

6. Juan hopes to fly jets for the United States AF.

7. The keynote speaker was Dr. David Hoyt, Ph.D.

8. Congress has designated holidays to honor the memory of such great Americans as Abraham Lincoln, George Washington, and Martin Luther King, Junior.

9. R. Reagan was the fortieth president of the United States.

10. The table on page 13 gives the measurement as "6 ft, 3 in deep."

> **Review A** **Correcting Sentences by Adding Periods, Question Marks, and Exclamation Points**

Write the following sentences, adding periods, question marks, and exclamation points as needed.

EXAMPLE   1. Does Pete come from New York City

            1. *Does Pete come from New York City?*

1. What a car that is

2. Whose car is that

3. I went to Washington, DC., to visit Patrick.

4. We asked who owned that boat

5. By AD. 1100, Moscow was already an important city

6. George Washington Carver, Jr, received the Spingarn Medal in 1923

7. Why do so many dogs enjoy playing fetch

8. Please explain why so many dogs enjoy playing fetch

9. When did Bill Bradley run for president

10. Terrific Here's another coin for my collection

Commas

Items in a Series

26f. Use commas to separate items in a series.

EXAMPLES   The basketball coach recommended that Désirée practice dribbling, shooting, weaving, and passing. [words in a series]

               We can meet before English class, during lunch, or after school. [phrases in a series]

COMPUTER TIP

Publishers usually print time abbreviations as small capitals—uppercase letters that are slightly smaller than standard uppercase letters. Your word processor may offer small capitals as a style option. If it does not or if you are writing by hand, you may use either uppercase or lowercase letters for time abbreviations, as long as you are consistent within each piece of writing.

MECHANICS

After school I must make sure that my room is clean, that my little brother is home from his piano lesson, and that the garbage has been emptied. [clauses in a series]

When *and, or,* or *nor* joins the last two items in a series, the comma is sometimes omitted before the conjunction if a comma is not needed to make the meaning of the sentence clear.

UNCLEAR Phyllis, Ken and Matt formed a rock band. [It looks as though Phyllis is being addressed.]

CLEAR Phyllis, Ken, and Matt formed a rock band. [Phyllis is clearly a member of the band.]

NOTE Some words—such as *bread and butter* and *law and order*—are paired so often that they may be considered a single item.

EXAMPLE For lunch we had soup, salad, **bread and butter,** and milk.

(1) If all the items in a series are joined by *and, or,* or *nor,* do not use commas to separate them.

EXAMPLES Tyrone **and** Earlene **and** Lily won awards for their sculptures.

Should we walk **or** ride our bikes **or** take the bus?

(2) Generally, a comma should not be placed before or after a series.

INCORRECT I enjoy, gymnastics, basketball, and wrestling.
CORRECT I enjoy gymnastics, basketball, and wrestling.

INCORRECT I'll meet Mr. Catalano, Mr. Lawson, and Mr. Liu, tomorrow afternoon.
CORRECT I'll meet Mr. Catalano, Mr. Lawson, and Mr. Liu tomorrow afternoon.

(3) Short independent clauses in a series may be separated by commas.

EXAMPLE I came, I saw, I conquered.

Julius Caesar

26g. Use commas to separate two or more adjectives preceding a noun.

EXAMPLE Lucia is an intelligent, thoughtful, responsible student.

STYLE | TIP

For clarity, some writers prefer always to use the comma before the conjunction in a series. Follow your teacher's instructions on this point.

STYLE | TIP

The abbreviation *etc.* (meaning "and so forth") at the end of a series should be followed by a comma unless it falls at the end of a sentence.

EXAMPLES
Al bought hamburger, buns, onions, etc., for the French Club's cookout.

For the French Club's cookout, Al bought hamburger, buns, onions, etc.

Reference Note

Independent clauses in a series can be separated by semicolons. For more about this use of the **semicolon,** see page 804.

MECHANICS

Do not use a comma before the final adjective preceding a noun if that adjective is thought of as part of the noun.

EXAMPLES   Let's play this new video game. [not *new, video game*]

I've finally found a decent, affordable used car. [not *affordable, used car*]

NOTE   An adverb may modify an adjective preceding a noun. Do not use a comma between the adverb and the adjective.

EXAMPLE   I think you should wear the **bright blue** shirt with that suit.

Independent Clauses

26h. Use a comma before a coordinating conjunction (*and, but, for, nor, or, so,* or *yet*) when it joins independent clauses.

EXAMPLES   I read a review of Charles Frazier's *Cold Mountain,* and now I want to read the book.

Amy followed the recipe carefully, for she had never made paella before.

NOTE   Always use a comma before *for, so,* or *yet* joining independent clauses. The comma may be omitted before *and, but, nor,* and *or* if the independent clauses are very short and if the sentence is not awkward or unclear without it.

CLEAR   The phone rang and I answered it.
             We can go in the morning or we can leave now.

AWKWARD   The teacher called on Maria and John began to answer.

CLEAR   The teacher called on Maria, and John began to answer.

Do not confuse a compound sentence with a simple sentence that has a compound verb.

SIMPLE SENTENCE   My stepsister had been accepted at Howard University but decided to attend Grambling State University instead. [one independent clause with a compound verb]

COMPOUND SENTENCE   My stepsister had been accepted at Howard University, but she decided to attend Grambling State University instead. [two independent clauses]

TIPS & TRICKS

A compound noun such as *video game* or *used car* is considered a single noun. You can use two tests to determine whether an adjective and a noun form a unit.

TEST 1
Change the order of the adjectives. If the order of the adjectives can be reversed sensibly, use a comma. *Affordable, decent used car* makes sense, but *used decent car* and *video new game* do not.

TEST 2
Insert the word *and* between the adjectives. If *and* fits sensibly between the adjectives, use a comma. *And* cannot be logically inserted between *new* and *video game. And* sounds sensible between *decent* and *affordable* but not between *affordable* and *used.*

MECHANICS

Also, keep in mind that compound subjects and compound objects are generally not separated by commas.

EXAMPLES   What he is saying today and what he said yesterday are two different things. [two subordinate clauses serving as a compound subject]

Television crews covered the women's triathlon and the awards ceremony. [compound object]

Reference Note

For more about **compound subjects** and **compound verbs,** see page 517. For more about **compound sentences,** see page 570.

Exercise 3   Using Commas Correctly

Write each of the following sentences, inserting or deleting commas wherever necessary. If a sentence is already correct, write *C.*

EXAMPLE   1. Salvatore is an eager, willing, and able, young man.

1. *Salvatore is an eager, willing, and able young man.*

1. Soon both coasts would be connected by huge coal-black "iron horses" traveling along the rails.
2. I'll draw the plans Clay will get the supplies and Kerry will build the fountain.
3. I can't decide what to order but I'm sure that I'll have something spicy, mild or sweet-and-sour.
4. I enjoy, guitar music, *Zarzuelas,* and light opera.
5. Dad had sent away for the new coat but then changed his mind and canceled the order.
6. The tenor sang his solo and the soprano sang hers.
7. The watch has been ordered from Europe, but will not be delivered until next month.
8. They will visit museums, shops, and art galleries, this week.
9. You'll be writing many addresses in your life so learn to use commas now and you won't have many problems later.
10. Blanche Kelso Bruce took a seat in the U.S. Senate in 1875 served six years, and so became the first African American to serve a full term as senator.

Exercise 4   Correcting Sentences by Adding Commas

For the following sentences, write each word that should be followed by a comma, and add the comma. If a sentence is already correct, write *C.*

EXAMPLE   1. Taylor Greer is the strong-minded unpredictable heroine of Barbara Kingsolver's novel *The Bean Trees.*

1. *strong-minded,*

1. The photograph showed a happy mischievous good-natured boy.
2. Barbara will bring potato salad to the picnic and Marc will bring the cold cuts and the volleyball net.
3. Alain Locke taught philosophy created one of the foremost collections of African art and mentored many black writers.
4. We studied the following authors in English class this semester: F. Scott Fitzgerald Lorraine Hansberry and Rudolfo Anaya.
5. The introduction of the hardy sweet potato helped the Chinese to alleviate the famines that plagued them.
6. The committee has suggested that the cafeteria serve a different selection daily that classes not be interrupted by announcements and that pep rallies always be held during sixth period.
7. Students will receive paper pencils rulers etc. at the beginning of the test.
8. April looked on the desk, under the chair, and in her purse.
9. Last winter was abnormally cold icy and snowy.
10. The concert consisted of African American music and featured jazz rhythm and blues spirituals and several gospel songs.

Review B **Proofreading for the Correct Use of End Marks and Commas**

Rewrite the sentences in the following paragraph, adding, deleting, or reordering end marks and commas as necessary.

EXAMPLE   [1] Do you know the name of the famous structure shown in the photograph on the next page

1. *Do you know the name of the famous structure shown in the photograph on the next page?*

[1] Known as Stonehenge, this great circle of stones is located in England, and remains one of the most mysterious structures of the ancient world. [2] Much of the riddle of Stonehenge concerns the transport of the awesome massive stones that stand in the monument's inner circle. [3] These rocks are indigenous to Wales and many people have asked, "How did these huge stones travel two hundred miles to England" [4] Do you remember Merlin from the stories of King Arthur's legendary court [5] This wily, and powerful sorcerer is said to have moved the stones by magic. [6] The story of Merlin may be fascinating but modern astronomers anthropologists, and other scientists are searching for a more rational explanation. [7] Some theorists believe that many of the incredibly heavy gigantic monoliths were shipped by raft through dangerous tidal waters, but other scientists

scoff and exclaim, "That's impossible"! [8] Still other theorists wonder whether glaciers may have lifted moved, and deposited the stones so far from their home? [9] Visitors to Stonehenge are no longer allowed within the monument and venturing inside the protected area will draw a polite but authoritative, "Will you please step back" [10] So far, Stonehenge has not yielded a solution to the mystery of the stones yet a section of the site remains unexplored and may contain clues as to how they got there.

Nonessential Clauses and Phrases

26i. Use commas to set off nonessential subordinate clauses and nonessential participial phrases.

Reference Note

For more about **subordinate clauses,** see page 559. For more about **participial phrases,** see page 541.

A *nonessential* (or *nonrestrictive*) subordinate clause or participial phrase adds information that is unnecessary to the basic meaning of the sentence.

NONESSENTIAL CLAUSES	Marie Curie, **who studied radioactivity,** won the Nobel Prize for chemistry in 1911.
	Did the 1998 Senate hearings, **which were televised,** attract a large audience?

NONESSENTIAL PHRASES	Monique, **carrying the heaviest load,** lagged far behind the others.
	Willie Herenton, **defeating the incumbent in 1991,** became the first African American mayor of Memphis.

Notice that the nonessential clause or phrase from each of the examples above can be left out without changing the basic meaning of the sentence.

EXAMPLES	Marie Curie won the Nobel Prize for chemistry in 1911.
	Did the 1998 Senate hearings attract a large audience?
	Monique lagged far behind the others.
	Willie Herenton became the first African American mayor of Memphis.

An *essential* (or *restrictive*) subordinate clause or participial phrase is not set off by commas because it contains information that cannot be left out without changing the basic meaning of the sentence.

ESSENTIAL CLAUSES	The juniors **who were selected for Boys State and Girls State** were named.
	Should material **that is quoted verbatim** be placed in quotation marks?
ESSENTIAL PHRASES	Those **participating in the food drive** should bring their donations by Friday at the latest.
	The election **won by Willie Herenton** was in October 1991.

Notice how leaving out the essential clause or phrase changes or restricts the basic meaning of each of the examples above.

EXAMPLES	The juniors were named. [Which juniors?]
	Should material be placed in quotation marks? [Which material?]
	Those should bring their donations by Friday at the latest. [Which those?]
	The election was in October 1991. [Which election?]

Some subordinate clauses and participial phrases may be either essential or nonessential. The presence or absence of commas tells the reader how the clause or phrase relates to the main idea of the sentence.

TIPS & TRICKS

A subordinate clause or a participial phrase that modifies a proper noun is generally nonessential.

EXAMPLES
The Eiffel Tower, **which Alexandre-Gustave Eiffel designed,** is in Paris.

Skipper, **barking at the mail carrier,** would not calm down.

TIPS & TRICKS

Adjective clauses beginning with *that* are nearly always essential.

EXAMPLE
The platypus and the spiny anteater are the only mammals **that** lay eggs.

MECHANICS

NONESSENTIAL CLAUSE	Una's cousin, **who wants to be an astronaut,** attended a space camp in Huntsville, Alabama, last summer. [Una has only one cousin, and that cousin attended the space camp.]
ESSENTIAL CLAUSE	Una's cousin **who wants to be an astronaut** attended a space camp in Huntsville, Alabama, last summer. [Una has more than one cousin. The one who wants to be an astronaut attended the space camp.]
NONESSENTIAL PHRASE	Your cat, **draped along the back of the couch,** seems contented. [You have only one cat, and it seems contented.]
ESSENTIAL PHRASE	Your cat **draped along the back of the couch** seems contented. [You have more than one cat. The one draped along the back of the couch seems contented.]

Exercise 5 Using Commas Correctly

Rewrite the following sentences, adding or deleting commas as necessary. If a sentence is already correct, write *C*.

EXAMPLE 1. The movie which is one of my favorites is about a friendly extraterrestrial.

1. *The movie, which is one of my favorites, is about a friendly extraterrestrial.*

1. Students, going on the trip tomorrow, will meet in the auditorium.
2. The White River Bridge which closed today for resurfacing will not be open for traffic until mid-October.
3. The symphony, that Beethoven called the *Eroica*, was composed to celebrate the memory of a great man.
4. From the composer's letters, we learn that the "great man" whom he had in mind was Napoleon Bonaparte.
5. Natalie Curtis Burlin always interested in the music of American Indians recorded their songs in the early 1900s.
6. The driver stopped on the side of the road had a flat tire.
7. The musician, who founded the annual music festival in Puerto Rico, was Pablo Casals.
8. Semantics which is concerned with the meanings of words is an interesting subject of study for high school students.
9. My parents' station wagon which is more than seven years old simply refuses to start on cold mornings.
10. All contestants, submitting photographs, must sign a release form.

Introductory Elements

26j. Use a comma after certain introductory elements.

(1) Use a comma to set off a mild exclamation such as *well, oh,* **or** *why.* **Other introductory words such as** *yes* **and** *no* **are also set off by commas.**

EXAMPLES   **Well,** I guess so.

              Yikes, are we late!

              Yes, I heard your question.

(2) Use a comma after an introductory participle or participial phrase.

EXAMPLES   **Exhausted,** the scouts took a break.

              Looking poised and calm, Jill walked to the podium.

NOTE Do not confuse a gerund phrase used as the subject of a sentence with an introductory participial phrase.

EXAMPLES   **Following directions** can sometimes be difficult.
[*Following directions* is a gerund phrase used as the subject of the sentence.]

              Following directions, I began to assemble the bike.
[*Following directions* is an introductory participial phrase modifying *I.*]

(3) Use a comma after two or more introductory prepositional phrases or after one long one.

EXAMPLES   **In the first round of the golf tournament,** I played against one of the best golfers in the state.

              In the secret chamber called "the crystal keep," the heroine found the missing map.

    A single short introductory prepositional phrase does not require a comma unless the sentence is awkward to read without one or unless the phrase is parenthetical.

EXAMPLES   **At the track,** meet me in front of the snack bar. [The comma is needed to avoid reading "track meet."]

              By the way, I need to borrow a quarter. [The comma is needed because *by the way* is parenthetical.]

STYLE TIP

Make sure that an introductory participial phrase modifies the subject of the sentence; otherwise, the phrase may be misplaced.

MISPLACED
Cracking and eating the seeds from the bird feeder, we enjoyed watching the playful cardinals.

REVISED
Cracking and eating the seeds from the bird feeder, the playful cardinals were a joy to watch.

Reference Note

For information on **participial phrases** and **gerund phrases,** see pages 541 and 544. For information on **prepositional phrases,** see page 536.

MECHANICS

(4) Use a comma after an introductory adverb clause.

An introductory adverb clause may appear at the beginning of a sentence or before any independent clause in the sentence.

EXAMPLES   **After I had locked the car door,** I remembered that the keys were still in the ignition.

I had a spare set of keys with me; **if I hadn't,** I would have had to walk home.

NOTE   An adverb clause that follows an independent clause is generally not set off by a comma.

EXAMPLE   Thousands of homes in the Philippines were destroyed **when Mount Pinatubo erupted in 1991.**

Review C   **Using Commas in a Paragraph**

For the sentences in the following paragraph, write each word that should be followed by a comma, and add the comma. If a sentence is already correct, write *C*.

EXAMPLE   **[1]** Well what do you think the clocks in the painting shown on the opposite page symbolize?

   1. *Well,*

[1] Have you ever had a dream that seemed absolutely real; then, as you awoke you realized how outlandish it was? [2] An artist painting a surrealistic picture can sometimes generate that same dreamlike feeling in an audience. [3] For example, this painting which is one of many surreal landscapes by Salvador Dali conveys the strange experience of a dream. [4] In a dream time has a different meaning, and the bizarre can seem ordinary. [5] While only five minutes may actually have passed events requiring hours or days may have taken place in a dream. [6] Dali's clocks drooping as limply as a sleeper show that the rigid march of time can relax in a dream. [7] In the liquid time and unearthly space of dreams not even solid reality can be certain.

[8] Objects far more fantastic and incredible than the creature who reclines on the sand can seem in dreams to be as familiar as your own face. [9] Sleeping peacefully Dali's strange creature does not seem to realize that it is saddled with the burden of time. [10] Well until the alarm clock wakes you from your own dreams you probably don't realize it either.

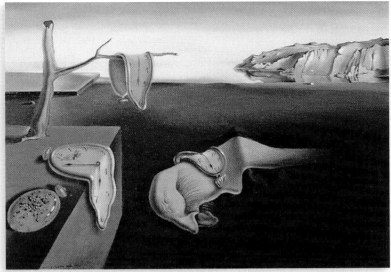

Interrupters

26k. Use commas to set off an expression that interrupts a sentence.

(1) Nonessential appositives and appositive phrases are set off by commas.

An *appositive* is a noun or pronoun placed beside another noun or pronoun to identify or describe it. An *appositive phrase* consists of an appositive and its modifiers.

A *nonessential* (or *nonrestrictive*) appositive or appositive phrase adds information that is unnecessary to the meaning of the sentence. In other words, the basic meaning of the sentence is clear and complete with or without the appositive or appositive phrase.

EXAMPLES   Ron Arias's first novel, **The Road to Tamazunchale,** was nominated for the National Book Award.

Tylan, **my oldest nephew,** plays the accordion.

Is that he, **the young man with the red hair**?

Notice that the basic meaning of each of the examples above remains clear and complete without the appositive or appositive phrase.

EXAMPLES   Ron Arias's first novel was nominated for the National Book Award.

Reference Note

For more about **appositives** and **appositive phrases,** see page 550.

MECHANICS

Tylan plays the accordion.

Is that he?

NOTE An **essential** (or **restrictive**) appositive or appositive phrase is not set off by commas because it adds information that is necessary to the meaning of the sentence. In other words, the basic meaning of the sentence is unclear or incomplete without the appositive or appositive phrase.

EXAMPLES   Does your friend **Joshua** have a part in the play, too?

The old saying **"Haste makes waste"** certainly applies to this situation.

Notice that without the appositive the meaning of the examples above is unclear or incomplete.

Reference Note
For information on **correcting misplaced modifiers,** see page 712.

(2) Words used in direct address are set off by commas.

EXAMPLES   **Mom,** have you called Mrs. Johnson yet?

Your painting, **Andy,** is very original.

Will you answer the question, **Monica**?

(3) Parenthetical expressions are set off by commas.

A *parenthetical expression* is a side remark that adds information or shows a relationship between ideas.

Reference Note
Some parenthetical expressions, such as *consequently, however, moreover,* and *therefore,* are **conjunctive adverbs.** See page 570.

Reference Note
Parentheses and **dashes** can also be used to set off parenthetical expressions. See page 809.

Commonly Used Parenthetical Expressions		
after all	I believe (hope, *etc.*)	naturally
at any rate	incidentally	nevertheless
by the way	in fact	of course
consequently	in general	on the contrary
for example	in the first place	on the other hand
for instance	meanwhile	that is
however	moreover	therefore

EXAMPLES   **Incidentally,** I won't be home for supper.

Exercise makes the heart and lungs more efficient, and, **moreover,** it contributes to an overall sense of well-being.

It's too late to call now, **I believe.**

MECHANICS

Sometimes the expressions in the preceding chart are not used parenthetically. When they are not, do not set them off with commas.

EXAMPLES **By the way,** she is in my vocal music class. [parenthetical, meaning "incidentally"]

You can tell **by the way** she sings that she enjoys the class. [not parenthetical, meaning "by the manner in which"]

NOTE A contrasting expression introduced by *not* is parenthetical and is set off by commas.

EXAMPLES Margaret Walker, **not Alice Walker,** wrote the novel *Jubilee.*

Exercise 6 Correcting Sentences by Adding Commas

For each of the following sentences, write each word that should be followed by a comma, and add the comma. If a sentence is already correct, write *C*.

EXAMPLE 1. Hania one of my cousins from Poland sent me a copy of our family tree.

1. *Hania, Poland,*

1. As a matter of fact your lateness is your own fault since you knew what time the bus would be leaving.
2. Have you seen Mr. Welch our new accounting teacher?
3. Zimbabwe's stone ruins once a stronghold for an ancient empire attest to the skill of those early stonemasons.
4. Please listen class while Jim makes an announcement.
5. Our friend Mrs. Kirby gets our mail when we are away.
6. Texans have a right to be proud of Sergeants José Mendoza López and Macario García Texan citizens who earned the Congressional Medal of Honor.
7. Daniel my twin brother just got a new job.
8. It is the pressure of getting work in on time not the work itself that gets on my nerves.
9. Mr. Beck the yearbook photographer always tries I think to place each person in the most flattering pose.
10. It's the phone that's ringing Suzanne not the doorbell.
11. Incidentally the green revolution a few decades ago was the direct result of improved technology and better seed.
12. Doesn't the word *aerobic* after all simply refer to an increase in the body's oxygen intake?

If you use a computer to write, you may want to create a file of the parenthetical expressions listed on page 794. Refer to this file as you proofread your writing, and be sure that you have punctuated these expressions correctly. Use the word-processing software's search function to speed up your proofreading. The computer will search for and highlight each occurrence of whatever expression you select.

MECHANICS

13. The Van Allen belt is to the best of my knowledge a layer of electrically charged particles over the earth's atmosphere.
14. My friend your accounting figures are on the contrary an oasis of certainty in a desert of unreliability.
15. This unproved theory moreover has formed the basis of much of modern thought.
16. We may have a vacancy late tomorrow evening however.
17. Tyler had been in first place not second for most of the race.
18. What are the employment possibilities in alternative energy industries for example geothermal energy?
19. In general mosquitoes seem to thrive in warm climates wherever there is standing water.
20. Actually, Stan, I'm not planning to enter the race; I'd be happy if this old jalopy ran at any rate at all.

Conventional Uses

26l. Use commas in certain conventional situations.

(1) Use a comma to separate items in dates and addresses.

EXAMPLES   On Monday, December 1, 1999, I bought my pet parakeet.

Contact the postmaster at 108 Griffith Lane, Bethesda, MD 20814-9997, if you need more information.

Notice in each example above that a comma separates the last item in a date or an address from the words that follow it.

    Do not use commas to set off

- the month from the day

    EXAMPLE   My grandparents celebrated their fiftieth wedding anniversary on **January 17,** 2000.

- the day from the month when the day is given before the month

    EXAMPLE   On **15 June** 1924, Congress granted U.S. citizenship to all American Indians.

- the month from the year when no day is given

    EXAMPLE   Will the new high school be open by **August 2004?**

- a house number from a street name

    EXAMPLE   The Espinozas' address is **236 Meadowlark Lane,** Omaha, NE 68108-0335.

- a state abbreviation from a ZIP Code

  EXAMPLE   Is 1410 Azalea Drive, Alpharetta, **GA 30005-9725,** the correct address?

- items joined by prepositions

  EXAMPLE   The play is at the Majestic Theater **on** Broad Avenue **in** Midland Heights.

(2) Use a comma after the salutation of a personal letter and after the closing of any letter.

EXAMPLES   Dear Dale and Amy,   Sincerely yours,

> NOTE   Use a colon after the salutation of a business letter.
>
> EXAMPLE   Dear Dr. Wong:

(3) Use commas to set off a title, such as *Jr.*, *Sr.*, or *M.D.*, that follows a person's name.

EXAMPLES   Coretta Jones, M.D.

Isaiah Walker, Sr., makes animated films.

Unnecessary Commas

26m. Do not use unnecessary commas.

Use a comma only if a rule requires one or if the meaning is unclear without one.

INCORRECT   The teacher in the room across the hall, is Cameron's aunt.
[There is no rule requiring a comma to separate the subject, *teacher*, from the verb, *is*.]

CORRECT   The teacher in the room across the hall is Cameron's aunt.

Review D   **Correcting Sentences by Adding Periods, Question Marks, Exclamation Points, and Commas**

Rewrite each of the following sentences, adding periods, question marks, exclamation points, and commas where they are needed.

EXAMPLE   **1.** Gina can you tell us how many American astronauts have walked on the moon

1. *Gina, can you tell us how many American astronauts have walked on the moon?*

Reference Note

For information on **writing business letters,** see "Writing" in the Quick Reference Handbook.

MECHANICS

1. Wow Rob who taught you to draw a bow like that
2. First performed on March 11 1959 on Broadway in New York City Lorraine Hansberry's most famous play *A Raisin in the Sun* was awarded the New York Drama Critics Circle Award
3. Grinning Dad said that if we all helped put away toys and books picked up all the clothes lying around dusted the furniture and vacuumed the rug the house might very well look presentable by the time Grandma arrived
4. After all you could look at the map to see whether there is an exit from Interstate 70 to a state road that will take us south to Greenville Illinois instead of just complaining because I don't know the way
5. On her way to work each morning she saw young people on their paper routes children waiting for school buses mail carriers beginning their deliveries and the inevitable joggers puffing along on their morning workouts
6. Why do buses run so infrequently and when they do arrive why are they in bunches of three or four or more
7. Gen Benjamin O Davis Jr the first African American who was promoted to the rank of lieutenant general in the U.S. Air Force was the grandson of a slave
8. If you are going to paint window frames cover the panes of glass with masking tape which will protect the glass from being spattered
9. On a beautiful fall day in New England it is wise to go for a walk play a game outdoors or go for a drive; for it won't be long until everything is bleak cold and dreary
10. If I had my way I would live in a climate where it would be warm not hot in the daytime and cool in the evening all year round

Chapter Review

A. Using Periods, Question Marks, Exclamation Points, and Commas Correctly

For each of the following sentences, write each word, numeral, or letter that should be followed by a punctuation mark. Then, add the correct punctuation. If a sentence is already correct, write *C*.

1. If you sign up as a volunteer for the Special Olympics you will find that you receive as much as you give

2. The task before us was challenging but we felt prepared to meet it

3. Because the dentist's office was decorated in subtle warm earth tones I felt very relaxed during my visit

4. Oh I didn't know we have the same birthday

5. Trailing in the fourth quarter, our school's football team won the game in the last ten seconds of play.

6. In fact on August 9 1974 Richard M Nixon made history by resigning from his position as president of the United States

7. Ms Rizzo wasn't W Averell Harriman one of the world's foremost experts on Russian society

8. Read *The Hobbit* one of my favorite books

9. When I began this science project I knew that I would have to spend hours researching the subject

10. Joe Croce Gina Jackson and Sonya Shavatski are all candidates in the primary so expect the vote to be very close

11. Everyone wanted to know who he was what he wanted and how long he intended to stay

12. Maria who is a lively enthusiastic worker began her job as an electrician yesterday

13. By running all the way to school Suke arrived at basketball practice on time

14. We need more volunteers I believe if we are going to finish on time

15. Kareem did you enjoy your sightseeing trip through Maine Vermont and New Hampshire

16. Wait until Saturday before you write the letter for the package will surely have arrived by then

MECHANICS

17. The student who maintains the highest average in school will receive the scholarship.

18. Watch out Lana

19. Having completed the painting I asked Dad whether I could go to the movie

20. According to the records Joseph Hardwicke Barrymore Jr. is the baby's full name

B. Using Periods, Question Marks, Exclamation Points, and Commas Correctly

Write the following sentences, adding, deleting, replacing, or reordering periods, question marks, exclamation points, and commas as necessary. If a sentence is already correct, write *C*.

21. Do you think that it will rain today Brian.

22. Before the start of the concert the musicians tuned their instruments.

23. When I joined the staff of the newspaper I was taught to write short powerful headlines

24. The essay, that Ms Hughes assigned yesterday, is due next Monday.

25. Lisette would you send me a postcard from Hawaii while you're there on vacation

26. Bravo What a great performance

27. Geometry which I took last year was not an easy subject for me.

28. Peg asked, "For example have you read *Animal Farm*"?

29. Please send this package to 116 East Elm Street, Allentown, PA 18001.

30. The letter was dated June 16 2000 and was mailed from Washington D.C..

31. Governor Jameston a Democrat does not plan to run.

32. Dear Rosaline

How are you. Drop me a line.

Yours

Viola

33. In 1998 NASA. sent Sen. John Glenn back into space on the shuttle *Discovery.*

34. Preston asked Callie if she had seen the play yet.

35. My father enjoyed a visit with Uncle John, Aunt Dee, and my cousin Nora, yesterday afternoon.

36. Will you be asking Dean to come to the movies with us.

37. The meadow was covered with tiny delicate flowers.

38. We told the man who brought us the menus that we wanted a pitcher of lemonade.

39. Vincente said, "Wait would you like to come with us."

40. The play by Oscar Wilde was witty, and also serious.

Writing Application

Using Commas in an Essay

Punctuating Interrupters   Next Friday, your English class will celebrate Literary Heroes Day. Your teacher has asked you to write a brief essay (two or three paragraphs long) about your favorite fictional character. Describe the character, and explain why the character is your hero. In your essay, use at least two appositives and three parenthetical expressions. Be sure to use commas correctly with each interrupter.

Prewriting   First, you will need to decide on a character. Choose the one that impressed or entertained you the most. In your notes, be sure to include the character's strongest and most interesting traits.

Writing   Use your notes to help you write your first draft. Begin by describing the character and noting some of the most important traits that make this person your hero. Illustrate these traits by giving at least two examples of things the character does or says.

Revising   Ask a friend or relative to read your essay. Does your description give a vivid picture of the character? Is it clear why this character is your hero? If not, add or revise details to make your point more clearly. Be sure that you have used at least two appositives and three parenthetical expressions.

Publishing   Proofread your essay for any errors in grammar, usage, and mechanics. Pay special attention to commas before and after parenthetical expressions. You and your classmates may want to celebrate Literary Heroes Day by creating a bulletin board display. Place a typed or neatly written copy of each essay on the bulletin board along with illustrations of the different characters.

CHAPTER

Punctuation
Other Marks of Punctuation

Diagnostic Preview

A. Proofreading Sentences for Correct Punctuation

The following sentences contain errors in the uses of semicolons, colons, dashes, parentheses, brackets, italics (underlining), quotation marks, ellipses, apostrophes, and hyphens. Rewrite the sentences, correcting the errors. If a sentence is already correct, write *C*.

EXAMPLE   1. Did you say "that you want to join us"?

             1. *Did you say that you want to join us?*

┌─HELP─┐

There may be more than one error per sentence in the Diagnostic Preview. You may have to add punctuation where it is needed, and you may have to delete punctuation that is used incorrectly. Some sentences have commas where other punctuation marks should be.

1. Ed's and Jim's essays were both titled Kwanzaa A Special Time for African Americans.
2. Heres my phone number, call me if you decide to see the movie.
3. The circus audience loudly applauded and cheered as the acro bats performed the perfectly-timed stunt.
4. Paula said in a desperate tone, "I know Sue's directions stated, "Turn right when you get to the gas station; but, unfortunately, I'm not sure which gas station she meant.
5. William Butler Yeats 1865–1939, an Irish poet and playwright who won the Nobel Prize in literature, was once a member of the Irish parliament.
6. At the end of the play, Macbeth concludes that life is only "a tale . . . . . signifying nothing."
7. Oh no, I think my driver's license has no, it says here it wo'nt expire for another two weeks.

8. "Well, I dont know," Lauren said. "Where do you think all this soot comes from?"

9. Several people whom I respect think Raintree County by Ross Lockridge, Jr., is a fantastic novel, I plan to read it soon.

10. "Among the writers in America today, he Galway Kinnell has earned his reputation as an outstanding poet," noted the critic in Newsweek.

B. Proofreading a Dialogue for Correct Punctuation

The following dialogue contains errors in the uses of semicolons, colons, dashes, parentheses, italics (underlining), quotation marks, apostrophes, and hyphens. Rewrite the dialogue, correcting the errors.

EXAMPLE   **[1]**   "You may like mystery, comedy, and science fiction movies, but, you know, my favorite movies are those about real peoples lives, Ben said."

1.   *"You may like mystery, comedy, and science fiction movies; but, you know, my favorite movies are those about real people's lives," Ben said.*

[11] Tell me we've got time some of your all time favorites," Tani replied to Ben.

[12] "I recently saw Mountains of the Moon for the first time I learned about the life of Sir Richard Burton from it," Ben replied.

[13] Whats his claim to fame"? Tani asked.

[14] "Sir Richard Burton was a man of many talents he was an explorer, an author, a scholar, a linguist, and a diplomat."

[15] "Did the movie try to show all his talents?" Tani asked. Doing so would be difficult."

[16] "The movie is mostly an African adventure its about Burtons search for the source of the Nile," Ben said. [17] "Some of my other favorites include: Gandhi, about the Indian independence leader, Amadeus, about Mozart's life, and The Spirit of St. Louis, a really old film about Charles Lindbergh."

[18] "I'll bet three-fourths of our friends have never heard of most of the movies youve seen," Tani said.

[19] "The downtown video store the one owned by Ross's brother has them all," Ben said.

[20] "Biographical movies well researched ones, anyway are a good way to learn about famous people," Tani said.

Semicolons

27a. Use a semicolon between independent clauses that are closely related in thought and that are not joined by a coordinating conjunction (*and, but, for, nor, or, so,* or *yet.*)

Reference Note

For more information about **coordinating conjunctions,** see page 505.

EXAMPLES   The rain had finally stopped; a few rays of sunshine were pushing their way through breaks in the clouds.

              Owning a dog is a big responsibility; a dog requires training, grooming, and regular exercise.

Do not use a semicolon to join independent clauses unless there is a close relationship between the main ideas of the clauses.

INCORRECT   For Ramón, oil painting is a difficult medium to master; when he was younger, he had quite enjoyed taking photographs.

CORRECT   For Ramón, oil painting is a difficult medium to master. When he was younger, he had quite enjoyed taking photographs.

27b. Use a semicolon between independent clauses joined by a conjunctive adverb or a transitional expression.

Reference Note

For more information on **conjunctive adverbs** and **transitional expressions,** see page 570.

A *conjunctive adverb* or a *transitional expression* indicates the relationship of the independent clauses that it joins.

EXAMPLES   The snowfall made traveling difficult; **nevertheless,** we arrived home safely.

              Denisa plays baseball well; **in fact,** she would like to try out for a major-league team.

Commonly Used Conjunctive Adverbs		
accordingly	however	moreover
besides	indeed	nevertheless
consequently	instead	otherwise
furthermore	meanwhile	therefore

Commonly Used Transitional Expressions		
in other words	for instance	as a result
for example	in fact	that is

MECHANICS

NOTE Use a comma after a conjunctive adverb or a transitional expression that is used directly after a semicolon joining independent clauses. When used within a clause, a conjunctive adverb or a transitional expression is set off by commas.

EXAMPLES   Most members of Congress favor the new tax bill; **however,** the president does not support it.

Most members of Congress favor the new tax bill; the president, **however,** does not support it.

Most members of Congress favor the new tax bill; the president does not support it, **however.**

27c. A semicolon (rather than a comma) may be needed before a coordinating conjunction to join independent clauses that contain commas.

EXAMPLES   Some monarch butterflies migrate all the way from Canada to California, to Florida, or to Mexico; and then, come spring, they head north again.

I wanted to register for biology, volleyball, and conversational Spanish; but only calculus, golf, and intermediate German were available during late registration.

27d. Use a semicolon between items in a series if the items contain commas.

EXAMPLES   The club's president has appointed the following people to chair the standing committees: Richard Stokes, planning; Rebecca Hartley, membership; Salvador Berrios, financial; and Ann Jeng, legal.

The collection of short stories includes "The Circuit," by Francisco Jiménez; "The Iguana Killer," by Alberto Ríos; and "Everybody Knows Tobie," by Daniel Garza.

Exercise 1 Using Semicolons Correctly

For the following sentences, write each word or numeral that should be followed by a semicolon, and add the semicolon. If a sentence is already correct, write *C*.

EXAMPLE   **1.** The great American humorist Will Rogers was proud of his Cherokee heritage he often referred to it in his talks and writings.

    1. heritage;

STYLE   TIP

In cases covered by Rule 27c, use semicolons only to prevent misreading. If a sentence is clear without a semicolon, do not add one just because the clauses contain commas.

EXAMPLE
Lana, you are the best musician I know, and you're a great dancer, too. [clear without semicolon]

MECHANICS

HELP

Some of the sentences in Exercise 1 require more than one semicolon. Also, in some of the sentences, you will need to change another punctuation mark to a semicolon.

1. William Penn Adair Rogers was born in 1879 in Oologah, Indian Territory, which is now Oklahoma, and he spent his childhood on his father's ranch, a rather prosperous holding of about sixty thousand acres.

2. As a youth, Will Rogers liked to learn and practice rope tricks he often could be found roping instead of attending to his chores.

3. Rogers was captivated by professional roping performers at the Chicago World's Fair in 1893; in fact, that experience probably marked the start of his interest in show business.

4. He went on to do some roping and humorous speaking at fairs and other public gatherings however, his actual show business debut came in 1902.

5. That year, Rogers joined Texas Jack's Wild West Show as a lasso artist he also rode horses and performed in various Western skits in the show.

6. Notice how confident the young Rogers appears in this publicity photo his expression, stance, and costume suggest an accomplished performer.

7. Rogers greatly enjoyed earning his living by doing what he most loved—roping consequently, he decided to take his act to New York City's vaudeville theaters.

8. Rogers's stage shows, combining his roping with humorous comments, were popular they led to starring roles in musicals, in the legendary Ziegfeld Follies, and in movies.

9. In Hollywood, Rogers made such films as *The Ropin' Fool,* in which he performed fifty-three rope tricks, *Steamboat, 'Round the Bend,* directed by John Ford, and *A Connecticut Yankee in King Arthur's Court,* based on the Mark Twain novel.

10. From 1922 until his death in 1935, Rogers wrote a syndicated newspaper column that Sunday column featured his unique and humorous insights into national and international news.

Colons

27e. Use a colon to mean "note what follows."

(1) Use a colon before a list of items, especially after expressions such as *as follows* and *the following.*

EXAMPLES	Prior to 1722, the Iroquois Confederation consisted of five American Indian nations: Mohawk, Oneida, Onondaga, Cayuga, and Seneca.
	My brother is working on a multimedia presentation featuring the following women: Mary Baker Eddy, Clara Barton, Maria Mitchell, Mary Church Terrell, Susan B. Anthony, and Sarah Winnemucca.

NOTE Do not use a colon between a verb and its complement(s) or between a preposition and its object(s).

INCORRECT	The emergency kit included: safety flares, jumper cables, and a flashlight.
CORRECT	The emergency kit included safety flares, jumper cables, and a flashlight.
INCORRECT	Each student taking the math test was provided with: two sharpened pencils, some paper, and a ruler.
CORRECT	Each student taking the math test was provided with two sharpened pencils, some paper, and a ruler.

(2) Use a colon before a long, formal statement or quotation.

EXAMPLE	Abraham Lincoln's Gettysburg Address begins with these famous words: "Fourscore and seven years ago our fathers brought forth on this continent a new nation, conceived in liberty, and dedicated to the proposition that all men are created equal."

Reference Note

For more about **using long quotations,** see page 818.

(3) Use a colon between independent clauses when the second clause explains or restates the idea of the first.

EXAMPLES	Lois felt that she had done something worthwhile: She had designed and sewn her first quilt.
	Thomas Jefferson had many talents: He was a writer, a politician, an architect, and an inventor.

NOTE Notice that the first word of a complete sentence following a colon is capitalized.

27f. Use a colon in certain conventional situations.

(1) Use a colon between the hour and the minute.

EXAMPLES	7:30 P.M.	8:45 in the morning

MECHANICS

(2) Use a colon between chapter and verse when referring to a passage from the Bible.

EXAMPLES   Proverbs 10**:**12   Luke 17**:**1–4

(3) Use a colon between a title and subtitle.

EXAMPLES   *Another View***:** *To Be Black in America* [book]

                *Superman IV***:** *The Quest for Peace* [movie]

                *Impression***:** *Sunrise* [painting]

(4) Use a colon after the salutation of a business letter.

EXAMPLES   Dear Mrs. Rodríguez**:**   To Whom It May Concern**:**

                Dear Sir or Madam**:**   Dear Service Manager**:**

> **NOTE** Use a comma after the salutation of a personal letter.
>
> EXAMPLE   Dear Mom and Dad**,**

Reference Note

For more information on **writing letters,** see "Writing" in the Quick Reference Handbook. For more about **using commas in letters,** see page 797.

Exercise 2 Using Colons Correctly

Rewrite each of the following sentences, inserting or deleting colons wherever necessary.

EXAMPLE   1. Did he mean 8 00 P.M. or 8 00 A.M.?

            1. *Did he mean 8:00 P.M. or 8:00 A.M.?*

1. The word *zone* is a multipurpose word that can be found in many disciplines It is used in mathematics, ecology, anatomy, geology, computer science, city planning, and also slang.
2. We stared dumbfounded, for never had we read such wordy prose "Due to the fact that consumers may now avail themselves of many forms of energy from both traditional and alternative sources, revenue from governmentally established sites has in the local vicinity been decreasing although provider costs have tended to rise; consequently, this has made it incumbent upon your local site to warrant a slight increase in concurrent fees for said service. We thank you for your continued cooperation."
3. Do you have a book called *Sarajevo The Road to Destiny*?
4. The following items should be included in any first-aid kit bandages, antibacterial ointment, and disinfectant.
5. In the Bible, the story of how God creates light appears in Genesis 1 1.

6. When I did the laundry yesterday, the contents of my little brother's pockets proved to be as follows a broken marble, a hunk of moss, a live beetle, four sticks of varying lengths, three cents, a quantity of dirt, a piece of aluminum foil, and a large pebble.

7. I began my letter with "Dear Mr. Engstrom Thank you for your assistance."

8. Wow! Look at all these thesaurus entries for *money scratch, moola, long green, dough,* and *lettuce.*

9. India shares its borders with: Pakistan, Afghanistan, Tibet, Nepal, Bangladesh, Myanmar, and Bhutan.

10. There's a show about Pancho Villa on PBS tonight at 9 00.

Parentheses

27g. Use parentheses to enclose informative or explanatory material of minor importance.

EXAMPLES   Amelia Earhart **(**1897– c.1937**)** was the first woman to pilot an airplane alone across the Atlantic Ocean.

A *roman à clef* **(**literally, "novel with a key"**)** is a novel about real people to whom the novelist has assigned fictitious names.

NOTE Be sure that the material enclosed in parentheses can be omitted without losing important information or changing the basic meaning and construction of the sentence.

IMPROPER USE   George Eliot (whose real name was Mary Ann
OF PARENTHESES   Evans) was one of many women in nineteenth-century England who wrote under a masculine pseudonym. [The information in parentheses clarifies that George Eliot was a woman. The parentheses should be replaced by commas.]

Follow these guidelines for capitalizing and punctuating parenthetical sentences.

(1) A parenthetical sentence that falls within another sentence

- should not begin with a capital letter unless it begins with a word that should be capitalized

- should not end with a period but may end with a question mark or an exclamation point

MECHANICS

EXAMPLES   The Malay Archipelago **(see the map on page 350)** includes the Philippines.

Legendary jazz musician Louis "Satchmo" Armstrong **(have you heard of him?)** was born in Louisiana.

When parenthetical material falls within a sentence, punctuation should not come before the opening parenthesis but may follow the closing parenthesis.

INCORRECT   The first professional baseball team, the Cincinnati Red Stockings, (the Reds) was formed in 1869.

CORRECT   The first professional baseball team, the Cincinnati Red Stockings **(**the Reds**),** was formed in 1869.

(2) A parenthetical sentence that stands by itself

- should begin with a capital letter
- should end with a period, a question mark, or an exclamation point before the closing parenthesis

EXAMPLES   The Malay Archipelago includes the Philippines. **(See the map on page 350.)**

Legendary jazz musician Louis "Satchmo" Armstrong was born in Louisiana. **(Have you heard of him?)**

Dashes

Sometimes words, phrases, and sentences are used *parenthetically;* that is, they break into the main thought of a sentence.

EXAMPLES   Ann, **however,** does not agree with him.

The decision **(which player should he choose?)** weighed on Coach Johnson's mind.

Most parenthetical elements are set off by commas or parentheses. Sometimes, however, parenthetical elements are such an interruption that a stronger mark is needed. In such cases, a dash is used.

27h. Use a dash to indicate an abrupt break in thought or speech.

EXAMPLES   The team's leading scorer——I can't remember her name——is also an excellent defensive player.

The real villain turns out to be——but I don't want to spoil the ending for those of you who have not yet seen the movie.

27i. Use a dash to mean *namely, in other words,* or *that is* before an explanation.

EXAMPLES   Amanda joined the chorus for only one reason——she loves to sing.

Very few people in this class——three, to be exact——have not completed their projects.

Brackets

27j. Use brackets to enclose an explanation within quoted or parenthetical material.

EXAMPLES   The newspaper article stated, "At the time of that Democratic National Convention **[in Chicago in 1968]** there were many protest groups operating in the United States." [*In Chicago in 1968* is in brackets to show that it is not part of the original quotation.]

I think that Hilda Doolittle (more commonly known as H. D. **[1886–1961]**) is best remembered for her imagist poetry. [*1886–1961* is in brackets because it is within parenthetical material.]

> **Exercise 3** **Using Parentheses, Dashes, and Brackets Correctly**

The following sentences have been punctuated incorrectly. Write each sentence, deleting incorrect punctuation and inserting correct dashes, parentheses, and brackets as necessary. Make sure that any parenthetical material is properly capitalized and punctuated.

EXAMPLE   **1.** One, no, two, fawns are with the doe.

      1. *One—no, two—fawns are with the doe.*

1. For a loan like this, a bank will need collateral something of value like a boat or a car.

2. Quinine, which is a common treatment for malaria, comes from the bark of the cinchona (a name said to honor the Countess of Chinchón (1576–1639).

3. *Laissez-faire* pronounced les-ay-FAIR is a French phrase that means "let do"; it is often used to describe a system of government with few or no controls on business.

4. That's not a broken lamp; it's a sculpture oops, now it's broken; maybe we can make a lamp out of it.

MECHANICS

5. The focal point of the Byzantine Empire, Constantinople [See map on page 781] is now Istanbul.
6. Looks as though we got here just in time hey, the curtain's going up.
7. The article continued, "Once the material reaches its critical mass the minimum amount of pressure required for a reaction, a chain reaction occurs."
8. There must have been a million well, at least a few hundred cars stopped on the highway.
9. As the joker is to a modern deck of cards, so a blank card was to the French hence the phrase, *carte blanche,* "a blank card."
10. The black history movement, which owes much to Melville Jean Herskovits he was my grandpa's professor at Northwestern University in 1951 began fifty years ago.

Reference Note

For examples of **titles** that are not italicized but are enclosed **in quotation marks,** see page 820.

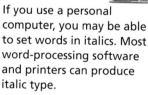

COMPUTER TIP

If you use a personal computer, you may be able to set words in italics. Most word-processing software and printers can produce italic type.

Italics

Italics are printed characters that slant to the right—*like this.* To indicate italics in handwritten or typewritten work, use underlining.

PRINTED *The Heart Is a Lonely Hunter* was written by Carson McCullers.

HANDWRITTEN *The Heart Is a Lonely Hunter was written by Carson McCullers.*

MECHANICS

27k. Use italics (underlining) for the titles and subtitles of books, plays, long poems, periodicals, works of art, movies, radio and TV series, videos, video games, long musical works and recordings, computer games, and comic strips.

Type of Title	Examples
Books	*The Princess Bride* *Aké: The Years of Childhood* *The Innocents Abroad*
Plays	*A Doll's House* *Death of a Salesman* *Harvey*
Long Poems	*Rubáiyát* *The Rime of the Ancient Mariner* *Don Juan*
Periodicals	*U.S. News & World Report* *The Dallas Morning News* *Sports Illustrated*
Works of Art	*Mona Lisa* *Nocturne in Black and Gold: The Falling Rocket*
Movies	*Hank Aaron: Chasing the Dream* *Antz*
Radio and TV Series	*Midnight Mystery Theatre* *Star Trek: Voyager*
Videos, Video Games	*Working Out at Home* *Moonwalker*
Long Musical Works and Recordings	*Rhapsody in Blue* *The Sounds of Nature*
Computer Games	*Raceway U.S.A.* *Flight Simulator*
Comic Strips	*Dennis the Menace* *Jumpstart* *Rose Is Rose*

TIPS & TRICKS

Long poems are poems that are long enough to be published as separate volumes. Such poems are usually divided into titled or numbered sections, such as cantos, parts, or books. Long musical works include operas, symphonies, ballets, oratorios, and concertos.

STYLE TIP

Generally, do not use italics for the title of your own paper. However, if your title contains a title that belongs in italics, you will need to use italics for that part of the title.

EXAMPLES
Rafe Buenrostro: A Soldier Comes Home [contains no title that belongs in italics]

Nathaniel Hawthorne's Use of Gothic Elements in *The Scarlet Letter* [contains a title that belongs in italics]

Be creative when giving your paper a title. Avoid using the title of another work as the complete title of your paper.

MECHANICS

Reference Note

For more information on **capitalizing titles,** see page 763.

STYLE TIP

Writers sometimes use italics (underlining) for emphasis, especially in written dialogue. The italic type shows how the sentence is supposed to be spoken. Read the following sentences aloud. Notice that by italicizing different words, the writer can change the meaning of the sentence.

EXAMPLE

"Did you read *that* book by Mark Twain?" asked Jennifer. [Did you read that book or some other book?]

"Did *you* read that book by Mark Twain?" asked Jennifer. [Did you read the book or did someone else?]

Italicizing (underlining) words for emphasis is a handy technique that should not be overused. It can quickly lose its impact.

NOTE An article (*a, an,* or *the*) before a periodical's title is not italicized or capitalized unless it is part of the official title, which is usually found on the editorial page or in the table of contents. The official title of a book appears on the title page of the book.

EXAMPLE   I found this information in *The New York Times,* not in t**he** *New York Post.*

Do not use italics for titles of religious texts or for titles of legal or historical documents.

RELIGIOUS TEXTS   Old Testament
    Talmud

LEGAL OR HISTORICAL DOCUMENTS   Treaty of Guadalupe Hidalgo
    United States Constitution

27l. Use italics (underlining) for the names of trains, ships, aircraft, and spacecraft.

Type of Title	Examples
Trains, Ships	*Sunset Express* *Andrea Doria*
Aircraft, Spacecraft	*Graf Zeppelin* *Voyager 2*

27m. Use italics (underlining) for words, letters, symbols, and numerals referred to as such, and for foreign words that have not been adopted into English.

EXAMPLES   Make sure to use the words **emigrate** and **immigrate** correctly in your essay.

I like the basic design of the poster, but the **$** looks too much like an **S.**

Is that an **8** or a **3**?

The word **fossil** derives from the Latin verb **fodere,** "to dig."

NOTE If you are not sure whether to italicize a foreign word, look it up in an up-to-date dictionary.

Exercise 4 **Correcting Sentences by Adding Underlining**

Underline all the words and word groups that should be italicized in the following sentences.

EXAMPLE   **1.** I try to watch Sixty Minutes every week.

        1. _Sixty Minutes_

1. According to tradition, The Red Vineyard is the only painting Vincent van Gogh ever sold during his lifetime.

2. The Fantasticks is the longest-running musical in history.

3. Jesse's birthday present was a subscription to Rolling Stone magazine.

4. The theater club will present Arsenic and Old Lace in the fall.

5. My sister missed the word xeriscape in the spelling bee.

6. Arlene reads Peanuts in the newspaper every day.

7. My uncle Bob remembers when the USSR first launched Sputnik 1 into orbit.

8. That last episode of Babylon 5 kept me on the edge of my seat!

9. In American literature, we are studying Stephen Crane's novel The Red Badge of Courage.

10. I get a little better at it every time I play Escape Velocity on my computer.

Quotation Marks

27n. Use quotation marks to enclose a *direct quotation*—a person's exact words.

Be sure to place quotation marks both before and after a person's exact words.

EXAMPLES   In his speech to the Virginia House of Burgesses in 1765, Patrick Henry said, "If this be treason, make the most of it."

        "The track meet is canceled because of the unusually cold weather," announced Coach Griffey.

Do not use quotation marks to enclose an *indirect quotation*—a rewording of a direct quotation.

DIRECT QUOTATION	Aaron said, "I can type seventy-five words per minute."
INDIRECT QUOTATION	Aaron said that he can type seventy-five words per minute.

(1) A direct quotation generally begins with a capital letter.

EXAMPLE   The poet Emily Dickinson wrote in a letter to Thomas Wentworth Higginson, her literary advisor, "**If** I feel physically as if the top of my head were taken off, I know *that* is poetry."

However, when the quotation is obviously only a fragment of the original quotation, it generally begins with a lowercase letter.

EXAMPLE   In her essay "On the Mall," Joan Didion describes shopping malls as "**t**oy gardens in which no one lives."

(2) When an expression identifying the speaker divides a quoted sentence, the second part begins with a lowercase letter.

EXAMPLE   "If you like board games," said Tyrone, "**y**ou should come to the party." [Notice that each part of a divided quotation is enclosed in quotation marks.]

When the second part of a divided quotation is a complete sentence, it begins with a capital letter.

EXAMPLE   "English and French are recognized as official languages of Canada," explained Ms. Hawkins. "**T**he French Canadians, most of whom live in Quebec, speak French and observe many of the customs of their French ancestors."

NOTE   When a direct quotation of two or more sentences is not divided, only one set of quotation marks is used.

EXAMPLE   **"**English and French are recognized as official languages of Canada. The French Canadians, most of whom live in Quebec, speak French and observe many of the customs of their French ancestors.**"**

(3) A direct quotation can be set off from the rest of the sentence by a comma, a question mark, or an exclamation point, but not by a period.

EXAMPLES   "I nominate Pilar for class president**,**" said Erin.

Erin said**,** "I nominate Pilar for class president."

"What is the capital of Thailand**?**" asked Mr. Klein.

"This chili is too spicy**!**" exclaimed Brian.

(4) When used with quotation marks, other marks of punctuation are placed according to the following rules:

- Commas and periods are placed inside the closing quotation marks.

EXAMPLE "By the way," he said, "we decided to go to the play."

- Semicolons and colons are placed outside the closing quotation marks.

EXAMPLES Winona said, "I need to study my lines tonight"; she has a major role in the community theater's next play.

Gina Berriault uses several types of figurative language in her short story "The Stone Boy": simile, metaphor, and personification.

- Question marks and exclamation points are placed inside the closing quotation marks if the quotation itself is a question or an exclamation. Otherwise, they are placed outside.

EXAMPLES "Dad, will you please call the doctor tomorrow morning?" I asked.

"Move those feet double-time!" ordered the drum major.

Did Langston Hughes write the line "My soul has grown deep like the rivers"?

I'm tired of hearing "This is boring"!

Notice in the last two examples given above that the end mark belonging with each quotation has been omitted. When a sentence ends with a quotation, only one end mark is necessary.

(5) When quoting a passage that consists of more than one paragraph, put quotation marks at the beginning of each paragraph and at the end of only the last paragraph of the passage.

EXAMPLE "The water was thick and heavy and the color of a mirror in a dark room. Minnows broke the surface right under the wharf. I jumped. I couldn't help it.

"And I got to thinking that something might come out of the water. It didn't have a name or a shape. But it was there."

Shirley Ann Grau, "The Land and the Water"

NOTE A long passage quoted from a printed source is often set off from the rest of the text. The entire passage may be indented and double-spaced. When a quotation is set off, quotation marks are used only if they appear in the printed source. Otherwise, quotation marks are unnecessary.

EXAMPLE

In Sabine Ulibarrí's story "My Wonder Horse," the young narrator, a fifteen-year-old boy, finally captures Mago, the legendary horse, and proudly brings him home. The following passage shows the reaction of the boy's father:

> My father saw me coming and waited for me without a word. A smile played over his face, and a spark danced in his eyes. He watched me take the rope from Mago, and the two of us thoughtfully observed him move away. My father clasped my hand a little more firmly than usual and said, "That was a man's job." That was all. Nothing more was needed. We understood one another very well.

(6) When writing *dialogue* (a conversation), begin a new paragraph every time the speaker changes, and enclose each speaker's words in quotation marks.

EXAMPLE

"But what kind of authentic and valuable information do you require?" asked Klapaucius.

"All kinds, as long as it's true," replied the pirate. "You never can tell what facts may come in handy. I already have a few hundred wells and cellars full of them, but there's room for twice again as much. So out with it; tell me everything you know, and I'll jot it down. But make it snappy!"

"A fine state of affairs," Klapaucius whispered in Trurl's ear. "He could keep us here for an eon or two before we tell him everything we know. Our knowledge is colossal!!"

"Wait," whispered Trurl, "I have an idea."

Stanislaw Lem, "The Sixth Sally"

(7) Use single quotation marks to enclose a quotation within a quotation.

EXAMPLES   Mr. Laveau said, "Please tell us what is meant by Benjamin Franklin's maxim ʻLost time is never found again.ʼ" [Notice that the period is placed inside the single quotation mark.]

Mr. Laveau asked, "Can anyone tell us what is meant by Benjamin Franklin's maxim ʻLost time is never found again'?" [The question mark is placed inside the double quotation marks, not the single quotation mark, because the entire quotation of Mr. Laveau's words is a question.]

Exercise 5   Using Quotation Marks with Other Marks of Punctuation

Add quotation marks and other punctuation marks where they are needed in the following dialogue. Also, correct any errors in the use of capitalization, and begin a new paragraph each time the speaker changes.

EXAMPLE   [1] You can tell from this picture Lloyd said that people have a lot of fun during the Juneteenth holiday. But I don't get it.

    1.   *"You can tell from this picture," Lloyd said, "that people have a lot of fun during the Juneteenth holiday, but I don't get it."*

[1] Do you mean Janelle asked that you don't understand having fun or you don't understand Juneteenth [2] Lloyd, who didn't like being misunderstood, quickly replied stop joking around [3] Janelle said I'll be glad to tell you what Juneteenth is; she hadn't meant to tease

Be sure to reproduce quoted material exactly as it appears in the original. If the original contains an error, write the Latin word *sic,* which means "thus so," in brackets directly after the error.

EXAMPLE
The writer continued, "The film is an excelent [*sic*] adaptation of a novel by Tom Clancy." [Notice that *sic* is italicized.]

MECHANICS

Lloyd. [4] Juneteenth is celebrated every year on June 19 she continued To mark the day in 1865 when a Union general proclaimed the slaves in Texas to be free. [5] It's celebrated not only in Texas but also throughout the rest of the South [6] Lloyd interrupted why were the Texas slaves proclaimed free so long after Lincoln's Emancipation Proclamation [7] Remember that Lincoln made his proclamation in 1863, but the Civil War continued until April 9, 1865 Janelle replied and then it took a while for news to spread [8] Janelle thought that her explanations had satisfied Lloyd, but then he asked Well, how is Juneteenth celebrated [9] Now that's a question you don't need to ask she replied Because you go to the Juneteenth parade every year. [10] It's celebrated much the same everywhere she added With families enjoying picnics, parades, games, and music.

27o. Use quotation marks to enclose titles (including subtitles) of short works such as short stories, poems, essays, articles and other parts of periodicals, songs, episodes of radio and TV series, and chapters and other parts of books.

Reference Note
The titles of long poems and long musical works are italicized. For examples of these titles and of other **titles that are italicized,** see page 813.

Type of Title	Examples
Short Stories	"The Open Boat" "The Necklace"
Poems	"The Dance" "Mending Wall"
Essays	"Of Friendship" "Self-Reliance"
Articles and Other Parts of Periodicals	"Choices: Careers in Graphic Arts" "Talk of the Town"
Songs	"Georgia on My Mind" "Wind Beneath My Wings"
Episodes of Radio and TV Series	"Phantom Footsteps: A Ghost Tale" "Arctic Encounter"
Chapters and Other Parts of Books	"The Civil War: The Eastern Campaign" "Epilogue"

MECHANICS

NOTE Use single quotation marks for the titles of short works within quotations.

EXAMPLE   "Class, please read 'Child of the Americas' by tomorrow."

Do not use quotation marks for titles of religious texts or for titles of legal or historical documents.

RELIGIOUS TEXTS   Holy Bible
                     Koran

LEGAL OR HISTORICAL   Treaty of Medicine Lodge
        DOCUMENTS   Declaration of Independence

27p. Use quotation marks to enclose slang words, invented words, technical terms, dictionary definitions of words, and any expressions that are unusual in standard English.

EXAMPLES   Chloe reached for a high note and hit a "clinker."

            Deanna calls Tyler's incessant punning "punishment"; he calls it "punnology."

            Although I am not familiar with computer jargon, I do know that "to boot" a disk does not mean to kick it.

            The verb *recapitulate* means "to repeat briefly" or "to summarize."

NOTE Avoid using slang words in formal speaking and writing. Also, when using technical terms, be sure to explain their meanings. If you are not sure whether a word is appropriate or whether its meaning is clear, consult an up-to-date dictionary.

Review A **Correcting Sentences by Adding Quotation Marks, Other Punctuation Marks, and Capitalization**

Revise the following sentences by correcting errors in the use of quotation marks, other marks of punctuation, and capitalization.

EXAMPLE   1. Mark Twain wrote it is easier to stay out than get out.

           1. *Mark Twain wrote, "It is easier to stay out than get out."*

1. The section called People in the News in this book has some interesting facts about celebrities.

STYLE   TIP

On the cover page or title page of a paper of your own, do not use quotation marks for the title of your paper. However, if your title contains a title that belongs in quotation marks, you will need to use quotation marks for that part of your title.

EXAMPLE
Miss Lottie in "Marigolds": A Character Sketch [contains a title that belongs in quotation marks.]

Be creative when giving your paper a title. Avoid using the title of another work as the complete title of your paper.

MECHANICS

Reference Note

For information on **using a dictionary,** see "The Dictionary" in the Quick Reference Handbook.

2. Are you going to the Greek Festival asked Mr. Doney or didn't you know that it's scheduled for this weekend

3. Our teacher quoted Willa Cather's words there are only two or three human stories, and they go on repeating themselves as fiercely as if they had never happened before.

4. How do I find out who wrote the poem Dream Deferred Jill asked her English teacher.

5. The expression icing on the cake is not literally about dessert it refers to something additional that is a pleasant surprise.

6. I'm still hungry complained Donna that baked apple looks tempting

7. When faced with a frightening situation, I often recite Psalm 23 4, which begins as follows Yea, though I walk through the valley of the shadow of death, I will fear no evil.

8. Perhaps the finest memorial to Abraham Lincoln is Walt Whitman's poem When Lilacs Last in the Dooryard Bloom'd.

9. Are you saying that I don't know the answer or that I don't understand the question

10. Ms. Hammer warned us that the movie was, to use her words, a parody of the novel furthermore, she advised us not to waste our money and time by seeing it.

11. Did she say guess or yes?

12. My older brother said that my new shoes were fly, meaning that they looked cool or stylish.

13. Please don't make me sing Jingle Bells another time, I begged my little sister.

14. One of the geologists pointed out chatter marks that indicated glacial action, and I asked her what the term meant.

15. Woody Guthrie wrote one of my favorite songs—This Land Is Your Land.

16. Did you read Cody's essay on dress codes, Shoelaces, Foolaces?

17. Here's the way I figure it: We're teaching the baby new words, so it's only fair that he teaches us new words like abot and fa-fa.

18. Why did she say, It's jake with me?

19. Are we supposed to read the story All Summer in a Day out loud? we asked.

20. The phrase ad hominem is Latin for to the man; the phrase refers to an argument that attacks one's opponent, not the issue.

21. The phrase putting the cart before the horse can be traced back to 61 B.C.

22. I'm sorry I couldn't talk on the phone last night Chris said but I was washing dishes.

23. Stephen Crane's poem War Is Kind is as topical today as it was one hundred years ago.

24. Who said To err is human, to forgive divine?

25. When Mr. Wilson said Put down your pencils, everyone sighed with relief.

Review B **Proofreading a Dialogue for Correct Punctuation**

Correct any errors in the use of quotation marks and other marks of punctuation in the following dialogue. Also, correct any errors in the use of capitalization, and begin a new paragraph each time the speaker changes.

EXAMPLE　**[1]** I think The Weeping Woman would be a good title for my new song Jim told Tomás. can you guess what it is about

　1.　*"I think 'The Weeping Woman' would be a good title for my new song," Jim told Tomás. "Can you guess what it's about?"*

[**1**] Well, I once read a magazine article titled *La Llorona* The Weeping Woman. It was about a popular Mexican American legend, Tomás replied. [**2**] That's the legend I'm talking about! Jim exclaimed I first heard it when I was a little boy growing up in southern California. [**3**] I think commented Tomás, People in the music business would call the song a tear-jerker because it tells a sad story. [**4**] I'll say it's sad Jim replied it's about a poor, wronged woman who goes crazy, drowns her children, and kills herself; then she returns as a ghost to look for them forever. [**5**] The legend is frightening to hear when you're young because *La Llorona* is usually described as a headless woman dressed all in white. [**6**] Isn't she usually seen around water Tomás asked. [**7**] Yes, Jim said but you didn't mention one of the scariest things: Her fingernails look like knives [**8**] Didn't your mother ever say, Don't believe ghost stories, son asked Tomás [**9**] Oh, sure Jim replied. to tell the truth, I never did really believe them. They are great stories, though. [**10**] Well, maybe, but give me a humorous story like The Catbird Seat any day Tomás said.

Ellipsis Points

27q. Use ellipsis points (. . .) to mark omissions from quoted material.

ORIGINAL   Sitting here tonight, many years later, with more time than money, I think about those faces that pass before my eyes like it was yesterday. They remind me of the chances and temptations to become an outlaw. I sure came through a tough mill. I see those men as they stood in those old days of the Golden West—some of them in the springtime of their manhood, so beautiful and strong that it makes you wonder, because their hearts are as black as night, and they are cruel, treacherous and merciless as a man-eating tiger of the jungle.

Andrew García, *Tough Trip Through Paradise*

(1) When you omit words from the middle of a sentence, use three spaced ellipsis points.

EXAMPLE   In his autobiography, *Tough Trip Through Paradise,* Andrew García reflects, "Sitting here tonight, **. . .** I think about those faces that pass before my eyes like it was yesterday."

NOTE Be sure to include space before and after each ellipsis point.

(2) When you omit words at the beginning of a sentence within a quoted passage, keep the previous sentence's end punctuation and follow it with the ellipsis points.

EXAMPLE   García writes, "They remind me of the chances and temptations to become an outlaw. I sure came through a tough mill**. . .** [T]heir hearts are as black as night, and they are cruel, treacherous and merciless as a man-eating tiger of the jungle."

NOTE Do not begin a quoted passage with ellipsis points.

INCORRECT   ". . . They remind me of the chances and temptations to become an outlaw. I sure came through a tough mill."

CORRECT   "They remind me of the chances and temptations to become an outlaw. I sure came through a tough mill."

(3) When you omit words at the end of a sentence within a quoted passage, keep the sentence's end punctuation and follow it with the ellipsis points.

—HELP—

Notice in the quotation to the right that *their* has been capitalized because it now begins the sentence. The *T* is in brackets to show that it was not capitalized in the original passage.

EXAMPLE García writes, "I think about those faces that pass before my eyes. . . . They remind me of the chances and temptations to become an outlaw."

(4) When you omit one or more complete sentences from a quoted passage, keep the previous sentence's end punctuation and follow it with the ellipsis points.

EXAMPLE Recalling his youth, Andrew García writes, "Sitting here tonight, many years later, with more time than money, I think about those faces that pass before my eyes like it was yesterday. . . . I sure came through a tough mill."

(5) To show that a full line or more of poetry has been omitted, use an entire line of spaced periods.

COMPLETE POEM

A single flow'r he sent me, since we met.
   All tenderly his messenger he chose;
Deep-hearted, pure, with scented dew still wet—
   One perfect rose.

I knew the language of the floweret;
   "My fragile leaves," it said, "his heart enclose."
Love long has taken for his amulet
   One perfect rose.

Why is it no one ever sent me yet
   One perfect limousine, do you suppose?
Ah no, it's always just my luck to get
   One perfect rose.

        Dorothy Parker, "One Perfect Rose"

POEM WITH OMISSION

A single flow'r he sent me, since we met.
   All tenderly his messenger he chose;

. . . .

Why is it no one ever sent me yet
   One perfect limousine, do you suppose?
Ah no, it's always just my luck to get
   One perfect rose.

27r. Use three ellipsis points (. . .) to indicate a pause in dialogue.

EXAMPLE "Well . . . I can't really say," hedged the company's representative.

—HELP—

Notice that the line of ellipsis points showing an omission in a poem is as long as the line of poetry above it.

MECHANICS

HELP

In Exercise 6, you may need to keep or omit punctuation, such as commas within a sentence, depending on whether that punctuation is necessary to the meaning or clarity of the sentence with the omission.

Exercise 6 — Using Ellipsis Points Correctly

Omit the italicized parts of the following passages. Use ellipsis points to punctuate each omission correctly.

EXAMPLE
1. In those days, *which is to say when the world was green*, a baseball was the core of my universe, and a bat its axis.

1. *In those days . . . a baseball was the core of my universe, and a bat its axis.*

1. Today's marathon runners race for a little more than twenty-six miles. *Why not twenty-five miles or thirty?* The distance commemorates the length of the plain of Marathon where, as legend has it, a long-distance runner once carried the news of the Athenian defeat of the Persian army.

2. The software, to my mind, is cumbersome at best, *a little like wearing an exceedingly large backpack on top of another backpack.* However, it may have some limited use for animation professionals and other high-resolution graphics users.

3. A globe, *translucent magenta and dotted with unfamiliar aqua-blue continents,* sat on his desk and spun slowly, powered by some unseen force.

4. She said, "Who am I?"
   I say, "Fie."
   I'm the pie in the sky of a dragon's eye.
   So, bye-bye, small fry.

5. How could I have known? *Could I have even guessed?* The events were so startling that even as I experienced them, they did not seem real.

6. The new highway, *which will reduce inner-city traffic,* will bypass the city by routing traffic to the west. This new freeway is scheduled to be completed in 2007. Residents who wish to comment on the proposed path may obtain a copy of the plans at the courthouse.

7. Movie fans, save your summer cash and skip this movie. The young actress Maisie Mills, *who plays the romantic lead, is very pretty but* is painfully unfunny and no friend to our friend the camera.

8. Persuasive essays demand a point of view; they require the writer to take a position and defend it. There is no place for objective reports or evenhanded considerations in a persuasive essay, *except insofar as they might reinforce the position being advanced.* The approach is entirely subjective.

MECHANICS

9. The tension between freedom and responsibility powers the plot of this novel, *as, indeed, it drives the lives of most readers.* Duty's demands conflict directly with Lei Lei's wish to become a doctor. To achieve her dreams, she must sacrifice her family; to help her family, she must sacrifice her dreams.

10. Myles lived in a plain one-story house of the kind known as a bungalow, *with the word's lingering nostalgia for horizons on which the sun never set.* It was at the bottom end of The Parade and commanded a view, *through the stone crosses of St. Colm's churchyard,* of the white sails of sailboats on the English Channel.

Apostrophes

Possessive Case

The ***possessive case*** of a noun or a pronoun shows ownership or possession.

EXAMPLES	the **performers'** costumes	Mr. **Elders'** dog
	Grandmother's recipe	ten **dollars'** worth
	the **team's** coach	**your** responsibility
	my best **friend's** sister	**our** cousins

27s. Use an apostrophe to form the possessive forms of nouns and indefinite pronouns.

(1) To form the possessive of most singular nouns, add an apostrophe and an *s.*

EXAMPLES	a bird**'s** nest	Louis**'s** opinion
	the principal**'s** office	a leader**'s** responsibility

NOTE When forming the possessive of a singular noun ending in an *s* sound, add only an apostrophe if the noun has two or more syllables and if the addition of an apostrophe and an *s* will make the noun awkward to pronounce. Otherwise, add an apostrophe and an *s.*

EXAMPLES	for conscience**'** sake	Ms. Schwartz**'s** car
	Xerxes**'** army	the witness**'s** testimony

Reference Note

Do not confuse **the pronouns** *its, your, their, theirs,* and *whose* with **the contractions** *it's, you're, they're, there's,* and *who's.* See "Words Often Confused" in Chapter 28 for more about these words. For more about **possessive pronouns,** see pages 606 and 613.

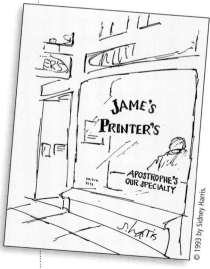

© 1993 by Sidney Harris.

MECHANICS

(2) To form the possessive of a plural noun ending in *s*, add only the apostrophe.

EXAMPLES   the girls' gym   the Joneses' house

                      the players' uniforms   the volunteers' efforts

     The few plural nouns that do not end in *s* form the possessive by adding an apostrophe and an *s*.

EXAMPLES   women's fashions   children's toys

                      geese's squawking   mice's nests

Reference Note

For information about using **apostrophes to form plurals of numerals, symbols, letters, and words referred to as words,** see page 832.

NOTE   In general, you should not use an apostrophe to form the plural of a noun.

INCORRECT   How many Olympic medal's did Carl Lewis win?
CORRECT   How many Olympic **medals** did Carl Lewis win?

(3) Do not use an apostrophe with possessive personal pronouns or with the possessive pronoun *whose*.

Possessive Personal Pronouns		
First Person	my, mine	our, ours
Second Person	your, yours	your, yours
Third Person	his, her, hers, its	their, theirs

INCORRECT   The leopard can't change it's spots.
CORRECT   The leopard can't change **its** spots.

INCORRECT   Marjorie is the girl who's mother I met.
CORRECT   Marjorie is the girl **whose** mother I met.

(4) To form the possessive of an indefinite pronoun, add an apostrophe and an *s*.

Indefinite Pronouns in the Possessive Case			
another's	each's	nobody's	other's
anybody's	everybody's	no one's	somebody's
anyone's	everyone's	one's	someone's

EXAMPLES   One runner got in the other's way.

He seems to need everybody's attention.

NOTE The correct possessive forms of *anyone else* and *somebody else*
are *anyone else's* and *somebody else's.*

Exercise 7 **Proofreading for Correct Possessive
and Plural Forms**

Most of the following items contain an incorrect possessive or plural
form. For each error, give the correct form of the word. If an item is
already correct, write *C.*

EXAMPLE   **1.** Chris' tapes
             1. Chris's tapes

1. It is her's.
2. womens' department
3. that boys' radio
4. leaves' color
5. a fly's wings
6. four dog's in a line
7. that spacecrafts' air lock
8. childrens' program
9. no ones' fault
10. the Harlem Globetrotters's game

11. San Jose's industries
12. a Buddhist's beliefs
13. Who's is it?
14. It is somebody's else.
15. a pair of shoe's
16. it's shiny surface
17. That is their's.
18. a churches' spire
19. mice's tails
20. a horses' hooves

**(5) Generally, in compound nouns, in names of organizations and
businesses, and in word groups showing joint possession, only
the last word is possessive in form.**

EXAMPLES   sister-in-law's shoes

Weber, Mendoza, and Stone's law office

Joe and Clara's song

NOTE The possessive of an acronym is formed by adding an apostrophe
and *s.*

EXAMPLES   NBC's latest sitcom

UNESCO's new headquarters

Reference Note

For more about **compound nouns,** see
page 486.

STYLE   TIP

Use a phrase beginning
with *of* or *for* to avoid
awkward possessive forms.

AWKWARD
  the Society for the
  Preservation of Historic
  Homes's advertisement

BETTER
  the advertisement **for** the
  Society for the Preservation of Historic Homes

MECHANICS

When a possessive pronoun is part of a word group showing joint possession, each noun in the word group is also possessive.

EXAMPLES   Chen's, Ramona's, and **my** project

                Juan's and **her** business

(6) Form the possessive of each noun in a word group showing individual possession of similar items.

EXAMPLES   Asimov's and Bradbury's stories

                the doctor's and dentist's fees

(7) When used in the possessive form, words indicating time, such as *minute, hour, day, week, month,* and *year,* and words indicating amounts in cents or dollars require apostrophes.

EXAMPLES   a day's rest   four weeks' vacation

                a dollar's worth   two cents' worth

Review C Forming Possessive Nouns and Pronouns

Each of the following phrases expresses a possessive relationship. Revise each word group so that a possessive noun or pronoun expresses the same relationship.

EXAMPLES   **1.** promise of my sister-in-law

             1. my sister-in-law's promise

             2. bikes of Jane and Mia

             2. Jane's and Mia's bikes

1. party of Juan and Geraldo
2. clothes of babies
3. singing of the birds
4. profits of ABC
5. pay of two weeks
6. restaurant of Charlie and Barney
7. worth of one dollar
8. coats of the gentlemen
9. jobs of my brothers-in-law
10. plans of the school board
11. victory of the players
12. languages of Spain and France
13. delay of six months
14. testimonies of the clerk and the customer
15. streets of West Baden
16. name of it
17. flooding of the Nile River
18. hope of everyone else
19. opinions of him
20. route of our mail carrier

Contractions

27t. **Use an apostrophe to show where letters, numerals, or words have been omitted in a contraction.**

A *contraction* is a shortened form of a word, word group, or numeral in which an apostrophe takes the place of all the letters, words, or numerals that are omitted.

27
t

STYLE TIP

Many people consider contractions informal. Therefore, it is generally best to avoid using them in formal writing and speech.

EXAMPLES			
I am . . . . **I'm**		they had . . . . . . **they'd**	
let us . . . . **let's**		where is . . . . . . **where's**	
of the clock . . **o'clock**		we are . . . . **we're**	
she would . . . . **she'd**		you will . . . . **you'll**	
1999 . . . . **'99**		Pat is . . . . **Pat's**	

The word *not* can be shortened to *n't* and added to a verb, usually without any change in the spelling of the verb.

EXAMPLES			
is not . . . . **isn't**		has not . . . . **hasn't**	
do not . . . . **don't**		should not . . . . **shouldn't**	
does not . . . . . **doesn't**		were not . . . . . . **weren't**	
would not . . . . **wouldn't**		could not . . . . . **couldn't**	
EXCEPTIONS will not . . . . **won't**		cannot . . . . **can't**	

Do not confuse contractions with possessive pronouns.

Contractions	Possessive Pronouns
It's [It is] late. **It's** [It has] been an exciting week.	**Its** wing is broken.
Who's [Who is] in charge? **Who's** [Who has] been keeping score?	**Whose** ticket is this?
You're [You are] a good student.	**Your** shoe is untied.
They're [They are] in the library. **There's** [There is] no one at home.	**Their** house is for sale. Those dogs are **theirs**.

MECHANICS

Using Possessive Forms and Contractions Correctly

Each of the following sentences contains at least one possessive form or contraction that has been written incorrectly. Rewrite each incorrect word, adding or deleting apostrophes as needed.

EXAMPLE   1. Its easy to see that youve been practicing.

    1. *It's, you've*

1. Their still in the gym going over there acrobatics routine.
2. Larry asked the woman whose in charge, and she said that the branch library doesnt have any of Octavio Paz's works.
3. If shes not here by six oclock, whose going to make the introduction?
4. Theirs plenty of potato salad and lemonade over their on the picnic table.
5. It look's as though I shouldve checked the lid more carefully before I shook this bottle.
6. Who wouldnt have laughed at that silly kitten chasing it's own tail?
7. Adam's busy; he cant help us with the script.
8. Lets go over their and see whose playing the flute.
9. Wed have gladly given the kids a puppet show if youd asked.
10. His bar mitzvah was in 99; what year was your's?

Plurals

27u. Use an apostrophe and an *s* to form the plurals of lowercase letters, symbols, numerals, some uppercase letters, and some words referred to as words.

EXAMPLES   The word *tomorrow* has two *r*'s but only one *m*.

The accountant added **$**'s and **%**'s to all of the figures in the columns on the annual report.

I have three **7**'s in my telephone number.

After the happy couple said their **I do**'s, everyone cheered.

Some writers add only an *s* to form the plurals of such items—except lowercase letters—when the plural forms will not cause misreading.

EXAMPLE   The U.S. economy expanded rapidly in the mid- and late-**1990s.**

| S T Y L E   T I P |

Use apostrophes consistently.

EXAMPLE
Several of her grades had improved from **B's** to **A's.**
[Without the apostrophe, the plural of *A* would spell *As*. The apostrophe in the plural of *B* is unnecessary but is included for consistency.]

Review D Proofreading for Errors in Possessives, Contractions, and Plurals

Correctly write each incorrect possessive, contraction, or plural in the following sentences.

EXAMPLE

1. Lets try to find a modern puzzle maze that wont be too difficult for us to explore.

1. *Let's; won't*

1. Your lucky if youve ever been through an old-fashioned hedge maze such as the one pictured below.
2. Its like a maze from an English castle; in fact, we cant help being reminded of the maze at Hampton Court Palace.
3. From above, some of the bushes look like *h*s, *t*s, and other letters.
4. Dont you wonder if these people will find they're way out by dusk or even ten o clock?
5. Ive read that mazes like this one became popular in Europe during the sixteenth and seventeenth centuries; however, my uncle said that hes read about mazes that were built two thousand years ago.
6. When a maze is architectural, *labyrinth*s the word to use for it.
7. Youll be surprised to know that the biggest labyrinth dates back over forty century's ago; the extreme complexity of this labyrinth protected the tomb of Amenehet III.
8. Indeed, other ancient labyrinths may have been defensive structures; after all, theirs no general in the world whose going to send an army single file through a tricky tangle of passageway's.

STYLE TIP

To form the plural of abbreviations that end with a period, add 's.

EXAMPLES
M.D.'s   B.A.'s

To form the plural of abbreviations not followed by periods, add either 's or s.

EXAMPLES
CD-ROM's or CD-ROMs
POW's or POWs

MECHANICS

9. Cant you just imagine a cartoon of the confused soldiers with *?*s and *!*s over there heads?
10. Today, the popularity of mazes drives sales of video game's on cartridges, disks, and CD-ROMs, where a maze can even have an upstairs and a downstairs, trapdoors, and all manner of deceptions.

Hyphens

27v. Use a hyphen to divide a word at the end of a line.

When dividing a word at the end of a line, remember the following rules:

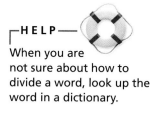

┌HELP──

When you are not sure about how to divide a word, look up the word in a dictionary.

- Do not divide a one-syllable word.

INCORRECT	The treaty that ended the war was sign-ed in Paris in 1783.
CORRECT	The treaty that ended the war was signed in Paris in 1783.

- Divide a word only between syllables.

INCORRECT	Shashona wrote a story about the enda-ngered gray wolf.
CORRECT	Shashona wrote a story about the endan-gered gray wolf.

- A word containing double consonants is usually divided between the double consonants.

INCORRECT	I couldn't believe that it was the beginn-ing of term.
CORRECT	I couldn't believe that it was the begin-ning of term.

- Divide an already hyphenated word at the hyphen.

INCORRECT	Among Elena's drawings were two self-por-traits.
CORRECT	Among Elena's drawings were two self-portraits.

- Do not divide a word so that one letter stands alone.

INCORRECT	Most of the buildings there are made of a-dobe.
CORRECT	Most of the buildings there are made of adobe.

MECHANICS

- Divide words with prefixes or suffixes between the prefix and the root or between the root and the suffix.

INCORRECT   Did you know that Uncle Silas bought a very depen-dable car?

CORRECT   Did you know that Uncle Silas bought a very depend-able car?

27w. Use a hyphen with compound numbers from *twenty-one* to *ninety-nine* and with fractions used as modifiers.

EXAMPLES   one hundred **fifty-five**

a **two-thirds** majority [Here, *two-thirds* is an adjective modifying *majority*.]

two thirds of them [Here, *two thirds* is not a modifier. *Thirds* is a noun modified by the adjective *two*.]

27x. Use a hyphen with the prefixes *ex–*, *self–*, *all–*, and *great–*; with the suffixes *–elect* and *–free*; and with all prefixes before a proper noun or proper adjective.

EXAMPLES   **ex-**mayor   **great-**uncle   **pre-**Waterloo

self-improvement   governor-**elect**   **mid-**Atlantic

all-star   sugar-**free**   **trans-**Siberian

27y. Hyphenate a compound adjective when it precedes the noun it modifies.

EXAMPLES   a **well-designed** engine   an engine that is **well designed**

a **world-famous** skier   a skier who is **world famous**

NOTE   Some compound adjectives are always hyphenated, whether they precede or follow the words they modify.

EXAMPLES   an **up-to-date** look   a look that is **up-to-date**

a **well-informed** man   a man who is **well-informed**

If you are unsure about whether a compound adjective is hyphenated, look up the word in a dictionary.

Do not use a hyphen if one of the modifiers before a noun is an adverb ending in *–ly*.

EXAMPLE   a **partly finished** research paper

Reference Note

For more about **adding prefixes and suffixes to words,** see page 846.

STYLE TIP

The prefix *half* often requires a hyphen, as in *half-life, half-moon,* and *half-truth.* However, sometimes *half* is used without a hyphen, either as a part of a single word (*halftone, halfway, halfback*) or as a separate word (*half shell, half pint, half note*). If you are not sure how to spell a word containing *half*, look up the word in a dictionary.

MECHANICS

Reference Note

For more information on **using the dictionary,** see "The Dictionary" in the Quick Reference Handbook.

27z. Use a hyphen to prevent awkwardness or confusion.

EXAMPLES   **de-emphasize** [The hyphen prevents the awkwardness of two identical vowels next to each other.]

anti-inflammatory [The hyphen prevents the awkwardness of two identical vowels next to each other.]

re-cover a chair [The hyphen prevents confusion with the word *recover.*]

a re-creation of the event [The hyphen prevents confusion with the word *recreation.*]

Exercise 9   Writing Sentences Using Hyphens

Write ten sentences according to the following guidelines. In your sentences, use a variety of subjects and verbs.

EXAMPLE   1. Write a sentence in which you divide a word at the end of a line.

1. *My brother would love to have the toy frog in the cat-alog.*

1. Write a sentence containing a compound number.
2. Write a sentence containing a fraction used as an adjective.
3. Write a sentence containing a word with the prefix *ex–*.
4. Write a sentence containing a compound adjective that precedes the word it modifies.
5. Write a sentence in which you divide a word at the end of a line.
6. Write a sentence containing a word with the prefix *self–*.
7. Write a sentence containing a word with double consonants; at the end of a line, correctly divide that word.
8. Write a sentence containing a word with the suffix *–elect*.
9. Write a sentence containing a word with the prefix *all–*.
10. Write a sentence in which you divide an already hyphenated word at the end of a line.

Review E   Using Apostrophes and Hyphens

Revise the following words or word groups by adding apostrophes and hyphens where needed. If a word or word group is already correct, write *C*.

EXAMPLE   1. post Reformation Europe

1. *post-Reformation Europe*

1. my sister in laws new truck
2. transAlaskan
3. Wheres the Shaker box you bought?
4. Youre from Peru, arent you?
5. one third of the class
6. Isnt soda bread Irish?
7. To whom do all of these *you*'s and *they*s refer?
8. one third finished with the project
9. There are three *as* in *alphabetical.*
10. Its theirs, not ours.
11. antiindustrial sentiment
12. politics in the 1890's
13. dotted all of your *is*
14. Didnt Anthony make your piñata?
15. my great grandmother
16. Its after five oclock.
17. part time job
18. Can you tell me, Denise, why no one an-swered the phone?
19. sugar free foods
20. Achilles heel

COMPUTER TIP

Some software programs can evaluate your writing for common errors in the use of punctuation marks. Such programs can help you proofread your writing.

MECHANICS

Review F   **Proofreading a Paragraph for Correct Punctuation**

Most of the sentences in the following paragraph contain at least one error in the use of punctuation. Rewrite each incorrect sentence, adding and deleting punctuation as necessary. If a sentence is already correct, write *C*.

┌**HELP**

Some sentences in Review F have commas where other punctuation marks should be.

EXAMPLE   [1] Can we be sure sports historians arent that Abner Doubleday invented baseball, that Princeton and Rutgers played the first football game, or that golf originated in China in the second century B.C.?

1. *Can we be sure (sports historians aren't) that Abner Doubleday invented baseball, that Princeton and Rutgers played the first football game, or that golf originated in China in the second century B.C.?*

[1] The origins of most sports are unknown try as we may, we cannot say exactly when or where or how such games as baseball, football, and golf were first played. [2] There is, however, one exception to this rule the game of basketball. [3] Historians of sports know precisely

where basketball began, they know precisely when it began, and perhaps the most interesting fact of all they know the name of the man who invented it Dr. James Naismith. [4] In the winter of 1891–1892, Naismith, who was then an instructor at the YMCA Training College now called Springfield College in Springfield, Massachusetts, had a problem on his hands. [5] The football season was over the baseball season had not yet begun. [6] His students wanted indoor exercise at a competitive sport however, no such sport existed. [7] Working with the materials at hand, Naismith decided to create a new indoor sport. [8] He fastened two peach basket's to the walls at opposite ends of a gymnasium and, using a soccer ball, devised the game that today we call basketball. [9] He started with eighteen available players, and the first rule he wrote read as follows There shall be nine players on each side. [10] Imagine eighteen players set loose on a modern basketball court!

Chapter Review

A. Using Semicolons and Colons Correctly

Rewrite each of the following sentences, adding semicolons and colons as necessary.

┌─HELP─
In Part A of
the Chapter Review, you
may need to replace a
comma with a semicolon or
colon in some sentences.

1. In the attic we found many interesting items an antique mirror, a World War II uniform, some silver bowls, and a chest full of letters.
2. Nicci gets up at six o'clock every weekday morning, consequently, she is never late for school.
3. On Thursday, the most hectic day of the week for me, my schedule includes band practice, 3 15 P.M. my part-time job, 5 00 P.M., and homework, 8 30 P.M.
4. Randy Newman is one of Hollywood's most successful film composers, he has composed the music for such films as *Toy Story*, *A Bug's Life*, and *James and the Giant Peach*.
5. In his 1961 presidential inaugural address, John Fitzgerald Kennedy delivered these famous words, "Ask not what your country can do for you—ask what you can do for your country."

B. Using Underlining and Quotation Marks Correctly

Rewrite each of the following sentences, using underlining (italics) and quotation marks correctly. Change punctuation and capitalization as necessary.

6. One of the books we read this summer was William Golding's Lord of the Flies.
7. "Your essays about the space shuttle Discovery," said Ms. Buchanan, will be due in class on Monday, November 3".
8. "For next Monday," said Mr. Tillinghast, "read the chapter titled The Gilded Age."
9. According to the librarian, Gita has the latest issue of Scientific American.
10. "These written exercises, Catalina complained, "are hard to do, even when you've studied the material."

MECHANICS

Rewrite each of the following sentences, using apostrophes, hyphens, dashes, brackets, and parentheses correctly. Replace any italicized sections with ellipsis points. Change spelling as necessary.

11. Mr. Jones states, "They the joint chiefs of staff favor an increase in the defense budget."

12. Everybodys street clothes are in the locker room, a few minutes walk from here.

13. The critic said, "The meaning of the essay if indeed it had any meaning has been lost through the writer's lack of coherence."

14. It will be warmer in mid April, wont it?

15. Is this Gillian and Matthews house?

16. For his courageous leadership, Dr. Martin Luther King, Jr. 1929–1968, received the Nobel Peace Prize.

17. Whose in the office now?

18. The War Between the States (better known as the Civil War 1861–1865) was one of the defining periods of American history.

19. The ex senator is a well respected commentator on foreign policy.

20. Since the book was too boldly new and strange to win the attention of reviewers or readers *who had fixed ideas about poetry,* it's publication went nearly unnoticed.

D. Proofreading a Dialogue for Correct Punctuation

The following dialogue contains errors in the use of semicolons, colons, dashes, parentheses, italics (underlining), quotation marks, apostrophes, and hyphens. Rewrite the dialogue, correcting the errors and dividing it into paragraphs where appropriate.

[**21**] What in the world please dont think me too uninformed is a Renaissance festival"? Leon asked. [**22**] "Its a fair that celebrates Europes Renaissance, which lasted from about A.D. 1300 to around A.D. 1600," Janice said. [**23**] "Well, I'm ready to go, I know what to expect because I've seen the movies Camelot and The Princess Bride," Leon said. [**24**] "Even so, youll be amazed Janice said, because youll see people dressed up as: kings and queens, jesters, peasants, and knights. [**25**] "I suppose Id better mind my ps and qs with knights around"! Leon exclaimed. [**26**] "Oh, all the fierce looking knights actually are

friendly," Janice said. **[27]** "There are many other sights to see jousts, mazes, elephants and camels, games of strength, music, and all kinds of crafts". **[28]** Leon asked, "isnt there any Renaissance food? **[29]** "Plenty!" Janice said. "My favorites are: bagels, which are sold from traveling carts, soup served in bowls made out of bread, which is freshly baked, and fruit fritters." **[30]** "I've been to several Renaissance fairs," Janice added. Including ones in Texas and Missouri, and I think theyre all great."

Writing Application
Using Contractions in Informal Dialogue

Using Contractions Correctly   You have decided to write and produce a short play and have already drafted a scene-by-scene outline of the play. In one scene, the two main characters have a heated discussion about something that's important to them. Write the dialogue for your scene. Use contractions to make the characters' speech sound natural and realistic.

Prewriting   First, brainstorm some ideas for your main characters. Once you decide who your characters are, think about the sort of discussion they might have. Decide how the characters will resolve their argument at the end of the scene.

Writing   Follow the form for presenting dialogue in a play. In your first draft, concentrate on getting down the basic content of your characters' conversation. You can polish the dialogue later as you evaluate and revise. Be sure that your dialogue focuses on a specific topic or issue and that you maintain a consistent tone throughout.

Revising   To help you evaluate the dialogue, ask two friends to read the parts aloud. As you listen, ask yourself these questions: Does each line of dialogue sound natural? Does the dialogue convey the proper tone? Do the characters resolve their argument in a realistic way? Use contractions to help your dialogue sound like an actual discussion between two people.

Publishing   Proofread your dialogue carefully for correct punctuation. Make sure you have begun a new paragraph each time the speaker changes. You may want to produce your scene for the class. Cast two volunteer actors for the roles, and work with them to get the dialogue just right.

Reference Note

For more about the differences between **formal and informal English,** see page 723.

MECHANICS

Spelling
Improving Your Spelling

Diagnostic Preview

A. Proofreading Sentences for Spelling Errors

Identify and correct each misspelled word in the following sentences.

EXAMPLE   1.   A chill but bracing wind blasted down through the vallies.

           1.   *vallies—valleys*

1. Six steaming loafs of bread sat on the counter in readyness for the family reunion.
2. Where did the superstition about cats' having nine lifes originate?
3. Arctic foxs romped in the snowdrifts in gloryous delight.
4. I must have counted at least three thousand sheeps before I finaly fell asleep.
5. No, they're not argueing; they enjoy shouting about foriegn policy.
6. Study these suffixs closely; you can use them to decode words.
7. It's not a new car, but it's perfectly servicable and the monthly payments are managable.
8. Let's rexamine your data on sea gull's.
9. You can judge the ripeness of a melon by its smell and by taping it and listening for a hollow sound.
10. With our senses, we can percieve only a small part of the world.

B. Proofreading Sentences for Words Often Confused

Proofread the following paragraphs, and replace each incorrectly used word. If a sentence is already correct, write *C*.

EXAMPLE   **[1]** In speaking or writing, few things in language are more satisfying then discovering and using just the right word—for example, *copacetic*.

    1. *than*

    [11] A friend of yours tells you about a peace of music by saying, "Man, it was copacetic." **[12]** Right away, you know your friend is paying the music a complement, because *copacetic* sounds to nice to be critical. **[13]** To state merely, as dictionaries do, that *copacetic* means "excellent" or "first class" would be selling the word short, because it connotes much more than simple superiority.

    [14] It is not a strait word; it's smooth and curved; it doesn't take the shortest rout. **[15]** Like the jazz musicians who used it in the late 1800s, it enjoys the scenery, and it does so with style and originality. **[16]** Some scholars say the word began in Harlem; others say it was borne in France. **[17]** Still others claim *copacetic* is Yiddish in derivation but Southern in accent.

    [18] In short, etymologists are all together stumped; consequently, the origin of *copacetic* is formerly listed as unknown. **[19]** For now, we don't know weather this adjective is French, Italian, Hebrew, or an invention of African Americans. **[20]** Therefore, its origin will have to stay a personnel opinion, but one thing's for sure—*copacetic* is an American English word.

Good Spelling Habits

Using the following techniques will improve your spelling.

1. Pronounce words carefully.

EXAMPLES   ath•lete [not *ath•e•lete*]

        ac•ci•den•tal•ly [not *ac•ci•dent•ly*]

        can•di•date [not *can•i•date*]

        mis•chie•vous [not *mis•chie•ve•ous*]

┌─HELP─

If you are not sure how to pronounce a word, look in a dictionary. In the dictionary, you will usually find the pronunciation given in parentheses after the word. The information in parentheses will show you the sounds used, the syllable breaks, and any accented syllables. A guide to the pronunciation symbols is usually found at the front of the dictionary.

2. Spell by syllables. A *syllable* is a word part that is pronounced as one uninterrupted sound.

EXAMPLES   per•ma•nent [three syllables]

op•ti•mis•tic [four syllables]

oc•ca•sion•al•ly [five syllables]

3. Use a dictionary. By using a dictionary, you will become familiar with the correct pronunciations and divisions of words. In fact, using a dictionary to check the spelling of one word may help you spell other words. For example, checking the spelling of *democracy* may help you spell other words ending in *–cracy*, such as *theocracy, autocracy,* and *aristocracy.*

4. Proofread for careless spelling errors. Always re-read what you have written so that you can eliminate careless spelling errors, such as typographical errors (*thier* for *their*), missing letters (*familar* for *familiar*), and the misuse of similar-sounding words (*than* for *then*).

5. Keep a spelling notebook. Divide each page into four columns.

COLUMN 1   Write correctly any word you find troublesome.
COLUMN 2   Write the word again, dividing it into syllables and marking the stressed syllable(s). (You will probably need to use a dictionary.)
COLUMN 3   Write the word again, circling the part(s) that cause you trouble.
COLUMN 4   Jot down any comments or mnemonics that will help you remember the correct spelling.

    Here is an example of how you might make entries for two words that are often misspelled.

Correct Spelling	Syllables and Accents	Trouble Spot	Comments
probably	prob'•a•bly	prob(ab)ly	pronounce clearly
desirable	de•sir'•a•ble	desi(ra)ble	Study Rule 28 f.

MECHANICS

Exercise 1 **Dividing Words into Syllables**

Without looking up the words in a dictionary, write the syllables of each of the following words, using hyphens between the syllables. Be sure that the division of each word includes all of the letters of the word. When you have finished, use a dictionary to check your work.

EXAMPLE   1. accommodate

       1. ac-com-mo-date

1. adversary
2. alias
3. barbarous
4. chimney
5. costume
6. deficit
7. genuine
8. incidentally
9. procrastinate
10. library

┌─HELP─

Rules 28a and 28b apply only when the *i* and the *e* are part of the same syllable.

EXAMPLES

de • i • ty

sci • ence

Spelling Rules

ie and *ei*

28a. **Write *ie* when the sound is long *e*, except after *c*.**

EXAMPLES   bel**ie**ve   f**ie**ld   n**ie**ce   conc**ei**t   c**ei**ling

EXCEPTIONS   **ei**ther   l**ei**sure   n**ei**ther   s**ei**ze   prot**ei**n

28b. **Write *ei* when the sound is not long *e*.**

EXAMPLES   forf**ei**t   fr**ei**ght   **ei**ght   n**ei**ghbor   w**ei**gh

EXCEPTIONS   anc**ie**nt   v**ie**w   fr**ie**nd   misch**ie**f   consc**ie**nce

Exercise 2 **Spelling *ie* and *ei* Words**

Spell each of the following words correctly by supplying *ie* or *ei*.

EXAMPLE   1. retr . . . ve

       1. retrieve

1. gr . . . f
2. th . . . r
3. v . . . l
4. h . . . r
5. bel . . . f
6. counterf . . . t
7. dec . . . ve
8. ch . . . ftain
9. perc . . . ve
10. rec . . . pt
11. p . . . rce
12. w . . . ld
13. th . . . f
14. sl . . . gh
15. bes . . . ge
16. shr . . . k
17. f . . . rce
18. . . . ght
19. cash . . . r
20. y . . . ld

BORN LOSER reprinted by permission of Newspaper Enterprise Association, Inc.

–cede, –ceed, and –sede

28c. The only English word ending in *–sede* is *supersede*. The only English words ending in *–ceed* are *exceed, proceed,* and *succeed.* Most other words with this sound end in *–cede.*

EXAMPLES   ac**cede**   con**cede**   inter**cede**

                  pre**cede**   re**cede**   se**cede**

Adding Prefixes

Reference Note

For a list of **prefixes,** see "Reading and Vocabulary" in the Quick Reference Handbook.

A *prefix* is a letter or group of letters added to the beginning of a word or a root to create a new word.

EXAMPLES   il + legible = **il**legible   pre + historic = **pre**historic

                  in + correct = **in**correct   un + certain = **un**certain

28d. When adding a prefix, do not change the spelling of the original word.

EXAMPLES   dis + satisfy = dis**satisfy**   im + mature = im**mature**

                  mis + spell = mis**spell**   re + adjust = re**adjust**

Adding Suffixes

Reference Note

For a list of **suffixes,** see "Reading and Vocabulary" in the Quick Reference Handbook.

A *suffix* is a letter or group of letters added to the end of a word to create a new word.

EXAMPLES   help + less = help**less**   worry + ed = worri**ed**

                  move + ment = move**ment**   hope + ful = hope**ful**

28e. When adding the suffix *–ness* or *–ly*, do not change the spelling of the original word.

EXAMPLES   open + ness = **open**ness   normal + ly = **normal**ly

                  gentle + ness = **gentle**ness   final + ly = **final**ly

EXCEPTION   For most words ending in *y*, change the *y* to *i* before adding *–ness* or *–ly*.

                  messy + ness = mess**iness**   merry + ly = merr**ily**

                  heavy + ness = heav**iness**   ready + ly = read**ily**

HELP

One-syllable adjectives ending in *y* generally do not change the *y* to *i* before a suffix.

EXAMPLES
shy + ness = shy**ness**
sly + ly = sly**ly**

Exercise 3 **Spelling Words with Prefixes and Suffixes**

Spell each of the following words, adding the prefix or suffix given.

EXAMPLE   **1.** in + active

           1. inactive

1. mis + inform   **6.** crafty + ly

2. habitual + ly   **7.** in + animate

3. il + legal   **8.** im + movable

4. dis + appear   **9.** happy + ness

5. stubborn + ness   **10.** dis + similar

28f. Drop the final silent *e* before adding a suffix that begins with a vowel.

EXAMPLES   create + ive = **creat**ive   rate + ing = **rat**ing

               achieve + able = **achiev**able   simple + er = **simpl**er

EXCEPTIONS   **1.** Keep the final silent *e* in most words ending in *ce* or *ge* before a suffix that begins with *a* or *o*: peac**eable,** courag**eous.** Sometimes the *e* becomes *i,* as in spac*i*ous and grac*i*ous.

                   2. To avoid confusion with other words, keep the final silent *e* in some words: *dye*ing, *singe*ing (to prevent confusion with *dying* and *singing*).

                   3. mile + age = mileage

28g. Keep the final silent *e* before adding a suffix that begins with a consonant.

EXAMPLES   fate + ful = fat**eful**   time + ly = tim**ely**

            care + less = car**eless**   place + ment = plac**ement**

EXCEPTIONS   awe + ful = aw**ful**   true + ly = tru**ly**

             argue + ment = argu**ment**   nine + th = nin**th**

28h. For words ending in *y* preceded by a consonant, change the *y* to *i* before any suffix that does not begin with *i.*

EXAMPLES   sunny + est = sunn**iest**

            accompany + ment = accompan**iment**

            modify + ing = modif**ying**

┌─HELP──

When adding *–ing* to words that end in *ie,* drop the e and change the *i* to *y.*

EXAMPLES

   die + ing = d**ying**

   lie + ing = l**ying**

   tie + ing = t**ying**

MECHANICS

┌─HELP──

Some words can be spelled with or without the silent e before a suffix.

EXAMPLES

   judg**ment** or judg**ement**

   acknowledg**ment** or acknowledg**ement**

28i. For words ending in *y* preceded by a vowel, keep the *y* when adding a suffix.

EXAMPLES   gray + est = gra**yest**   obey + ing = obe**ying**

                 play + ed = pla**yed**   enjoy + ment = enjo**yment**

EXCEPTIONS   day—da**ily**   lay—la**id**   pay—pa**id**   say—sa**id**

Exercise 4   **Spelling Words with Suffixes**

Spell each of the following words, adding the suffix given.

EXAMPLE   1. delay + ed

              1. *delayed*

1. employ + ment
2. thrifty + ness
3. beauty + fy
4. abate + ment
5. sure + ly

6. notice + able
7. share + ing
8. glide + ed
9. loose + est
10. tie + ing

28j. Double the final consonant before a suffix that begins with a vowel if the word both (1) has only one syllable or has the accent on the last syllable and (2) ends in a single consonant preceded by a single vowel.

EXAMPLES   win + er = wi**nner**

               occur + ence = occu**rrence**

               snap + ing = sna**pping**

               refer + ed = refe**rred**

Do not double the final consonant unless the word satisfies both of the conditions.

EXAMPLES   prevent + ing = preven**ting** [*Prevent* has the accent on the last syllable but does not end in a single consonant preceded by a single vowel.]

               falcon + er = falco**ner** [*Falcon* ends in a single consonant preceded by a single vowel but does not have the accent on the last syllable.]

               refer + ence = refe**rence** [*Refer* satisfies both conditions, but the addition of a suffix causes a shift in the accent.]

⌐HELP—

The final consonant of some words may or may not be doubled. Either spelling is acceptable.

EXAMPLES
cancel + ed =
cance**led** or cance**lled**

travel + er = trave**ler** or trave**ller**

If you are not sure whether to double a final consonant, look up the word in a dictionary.

MECHANICS

Review A **Spelling Words with Suffixes**

Spell each of the following words, adding the suffix given.

EXAMPLE   **1.** exact + ly

        1. *exactly*

1. plan + ed
2. stop + er
3. friendly + er
4. achieve + ment
5. propel + er
6. seize + ure
7. definite + ly

8. joy + ful
9. argue + ment
10. prepare + ed
11. sly + ly
12. trace + able
13. wed + ing
14. happy + ly

15. sudden + ness
16. satisfy + ed
17. day + ly
18. prefer + ence
19. gentle + ly
20. steady + ing

Review B **Proofreading a Paragraph for Spelling Errors**

Proofread the following paragraph, and correct each misspelled word.

EXAMPLE   **[1]** The sceintist Granville T. Woods was quite an inventor.

        1. *sceintist—scientist*

[1] After leaveing school at the age of ten, Woods worked on the railroads in Missouri. [2] However, his love of electrical and mechanical devices led him to study engineering and later to open a factory where his managment skills and knowledge served him well. [3] Later, Woods succeded in devising a telegraph that allowed stationmasters to communicate with engineers on moving trains. [4] With this device, speeding trains could be notified of any problems along the track, and train engineers could quickly alert stations to dangerous situations. [5] His successes permitted Woods to relocate to New York City. [6] There he learned that the method the-aters used for diming lights was responsible for many fires. [7] Woods revaluated the design and devised a new system. [8] This new lighting system operated safly and was, at the same time, 40 percent more efficient than the old one. [9] Not surprisingly, com-panies like American Bell Telephone and General Electric payed generous sums for Woods's inven-tions. [10] In all, Woods recieved more than 150 patents for his inventions, and many of those inven-tions, such as the electrified rail for New York City's subway, are still in use.

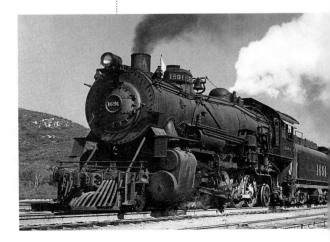

Forming the Plurals of Nouns

28k. Remembering the following rules will help you spell the plural forms of nouns.

(1) For most nouns, add _s_.

SINGULAR	dancer	beagle	ship	lake	parasol	Morrison
PLURAL	dancer**s**	beagle**s**	ship**s**	lake**s**	parasol**s**	Morrison**s**

(2) For nouns ending in _s, x, z, ch,_ or _sh_, add _es_.

SINGULAR	dress	fox	waltz	march	brush	Katz
PLURAL	dress**es**	fox**es**	waltz**es**	march**es**	brush**es**	Katz**es**

> **NOTE** Some one-syllable words ending in _z_ double the final consonant when forming plurals.
>
> EXAMPLES quiz—qui**zz**es   fez—fe**zz**es

(3) For nouns ending in _y_ preceded by a vowel, add _s_.

SINGULAR	essay	journey	Friday	decoy	tray	Bailey
PLURAL	essay**s**	journey**s**	Friday**s**	decoy**s**	tray**s**	Bailey**s**

(4) For nouns ending in _y_ preceded by a consonant, change the _y_ to _i_ and add _es_.

SINGULAR	sky	folly	comedy	trophy	cavity	theory
PLURAL	sk**ies**	foll**ies**	comed**ies**	troph**ies**	cavit**ies**	theor**ies**

EXCEPTION For proper nouns, simply add _s_.

Brodsky—Brodsky**s**   Gregory—Gregory**s**

(5) For some nouns ending in _f_ or _fe_, add _s_. For others, change the _f_ or _fe_ to _v_ and add _es_.

SINGULAR	gulf	roof	safe	leaf	shelf	knife
PLURAL	gulf**s**	roof**s**	safe**s**	lea**ves**	shel**ves**	kni**ves**

(6) For nouns ending in _o_ preceded by a vowel, add _s_.

SINGULAR	studio	radio	cameo	video	igloo	Antonio
PLURAL	studio**s**	radio**s**	cameo**s**	video**s**	igloo**s**	Antonio**s**

(7) For nouns ending in _o_ preceded by a consonant, add _es_.

SINGULAR	torpedo	tomato	hero	veto	potato
PLURAL	torpedo**es**	tomato**es**	hero**es**	veto**es**	potato**es**

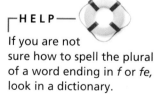

┌**HELP**──
If you are not sure how to spell the plural of a word ending in _f_ or _fe_, look in a dictionary.

MECHANICS

For proper nouns ending in *o* preceded by a consonant and for some common nouns, especially those referring to music, add only *s*.

SINGULAR	Alvarado	taco	photo	piano	solo
PLURAL	Alvarado**s**	taco**s**	photo**s**	piano**s**	solo**s**

NOTE For some nouns ending in *o* preceded by a consonant, you may add either *s* or *es*.

SINGULAR	motto	tornado	cargo	lasso	banjo
PLURAL	motto**s**	tornado**s**	cargo**s**	lasso**s**	banjo**s**
	or	*or*	*or*	*or*	*or*
	motto**es**	tornado**es**	cargo**es**	lasso**es**	banjo**es**

(8) The plurals of a few nouns are formed in irregular ways.

SINGULAR	tooth	goose	woman	mouse	ox	child
PLURAL	t**ee**th	g**ee**se	wom**en**	m**ice**	ox**en**	child**ren**

(9) For a few nouns, the singular and the plural forms are the same.

SINGULAR AND PLURAL	sheep	deer	Chinese
	moose	species	Japanese

(10) For most compound nouns, form the plural of only the last word of the compound.

SINGULAR	notebook	blueprint	disc jockey	two-year-old
PLURAL	notebook**s**	blueprint**s**	disc jockey**s**	two-year-old**s**

(11) For compound nouns in which one of the words is modified by the other word or words, form the plural of the noun modified.

SINGULAR	brother-in-law	passerby	rock garden
PLURAL	brother**s**-in-law	passer**s**by	rock garden**s**

NOTE Some compound nouns have two acceptable plural forms.

SINGULAR	attorney general	court-martial	notary public
PLURAL	attorney general**s**	court-martial**s**	notary public**s**
	or	*or*	*or*
	attorney**s** general	court**s**-martial	notar**ies** public

---

HELP

If you are ever in doubt about the plural form of a noun ending in *o* preceded by a consonant, check the spelling in a dictionary.

STYLE TIP

When it refers to a computer device, the word *mouse* can be made plural in either of two ways—*mouses* or *mice*. Someday, one of these forms may be the preferred style. For now, either is correct.

MECHANICS

HELP

Check an up-to-date dictionary whenever you are in doubt about the plural form of a compound noun.

28 k

Spelling Rules **851**

STYLE TIP

The plural form *alumni* is used to refer to graduates of a coeducational school.

(12) **For some nouns borrowed from other languages, the plural is formed as in the original languages.**

SINGULAR	alumnus [male]	alumna [female]	phenomenon
PLURAL	alumn**i** [male]	alumn**ae** [female]	phenomen**a**

A few nouns borrowed from other languages have two plural forms. For each of the following nouns, the plural form preferred in English is given first.

SINGULAR	index	appendix	formula	cherub	cactus
PLURAL	index**es**	appendix**es**	formula**s**	cherub**s**	cactus**es**
	or	*or*	*or*	*or*	*or*
	ind**ices**	append**ices**	formul**ae**	cherub**im**	cact**i**

TIPS & TRICKS

It is not incorrect to add both an apostrophe and an *s* to form the plurals of numerals, letters, symbols, and words used as words. Therefore, if you have any doubt about whether or not to use the apostrophe, use it.

(13) **To form the plural of numerals, most uppercase letters, symbols, and words used as words, add either an *s* or both an apostrophe and an *s*.**

SINGULAR	8	1760	Q	&	and
PLURAL	8**s**	1760**s**	Q**s**	&**s**	and**s**
	or	*or*	*or*	*or*	*or*
	8**'s**	1760**'s**	Q**'s**	&**'s**	and**'s**

To prevent confusion, add both an apostrophe and an *s* to form the plural of all lowercase letters, certain uppercase letters, and some words used as words.

EXAMPLES   The word *Mississippi* contains four *s***'s** and four *i***'s.** [Without an apostrophe, the plural of *s* would look awkward, and the plural of *i* could be confused with *is.*]

Sebastian usually makes straight A**'s.** [Without an apostrophe, the plural of *A* could be confused with *As.*]

Because I mistakenly thought Evelyn Waugh was a woman, I used *her***'s** instead of *his***'s** in my paragraph. [Without an apostrophe, the plural of *her* would look like the possessive pronoun *hers* and the plural of *his* would look like the word *hiss.*]

NOTE   To form the plural of an abbreviation that includes periods, add both an apostrophe and an *s.* To form the plural of an abbreviation that does not include periods, add an apostrophe and an *s,* or add only an *s.*

EXAMPLES   Ph.D.—Ph.D.**'s**   CD—CD**'s** *or* CD**s**

Exercise 5 Spelling the Plural Forms of Nouns

Spell the plural form of each of the following nouns.

EXAMPLE **1.** shelf

    1. shelves

1. elk   **8.** box   **15.** Murphy
2. *o*   **9.** half   **16.** gulf
3. turkey   **10.** echo   **17.** penny
4. niece   **11.** soprano   **18.** father-in-law
5. politics   **12.** life   **19.** merry-go-round
6. valley   **13.** phenomenon   **20.** 1700
7. try   **14.** bunch

Review C Proofreading for Spelling Errors

Correct each misspelled word in the following sentences.

EXAMPLES **1.** After we renter the program, the cursor vanishs.

    1. reenter, vanishes

    2. David displays his trophys on a shelf in his room.

    2. trophies

1. Many varietys of fish thrive near continental shelfs.
2. Be more careful; your *a*s look like *o*s.
3. At center stage, two identical black grand pianoes stood facing each other like dinosaures.
4. What a horrific three-year struggle Hernando De Soto and his mans must have had as they made thier way through swamps and mosquitos and past alligatores and rattlesnakes.
5. Gracefuly, the mountain goats leap from rock to rock.
6. Not everyone succedes in mastering the art of *chanoyu*, the Japanese tea ceremony.
7. Walter E. Massey, Ph.D., a physicist, did much to bring the sceinces to both private industryies and schools.
8. These bootes are woven with a special material that keeps your foots warm.
9. Three sharp buzzs startled the workers who were eating their lunchs in the lounge.
10. Each of the runner-ups uneasly shifted from one foot to the other as she awaited the announcment.

┌─HELP─

No proper nouns or foreign words in Review C are misspelled.

MECHANICS

┌HELP─┐

Generally, you should not spell out some numbers and use numerals for others in the same context. Be consistent by using numerals to express all of the numbers.

INCONSISTENT
Shakespeare wrote thirty-seven plays and 154 sonnets.

CONSISTENT
Shakespeare wrote **37** plays and **154** sonnets.

However, to distinguish between numbers that appear beside each other but that count different things, spell out one number, and use numerals for the other.

EXAMPLE
I need to buy **ten 33**-cent stamps.

┌STYLE   TIP┐

In sentences, spell out the names of units of measurement (such as *ounces* and *feet*) whether they stand alone or follow numerals or spelled-out numbers. In charts and tables, however, you may use the abbreviations for units of measurement (such as *oz* and *ft*) when they follow numerals.

Writing Numbers

28l. Spell out a *cardinal number*—a number that shows how many—if it can be expressed in one or two words. Otherwise, use numerals.

EXAMPLES	**seven** juniors	**203** juniors
	fifty-one votes	**421** votes
	one thousand miles	**1,242** miles

28m. Spell out a number that begins a sentence.

EXAMPLES **Eighty-eight** senators voted in favor of the bill.

Three hundred thirty-two wreaths were sold.

If the number appears awkward when spelled out, revise the sentence so that it does not begin with the number.

AWKWARD Two thousand five hundred sixty-four pounds is the combined weight of those sumo wrestlers.

IMPROVED The combined weight of those sumo wrestlers is **2,564** pounds.

28n. Spell out *ordinal numbers*—numbers that express order.

EXAMPLES Thurgood Marshall was the **first** [not *1st*] African American to serve on the U.S. Supreme Court.

The Rio Grande is the **twenty-second** [not *22nd*] longest river in the world.

28o. Use numerals to express numbers in conventional situations.

Conventional situations include

• identification numbers

EXAMPLES	Chapter **26**	pages **41–54**
	Interstate **20**	lines **10–14**
	Act **5**	Channel **8**

• measurements/statistics

EXAMPLES	**98.6** degrees	**42** years old
	14.3 ounces	**4 1/2** feet
	8 percent	ratio of **5** to **1**

- addresses

EXAMPLE   **512** Willow Drive
            Arrowhead, DE **34322-0422**

- dates

EXAMPLES   July **7, 1999**   **44** B.C.   A.D. **145**

- times of day

EXAMPLES   **6:20** P.M.   **8:00** A.M.

NOTE   Spell out a number used with *o'clock.*

EXAMPLE   **nine** o'clock

Exercise 6   Proofreading for Spelling Errors

Proofread the following sentences, and correct each misspelled or
incorrectly written numerical expression.

EXAMPLE   1. 50 dollars for a pair of socks—let's get out of here!
            1. *50—Fifty*

1. Not all Viking funerals involved burning a ship; a 30-foot vessel
   replete with thirty-two shields has been found buried in Norway.
2. Take State Road Seventeen straight down to Arcadia, and you'll be
   there by three P.M.
3. Pearls are weighed by grains, with 128,000 grains (that's about
   fourteen pounds) belonging to the heaviest pearl, which happened
   to be produced by an abalone.
4. I am not sure, but I think that Sergio and I are the 19th and 20th
   players to register.
5. The honor of being the 1st African American novelist belongs to
   William Wells Brown, whose novel *Clotel* was published in 1853.
6. Mom, for the third time in 2 days, Channel thirty-eight isn't
   coming in again.
7. On the Fahrenheit scale, two hundred twelve degrees is the boiling
   point of water; this temperature equals one hundred degrees on
   the Celsius scale.
8. On page twelve, you'll find a map of what the Bering Land Bridge
   might have looked like at that time.
9. Meet us at 10 o'clock Saturday morning at 459 Keeshond Drive.
10. 1 was delivered yesterday; the other 3 should be here tomorrow.

STYLE   TIP

Do not use *A.M.* or *P.M.*
with a spelled-out number
or as a substitute for the
word *morning, afternoon,*
or *evening.*

EXAMPLES
Soccer practice begins
at **4:00 P.M.**

Come home at **four
o'clock in the afternoon.**

We'll go fishing early in
the **morning.**

Reference Note

For information about
hyphenating numbers,
see page 835.

STYLE   TIP

For large round numbers,
you may use words or a
combination of words and
numerals.

EXAMPLES
13,700,000 people *or*
13.7 million people

MECHANICS

Review D Proofreading a Paragraph for Spelling Errors

Proofread the following paragraph, and correct each misspelled word or incorrectly written numerical expression.

EXAMPLE   [1] What is the 1st thing that comes to mind when you hear the name Hermann Rorschach?

1. 1st—first

[1] Does this inkblot remind you of monkies? [2] Maybe you see faces and bodies of several people and animals, some faceing toward you and others facing in different directions. [3] Then again, maybe four geese chasing a dozen mice down Interstate Four is the image that comes to your mind as you gaze at the shapes in this inkblot. [4] To psychiatrists and psychologists who have taken special class's, the pictures that you imagine are really images of your own mind. [5] 1 of ten standard inkblots, this design is part of a special psychological test devised by Hermann Rorschach. [6] Although Rorschach was not the 1st to study inkblots and the imagination, his inkblots are one of the most famous methods of gaining insights into people's minds. [7] As you might suspect, a group of five-years-olds will see very different images in these inkblots than a group of adults will. [8] By having a person describe what he or she saw in each inkblot, Rorschach was able to infer a great deal about that person's fears, beliefes, desires, and hopes. [9] For example, what does it mean if you see seven tacos playing banjos made of white potatos, waltzing with two walruses on loaves of bread? [10] Maybe you're hungry, or maybe you feel like danceing and it's time to put on your tap shoe's.

Words Often Confused

You can prevent many spelling errors by learning the difference between the words grouped together in this section. Some of them are confusing because they are *homonyms*—that is, they are pronounced alike. Others are confusing because they are spelled the same or nearly the same.

Reference Note

If there is a word you cannot find in the list of words often confused, refer to the **Glossary of Usage** in Chapter 24, or look up the word in a dictionary.

all ready	[adjective] *all prepared* The players were *all ready* for the game.
already	[adverb] *previously* Jenna has *already* studied that chapter.
all right	[adjective] *satisfactory;* [adverb] *satisfactorily* The text was difficult, but Sam's translation was *all right.* I think I did *all right* on the quiz. [Although the spelling *alright* appears in some dictionaries, it has not become standard usage.]
all together	[adjective] *in the same place;* [adverb] *at the same time* My family will be *all together* for Thanksgiving. Please sing *all together* now.
altogether	[adverb] *entirely* Ms. Shapiro is *altogether* in favor of having a referendum.
altar	[noun] *a table or stand at which religious rites are performed* This is the *altar* used in the Communion service.
alter	[verb] *to change* Do not *alter* your plans on my account.
ascent	[noun] *a rise; a climb* The climbers' *ascent* was a slow one.
assent	[verb] *to agree;* [noun] *consent* Will they *assent* to our proposal? Our last proposal won their *assent.*
born	[verb form] *given life* Ynes Mexia was *born* in Washington, D.C.
borne	[verb form] *carried; endured* They have *borne* their troubles better than we thought they would.

(continued)

(continued)

brake	[verb] *to stop or slow down;* [noun] *a device for stopping or slowing down* He *braked* and swerved to avoid hitting the child. An automobile *brake* will overheat if used too often.
break	[verb] *to cause to come apart; to shatter;* [noun] *a fracture* If you're not careful, you'll *break* the mirror. The *break* in the bone will heal in six weeks.
capital	[noun] *a city that is the seat of government of a country or state; money or property;* [adjective] *punishable by death; an uppercase letter; important, serious* Manila is the *capital* of the Philippines. The company has *capital* of $100,000. *Capital* punishment was the subject of the debate. A proper noun begins with a *capital* letter. That is an issue of *capital* concern.
capitol	[noun] *building in which a legislature meets* [capitalized when it refers to the building where the U.S. Congress meets] The *capitol* in Austin is a tourist attraction. Meet us in front of the *Capitol* in Washington, D.C.
clothes	[noun] *apparel* I'd like to buy some summer *clothes*.
cloths	[noun] *pieces of fabric* Please use these *cloths* to clean the car.

┌**HELP**──
To remember
the spelling of *capitol,* use
this sentence: The capit**o**l
has a d**o**me.

Exercise 7 Distinguishing Between Words Often Confused

From the choices in parentheses, select the correct word or words for each of the following sentences.

EXAMPLE   **1.** My sister Lela was (*born, borne*) on March 5, 1985.

        1. born

1. Your arguments are not (*all together, altogether*) convincing.
2. We have finished packing and are (*all ready, already*) to go.
3. Saying nothing, the major gave a nod of (*ascent, assent*).
4. At night, Tokyo, the (*capital, capitol*) of Japan, is filled with vivid neon lights advertising all sorts of shops, clubs, and products.

5. The little boy was scared but otherwise (*all right, alright*).

6. Slow down! Please keep your foot on the (*brake, break*).

7. The expenditures will be (*born, borne*) by the taxpayers.

8. Seminole jackets are made from long, narrow strips of different-colored (*cloths, clothes*) carefully sewn together to make one garment.

9. The new dam will (*altar, alter*) the course of the river.

10. The governor said the roof of the (*capital, capitol*) needs repair.

coarse	[adjective] *rough, crude* The driveway was covered with *coarse* sand. His *coarse* language and manners prevented him from getting the job.
course	[noun] *path of action, passage, or way; study or group of studies; part of a meal;* [also used with *of* to mean *naturally* or *certainly*] What *course* do you think I should follow? The *course* in world history lasts a full year. My favorite main *course* is bolichi. Of *course*, you may go with us.
complement	[noun] *something that makes whole or complete;* [verb] *to make whole or complete* The diagram shows that the angle *WXY* is the *complement* of the angle *YXZ*. A good shortstop would *complement* the team.
compliment	[noun] *praise; respect;* [verb] *to express praise or respect* The performer was pleased and flattered by the critic's *compliments*. Did the critics *compliment* all of the other performers, too?
consul	[noun] *a person appointed by a government to serve its citizens in a foreign country* The Israeli *consul* held a press conference to pledge his support for the peace talks.
council	[noun] *a group assembled for conferences or legislation* The student *council* meets this afternoon.
counsel	[noun] *advice;* [verb] *to advise* Shandra sought *counsel* from Mr. Nakai. Mr. Nakai *counseled* her to apply for the scholarship.

—HELP—

To remember the spelling of *complement,* keep in mind that a complement completes.

MECHANICS

(continued)

(continued)

councilor	[noun] *a member of a council* The city *councilors* met together for several hours but could not agree.
counselor	[noun] *one who gives advice* Shandra's guidance *counselor* helped her complete the application.
desert	[noun, pronounced des'•ert] *a dry region* Irrigation has brought new life to the *desert*.
desert	[verb, pronounced de•sert'] *to leave or abandon* A good soldier never *deserts* his or her post.
dessert	[noun, pronounced des•sert'] *a sweet, final course of a meal* My favorite *dessert* is frozen yogurt with strawberries on top.
formally	[adverb] *in a strict or dignified manner* Mayor Pérez will *formally* open the new recreation center on Wednesday.
formerly	[adverb] *previously* Mrs. Ling was *formerly* the head of the math department at Leland High School.
ingenious	[adjective] *clever, resourceful, skillful* Carla has an *ingenious* plan to earn some money this summer.
ingenuous	[adjective] *innocent, trusting, frank* Ian is as *ingenuous* as a five-year-old child.
its	[possessive form of the pronoun *it*] *belonging to it* Our city must increase *its* water supply.
it's	[contraction of *it is* or *it has*] *It's* almost time for the bell to ring. *It's* been nice talking to you.
later	[adjective] *more late;* [adverb] *at a subsequent time* I wasn't on time, but you were even *later*. I'll see you *later*.
latter	[adjective] *the second of two* (as opposed to *former*) Dr. Edwards can see you in the morning or the afternoon, but the *latter* time is more convenient for her.

MECHANICS

lead	[verb, pronounced "leed"] *to go first; to guide*
	Who will *lead* the discussion group?
led	[verb, past tense of *lead*]
	Elaine *led* the band onto the field.
lead	[noun, pronounced "led"] *a heavy metal; graphite in a pencil*
	The mechanic used small weights made of *lead* to balance the wheel
	My pencil *lead* broke during the test.

Exercise 8 **Distinguishing Between Words Often Confused**

For each of the following sentences, select the correct word from the pair in parentheses.

EXAMPLE   1. Are you taking a (*coarse, course*) in computer programming?

1. *course*

1. Court is (*formally, formerly*) opened with a bailiff's cry of "Oyez, Oyez!"
2. When her painting was displayed in the museum, the artist received many (*complements, compliments*).
3. After dinner, my new stepfather sometimes says, "What's next—(*desert, dessert*) or (*desert, dessert*) the table?"
4. The development of synthetic fibers must have required an (*ingenious, ingenuous*) mind.
5. I enjoy both chicken and fish but prefer the (*later, latter*).
6. One of the guidance (*councilors, counselors*) (*lead, led*) me to information on a new (*coarse, course*) of study.
7. Do you find the texture rather (*coarse, course*)?
8. Ebenezer D. Basset, the first African American diplomat, was appointed minister to Haiti by President Grant; Basset later served as Haiti's (*consul, council*) general.

I'M SORRY, DID I SAY "DESERT"? I MEANT "DESSERT" TRAY.

MECHANICS

9. Do you know the song "(*Its, It's*) Later Than You Think"?

10. The stark simplicity of the sand painting forms a perfect (*complement, compliment*) to its complex spiritual meaning.

loose	[adjective, rhymes with *noose*] *not firmly fastened; not tight* The front wheel on your bike is *loose*. Clothes with a *loose* fit are stylish now.
lose	[verb, rhymes with *shoes*] *to suffer loss* The trees will *lose* their leaves soon.
miner	[noun] *a worker in a mine* American *miners* lead the world in the production of coal.
minor	[noun] *a person under legal age;* [adjective] *of small importance* (as opposed to *major*) A *minor* is not permitted to sign the form. Let's not list any of the *minor* objections to the plan.
moral	[adjective] *good, virtuous;* [noun] *a lesson of conduct derived from a story or event* Good conduct is based upon *moral* principles. The *moral* of this old folk tale is "Be true to yourself."
morale	[noun] *spirit; mental condition* Teamwork is impossible without good *morale*.
passed	[verb, past tense of *pass*] *went by* The deadline for applications *passed* already.
past	[adjective] *ended;* [noun] *time gone by;* [preposition] *farther than, beyond* This *past* week has been a nightmare. History is the study of the *past*. We walked *past* the bookstore.
peace	[noun] *calmness* (as opposed to *strife* or *war*) Disarmament is an important step toward *peace*.
piece	[noun] *a part of something;* [verb] *to assemble slowly* Four *pieces* of the puzzle are missing. The detective *pieced* the clues together.

TIPS & TRICKS

To remember the spelling of *piece*, use this sentence: I'd like a **pie**ce of **pie.**

personal	[adjective] *individual; private* My *personal* opinion has nothing to do with the case. Do you truly feel that details of the candidates' *personal* lives should be made public?
personnel	[noun] *a group of people employed in the same work or service* Most companies prefer to recruit executive *personnel* from among college graduates.
plain	[adjective] *not fancy, undecorated; clear;* [noun] *a large area of flat land* The new uniforms are *plain,* but quite attractive. Does my explanation make things *plain* to you? Many Western movies are set in the Great *Plains.*
plane	[noun] *a flat surface; a woodworking tool; an airplane* Some problems in physics deal with the mechanical advantage of an inclined *plane.* Use this *plane* to make the wood smooth. We watched the *plane* circle for its landing.
principal	[noun] *the head of a school;* [adjective] *main, most important* The *principal* will address the entire student body. Florida and California are our *principal* citrus-growing states.
principle	[noun] *a rule of conduct; a fact or a general truth* The *principle* of the Golden Rule is found in many religions. The author was trying to convey a *principle.*
quiet	[adjective] *still, silent* The library is usually a *quiet* place to study.
quite	[adverb] *completely; rather; very* Are you *quite* finished? We are *quite* proud of Angel's achievements.
rout	[noun] *a disorderly flight;* [verb] *to put to flight; to defeat overwhelmingly* What began as an orderly retreat ended as a *rout.* The coach predicts that his Bears will *rout* the Wildcats in the playoffs.
route	[noun] *a road; a way to go* This highway is the shortest *route.*

TIPS & TRICKS

To remember the spelling of *principal,* use this sentence: The princi**pal** is your **pal.**

MECHANICS

For each of the following sentences, select the correct word from the pair in parentheses.

EXAMPLE 1. Have you met Ms. Cordero, our new (*principal, principle*)?

1. *principal*

1. The (*principal, principle*) duty of Surgeon General Antonia Novello was to safeguard the health of Americans.
2. In the recent (*passed, past*), automated methods of extracting ore have put thousands of (*miners, minors*) out of work.
3. Coral has a sign on her desk in the library: "(*Quiet, Quite*) please. Genius at work."
4. When Kurt's (*plain, plane*) failed to return, the (*moral, morale*) of his squadron sank to zero.
5. The accident that completely demolished the car was caused by a (*loose, lose*) cotter pin worth ten cents.
6. Follow the marked (*rout, route*), or you will surely (*loose, lose*) your way.
7. The (*principal, principle*) that underlies that company's choice of (*personal, personnel*) is "An educated person is usually willing to learn more."
8. The columnist described the game as a (*rout, route*) for our team.
9. To prevent infection, always apply first aid to (*miner, minor*) cuts.
10. For his contributions toward ending the first Arab-Israeli war, Dr. Ralph J. Bunche received the Nobel Prize for (*piece, peace*) in 1950.

┌ TIPS & TRICKS ┐

To remember the spelling of *stationery,* use this sentence: You write a letter on station**e**ry.

stationary	[adjective] *in a fixed position* The new state power plant contains large *stationary* engines.
stationery	[noun] *writing paper* I save my best *stationery* for important letters.
straight	[adjective] *not crooked or curved; direct* Draw a *straight* line that connects points A and B.
strait	[noun] *channel connecting two large bodies of water;* [noun, usually plural] *difficulty; distress* The *Strait* of Gibraltar links the Atlantic Ocean and the Mediterranean Sea. His family helps him when he is in bad *straits.*

MECHANICS

than	[conjunction, used for comparisons] Loretta is taller *than* I am.
then	[adverb] *at that time; next* We lived on Garden Street until last year; *then* we moved to our new house.
their	[possessive form of the pronoun *they*] *belonging* *to them* The singers are practicing *their* parts.
there	[adverb] *at that place;* [also an expletive, used to begin a sentence] The chorus director will be *there* soon. *There* will be two performances of the concert.
they're	[contraction of *they are*] *They're* presenting the concert next weekend.
theirs	[possessive form of the pronoun *they*] *something* *belonging to them* The fence separates our property from *theirs*.
there's	[contraction of *there is* or *there has*] *There's* one other way to solve the problem. *There's* been a change in the softball team's starting lineup.
to	[preposition; sign of the infinitive form of a verb] Let's go *to* the movies. After the rain, the birds began *to* sing.
too	[adverb] *more than enough; also* Is it *too* far to walk? You, *too*, are invited to the sports banquet.

two	[adjective] *one plus one;* [noun] *the number*
	    between one and three; a pair
	They serve *two* flavors: vanilla and chocolate.
	
	Two of my favorite writers are Nadine Gordimer
	    and Ntozake Shange.

waist	[noun] *the midsection of the body* These slacks are too tight at the *waist*.

waste	[noun] *useless spending; unused or useless material;*
	    [verb] *to use foolishly*
	The movie last night was simply a *waste* of two hours
	    of my time.
	
	Don't *waste* your money on movies like that.

(continued)

MECHANICS

(continued)

weather	[noun] *atmospheric conditions* We had good *weather* for the picnic.
whether	[conjunction indicating an alternative or doubt] I don't know *whether* Denzel will help us.
who's	[contraction of *who is* or *who has*] *Who's* [Who is] going to take the dog to the vet's office? *Who's* [Who has] been tutoring you?
whose	[possessive form of *who*] *belonging to whom* *Whose* earrings are these?
your	[possessive form of the pronoun *you*] *belonging to you* Is *your* sister still in college?
you're	[contraction of *you are*] If *you're* not busy, let's discuss the assignment.

Exercise 10 **Distinguishing Between Words Often Confused**

For each of the following sentences, select the correct word or words from the choices given in parentheses.

EXAMPLE   **1.** (*Who's, Whose*) golf clubs are these?

   1. Whose

1. (*Their, There*) Great Dane is even taller and heavier (*than, then*) (*your, you're*) Irish wolfhound.
2. Since the roof of the stadium is not (*stationary, stationery*), we can put it up or take it down as needed.
3. If the (*weather, whether*) isn't (*to, too, two*) awful, we will go (*to, too, two*) the game.
4. The women over (*there, their, they're*) are wearing *rebozos,* versatile shawls worn over the head, around the shoulders, or about the (*waist, waste*).
5. (*Who's, Whose*) planning to write a term paper about Ida Tarbell?
6. That is not (*your, you're*) car; (*who's, whose*) is it—(*there's, theirs*)?
7. I wonder how many tons of food are (*waisted, wasted*) every year in the United States.
8. What did (*your, you're*) family say when you told them about the scholarship (*your, you're*) going to get?

9. What styles of (*stationary, stationery*) did you order for the class pen-pal project?

10. Deep in the jungles of Cambodia lies a maze of (*straight, strait*) roads and canals that were part of the ancient Khmer capital of Angkor Thom.

Review E **Proofreading Paragraphs for Errors in Spelling and Words Often Confused**

Proofread the following paragraphs, and correct each misspelled or misused word. If a sentence is already correct, write *C*.

EXAMPLE **[1]** On my trip to Peru, I learned a great deal about the anceint Nazca people.

1. *anceint—ancient*

┌HELP┐

No proper nouns or proper adjectives in Review E are misspelled.

[1] Last winter, as we flew over the Nazca Plains of Peru, I took photographs of the eighteen famous images that have puzzled archaeologists for years. [2] Excitement rippled through the aircraft as the dessert seemed to come alive with mysterious images like this one. [3] Although the group of figures covers two hundred square miles, each figure is made only of lose mounds of rocks and pebbles. [4] The dry whether in the region has preserved these fragile images for more than fifteen hundred years.

[5] Because many of the designs cannot be perceived from the ground, some people believe that the Nazca had aircraft, perhaps balloons or huge kites, capable of an assent to a thousand feet or more. [6] To test this hypothesis, one group of investigators actually

MECHANICS

constructed a crude hot-air balloon made of course vegetable fiber. [7] A violent gust threw the balloon and it's passengers to the ground before a strong wind carried them some three miles away.

[8] One of the more astounding theories about the designs is that the strait lines were landing strips for spaceships. [9] Other theorists wonder whether the flight routs of the birds represented by some of the patterns helped warn the Nazca of cold winds and rain. [10] Maria Reiche, an astronomer and mathematician who has studied the area, believes that the lines form an ingenuous calendar. [11] However, a computer analysis of lunar and solar patterns has lead other astronomers to doubt this theory.

[12] As our plane landed, we tourists were already for a closer look at these weird figures. [13] Early the next day, we met our tour guide in front of the hotel and boarded a small bus; than we headed for the Nazca lines.

[14] Our guide told us that parts of the fragile figures have all ready been ruined by car and foot traffic. [15] Following the consul of Maria Reiche, the Peruvian government no longer allows tourists to walk or drive over the area. [16] Consequently, we could view the figures only from an observation tower that had been built close too them. [17] Nevertheless, we were quiet impressed by the amount of planning and work that must have been required to create these fascinating lines.

[18] When our guide signaled us back to the bus, I picked up a stone and, for a moment, wondered whether I held a peace of history in my hand; then I carefully placed the stone back where I had found it. [19] Latter, I sat in my hotel room and thought about the Nazca and the unusual images they had made. [20] Who, I wondered, were these ancient people who's achievements continue to baffle modern science?

Chapter Review

A. Recognizing Misspelled Words

Correctly write the word in each group that is spelled incorrectly.

1. modifying, trodden, recieve
2. studios, disimilar, craftily
3. emptiness, handkerchiefs, desireable
4. journies, runners-up, freight
5. formaly, relief, illegible
6. surely, propeller, excede
7. alumna, iciness, managable
8. secede, indices, infered
9. precede, dareing, unforgettable
10. nineth, loneliness, adorable
11. gently, merryment, referral
12. kindlyness, adjustment, carefully
13. frayed, winning, dissappear
14. conceed, conceited, considered
15. rueful, augmented, earlyest

B. Proofreading a Paragraph for Spelling Errors

Correctly write each misspelled or incorrectly used word or numeral in the following paragraph.

[16] 150 people attended the program on San Francisco, and I'm sure no one was disappointed. [17] We learned many facts about the "City by the Bay" and discovered that it is an enchantting place. [18] In the 1st part of the program, the speaker showed slides of various landmarks, including the Golden Gate Bridge, Telegraph Hill, and The Palace of Fine Arts. [19] The size of Golden Gate Park surprised me; it covers more than 1,000 acres! [20] We also saw many photoes of the city's famous cable cars and of Lombard Street. [21] I could understand why Lombard Street is called the Crookeddest Street in the World! [22] Everyone enjoied seeing pictures of San Francisco's colorful Chinatown, as well. [23] Finally, the speaker told us about Union Square, a famous shopping area, and said that shoppers would not be

disatisfied there. [24] I would like time to explore the city's sights and sounds at my liesure. [25] Because of the presentation, my previous travel desires have been superceded by a longing to go to San Francisco.

C. Forming the Plural Forms of Words

Write the correct plural form of each of the following words.

26. 1980

27. species

28. phenomenon

29. two-year-old

30. dictionary

31. Getty

32. president-elect

33. lynx

34. calf

35. Coronado

36. boxer

37. array

38. zero

39. goose

40. house

D. Distinguishing Between Words Often Confused

In each of the following sentences, write the correct word of the pair in parentheses.

41. The ancient Egyptians developed an (*ingenuous, ingenious*) method of irrigating crops.

42. "I have trouble remembering whether Abraham Lincoln was (*borne, born*) in Illinois or in Kentucky," William said.

43. "Both states are important in Lincoln's life, but he was born in the (*later, latter*) state," Mr. Gallegos said.

44. Many places are named for famous explorers, such as the (*Straight, Strait*) of Magellan, named after Ferdinand Magellan.

45. That ornate (*altar, alter*) was made by a Bavarian woodcarver.

46. Let's ask the team members if (*they're, their*) willing to participate in the highway cleanup project.

47. Congress must give its (*ascent, assent*) before a bill can become a law.

48. Which (*rout, route*) to the stadium has fewer traffic lights?

49. The trail to the ruins is longer (*than, then*) it looks.

50. "I don't buy much (*stationary, stationery*) now that I use e-mail," Mandy said.

Writing Application
Using Correct Spelling in a Paragraph

Words Often Confused   Write a paragraph about your favorite CD or television show. Be sure to use correctly at least five of the words that are listed in this chapter as Words Often Confused.

Prewriting   Pick a favorite CD or television show and make a list of the reasons you prefer it over other music or shows. If you decide to write about a television show, for example, you may want to compare it to a similar television show.

Writing   As you write your first draft, be sure to include information about the CD or television show, such as who wrote the music or the show, who directed or produced it, or who performed the music or acted on the program. Remember to use a dictionary to help with correct spelling.

Revising   As you read your draft, make sure you have used enough details to support your reasons. Check the organization of your comparisons. Are they in a clear and logical order?

Publishing   Check your paragraph for spelling mistakes. Use a computer spellchecker, if one is available, but remember that spellcheckers will not recognize a misused word (for example, *principle* for *principal*), as opposed to a misspelled word. Also, pay attention to the spelling of foreign words, and consult a dictionary if you have any doubt. Exchange your report with a partner, and check each other's spelling. Read your report aloud to the class and compare each other's favorite CDs and television shows.

MECHANICS

300 Spelling Words

The following list contains three hundred commonly misspelled words. To master any words that give you difficulty, follow the procedure given at the beginning of this chapter.

accidentally
accommodate
accurate
acknowledgment *or*
    acknowledgement
acquaintance
across
aerial
aisle
all right
always
amateur
analyze
announce
anonymous
apologize
appearance
appreciate
approaching
appropriate
approval
arctic
argument
arrangement
assassinate
association
athletics
atomic
attach
attention
attitude
auxiliary
awful
awkward

bachelor
background

banana
bargain
beggar
beginning
believe
benefited
bicycle
biscuit
bookkeeper
bracelet
breathe
bruise
bulletin
bureau
business

calendar
campaign
candidate
catastrophe
cellophane
cemetery
ceremony
challenge
chaperon *or*
    chaperone
classroom
college
colonel
colossal
column
commission
committee
comparatively
compel
competition
completely

complexion
concentrate
conscience
conscientious
contemptible
convenience
copies
cordially
corps
correspondence
corroborate
courageous
courteous
criticism
criticize
cylinder

decide
decision
defense
definitely
dependent
descendant
descent
description
desirable
develop
dictionary
different
dining
dinosaur
disappear
disappoint
discipline
discuss
disease
dissatisfied

divided
doesn't

economical
efficient
eighth
elementary
eligible
embarrass
emphasize
endeavor
environment
equipment
especially
etiquette
exaggerate
excellent
excitement
exercise
exhausted
existence
expense
experienced
extraordinary

familiar
fascinating
fatigue
February
feminine
fiery
financial
foreign
forfeit
fourth
fragile

generally

genius
government
governor
grammar
grateful
guarantee
guard
gymnasium

handkerchief
happened
harass
haven't
height
heroes
hindrance
hoping
horizon
hospital
humorous

imitation
immediately
incident
inconvenience
indispensable
inevitable
influence
initial
interpreted
interrupted
irrelevant
irresistible

jewelry

laboratory
leisure
license
lightning
likelihood
literacy
loneliness
losing

luxurious

maintenance
maneuver
marriage
matinee *or*
    matinée
meant
medicine
medieval
mentioned
microphone
minimum
mischievous
missile
misspelled
movable *or*
    moveable
municipal

necessary
neighbors
nickel
ninety
ninth
nonsense
noticeable
nuclear
nuisance

occasionally
occur
occurred
omitted
opinion
opportunity
optimistic

pamphlet
parallel
parliament
particularly
pastime
permanent

permissible
perseverance
personally
personnel
perspiration
persuade
playwright
pleasant
pneumonia
possess
possibility
potato
practice
preference
prejudice
privilege
probably
procedure
professor
pronunciation
propaganda
propeller
prophecy
psychology
pursue

questionnaire

realize
receive
recognize
recommend
referral
rehearse
reign
relief
repetition
representative
restaurant
rhythm

satisfactorily
schedule
scissors

seize
semester
separate
sergeant
shiny
siege
similar
sincerely
souvenir
straight
strategy
subtle
successful
sufficient
suppress
surprised
suspension
syllable
sympathy
synonym

tariff
television
temperament
temperature
thoroughly
tomorrow
tournament
traffic
tragedy
transferred
twelfth
tyranny

undoubtedly
unforgettable
unfortunately
unnecessary

vacuum
valuable
villain

weird

Correcting Common Errors

Key Language Skills Review

This chapter reviews key skills and concepts that pose special problems for writers.

- **Sentence Fragments and Run-on Sentences**
- **Subject-Verb and Pronoun-Antecedent Agreement**
- **Clear Pronoun Reference**
- **Verb Forms**
- **Comparison of Modifiers**
- **Misplaced and Dangling Modifiers**
- **Standard Usage**
- **Capitalization**
- **Punctuation—End Marks, Commas, Semicolons, Colons, Quotation Marks, and Apostrophes**
- **Spelling**

Most of the exercises in this chapter follow the same format as the exercises found throughout the grammar, usage, and mechanics sections of this book. You will notice, however, that two sets of review exercises are presented in standardized test formats. These exercises are designed to provide you with practice not only in solving usage and mechanics problems but also in dealing with such problems on standardized tests.

Exercise 1 — Identifying and Revising Sentence Fragments

Decide which of the following word groups are sentences and which are sentence fragments. If an item contains a sentence fragment, revise the fragment to make it a complete sentence. If it contains a complete sentence, write *C*.

EXAMPLE   **1.** While she was preparing the score for the video.

1. While she was preparing the score for the video, they shot the scenes.

1. Consider this.
2. Such as monarchies, aristocracies, oligarchies, and democracies.
3. The first to exploit the assembly line's potential for profit.
4. However, this boy who stammered became one of the great actors of our time—James Earl Jones.
5. Twisting thousands of strips of crepe paper into flowers.
6. In an antique tin box inside a trunk buried under a dozen boxes.
7. To attend the display of archaeological artifacts at the museum.
8. He, not I, would carry the project to its completion.
9. Subsequently, produced some of the finest ceramic pieces ever created in North America.
10. Eventually finished the house and made plans for a deck.

Reference Note

For information on **sentence fragments,** see page 513.

Exercise 2 — Identifying and Revising Run-on Sentences

Most of the following items are run-on sentences. Revise each run-on sentence to make at least one complete sentence. Add or delete words wherever necessary. Be sure to check your revised version for correct capitalization and punctuation. If a sentence is already correct, write *C*.

EXAMPLE   **1.** Time travel may be theoretically possible it does pose some practical difficulties.

1. Time travel may be theoretically possible; however, it does pose some practical difficulties.

or

Although time travel may be theoretically possible, it does pose some practical difficulties.

1. Fortunately, the program will run under your operating system, you will need a software patch first.

—HELP—

Although the example in Exercise 2 shows two possible revisions, you need to give only one for each item.

COMMON ERRORS

Reference Note

For information on **run-on sentences,** see page 432.

2. Those small bumps on the elevator's control panel are Braille letters, after all, people who are visually impaired need to use the elevators, too.

3. For two years, Ron had been working on the old jalopy, now it was finally ready for a test drive.

4. Even simple household repairs can be expensive publishers do a brisk business in do-it-yourself books.

5. Squirrels played tag among the branches, we watched from our upstairs window.

6. You should have some fun with math look at factoring as play.

7. We were unfamiliar with the customs of our neighbors from India, so they explained some of their traditions to us.

8. These birds above us, however, are on their way to Mexico spring will bring them back again.

9. Low-flying planes over Bristol Bay frightened the walruses the Marine Mammal Protection Act now forbids such flights.

10. Finding my little sister's runaway lizard in the house is easy capturing him is the hard part.

Exercise 3 Revising Sentence Fragments and Run-on Sentences

Reference Note

For information on **sentence fragments,** see page 513. For information about **run-on sentences,** see page 432.

Each of the following items contains a sentence fragment or a run-on sentence. Revise each item to correct the sentence fragment or run-on sentence. Be sure to check your revisions for correct capitalization and punctuation.

EXAMPLE
1. Musicians, clowns, mimes, and a juggler entertained the crowd at the carnival. Which began on my birthday.

1. *Musicians, clowns, mimes, and a juggler entertained the crowd at the carnival, which began on my birthday.*

1. To protect the seedlings from the damaging effects of the summer sun. We shaded the young plants in a makeshift greenhouse.

2. Many prospectors were deceived by the glittering mineral pyrite. Which became known as fool's gold.

3. Next door, a new building was under construction consequently, trucks and construction materials covered much of the parking lot.

4. The children sat on the floor. And laughed at the kittens playing with a ball of yarn that had tumbled down from Mother's lap.

5. After he worked on my computer. The technician assured me that it would work more efficiently.

6. The Chippewa mastered the art of harvesting birch bark, properly stripped trees do not die.

7. Sara gave her updated photography portfolio to Mrs. Strunz. Her photojournalism professor.

8. The baseball coach said he thought I would make the team next year he intends to train some students over the summer.

9. As in agricultural communities everywhere. The cycle of the seasons governs much of life in rural Africa.

10. Uncle Joseph's favorite class in high school was creative writing, no wonder he's chosen writing as his profession!

Exercise 4 **Revising Sentence Fragments and Run-on Sentences**

The following paragraphs contain sentence fragments and run-on sentences. Revise the sentence fragments and run-on sentences, changing the punctuation and capitalization as necessary to make each sentence clear and complete.

Reference Note

For information on **sentence fragments,** see page 513. For information on **run-on sentences,** see page 432.

EXAMPLE   [1] Pablo Picasso was born in Spain in 1881, he moved to France in 1904.

1. *Pablo Picasso was born in Spain in 1881. He moved to France in 1904.*

[1] Generally recognized as one of the greatest painters of the twentieth century. [2] Picasso stands among the masters of art, his work reveals the full range of human emotion. [3] From the calm restraint of his line drawings to the harsh drama of *Guernica*. [4] Picasso's work encompasses many of the artistic trends of the century he is perhaps best known for his abstract, neoclassical, and cubist works.

[5] Always moving ahead, never settling on any one style. [6] Picasso created in various mediums, not just paint, these include ceramics, sculpture, and engraving, he also developed a new collage technique with Georges Braque. [7] Whose fame partly rests on the famous collages that emerged from this period.

[8] Reflecting the confusion and fragmentation of life in the modern world. [9] Picasso's cubist works offer viewers multiple viewpoints on people and objects, indeed, these works cannot be fully appreciated from only one perspective. [10] Picasso teaches us to "see," he challenges us to look at the world from many vantage points.

COMMON ERRORS

Reference Note

For information on **subject-verb agreement,** see page 578.

Exercise 5 **Choosing Verbs That Agree in Number with Their Subjects**

For each of the following sentences, choose the correct form of the verb in parentheses.

EXAMPLE
1. Two thousand years (*is, are*) a long time for a tool to resist improvement, yet the blacksmith's anvil has retained the same general shape all that time.

1. *is*

1. Since ancient times, blacksmiths (*has, have*) provided a valuable service to people all over the world.
2. In the past, all necessary nails, pliers, and shears (*was, were*) made by blacksmiths.
3. By the mid-1800s, U.S. factories (*was, were*) producing such items; hence, blacksmiths made their livings more by servicing than by producing these and other items made of iron.
4. Nevertheless, blacksmiths throughout the country (*has, have*) continued to produce many types of ironwork.
5. Travelers in the South often (*notice, notices*) the elegant ironwork decorating architecture there.
6. In South Carolina many of the homes and historical buildings (*feature, features*) the work of several generations of African American blacksmiths.
7. Similarly, New Orleans (*is, are*) filled with impressive grillwork.
8. Today, one of the best-known smiths is Philip Simmons, who (*has, have*) been named a National Heritage Fellow.
9. The animal shapes in his ironwork (*is, are*) a prominent feature.
10. The news of Simmons's selection by the National Endowment for the Arts (*was, were*) welcomed by those who knew his work.

Exercise 6 **Proofreading for Subject-Verb Agreement**

Most of the following sentences contain an error in subject-verb agreement. Identify each incorrect verb, and write the correct form. If a sentence is already correct, write *C*.

EXAMPLE
1. Anyone who eats in the presence of others are well-advised to learn the local etiquette.

1. *are—is*

1. Most of the following dining guidelines is simply common courtesy in our country.

Reference Note

For information on **subject-verb agreement,** see page 578.

2. A thoughtful host always try to seat guests with similar interests near one another.
3. After sitting down, guests places their napkins on their laps to protect their clothing.
4. During the meal both men and women avoids placing their elbows on the table.
5. They eat bread in a polite manner, breaking off bite-sized pieces one at a time.
6. Neither a gentleman nor a lady drink from his or her bowl or saucer.
7. Generally speaking, the rules of proper etiquette dictates that only someone expecting an urgent call should wear a pager at a party.
8. Aren't the ringing of mobile phones also likely to disturb the people at the table?
9. A woman who put on makeup at the dinner table is not following proper etiquette.
10. Following rules of dining etiquette are one way to show respect for others.

Exercise 7 **Proofreading for Subject-Verb Agreement**

Reference Note

For information on **subject-verb agreement,** see page 578.

Most of the following sentences contain an error in subject-verb agreement. Identify each incorrect verb, and write the correct form. If a sentence is already correct, write *C*.

EXAMPLE   1. Genetics have become an active area of medical research.
            1. have—has

1. Solutions to any problem is usually the result of serious reflection and action.
2. Many a child around here imagine the lives of the Pueblos of long ago.
3. Don't she know the address of the new florist?
4. There before them stand the awesome sight of Angel Falls.
5. Have the news been on yet, Alexandra?
6. Either Mrs. Jordan or the Wright twins visits the nursing home on the weekend.
7. *Green Mansions* is the only movie on tonight.
8. Here's the answers to that crossword puzzle.
9. That's right—the band playing the best salsa tunes receive a recording contract!
10. Are Jackson's Sporting Goods still having that sale on backpacks?

COMMON ERRORS

Reference Note

For information on **pronoun-antecedent agreement**, see page 593.

Exercise 8   Supplying Pronouns That Agree with Their Antecedents

Complete each of the following sentences by supplying at least one pronoun that agrees with its antecedent. Use standard, formal English.

EXAMPLE   1. Everyone in the class will do _____ part to make the play a success.

   1. *his or her*

1. Cindy has the best plan for the castle, so _____ will supervise the construction of the set.
2. Melissa or Elena has offered _____ time on Tuesday afternoon to call several companies about donating the cardboard.
3. If Kyle and Larry can borrow a van, _____ will bring the cardboard to school.
4. Both of the twins are artists, so _____ will draw architectural details.
5. One of the boys will bring _____ keyboard and play the background music.
6. Each of my sisters has volunteered to bring _____ video equipment to tape the play.
7. Several members of the industrial arts class will contribute _____ time to build a castle on the stage.
8. Mr. Faust is a tailor, and _____ has offered to let us use his sewing machines to create costumes.
9. If someone doesn't have an assignment, _____ will need to see me.
10. Anybody who can supply paint should talk to _____ team leader.

Exercise 9   Proofreading for Pronoun-Antecedent Agreement

Most of the following sentences contain an error in pronoun-antecedent agreement. Identify each incorrect pronoun, and supply the correct pronoun form. If the sentence is already correct, write *C*.

Reference Note

For information on **pronoun-antecedent agreement**, see page 593.

EXAMPLE   1. Do you know the tale of William Tell and their crossbow?

   1. *their—his*

1. The bow, together with the arrows it shoots, has made their mark on history.
2. People in Asia and Europe used the bow, just as people in Africa and the Americas used them.
3. Many American Indians armed themselves with bows and arrows to obtain food and to defend themselves.

4. The reputations of the conquerors Genghis Khan and Attila the Hun were based largely on his troops' skill with bows.

5. European history is full of stories about famous archers and his or her exploits, including tales of Robin Hood.

6. Of Robin Hood's men, was Friar Tuck or Little John more famous for their skill with a bow?

7. Today, archery is practiced around the world, and an archer can choose their bow from among many styles.

8. In Japan the art of archery attracts students who consider it a form of meditation.

9. One of the twentieth century's greatest female archers was Janina Spychajowa-Kurkowska from Poland; in the 1930s and 1940s, they won seven world titles.

10. If anyone has an interest in this sport, they should contact local schools that offer archery classes.

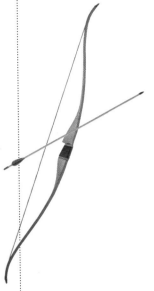

Exercise 10 Proofreading for Subject-Verb and Pronoun-Antecedent Agreement

Most of the following sentences contain at least one error in subject-verb agreement or pronoun-antecedent agreement. Identify and correct each error. If a sentence is already correct, write *C*.

EXAMPLE   [1] A goldsmith in the Ashanti Empire has a long and distinguished history behind them.

     1. *them—him*

[1] The Ashanti King Otumfuo Opoku Ware II has adorned himself with weighty golden ornaments for a celebration of its twenty-fifth year on the throne. [2] So important is this event that they have lasted a whole year. [3] Several men, perhaps bodyguards, look warily around; the sword bearers and they wear wondrous golden caps on their heads. [4] The king's advisors and ministers conducts himself with great solemnity. [5] One wealthy young woman has actually dusted their face with gold. [6] Her spouse and she will pass on the gold to their children. [7] Wives or princesses who are of the royal bloodline have merely borrowed her finery from the royal treasury. [8] Wearing lively *kente* cloth, some of the women dance; each of them can explain the meaning of every move she makes. [9] One woman draw particular attention; friends smile and admire the dancers and her. [10] None of the onlookers remains unimpressed by the festivities, and all of them will forever keep this moment in his or her memories.

Reference Note

For information on **pronoun-antecedent agreement,** see page 593.

COMMON ERRORS

Reference Note

For information on **subject-verb agreement,** see page 578. For information on **pronoun-antecedent agreement,** see page 593.

Exercise 11 Proofreading for Subject-Verb Agreement and Pronoun-Antecedent Agreement

Rewrite each of the following sentences to correct any errors in subject-verb agreement and pronoun-antecedent agreement.

EXAMPLE   **[1]** Our club at school help elementary students.

1.   *Our club at school helps elementary students.*

[1] Each Friday afternoon, we and our sponsor goes to Alcott Elementary where we tutor younger students. [2] Either Mrs. de Salvo or Mr. Newman drive her or his van on the ride over. [3] The fifth-graders usually meets us high school students in the library. [4] All of the younger students enjoy seeing his or her tutors, and of course we look forward to seeing them. [5] Mathematics, especially fractions, are a problem for some of the students. [6] Karen or Elena usually teach that subject. [7] Mike is probably the most popular tutor; none of the other tutors gets along better with the ten-year-olds than he does. [8] English is easy for me, so I usually takes the language arts students. [9] During the week, Mike and Elena often prepare a special activity, such as making mobiles or playing games, for his or her students. [10] Somebody in the group usually bring a snack for our break, and, to tell the truth, the break is the part we all like most—just talking, snacking, and laughing together.

Exercise 12 Selecting Correct Forms of Pronouns

Choose the correct form of the pronoun in parentheses in each of the following sentences. Use standard, formal English.

EXAMPLE   1.   Do you know (*who, whom*) your lab partner in chemistry class is?

1.   *who*

1. The runoff election will be between Barbara and (*she, her*).
2. When ducklings hatch, they will follow (*whoever, whomever*) they see first.
3. By the time we arrived, the only ones left at the party were Joe, Stephen, and (*he, him*).
4. Please ask Nicole and (*she, her*) about the entrance fee.
5. Red Cloud, (*who, whom*) died in 1909, was a principal chief of the Oglala Sioux.
6. This new exercise program has been designed for people like (*me, myself*).

7. I never dreamed that the winner would be (*I, me*).
8. The museum director arranged a private tour for (*we, us*) art history students.
9. Samuel Clemens, (*who, whom*) readers know as Mark Twain, wrote works that from time to time become subjects of controversy.
10. Did Jason and (*you, yourself*) do all the computer programming for the project?

Exercise 13 Proofreading for Correct Pronoun Usage

Most of the following sentences contain an error in pronoun usage. Identify and correct each error, using the rules of standard, formal English. If a sentence is already correct, write *C*.

EXAMPLE   1. Sean still corresponds with his former teachers, Mr. Finn and she.

    1. *she—her*

1. Even for native Spanish speakers like myself, translations are not always easy.
2. Actually, this is something that I'm doing for me.
3. I believe that Christy earned as much money as her.
4. No, him practicing the scales never bothers me.
5. Why don't we give Rhonda and they a going-away party?
6. Nobody, at least nobody I know, is more talented than him.
7. Who would have guessed that this year's candidates would be us two?
8. The oldest siblings in the family, Ted and me, usually help take care of the younger kids.
9. Surely you are familiar with the Marsalis family, many of whom are well known for their musical abilities.
10. Him making kites from scratch inspired Althea to do the same.

Exercise 14 Revising Sentences by Correcting Faulty Pronoun References

Most of the following sentences contain ambiguous, general, weak, or indefinite pronoun references. Revise each sentence that contains a faulty pronoun reference. If a sentence is already correct, write *C*.

EXAMPLE   1. Over the door, it read "No Admittance."

    1. *Over the door, a sign read "No Admittance."*

1. When foods are high in calories but low in nutrients, this leads to their being called junk foods.
2. When the limousine passed the bus, it swerved sharply to the right.

Reference Note

For information on **using pronouns correctly,** see Chapter 19.

┌ H E L P ─

Although sentences in Exercise 14 can be corrected in more than one way, you need to give only one revision for each item.

Reference Note

For information on **clear pronoun reference,** see Chapter 20.

COMMON ERRORS

3. The fans began leaving the bleachers and heading toward their cars when it started raining harder.
4. In reports to the United Nations, they concentrated on regions that had suffered drought.
5. Karen talked to Eileen about her plans for college.
6. Bill enjoys shopping in secondhand clothing stores, where he often finds very nice ones.
7. Several inexperienced hikers were late returning to the trailhead, which worried the rangers.
8. On the notice, it does not give a specific time and place for the meeting.
9. The traffic on Highway 183 was brought to a crawl by the road construction; this is expected to continue until next fall.
10. Officials told members of the council that they did not need to attend the conference.

┌─HELP─┐

Although sentences in Exercise 15 can be corrected in more than one way, you need to give only one revision for each item.

Reference Note

For information on **clear pronoun reference,** see Chapter 20.

COMMON ERRORS

Exercise 15 Revising Sentences by Correcting Faulty Pronoun References

Most of the following sentences contain ambiguous, general, weak, or indefinite pronoun references. Revise each sentence that contains a faulty pronoun reference. If a sentence is already correct, write *C.*

EXAMPLE
1. Sergeant Wu taught Lisa fingerprinting techniques, and she will demonstrate them to our class.

1. *Sergeant Wu taught Lisa fingerprinting techniques, and Lisa will demonstrate them to our class.*

or

Sergeant Wu taught Lisa fingerprinting techniques and will demonstrate them to our class.

1. No two people ever have exactly the same fingerprints, which Sir Francis Galton discovered.
2. For instance, Marcie's fingerprints are different even from those of her identical twin.
3. Also, even as a person ages, they say all ten fingerprints will stay the same.
4. Sir Edward Henry, who later became the commissioner of Scotland Yard, analyzed the characteristics of fingerprints, and it has helped police the world over.
5. He noticed patterns such as arches and loops, which is how he created a system for filing and classifying fingerprints.

6. Although fingerprinting is common today, it has helped police solve crimes for only about a hundred years.

7. Today, police use fingerprints left at crime scenes to identify suspects—and they are not always easy to find.

8. In many detective stories, they tell of the clever techniques that criminals devise to avoid leaving fingerprints.

9. Mario asked Mr. Lincoln about a field trip to the police station; he said the whole class would enjoy it.

10. Mario's dad, who is on the police force, told us about fingerprints, and it was quite interesting.

Exercise 16 Using the Past and Past Participle Forms of Irregular Verbs

Give the correct form (past or past participle) of the irregular verb in parentheses in each of the following sentences.

EXAMPLE
1. Could a huge island like Atlantis have (*sink*) without a trace?
1. *sunk*

Reference Note

For information on **using irregular verbs correctly,** see page 646.

1. The mongoose (*strike*) the cobra.
2. A sudden gust had (*take*) the kite into the trees.
3. Resolutely, General MacArthur (*swear*) that he would return to the Philippines.
4. What an interesting essay you have (*write*)!
5. Dress gloves are rarely (*wear*) nowadays, even on formal occasions.
6. Holding her breath, Lawanda (*swim*) the entire length of the pool.
7. The tornado (*tear*) the roof off the shed.
8. Oh, yes, they have (*speak*) of you often.
9. Hey! These new jeans have (*shrink*)!
10. Because Prometheus had (*steal*) fire from the gods, he was savagely punished.

Exercise 17 Proofreading Sentences for the Correct Use of Irregular Verbs

Most of the following sentences contain an error in the use of irregular verbs. If a verb is incorrect, supply the correct form. If a sentence is already correct, write *C*.

EXAMPLE
1. The developers of Starbright World have maked a computer game especially for hospitalized children.
1. *made*

Reference Note

For information on **using irregular verbs correctly,** see page 646.

COMMON ERRORS

1. Starbright World, a sophisticated computer playground, has gave children who are in the hospital a chance to play together in a computerized wonderland.
2. The Starbright team has strove to create sophisticated input devices that can be operated by tiny movements—even by breaths of air.
3. Once inside the program, a child chooses a character and then controls that character's actions and interactions with others in the Starbright World.
4. As the Starbright project has progressed, it has growed.
5. Multiple virtual worlds becomed part of the plans.
6. Soon several major companies seen the potential of the project and made significant contributions.
7. In fact, some of the most imaginative people in the country, including Steven Spielberg, finded the project irresistible.
8. At one presentation, Spielberg speaked of creating virtual toy stores and team sports.
9. He also redesigned some of the carts that house the computers and made the carts look like fanciful toys.
10. By 1995, some children's hospitals had began testing the Starbright network.

Exercise 18 Proofreading Sentences for Correct Verb Forms

Give the correct form for each incorrect verb in the following sentences. If a sentence is already correct, write C.

EXAMPLE   1. Has anyone wrote a book about Africa's traditional fabrics?

1. *written*

1. Clothing with traditional African colors and patterns has growed quite popular in the United States.
2. Have you ever buyed any garments made of raffia or cut-pile cloth?
3. For another type of African cloth, bark is cutted from trees and then soaked in water or steamed.
4. Later, the bark is beaten with a mallet.
5. Gradually, after the bark has been striked many times, the softened fibers mat together and become pliable material.
6. This material is knowed as bark cloth.

Reference Note

For information on **using verbs correctly,** see Chapter 21.

7. Other cloth is made on a loom, sometimes from thread that has been spinned by hand.
8. After cloth has laid in dye baths for a time, it is removed and washed.
9. Many an African woman has holded her baby in a sling made from traditional African cloth.
10. Quite a few women in the United States have adopted this practice, and today, many babies in this country have rode in these slings.

Exercise 19 Proofreading a Paragraph for Consistent Verb Tenses

Decide whether the following paragraph should be written in present or past tense. Then, change the verbs to correct any unnecessary shifts in tense.

EXAMPLE   **[1]** Because it is a beautiful day, I wanted to be outside.

     1. *Because it is a beautiful day, I want to be outside.*

or

     Because it was a beautiful day, I wanted to be outside.

[1] I am hanging laundry out to dry. [2] Our playful new puppy ran around in circles under the clothesline. [3] Too busy for games, I just ignored him and continue my work. [4] However, he won't take no for an answer and jumped up and bit the corner of a clean, white sheet. [5] Of course, I tell him to stop, but he has his mind made up. [6] He growls, shakes his shaggy head, and tears the sheet from the line. [7] Gleefully, he dragged the sheet through the yard. [8] He is really enjoying himself and evidently thinks that I am, too! [9] Angry, I chase him but accidentally step on the sheet and fall into the tangle of wet fabric. [10] Ecstatic, the puppy jumps on my stomach and licked my face.

Exercise 20 Proofreading Sentences for Correct Verb Tenses

Each of the following sentences contains an error in the use of tenses. Revise each sentence, using the correct verb form.

EXAMPLE   1. As technology changes, our pace of life has changed.

     1. *As technology has changed, our pace of life has changed.*

or

     As technology changes, our pace of life changes.

┌HELP─

Although the example in Exercise 19 gives two revisions, you need to give only one for each item.

Reference Note
For information on **verb tense,** see page 664.

┌HELP─

Although the example in Exercise 20 gives two revisions, you need to give only one for each item.

Reference Note
For information on **using verb tenses correctly,** see page 664.

COMMON ERRORS

1. Did you restart the computer after you change the start-up file?
2. Although the Nakayamas left before noon, they didn't arrive until very late at night.
3. Carlos finished the book before Marcel started reading it.
4. Everyone applauded as the floats pass by.
5. If you would have done what I asked you to do, we would not have been in all that trouble.
6. We always remembered to wash the vegetables carefully before we cook them.
7. The House of Representatives is going to study the bill before the representatives are voting on it.
8. By the time I take the test tomorrow, I will surely memorize every date that appears in Chapter 13.
9. We would have made reservations if they would have told us about the convention.
10. Although his new car goes more than one hundred miles an hour, Mr. Reynolds never exceeded the speed limit.

(Exercise 21) **Proofreading Sentences for Correct Comparison**

Reference Note

For information about **using comparative and superlative forms correctly,** see page 701. For information on **comparison within a group,** see page 702.

Most of the following sentences contain an error in comparison of modifiers. Revise each sentence that contains an error. If a sentence is already correct, write *C.*

EXAMPLE
1. Of all the cars on the market, which one runs more economically?

1. *Of all the cars on the market, which one runs most economically?*

1. My best friend sings better than anybody I know.
2. Which was more hard for you to learn, tennis or racquetball?
3. Too late, we discovered that we should have tied the boat most securely than we did.
4. Exercise sometimes makes an injury worse.
5. That dog can bark louder than any dog I've ever heard!
6. Please identify the modern city that is most closest to the site of the ancient city Pompeii.
7. Of all the varieties of trees that were damaged last winter, the orange trees were hurt worse.
8. Keisha and Tommie have promised that this year's prom will be the elegantest ever.
9. Of the two possibilities, Pat's is the best solution to the problem.

10. At that moment, the mountain climbers seemed to be the least fearfulest people on earth.

Exercise 22 Proofreading Sentences for Correct Use of Modifiers

Revise the following sentences by correcting errors in the use of modifiers.

EXAMPLE
1. Which do you like best to sleep under, a blanket or a quilt?

1. *Which do you like better to sleep under, a blanket or a quilt?*

1. On a cold night in January, you may find yourself searching for a more warmer blanket.
2. For many people an old quilt may be the better cover of any in the house.
3. To a quilter a seemingly worthless scrap of cotton may be worth more than any piece of cloth.
4. In fact, many quilts are made out of the inexpensivest materials that a person has at hand, such as strips of cloth salvaged from a family's old clothes.
5. These quilts are often more valuable than ordinary covers, for they may help recall the quilter's most fond memories.
6. The stitches in a quilt may be arranged as precise as the rows in an accountant's ledger.
7. The hand stitching of bygone days is sometimes replaced by efficienter machine-made stitches now.
8. With computer programs, designing quilts is now even more easier.
9. Some of the most beautifulest quilts hang in museums.
10. Harriet Powers sewed good, and one of her pictorial quilts hangs in the Smithsonian.

Exercise 23 Proofreading for the Correct Use of Modifiers

Most of the sentences in the following paragraph contain an error in the use of modifiers. Correct each error. If a sentence is already correct, write C.

EXAMPLE
[1] Few places in the world are more beautifuler than Cuba.

1. *more beautiful*

Reference Note

For information on **using modifiers correctly,** see Chapter 22.

Reference Note

For information on **using modifiers correctly,** see Chapter 22.

COMMON ERRORS

[1] Perhaps no Cuban has had as rich and varied a career as the Cuban writer José Martí. [2] Martí is most famous for his revolutionary politics than for his writing. [3] However, it is his writing that gives more deeper dimension to the man. [4] Without it, he would be just another revolutionary. [5] Martí took the formal style of a sermon, added the more angrier, colorful phrases of the street, and arrived at a persuasive appeal strong enough to spark a revolution. [6] Although that kind of prose power might be enough for anybody, it was not enough for Martí. [7] Worldy and well traveled, Martí knew that life itself is more important than politics. [8] Heart and soul matter, too, so he wrote stories for children as well as poetry that is more directer than flowery, romantic verse. [9] Martí was both a writer and revolutionary; his range was wider than almost any other person. [10] No one can say which life is better—that of a poet, a revolutionary, or a sociopolitical analyst; Martí was all of these.

Exercise 24 Proofreading Sentences for Misplaced Modifiers

Reference Note

For information on **misplaced modifiers,** see page 712.

The following sentences each contain an error in the placement of modifiers. Revise each sentence so that its meaning is clear and correct.

EXAMPLE   1. He dreamed of competing in the Olympics in the barn.

         1. *In the barn, he dreamed of competing in the Olympics.*

1. The snow was piled in deep drifts on the mountainside that had fallen in the night.
2. The community recreation center only will admit people with valid memberships.
3. The airline clerk told me that my flight would be boarding at 2:00 P.M. on the telephone.
4. The meteor shower was the most spectacular one I had ever seen that occurred last night.
5. After bucking off every rider, the ranch hands wearily sat on the fence as the mustang grazed peacefully.
6. The largest branch of the grapefruit tree touched the ground, which was heavy with fruit.
7. The general reported that three thousand troops were awaiting supplies during the briefing.
8. Only break glass in case of fire.
9. The firefighters quickly rescued the little boys with the tall ladder.
10. The scouts found several plants and vines in the woods that are poisonous.

Exercise 25 Correcting Dangling Modifiers in Sentences

Most of the following sentences contain a dangling modifier. Revise each incorrect sentence so that its meaning is clear and correct. If a sentence is already correct, write *C*.

Reference Note

For information about **dangling modifiers,** see page 714.

EXAMPLE 1. To play better, more practice is necessary.
    1. *To play better, you need to practice more.*

1. Having studied all weekend, the test was easy.
2. While standing in the moonlight, hundreds of fireflies appeared.
3. After watching the eclipse for a while, its novelty waned.
4. When making arrangements for the play, access for people using wheelchairs should not be forgotten.
5. Traveling to stars light-years away, new life forms might be found.
6. After loading the lumber onto the flatbed, the truck drove away.
7. While replacing the battery in the smoke detector, the alarm went off.
8. To manage your finances, a budget will definitely be needed.
9. Dressed as if they were going to a fancy restaurant, the family sat down at their own dining table.
10. Having already seen the movie that was playing, a game of chess seemed more inviting.

Exercise 26 Identifying Correct Usage

Choose the correct word or words in parentheses in each of the following sentences.

Reference Note

For information on **common usage errors,** see Chapter 24.

EXAMPLE 1. Wow! You're playing (*good, well*) today.
    1. *well*

1. Ask for directions from (*those, them*) people over there, Dad.
2. (*Lay, Lie*) down and rest for a while, Samantha.
3. She (*done, did*) the first part, and then she got a phone call and left.
4. (*Let, Leave*) him have a turn at bat, Orson.
5. Is the home team playing very (*bad, badly*)?
6. Well, the joke was based on an (*illusion, allusion*) to *Don Quixote*.
7. Use a comma with (*these types, this type*) of expression.
8. You (*ought, had ought*) to give yourself a chance to like sushi.
9. Will similes, metaphors, (*etc., and etc.*) be covered on the test?
10. Yes, sir, (*this, this here*) old guitar was once played by the legendary Muddy Waters.

Reference Note

For information on **common usage errors,** see Chapter 24.

Reference Note

For information on **common usage errors,** see Chapter 24.

Exercise 27 Correcting Errors in Usage

Most of the following sentences contain an error in usage. Revise each sentence that contains an error. If a sentence is already correct, write *C*.

EXAMPLE   1. These noodles taste well with this sauce.

1. *These noodles taste good with this sauce.*

1. One of Japan's most popular dining attractions is the *yatai*, a type of small food shop that can be found almost everywheres in Japanese cities.
2. On the way home from work, many Japanese they stop to get a bite to eat at one of these street stalls.
3. These type of stalls is equipped with a kitchen and is movable.
4. A large amount of these stalls appear on back or side streets after sunset.
5. Being as people are tired and hungry after a day's work, they appreciate the convenience of these stalls.
6. Choosing among braised chicken, stewed vegetables, and one of the other main dishes is often difficult.
7. One reason people stop at the *yatai* is because they enjoy the companionship of new and old acquaintances.
8. Sitting besides strangers from all walks of life can be fun.
9. No doubt, Japanese who emigrate to the United States miss the food, atmosphere, and camaraderie at the *yatai*.
10. Although fast-food restaurants in the United States are places where people can gather, customers usually visit them primarily for convenience rather then for companionship.

Exercise 28 Correcting Errors in Usage

Each of the following sentences contains an error in usage. Revise each sentence.

EXAMPLE   1. I'm going to join the navy, like my father did.

1. *I'm going to join the navy, as my father did.*

1. Do you want to try one of these free samples that I got off of the man at the bakery counter?
2. Neither the museum or the art school has information on him.
3. Oh, no! I must of locked the keys in the car again.
4. This answer don't make sense to me, Mr. Washington.
5. The reason for the delay is because severe thunderstorms have grounded all flights.

6. The baseball that busted the living room window had Patrick's name on it.
7. Where will the party be at tonight?
8. Did you read where a faster computer chip has been created?
9. The engine sounded like it had been filled with gravel, not gasoline.
10. A warm boot is when a computer is restarted by keyboard strokes.

Exercise 29 Correcting Double Negatives and Other Errors in Usage

Eliminate the double negatives and other errors in usage in the following sentences.

EXAMPLES
1. The musicians couldn't hardly wait for the concert to begin.
1. *The musicians could hardly wait for the concert to begin.*

2. Our lunch break was so short that we didn't scarcely have time to eat.
2. *Our lunch break was so short that we scarcely had time to eat.*

1. What affect does the gravitational pull of the moon have on the tides of the Atlantic Ocean?
2. They said that they didn't know nothing about the school dance on Friday night.
3. The concert hall was so crowded that the management wouldn't let no one else in.
4. I read where this movie theater no longer accepts discount passes for new releases.
5. Arturo and Jason should of realized that their voices would echo loudly in that deep, narrow canyon.
6. Isn't nobody going to help me bring in the groceries?
7. In the early nineteenth century, Robert Owen tried to create an utopia—an ideal or perfect place—in New Harmony, Indiana.
8. His fingers moved so fast that I couldn't hardly see all the chords he played.
9. Less species of fish live in the Arctic and Antarctic Oceans than in other, warmer oceans.
10. Don't you wash no dog in my clean bathtub!

┌─H E L P─
Although some of the sentences in Exercise 29 can be corrected in more than one way, you need to give only one revision for each item.

Reference Note

For information on **common usage errors,** see Chapter 24.

COMMON ERRORS

Grammar and Usage Test: Section 1

DIRECTIONS Read the paragraph below. For each numbered blank, select the word or word group that best completes the sentence. Indicate your response by shading in the appropriate oval on your answer sheet.

EXAMPLE Until the early twentieth century, the nations of the world __(1)__ no strategy for collectively solving international problems.

  1. **(A)** they had
     (B) didn't have
     (C) have
     (D) had
     (E) having

ANSWER 1. Ⓐ Ⓑ Ⓒ ⬤D Ⓔ

   With the horrors of World War I fresh in their minds, representatives from around the world __(1)__ in Geneva, Switzerland, to find a peaceful way to solve __(2)__ disputes. The solution that they reached __(3)__ to form an international organization. Established in 1920, the League of Nations __(4)__ to resolve conflicts through arbitration. However, the League __(5)__ power to make countries comply with __(6)__ decisions. Moreover, the refusal of the United States to join __(7)__ weakened what little authority the League did have. Ironically, it was U.S. President Woodrow Wilson __(8)__ first suggested forming the League. __(9)__ the League was so weak, it could do nothing in the 1930s to stop Japan, Italy, and Germany's mounting aggression, which led to the outbreak of World War II. In 1946, the League of Nations __(10)__ apart, and the United Nations took its place.

---

1. (A) was meeting
   (B) meeted
   (C) meets
   (D) met
   (E) would have met

2. (A) them
   (B) his or her
   (C) their
   (D) they're
   (E) these kind of

3. (A) it was
   (B) has been
   (C) were
   (D) being
   (E) was

4. (A) were formed
   (B) was formed
   (C) was forming
   (D) forming
   (E) forms

5. **(A)** had no
   (B) didn't have no
   (C) scarcely had no
   (D) had barely no
   (E) never had no

6. **(A)** it's
   (B) its
   (C) their
   (D) his or her
   (E) them

7. **(A)** greater
   (B) more greater
   (C) more greatly
   (D) greatly
   (E) greatlier

8. **(A)** whom
   (B) which
   (C) whose
   (D) whoever
   (E) who

9. **(A)** Being as
   (B) Although
   (C) Because
   (D) Being that
   (E) Until

10. **(A)** broke
    (B) breaked
    (C) broken
    (D) break
    (E) busted

Grammar and Usage Test: Section 2

DIRECTIONS Using the rules of standard written English, choose the answer that most clearly expresses the meaning of the underlined portion of each of the following sentences. If the sentence is best written as is, choose A. Indicate your response by shading in the appropriate oval on your answer sheet.

EXAMPLE 1. Romare Bearden gained artistic fame for his <u>collages his works are made of pieces of paper that have been cut or torn</u>.

    (A) collages his works are made of pieces of paper that have been cut or torn

    (B) collages, his works are made of pieces of paper that have been cut or torn

    (C) collages, which are made of pieces of paper that have been cut or torn

    (D) collages, his works being made of pieces of paper that have been cut or torn

    (E) collages, collages are made of pieces of paper that have been cut or torn

ANSWER 1. A B C D E

1. Raiding the garden, Dad hollered at the raccoon.
   (A) Raiding the garden, Dad hollered at the raccoon.
   (B) While raiding the garden, Dad hollered at the raccoon.
   (C) Dad, raiding the garden, hollered at the raccoon.
   (D) Dad hollered at the raccoon while he was raiding the garden.
   (E) Dad hollered at the raccoon raiding the garden.

2. In this article it says that Sir Arthur Conan Doyle was a doctor.
   (A) In this article it says
   (B) This article says
   (C) This article it says
   (D) In this article says
   (E) In this article they say

3. That violinist Midori, whom audiences all over the world admire.
   (A) That violinist Midori, whom audiences all over the world admire.
   (B) That violinist is Midori, who audiences all over the world admire.
   (C) That violinist is Midori, audiences all over the world admire her.
   (D) That violinist is Midori, whom audiences all over the world admire.
   (E) That violinist Midori, admired by audiences all over the world.

4. The Chinese poet T'ao Ch'ien liked to work in his garden, Li Po preferred to travel.
   (A) garden, Li Po preferred to travel
   (B) garden; Li Po preferred to travel
   (C) garden Li Po preferred to travel
   (D) garden, so Li Po preferred to travel
   (E) garden; moreover, Li Po preferred to travel

5. After she had a nightmare about a scientist's monstrous experiment, Mary Shelley writes her novel *Frankenstein*.
   (A) writes her novel *Frankenstein*
   (B) writing her novel *Frankenstein*
   (C) had written her novel *Frankenstein*
   (D) she wrote her novel *Frankenstein*
   (E) wrote her novel *Frankenstein*

6. E. G. Valens's book *The Other Side of the Mountain,* which tells the story of Jill Kinmont's remarkable life.

    (A) E. G. Valens's book *The Other Side of the Mountain,* which tells the story of Jill Kinmont's remarkable life.

    (B) E. G. Valens's book *The Other Side of the Mountain* tells the story of Jill Kinmont's remarkable life.

    (C) The remarkable E. G. Valens wrote the book *The Other Side of the Mountain,* it tells the story of Jill Kinmont's life.

    (D) E. G. Valens's book *The Other Side of the Mountain* telling the story of Jill Kinmont's remarkable life.

    (E) E. G. Valens wrote the book *The Other Side of the Mountain* it tells the story of Jill Kinmont's remarkable life.

7. Soon after the Worthingtons had moved to the neighborhood, the Smiths invited them to a barbecue.

    (A) Soon after the Worthingtons had moved to the neighborhood, the Smiths invited them to a barbecue.

    (B) The Smiths invited the Worthingtons to a barbecue soon after they had moved to the neighborhood.

    (C) Soon after they had moved to the neighborhood, the Smiths invited the Worthingtons to a barbecue.

    (D) Having just moved to the neighborhood, the Smiths invited the Worthingtons to a barbecue.

    (E) Soon after the Smiths had moved to the neighborhood, the Worthingtons invited them to a barbecue.

8. Many woodcarvers in Mexico's Oaxaca Valley make colorful figures, they sell them to visitors from all over the world.

    (A) Many woodcarvers in Mexico's Oaxaca Valley make colorful figures, they sell them to visitors from all over the world.

    (B) Many woodcarvers in Mexico's Oaxaca Valley, who make colorful figures, they sell them to visitors from all over the world.

    (C) Many woodcarvers in Mexico's Oaxaca Valley make colorful figures, and they are sold to visitors from all over the world.

    (D) Many woodcarvers in Mexico's Oaxaca Valley make colorful figures and sell them to visitors from all over the world.

    (E) Many woodcarvers in Mexico's Oaxaca Valley made colorful figures that they will sell to visitors from all over the world.

9. While excavating the ruins, pieces of jewelry made of lapis lazuli were discovered by the archaeologists.

   (A) While excavating the ruins, pieces of jewelry made of lapis lazuli were discovered by the archaeologists.

   (B) While excavating the ruins, pieces of jewelry were discovered by the archaeologists, made of lapis lazuli.

   (C) The archaeologists discovered pieces of jewelry made of lapis lazuli excavating the ruins.

   (D) The archaeologists discovered pieces of jewelry while excavating the ruins made of lapis lazuli.

   (E) While excavating the ruins, the archaeologists discovered pieces of jewelry made of lapis lazuli.

10. While studying bristlecone pines, their great age was discovered.

   (A) While studying bristlecone pines, their great age was discovered.

   (B) While scientists were studying bristlecone pines, their great age was discovered.

   (C) While studying bristlecone pines, scientists discovered these trees' great age.

   (D) While studying bristlecone pines, scientists discovered their great age.

   (E) While studying bristlecone pines, their great age were discovered.

WORD FOR WORD reprinted by permission of Associated Press.

Exercise 30 Proofreading for Correct Capitalization

Most of the sentences in the following paragraph contain at least one error in capitalization. Correct each error. If a sentence is already correct, write *C*.

EXAMPLE   **1.** Whether it's just a bend in the Road or New York city, almost everyone loves his or her hometown.

    1. *road, City*

[**1**] However, many of us at Marshall high school don't want to spend our whole lives sitting in a red vinyl booth at Angie's restaurant, sipping an iced tea after services at Trinity church. [**2**] In the old days, some students used to go to europe after they graduated; doing so was a tradition. [**3**] Of course, not everybody wants to go that far; but some of our class do have dreams that take us all around the Earth. [**4**] bob and Alma would love to see Ireland, where their Grandmother agnes was born. [**5**] Jomo, dr. Henry's son, actually wants to make Kenya his home after he finishes up at river city junior college. [**6**] As for me, i want to see the East—the far East, that is—the one with the great wall of China, Chinese new year, the Yellow river, and those little oranges. [**7**] If the *orient-express* is still rolling down the tracks, maybe I'll just keep going east until I reach the west again. [**8**] On the way, I'll be sure to sail the Mediterranean sea, check out the temple of apollo, visit the land of the talmud, stand beside the Eiffel tower, and, in general, make sure that *National Geographic Explorer* has its facts straight. [**9**] Hey! Maybe I'll even write up my adventures and call them "the Grand Tour In The Twenty-First Century." [**10**] Imagine that—me published in *National Geographic*!

Exercise 31 Correcting Errors in Capitalization

Correct any error in capitalization in each of the following items. If an item is already correct, write *C*.

EXAMPLES   **1.** "Secret World Of A Pond"

    1. *"Secret World of a Pond"*

    2. a hindu tradition

    2. *a Hindu tradition*

1. the Restaurants of New York city
2. polynesian music
3. my Cousin's shoe store
4. in san francisco
5. ms. julia child

Reference Note

For information on **capitalization rules,** see Chapter 25.

Reference Note

For information on **capitalization rules,** see Chapter 25.

COMMON ERRORS

6. Russian dressing on my salad
7. dates and figs from israel
8. salmon from the pacific area
9. the fair at central park
10. home economics II
11. the board of health
12. the snack bar in the Regal hotel
13. celebrating kwanzaa
14. a cup of Lipton® Tea
15. during the dark ages
16. brought to spain by Columbus
17. astronauts aboard the *Discovery*
18. the summer issue of *Native peoples* magazine
19. stop the presses, alice!
20. a cherokee name
21. a baptist minister
22. *The big Book Of Tell me Why*
23. Enlighten us, o Athena!
24. named for the god jupiter
25. the house of representatives

Reference Note

For information on **using commas,** see page 783.

COMMON ERRORS

Exercise 32 Correcting Sentences by Adding Commas

Rewrite each of the following sentences, inserting commas where they are needed.

EXAMPLE
1. Paul why don't you come over tonight and see our new computer?

1. *Paul, why don't you come over tonight and see our new computer?*

1. Saturday August 5 2000 was a big day for everyone in our family.
2. When we first got the computer no one in the family knew much about how to use it.
3. Mom read the directions for setting up the hardware and I hooked up the monitor keyboard and speakers.
4. When we turned on the computer we hadn't realized that the volume was turned up very high.
5. Naturally we all jumped when the computer blasted out a musical welcome.
6. My youngest brother Derek who has played with computers since he was in nursery school knew just what to do.

7. With hardly a moment of hesitation he reached out and turned down the volume and then pushed a button.
8. The CD drawer slid out in one smooth sudden motion.
9. He picked up a shiny silver disc that had a program about dinosaurs popped it in and pressed the button again.
10. After reading the directions for a few minutes Dad typed in a short command, pressed a key, and entered a virtual prehistoric world.

Exercise 33 **Correcting Sentences by Adding Periods, Question Marks, Exclamation Points, and Commas**

Rewrite the following sentences, adding periods, question marks, exclamation points, and commas as needed. If a sentence is already correct, write *C*.

EXAMPLE
   1. Mr Cross please fax this to headquarters immediately
   1. *Mr. Cross, please fax this to headquarters immediately.*

or

   Mr. Cross, please fax this to headquarters immediately!

1. Mike Joe and I will meet at 8:00 P.M. at the corner of Elk St. and Fifth Ave
2. "Don't you dare" I yelled to my sister when she turned on the water picked up the garden hose and pointed it at me.
3. Doesn't your oldest sister Susan go to that junior college Tim
4. On the wall were three large glossy photographs—one of General Colin Powell one of President John F Kennedy and one of Dr. Martin Luther King Jr
5. Oh what a beautiful sunset this is
6. No person who has purchased a ticket will be excluded from the school carnival.
7. In the fall of last year archaeologists I believe found a site that dates back to 200 B C
8. For example many of the pesticides that are used in agriculture can eventually filter into our water supply.
9. I wondered moreover whether the shipment would even arrive by July 10 2002.
10. Remember to ask Dr Franklin about whether you should exercise your knee

┌─ **HELP** ─

Although the example in Exercise 33 gives two possible revisions, you need to give only one for each sentence.

Reference Note

For information on **using commas,** see page 783. For information on **using end marks,** see page 776.

COMMON ERRORS

Some sentences
in Exercise 34 have a
comma where a semicolon
or a colon should be.

Reference Note
For information on **using
semicolons and colons,**
see pages 804 and 806.

Exercise 34 Proofreading Sentences for the Correct Use
of Semicolons and Colons

Rewrite the following sentences, adding or deleting semicolons and
colons as needed.

EXAMPLE
1. Only fragments of these ancient scrolls exist, however,
scholars are attempting to piece the text together.

1. *Only fragments of these ancient scrolls exist; however,
scholars are attempting to piece the text together.*

1. The President did not veto the bill, in other words, he allowed it to
become law.
2. There are many possible titles for your paper for example, you
could use "Legacy of Laughter The Stories of Toni Cade Bambara."
3. By 8 00 at night, a dense fog had obscured our view only the lights
of the house next door were visible.
4. The vase was filled with flowers daisies, irises, daffodils, and tulips.
5. The following materials are necessary to assemble the cart, a screw-
driver, eighteen half-inch screws, and eighteen nuts.
6. My uncle loves to fish, in fact, he goes fishing every weekend.
7. Her choice was clear, Find a way out of the jungle or die.
8. We set out with: a compass, a canteen of water, a blanket, and a
tattered copy of Psalm 23 1–6.
9. The film will be shown three times: Sunday, March 15, Friday,
April 3, and Saturday, April 25.
10. Her mother was, I think, originally from Veracruz, Mexico but she
has lived in Sacramento, California, for more than thirty years.

Exercise 35 Proofreading a Dialogue for
Correct Punctuation

Rewrite the following dialogue, correcting any errors in the use of quotation marks and other marks of punctuation. Also, correct any errors
in the use of capitalization, and begin a new paragraph each time the
speaker changes.

EXAMPLE
[1] I have two very important papers due next week! Eric
sighed. "Have you started on them yet? Rita asked.

1. *"I have two very important papers due next week,"
Eric sighed.
"Have you started on them yet?" Rita asked.*

[1] "Well, I've decided," Eric answered, "On a topic for one, and I've
done research for another one."

Reference Note
For information about
punctuating dialogue,
see page 818.

COMMON ERRORS

[2] "You do have a lot of work to do! Rita exclaimed. I guess you won't be going out this weekend."

[3] How are you doing on your papers? Eric asked. Rita answered "I still have to edit, print, and proofread one." The other is almost done, too."

[4] "How do you manage to get it all done"? Eric asked.

[5] "Every time I get a big assignment, I make a list of all the things I'll need to do. Then I estimate how long each step will take me." she replied.

[6] Eric said, shaking his head, "that sounds like extra work to me."

[7] "Well, it keeps me on schedule and helps me avoid having to rush through the writing process.

[8] Hmm, I see what you mean," Eric mused. "I guess it's too late for me to get organized now." "Rita replied, I don't think so."

[9] "It's not too late. Never say "never"." Just take the time you have left, and figure out what needs to be done each day.

[10] "Okay, I think I'll give your plan a try in study hall. Eric said.

(Exercise 36) Proofreading a Dialogue for Correct Punctuation

Rewrite the following dialogue, correcting any errors in the use of quotation marks and other marks of punctuation. Also, correct any errors in the use of capitalization, and begin a new paragraph each time the speaker changes.

Reference Note

For information about **punctuating dialogue,** see page 818.

EXAMPLE   [1] I understand that you began flying in the 1930s, Colonel Scott, the interviewer stated. "Yes, that's right, Scott agreed.

1.   *"I understand that you began flying in the 1930s, Colonel Scott," the interviewer stated.*
"Yes, that's right," Scott agreed.

[1] In those days, flying was the hottest thing around. Being a pilot then was better than being a rock star today, for me, anyway. All I ever wanted to do was fly. I used to hang around the field doing odd jobs, hoping to get some flight time in.

[2] Was that how you met Jackie Cochran? Were you working for her?" the interviewer questioned.

[3] "I was just a kid. I ran a few errands for her. Later, we became good friends in Europe. We'd be "socked in" and get to talking."

[4] Excuse me, but what's "socked in?"

[5] "When bad weather grounds a plane, the pilots are "socked in". Lots of times I'd see her when she ferried a plane. You know, Jackie was the one who really got the WASPs going." "The Women Airforce Service Pilots"? the interviewer interrupted.

[6] "That's right. Jackie liked being first. She was a competitor from the word go. Jackie didn't really have much of a childhood," Scott mused. "Maybe she took all that kid's excitement and funneled it into flying. I don't know."

"I do know that she grew up in a foster home. She was working in a cotton mill when she was nine or so. She quit school—such things weren't unusual in those days".

[7] "How old was she when she got her pilot's license"? "Around twenty. She wasn't much more than that when she set her sights on that Bendix Transcontinental Air Race and wouldn't let up. I was with her when she took off in '38".

[8] "That was the year she won, wasn't it", the interviewer continued.

[9] "Sure was. Nobody could beat her—and, believe me, there were some very good pilots around. Whether it was altitude, speed, or endurance records, it didn't matter. She won them all.

[10] 'Thank you, Colonel, for sharing your memories of Jacqueline Cochran, a member of the National Aviation Hall of Fame.'

Exercise 37 Using Apostrophes Correctly

Most of the following items contain at least one error in the use of apostrophes. Correct each error. If an item is already correct, write *C.*

EXAMPLE
 1. Its easy.
 1. *It's easy.*

1. The rest is her's.
2. Lets dance!
3. Kim wont be late.
4. We were reading Jo's essay.
5. Im not finished.
6. Is this your's?
7. nobodys fool
8. my sister's-in-law house
9. six day's time
10. P. J. and Tims treehouse
11. two o clock
12. Follow it's trail.
13. mens' clothing
14. Youll be fine.
15. Were home!
16. too many *and*s
17. Who's keys' are these?
18. Theres the girls' team.
19. You're right.
20. cat and dogs' ears
21. somebodys' wallet
22. Theyre here!
23. Jon made three As.
24. Ada hasnt sneezed.
25. Wasn't 99 a great year?

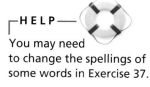

┌HELP─

You may need to change the spellings of some words in Exercise 37.

Reference Note

For information about **apostrophes,** see page 827.

COMMON ERRORS

Exercise 38 Proofreading Sentences for Correct Punctuation

Rewrite the following sentences, adding, deleting, or changing punctuation as necessary.

EXAMPLE
1. Langston Hughes, 1902–1967, was one of many poets and artists to gain fame during the Harlem Renaissance.

1. *Langston Hughes (1902–1967) was one of many poets and artists to gain fame during the Harlem Renaissance.*

1. Oh, I dont mind", Hazel replied.
2. The dog on the fire engine was the firefighters' traditional mascot the Dalmatian.
3. Roseannes presentation required twenty seven visuals.
4. Engraved inside the ring was the Latin expression imo pectore which means "from the bottom of the heart.
5. Mr Hilliard your team will include these players, Barbara, Trang, Kyle, and Tracy.
6. The hugely-successful strategy was worth the time we took.
7. Carrie won the election with a three fourths majority.
8. Ms. Levine [Kathy's mother] will speak to our class on career choices in medicine.
9. The hull of the sleek new space shuttle Atlantis gleamed as the spacecraft glided into orbit.
10. We've studied skeletal structure, we'll study circulation next week.

Exercise 39 Proofreading Sentences for Spelling Errors

Correct each misspelled word in the following sentences.

EXAMPLE
1. Why do truck's have to pull over along highways to be wieghed?

1. *trucks, weighed*

1. Slowly, the waters receeded, and we carefully made our way across the creek.
2. The puppy was so adoreable that we didn't mind doing the extra dayly chores that caring for it required.
3. Forty-two students have applied for the scholarship and have recieved replies from the scholarship committee.
4. As soon as our nieghbor's lawn mower stoped, I napped for a few minutes.

5. We could see geeses, deer, and other wildlife on the shore of the lake.

6. The knife's blade was dull, so I checked the drawers and shelfs, but I couldn't find anything to open the box except a few more dull table knifes.

7. The O'Grady twins always seem to be up to mischeif and keep the O'Gradies wondering what the next disaster will be.

8. Both of my brother-in-laws prefered raising sheeps to raising chickens.

9. On September seventh at 4:00 P.M., the temperature exceded ninety-five degrees.

10. Dozens of monkies chattered among the branchs of the trees.

Exercise 40 Proofreading for Spelling Errors and Words Often Confused

Correct each misspelled or incorrect word in the following sentences.

EXAMPLES
[1] The capitol of Pennsylvania, the 5th most populous state, is Harrisburg.

1. *capital, fifth*

[2] While Pennsylvania is often thought of for its manufactureing and industry, another area of commerce is also interesting.

2. *manufacturing*

[1] Pennsylvania's history and it's economy intersect in the feild of communication. [2] In 1719, the *American Weekly Mercury* became the 1st newspaper in the colony; a few years latter, another paper destined to make history, the *Pennsylvania Gazette,* became the property of Ben Franklin. [3] A strong tradition of communication is the heritage of the Keystone State, and in 1920, Pittsburgh renewed Pennsylvania's heritage and claimed quiet a prize when it became the site of the first commercialy operated radio station in the whole world.

[4] Today, of coarse, radio and newspapers have been joined by television stations, but the principle economic activity is manufacturing. [5] Farms also play an economic role; although livestock, such as cattle, contributes the most income, agricultureal crops, such as peaches and tomatos, are also important to the economy. [6] Interestingly enough, for some time the countys of Delaware and Chester have lead the nation in the production of mushrooms.

┌─H E L P ───
No proper nouns are misspelled or misused in Exercise 40.

Reference Note
For information on **words often confused,** see page 857.

COMMON ERRORS

[**7**] Although forestry once thrived their, the state is now expereincing a drop in lumber production. [**8**] Unfortunatly, overcuting forests in the 1800s is still having an effect.

[**9**] From Valley Forge too Gettysburg, the cities of Pennsylvania offer a veiw straight into American history. [**10**] However, as spectacular as this state's history is, for many people nothing could be more glorious then the sight of Pennsylvania's colorful fall leafs.

Exercise 41 **Distinguishing Between Words Often Confused**

Choose the correct word or word group from each pair in parentheses in the following sentences.

EXAMPLES 1. Soldiers who decided to (*desert, dessert*) had to cross the hot and endless sands of the (*desert, dessert*).

1. *desert, desert*

2. We could see the dome of the (*capital, capitol*) during our trip to the nation's (*capital, capitol*).

2. *capitol, capital*

Reference Note

For information on **words often confused,** see page 857.

1. Three sky divers jumped out of the (*plain, plane*).
2. (*Who's, Whose*) going to decide (*who's, whose*) plan for the party is the best one?
3. From the edge of the cliff, (*it's, its*) difficult to see the eagle in (*it's, its*) nest.
4. What (*led, lead*) to the discovery of the poisonous nature of (*led, lead*)?
5. The kindergartners grew (*quite, quiet*) as the teacher began to read the story.
6. (*There, Their, They're*) is the new lantern that (*there, their, they're*) taking with them.
7. (*You're, Your*) going to have to make up (*you're, your*) mind sooner or later.
8. Mike said that he would go to the movies rather (*then, than*) to the skating rink.
9. This math question is (*altogether, all together*) too easy to put on the final exam.
10. If the chickens get (*lose, loose*) again, we will almost certainly (*lose, loose*) a few.

Exercise 42 Proofreading for Mechanics

Correct any errors in mechanics in each of the following items.

EXAMPLE   **[1]** 933 West Forty fifth St

   1. *933 West Forty-fifth St.*

[1] New York, NY, 10023
February 3, 2001

[2] Ms Annelise Wilson
Widgets and Gadgets, Inc.
87 Beaumont Ave.
New York, NY 10027

[3] Dear Ms. Wilson,

[4] Thank you for coming to speak to our local
chapter of the young entrepreneurs club.

[5] My fellow club members and I hope that you
enjoyed the reception as much as we
enjoyed hearing you're advice. **[6]** Your
word's were a great help to those of us
who hope to have careers in business.
[7] Thank you for giving us students a
chance, to learn about many of the challenges of starting a business.

[8] Please except the enclosed certificate as a
small token of our appreciation. **[9]** We
look forward to seeing you at the upcoming
convention at the Seacrest hotel.

[10] Sincerely:

Rodney Alvarez

Rodney Alvarez
President,
Young Entrepreneurs
Club

Enclosure

COMMON ERRORS

Mechanics Test: Section 1

DIRECTIONS   For each of the following sentences, choose the answer that shows the correct capitalization, punctuation, and spelling of the underlined part. If there is no error, choose answer E (*Correct as is*). Indicate your response by shading in the appropriate oval on your answer sheet.

EXAMPLE   1. It <u>would, of coarse, be</u> wise to bring a flashlight for exploring the caves.

        (A) would of coarse be

        (B) would, of course be

        (C) would of course, be

        (D) would, of course, be

        (E) Correct as is

ANSWER   1.

---

1. "Have you seen Spielberg's latest <u>movie," asked Tasha.</u>

    (A) movie"? asked Tasha.

    (B) movie? asked Tasha.

    (C) movie,"? asked Tasha.

    (D) movie?" asked Tasha.

    (E) Correct as is

2. On the corner, musicians from <u>the Salvation army</u> were playing Christmas carols.

    (A) the salvation army

    (B) the Salvation army,

    (C) the Salvation Army

    (D) the salvation Army

    (E) Correct as is

3. These engine parts are manufactured in <u>Detroit Mi.</u>

    (A) Detroit, MI.

    (B) Detroit MI.

    (C) Detroit Michigan

    (D) Detroit, Michigan.

    (E) Correct as is

4. Did you know that both of my <u>brother-in-laws repair their</u> own cars?

    (A) brothers-in-laws repair thier

    (B) brother-in-law's repair their

    (C) brothers-in-law repair their

    (D) brothers-in-law repair they're

    (E) Correct as is

5. Gerry announced that the refreshment committee still <u>needs cups, plates, and napkins.</u>

    (A) needs: cups, plates, and napkins.

    (B) needs cups plates and napkins.

    (C) needs—cups, plates, and napkins.

    (D) needs, cups, plates, and napkins.

    (E) Correct as is

6. Did you <u>say "That</u> Michelangelo began painting the ceiling of the Sistine Chapel in 1508?

    (A) say that

    (B) say, "that

    (C) say that,

    (D) say, "That

    (E) Correct as is

7. The green ice chest in the back of the truck is <u>their's; the</u> red one is mine.

    (A) there's; the

    (B) theirs; the

    (C) thiers; the

    (D) theirs; The

    (E) Correct as is

8. The names of the <u>students, who made the honor roll, are</u> posted on that bulletin board.

    (A) students who made the honor roll, are

    (B) students who made the honor roll are

    (C) students (who made the honor roll) are

    (D) students, who made the honor roll are

    (E) Correct as is

9. I haven't read *Hamlet* yet, consequently, I don't understand Ms. Klein's references to Ophelia.

(**A**) *Hamlet* yet; consequently, I

(**B**) *Hamlet* yet consequently, I

(**C**) *Hamlet* yet consequently I

(**D**) *Hamlet* yet; consequently I

(**E**) Correct as is

10. On my cousins' farm in Texas, the peach trees are covered with blossoms each spring.

(**A**) cousins farm in Texas,

(**B**) cousins farm in Texas

(**C**) cousins' farm in texas

(**D**) cousins' farm in texas,

(**E**) Correct as is

Mechanics Test: Section 2

DIRECTIONS   Each numbered item below contains an underlined group of words. Choose the answer that shows the correct capitalization, punctuation, and spelling of the underlined part. If there is no error, choose answer E (*Correct as is*). Indicate your response by shading in the appropriate oval on your answer sheet.

EXAMPLE   **[1]** <u>41, Maple Ridge Road</u>

     1. **(A)** Forty one, Maple Ridge Road

        (B) Forty One Maple Ridge Road

        (C) 41, Maple ridge road

        (D) 41 Maple Ridge Road

        (E) Correct as is

ANSWER   1.  Ⓐ Ⓑ Ⓒ **Ⓓ** Ⓔ

---

[1] <u>October 17, 2001</u>

[2] <u>Dr Maria H. Ramirez</u>
Grove Health Center

[3] 2104 <u>Fifty-Third</u> Street, #14
Des Moines, IA 50318

[4] <u>Dear Dr. Ramirez,</u>

Thank you for agreeing to speak to our **[5]** <u>high school's Brainstormers'</u> <u>club</u>. We have reserved the auditorium for the afternoon of **[6]** <u>Thursday,</u> <u>November, 9</u>. As you requested, I will introduce you at **[7]** <u>300 P.M.</u> Our vice president, Julie Jackson, will meet you at the school's front office fifteen minutes beforehand. Please let me know **[8]** <u>weather we need to alter</u> these arrangements. **[9]** <u>37 students</u> have **[10]** <u>already signed up for you're</u> talk! We all look forward to seeing you soon.

Yours truly,

George Karras

George Karras
President, Brainstormers' Club

---

1. **(A)** October, 17, 2001
   (B) October 17 2001
   (C) October 17th, 2001
   (D) Oct 17, 2001
   (E) Correct as is

2. **(A)** Dr. Maria H Ramirez
   (B) Dr Maria H Ramirez,
   (C) Dr Maria H. Ramirez
   (D) Dr. Maria H. Ramirez
   (E) Correct as is

3. **(A)** Fifty-third
   (B) Fiftythird
   (C) Fifty Third
   (D) fifty third
   (E) Correct as is

4. **(A)** Dear Dr. Ramirez:
   (B) Dear Dr Ramirez:
   (C) Dear Dr Ramirez,
   (D) Dr Ramirez:
   (E) Correct as is

5. **(A)** high schools
       Brainstormers' club
   (B) High School's
       brainstormers' Club
   (C) high school's
       Brainstormers' Club
   (D) High schools
       Brainstormers' club
   (E) Correct as is

6. **(A)** Thursday November 9
   (B) Thursday, November 9th
   (C) Thursday, Nov. 9th
   (D) Thursday, November 9
   (E) Correct as is

7. **(A)** 3:00 o'clock P.M.
   (B) 3:00 P.M.
   (C) 3 oclock P.M.
   (D) three P.M.
   (E) Correct as is

8. **(A)** weather we need too alter
   (B) whether we need to alter
   (C) weather we need to altar
   (D) whether we need to altar
   (E) Correct as is

9. **(A)** Thirty-seven students
   (B) 37 Students
   (C) Thirty seven students
   (D) Thirty-seven student's
   (E) Correct as is

10. **(A)** all ready signed up
        for you're
    (B) already signed up
        for youre
    (C) allready signed up
        for your
    (D) already signed up
        for your
    (E) Correct as is

PART 4

Quick Reference Handbook

The Dictionary

Information About Words

Contents of a Dictionary

Dictionaries record how words are used in language. A dictionary of the English language shows how most English speakers spell and pronounce a word and what the word means in various contexts or circumstances. In a dictionary, you will also find information such as word histories and the various forms in which a word may appear.

Dictionary Entry   A *dictionary entry* lists a word and information about it. The entry on the next page is from an abridged dictionary. (See also **Abridged** on page 919.) The parts of the entry are labeled and explained below.

1. **Entry word.** The boldface entry word shows how the word is spelled and how it is divided into syllables. The entry word may also show capitalization and list alternate spellings.
2. **Pronunciation.** Accent marks and either phonetic spellings or diacritical marks show the word's pronunciation. A pronunciation

key, usually located in the front of the dictionary or at the bottom of each page, explains the meaning of diacritical marks or phonetic symbols.
3. **Part-of-speech labels.** The part-of-speech labels (usually in abbreviated form) indicate how the entry word is used in a sentence. Some words may be used as more than one part of speech. In this case, a part-of-speech label is given in front of each numbered or lettered series of definitions.
4. **Etymology.** The etymology is the origin and history of a word. It tells how the word (or its parts) came into English, tracing the word from its earliest known form in the language from which it came. A key for understanding the symbols used in etymologies is usually found in the front or back of a dictionary.
5. **Definitions.** If the word has more than one meaning, definitions are numbered or lettered. Most dictionaries list definitions in order of frequency of use, but some order

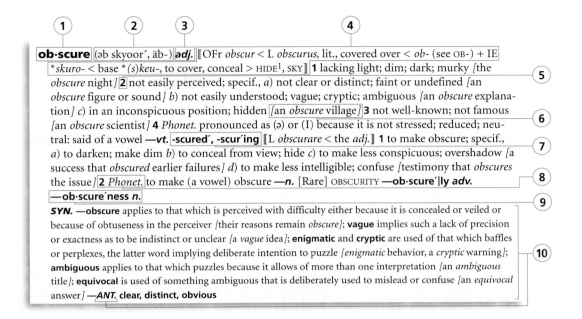

① **ob·scure** **②** (əb skyoor′, äb-) **③** *adj.* **④** ⟦OFr *obscur* < L *obscurus,* lit., covered over < *ob-* (see OB-) + IE **skuro-* < base **(s)keu-,* to cover, conceal > HIDE¹, SKY⟧ **1** lacking light; dim; dark; murky *[the obscure* night] **2** not easily perceived; specif., *a)* not clear or distinct; faint or undefined *[an obscure* figure or sound] *b)* not easily understood; vague; cryptic; ambiguous *[an obscure* explanation] *c)* in an inconspicuous position; hidden *[an obscure* village] **3** not well-known; not famous *[an obscure* scientist] **4** *Phonet.* pronounced as (ə) or (I) because it is not stressed; reduced; neutral: said of a vowel **—*vt.*** **-scured′, -scur′ing** ⟦L *obscurare* < the *adj.*⟧ **1** to make obscure; specif., *a)* to darken; make dim *b)* to conceal from view; hide *c)* to make less conspicuous; overshadow *[a* success that *obscured* earlier failures] *d)* to make less intelligible; confuse *[testimony that obscures* the issue] **2** *Phonet.* to make (a vowel) obscure **—*n.*** [Rare] OBSCURITY **—ob·scure′ly** *adv.* **—ob·scure′ness** *n.*

SYN. **—obscure** applies to that which is perceived with difficulty either because it is concealed or veiled or because of obtuseness in the perceiver *[their reasons remain obscure];* **vague** implies such a lack of precision or exactness as to be indistinct or unclear *[a vague idea];* **enigmatic** and **cryptic** are used of that which baffles or perplexes, the latter word implying deliberate intention to puzzle *[enigmatic* behavior, a *cryptic* warning]; **ambiguous** applies to that which puzzles because it allows of more than one interpretation *[an ambiguous* title]; **equivocal** is used of something ambiguous that is deliberately used to mislead or confuse *[an equivocal* answer] **—*ANT.*** clear, distinct, obvious

the definitions according to the date when the word came to have each meaning. Read the dictionary's introduction to confirm how the word's definitions are listed.

6. **Examples.** Phrases or sentences may illustrate the word as it has just been defined.

7. **Other forms.** A dictionary may list spellings for other forms of the word, such as full or partial spellings of plural forms of nouns, different tenses of verbs, or the comparison forms of adjectives and adverbs.

8. **Special usage labels.** These labels may show that a definition is limited to certain forms of speech (such as [Archaic] or [Slang]). Or, the labels may indicate that a definition is used only in a certain field, such as *Law, Med.* (medicine), or *Chem.* (chemistry). Every dictionary will have a key for abbreviations used.

9. **Related word forms.** These are various forms of the entry word, usually created by adding suffixes or prefixes.

10. **Synonyms and antonyms.** Synonyms and antonyms may appear at the end of some word entries. Synonyms may also be included within the list of definitions, printed in capital letters.

Although not illustrated in the above entry, many dictionary entries give additional information specific to that entry.

■ **Homographs** Words that are spelled alike but have different meanings usually are listed as separate entry words and often are identified by superscripts.

flue¹ (flo͞o) *n.* ⟦< ? OFr *fluie,* a flowing, stream⟧ **1** a tube, pipe, or shaft for the passage of smoke, hot air, exhaust fumes, etc. esp. in a chimney **2** ⟦ME, mouthpiece of a hunting horn⟧ *a)* a flue pipe in an organ *b)* the opening or passage for air in such a flue pipe

flue² (flo͞o) *n.* ⟦altered < ? FLUKE²⟧ a barbed point; fluke

- **Illustrations** Pictures and diagrams help to simplify difficult concepts.
- **Subentries** Phrases that use the main entry word have their own definitions but appear under the overall heading of the main entry word. In the following example "meet halfway" is a subentry of *halfway*.

  half•way (haf′ wā′, -wā′) **adj. 1** equally distant between two points; states, etc.: midway **2** incomplete; partial [*halfway* measures] **—adv. 1** half the distance; to the midway point **2** incompletely; partially **—meet halfway** to compromise or be willing to compromise (with)

Other Parts of a Dictionary In addition to entry words, most dictionaries also include the following parts or elements.

- **Abbreviations** Many dictionaries include a chart of common abbreviations, including those for governmental agencies, weights and measurements, and the names of states or geographical regions.
- **Biographical and Geographical Entries** Some dictionaries include a section that identifies famous or influential figures in history, including writers, politicians, scientists, inventors, and explorers. The entries identify the person's profession and provide the dates of his or her birth and death. In other dictionaries, biographical entries are included in the regular listing of words. Some dictionaries have a geographical section, while others include geographical names in the regular listing of words. The geographical section is a list of most of the populated places in the world and includes the pronunciation of the place name and the population size at the time of the dictionary's publication.

- **Colleges and Universities** Many dictionaries, particularly school or college editions, list all the colleges and universities in the United States and Canada. The entries provide the school's location, the date of its establishment, and the number of students attending at the time of the dictionary's publication.
- **Copyright** A copyright is the exclusive right of ownership, granted by law for a specific period of time, for a publication. A copyright page, often found in the front of a dictionary, indicates when a dictionary was published. Each updated edition shows the new copyright date on its copyright page and includes recent words and new meanings of old words.
- **Guide to the Dictionary** Most dictionaries have a few pages that explain how the material is organized and what the abbreviations and different typefaces mean.
- **Index** Some dictionaries have an index that indicates where to find the dictionary features listed here, including the pronunciation key, the pages dedicated to word entries, and, in some cases, the biographical and geographical entries if they are separate from the word entries.
- **Pronunciation Key** A pronunciation key is provided at the front of any dictionary and often at the bottom of each page or pair of pages within the dictionary.
- **Scholarly Essays** The scholarly essays are written by language experts and provide information about subjects such as the history and growth of the English language, the way a new edition of the dictionary differs from a previous one, and how the dictionary was researched and prepared.

Types of Dictionaries

Different types of dictionaries provide various kinds and amounts of information about the words they contain. The dictionary you choose should be determined by the kind of information that you need.

Abridged An *abridged,* or shortened, *dictionary* is the most common type of dictionary. It contains *most* of the words the average person uses or encounters in writing or reading. For this reason, an abridged dictionary (also called a *college* dictionary) is the kind of dictionary most commonly found in homes, classrooms, and workplaces. One advantage of abridged dictionaries is that they are frequently updated, so they can provide the most recent information on meanings and uses of words. Abridged dictionaries arrange their word listings in alphabetical order and include basic information, such as the spelling, definition, pronunciation, part of speech, and source of a word. Most abridged dictionaries also include tables of commonly used abbreviations, selected biographical entries, and tables of signs and symbols.

Specialized *Specialized dictionaries* contain entries that relate to a specific subject or field. Specialized dictionaries also provide *specialized information* about a word or term— word meanings for a particular context perhaps not included in a general dictionary. For example, specialized dictionaries collect and define terms as they are used in art, music, sports, filmmaking, gardening, mythology, and many other subjects. Some specialized dictionaries define slang words and idioms. Another type of specialized dictionary contains ordinary words grouped or arranged to suit a particular purpose, such as rhyming dictionaries (often consulted by poets) that group rhyming words.

Foreign language dictionaries define words and phrases from other languages and sometimes contain lists of irregular verbs and rules of grammar or punctuation.

Unabridged An *unabridged dictionary* is the most comprehensive source for finding information about a word. Unabridged dictionaries offer more word entries than abridged or specialized dictionaries and include words that are relatively rare. In addition, they usually provide more information, such as extensive word histories and longer lists of synonyms and antonyms. The largest unabridged dictionary of the English language is the *Oxford English Dictionary* (*OED*), which attempts to list and define every word in the English language. The present twenty-volume edition of the *OED* contains definitions and/or illustrations for over 600,000 word forms. Each entry gives detailed descriptions of a word's source, its first appearance in the language (with a specific citation as an example), its various forms, and the way its meaning has changed over time. Quotations from historical and literary sources document a word's meaning and usage since the year 1150. The entries of the *OED* emphasize a word's history instead of its current meaning and are much longer than those found in abridged or specialized dictionaries. For these reasons, the *OED* is not used like other dictionaries.

Aside from the *OED,* most other unabridged dictionaries commonly consist of one large volume. One well-known, single-volume unabridged dictionary is *Webster's Third New International Dictionary.* It is called an *international* dictionary because it contains words (with variations in spelling and meaning) used in several English-speaking countries. Another widely used unabridged dictionary is the *Random House Dictionary of the English Language.*

Document Design

Manuscript Style

Not all documents or compositions are designed on a computer—or even need to be. The way your paper looks, however, makes an impression on your readers, and you probably want that impression to be a favorable one. Teachers, for the most part, require only a neat and legible manuscript from you. The following chart provides guidelines for preparing papers, whether you type on a typewriter, use a computer, or write out your compositions by hand. (See also **Writing** on page 1023.) Your teacher may have additional guidelines for you to follow. Remember that these guidelines will help improve the appearance of your papers.

Guidelines for Submitting Papers

1. Use only one side of a sheet of paper.

2. Use standard size, white, ruled paper if you are handwriting or standard size, white, unruled paper if you are typing. Do not use legal size or spiral-notebook paper.

3. Write in blue or black ink, or **type your paper.** If you type, use a blue or black ribbon that prints legibly. If you prepare your paper on a computer, try to use a letter-quality printer.

4. If you write by hand, do not skip lines, unless your teacher directs you otherwise. If you type, double-space the lines.

5. Leave one-inch margins at the top, sides, and bottom of each page.

6. Indent the first line of each paragraph (about five letter spaces).

7. Number all the pages except the first page. Place the number in the upper right-hand corner of the page.

8. Keep all pages neat and clean. You may make a few corrections with correction fluid. If you have several errors on a page and the page is difficult to read, write out or type the page again.

9. Follow your teacher's instructions for placing your name, the date, your class, and the title of your paper. Your teacher may also request that information be placed on a separate title page.

Desktop Publishing

Page Design or Layout

Before the widespread use of computers changed the printing industry, documents were designed by hand. Page designers worked page by page, cutting up, arranging, and pasting down strips of text (words), illustrations, headings, and captions. Now almost anyone with a computer can design an entire document. Effective design entails setting text on a page with images and graphics in a way that communicates a coherent message and attracts readers' attention. The following section explains some key concepts for designing professional-looking pages. (Remember that these principles of design may apply also to pages that you write and lay out manually. Using a computer provides you with a wealth of design options, but you still may use space effectively when you arrange text and graphics by hand.)

Alignment *Alignment* refers to how lines of text are arranged on a page. There are several ways text can be aligned.

- **Left aligned** Text that is *left aligned* is set so that each line begins against the left margin. Most printed documents are set left aligned to facilitate reading from left to right.

  EXAMPLE

  This text is left aligned.
  Notice how the lines form
  a straight edge along the
  left margin.

- **Right aligned** Text that is *right aligned* has lines that end against the right margin. Right-aligned text is usually used in small

doses because it is not easy to read. Pull-quotes and poetry are occasionally aligned right. (See also **Pull-quote** on page 924.)

  EXAMPLE

  This text is right aligned.
  Notice how it forms a straight
  edge along the right margin.

- **Center aligned** Text that is *center aligned*, or *centered*, is set in the middle of the page. Center-aligned text usually appears in invitations, posters, or advertisements.

  EXAMPLE

  This text is center aligned.
  Notice how each line is evenly spaced
  on both sides of an invisible, vertical line
  in the center of the page.

- **Justified alignment** means that both ends of several lines of text form a straight edge. Extra spaces may be added between words to ensure that the lines are equal in length.

  EXAMPLE

  This sample text is left and right aligned, or *justified*. Notice how the lines of text form two neat edges.

- **Ragged alignment** means that the lines of the text do not create a straight edge on both sides. Usually the right-hand side of the text is ragged in alignment.

  EXAMPLE

  This sample text is left aligned and also *ragged*. Notice how the lines form a neat edge on the left but not on the right.

Bullet A *bullet* (•) is a symbol used to high-light information in a text. Bullets are often used to separate information into lists. Bullets attract attention and help readers remember the information included in lists. When you use bulleted lists, keep in mind the following tips.

- Always indent your bulleted list from the main body of the text.
- Use plain bullets in formal documents. Decorative symbols (for example, ¶, Δ, ◊, *, or +) may be used as bullets in other forms of writing, such as journal entries and poems.
- Make sure that the items in your list are parallel both in the type of information they contain and in construction. For example, use all nouns or all imperative sentences, as in this bulleted list.

Callout A *callout* is a line or phrase of text that describes some aspect of a graphic image. Usually the callout is connected to the illustration by an arrow or line. Notice in the following diagram how the callouts identify the various parts of the illustration.

EXAMPLE

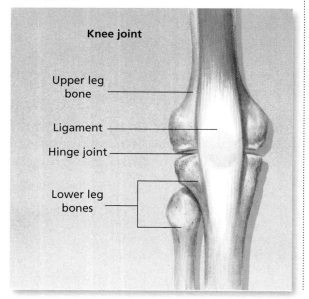

Knee joint

Upper leg bone

Ligament

Hinge joint

Lower leg bones

Columns and blocks of text Text is easier to read when it is contained in rectangular-shaped areas, such as in *columns* or *blocks*. The width of a column or block of text varies, depending on the length of the text and the format of the document. The text in posters, advertisements, and fliers is usually set in horizontal blocks so that it may be read quickly. Text in reference books and newspapers, which contain large quantities of information, usually appears in vertical columns. (See also **Line length** on page 924.)

Contrast *Contrast* refers to the balance of light and dark areas on a page. Dark areas are those that contain blocks of text or graphics. Light areas have little type. A page with high contrast, or roughly balanced light and dark areas, is easier to read than a page with low contrast—one mostly light or one filled with text and images. (See also **White space** on page 925.)

Emphasis In page design, *emphasis* is the way a writer indicates to a reader which information on a page is most important. For example, the front page of a newspaper uses bold or large headlines and photographs to place emphasis on a particular story. Because readers' eyes are drawn naturally to color, large or bold print, and graphics, these elements are commonly used to create emphasis.

Graphic A *graphic* is a picture, chart, illustration, or piece of artwork that is used to convey information visually. Short sections of text, such as headings, subheadings, titles, headers, and footers, may also be considered graphics because they serve a visual function. (See also **Types of Graphics** on page 930; **Headings and subheadings** and **Headers and footers** on the following page.)

Gray page   A *gray page* contains text almost exclusively. It has few or no graphics to indicate visually the organization or structure of the material on the page. As a result, reading and understanding the information contained on a gray page may take more time than reading the information on a page that uses some graphics. Textbooks, such as the one you are now reading, have moved away from gray pages to a page layout that balances text and graphics. (See also **Contrast** on pages 922 and 926.)

Grid lines   *Grid lines* are vertical and horizontal intersecting lines that provide structure to a page by dividing it into sections. Often, grid lines are used to plan the layout, or final appearance, of a page. In some computer software programs, grid lines are visible in a document when it appears on a computer monitor, but they do not appear in the printed version.

Gutter   A *gutter* is the inner margin of space from a page's printed area to the binding.

Headers and footers   *Headers* and *footers* are like signposts that provide information about a printed document. Headers appear in the top margin of a page, and footers appear in the bottom margin. Most documents—whether articles, books, magazines, or newspapers—do not have both. Headers and footers may include some or all of the following information.

- the name of the author
- the name of the publication
- chapter or section titles
- the date of the publication
- page numbers

Headings and subheadings   *Headings* and *subheadings* (also called *heads* and *subheads*) are lines of text used graphically to give readers clues about the content and organization of a document.

- **Headings**   A *heading* functions as a title or headline; it gives readers an immediate general idea of what a book, article, or chapter is about. Headings appear at the beginning of a text and are usually set in large, bold capital letters. Often they appear in a typeface different from that of the body of the text.

- **Subheadings**   A *subheading* links the heading and the text. It is more specific than a heading and indicates a new section or idea in the text. Several subheadings usually appear under one heading. To distinguish them from the headings and the text, subheadings may be set in letters larger than the regular type, in boldface or italic, or in a different typeface.

EXAMPLE

Language Loss Spells End of Culture — heading
The Demise of the — subheading
Chamicuro Language
Chamicuro, the language of the — text
Chamicuro people in the jungle
areas of Peru, is still spoken only
by a handful of elderly people.

Indentation   An *indentation* is the space skipped over from the left margin—usually a few letter spaces—to indicate the beginning of a new paragraph in a text. Whether you are preparing text on a computer or writing your work by hand, the indentation should be one-half of an inch from the left margin. If you are working on a computer or typewriter, one-half of an inch is roughly equivalent to five letter spaces. Block quotations should be indented one inch or ten letter spaces from the left margin. Indentation is also used with bulleted lists (see page 922).

Line length *Line length* is the number of characters (letters, spaces between words, and punctuation marks) a line contains. (Remember, a line is not a sentence; it is a single line of text that may or may not form a complete thought.) The best line length for a document depends on the size of the type and the format of the document. In general, limit line length to nine or ten words, about sixty-five characters. Doing so will make the text easier to read. Always keep in mind that a major goal of desktop publishing is to design texts that are clear and accessible to readers.

Margins *Margins* are the space that surrounds the text on a page—whether typed on a typewriter, word processor, or computer. Most computer word-processing programs automatically set the side margins at 1.25 inches and the top and bottom margins at 1 inch. Margins are flexible, however. If your teacher recommends a different set of measurements for the margins of your papers, use them instead. (See also **White space** on the next page and **Guidelines for Submitting Papers** on page 920.)

Pull-quote A *pull-quote* is a quotation from a text, such as a magazine article or story, that has been turned into an eye-catching graphic and set in the margin. Pull-quotes should be short and concise; often they are excerpts from a longer thought in the text. You can use a pull-quote from your text to catch the reader's interest.

EXAMPLE

> Trust thyself; every heart vibrates to that iron string. Accept the place the divine providence has found for you, the society of your contemporaries, the connection of events. Great men have always done so, and confided themselves childlike to the genius of their age, betraying their perception that the absolutely trustworthy was seated at their heart. . . .

"Trust thyself."
— R.W. Emerson

Rule lines *Rule lines* are lines used graphically to create visual effects on a page. Rule lines may be thick or thin, vertical or horizontal. They may set text off from a headline or caption, separate columns, or draw your eye to something on the page. This page, in fact, has a rule line running down its center.

Title and subtitle A *title* is the name of an entire document, whether a book, article, or essay. A *subtitle* is more descriptive than the title and sometimes longer. Sometimes subtitles appear in a smaller typeface; alternatively, they may be attached to a title by a colon. In books, titles (often with the accompanying subtitles) appear alone on a separate page (the title page) at the very beginning of a book.

EXAMPLES

The Norton Anthology of Literature by Women
The Tradition in English

Exploring the Moon: The Apollo Expeditions

Visuals *Visuals,* like *graphics,* are pictures, charts, illustrations, or artwork that convey information. (See also **Types of Graphics** on page 930.)

White space *White space* is any area on a page where there is little or no text or graphics. White space contrasts to the dark ink on a page and makes the print more readable. Usually, white space is limited to the margins, the gutter, and the spaces between words, lines, and columns. (See also **Contrast** on page 922.)

Typography

Typography refers to the letters and markings used in printing and publishing. When Johannes Gutenberg introduced his printing press over 500 years ago, the letters of the movable type were cut out of wood and modeled on handwritten characters or the lettering in manuscript books. Today, computers have made printing considerably easier. With practice, working with typography can become an art form, but your document design will most likely focus on function—communicating information clearly. The following section provides basic information about typography.

Capital letters *Capital* (or *uppercase*) *letters* help readers identify the beginning of a new sentence or idea. Capital letters command readers' attention and may be used in the following ways to create emphasis in a document.

■ **Headings or titles** When **headings** or **titles** appear in the same typeface as the text, setting them in all capital letters creates emphasis and draws the reader's eye. (See also **Contrast** and **Emphasis** on page 922.)

STUDENT NEWSPAPER WINS NATIONAL AWARD

THE BASIC ELEMENTS OF PERSUASIVE WRITING

■ **Initial cap** An *initial cap* is an artistic use of a capital letter in the first word of a first paragraph. Initial caps may emphasize important section breaks, such as chapter openers, within a long text. Originally initial caps derived from medieval illuminated manuscripts in which the first letter of a section or chapter was enlarged and transformed into a colorful drawing. Generally, there are two kinds of initial caps: *drop caps,* which descend below the line, and *stickup caps,* which rise above the line. Some computer software may use only one term in its menu, such as *drop cap,* to indicate the variety of ways you may design the initial cap.

EXAMPLE

O nce upon a time in
the middle of winter . . .

■ **Small caps** *Small caps* are uppercase letters that are reduced in size. Usually they appear in abbreviations of time, such as 9:00 A.M. and A.D. 1500, or of the names of organizations, such as NASA or NATO. Small caps may also be combined with true capital letters for an artistic effect.

NOTE Because of their uniform shapes, capital letters can be difficult to read, especially in long sections of type. Use capital letters for contrast or emphasis, not for large bodies of text.

Captions *Captions* are lines of text that appear under photographs or illustrations. They

QUICK REFERENCE HANDBOOK

explain the meaning or importance of a visual and connect it to the text. Because readers usually look first at the graphics on a page, captions are often the first text they read. Therefore, captions should be concise, accurate, and interesting. Captions may appear in a smaller size type (usually two point sizes smaller) than the text or in italicized type of the same size. (See also **Font size** on page 927.)

Contrast   In terms of typography, *contrast* refers to the visual effect of using different fonts in a document. In general, use only two different fonts in a single document—one for the body of your text and captions and one for the headings and subheadings. Three or more typefaces in a document make it difficult to read. (For an example of contrast between headings and subheadings, see **Headings and subheadings** on page 923.)

Font   A *font* is one complete set of characters (such as letters, numbers, and punctuation marks) of a given design. Thanks to computer technology there are now more than ten thousand available fonts. (Usually, the terms *typeface* and *font* are used interchangeably, although those in the printing industry make a distinction between the two terms.) The best font is easy to read and appropriate to the subject matter. (See also **Fonts, categories of** below; **Font size** and **Fonts, styles of** on page 927.)

Fonts, categories of   There are thousands of fonts available, each with its own name and unique appearance. In general, though, all fonts belong to one of the three following categories.

- **Decorative, or script**   *Decorative* fonts are elaborately designed characters that convey a distinct mood or feeling. *Script* fonts simulate

handwriting: The letters touch each other. Because they are too difficult to read as regular text, decorative fonts should be used sparingly for an artistic effect. They are most commonly used in wedding invitations or graduation announcements.

EXAMPLES
This is an example of Zapf Chancery typeface.
This is an example of Linoscript typeface.
This is an example of Fresh Script typeface.

- **Sans serif**   The characters in *sans serif* fonts are formed by neat straight lines, with no small strokes at the ends of the letters. (*Sans serif* means "without serifs, or strokes.") This font—characterized by letters and symbols simplified to their bare essentials—was invented in the nineteenth century. Sans serif typefaces work well as headings and subheadings, pull-quotes, and captions because they have clean edges and are easy to read. (See also **Serif** below.)

EXAMPLES
Helvetica is a sans serif font.
Franklin Gothic is a sans serif font.
Futura is a sans serif font.

- **Serif**   The characters in serif fonts have little strokes (*serifs*) attached at each end. Serif fonts were the first styles of typeface used when printing was invented. The serifs, or strokes, are believed to be modeled on the connectors between characters in handwritten writing, on which serif type was based. As in handwriting, the little strokes help guide the reader's eyes from letter to letter and word to word. Serif type—such as the Minion typeface you see in this book—is still commonly used to set large bodies of type because of its readable quality. The font does not call attention to itself and makes it easier to read large amounts of text. (See also **Readability** on page 928.)

EXAMPLES
Palatino is a serif font.
New Century Schoolbook is a serif font.
Times is a serif font.

NOTE Mixing decorative, sans serif, and serif fonts on a page creates high contrast; however, you should not use more than one font from each category. Too many fonts on a page may confuse readers.

Font size or point size The size of the type in any document is called the *font size* or *point size*. Every font comes in varying sizes, which are determined by measuring a sample of type (a capital letter) against a scale of 72 points (there are 72 points to an inch). Word-processing software provides many options for sizing text. Many newspapers and textbooks use type measured at 12 points. Type for headings and headlines may range anywhere from 18 to 48 points. Captions usually appear in 9- to 11-point type.

EXAMPLES

Exploring
28 point type

He never actually did much hiking.
9 point type

Fonts, styles of In addition to the various categories of fonts, there are also several different styles. Such styles can be applied to most fonts to provide emphasis and contrast. For example, titles of books or films and captions are often set in *italics*. **Boldface** or ***boldface italic*** can highlight new or important concepts. In addition, computers and desktop publishing software have made more elaborate styles from the printing industry available on computers.

The most common differences between font styles are between roman (meaning, in this case, "not slanted") and italic, or between capital letters and lowercase letters. Look at the following examples of eye-catching fonts. (See also **Font, categories of** on page 926.)

EXAMPLES
roman boldface
roman outline font
roman underscored
roman condensed
italic lowercase
italic boldface

roman shadow font
r o m a n   e x p a n d e d
roman lowercase letters
ROMAN CAPITALS
ITALIC CAPITALS

NOTE Select font styles that will help readers understand your text, and avoid using too many fonts in the same document. Also be consistent in your use of font styles. For example, if you use italic boldface for one heading, use it for all the other headings as well. Remember that your reader may be confused if you change font styles in the middle of your text.

Knockout type *Knockout,* or *reversed, type* is the technique of setting light type against a contrasting, dark background. Use this technique sparingly, for white text on a black background is harder to read than black on white. You might try using knockout type in a chapter heading or title.

EXAMPLES
Here is dark type set against a light background.
Here is type set in knockout, or reversed, type.

Leading or line spacing *Leading* (rhymes with *sledding*), or *line spacing,* is the distance measured in points between lines of text. Most word processors and typewriters allow you to adjust the amount of line spacing to single-, double-, or even triple-space measurements. For formal documents, use double-spacing because documents that are double-spaced are easier to read and allow room for handwritten edits.

Legibility   *Legibility* refers to the ease with which a reader can decipher a short section of text like a headline or cross reference. Clear typefaces and simple fonts in readable sizes make a text more legible.

Lowercase   *Lowercase* type is the set of letters that are not capital letters. Lowercase letters are characterized by *ascenders* (rising strokes, as in the letters *b* and *h*) and *descenders* (dropping strokes, as in the letters *g* and *y*). When type was set by hand, these letters were placed in a case below a case holding the capital letters, thus the terms *lowercase* and *uppercase*. Most text that you read or write will appear in lowercase type because it is easier to read and because it conforms with the conventions of written language. (See also **Capital letters** on page 925 and **Readability** below.)

Readability   *Readability* refers to how easily a text can be read. Unlike legibility, readability refers to the ease of reading long sections of text. A document with high readability contains text set in simple fonts (generally in a classic serif typeface) and in appropriate point sizes. Document pages with high readability often have high contrast, or roughly balanced light and dark areas. (See also **Contrast** on pages 922 and 926; **Fonts, categories of** on page 926; **Font size** and **Fonts, styles of** on page 927.)

Graphics

Graphics organize and communicate information visually. They may be used to display data or information; explain a process; illustrate how something looks, works, or is organized; or show trends or relationships over time. Select and develop your graphics carefully. They must always convey information clearly and support the text that appears on the page. Text and graphics should fit together nicely, like the pieces of a jigsaw puzzle, so that readers understand the overall design of your document, whether computer-generated or written by hand. (For more on reading graphics, see **Interpreting Graphics** on page 961.)

Arrangement and Design

The challenge of designing a document that contains text and graphics is to place all the components in a balanced and organized way. The following elements should be considered when you design a document with graphics.

Accessibility   *Accessibility* refers to the ease with which readers can find information in a document. You can increase a document's accessibility by using bulleted lists, headers, headings, footers, and subheadings.

Accuracy   All graphics must contain *accurate,* or true, information. Never manipulate or change images or the data shown in charts, graphs, or tables. Readers must be able to trust the information in the graphics you include in your document.

Color   *Color* naturally attracts a reader's eye, especially when it contrasts with the black and white of text and white space. Color may be used to command the reader's attention, highlight a piece of information, indicate that certain items on a page belong together, or show the organization of the parts of a document or page.

■ **Choosing color**   When you choose colors for graphics, remember the following guidelines.

1. **Colors are for emphasis in images or backgrounds, not for text.** Text may look more appealing in color, but readers find such text difficult to read and remember.
2. **Use colors in pairs or schemes.** Color schemes provide contrast; a single color may simply look out of place. However, avoid an overabundance of color.
3. **Choose colors that complement each other.** The colors that appear opposite one another on the color wheel (shown on this page) are always complements.
4. **Use warm colors, such as red and orange, sparingly.** These colors appear to expand or jump off the page.
5. **Use cool colors, such as blue and green, as background.** Because of their calming effect, blue and green will not compete with your text.

■ **Color wheel**   The *color wheel* shows the relationships colors have to one another. The primary colors are yellow, red, and blue; all other colors are the result of combining these colors or mixing them with white or black. Colors that complement each other appear opposite each other on the wheel. To create a color scheme, choose three complementary colors, one from each of the primary color families and equidistant from one another on the color wheel.

Contrast   *Contrast* is the quality of standing out. Create contrast within graphics by using

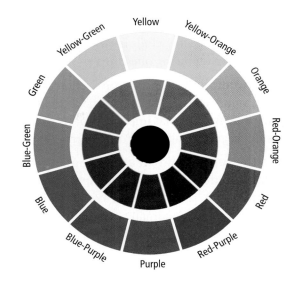

different visual cues for different kinds of information. For example, set important terms in boldface type or in bulleted lists. Use color in your charts, graphs, and tables to make it easy to distinguish bits of information. For example, use different colors for each of the wedges of a pie chart. Contrast makes it easier for your reader to understand your graphic. (See also **Contrast** on pages 922 and 926; **Fonts, styles of** on page 927.)

Emphasis   *Emphasis* draws the readers' attention to what you want them to see. It is achieved with the use of visual cues such as color, capital letters, boldface or italic fonts, and large type size. Graphics provide emphasis because they usually attract a reader's attention first. (See also **Emphasis** on page 922.)

Focus   *Focus* refers to the most important part of an illustration, photograph, or drawing—what a reader looks at first. Usually photographs, illustrations, or drawings depict a subject, whether a person, an event, or a thing, as seen through the artist's, photographer's, or creator's eyes. The focus of a graphic should always reinforce the text. When you design or choose an image to include in your document, ask yourself the following questions about its focus.

- **Is the subject of the graphic clear?** Choose a graphic whose subject is immediately recognizable. Be sure that important parts of the subject are not obscured or hidden from view.

- **Is the subject shown at the angle that you intend?** If you wish to emphasize a subject's height, show it from a low angle; if you want to show how small a subject is, show it from above. Always ask, "Will this graphic give readers a clear sense of what the text describes?"

- **Does the graphic include any distracting details?** Crop or trim the graphic so that its focus is clear.

- **Will you need to add labels to the graphic so readers will understand?** If the meaning of the graphic is unclear, add labels or captions. Remember, however, that too many labels make a graphic hard to understand. If the graphic becomes too cluttered, group labels into larger categories or find a better, simpler visual expression.

Font and font size   Text, such as labels and captions, that appears in graphics should be small, between 9.5 and 11 points. The type may appear in the same font as the main text, but smaller or in italics. You may also provide a visual contrast by setting all labels and captions in a contrasting font. (See also **Labels and captions** on this page.)

Integration   *Integration* refers to the way the content of graphics and text fit together on the page. Place close together graphics and text that are related or cover the same material. In addition, the text should direct the reader's attention to the visual and explain its content.

Labels and captions   To promote understanding, many graphics need *labels* or *captions.* Labels briefly identify the content of charts, tables, and diagrams. Usually they appear within the body of the graphic, but often they are attached to the graphic by thin rule lines. Captions are usually full sentences that describe a graphic such as a photograph or illustration. They appear directly under, beside, or above the graphic. (For an example of a label, see the diagram on page 932. See also **Callout** on page 922.)

Organization   *Organization*, or arrangement, refers to the placement or grouping of the text and graphics on a page. All the elements that deal with a similar subject should be grouped together. Use visual cues such as headings and subheadings, similar fonts, color, and rule lines to show that certain text and visual elements are related. (See also **Integration** on this page.)

Tone   Graphics, like words, can express many different attitudes and feelings, or *tones.* Because the text and the graphics support one another, the tone of one element should match the other. In other words, if the text is about a serious topic, then the graphic should be clear and unobtrusive, not cartoonish. (See also **Tone** on page 1044.)

Types of Graphics

Graphics can take various forms. Designing or choosing the right kind of graphic may be a challenge. However, the following list will help you decide among some of the most common and helpful types.

Chart   A *chart* shows relationships among ideas or data. Three types of charts you are likely to use are flow charts, pie charts, and tables.

- **Flow charts**   A **flow chart** shows a sequence of events. Notice how the boxes below are set so that you read them from left to right. In flow charts, all text is contained in boxes and direction arrows are used between the boxes to indicate the direction of movement.

How to Build a Fire in the Woods

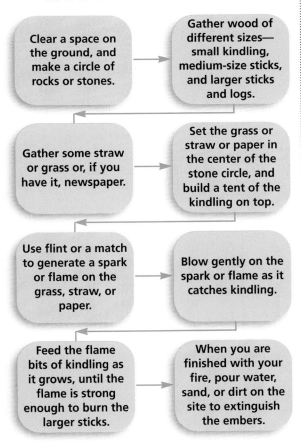

- **Pie charts**   A **pie chart** shows the relationships of the parts of a whole to one another. It is composed of wedges, arranged so that readers can perceive how each wedge compares to the others. (Usually pie charts are arranged with the largest wedge at the top and the other wedges descending clockwise.) Pie charts also usually contain labels and percentages for each wedge.

What Creates Solid Wastes?
(Percentage of solid waste)

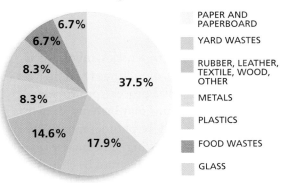

- **Tables or simple charts**   A *table* organizes information in horizontal and vertical grids. Usually the categories of a table are identified above and along the left-hand side of the grid. Tables display information, leaving interpretation to the reader; therefore, they need to be organized so that the information is clear and distinct. (See also **Tables** on page 963.)

EXAMPLES

Two-column Table

Largest National Parks in the United States	
National Parks	**Size in Million Acres**
Wrangell-St. Elias, Alaska	7.6
Gates of the Arctic, Alaska	7.0
Denali, Alaska	4.7
Katmai, Alaska	3.5
Glacier Bay, Alaska	3.2

Source: U.S. National Park Service

Three-column Table

Five Largest American Indian Tribes		
Tribe	Number	Percent
Cherokee	369,035	19.0
Navajo	225,298	11.6
Sioux	107,321	5.5
Chippewa	105,988	5.5
Choctaw	86,231	4.5

Source: Bureau of the Census, U.S. Dept. of Commerce, 1990 Census

Diagram A *diagram* uses symbols, such as circles or arrows, or pictures to compare abstract ideas, show a process, or provide instruction. Diagrams may be hand-drawn, computer-generated, or photographed. They are usually spare, showing only the important details. Sometimes the diagram has labels to explain its various parts. (See also **Callouts** on page 922.)

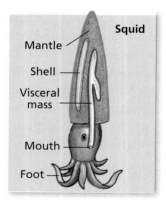

Squid
Mantle
Shell
Visceral mass
Mouth
Foot

Graph A *graph* can either show a comparison of quantities, or reveal changes or trends over time, allowing readers to see a "big picture" in one glance. Notice in the following examples how the horizontal axis in a line or bar graph indicates points in time or categories of things, and the vertical axis shows quantities.

Line Graph

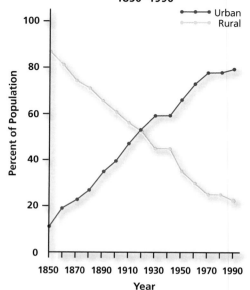

Changes in the Urban and Rural Population, 1850–1990

Urban
Rural

Percent of Population
Year

Source: *Statistical Abstract of the United States*

Bar Graph

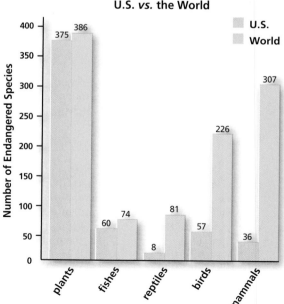

Endangered Species, 1994
U.S. *vs.* the World

U.S.
World

Number of Endangered Species

plants 375 386
fishes 60 74
reptiles 8 81
birds 57 226
mammals 36 307

Source: U.S. Fish and Wildlife Service

Illustration *Illustrations*, such as drawings, photographs, and other artwork, may be used to show readers something new, unfamiliar, or indescribable; what something or someone looks like; or how something works. (See also **Diagram** on previous page.)

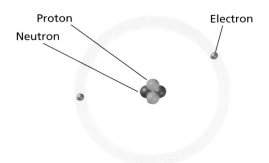

A helium nucleus must have neutrons in it to keep the protons from moving apart.

Storyboard A *storyboard* illustrates the course of an event or the scenes of a story. Storyboards may be used to plan a video or to map out the events in a story. The boxes in a storyboard contain drawings as well as text; text may also appear outside and under the boxes.

Time line A *time line* identifies events that occurred during a particular period of time. Usually, the horizontal axis, or line, of a graph shows the dates or time periods, and the events which correspond to these dates are identified or described above or below the horizontal line. Some time lines are illustrated with small photos or drawings appearing above each date.

EXAMPLE

Life of Ralph Waldo Emerson

| 1803 | 1817 | 1826 | 1831–32 | 1836 | 1842–44 | 1847 | 1882 |

Enters Harvard

Resigns position; then travels to Europe after wife's death

Edits the journal *The Dial*

Publishes *Poems* and delivers lectures in Europe

Born May 25 in Boston, Massachusetts

Publishes *Nature*, becomes center of Transcendentalist movement

Becomes associate pastor at Boston's Second (Unitarian) Church

Dies in Concord, Massachusetts

Shot: Close-up
Voice-over: "Livingston High School first opened in 1923. . . ."

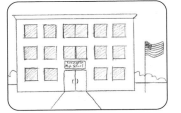

Shot: Pull back to long view of school
Voice-over: "It was built to accommodate the city's growing number of immigrants. . . ."

Shot: Close-up of photograph; pan slowly from left to right
Voice-over: "and its first graduating class had fifty students. . . ."

English Origins and Uses

History of English

A Historical Overview

The English language was first written about 1,300 years ago but was spoken long before that. Since its beginnings, the language has changed so much that English speakers today find it difficult to recognize its earlier forms. Still, there is continuity across the ages. The history of the English language may be divided into four major periods: *Pre-English, Old English, Middle English,* and *Modern English.* The time line below shows approximately when English moved from one period to the next and when other languages influenced the development of English. It also indicates how the number of English speakers has grown over the centuries.

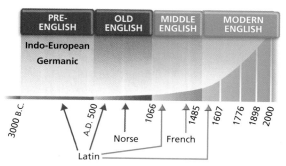

Pre-English   About five thousand years ago, *Proto-Indo-European,* an ancestor of English and other languages, was spoken by peoples in Asia Minor and southeast Europe. Most of the languages of Europe, as well as many of those spoken in northern India and Iran, come from Proto-Indo-European. (*Proto–* means "first or earliest.")

As people who spoke Proto-Indo-European migrated and settled, they developed their own *dialects,* or different ways of speaking the language. One of the groups settled in what is now northern Germany, along the coast of the North Sea. This group organized into several tribes— the Jutes, the Angles, and the Saxons. Their version of Proto-Indo-European, called *Germanic,* is the language from which Modern English is descended.

The Germanic-speaking tribes in northern Europe, known generally as the *Anglo-Saxons,* eventually mingled with Latin-speaking Romans of southern Europe. From the Romans, the Anglo-Saxons took words, called *loanwords,* into their language. Words such as *street, dish, mile,* and *wall* are loanwords borrowed from Latin. Although early English speakers probably took words from other languages, the Latin words borrowed on the continent of Europe more than two thousand years ago are the first loanwords we can be sure about.

Old English Around A.D. 450, the Anglo-Saxons invaded Britain, taking over land that had been settled earlier by the Celts and colonized for centuries by the Romans. The Anglo-Saxons called the island after themselves, *Englaland*—the land of the Angles—or, as it is known today, England. They called their language *Englisc,* which is now referred to as **Old English.** The invading Anglo-Saxons incorporated very few Celtic words into their language, though several words that referred to features of the British landscape—*crag* and *tor* (a high rock), and *combe* (a deep valley)—became part of Old English. The language was further enriched over the years when the English were converted to Christianity by Latin-speaking missionaries. Latin provided words associated with religious matters, such as *church* and *bishop,* as well as other things, such as *school* and *butter.* Then, from the ninth to eleventh centuries Norse invaders from Scandinavia settled in Britain. The Norse provided English with the pronouns *they, their,* and *them,* as well as many English words that begin with *sc* or *sk,* such as *scared, skirt,* and *sky.*

In many ways, the English spoken by the Anglo-Saxons was very different from Modern English. They used sounds that have been lost over time, as in their word *hnutu,* which became *nut.* When they wrote at all, the alphabet they used was an angular-looking system of characters called runes. Also, Old English words had endings or alternative forms to show how they fit together in a sentence. The order of most words in the sentence could stay the same, while the forms of the words changed to express different meanings. Below is an example of how word endings affected the meanings of sentences. (The Old English word *guma* means "man" and *boda* means "messenger.")

Modern English	The man gave the messenger an answer.
	The messenger gave the man an answer.
Old English	Se guma geaf **thæm** bod**an** andsware.
	Thæm gum**an** geaf **se** boda andsware.

Although the English language has changed over the centuries, a number of Old English words have survived with little alteration in spelling or meaning. The following lists show the Old English and Modern English forms of several everyday words.

Old English	Modern English
cnif	knife
hus	house
modor	mother
æppel (meaning "fruit")	apple
wyrm (meaning "serpent")	worm

Middle English In 1066, another group of Norse seized control of England. For the next 150 years, the French-speaking Normans ("north men") made French the language of government, business, and law in England. Because of this, many English words that are connected with wealth and power come from the French, such as *governor, attorney,* and *fashion.* The common people of England, however, still spoke English—a changing form of the language now called **Middle English.**

The English language did not die out under French rule for three reasons. First, the English-speaking commoners outnumbered the French-speaking rulers. Second, the French-speaking rulers in England gradually lost contact with the French culture and language. Third, a shift was triggered when, in 1204, King John of England lost Normandy, the largest of the English possessions in France. Although England still owned large possessions in France, the loss of Normandy forced the King and his nobles to make England their first priority. Noble families possessing lands in England and France found that they had to choose between the two countries. Later, acts by the kings of England and France made it necessary for the nobility to declare their loyalty to one kingdom or the other. As a result, those nobles who chose England became English-speaking Englishmen.

Three hundred years after the French invasion, English was re-established as the national language of England. By this time, however, it had developed a grammar and structure similar to the English spoken today. In addition, many English words had been replaced with French and Latin vocabulary. For example, the native English word *leorningcild* ("learning child") was replaced by the Latin *studiante* ("student"). Here are some other French and Latin loanwords that entered English in the Middle English period.

French	armée	lettre	palais	prière
Modern English	army	letter	palace	prayer
Latin	alphabetum	ecclesiasticus		
Modern English	alphabet	ecclesiastical		

Modern English (1500–Present) Despite the Scandinavian and Norman French invasions of England, the English were relatively isolated from the continent of Europe for nearly 1,200 years. Living in small villages, the English were also isolated from one another; consequently, speakers and writers in different parts of the country used different versions of the language. However, as London became the center of commerce and government, the kind of English pronunciation, grammar, and spelling spoken and used there became the standard. Equally important to the development of modern English was William Caxton's printing press, introduced in 1496. Books, previously handwritten and affordable only to the rich, became more available to the masses. Early printers standardized spelling and grammar to the kind of English spoken and written in London. The availability of cheap books meant that more people learned to read and to speak using the new standardized language. The first dictionary showing English usage, spelling, and pronunciation was prepared in 1604 by Robert Cawdrey.

Once standardized, however, the English language did not stop changing. In fact, it expanded into an international language. From the sixteenth century to the nineteenth century, English merchants, explorers, and settlers spread English to other parts of the globe. For example, the first English settlement in North America was established in Jamestown, Virginia, in 1607 and was followed thirteen years later by the more successful settlement in Plymouth, Massachusetts. Later, English settlers and traders ventured to Canada, the Caribbean, India, Australia, New Zealand, South Africa, and other places. The introduction of the English language and culture would permanently influence the native languages and cultures of all these places. At the same time, English people's interaction with other cultures brought many new loanwords into English.

American English

A Brief History

Immigration to the North American colonies by the English in the seventeenth and eighteenth centuries brought about a new version of the language—American English. Separated by an ocean, the two strains of English—British and American—developed into recognizably different varieties. The history of American English is divided into three periods: *Colonial, National,* and *International.*

The Colonial Period (1607–1776)   One of the many problems faced by English settlers in North America was to find words to describe things and experiences that had never been seen or described by an English speaker. Often they had to borrow words from the Native Americans or to adapt old words for their new situations. For example, to describe the unfamiliar mammal with the single white stripe down its back, settlers used its Algonquian name, *skunk.* In another example, settlers had no word for the slope that leads down to a running river, characteristic of the deep-cut rivers in America, because in England rivers are mostly level with the land through which they run. Therefore, the settlers adapted the word *bank,* which in England described a hill or mound of earth, and created the expression "river bank." In short, the early English colonists had language changes forced on them almost immediately because of the new conditions under which they lived.

The National Period (1776–1898)

As settlers began to spread westward, more and more words entered the language, and American English became increasingly different from British. When the thirteen original British colonies declared their independence from England in 1776, American English emerged as a separate national standard. A number of the new nation's founders, including Thomas Jefferson, John Adams, and Benjamin Franklin, recognized that the United States had to be independent not only in government, but also in literature, language, and thought. However, the man who did the most toward standardizing American English was Noah Webster, who took the initiative in choosing single American spellings from multiple British ones. (In the eighteenth century, many British words were spelled more than one way.) As a result, British words ending in *–re, –our,* and *–ise,* such as *centre, humour,* and *realise,* became the Americanized *center, humor,* and *realize.* Generations of American schoolchildren learned Webster's spellings in his "Blue-Backed Spellers" and in the many dictionaries he prepared. By the end of the nineteenth century, American English was distinctly American, not British—the differences were documented in dictionaries and grammar books and recorded in its own literature.

The International Period (1898 to the Present)   During the twentieth century, American English spread all over the world through the influence of U.S. business, wars and political affairs, popular culture, and technology. The location of the United Nations headquarters in New York City, the presence of U.S. military bases in various international places, and professional and amateur athletes from the United States playing sports around the world have helped spread American English to other lands. Now the French may *golfer* on *le weekend* (play golf on the weekend), the Danes may *zappe* from one television channel to the next, and the Japanese may eat a *hotto doggu* (hot dog) while watching *futtobooru* (football) on the *terebi* (television).

At the same time, of course, American English has also changed. Immigrants to the United States have contributed their vocabulary to the language, and the media have brought various products and ideas from other cultures into U.S. homes. Look at some of the following words that English has borrowed from other cultures in the twentieth century.

Afrikaans: apartheid
Arabic: falafel
Chinese: chow mein
Czech: robot
French: discothèque
German: moped
Greek (classical): cybernetics
Greek (modern): pita
Italian: pepperoni
Japanese: honcho

Latin: spelunking
Mexican
Spanish: bronco
Norwegian: slalom
Portuguese: bossa nova
Russian: perestroika
Spanish: rumba
Swedish: smorgasbord
Swiss German: muesli
Tagalog: boondocks
Yiddish: schmaltz

American and British English

In some respects, American English has changed less than British English. Those who traveled to the U.S. were more conservative in the way they talked than those who stayed in England. For example, most Americans pronounce *r* where it is spelled, as in *roar* and *card*. However, many English people do not pronounce *r* unless it is immediately followed by a vowel, so their pronunciation of *roar* sounds like *raw* and *card* sound like *cod*. The American pronunciation is older, as the spelling suggests.

Similarly, Americans say both "She's got an idea" and "She's gotten an idea" but mean different things by them. "She's got an idea" is equiva-lent to "She has an idea," whereas "She's gotten an idea" means "An idea has occurred to her." *Got* and *gotten* are both past participles of the verb *get*, but *gotten* is the older form. In England today, people do not generally use *gotten* anymore. They have lost one of the forms of the verb, while Americans have kept it.

On the other hand, Americans have added many words to the English language, perhaps more than the British have. Here is a sample of words—both older and newer ones—that Americans have contributed to English.

American Words Added to English		
avocado	kerosene	T-shirt
belittle	lipstick	upside-down cake
cedar chest	mileage	
disc jockey	nifty	volleyball
eggbeater	ouch!	waffle
glitzy	parking lot	xerography
hamburger	quarterback	yo-yo
inchworm	road hog	zipper
jampacked	shack	

NOTE American English has also contributed the popular word *OK*. It came into the language first in 1838–39 as an abbreviation for "oll korrect," a comic misspelling used in Boston newspapers. Then, in 1840, a political organization called the "O.K. Club" was formed to support Martin Van Buren's reelection as President of the United States. Van Buren was nicknamed "Old Kinderhook" after his hometown of Kinderhook, New York, and the club adopted the initials *O.K.*, which punned on the newspaper term and Van Buren's nickname. During the election campaign of 1840, the expression *OK* changed from a regional to a national expression. Now, of course, the term *OK* is used internationally to mean "all correct."

English in the Twenty-first Century

English—both the American and British forms—has become the most widely used language in the world. In fact, it is the official language in more than eighty-seven nations and territories. Several countries, such as India, which have more than one native language, use English as a second language for government and education. English is also the world language of diplomacy, science, technology, aviation, and international trade.

As people around the world use and contribute to the language, it continues to grow and diversify. In fact, some people fear that as English is used in different regions around the world, it will break up into many local languages, just as Latin developed into Italian, French, Spanish, Portuguese, and Romanian at the end of the Roman Empire. Local varieties of English are developing, but so is an international standard of English usage. Airplane travel, television, movies, computers, and other forms of mass communication promote uniformity in the language and keep it from changing too quickly.

> **NOTE** The English language is accompanied by hundreds of **gestures,** or "body language," that reinforce, or contradict, what we are saying. Many gestures are universal. For example, when people—no matter what language they speak—are puzzled, they tend to lift their eyebrows and open their eyes wide. Other gestures are particular to a specific language. For example, English speakers say goodbye with an upraised hand, palm extended outward, fingers moving together up and down. In another culture, people wave goodbye similarly, but they turn their palms toward themselves. They say "Goodbye" with a gesture that to English speakers usually means "Come here."

Varieties of American English

Dialects of American English

Like all languages, American English has many distinct versions of speech, called *dialects.* Everyone uses a dialect, and no dialect is better or worse than another. Dialects can communicate much about us—our home locality, education, gender, and age. Each has unique features of grammar, vocabulary, and pronunciation.

Ethnic Dialects *Ethnic dialects* are the speech patterns of special communities that have preserved some of their heritage from the past. Every group of people that has come to the United States has brought something characteristic of its original homeland and culture. For example, English, Scottish, Irish, Dutch, Welsh, French, Spanish, Scandinavian, German, Yiddish, Polish, Czech, Italian, Greek, Armenian, Indic, Chinese, Japanese, Korean, and Vietnamese have all influenced American English.

One of the most prominent ethnic dialects in the United States is African American dialect. This dialect unites some of the features of West African languages with some features of early Southern speech and yet other usages developed by African American communities themselves. Some features are *aunt* pronounced "ahnt," *He be sick* meaning a continuing rather than temporary illness, and *tote* meaning "carry" ("tote" is of African origin but now is common in all Southern use).

Another prominent ethnic dialect is Hispanic English, which has three subvarieties: Mexican-influenced English in the Southwest, Cuban-influenced English in Florida, and

Puerto Rican-influenced English in New York City and, of course, in Puerto Rico. Early Hispanic influence in the West introduced such words as *vamoose* (from Spanish *vamos,* "let's go") and *mesa* ("table"). Today, Spanish-influenced English uses English words with meanings similar to Spanish words. For example, the English word *direction* is used to mean "address," the meaning of the Spanish word *direccion.* The number of speakers of Hispanic English has grown in recent years and so has the importance of their dialect.

Of course, not all African Americans or Hispanic Americans use the dialect associated with their groups, and some features of these dialects turn up in other speech communities, too. Obviously, the boundaries of ethnic and regional dialects are fluid and ever-changing.

Regional Dialects The United States has four major *regional dialects:* the *Northern,* the *Midland,* the *Southern,* and the *Western.* Remember, however, that not everyone in a region speaks the dialect of that region, just as all members of a particular ethnic group do not speak the same way.

The pronunciations of words often vary from one dialect to another. For example, some

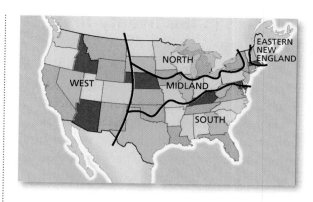

Southerners pronounce the words *ten* and *tin* the same way—"tin." Some Northerners tend to drop the *r* sound from words and lengthen the /a/ sound, so that *farm* sounds like "fahm."

Similarly, regional dialects differ in grammar and vocabulary. For example, someone from the South might say "sick at my stomach," while someone from the North might say "sick to my stomach." You might drink *soda, tonic,* or *pop* depending on the part of the country in which you reside. Furthermore, dialects often vary within each of the four major regions. The following table shows some of the distinctive features of pronunciation, vocabulary, and grammar that distinguish regional dialects. (According to linguists, the Western dialect is still developing and is not yet as well defined as other regional dialects.)

Features of Regional Dialects				
	Northern	**North Midland**	**South Midland**	**Southern**
Pronunciation	"greassy"	"greassy"	"greazy"	"greazy"
	"hahg"	"hahg" or hog	hog	"hawg"
	"pahked cah"	parked car	parked car	"pawked caw"
Word Choice	burlap bag or gunny sack	burlap bag	burlap bag	burlap bag or croker sack
	pail	bucket	bucket	bucket
Grammar	quarter of/to you, youse	quarter to you	quarter til you, you'uns	quarter til/to you, y'all

Standard English

Standard English   Standard English is a variety of language that is not limited to a particular place or ethnic group. It is the one variety of English that is more widely used and accepted than any other in the United States. Because it is commonly understood, people from many different regions and cultures can communicate with one another clearly. In the U.S., standard English is usually more a matter of writing than of speech. It is used for treating important matters seriously, and it is especially appropriate for talking with or writing to people we don't know well. It is the language of public affairs and education, of publications and television, of science and technology, and of business and government. People are expected to use standard English in most school and business situations. It is also the variety of English recorded in dictionaries and grammar books.

This textbook presents and illustrates many of the rules and guidelines for using standard English. To identify the differences between standard English and other varieties of English, this book uses the labels *standard* and *nonstandard*. Nonstandard does not mean wrong language. It means language that is inappropriate in situations where standard English is expected. Nobody needs to use standard English all the time, but everybody should be able to use it when it is the right variety to use.

Standard English—Formal to Informal

Depending on your audience and purpose, the language you use can be formal, informal, or somewhere in between.

Formal English, like formal dress and formal manners, is for special occasions, such as writing serious papers and reports or speaking at formal, dignified occasions. The sentence structure of formal English is long and complex; word choice is precise, often technical or scientific; and the tone is serious and dignified.

Informal English is everyday English. Used for writing personal letters, journal entries, and many newspaper and magazine articles, informal English has a short and easy sentence structure and simple, ordinary word choices. Informal English often includes contractions, colloquialisms, slang, and a conversational tone.

- *Colloquialisms* are the informal words and phrases of conversational language. (The word *colloquial* derives from a Latin word meaning "conversation.") They bring flavor and color to everyday speech and a friendly, conversational tone to writing. Many are figures of speech or **idioms** that are not meant to be taken literally.

  EXAMPLE   When my computer crashed the night before my paper was due, I thought I would **lose my mind**.

- *Slang* is newly coined language or old words used in unconventional ways. Often special language used by specific groups of people, such as students, musicians, and military personnel, slang is sometimes an indication that the speaker is in tune with a particular group.

  EXAMPLES
  yo!—hello
  hot—pleasing, excellent
  cool—pleasing, excellent
  code red—an emergency situation
  punt—to give up on further action

Don't be surprised if many of these slang words seem outdated. Most slang is popular for a short time and then dies out quickly. A few slang words, however, have been around for centuries. The word *duds,* meaning "clothing," dates back to the sixteenth century.

The Library/ Media Center

Using Print and Electronic Sources

The library or media center in your school or community provides a range of print and electronic sources to help you find and use information. *Print sources* include books, periodicals (magazines, newspapers, and journals), and specialized sources (such as microforms or vertical files). *Electronic sources,* or sources accessed with a computer, include CD-ROMs, the Internet, and online databases.

> **TIP** In addition to these sources, go beyond the library walls to find information in real-world documents—maps, technical instructions, contracts, glossaries, and a variety of other consumer, business, and public texts.

Call Number A *call number* is a code that indicates how a book is classified and where it is shelved in the library. The two systems of classification are the Dewey decimal system and the Library of Congress system.

■ **Dewey decimal system** The *Dewey decimal system* classifies books according to ten general subject areas. Each of these ten

categories is then subdivided into more specific fields. The ten general subject areas and corresponding numbers are as follows:

000–099 Generalities (encyclopedias, bibliographies)

100–199 Philosophy and related disciplines

200–299 Religion

300–399 Social sciences (economics, sociology)

400-499 Language (dictionaries, grammar)

500–599 Pure sciences (mathematics, biology)

600–699 Technology and applied sciences (television, aviation)

700–799 The Arts (sculpture, music)

800–899 Literature (novels, poetry, plays)

900–999 Geography, history, and related disciplines

■ **Library of Congress system** The *Library of Congress system* uses code letters to identify subject categories. The first code letter of a book's call number identifies its general category (such as history); the second letter identifies the subcategory (such as American).

Card Catalog A traditional **card catalog** is a collection of index cards arranged in alphabetical order in a cabinet of drawers. For each book in the library, the card catalog contains a **title card,** an **author card,** and if the book is nonfiction, a **subject card**. In addition, **cross-reference cards** advise you where to look for additional information. Each card contains most of the following information:

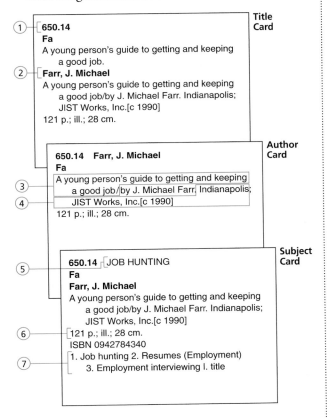

1. the **call number** assigned to a book by the Dewey decimal system or the Library of Congress classification system
2. the **author's full name,** last name first
3. the full **title** and **subtitle** of a book
4. the place and date of **publication**
5. the general **subject** of a book; a subject card may show specific headings

6. a **description** of the book, such as its size and number of pages and whether it is illustrated
7. **cross-references** to other headings or related topics under which a book is listed

As libraries acquire computer technology, card catalogs are being converted to electronic or online formats. (See also **Online Card Catalog,** page 944.)

CD-ROMs A **CD-ROM** (**C**ompact **D**isc **R**ead **O**nly **M**emory) is a compact disc designed to hold visual as well as audio information. The data is encoded digitally and can be accessed only by a computer with a CD-ROM drive. A single CD-ROM may contain the equivalent of 250,000 pages of printed text. Many reference tools—such as encyclopedias, dictionaries, and indexes—are now available on CD-ROMs. CD-ROMs contain the same text as the printed versions but have the added attractions of searching capabilities, interactive graphics, and audio. (See the **Reference Sources chart** on page 946.)

Internet The **Internet** is a global network of computers. With the Internet, a computer user may access information from another computer or a network of computers anywhere in the world. Created in the late 1960s, the Internet was originally used by research scientists to share data electronically with each other. The content exchanged on the Internet has since expanded beyond scientific matters to include nearly any topic. In fact, almost anyone who has a computer equipped with a modem may use the Internet. Information transfer systems—such as Gopher, Telnet, and FTP (File Transfer Protocol)—allow you to view material on the

Internet, and *World Wide Web browsers* provide access to files and documents, news and discussion groups, bulletin boards, and e-mail. The *World Wide Web* is the place on the Internet you are most likely to go for your research. (See also *World Wide Web* on page 949; *World Wide Web, Web Site Evaluation* on page 952.)

Microforms   *Microforms* are the photographically reduced pages of newspaper or magazine articles. The two most common kinds of microforms are *microfilm* (a roll or reel of film) and *microfiche* (a sheet of film). Special machines provided at the library enlarge microfilm and microfiche images and project them onto a screen for reading.

Online Card Catalog   An *online card catalog* is an electronic or computerized version of the card catalog. Instead of searching through individual cards, you may find a book by typing in a book's title, author, or subject. (If you do not have a specific book in mind, type in **key words** that may appear in the title or description of the book.) The online catalog quickly retrieves information based on your request and provides you with a screen like the one shown in the next column. The online catalog can also tell you if the book has been checked out or if it is available at another library.

Online Databases   An *online database* is a contained system of electronic information that may be accessed only by computer. In most cases, organizations such as universities, libraries, or businesses create or subscribe to databases that are of specific interest to the people in the organizations. LEXIS–NEXIS is an example of a subscription-only database. Users must have an identification number that allows

Online
AUTHOR: Neasel, Carla.
CALL NUMBER: 610.9/Friedman
AUTHOR: Friedman, Meyer, 1910
TITLE: Medicine's 10 greatest discoveries
PUBLISHER: New Haven, Conn.: Yale University Press, 1988.
DESCRIPTION: 263 p. ill.
NOTES 1: Includes bibliographic references and index.
SUBJECT 1: Medicine—History
SUBJECT 2: Medical scientists
AUTHOR 2: Friedland, Gerald W.
TITLE 2: Medicines ten greatest discoveries
ISBN: 0300075987

them to read the information. However, some databases are public and may be accessed through the World Wide Web.

Online Sources   An information source located and accessed by using computers is called an *online source*. Computers that are online are able to communicate with each other over telecommunication lines, such as telephone lines and fiber-optic cables, and via satellite. When computers are linked, they form a *network*. Computer networks make the Internet and the World Wide Web possible.

Radio, Television, and Film   *Radio* and *television* are important sources of news and information. Newscasts, newsmagazines, and documentaries are regular features of these media. In turn, descriptive listings of radio and television programs appear in newspapers and, in some cases, on the Internet. Documentaries and educational materials are also often produced on *film* or *video*. Indexes of educational films and videos, such as *The Video Source Book* (Gale, 1998) are available at libraries and book stores. Be sure to check the ratings provided for the films and videos before viewing them. (See also **Critical Viewing** on page 1016 and **Critical Listening** on page 991.)

Readers' Guide to Periodical Literature

The *Readers' Guide to Periodical Literature* is an index of articles, poems, and stories from more than two hundred magazines and journals. Throughout the year, paperback editions of the *Readers' Guide* list materials published two to four weeks earlier. At the end of each year, the paperback issues are bound into a single hardcover volume.

As the following sample entry shows, the articles are listed alphabetically by author and by subject, but not by title. The headings are set in boldface type. The *Readers' Guide* also gives "see" and "see also" references. A key located in the front of the *Readers' Guide* explains the meanings of the abbreviations used in the entries.

Some libraries subscribe to an online version of the *Readers' Guide*, shown on the next page. To use this version, enter a search word or phrase into the computer and choose the records that interest you from the search results. The record on the next page was selected from a list of fifteen articles found by a researcher using the search words *water conservation* and *water pollution*.

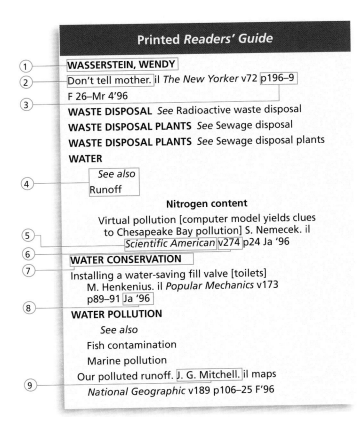

Printed *Readers' Guide*

① **WASSERSTEIN, WENDY**
② Don't tell mother. il *The New Yorker* v72 p196–9
③ F 26–Mr 4'96
WASTE DISPOSAL *See* Radioactive waste disposal
WASTE DISPOSAL PLANTS *See* Sewage disposal
WASTE DISPOSAL PLANTS *See* Sewage disposal plants
WATER
④ *See also*
Runoff
Nitrogen content
⑤ Virtual pollution [computer model yields clues to Chesapeake Bay pollution] S. Nemecek. il *Scientific American* v274 p24 Ja '96
⑥ **WATER CONSERVATION**
⑦ Installing a water-saving fill valve [toilets] M. Henkenius. il *Popular Mechanics* v173 p89–91 Ja '96
⑧ **WATER POLLUTION**
See also
Fish contamination
Marine pollution
⑨ Our polluted runoff. J. G. Mitchell. il maps *National Geographic* v189 p106–25 F'96

① Author entry
② Title of article
③ Page reference
④ Subject cross-reference
⑤ Name of periodical
⑥ Volume number of periodical
⑦ Subject entry
⑧ Date of periodical
⑨ Author of article

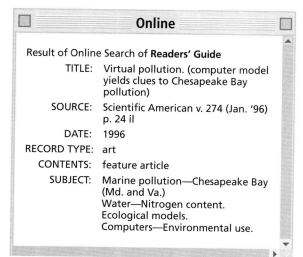

Online

Result of Online Search of **Readers' Guide**

TITLE:	Virtual pollution. (computer model yields clues to Chesapeake Bay pollution)
SOURCE:	Scientific American v. 274 (Jan. '96) p. 24 il
DATE:	1996
RECORD TYPE:	art
CONTENTS:	feature article
SUBJECT:	Marine pollution—Chesapeake Bay (Md. and Va.) Water—Nitrogen content. Ecological models. Computers—Environmental use.

Recorded Materials   Your library may have *recorded materials* such as *audiocassettes* of famous speeches, readings by well-known authors, and *videotapes* of documentaries or other educational programs. These materials can be helpful as research sources.

Reference Books   Reference sources are books of specialized information. They contain facts and information organized in a logical way, such as alphabetical or chronological order or by category. (Some reference books are set aside in a separate section of the library—called the *reference section*.) Examples of reference books include encyclopedias, dictionaries, thesauri, indexes, books of quotations, atlases, and almanacs. (See also the **Reference Sources chart** below.)

Reference Sources   There are many different kinds of reference sources that you can use to find specific kinds of information. The following chart identifies and describes common reference sources and provides examples of print and electronic reference sources.

Reference Sources		
Type of Reference Source	**Description**	**Examples**
ALMANACS	Up-to-date information about current events, facts, statistics, and dates	• *Information Please Almanac* • *TIME Almanac—The Reference Edition* (CD-ROM)
ATLASES	Maps and geographical information	• *Hammond Atlas of the World* • *Microsoft Encarta World Atlas* (CD-ROM)
ATLASES (HISTORICAL)	Maps and graphic representations of significant historical changes	• *The American Heritage Pictorial Atlas of United States History* • *Historical Atlas of the Holocaust* • *Small Blue Planet: Time City Flashback Atlas* (CD-ROM) • *The Times Atlas of World History*

Reference Sources

Type of Reference Source	Description	Examples
BIOGRAPHICAL REFERENCES (GENERAL)	Information about birth, nationality, and major accomplishments of prominent people (past and present). Biographical indexes tell where to find books and periodicals with information about specific people.	• *Biography Index* • *Biography Index* (CD-ROM) • *Dictionary of American Biography on CD-ROM* • *The International Who's Who* • *Who's Who in America*
BIOGRAPHICAL REFERENCES (LITERARY)	Information about authors; usually contains details of birth, death, publications, and awards or honors	• *American Authors 1600–1900* • *Contemporary Authors® on CD-ROM* • *Twentieth Century Authors* • *World Authors 88 BC–1996* (CD-ROM)
BIOGRAPHICAL REFERENCES (SPECIALIZED)	Information about people noted for accomplishments in a specific field or for membership in a specific group	• *American Men and Women of Science 1998–1999* • *The Multimedia Encyclopedia of the American Indian* (CD-ROM) • *Who's Who Among African Americans*
BOOKS OF QUOTATIONS	Famous quotations indexed or grouped together by subject or source	• *American Heritage Dictionary of American Quotations* • *Bartlett's Familiar Quotations* (CD-ROM) • *Gale's Quotations: Who Said That?* (CD-ROM) • *The Oxford Dictionary of Quotations*
BOOKS OF SYNONYMS	Lists of exact or more interesting words to express ideas; may use a categorized index or alphabetical order as in a dictionary	• *Oxford Thesaurus on CD-ROM* • *Roget's International Thesaurus* • *Webster's New Dictionary of Synonyms*
CAREER GUIDES	Information about various industries and occupations, such as job descriptions and educational requirements	• *Ace the Interview: The Multimedia Job Interview Guide* (CD-ROM) • *Peterson's Career & College Quest* (CD-ROM) • *The Dictionary of Occupational Titles*
COLLEGE REFERENCE SOURCES	Profiles of colleges and information about finding and applying to colleges and vocational schools	• *Barron's Profile of American Colleges on CD-ROM* • *Peterson's College Database CD-ROM* • *The Directory of Educational Institutions*

(continued)

(continued)

Reference Sources

Types of Reference Sources	Description	Examples
CURRENT EVENT RESOURCES	Up-to-date information on topics such as crime and family issues, scientific discoveries, and documents from the National Archives	• *Social Issues Resources Series (SIRS)* (audiotapes, videotapes, reprints of newspaper and magazine articles, photographs, letters, and posters)
Encyclopedias	Articles of general information arranged alphabetically by subject in a single volume or in several volumes; multi-volume sets may also contain an index that lists broader topics	• *The Columbia Encyclopedia* • *The Columbia Encyclopedia on CD-ROM* • *New Encyclopaedia Britannica* • *The World Book Multimedia Encyclopedia*™
Indexes	Information in list form of articles found in periodicals or other information sources	• *Art Index* (CD-ROM) • *Biography Index* • *Book Review Index on CD-ROM* • *Gale's Literary Index CD-ROM* • *New York Times Index*
Literary References	Information about where to locate various works of literature; information about authors and about individual literary works, such as plot summaries and book reviews	• *The Columbia Granger's Index to Poetry* • *The Columbia Granger's World of Poetry on CD-ROM* • *Contemporary Authors*™ series • *Masterplots Nonfiction, Drama, Poetry* (CD-ROM)
Special Reference Sources for Specific Subjects	Information related to specific subjects or topics of interest to researchers in specific fields	• *The Dictionary of Science and Technology* (CD-ROM) • *The Encyclopedia of American Facts and Dates* • *Encyclopedia of North American Sports History* (Facts on File) • *History of Music CD-ROMs* • *The Lives of the Artists*
Style and Writing Manuals	Information about proper writing style and preparation of research papers	• *The Chicago Manual of Style* • *Harbrace College Handbook* (CD-ROM) • *MLA Style Manual for Writers of Research Papers* • *The Elements of Style,* by Strunk and White

Vertical File   A *vertical file* is a set of file drawers containing up-to-date materials, such as pamphlets, newspaper clippings, and photographs, that are not likely to be cataloged anywhere else. Organized by subject, these materials often consist of government, business, or educational publications. As the use of electronic or online resources (such as the World Wide Web) increases, vertical files are less likely to be maintained by libraries in the future.

World Wide Web (*WWW* or the *Web*)
The *World Wide Web* is one part of the Internet. It is an enormous system of connected, or linked, documents that contain text, graphics and visuals, sounds, and video. Documents (*Web sites* or *Web pages*) on the World Wide Web are connected by *hyperlinks,* underlined or color-coded text that provides a link to another section within the document (*internal link*) or another site altogether (*external link*). When you click on a hyperlink, the new site quickly appears on your screen. To navigate or view the World Wide Web, you must have *browser* software installed on the computer you are using.

World Wide Web, Key Terms   These terms will help you understand the Web.

■ **Browser**   A *browser* is a software application that allows you to find and access information on the Web. The software allows you to explore, read, save, and download documents, images, sounds, and videos that you may find on Web sites. Using a browser to locate and read documents is called *browsing.* (See also **Web Site** on page 950.)

■ **Domain**   A *domain* is the name of a computer or server on the Internet from which you may access information. Every Web address specifies a domain, or particular server. (See also **URL** on page 950.)

■ **Home page**   A *home page* is the first screen or page of a Web site. Usually, it identifies the person or organization that sponsored or created the site, provides an index or table of contents for the site, and often includes hyperlinks to related sites on the Web. (See also **Web Site** on page 950.)

■ **Hyperlink**   A *hyperlink* is a specially coded text or image that allows a user to move from one place or page on the World Wide Web to another. On-screen, hyperlinks usually appear in a contrasting color and are underlined; sometimes, they may appear as shaded "buttons." *Internal hyperlinks* send you to other, more specific sections of the same page; *external hyperlinks* send you to other Web sites. (See also **Hypertext Markup Language** on this page.)

■ **Hypertext**   *Hypertext* is a system that allows a user to find and open related files and documents on the Web without having to quit or close the original file. A user can move in a nonlinear way from one document to another via hyperlinks. Hypertext is the basic organizing principle of the World Wide Web.

■ **Hypertext Markup Language (HTML)**
Hypertext markup language is the formatting language used to create documents on the World Wide Web.

■ **Hypertext Transfer Protocol (HTTP)**
Hypertext Transfer Protocol is the language, or set of communication rules, used by browser software to transmit the information of different sites or documents on the World Wide Web from one computer to another.

■ **Search engine**   A search engine is a tool for finding specific information on the Web. (See also **World Wide Web, Searching** on page 950.)

■ **URL (*Uniform Resource Locator*)**   A *URL* is the address of a specific document or resource on the Web. A typical URL includes words, abbreviations, numbers, and specific kinds of punctuation. The following example of a URL would connect you to the listings of science programs that are broadcast on National Public Radio. The parts of the address are explained below.

```
         1           2              3
http://www.npr.org/programs/science
```

1. The *protocol,* or how the site is formatted
2. The *domain name*. Domain names have at least two parts. The part on the left is the name of the company, institution, or other organization. The part on the right is a general domain. A list of the most common domain abbreviations follows. (See also *Domain* on page 949.)

Common Domains on the World Wide Web	
com	commercial
edu	educational
gov	governmental
net	administrative
org	nonprofit organization

3. The *subdirectory name* shows where a specific piece of information is stored. (Each word following a slash requests a narrower search into the site.) Not all addresses will have this part.

■ **Web Site (or Web Page)**   A *Web site* or *Web page* is a document or location on the Web that is linked to other locations on the Web. A site may contain several Web pages. The screen on the next page shows the most important parts of a browser and a typical Web site.

World Wide Web, Plagiarism   Taking another person's idea or work and presenting it as your own is called *plagiarism.* Because the World Wide Web is such a vast source of information and because it is easy to download or copy information, plagiarism of electronic material has become a serious concern. Therefore, treat any information you find on the World Wide Web as if it were from a printed or published source. Avoid plagiarism by paraphrasing information you find on the World Wide Web, and **be sure that you cite the sources of your information.** (For more about documenting sources see page 268.)

World Wide Web, Searching   There are three ways to search for information on the World Wide Web: *direct address, search engines,* and *subject catalogs.* Each type of search has benefits and drawbacks. A combination of all three types of searches usually works best. Most search services on the Web allow you to use all three. The following list gives you more information about each kind of search.

■ **Direct address**   The most direct way to find a Web site is to type in the Web site's *direct address,* or URL, in the location box. The address must be typed exactly, using the proper case and punctuation. This strategy does not work, of course, if you do not have the site's address.

NOTE   When sites are protected by a special security system, you will see an icon on your screen that looks like a lock. If the site is not protected, the icon will appear as a broken lock.

1. **Toolbar** The buttons on the toolbar allow you to complete different functions, such as moving to different pages, searching, printing out information, and seeing or hiding images.

2. **Location window** This box shows you the URL, or address, of the site you are seeing before you.

3. **Content area** This is the area of the screen where the text, images, hyperlinks, and other parts of a Web page appear.

4. **Hyperlinks** By clicking these buttons, you can connect to other Web pages or sites. Internal hyperlinks send you to different parts of this site; external hyperlinks send you to other addresses (or URLs).

5. **Scroll bar** This bar allows you to scroll left and right. The scroll bar on the right-hand side allows you to scroll up and down.

① Back Forward Reload Home Search

② Location: http://www.spiderweb.com/~japrufrock

③ *Our Motto: "Education for All"*

Welcome to
"You Shall Know the Truth"
College Overview

Simplify your higher education search by choosing one of the directory items below. Still confused about what to choose? After your preliminary search, click on information collation. You will see a complete listing of categories and the colleges/universities which fit them.

④ State Name   Student Activities/Campus Photos

Annual Cost of Education   Sports Programs

See also: GED in Hand, International Opportunity Search, Advanced Degrees

■ **Search engines** *Search engines* allow you to search *databases* that contain information about the millions of sites on the Web. These databases are compiled automatically by computer programs called *robots*. (See also **World Wide Web, Using Search Engines** on this page.)

■ **Subject catalogs** A *subject catalog* provides an extensively organized table of contents of the World Wide Web. Information from Web sites is organized in broad categories, such as *Education* and *Entertainment*. (Unlike search engines, subject catalogs are organized by humans, not by machines.) Each category in the catalog contains many specific subcategories, which in turn break down into even more specific sub-subcategories. A subject catalog is searched by narrowing down from a general topic to a specific one.

World Wide Web, Using Search Engines
Unlike subject catalogs, *searchable indexes* and *search engines* allow you to search for Web sites that contain keywords or phrases. These search tools also allow you to refine your searches.

■ **Keyword search** A *keyword search* lets you look for sites that contain specific words or phrases. Type keywords in the space provided on the search engine screen and press the Return key or the Search or Find button. The search engine analyzes each Web site indexed in its database for the frequency and importance of the words you specified. The results appear in the form of a list. The sites that contain all your keywords should appear at the top of the list, followed, in descending order, by other relevant matches. Most search engines assign each item on the list a percentage or rank number to indicate how well the site matched your request. The keyword search works best when you have a very clear or specific topic to research.

■ **Refining a Keyword Search**   Because search engines may identify hundreds or thousands of Web sites that contain your keywords—or no sites at all—you should always consider *refining* or focusing your search. Look at the following chart for some strategies that may help you. Keep in mind, however, that different search engines may require slightly different commands than those listed here. Consult the "help" section of your search engine for specific commands.

World Wide Web, Web Site Evaluation

The content of the World Wide Web is not monitored for accuracy in the way that most newspapers, books, and magazines are.

Refining Keyword Search	
Tip	**How It Works**
Replace general terms with more specific ones.	A keyword that is common or used in ways you do not expect can result in irrelevant matches. EXAMPLE If you are interested in cave exploration, enter *spelunking* instead of *caving*.
Use quotation marks.	By placing your keywords in quotation marks, the search engine will find sites that use the words exactly as you have typed them. EXAMPLE Enter "New Mexico" to find sites specific to the state rather than sites about the country of Mexico or any sites that contain the word *new*.
Use *and* and *not*.	Narrow your search by putting the word *and* between your keywords. The search engine will find only Web sites that contain all words connected by *and*. EXAMPLE For sites that mention crystal caverns in both New Mexico and Virginia, enter *New Mexico and Virginia and crystal caverns*. Use *not* between keywords to ensure that the search engine does not pull up sites that deal with similar but unrelated topics. EXAMPLE Enter *crystal caverns not glassware* to avoid Web sites about handmade crystal drinking glasses.
Use *or*.	To broaden your search, use *or* to let the search engine know that you would accept sites that contain any of your key words. EXAMPLE If you want sites that discuss either the caverns in New Mexico or in Virginia, enter *New Mexico caverns or Virginia caverns*.

Anyone can publish on the Web, and huge numbers of Web pages undergo no review process before publication. Consequently, you must think critically about the information you find on the Web to make sure it is reliable and authoritative. Use the questions in the following chart to help you *evaluate* a Web site's value as a source of information. You may be surprised to find how few sites actually meet all the criteria. Keep in mind the newness of the World Wide Web; standards for Web sites are still evolving.

Evaluating Web Sites	
Questions to Ask	**Why You Should Ask**
Who created or sponsored the Web site?	The kind of information on a Web site is determined by the site's creator or sponsor, which the Web site's home page should identify. The author or organization should be recognized in the field the site covers. Use Web sites that are affiliated with reputable organizations, such as government agencies, universities, museums, and national news organizations. Such Web sites will usually belong in the *edu, gov,* or *org* domains.
What is the purpose of the Web site?	People and groups have various reasons for publishing on the Web, such as to provide information, to market a product, or to promote a cause. Determining the site's purpose will help you to assess its reliability and to detect any bias.
Does the Web site offer adequate coverage of the subject?	If the site contains a type and depth of coverage not available elsewhere, being online is probably worth your time. Otherwise, you might want to rely on alternative reference sources.
When was the page first posted, and is it frequently updated?	This information usually appears at the end of a home page. Most often, it includes a copyright notice, the date of the most recent update, and a link to the creator's e-mail address. As with any reference source, you want your information to be up-to-date.
What other Web pages is the site linked to?	Looking at the links provided in a Web site can help you determine how legitimate it is. If a site is a source of accurate information, it will have links to other reputable Web sites.
Does the Web site present information objectively?	Look for signs of bias, such as strong language or statements of opinion. If the site is trying to be objective, it will present facts and ideas from both sides of an issue or debate. Beware of a site that uses fictional support for ideas.
Is the Web site well designed?	A well-designed Web site has legible type, clear graphics, and working links. It is easily searched or navigated. The written content of the site should be well organized and use proper spelling, punctuation, and grammar.

Reading and Vocabulary

Reading

Skills and Strategies

The following skills and strategies can help you to become a more effective reader.

Author's Purpose and Point of View, Determining
An author always has a reason, or *purpose*, for writing, whether to inform, persuade, express himself or herself, or entertain. (Some forms of writing fit only one purpose—business writing and policy statements, for example—while others, such as Web sites, are suited to nearly any purpose.) In addition, an author has a *point of view*, an opinion or attitude, about his or her subject. A strong opinion, or bias, may lead an author to provide unclear or inaccurate information. Determining an author's purpose and point of view will help you to find more meaning in any text you read. (See also page 291.)

> EXAMPLE Composting is an excellent way to replenish the soil. All you need is a ventilated bin or crate. Fill the bin with layers of dead leaves, grass clippings, and vegetable peelings. Turn the mixture over once a month, and in a few months you will have a natural source of high-powered fertilizer for your garden.
>
> Author's purpose: To explain composting
>
> Author's point of view: Composting is a good, natural way to fertilize a garden.

Cause-and-Effect Relationships, Analyzing
A *cause* makes something happen. An *effect* is what happens as a result of a cause. Ask, "Why?" and "What are the effects?" as you read to examine causes and effects.

> EXAMPLE In 1904, a fungus inadvertently introduced to the United States at a botanical exhibit proved almost fatal to the American chestnut tree. Within forty years, nearly every chestnut tree in the United States was killed or damaged by the fungus. The demise of the chestnut affected the lumber industry and chestnut farmers as well as future generations of the trees. Even today, chestnut seedlings cannot mature in nature. Only in those parts of the country where the fungus does not exist do cultivated chestnuts flourish.
>
> Analysis: A fungus was the cause of the virtual extinction of the American chestnut. One effect of the fungus's spread was the demise of nearly every chestnut tree in the U.S.

Clue Words				
Cause-and-Effect	Chronological Order	Comparison-and-Contrast	Listing	Problem-and-Solution
as a result	after	although	also	as a result
because	as	as well as	for example	nevertheless
consequently	before	but	in fact	therefore
if . . . then	finally	either . . . or	most important	this led to
nevertheless	first	however	to begin with	thus
since	not long after	not only . . . but also		
so that	now	on the other hand		
therefore	second	similarly		
this led to	then	unless		
thus	when	yet		

Clue Words Writers use certain words to connect their ideas or to show relationships between ideas. Readers can use these *clue words* to help them identify a text's organizational pattern. Look at the chart above. (See also **Text Structures, Analyzing** on page 959.)

Drawing Conclusions A *conclusion* is a judgment you make by combining information in a text with information you already know. As you read, you gather information, connect it to your experiences, and then draw conclusions that are specific to the text. (See also page 237.)

EXAMPLE The air had become too thin to breathe, and the weather was turning ominous. I strapped on an oxygen tank and looked down from one of the highest peaks in the world. I was not used to such a climate, of course, but the hardship was worth such a rare view of the world. "Only astronauts go higher," I thought.
Conclusion: The narrator has climbed to the top of one of the world's highest mountain peaks.

Fact and Opinion, Distinguishing A *fact* is information that can be proven by testing, personal experience, or reliable sources. An

opinion expresses a personal belief or attitude that cannot be proven true or false. Only opinions that are supported by factual evidence are considered **valid.** (See also page 332.)

EXAMPLE
Fact: Queen Elizabeth I of England ruled from 1558 to 1603. [Reference works support this as a true statement.]

Opinion: Queen Elizabeth I was the most effective ruler in English history. [This is what one writer thinks or believes; the statement cannot be proved true or false.]

Generalizations, Forming A reader forms a *generalization* by combining information in a text with personal experience to make a judgment about the world. (See also page 345.)

EXAMPLE Even if you do not own a computer or use one in your daily life, you are affected by them every day. Computers are in use at the grocery store checkout counter, gas pumps, and the doctor's office. The people who ticket your parked car, read your electric meters, and fix your telephones use computers as well.
Generalization: Computers are everywhere even if we do not think that we use them.

Implied Main Idea, Identifying   Some writers do not directly state their main ideas; instead, they choose to *imply,* or suggest, them. As a reader, you must analyze the meaning of the details in the text to identify main ideas that are *implied,* or expressed indirectly. (See page 153 and **Stated Main Idea** on page 958.)

EXAMPLE   In 1796, English physician Edward Jenner created the first smallpox vaccine from a related cowpox virus. He tested the vaccine on children whom he then exposed to smallpox. The success of Jenner's experiment marked the first step in the development of effective vaccines.

Implied main idea: Edward Jenner invented the first effective vaccine.

Inferences, Making   An *inference* is an educated guess about ideas a text does not state directly. You make an inference by combining information in a text with your prior knowledge and experience. (See also page 157.)

EXAMPLE   Six million American women went to work outside the home between 1941 and 1945. They took on jobs normally reserved for men, making up about 12 percent of shipyard workers and 40 percent of aircraft plant workers. Assuming more responsibility than ever before, women workers hoped to keep working after the war. Yet in 1946, two million women lost their industry jobs to male workers returning from the war.

Inference: When many men were at war, women significantly expanded their traditional roles.

Paraphrasing   When you *paraphrase,* you restate in your own words the ideas and information in a text. Paraphrasing is a good way to check your understanding of a complex text such as a poem—if you can paraphrase it, you probably understand it. Unlike a summary, a paraphrase is not a condensed version of the text; often, it is the same length. (See the chart on page 192 for paraphrasing guidelines.)

EXAMPLE   The use of punctuation, particularly the period, in writing is a relatively recent development. Ancient writers were not consistent, relying on blank spaces, dots, and slashes to indicate the end of an idea. When a period like mark was introduced in the eighth century, it served as both a comma and an end mark. It was not until 1566 that Aldus Manutius the Younger made the period an official end mark that has been used by printers ever since.

Paraphrase: Punctuation has not always been used in writing. Ancient writers used spaces, dots, and slashes to end sentences. When the period was first introduced, it worked as both a comma and an end mark. In 1566, the period was established by Aldus Manutius the Younger as the correct way to end a sentence.

Persuasive Techniques, Analyzing   An author uses *persuasive techniques* to convince readers to think or act in a certain way. As you read persuasive writing, look for logical reasoning and facts. Also look for emotional and ethical appeals, which add force to writing, but which should never be a substitute for logical reasoning. (See also page 293.)

EXAMPLE   Our town is growing at an alarming pace, and we need to prepare for its citizens' future needs. Our population has grown by 40 percent in the last fifteen years. Those who have lived here long enough see the negative effects of growth—traffic, pollution, and increased crime. There are benefits, such as the new hospital, but they are outweighed by the problems that will result if we do not upgrade our police and fire-fighting units. Imagine the shame we will feel in ten years if someone is hurt or dies because we did not act now to make our city a safe place to live.

Analysis: The second, third, and fourth sentences provide evidence to support the opinion in the first sentence. The final sentence contains an emotional and an ethical appeal.

Predicting When a reader makes an educated guess about what will happen next in a text, he or she is *predicting.* To make predictions, use information in the text, including key words, headlines, subheadings, and illustrations or graphics, plus your own knowledge and experience. (See also page 5.)

EXAMPLE

Principal Jill Feldman met Wednesday with the school board to discuss the future of an after-school program that provides extra study time for students in grades 5–8. Because of needed repairs to the school's roof, which suffered water damage, the school board suggested cutting back on the hours of the program. Principal Feldman argued that since the program had been in effect, students' scores on state reading tests had risen slightly.

Prediction: The article will reveal whether the program lost its funding.

Problem-Solution Relationships, Analyzing A *problem* is often an unanswered question. A *solution* is an attempt to answer the question. Think about a problem as you read by asking three questions:

- What is the problem?
- Who is affected by the problem?
- What are the effects of the problem?

Then, you can analyze and evaluate the solution by asking:

- What are the advantages and disadvantages of each proposed solution?
- What is the outcome of each attempted solution?
- What is the final result of the solution? (In other words, was the problem solved?)

(See also page 151.)

EXAMPLE When war erupted in Anna Aliu's grandparents' homeland, she felt torn between her American identity and her heritage. None of her friends had any interest in the conflict. Anna had several options. She could look on the Web for chat rooms and discuss the issues there, but she felt that that alone was too passive. She considered a hunger strike, but thought it was too extreme. Finally, she used the Web and the library to find names of organizations and officials to whom she and her friends could write about ending the conflict.

Analysis: *What is the problem?* The problem is that no one but Anna thinks a war in Anna's grandparents' homeland *is* a problem. *Who is affected by the problem?* Anna, her grandparents, and all the people in the war-torn country. *What are the effects of the problem?* Aside from the effects felt by the victims of the conflict, Anna feels frustrated by the lack of concern expressed in the United States. *What are the advantages and disadvantages of each proposed solution?* The first two may not be very effective; the last solution has the best chance of succeeding. *What outcome might be expected of each possible solution?* and *What is the final result of the solution?* The solution—to make contact with people who care about the issue and to make a call for peace—hasn't been in effect long enough to gauge its effect.

Reading Log, Using A *reading log* is a notebook, or a section of a notebook, in which you simply write about your reading. As you read, jot down your honest reactions to the text—ask questions, make connections to your own experience, and note especially important passages. You can also use a reading log to record any prereading or postreading ideas. Because readers have different experiences, interests, beliefs, and opinions, no two reading logs will be alike.

Reading Rate, Adjusting *Reading rate* is the speed at which you read a text. How quickly or how slowly you read depends upon a combination of things: your purpose for reading, the difficulty of the text, and your prior knowledge.

Reading Rates According to Purpose		
Reading Rate	**Purpose**	**Example**
Scanning	Reading for specific details	Hunting for a quotation that best expresses the theme of a story
Skimming	Reading for main points	Reviewing chapter headings, subheadings, and graphic organizers in a textbook in preparation for a test
Reading for mastery	Reading to understand and remember	Taking notes and outlining a section in a textbook before beginning an assignment
Reading for enjoyment	Reading at the speed you find most comfortable	Reading a magazine article about an interest or hobby

Always adjust your reading rate to suit your purpose as well as the text's level of difficulty. The chart above shows how purpose can affect reading rate.

SQ3R Long a popular reading-study strategy, *SQ3R* can help you read more effectively.

S *Survey* the entire text. Look briefly at each page—headings, titles, illustrations, charts, and material in boldface and italics.

Q *Question* yourself as you do your survey. What should you know after completing your reading? List questions to be answered.

R *Read* the entire selection. Think of answers to your questions as you read.

R *Recite* in your own words answers to each question.

R *Review* the material by re-reading quickly, looking over questions, and recalling answers.

Stated Main Idea and Supporting Details, Identifying A *main idea* is the focus or key idea in a piece of writing. Main ideas often appear as topic sentences of

paragraphs or, in a longer piece of writing, as a thesis statement in an introductory or concluding paragraph. *Supporting details* prove or explain the main idea.

EXAMPLE With patience, consistency, and confidence, you can train any dog. Dog training takes time, at least half an hour a day of concentrated practice. Each time you give the dog a command, make sure that it obeys. For example, if it does not sit, correct the dog with a firm pull on its collar. Letting the dog get away with disobedience is sending the wrong message. Be confident in your treatment of the dog, and it will always respect and respond to you.

Stated main idea: Training a dog requires patience, consistency, and confidence.

Supporting details: Dog training takes time. Lack of consistency sends the wrong message. Dogs respect and obey a confident trainer.

NOTE A stated main idea is also called an *explicit* main idea. (See also page 153 and **Implied Main Idea** on page 956.)

Summarizing A *summary* is a short restatement of the main points of a selection. Summarizing is a useful reading skill. It allows you to identify the basic meaning of any article or passage you are studying. It also helps you think critically by requiring you to analyze the material, isolating main ideas and identifying details that can be omitted. When you *summarize,* try to present a complete picture using as few words as possible. (See the chart on page 111 for summarizing guidelines.)

EXAMPLE   One way to determine the age of an archaeological ruin is to take a sample of timber from the structure and examine its tree rings. Tree rings reflect the growth patterns of the tree, creating a sort of map of the tree's life span. Comparing the rings to a series that has already been dated is one of the most reliable ways to date prehistoric sites.

Summary: The age of an archaeological ruin can be estimated by looking at the ring patterns of the structure's wood.

Text Structures, Analyzing   A *text structure* is the pattern a writer uses to organize ideas or events. Writers commonly use five major patterns of organization: *cause and effect, chronological order, comparison and contrast, listing,* and *problem and solution.* Being able to recognize the way people, things, events, and ideas are related will help you to understand a text. Use the following guidelines to analyze a text structure:

1. **Search the text for the main idea.** Look for clue words that signal a specific pattern of organization (See also **Clue Words** on page 955).

2. **Study the text for other important ideas.** Think about how the ideas connect, and look for an obvious pattern.

3. **Remember that a writer might use one organizational pattern throughout an entire text or might combine patterns.** Often a text has an overall pattern, but

different patterns within sections or paragraphs.

4. **Use a graphic organizer to map the relationships among the ideas.** The five common text structures, or organizational patterns, are illustrated by the following graphic organizers.

- *Cause-and-effect pattern* shows the relationship between results and the ideas or events that made the results occur. (See also page 114.) One type of cause-and-effect pattern is the *causal chain.* In a causal chain, one thing leads to the next. The following example shows the positive and negative effects of affordable computers.

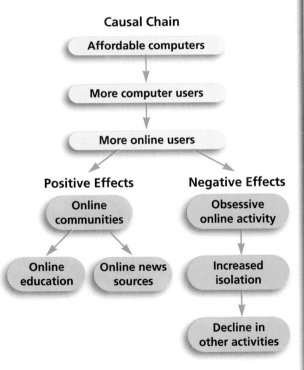

Causal Chain

Affordable computers

More computer users

More online users

Positive Effects

Online communities

Online education

Online news sources

Negative Effects

Obsessive online activity

Increased isolation

Decline in other activities

- *Chronological order* shows events or ideas happening in sequence. (See also page 23.) The following example shows the sequence for fixing a flat bicycle tire.

Sequence chain

> **Remove wheel from bike frame**
>
> ↓
>
> **Remove tire and inner tube from wheel**
>
> ↓
>
> **Pump up inner tube**
>
> ↓
>
> **Submerge inner tube in water to identify location of leak**
>
> ↓
>
> **Place glue around leak hole**
>
> ↓
>
> **Wait one minute before placing patch over glue**

- *Comparison-and-contrast* points out similarities and differences. The following example shows a comparison of the ancient classical languages of Greek and Latin.

- *Listing* presents material according to certain criteria, such as size, location, or importance. The following example lists the visual elements of Impressionist paintings in order of importance.

List

1. Harmony of line, color, form
2. Appearance of color patches rather than long, firm brush strokes
3. Attention to depiction of light
4. Depiction of entertainment scenes, such as cafes, theaters, and concerts

- *Problem-solution pattern* identifies at least one problem, offers one or more solutions to the problem, and explains or predicts the outcomes of the solutions. (See also page 151.) The example at the top of the next page is based on an article that shows how scientists and the inhabitants of an island dealt with a problem caused by nonnative pests on the island.

Venn Diagram

Classical Greek   **Classical Latin**

Differences   **Similarities**   **Differences**

- Ancestor of Modern Greek
- Greek alphabet (24 symbols), some of which are used in mathematical equations

- Dead language
- Indo-European language
- Language of classical texts

- Ancestor of Romance languages, such as French, Italian, and Spanish
- Roman alphabet (23 letters), on which modern western European alphabets are based

Problem-Solution Chart

Problem

- **What is the problem?**
- **Who has the problem?**

- **Why is it a problem?**

- The island is overrun by nonnative animals.
- The people of the island must deal with the damage caused by the proliferation of nonnative animals.
- The populations of nonnative animals are exploding because they have no natural enemies on the island.

Attempted solutions

- Extermination of nonnative animals
- Import natural enemies of the pests
- Study the problem

Outcomes of attempted solutions

- Difficult to destroy all the animals
- No guarantee; a similar problem may arise
- Does not produce any immediate results

Final results

Scientists study and discuss the problem further. Islanders enforce stricter inspections for aircraft, ships, and travelers from the outside.

Transitional Words and Phrases, Using

Transitions are used by writers to connect ideas and create coherence. As a reader, your ability to recognize transitions will help you to understand how all the ideas in a selection fit together. (See also the **Transitional Expressions** chart on pages 461 and 1045.)

Interpreting Graphics

Graphics convey ideas in a visual format. They can be used to organize and display information, to explain a process, to describe relationships among things, or to illustrate concepts or things. Most often, graphics provide a clear comparison of different but related points of information. As a reader, begin by reading any sentences, titles, captions, labels, or keys that explain the graphic and relate it to the text. The most common forms of graphics in informational writing are *charts, diagrams, graphs, tables,* and *time lines.* (See also **Graphics** on page 928.)

Charts   *Charts* show the relationships among ideas or data. Two types of charts you are likely to find in your reading are *flow charts* and *pie charts.* **Flow charts** use geometric shapes linked by arrows to show the sequence of events in a process (see the chart on the next page). The direction of the flow is always from left to right or top to bottom. *Pie charts* show the relationships of the parts of a whole. When percentages are given, they total one hundred percent. Look for labels within the pie chart or a color-coded legend nearby. The following pie chart shows the distribution of a company's time and resources in the production of a computer game.

Costs in Production of Computer Game #1

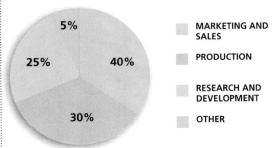

5%

25%

40%

30%

MARKETING AND SALES

PRODUCTION

RESEARCH AND DEVELOPMENT

OTHER

Diagrams *Diagrams* use symbols (such as circles, arrows, or simple pictures) to illustrate something, show a process, compare abstract ideas, or provide instruction. (Usually, diagrams are *not* used to present numerical data; a diagram's shapes are unable to represent amounts accurately.) Look at the diagram to the right illustrating how viruses reproduce.

A ***Venn diagram*** uses intersecting circles to compare two ideas or things. The section of the diagram in which the circles overlap contains the elements shared by the two things. The Venn diagram below illustrates the similarities and differences between two different styles of the sport of fencing.

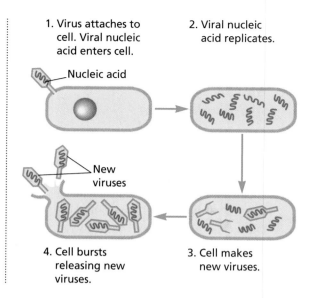

1. Virus attaches to cell. Viral nucleic acid enters cell.
   Nucleic acid
   New viruses
2. Viral nucleic acid replicates.
3. Cell makes new viruses.
4. Cell bursts releasing new viruses.

Venn Diagram

Saber

Epee

Differences

Similarities

Differences

- Requires a light, flat-bladed sword
- Points only count if opponent is hit above the waist
- Points are scored by hitting opponent with point or edge of blade

- Traditional, competitive sport involving swordplay
- Requires protective equipment, such as mask and padding
- Is played on long, narrow playing area
- Points may be recorded electronically

- Requires a thin, stiff sword
- Points only count if scored with point of epee
- Points are made by touching opponent anywhere on the body

Line and bar graphs   *Line and bar graphs* show how one variable changes in relation to another. Usually, the horizontal axis, or line, indicates points in time, and the vertical axis shows quantities. The following line and bar graphs illustrate the sales trends of two computer games.

Line Graph

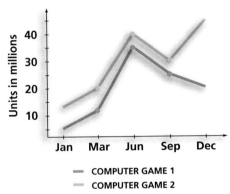

Sales of Two Computer Games

Bar Graph

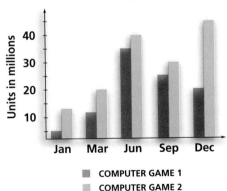

Sales of Two Computer Games

Notice how the vertical axes on both graphs begin at zero. When reading graphs, check to see that the vertical axis begins with zero; if it does not, the ratios suggested by the graph may be misleading. Also, be wary of any graph that switches the vertical and horizontal axes. If the vertical axis indicates time passing, the resulting peaks and valleys shown on the graph may be unclear or ambiguous. In the following line graph, the vertical axis indicates time. Notice how difficult it is to draw any conclusions from the graph.

Misleading Graphic

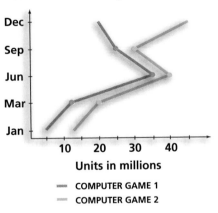

Sales of Two Computer Games

Tables   *Tables* are lists of related data arranged in rows and columns. A table presents data, but does not interpret it. Readers must draw their own conclusions about any relationships among the data. Look at how the table below is arranged.

Sale of Three Computer Games in Units of Millions					
Game	January	March	June	September	December
Computer Game X	5	12	35	20	25
Computer Game Y	11	20	45	28	40
Computer Game Z	18	22	35	32	40

Time Lines *Time lines* identify events that take place over the course of a specific period of time. Usually events are identified or described above the time line and the time demarcations are indicated below it. The following time line indicates some key events in the first fifty years of American space exploration.

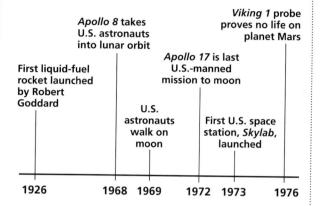

Reading Graphics Critically As a reader, you should always read graphics with a critical eye. Keep in mind the following tips.

1. **Read the title, labels, and legend** of any graphic before analyzing the data. A *title* identifies the subject or main idea of the graphic. *Labels* identify and give meaning to the information shown in the graphic. A *legend* identifies special symbols, color-coding, scale, or other features you need in order to read the graphic; it appears as a small box placed near the body.

2. **Draw your own conclusions,** and compare them to those of the writer. Often, drawing on your own prior knowledge, as well as formulating an interpretation of the text surrounding the graphic, can help you think

more critically about a graphic. For example, does the graphic oversimplify a concept—or present it as overly complex?

3. **Think about what information is *not* included** in the graphic. Often, important information is left out because it does not match the author's conclusions.

4. **Watch out for optical illusions in graphs.** For example, bar graphs and pie charts that are shown in three dimensions are easily misread because some sections look more dense than others. Also, pie charts are often "exploded" (one segment is pulled away from the others). Your eye naturally will be drawn to the exploded piece, but you should still pay attention to the whole picture.

5. **Look for manipulated data** by making sure that the horizontal axis of any graph indicates time, not amount. Also, make sure that the axes of a graph or sections of a pie chart are clearly labeled and consistently marked.

6. **Look for the source.** The *source* is a citation; it identifies where the information contained in the graphic was obtained and how current it is. Knowing the source helps you evaluate the accuracy of the graphic. For example, if the source for information about a quickly changing topic, such as the World Wide Web, is more than a few years old, you might question the relevance of the information. If no source is given, you must question the accuracy of the information.

You can also use the *4R test* to evaluate the source of the information in a graphic. Ask yourself if the source is **relevant, recent, reliable,** and **representative.** (See also page 251.)

Vocabulary

Context Clues   Often you can figure out the meaning of an unfamiliar word by examining its *context,* the group of words or sentences surrounding the unfamiliar word. Examining surrounding words, phrases, and sentences is called using *context clues.* The following chart shows examples of some of the common types of context clues. Note that the difficult vocabulary words are printed in italics and the clue word or words are printed in boldface. (See also pages 27, 68, 114, and 242.)

How to Use Context Clues
Types of Clues
Antonyms: Look for clues that indicate an unfamiliar word is opposite in meaning to a familiar word or phrase.
Example:
During the 1930s, many American farmers abandoned their **unproductive fields** in search of *arable* farmland.
Cause and Effect: Look for clues that indicate an unfamiliar word is the cause of or the result of an action, feeling, or idea.
Example:
Constant drought and windstorm conditions caused the *erosion* of fertile topsoil that crops needed to grow.
Comparison: Sometimes an unknown word may be compared with a more familiar word.
Example:
Impromptu camps of emigrants would spring up **like mushrooms** near farms that had crops to be harvested.

Contrast: An unfamiliar word may sometimes be contrasted with a more familiar word or concept.

Example:

Unlike the displaced farmers and others who were suddenly unemployed, the *affluent* were not much affected by the economic depression.

Definitions and Restatements: Look for words that define the term or restate it in other words.

Example:

Entire families often became *transient,* **moving from place to place in order to find work.**

Examples: Look for examples used in context that reveal the meaning of an unfamiliar word.

Example:

Archives, **such as the Library of Congress,** contain documents that describe the troubles many people experienced during the 1930s.

Synonyms: Look for clues that indicate an unfamiliar word is similar in meaning to a familiar word or phrase.

Example:

Many memoirs describe the feeling of *camaraderie* between people, **the friendship** they felt when they shared what little they had with others.

Word Bank   One way of increasing your vocabulary is to collect words in a *word bank,* a list of words created from your own reading, listening, and viewing. Each time you encounter a new word, enter it into your word bank—usually a separate notebook or computer file. Check a dictionary to make sure you understand the meaning and use of each new word.

Word Formations

Process	Description	Examples
Combining	Combining two base words to make a compound or combining a word with a prefix or suffix	doorway, high-rise, unfold, wonderful
Shortening	Omitting part of an original word to shorten it or to change it to another part of speech	telephone > phone information > info nuclear > nuke
Blending	Shortening and combining two words	breakfast + lunch = brunch smoke + fog = smog
Shifting	Changing the meaning or usage of a word	host (n.) > host (v.) farm (n.) > farm (v.)

Word Formations   New words are constantly added to the English language. The most common way new words are formed is by combining words or word parts. Prefixes and suffixes are usually added to a ***base word,*** or a word ***root,*** to make a new word. Sometimes, however, two base words can be combined (with or without a hyphen) to make a new word. The table at the top of the page shows the most common ways new words are formed. (See also **Word Parts** on page 970.)

Word Meanings   Words have many layers of meanings. Their messages can change depending on the time, the place, or the situation in which they are used. Use the following definitions and examples to make sure that your words say what you want them to say.

■   Analogies are comparisons of two things. In ***analogy questions,*** you are asked to analyze the relationship between two words and then identify another pair of words that have the same relationship. Analogy questions often appear on standardized tests because they measure your knowledge of vocabulary as

well as your ability to identify relationships and patterns between words.

EXAMPLE
1. INCH: FOOT : _____
   A. quart : measure
   B. weight : peck
   C. ounce : pound
   D. meter : yard

■   *Clichés* are tired expressions. A cliché's message has been made weak and boring by overuse. Some clichés began as apt phrases that became fashionable sayings. For instance, the phrase "Footprints on the sands of time" helped make Henry Wadsworth Longfellow a popular poet, but overuse has made the expression trite and almost meaningless.

EXAMPLES   light as a feather, slow as molasses, the heart of the matter, time will tell, sings like a bird

■   *Colloquialisms* are words and phrases of conversational language. In fact, *colloquial* derives from a Latin word meaning "conversation." Used appropriately and sparingly in informal writing, colloquialisms can give your writing a lively, personal tone.

EXAMPLES

We are all *pulling* for Rhonda to win the race tonight.

I'm *fixing to* drive out to San Francisco one of these days.

Morris *put in* for the Saturday shift.

■ **Denotation and Connotation** are vital in understanding levels of word meaning. **Denotation** refers to a word's literal meaning—the meaning given in a dictionary's definition of a word. **Connotation** is the emotional meaning or association that people may connect to the word. Because connotations often stir people's feelings, they can have powerful effects on the listener or reader.

EXAMPLE   The adjectives *impromptu* and *impetuous* share the denotative meaning "spontaneous," but they suggest different ideas or feelings. *Impromptu* usually suggests a speech or other action done with little rehearsal or preparation. *Impetuous*, on the other hand, has the negative connotation of a hasty and ill-advised action.

■ **Euphemisms** are indirect, agreeable terms used in place of more direct, less appealing ones. Some euphemisms are used as a courtesy to avoid offending people; others, however, are used to mislead people—to hide unpleasant truths or misrepresent the facts.

Euphemism	More Direct Term
memorial garden	cemetery
socially maladjusted	rude
faux	imitation
misrepresentation	lie
casualties	dead

■ **Figurative language** goes beyond the literal meaning of the words to create a special effect or feeling. The following chart shows the most common types of figurative language.

Types of Figurative Language

A **simile** compares two basically unlike things, using a connective word such as *like* or *as*.

Example

The engine started up like a grumpy old man getting out of bed.

A **metaphor** equates two things without using a connective word such as *like* or *as*.

Example

The wait was an eternity.

Personification gives human characteristics to a nonhuman thing.

Example

The soft wind outside sang me to sleep.

■ **Gobbledygook** is wordy, puffed-up language. Gobbledygook results in long, rambling sentences that make little sense but may seem impressive because they contain difficult words. Sometimes, gobbledygook is used to confuse readers or listeners.

EXAMPLE   Experience indicates that the characteristic of tardiness is overall more felicitous than the fact of total avoidance or absence.
Translation: Better late than never.

■ **Idioms** are conversational phrases that mean something different from the literal meanings of the words. Idioms often cannot be explained grammatically, and they make no sense if translated word-for-word into another language. In many idioms, the change of a word or two can alter completely the meaning of the expression. Think, for example, about the idiom *up a creek*. If you are up a creek (without a paddle) you are generally in trouble. What if you were down a creek? Look at the following examples for familiar idioms.

EXAMPLES

Max could not concentrate on his work; he was really *out to lunch.*

My friend explained the joke twice, but I just didn't *get it.*

We can't reach a solution when you *dance around* the problem.

I *hit the road* around noon and got home in time for dinner.

■ ***Jargon*** is a special language used by groups of people in a particular occupation, hobby, or field of study. Jargon is effective only if the reader or listener is familiar with its special meanings. Note in the following example how the single word *cast* can mean different things to different groups.

EXAMPLE: **cast**

Theater—the actors in a stage production
Sculpture—the molding of liquefied metal into a specific shape
Medicine—the plaster dressing used to set a broken bone
Fishing—the throwing of a baited fishing line into water

■ ***Loaded words*** are used to provoke strong feeling, either positive or negative. A writer or speaker who wants to prejudice you for or against something may appeal to your emotions with loaded words. Politicians, advertisers, and writers of newspaper editorials all know and use the power of loaded language to influence their audiences. Notice the difference between the following two sentences; the tone of the first sentence changes dramatically

when neutral words are replaced by loaded ones.

EXAMPLE

The audience received the administrator's *fair-minded* comments with *restrained attention.*
The audience received the administrator's *mealy-mouthed* comments with *rude indifference.*

■ ***Malapropisms*** are words that sound like the correct words but are not. The term comes from the name of a character, Mrs. Malaprop, in British playwright Richard Sheridan's comedy *The Rivals.* Mrs. Malaprop's name is a joke (it is based on the French expression *mal à propos*, which means "not appropriate"). She pretends to know more than she does, and her misuse of words is so humorous that similar blunders are now called "malapropisms" in her honor. For example, mistaking the word *pineapple* for *pinnacle*, Mrs. Malaprop exclaims, "He is the very pineapple of politeness!" You can avoid malapropisms by familiarizing yourself with the precise meanings of easily confused words, such as *anecdote* and *antidote, effect* and *affect,* or *infer* and *imply.*

EXAMPLES

The perfect *anecdote* for a broken heart is a new romance. [*Anecdote* should be *antidote.*]
Am I to *imply* that you are angry with me? [*Imply* should be *infer.*]

■ ***Multiple meaning words*** have more than one meaning and often function as more than one part of speech. When you use a dictionary to find a word's meaning, look at all the word's definitions and keep in mind the context in which you read or heard the word. Then, try the various definitions in that context until you find the one that fits. Look at the italicized multiple meaning word in the example on the next page.

EXAMPLE

Historically, injustice to a particular group of people has become the *grounds* for changing the law.

grounds (groundz) *n.* **1.** an area set aside for a specific purpose or event **2.** the cause for an action **3.** the solid or sediment at the bottom of a liquid [The second definition best fits the meaning in context.]

■ *Nonsexist language* is language that applies to people in general, both male and female. For many years, it was acceptable practice to use gender-specific terms, such as *man* or *mankind*, to describe groups that included both genders. In recent years, writers have learned to use nonsexist terms instead—using, for example, *humanity* and *humankind* in place of the gender-specific *mankind*. In addition, many occupations that once were limited only to men or to women are now open to both. As a result, many job titles have been adjusted to reflect the change. Below are some widely used nonsexist terms that you may use to replace older, gender-specific ones.

Gender-specific terms	Nonsexist terms
chairman	chairperson (or chair)
deliveryman	delivery person
fireman	firefighter
mailman	mail carrier
man-made	synthetic
policeman	police officer
salesman	sales representative
steward, stewardess	flight attendant
watchman	security guard

■ *Slang* is highly informal language that consists of made-up words or words used in new ways. It is often lively, imaginative, and entertaining but is usually short-lived, as it rides a crest of popularity and then dies out quickly. For instance, in the 1950s, the word *shoe* briefly replaced the slang words *neat* and *cool*. Of course, *neat* and *cool* have been around a long time, but not as long as *duds*, which means "clothing" and dates back to the sixteenth century. Sometimes slang words become so widely used that they are integrated into the language. Words such as *nice*, *pants*, and *nickel* were all once considered slang words. Interestingly enough, sometimes word opposites have exactly the same slang meaning. For example, *hot* and *cool* both mean "excellent" or "very pleasing."

■ *Synonyms* are words that have the same or nearly the same meaning. However, synonyms often have subtle shades of or differences in meaning. Use a dictionary or thesaurus to make sure that you understand the exact differences in meanings between synonyms. Often the difference between two synonyms is a matter of connotation. In the sentences below, it is clear that *strolled* and *wandered* are synonyms for *walked*, but while *walked* is a general verb, *strolled* and *wandered* describe specific ways of moving. *Strolled* suggests a casual, easy gait, and *wandered* suggests a lack of aim or direction. (See also **Denotation and Connotation** on page 967.)

EXAMPLES

Nicole *walked* along the crowded street.
Nicole *strolled* along the crowded street.
Nicole *wandered* along the crowded street.

■ *Tired words* have lost their freshness and force. They have been used so often and so carelessly that they have become worn-out and almost meaningless.

EXAMPLES   *nice, fine, pretty, wonderful, terrific,* and *great*

Word Origins

Words always originate, or come into a language, at some time and from some place. The origin and history of a word—its *etymology*—often appears in brackets in the dictionary entry. The following etymology indicates that the origin of *fidelity* is Latin and that it came into modern use by way of Old French (OFr) and Middle English (ME). The symbol < means "comes from."

EXAMPLE   **fidelity** [ME < OFr < L *fidelitas* < *fidelis,* faithful < *fides,* faith *fidelite*]

Word Parts

English words can be classified into two types: those that cannot be subdivided into parts, and those that can. Words that cannot be subdivided, like *graph, straight,* and *please,* are called **base words.** Words that can be subdivided, such as *childhood, replacement,* and *acknowledge,* are made up of **word parts.** The three types of word parts are **roots, prefixes,** and **suffixes.** Knowing the meanings of roots, prefixes, and suffixes can help you determine the meanings of many unfamiliar words.

■ *Roots* are the foundations on which words are built. A root carries the word's core meaning, and it is the part to which prefixes and suffixes are added. Some roots come from base words, such as *–see–* in *foreseeable,* and are relatively easy to define. Other roots may be more difficult to define, such as those in *diversion* (*–vers–,* "turn") and *inspiration* (*–spir–,* "breathe"). These roots and others come from Greek and Latin.

Commonly Used Roots

Roots	Meanings	Examples
Greek		
–anthrop–	human	anthropology, anthropomorphic
–bio–	life	biography, bionic
–chrom–	color	chromatic, monochrome
–dem–	people	demagogue, democratic
–derm–	skin	dermatology, epidermis
–graph–	write, writing	calligraphy, autograph
–hydr–	water	hydrant, hydroelectric
–log–, –logy–	study, word	logic, theology
–ortho–	straight	orthodox, orthography
–phil–	like, love	philosophy, philanthropy
–zo–	life, animal	zoo, zoology
Latin		
–audi–	hear	audio, auditorium

Commonly Used Roots

Roots	Meanings	Examples
Latin continued		
–ben–, –bene–	good	benign, beneficial
–cent–	hundred	centennial, century
–cogn–	know	recognize, cognizant
–duc–, –duct–	draw, lead	induce, deduct
–loc–	place	locality, locate
–magn–	large, grand	magnitude, magnify
–man–	hand	manicure, manual
–mater–, –matr–	mother	maternal, matriarch
–mor–, –mort–	death	moribund, mortal
–omni–	all	omnipresent, omniscient
–pater–, –patr–	father	paternal, patriarchy
–prim–	early	primeval, primitive
–solv–	loosen, accomplish	dissolve, solvent
–spir–	breath	expire, inspire
–vid–, –vis–	see	video, vision

■ **Prefixes** are word parts added before a root. The word that is created from a prefix and a root combines the meanings of both of its parts. The chart below includes some common prefixes, their meanings, and examples of each. (See also page 196.)

Commonly Used Prefixes

Roots	Meanings	Examples
Greek		
a–	lacking, without	amorphous, asymmetry
anti–	against, opposing	antipathy, antithesis
dia–	through, across, between	diagnose, diameter
hyper–	excessive	hypersensitive, hypertension
hypo–	under, below	hypodermic, hypothermia
mon–, mono–	one	monanthous, monotheism
para–	beside, beyond	paradox, paralegal
peri–	around	perimeter, periscope
psych–, psycho–	mind	psychic, psychopath
sym–	together, with	sympathy, symphony

(continued)

Commonly Used Prefixes		
Roots	**Meanings**	**Examples**
Latin and French		
ab–	from, away	abdicate, abjure
co–, col–, com–, con–, cor–	together, with	coexist, collide, compose, convene, correspond
contra–	against	contradict, contravene
de–	away, from, off, down	deflect, defrost
dif–, dis–	away, not, opposing	differ, disappoint
e–, ef–, ex–	away, from, out	emigrate, effrontery, extract
in–, im–	in, into, within	infer, insurgent, impression
inter–	between, among	intercede, international
intra–	within	intramural, intrastate
non–	not	nonsense, nonprofit
per–	through	perceive, permit
post–	after, following	postpone, postscript
pre–	before	preclude, predisposed
pro–	forward, favoring	produce, pronoun
re–	back, backward, again	revoke, regenerate, recur
retro–	back, backward	retrograde, retrospective
semi–	partly	semiofficial, semiprivate
sub–, suf–, sum–, sup–, sus–	under, beneath	subjugate, suffuse, summon, suppose, suspect
ultra–	beyond, excessively	ultramodern, ultraviolet
Old English		
be–	around, about	belay, bemoan
for–	away, off, from	forgo, forswear
mis–	badly, not, wrongly	miscalculate, mismatch
over–	above, excessively	oversee, overdo
un–	not, reverse of	unhappy, unlock

■ **Suffixes** are word parts added after a root. Often, adding or changing a suffix will change both a word's meaning and its part of speech. There are two main types of suffixes. The first type provides a grammatical signal of some kind but does not greatly change the basic meaning of the word (*–s, –ed, –ing*). The second type of suffix creates new words. The suffixes listed on the next page are primarily those that create new words.

Commonly Used Suffixes

Roots	Meanings	Examples
Greek, Latin, and French		
Nouns		
–ance, –ancy, –ence	act, condition	acceptance, hesitancy, turbulence
–cy	state, condition	accuracy, currency
–ism	act, doctrine, manner	barbarism, cubism, patriotism
–ity	state, condition	possibility, ability
–tion	action, condition	selection, relation
–ty, –y	quality, state, action	beauty, enmity, inquiry
–ure	act, results, means	culture, signature
Adjectives		
–able, –ible	able, likely	tolerable, possible
–ate	having, characteristic of	desolate, separate
–ous	marked by, given to	religious, riotous
Adjectives or Nouns		
–ant, –ent	actor, showing	servant, confident
–ite	formed, showing	composite, favorite
Verbs		
–ate	become, cause to be	animate, sublimate
–esce	become, grow, continue	acquiesce, obsolesce
–fy	make, cause to have	fortify, glorify
–ize	make, cause to be	criticize, motorize
Old English		
Nouns		
–dom	state, rank, condition	kingdom, wisdom
–hood	state, condition	statehood, falsehood
–ness	quality, state	kindness, tenderness
Adjectives		
–en	made of, like	wooden, ashen
–ful	full of, marked by	thankful, zestful
–less	lacking, without	countless, hopeless
–ly	like, characteristic of	yearly, positively
–some	apt to, showing	lonesome, tiresome
Verbs		
–en	cause to be, become	blacken, weaken

Words to Learn The three hundred words in the list below may be used as the basis of your vocabulary study for this year. Make it a habit to learn unfamiliar words from this list regularly.

abash
abate
abominable
abridge
abstain
abut
accentuate
accost
acquiesce
acquisition
adamant
affable
affinity
affluent
allegory
alleviate
allure
altercation
ambiguous
ambivalent
anagram
anecdote
antagonize
appraisal
apprise
arable
arbitrary
archives
arduous
array
askew
assail
assay
assertion
attrition
audacious
augment
auspicious

austere
autocrat

baleful
bandy
banter
beleaguer
beneficent
bestow
betrothed
bilateral
blithe
bolster
brevity
browbeat
brunt
brusque
bulwark
bumptious
bureaucracy

camaraderie
catharsis
cede
chagrin
cite
climactic
coalition
coherent
comely
comprehensive
concerted
congenital
conjecture
connotation
consensus
consonant
contraband
contrition

convivial
correlate
credence

debacle
debonair
decadence
deference
defile
degenerate
deign
deluge
demeanor
deprecate
derogatory
despicable
dissipate
dissolute
diverge

effete
efficacious
elation
embellish
emendation
encroach
enormity
enthrall
entity
entomology
entourage
epicure
epilogue
epithet
equestrian
erroneous
evasive
evoke
exhaustive
exodus
exonerate
expedite
expletive
extemporaneous

faction
factious
fallible
fastidious
felicitous
felony
ferocity
fidelity
filial
finality
fiord
flail
flaunt
flay
foreshadow
forgo
forte
frustrate
fulminate
furor
furtive

garrulous
gibe
gird
goad
gradation
grandiose
guise

haggard
heinous
hypercritical
hypochondriac

idiomatic
idyll
imbibe
immemorial
imperious
impetuous
impromptu
impunity
inane
incise

QUICK REFERENCE HANDBOOK

incoherent
incongruous
incredulous
indigenous
indolence
inexplicable
infer
ingratiate
inherent
innocuous
insatiable
insidious
insular
intangible
integral
interminable
interpose
intrepid
intricacy
intrinsic
introspective
inure
invidious
invoke
irascible

laudable
lucid
lucrative

malevolent
martyr
mercenary
microcosm
misanthrope
miscreant

noncommittal
nostalgic
novice
nurture

omnivorous
oracular
orient

oscillate
ostentatious

palliate
panacea
peripheral
permeate
pernicious
perpetuate
phalanx
platitude
plebeian
politic
populace
precipitate
predecessor
preemptory
premeditated
presumptuous
pretentious
proboscis
procrastinate
prodigy
proficient
proletarian
prologue
propagate
protagonist
prototype
protract
provocation
provocative
proxy
purport

query
quixotic

rapacious
rationalize
recalcitrant
reciprocate
recrimination
redress

reiterate
relent
remission
repartee
repression
repugnant
resilient
rhetorical
rigorous
rudiment

sallow
sanction
satiate
scapegoat
scrutinize
secular
shibboleth
shrew
sluice
solstice
somnolent
sortie
staunch
stereotype
stigma
stint
stipend
stoic
subservient
subside
subterfuge
supercilious
supplication
surmise
symposium
synchronize
syndicate

taint
tawdry
tenacity
tepid
terse

thwart
transient

ulterior
undermine
unremitting
usurp

vanquish
vegetate
verbose
vernacular
vilify
vivacious
vogue

waive
wily
wistful
wrest

Speaking and Listening

Speaking

You speak most often in conversational situations—with family members, friends, classmates, teachers, co-workers, and so on. Frequently, however, you are required to speak on occasions that require more careful communication than the ordinary conversation. No matter what the speaking occasion, there are strategies and techniques you can use to become a better speaker.

Debate

A formal *debate* involves two groups or teams who publicly discuss a controversial topic in a systematic way. The topic under discussion is called the *proposition.* One team, the *affirmative team,* argues that the proposition should be accepted or adopted. The other side, the *negative team,* argues that the proposition should be rejected. To win the debate, the affirmative side must present enough proof to establish its case; alternatively, the negative side must refute, or prove wrong, the affirmative case by defending the status quo (the present state of affairs) or by presenting a counterplan.

Features of a Debate   While there are different formats for debates, some features are common to all of them.

- **Debate proposition**   The central issue in a debate is a proposition that is phrased as a resolution and limited to a specific idea. The proposition should be an issue that is actually debatable, and should offer each side an equal chance to build a reasonable case. The proposition should be clearly stated in language that is understandable to the debaters and to the audience.

  One of two types of debate propositions is used in formal debate.
- The *proposition of value* asserts the value of a particular person, place, or thing. Here is an example of a proposition of value: "Resolved: That students from the United States compete with foreign students in all areas of study."
- The *proposition of policy* asserts that a particular action should be taken. Here is an example of a proposition of policy: "Resolved: That the United States should

adopt a national health insurance plan for all citizens."

■ **Debate etiquette** An important feature of debate is the etiquette, or manners, required of debaters. Ridicule, sarcasm, or personal attacks are not acceptable. Deliberately misquoting or attempting to distract or disturb opponents is also unacceptable. A debate should be won or lost only on the basis of reasoned argument and convincing delivery. Also, it is customary to refer to participants in a debate by using polite terms such as "the first affirmative speaker," "my worthy opponent," "my colleagues," or "my teammates."

■ **Debate officials** A chairperson often presides during the debate. A speaker may appeal to the chairperson if he or she believes that any debating procedures or time limits have been violated by the opposing team. The most common method of determining the winner of a debate is by the decision of three appointed judges. The judges are expected to base their decision on the merits of the debate and not on their own views of the proposition. Occasionally, an audience may vote to determine the winning team.

Formats of Debate Most debates are divided into two parts. In the first part, both sides make constructive speeches, attempting to build their cases by presenting their arguments for or against the proposition and attempting to *refute,* or disprove, the points of the opposing side. Then, after an intermission, both sides make *rebuttal speeches,* replying to damaging arguments raised by the opposing side. Specific time limits are assigned for each speech, although these limits vary, depending on the type of debate.

■ **Traditional, or formal, debate** This debate format has two speakers on a team. One team takes the affirmative position and the other takes the negative position on a proposition of policy. Each member of each team speaks twice within set time limits. The following chart shows the speaking order and the time limits of a typical traditional, or formal, debate.

The Traditional Debate

1. Constructive Speeches (all 10 minutes)
   a. First affirmative
   b. First negative
   c. Second affirmative
   d. Second negative

2. Rebuttal speeches (all 5 minutes)
   a. First negative
   b. First affirmative
   c. Second negative
   d. Second affirmative

■ **Cross-examination debate** This type of debate also features two affirmative and two negative speakers. The difference between this debate format and the traditional debate is that participants are allowed the opportunity to question opponents. During this cross-examination period, a speaker can clarify issues and point out weaknesses in an opponent's position. The following chart shows the speaking order of a typical cross-examination debate with typical time limits. Time limits can vary.

The Cross-Examination Debate	
Order of Speakers	Typical Time Limits
1. Constructive Speeches	
a. First affirmative	8 minutes
b. Cross-examination by second negative	3 minutes
c. First negative	8 minutes
d. Cross-examination by first affirmative	3 minutes
e. Second affirmative	8 minutes
f. Cross examination by first negative	3 minutes
g. Second negative	8 minutes
h. Cross-examination by second affirmative	3 minutes
2. Rebuttal speeches	
a. First negative	5 minutes
b. First affirmative	5 minutes
c. Second negative	5 minutes
d. Second affirmative	5 minutes

The Lincoln–Douglas Debate	
Speaker	Time Limits
Affirmative	6-minute constructive speech
Negative	3-minute questioning of the Affirmative
Negative	7-minute constructive speech and refutation
Affirmative	3-minute questioning of the Negative
Affirmative	4-minute rebuttal speech
Negative	6-minute rebuttal speech and summary
Affirmative	3-minute rebuttal speech and summary

■ **Lincoln-Douglas debate** This type of debate commemorates the famous debates between two candidates for senator from Illinois in 1858—Abraham Lincoln and Stephen A. Douglas. This format features an affirmative speaker and a negative speaker debating a proposition of value. The affirmative speaker argues that the proposition is a true and worthy statement; the negative speaker argues the opposite. This format is well-suited for debates on matters of values and beliefs. It encourages logical analysis of abstract concepts. The following chart shows the speaking order and the time limits of a typical Lincoln-Douglas debate.

Preparing for Debate To be an effective debater, you must prepare thoroughly. Follow the steps below to research the proposition and plan a strategy for the debate.

1. **Research the proposition.** Consult reference books and other sources to obtain information. Record facts and evidence.
2. **Identify specific issues.** The *issues* in a debate are the main differences between the affirmative and the negative positions. Every debatable proposition rests on several issues. To prove your proposition, list all the arguments you have for supporting your side of the proposition. To refute your opposition, list all the reasons you think your opponents will give for disagreeing with your views.
3. **Support your arguments.** Based on the information gathered during your research, identify evidence that supports your arguments—examples, quotations, statistics, expert opinions, analogies, and logical reasons. Also, find evidence that will refute arguments your opponents are likely to use.

4. **Build a brief.** A *brief* is an outline for a debate. It is like a formal outline for an argumentative essay. The affirmative side in a debate creates a brief that contains a logical arrangement of all the arguments needed to prove the proposition, as well as the evidence necessary to support its arguments. The negative side creates a brief to disprove the proposition.

■ **Refuting opposing arguments**   In addition to building a strong case for or against the proposition, each team must argue against its opponents' case. An attack on the opposition's argument is known as *refutation.* To refute your opposition's case you can attack in one or more of the following three ways.

  ■ **Refute the *quantity* of their evidence.** Look for places in your opposition's case where there is little or no supporting evidence.
  ■ **Refute the *quality* of their evidence.** Your opposition's case may be built on many poor pieces of supporting evidence. Arguments supported by weak evidence are vulnerable to attack.
  ■ **Refute their *reasoning* from their evidence.** Your most effective way to refute is to point out flaws in your opposition's reasoning or logic. Look for places where their case is based on faulty conclusions.

  Follow these steps to refute your opponents' arguments.
  1. State clearly the arguments you are going to refute.
  2. Tell the audience how you plan to refute the argument.
  3. Present proof to refute the argument by using facts, statistics, quotations, and other supporting data or evidence.
  4. Explain how your proof effectively refutes your opponents' arguments.

■ **Building a rebuttal**   The *rebuttal* should attempt to rebuild your case. This part of the debate allows each of the opposing sides a chance to repair the arguments that have been attacked by their opponents during the refutation. An effective rebuttal should

  1. restate your original arguments
  2. state your position on the issues your opponents have already attacked
  3. present proof that supports your arguments
  4. point out any weaknesses in your opponents' arguments
  5. summarize your original documents and present any additional evidence you have gathered that supports your position

Formal Speaking Occasions

There are several kinds of formal speaking occasions: delivering formal speeches, participating in formal group discussions, conducting interviews, and being the subject of an interview. Each requires more preparation than an informal speaking occasion.

Formal Speeches   Formal speeches do not simply happen; they require time and thoughtful preparation. You can follow the steps below to prepare a formal speech.

1. **Identify Task, Occasion, and Purpose** Thoroughly understand your *task,* or the job you are required to do. For example, a formal speech requires advanced planning, formal structure, and appropriate language. The task may also require that your speech be a certain length, or you may have limitations on time or topic. Then, think of the *occasion* for your speech. What has motivated you to speak and what will be the setting of the speech? Your general *purpose* is the overall

General Types of Speeches		
General Type of Speech	**Purpose**	**Examples**
Informative Speeches	To present new information to an audience or to provide a new view of old information	• Lecture • News broadcast • Orientation • Instruction
Persuasive Speeches	To change an attitude or belief or to move an audience to action	• Campaign speech • Advertisement • Debate
Special Occasion Speeches	To entertain or amuse an audience or acknowledge a special reason for the audience's presence	• Anecdote • Oral interpretation of a piece of literature • Valedictorian addressing classmates and parents • Speech dedicating a new library

intent of your speech. Most often, the purpose of a speech is to inform or to persuade an audience. Common purposes for giving speeches appear in the chart above.

2. **Select a Topic**   If the topic of your speech is not assigned, choose something that interests you. If you show no enthusiasm for your subject, your audience will quickly lose interest. Consider the answers to the following questions when selecting your topic.

- *What is the general purpose of your speech?* Do you want to inform, persuade, or entertain your listeners?
- *What is the occasion of your speech?* What, in other words, prompts you to speak? Are you, for example, speaking to protest a curfew law the city council is considering? Think about how your topic will fit the occasion of your speech and how the setting affects your choice of topic. For example, if

you are to give a speech at your state capitol, you may choose to speak on current legislation or on our nation's political ideals.

- *How much time will you have to speak?* Have you limited your speech topic so that you can deliver it within the prescribed time frame?

3. **Analyze the Audience**   Once you select your topic, you must think about how to tailor your speech to your audience's needs or interests. You might know the people in your audience quite well or not at all. Either way, find out as much as you can about

- how you can relate your thesis to your audience members' lives and experiences
- how familiar audience members are with your subject
- what their expectations of you are

If possible, poll some members of your audience before you begin writing your speech.

Analyzing Your Audience

Questions about audience	Evaluation	Your speech should include
Who are the people in your audience?	• Mostly younger than you • Mostly older than you	• Simple language, short sentences, age-specific examples, and clear explanations • A respectful tone, general examples that all people will understand, and no slang or jargon
What does the audience already know about the topic?	• Very little • A little • A good deal	• Basic background or details to inform your listeners • Some background • A more advanced discussion that focuses on interesting issues or aspects of the topic
How interested will the audience be in your topic?	• Very interested • Somewhat interested • Uninterested	• Details about the topic to maintain the audience's interest • A discussion of aspects that are most interesting to the audience • Material that persuades the audience that the topic is important

The chart above provides some questions and strategies for adapting material to a particular audience.

4. **Create a Formal Tone** Your *tone* is the feeling that you reveal or convey to your audience about your topic. Although your speech and your tone are formal, you should avoid making your speech unbearably dull, dry, and serious. Here is how you can achieve an appropriate formal tone.

- Present serious ideas. The content of your speech is often a great indicator of your tone.
- Use good vocabulary, grammar, and syntax, making sure to use complete sentences.
- Do not use slang or idiomatic expressions.
- Insert an appropriate amount of humor. Have enough humor to keep your audi-

ence's interest, but not so much as to detract from the seriousness of your ideas.
- Pay close attention to the structure of your speech (detailed on the next page).

5. **Gather Material and Organize Content** The next step in preparing a speech is to research the topic you have selected. (For information about how to use the **library** or **media center** for research, see page 942. For information on **taking notes** and **preparing outlines,** see pages 253 and 1037.)

6. **Write the Speech** In writing your speech, you must consider the structure of your speech, the language you use, and the way that you involve your audience with your material. The chart on the next page provides some basic guidelines.

Features of a Formal Speech

Structure

The speech should be composed of three parts: an *introduction* with a thesis statement or main idea, a *body,* and a *conclusion.*

(For information about **composition structure** and the **writing process,** see page 465.)

Language

The language you use should be appropriate for your audience. Keep in mind the following points:

1. Use formal, standard English.

2. Use technical terms sparingly, and be sure to define them.

3. Avoid slang, jargon, and euphemisms in your speech.

Audience Involvement

It is important to remember that written English sounds different when it is read aloud. Make your speech more "listener-friendly" by doing the following:

1. Use personal pronouns. For example, say "you may think" or "we believe" instead of "one may think" or "people believe."

2. Instead of making statements, ask rhetorical questions, questions not meant to be answered but asked only for effect. For example, instead of telling the audience a fact or statistic about accidental death among children in the United States, ask them "Did you know that accidental deaths account for . . . ?"

---

7. Determine Method of Delivery Now you need to decide which method you will use to deliver your speech. The following chart describes the basic methods of delivering a speech and the advantages and disadvantages of each.

Methods of Delivering a Speech

Method	Advantages	Disadvantages
Manuscript speech (read to audience word for word from a prepared script)	Provides exact words you wish to say; less chance of errors or omissions	Does not permit audience feedback; tends to be dull for audience
Memorized speech (memorized word for word from a script and recited to the audience)	Gives speaker freedom to move around and look at the audience	May not sound natural; requires much practice and memorization; risk of forgetting speech
Extemporaneous speech (outlined and carefully prepared, but not memorized; speech notes often used)	Sounds natural; allows speaker to respond to audience in a natural, less formal manner	Requires practice and preparation

If you are delivering a prepared speech to a live audience, the extemporaneous method is usually the most effective. To organize your materials for an extemporaneous speech, first write out a complete outline. Then, using the guidelines below, prepare note cards that you may refer to as you present your speech.

Guidelines for Extemporaneous Speech Notecards

1. Put only one key idea, possibly accompanied by a brief example or detail, on each card.

2. Make a special notecard for material that you plan to read word for word, such as a quotation, a series of dates, or a list of statistics.

3. Make a special notecard to indicate when you should pause to show a visual, such as a chart, diagram, graph, picture, or model.

4. Number your completed cards to keep them in order.

8. Rehearse the Speech You will give a better and more convincing presentation if you rehearse it. Your audience can evaluate your speech on the basis of your ideas, of course, but they can also evaluate it on the basis of certain **nonverbal** and **verbal signals** you use in delivering your speech. You use nonverbal and verbal signals anytime you speak, but because they are especially obvious to an audience when you speak formally, it is wise to rehearse them.

- *Nonverbal Signals* In addition to communicating with words, you can communicate with nonverbal signals, like those described in the following chart, when you deliver your speech.

Communicating With Nonverbal Signals

Nonverbal signals	Tips and Effects
Eye Contact	Look directly into the eyes of as many members of the audience as you can. Eye contact communicates honesty and sincerity. It makes the audience feel as if you are speaking *with* them rather than *to* them.
Facial Expression	The entire range of facial expressions—smiling, frowning, sneering, raising an eyebrow, and so on—can reveal your feelings and enhance or even take the place of a verbal message. Be sure your facial expression matches your words and feelings.
Gesture	Making relaxed and natural gestures with your head, hands, or arms as you speak emphasizes verbal messages. Nodding the head for *yes* or shaking it for *no,* using the hands to indicate size or shape, or pointing with the index finger can effectively punctuate your speech.
Posture	Stand erect and look alert to communicate an air of confidence and authority to your audience.

- *Verbal Signals* Use your voice expressively when you deliver a speech. The following verbal signals will help you communicate your message to an audience.

Communicating With Verbal Signals	
Verbal signals	**Tips**
Diction (the clarity of your pronunciation)	Always speak clearly and carefully so that your listeners can understand you.
Emphasis (the stress put on a word or phrase)	If you were arguing that the jury system in United States courts is too inefficient and costly and should be updated, you would probably want to place emphasis on the words *time* and *efficiency.*
Pause (small silences in your speech)	Use pauses to help listeners catch up or to suggest that what you have said or are about to say is important.
Pitch (how your voice sounds)	When speakers are nervous, the pitch in their voices tends to become higher. Take a deep breath and relax before you speak to keep your voice's pitch at its most natural.
Rate (the speed with which you talk)	Normal speed is about 120 to 160 words per minute. When delivering a speech, you should speak at a slower-than-normal rate.
Volume (the level of sound you create)	Although it may sound unnatural to you to speak loudly when giving a speech, your audience appreciates the extra volume. Be sure to ask listeners if they can hear you before you begin your speech.

9. **Deliver the Speech** If you are like most people, you will feel nervous before you deliver your speech. You should not, however, allow your normal nervousness to affect your delivery. Here are some suggestions that can help.

- *Be prepared.* Avoid excessive nervousness by organizing and being familiar with your speech notes and audiovisual devices.
- *Practice your speech.* Rehearse as if you are actually delivering your speech.
- *Focus on your purpose for speaking.* Think about what you want your listeners to do, believe, or feel as a result of your speech.
- *Pay attention to audience feedback.* Different audiences will react differently to your speech. Pay attention to the messages the audience sends you. Are people in the audience alert or are they yawning and inattentive? Are they shaking their heads in disagreement or nodding in agreement? Depending upon the feedback you receive from the audience you might need to adjust your pace, use more emphatic gestures, or speak more loudly to keep their attention.

10. **Use Audiovisual Devices (if appropriate)** Audiovisual devices can contribute to the effectiveness of your presentation. Under the right circumstances, you can use audio or video recordings, films or filmstrips, charts, graphs, illustrations, or diagrams to enhance or clarify your speech. Use the following questions to determine if your presentation could benefit from the use of one or more audiovisual devices.

- *Will using audiovisual devices help you clarify a point?* Some ideas are easily explained verbally, but others need visual clarification. In those cases, using a chart or a poster will help you keep the audience on track.

- *Will using audiovisual devices make an idea more memorable for the audience?* Not every point in your speech is equally important. Decide which points will benefit from audio emphasis, visual emphasis, or both.
- *Will using audiovisual devices distract the audience while you are speaking?* Make sure that any audiovisual device you use is essential to your presentation but not so engaging that it replaces you as the focal point of the audience's attention.

NOTE Make certain that your choice of audiovisual materials is visible, legible, or audible to the audience. Audiovisual materials such as audiotapes or videotapes should be cued up and ready to play. Visuals should be large enough to read or see. (See also **Types of Graphics** on page 930.)

Group Discussion A *formal group discussion* occurs when clubs, organizations, and other groups meet on a regular basis to discuss issues of importance to the entire group. To conduct effective meetings, formal groups often follow an established set of rules known as *parliamentary procedure.* The basic principles of parliamentary procedure, listed below, protect the rights of the individual members of the group while providing a system for dealing with issues that come before the group.

- The majority decides.
- The minority has the right to be heard.
- Decisions are made by voting.
- Only one issue is decided at a time.
- Everyone is assured of the chance to be heard and has the right to vote.
- All votes are counted as equal.
- All sides of an issue are debated in open discussion.

The best source for information about parliamentary procedure is a book by Henry Robert called *Robert's Rules of Order, Newly Revised.* It is the source for the order of business and the procedures for the discussion of business presented below and on the next page.

Order of Business

A formal meeting usually follows the standard order of business suggested in *Robert's Rules of Order:*

1. Call to order: The chairperson says, "The meeting will come to order."

2. Reading and approval of the minutes: The chairperson says, "The secretary (or recorder) will read the minutes from our previous meeting." The secretary reads the minutes, and the chairperson inquires, "Are there any additions or corrections to the minutes?" The minutes are then approved, or they are corrected and then approved.

3. Officers' reports: The chairperson calls for a report from other officers who need to report, by saying, for example, "Will the treasurer please give us a report?"

4. Committee reports: The chairperson may ask the presiding officers of standing committees to make reports to the group.

5. Old business: Any issues that have not been fully resolved at the last meeting may now be discussed. The chairperson may ask the group, "Is there any old business to be discussed?"

6. New business: Any new issues that have not been previously discussed may now be addressed.

7. Announcements: The chairperson may ask the members, "Are there any announcements?"

8. Adjournment: The chairperson ends the meeting, saying, "The meeting is now adjourned."

Procedures for Discussion of Business

1. Anyone who wishes to speak must raise his or her hand and wait to be recognized by the chairperson.

2. A participant may introduce a motion, or proposal, for discussion, by saying "I move that . . ."

3. To support a motion, another member must second it by saying "I second the motion." A motion that is not seconded must be dropped from discussion.

4. A motion that has been seconded may be discussed by the group.

5. Other motions made by members may amend the motion under consideration; may postpone, limit, or extend debate or discussion; or may refer the motion to a committee for further research.

6. After discussion, the group votes on the motion. The chairperson usually votes only to break a tie.

Interviewing An *interview* is a formal communication situation in which one person, the *interviewer,* gathers ideas or information from another person, the *interviewee.* When you are preparing a research paper, a class report, or a newspaper article, you may need to be an interviewer to obtain firsthand information from certain people. When you are questioned by a potential employer or a school's admissions officer as part of the application process, you become the interviewee.

- **Conducting an Interview** Successful interviews require careful planning. Begin first by finding a knowledgeable and reliable source—someone who will give you accurate and dependable information. The following chart provides additional useful suggestions for planning and conducting an interview.

Conducting an Interview

Preparing for the Interview	- Make arrangements well in advance. Set up a time that is convenient for the other person to meet with you. - Make a list of questions to ask. Make sure the questions are arranged in a logical order and require more than yes or no answers.
Participating in the Interview	- Arrive on time, and be polite and patient. - Ask the other person's permission to take notes or use a tape recorder. - Avoid argument. Be tactful and courteous. Remember the interview was granted at your request. - Listen carefully, and ask follow-up questions if you do not understand an answer or if you think you need more information.
Following up on the Interview	- Review your notes to refresh your memory, and then make a summary of the material you have gathered. - Send a note expressing your appreciation for the interview.

- **Interviewing for a Job** A job interview can be a nerve-racking situation; being thoroughly prepared to be interviewed can relieve some of the anxiety. The following chart tells you how to be a successful interviewee.

1. Arrange an appointment. Write a business letter of application in which you request an interview for the job. If you are granted an interview, be prompt for your appointment.

2. Bring a résumé. If you have not already submitted a résumé, take one to the interview and give it to the interviewer. (For information about **preparing a résumé,** see page 1043.)

3. Be neat and well-groomed. It is important to look your best when you are interviewing for any type of job.

4. Answer questions clearly and honestly. Answer the questions the interviewer asks, adding any additional information that might inform the employer that you are the right person for the job.

5. Ask questions. Questions that job applicants usually ask include requests for information about work hours, salary, or chances for advancement. By your questions, show that you know something about the company or business.

6. Be prepared to be tested. The employer may require you to take tests that demonstrate your skills, intelligence, or personality.

7. Follow up the interview. After the interview, write a short thank-you note. Tell the interviewer that you appreciated the opportunity for the interview and that you look forward to hearing from the company in the near future.

Informal Speaking Occasions

Informal communication involves asking for and sharing information in casual situations. Unlike formal speaking situations, in which you are usually at a distance from your audience, informal speaking situations allow you to have personalized contact. Informal speaking situations tend to be either informative or social in nature. The chart below describes some common informal speaking situations.

Informal Speaking Situations		
Situation	**Purpose**	**Preparation and Presentation**
Directions	To explain how to get to a particular place (Informational situation)	Choose the easiest route. Divide the route into logical steps. Use terms that are accurate or visual. If necessary, draw a map. Repeat any steps if necessary.
Impromptu speech	To speak for five minutes on a particular topic without any previous preparation (Informational situation)	If you must choose the topic, think of one that is appropriate for your audience. Think of a main idea, an attention-getting beginning, and some supporting ideas. Speak clearly and in a confident voice. Use a tone that is appropriate to the topic.

(continued)

Informal Speaking Situations		
Situation	**Purpose**	**Preparation and Presentation**
Instructions	To give information on how to do a particular task (Informational situation)	Divide the information into clear, logical steps. Give the steps in order. Make sure your listener understands; ask to be sure.
Introductions	To introduce yourself or another person to a person or group (Social situation)	Take the initiative, and introduce yourself if no one else does. When introducing another person, identify the person by name. When introducing another person, it is customary to address first • a person of higher status • an older person before a younger one • the person you know better.
Critiques	To give criticism in a constructive manner (School or business situation)	Think about the effect you want to achieve. Clearly state the problem and the solution. Praise things the person does well, if appropriate. Speak truthfully and positively.
Telephone conversations	To communicate via telephone (Social situation)	Call people at appropriate times of day. Identify yourself, and state the reason for your call. Be polite and patient. Keep your call to an appropriate length.

Informal Group Discussion An *informal group discussion* is one that usually takes place among members of a group small enough to allow everyone to participate. Effective informal group discussions require that each participant play a role and take on certain responsibilities, which are described on page 989. In its discussion, a group may follow a prepared *agenda,* or outline, of the topics in the order they will be discussed. In some groups, the chairperson sets the agenda; in others, the agenda is established by the group members. The following charts show typical purposes for informal group discussions and the responsibilities of group members.

Purposes for Discussion

• to brainstorm and share ideas
• to learn cooperatively
• to make a decision, evaluation, or recommendation
• to make plans
• to negotiate agreements
• to resolve conflicts
• to solve a problem

Group Members' Responsibilities

All Group Members

1. Take part in the discussion.
2. Cooperate with other members, being courteous, impersonal, and fair.
3. Stick to the subject under discussion.

Chairperson

1. Announces the topic and explains the agenda.
2. Follows the agenda, keeping the discussion on the topics to be considered.
3. Encourages member participation.
4. Avoids disagreements by being objective and settling conflicts or confusions fairly.

Group Secretary or Recorder

1. Makes notes of significant information or actions.
2. Prepares a final report.

Oral Interpretation

Oral interpretation involves the presentation of a work of literature to a group of listeners in order to express your interpretation of the literary work. You might use acting as well as speaking skills—vocal techniques, facial expressions, body language, and gestures—to express the overall meaning of the literary work. Use the following steps to prepare an oral interpretation.

1. **Find and cut material.** When you research material for an oral interpretation, you usually have a specific purpose and audience in mind. Every occasion has its own requirements. Be sure that you have thought about factors such as length of time allotted for your presentation and your audience's interest. As a general rule, no props or costumes are required for oral interpretation; instead, performers rely on the imagination of the audience to provide the scenery and other dramatic enhancements. For your oral interpretation, you will need to make a *cutting,* or abbreviated version, of a work of fiction, nonfiction, poetry, or drama. To make a cutting of your work:

   - Follow the story line of the literary work in time order.
   - Delete tag lines such as *she replied sadly.* Instead, use clues to tell you how to interpret the character's words as you express them.
   - Delete passages that do not contribute to the overall effect or impression you intend to create with your oral interpretation.

2. **Prepare the reading script.** A reading script is usually typed (double-spaced) and can be marked to assist you in your interpretive reading. For example, you might underline words to remind you to use special emphasis, or make a slash (/) to indicate where you would like a dramatic pause.

3. **Rehearse your interpretation.** Once you have developed a reading script, rehearse different interpretations until you think that you have chosen the most effective one to express the meaning of your selection. Use your voice in a manner that suits your presentation. Pronounce words carefully. You can use your body and your voice to portray different characters. Use body language and gestures to emphasize meaning or to reveal traits of major characters in the story as you present your interpretation.

4. **Deliver your presentation.** To begin your presentation, introduce the piece of literature you are interpreting. Give your audience information that sets the scene, tells something about the author, or gives some necessary details about what has already taken place in the story.

Listening

Listening involves more than simply hearing a speaker's words. It requires you to take part in an active process. When you listen actively, you receive verbal and nonverbal messages, construct meanings for those messages, and respond to those meanings.

Basics of the Listening Process

Listening is an indispensable part of communication. Active, effective listening, like active reading, is a process. The stages in that process are explained in the following chart.

The Three Stages of the Listening Process

Before you listen

- **Be physically and mentally prepared to listen.** To be an effective listener, you should be physically comfortable and free of mental distractions that will interfere with your ability to focus.
- **Determine your reason for listening.** Are you listening to be entertained? to be informed? to provide support or understanding? to receive instructions or directions? Identifying a reason for listening sets you up as an active listener.
- **Decide what you already know about the speaker and the subject.** Bringing your prior knowledge of a subject or of a speaker to the surface can make your listening experience more productive.
- **Add to your prior knowledge of the speaker and the subject.** Brainstorming with others or doing individual research to increase your knowledge of the speaker and the subject will enhance your ability to understand and evaluate both.
- **Keep an open mind.** Set aside any biases, prejudices, or preconceived notions you might have concerning the speaker or the topic of the speech. Make your judgments after listening to what the speaker has to say.

As you listen

- **Make connections to prior knowledge and experience.** Try to relate what the speaker is saying to what you know from any source—experience, books and magazines, television, school, and so on.
- **Think of questions you would like to ask the speaker.** You may or may not have an opportunity to ask the speaker to clarify a point or expand upon an idea, but making yourself think of questions helps you to focus on the **speaker's message.**
- **Make educated guesses about what a speaker will say next.** If you are wrong, try to determine what misled you.
- **Find meaning behind what the speaker says directly.** Make inferences about a speaker's attitudes or opinions by paying attention to what he or she does not say.

After you listen

- **Discuss the speaker and message with others.** Get together with others to exchange ideas, agree or disagree with the speaker's opinions, and relate what the speaker has said to what you have experienced, seen, and read.
- **Write a summary and evaluation of the speaker and the presentation.** Writing about a presentation while it is fresh in your mind can help you clarify and solidify your thoughts and opinions.

Evaluating Yourself as a Listener

For oral communication to be effective, you must be a good listener. In fact, the listener carries as much of the responsibility for communicating a message as the speaker does. The following chart gives several of the points you should look for when you evaluate how well you listen.

Evaluating Yourself as a Listener

A good listener should

- be mentally and physically prepared to listen
- be able to ignore distracting behavior by the speaker and members of the audience
- focus on the speaker throughout the presentation
- follow the organization of the speaker's presentation
- distinguish between facts and opinions
- think of questions to ask the speaker
- determine the **speaker's message,** his or her main idea, and primary supporting details
- withhold judgment until the presentation is over
- listen for bias or prejudice on the speaker's part
- reflect upon the presentation after it is over
- discuss the presentation with others
- ask questions of the speaker if given the opportunity
- write a summary or evaluation of the presentation

Four Types of Listening

There are four basic types of listening and a number of purposes or reasons for listening associated with each type.

Appreciative (or Aesthetic) Listening

The purpose of this type of listening is enjoyment. When you listen to someone read a story or a poem, you are engaged in appreciative listening. There are certain strategies that can make this type of listening experience more rewarding.

- **Before you listen, activate what you know about the literary work** that you will hear presented. What do you know about the work, the author, or other works by the same author? To what literary *genre,* or type, does the work belong? What literary elements—conflict, imagery, character, figurative language, climax, rhyme—figure prominently in this type of literature? Make predictions about what you might hear.

- **While you listen, make connections to other literary works you know and to your personal experiences.** Does the presentation remind you of something else you have read, seen, or heard? Do any of the descriptions remind you of places you have been, people you have known, or feelings you have had? Try to visualize—see in your mind's eye—what you are hearing.

- **After you listen, discuss the presentation with others and evaluate it.** Were your predictions correct or incorrect? Can you determine the reason for any incorrect predictions? What literary and artistic qualities were prominent? Was the speaker's presentation clear? Did the speaker use the appropriate body language? Did the speaker use his or her voice effectively? Write what you liked and did not like about the presentation and why.

Critical Listening In this type of listening, you attempt to comprehend, analyze, and evaluate the speaker's points and the value of the ideas. Critical listening should be applied to messages heard in school, in the workplace, or in the media. You can use the strategies in the following chart to analyze and evaluate media presentations as well as live presentations.

How to Listen Critically

What to do	What to listen for
Identify the speaker's purpose.	Does the speaker make clear why he or she is giving the speech?
Distinguish between facts and opinions.	Does the speaker make statements with which you agree or disagree? Ask yourself why you disagree. (Such statements are opinions. An opinion is a belief or a judgment about something that cannot be proved. A fact is a statement that can be proved true.)
Identify the speaker's message, his or her main ideas.	What are the most important points? (Listen for clue words or phrases, such as *major, main,* and *most important.*)
Identify significant or supporting details.	What dates, names, or facts does the speaker use to support the main points of the speech? What kinds of examples or explanations are used to support the main ideas?
Identify the order of organization.	What kind of order does the speaker use to present the information—time sequence, spatial order, order of importance, or logical order?
Listen to detect bias.	Is the speaker biased, or prejudiced, toward one point of view? Does the speaker use extreme or all-inclusive words such as *never* or *always*? Does the speaker acknowledge that there are other points of view?
Evaluate the speaker's credibility.	Is the speaker an authority on the subject? Does the speaker refer to sources of information? Are the sources respectable or credible, such as newspaper and journal articles or reference materials?
Note comparisons and contrasts.	Are some details compared or contrasted with others? Why?
Predict outcomes and draw conclusions.	What can you reasonably conclude from the facts and evidence presented in the speech?
Look for logic.	Does the speaker build his arguments in a logical way? Does the speaker use false logic such as hasty generalization, false cause and effect, or circular reasoning?
Look for emotional appeals.	Does the speaker use the bandwagon appeal? the glittering generality? snob appeal? plain folks appeal? the veiled threat?
Understand cause and effect.	Do some events described by the speaker relate to or affect others? Does the speaker make the logical connections between cause and effect?

Comprehensive Listening When you listen for the content of a message, you are engaged in *comprehensive listening*. Some people call this type of listening **informational listening**. Much of the listening you do in school is of this type. Below are some techniques for effective comprehensive listening:

■ **Listening for Information** You are often in situations where you listen to acquire information. When a doctor describes the symptoms of a certain disease, for example, he or she is delivering information you need to understand, not attempting to be persuasive or entertaining. The following strategies are helpful in these situations.

1. **The LQ2R Method** helps you when you listen for information from a speaker:

   L Listen carefully to material as it is being presented.

   Q Question yourself as you listen. Mentally or in your notes, make a list of questions as they occur to you.

   R Recite in your own words the information as it is being presented. Summarize the material in your mind.

   R Review the whole presentation, restating or reemphasizing major points.

2. **Note Taking** You cannot possibly write down every word the speaker says. Develop an effective way to jot down the speaker's main points and supporting details as well as your own thoughts, questions, or comments. For example, you could use split-page notes—you divide your paper so that forty percent of the pages lies to the left and sixty percent lies to the right. Take brief notes on the left-hand side only, leaving the right-hand side for reorganizing and expanding your notes after listening. (See also **taking notes** on page 253.)

■ **Listening to Instructions** Because instructions are usually made up of a series of steps, you can easily misunderstand them. The following steps can help you make sense of instructions.

1. **Listen for the order of the steps.** Listen for words such as *first, second, next, then,* and *last* to tell you when one step ends and the next one begins.

2. **Identify the number of steps in the process.** Take notes if the instructions are long or complicated. Do not hesitate to ask for clarification or for the speaker to slow down as you take notes.

3. **Visualize each step.** Imagine yourself actually performing each step. Try to get a mental image of what you should be doing at every step in the process.

4. **Review the steps.** When the speaker is finished, be sure you understand the process from beginning to end. Ask questions if you are unsure.

NOTE When you take a message on the telephone, you are listening for information that answers the basic *5W-How?* questions—*Who? What? When? Where? Why?* and *How?* Take down details that answer questions such as *Who* is calling? *What* is the message or purpose for the call? *Where* can the caller be reached? *When* can the caller be reached? and *How* may you help the caller?

Empathic (or Reflective) Listening

This is the kind of listening you do when you want to help a friend understand a difficult problem or when you want to show someone your understanding and acceptance. Show empathic listening through your facial expressions and body language and through your responses to the speaker. Here are some strategies to use.

- Do much more listening than talking.
- Show genuine warmth and concern.
- Paraphrase what the speaker says to show your understanding.
- Respond to the speaker's feelings rather than analyzing the facts.
- Keep your opinions to yourself.

Special Listening Situations

Some situations require that you participate as both a careful listener and a speaker. **Interviews** and **group discussions** are two such situations.

Listening in an Interview An interview is a unique listening situation that usually takes place between two people, the interviewer and the interviewee. Use these listening techniques to make the most of an interview.

- **As interviewer**
  1. **When you ask a question, listen to the complete answer.** Be courteous and patient as your interviewee answers. Think of related follow-up questions as he or she responds.
  2. **Respect the interviewee's opinions, even if you do not agree.** You may state your disagreement politely only if your comment will serve to prompt the interviewee to clarify, expand, or provide support for a statement or claim. Do not express your disagreement if it is likely to upset your interviewee and disrupt the interview.

  3. **Monitor your nonverbal communication.** Make sure that your nonverbal reactions reflect a respectful tone. Maintain good eye contact, nod to show understanding, and smile to indicate your interest.
  4. **Always thank the interviewee at the end of your interview.**

- **As interviewee**
  1. **Listen to the interviewer's complete question before answering.** If you start answering the question before the interviewer finishes asking it, you might answer the wrong question.
  2. **Answer the question.** Stick to the point the interviewer is addressing. Do not simply ignore a question and respond with something totally off track.

Listening in a Group Discussion

Listening as a member of a group discussion is different from listening as part of a large audience. The setting is more intimate, and it is more likely that you will participate as both a listener and a speaker. The following tips should help you listen effectively in a group discussion.

- Maintain nonverbal communication by sitting up, looking attentively at each speaker, and nodding to register agreement or understanding.
- Demonstrate respect for the other group members by paying attention and refraining from making comments while they speak.
- Take notes on each speaker's points, and list questions or comments you have.
- Concentrate on what the speaker is saying, not on what you intend to say.
- When you are ready to speak, raise your hand and wait to be recognized.

Studying and Test Taking

Study Skills and Strategies

The **purpose** of studying is not just to do well on tests and to get good grades. It is also to help you understand and remember information you may need later. (See also **Test-Taking Skills and Strategies** on page 999 and **Reading and Vocabulary** on page 954.)

Making a Study Plan

The following suggestions may help you make effective use of your study time.

1. **Know your assignments before you study.** Use a calendar or planner to record your assignments and their due dates. Make sure that you understand what you are expected to do or to know.
2. **Select a time and make a plan to study.** Break larger assignments, such as writing a research report, into smaller steps. Schedule time to complete each step.
3. **Concentrate when you study.** Set aside a regular time and place strictly for studying. Some people find it helps to listen to music or to study with others; other people prefer quiet and solitude. Find out what method works best for you, and then stick with it.

Organizing and Remembering Information

The following strategies can help you organize and remember information as you study.

Classifying *Classification* is a method of organizing by arranging items into categories. For example, you use classification when you make an outline, determining the ideas that fit together under a specific heading. When you classify items, you identify relationships among them.

> EXAMPLE   What do each of the following cities have in common?
> Austin, Baton Rouge, Bismarck, Tallahassee, Sacramento
>
> ANSWER   They are all state capitals.

You also classify when you recognize patterns. For example, look at the sequence of numbers on the next page.

What is the next number in the series?
4   4   8   24   96   <u>?</u>

Answer: The first number (4) is multiplied by *1* to produce the second number (4). The second number is multiplied by *2* to produce the third number (8); the third number is multiplied by *3*, and the fourth number (24) is multiplied by *4*. So, the fifth number (96) should be multiplied by *5* to produce the answer, which is *480*.

Graphic Organizers   You may find it helpful to reorganize information into a visual form such as a chart, map, or diagram. *Graphic organizers* like these give you another way to think about your subject. (See also **Graphic Organizers** on page 1034.)

Memorization   Memorize and remember what you have learned by practicing in frequent, short, focused sessions.

Notes on Reading or Lectures   Taking careful *notes* while reading or listening to a lecture will help you organize and remember information for later when you are studying for tests or writing research papers. The steps below explain how to take study notes.

How to Take Study Notes

1. Recognize main points, and record them as headings in your notes.

- In a lecture, listen for **key words** and **phrases,** such as *major* or *most important*. Key words like these indicate points that you should remember.
- In a textbook, pay attention to chapter headings, subheadings, lists, charts, time lines, and illustrations.

2. Summarize what you hear or read. Don't record every detail. Summarize, abbre-viate, and condense information about key ideas. Indent supporting points in your notes to distinguish them from the main points.

3. Note important examples. Make note of examples that illustrate the main points. Jotting the word *mitosis* or sketching a divided cell in your notes may help jog your memory later.

Look at the organization of the following student notes. Each group of details has been given a heading that indicates the key idea.

Marian Anderson

<u>Biography</u>
- African American; born 1902 in Philadelphia, PA
- sang in church choir; supporters paid for opera training

<u>Discriminatory Treatment</u>
- many music schools and some concert halls closed to her
- segregated railroad coaches and hotels
- Daughters of the American Revolution (DAR) refused to let her perform at Constitution Hall

<u>Successes</u>
- DAR ban protested; many resigned DAR (e.g., Eleanor Roosevelt)
- in 1930s, studied in Europe; concerts praised
- Cabinet member invited her to sing at Lincoln Memorial on Easter Sunday, 1939; over 75,000 attended
- 1st black soloist at Metropolitan Opera
  - some called her greatest contralto of 20th century
  - 1958, delegate to U.N.; 1963 Pres. Medal of Freedom

Outlines   An *outline* can help you organize ideas by grouping them in a pattern that shows their order and their relationship to one another. (See also **Outlines** on page 1037.)

Paraphrasing   To *paraphrase* is to restate someone else's words in your own words. You are more likely to remember an idea if you state it in your own words. Also, paraphrasing helps you understand what you read, especially if the original is written in poetic or elaborate language. A paraphrase is usually about the same length as the original reading passage, so paraphrasing is rarely used for long passages. (See also **Paraphrasing** on page 956.)

SQ3R   *SQ3R* stands for *Survey, Question, Read, Recite,* and *Review* and is a strategy designed to help you study from a book or textbook. (See also **SQ3R** on page 958.)

Summarizing   *Summarizing* is a way to condense information from a lecture, book, or notes. When you summarize, you record the basic meaning of the material you are studying. Writing a summary helps you think critically; you have to analyze the material, identify the most important ideas, and eliminate details that are less important. (See also **Summarizing** on page 958.)

Writing a Précis   A *précis* is a formal written summary. When you write a précis, you shorten a piece of writing—such as a reading passage, a chapter, an article, or a report—to its bare essentials. Most of the techniques that you use for writing a précis are the same as summarizing skills. The following are certain standard practices that you should follow when writing a précis.

How to Write a Précis

1. Be brief. A précis is seldom more than a third as long as the material being summarized, often less.

2. Do not paraphrase. If you merely put each sentence of the original in slightly different words, you will wind up with as much material as the original.

3. Stick to the central points. Avoid examples, unnecessary adjectives, and repetitions.

4. Use your own wording. Don't just take phrases or sentences from the original.

5. Be faithful to the author's points and views. Do not add your own comments, and do not use expressions such as "the author says" or "the passage means."

The passage below is followed by a sample précis on the next page.

Sample Passage

Rapidity in reading has an obvious, direct bearing on success in college work because of the large amount of reading which must be covered in nearly all college courses. However, it is probably also a direct measure of the special kind of aptitude that can be called "bookish," because rapidity of reading usually correlates with comprehension and retention. Generally speaking, the more rapidly a reader reads, the more effectively he or she grasps and retains. The normal reading speed of first-year college students has been found to be around 250 words a minute on ordinary reading matter. Students who read more slowly than that will certainly have difficulty in completing their college tasks within reasonable study periods. To be a really good college risk under this criterion, one should readily and habitually cover not fewer than 300 words a minute on ordinary reading matter. [144 words]

Common Errors in Précis Writing	
Error	**Example from Faulty Précis**
Précis uses phrases taken directly from original.	Reading speed has a <u>direct bearing on success in college</u> since college classes often demand much reading. <u>Rapidity of reading</u> usually means a student has better <u>comprehension and retention</u>.
Précis misses the point of the original; emphasizes unimportant points.	<u>Great amounts of reading are required in most college courses</u>. The more you read now, the better prepared you will be for college.
Writer of précis injects own ideas.	For college success, reading speed is important since college classes, <u>such as history and English</u>, often demand much reading. <u>Surprisingly</u>, students who read quickly retain and recall material better than slower readers, <u>who may fail if they cannot complete their work</u>.

Sample Précis

For college success, reading speed is important; college classes demand much reading. Quick readers retain and recall material better than slower readers. The average first-year student's speed is 250 words a minute, but higher achievers read at least 300 words a minute. [42 words]

The chart above shows errors you should avoid when writing a précis. Examples in the right-hand column are taken from a faulty précis based on the sample passage.

Writing to Learn Writing is a valuable study tool. By writing, you may focus your thoughts, respond to ideas, record your observations, and plan your work. The chart below shows the ways different types of writing can help you study.

Type of Writing	How It Helps	Example
Diaries	• help you recall your impressions and express your feelings	Write about your reactions to issues raised during a lecture or in a chapter you read for class.
Freewriting	• helps you focus your thoughts	Write for three minutes after class or after reviewing your notes in order to focus on the most important points.
Journals and Learning Logs	• help you to record your observations, descriptions, solutions, and questions • help you present a problem, analyze it, and propose a solution	Write about problems or successes you had in solving a problem in a science experiment. Write about the way you will incorporate a source or piece of information in a research paper for your history class.
Précis	• helps you identify what is essential in a piece	Write a précis based on a chapter in a novel.

Test-Taking Skills and Strategies

Classroom Tests

The purpose of the typical *classroom test* is to measure your ability to use key academic skills or to demonstrate your knowledge of specific academic subjects. Classroom tests often combine several types of test questions. For example, a test might be made up of twenty multiple-choice questions worth four points each and two essay questions worth ten points each. Many different combinations of test questions and scoring methods may be used. The best way to prepare for classroom tests is to be sure that you are familiar with the material or that you have practiced the skill you must demonstrate at the time of testing. It is also helpful to be familiar with the kinds of questions that appear on classroom tests.

Essay Questions   When you answer an *essay question,* you must demonstrate two things. First, you must show that you can think critically about material you have learned. Second, you must be able to express your understanding of the material in a well-written, organized composition of one or more paragraphs. Essay questions are challenging because they may ask you to discuss several ideas in your answer.

NOTE   To study for the essay portion of any test, follow these steps:

- Read your study materials carefully. Take notes on key ideas and examples.
- Outline the material. Identify main points and important details.

- Make a practice set of possible questions. Prepare an answer for each question.
- Check your notes and textbook to confirm the accuracy of your answers. Evaluate and revise your answers.

How to Answer Essay Questions

1. Scan the questions on the test. Determine how many questions you are expected to answer. If you can choose from several items, decide which ones you think you can answer best. Then, plan how much time to spend on preparing and writing each answer. (Remember, some essay tests have a time limit.)

2. Read the questions carefully. There may be several parts to each question. Use a highlighter or pen to highlight or circle the key terms in each question.

3. Pay attention to the key verbs in the questions. The questions will use verbs to ask you to do specific tasks. Familiarize yourself with the key verbs that commonly appear on essay tests. (See the chart, **Key Verbs That Appear in Essay Questions,** on the following page.)

4. Take time to plan your answers, using prewriting strategies. Brainstorm, jot down notes, or create an outline of what you want to say in your answers. (See also **Prewriting Techniques** on page 1039.)

5. Evaluate and revise your answers as you write. Because you are in a test situation, you will not have time for more than one draft of your answers. Leave yourself time to proofread your answers, correcting any spelling, punctuation, or grammatical errors.

Key Verbs That Appear in Essay Questions		
Key Verb	**Task**	**Sample Question**
Analyze	Look carefully at the parts of something to see how each part works and how the parts are related.	**Analyze** the main character in Nathaniel Hawthorne's "The Minister's Black Veil."
Argue	Take a stand on an issue, and give reasons and evidence to support your viewpoint or opinion.	**Argue** whether your school should discourage students from working on weekday evenings.
Compare or **Contrast**	Point out similarities or differences between things, people, or ideas.	**Compare** the British Parliament with the U.S. Congress as lawmaking bodies.
Define	Give specific characteristics that make something or some idea unique.	**Define** the term *osmosis* as it relates to the permeability of membranes.
Demonstrate	Provide examples to support a point.	**Demonstrate** how an electrical charge is conducted by metal.
Describe	Give a picture in words.	**Describe** the critical reception of Walt Whitman's *Leaves of Grass*.
Discuss	Examine in detail.	**Discuss** the term *Romanticism*.
Explain	Give reasons or make the meaning clear.	**Explain** why congruent angles are complementary.
Identify	Point out specific persons, places, things, or characteristics.	**Identify** members of the presidential cabinet and their duties.
Interpret	Give the meaning or significance of something.	**Interpret** the importance of the dismantling of the Berlin Wall.
List	Give all the steps in order or all details about a subject.	**List** events leading to the ratification of the 19th Amendment.
Summarize	Give a brief overview of the main points.	**Summarize** the greenhouse effect.

Although there are a wide variety of essay questions, nearly all good answers contain the same qualities. The following are characteristics of a good essay answer.

- The essay answers the question.

- The essay has an introduction, a body, and a conclusion.
- The main ideas and supporting points are clearly presented and organized in the body.
- The sentences are complete and well written.

- There are no errors in spelling, punctuation, or grammar.

(For more about **essay questions,** see page 315.)

Matching Questions
In matching questions, your goal is to match up the items on two lists.

EXAMPLE

Directions: Match the items in the two columns by writing the letter of each title in the space preceding the name of the work's author.

C	**1.** Hawthorne	**A.**	"I'm Nobody!"
E	**2.** Emerson	**B.**	*Little Women*
D	**3.** Whitman	**C.**	*The Scarlet Letter*
B	**4.** Alcott	**D.**	*Leaves of Grass*
A	**5.** Dickinson	**E.**	"Self-Reliance"

How to Answer Matching Questions

1. Read the directions carefully. Sometimes answers may be used more than once.

2. Scan the columns and match items you know first. That way, you can gain some time for evaluating the answers of which you are less sure.

3. Complete the matching process. Make your best guess on any remaining items.

Multiple-Choice Questions
Multiple-choice questions ask you to select a correct answer from among a number of choices.

EXAMPLE

1. Which of the following items did *not* take place in 1912?
- **A.** The *Titanic* struck an iceberg and sank in the North Atlantic.
- **B.** New Mexico and Arizona were admitted as states to the United States.
- **C.** The United States entered World War I.
- **D.** Woodrow Wilson was elected president of the United States.

How to Answer Multiple-Choice Questions

1. Read the initial statement carefully. Make sure you understand the statement completely before looking at your choices.

2. Look for qualifiers, such as *not, always,* or *never,* because these words limit or affect the answer. In the previous example, you must choose the event that did *not* take place in the year 1912.

3. Read all the answers before making a choice. Sometimes the answer includes two or more choices, such as "Both A and B" or "All of the above." Remember, in the preceding example, you are looking for one event that did not take place, so you must consider the possible answers carefully.

4. Narrow your choices by eliminating answers you know are incorrect. Some answers are clearly wrong, while others are somewhat related to the correct answer. If you already know that the *Titanic* sank in 1912, and you are looking for the event that did *not* happen in 1912, you can easily rule out Answer A.

5. From the remaining choices, select the answer that makes the most sense. The answer is C.

Short-Answer Questions
Short-answer questions ask you to explain what you know about a subject in a brief, written reply. In general, short-answer questions require a specific answer of one or two sentences. (Some short-answer questions, such as maps or diagrams that you are supposed to label, or fill-in-the-blank questions, can be answered with one or a few words.)

EXAMPLE

1. What were some of the effects of the electrification of cities in the United States?

1. Electrification produced a higher standard of living for people. Electrification allowed people to rely more on machines and to work and read even at night so that they were more productive workers.

True/False Questions *True/False questions* ask you to determine whether a given statement is true or false.

EXAMPLE

1. (T) F *Claves* are percussion instruments that maintain various fixed rhythmic patterns in Latin-American dance bands.

How to Answer True/False Questions

1. Read the entire statement carefully.

2. Check for qualifiers. Words such as *always* or *never* qualify, or limit, a statement's meaning.

3. Choose an answer based on the following principles:

- If any part of the statement is false, the entire statement is false.
- A statement is true only if it is entirely and always true.

Standardized Tests

A *standardized test* is one in which your score is evaluated according to a standard or norm compiled from the scores of other students who have taken the same test. Some standardized tests may be developed by a school district or state. The best-known tests of this type, such as the *Scholastic Assessment Tests (SAT)* and the *American College Testing Program (ACT)*, are given to students across the entire United States. There are two basic types of standardized tests: aptitude tests and achievement tests. The differences are explained in the following chart.

Types of Standardized Tests

Aptitude (or Reasoning) Tests	• intended to evaluate basic skills or reasoning abilities needed in general areas of study • often cover material learned during many years of study (such as verbal expression and critical-thinking skills)
Achievement (or Academic Subject) Tests	• intended to measure knowledge of specific subjects (such as history, literature, sciences, mathematics, or foreign languages) • some achievement tests, such as **advanced placement** tests, are used to obtain college credit

When preparing for standardized tests, keep in mind the following tips:

How to Prepare for Standardized Tests

1. Learn what specific abilities will be tested and what kinds of questions will be asked. Information booklets may be provided. Practice with these or with published study guides.

2. Know what materials you will need. On the day of the test, you may need to bring specific materials, such as your official test registration card, number-two pencils, or lined paper for writing an essay.

3. Determine how the test is evaluated. If there is no penalty for wrong answers, make your best guess on all questions possible. If wrong answers are penalized, however, make guesses only if you are fairly sure of the correct answer.

Analogy Questions   *Analogy questions* are questions that measure your ability to recognize kinds of relationships. Specifically, they ask you to analyze the relationship between a pair of words (called a **stem pair**) and then to identify a second pair of words that has the same relationship. Analogy questions usually appear on standardized tests in multiple-choice form. (Be sure to note the symbols often used in analogy questions; the symbol **:** means "is related to," while **::** means "equals" or "is equivalent to.")

EXAMPLE

1. Select the appropriate pair of words to complete the analogy.

   ROBIN : BIRD :: _____

   A. paint : artist

   B. willow : tree

   C. plaster : break

   D. wind : moan

   Sometimes, however, analogies are written as fill-in-the-blank questions, which ask you to fill in the missing item.

EXAMPLE

2. Complete the following analogy.

   INCH : YARD :: ounce : _*pound*_

How to Answer Analogy Questions

1. Identify the relationship between the words in the stem. In Example 1, a *robin* is a class of *bird;* the relationship is one of classification. Express the relationship in a short sentence: "A robin is a class of bird, just as a _____ is a kind of _____." Example 2 shows a relationship of part to whole—a yard is made up of inches, and a pound is made up of ounces. (See also the **Types of Analogies** chart on page 1004.)

2. Look for a similar relationship in each possible answer. Paint is not a class of artist; **A** is incorrect. A willow is a class of

tree; **B** could be correct. Plaster is not a class of break; **C** is incorrect. Wind is not a class of moan; **D** is incorrect.

3. Find the best available choice to complete the analogy. If multiple-choice answers are provided, select the pair of words that shares the same relationship as the stem pair. If you must fill in a word, look closely at the stem pair and then select a word that has the same relationship to the word to the right of the double colons (::) as the two words to the left of the colons.

In addition to the previous three steps, remember the following helpful tips for solving analogies. (See also page 69.)

- **Consider the parts of speech.** Some of the words may be used as more than one part of speech. Thinking about a word as a noun, a verb, or an adjective might help unlock the relationship in the analogy.

- **Familiarize yourself with the most common relationships.** Think about the simplest relationship first and then proceed to more complex or more specific relationships. (See the **Types of Analogies** chart on page 1004.)

- **Remember: The relationship between the words is important, not the meanings of the individual words.** Look again at the first example. A *robin* and a *willow* have nothing in common, but the relationship a *robin* has to a *bird* is the same as the relationship a *willow* has to a *tree:* classification.

Although there are many different relationships that can be represented in analogies, a smaller number of specific relationships are fairly common. Examples of these common types are shown in the chart on the next page.

Types of Analogies		
Type	Example	Solution
Action to Performer or **Performer to Action**	PAINTING : ARTIST : : paddling : canoeist	*Painting* is performed by an *artist*, just as *paddling* is performed by a *canoeist*.
Antonyms or **Synonyms**	RECKLESS : CAUTIOUS : : rash : prudent	*Reckless* behavior is the opposite of *cautious* behavior, just as *rash* behavior is the opposite of *prudent* behavior.
Cause or **Effect**	VIRUS : FLU : : tension : headache	A *virus* causes a *flu*, just as *tension* causes a *headache*.
Characteristic	HOT : LAVA : : cold : ice	*Lava* is always *hot*, just as *ice* is always *cold*.
Classification	ALLIGATOR : REPTILE : : mosquito : insect	An *alligator* is part of the *reptile* class, just as a *mosquito* is part of the *insect* class.
Degree	CHUCKLE : LAUGH : : whimper : cry	A *chuckle* is less pronounced than a *laugh*, just as a *whimper* is less pronounced than a *cry*.
Measure	RULER : DISTANCE : : thermometer : temperature	A *ruler* is used to measure *distance*, just as a *thermometer* is used to measure *temperature*.
Part to Whole or **Whole to Part**	FLOOR : BUILDING : : step : staircase	A *floor* is a part of a *building*, just as a *step* is a part of a *staircase*.
Place	MADISON : WISCONSIN : : Washington, D.C. : United States	*Madison* is the capital of *Wisconsin*, just as *Washington, D.C.* is the capital of the *United States*.
Time Sequence	TUESDAY : THURSDAY : : June : August	*Tuesday* comes before *Thursday*, just as *June* comes before *August*.
Use	PENCIL : WRITING : : chisel : sculpting	A *pencil* is used for *writing*, just as a *chisel* is used in *sculpting*.

Critical-Reading Questions Standardized tests may contain a number of questions that measure your ability to analyze and interpret a piece of writing. These ***critical-reading questions*** (sometimes called ***on-demand reading questions***) require you to look critically at a particular piece of writing and to find the meaning, purpose, or organization of the selection. In addition, these questions may require you to evaluate the effectiveness of the passage in conveying the meaning intended by the writer. Critical-reading questions focus either on a particular approach to the passage or on an element within it. The following chart shows types of critical-reading questions and the actions you must take to answer them. For more information and practice with any of the bulleted elements indicated, see the pages referred to in parentheses after each item.

Critical-Reading Test Questions

In **rhetorical strategy questions,** or **evaluation questions,** you judge the effectiveness of techniques used by the author of a passage. These test items often cover identification and analysis of
- the author's intended audience
- the author's opinions (page 291)
- the author's purpose (page 954)
- the author's tone or point of view (pages 296 and 291)

(See also page 243.)

In **inference questions,** or **interpretation questions,** you draw conclusions or make inferences about the meaning of information presented in a passage. These test items often cover identification of
- conclusions or inferences based on given material (page 157)
- specific conclusions or inferences that can be drawn about the author or the topic of a passage (page 157)

(See also page 956.)

In **organization questions,** or **main idea** or **detail questions,** you identify the organizational techniques used by the writer of a passage. These test items often cover identification of
- the main idea of a passage (page 376)
- arrangement of supporting details (page 1029)
- the author's use of particular writing strategies (page 243)
- techniques used to conclude the passage (page 1030)
- transitional devices that make the passage coherent (page 1045)

(See also page 461 and page 959.)

In **style questions,** or **tone questions,** you analyze a passage to evaluate the author's use of style. These test items often cover identification of
- the author's intended audience
- the author's style
- the author's voice and tone (page 1045)

(See also page 296.)

In **synthesis questions,** you demonstrate knowledge of how parts of a passage fit together into a whole. These are, then, inference questions of a kind, though more general. These test items often cover interpretation of
- the cumulative meaning of details in a passage (page 62)
- techniques used to unify details (page 460)

In **vocabulary-in-context questions,** you infer the meaning of an unfamiliar word by using context clues (page 28).

(See also page 965.)

Here is a typical **reading passage** followed by sample test questions based on this passage.

By the end of 1855, Walt Whitman was seeing his "wonderful and ponderous book," *Leaves of Grass,* through its final stages. He read the typeset pages by candlelight. When the poet Hart Crane began working on *The Bridge* some sixty years later, he worked under an electric light. Before 1920, few major American cities had been electrified. By the 1930s, nearly every city was illuminated.

Henry Adams saw his first electric generator, or dynamo, in Paris at the Great Exposition of 1900. Because they could produce cheap electricity, these dynamos had commercial use. In time they were used to

(continued)

generate the brilliant arc lights of San Francisco, New York, and Philadelphia, thus replacing gas street lamps that were the hallmark of American cities in the nineteenth century.

Yet arc lights were simply unsuitable for home use because of their intense brightness. Credit for the discovery and promotion of the incandescent light used in household lightbulbs must go to Thomas Alva Edison. Financed by a group of wealthy backers, Edison and his team designed an entire system to provide electricity: filaments, wiring, efficient dynamos, safety features, and even the sockets themselves. In 1881, Edison unveiled his famous Pearl Street Station in New York City. Edison's workers laid wires to the square mile around 257 Pearl Street, and they wired individual households and installed meters to measure electricity use. Edison's stations would eventually supply power to over 400,000 lamps in places such as Chicago, New Orleans, Milan, and Berlin.

At the outset, electricity for the home was an expensive luxury for the elite. In 1907, for example, only eight percent of American homes had electricity. However, large-scale generators and greater consumption gradually allowed costs to drop. By 1920, thirty-four percent of American homes had electricity, and by 1941, nearly eighty percent were supplied with electricity. Today, we simply take electricity for granted.

By candlelight, Whitman wrote his poetry by hand. By fluorescent light, a modern poet keystrokes poetry into a computer. Electrification, communication, urbanization—all are processes and systems that affect our lives. Only by understanding the history of these technological developments can we truly understand their importance.

Sample Critical-Reading Questions

1. According to the passage, in which order (from earliest to latest) did the following events occur?

   I. Eighty percent of American homes have electricity.

   II. Walt Whitman writes *Leaves of Grass.*

   III. Henry Adams sees the dynamo at the Great Exposition.

   IV. Edison begins operation of the Pearl Street Station in New York.

   A. II, IV, III, I

   B. II, III, IV, I

   C. II, I, III, IV

   D. II, IV, I, III

[This is an organization question; it requires you to identify the time sequence of these events and to arrange them in chronological order.]

2. The word *elite* in the fourth paragraph may be defined as

   A. a variety of type found on the typewriter

   B. a group of arrogant, stubborn people

   C. the last people to agree to an idea

   D. the wealthiest members of a social group

[This is a vocabulary-in-context question; it requires you to examine the context in which the word appears in the passage in order to determine the appropriate definition.]

3. After reading the passage, one of your classmates wrote the following paragraph.

   In the home, women were thought to be the ones to benefit from electrification. Irons, vacuum cleaners, hot water heaters, clothes washers, and refrigeration—all were hailed as inventions that would make women's lives easier. However, they also reinforced the idea that the woman's place was in the home. These gadgets were indeed labor-saving devices, but only if someone remained at home to use them. Only recently have we questioned whether these so-called technological advances were advantages at all.

To make her point, your classmate criticizes the idea that technological advances

   A. are often invisible

   B. are often expensive

   (**C.**) are beneficial to everyone

   D. exist independently of each other

[This is a rhetorical strategy question; it requires you to identify the main points of the passage and to recognize which of these points your classmate disputed.]

4. The phrase "keystrokes poetry into a computer" is best taken to mean that electrification is a form of progress that

   A. jeopardizes our historical awareness

   (**B.**) influences daily the way we live our lives

   C. improves our ability to compose poetry

   D. most affects students

[This is an inference question; you are asked to examine the context of the words in order to explain their meaning in the passage.]

5. It can be inferred from the description of Thomas Alva Edison that he was

   A. a man who represented the nineteenth century

   B. a man who changed his ideas frequently

   (**C.**) an organized, creative man

   D. a capitalist concerned only for his own welfare

[This is a synthesis question; it requires you to read, in the passage as a whole, about the efforts needed to electrify a small urban area. Then, adding up all the details, you might infer that Edison, the project director, was a driven man of great organizational powers.]

6. Readers of the reading passage are likely to describe it as

   A. informal

   (**B.**) informative

   C. inspirational

   D. biographical

[This is a style question; it requires you to analyze the passage to determine the type of writing it represents.]

NOTE At times it will help you to compare words and phrases in the question to words and phrases in the reading passage. If, however, the words in the prompt are not used in the reading passage, you must draw your own conclusions. For example, question 2 in the preceding chart cites a word (*elite*) that is used in the fourth paragraph of the reading passage. Question 6, however, does not lead you to a specific section of the passage. Instead you must draw your own conclusion about the passage as a whole.

Multiple-Choice Questions Many of the questions in standardized tests are *multiple-choice questions* similar to those found on classroom tests. Standardized tests, however, generally begin with easier questions, and become progressively more difficult. Because each question is worth the same amount, be sure to answer all the easy questions you can before tackling the difficult ones. Also, be sure to keep track of your time. Don't spend too much time on one question, but don't let the time constraints pressure you into making careless mistakes. (See also **Multiple-Choice Questions** on page 1001.)

On-Demand Writing Prompts

On-demand writing prompts are similar to essay questions because they require you to write several paragraphs in a limited amount of time. The key difference is that you have no prior knowledge about the writing topic for an on-demand writing prompt. On-demand writing prompts are the core of many state writing tests. These prompts may ask you to write a persuasive, informative, or descriptive composition in answer to a prompt on a broad topic.

EXAMPLE
Many schools are requiring students to sign an honor code at the beginning of each school year. The document is a contract between the student and the school in which the student agrees never to cheat on tests and never to plagiarize writing assignments. Write a persuasive essay in which you argue for or against the use of honor codes in school.

Another variation of the on-demand writing prompt is found in placement tests. The essays written from these prompts use details pulled from your knowledge of a specific subject area. For example, a prompt on a placement test for English might require you to know literary elements and to have knowledge from reading certain novels or plays. Here is one example:

Select a minor character who plays an important part in a distinguished literary work. In a well-organized essay, describe how the author strengthens the message of his or her work through this character. Avoid plot summary.

Do not base your essay on a movie, television program, or any other adaptation of a work.

How to Respond to an On-Demand Writing Prompt

1. Read the prompt carefully and determine what it is asking. Look for key verbs to indicate whether your answer should be persuasive, informative, or descriptive. (See also the **Key Verbs That Appear in Essay Questions** chart on page 1000.)

2. Plan your answer using prewriting strategies such as brainstorming and clustering. (See also **Prewriting Techniques** on page 1039.)

3. Evaluate and revise your answer as you write. Make sure that your answer has a topic sentence, supporting details, transitions between ideas, and a clear conclusion.

NOTE It's a good idea to become familiar with the kinds of writing that on-demand writing prompts require and to practice writing responses. If possible, practice with questions that have appeared on standardized tests administered at your school in the past—usually available through your school counselors or library. Use a timer to simulate the time constraints of an actual test.

Reasoning or Logic Questions

Reasoning or logic questions (sometimes called *sentence completion questions*) are multiple-choice questions that measure your ability to recognize relationships. These questions may ask you to analyze a sentence or a brief passage and to fill in one or more blanks with the most appropriate word or words given. (See also page 197.)

EXAMPLE

The fact that electrification began to gain
_____ at the turn of the twentieth century
signaled an important _____ in the development of cities in the United States.

A. mediocrity . . . collapse

B. popularity . . . rendezvous

C. patents . . . tragedy

(D.) momentum . . . juncture

How to Answer Reasoning or Logic Questions

1. Analyze the meaning implied in the question. The example question suggests a cause-and-effect relationship between electrification and U.S. cities at the turn of the twentieth century.

2. Insert each of the pairs of words to see if they make sense. Remember that even though the first word in a suggested pair may make sense, the second may not. For example, the first word in answer B, *popularity*, seems like a good possibility, but the second word, *rendezvous*, makes no sense in the context of the sentence.

Verbal-Expression Questions   *Verbal-expression questions* measure your understanding of written expression and grammatical correctness. Below is a chart showing the kinds of verbal-expression questions. For more information and practice with any of the grammar, usage, and mechanics items listed, see the pages referred to in parentheses after each item.

Types of Verbal-Expression Questions

Grammar Questions   You demonstrate your knowledge of standard grammar and usage. These test items often cover use of

Verbal Expression Questions

- principal parts of verbs (page 644)
- pronouns (page 604)
- subject-verb agreement (page 578)

Punctuation Questions   You identify the use of correct punctuation. These test items often cover correct use of

- apostrophes and hyphens (pages 827 and 834)
- end marks and commas (page 774)
- parentheses and quotation marks (pages 809 and 815)
- semicolons, colons, and dashes (pages 804, 806, and 810)

Sentence Structure Questions   You demonstrate knowledge of what is (and what is not) a complete sentence. These test items often cover

- combining sentences (page 436)
- fragments and run-ons (pages 427 and 432)
- parallel structure (page 424)
- transitional words (page 474)
- verb usage (page 642)

Revision-in-Context Questions   You show appropriate revision to a part of or to an entire composition. These test items often cover correct use of

- arranging ideas (pages 474 and 461)
- composition structure (page 465)
- tone (page 1045)
- unity and coherence (page 474)

Multiple-choice verbal-expression questions usually accompany a reading passage in which several words and phrases are underlined and numbered. The following chart describes the two most common types of verbal-expression test items.

QUICK REFERENCE HANDBOOK

Most Common Types of Verbal-Expression Test Items

"NO CHANGE" Items
- give a list of suggested revisions of under-lined, numbered portions of a passage.
- always contain one "NO CHANGE" choice (these words are often printed in capital letters) among choices; selected if indicated part is correct as is

Critical-Thinking Items
- ask you to analyze and evaluate the passage as a whole
- ask you to make inferences about portions of a passage as related to the whole

Following is a passage with sample verbal-expression questions.

In an Age of Science—and of all the periods in history, none of them merits(1) the name better than our own—trained scientists are fortunate people. Their training is a matter of national concern, because(2) the nation badly needs more scientists than it has. Scientists can often advance quickly. They can climb as far in science as their ambitions and talents permit. Most important is that they stand(3) at the very center of the forces that are conquering and remaking the world around us. Their futures are bright. It is small wonder that so many young people dream of entering one of the scientific professions.

Sample Verbal-Expression Questions

1. **A.** NO CHANGE
   B. are meriting
   C. meriting
   D. merit

[This is a grammar question; it requires you to know the correct subject-verb agreement.]

2. **A.** NO CHANGE
   B. concern; because
   C. concern. Because
   D. concern because

[This is a punctuation question; it requires you to know which mark of punctuation is appropriate here.]

3. How should the third and fourth sentences be combined?
   A. In science, because they can often advance quickly, they can climb as far as their ambitions and talents permit.
   B. They can often advance as fast and as far in science as their ambitions and talents permit.
   C. They can often advance quickly and far in science, because of their ambitions and talents.
   D. As quickly and as far in science as their ambitions and talents will permit them, they can advance.

[This is a question about sentence structure; it requires you to know how to combine sentences effectively.]

4. Which is the best revision of the portion of the passage indicated by the number 3?
   A. Most importantly, they stand
   B. It is most important that they stand
   C. It is most important; they stand
   D. Most importantly that they stand

[This is a revision-in-context question; it requires you to use revision skills to best express the ideas in the passage.]

Viewing and Representing

Media Terms

Because media messages, such as advertise-ments, television programs, music videos, and movies, are a constant part of life, it is impor-tant to be able to understand, interpret, analyze, evaluate, and create media messages. The terms defined below refer to many different areas of media communication, including television and film production, advertising, and jour-nalism. The terms are grouped into three lists: **electronic media terms** (below), **general media terms** (page 1015), and **print media terms** (page 1020). (Terms relating to the Internet and the World Wide Web can be found in the **Library/Media Center** section on page 942; terms relating to the use of type and graphics can be found in **Document Design** on page 920.)

Electronic Media Terms

Advertising   (See **Advertising** on page 1020.)

Affiliate   An *affiliate* is a privately owned, local television or radio station that presents the programming of a national network. (See also **Network** on page 1013.)

Animation   *Animation* is the film art of making drawings appear to move. An animated film may combine drawing, painting, sculpture, or other visual arts. Animators take film or video pictures of a scene at a rate of twenty-four frames per second, making small changes as they go. When viewed, the frames create the illusion of movement. Animation is used in many different types of media messages, including advertising and cartoons. (See also **Advertising** on page 1020.)

Broadcasting   *Broadcasting* means using airwaves to send television or radio content over a wide area of potential viewers or listeners. **Commercial broadcasting** is for profit. Adver-tisers pay broadcasters for airtime in which to persuade the audience to buy their products or services. **Public broadcasting** is not-for-profit. In the United States, the Public Broadcasting Service (PBS) has more than three hundred affiliates, or member stations. The service is funded mostly by the federal government, cor-porations, and individual viewers and listeners. (See also **Affiliate** on this page.)

Byline   (See **Byline** on page 1020.)

Cable Television   *Cable television* is a method of distributing TV signals using cables and wiring instead of airwaves to bring messages into people's homes. There are two principal types of cable TV companies. Some companies *create* original programming in the form of channels or networks, such as all-cartoon networks or all-weather channels. Other companies *distribute* packages, or groups, of many different channels into homes.

Camera Angle   The *camera angle* refers to the angle at which a camera is set when it is pointed at its subject. The angle may be low, high, or tilted. The effect of a low angle is to make the subject look tall and powerful. The high angle makes the subject look small. The tilt angle may suggest that the subject is not balanced.

Camera Shots   A *camera shot* is what the viewer sees in a movie or video. Just as a story needs many words, a film or video needs many shots in order to create a scene or story. Below are the most common shots used in film production.

- **Close-up shot**   A *close-up shot* is a shot of only the subject, usually a person's face.

- **Extreme close-up shot**   An *extreme close-up shot* is a very close shot, usually of only part of a person's face or part of the subject.

- **Medium shot**   A *medium shot* is a shot that shows the subject, usually a person from the waist up, and perhaps some of the background.

- **Long shot**   A *long shot* is a shot that shows a scene from far away, usually to show a place or setting of a scene.

- **Reverse angle shot**   A *reverse angle shot* is a view of the opposite side of a subject or of another person in the scene.

Channel   In general communication, a *channel* is the means by which a message is communicated. For example, if you are communicating verbally (such as by talking or singing), the channel is sound waves. If you communicate nonverbally (for instance, by gestures, expressions, or sounds such as laughter, clapping, or whistling), the channel is waves of light, sound waves, or the sense of touch. In television and radio, a channel is a fixed band of frequencies used for the transmitting of television or radio broadcasts. (See also **Medium** and **Message,** both on page 1021.)

Copy   (See **Copy** on page 1020.)

Credits   *Credits* refer to the list of names of people who worked to produce a program. This list usually appears at the end of a television program, film, or video or on the back of a compact disc case.

Demographics   (See **Demographics** on page 1020.)

Digital Editing   (See **Digital Editing** on page 1020.)

Docudrama   *Docudrama* is a type of documentary that blends elements of both documentary and drama to explore an actual historical, political, or social event. For example, docudramas may use actors and scripted dialogue to re-create historical events.

Documentary   *Documentary* is a genre of film and television programming which uses language, sounds, and imagery to provide an interpretation of real-life events. Although documentaries attempt to relate factual information, they may show only one producer's perceptions or point of view. Documentaries often have informative, persuasive, and artistic purposes.

Drama   *Drama* is an art form that tells a story through the speech and actions of the characters in the story. Most dramas use actors who impersonate the characters. Some dramas are performed in a theater, while others are presented on film.

Electronic Media   The term *electronic media* refers to the forms of mass media products that are available to consumers through some type of electronic technology such as a computer or a television. Electronic media products can be found on the Internet, on the radio, and on television.

Feature News   (See **Feature News** on page 1021.)

Hard News   (See **Hard News** on page 1021.)

In-Camera Editing   *In-camera editing* refers to any editing that is performed through the operation of a video or film camera and not by the cutting and shaping of an editor. The sequence of shots and scenes remains exactly as they were gathered by the camera operator. In-camera editing is an effective method of creating video when editing equipment is unavailable or time-consuming. To create an effective work using in-camera editing, a great deal of preproduction planning is required, including a complete shot list and storyboards.

In most cameras, sound can be added after the images have been shot.

Internet   The *Internet* is a global network of computers. With the Internet, a computer user may access information from another computer or a network of computers anywhere in the world. The Internet may be used by almost anyone who has a computer equipped with a modem.

Lead   (See **Lead** on page 1021.)

Marketing   (See **Marketing** on page 1021.)

Medium   (See **Medium** on page 1021.)

Message   (See **Message** on page 1021.)

Multimedia Presentation   A *multimedia presentation* is any presentation that involves two or more forms of media. For example, when you give an oral presentation including visuals (such as photographs, handouts, or overheads), you are giving a multimedia presentation, one medium being your voice, the other being the visuals you use to support your presentation. A multimedia presentation that involves the use of presentation software or Web sites is sometimes called a **technology presentation.**

Network   A *network* is a company that obtains and distributes programming to affiliated local stations or cable systems. Networks are not TV stations, but nearly 85 percent of all TV stations are affiliated with a network. Examples of networks include CBS, ABC, NBC, FOX, and WB. Each local station is responsible for its own programming, but a station that is affiliated with a network receives morning news programs, talk shows, soap operas, national news programs, situation comedies, dramas, and late-night programming. The networks provide the programs free to stations in exchange for the right to sell advertising. (See also **Affiliate** on page 1011.)

News   (See **News** on page 1021.)

Newsmagazine   (See **Newsmagazine** on page 1022.)

Nielsen Rating   *Nielsen rating* refers to the ratings system invented by the A. C. Nielsen Company, one of the largest marketing research companies in the United States. Nielsen ratings gather information about household television viewing choices from a sample of five thousand households selected to represent the population as a whole. Using a device called a peoplemeter, the firm gathers and later distributes information including the program watched, who was watching it, and the amount of time each viewer spent watching. Nielsen ratings are used to measure a program's popularity and to pinpoint target audiences for shows. Advertisers make decisions about buying airtime for their commercials during specific shows based in part on Nielsen ratings.

Photography   (See **Photography** on page 1022.)

Political Advertising   (See **Political Advertising** on page 1022.)

Producer   A *producer* is the person responsible for overseeing the creation of a movie or television or radio program. He or she is responsible for the following tasks:

- developing the overall message
- finding appropriate materials
- organizing a crew or staff
- finding and budgeting funding
- keeping the production on a timetable

Public Access   *Public access* refers to the channels on a cable television system that are set aside specifically for use by the public to create a variety of programs. These channels are often controlled by education officials or government leaders.

Public Relations   (See **Public Relations** on page 1022.)

Ratings   *Ratings* are the system of categorizing films, TV programs, or video games by considering whether the content is appropriate for people of different ages. Ratings help adults and children evaluate the content of a message before viewing. (See also **Nielsen Rating** on this page.)

Reality TV   *Reality television* is the presentation of actual video footage taken by amateurs with police monitors and by surveillance cameras. Usually the footage is highly edited; but because reality TV is presented as an eyewitness account, people tend to find it believable.

Reporter   (See **Reporter** on page 1022.)

Script   A *script* is the text or words of a film, play, or television or radio show. The format for film and TV scripts often includes information about the images to be shown. The script for news broadcasts is called *copy*. (See also **Copy** on page 1020.)

Sequencing *Sequencing* is the order in which scenes or images appear in a narrative. In television, film, and video, sequencing is enhanced in the editing process, in which scenes, usually filmed separately and in different locations, are spliced or joined together to create a sense of flow or sequence. The duration of each scene sets the mood for the entire sequence. For example, grouping together several long, slow scenes can create a feeling of suspense. On the other hand, rapidly changing from one short scene to another can create a feeling of urgency. Choosing whether to use long or short scenes in a sequence is called *editing for rhythm.*

Soft News   (See **Soft News** on page 1022.)

Source   (See **Source** on page 1022.)

Sponsorship A *sponsorship* takes place when a business gives money to support a particular TV or radio program in return for commercial airtime. Sponsorship is different from advertising because in sponsorship, a company's name is acknowledged but usually the product is not promoted. Even though public broadcasting does not include commercials, it may include sponsors' names and slogans. (See also **Broadcasting** on page 1011.)

Storyboard   A *storyboard* is a visual script, or series of drawings, that indicates the appearance and order of shots and scenes in a script as well as audio and visual cues. (For an example of a **Storyboard,** see pages 225 and 413.)

Target Audience   (See **Target Audience** on page 1022.)

Text   (See **Text** on page 1022.)

General Media Terms

Audience   An *audience* is a group of receivers of a media message. Audiences may receive a message by listening, reading, or viewing. The audience is important to understanding the economics of the mass media business, since advertisers pay to reach specific audiences when they place ads in newspapers or magazines, or on radio, television, or the Internet. Audiences are often identified by specific characteristics, or demographics. (See also **Demographics** on page 1020.)

Authority   *Authority* refers to the believability of a message. When a message seems believable because it comes from a trustworthy and knowledgeable individual, the message has authority. For example, we would say a message about how to grow corn would have more authority coming from a farmer than from a city-dweller. (See also **Credibility** below and **Source** on page 1022.)

Bias   A *bias* is a negative connotation or point of view. An editorial writer with a bias may present only one side of an issue or ignore information that does not support his or her position. (See also **Point of View** on page 1019.)

Communicator   A *communicator* is a person involved in the act of communicating or sharing messages with another person or persons. The communicator is the person who sends the message to the audience. The receiver takes on the role of communicator when he or she returns the message.

Credibility   *Credibility* is the willingness to believe in a person or to trust what a person says and does. Credibility is not a characteristic of a speaker. It is a perception that exists in the minds of a listener or viewer. (See also **Authority** on page 1015.)

Critical Viewing   *Critical viewing* is the ability to use critical thinking skills to view, question, analyze, and understand issues presented in visual media, including photography, film, television, and other mass media. Critical viewers use **media literacy concepts** to access, analyze, evaluate, and communicate media messages. Below are five key concepts of media literacy and some questions to help you evaluate media messages.

Media Literacy Concepts	Evaluation Questions
1. All messages are made by someone. Every message sent out by the media is written, edited, selected, illustrated, or composed by someone or by a group of individuals. Writers, photographers, artists, illustrators, and TV and radio producers all make decisions about which elements (words, images, sounds) to include in a media message, which ones to leave out, and how to arrange and sequence the chosen elements. Knowing how media messages are constructed will help you better interpret the meaning of a message.	Ask yourself: "What words, images, or sounds are used to create the message?" and "What words, images, or sounds may have been left out of the message?"
2. Media messages are not reality. Media messages are *representations* of reality that in turn shape people's ideas of the world. Fictional stories in the media can seem realistic if characters act in ways that seem authentic, but, of course, the stories are not real. Even an eyewitness news account of a robbery can seem real, but it usually reflects only one person's point of view, filtered through a TV camera and carefully edited down to a few images and words. Media messages can never perfectly match the complexity of the real world. Every media message also affects the way you think about the world. It is important that you judge the accuracy of media messages and whether or not you think the messages reflect reality.	Ask yourself: "What is the point of view or experience of the message maker?" and "How does this message affect the way I think about a particular topic or idea?"
3. Each person interprets media messages differently. Your interpretation of a media message is based on your knowledge of the world in which you live. You can use your prior knowledge and experience to examine the many different stylistic features of a message and to evaluate the message within its context.	Ask yourself: "How does the message make me feel?" or "What does the message make me think of?"
4. People have a wide range of purposes for creating media messages. People create and share messages for many reasons, but making money is one of the most important reasons that message making is so important in modern culture. When people have political purposes, they use messages to gain power or authority over others. Understanding how messages operate in terms of their economic, political, social, and aesthetic purposes will help you better understand the context of a work.	Ask yourself: "Who created the message and why?" or "Is the producer's purpose to inform, to influence, to present ideas, to make money, to gain power, or to express ideas?

5. Each mass medium—from TV to the newspaper to the Internet—has unique characteristics. Media messages come in different forms. A media producer makes choices about which kinds of media are most appropriate to convey a particular message. For example, TV news favors messages that are immediate and visual, while news photographs favor messages that have an emotional component. Knowing how the medium shapes the message will help you understand why its creator used certain elements and why the message makes you feel the way it does.

Ask yourself: "Through what medium is the message delivered?" and "How does the form affect the message?"

Decoding   *Decoding* is the making of meaning from verbal and nonverbal signals. For example, audiences decode symbols, such as words and pictures, when they watch TV or read a newspaper. *Encoding,* the opposite of decoding, refers to the process of turning ideas and feelings into verbal and nonverbal messages. For example, reporters encode when they write news stories.

Deconstruction   *Deconstruction* is the process of analyzing, or taking apart, the pieces of a media message to understand its meaning. The process of deconstruction involves looking at both what is stated, such as the words and images printed on a page, and what is not directly stated, including elements of the historical, economic, and political context in which the message was created.

Desensitization   *Desensitization* is a decrease in the level of emotional reaction to media messages as a result of repeated exposure to those media messages. For example, you may feel upset after learning about a crime in the news, but after seeing reports of the same crime many times (on TV, in the newspaper, and on the Internet) it doesn't bother you as much to hear about the crime. The *bystander effect* suggests that people who have been desensitized to violence are less likely to help others in real-life violent situations.

Feedback   *Feedback* is a response from an audience to the sender of a message. It can be immediate or delayed. Applause and asking questions are typical forms of **immediate audience feedback.** Writing a letter to the editor to respond to a newspaper editorial and filling out a questionnaire on a Web page are forms of **delayed feedback.**

Formula   A *formula* is an established or conventional model or approach. In television and film, it refers to a typical combination of characters or presentation of material. Local news broadcasts, for example, often present news first, then a weather report, and finally sports.

Genre   A *genre* is a category of artistic forms or media products that share **conventions,** or commonly accepted ways of presenting messages. For example, mysteries usually include the presentation of a problem, the search to find an answer to the problem, and the resolution of the problem. Each genre has a particular audience and conventions. See the chart on the next page. (See also **Docudrama, Documentary,** and **Drama** on pages 1012 and 1013.)

QUICK REFERENCE HANDBOOK

Genre Categories: Film and Television

Genre	Explanation
Action Adventure	Action adventure programming offers the viewer excitement, suspense, and escape. Most action adventure films or TV shows feature the hero in a series of physical feats, fights, and chases, sometimes in unusual or exotic settings.
Comedy	Comedies give viewers the opportunity to laugh and feel comforted by a happy ending. Most comedies show the ludicrous in human behavior and affairs. Comedies allow audiences to laugh at the mistakes and misfortunes of people a little less smart or less secure than themselves. A **situation comedy** is a television format that involves stories about a regular set of characters in either a home or work setting. Situation comedies focus on life's ordinary problems and solutions.
Fantasy	A fantasy features improbable and impossible characters and events. Fantasies create an unreal world in which the laws of physics and biology do not apply. Fantasies satisfy the audience's desire for highly imaginative storytelling.
Farce	A farce is a type of comedy which features exaggerated characters in exaggerated situations to evoke laughter. Farces often feature absurdly funny plots, physical action including slapstick, and ridiculous character types.
Horror	Works of horror seek to cause fright and even terror in viewers. Horror offers the audience the chance to experience extreme feelings of revulsion, disgust, and fear as entertainment since viewers sit comfortably and safely while watching. Horror often deals with anything which unsettles, disturbs, and threatens us— including violence, death, the unknown, and even science and outer space.
Parody	Parodies are humorous imitations (and often exaggerations) of another work or group of works. Some parodies are good-natured, while others are satirical.
Romance	Romance is about love relationships. The love relationship is usually presented in a positive, emotional, and sometimes sentimental manner. Romances allow the viewer to see love as the saving grace of human existence.
Romantic Comedy	Romantic comedies show comic misunderstandings, obstacles, and difficulties in a relationship between two people. Usually, they end happily.
Science Fiction	Science fiction is a subgroup of the fantasy genre. Often science fiction offers a futuristic vision of life based on some elements of contemporary society. Science fiction stories often involve space exploration and alien encounters.
Slapstick	Slapstick refers to any comic action that involves an aggressive or violent action as a source of humor.
Soap Opera	A soap opera is a genre of television programming that uses a serial structure: Each daily program continues an ongoing story. Soap operas feature sentimental, romantic, melodramatic, and escapist events among a group of related individuals.

Interpretation   *Interpretation* is the process of creating meaning from exposure to a message through reading, viewing, or listening. People's interpretations of messages differ, depending on their life experiences, backgrounds, and points of view.

Media Law   Various government structures, laws, and policies regulate access, content, delivery, and use of the mass media. For example, the *First Amendment* to the Constitution forbids Congress to set up or in any way pass laws limiting speech or the press. *Copyright law* protects the rights of authors and other media owners against the unauthorized publishing, reproduction, and selling of their works. *Censorship* is any governmental attempt to suppress or control people's access to media messages. Some censorship, however, may be used to protect citizens against damage to their reputations (*libel*) or against invasions of their privacy.

News Values   *News values* are the set of criteria journalists use to determine whether information is newsworthy. News values include

- **timeliness**   events or issues that are happening now
- **conflict**   unresolved events or issues that are interesting to the public
- **novelty**   stories that contain unique, interesting elements
- **relevance**   stories that are of interest to local readers
- **human interest**   stories that touch people's emotions
- **prominence**   stories about celebrities, politicians, or other noteworthy people
- **impact**   stories that make a difference in people's lives

If a news event has these features, it is more likely to be covered by the news media.

Newsworthiness   *Newsworthiness* is the quality of an event that is worthy of being reported in a newspaper or news broadcast. An event must be of interest or importance to the public in order to be considered newsworthy. (See also **News Values** on this page.)

Omission   An *omission* is what is left out of a media message. All messages are selective and incomplete. For example, some documentaries present only one point of view of a historical event, omitting all other possible points of view. Some press releases present only one side of an issue, omitting facts and opinions that are contrary to the writer's opinion. Noticing what is not included in a message helps to identify the author's point of view. (See also **Point of View** below.)

Point of View   *Point of view* can refer to the position or view of the person reporting a story or telling a tale in the mass media. Point of view is also a literary concept which can be used to interpret mass media texts ranging from news photographs to situation comedies. In the electronic media, point of view can be indicated by the type of narration used or by the type of camera shot used. There are many possible points of view. (See also **Bias** on page 1015.)

Propaganda   *Propaganda* is any form of communication that uses persuasive techniques to reach a mass audience. Propaganda was originally defined as the spreading of biased ideas and opinions through lies and deception. This definition gave the concept of propaganda a negative connotation. However, as scholars began to study the topic in the 1940s, they came to realize that propaganda was everywhere. Over time, the concept of propaganda has lost some of its negative connotation. Propaganda is now thought of as the communication of a point of view with the goal of having audience members come to voluntarily accept this position as one of their beliefs. Advertising is one of the major forms of propaganda. (See also **Advertising** on this page.)

Purpose   The *purpose* of a media message is what its sender or creator intends to achieve. Usually, the purpose of a message is to inform, to educate, to persuade, to entertain, to express oneself, or to make money. A message may have a primary and a secondary purpose at the same time.

Sensationalism   *Sensationalism* is the media's use or portrayal of material that is intended to generate curiosity, fear, or other strong responses. The material can be exaggerated or shocking in content. Content that refers to romance, death, children, or animals is often sensational. (See also **Reality TV** on page 1014 and **Tabloid** on page 1022.)

Stereotypes   *Stereotypes* are generalized beliefs based on misinformation or insufficient evidence about an entire group of individuals. Stereotypes often misrepresent the complexities of human relationships, ideas and cultures. A stereotype about professors, for example, would be that all professors are absent-minded. (For more on **Stereotypes,** see page 140.)

Visual Literacy   *Visual literacy* is a person's awareness of how meaning is communicated through visual media, including the use of color, line, shape, and texture.

Print Media Terms

Advertising   *Advertising* is the use of images or text to promote or sell a product, service, image, or idea. Advertising is a marketing technique that is designed to persuade an audience. Typical advertising formats include print advertisements in newspapers and magazines, billboards, radio and television commercials, and electronic billboards on the World Wide Web. (See also **Marketing** on page 1021 and **Sponsorship** on page 1015.)

Byline   A *byline* is the name of the reporter or writer of a report published in a newspaper or magazine or presented on television or radio.

Circulation   *Circulation* is a measurement of the size of the audience for print media. It includes the total number of copies of a publication, such as a magazine, that is delivered to subscribers, newsstands, and vendors.

Copy   *Copy* is the text in a media message.

Demographics   *Demographics* are the characteristics that define a particular audience. They include gender, age, educational background, cultural heritage, and income. Advertisers use demographics to target certain audiences. For example, advertisers will advertise computer software in technology magazines computer programmers read.

Digital Editing   *Digital editing* is the use of computer technology to alter or change an image before it is presented to an audience. Photo editors often edit out distracting elements from photo illustrations. However, extensive digital editing of hard-news photographs is considered unethical.

Elements of Design   *Elements of design* give meaning to visual representations in the following ways. (See also **Document Design** on page 920.)

- **Color** creates mood and can also designate areas of space by separating and emphasizing parts of a visual.
- **Line** determines the direction and speed of the viewer's eye movement. For example, curvy lines suggest gracefulness.
- **Shape** emphasizes elements in the visual, adds interest, and communicates concepts. For example, a square represents solidness; a circle, completeness.
- **Texture** appeals to a viewer's sense of touch. For example, a grainy visual suggests roughness.

Feature News   *Feature news,* or soft news, refers to news stories whose primary purpose is to entertain. Feature stories usually are not timely. Stories about celebrities and ordinary people, places, animals, events, and products are considered feature news because they generate sympathy, curiosity, or amazement in viewers, readers, or listeners. (See also **Hard News** below and **Soft News** on page 1022.)

Font   A *font* is a style of lettering used for printing text. (For more on **Fonts,** see page 926.)

Hard News   *Hard news* refers to fact-based reporting of breaking news stories. Hard news answers the basic *5W-How?* questions about timely subjects, such as national and international politics, economics, social issues, the environment, and scientific discoveries. An example of hard news would be a story reporting on the aftermath of a tornado. (See also **Feature News** above and **Soft News** on page 1022.)

Headline   A *headline* is the title of a newspaper or magazine article, usually set in large or bold type. It has two purposes: to inform the reader of the content of the article and to get the reader's attention.

Lead   A *lead* is the introduction to a newspaper article or a broadcast report. It ranges from one sentence to several paragraphs in length. A lead contains information that motivates a reader or viewer to continue with the story. A lead usually contains the major facts of a story, and may describe a curious or unusual situation to attract reader or viewer attention.

Marketing   *Marketing* is the process of moving goods or services from the producer to the consumer. It includes identifying consumer wants or needs; designing, packaging, and pricing the product; and arranging for locations where the product will be sold. Marketing also includes promoting the product to a target audience through advertising or other means. (See also **Advertising** on page 1020.)

Medium   The *medium* of a message is the form in which it is presented or distributed, including film, video, radio, television, the Internet, and print.

Message   A *message* is a combination of symbols that is communicated to one or more people. Messages are created by people who use symbols, including language, gestures, images, sounds, and electronic forms. Media messages are communicated through various mass media. (See also **Medium** above.)

News   *News* is the presentation of current and interesting information that will interest or affect an audience. Local news is produced by local newspapers and radio and TV stations, which use their own equipment, reporters, and resources. The focus of local news is information that affects a small audience with regional interests. National news is produced by large newspapers and radio and TV stations. Because their resources are greater, national news organizations may cover more national and world issues or events.

Newsmagazine   A *newsmagazine* is a weekly, biweekly, monthly, or bimonthly printed journal that focuses on news issues. On TV, a newsmagazine is a news program divided into several news segments or stories.

Photography   *Photography* is a process of making pictures by using cameras to record patterns of light and images on film or on computer disks. People may think that "a photograph never lies," but a photograph, like all media messages, is selective and incomplete. Photographers use many techniques to communicate their points of view, including the framing and composition of an image and the use of filters or digital editing. (See also **Digital Editing** on page 1020 and **Point of View** on page 1019.)

Political Advertising   *Political advertising* is the use of the mass media to persuade listeners and viewers about a political candidate's ideas or opinions. Political candidates who use advertising must use techniques similar to those used to sell products. Their messages must be simple and attention-getting. (See also **Advertising** on page 1020.)

Print Media   *Print media* refers to the hard copies of mass media products that are printed on paper to be read or looked at by consumers. Examples of print media are newspapers, magazines, pamphlets, and fliers.

Public Relations   A *public relations* department is responsible for shaping and responding to public opinion about the company's products, services, image, or individual staff. A public relations department acts as a go-between between the company, the mass media, and the public. Public relations departments write press releases to try to persuade the mass media to report on their issues in a favorable light. (See also **Marketing** on page 1021.)

Reporter   A *reporter* is a journalist who is responsible for gathering information. Reporters gather information and work with editors to create TV and print news.

Soft News   *Soft news,* or feature news, is the presentation of general interest material, such as celebrities and sports, in a news format. (See also **Feature News** and **Hard News** on page 1021.)

Source   A *source* is the person who first supplies information or ideas that are then shared with others. Journalists rely on sources for the information they report, and select individuals that they believe are credible and have authority. (See also **Authority** on page 1015.)

Tabloid   A *tabloid* is a publication with a newspaper format that provides sensational news items and photographs. Tabloid producers often admit that the stories they report are either false or exaggerations of the truth.

Target Audience   A *target audience* is a segment of the population for which a product or presentation is designed. (See also **Demographics** on page 1020.)

Text   *Text* refers to the symbols used to create a message such as a book or a TV show.

Writing

Skills, Structures, and Techniques

Good writing takes enthusiasm and practice. It also takes an understanding of some basic forms and strategies. Use the following ideas and information to become a more successful and effective writer.

Business Letters   The purpose of a *business letter* is to take action in some business-related matter, such as applying for a job or requesting goods or services. A business letter not only must sound professional—but also must look professional. Use the following guidelines.

Business Letter Guidelines

Use white, unlined 8 1/2" × 11" paper.

Type your letter or prepare your letter on a computer, using single-spacing and an extra line between paragraphs. If you must write by hand, neatly write the letter, using black or blue ink. Check for typing errors and misspellings.

Center your letter with equal margins on the sides and at the top and bottom.

Use only one side of the paper. If your letter will not fit on one page, leave a one-inch margin at the bottom of the first page and carry over at least two lines onto the second page.

Avoid mark-outs, erasures, and other careless marks.

Use a polite, respectful, professional tone.

Use formal, standard English. Avoid slang, contractions, and most abbreviations.

Include all necessary information, but get to the point quickly. Be sure that your reader knows why you wrote and what you are asking.

■ **Parts of a business letter**   There are six parts of a business letter, usually arranged on the page in one of two styles. In *block form,* all six parts begin at the left margin, and paragraphs are not indented. In *modified block form,* the heading, the closing, and your signature begin to the right of the center of the page. All the other parts begin at the left margin, and all paragraphs are indented.

Block Style

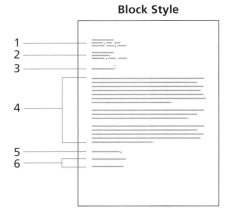

Modified Block Style

1. The *heading* usually has three lines:
   - your street address (or post office box number)
   - your city, state, and ZIP Code
   - the date the letter was written

2. The *inside address* gives the name and address of the person or organization to whom you are writing. Use a courtesy title (such as *Mr., Mrs., Ms.,* or *Miss*) or a professional title (such as *Dr.* or *Professor*) in front of the person's name. Include the person's business title (such as *Director* or *Editor*) after the name. Finally, follow the name with the name of the company or organization and its address. If you do not know the name of the person who will read your letter—for example, if you are writing to the station manager of your favorite radio station to commend the morning DJs—put the position title (Manager, for example) in the place of the name.

3. The *salutation* is your greeting. If you are writing to a specific person, begin with *Dear* followed by his or her courtesy title or professional title, and the person's last name. End with a colon. If you do not have the name of a specific person, use a general salutation such as *Dear Sir or Madam.* Another option is to use a department name or a position title, with or without the word *Dear.*

4. The *body,* the main part of your letter, contains the message. If this message requires more than one paragraph, leave an extra line between paragraphs.

5. The *closing* is your ending. You should always end your letter in a courteous manner. Appropriate closings are *Yours truly, Sincerely,* or *Respectfully yours.* Capitalize only the first word of the closing. End the closing with a comma.

6. Your *signature* should be handwritten in ink, directly below the closing and above your typed or printed name. Always sign your full name with no titles.

NOTE If you are including more in your envelope than just your letter—for example, a résumé, brochure, or writing sample—leave two lines blank after the signature, then type "enclosure" or "encl.," plus the type of item you are enclosing. "Enclosure" should be left aligned.

- **Types of business letters** There are four main types of business letters.

  1. **Appreciation or commendation letters**
     An *appreciation* or *commendation letter*

is written to compliment or express appreciation to an individual, a company, or an organization. For example, you might write to a television network, noting how much you like a particular program and encouraging the network not to cancel it. Your appreciation or commendation letters are most effective when you explain exactly why you are pleased. Here is an example.

```
    On Tuesday, June 13, I watched
the first show of the series Teens
Beyond 2000. I especially enjoyed
watching the show because it accu-
rately portrayed some of the prob-
lems we teenagers face today. I
appreciated the fact that teens
wrote and produced the show, which
explains why it did not just focus
on the problems but also provided
some suggestions about where young
people can go for information,
resources, or support.

    I think that a lot of people,
including my mother and step-
father, rarely hear about teen
issues from an unbiased source. We
need more programs like this one
that contribute to honest and open
talks about serious issues that
affect young and old people alike.
```

2. **Complaint or adjustment letters** The purpose of a *complaint* or *adjustment letter* is to report an error or problem, or to state that you have not received services or products that you have reason to expect. In a calm, courteous tone, tell why you are displeased. Then, request the solution that you believe will correct the problem. Keep the tone of your letter polite. Despite your frustration, your letter will be more effective if you are coolheaded and communi-

cate the problem clearly. Here is the body of a sample adjustment letter.

```
    On October 25, 2000, I bought a
down-filled ski parka at your store
for $79.99. The parka was charged
to my mother's account. Since the
size I needed was not in stock, the
parka was delivered to my home.
When it arrived on October 28, the
packing envelope looked like it had
been sliced with a knife. When I
opened the package, there were
feathers everywhere and the jacket
had a two-inch gash in the back.

    I am returning the parka and
would like another in its place. If
that is not possible, then I would
like the full amount of $79.99 to
be credited to my mother's account.
The account is under the name of
Sabrina Tallwood, and her account
number is 55-432-6591-2.
```

When you write a complaint or adjustment letter, remember to register your complaint as soon as possible after noticing the problem and explain exactly what is wrong. Include information such as

- what product or service you ordered or expected
- why you are not satisfied (for example, the goods were damaged)
- how you were affected (for example, you lost time or money)
- what you want the individual, company, or organization to do about the problem

NOTE Some complaint letters include informative headings to emphasize the main points in the letter. Headings show at a glance how the letter is organized. If you use headings in your letter, be sure they are specific and parallel.

3. Letters of Application

Letters of application, sometimes called *cover letters,* provide a selection committee or a possible employer with enough information to determine whether you are a good candidate for a position. This position may be a job, a membership in an organization, or a scholarship.

Guidelines for Letters of Application

1. Identify the job or position for which you are applying and mention how you heard about it.

2. Depending on the position you are applying for, you might mention

- your classification in school
- your grade-point average
- your experience, activities, awards, or honors
- personal qualities or characteristics that make you a good choice for the position
- the date or times you are available for the position

3. Always offer to provide references. Your references should include two or three responsible adults (usually not relatives) who have agreed to recommend you. Be prepared to supply their titles, addresses, and telephone numbers.

4. As shown in the example, letters of application include your full address and a date in the heading. Your phone number is optional because it is included in the body of the letter.

5. Use a salutation, followed by a colon. Do not use *Mr., Mrs.,* or *Ms.* unless you are sure of your reader's preference.

6. It is a good idea to use lists to highlight key points in your letter.

Below is an example of an application letter.

```
                    1632 Garden View Terrace
                    Allentown, PA 18103
                    May 20, 2001

Personnel Director
Value Insurance Company
10 Central Avenue
Allentown, PA 18102

Dear Personnel Director:

    Please consider me for the
position of summer intern adver-
tised in Sunday's Morning Call.

    As a junior at Jefferson High
School, I have completed courses
in word processing, bookkeeping,
and business English, in addition
to the required courses. I am
familiar with the most recent
word-processing programs, and I
can type fifty words per minute.

    Last summer I was employed as
a fill-in receptionist at Quality
Supply, where I took telephone
messages, filed orders, prepared
billing statements, and entered
data into the company database.

    My résumé lists references who
can tell you about my work and my
personal characteristics.

    I believe that my background
qualifies me for the summer
intern position. Please call me
at 555-7023 if you would like to
schedule an interview.

            Sincerely,

            Veronica Harjo

            Veronica Harjo
```

4. Request or order letters A *request letter* asks for information about a product or asks for someone's time or services. An *order letter* requests something specific, such as a free brochure or an item in a catalog. Here is a sample request letter.

```
Northfield High School
36 Michigan Avenue
Northfield, NJ 07973
January 28, 2001


Ms. Erika Lehman
511 Chestnut Street
Willmington, NJ 07990

Dear Ms. Lehman:

I would like to invite you to
serve as one of the judges at the
Northfield High School Arts Fair.
This year's fair will be held on
April 14, 2001, from 9:00 A.M. to
3:00 P.M. on the Northfield High
School campus.

Please let me know if you would
be interested in judging one hun-
dred submitted student artworks,
including paintings, sculpture,
ceramics, and photography. You
would be on a panel with four
other judges, who are also pro-
fessional artists from our commu-
nity. I have enclosed a schedule
of events for the fair as well as
an article from the school paper
about last year's fair.

I look forward to hearing from you.

Yours truly,

Marco Day

Marco Day
Arts Fair Coordinator

Encl. schedule, article
```

Compositions A composition is a longer piece of writing composed of paragraphs. A composition usually has three main parts: an *introduction, body,* and *conclusion.* Each has a specific function, yet they all work together to communicate the writer's main idea, usually stated in the *thesis.*

- **Introduction** Often introductions begin with general information and then grow more specific, ending with the thesis. The following graphic may help you to visualize the organization.

Introduction

General

**Specific
(Thesis)**

The *introduction* of a well-written composition should do three things:

1. **Catch the reader's attention.** An introduction should pique your readers' curiosity and make them want to read on.
2. **Set the tone or indicate your attitude toward the topic.** The *tone* of your composition may be formal, informal, serious, humorous, critical—even angry.
3. **Present the thesis.** A *thesis statement* is a sentence or two that announces your limited topic and your main, or unifying, idea about it. A thesis statement is a little like a topic sentence in a paragraph—it's the glue that holds details together. It also lets your readers know exactly what will be covered in your composition. Some strategies for writing a thesis statement are listed on the following page.

- Review the facts and details in your prewriting notes. Identify the main or unifying idea and begin thinking about how the details support it.
- Check your thesis statement by asking these two questions: What is my topic? What am I trying to say about my topic?

- Sharpen your focus and present a clear, specific idea.
- Evaluate your thesis with your audience in mind. Will your readers care about your topic and arguments?

To write an effective *introduction*, try one of the following techniques. The examples show

Technique	Example
Begin with an anecdote or example.	Each person entering the canopy where my cousin Louise was getting married was handed a small paper box and given the warning not to open it until the end of the ceremony. I shook the box but heard nothing inside. It couldn't be rice or confetti. Finally, after the words *I do,* I learned that each box contained a butterfly. When the butterflies were released into the air, they created a spectacular effect.
Begin with a startling fact or by adopting an unusual position.	Scientists have yet to clone a butterfly, but, as it turns out, ordinary people can breed thousands of dollars worth of butterflies right at home. The question is, is the practice as good for the environment as people think?
Use an appropriate quotation.	"Although most people consider butterflies to be beautiful creatures, the practice of releasing hundreds at a time into a new environment troubles me," says Dr. Gwyneth Monroe, of Valley College. Dr. Monroe's comment raises several important questions about the breeding and releasing of butterflies.
Start with background information.	In just the last few years, more than sixty butterfly breeding companies have started operations. They breed tens of thousands of butterflies each season for the purpose of releasing them into the wild. Scientists are worried that the released butterflies will bring disease to the populations of wild butterflies.
Begin with a simple statement of your thesis.	Now that people are releasing butterflies on special occasions instead of balloons, rice, or confetti, the impact of butterfly breeding on the environment is only just being examined. On the one hand, breeders believe that they are benefiting the environment; on the other hand, scientists are worried about widespread outbreaks of disease.
Begin by addressing the reader in a question or a challenge.	Is there anyone who can deny the simple beauty of a butterfly in flight? How about hundreds at a time? The sight is a common one these days at weddings and other special occasions. We must ask ourselves, though, are these butterflies a harmless pleasure?

how you might introduce a composition about breeding and releasing butterflies.

■ **Body** The *body* develops and elaborates the composition's main points. In short compositions, such as most of the essays you write in school, each main point is developed in one paragraph. In longer, more complex compositions, more than one paragraph may be required to develop a main point. Together, all the paragraphs in the body support the thesis statement—the composition's one main idea. Keep in mind the following guidelines as you write the body of your composition.

1. **Arrange your information** in a way that makes sense to your readers and is appropriate to your topic. A thoughtful organization gives your composition **coherence.** The table below indicates four common ways to arrange ideas in a composition.

2. **Eliminate any details that do not support your thesis.** This gives your paper *unity*—all details relate to one central idea.

3. **Show how your ideas are connected** by using *direct references* and *transitional expressions.* These serve as signposts to guide the reader through the composition. (See also **direct references** and **transitional expressions** on pages 461, 961, and 1045.)

See also page 474.

■ **Conclusion** The *conclusion* is the final part of your paper. A good conclusion is one that is a satisfying and appropriate end to your particular essay. Often a conclusion begins with a specific restatement of the thesis and then moves to a broader view, sometimes ending with a thought-provoking question or speculation about the future. The following graphic may help you to visualize the organization.

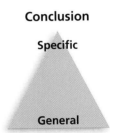

Conclusion

Specific

General

Arranging Ideas		
Type of Order	**Definition**	**Examples**
Chronological	Order that presents events as they happen in time	Explanation of a process; personal narrative; story
Spatial	Order that describes objects according to their location	Descriptions (near to far, left to right, top to bottom, and so on)
Importance	Order that gives details from least to most important or the reverse	Descriptions, evaluative writing; explanations (main idea and supporting details); persuasive writing
Logical	Order that relates groups and items	Comparison and contrast; explanations of cause and effect or problem-solution; definitions

For conclusions, follow these tips:

1. **Provide readers with a sense of completion.** Your readers have invested in your ideas by reading your entire composition. Be fair to readers by bringing together all the ideas you mentioned earlier.

2. **Reinforce your main idea.** Remember, your thesis statement was intended to state your main idea and show readers the direction in which your writing would go. A final restatement or summary of the thesis confirms that you have arrived at the place you wanted to be.

3. **Summarize your major points.** By summarizing the main points of your composition, you help your readers remember what they read.

4. **Offer a solution or make a recommendation.** If you have taken a stand on an issue in your composition, you should emphasize your point by offering a solution or recommending a point of action in the conclusion. Including a stand or recommendation in the conclusion will make it clear how much you care about the issue.

Look at how different strategies were used for concluding a paper on the trend of butterfly breeding.

Technique	Example
Restate your main idea.	Breeding butterflies and releasing them into the air on special occasions has become a trend that both intrigues and troubles environmentalists.
Summarize your major points.	The breeding of butterflies increases the chance of introducing disease into the population of wild butterflies. In addition, releasing butterflies into the wild ruins scientific studies of certain butterflies' migration.
Close with a final idea or example.	Last week I went to yet another wedding. At this one, the bride and her mother wore small, lacquered pins in the shapes of butterflies. The bride said she did not have the heart to release real ones at the ceremony.
End with a comment on the topic (a thoughtful observation or a look to the future).	By releasing butterflies, the butterfly goes free, and we enjoy its beauty. Scientists, however, say that we may pay a price later.
Call on your readers to take action.	If you must order butterflies, make sure that the breeder has followed all the required regulations before you release the insects in your neighborhood.
Refer to your introduction.	The next time you see a butterfly, ask yourself where it came from—nature or the farm?

E-mail *Electronic mail*, or *e-mail*, is correspondence sent by the computer rather than through your local post office. The use of computers and the Internet to conduct personal and business correspondence has proliferated in recent years. Because this growth promises to continue, it is important that you know how to use e-mail properly. E-mail can be used to write personal, informal letters or to send business messages. Because e-mails are easy to write, send, and receive, many e-mail users ignore the guidelines associated with writing letters. Informal content and format are often acceptable when you write to a close friend or send comments to a newsgroup or chat group where the discussions are clearly relaxed. However, if you are writing to someone you do not know well for business or research purposes, you should follow the guidelines listed below. Online etiquette, or "Netiquette," stresses the importance of good manners and common sense in cyberspace, just as etiquette does in the real world.

E-mail Guidelines

- Always be polite in your messages—even if you know the person to whom you are writing. Being rude to someone in an e-mail is called *flaming.* Flaming often backfires because there is always the chance that your angry message could be forwarded and read by someone you did not intend to see it.

- Avoid using capital letters in your messages. CAPITALS CONVEY SHOUTING. No one wants to be shouted at in cyberspace. (If you want to show emphasis, place asterisks (*) on either side of the important word or term instead. For example, "What do you think about the *metaphor* in chapter 2?")

- Use emoticons sparingly and never use them in formal e-mails. *Emoticons* are combinations of symbols that, when you tilt your head to the left, look like faces and suggest feelings. For example, the emoticon :-) suggests laughter or "I'm just kidding." Use them in informal e-mails only.

- Always pay attention to the addresses entered in your address line. Make sure that you are sending appropriate messages to the right people.

- Always fill in the subject line before you send a message. Providing a subject will help your readers prioritize your message, which could be one of many they receive.

- Avoid forwarding an e-mail without asking the permission of the original sender. Private e-mails are usually intended for your eyes only.

- Keep your message concise and to the point. Limit yourself to one full screen or less of text. Scrolling through long e-mail messages can be tedious.

- Use bulleted lists and indentation to make the document easy for your readers to read on-screen. Bulleted lists are especially helpful if you are raising more than one question or point.

- Use standard English and always make sure that your spelling, grammar, and punctuation are correct.

- Include salutations such as "Dear Dr. Brunelli" if you are writing for the first time to someone you do not know. Also, a closing, such as "Sincerely" or "Thank you," followed by your full name is always considered polite.

Envelopes   If you expect a letter to arrive promptly at its destination, the letter's envelope must be addressed correctly. Write or type your complete return address in the top left-hand corner of the envelope. Then, place the name and address of the person or organization to whom you are writing in the center of the envelope. For a business letter, the addressee's name and address should exactly match the inside address. Use the two-letter state code on the envelope—TX or CA, for example, rather than writing out the state name. Business letters should always be sent in plain 9 1/2" × 4 1/4" business envelopes. Special notations, for example, the word *Confidential,* should be above and slightly to the right of the address on your envelope.

The optical scanning equipment used by the Postal Service reads envelopes from the bottom up. If you want a letter to be delivered to a post office box rather than a street address, enter the post office box number on the line above the city and state.

```
Return
Address

        Mailing Address
        (type in block format)
```

Forms   As you enter the work force or begin applying to colleges, you will be asked to fill out forms and applications. The following techniques will help you fill out any form accurately and completely.

- Read all of the instructions carefully before you start.
- Type or write neatly. Unless a pencil is specified, type or print your information in either blue or black ink.
- Include all information requested. If a question does not apply to you, write *N/A* or *not applicable* instead of leaving the space blank.
- Be careful to put the information requested in the correct space on the form. For example, some forms want last name first. Others want first name first.
- Proofread your completed form and correct errors neatly.
- Submit the form to the correct person.
- Keep the form neat and clean. Avoid cross-outs.

Look at the example application form printed on the opposite page.

Application for Employment

Personal Information

1. Social Security Number   012-34-5678
2. Name   Harjo   Veronica   Elena
           last   first   middle
3. Present Address   1632 Garden View Drive   Allentown,   PA   18103
                     street   city   state   zip
4. Permanent Address   same as above
5. Phone No. (215) 555-7023
6. If related to anyone in our employ, state name and department.
   N/A
7. Referred by   Ms. Bernie Schulman

Employment Desired

8. Position   Summer Intern   Date you can start 6/8/99   Salary desired $5.50/hour
9. Are you employed now?   No
   If so, may we inquire of your present employer?   N/A
10. Ever applied to this company before?   No
    Where?   N/A   When?   N/A

Education

11. Name and Location of Last School   Jefferson H.S., Allentown, PA
    Subjects Studied   Business and foreign languages
12. Graduated? Yes _____   No   X

Former Employers

(List below last two employers, beginning with most recent.)

13. Date Month/Year	Name and Address of Employer	Salary	Position	Reason for leaving
6/98	Quality Supply Co. Allentown, PA	$4.75/hr	Fill-in receptionist	Back to school
6/97	YWCA Allentown, PA	N/A	Volunteer office worker	Back to school

References: List the names of three persons not related to you whom you have known at least one year.

Name/Business Address	Business Phone	Years Acquainted
14. Dr. Walter A Smith, Principal Jefferson H.S., Allentown, PA	(215) 555-1019	3
15. Ms. Mary Frances Tate, Teacher Jefferson H.S., Allentown, PA	(215) 555-1019	3
16. Mr. Glen Ramos, Owner Quality Supply Co., Allentown, PA	(215) 555-4593	2

Signature: Veronica Harjo   **Date:** 6/3/99

Graphic Organizers   A *graphic organizer* is a visual that helps you "see" what you are thinking. You can use graphic organizers to find a subject to write about, to gather information, and to organize your information. In your final writing, graphics can also help your readers visualize what you are discussing in your text.

▪ **Charts**   *Charts* group related pieces of information, allowing you to see the overall arrangement clearly. By dividing a subject into its logical parts, you can analyze and organize your details. In the following chart, a writer who is describing Mexico's major historic cultures in 1500 has organized information in three columns. Notice that the chart has both horizontal and vertical headings.

Major Cultures of Mexico in 1500		
People	Location	Characteristics
Aztecs	Central Mexico	centralized government; large, efficient army; 365-day calendar; advanced engineering and architectural skills
Mayas	Yucatán peninsula	written language; base-20 mathematical system; 365-day calendar; sophisticated artistry, especially sculpture
Mixtecs	Southwest Mexico	fine stone and metal work; beautiful carvings in wood; painted polychrome pottery
Zapotecs	Oaxaca and Isthmus of Tehuantepec	priestly hierarchy; ancestor worship, artistic heritage influenced by early Maya

▪ **Clustering**   See **Prewriting Techniques** on page 1040.

▪ **Mapping**   See **Prewriting Techniques** on page 1041.

▪ **Sequence chain**   A *sequence chain* is a diagram that helps you see how one event leads to another. It works well when you are narrating or explaining a process. In the following example, the writer uses a sequence chain to show the general steps for making bread.

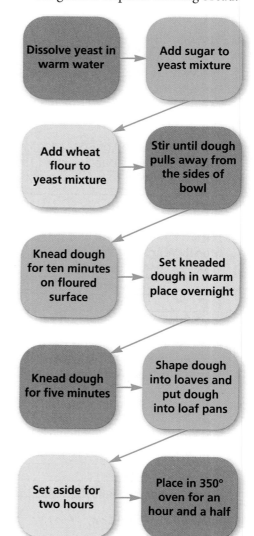

■ **Time line** A *time line* organizes information chronologically on a horizontal line, with the first or earliest events on the left end and the most recent or latest events on the right end of the line. Time lines are most often used in compositions which discuss a series of events that occurred over a relatively long period.

Stages of Pre-Columbian Cultures of Mexico

See also also **time lines** on pages 933 and 964.

■ **Venn diagram** A *Venn diagram* uses intersecting circles to show the similarities and differences between two subjects. The area of overlap between the two circles shows how the two subjects are similar; the remaining areas show how they are different. (See also page 962.)

Informal or Personal Letters The content and appearance of a personal, or social, letter is less formal than a business letter because the purpose is less formal. Personal letters are usually handwritten rather than typed. When you write a personal letter, use the modified block form, but do not include an inside address. Also follow the tips in the following chart. (See also **Business Letters** on page 1023.)

Informal Letter Guidelines

1. Include the five parts of an informal letter: heading, salutation, body, closing, and signature.

2. Position the heading, which contains your street address and the date, in the upper right-hand corner.

3. Place a comma after both the salutation and the closing, and line up the closing with the heading.

4. Written letters should be neat and clear. If you type your letter, be sure to sign by hand.

5. An informal letter should have a friendly tone, stemming from informal language.

6. Indent each of your body paragraphs.

There are three common types of informal or personal letters that you will probably write on a regular basis. Each is considered important by most standards of etiquette.

■ **Invitations** An informal *invitation* should contain specific information about the occasion, the time and place (with directions for getting there), and other details your guest will need to know.

■ **Letters of regret** Send a *letter of regret* if you have been invited somewhere and are unable to go. A written reply is especially appropriate if you were sent a written invitation with the letters *R.S.V.P.* (French abbreviation for *please reply*).

■ **Thank-you letters** A *thank-you letter* tells someone that you appreciate his or her gift of time, effort, or expense on your behalf. Try to say more than just "thank-you": Give details about how the person's present or efforts were helpful or appreciated.

Manuscript Form   When you formally share your composition with others, remember that its appearance is important. The guidelines below will help improve the appearance of your paper.

Guidelines for Manuscript Form

Use only one side of a sheet of 8 1/2″ × 11″ paper.

Write in blue or black ink, or type.

If you write by hand, do not skip lines. If you type, double-space the lines.

Leave margins of about one inch at the top, sides, and bottom of a page.

Indent the first line of each paragraph.

Number all pages except the first page. Place the number in either the upper or lower right-hand corner.

All pages should be neat and clean. You may make a few small, subtle corrections with correction fluid.

Follow your teacher's instructions for placing your name, the date, your class, and the title of your paper.

(See also page 920.)

Memos   A memorandum, or *memo,* is a written message for conducting business within an organization. Most memos are for announcing meetings, sharing summaries of meetings, or requesting action or information. Memos are concise messages that generally cover only one topic, and, although they do not include all parts of a letter, they still tell the reader *who, what, when, where, why,* and *how.* Electronic mail (e-mail) is used in many businesses for memos because of its speed and the ease of record keeping. (See also **E-mail** on page 1031.)

Memo Guidelines

Use the words *DATE, TO, FROM,* and *SUBJECT* to guide you as you write your memo.

State your request clearly and briefly.

If you are asking for action or information, include a deadline.

Include your phone number so the recipient of the memo may call you with questions.

Send a copy (cc) of the memo to people who need to know about the meeting but do not need to attend. The abbreviation *cc* stands for "carbon copy," a reference to a method of making copies by using carbon paper.

```
   DATE: March 2, 2000
     TO: Production Control Staff
   FROM: Victor Jones, Production
         Manager, ext. 7890
     cc: Leo Park, Production
         Director
SUBJECT: New circuit board

There will be a meeting Friday,
March 6, from 2:00 to 3:00 P.M.
in Room 3A to discuss the new
circuit board.
```

(See also page 134.)

Messages   Taking a *message* requires listening to information, usually by telephone, and then communicating that information to someone else. Think of the five "W" questions when writing a message.

Who is the message from and for **whom**?
What is the message?
When was the message written (date and time)?
Where can the sender be reached, if necessary?
Why is the message important?

Outlines An *outline* is a plan—a way of grouping and organizing information to show relationships among ideas so that writers can present ideas clearly as they draft. When a paper is finished, a formal outline can act as a sort of table of contents that also summarizes.

■ **Formal outlines** A *formal outline* is a highly structured, clearly labeled list of an essay's contents. It has a set pattern, using letters and numbers to label main headings and subheadings or levels of subordination among ideas. It may be a **topic outline,** which uses single words and phrases, or a **sentence outline,** which uses complete sentences for each item. Formal outlines may be used for planning, but they are also written after the essay is complete to provide an overview for the reader. Here is a portion of a formal outline about how to look for a job.

```
Title: How to Find Work
Thesis statement: If you want to
be among the millions of teens
who are employed part time, fol-
low these tips on finding and
landing a job to increase your
chances of success.
  I. Job leads
     A. Employer leads
        1. Signs
        2. Newspaper advertisements
        3. Employment agencies
     B. Contacts
        1. Former employers
        2. Friends and family
           members
        3. Business acquaintances
        4. School counselor
 II. Job applications
     A. Purpose
     B. Techniques
        1. First impression
        2. Skills and accomplishments
     C. Follow-up
```

■ **Informal outlines or early plans** An *early plan,* sometimes called a *rough outline,* gives you a rough idea of the kinds and the order of information you want in your composition. Early plans do not have a set form. You simply sort your ideas or facts into groups and arrange the groups in order. To sort your information into groups, ask yourself:

■ *Which items belong together?*
■ *What do they have in common?*
■ *Which items don't fit anywhere?*

Then, give each group a heading that shows how the items in it are related. Next, arrange your information in a way that will make sense to your readers: *chronological order, spatial order, logical order,* or *order of importance.* (See also page 474.) Some papers will fit easily into one of these organizational patterns; others will combine two or more types of order. Ask yourself: "Is the purpose and the order of each grouping of details understandable?"

Informal outlines can be lists, concept maps, or boxes. The important thing is to show how ideas relate to each other. Remember, too, that your thesis and details drive the type of organization you choose to order your ideas. The map below is one example of an informal outline for an essay on teenagers finding jobs.

Paragraphs A paragraph is a group of sentences that presents and supports a main idea, often stated in a topic sentence. Paragraphs are the primary building blocks in a composition. Paragraphs that present and support a main idea often have a three-part structure like this one.

Topic Sentence

Body

Clincher Sentence

Although most of the paragraphs in a single composition will often be of one major type, many compositions contain more than one type of paragraph. The four types of paragraphs vary according to their purpose.

■ **Descriptive paragraphs** A *descriptive paragraph* lets your readers "see" your topic, whether it is a person, an object, or a scene. Specific details help to create a clear picture for the reader. Often, descriptive paragraphs do not have a stated main idea—a topic sentence. Instead, the details provide clues to an implied main idea, sometimes referred to as a dominant impression. Descriptive paragraphs often use a **spatial order** and usually contain **sensory details** (appeals to the senses).

Sensory details   The old store, lighted only by three fifty-watt bulbs, smelled of coal oil and baking bread. In the middle of the rectangular room, Spatial details   where the oak floor sagged a little, stood an iron stove. To the right was a wooden table with an Spatial details   unfinished game of checkers and a stool made from an apple-tree stump.

William Least Heat-Moon,
Blue Highways

■ **Expository paragraphs** An *expository paragraph* is used to explain and inform. It may explain how to do something or how something works. It may also explain facts or ideas. Because explanations are clarified by organizing information into categories, expository paragraphs frequently use **logical order.** They also frequently contain factual and statistical information. Expository paragraphs are the kinds of paragraphs you will use most often on essay examinations and in essays for your English class. An expository paragraph often has a stated main idea in the form of a topic sentence. The following expository paragraph discusses the impact that central Italian earthquakes in 1997 had on national art treasures and monuments. Notice the author's use of specific facts and details to explain the main idea to readers.

Although the city of Assisi garnered most of the publicity, the impact of the earthquake was far more widespread. It left cracks in the frescoes by Filippo Lippi in the cathedral of Spoleto and caused serious structural damage to the cathedrals in Urbino and Perugia. It also brought on the partial collapse of important buildings in many other towns within a 50-mile radius of Assisi. The domed 18th-century clock tower of the town hall in Foligno became the national symbol for the disaster. Throughout October, successive tremors undermined it, brick by brick, until, as though timed for the evening news, the tower toppled. The spectacular collapse was shown live on television at 5:30 on October 14.

Jonathan Turner, "Culture Shock,"
ARTnews

- **Narrative paragraphs**   A *narrative paragraph* tells a story or illustrates events, usually in **chronological order.**

Event 1

Event 2

Event 3

Event 4

> First came a drizzle. Then groundwater poured from the walls, and I was plunging through a waterfall. The darkest darkroom doesn't compare to the pitch black inside the mine shaft. I couldn't look upward at the patch of daylight above for fear of drowning. After about three minutes—an eternity—the unseen operator threw on the brake, jerking me to a stop two feet above the mud. To no one in particular, I sighed, "Welcome to the glamorous world of emeralds."
>
> Fred Ward, "The Timeless Mystique of Emeralds," *National Geographic*

- **Persuasive Paragraphs**   A *persuasive paragraph* expresses a writer's opinion or issues a call to action. Such paragraphs are usually arranged by **order of importance** or **logical order.**

> I only ask of the government to be treated as all other men are treated. If I cannot go home, let me have a home in some country where my people will not die so fast. . . . Let me be a free man—free to travel, free to stop, free to work, free to trade where I choose, free to choose my own teachers, free to follow the religion of my fathers, free to think and talk and act for myself—and I will obey every law, or submit to the penalty.
>
> Chief Joseph (In-Mut-Too-Yah-Lat-Lat), "An Indian's Views of Indian Affairs"

Prewriting Techniques   You may use the following techniques to find a topic to write about, to gather information about a topic, or to explore and learn about the topic. Although the prewriting techniques are presented separately, you may often use more than one technique at a time. You may also find that you prefer to use some techniques more than others.

- **Asking the *5W-How?* questions**   Ask yourself the reporter's questions—*Who? What? When? Where? Why?* and *How?*—to explore further. Although not every question applies to every situation, the *5W-How* questions are a good basic approach. You can also ask the *5W-How* questions more than once about various aspects of your topic.

  EXAMPLE

  Who are some local gardeners?

  What kinds of plants do they grow?

  When do they plant their gardens?

  Where did they learn to garden?

  Why do they prefer certain plants?

  How do they fertilize the soil?

- **Asking *What if?* questions**   To prompt some creative thinking, ask a series of *What if?* questions about a topic. Imagine everyday situations that pique interest or curiosity.

  EXAMPLE

  What if I could change my circumstances? (What if I were an only child or what if I were *not* an only child? What if I had lived during the Middle Ages?)

  What if a familiar thing no longer existed? (What if we had no music? What if we had no public schools?)

  What if major social changes were made overnight? (What if racial prejudice no longer existed? What if everyone earned the same amount of money?)

■ **Brainstorming** *Brainstorming* is simply letting your mind wander freely. Write down a topic, and then list as quickly as you can all the ideas that come into your mind. Resist the urge to evaluate your ideas; remember that you are trying to come up with as many ideas as possible. Even ideas that seem off the topic may be valuable later. Keep going until you run out of ideas. (Brainstorming is also a good group activity. When you brainstorm in a group, it is helpful to have just one person recording ideas.)

■ **Clustering** *Clustering* (also called **webbing**) is another technique useful for spurring creative ideas. First, write a topic in the middle of your paper and circle it. Then, in the space around the topic, write whatever related ideas occur to you. Circle the new ideas and draw lines to connect the new ideas with the original topic. Continue to branch off as necessary.

EXAMPLE

■ **Cubing** Investigate a topic by imagining a cube that has one of the following directions on each of its six sides: *Describe it. Compare it. Associate it. Analyze it. Apply it. Argue for or against it.* Focus on your topic, writing for three minutes about each side of the cube.

EXAMPLE

Garlic

Describe it. (Tell how it can be used or what you can do with it.)

Garlic is a bulb-shaped herb related to onions and leeks. It is used in cooking, particularly in Mediterranean-style recipes. It was often used in ancient and medieval times for medicinal purposes. Ancient Egyptians considered garlic to be a sacred plant and placed it in the tombs of their kings. Newborn English princes in the fourteenth and fifteenth centuries had their lips dabbed with its juice—for luck or for their health?

■ **Freewriting** When you *freewrite,* you write whatever pops into your head. Think of a word or topic that interests you, and write about it for three to five minutes. Do not worry about using complete sentences or proper punctuation. Just write as much as you can. If you cannot think of anything new to write, copy the same word or phrase until something comes to mind.

EXAMPLE

> JOGGING. Why jog? The gym teacher says it's better just to walk fast. Nora jogs and Fumiyo speed walks. I bought running shoes. Jogging. Jogging. Maybe jogging hurts your knees. How? First time I jogged—sore legs for a week. Some guy made jogging popular. Don't know his name. Must have good running shoes. Ran three miles last week and still my legs hurt. Jog tomorrow.

- **Listening with a focus**   Your ears are another pair of powerful prewriting tools. You can gather ideas for writing by listening to radio and television programs, audiotapes, and experts during personal or telephone interviews. You must *prepare* to listen, though. Write down your topic, and then brainstorm what you already know about it. Make a list of questions that you would like to have answered as you listen. This list of questions should help guide and focus your listening. Listen carefully with your questions in front of you. As much as possible, eliminate mental and physical distractions.

As you listen, take careful notes. Listen especially for the speaker's message. However, don't try to write every word—use phrases and abbreviations and listen for main ideas and significant details.

When you are through listening, ask questions if possible. Then, while what you have heard is fresh on your mind, consult your notes and write a summary of them. (See also **Listening** on page 990.)

- **Mapping**   *Mapping* resembles clustering in form but is used to organize your ideas. It is a helpful graphic for determining whether you have enough support for each main idea. Notice how the following map groups main ideas and supporting details.

EXAMPLE

RESEARCHING
(what is out there?)
- bike magazines
- bike stores
- friends' bikes
- World Wide Web

shopping for a new bicycle

PURPOSE
- transport to school and town
- off-road trail riding
- night riding
- all kinds of weather

FINANCING
- weekend job to raise money
- last year's models are usually marked down
- reflectors and lights taken from old bike to save money
- used bikes are cheaper

- **Pentad**   Investigate a topic by imagining a five-pointed star. Each of its points has one of the following questions: *What is happening? Who is causing it to happen? How is it being done? Where and when is it being done? Why is it happening?* After answering each question, determine a focus. You can find a focus by considering the points you wrote about most and then identifying an interaction between those points. This focus will probably be your thesis statement. A pentad is a particularly good prewriting technique to use when you are writing about literature.

EXAMPLE

What is happening?
A monument is being dedicated at a battle site in Concord, Massachusetts.

Why is it happening?
It is to remind future generations of the sacrifice made by the colonists to fight for independence.

Poem:
"Concord Hymn"
by Ralph Waldo Emerson

When and where is it being done?
April 19, 1836, in Concord, Massachusetts.

How is it being done?
The poem is a hymn; perhaps it is being sung at the commemoration.

Who is causing it to happen?
It is not clear; the poem is set in April 1836, so it could be the descendants of the American colonists who fought the battle.

■ **Reading with a focus**   Reading books, newspapers, or magazines can also help you gather ideas for writing. When you read to determine a topic, use the index and table of contents to narrow your search. Skim the material, searching only for information about your topic. When you find relevant information, read carefully and take notes.

■ **Using your five senses**   Observe your topic through all five senses: sight, hearing, smell, taste, and touch. If you take the time to focus on all the sensory details around you, you will have an almost limitless supply of specific details that will make your writing come alive for your readers.

EXAMPLE

Camping Trip

sight: trout leaping from the water; moonlit nights around the campfire
sound: rush of the water; chatter of the crickets; crackling fire; campers shouting and laughing

smell: tangy odor of wet leaves and grass; musty smell of wet swimsuits drying; savory odor of fish frying
taste: toasted marshmallows; tart lemonade; salty trail mix
touch: rough, splintery firewood; shoulders aching from carrying backpacks

■ **Visualizing**   *Visualizing* means making mental images of something in your "mind's eye." As you "see" your scene, try to use other senses as well.

EXAMPLE

I am inside an airplane. Outside the oval window I can see the clouds we will have to break through on takeoff. The engines roar, giving off a sickening smell of fuel. The plane sways as it travels down the runway, and I feel giddy as the plane lifts up from the ground. Immediately the plane climbs, through the clouds into brilliant sunshine where we will stay for two hours. I push my seat back and relax.

■ **Writer's notebook, log, or journal**   Use a special notebook or file folder to record your experiences and observations, feelings and opinions, brilliant ideas, and questions. You can also collect print material that has special meaning to you, such as poems, songs, cartoons, and newspaper articles. For paste-in entries, write notes beside them. Why did you like a particular quotation or cartoon? Try to write in your notebook daily, and date your entries. Don't worry about punctuation, grammar, or usage. This journal is for you. Soon your journal will be a sourcebook full of ideas for you to use in future compositions.

■ **Writer's notebook, log, or journal**

Résumé   A *résumé* is a summary of your background and experience. For many job positions, you submit a résumé along with your letter of application. There are many ways to arrange the information on a résumé. Whatever style you select, be sure that your résumé looks neat and businesslike. The example below shows a typical résumé form.

VERONICA HARJO
1632 Garden View Drive
Allentown, PA 18103
Telephone: (215) 555-7023
E-mail: Veronic@allentwn.net

EDUCATION:
Junior, Jefferson High School
Grade-point average: 3.0 (B)
Major studies: Business and foreign language courses

WORK EXPERIENCE:
Summer 1999   Fill-in Receptionist
               Quality Supply Company
               Allentown, PA
Summer 1998   Volunteer office worker, YWCA
               Allentown, PA

SKILLS:
Typing: 50 words per minute
Business: Dictating and calculating machines and copy machines;
               personal computers and word processors; fax machine
Languages: Spanish (fluent reading, writing, and speaking)

EXTRACURRICULAR ACTIVITIES:
Vice President, Future Business Leaders of America; member of Spanish Club

REFERENCES:
Dr. Walter A. Smith, Principal
(215) 555-1019
Jefferson High School
Allentown, PA

Ms. Mary Frances Tate, Teacher
(215) 555-1019
Jefferson High School
Allentown, PA

Mr. Glen Ramos, Owner
(215) 555-4593
Quality Supply Company
Allentown, PA

Symbols For Revising And Proofreading

Symbol	Example	Meaning Of Symbol
≡	Spence college	Capitalize a lowercase letter.
/	our Best friend	Lowercase a capital letter.
∧	on the Fourth of July	Insert a missing word, letter, or punctuation mark.
∧	endurance (a)	Change a letter.
⌐	the capital lake of Iowa	Replace a word.
ℓ	hoped for to go	Leave out a word, letter, or punctuation mark.
ℨ	on that occassion	Leave out and close up.
⌒	today's home work	Close up space.
∪	nieghbor	Change the order of letters.
tr	the counsel general of the corporation	Transpose the words. (Write *tr* in nearby margin.)
¶	¶ "Wait!" I shouted.	Begin a new paragraph.
⊙	She was right	Add a period.
∧	Yes that's true.	Add a comma.
#	centerfield	Add a space.
⊙	the following items	Add a colon.
∧	Evansville, Indiana Columbus, Ohio	Add a semicolon.
=	self control	Add a hyphen.
∨	Ms. Ruiz's office	Add an apostrophe.
stet	a very tall building	Keep the crossed-out material. (Write *stet* in nearby margin.)

Revising and Proofreading Symbols

When you are revising and proofreading, indicate any changes by using the symbols in the chart above.

Tone   *Tone* refers to the feelings you convey through your voice when you write or speak. It lets your readers or listeners know how you feel about them as well as about your subject. In writing, tone is conveyed three ways—through choice of details, sentence length and structure, and word choice.

■ **Choice of Details**   The *choice of details* in your writing lets your reader know what is important to you as a writer. For example, providing readers with lists of facts or statistics sets the tone as serious and objective, while writing about childhood memories of a place conveys a more intimate tone.

■ **Sentence Length and Structure**   The *length* and *structure* of the sentences in your writing also influences your tone. If your writing is full of long, complex sentences, then it is clear to readers that you are writing about a serious subject in a formal way. Short, snappy sentences often suggest a sense of playfulness.

■ **Word Choice**   Your *word choice* lets your readers know how seriously you take the subject and what relationship you have established with the audience. For example, the choice of formal language conveys a more serious, concerned tone and a more detached relationship with readers than informal language. Conversely, the use of informal language, such as contractions and colloquialisms, suggests a more friendly, personal tone. The **connotations** of the words you choose also greatly inform your readers about your tone. For example, "that guy" is informal or casual, while "the gentleman" is polite and respectful.

Keep in mind that the *occasion* for which you are writing always affects your tone. The occasion is the reason for writing. Often the occasion is to fulfill an assignment for school, but it might also be to communicate with a friend or family member or to instruct someone younger than yourself. In thinking about occasion, ask yourself these three questions:

1. Why am I writing—for school, fun, or brainstorming ideas?
2. Who will read my writing—a teacher, a friend, or myself?
3. When or where will the reader read my writing—in front of the class, alone at home, or on a bus?

Transitions   *Transitions,* or *transitional expressions,* are words and phrases that show readers how ideas and details fit together. To connect your ideas within paragraphs and between paragraphs, learn to use transitional expressions such as these.

time	at last, meanwhile, then, now, later, at first, by this time
place	here, there, beyond, farther on, to the left, next, over, between
addition	and, besides, for example, furthermore
contrast	but, still, although, however, nevertheless
conclusion	thus, consequently, in conclusion, looking back, in review, finally

(See also pages 461 and 961.)

Voice   The way a piece of writing "sounds," or its *voice,* is determined by sentence structure, word choice, and tone. Although audience and purpose influence your writing voice, always try to sound honest and natural. Ultimately, your voice is unique, your own, no matter what you are writing.

Writing to Learn   You can use your writing skills for more than just writing essays. Writing can help you to understand the relationships of ideas in the texts that you read; for example, you can use mapping to see relationships between main ideas and details. Writing can also be a way of learning. For example, if you freewrite about information from one of your classes, you will see what you know and what you need to review.

Grammar at a Glance

┌─HELP─┐

Grammar at a Glance is an alphabetical list of special terms and expressions with examples and references to further information. When you encounter a grammar or usage problem in the revising or proofreading stage of your writing, look for help in this section first. You may find all you need to know right here. If you need more information, **Grammar at a Glance** will show you where in the book to turn for a more complete explanation. If you do not find what you are looking for in **Grammar at a Glance,** turn to the index.

abbreviation An abbreviation is a shortened form of a word or a phrase.

■ **capitalization of**

TITLES USED WITH NAMES	**M**s.	**L**t. **C**ol.	**S**r.	**RN**
KINDS OF ORGANIZATIONS	**L**td.	**I**nc.	**D**ept.	**C**orp.
PARTS OF ADDRESSES	**A**ve.	**S**t.	**D**r.	**P.O. B**ox
NAMES OF STATES	[without ZIP Codes]		**L**a.	**F**la.
			Mich.	**S. D**ak.
	[with ZIP Codes]		**LA**	**FL**
			MI	**SD**
TIMES	**A.M.** **P.M.** **B.C.** **A.D.**			

■ **punctuation of** (See page 779.)

WITH PERIODS	(See preceding examples.)
WITHOUT PERIODS	SAT DNA NCAA IRS
	DC (D**.**C**.** without ZIP Code)
	ml mi gal °F mm
	[Exception: inch = in**.**]

action verb An action verb expresses physical or mental activity. (See page 495.)

EXAMPLE   The herd of zebra **galloped** across the plains.

active voice Active voice is the voice a verb is in when it expresses an action done by its subject. (See page 676. See also **voice.**)

EXAMPLE   Mr. Intrator, the museum director, gingerly **handled** the Limoges vase.

adjective An adjective modifies a noun or a pronoun. (See page 491.)

EXAMPLE   **The** Schmidts live in **a magnificent, spacious** apartment.

adjective clause An adjective clause is a subordinate clause that modifies a noun or a pronoun. (See page 560.)

EXAMPLE   The years **that Mom likes to remember** are the late 1970s.

adjective phrase A prepositional phrase that modifies a noun or a pronoun is called an adjective phrase. (See page 536.)

EXAMPLE   Cars **in Europe and Asia** are generally smaller than cars **in North America.**

adverb An adverb modifies a verb, an adjective, or another adverb. (See page 499.)

EXAMPLE   "I **really** like that desk," said Emily. "It's **almost** perfect."

adverb clause An adverb clause is a subordinate clause that modifies a verb, an adjective, or an adverb. (See page 565.)

EXAMPLE   **While he was driving,** Jerry listened to news reports on the radio.

adverb phrase A prepositional phrase that modifies a verb, an adjective, or an adverb is called an adverb phrase. (See page 537.)

EXAMPLE   **Before dinner,** Dr. Laplace was called away.

agreement Agreement is the correspondence, or match, between grammatical forms. Grammatical forms agree when they have the same number, gender, and person.

■ **of pronouns and antecedents** (See page 593.)

SINGULAR   **Nathan** cannot find **his** driver's license.
PLURAL   The **dancers** train hard every day, striving to perfect **their** performances.

SINGULAR   Does **everyone** in the cast know **his or her** lines?
PLURAL   Do **all** of the actors know **their** lines?

SINGULAR	Neither **Mariah** nor **Claire** has decided whether **she** will play basketball this season.
PLURAL	**Mariah** and **Claire** have not decided whether **they** will play basketball this season.

- **of subjects and verbs** (See page 578.)

SINGULAR	The **chief executive officer is** confident that the corporation will remain competitive.
	The **chief executive officer,** along with the stockholders, **is** confident that the corporation will remain competitive.
PLURAL	The **stockholders are** confident that the corporation will remain competitive.
	The **stockholders,** along with the chief executive officer, **are** confident that the corporation will remain competitive.
SINGULAR	**Each** of the planets **revolves** around the sun.
PLURAL	**All** of the planets **revolve** around the sun.
SINGULAR	Normally, **Matthew or Julia writes** the club's monthly newsletter.
PLURAL	Normally, **Matthew and Julia write** the club's monthly newsletter.
SINGULAR	Here **is** my **report** on the history of the Japanese theater.
PLURAL	Here **are** my **notes** on the history of the Japanese theater.
SINGULAR	**One hundred dollars is** what we paid for this painting.
PLURAL	**One hundred dollars** with consecutive serial numbers **were found** in an old shoe box.
SINGULAR	*Clubhouse Detectives* **is** a good movie.
PLURAL	The young **detectives are investigating** the disappearance of a neighbor.
SINGULAR	**Is physics offered** at your school?
PLURAL	**Are** my **sunglasses** in your car?
SINGULAR	Soledad is one applicant **who qualifies** for the job.
PLURAL	Soledad is one of the applicants **who qualify** for the job.
SINGULAR	Soledad is the only one of the applicants **who qualifies** for the job.

ambiguous reference Ambiguous reference occurs when a pronoun incorrectly refers to either of two antecedents. (See page 630.)

AMBIGUOUS   One difference between coniferous trees and broadleaf trees is that they produce cones instead of flowers.

CLEAR   One difference between coniferous trees and broadleaf trees is that coniferous trees produce cones instead of flowers.

antecedent An antecedent is the word or words that a pronoun stands for. (See page 630.)

EXAMPLE   At **Patti** and **Paul**'s anniversary dinner, **Adrianna** sang a song that **she** had written especially for **them.** [*Patti* and *Paul* are the antecedents of *them*. *Adrianna* is the antecedent of *she*.]

apostrophe

■ **to form contractions** (See page 831. See also **contraction.**)

EXAMPLES   shouldn't   you'll   let's   '99

■ **to form plurals of letters, numerals, symbols, and words used as words** (See page 832.)

EXAMPLES   *x*'s and *o*'s   too many *and*'s and *so*'s

1990's [*or* 1990s]   CD's [*or* CDs]

■ **to show possession** (See page 827.)

EXAMPLES   the farmer's wheat crop

the farmers' wheat crops

men's fashions

someone's keys

during the President and the First Lady's trip to South Africa

one week's [*or* five days'] wages

appositive An appositive is a noun or a pronoun placed beside another noun or pronoun to identify or explain it. (See page 550.)

EXAMPLE   I like the novels of the writer **James Jones.**

appositive phrase An appositive phrase consists of an appositive and its modifiers. (See page 551.)

EXAMPLE James Jones, **the author of _From Here to Eternity_,** lived for many years in Paris.

article The articles, _a_, _an_, and _the_, are the most frequently used adjectives. (See page 492.)

EXAMPLE **The** watch, **an** old possession of my mother's, was **a** fine example of Swiss workmanship.

**bad, badly** (See page 696.)

NONSTANDARD Do you think this sushi smells badly?
STANDARD Do you think this sushi smells **bad**?

base form The base form, or infinitive, is one of the four principal parts of a verb. (See page 644.)

EXAMPLE We thought we heard something **move** downstairs.

brackets (See page 811.)

EXAMPLES In his introduction to Victorian poetry, the teacher explained, "Many people mistakenly attribute **[Elizabeth Barrett]** Browning's 'Sonnet 43,' which begins with the famous line 'How do I love thee? Let me count the ways,' to William Shakespeare."

Of all of the Navajo gods, the most revered is Changing Woman (often called Earth Woman **[**the belief is that her spirit inhabits the earth**]**).

capitalization

- **of abbreviations and acronyms** (See page 766. See also **abbreviation.**)

- **of first words** (See page 751.)

EXAMPLES **M**y sister writes in her journal every night.

Omar asked, "**W**ould you like to play on my team?"

Dear Ms. Reuben:

Sincerely yours,

■ of proper nouns and proper adjectives (See page 753.)

Proper Noun	Common Noun
Richard the Lion-Hearted	leader
Australia	continent
Costa Rica	country
Santa Clara County	county
Quebec Province	province
Liberty Island	island
Narragansett Bay	body of water
Mount Makalu	mountain
Mesa Verde National Park	park
Petrified Forest	forest
Timpanogos Cave	cave
the Northwest	region
Twenty-fourth Street	street
Parent-Teacher Association (PTA)	organization
Democratic Party (or party)	political party
Industrial Revolution	historical event
Middle Ages	historical period
World Series	special event
Labor Day	holiday
January, Saturday	calendar items
Oglala Sioux	people
Shinto	religion
God (*but* the god Thor)	deity
Rosh Hashana	holy days
Veda	sacred writing
First Interstate World Center	building
Presidential Medal of Freedom	award
Uranus	planet
Beta Centauri	star
Corona Borealis	constellation
Dona Paz	ship
Discovery	spacecraft
Chemistry I (*but* chemistry)	school subject
Hindi	language

■ **of titles** (See page 762.)

EXAMPLES   **M**ayor Biondi [preceding a name]

Bill Biondi, the **m**ayor of our town [following a name]

Thank you, **M**ayor. [direct address]

Aunt Katarina [*but* my aunt Katarina]

*Glow-in-the-**D**ark **C**onstellations: **A** **F**ield **G**uide for **Y**oung **S**targazers* [book]

A River Runs Through It [movie or book]

Planet Safari [TV program]

*Landscape with the **F**light into **E**gypt* [work of art]

*Hymns from the **R**ig **V**eda* [musical composition]

"**W**onderful **W**orld" [song]

"**T**he **J**ilting of **G**ranny **W**eatherall" [short story]

"**S**topping by **W**oods on a **S**nowy **E**vening" [poem]

National Geographic World [magazine]

the *Denver Rocky Mountain News* [newspaper]

Hi and Lois [comic strip]

case of pronouns Case is the form a pronoun takes to show how the pronoun is used in a sentence. (See page 606.)

NOMINATIVE   Last summer, **she** and **I** traveled to Boston and walked the Freedom Trail.

The only juniors on the prom committee are Chiaki and **he.**

Either one, Margo or **she,** will be glad to accompany you.

We senior citizens are organizing a community walkathon.

Is Gioacchino Rossini the composer **who** wrote the opera *The Barber of Seville*?

Do you know **who** the guest speaker will be?

I helped Simon more than **she.** [meaning *more than she helped Simon*]

OBJECTIVE   Quincy accompanied **her** to Freedom Hall to see the African Heritage exhibit.

Miguel taught **them** some traditional Mexican folk songs.

The first tennis match was between Lupe and **me.**

The Nobel Peace Prize was awarded to both leaders, John Hume and **him.**

Our math teacher explained to **us** students what a magic square is.

Then the math teacher asked **us** to create some magic squares.

My neighbor Mr. Mukai often quotes Shakespeare, **whom** he considers the greatest writer of all time.

One ruler about **whom** I would like to learn more is Hatshepsut, the first woman pharaoh.

I helped Simon more than **her.** [meaning *more than I helped her*]

POSSESSIVE **Your** computer can process data faster than **mine** can.

Her sliding safely into home plate in the bottom of the ninth inning tied the game.

clause A clause is a group of words that contains a verb and its subject and that is used as a sentence or as part of a sentence. (See page 558.)

INDEPENDENT CLAUSE Robert Graves was an English poet and writer

SUBORDINATE CLAUSE who was famous for the novel *I, Claudius*

colon (See page 806.)

■ **before lists**

EXAMPLES Central America comprises the following nations**:** Belize, Costa Rica, El Salvador, Guatemala, Honduras, Nicaragua, and Panama.

Today, the discussion in our world history class focused on the beliefs and teachings of three philosophers of ancient Greece**:** Socrates, Plato, and Aristotle.

■ **in conventional situations**

EXAMPLES 8**:**45 P.M.

Genesis 7**:**1–17

*Bulfinch's Mythology***:** *The Age of Fable, The Age of Chivalry, Legends of Charlemagne*

Dear Dr. Sabatini**:**

comma (See page 783.)

■ **in a series**

EXAMPLES   Ms. Camara explained the differences between a meteor, a meteoroid, and a meteorite.

On his vacation in Alaska, Jason went kayaking, bob-sledding, and rock climbing.

■ **in compound sentences**

EXAMPLES   Alberto has written three drafts of his essay on transcendentalism, and he is not satisfied with any of them.

I nominated my best friend, Elena, for junior class president, but she surprised me by declining the nomination.

■ **with nonessential phrases and clauses**

EXAMPLES   Pa-out-She, an ancient Chinese scholar, is credited with compiling the first dictionary.

Carlos Chavez, who composed symphonies and ballets, founded the Symphony Orchestra of Mexico.

■ **with introductory elements**

EXAMPLES   On the surface of the moon, a person would weigh about one sixth of what he or she weighs on the earth's surface.

After they had read several of the fables attributed to Aesop, the students discussed the moral lessons that the fables teach.

■ **with interrupters**

EXAMPLES   The most fascinating exhibit in the museum, in my opinion, is the huge Egyptian tomb that visitors are allowed to explore.

Nocturnal animals, such as armadillos, hunt and feed at night and rest during the day.

■ **in conventional situations**

EXAMPLES   On Friday, July 9, 1999, the Wilsons set out on a road trip from Bangor, Maine, to Seattle, Washington.

I mailed the letter to 645 Pinecrest Ave., Atlanta, GA 30328-6645, on 16 October 2000.

comma splice A comma splice is a run-on sentence in which sentences have been joined with only a comma between them. (See page 432. See also **fused sentence** and **run-on sentence.**)

COMMA SPLICE	I asked the librarian to suggest a contemporary novel about family values, she highly recommended *Mama Flora's Family* by Alex Haley and David Stevens.
REVISED	I asked the librarian to suggest a contemporary novel about family values**, and** she highly recommended *Mama Flora's Family* by Alex Haley and David Stevens.
REVISED	I asked the librarian to suggest a contemporary novel about family values**;** she highly recommended *Mama Flora's Family* by Alex Haley and David Stevens.
REVISED	I asked the librarian to suggest a contemporary novel about family values**. S**he highly recommended *Mama Flora's Family* by Alex Haley and David Stevens.

comparison of modifiers (See page 698.)

◾ **comparison of adjectives and adverbs**

Positive	Comparative	Superlative
soft	soft**er**	soft**est**
early	earl**ier**	earl**iest**
effective	**more (less)** effective	**most (least)** effective
rapidly	**more (less)** rapidly	**most (least)** rapidly
far	**farther/further**	**farthest/furthest**

◾ **comparing two**

EXAMPLES   Our science teacher asked us, "Which is **heavier,** a pound of feathers or a pound of lead?"

Which of these two automobiles do you think operates **more efficiently**?

◾ **comparing more than two**

EXAMPLES   Founded in 1636, Harvard is the **oldest** university in the United States.

Of the four debaters on the team, Yosuke argued **most persuasively.**

complement A complement is a word or word group that completes the meaning of a verb. (See page 520.)

EXAMPLES   Papa sent **me letters** and **postcards.**

This room is **quiet;** it will be my **study.**

complex sentence A complex sentence has one independent clause and at least one subordinate clause. (See page 571.)

EXAMPLES   Angel Falls, which is the world's highest waterfall, was named for the aviator James Angel, who crash-landed near the falls in 1937.

As we read the historical play by Shakespeare, the teacher pointed out several anachronisms, which are things that are out of their proper time in history.

compound-complex sentence A compound-complex sentence has two or more independent clauses and at least one subordinate clause. (See page 571.)

EXAMPLES   Animals that live in the desert, such as the camel, the mule deer, and the kangaroo rat, require very little water to survive; in fact, most desert animals can go several days without drinking any water.

Maya Angelou, who is one of our country's most gifted authors, has written short stories, novels, plays, and poems; but she is perhaps best known for her autobiographical work *I Know Why the Caged Bird Sings.*

compound sentence A compound sentence has two or more independent clauses but no subordinate clauses. (See page 570.)

EXAMPLES   The African elephant is the largest land animal, and the Savi's pygmy shrew, also indigenous to Africa, is the smallest.

The first Women's Rights Convention was held in 1848 in Seneca Falls, New York; today, the city is the home of the National Women's Hall of Fame.

conjunction A conjunction joins words or groups of words. (See page 505.)

EXAMPLES   The long line of moviegoers **and** their families **or** friends stretched around the block, **for** it was **not only** a beautiful night **but also** a national holiday.

Turn off the lights **before** you leave.

contraction A contraction is a shortened form of a word, a numeral, or a group of words. Apostrophes in contractions indicate where letters or numerals have been omitted. (See page 831. See also **apostrophe.**)

EXAMPLES	you're [you are]	here's [here is]
	who's [who is *or* who has]	they're [they are]
	wasn't [was not]	it's [it is *or* it has]
	can't [cannot]	don't [do not]
	'14–'18 war [1914–1918 war]	o'clock [of the clock]

dangling modifier A dangling modifier is a modifying word, phrase, or clause that does not clearly and sensibly modify a word or a word group in a sentence. (See page 714.)

DANGLING	Proofreading his report on mummification and other ancient Egyptian practices, a few errors, including a dangling modifier, were discovered. [Who is proofreading his report?]
REVISED	Proofreading his report on mummification and other ancient Egyptian practices, **Richard** discovered a few errors, including a dangling modifier.

dash (See page 810.)

EXAMPLE	My grandparents——my mother's parents, that is——moved to California before my mother was born.

declarative sentence A declarative sentence makes a statement and is followed by a period. (See page 527.)

EXAMPLE	Euripides was a famous Greek playwright.

direct object A direct object is a word or word group that receives the action of the verb or shows the result of the action, answering the question *Whom?* or *What?* after a transitive verb. (See page 521.)

EXAMPLE	Every Friday night, we eat **fish.**

double comparison A double comparison is the use of two comparative forms (usually *more* and *–er*) or two superlative forms (usually *most* and *–est*) to express comparison. In standard usage, the single comparative form is correct. (See page 702.)

NONSTANDARD	This salsa is more spicier than the salsa that you normally make.
STANDARD	This salsa is **spicier** [*or* **more spicy**] than the salsa that you normally make.

double negative A double negative is the nonstandard use of two or more negative words to express a single negative idea. (See page 743.)

NONSTANDARD   When I met the President, I was so nervous that I couldn't hardly speak.

STANDARD   When I met the President, I was so nervous that I **could hardly** speak.

NONSTANDARD   The field trip to the petting zoo won't cost the children nothing.

STANDARD   The field trip to the petting zoo **won't cost** the children **anything.**

STANDARD   The field trip to the petting zoo **will cost** the children **nothing.**

double subject A double subject occurs when an unnecessary pronoun is used after the subject of a sentence. (See page 734.)

NONSTANDARD   Kiyoshi and his sister, although they are twins, they do not have the same birthday.

STANDARD   **Kiyoshi and his sister,** although they are twins, **do** not have the same birthday.

elliptical construction An elliptical construction is a clause from which words have been omitted. (See pages 566 and 616.)

EXAMPLE   Aunt Zita is much more outgoing **than Mother [is].**

end marks (See page 776.)

- **with sentences**

EXAMPLES   Spanakopita, a delicious Greek dish, is a thin shell of pastry dough filled with spicy spinach and feta cheese. [declarative sentence]

Do you have a recipe for spanakopita? [interrogative sentence]

Yum! [interjection] What a tasty dish this is! [exclamatory sentence]

Please give me your recipe. [imperative sentence]

- **with abbreviations** (See **abbreviation.**)

EXAMPLES   The first American in space was Alan B. Shepard, Jr.

Was the first American in space Alan B. Shepard, Jr.?

essential clause/essential phrase An essential, or restrictive, clause or phrase is necessary to the meaning of a sentence; it is not set off by commas. (See page 788.)

EXAMPLES   Any pilots **who have already logged more than two hundred hours** will be excused from training. [essential clause]

Students **competing for the first time** must report to Mr. Landis. [essential phrase]

exclamation point (See **end marks.**)

exclamatory sentence An exclamatory sentence expresses strong feeling and is followed by an exclamation point. (See page 528.)

EXAMPLE   That's absolutely fantastic**!**

faulty coordination Faulty coordination occurs when unequal ideas are presented as though they were coordinated. (See page 424.)

FAULTY   At the age of sixty-five, my grandmother retired from teaching school, but within a year she grew restless and bored, for she missed the camaraderie of her colleagues and the exuberance of the students, so she decided to become a substitute teacher, and now she is back in the classroom nearly every day, and she is enjoying life again.

REVISED   At the age of sixty-five, my grandmother retired from teaching school. Within a year, however, she grew restless and bored, for she missed the camaraderie of her colleagues and the exuberance of the students. As a result, she decided to become a substitute teacher. Now she is back in the classroom nearly every day and is enjoying life again.

fragment (See **sentence fragment.**)

fused sentence A fused sentence is a run-on sentence in which sentences have been joined together with no punctuation between them. (See page 432. See also **comma splice** and **run-on sentence.**)

FUSED   Last night, a heavy snowfall blanketed our community consequently, all schools and many businesses in the area were closed today.

REVISED   Last night, a heavy snowfall blanketed our community**;** consequently, all schools and many businesses in the area were closed today.

REVISED   Last night, a heavy snowfall blanketed our community.
           Consequently, all schools and many businesses in the area
           were closed today.

general reference A general reference is the incorrect use of a pronoun to refer to a general idea rather than to a specific noun. (See page 631.)

GENERAL   To make food called glucose, a green plant uses water from its
           roots, a chemical called chlorophyll, and the energy from the
           sun. This is called photosynthesis.
REVISED   To make food called glucose, a green plant uses water from its
           roots, a chemical called chlorophyll, and the energy from the
           sun. **This process** is called photosynthesis.

gerund A gerund is a verb form ending in *–ing* that is used as a noun. (See page 543.)

EXAMPLE   **Procrastinating** leads nowhere, as my mom always says.

gerund phrase A gerund phrase consists of a gerund and its modifiers and complements. (See page 544.)

EXAMPLE   **Collecting Beatles memorabilia** is my uncle's hobby.

good, well (See page 696.)

EXAMPLES   Paul is a **good** employee.
           Paul works **well** [not *good*] with others and performs his
           duties effectively.

hyphen (See page 834.)

■ **to divide words**
   EXAMPLE   Both Ming and I wish that our school offered com-
              puter courses earlier in the day.

■ **in compound numbers**
   EXAMPLE   Ms. Hughes served as president of the company for
              twenty-one years.

■ **with prefixes and suffixes**
   EXAMPLES   The football season begins in mid-August.
              I think this salsa is fat-free.

imperative mood The imperative mood is used to express a direct command or request. (See page 680.)

EXAMPLES   **Name** and **describe** the Seven Wonders of the ancient world.

Ladies and gentlemen, please **stand** for the singing of our national anthem.

imperative sentence An imperative sentence gives a command or makes a request and is followed by either a period or an exclamation point. (See page 527.)

EXAMPLES   Please return this map to Mr. Miller.

Get out of that tree now!

indefinite reference An indefinite reference is the incorrect use of the pronoun *you, it,* or *they* to refer to no particular person or thing. (See page 635.)

INDEFINITE   In this week's edition of our community newspaper, it shows the official ballot that will be used for the upcoming local election.

REVISED   This week's edition of our community newspaper shows the official ballot that will be used for the upcoming local election.

REVISED   In this week's edition of our community newspaper is a reproduction of the official ballot that will be used for the upcoming local election.

independent clause An independent clause (also called a *main clause*) expresses a complete thought and can stand by itself as a sentence. (See page 558.)

EXAMPLES   **The game was afoot,** as Holmes would say, and **no dawdling would be tolerated.**

indicative mood The indicative mood is used to express a fact, an opinion, or a question. (See page 680.)

EXAMPLES   Denzel Washington **has received** considerable praise for his performance in the movie.

Denzel Washington, in my opinion, **deserves** an Academy Award.

Didn't Denzel Washington **win** an Oscar for his performance?

indirect object An indirect object is a noun, pronoun, or word group that often appears in sentences containing direct objects. An indirect object tells *to whom* or *to what* (or *for whom* or *for what*) the action of a transitive verb is done. Indirect objects generally precede direct objects. (See page 522.)

EXAMPLE   In Roman mythology, Mercury gave **gods** messages from humans.

infinitive An infinitive is a verb form, usually preceded by *to,* used as a noun, an adjective, or an adverb. (See page 546.)

EXAMPLE   **To understand,** read the book.

infinitive phrase An infinitive phrase consists of an infinitive and its modifiers and complements. (See page 547.)

EXAMPLE   **To play the piano well** has long been an ambition of mine.

interjection An interjection expresses emotion and has no grammatical relation to the rest of the sentence. (See page 507.)

EXAMPLE   **Oh no!** The whole freeway's backed up for miles!

interrogative sentence An interrogative sentence asks a question and is followed by a question mark. (See page 527.)

EXAMPLE   Ma'am, are you sure you spoke to Dr. Ryan in person**?**

intransitive verb An intransitive verb is a verb that does not take an object. (See page 498.)

EXAMPLE   The dogs **barked** as the camels **passed.**

irregular verb An irregular verb is a verb that forms its past and past participle in some way other than by adding *d* or *ed* to the base form. (See page 646. See also **regular verb.**)

Base Form	Present Participle	Past	Past Participle
be	[is] being	was, were	[have] been
become	[is] becoming	became	[have] become
begin	[is] beginning	began	[have] begun

Base Form	Present Participle	Past	Past Participle
catch	[is] catching	caught	[have] caught
put	[is] putting	put	[have] put
take	[is] taking	took	[have] taken
throw	[is] throwing	threw	[have] thrown

italics (See page 812.)

■ **for titles**

EXAMPLES   *A History of the Supreme Court* [book]

           Scientific American [periodical]

           Perseus with the Head of Medusa [work of art]

           A Little Night Music [long musical composition]

■ **for words, letters, and symbols used as such and for foreign words**

EXAMPLES   You misspelled ***exhilaration*** by leaving out the ***h.***

           A ***cause célèbre*** is a scandal or a controversial incident.

its, it's (See page 860.)

EXAMPLES   **Its** [Canada's] capital is Ottawa.

           Brrr! **It's** [It is] cold outside.

           It's [It has] been snowing here since early this morning.

lie, lay (See page 659.)

EXAMPLES   For several weeks, straw **lay** over all of our backyard.

           We **laid** straw on the ground to cover the grass seed.

linking verb
A linking verb connects its subject with a word that identifies or describes the subject. (See page 495.)

EXAMPLE   As she **grew** older, her ambitions changed.

QUICK REFERENCE HANDBOOK

M

misplaced modifier A misplaced modifier is a word, phrase, or clause that seems to modify the wrong word or words in a sentence. (See page 712.)

MISPLACED   Chicle is the main ingredient in chewing gum made from the sap of the sapodilla tree. [Chicle, not chewing gum, is made from the sap of the sapodilla tree.]

REVISED   Chicle, **made from the sap of the sapodilla tree,** is the main ingredient in chewing gum.

modifier A modifier is a word or word group that makes the meaning of another word or word group more specific. (See page 692.)

EXAMPLE   Ronald is **a prominent** attorney **in a small Kansas town.**

mood Mood is the form a verb takes to indicate the attitude of the person using the verb. (See page 680. See also **imperative mood, indicative mood,** and **subjunctive mood.**)

N

nonessential clause/nonessential phrase A nonessential, or nonrestrictive, clause or phrase adds information not necessary to the main idea in the sentence and is set off by commas. (See page 788.)

EXAMPLES   The tourists on the pier, **who had all agreed to wear the same color combinations,** were becoming restless. [nonessential clause]

Our cats Boots and Bandit, **those two scamps,** are hiding behind the curtains. [nonessential phrase]

noun A noun names a person, place, thing, or idea. (See page 485.)

EXAMPLE   **Tyrell** is a **musician** of great **skill.**

noun clause A noun clause is a subordinate clause used as a noun. (See page 562.)

EXAMPLE   The prize goes to **whoever comes in first.**

number Number is the form a word takes to indicate whether the word is singular or plural. (See page 578.)

SINGULAR	door	I	loaf	mouse
PLURAL	doors	we	loaves	mice

objective complement An objective complement is a word or word group that helps complete the meaning of a transitive verb by identifying or modifying the direct object. (See page 523.)

EXAMPLE   The Hartleys painted their bookcases **black.**

object of a preposition An object of a preposition is the noun or pronoun that ends a prepositional phrase. (See page 502.)

EXAMPLE   In the **general store** she found a battery for her **watch.** [*In the general store* and *for her watch* are prepositional phrases.]

parallel structure Parallel structure is the use of the same grammatical forms or structures to balance related ideas in a sentence. (See page 424.)

NONPARALLEL   The job requires someone with a college degree in computer programming and who has excellent communication skills.

PARALLEL   The job requires someone **with a college degree in computer programming** and **with excellent communication skills.** [two prepositional phrases]

PARALLEL   The job requires someone **who has a college degree in computer programming** and **who has excellent communication skills.** [two adjective clauses]

parentheses (See page 809.)

EXAMPLES   The seven colors of the spectrum **(**think of a rainbow**)** are as follows: red, orange, yellow, green, blue, indigo, and violet. **(**See diagram C.**)**

participial phrase A participial phrase consists of a participle and any complements and modifiers it has. (See page 541.)

EXAMPLE   The kangaroo, **leaping ever farther and higher,** was soon out of sight.

participle A participle is a verb form that can be used as an adjective. (See page 540.)

EXAMPLE   **Astounded,** Mother could only nod her head in assent.

passive voice The passive voice is the voice a verb is in when it expresses an action done to its subject. (See page 676. See also **voice.**)

EXAMPLE   Emile **has been given** a great responsibility.

period (See **end marks.**)

phrase A phrase is a group of related words that does not contain a verb and its subject and that is used as a single part of speech. (See page 535.)

EXAMPLES   Goethe, **probably Germany's greatest writer,** represents the best **of the classical and romantic traditions.**
[*Probably Germany's greatest writer* is an appositive phrase. *Of the classical and romantic traditions* is a prepositional phrase.]

     Always to tell the truth requires courage. [*Always to tell the truth* is an infinitive phrase.]

     Sitting in the bleachers, we cheered our team. [*Sitting in the bleachers* is a participial phrase.]

predicate The predicate is the part of a sentence that says something about the subject. (See page 515.)

EXAMPLE   Ed **throws an unforgettable fastball.**

predicate adjective A predicate adjective is an adjective that completes the meaning of a linking verb and modifies the subject of the verb. (See page 525.)

EXAMPLE   The White House aides seemed **worried** and **uncertain** about the latest developments.

predicate nominative A predicate nominative is a word or word group that completes the meaning of a linking verb and that identifies the subject or refers to it. (See page 524.)

EXAMPLE   My younger brother John is turning into a very influential **reporter.**

prefix A prefix is a word part that is added before a base word or root. (See page 846.)

EXAMPLES   un + usual = **un**usual   il + logical = **il**logical

re + write = **re**write   pre + mature = **pre**mature

self + discipline = **self**-discipline   ex + senator = **ex**-senator

mid + October = **mid**-October   pre + Columbian = **pre**-Columbian

preposition A preposition shows the relationship of a noun or a pronoun to some other word in a sentence. (See page 502.)

EXAMPLE   The house **in** the valley, built **by** my grandfather Ernesto, has a view **of** the forest.

prepositional phrase A prepositional phrase includes a preposition, its object (a noun or a pronoun), and any modifiers of that object. (See page 536. See also **object of a preposition.**)

EXAMPLE   Finally, someone went **for additional refreshments.**

pronoun A pronoun is used in place of one or more nouns or pronouns. (See page 487.)

EXAMPLES   **My** cousin Rich, **who** worked in the Peace Corps when **he** was younger, wants to devote **his** life to helping people.

Everyone should introduce **himself** or **herself** to the group.

question mark (See **end marks.**)

quotation marks (See page 815.)

■ **for direct quotations**

EXAMPLE   **"**Before I make my ruling,**"** said the judge, **"**I want to meet with both counsels in my chambers.**"**

■ **with other marks of punctuation** (See also preceding example.)

EXAMPLES   **"**In what year was the Great Wall of China completed**?"** asked Neka.

Is Robert Frost the poet who said that a poem should **"**begin in delight and end in wisdom**"?**

The teacher asked, **"**Who are the speakers in Gwendolyn Brooks's poem **'**We Real Cool**'?"**

■ **for titles**

EXAMPLES   ❝The Bells of Santa Cruz❞ [short story]

                   ❝Mother to Son❞ [short poem]

                   ❝Backwater Blues❞ [song]

R

regular verb A regular verb is a verb that forms its past and past participle by adding *d* or *ed* to the base form. (See page 645. See also **irregular verb.**)

Base Form	Present Participle	Past	Past Participle
ask	[is] asking	asked	[have] asked
drown	[is] drowning	drowned	[have] drowned
receive	[is] receiving	received	[have] received
risk	[is] risking	risked	[have] risked
suppose	[is] supposing	supposed	[have] supposed
use	[is] using	used	[have] used

rise, raise (See page 662.)

EXAMPLES   A dense cloud of dust **rose** behind the wild horses as they galloped into the canyon.

                  As soon as she **raised** the hood of the car, she saw what was causing the noise.

run-on sentence A run-on sentence is two or more complete sentences run together as one. (See page 432. See also **comma splice** and **fused sentence.**)

RUN-ON   Barney Oldfield (1877–1946) was the first race-car driver to go at a speed of a mile per minute, he won his first race at Detroit in 1902.

REVISED   Barney Oldfield (1877–1946) was the first race-car driver to go at a speed of a mile per minute. **H**e won his first race at Detroit in 1902.

REVISED   Barney Oldfield (1877–1946) was the first race-car driver to go at a speed of a mile per minute; he won his first race at Detroit in 1902.

semicolon (See page 804.)

- **in compound sentences with no conjunctions**

  EXAMPLE More than six hundred paintings were created by the Dutch artist Rembrandt; nearly one hundred of them were self-portraits.

- **in compound sentences with conjunctive adverbs**

  EXAMPLE Usually, the planet farthest from the sun is Pluto; **however,** because of its orbit, Pluto is at times closer to the sun than Neptune is.

- **between a series of items containing commas when the items contain commas**

  EXAMPLE For her research paper Marva wrote about three women who were awarded the Nobel Peace Prize: Jane Addams, a cofounder of the American Civil Liberties Union; Mother Teresa, the founder of Missionaries of Charity in Calcutta, India; and Rigoberta Menchú, a human rights activist from Guatemala.

sentence A sentence is a group of words that contains a subject and a verb and expresses a complete thought. (See page 513.)

EXAMPLE At sunrise the bats returned to the cave.

sentence fragment A sentence fragment is a group of words that is punctuated as if it were a complete sentence but that does not contain both a subject and a verb or that does not express a complete thought. (See pages 427 and 513.)

FRAGMENT A beautiful cantata composed by George Frideric Handel.

SENTENCE The chorus sang a beautiful cantata composed by George Frideric Handel.

FRAGMENT The scene in which an ocean current sweeps the swimmers into an underwater cave.

SENTENCE The scene in which an ocean current sweeps the swimmers into an underwater cave is the most exciting part of the movie.

simple sentence A simple sentence has one independent clause and no subordinate clauses. (See page 569.)

EXAMPLES The relatively long word *sesquipedalian* means "a long word."

Are Justin and Suzanne going with you to Autumn Applefest this weekend?

sit, set (See page 661.)

EXAMPLES The children **sat** spellbound as the storyteller narrated the Russian folk tale "Baba Yaga."

Dad requested, "Please **set** these crates of aluminum cans in the back of the truck, and take them to the recycling center."

slow, slowly (See page 696.)

EXAMPLE Led by the school's marching band, the homecoming parade proceeded **slowly** [not *slow*] through town.

subject The subject tells whom or what a sentence is about. (See page 515.)

EXAMPLE The **aquarium** contains a fascinating array of tropical fish.

subject complement A subject complement is a word or word group that completes the meaning of a linking verb and identifies or describes the subject. (See page 524.)

EXAMPLES Biarritz is a very popular **resort.**

Biarritz is very **popular.**

subjunctive mood The subjunctive mood is used to express a suggestion, a necessity, a condition contrary to fact, or a wish. (See page 681.)

EXAMPLES Brad recommended that Katie **be appointed** chairperson. [suggestion]

If I **were** you, Sinan, I would call Yori and apologize. [condition contrary to fact]

Kelly wishes she **were** taller. [wish]

subordinate clause A subordinate clause (also called a *dependent clause*) does not express a complete thought and cannot stand alone as a sentence. (See page 559. See also **noun clause, adjective clause, adverb clause.**)

EXAMPLES **What you need** is a nap. [noun clause]

The kitten **that Sally wants** is over there. [adjective clause]

The firefighters had to wait **until the wind died down.** [adverb clause]

suffix A suffix is a word part that is added after a base word or root. (See page 846.)

EXAMPLES   love + ly = love**ly**   ready + ly = readi**ly**

                plain + ness = plain**ness**   delay + ing = delay**ing**

                remove + able = remov**able**   notice + able = notice**able**

                win + er = win**ner**   perform + er = perform**er**

tense of verbs The tense of verbs indicates the time of the action or of the state of being expressed by the verb. (See page 664.)

Present Tense

I drive	we drive
you drive	you drive
he, she, it drives	they drive

Past Tense

I gave	we gave
you gave	you gave
he, she, it gave	they gave

Future Tense

I will (shall) drive	we will (shall) drive
you will (shall) drive	you will (shall) drive
he, she, it will (shall) drive	they will (shall) drive

Present Perfect Tense

I have driven	we have driven
you have driven	you have driven
he, she, it has driven	they have driven

Past Perfect Tense

I had driven	we had driven
you had driven	you had driven
he, she, it had driven	they had driven

Future Perfect Tense

I will (shall) have driven	we will (shall) have driven
you will (shall) have driven	you will (shall) have driven
he, she, it will (shall) have driven	they will (shall) have driven

QUICK REFERENCE HANDBOOK

transitive verb A transitive verb is an action verb that takes an object. (See page 498.)

EXAMPLE   Pete **drove** the bus.

underlining (See **italics**.)

verb A verb expresses an action or a state of being. (See page 495.)

EXAMPLES   An interpreter **translates** languages orally.

                Bern **is** the capital of Switzerland.

verbal A verbal is a form of a verb used as a noun, an adjective, or an adverb. (See page 540. See also **gerund, infinitive,** and **participle.**)

EXAMPLES   **Thrilling** as the balloon ride may have been for you, it was certainly **tiring** for me. [participles]

                I intend **to win.** [infinitive]

verb phrase A verb phrase consists of a main verb and at least one helping verb. (See page 516.)

EXAMPLE   He **has** rarely **been** so cheerful in the morning.

verbal phrase A verbal phrase consists of a verbal and its modifiers and complements. (See page 540. See also **gerund phrase, infinitive phrase,** and **participial phrase.**)

EXAMPLES   **Uprooted by the storm,** the oak lay across the path. [participial phrase]

                Our dog Scooter loves **meeting new people.** [gerund phrase]

voice Voice is the form a transitive verb takes to indicate whether the subject of the verb performs or receives the action. (See page 676.)

ACTIVE VOICE   Wolfgang Amadeus Mozart **composed** the opera *The Magic Flute.*

PASSIVE VOICE   The opera *The Magic Flute* **was composed** by Wolfgang Amadeus Mozart.

weak reference A weak reference is the incorrect use of a pronoun to refer to an antecedent that has not been expressed. (See page 634.)

WEAK   The art teacher explained surrealism, but not until he showed me one did I fully understand his explanation.

REVISED   The art teacher explained surrealism, but not until he showed me **a surrealist painting** did I understand his explanation.

well (See **good, well.**)

who, whom (See page 619.)

EXAMPLES   Among the American artists **whom** we have studied is Frederic Remington, **who** is famous for works that depict life on the American plains.

wordiness Wordiness is the use of more words than necessary or the use of fancy words where simple ones will do. (See page 452.)

WORDY   One of the articles in this magazine provides a number of suggestions that are practical for helping a person to make better his or her ability to concentrate.

REVISED   This magazine article provides several practical suggestions for improving concentration.

QUICK REFERENCE HANDBOOK

Diagramming Appendix

The Sentence Diagram

A *sentence diagram* is a picture of how the parts of a sentence fit together and how the words in a sentence are related.

Subjects and Verbs

Reference Note

For more information about **subjects** and **verbs,** see page 515.

Every sentence diagram begins with a horizontal line intersected by a short vertical line, which divides the subject from the verb.

EXAMPLE   **Judy Garland sang** "Over the Rainbow."

Judy Garland	sang

Understood Subjects

Reference Note

For more information about **understood subjects,** see page 528.

EXAMPLE   Close the door.

(you)	Close

Nouns of Direct Address

Reference Note

For more information about **nouns of direct address,** see page 518.

EXAMPLE   Hand me the dictionary, **George.**

George

(you)	Hand

Compound Subjects

EXAMPLE   **Ryan** and **Maria** are running a marathon.

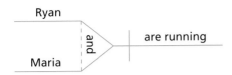

Reference Note

For more information about **compound subjects,** see page 517.

Compound Verbs

EXAMPLE   Eileen **sings** and **dances.**

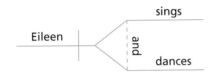

Reference Note

For more information about **compound verbs,** see page 517.

Compound Subjects and Compound Verbs

EXAMPLE   **Art** and **literature can entertain** and **inspire**.

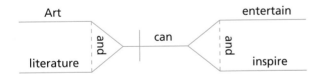

When the parts of a compound subject or a compound predicate are joined by a correlative conjunction, diagram the sentence this way:

EXAMPLE   **Both** Amy **and** Megan have **not only** called **but also** visited.

Reference Note

For more information about **correlative conjunctions,** see page 505.

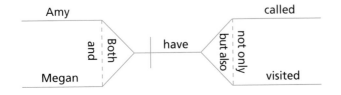

Modifiers

Adjectives and Adverbs

Reference Note

For more information about **adjectives,** see page 491. For more about **adverbs,** see page 499.

Adjectives and adverbs are written on slanting lines beneath the words they modify.

EXAMPLE   **The large** fish **slowly** turned **upstream.**

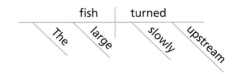

An adverb that modifies an adjective or an adverb is placed on a line connected to the word it modifies.

EXAMPLE   The time passed **incredibly** quickly.

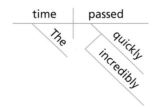

Here, There, and *Where* as Modifiers

Reference Note

For more about questions and sentences beginning with **here** and **there,** see page 519.

EXAMPLES   **Here** comes the rain!

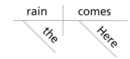

There goes the American cycling team.

Where has the boat docked?

Phrases

Prepositional Phrases

The preposition is placed on a slanting line leading down from the word that the phrase modifies. The object of the preposition is placed on a horizontal line connected to the slanting line.

Reference Note

For more information about **prepositional phrases,** see page 536.

EXAMPLES   The shallow pool **in the cave** was filled **with microorganisms.** [adjective phrase modifying the subject; adverb phrase modifying the verb]

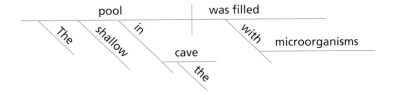

We awoke early **in the morning.** [adverb phrase modifying an adverb]

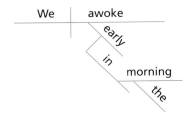

Grandpa told an old joke to **Brian** and **Sam.**
[compound object of preposition]

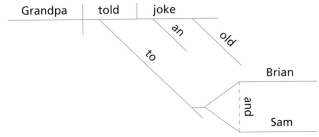

Around the sun and **beyond the planets** orbit many comets. [two phrases modifying the same word]

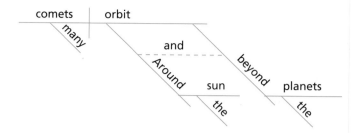

The hermit lived **in a hut by the lake.** [phrase modifying the object of another preposition]

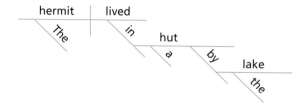

Reference Note

For more information about **participles** and **participial phrases,** see page 540.

Participles and Participial Phrases

Participles and participial phrases are diagrammed as follows.

EXAMPLES   He saw her **waving.**

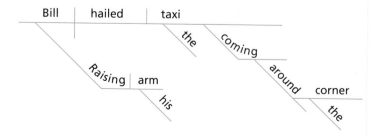

Raising his arm, Bill hailed the taxi **coming around the corner.**

Notice above that the participle *Raising* has a direct object (*arm*), which is diagrammed in the same way that a direct object of a main verb is.

Gerunds and Gerund Phrases

Gerunds and gerund phrases are diagrammed as follows.

EXAMPLES   **Diving** is not risk-free. [gerund used as subject]

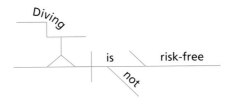

Exercising regularly with friends is definitely a good
plan for **developing healthy habits.** [gerund phrases used
as subject and as object of a preposition]

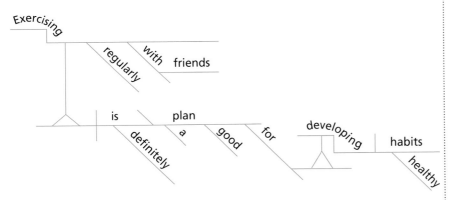

Notice above that the gerund *developing* has a direct object (*habits*).

Infinitives and Infinitive Phrases

Infinitives and infinitive phrases used as modifiers are diagrammed in
the same way as prepositional phrases.

EXAMPLE   They fought **to survive.** [infinitive used as adverb]

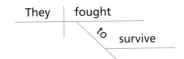

Reference Note

For more information
about **gerunds** and
gerund phrases, see
page 543.

Reference Note

For more information
about **infinitives** and
infinitive phrases, see
page 546.

Infinitives and infinitive phrases used as nouns are diagrammed as follows.

EXAMPLES **To reach the highest peak** requires great determination. [infinitive phrase used as subject]

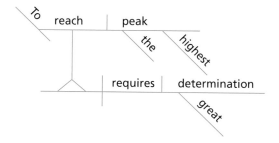

We are planning **to leave New York tomorrow.** [infinitive phrase used as direct object]

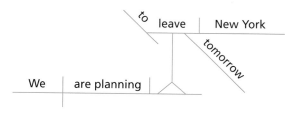

My friend helped **me find my dog.** [infinitive clause with subject, *me*, and with *to* omitted]

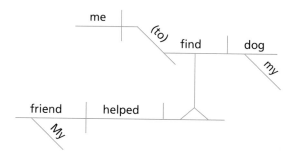

Reference Note

For more information about **appositives** and **appositive phrases,** see page 550.

Appositives and Appositive Phrases

Place the appositive in parentheses after the word it identifies or describes.

My sister **Joan** is a surgeon.

Seamus traveled to Kilkenny, **a town in Ireland.**

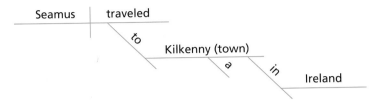

Subordinate Clauses

Adjective Clauses

An adjective clause is joined to the word it modifies by a broken line leading from the modified word to the relative pronoun.

EXAMPLES   The bird **that he spotted** was very beautiful.

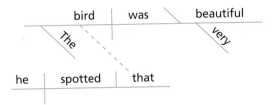

Those dark clouds, **which brought the rain,** were thunderheads.

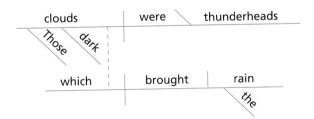

Reference Note

For more information about **adjective clauses,** see page 560.

He is the man **from whom I heard the strange tale.**

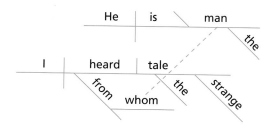

Adverb Clauses

Reference Note

For more information about **adverb clauses,** see page 565.

Place the subordinating conjunction that introduces the adverb clause on a broken line leading from the verb in the adverb clause to the word the clause modifies.

EXAMPLE   **If a drought occurs,** many plants may die.

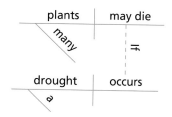

Noun Clauses

Reference Note

For more information about **noun clauses,** see page 562.

Noun clauses often begin with the word *that, what, who,* or *which.* These words may have a function within the subordinate clause or may simply connect the clause to the rest of the sentence. How a noun clause is diagrammed depends on how it is used in the sentence and whether or not the introductory word has a grammatical function in the noun clause.

EXAMPLES   **What he did** surprised us. [The noun clause is used as the subject of the independent clause. *What* functions as the direct object in the noun clause.]

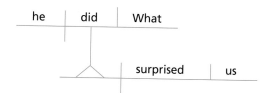

Sam forgot **that Mike needed a ride.** [The noun clause is the direct object of the independent clause. *That* has no grammatical function in the noun clause.]

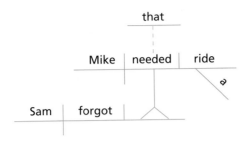

If the introductory word were omitted from the preceding sentence, the diagram would look like this.

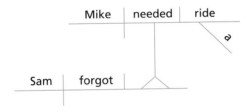

Sentences Classified According to Structure

Simple Sentences

EXAMPLES   The Grand Canyon is a national treasure. [one independent clause]

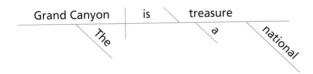

Meredith took a photograph. [one independent clause]

Meredith | took | photograph
a

Reference Note

For more information about **simple sentences,** see page 569.

Reference Note

For more information about **compound sentences,** see page 570.

Compound Sentences

EXAMPLE The enormous icebergs frightened us, but our ship sailed around the danger. [two independent clauses]

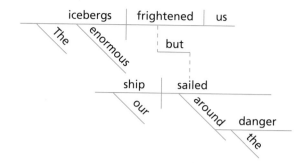

If the compound sentence has a semicolon and no conjunction, a straight broken line joins the two verbs.

EXAMPLE Svetlana Savitskaya made history in the 1980s; she was the first Russian female spacewalker.

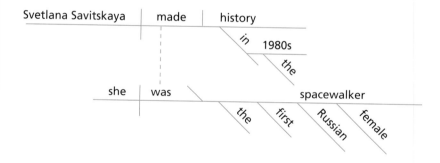

Reference Note

For more information about **conjunctive adverbs,** see page 570.

If the clauses of a compound sentence are joined by a semicolon and a conjunctive adverb (such as *consequently, therefore, nevertheless, however, moreover,* or *otherwise*), place the conjunctive adverb on a slanting line below the verb it modifies.

EXAMPLE   Juan runs daily before sunrise; **therefore,** he can hope to win the big race.

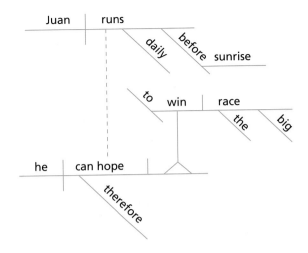

Complex Sentences

EXAMPLE   Before he arrived, the party was dull. [one independent clause and one subordinate clause]

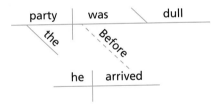

Reference Note

For more information about **complex sentences,** see page 571.

Compound-Complex Sentences

EXAMPLE   The museum that Felicia visited was small, but she enjoyed the collection. [two independent clauses and one subordinate clause]

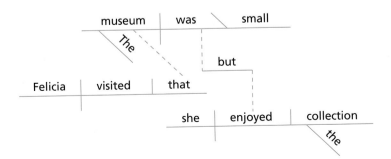

Reference Note

For more information about **compound-complex sentences,** see page 571.

definition of, 183
as illustrations, 122–23
Barely, 743
Base form
definition of, 1050
as principal part of verb, 644
Baym, Nina, 189–91
Be
always with passive voice, 676
conjugation of, 667–68
as helping verb, 497, 644
as linking verb, 496
principal parts of, 650
progressive form of verbs and, 666
Bear, **principal parts of,** 650
Beat, **principal parts of,** 650
Because, 728
Become, **principal parts of,** 650
Begin, **principal parts of,** 650
Being as, being that, 728
Bend, **principal parts of,** 647
Beside, besides, 728
Between, among, 728–29
Bias
definition of, 1015
determining point of view and bias in writing, 292, 954
in editorials, 288, 291–92
in media coverage, 100
of sources, 251
techniques signaling biased writing, 291
Bibliography. *See* Works Cited list.
Billboards, advertisement and, 378
Bind, **principal parts of,** 647
Biographical and geographical references
in dictionaries, 918
as library source, 946–47
Biographical poster, 285
Bite, **principal parts of,** 650
Block quotations, punctuation of, 278
Blow, **principal parts of,** 650
Body, of compositions, 473–75, 1029
Body language, 360
Bookmark, 284
Book review (reading)
criteria for evaluating, 328, 334–36
distinguishing fact and opinion, 328, 332–34
reading selection, 329–31
Book review (writing)
audience, 340–41
evaluating and revising, 353–55
prewriting, 339–47
proofreading and publishing, 357–58
purpose, 340
student's model, 352
support, 346–47
topic, 339–40

writer's model, 349–51
writing first draft, 348
Born, borne, 857
Borrow, lend, 729
Brackets, 267, 811, 1050
Brainstorming
about analyzing novels, 187
about autobiographical narratives, 17
definition of, 1040
about editorial piece, 287
about poetic topics, 91
about problem-solution explanations, 145
about progress reports, 105
about research, 229
topics for book review, 339
Brake, break, 858
Break, brake, 858
Break, **principal parts of,** 650
Bring, **principal parts of,** 644, 647
Bring, take, 729
British English language, 938
Broad, William J., 329–31
Broadcasting, definition of, 1011
Browser, 949
Build, **principal parts of,** 647
Bullets, using bullets, 176, 922
Burn, **principal parts of,** 645
Burst, **principal parts of,** 647, 654
Business and marketing Web pages, 281
Business letters. *See also* Business texts.
addressing envelopes, 1032
application letters, 1026
appreciation letter, 1024–25
closing, 1024
commendation letter, 1024–25
complaint letters, 1025
heading for, 1024
inside address and, 1024
parts of, 1023–24
punctuation of, 797, 808
request or order letters, 1027
sales letters, 316–17
salutation, 1024
types of, 1024–27
Business texts. *See also* Business letters; Letters (correspondence).
appreciation letter, 1024–25
committee reports in formal meetings, 985
complaint letters, 1025
forms, 1032, 1033
résumé writing, 53
summarizing job descriptions, 143
Bust, busted, 729
But, only, 743

Buy, **principal parts of,** 647
Byline, definition of, 1020

Cable television, definition of, 1012
Callouts, definition of, 922
Camera angles, 226, 1012
Campaign. *See* Ad campaigns.
Can't hardly, can't scarcely, 743
Capital, capitol, 858
Capital letters, in document design, 925
Capitalization
    of abbreviations, 754, 755, 1046
    of acronyms, 767, 1050
    in addresses, 755
    of brand names, 757
    of businesses, 757
    after colons, 807
    of comic strips, 764
    of compound words, 753
    of computer games, 764
    in dates, 768–69
    in dialogue, 752
    direct quotations and, 816
    of first words, 751–52, 1050
    of geographical terms, 754–55, 767–68
    of historical events and periods, 758
    of holidays and other calendar items, 758
    of interjection *O,* 752
    in letters (correspondence), 752
    of monuments and memorials, 758
    of musical works, CDs, audio tapes, 764
    of names of persons, 754, 766
    of nationalities, races, peoples, 758
    parenthetical sentences and, 809–10
    of particular buildings and structures, 757
    of planets and heavenly bodies, 756
    in poetry, 752
    of pronoun *I,* 752
    of proper adjectives, 753, 1051
    of proper nouns, 753, 1051
    of religions and their followers, holy days, etc., 759
    of school subjects, 760
    of ships, trains, aircraft, spacecraft, 759
    of special events, 758
    of subtitles of publications, 763
    of time of day, 768–69
    of titles of movies, works of art, etc., 763–64, 1052
    of titles of persons, 762, 766–67, 1052
    of titles of publications, 763–64, 1052
    of units of measurement, 769
    of words showing family relationships, 762
Capitol, capital, 858
Captions, 925–26

Card catalogs, 249, 943
Career development activities
    compile booklet of job reviews, 365
    create dictionary of college application terms, 103
    create résumé with autobiographical experience, 53
    interviewing marketing researcher, 415
    interviewing speech writer or ad writer, 325
    interviewing professionals and writing reports, 285
    presenting problems from different perspectives, 185
    summarizing job descriptions, 143
    teach about analysis of novel, 227
    writing as career, 15
Career guides, as library source, 947
Cartoons. *See* Editorials.
Case forms
    definition of, 606
    nominative case, 607–608, 1052
    objective case, 610–12, 1052–53
    possessive case, 613–14, 1053
Catch, **principal parts of,** 647
Cause-and-effect relationships
    analysis of, 954
    causal chain, 959
    clue words for, 955
    context clues for, 114, 965
CD-ROM databases, 943. *See also* Reference sources.
–cede, –ceed, –sede, 846
Censorship, 1018
Center aligned, 921
Central idea. *See* Main idea.
Channel, definition of, 1012
Character of Pearl, The (Baym), 189–91
Charts
    definition of, 1034
    types of, 931–32
Chicago Manual of Style, The (CMS), 252
Chief Joseph, 1039
Choice of details, 1044
Choose, **principal parts of,** 650
Chronological order
    clue words for, 955
    coherence in paragraphs and, 461
    as order of ideas, 33, 78, 121–22, 167, 205
    sequence chain, 959–60
Circulation, definition of, 1020
Citations
    punctuating correctly, 278
    Works Cited list, 252, 270–73
    Works Consulted list, 252
Clarity. *See* Sentence clarity.
Classifying
    as definition tool, 56, 64–67
    steps in classifying, 66
    as study strategy, 995–96
    techniques for, 65
Clauses
    adjective clauses, 422, 444–45, 560–61, 1047

Tables

W

ACKNOWLEDGMENTS

For permission to reprint copyrighted material, grateful acknowledgment is made to the following sources:

Janet Alexander & Marsha Ann Tate of Widener University, Chester, PA: Adapted from "Evaluating Web Resources" of the *Widener University* Web site accessed July 19, 2002, at http://www2.widener.edu/Wolfgram-Memorial-Library/webevaluation/webeval.htm, which complements the book *Web Wisdom: How to Evaluate and Create Information Quality on the Web* by Janet Alexander and Marsha Ann Tate. Copyright © 1999 by Janet Alexander and Marsha Ann Tate.

Georges Borchardt, Inc., for Carol Bly: From "To Unteach Greed" from *Letters from the Country* by Carol Bly. Copyright © 1977 by Carol Bly. Published by Harper & Row, New York, 1981.

Chronicle Books, LLC, San Francisco: From "Oranges" from *New and Selected Poems* by Gary Soto. Copyright © 1995 by Gary Soto.

Andrea Gabor: From "Even our most loved monuments had a trial by fire" by Andrea Gabor from *Smithsonian*, May 1997. Copyright © 1997 by Smithsonian Institution.

The Gale Group: From "Pearl" from *The Scarlet Letter: A Reading* by Nina Baym. Copyright © 1986 by G. K. Hall & Co. From "The Jazz Tradition" from *The African American Almanac*, Seventh Edition, edited by L. Mpho Mabunda. Copyright © 1997 by Gale Research Inc. All rights reserved.

Harcourt, Inc.: From "The Jilting of Granny Weatherall" from *The Flowering Judas and Other Stories* by Katherine Anne Porter. Copyright 1930 and renewed © 1958 by Katherine Anne Porter.

HarperCollins Publishers, Inc.: From *Their Eyes Were Watching God* by Zora Neale Hurston. Copyright 1937 by Harper & Row, Publishers, Inc.; copyright renewed © 1965 by John C. Hurston and Joel Hurston.

Harvard University Press and the Trustees of Amherst College: "479: Because I could not stop for Death" and "598: The Brain" from *The Poems of Emily Dickinson*, edited by Ralph W. Franklin. Copyright © 1951, 1955, 1979, and 1983 by the President and Fellows of Harvard College. Published by The Belknap Press of Harvard University Press, Cambridge, MA.

Houghton Mifflin Company: From *Tough Trip Through Paradise* by Andrew García. Copyright © 1967 by the Rock Foundation. All rights reserved.

Alfred A. Knopf, Inc.: From *Alistair Cooke's America* by Alistair Cooke. Copyright © 1973 by Alistair Cooke.

Harold Matson Company, Inc.: From *All Creatures Great and Small* by Daniel Mannix. Copyright © 1963 by Daniel P. Mannix.

National Audubon Society: From "Environmentalism's New Wave" by Dan Koeppel from *Audubon*, Nov.-Dec. 1995. Copyright © 1998 by Dan Koeppel. To subscribe to *Audubon*, call 800-274-4201.

National Geographic Society: From "Amelia Earhart" by Virginia Morell from *National Geographic*, vol. 193, no. 1, January 1998. Copyright © 1998 by National Geographic Society.

National Wildlife Federation: From "Single, Lonely Parrot Seeks Companionship" by Mac Margolis from *International Wildlife*, vol. 26, no. 1, January/February 1996. Copyright © 1995 by National Wildlife Federation.

The New York Times Company: From "Hot Rocks" (retitled "Hot Topic") by William J. Broad from *The New York Times*, July 20, 1997. Copyright © 1997 by The New York Times Company. "Students' Test Scores Show Slow but Steady Gains of Nation's Schools" by Peter Appleborne from *The New York Times*, September 3, 1997. Copyright © 1997 by The New York Times Company. From "Bananas for Rent" by Michiko Kakutani from *The New York Times Magazine*, November 9, 1997. Copyright © 1997 by The New York Times Company. From "School Uniforms, the $80 Million Boondoggle" by Micah C. Lasher from *The New York Times*, February 21, 1998. Copyright © 1998 by The New York Times Company. "Cleaning Up College Basketball" by Lee C. Bollinger and Tom Goss from *The New York Times*, September 5, 1998. Copyright © 1998 by The New York Times Company.

Newsweek, Inc.: From "Rockets" by Russell Watson and John Barry from *Newsweek Extra: 2000*, Winter 1997–98. Copyright © 1997 by Newsweek, Inc. All rights reserved.

Leslie Norris: From "A Flight of Geese" from *Collected Stories* by Leslie Norris. Copyright © 1996 by Leslie Norris.

G. P. Putnam's Sons, a division of Penguin Putnam Inc.: From "Rules of the Game" from *The Joy Luck Club* by Amy Tan. Copyright © 1989 by Amy Tan.

Random House, Inc.: Slightly adapted from *A Raisin in the Sun, Expanded 25th Anniversary Edition,* by Lorraine Hansberry. Copyright © 1958 by Robert Nemiroff as an unpublished work; copyright © 1959, 1966, 1984, 1987 by Robert Nemiroff.

Scribner, an imprint of Simon & Schuster Adult Publishing Group: From *The Great Gatsby* by F. Scott Fitzgerald. Copyright 1925 by Charles Scribner's Sons; copyright renewed 1953 by Frances Scott Fitzgerald Lanahan.

Time Inc.: From "Seeking the Roots of Violence" by Anastasia Toufexis from *Time,* April 19, 1993. Copyright © 1993 by Time Inc. From "Welcome to Cyberspace: What is it? Where is it? And how do we get there?" by Philip Elmer De-Witt from *Time,* Spring 1995, pp. 4-8. Copyright © 1995 by Time Inc.

Jonathan Turner: From "Culture Shock" by Jonathan Turner from *ARTnews,* February 13 - March 14, 1998. Copyright © 1998 by Jonathan Turner.

Sabine Ulibarrí: From "My Wonder Horse" from *Tierra Amarilla: Stories of New Mexico* by Sabine Ulibarrí. Copyright © 1971 by The University of New Mexico Press.

Viking Penguin, a division of Penguin Putnam Inc.: "One Perfect Rose" from *The Portable Dorothy Parker.* Copyright 1926 and renewed © 1954 by Dorothy Parker.

Villard Books, a division of Random House, Inc.: From "The Stikine Ice Cap" (retitled "Reaching the Summit") from *Into the Wild* by Jon Krakauer. Copyright © 1996 by Jon Krakauer.

Vintage Books, a division of Random House, Inc.: From *A Natural History of the Senses* by Diane Ackerman. Copyright © 1990 by Diane Ackerman.

Fred Ward: From "The Timeless Mystique of Emeralds" by Fred Ward from *National Geographic,* July 1990. Copyright © 1990 by Fred Ward.

Washington Post Writers Group: From "The Assembly Line" by Robert J. Samuelson from *Newsweek Extra,* Winter 1997-98. Copyright © 1998 by Newsweek.

Bruce Watson: Adapted from "A Wizard's Scribe" from *Smithsonian,* vol. 29, no. 5, August 1998. Copyright © 1998 by Bruce Watson.

WNUR-FM Northwestern University: From *WNUR-FM Jazz* Web site, accessed March 8, 1999, at http://www.nwu.edu.WNUR/jazz/. Copyright © by WNUR-FM, Northwestern University.

SOURCES CITED:

Quote by Tridas Mukophadhyay from "Carnegie Mellon Study Reveals Negative Potential of Heavy Internet Use on Emotional Well Being" by Teresa S. Thomas and Anne Watzman from *Science Daily,* September, 1998. Published by Carnegie, Mellon, Pittsburgh, 1998.

From "The Sixth Sally" from *The Cyberiad: Fables for the Cybernetic Age* by Stanislaw Lem, translated by Michael Kandel. Published by The Contiuum Publishing Company, New York, NY, 1974.

From *A Rare Bird* by Max Harrison. Published by Da Capo Press, Ltd., New York, 1997.

Quote by Jay McShann from *Bird Lives!* by Gary Giddins. Published by Da Capo Press, Ltd., New York, 1987.

From *Blue Highways: A Journey into America* by William Least Heat-Moon. Published by Little, Brown and Company, Boston, 1982.

Quote by Benny Green from "Musical Forms and Genres: Jazz as a Social Force" from *The New Encyclopedia Britannica.* Published by Encyclopedia Britannica, Inc., Chicago, IL, 1995.

From "No Bop Roots in Jazz: Parker," by Michael Levin and John S. Wilson from *DownBeat,* September 9, 1949. Published by John Maher Printing Company, Chicago, IL, 1949.

From *Jazz Is* by Nat Hentoff. Published by Random House, Inc., New York, NY, 1976.

"The Color Circle" from *World Book Encyclopedia.* Published by World Book, Inc., Chicago, IL, 1995.

PHOTO CREDITS

Abbreviations used: (tl)top left, (tc)top center, (tr)top right, (l)left, (cl)center left, (c)center, (cr)center right, (r)right, (bl)bottom left, (bc)bottom center, (br)bottom right.

COVER: Scott Van Osdol/HRW Photo.

TABLE OF CONTENTS: Page ix, Art Valero/The Stock Illustration Source; x, Rob Colvin/Stock Illustration Source; xi, Paul Anderson/The Stock Illustration Source, Inc.; xii, AKG Photo, London; xiii, (astronaut) (chief), CORBIS; xiii (soldiers), National Archives (NARA); xiii (Tubman) (family), Bettmann/CORBIS; xiii (flappers) Underwood & Underwood/CORBIS; xiv, CORBIS; xvi, Sam Dudgeon/HRW Photo; xvii, Rick Havner/AP Photo; xix, David Parker/Science Photo Library/Photo Researchers, Inc.; xx, Gene Stein/CORBIS; xxi, Ron Watts/CORBIS; xxii, Ken Reid/Getty Images/FPG; xxiii, TravelPix/Getty Images/FPG; xxiv, Vicki Ragan/Folkart Carvings by Ventura Fabian; xxvi, Anthony Howarth/Woodfin Camp & Associates, Inc.; xxviii, Image Copyright ©2001 Photodisc, Inc.; xxix, Tom McHugh/Photo Researchers, Inc.; xxx, Getty Images/Stone; xxxi, John Elk, III.

PART OPENERS: Page xxxiv, 1, 318, 319, 372, 373, 802, 803 ©Dave Cutler/The Stock Illustration Source, Inc.

TAKING TESTS: Page 2, Digital Image copyright ©2004 EyeWire; 4, Kevin Schafer/CORBIS; 7, Lynda Richardson/CORBIS.

CHAPTER 1: Page 21, Corbis Images; 38, Image Copyright ©2001 Photodisc, Inc.; 44, Bill Silliker, Jr./Animals Animals.

CHAPTER 2: Page 54, Art Valero/SIS; 57, Image Copyright ©2001 Photodisc, Inc.

CHAPTER 3: Page 104, Rob Colvin/Stock Illustration Source.

CHAPTER 4: Page 144, Paul Anderson/The Stock Illustration Source, Inc.

CHAPTER 5: Page 186, AKG Photo, London.

CHAPTER 6: Page 228 (tl) (c), CORBIS; 228 (tc), National Archives (NARA); 228 (cl) (br), Bettmann/CORBIS; 228 (bl) Underwood & Underwood/CORBIS; 231, James P. Blair/CORBIS; 233, Image Copyright ©2001 PhotoDisc, Inc.; 236, James P. Blair/CORBIS; 283, Image Copyright ©2001 PhotoDisc, Inc.

CHAPTER 7: Page 286, CORBIS.

CHAPTER 9: Page 366, Sam Dudgeon/HRW Photo; 378, National Fluid Milk Processor/Bozell Advertising Agency.

CHAPTER 10: Page 421, Orion Press/Getty Images/Stone; 422, CORBIS/Ted Spiegel; 423, David Burckhalter; 425, Photoworld/Getty Images/FPG; 427, Stan Osolinski/Getty Images/FPG; 428, Culver Pictures, Inc.; 429, The Granger Collection, New York; 430 (tr), Courtesy Museum of New Mexico, #30263; 430 (bl), Rick Havner/AP Photo; 431, Culver Pictures, Inc.; 432, Montana Historical Society, Helena; 435, Culver Pictures, Inc.

CHAPTER 11: Page 436, Tsantes Photography 1999; 439, Library of Congress; 440, NASA/Science Photo Library/Photo Researchers, Inc.; 441, Schomburg Center for Research in Black Culture; 446, David Parker/Science Photo Library/Photo Researchers, Inc.; 447, Culver Pictures, Inc.

CHAPTER 12: Page 448, Michael Fogden/Bruce Coleman, Inc.; 452, SuperStock; 455, The Granger Collection, New York.

CHAPTER 13: Page 458, Paul S. Howell/Liaison International; 459, CORBIS; 464, Courtesy of Rudolfo Anaya. Photographer: Mimi; 468, NASA/Science Photo Library/Photo Researchers, Inc.; 472, Dr. Joan Oates/The McDonald Institute for Archaeological Research; 475, Schomburg Center for Research in Black Culture/The New York Public Library, Astor, Lenox and Tiden Foundations/Photographed by Andrew J. Figueroa; 480, Peter Van Steen/HRW Photo; 481, Pool Mondial 98/Gamma.

CHAPTER 14: Page 502, John Langford/HRW Photo.

CHAPTER 15: Page 527, Ken Reid/Getty Images/FPG.

CHAPTER 16: Page 537, Tom McHugh/Photo Researchers, Inc.; 539, Joe Jawarski/HRW Photo; 549, John Elk, III; 552, Image Copyright ©2001 Photodisc, Inc.

CHAPTER 17: Page 559, 560 (tl) Lisa Davis/HRW Photo; 560 (tc), J.C. Allen & Sons, Inc.; 565, Ric Ergenbright/CORBIS.

CHAPTER 18: Page 580, J. Nettis/H. Armstrong Roberts; 590, Grant Heilman Photography.

CHAPTER 19: Page 612, Vicki Ragan/Folkart Carvings by Ventura Fabian.

CHAPTER 20: Page 633, Courtesy of the Southern Poverty Law Center in Montgomery, Alabama. Photo: Paul Roberson Photography; 637, Everett Collection, Inc.

CHAPTER 21: Page 653, Wata Nabe/Sony Classical; 655, Stuart Dike/Getty Images/FPG.

CHAPTER 22: Page 695 (c) (br), Jerry Jacka Photography; 698, Robert Reiff/Getty Images/FPG; 706, Porterfield/Chickering/Photo Researchers, Inc.

CHAPTER 23: Page 718, Ron Watts/CORBIS; 727, 728, PaceWildenstein.

CHAPTER 24: Page 732, Gene Stein/CORBIS; 733, Daniel Westergren/National Geographic Society Image Collection.

CHAPTER 25: Page 761, TravelPix/Getty Images/FPG.

CHAPTER 26: Page 788, Anthony Howarth/Woodfin Camp & Associates, Inc.

CHAPTER 27: Page 806, Culver Pictures, Inc.; 819, Bob Daemmrich Photography; 833, Mark Hess/Getty Images/The Image Bank; 838, Image Copyright ©2001 Photodisc, Inc.

CHAPTER 28: Page 849, Santa Fe Railway Photo/HRW Photo Research Library; 856, Getty Images/Stone; 867, Alejandro Balaguer/Getty Images/Stone.

CHAPTER 29: Page 877, 879, Image Copyright ©2001 Photodisc, Inc.; 881, ©1997 Radlund & Associates for Artville; 884, 887, Image Copyright ©2001 Photodisc, Inc.; 889, Sam Dudgeon/HRW Photo; 892, HRW Photo Research Library; 899, Sam Dudgeon/HRW Photo; 901, Corbis Images; 906, 907, Image Copyright ©2001 Photodisc, Inc.

ILLUSTRATION CREDITS

TABLE OF CONTENTS: Page viii, Matt Manley/Corey Graham Represents; xiii (cl), Kenneth William Kotik; xv (cl), Gillie Schattner/Mendola.

CHAPTER 1: Page 16 (all), Matt Manley/Corey Graham Represents.

CHAPTER 3: Page 182 (c), MapQuest.com, Inc.

CHAPTER 5: Page 224 (b), Leslie Kell; 226 (c), HRW.

CHAPTER 6: Page 228 (all), Kenneth William Kotik; 246 (tc), 248 (c), 254 (c), 283 (c), Leslie Kell.

CHAPTER 8: Page 326 (all), Gillie Schattner/Mendola.

CHAPTER 9: Page 366 (all), 407 (c), 413 (b), HRW.

CHAPTER 11: Page 442 (cl), Yoshi Miyake; 442 (bl), Linda Blackwell.

CHAPTER 12: Page 451 (tr), HRW.

CHAPTER 13: Page 463 (bc), Network Graphics.

CHAPTER 15: Page 520 (tl), Eve Steccati; 524 (c), Uhl Studios, Inc.

CHAPTER 19: Page 609 (br), Ortelius Design.

CHAPTER 21: Page 658 (bl), Ortelius Design.

CHAPTER 25: Page 765 (br), HRW.

CHAPTER 28: Page 844 (cl), Leslie Kell; 867 (br), Ortelius Design.

QRH: Page 922 (bl), David Fischer; 932 (bl), Don Collins; 933 (tl), Stephen Durke/Washington-Artists' Represents; 933 (b), 934 (bl), HRW; 940 (bl), MapQuest.com, Inc.; 951 (tr), Leslie Kell; 962 (tr), George Kelvin; 1040 (cr), HRW.